DELAWARE

Laws Governing
BUSINESS ENTITIES

Annotations from
All State and Federal Courts

Includes Full Text of Selected Opinions

SPRING 2008 EDITION
VOLUME 2

Corporation Service Company® and LexisNexis®

Corporation Service Company and LexisNexis work in partnership to provide you with the highest quality publications and services you need.

For questions regarding content, billing, or subscriptions for this and other CSC® publications, contact LexisNexis at 1.800.833.9844, or visit us on the web at **www.lexisnexis.com/PrintCDSC**.

To learn more about the products and services of Corporation Service Company, call us at 1.800.927.9800, fax us at 302.636.5454, or visit our website at **www.cscglobal.com**.

> **This book is now online at no extra cost** for subscribers to the Fall and Spring Editions. To learn more, visit our website at **http://cscde@lexisnexis.com**.

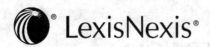

Table of Contents

———

Publisher's Note

———

The annotations in this publication include cases decided under Delaware business entity law in all U.S., state and federal courts, providing you with a single source for all case law applying Delaware business entity statutes.

Please note that annotations from federal courts based in Delaware are part of the Delaware portion of the annotations for each relevant statute. They are not included as part of the notes set out under the Third Circuit headings throughout the volume. New annotations that have been added since the Fall 2007 edition of this title are indicated by a gray sidebar for your convenience.

CORPORATIONS

——

TITLE 8
CORPORATIONS

CHAPTER 1.
GENERAL CORPORATION LAW

Subchapter I.
Formation

§ 101. Incorporators; how corporation formed; purposes

DELAWARE CASE NOTES — REPORTED

Enabling statute. — Delaware's General Corporation Law, like most general laws of incorporation, is an enabling statute; that is, the philosophy that underlies it is that the public good is advanced by the provision of an inexpensive mechanism that allows all individuals to achieve the benefits that the corporate form provides through establishing management and governance terms that appear advantageous to those designing the organization. *In re Ford Holdings, Inc. Preferred Stock, 698 A.2d 973 (Del. Ch. 1997).*

Corporation is artificial being created by law and acting under the authority of law for designated purposes and being artificial and the mere creature of the law, it can only act by its officers and agents. *Joseph Greenspon's Sons Iron & Steel Co. v. Pecos Valley Gas Co., 34 Del. 567, 156 A. 350 (1931).*

With same status as if created by special act. — Corporations organized under the general corporation law have the same legal status as if they had been created by a special act of the *General Assembly. State ex rel. Cochran v. Penn-Beaver Oil Co., 34 Del. 81, 143 A. 257 (1926).*

And corporation is entity distinct from its stockholders. *Bird v. Wilmington Soc'y of Fine Arts, 28 Del. Ch. 449, 43 A.2d 476 (1945).*

Even if there is only 1 stockholder. — The fact that 1 person owns all of the stock of a corporation does not make such person and the corporation 1 and the same person. *Martin v. D.B. Martin Co., 10 Del. Ch. 211, 88 A. 612 (1913).*

But this fiction should be ignored when used for fraudulent acts. — The fiction of a legal corporate entity should be ignored when it has been used as a shield for fraudulent or other illegal acts. *Martin v. D.B. Martin Co., 10 Del. Ch. 211, 88 A. 612 (1913).*

Cemetery corporation operated for profit not forbidden. — The public policy of this State does not forbid the operation of a cemetery corporation for private profit. *Wilmington Mem. Co. v. Silverbrook Cem., 287 A.2d 405 (Del. Ch.), aff'd, Wilmington Mem. Co. v. Silverbrook Cem., 297 A.2d 378 (Del. 1972).*

CASE NOTES — FEDERAL COURTS

First Circuit

Entity distinct from stockholders. — A duly organized corporation enjoys a legal identity separate and apart from its shareholders, directors and officers. Certainly in the normal course of events a corporate entity must be regarded as more than a mere formality. It is an entity distinct from its stockholders. *Enterasys Networks, Inc. v. Gulf Insurance Co., 364 F. Supp. 2d 28 (D.N.Hamp. 2005).*

Piercing the corporate veil. — Under Delaware law, the corporate veil may be pierced where there is fraud or where a subsidiary is in fact a mere instrumentality or alter ego of the parent. Similar to the factors under Virginia law, relevant factors under Delaware law in determining whether the subsidiary is merely an instrumentality or alter ego include (1) whether the dominant shareholders siphoned corporate funds, (2) whether the corporation is a facade for the dominant shareholders, (3) whether the corporation was solvent and adequately capitalized, and (4) whether corporate formalities were followed, including payment of dividends and separate corporate records. Piercing the corporate veil may only be done if it is in the interest of justice when such matters of fraud, contravention of law or contract, public wrong, or where equitable consideration among members of the corporation are involved. *CCBN.com, Inc.*

v. Thomson Financial, Inc., 270 F. Supp. 2d 146 (D.Mass. 2003).

Persuading a Delaware court to disregard the corporate entity is a difficult task. To state a cognizable claim for piercing the corporate veil under Delaware law, the plaintiff must allege facts that, if taken as true, demonstrate the defendant's complete domination and control over the corporation. This degree of control requires exclusive domination and control to the point that the corporation no longer has legal or independent significance of its own. Piercing the corporate veil under the alter ego theory requires that the corporate structure cause fraud or similar injustice. *Northern Laminate Sales, Inc. v. Matthews, 249 F. Supp. 2d 130 (D.N.H. 2003).*

Second Circuit

Piercing the corporate veil. — A securities fraud plaintiff seeking to persuade a Delaware court to disregard the corporate structure faces a difficult task. Courts have made it clear that the legal entity of a corporation will not be disturbed until sufficient reason appears. *Gabriel Capital, L.P. v. NatWest Fin., Inc., 122 F. Supp. 2d 407 S.D.N.Y. 2000).*

To pierce the corporate veil under Delaware law, the plaintiff must show that the controlling corporation wholly ignored separate status of controlled corporation and so dominated and controlled its affairs that separate existence was a sham. *Harrison v. NBD Inc., 990 F. Supp. 179 (E.D.N.Y. 1998).*

Under Delaware law, a corporate veil may be pierced in the interest of justice, when there are such matters as fraud, contravention of law or contract, public wrong, or where equitable consideration among members of the corporation require it, are involved. *S.J. Berwin & Co. v. Evergreen Entertainment Group, 1995 U.S. Dist. LEXIS 15155 (S.D.N.Y. 1995).*

To prevail on an alter ego claim, a plaintiff must show (1) that the parent and the subsidiary operated as a single economic entity and (2) that an overall element of injustice or unfairness is present. Under an alter ego theory, no showing of fraud is required. Rather, the injustice or unfairness must arise from the defendant's use of the corporate form, and may include factors such as contravention of law or contract, public wrong, or equitable considerations. Beyond formally piercing the corporate veil, when evaluating the effect of a corporate transaction, courts will look behind the form of the transaction to the substance because the term or title given by the parties to a particular transaction or agreement is not conclusive as to what it may actually be in practical operation. To this end, while the parties to a transaction may intend that, as between themselves, their relationship is to be governed by the labels they affix, that label neither governs the rights of third parties nor affects the legal consequences of the parties' agreement. *SR International Business Insurance Co. v. World Trade Center Props., LLC, 375 F. Supp. 2d 238 (S.D.N.Y. 2005).*

In order to state an alter ego claim, a plaintiff must plead that the parent and subsidiary operated as a single economic entity, and must demonstrate an overall element of injustice or unfairness. Where a subsidiary is in fact a mere instrumentality or alter ego of its owner, a court can pierce the corporate veil. Plaintiff must show that the owners exercised complete domination of the corporation in respect to the transaction attacked. *Union Carbide Corp. v. Montell N.V., 944 F. Supp. 1119 (S.D.N.Y. 1996).*

Under Delaware law, a court may pierce the corporate veil where there is fraud or where it is in fact a mere instrumentality or alter ego of its owner. To demonstrate alter ego, a plaintiff need plead or prove, only that the two corporations operated as a single economic entity such that it would be inequitable to uphold a legal distinction between them. *Motown Record Co., L.P. v. iMesh.com, Inc., 2004 U.S. Dist. LEXIS 3972 (S.D.N.Y. 2004).*

According to Delaware law, courts can pierce the corporate veil of a company where there is fraud or where it is in fact a mere instrumentality or alter ego of its owner. There is no requirement of fraud under the alter ego theory. To prove an alter ego claim, a plaintiff must satisfy the two-prong test (1) that the parent and the subsidiary operated as a single economic entity and (2) that an overall element of injustice or unfairness is present. Piercing the corporate veil under the alter ego theory requires that the corporate structure cause fraud or similar injustice. Thus, a court may pierce the corporate veil if (1) there are alter ego factors including whether the corporation was adequately capitalized for the corporate undertaking; whether the corporation was solvent; whether dividends were paid, corporate records kept, officers and directors functioned properly, and other corporate formalities were observed; whether the dominant shareholder siphoned corporate funds; and whether, in general, the corporation simply functioned as a facade for the dominant shareholder and (2) there is an element of injustice or unfairness. Although no single factor could justify a decision to disregard the corporate entity, some combination of them is required, and an overall element of injustice or unfairness must always be present. *Acciai Speciali Terni USA, Inc. v. Momene, 202 F. Supp. 2d 203 (S.D.N.Y. 2002).*

Delaware law permits a court to pierce the corporate veil of a company where there is fraud or where it is in fact a mere instrumentality or alter ego of its owner. Thus, under an alter ego theory, there is no requirement of a showing of fraud. To prevail on an alter ego claim under Delaware law, a plaintiff under § 10(b) of the Securities Exchange Act of 1934, 15 U.S.C.S. § 78j(b), must show (1) that the parent and the subsidiary operated as a single economic entity and (2) that an overall element of injustice or unfairness is present. *Gabriel Capital, L.P. v. NatWest Fin., Inc., 122 F. Supp. 2d 407 S.D.N.Y. 2000).*

Delaware law permits a court to pierce the corporate veil of a company where there is fraud or where it is in fact a mere instrumentality or alter ego of its owner. Under an alter ego theory, there is no requirement of a showing of fraud. To prevail on an alter ego claim under Delaware law, a plaintiff must show (1) that the parent and the subsidiary operated as a single economic entity and (2) that an overall element of injustice or unfairness is present. *Fletcher v. Atex, Inc., 68 F.3d 1451 (2d Cir. 1995).*

A showing of fraud or wrongdoing is not necessary under an alter ego theory of liability, but the plaintiff must demonstrate an overall element of injustice or unfairness. *Fletcher v. Atex, Inc., 68 F.3d 1451 (2d Cir. 1995).*

The fact that a parent and a subsidiary have common officers and directors does not necessarily demonstrate that the parent corporation dominates the activities of the subsidiary in terms of finding liability under the theory of alter ego. *Fletcher v. Atex, Inc., 68 F.3d 1451 (2d Cir. 1995).*

Single economic entity analysis. — The factors to be considered in determining whether a parent and subsidiary are a single economic entity under Delaware law are: whether the corporation was adequately capitalized for the corporate undertaking; whether the corporation was solvent; whether dividends were paid, corporate records kept, officers and directors functioned properly, and other corporate formalities were observed; whether the dominant shareholder siphoned corporate funds; and whether, in general, the corporation simply functioned as a facade for the dominant shareholder. *Gabriel Capital, L.P. v. NatWest Fin., Inc., 122 F. Supp. 2d 407 S.D.N.Y. 2000).*

Fiduciary duty. — Under Delaware law, a corporation does not owe a fiduciary duty to its shareholders nor may it be held vicariously liable for breaches of fiduciary duty that are committed by its officers. *Onex Food Servs. v. Grieser, 1996 U.S. Dist. LEXIS 2797 (S.D.N.Y. 1996).*

Third Circuit

Piercing the corporate veil. — Under Delaware law, piercing the corporate veil is appropriate where the corporation is merely an instrumentality or alter ego of its owners. Although the term "alter ego" is often used synonymously with "piercing the corporate veil," it is but one basis for bypassing the corporate shield. Other relevant factors in determining whether to disregard the corporate entity include whether it is in the interest of justice, when such matters as fraud, contravention of law or contract, public wrong, or where equitable considerations among members of the corporation are involved. Also to be considered are whether the dominant shareholders siphoned corporate funds; whether the corporation is a facade for the dominant shareholders; whether a corporation was adequately capitalized and solvent; and whether corporate formalities were followed, including payment of dividends and upkeep of corporate records. *Terranova, Inc. v. S/Y Terra-Nova, 2003 U.S. Dist. LEXIS 5134 (D.V.I. 2003).*

Under Delaware law, piercing the corporate veil is appropriate where the corporation is merely an instrumentality or alter ego of its owners. Although the term "alter ego" is often used synonymously with "piercing the corporate veil," it is but one basis for bypassing the corporate shield. Other relevant factors in determining whether to disregard the corporate entity include whether

it is in the interest of justice, when such matters as fraud, contravention of law or contract, public wrong, or where equitable considerations among members of the corporation are involved. Also to be considered are whether the dominant shareholders siphoned corporate funds; whether the corporation is a facade for the dominant shareholders; whether a corporation was adequately capitalized and solvent; and whether corporate formalities were followed, including payment of dividends and upkeep of corporate records. *Virgin Islands v. Lansdale, 172 F. Supp. 2d 636 (D.V.I. 2001).*

Control over subsidiary. — Liability for direct patent infringement cannot be imposed on a parent corporation if it exercises only basic directional control over a subsidiary. Every parent corporation, and indeed every majority stockholder in a corporation, exercises this degree of control. In fact, stockholder control over major decisions is required by law. Parent corporations cannot be held liable for merely exercising a basic level of control that is inherent in stock ownership. *Ronald A. Katz Technology Licensing, L.P. v. Verizon Communications, Inc, 2002 U.S. Dist. LEXIS 24117 (E.D.Pa. 2002).*

Fourth Circuit

The degree of control required to pierce the veil is exclusive domination and control to the point that the corporation no longer has legal or independent significance of its own. Thus, to state a veil-piercing claim, the plaintiff must plead facts supporting an inference that the corporation, through its alter ego, has created a sham entity designed to defraud investors and creditors. Piercing the corporate veil under the alter ego theory requires that the corporate structure cause fraud or similar injustice. Effectively, the corporation must be a sham and exist for no other purpose than as a vehicle for fraud. Further, the alleged fraud or inequity must be distinct from the tort alleged in the complaint. *Richmond v. Indalex Inc., 308 F. Supp. 2d 648 (M.D.N.Car. 2004).*

Fifth Circuit

Piercing the corporate veil. — Persuading a Delaware court to disregard the corporate entity is a difficult task. For a court to pierce the corporate veil, the plaintiffs must allege facts that, if taken as true, demonstrate complete domination or control of a corporation. The degree of control required to pierce the veil is exclusive domination and control to the point that the entity no longer has legal or independent significance of its own. A court can pierce the corporate veil of an entity where there is fraud or where a subsidiary is in fact an alter ego or mere instrumentality of its owner. Common management of two entities does not, by itself, justify piercing the corporate veil. The corporation must be a sham and exist for no other purpose than as a vehicle for fraud. If two entities, parent and subsidiary, fail to follow legal formalities when contracting with each other, it would be tantamount to declaring that they are indeed one in the same. *Sanderson v. H.I.G. P-Xi Holding, Inc., 2001 U.S. Dist. LEXIS 5074 (E.D.La. 2001).*

In determining whether to allow veil piercing under Delaware law, a court may look to the following factors:

Corporations

Whether a corporation is adequately capitalized and solvent; whether corporate formalities are followed, including payment of dividends and upkeep of corporate records; whether the dominant shareholders siphon corporate funds; and whether the corporation is a facade for the dominant shareholders. *Weaver v. Kellogg, 216 B.R. 563 (S.D.Tex. 1997).*

In order for Delaware's alter ego doctrine to apply, the corporation must be a sham and exist for no other purpose than as a vehicle for fraud. Under Delaware law, the prominent factors to consider under alter ego analysis are: whether the corporation was adequately capitalized for the corporate undertaking; whether the corporation was solvent; whether dividends were paid, corporate records kept, officers and directors functioned properly, and other corporate formalities were observed; whether the dominant shareholder siphoned corporate funds; and whether in general the corporation simply functioned as a facade for the dominant shareholder. *DDH Aviation, L.L.C. v. Holly, 2005 U.S. Dist. LEXIS 5362 (N.D.Tex. 2005).*

Under Delaware law, numerous factors are pertinent to an alter ego analysis, but no single factor can justify a decision to disregard the corporate entity. These factors include whether the corporation was adequately capitalized for the corporate undertaking; whether the corporation was solvent; whether dividends were paid, corporate records kept, officers and directors functioned properly, and other corporate formalities were observed; whether the dominant shareholder siphoned corporate funds; and whether, in general, the corporation simply functioned as a facade for the dominant shareholder. *Alberto v. Diversified Group, 55 F.3d 201 (5th Cir. 1995).*

Delaware law makes clear that to pierce the corporate veil on an alter ego theory, a plaintiff must demonstrate a misuse of the corporate form or an overall element of injustice or unfairness. This is because Delaware courts of chancery will not disregard the corporate form of a subsidiary unless equity so demands. Although this equitable power is broad and can be invoked whenever justice demands, Delaware courts require a strong case to induce a court of equity to consider two corporations as one. *Alberto v. Diversified Group, 55 F.3d 201 (5th Cir. 1995).*

Seventh Circuit

Piercing the corporate veil. — In Delaware, as in other states, the protection offered shareholders by the corporate form is not absolute. Still, Delaware courts will allow the corporate veil to be pierced only under the most exceptional of circumstances. It may be done only in the interest of justice, when such matters as fraud, contravention of law or contract, public wrong, or where equitable consideration among members of the corporation require it, are involved. *Heyman v. Beatrice Co., 1995 U.S. Dist. LEXIS 4135 (N.D.Ill. 1995).*

Under Delaware law, a court can pierce the corporate veil of an entity where there is fraud or where the entity is in fact a mere instrumentality or alter ego of its owner. Delaware courts consider numerous factors when determining whether separate legal entities such as a parent and its subsidiary should be regarded as alter egos. An alter ego analysis must start with an examination of factors which reveal how the corporation operates and the particular defendant's relationship to that operation. These factors included whether the corporation was adequately capitalized for the corporate undertaking; whether the corporation was solvent; whether dividends were paid, corporate records kept, officers and directors functioned properly, and other corporate formalities were observed; whether the dominant shareholder siphoned corporate funds; and whether, in general, the corporation simply functioned as a facade for the dominant shareholder. No single one of these factors alone is enough to justify disregarding the corporate entity. A combination of factors demonstrating that the subsidiary was misused as a mere instrumentality of the parent is essential. An overall element of injustice or unfairness must always be present, as well. *Heyman v. Beatrice Co., 1995 U.S. Dist. LEXIS 4135 (N.D.Ill. 1995).*

Alter ego analysis. — Under Delaware law, the corporate veil may be pierced where there is fraud or where a subsidiary is in fact a mere instrumentality or alter ego of the parent. Relevant factors in determining whether the subsidiary is merely an instrumentality or alter ego include: (1) whether the dominant shareholders siphoned corporate funds; (2) whether the corporation is a facade for the dominant shareholders; (3) whether the corporation was solvent and adequately capitalized; and (4) whether corporate formalities were followed, including payment of dividends and separate corporate records. Piercing the corporate veil may only be done if it is in the interest of justice when such matters of fraud, contravention of law or contract, public wrong, or where equitable consideration among members of the corporation are involved. *Caccamo v. Greenmarine Holdings L.L.C., 2002 U.S. Dist. LEXIS 12933 (N.D.Ill. 2002).*

An alter ego relationship might exist where a corporate parent exercises complete domination and control over its subsidiary. A subsidiary corporation may also be deemed the alter ego of its corporate parent where there is a lack of attention to corporate formalities, such as where the assets of two entities are commingled and their operations intertwined. Furthermore, fraud or something like it is required. *Binder v. Bristol-Myers Squibb, Co., 184 F. Supp. 2d 762 (N.D.Ill. 2001).*

Acts of subsidiary. — Delaware courts have consistently held that a corporate parent cannot be held liable for the acts of its subsidiary, unless it can be shown that the corporate partner both exercised control and used that control to benefit itself wrongfully in some fashion. *Niki Development Corp. v. HOB Hotel Chicago Partners, L.P., 2003 U.S. Dist. LEXIS 4949 (N.D.Ill. 2003).*

Essentially, two general theories of liability exist under which a parent corporation may be held responsible for the obligations of its subsidiaries: alter ego and agency principles. *Binder v. Bristol-Myers Squibb, Co., 184 F. Supp. 2d 762 (N.D.Ill. 2001).*

Ninth Circuit

The corporate form protects shareholders by limiting their liability and their direct control over the corporation. Indeed, courts are reluctant to disregard the separate existence of related corporations by piercing the corporate veil, and have consistently given substantial weight to the presumption of separateness. The corporate entity may be disregarded only in exceptional circumstances. *McKesson HBOC, Inc. v. New York State Common Retirement Fund, Inc., 339 F.3d 1087 (9th Cir. 2003).*

Alter ego analysis. — The factors to be considered in an alter ego analysis include whether the corporation was adequately capitalized for the corporate undertaking; whether the corporation was solvent; whether dividends were paid, corporate records kept, officers and directors functioned properly, and other corporate formalities were observed; whether the dominant shareholder siphoned corporate funds; and whether, in general, the corporation simply functioned as a facade for the dominant shareholder. *Trans-World Int'l v. Smith-Hemion Productions, 972 F. Supp. 1275 (C.D.Cal. 1997).*

Under the law of Delaware, a court may hold other individuals or entities liable as alter egos for a corporation's debts where those individuals (1) completely dominate and control the corporation, and (2) use the corporate form to perpetrate fraud or something like it. *Occidental Fire & Casualty Co. v. Great Plains Capital Corp., 1997 U.S. App. LEXIS 5333 (9th Cir. 1996).*

Tenth Circuit

Piercing the corporate veil. — There are two bases for disregarding the corporate form: A court can pierce the corporate veil of an entity where there is fraud or where a subsidiary is in fact a mere instrumentality or alter ego of its owner. This second ground for disregarding the separateness of corporate entities is consistent with the general principle that a court may regard a corporate parent as the sole party in interest where equitable considerations require it. *Old Colony Ventures I v. SMWNPF Holdings, 1996 U.S. Dist. LEXIS 18305 (D.Kan. 1996).*

Persuading a Delaware court to disregard the corporate entity is a difficult task. In order to prevail on a claim to pierce the corporate veil and hold the corporation's shareholders liable, a plaintiff must prove that the corporate form causes fraud or similar injustice. *Salt Lake Tribune Publishing Co., LLC v. AT&T Corp., 2002 U.S. Dist. LEXIS 27804 (D.Utah 2002).*

Parent and subsidiary. — Under Delaware law, the separate corporate existences of parent and subsidiary will not be set aside merely on a showing of common management of the two entities, nor on a showing that the parent owned all the stock of the subsidiary. Persuading a Delaware court to disregard the corporate entity is a difficult task. *Old Colony Ventures I v. SMWNPF Holdings, 1996 U.S. Dist. LEXIS 18305 (D.Kan. 1996).*

§ 102. Contents of certificate of incorporation

DELAWARE CASE NOTES — REPORTED

Corporation possesses only those properties which charter of its creation confers upon it, either expressly, or as incidental to its very existence. *Federal Mining & Smelting Co. v. Wittenberg, 15 Del. Ch. 409, 138 A. 347 (1927).*

And by appropriate language in charter, Delaware corporation may deny to itself action permitted by Delaware law. *Weinberg v. Baltimore Brick Co., 34 Del. Ch. 586, 108 A.2d 81 (1954),* aff'd, *35 Del. Ch. 225, 114 A.2d 812 (1955).*

Corporate charter is a contract between the State and the corporation and its stockholders, between the corporation and its stockholders and between the stockholders inter sese. *Morris v. American Pub. Util. Co., 14 Del. Ch. 136, 122 A. 696 (1923).*

A certificate of incorporation evidences a contract between the State and the corporate entity created thereby. *State ex rel. Southerland v. U.S. Realty Imp. Co., 15 Del. Ch. 108, 132 A. 138 (1926); Lawson v. HFC, 17 Del. Ch. 1, 147 A. 312 (1929),* aff'd, *17 Del. Ch. 343, 152 A. 723 (1930).*

A corporate charter, together with the pertinent constitutional and statutory law, forms a contract. *Corbett v. McClintic-Marshall Corp., 17 Del. Ch. 165, 151 A. 218 (1930).*

The charter of a corporation is a contract both between the corporation and the State and the corporation and its stockholders. *Lawson v. HFC, 17 Del. Ch. 343, 152 A. 723 (1930).*

A corporate charter in 1 of its aspects has often been referred to as a contract between the stockholders. *Holland v. National Automotive Fibres, Inc., 22 Del. Ch. 386, 2 A.2d 124 (1938).*

A corporate charter is a contract between the corporation and the State. It also regulates and defines the rights of its stockholders and is, therefore, in some respects a contract between them individually. *Aldridge v. Franco Wyo. Oil Co., 24 Del. Ch. 126, 7 A.2d 753 (1939),* aff'd, *24 Del. Ch. 349, 14 A.2d 380 (1940).*

Charter constitutes contract between corporation and its stockholders, and between shareholders inter sese. *Voege v. American Sumatra Tobacco Corp., 241 F. Supp. 369 (D. Del. 1965).*

Therefore rights of stockholders are contract rights. *Gaskill v. Gladys Belle Oil Co., 16 Del. Ch. 289, 146 A. 337 (1929).*

The rights of stockholders are contract rights and it is necessary to look to the certificate of incorporation to ascertain what those rights are. *Ellingwood v. Wolf's Head Oil Ref. Co., 27 Del. Ch. 356, 38 A.2d 743 (1944).*

Provisions of certificate are upheld if they do not violate statutory or decisional law. — Certificate provisions which facilitate corporate action and to which a stockholder assents by becoming a stockholder are normally upheld by the court unless they contravene a principle implicit in statutory or settled decisional law governing corporate management. *Frankel v. Donovan, 35 Del. Ch. 433, 120 A.2d 311 (1956).*

Or are not against public policy. — A certificate of incorporation may contain any provision with respect to the stock to be issued by the corporation, and the voting rights to be exercised by said stock, that is agreed upon by the stockholders, provided that the provision agreed to is not against public policy. *Ellingwood v. Wolf's Head Oil Ref. Co., 27 Del. Ch. 356, 38 A.2d 743 (1944).*

"Laws of this state" in subsection (b)(1) does not include common law. *Sterling v. Mayflower Hotel Corp., 33 Del. Ch. 293, 93 A.2d 107 (1952).*

Construction rules applicable to charters. — The same rules which govern the construction of statutes, contracts and other written instruments are made use of in construing the provisions and determining the meaning of charters and grants of corporate powers and privileges. *Lawson v. HFC, 17 Del. Ch. 343, 152 A. 723 (1930).*

In interpreting the meaning of charter provisions the same method is applied as that which is followed in interpreting written contracts generally and the instrument should be considered in its entirety, and all of the language reviewed together in order to determine the meaning intended to be given to any portion of it. *Ellingwood v. Wolf's Head Oil Ref. Co., 27 Del. Ch. 356, 38 A.2d 743 (1944).*

Words and phrases of certificate to be given common meaning. — Words and phrases employed by incorporators in drafting a certificate of incorporation should be given their common accepted meaning, unless the context clearly requires otherwise or unless legal phrases having a special meaning are used. But where the language is not expressed with that clarity of expression which permits of but 1 reasonable interpretation, the language must be said to be ambiguous, and resort must be had for assistance to well-established legal rules of construction. *Standard Power & Light Corp. v. Investment Assocs., 29 Del. Ch. 593, 51 A.2d 572 (1947).*

But when provision of certificate attempts to change common law, provision must be strictly construed. *Investment Assocs. v. Standard Power & Light Corp., 29 Del. Ch. 225, 48 A.2d 501 (1946), aff'd, 29 Del. Ch. 593, 51 A.2d 572 (1947).*

Certificate provision cannot deny access to corporate books by stockholders. — Provisions in a corporate charter which permit the directors to deny any examination of the company's records by a stockholder is unauthorized and ineffective. *State ex rel. Cochran v. Penn-Beaver Oil Co., 34 Del. 81, 143 A. 257 (1926).*

As a matter of law, subdivision (b)(7) of this section bars a claim only if there is an unambiguous, residual due care claim and nothing else. *In re Walt Disney Co. Derivative Litig., 825 A.2d 275 (Del. Ch. 2003).*

The protective ambit of subsection (b)(7) of this section does not include acts or omissions undertaken dishonestly such as: breach of the director's duties of loyalty; acts not in good faith involving intentional misconduct or knowing violation of the law; transactions creating improper personal gain for the director; or liability covered under *8 Del. C. § 174. In re Walt Disney Co. Derivative Litig., 825 A.2d 275 (Del. Ch. 2003).*

Limiting liability of directors. — Claims against directors can be dismissed pursuant to certificate of incorporation provisions tracking subsection (b)(7) only where the complaint fails to plead sufficiently that the directors' conduct falls into at least one of the exceptions under which the directors are not afforded the provisions' protection. *O'Reilly v. Transworld Healthcare, Inc., 745 A.2d 902 (Del. Ch. 1999).*

Judicial determination on the issue of entire fairness was a condition precedent to any consideration of damages; defendant directors' request for exculpation should then have been examined in the context of the completed judicial analysis that resulted in a finding of unfairness, and the directors could avoid personal liability for paying monetary damages only if they had established that their failure to withstand an entire fairness analysis was exclusively attributable to the violation of the duty of care. *Emerald Partners v. Berlin, 787 A.2d 85 (Del. 2001).*

Despite a limited liability company agreement containing an exculpatory clause protecting the company's directors from a breach of the duty of care, a motion to dismiss filed by the company and the directors was denied, in a former equity unit holders' suit asserting breach of fiduciary duty, because the former equity unit holders alleged sufficient facts in the complaint to support a claim for disloyal conduct, which was enough to survive the motion to dismiss; the complaint alleged that the approval of a transaction that resulted in the distribution to the company's creditors of 100 percent of available funds — an amount that exceeded the total amount of their claims and which rendered the equity units of the company worthless — was violative because the directors failed to consider alternative transactions that would have provided a better result for the company's equity holders, particularly in light of the alleged fact that the company was in no way insolvent at the time of the transaction. *Blackmore Partners, L.P. v. Link Energy LLC, 864 A.2d 80 (Del. Ch. 2004).*

Provisions purporting to shield directors from liability. — A provision in the certificate of incorporation, authorized by subdivision (b)(7), which purports to protect directors from monetary liability for breaches of fiduciary duty, does not shield directors from liability for equitable fraud. *Zirn v. VLI Corp., 621 A.2d 773 (Del. 1993).*

The legislative history of subdivision (b)(7) indicates that corporations are empowered to shield directors from breaches of the duty of care, not the duty of loyalty or the duty of disclosure. *Zirn v. VLI Corp., 621 A.2d 773 (Del. 1993).*

Claims alleging disclosure violations that do not otherwise fall within any exception are protected by subsection (b)(7) and any certificate of incorporation provision adopted pursuant thereto. *Arnold v. Society for Sav. Bancorp, 650 A.2d 1270 (Del. 1994).*

Where the complaint did not include anything specific about the alleged illegal scheme suggesting that the directors must have known of it, but did plead with particularity what obvious danger signs were ignored or what additional measures the directors should have taken, defendant directors' motion to dismiss for failure to comply with rules of pleading was granted. *In re Baxter Int'l Inc., 654 A.2d 1268 (Del. Ch. 1995).*

The term "monetary damages" in subsection (b)(7) does not mean that directors may be liable for an equitable remedy such as rescissory damages; directors are free from personal financial liability whether monetary damages arise out of legal or equitable theories. *Arnold v. Society for Savs. Bancorp., 678 A.2d 533 (Del. 1996).*

Notwithstanding subsection (b)(7) of this section, monetary damages are available for wrongful conduct going beyond duty of care violations, and equitable remedies not involving monetary damages, such as injunction or corrective disclosure, are also permitted. *Arnold v. Society for Savs. Bancorp., 678 A.2d 533 (Del. 1996).*

A good faith erroneous judgment as to the proper scope or content of required disclosure implicates the duty of care rather than the duty of loyalty and, thus, falls within the protection of subsection (b)(7). *Zirn v. VLI Corp., 681 A.2d 1050 (Del. 1996).*

The shield from liability provided by a provision adopted pursuant to subsection (b)(7) is in the nature of an affirmative defense, and defendants seeking exculpation under such a provision will normally bear the burden of establishing each of its elements. *Emerald Partners v. Berlin, 726 A.2d 1215 (Del. 1999).*

Where the factual basis for a claim solely implicates a violation of the duty of care, the protections afforded by a provision adopted pursuant to subsection (b)(7) may properly be invoked and applied. *Emerald Partners v. Berlin, 726 A.2d 1215 (Del. 1999).*

A breach of loyalty claim requires some form of self-dealing or misuse of corporate office for personal gain. *Graham v. Taylor Capital Group, Inc., 91 F. Supp. 2d 706 (D. Del. 2000).*

To show a breach of the duty of care, plaintiffs must overcome the presumption, known as the business judgment rule, that the defendant directors have acted on an informed basis and in the honest belief they acted in the best interest of the corporation. *Graham v. Taylor Capital Group, Inc., 91 F. Supp. 2d 706 (D. Del. 2000).*

Where plaintiffs averred sufficient evidence to permit the inference that defendants may have knowingly withheld material information from company's shareholders, the court permitted plaintiffs to conduct additional discovery on the issue, as such conduct could be a violation of loyalty which would not be immune under the exculpatory clause. *Graham v. Taylor Capital Group, Inc., 91 F. Supp. 2d 706 (D. Del. 2000).*

Creditor's complaint against a company pleaded non-exculpated fiduciary duty claims with particularity, and these aspects of the fiduciary duty claims survived a motion to dismiss filed by the company and its officers; the creditor's complaint alleged the company's board had taken particular steps to disadvantage the creditor and to frustrate its efforts at collection, including causing the company to issue or pledge billions of shares more than were authorized by its charter, and permitting the controlling shareholder to obtain liens on the company's assets. *Prod. Res. Group, L.L.C. v. NCT Group, Inc., 863 A.2d 772 (Del. Ch. 2004).*

Waiver of shield. — Shield provided by subsection (b)(7) can be waived, but waiver must be clear and unambiguous. *Arnold v. Society for Sav. Bancorp, 650 A.2d 1270 (Del. 1994).*

Increase in majority vote requirements. — In the case of a corporation which has designated a vote of a large portion for corporate action, the majority rule of *8 Del. C. § 242* is supplanted by the designated voting rule contained in the certificate when the stock class to be affected by a proposed amendment is called upon to vote with respect to matters adversely affecting the specified rights to which the voting rule is applicable. *Sellers v. Joseph Bancroft & Sons Co., 23 Del. Ch. 13, 2 A.2d 108 (1938).*

The general rule is that a majority of the votes cast at a stockholders' meeting, provided a quorum is present, is sufficient to elect directors, and if this rule is not to be observed, then the certificate of incorporation provision must not be couched in ambiguous language, rather the language employed must be positive, explicit, clear and readily understandable and susceptible to but 1 reasonable interpretation, which would indicate beyond doubt that the rule was intended to be abrogated. *Standard Power & Light Corp. v. Investment Assocs., 29 Del. Ch. 593, 51 A.2d 572 (1947).*

Rights and attributes of stock are determined by corporate charter. — Because of the contractual nature of a corporate charter, special rights and attributes of the stock issue, pursuant to its provisions, can only be given and defined by that instrument as originally drawn or subsequently amended. *Aldridge v. Franco Wyo. Oil Co., 24 Del. Ch. 126, 7 A.2d 753 (1939), aff'd, 24 Del. Ch. 349, 14 A.2d 380 (1940).*

Authority to issue special kinds of stock must be express in charter. — The authority of a corporation to issue special kinds of stock must be express authority in the charter. *Standard Scale & Supply Corp. v. Chappel, 16 Del. Ch. 331, 141 A. 191 (1928).*

If the stockholders wish to confer special rights upon a given class of stock they must express their wish in the instrument which this section designates as the place for its recordation and that place is the certificate of incorporation. *Gaskill v. Gladys Belle Oil Co., 16 Del. Ch. 289, 146 A. 337 (1929).*

Thus holder of preferred stock must look to charter for his or her rights. — The mere word "preferred" unless it is supplemented by a definition of its significance conveys no special meaning. The holder of preferred stock must therefore refer to the appropriate language of the corporate contract for the ascertainment

Corporations

of his or her rights. *Gaskill v. Gladys Belle Oil Co., 16 Del. Ch. 289, 146 A. 337 (1929).*

At common law all stockholders had equal rights. — At common law, and in the absence of any statute or agreement to the contrary, all stock enjoys equal rights and privileges, and claims for special preferences must be clearly provided by the charter contract. *Penington v. Commonwealth Hotel Constr. Corp., 17 Del. Ch. 394, 155 A. 514 (1931).*

Thus preferences must be made clear in certificate. — Where in the original certificate of incorporation 2 classes of stock were created, a preferred with a par value and a common with no par value, but the preferred was simply called such and any description of preferences was omitted, the word "preferred" meant nothing. *Rice & Hutchins, Inc. v. Triplex Shoe Co., 16 Del. Ch. 298, 147 A. 317 (1929), aff'd, 17 Del. Ch. 356, 152 A. 342 (1930).*

Nothing is to be presumed in favor of preferences attached to stock, and when a corporate charter attempts to confer preferences upon any class of stock provided for by it the same should be expressed in clear language. *Ellingwood v. Wolf's Head Oil Ref. Co., 27 Del. Ch. 356, 38 A.2d 743 (1944).*

No corporation can create preferred stock by bylaw provision. *Gaskill v. Gladys Belle Oil Co., 16 Del. Ch. 289, 146 A. 337 (1929).*

Unanimous stockholder consent said to have authorized the creation of new stock preferences by bylaw action is ineffectual to do so in the face of such statutory provisions as are found in this section and *8 Del. C. § 151. Gaskill v. Gladys Belle Oil Co., 16 Del. Ch. 289, 146 A. 337 (1929).*

Preferred stock may vote unless it is denied in certificate. — Unless a preferred stock is denied the right to vote in the certificate of incorporation, it has such right. *Rice & Hutchins, Inc. v. Triplex Shoe Co., 16 Del. Ch. 298, 147 A. 317 (1929), aff'd, 17 Del. Ch. 356, 152 A. 342 (1930).*

Certificate cannot authorize no par stock without stating number of shares. — The provision in the certificate of incorporation that a certain part of the capital of the incorporation is in shares of common stock without any par value, without stating the number of shares, is unauthorized by any law of the *State. Triplex Shoe Co. v. Rice & Hutchins, Inc., 17 Del. Ch. 356, 152 A. 342 (1930).*

No par value stock attempted to be issued under the certificate of incorporation was invalid stock for the reason that the certificate of incorporation must state the total number of shares authorized. *Triplex Shoe Co. v. Rice & Hutchins, Inc., 17 Del. Ch. 356, 152 A. 342 (1930).*

Cumulating of votes is allowed only when certificate of incorporation so provides. *Chappel v. Standard Scale & Supply Corp., 15 Del. Ch. 333, 138 A. 74 (1927), rev'd on other grounds, 16 Del. Ch. 331, 141 A. 191 (1928).*

Original incorporators have no right to select name either intended or directly calculated to work a wrong. *Philadelphia Trust, Safe Deposit & Ins. Co. v. Philadelphia Trust Co., 123 F. 534 (C.C.D. Del. 1903).*

And equity will enjoin use of confusing trade name. — If by the choice of a name for a corporation it is the manifest purpose of its incorporators to pirate the goodwill and trade name of another, a court of equity ought, when appealed to, afford its protection to the aggrieved party. *Liberty Life Assurance Soc'y v. Heralds of Liberty, Inc., 15 Del. Ch. 369, 138 A. 634 (1927).*

Where the use by a defendant of the name selected by it was calculated to produce confusion in the business of the 2 corporations, mislead the public as to the identity of the corporation intended to be dealt with and also produce unfair competition in business, a preliminary injunction was issued against the use of its corporate name by the defendant. *Liberty Life Assurance Soc'y v. Heralds of Liberty, Inc., 15 Del. Ch. 369, 138 A. 634 (1927).*

So valuable does the law consider the business which an individual has built up and identified with a name, mark or device at the expenditure of much time, labor and money, and which is the sign-manual of a particular quality or superior excellence of product attributable to the producer's efforts, that notwithstanding the general policy of the law which abhors monopoly and favors the freedom of competition, any attempt by another to take away the business by imitating the name of its owner or by simulating the owner's distinctive marks, will be enjoined. *Standard Oilshares, Inc. v. Standard Oil Group, Inc., 17 Del. Ch. 113, 150 A. 174 (1930).*

Danger to reputation and to credit, as well as damage to sales, are among the sorts of injuries which courts will consider in determining whether an injunction should issue against the use by a defendant of a name which confuses its identity with the complainant. *American Radio Stores, Inc. v. American Radio & Television Stores Corp., 17 Del. Ch. 127, 150 A. 180 (1930).*

Thus action of secretary of state in accepting and filing certificate is not conclusive upon the question of distinguishableness of the corporate names. *Drugs Consol., Inc. v. Drug Inc., 16 Del. Ch. 240, 144 A. 656 (1929).*

Only statutory restriction in choice of corporate name is that it must be distinguishable on records in office of secretary of state; the question of distinguishableness would rest largely in the Secretary's discretion. *Standard Oilshares, Inc. v. Standard Oil Group, Inc., 17 Del. Ch. 113, 150 A. 174 (1930); Trans-Americas Airlines v. Kenton, 491 A.2d 1139 (Del. 1985).*

So it must meet standards of unfair competition law. — In a matter involving the rivalry of corporate names, judicial cognizance of the controversy is not amplified by statutory provisions, but rests solely in the field of general law dealing with unfair competition. *Standard Oilshares, Inc. v. Standard Oil Group, Inc., 17 Del. Ch. 113, 150 A. 174 (1930).*

A corporate name being categorized as either a trade name or trademark, more properly the former, the right to the exclusive use of such a name is to be tested by the principles which govern in the law of unfair competition, so that one cannot by the device of a corporate title dignify a nonappropriable common or descriptive name with some sort of exclusiveness. *Standard Oilshares, Inc.*

v. Standard Oil Group, Inc., 17 Del. Ch. 113, 150 A. 174 (1930).

But corporation is entitled to protection from unfair use or simulation of its name. — If an existing corporation is in fact engaged in the business for the conducting of which it was incorporated, it seems to be settled as a general proposition that it is entitled to be protected, even in the absence of statute, in the enjoyment of its corporate name against an unfair use or simulation thereof by another corporation if such use or simulation is misleading and calculated to injure the former's business. *Drugs Consol., Inc. v. Drug Inc., 16 Del. Ch. 240, 144 A. 656 (1929).*

Courts of equity must assume that public will use reasonable intelligence and discrimination with reference to names of corporations with which they are dealing or intend to deal, the same as in cases of individuals bearing the same or similar names. *Drugs Consol., Inc. v. Drug Inc., 16 Del. Ch. 240, 144 A. 656 (1929).*

And court should not pay too meticulous regard to confusion that may arise in minds of ignorant or careless people occasioned by similarity of corporate names. *Delaware Charter Co. v. Delaware Charter Serv. Co., 16 Del. Ch. 246, 144 A. 659 (1929).*

Testing for distinguishableness. — In examining 2 corporate names, the Chancellor is confined to a mere inspection and pronouncing of them for a discovery of their distinguishableness, where there is no evidence showing by actual experience that the public will be misled by similarity into confusing the 2. *Drugs Consol., Inc. v. Drug Inc., 16 Del. Ch. 240, 144 A. 656 (1929).*

"Drugs Consolidated, Inc.," upon the mere pronouncing of it, as well as from the look of it to the eye when printed, is sufficiently different from "Drug Incorporated" as to warrant the view that they are reasonably distinguishable. *Drugs Consol., Inc. v. Drug Inc., 16 Del. Ch. 240, 144 A. 656 (1929).*

There is enough similarity between "Delaware Charter Company" and "Delaware Charter Service Company" to lead to a probable confusion in the mind of the public. This being so, an injunction will issue restraining the defendant from doing business under its corporate name, with sufficient time allowed the defendant to effect a change in its name if desired. *Delaware Charter Co. v. Delaware Charter Serv. Co., 16 Del. Ch. 246, 144 A. 659 (1929).*

Use of name is not required. — Paragraph (1) of subsection (a) of this section removes the necessity of showing actual use in business of the name, a use which many cases dealing with the general law of unfair competition require as a prerequisite to relief in trade name and trademark controversies. *Drugs Consol., Inc. v. Drug Inc., 16 Del. Ch. 240, 144 A. 656 (1929).*

Disclosure obligations of directors under (b)(7). — Directors' disclosure obligations arise out of both the fiduciary duty of care and the duty of loyalty. A claim for breach of the fiduciary duty of disclosure implicates only the duty of care when the factual basis for the alleged violation suggests that the violation was made

as a result of a good faith, but nevertheless, erroneous judgment about the proper scope or content of the required disclosure; however, where a complaint alleges or pleads facts sufficient to support the inference that the disclosure violation was made in bad faith, knowingly or intentionally, the alleged violation implicates the duty of loyalty. *O'Reilly v. Transworld Healthcare, Inc., 745 A.2d 902 (Del. Ch. 1999).*

The court did not dismiss the shareholder's disclosure claim regarding the fair market value of a building under the corporation charter's exculpatory provision for breach of a duty of care in subdivision (b)(7) of this section, since the court determined that the shareholder had properly - led breach of the duty of loyalty which was not exculpated by the provision. *Orman v. Cullman, 794 A.2d 5 (Del. Ch. 2002).*

Exculpation provision in (b)(7) an affirmative defense. — Where plaintiff sufficiently pleaded that the corporate directors' alleged disclosure violations implicated the duty of loyalty, the Exculpation Provision in (b)(7), now known to be an affirmative defense, did not act as a bar as a matter of law. *O'Reilly v. Transworld Healthcare, Inc., 745 A.2d 902 (Del. Ch. 1999).*

Exculpatory clauses in charters. — Although the exculpatory clause that is authorized by this section to be included in charters does not release directors from liability for claims based on breaches of the duty of loyalty or for intentional misconduct done in bad faith, the clause shields directors from liability for claims based on a breach of the duty of care made in good faith. *Graham v. Taylor Capital Group, Inc., 135 F. Supp. 2d 480 (D. Del. 2001).*

Corporation not for profit may be organized without any capital stock, even though such corporations are neither religious, charitable, social, literary, educational or eleemosynary in nature; the test to be applied in each case, when the proposed corporation assumes to organize with no capital stock, is whether it is as a matter of fact conducted for profit. *Read v. Tidewater Coal Exch., Inc., 13 Del. Ch. 195, 116 A. 898 (1922).*

And social organization may be incorporated under nonprofit provisions of subsection (a)(4) of this section and within reasonable and proper limits engage in an activity to make profit. *Southerland ex rel. Snider v. Decimo Club, Inc., 16 Del. Ch. 183, 142 A. 786 (1928).*

Nonprofit corporations may engage in doing business. — A nonprofit or membership corporation may be permitted to engage in business to some extent for this section does not mean to prohibit absolutely and entirely such corporations from doing business. *Southerland ex rel. Snider v. Decimo Club, Inc., 16 Del. Ch. 183, 142 A. 786 (1928).*

As long as profit making does not become principal object. — If the facts and circumstances show a business to be such in character and volume as to indicate that the engaging in business and the making of profits therefrom for the benefit of its members is the principal or 1 of the principal objects of the corporation, rather than a thing which is subordinate and merely incidental to the principal object of its existence, it is reasonable to conclude that the corporation cannot be called one which is organized "not for profit." *Southerland ex rel. Snider v. Decimo Club, Inc., 16 Del. Ch. 183, 142 A. 786 (1928).*

It was not the intention of the General Assembly to allow the easy and liberal provisions of the corporation and revenue statutes applicable to corporations organized not for profit to be enjoyed by corporations whose purpose is in fact to engage in business for profit to such an extent that the desire for profits constitutes a conspicuous object of its existence. *Southerland ex rel. Snider v. Decimo Club, Inc., 16 Del. Ch. 183, 142 A. 786 (1928).*

But charter will be revoked if it abuses right. — Where the evidence shows the defendant, organized as a nonprofit corporation, is engaged in misusing and abusing its corporate powers, privileges, and franchises by seeking as 1 of the principal objects of its existence to make profits for the use of itself and members, a decree of revocation and forfeiture as authorized by *8 Del. C. § 283* must be entered. *Southerland ex rel. Snider v. Decimo Club, Inc., 16 Del. Ch. 183, 142 A. 786 (1928).*

Bylaw in conflict with certificate of incorporation is nullity. *Burr v. Burr Corp., 291 A.2d 409 (Del. Ch. 1972).*

DELAWARE CASE NOTES — UNREPORTED

Commitment to private ordering by charter. — Delaware's corporate statute is widely regarded as the most flexible in the nation because it leaves the parties to the corporate contract (managers and stockholders) with great leeway to structure their relations, subject to relatively loose statutory constraints and to the policing of director misconduct through equitable review. Subdivision (b)(1) of this section and subsection (a) of Section 141 are therefore logically read as important provisions that embody Delaware's commitment to private ordering in the charter. By their plain terms, they are sections of broad effect, which apply to a myriad of issues involving the exercise of corporate power. *Jones Apparel Group v. Maxwell Shoe Co., 2004 Del. Ch. LEXIS 74, No. 365-N (May 27, 2004).*

Exculpation. — The vast majority of Delaware corporations have a provision in their certificate of incorporation that permits exculpation to the extent provided for by subdivision (b)(7) of this section. This provision prohibits recovery of monetary damages from directors for a successful shareholder claim, either direct or derivative, that is exclusively based upon establishing a violation of the duty of due care. The existence of an exculpation provision authorized by subdivision (b)(7) does not, however, eliminate a director's fiduciary duty of care, because a court may still grant injunctive relief for violations of that duty. *In re Walt Disney Co. Derivative Litig., 2005 Del. Ch. LEXIS 113, No. 15452 (Aug. 9, 2005).*

Good faith standard. — Upon long and careful consideration, the chancery court is of the opinion that the concept of intentional dereliction of duty, a conscious disregard for one's responsibilities, is an appropriate (although not the only) standard for determining whether fiduciaries have acted in good faith. Deliberate indifference and inaction in the face of a duty to act is conduct that is clearly disloyal to the corporation. It is the epitome of faithless conduct. *In re Walt Disney Co. Derivative Litig., 2005 Del. Ch. LEXIS 113, No. 15452 (Aug. 9, 2005).*

Bad faith standard. — A corporation can exculpate its directors from monetary liability for a breach of the duty of care, but not for conduct that is not in good faith. To adopt a definition of bad faith that would cause a violation of the duty of care automatically to become an act or omission "not in good faith," would eviscerate the protections accorded to directors by the General Assembly's adoption of subdivision (b)(7) of Section 102. *Brehm*

v. Eisner (In re Walt Disney Co. Derivative Litig.), 2006 Del. LEXIS 307 (Del. June 8, 2006).

Subdivision (b)(7) on its face seems to equate bad faith with intentional misconduct. In re Walt Disney Co. Derivative Litig., 2005 Del. Ch. LEXIS 113, No. 15452 (Aug. 9, 2005).

Charter provision was valid and its plain terms establish the record date for consent solicitation. Both subdivision (b)(1) of this section and subsection (a) of Section 141 of the Delaware Corporations Law (DGCL) provide authority for charter provisions to restrict the authority that directors have to manage firms, unless those restrictions are "contrary to the laws of this State." The charter provision is a valid exercise of authority under those sections and is not contrary to law, in the sense that courts have interpreted that phrase. A consideration of subsection (b) of Section 213's terms and legislative history, as well as of the related statutory section governing consent solicitations, Section 228, reveals that no public policy set forth in the DGCL (or in Delaware's common law of corporations) is contravened by the charter provision at issue. Given the absence of any conflict with a mandatory aspect of Delaware corporate law, the charter provision's restriction on the board's authority to set a record date was valid. *Jones Apparel Group v. Maxwell Shoe Co., 2004 Del. Ch. LEXIS 74, No. 365-N (May 27, 2004).*

Private club may expel members. — Private club may enact governance procedures allowing the expulsion of a member for cause; where the club is organized as a non-stock corporation, the expulsion provision may be contained in the certificate of incorporation or the by-laws. *Capano v. Wilmington Country Club, 2001 Del. Ch. LEXIS 127 (Oct. 31, 2001).*

Limitation of liability. — A charter provision pursuant to subsection (b)(7) can eliminate or limit personal liability of a corporate director for breaches of the duty of care; however, liability for duty of loyalty breaches cannot be eliminated or limited. *Rosser v. New Valley Corp., — A.2d —, 2000 Del. Ch. LEXIS 115 (Del. Ch. Aug. 15, 2000).*

Although subsection (b)(7) generally shields directors from monetary liability for a breach of their duty of due care, it does not shield directors from personal liability for breach of their duty of loyalty. *In re Ply Gem Indus. Inc., 2001 Del. Ch. LEXIS 84 (June 26, 2001).*

Corporate merger with its majority shareholder was found to be unfair and, upon a fairness analysis being conducted, it was concluded that various corporate directors and officers had breached their fiduciary duties of care, good faith and/or loyalty by engaging in nondisclosure of material information, not adequately representing the minority interests, and not disclosing their interested status in the negotiations; accordingly, they were not protected from liability by an exculpatory clause, pursuant to subdivision (b)(7) of this section, although one director that had, at most, only violated the duty of care was insulated from liability. In re Emerging Communs., Inc. S'holders Litig., *2004 Del. Ch. LEXIS 70 (May 3, 2004).*

Provisions purporting to shield directors from liability. — Claims against corporate directors were dismissed for failure to state a claim, except as to one outside director who uniquely benefited from transactions; the remaining directors were protected by the business judgment rule and an exculpation clause in the corporate certificate. *Continuing Creditors' Comm. of Star Telecomms. Inc. v. Edgecomb, 2004 U.S. Dist. LEXIS 25807 (D. Del. Dec. 21, 2004).*

As to an option grant, while the complaint of a committee of unsecured creditors against a company's directors alleged that a compensation consultant was asked to provide an after-the-fact supporting report, the complaint did not allege that previous discussion of the option grant was improper; the directors did not intentionally disregard their responsibilities with regard to this option grant, and the company's 8 Del. C. § 102(b)(7) provision insulated the directors from liability. *Official Comm. of Unsecured Creditors of Integrated Health Servs. v. Elkins, 2004 Del. Ch. LEXIS 122 (Aug. 24, 2004).*

Claims of a committee of unsecured creditors against two corporate directors arising out of the ex post approval of a loan to a former company president survived motions to dismiss, as the directors were denied protection under 8 Del. C. § 102(b)(7); director testified as to knowledge that the former president was receiving the proceeds of the $ 2.088 million loan prior to the compensation committee's approval. *Official Comm. of Unsecured Creditors of Integrated Health Servs. v. Elkins, 2004 Del. Ch. LEXIS 122 (Aug. 24, 2004).*

Standard of review in waste claim. — With respect to an argument that subdivision (b)(7) of this section bars a claim, that argument is without merit where the plaintiffs are seeking rescission of a stock option plan, not monetary damages; with respect to the adoption of a stock option plan, the appropriate standard of care that must be demonstrated to state a claim is waste: to state a claim for waste, the plaintiffs must demonstrate that (1) the directors authorized an exchange that was so one sided that no business person of ordinary, sound judgment could conclude that the corporation has received adequate consideration, and (2) that the transaction served no corporate purpose or was so completely bereft of consideration that such transfer was in effect a gift, and (3) that the alleged facts established a complete failure of consideration. *President & Fellows of Harvard Coll. v. Glancy, 2003 Del. Ch. LEXIS 25 (Mar. 21, 2003).*

Exculpatory provision did not cure breach of duty of loyalty. — Defendants' motion to dismiss a shareholder's action on the basis of an exculpatory provision in the corporation's certificate of incorporation was denied, as the provisions in the certificate of incorporation could limit the liability of directors for money damages for breaches of fiduciary duties, but such provisions could not exculpate a director for the breach of the duty of loyalty to the corporation or its stockholders under subdivision (b)(7) of this section. *Cal. Pub. Employees Ret. Sys. v. Coulter, 2002 Del. Ch. LEXIS 144 (Dec. 18, 2002).*

Exculpation from personal liability. — Under 8 Del. C. § 102(b)(7), directors may be exculpated from personal liability for monetary damages arising out of their breach of their duty of care; if the loyalty or good faith of a director is in doubt, however, the protection of 8 Del. C. § 102(b)(7) is not available. *Gentile v. Rossette, 2005 Del. Ch. LEXIS 160 (Del. Ch. Oct. 20, 2005).*

It was premature to determine whether an exculpatory charter provision protected a controlling shareholder and certain other directors from liability on motion to dismiss for failure to state a claim; it would be necessary to determine, first, under the entire fairness rule, whether violations of the duties of loyalty and good faith were in fact implicated and then, only at that point, could there be a determination as to whether (if the directors were at worst culpable for negligence) the exculpatory provision could be applied. *In re LNR Prop. Corp. S'holders Litig., 2005 Del. Ch. LEXIS 171 (Del. Ch. Nov. 4, 2005).*

Applicability of preemptive rights language. — Language concerning preemptive rights in a corporation's certificate of incorporation (stating that "no stockholder shall have any preemptive right to subscribe to or purchase any issue of stock or other securities of the corporation, or any treasury stock or other treasury securities") applied only to common law preemptive rights and not to contractually granted preemptive rights; thus, the corporation's board had the authority to issue preferred stock with preemptive rights, pursuant to 8 Del. C. § 102(b)(3). *Benihana of Tokyo, Inc. v. Benihana, Inc., 2005 Del. Ch. LEXIS 191 (Del. Ch. Dec. 8, 2005).*

Failure to plead with particularity. — Shareholder's derivative action for corporation to recover overpaid officer bonuses was dismissed; the shareholder failed to plead with particularity why the board members were unprotected by the corporation's 8 Del. C. § 102(b)(7) provision and could personally liable for wasteful inactions such that a Ch. Ct. R. 23.1 demand on them would be futile. *Laties v. Wise, 2005 Del. Ch. LEXIS 196 (Del. Ch. Dec. 14, 2005).*

Timing of exculpation defense. — Although in the chancery court's opinion, the better view is that an exculpatory charter provision is best viewed as a statutorily-authorized immunity, our Supreme Court has viewed it somewhat differently, terming it "in the nature of an affirmative defense." Given that reality, it is important for defendants to raise the exculpation clause

Corporations

defense early in a case. Here, the defendants waited until after the plaintiffs had shaped their trial plans to inject this defense into the case. That was prejudicial. *In re PNB Holding Co. S'holders Litig.*, 2006 Del. Ch. LEXIS 158 (Aug. 18, 2006).

There remained a genuine issue of material fact whether majority shareholder/director and other director were entirely fair as provided in 8 Del. C. § 102(b)(7), when the majority shareholder/director arranged for, and the other director approved, not only the conversion of the majority shareholder/director's debt to shares at one-tenth of the employee stock option conversion price and about one-fifteenth of the price under the merger that was concluded six months later. *Gentile v. Rossette*, 2005 Del. Ch. LEXIS 160 (Del. Ch. Oct. 20, 2005).

Director's approval insufficient validation. — Assuming that a director was independent and disinterested, since the director was one-half of a board and not a majority of the board, the director's approval of the corporation's merger was insufficient to validate the controlling shareholder/director's self-interested transaction under 8 Del. C. § 102(b)(7). *Gentile v. Rossette*, 2005 Del. Ch. LEXIS 160 (Del. Ch. Oct. 20, 2005).

Merger information statement was insufficient to validate the controlling shareholder/director's self-interested transactions under 8 Del. C. § 102(b)(7), because the statement did not provide adequate disclosures of the self-interested transactions; that omission also raised questions as to whether the directors had exercised the degree of care required by 8 Del. C. § 102(b)(7). *Gentile v. Rossette*, 2005 Del. Ch. LEXIS 160 (Del. Ch. Oct. 20, 2005).

Under 8 Del. C. § 102(b)(7), the minority shareholders had every right to expect the other director to try to find out whether the controlling shareholder/director had negotiated any significant specific favorable terms for an exclusive benefit in the merger. *Gentile v. Rossette*, 2005 Del. Ch. LEXIS 160 (Del. Ch. Oct. 20, 2005).

Personal liability not found. — In short, the evidence adduced at trial shows that director attempted to fulfill his responsibilities as the sole member of the special committee, but failed to do so effectively in part as a result of carelessness and negligence, through which he failed to fulfill his duty of due care, and in part because of the manipulative efforts of the controlling stockholder and its agents to squeeze out the minority at an unfair price. In other words, director did nothing during the merger process to cover himself in glory, or merit commendation. But it is equally true that negligent or even gross negligent conduct does not equate to disloyalty or bad faith, and nothing in the record in this case suggests that director intentionally conspired to engage in a process that would create the illusion, but avoid the reality, of arm's length bargaining to obscure the true purpose of benefitting holding company at the expense of the minority. As such, holding director personally liable in this case would be fundamentally inconsistent with the purpose and language of subdivision (b)(7) of this section. *Gesoff v. IIC Indus.*, 2006 Del. Ch. LEXIS 91 (Del. May 18, 2006).

Plaintiff's allegations fall into the bad faith exception to certificate of incorporation exculpatory clause. Plaintiff alleges that the defendants here acted with knowing and deliberate indifference when they stopped examining delinquent accounts. Further, he alleges that the defendants consciously disregarded red flags when the defendants paid no attention to the warnings allegedly contained in the auditor's and SEC's letters. Plaintiff has sufficiently pled breach of the duties of loyalty and good faith. As a result, the certificate of incorporation cannot operate to insulate the defendants from a breach of fiduciary duty claim. Consequently, the claim will proceed on the merits. *Buckley v. O'Hanlon*, 2007 U.S. Dist. LEXIS 22211 (D. Del. March 28, 2007).

CASE NOTES — OTHER STATES

Illinois

A corporate charter is a contract having a three-fold nature, it operates to create rights and duties between the state and the corporation, between the corporation and its shareholders, and among the shareholders themselves. *McCormick v. Statler Hotels Delaware*, 30 Ill. 2d 86, 195 N.E.2d 172 (1963).

Massachusetts

It would be permissible for the certificate of incorporation to require an 80% vote for approval of a merger under the authority of §102(b)(4) as opposed to the simple majority vote required by §251(c). This would simply be calling for "the vote of a larger portion of the stock" than is required by other parts of the chapter. However, the plaintiff argued that the statutory language — "larger portion of the stock" — means a fixed percentage greater than a majority and that §102(b)(4) cannot be read to permit a shifting vote requirement. *Seibert v. Milton Bradley Company*, 380 Mass. 656, 405 N.E.2d 131 (1980).

Issuance of stock without required consideration. — Delaware law appears to draw a distinction between a case where the issuance of a company's stock itself violates a provision of Delaware's Constitution, its corporation law, or the company's own corporate charter, and one where the company has the power and authority to issue stock but does so without receiving the required consideration. *Biotrack, Inc. v. Muni*, 12 Mass. L. Rep. 244 (Super. 2000).

Missouri

Three-way contract. — The law of Delaware supplies the terms of a contract among shareholders inter sese and among the shareholders and corporations. The corporate structure has been described as a three-way contract, representing the relations among shareholders, between shareholders and corporations, and between corporations and the state. The shareholders may be said to have constructively agreed to the terms of the Delaware law, including the restrictions upon the forum for the enforcement of appraisal rights. *Wilson v. Celestial Greetings, 896 S.W.2d 759 (Mo. App. 1995).*

New York

Authorized sale. — Del. Corp. Law § 64-a provides for the sale of the assets and franchises of a corporation when and as authorized by the affirmative vote of the holders of a majority of the stock issued and outstanding, or when authorized by the written consent of the majority thereof. The addendum provision allows the company to require in its certificate for said action the vote or written consent of a larger proportion of the stockholders. *Wattley v. National Drug Stores Corp., 122 Misc. 533, 204 N.Y.S. 254 (Sup. 1924).*

Pennsylvania

Principal place of business. — The Delaware laws required that the certificate of incorporation should set forth the name of the county, and the city, town, or place within the county in which the principal office or place of business of the corporation is located. Such laws required also that every corporation should maintain a principal office or place of business in the state. The certificates of incorporation of the corporations in question stated the location of their principal offices but were silent in respect of their places of business. The principal place of business of a corporation is where its actual business is conducted or transacted. *Wojdak v. Greater Philadelphia Cablevision, Inc., 550 Pa. 474, 707 A.2d 214 (1998).*

Delaware law does not require a corporation's certificate of incorporation to authorize a corporation to repurchase shares of its own stock. *Wyatt v. Phillips, 2004 Phila. Ct. Com. Pl. LEXIS 89 (2004).*

Inequitable action does not become permissible simply because it is legally possible. *Jewelcor Management, Inc. v. Thistle Group Holdings, Co., 2002 Phila. Ct. Com. Pl. LEXIS 79 (2002).*

CASE NOTES — FEDERAL

First Circuit

Subdivision (b)(7). — By its terms, Del. Code Ann. tit. 8, § 102(b)(7) insulates individual corporate directors from personal liability for money damages unless they have breached the duty of good faith and loyalty, violated Del. Code Ann. tit. 8, § 174, or authorized a transaction in which they derive improper personal benefit. *Growe v. Bedard, 2004 U.S. Dist. LEXIS 23746 (D.Me. 2004).*

Although a Del. Code Ann. Tit. 8, § 102(b)(7), provision does not operate to defeat the validity of a plaintiff's claim on the merits, it can operate to defeat the plaintiffs ability to recover monetary damages. Accordingly, if the shareholder complaint only alleges a duty of care violation, the entry of a monetary judgment following a finding of unfairness would be uncollectable. Consequently, a trial pursuant to the entire fairness standard of review would serve no useful purpose. Thus, under those specific circumstances, when the presumption of the business judgment rule has been rebutted in the shareholder complaint solely by successfully alleging a duty of care violation, the director defendants do not have to prove entire fairness to the trier of fact, because of the exculpation afforded to the directors by the § 102(b)(7) provision inserted by the shareholders into the corporation's charter. *Growe v. Bedard, 2004 U.S. Dist. LEXIS 23746 (D.Me. 2004).*

When entire fairness is the applicable standard of judicial review, injury or damages becomes a proper focus only after a transaction is determined not to be entirely fair. A fortiori, the exculpatory effect of a Del. Code Ann. Tit. 8, § 102(b)(7) provision only becomes a proper focus of judicial scrutiny after the directors' potential personal liability for the payment of monetary damages has been

established. Accordingly, although a § 102(b)(7) charter provision may provide exculpation for directors against the payment of monetary damages that is attributed exclusively to violating the duty of care, even in a transaction that requires the entire fairness review standard ab initio, it cannot eliminate an entire fairness analysis by the court. *Growe v. Bedard, 2004 U.S. Dist. LEXIS 23746 (D.Me. 2004).*

Limitation on reach of exculpatory provision. — Unless a breach of good faith or loyalty is made out on the part of a director, an exculpatory provision in the articles will prevent a plaintiff from recovering money damages from that director and, by extension, obviates the need for said director to prove entire fairness to the trier of fact, even if a breach of the duty of care is made out. However, where a question is raised with regard to loyalty, an exculpatory provision will not justify a summary disposition. *Growe v. Bedard, 2004 U.S. Dist. LEXIS 23746 (D.Me. 2004).*

The Delaware law that allows a certificate of incorporation to include a provision limiting or eliminating personal liability of the directors explicitly excludes acts or omissions not in good faith or which involve intentional misconduct or a knowing violation of the law. *Landy v. D'Alessandro, 316 F. Supp. 2d 49 (D.Mass. 2004).*

Second Circuit

The rights of preferred stockholders are governed by the charter, and resolutions adopted by the board of directors pursuant to authority vested in it thereby. These have the legal effect of a contract defining the rights and liabilities as between the preferred stockholders and the corporation. *In re Schenker, 1963 U.S. Dist. LEXIS 9993 (S.D.N.Y. 1963).*

Corporations

Rules of construction. — The interpretation of language in a certificate of incorporation of a Delaware corporation is viewed as a contract among shareholders, so that the general rules of contract interpretation should apply to its terms. In interpreting the rights accorded to preferred shareholders, the courts must apply a strict construction, without presuming in favor of the preferred shares because preferences are regarded by Delaware courts as in derogation of the common law. The certificate of incorporation should be construed in its entirety, and all of the language reviewed together in order to reconcile all of the certificate's provisions so as to determine the meaning intended to be given to any portion of it. *Lacos Land Co. v. Lone Star Industries, Inc., 141 B.R. 815 (Bankr. S.D.N.Y. 1992).*

Subdivision (b)(7). — As authorized by Delaware corporate law, a certificate of incorporation can eliminate directors' personal liability for breaches of their fiduciary duties. To overcome this protection, plaintiff must demonstrate that his or her claim against the director defendants falls outside of § 102(b)(7) by showing bad faith, intentional misconduct, or a knowing violation of the law on the part of the defendants. *Karpus v. Borelli, 2004 U.S. Dist. LEXIS 21429 (S.D.N.Y. 2004).*

Del Code Ann. tit. 8, § 102(b)(7) allows a corporation to limit or eliminate directors' liability for monetary damages for breach of fiduciary duty by including an exculpatory provision in its certificate of incorporation. However, the statute is strictly limited, prohibiting indemnification for any breach of the director's duty of loyalty to the corporation or its stockholders, for acts or omissions not in good faith or involving intentional misconduct or for any transaction for which the director derived an improper personal benefit. *In re Trump Hotels Shareholder Derivative Litig., 2000 U.S. Dist. LEXIS 13550 (S.D.N.Y. 2000).*

Del. Code Ann. tit. 8, § 102(b)(7) allows amendment to corporate charters to exonerate directors from monetary liability for breaches of fiduciary duty of care not involving bad faith, intentional misconduct, improper payment of dividends, improper stock purchase or redemption, or breach of duty of loyalty. Where the factual basis for a claim solely implicates a violation of the duty of care, the protections of such a charter provision may properly be invoked and applied. *Official Committee of the Unsecured Creditors v. Investcorp, S.A., 137 F. Supp. 2d 502 (S.D.N.Y 2001).*

Del. Code Ann. tit. 8, § 102(b)(7) (2005) authorizes corporations to adopt a charter provision shielding directors from the payment of monetary awards based on breaches of the duty of care. *Pereira v. Farace, 413 F.3d 330 (2d Cir. 2005).*

Standing. — That the equity committee is neither a "stockholder" nor a "director" within the meaning of Delaware General Corporation Law tit. 8, § 211(c) does not detract from its standing in this court for an order directing the debtor to conduct an annual shareholders' meeting in accordance with its corporate bylaws. *Official Committee of Equity Sec. Holders of Lone Star Industries,*

Inc., v. Lone Star Industries, Inc., 138 B.R. 420 (Bankr. S.D.N.Y. 1992).

Director disclosure. — Delaware does not prohibit a provision in the corporation's charter stating that interested directors did not have to disclose their interest or refrain from participation in settlement negotiations and agreements. *Piccard v. Sperry Corp., 48 F. Supp. 465 (S.D.N.Y. 1943).*

Proof of amendment. — Under Delaware law, the amendment of fundamental corporate documents by implication, acquiescence, or any informal method must be established by clear proof of a definite and uniform custom or usage, not in accord with the bylaws regularly adopted, and by acquiescence therein. *Management Techs. v. Morris, 961 F. Supp. 640 (S.D.N.Y. 1997).*

Applicable claims. — Although the statute does not mention creditors specifically, its plain terms apply to all claims belonging to the corporation itself, regardless of whether those claims are asserted derivatively by stockholders or by creditors. *Pereira v. Farace, 413 F.3d 330 (2d Cir. 2005).*

Third Circuit

Consideration of demand. — Under Delaware law, when a certificate of incorporation exempts directors from liability, the risk of liability does not disable them from considering a demand fairly unless particularized pleading permits the court to conclude that there is a substantial likelihood that their conduct falls outside the exemption. *Amalgamated Bank v. Yost, 2005 U.S. Dist. LEXIS 1280 (E.D.Pa. 2005).*

Amendment by course of conduct. — Generally, Delaware law holds that corporate charters and bylaws are interpreted using the same principles used to interpret statutes and contracts, and, therefore, when a court finds that a bylaw's language is unambiguous, it does not proceed to interpret it or to search for the parties' intent behind the bylaw. Notwithstanding this general rule, however, bylaws may be amended or established by custom or by acquiescence in a course of conduct by those authorized to enact them. Usually the course of conduct relied on to effect the change must have continued for such a period of time as will justify the inference that the stockholders had knowledge thereof and impliedly consented thereto. *Franklin v. SKF USA, Inc., 126 F. Supp. 2d 911 (E.D.Pa. 2001).*

Merger and consolidation. — It is elementary that the substantial elements of the merger and consolidation provisions of the General Corporation Law are written into every corporate charter. The shareholder has notice that the corporation whose shares he or she has acquired may be merged with another corporation if the required majority of the shareholders agree. He or she is informed that the merger agreement may prescribe the terms and conditions of the merger, the mode of carrying it into effect, and the manner of converting the shares of the constituent corporations into the shares of the resulting corporation. A well-understood meaning of the word "convert" is to alter in form, substance, or quality. Substantial rights of shareholders, as is well known, may include rights in respect of voting, options, preferences, and dividends. The average intelligent mind must be held to know that dividends may accumulate on preferred stock, and that in the event of a merger of the corporation issuing the stock with another corporation, the various rights of shareholders, including the right to dividends on preference stock accrued but unpaid, may, and perhaps must, be the subject of reconcilement and adjustment. *Langfelder v. Universal Laboratories, Inc., 163 F.2d 804 (3d Cir. 1947).*

Fourth Circuit

Limitation on reach of exculpatory provision. — While Delaware courts have allowed dismissal of a complaint for failure to make a pre-suit demand when the pleadings alleged solely a violation of the fiduciary duty of care on the grounds that the claim was barred by the corporation's exculpatory provision in its charter, indemnification provisions in corporate governing documents issued pursuant to Del. Code Ann. tit. 8, § 102(b)(7) cannot be invoked to bar duty of loyalty and good-faith claims. Thus, where the complaint alleges well-pleaded facts that implicate the duty of loyalty and good faith, as well as the duty of care, the indemnification provision will not subject the complaint to dismissal. *Miller v. U.S. Foodservice, Inc., 361 F. Supp. 2d 470 (D.Md. 2005).*

Under the standard for liability based on a director's failure to act and Delaware law, a director need not have acted intentionally to harm the corporation in order to be liable for breach of the duty to exercise appropriate attention to potentially illegal corporate activities. Behavior other than intentional conduct can subject a director to liability. To the extent that recklessness involves a conscious disregard of a known risk, it can be argued that such an approach is not one taken in good faith and thus could not be liability exempted under Del. Code Ann. tit. 8, § 102(b)(7). *Miller v. U.S. Foodservice, Inc., 361 F. Supp. 2d 470 (D.Md. 2005).*

Waiver clause. — Under Delaware law, when the validity of a waiver clause in a certificate of incorporation is not contested and where the plaintiffs allege only a breach of the duty of care, with no claims of bad faith, intentional misconduct, knowing violation of law, or any other conduct for which the directors may be liable, the waiver provision may be considered and applied in deciding a motion to dismiss. *Miller v. U.S. Foodservice, Inc., 361 F. Supp. 2d 470 (D.Md. 2005).*

While it is true that duty of care claims alleging only grossly negligent conduct are precluded by a Del. Code Ann. tit. 8, § 102(b)(7) waiver provision, it appears that duty of care claims based on reckless or intentional misconduct are not. *Miller v. U.S. Foodservice, Inc., 361 F. Supp. 2d 470 (D.Md. 2005).*

Business judgment analysis. — Under Delaware law, corporate officers and directors owe their corporation the fiduciary duties of due care, good faith, and loyalty. The duty of care requires that corporate officers and directors exercise an informed business judgment to make decisions reasonably determined to be in the best interests of the corporation and its shareholders. Officers and directors are protected from liability for their decisions under the rebuttable presumption of the business judgment rule, that is, that in making a business decision the directors of a corporation acted on an informed basis, in good faith and in the honest belief that the action taken was in the best interests of the company. The business judgment rule focuses on the process by which directors and officers make informed decisions, not on the substance of the decision itself. *Miller v. U.S. Foodservice, Inc., 361 F. Supp. 2d 470 (D.Md. 2005).*

While generally courts do not second-guess corporate decisionmaking and directors and officers enjoy the presumption of the business judgment rule, the rule can be overcome by allegations of gross negligence. *Miller v. U.S. Foodservice, Inc., 361 F. Supp. 2d 470 (D.Md. 2005).*

Failure to act. — There is a standard for liability based on a director's failure to act. When a loss eventuates not from a decision but, from unconsidered inaction, only a sustained or systematic failure of the board to exercise oversight—such as an utter failure to attempt to assure a reasonable information and reporting system exists—will establish the lack of good faith that is a necessary condition to liability. This is a "demanding test" to meet. Absent grounds to suspect deception, neither corporate boards nor senior officers can be charged with wrongdoing simply for assuming the integrity of employees and the honesty of their dealings on the company's behalf. However, corporate boards cannot satisfy the standard without assuring themselves that information and reporting systems exist in the organization that are reasonably designed to provide to senior management and to the board itself timely, accurate information sufficient to allow management and the board, each within its scope, to reach informed judgments concerning both the corporation's compliance with law and its business performance. It is important that the board exercise a good faith judgment as to whether its reporting systems are "adequate" to assure that the board could satisfy its responsibility. *Miller v. U.S. Foodservice, Inc., 361 F. Supp. 2d 470 (D.Md. 2005).*

Information and reporting systems. — There is a requirement that corporate directors and officers ensure that an adequate information and reporting system exists. *Miller v. U.S. Foodservice, Inc., 361 F. Supp. 2d 470 (D.Md. 2005).*

It is an elementary fact that the provision of relevant and timely information is an essential predicate for satisfaction of a board of director's supervisory and monitoring role. In other words, first and foremost, directors and officers must assure that a reporting system exists which is "in concept and design adequate" to provide appropriate and timely information to them so that they may satisfy their monitoring responsibility. Therefore, questions as to whether a director had grounds to suspect wrongdoing by other officers or directors presume the existence of an adequate reporting system. *Miller v. U.S. Foodservice, Inc., 361 F. Supp. 2d 470 (D.Md. 2005).*

Adequacy of consideration. — Directors are only liable for corporate waste claims when they authorize an exchange that is so one sided that no business person of ordinary, sound judgment could conclude that the corporation has received adequate consideration. Generally, courts grant broad discretion to directors in matters of executive compensation. Accordingly, if reasonable, informed minds might disagree on the question, then in order to preserve the wide domain over which knowledgeable business judgment may safely act, a reviewing court will not attempt to itself evaluate the wisdom of the bargain or the adequacy of the consideration. *Miller v. U.S. Foodservice, Inc., 361 F. Supp. 2d 470 (D.Md. 2005).*

Fifth Circuit

Del. Code Ann. tit. 8, § 102(b)(7) permits a corporation to limit or eliminate directors' liability for monetary damages for breach of fiduciary duty via inclusion of an exculpatory provision in a certificate of incorporation. *Cohn v. Nelson, 375 F. Supp. 2d 844 (E.D.Miss. 2005).*

Sixth Circuit

Under Delaware law, courts can pierce the corporate veil of an entity where there is fraud or where a subsidiary is in fact a mere instrumentality or alter ego of its owner. Fraud is not an absolute prerequisite for piercing the corporate veil. *General Electric Co. v. Advance Stores Co., 285 F. Supp. 2d 1046 (N.D.Ohio 2003).*

Waiver-of-liability provisions contained in a corporate charter are authorized pursuant to Del. Code Ann. tit. 8, § 102(b)(7). *Salsitz v. Nasser, 208 F.R.D. 589 (E.D. Mich. 2002).*

When the validity of a waiver of liability provision is not contested and the factual basis for the claims implicates only a breach of the duty of care, the waiver may properly be considered and applied in deciding a motion to dismiss for failure to make a pre-suit demand. *McCall v. Scott, 239 F.3d 808 (6th Cir. 2001).*

Del. Code Ann. tit. 8, § 102(b)(7) allows a corporation to amend its certificate of incorporation to protect its directors against claims for gross negligence. When the validity of such a provision is not contested and the factual basis for the claims implicates only a breach of the duty of care, the waiver may properly be considered and applied in deciding a motion to dismiss for failure to make a pre-suit demand. *McCall v. Scott, 250 F.3d 997 (6th Cir. 2001).*

Seventh Circuit

Parent and subsidiary. — A corporation is an entity distinct from its shareholders, even if they consist solely of a single individual or corporation. Allegations of total ownership, common management, and common officers and directors are insufficient to warrant disregard of the corporate form between a corporate subsidiary and its parent. This is particularly true when the subsidiary corporation has a function and purpose peculiar to it which it fulfills, and corporate formalities between parent and subsidiary are respected. Absent a showing of fraud or that the subsidiary is the alter ego of the parent, the Delaware courts will not disregard the corporate fiction between subsidiary and parent. *Pinellas County v. Great American Industrial Group, Inc., 1991 U.S. Dist. LEXIS 17517 (N.D.Ill. 1991).*

Creditor control. — Under the control and instrumentality theory, a plaintiff seeking to pierce the corporate veil need not show an active intent to deceive on the part of those controlling the corporation if the corporation has been ignored as a distinct legal entity and treated as a mere instrumentality. In particular, a corporate creditor may hold another corporate creditor liable for the corporation's debts to it if the second corporate creditor assumed actual participatory total control of the debtor corporation. The observation of corporate formalities is one important factor in making this determination. Where the party controlling the corporation is another creditor, the creditor must have been active in the formation of the corporation, and not merely an arm's length extender of credit, and the corporation must have been operated merely as an arm of the creditor's business. *Pinellas County v. Great American Industrial Group, Inc., 1991 U.S. Dist. LEXIS 17517 (N.D.Ill. 1991).*

The statute eliminates personal liability of the directors for damages for breaches of the duty of care. *In re Abbott Labs. Derivative Shareholders Litigation, 325 F.3d 795 (7th Cir. 2003).*

Limitation on reach of exculpatory provision. — Directors' fiduciary duties include not only the duty of care but also the duties of loyalty and good faith; although duty-of-care claims alleging only grossly negligent conduct are precluded by the Del. Code. Ann. tit. 8, § 102(b)(7) waiver provision, duty-of-care claims based on reckless or intentional misconduct are not. To the extent that recklessness involves a conscious disregard of a known risk, it could be argued that such an approach is not one taken in good faith and thus could not be liability exempted under the statute. Under Delaware law, the duty of good faith may be breached where a director consciously disregards his duties to the corporation, thereby causing its stockholders to suffer. A certificate of incorporation which exempts the directors from personal liability, a conscious disregard of known risks, which conduct, if proven, cannot have been undertaken in good faith; thus, claims are not precluded by the company's § 102(b)(7) waiver provision. *In re Abbott Labs. Derivative Shareholders Litigation, 325 F.3d 795 (7th Cir. 2003).*

Ninth Circuit

Construction with other law. — It is not improper for the court to consider the effect of a Del. Code Ann. tit. 8, § 102(b)(7) exculpatory provision on a Fed. R. Civ. P. 12(b)(6) motion to dismiss. *In re Sagent Technology, Inc, 278 F. Supp. 2d 1079 (N.D.Cal 2003).*

Judicial notice. — The certificate of incorporation of a Delaware corporation is a publicly filed document, and as such, can be judicially noticed. *McMichael v. United States Filter Corp., 2001 U.S. Dist. LEXIS 3918 (C.D.Cal. 2001).*

Exculpatory clauses. — Under Delaware law, corporations are authorized to adopt exculpatory clauses regarding directors' duty of care. *In re McKesson HBOC,*

Inc. Securities Litigation, 126 F. Supp. 2d 1248 (N.D.Cal. 2000).

Directors are protected against general claims for breach of the duty of care when pursuant to state law a corporation adopts a director protection provision into its articles of incorporation. However, if directors breach the duty of care intentionally, knowingly, or in bad faith, the director protection statutes will not shield them from personal liability. Furthermore, when directors breach the duty of loyalty or act in bad faith they are not shielded by the director protection statutes. Therefore, to successfully plead breach of fiduciary duty against the directors of a corporation, a plaintiff must sufficiently plead breach of the duty of loyalty, bad-faith performance of duties, or intentional or knowing breach of the duty of care. *Grassmueck v. Barnett, 281 F. Supp. 2d 1227 (W.D.Wash. 2003).*

Tenth Circuit

Judicial notice. — Delaware courts have taken judicial notice of a corporate exculpatory charter provision where the defendant has presented a certified copy of such a provision on file with the secretary of state. *Grogan v. O'Neil, 292 F. Supp. 2d 1282 (D.Kan. 2003).*

Eleventh Circuit

Veto right. — Under the Delaware Corporation Law, the holders of the preferred stock had the right as a class to vote upon and veto any proposed amendment of the charter which would alter or change the preferences, special rights, or powers of the preferred so as to affect the preferred adversely, or which would increase or decrease the amount of preferred or the par value. *Penfield v. Davis, 105 F. Supp. 292 (N.D. Ala. 1952).*

District of Columbia Circuit

Voidable shares. — Under Delaware law, shares of corporate stock that have not been initially authorized in full compliance with the requirements of the Delaware General Corporate Law, prior to ratification, are merely voidable, not void, because only voidable acts would be open to ratification. *CarrAmerica Realty Corp. v. Kaidanow, 321 F.3d 165 (D.C. Cir. 2003).*

§ 103. Execution, acknowledgment, filing, recording and effective date of original certificate of incorporation and other instruments; exceptions

DELAWARE CASE NOTES — REPORTED

Date stamp on filing. — Subdivision (c)(3) of this section mandated that the Secretary of State's office certify the date and hour of a filing, a requirement that clearly contemplated a good faith effort to record the actual time at which a document was filed; the Secretary of State's practice of permitting parties to ask for a particular filing date, and of honoring their requests, conflicted with the plain language of the statute and created the potential for abuse. *Liebermann v. Frangiosa, 844 A.2d 992 (Del. Ch. 2002).*

DELAWARE CASE NOTES — UNREPORTED

"Shall" in the context of § 103(c)(3) is not mandatory, but rather directory. *Harvard Bus. Servs. v. Coyle, 1997 Del. Super. LEXIS 70 (1997).*

Soliciting advice of Bank Commissioner. — Secretary's policy of soliciting the advice of the Bank Commissioner with regard to proposed filing of certificates of incorporation using the word "bank" in their corporate names is an example of the appropriate careful exercise of discretion, especially given the prohibition of 8 Del. C. § 126 that denies the power to engage in the business of banking to corporations organized under the DGCL. *Harvard Bus. Servs. v. Coyle, 1997 Del. Super. LEXIS 70 (1997).*

Secretary of State did not have a clear or obvious legal duty to accept for filing the restated certificate of incorporation with the word "bank" in its name, especially over the objections of the Bank Commissioner. *Harvard Bus. Servs. v. Coyle, 1997 Del. Super. LEXIS 70 (1997).*

CASE NOTES — OTHER STATES

Indiana

Effective date of merger. — Under Delaware law, a corporate merger with a foreign corporation becomes effective when adopted, approved, certified, executed, and acknowledged by each of the constituent corporations in accordance with the laws under which it is formed, and is evidenced by an agreement of merger or a certificate of merger filed with the secretary of state. The statute provides the method for a merger. Corporate instruments are effective upon the filing date. *Keybank National Association v. Mochael, 737 N.E.2d 834 (Ind 2000).*

CASE NOTES — FEDERAL

Second Circuit

Dissolution under Delaware law is authorized by an appropriate vote of the stockholders and becomes effective upon the proper filing of a certificate of dissolu-

tion. *New York v. Panex Industries, Inc., 1996 U.S. Dist. LEXIS 9418 (W.D.N.Y. 1996).*

Attestation. — The Delaware General Corporation Law does not, in any instance, require attestation of a business document as a requisite to the validity of that document as a corporate act. It specifies attestation as one means of affirming the authenticity of a document only in the case of organic corporate instruments, which are required to be filed with the Secretary of State. *Stewart* *Capital Corp. v. Andrus, 468 F. Supp. 1261 (S.D.N.Y. 1979).*

§ 104. Certificate of incorporation; definition

CASE NOTES — OTHER STATES

Illinois

A corporate charter is a contract having a three-fold nature, it operates to create rights and duties between the state and the corporation, between the corporation and its shareholders, and among the shareholders themselves. *McCormick v. Statler Hotels Delaware, 30 Ill. 2d 86, 195 N.E.2d 172 (1963).*

Missouri

Three-way contract. — The law of Delaware supplies the terms of a contract among shareholders inter sese and among the shareholders and corporations. The corporate structure has been described as a three-way contract, representing the relations among shareholders, between shareholders and corporations, and between corporations and the state. The shareholders may be said to have constructively agreed to the terms of the Delaware law, including the restrictions upon the forum for the enforcement of appraisal rights. *Wilson v. Celestial Greetings, 896 S.W.2d 759 (Mo. App. 1995).*

§ 105. Certificate of incorporation and other certificates; evidence

CASE NOTES — OTHER STATES

Minnesota

A filed certificate of incorporation is prima facie evidence of validity. *Erickson v. Horing, 2002 Minn. App. LEXIS 1137 (2002).*

§ 106. Commencement of corporate existence

DELAWARE CASE NOTES — REPORTED

The corporation is an entity distinct from its shareholders even if its stock is wholly owned by 1 person or corporation. *Scott-Douglas Corp. v. Greyhound Corp., 304 A.2d 309 (Del. Super. Ct. 1973).*

§ 107. Powers of incorporators

DELAWARE CASE NOTES — REPORTED

Promoters have right to organize company and to make profit in sale to company of property they brought, even though they secured it for the company, provided it is worth the stock given for it, and provided also they disclose the profit they will make, and the company, with full knowledge of all the facts, consented before the rights of the complainants intervened. In such case there was no secret or undisclosed profit. *Henderson v. Plymouth Oil Co., 16 Del. Ch. 347, 141 A. 197 (1928).*

Or to sell entire share capital to outside parties. — If the promoters themselves take the entire share capital of the corporation and then sell the shares to outside parties, there is no fraud upon the corporation, and no basis of complaint by it, no matter what profits the promoters may derive from the transaction. If there is any fraud in subsequent sale of shares the cause of action arising therefrom is personal to the purchasers. The matter is between these purchasers and their vendor, and no cause of action results to the corporation therefrom. *Henderson v. Plymouth Oil Co., 16 Del. Ch. 347, 141 A. 197 (1928).*

But there is fiduciary relationship. — If the promoters were under fiduciary obligations to a proposed corporation at the moment they acquired properties or rights to property which the corporation was to take over, and the circumstances are such as to show that they were acting in the capacity, actual or quasi, of agents purchasing for and on behalf of the proposed corporation, the rules prevail which are applicable to the dealings of an agent for his or her principal. The promoters in such case are bound to account according to the settled principles of law attaching to that relationship. *Henderson v. Plymouth Oil Co., 15 Del. Ch. 231, 136 A. 140 (1926), aff'd, 16 Del. Ch. 347, 141 A. 197 (1928).*

Strictly speaking, the promoters of a corporation are not trustees, but they, nevertheless, occupy a fiduciary or quasi trust relation toward the corporation, when organized, and prior thereto toward those who have subscribed for its stock. *Bovay v. H.M. Byllesby & Co., 25 Del. Ch. 1, 12 A.2d 178 (1940).*

There is a fiduciary relationship between the promoters of a corporation and the corporation itself. Those who undertake to form a new corporation, to procure for it the capital through which it may carry out the purpose or purposes for which it was formed, are necessarily charged with the duty to act in good faith in dealing with it. *Gladstone v. Bennett, 38 Del. Ch. 391, 153 A.2d 577 (1959).*

And promoters would be liable for secret profits. — If there are existing stockholders at the time the promoters deal with the corporation, and the transaction is such as to give to the promoters a secret profit, the corporation at that time being in their control, then the promoters are liable for such profits. *Henderson v. Plymouth Oil Co., 15 Del. Ch. 40, 131 A. 165 (1925).*

A corporation may recover secret profits from a promoter where there are, at the time of the contract, any stockholders or subscribers for stock who are without knowledge of the profits made by the promoter. *Nye Odorless Incinerator Corp. v. Felton, 35 Del. 236, 162 A. 504 (1931).*

Incorporators will not be permitted to benefit by any secret profit which they may receive at the expense of the corporation or of its members. Where the corporation deals with a promoter with full knowledge of all facts, this transaction will not be set aside since there is no secret or undisclosed property. *Gladstone v. Bennett, 38 Del. Ch. 391, 153 A.2d 577 (1959).*

But promoter may sell his or her property to corporation. — A promoter owes a fiduciary duty to the corporation which he or she procures to be organized, the obligations of which continue to rest upon the promoter so long as the corporation is in his or her control. An owner of property who wishes to form a corporation to take over the property is not restrained by the obligations of that duty from making the sale. The owner of property may "innocently" organize a company to buy it at an advance. *Henderson v. Plymouth Oil Co., 15 Del. Ch. 40, 131 A. 165 (1925).*

And need not sell it for price he paid for it. — If a person is the owner of property and promotes a corporation to buy it while under his or her control, such person need not, as in the case of an agent acting for his or her principal, turn the property over to the corporation at exactly the same figure he or she gave for it, or for nothing if he or she was so fortunate as to have received it as a gift. *Henderson v. Plymouth Oil Co., 15 Del. Ch. 40, 131 A. 165 (1925).*

As long as the promoter sells it to corporation for what it is fairly worth. — If a person receives valuable property, and then turns it over to a corporation of his or her creation and under his or her control for a large sum but for no more than it is fairly worth, he or she taking the stock and it being his or her property in fair exchange, he or she need not forfeit all his or her interest in it if he or she fails to disclose to every future stockholder he or she invites into it that it cost him or her nothing. In such case, while he or she has secured a profit, it has not been at the expense of the corporation nor any of its stockholders. *Henderson v. Plymouth Oil Co., 15 Del. Ch. 40, 131 A. 165 (1925).*

Promoter's contract antecedent to corporate existence does not bind the corporation. — Where a promoter of a corporation makes a promise, amounting to a contract obligation, that the corporation when formed will do certain things, there is no statute in this State which fastens the obligation of a promoter's antecedent contract on the corporation. *Stringer v. Electronics Supply Corp., 23 Del. Ch. 79, 2 A.2d 78 (1938).*

But corporation may adopt contract made by its promoters for its benefit, even though such contract antedates its existence. *Commissioners of Lewes v. Breakwater Fisheries Co., 13 Del. Ch. 234, 117 A. 823 (1922), aff'd, 128 A. 920 (Del. 1923).*

Corporation is competent to adopt and ratify an agreement made by the organizer and promoter in contemplation of its organization. *In re Acadia Dairies, Inc., 15 Del. Ch. 248, 135 A. 846 (1927).*

Clear duty rests on promoters to provide corporation with independent board of directors; a board, which, in dealing with such promoters, will act for the best interest of the corporation, and will not be dominated or controlled by them. *Bovay v. H.M. Byllesby & Co., 25 Del. Ch. 1, 12 A.2d 178 (1940).*

DELAWARE CASE NOTES — UNREPORTED

Where plaintiff incorporator named an initial board of directors comprised of himself or herself and defendant, his or her later attempt to name himself or herself as sole director of the incorporation was invalid, and any actions he or she took as sole director of the corporation were equally invalid. *Grant v. Mitchell, 2001 Del. Ch. LEXIS 23 (Feb. 23, 2001).*

CASE NOTES — FEDERAL

Second Circuit

Appointment of president. — Incorporators have no power to appoint a president and fix his or her salary before a board of directors is appointed. *Kenyon v. Holbrook Microfilming Service, Inc., 155 F.2d 913 (2d Cir. 1946).*

§ 108. Organization meeting of incorporators or directors named in certificate of incorporation

DELAWARE CASE NOTES — UNREPORTED

Single incorporator can hold meeting with himself or herself. — Although it is odd to think of a single incorporator holding a meeting with himself or herself, this section does not preclude a single incorporator from meeting with himself or herself to make such a decision, and the first sentence of subsection (a) explicitly contemplates a meeting of "the incorporator;" therefore, it is not inconceivable to think that a single incorporator could decide on the initial board of directors but fail to document that decision immediately. *Grant v. Mitchell, 2001 Del. Ch. LEXIS 23 (Feb. 23, 2001).*

§ 109. Bylaws

DELAWARE CASE NOTES — REPORTED

Bylaw which is repugnant to statute must always give way to the statute's superior authority. *Kerbs v. California E. Airways, Inc., 33 Del. Ch. 69, 90 A.2d 652 (1952).*

As must one in conflict with charter. — A bylaw that restricts or alters the voting power of stock of a corporation as established by the law of its charter is void. *Brooks v. State ex rel. Richards, 26 Del. 1, 79 A. 790 (1911); Gaskill v. Gladys Belle Oil Co., 16 Del. Ch. 289, 146 A. 337 (1929).*

Where, at a special meeting of a corporate board, a bylaw provision was adopted but the charter was never amended to change the terms, the bylaw provision is in conflict with the charter and it is therefore void. *Prickett v. American Steel & Pump Corp., 253 A.2d 86 (Del. Ch. 1969).*

A bylaw in conflict with the certificate of incorporation is a nullity. *Burr v. Burr Corp., 291 A.2d 409 (Del. Ch. 1972); Centaur Partners, IV v. National Intergroup, Inc., 582 A.2d 923 (Del. 1990).*

Bylaw cannot unreasonably restrain power of stock transfer. — A corporate bylaw which unreasonably restrains the power of a stockholder to transfer his or her stock will be held invalid as against public policy. *Lawson v. HFC, 17 Del. Ch. 343, 152 A. 723 (1930).*

Nor can bylaw completely restrict stockholder's right to inspect corporate records. — A bylaw giving stockholders the right to inspect corporate books only at directors' discretion is unreasonable and unlawful. *State ex rel. Brumley v. Jessup & Moore Paper Co., 24 Del. 379, 77 A. 16 (1910).*

But stockholders can amend bylaws to give themselves exclusive right to create additional directors and to elect them, and no amending of the certificate of incorporation is required. *Richman v. DeVal Aerodynamics, Inc., 40 Del. Ch. 389, 183 A.2d 569 (1962).*

Bylaws must be adopted by method prescribed by bylaws. — If bylaw provides directors can adopt new bylaws only at regular meetings and they adopt bylaws at a meeting other than a regular meeting, then the adopted bylaws are invalid. *Moon v. Moon Motor Car Co., 17 Del. Ch. 176, 151 A. 298 (1930).*

Stockholders can act on stockholder's proposal to amend bylaws. — Stockholders of a Delaware corporation can act validly on a stockholder's proposal to amend bylaws. *Securities & Exch. Comm'n v. Transamerica Corp., 163 F.2d 511 (3d Cir. 1947), cert. denied, 332 U.S. 847, 68 S. Ct. 351, 92 L. Ed. 418 (1948).*

Existence of corporate bylaws may be established by custom, or by acquiescence in course of conduct by those authorized to enact them; and this principle equally applies to an amendment. *In re Ivey & Ellington, Inc., 28 Del. Ch. 298, 42 A.2d 508 (1945).*

Unanimous consent by the stockholders to a regular course of action, inconsistent with the bylaws regularly adopted, may, therefore, justify the conclusion that an amendment thereto was intended. *In re Ivey & Ellington, Inc., 28 Del. Ch. 298, 42 A.2d 508 (1945).*

Ordinarily, a corporate bylaw may be amended by implication and without any formal action being taken by clear proof of a definite and uniform custom or usage, not in accord with the bylaws regularly adopted, and by acquiescence therein; but usually the course of conduct relied on to effect the change must have continued for such a period of time as will justify the inference that the stockholders had knowledge thereof and impliedly consented thereto. *In re Ivey & Ellington, Inc., 28 Del. Ch. 298, 42 A.2d 508 (1945).*

Courts have long held that bylaws may be amended or established by custom or by acquiescence in a course of conduct by those authorized to enact them. *In re Osteopathic Hosp. Ass'n, 41 Del. Ch. 369, 195 A.2d 759 (1963).*

Effect of certificate of incorporation. — Although bylaws are a contract between the corporation and its shareholders, where company's certificate of incorporation expressly authorized the directors to amend or repeal the bylaws without obtaining shareholder approval, the board had the power to amend the bylaws unilaterally. *Kidsco Inc. v. Dinsmore, 674 A.2d 483 (Del. Ch. 1995).*

Insulation of directors. — The fact that charter or bylaw provisions may technically permit an action contemplated by the directors does not automatically insulate directors against scrutiny of purpose. *Petty v. Penntech Papers, Inc., 347 A.2d 140 (Del. Ch. 1975).*

Corporate structure of foundation. — Where members were responsible for the foundation's creation and continued endowment and electing its directors, the members' power was intended to resemble that of stockholders, and as a result, the foundation's members could not be ousted by the very directors whom they had elected, for any other interpretation would render the foundation's corporate structure fundamentally unstable. *Oberly v. Kirby, 592 A.2d 445 (Del. 1991).*

CASE NOTES — OTHER STATES

Illinois

Construction. — A corporation's bylaws are construed according to the rules used to interpret statutes, contracts, and other written instruments. Pursuant to those rules, if the bylaw's language is unambiguous, the bylaw will be construed as written and the court need not resort to extrinsic aids to determine the corporation's intent. *Truserv Corporation v. Bess Hardware and Sports, Inc., 346 Ill. App. 3d 194, 804 N.E.2d 611 (2004).*

New York

By-laws are unenforceable as contravening applicable Delaware law where they preclude trustees of a not-for-profit corporation from binding themselves in advance to elect a particular individual to the board because the trustees have a duty to use their best judgment in filling a vacancy on the board of trustees as of the time the need arises. *Nesbeda v. Edna McConnell Clark Foundation, 266 A.D.2d 72, 698 N.Y.S.2d 627 (1999).*

Pennsylvania

Inequitable action does not become permissible simply because it is legally possible. *Jewelcor Management, Inc. v. Thistle Group Holdings, Co., 2002 Phila. Ct. Com. Pl. LEXIS 79 (2002).*

CASE NOTES — FEDERAL

First Circuit

Quorum. — Under Delaware law, a corporation's bylaws may specify the requisites of a quorum. Any action purportedly taken at a meeting lacking a quorum is a nullity. The court may, moreover, inquire into the underlying facts to determine the existence of a quorum despite the records of that meeting. But the parties challenging the validity of the meeting must prove the lack of quorum in the face of a presumption of validity. *Feldman v. Detarando, 1980 U.S. Dist. LEXIS 14272 (D.Mass 1980).*

Second Circuit

Proof of amendment. — Under Delaware law, the amendment of fundamental corporate documents by implication, acquiescence, of any informal method must be established by clear proof of a definite and uniform custom or usage, not in accord with the bylaws regularly adopted, and by acquiescence therein. *Management Techs. v. Morris, 961 F. Supp. 640 (S.D.N.Y. 1997).*

Third Circuit

Rules of construction. — Generally, Delaware law holds that corporate charters and bylaws are interpreted using the same principles used to interpret statutes and contracts, and, therefore, when a court finds that a bylaw's language is unambiguous, it does not proceed to interpret it or to search for the parties' intent behind the bylaw. Notwithstanding this general rule, however, bylaws may be amended or established by custom or by acquiescence in a course of conduct by those authorized to enact them. Usually the course of conduct relied on to effect the change must have continued for such a period of time as will justify the inference that the stockholders had knowledge thereof and impliedly consented thereto. *Franklin v. SKF USA, Inc., 126 F. Supp. 2d 911 (E.D.Pa. 2001).*

Proof of amendment custom. — Clearly, one who contends that a written bylaw has been amended by custom inconsistent therewith has the burden of establishing the existence of such a custom. *Franklin v. SKF USA, Inc., 126 F. Supp. 2d 911 (E.D.Pa. 2001).*

Seventh Circuit

Delaware corporate law permits a board of directors to adopt corporate bylaws before the corporation has received payment for its stock. *Heffernan v. Pacific Dunlop GNB Corp., 1993 U.S. Dist. LEXIS 5 (N.D.Ill. 1993).*

§ 111. Jurisdiction to interpret, apply, enforce or determine the validity of corporate instruments and provisions of this title

DELAWARE CASE NOTES — UNREPORTED

Legislative intent. — In order to "interpret, apply, enforce or determine the validity" of any "instrument, document or agreement," it is necessary first to determine the existence of that instrument, document or agreement. That determination may be less or more difficult depending on the facts of each case. When drafting § 111, however, the Delaware General Assembly did not intend that a plaintiff seeking redress petition one court to determine the existence of an agreement and then petition yet another court to interpret, apply, enforce or determine the validity of the same agreement. Stated differently, the General Assembly does not entrust the Court of Chancery with the jurisdiction to "interpret, apply, enforce or determine the validity" of any "instrument, document or agreement" by which a corporation creates options but then deprive it of the jurisdiction to determine the existence of the same. Defendant's reading of the statute is counter-intuitive in the context of Delaware corporate law where the General Assembly and the judicial branch seek to efficiently and expeditiously resolve corporate conflicts. Defendant cannot divest this court of jurisdiction by simply restating the ultimate issue in this case. *Cornerstone Brands, Inc. v. O'Steen, 2006 Del. Ch. LEXIS 172 (Sept. 20, 2006).*

Certificates of merger. — Chancery Court of Delaware had subject matter jurisdiction under *8 Del. C. § 111(b)* over a case for specific performance as to the redemption of corporate notes following a merger, because the resolution of the case required the Court to interpret and apply the Delaware General Corporation Law, *8 Del. C. § 101* et seq.; moreover, the Court had subject matter jurisdiction under *8 Del. C. § 111(a)*, because the Court was to interpret, apply, enforce, or determine the validity of the provisions of a certificate of merger. *Law Debenture Trust Co. v. Petrohawk Energy Corp., 2007 Del. Ch. LEXIS 113 (Del. Ch. Aug. 1, 2007).*

Dismissal without prejudice. — In a case where plaintiffs sought declarations under 8 Del. C. §§ 111 and 225, relating to the corporation's board elections, plaintiffs' motion for dismissal without prejudice under Del. Ch. Ct. R. 41(a)(2) was granted because the court found that the interests of justice were best served if the

dismissal was without prejudice. *Messina v. Klugiewicz, 2004 Del. Ch. LEXIS 47 (Apr. 30, 2004).*

Failure to state a claim. — In a case where plaintiffs sought a summary declaration relating to the corporation's bylaws, the case was dismissed without prejudice for failure to state a claim because this section did not provide a cause of action for plaintiffs; in addition, under 8 Del. C. § 229, the director had no grounds to sue for the corporation's failure to provide the director with 60 days' notice of proposed bylaws changes because the director attended the relevant meetings, but did not attend for the sole purpose of objecting to lack of notice. *Messina v. Klugiewicz, 2004 Del. Ch. LEXIS 47 (Apr. 30, 2004).*

Declaration as to a proposed corporate merger. — Corporation was entitled to summary judgment in its declaratory judgment action because the corporation's preferred stockholders were not entitled to a series vote on a proposed merger and, under the business judgment rule, the corporation's board did not breach any fiduciary duty in recommending the proposed merger and financing proposal. *WatchMark Corp. v. ARGO Global Capital, LLC, 2004 Del. Ch. LEXIS 168 (Nov. 4, 2004).*

CASE NOTES — FEDERAL

Third Circuit

Rules of construction. — Generally, Delaware law holds that corporate charters and bylaws are interpreted using the same principles used to interpret statutes and contracts, and, therefore, when a court finds that a bylaw's language is unambiguous, it does not proceed to interpret it or to search for the parties' intent behind the bylaw. Notwithstanding this general rule, however, bylaws may be amended or established by custom or by acquiescence in a course of conduct by those authorized to enact them.

Usually the course of conduct relied on to effect the change must have continued for such a period of time as will justify the inference that the stockholders had knowledge thereof and impliedly consented thereto. *Franklin v. SKF USA, Inc., 126 F. Supp. 2d 911 (E.D.Pa. 2001).*

Proof of amendment custom. — Clearly, one who contends that a written bylaw has been amended by custom inconsistent therewith has the burden of establishing the existence of such a custom. *Franklin v. SKF USA, Inc., 126 F. Supp. 2d 911 (E.D.Pa. 2001).*

Subchapter II.
Powers

§ 121. General powers

DELAWARE CASE NOTES — REPORTED

Corporations are given express specific and general powers. — A Delaware corporation, except perhaps in those instances when mandatory restrictive language is deliberately incorporated into its charter, is liberally endowed by the general corporation law of Delaware not only with express specific powers but also with express general powers. *Leibert v. Grinnell Corp., 41 Del. Ch. 340, 194 A.2d 846 (1963).*

By certificate of incorporation or law. — A corporation possesses all the powers conferred upon it not only by its certificate of incorporation, but as well those which

the act itself conferred upon all corporations created under it. *Davis v. Louisville Gas & Elec. Co., 16 Del. Ch. 157, 142 A. 654 (1928).*

No power or authority can be conferred upon a corporation by its charter, which was not provided by the statute under which it was created. *Lawson v. HFC, 17 Del. Ch. 343, 152 A. 723 (1930).*

Board of directors have no power conferred upon them by this section to remove one of their own number. *Bruch v. National Guar. Credit Corp., 13 Del. Ch. 180, 116 A. 738 (1922).*

CASE NOTES — OTHER STATES

Massachusetts

Under Delaware law, a corporate entity does not owe a fiduciary duty to shareholders. *Gerzof v. Cignal Global Communications, Inc., 13 Mass. L. Rep. 429 (Super. 2001).*

§ 122. Specific powers

DELAWARE CASE NOTES — REPORTED

One corporation may act as agent for another corporation. *Philadelphia Storage Battery Co. v. RCA, 22 Del. Ch. 211, 194 A. 414 (1937), aff'd, 6 A.2d 329 (Del. 1939).*

Corporation can only make an affidavit by natural person as its agent. *John R. Hitchens, Inc. v. Phillips Packing Co., 42 Del. 393, 35 A.2d 502 (1943).*

Corporation can only act through its agents, employees, and servants. — Corporations like people, may sue or be sued but since a corporation is an artificial entity and not itself a living being, it can act only through its servants, agents or employees. *Guthridge v. Pen-Mod, Inc., 239 A.2d 709 (Del. Super. Ct. 1967).*

Directors cannot make gifts except as authorized by this section. *Taussig v. Wellington Fund, Inc., 187 F. Supp. 179 (D. Del. 1960), cert. denied, 374 U.S. 806, 83 S. Ct. 1693, 10 L. Ed. 2d 1031 (1962).*

All other gifts require unanimous stockholder approval. — Gifts of corporate assets, except as authorized by this section, require unanimous stockholder approval. *Frankel v. Donovan, 35 Del. Ch. 433, 120 A.2d 311 (1956).*

Corporate gifts may be made solely for public welfare or for charitable, scientific or educational purposes but there is also an accepted corporate rule that majority stockholders have no power to give away corporate property against the protest of the minority. *Frankel v. Donovan, 35 Del. Ch. 433, 120 A.2d 311 (1956).*

Test to be applied in passing on validity of gift is that of reasonableness, a test in which the provisions of the Internal Revenue Code pertaining to charitable gifts by corporations furnish a helpful guide. *Theodora Holding Corp. v. Henderson, 257 A.2d 398 (Del. Ch. 1969)Kahn v. Sullivan, 594 A.2d 48 (Del. 1991).*

This section contains no limiting language as to donee or size of gift and must be construed to authorize any reasonable corporate gift of a charitable or educational nature. *Theodora Holding Corp. v. Henderson, 257 A.2d 398 (Del. Ch. 1969).*

Corporate payments in lieu of taxes, where reasonably incidental to the carrying on of the company business for its benefit, are permissible corporate disbursements as "donations for the public welfare." *Kelly v. Bell, 254 A.2d 62 (Del. Ch. 1969), aff'd, 266 A.2d 878 (Del. 1970).*

Compensation levels. — Generally, directors have the sole authority to determine compensation levels, and this determination is protected by the presumption of the business judgment rule in the absence of a showing that the business judgment rule does not apply because of a disabling factor. *Haber v. Bell, 465 A.2d 353 (Del. Ch. 1983).*

Adoption of "poison pill" plan, by which shareholders receive the right to be bought out by the corporation at a substantial premium on the occurrence of a stated triggering event, was consistent with the directors' fiduciary duty in facing a takeover threat perceived as detrimental to corporate interests. *Revlon, Inc. v. MacAndrews & Forbes Holdings, Inc., 506 A.2d 173 (Del. 1985).*

Corporation within its powers may contract without use of corporate seal the same as a natural person, unless the seal is required by the corporate charter or by statute. *Peyton-du Pont Sec. Co. v. Vesper Oil & Gas Co., 33 Del. 124, 131 A. 566 (1925).*

Corporation having corporate seal may adopt pro hac vice, for particular transaction, any other seal, or any device bearing semblance to a seal, as its own corporate seal, but the law does require that the seal or device, whatever it may be, shall be used and intended as the seal of the corporation, and not of the individual. *Rabinovich v. Liberty Morocco Co., 32 Del. 426, 125 A. 346 (1924).*

Instrument under corporate seal is admissible in evidence and presumptively binds corporation. *Italo-Petro. Corp. of Am. v. Hannigan, 40 Del. 534, 14 A.2d 401 (1940).*

Presence of seal is prima facie evidence of authority of affix. — When the common seal of a corporation appears to be affixed to an instrument and the signature of a proper officer is proved or admitted, the court is bound to presume that the officer did not exceed his or her authority, and the seal itself is prima facie evidence that it was affixed by proper authority. *Conine v. Junction & B.R.R., 8 Del. 288 (1866).*

It is implied from the corporate seal that the corporation, through its directors or those empowered to conduct the corporate business, authorized the president, secretary or other official acting in the particular case to make the contract evidenced by the instrument on which the seal is placed, and the instrument thus sealed, in the absence of opposing proof, is to be regarded as the binding act and deed of the corporation. *Italo-Petro. Corp. of Am. v. Hanningan, 40 Del. 534, 14 A.2d 401 (1940).*

Burden of showing that corporate seal is wrongfully used rests upon the party objecting to it. *Conine v. Junction & B.R.R., 8 Del. 288 (1866).*

It is jury question whether presumption of corporate act is rebutted. — In an action on notes executed on behalf of a corporation by its president, the question whether its president had authority to bind the corporation by executing the notes was for the jury if evidence to overcome the presumption of the execution by the corporate seal was, in fact, introduced. *Italo-Petro. Corp. of Am. v. Hanningan, 40 Del. 534, 14 A.2d 401 (1940).*

Corporation answers complaint under its corporate seal, that being the most solemn form of authentication which it is capable of adopting. *Hopper v. Fesler Sales Co., 11 Del. Ch. 255, 100 A. 791 (1917).*

Until legally dissolved, corporation is absolute owner of all of its property. *Wilmington Trust Co. v.*

Corporations

Wilmington Soc'y of Fine Arts, 27 Del. Ch. 243, 34 A.2d 308 (1943), aff'd, *28 Del. Ch. 449, 43 A.2d 476 (1945).*

Deed with seal is presumed valid. — In the absence of some notice to the contrary, a deed which appears to be regularly executed and to which the corporate seal is affixed, is ordinarily presumed to be a valid and binding corporate conveyance. Under such circumstances, the burden of showing lack of authority to execute that instrument is on the person attacking it. *Bethel M.E. Church v. Dagsboro Council No. 30 Junior Order United Am. Mechanics, 27 Del. Ch. 64, 30 A.2d 273 (1943).*

Misnomer of corporate grantee of property. — The inclusion or exclusion of the word "the," where it is, or is not properly, a part of the corporate name, will not vitiate a grant of lands either to or by the corporation. *Elbert v. Wilmington Turngemeinde, 30 Del. 355, 107 A. 215 (1919).*

Failure to perform duty by nonresident officer. — A corporation existing under the laws of this state cannot escape liability for failure to perform a legal duty by showing that the duty is that of nonresident officers. *State ex rel. Brumley v. Jessup & Moore Paper Co., 24 Del. 379, 77 A. 16 (1910).*

Immunity. — The State waived sovereign immunity in connection with its management of a school for juvenile delinquents where the school corporation had the power to sue and be sued. *Masten v. State, 626 A.2d 838 (Del. Super. Ct. 1991),* aff'd, *616 A.2d 1214 (Del. 1992).*

CASE NOTES — OTHER STATES

Alaska

Lawsuit capacity. — A corporation organized and under the law of Delaware has the capacity to sue or be sued, then it can be sued or sue anywhere, and if it has not any capacity to sue or be sued under the law of its domicile, it cannot sue or be sued anywhere. *University of Alaska v. Thomas Architectural Prods., 907 P.2d 448 (Alaska 1995).*

Illinois

Disregarding the corporate fiction. — In Delaware, piercing the corporate veil is an equitable remedy and is considered only in the court of chancery, Delaware's court of equity. As a general rule, the corporation is an entity distinct from its shareholders, even if its stock is wholly owned by one corporation. However, the corporate fiction may be disregarded to prevent fraud. Sole ownership of stock and common directors and officers between parent and subsidiary are only some of the factors to be considered by the courts in determining whether or not the corporate fiction should be disregarded and the shareholders held liable. It requires a strong case to induce a court to consider two corporations as one on account of one owning all the capital stock of the other. *Retzler v. The Pratt and Whitney Company, 309 Ill. App. 3d 906, 723 N.E.2d 345, 243 Ill. Dec. 313 (1999).*

CASE NOTES — FEDERAL

Third Circuit

Limitations on power of delegation. — An officer broadly charged with managing the affairs of a corporation impliedly possesses the authority to appoint subordinate agents under his control to act on behalf of the corporation. Nevertheless, the power of delegation is not without limits, and in determining such limits, the focus is on whether the delegated authority involves ministerial functions or acts that require the exercise of discretion by the sub-agent. As the very term management connotes, however, corporate officers and subordinate agents must be afforded some level of discretion when faced with the demands of supervising a modern corporation. Thus, given the necessities of the case and usage, corporate law recognizes that many discretionary acts will be carried out by officers and other subordinates. The critical factors are often the complexity of the corporation, the intent of the board, and the corporation's implied course of conduct. *Schoonejongen v. Curtiss-Wright Corp., 143 F.3d 120 (3d Cir. 1998).*

§ 123. Powers respecting securities of other corporations or entities

DELAWARE CASE NOTES — REPORTED

Purchasing corporation under this section has status of stockholder of the corporation whose shares it has purchased and nothing more. *Orzeck v. Englehart, 41 Del. Ch. 361, 195 A.2d 375 (1963).*

If corporation has power to hold stock, it has incidental power to vote it notwithstanding its certificate of incorporation confers no special power to that end. *Bouree v. Trust Francais, 14 Del. Ch. 332, 127 A. 56 (1924).*

Special and legal interest in stock. — This section does not merely relate to an absolute and unqualified ownership of stock, but also to a special and legal interest. *Aldridge v. Franco Wyo. Oil Co., 24 Del. Ch. 126, 7 A.2d 753 (1939),* aff'd, *24 Del. Ch. 349, 14 A.2d 380 (1940).*

Shares owned by corporation and not its stockholders. — Where shares of 1 corporation are owned by another corporation, they are owned by the other corporation and not its stockholders. *Bird v. Wilmington Soc'y of Fine Arts, 28 Del. Ch. 449, 43 A.2d 476 (1945).*

Corporation identities do not merge solely by reason of purchase by one of all of other's stock. *Orzeck v. Englehart, 41 Del. Ch. 361, 195 A.2d 375 (1963).*

Valid purchase of stock under this section need not comply with merger sections. *Orzeck v. Englehart, 41 Del. Ch. 361, 195 A.2d 375 (1963).*

For it has independent legal significance. — A valid purchase of stock under the authority of this section has independent legal significance unrelated to the merger sections. *Orzeck v. Englehart, 41 Del. Ch. 361, 195 A.2d 375 (1963)*.

Control of corporation's stock does not constitute "doing business" in a state. — Even direct domination and control of a domestic corporation by a foreign corporation by stock acquisition does not result in the conclusion that the foreign corporation is doing business in the state of the domestic corporation. *Mazzotti v. W.J. Rainey, Inc., 31 Del. Ch. 47, 77 A.2d 67 (1950)*.

§ 124. Effect of lack of corporate capacity or power; ultra vires

DELAWARE CASE NOTES — REPORTED

Assignee's action dismissed. — In an action by an assignee against a director, investment fund, and partner alleging that a corporation's stock redemption plan violated *8 Del. C. § 160*, and that the redemption transactions were fraudulent transfers of property under *11 U.S.C. § 548*, the motions to dismiss under *Fed. R. Civ. P. 12(b)(6)* filed by the director, investment fund, and partner were granted where (1) this section did not provide the assignee with a remedy for violations of *8 Del. C. § 160* because the assignee was not a stockholder, (2) *8 Del. C. § 174* did not provide the assignee with a cause of action against the director, investment fund, and partner because they redeemed their stock in good faith, (3) the assignee did not have an implied remedy against shareholders for the corporation's violation of *8 Del. C. § 160*, (4) the assignee lacked standing under *11 U.S.C.* § 544(b) because violations of *8 Del. C. § 160* were general claims that accrued to all creditors, not assignees, and (5) the assignee could not show fraudulent transfer under *11 U.S.C. § 548* because the assignee failed to show that the corporation did not receive reasonably equivalent value in the stock redemption transaction, or that the corporation had actual intent to defraud investors. *PHP Liquidating, LLC v. Robbins, 291 B.R. 592 (D. Del. 2003)*.

Redemption. — This section explicitly disallowed the liquidating entity from using the corporation's violation of *8 Del. C. § 160* to invalidate the redemption transactions; thus, the entity could not obtain relief from former stockholders based on the corporation's violation of § 160. *PHP Liquidating, LLC v. Robbins, 291 B.R. 603 (D. Del. 2003)*.

DELAWARE CASE NOTES — UNREPORTED

Apparent authority of principal. — Principal could not deny the validity of the sale-leaseback where he had apparent authority to bind the lessee because he served as president, sole director, and sole shareholder of a corporation. *Carriage Realty P'ship v. All-Tech Auto Auto., Inc., 2001 Del. Ch. LEXIS 144 (Nov. 27, 2001)*.

CASE NOTES — FEDERAL

Seventh Circuit

Standing to challenge. — When a corporation acts ultra vires, the action can be only be challenged by one of three persons: (1) a stockholder to enjoin the act; (2) the corporation itself, acting directly or acting through a receiver, trustee or other legal representative or through a stockholder derivative action against an officer or director for an unauthorized act; or (3) the Attorney General to dissolve the corporation or enjoin the act. *Kelly v. Apollo Travel Services Partnership, 2000 U.S. Dist. LEXIS 12017 (N.D.Ill. 2000)*.

Ninth Circuit

This section is a provision that limits the doctrine of ultra vires. A corporation may exercise only those powers that are granted to it by law, by its charter or articles of incorporation, and by any bylaws made pursuant to the laws or charter; acts beyond the scope of the power granted are ultra vires. An ultra vires act or contract, as the term is used in this chapter and according to the strict construction of the term, is one not within the express or implied powers of the corporation as fixed by its charter, the statutes, or the common law. *Patriot Sci. Corp. v. Korodi, 2007 U.S. Dist. LEXIS 38279 (D. Cal. May 5, 2007)*.

District of Columbia Circuit

Void versus voidable. — The law of Delaware distinguishes between those improper acts of a corporate board which are "void" and those which are merely "voidable." As the Delaware courts have explained, the essential distinction between voidable and void acts are that those acts which the corporation could accomplish lawfully but which it has undertaken to accomplish in an inappropriate manner are voidable. Acts which the corporation could not accomplish lawfully, no matter how undertaken, are void and cannot be cured. *CarrAmerica Realty Corp. v. Kaidanow, 321 F.3d 165 (D.C. Cir. 2003)*.

Under Delaware corporation law, a void result occurs when a corporate board acts without authorization, while the result of an authorized act improperly accomplished may be merely voidable. *CarrAmerica Realty Corp. v. Kaidanow, 321 F.3d 165 (D.C. Cir. 2003)*.

Under Delaware law, shares of corporate stock that have not been initially authorized in full compliance with the requirements of the Delaware General Corporate Law, prior to ratification, are merely voidable, not void, because only voidable acts would be open to ratification. *CarrAmerica Realty Corp. v. Kaidanow, 321 F.3d 165 (D.C. Cir. 2003)*.

§ 126. Banking power denied

DELAWARE CASE NOTES — UNREPORTED

Soliciting advice of Bank Commissioner. — Secretary's policy of soliciting the advice of the Bank Commissioner with regard to proposed filing of certificates of incorporation using the word "bank" in their corporate names is an example of the appropriate careful exercise of discretion, especially given the prohibition of 8 Del. C. § 126 that denies the power to engage in the business of banking to corporations organized under the DGCL.

Harvard Bus. Servs. v. Coyle, 1997 Del. Super. LEXIS 70 (1997).

Secretary of State did not have a clear or obvious legal duty to accept for filing the restated certificate of incorporation with the word "bank" in its name, especially over the objections of the Bank Commissioner. *Harvard Bus. Servs. v. Coyle, 1997 Del. Super. LEXIS 70 (1997).*

Subchapter IV.
Directors and Officers

§ 141. Board of directors; powers; number, qualifications, terms and quorum; committees; classes of directors; nonprofit corporations; reliance upon books; action without meeting; removal.

DELAWARE CASE NOTES — REPORTED

I. General Consideration.
II. Officers.
A. In General.
B. Powers and Duties.
C. Election.
D. Removal.
III. Sale or Purchase of Assets or Control.
IV. Stockholders.

I. GENERAL CONSIDERATION.

Level of culpability required. — Level of due care that is the litmus test for director liability, absent an exculpatory charter provision, is gross negligence; pleading it successfully requires the articulation of facts that suggest a wide disparity between the process the directors use to ensure the integrity of the company's financial statements and that which is rational. *Guttman v. Jen-Hsun Huang, 823 A.2d 492 (Del. Ch. 2003).*

Applicability. — Where there is no clear contractual language that preempts default fiduciary duty rules, the courts of Delaware will continue to apply them. *Werner v. Miller Tech. Mgmt., L.P., 831 A.2d 318 (Del. Ch. 2003).*

Pleadings. — To state a claim for a breach of the duty of care, a plaintiff must allege more than simple negligence. *Werner v. Miller Tech. Mgmt., L.P., 831 A.2d 318 (Del. Ch. 2003).*

Specificity of pleading cognizable breach of duty. — Precisely because the business judgment rule serves an important purpose, our law requires that a plaintiff plead facts supporting an inference that directors committed a cognizable breach of duty. To state a claim for gross negligence, a complaint might allege, by way of example, that a board undertook a major acquisition without conducting due diligence, without retaining experienced advisors, and after holding a single meeting at which management made a cursory presentation. To state a claim of disloyalty, a complaint might allege that a board undertook an acquisition of a company controlled by one of its directors because that director was having financial problems and the board, in bad faith, decided to prefer his interests to that of the company. What a plaintiff may not do, however, is simply allege that a majority independent board undertook a business strategy that was "all consuming and foolhardy" and that turned out badly and thereby seek to have the court infer that the later failure resulted from a grossly deficient level of effort or from disloyal motives. *Trenwick Am. Litig. Trust v. Ernst & Young, L.L.P., 906 A.2d 168, 2006 Del. Ch. LEXIS 139 (Aug. 10, 2006).*

II. OFFICERS.

A. IN GENERAL.

Control and management rest in officers and board of directors. — While the corporation is the owner of the assets, yet their control and management rest in the officers and directors, whose relation to the assets is one of fiduciary character. *Harden v. Eastern States Pub. Serv. Co., 14 Del. Ch. 156, 122 A. 705 (1923).*

In certain areas the directors rather than the stockholders or others are granted the power by the State to deal with questions of management policy. *Abercrombie v. Davies, 35 Del. Ch. 599, 123 A.2d 893 (1956),* rev'd on other grounds, *36 Del. Ch. 371, 130 A.2d 338 (1957).*

Corporations

The board of directors acting as a board must be recognized as the only group authorized to speak for "management" in the sense that under this section they are responsible for the management of the corporation. *Campbell v. Loew's, Inc., 36 Del. Ch. 563, 134 A.2d 852 (1957).*

The business of every corporation "shall be managed by a board of directors." Whether that business consists of the operations of the usual going concern or but a single task, the corporation requires management, that is, a board of directors and such officers as may be necessary to accomplish its purpose or purposes. *Olson Bros. v. Englehart, 42 Del. Ch. 348, 211 A.2d 610 (1965),* aff'd, *245 A.2d 166 (Del. 1968).*

Under Delaware law, board of directors comprises the management of the corporation. *Gould v. American Hawaiian S.S. Co., 351 F. Supp. 853 (D. Del. 1972).*

The directors, not the stockholders, are the managers of the business affairs of the corporation. *Maldonado v. Flynn, 413 A.2d 1251 (Del. Ch. 1980),* rev'd on other grounds, *430 A.2d 779 (Del. 1981).*

Relying on the General Assembly's determination under subsection (a) of this section that the business and affairs of every corporation shall be managed by or under the direction of a board of directors, courts defer to decisions made by boards of directors on how to run the corporation's affairs; generally, shareholders have only 2 protections against perceived inadequate business performance, they may sell their stock or they may vote to replace incumbent board members. *In re MONY Group Inc. S'holder Litig., 853 A.2d 661 (Del. Ch. 2004).*

Delaware has no public policy interest in shielding corporate advisors from responsibility for consciously assisting the managers of Delaware corporations in breaching their fiduciary duties. If well-pled facts can be pled that support the inference that a corporate advisor knowingly assisted corporate directors in breaching their fiduciary duties, Delaware has a public policy interest in ensuring that its courts are available to derivative plaintiffs who wish to hold that advisor accountable to the corporation. The precise circumstances when corporate advisors should be deemed responsible to the corporation or its stockholders for their role in advising directors and officers should be determined by decisions addressing the merits of aiding and abetting claims, not by decisions about motions to dismiss for lack of personal jurisdiction. *Sample v. Morgan, 935 A.2d 1046, 2007 Del. Ch. LEXIS 166 (November 27, 2007). [For the full text of this case opinion, please see the Appendix at the end of this Volume.]*

Call of directors' meeting by illegally elected president is nullity. — Where election of president of the corporate board was illegal, it follows that the purported calls for meetings by him as president were invalid and the subsequent meetings insofar as their validity depended upon such calls were nullities. *Young v. Janas, 34 Del. Ch. 287, 103 A.2d 299 (1954).*

Telephonic directors meeting without prior notice. — When the new board members of a corporation met and agreed to send certain instructions to the previous board members, the fact that they met telephoni-

cally and without prior written notice was not important, under subsection (i) of this section. *Liebermann v. Frangiosa, 844 A.2d 992 (Del. Ch. 2002).*

Directors of corporation cannot act by proxy. *Stevens v. Acadia Dairies, Inc., 15 Del. Ch. 248, 135 A. 846 (1927).*

Directors as agents. — Directors, in the ordinary course of their service as directors, do not act as agents of the corporation; it would be an analytical anomaly to treat corporate directors as agents of the corporation when they are acting as fiduciaries of the stockholders in managing the business and affairs of the corporation. *Arnold v. Society for Savs. Bancorp., 678 A.2d 533 (Del. 1996).*

De facto directors. — Where the corporate director was not a legally elected director but had acted as such under color of right at various directors' meetings since the action of the board purporting to elect him, he must therefore be regarded as a de facto officer. *Drob v. National Mem. Park, 28 Del. Ch. 254, 41 A.2d 589 (1945).*

The status of an illegally elected director who has acted in his or her position for some time after his or her election is not insulated from direct attack in subsequent proceedings by some extension of the de facto theory. *Young v. Janas, 34 Del. Ch. 287, 103 A.2d 299 (1954).*

Director who lawfully is in office before election which later is found invalid continues in office until a successor is duly elected and qualified. *Halle & Stieglitz, Filor, Bullard, Inc. v. Empress Int'l, Ltd., 442 F. Supp. 217 (D. Del. 1977).*

Amendment of charter. — The board of directors alone is empowered to act on behalf of the corporation, including taking action to initiate an amendment to the corporation's charter. *AGR Halifax Fund, Inc. v. Fiscina, 743 A.2d 1188 (Del. Ch. 1999).*

Validity of indefinite class-designated directorships. — It was neither the intended nor the unintended effect of the 1974 amendment to subsection (d) to invalidate certificate provisions creating class-designated directorships that do not state the term of such directorships or their voting power. *Insituform of N. Am., Inc. v. Chandler, 534 A.2d 257 (Del. Ch. 1987).*

B. POWERS AND DUTIES.

Duties of directors are administrative and relate to supervision, direction and control, the details of the business being delegated to inferior officers, agents and employees and this is what is meant by management. *Cahall v. Lofland, 12 Del. Ch. 299, 114 A. 224 (1921),* aff'd, *13 Del. Ch. 384, 118 A. 1 (1922).*

Agreements by stockholders cannot substantially limit this power. — The Delaware corporation law does not permit actions or agreements by stockholders which would take all power from the board to handle matters of substantial management policy. *Abercrombie v. Davies, 35 Del. Ch. 599, 123 A.2d 893 (1956),* rev'd on other grounds, *36 Del. Ch. 371, 130 A.2d 338 (1957).*

If an agreement between stockholders and directors tends to limit in a substantial way the freedom of director decisions on matters of management policy it violates the duty of each director to exercise his or her own best judgment on matters coming before the board. *Abercrombie v. Davies, 35 Del. Ch. 599, 123 A.2d 893 (1956)*, rev'd on other grounds, *36 Del. Ch. 371, 130 A.2d 338 (1957)*.

The Court of Chancery cannot give legal sanction to agreements which have the effect of removing from directors in a very substantial way their duty to use their own best judgment on management matters. *Abercrombie v. Davies, 35 Del. Ch. 599, 123 A.2d 893 (1956)*, rev'd on other grounds, *36 Del. Ch. 371, 130 A.2d 338 (1957)*.

Some powers of the board are delegated to officers. — The powers of a president of a corporation over its business and property are merely the powers of an agent, for a corporation can speak in no other manner. The control over the company's business and property is vested in the board of directors, but subject to this control certain powers are delegated by implication to certain officers. *Joseph Greenspon's Sons Iron & Steel Co. v. Pecos Valley Gas Co., 34 Del. 567, 156 A. 350 (1931)*.

Delegation of duty to manage may be made in certificate of incorporation. — There is no conflict with the general principle that directors may not delegate their duty to manage the corporate enterprise where the delegation of duty, if any, is made not by the directors but by stockholder action via the certificate of incorporation. *Lehrman v. Cohen, 43 Del. Ch. 222, 222 A.2d 800 (1966)*.

But directors may not delegate their duty to manage corporate enterprise. *Adams v. Clearance Corp., 35 Del. Ch. 459, 121 A.2d 302 (1956)*.

The general rule forbidding the directors to delegate managerial duties applies as well to a delegation of a single duty as to the delegation of several or of all duties. *Adams v. Clearance Corp., 35 Del. Ch. 459, 121 A.2d 302 (1956)*.

Delegation of task to one-person committee. — The setting of a record date for a stockholder vote must be accomplished by a board resolution adopted before the record date, and under subsection (c)(2), a board may delegate this task to a one-person board committee, but this board committee must itself comply with § 213(a) of this title by adopting a resolution fixing a future record date. *In re Staples, Inc. Shareholders Litig., 792 A.2d 934 (Del. Ch. 2001)*.

Committee to be of directors. — Delegation by the board of directors to its president and secretary to determine whether a sale of assets of the corporation would be made, and if so upon what terms, is a violation of *8 Del. C. § 271* and of the stockholders' resolution empowering the board to sell, because subsection (c) of this section authorizes delegation of directors' powers to directors, not to officers. *Clarke Mem. College v. Monaghan Land Co., 257 A.2d 234 (Del. Ch. 1969)*.

Options committee not covered by section. — Where committee was not empowered to grant options, but only to recommend to the board the grant of options to employees, thereafter, the board in its discretion, and in the exercise of its business judgment, was required to approve the grant of options, the options committee was not the type of committee subject to subsection (c) of this section which governs the creation of committees authorized to exercise the powers of the board of directors in the management of the business and affairs of the corporation. *Elster v. American Airlines, 39 Del. Ch. 476, 167 A.2d 231 (1961)*.

Authority delegated to compensation committee to grant stock options. — Corporate directors do not breach their fiduciary duty by delegating authority to a compensation committee to grant stock options. *Michelson v. Duncan, 386 A.2d 1144 (Del. Ch. 1978)*, aff'd in part and rev'd in part, *407 A.2d 211 (Del. 1979)*.

Authority relating to merger. — The question of the independence of the members of a special committee that recommended a merger turned upon the reality of the interests and incentives affecting the independent directors; as the full board of directors had to act to approve a merger agreement and recommend the merger to the stockholders for approval, a committee could not be empowered to perform that necessary board function, under subsection (c) of this section and *8 Del. C. § 251(b)*. *Krasner v. Moffett, 826 A.2d 277 (Del. 2003)*.

The court did not conclude that the 9 independent directors of 10 total directors were either too enamored with the opportunity of reaping the gains that would flow to them from their accelerated options that became vested in the event of a change of control merger, or too poorly informed to step forward and demand a better process, because the 9 directors: (1) did not have improper motives; (2) engaged in a reasonable corporate process to determine afair whole-company sale value; and (3) made a reasonable decision to execute a merger agreement containing the challenged termination fee and matching rights. *In re Toys "R" Us, Inc., Shareholder Litig., 877 A.2d 975 (Del. Ch. 2005)*.

Board's procedure to remain as independent as it could while it considered merger proposals included that the board and the executive committee be committed to avoiding discussion of future management equity, cash compensation, or positions with bidders early in the process; as a means of enforcing that commitment, meetings with bidders were held only in the presence of the investment banker and with all of the final 4 bidders. *In re Toys "R" Us, Inc., Shareholder Litig., 877 A.2d 975 (Del. Ch. 2005)*.

Authority to bind corporation through settlement agreements. — Settlement agreement negotiated by corporation's attorney was enforceable as it contained agreement (through the eyes of a reasonable negotiator) on all of the essential terms, including the payment of attorney fees in the event of a breach of the agreement; the agreement was not contingent upon the corporation's board's approval, based upon the presumption that an attorney had that authority and based upon lack of any statement or indication by the corporation's attorney to the contrary. *Loppert v. Windsortech, Inc., 865 A.2d 1282 (Del. Ch. 2004)*, aff'd, *867 A.2d 903 (Del. 2005)*.

Purpose of independent committee, delegated authority to decide whether to pursue pending derivative action, is to act as an independent arm of the ultimate power given to a board of directors under subsection (a) of this section to determine whether or not derivative plaintiff's pending suit brought on behalf of the corporation should be maintained when measured against the overall best interests of the corporation. *Abbey v. Computer & Communications Technology Corp., 457 A.2d 368 (Del. Ch. 1983).*

Bylaw construed so as not to limit board's power. — A bylaw giving the president the power to submit matters for stockholder action presumably only embraces matters which are appropriate for stockholder action. So construed the bylaws do not impinge upon the statutory right and duty of the board to manage the business of the corporation. *Campbell v. Loew's, Inc., 36 Del. Ch. 563, 134 A.2d 852 (1957).*

Courts will not interfere with directors' business judgment. — Courts will not upset the decisions of either directors or stockholders as to questions of policy and business management. *Mercantile Trading Co. v. Rosenbaum Grain Corp., 17 Del. Ch. 325, 154 A. 457 (1931).*

Unwise business management, while a source of irritation to disappointed stockholders, does not in itself necessarily show recoverable grounds of action against those responsible therefor. *Freeman v. Hare & Chase, Inc., 16 Del. Ch. 207, 142 A. 793 (1928).*

In stockholders' suit to cancel a voting trust, where the directors of the corporation produced evidence that they had acted in good faith and free from disqualifying interest in settling the complaint, the suit will be defeated, and with that finding on the corporation's behalf, equity court will not inquire into the merits of the settlement. *Perrine v. Pennroad Corp., 28 Del. Ch. 342, 43 A.2d 721 (1945),* aff'd, *29 Del. Ch. 531, 47 A.2d 479 (1946),* cert. denied, *329 U.S. 808, 67 S. Ct. 620, 91 L. Ed. 690 (1946).*

In the absence of a showing of bad faith on the part of the directors or of a gross abuse of discretion, the business judgment of the directors will not be interfered with by the courts. *Kaplan v. Centex Corp., 284 A.2d 119 (Del. Ch. 1971).*

Wide discretion in the matter of valuation is confided to directors, and as long as they appear to act in good faith, with honest motives, and for honest ends, the exercise of their discretion will not be interfered with. *Muschel v. Western Union Corp., 310 A.2d 904 (Del. Ch. 1973); Kaplan v. Goldsamt, 380 A.2d 556 (Del. Ch. 1977).*

Board's actions, taken as defensive measures to take-over threat, were entitled to the protection of the business judgment rule. *Ivanhoe Partners v. Newmont Mining Corp., 535 A.2d 1334 (Del. 1987).*

Power of court to limit contract terms. — Central purpose of *Revlon, Inc. v. MacAndrews & Forbes Holdings, Inc., Del. Supr., 506 A.2d 173 (1985),* is to ensure the fidelity of fiduciaries, not to serve as a license for the judiciary to set arbitrary limits on the contract terms that fiduciaries acting loyally and carefully can shape in the pursuit of their stockholders' interest; even less is it the purpose of Revlon to push the pricing of sales transactions to the outer margins (or beyond) of their social utility. *In re Toys "R" Us, Inc., Shareholder Litig., 877 A.2d 975 (Del. Ch. 2005).*

Unless there is fraud or illegal misconduct. — Fraud, actual or presumed, or illegal or ultra vires misconduct must be shown to justify an interference by the courts with questions of corporate policy and management. *Mercantile Trading Co. v. Rosenbaum Grain Corp., 17 Del. Ch. 325, 154 A. 457 (1931).*

In the absence of fraud, either express or implied, the action of the governing body of a corporation, in matters of internal management of this nature, will not be disturbed by a court of equity. *Hartford Accident & Indem. Co. v. W.S. Dickey Clay Mfg. Co., 26 Del. Ch. 16, 21 A.2d 178 (1941),* aff'd, *26 Del. Ch. 411, 24 A.2d 315 (1942).*

Courts will not undertake, in the absence of fraud, to review the exercise by a corporation's directors of their business judgment as to what is required for the best interests of the corporation. *Sandler v. Schenley Indus., Inc., 32 Del. Ch. 46, 79 A.2d 606 (1951).*

It is not the proper function of the Court of Chancery to overturn a business transaction duly ratified by the stockholders absent a showing of fraud, a gift of assets, illegality, or ultra vires action. *Lewis v. Hat Corp. of Am., 38 Del. Ch. 313, 150 A.2d 750 (1959).*

Rule applies where no showing of fraud or domination of outside directors. — The business judgment rule, rather than the rule of fairness, was applied to test the validity of a stock transaction between the corporation and a stockholder group which included insider directors, where there was no showing of fraud, no showing of domination of the outside directors, and no testimony which even tended to show that the terms of the transaction had been dictated by the group or any member thereof. *Puma v. Marriott, 283 A.2d 693 (Del. Ch. 1971).*

"Control" and "domination" may be exercised directly or through nominees. But, at minimum, the words imply (in actual exercise) a direction of corporate conduct in such a way as to comport with the wishes or interests of the corporation (or persons) doing the controlling. *Kaplan v. Centex Corp., 284 A.2d 119 (Del. Ch. 1971).*

Allegation of domination of board must be proved. — A plaintiff who alleges domination of a board of directors and/or control of its affairs must prove it. *Kaplan v. Centex Corp., 284 A.2d 119 (Del. Ch. 1971).*

Stock ownership alone, at least when it amounts to less than majority, is not sufficient proof of domination or control. *Kaplan v. Centex Corp., 284 A.2d 119 (Del. Ch. 1971).*

Plaintiff has burden to show breach of duty. — To rebut the business judgment rule, a shareholder plaintiff assumes the burden of providing evidence that directors, in reaching their challenged decision, breached any one of the triads of their fiduciary duty — good faith, loyalty or due care; if a shareholder plaintiff fails to meet this evidentiary burden, the business judgment rule attaches to protect corporate officers and directors and the decisions they make. *Cede & Co. v. Technicolor, Inc., 634 A.2d 345 (Del. 1993).*

Good faith must be present in business judgments of directors. — Good faith may always be brought in question where it appears that the settlement of a dispute between stockholders of a corporation is so grossly inadequate that one is required to reach the decision that the directors were reckless and indifferent as to the rights

Corporations

of the stockholders and did not exercise reasonable business judgment. *Perrine v. Pennroad Corp., 29 Del. Ch. 531, 47 A.2d 479*, cert. denied, *329 U.S. 808, 67 S. Ct. 620, 91 L. Ed. 690 (1946).*

Determination of breach of duty not outcome-determinative per se. — An initial judicial determination that a given breach of a board's fiduciary duties has rebutted the presumption of the business judgment rule does not preclude a subsequent judicial determination that the board action was entirely fair, and is, therefore, not outcome-determinative per se. *Cinerama, Inc. v. Technicolor, Inc., 663 A.2d 1156 (Del. 1995)*, aff'd, *663 A.2d 1156 (Del. 1995).*

It is presumed that directors form their business judgment in good faith. *Kors v. Carey, 39 Del. Ch. 47, 158 A.2d 136 (1960).*

Attempting action without meeting does not prove bad faith. — An attempt to take corporate action without a directors' meeting when all the directors did not approve of that action, while apparently in violation of this section, did not compel an inference of bad faith, where there was nothing surreptitious about the proceedings; those holding the minority view were informed of the proposed action, were given the opportunity to record their dissent, and approved in the procedure, apparently in the interest of saving the expense of getting the directors together for a meeting. *Bowers v. Columbia Gen. Corp., 336 F. Supp. 609 (D. Del. 1971).*

Directors, not corporation, are charged with liability for fraud and ultra vires acts. — In cases of fraud, ultra vires acts or acts of negligence on the part of those charged with the duty of managing the affairs of a corporation, the offending officers, and not the aggrieved corporation, are the proper parties to account. *Harden v. Eastern States Pub. Serv. Co., 14 Del. Ch. 156, 122 A. 705 (1923).*

Honest mistake of business judgment on part of directors is not reviewable by courts. *Karasik v. Pacific E. Corp., 21 Del. Ch. 81, 180 A. 604 (1935).*

In the settlement of disputes in which corporations are interested, the directors of the corporation, who are its duly accredited managers, are called upon to exercise honest business discretion, and if it appears that they acted honestly, they are not responsible for mere mistakes, and under such circumstances courts will not interfere with their action or attempt to assume their authority to act. *Perrine v. Pennroad Corp., 29 Del. Ch. 531, 47 A.2d 479 (1946)*, aff'd, *57 A.2d 63* (Del.), cert. denied, *329 U.S. 808, 67 S. Ct. 620, 91 L. Ed. 690 (1947).*

In a suit alleging that defendant board of directors breached their fiduciary duties in a series of note transactions, defendants were entitled to summary judgment as to the allegations of accounting abuses because the board of directors relied upon a clean accounting report (shielding them from liability under subsection (e) of this section). *Cantor v. Perelman, 235 F. Supp. 2d 377 (D. Del. 2002).*

But error in law is reviewable. — When a board acts under misconception of the law on a vital point, judicial review is in order, without there being any question of bad faith. *Gottlieb v. Heyden Chem. Corp., 33 Del. Ch. 82, 90 A.2d 660 (1952).*

Directors of corporation are trustees for the stockholders, and their acts are governed by the rules applicable to such a relation, which exact of them the utmost good faith and fair dealing, especially where their individual interests are concerned. *Lofland v. Cahall, 13 Del. Ch. 384, 118 A. 1 (1922); Finch v. Warrior Cement Corp., 16 Del. Ch. 44, 141 A. 54 (1928); Keenan v. Eshleman, 23 Del. Ch. 234, 2 A.2d 904 (1938); Bovay v. H.M. Byllesby & Co., 27 Del. Ch. 381, 38 A.2d 808 (1944).*

Directors of a corporation stand in a position of trustees with the stockholders. As such, the utmost good faith and fair dealing are required of directors, especially where their individual interests are concerned. *Petty v. Penntech Papers, Inc., 347 A.2d 140 (Del. Ch. 1975).*

And directors of corporation stand in fiduciary relation to corporation and its stockholders. Their acts are subject to be tested by the familiar rules that govern the relations of a trustee to the trustee's beneficiary. *Loft, Inc. v. Guth, 23 Del. Ch. 138, 2 A.2d 225 (1938)*, aff'd, *23 Del. Ch. 255, 5 A.2d 503 (1939); Bovay v. H.M. Byllesby & Co., 27 Del. Ch. 381, 38 A.2d 808 (1944).*

A director will be held as a trustee for the corporation he or she has undertaken to represent, and must account for the profits resulting from an unlawful act done to promote his or her own interest, because he or she cannot derive any personal benefit or advantage by reason of his or her position distinct from other stockholders. *Loft, Inc. v. Guth, 23 Del. Ch. 138, 2 A.2d 225 (1938)*, aff'd, *23 Del. Ch. 255, 5 A.2d 503 (1939).*

Corporate officers and directors are not permitted to use their position of trust and confidence to further their private interests and while technically not trustees, they stand in a fiduciary relation to the corporation and its stockholders. *Gottlieb v. McKee, 34 Del. Ch. 537, 107 A.2d 240 (1954).*

Under Delaware law a stockholder who in fact controls the management of a Delaware corporation owes a fiduciary duty to that corporation and its shareholders. *Harriman v. E.I. DuPont De Nemours & Co., 372 F. Supp. 101 (D. Del. 1974).*

Their acts are scanned in light of principles which define trust relationship. — Directors of a corporation are spoken of as its trustees; their acts are scanned in the light of those principles which define the relationship existing between trustee and cestui que trust. *Bowen v. Imperial Theatres, Inc., 13 Del. Ch. 120, 115 A. 918 (1922).*

The law imposes upon the directors the duty of disposing of the shares in the interest of the corporation; the manner in which they perform that duty must meet the exacting standards required of a fiduciary acting in an office of trust and confidence. *Cahall v. Burbage, 14 Del. Ch. 55, 121 A. 646 (1923).*

Each case of director's breach of fiduciary duty must be decided on its own facts. *Kors v. Carey, 39 Del. Ch. 47, 158 A.2d 136 (1960).*

Public policy demands of directors undivided loyalty to corporation to the end that there shall be no conflict between duty and self-interest. *Italo-Petro. Corp. of Am. v. Hannigan, 40 Del. 534, 14 A.2d 401 (1940); Guth v. Loft, Inc., 23 Del. Ch. 255, 5 A.2d 503 (1939)*, aff'd, *25 Del. Ch. 363, 19 A.2d 721 (1941)*.

A public policy, existing through the years, and derived from a profound knowledge of human characteristics and motives, has established a rule that demands of a corporate officer or director, peremptorily and inexorably, the most scrupulous observance of his or her duty, not only affirmatively to protect the interests of the corporation committed to his or her charge, but also to refrain from doing anything that would work injury to the corporation, or to deprive it of profit or advantage which his or her skill and ability might properly bring to it, or to enable it to make in the reasonable and lawful exercise of its powers. *Guth v. Loft, Inc., 23 Del. Ch. 255, 5 A.2d 503 (1939)*, aff'd, *25 Del. Ch. 363, 19 A.2d 721 (1941)*.

Corporate officers and directors are not permitted to use their position of trust and confidence to further their private interests. While technically not trustees, they stand in a fiduciary relation to the corporation and its stockholders. *Guth v. Loft, Inc., 23 Del. Ch. 255, 5 A.2d 503 (1939)*, aff'd, *25 Del. Ch. 363, 19 A.2d 721 (1941)*.

Directors are required to demonstrate both their utmost good faith and the most scrupulous inherent fairness of transactions in which they possess a financial, business or other personal interest which does not devolve upon the corporation or all stockholders generally. *Mills Acquisition Co. v. Macmillan, Inc., 559 A.2d 1261 (Del. 1988)*.

Judgment of directors of corporation enjoys benefit of presumption that it was formed in good faith and was designed to promote the best interests of the corporation they serve. *Davis v. Louisville Gas & Elec. Co., 16 Del. Ch. 157, 142 A. 654 (1928); Karasik v. Pacific E. Corp., 21 Del. Ch. 81, 180 A. 604 (1935)*.

Insulation of directors. — The fact that charter or bylaw provisions may technically permit an action contemplated by the directors does not automatically insulate directors against scrutiny of purpose. *Petty v. Penntech Papers, Inc., 347 A.2d 140 (Del. Ch. 1975)*.

Obligations to spin off company. — Prior to the date of distribution, the interests held by a spin off subsidiary's prospective stockholders were insufficient to impose fiduciary obligations on the parent and the subsidiary's directors, thus, corporate parent and directors of a wholly-owned subsidiary did not owe fiduciary duties to the prospective stockholders of the subsidiary after the parent declares its intention to spin-off the subsidiary. *Anadarko Petro. Corp. v. Panhandle E. Corp., 545 A.2d 1171 (Del. 1988)*.

Nonstockholder usurping function of directors assumes fiduciary duty. — A nonstockholder who usurps the function of the board of directors of a Delaware corporation or otherwise directs its activities assumes the same fiduciary duty as its directors have. *Harriman v. E.I. DuPont De Nemours & Co., 372 F. Supp. 101 (D. Del. 1974)*.

One who exercises control over a corporation which in turn exercises control over a Delaware corporation may have a fiduciary duty to the latter corporation. *Harriman v. E.I. DuPont De Nemours & Co., 372 F. Supp. 101 (D. Del. 1974)*.

Fiduciary duty arises from exercise of power with respect to corporation. — Under the Delaware cases which speak of fiduciary duty to a corporation or its stockholders, that duty arises from the exercise of power with respect to that corporation. *Harriman v. E.I. DuPont De Nemours & Co., 372 F. Supp. 101 (D. Del. 1974)*.

Such as exercise of stockholder power by majority stockholder. — A fiduciary duty may arise from the exercise of a stockholder power by a majority stockholder in his or her capacity as such, absent any intrusion in the affairs of the board of directors. *Harriman v. E.I. DuPont De Nemours & Co., 372 F. Supp. 101 (D. Del. 1974)*.

Affirmative undertaking necessary. — It is only when a person affirmatively undertakes to dictate the destiny of the corporation that he or she assumes such a fiduciary duty. *Harriman v. E.I. DuPont De Nemours & Co., 372 F. Supp. 101 (D. Del. 1974)*.

Directors derive their managerial decision making power from subsection (a) of this section. *Zapata Corp. v. Maldonado, 430 A.2d 779 (Del. 1981)*.

Good faith presumption has been consistently reaffirmed. — The presumption that boards of directors act in good faith has been consistently reaffirmed and broadened with respect to the sale of corporate assets over the past several decades. *Gimbel v. Signal Cos., 316 A.2d 599* (Del. Ch.), aff'd, *316 A.2d 619 (Del. 1974)*.

"Business Judgment Rule" is important aspect of presumption. — An important aspect of the presumption that boards of directors act in good faith has generally come to be known as the "business judgment rule." *Gimbel v. Signal Cos., 316 A.2d 599* (Del. Ch.), aff'd, *316 A.2d 619 (Del. 1974)*.

Business judgment rule is merely presumption of propriety accorded decisions of corporate directors. *Maldonado v. Flynn, 413 A.2d 1251 (Del. Ch. 1980)*, rev'd on other grounds, *430 A.2d 779 (Del. 1981)*.

And rule permits directors to exercise their discretion in managing corporation's business affairs in the manner they deem in the corporation's best interests. *Maldonado v. Flynn, 413 A.2d 1251 (Del. Ch. 1980)*, rev'd on other grounds, *430 A.2d 779 (Del. 1981)*.

When a stockholder's derivative suit challenges the propriety of a decision of the directors, the business judgment rule protects the directors from liability by a presumption that the decision is proper. *Maldonado v. Flynn, 413 A.2d 1251 (Del. Ch. 1980)*, rev'd on other grounds, *430 A.2d 779 (Del. 1981)*.

"Business Judgment Rule" evolved to give recognition and deference to directors' business expertise when exercising their managerial power. *Zapata Corp. v. Maldonado, 430 A.2d 779 (Del. 1981)*.

Business judgment rule requires utmost loyalty from directors to corporation and its interests. *Maldonado v. Flynn, 413 A.2d 1251 (Del. Ch. 1980)*, rev'd on other grounds, *430 A.2d 779 (Del. 1981)*.

The concept of reasonable doubt in corporate derivative jurisprudence is akin to the concept that the stockholder has a reasonable belief that the board lacks

Corporations

independence or that the transaction was not protected by the business judgment rule. *Grimes v. Donald, 673 A.2d 1207 (Del. 1996).*

Determining whether self-interest of directors overcome loyalty. — A court must determine whether the particularized factual allegations of a derivative stockholder complaint create a reasonable doubt that, as of the time the complaint is filed, the board of directors could have properly exercised its independent and disinterested business judgment in responding to a demand; if the derivative plaintiff satisfies this burden, then demand will be excused as futile. *Rales v. Blasband, 634 A.2d 927 (Del. 1993).*

A director is being independent only when the director's decision is based entirely on the corporate merits of the transaction and it not influenced by personal or extraneous considerations; by contrast, a director who receives a substantial benefit from supporting a transaction cannot be objectively viewed as disinterested or independent. *Cede & Co. v. Technicolor, Inc., 634 A.2d 345 (Del. 1993).*

One director's colorable interest in a challenged transaction is not sufficient, without more, to deprive a board of the protection of the business judgment rule presumption of loyalty. *Cede & Co. v. Technicolor, Inc., 634 A.2d 345 (Del. 1993).*

In assessing a challenge to defensive actions by a target corporation's board of directors in a takeover context, the Court of Chancery should evaluate the board's overall response, including the justification for each contested defensive measure and the results achieved thereby. *Unitrin, Inc. v. American Gen. Corp., 651 A.2d 1361 (Del. 1995).*

A material interest of one or more directors less than a majority of those voting would rebut the application of the business judgment rule if the plaintiff proved that the interested director controls or dominates the board as a whole or the interested director failed to disclose an interest in the transaction to the board and a reasonable board member would have regarded the existence of the material interest as a significant fact in the proposed transaction. *Cinerama, Inc. v. Technicolor, Inc., 663 A.2d 1156 (Del. 1995),* aff'd, *663 A.2d 1156 (Del. 1995).*

Duty of care. — The duty of the directors of a company to act on an informed basis forms the duty of care element of the business judgment rule; duty of care and duty of loyalty are of equal and independent significance. *Cede & Co. v. Technicolor, Inc., 634 A.2d 345 (Del. 1993).*

Loyalty-based standard. — The standard for liability for failures of oversight requires a showing that the directors have breached their duty of loyalty by failing to attend to their duties in good faith; the directors should be conscious of the fact that they are not doing their jobs under this standard set out in *In Re Caremark Int'l Derivative Litig., 698 A.2d 959 (Del. Ch. 1996). Guttman v. Jen-Hsun Huang, 823 A.2d 492 (Del. Ch. 2003).*

Duty of loyalty. — Disclosure of conflicts of interest may preclude a claim for breach of the duty of loyalty; a stockholder cannot complain of corporate action in which, with full knowledge of all the facts, he or she has concurred; nonetheless, it cannot be said that certain boilerplate

disclosures convey full knowledge of all of the facts. *Werner v. Miller Tech. Mgmt., L.P., 831 A.2d 318 (Del. Ch. 2003).*

The fiduciary duty of loyalty is not limited to cases involving a financial or other cognizable fiduciary conflict of interest. It also encompasses cases where the fiduciary fails to act in good faith. As the Court of Chancery aptly put it in *Guttman,* a director cannot act loyally towards the corporation unless she acts in the good faith belief that her actions are in the corporation's best interest. *Stone v. Ritter, 911 A.2d 362, 2006 Del. LEXIS 597 (Nov. 6, 2006).*

A failure to act in good faith is not conduct that results, *ipso facto,* **in the direct imposition of** fiduciary liability. The failure to act in good faith may result in liability because the requirement to act in good faith "is a subsidiary element[,]" i.e., a condition, "of the fundamental duty of loyalty." It follows that because a showing of bad faith conduct, in the sense described in *Disney* and *Caremark,* is essential to establish director oversight liability, the fiduciary duty violated by that conduct is the duty of loyalty. *Stone v. Ritter, 911 A.2d 362, 2006 Del. LEXIS 597 (Nov. 6, 2006).*

The obligation to act in good faith does not establish an independent fiduciary duty that stands on the same footing as the duties of care and loyalty. Only the latter two duties, where violated, may directly result in liability, whereas a failure to act in good faith may do so, but indirectly. *Stone v. Ritter, 911 A.2d 362, 2006 Del. LEXIS 597 (Nov. 6, 2006).*

Oversight liability. — *Caremark* articulates the necessary conditions predicate for director oversight liability: (a) the directors utterly failed to implement any reporting or information system or controls; *or* (b) having implemented such a system or controls, consciously failed to monitor or oversee its operations thus disabling themselves from being informed of risks or problems requiring their attention. In either case, imposition of liability requires a showing that the directors knew that they were not discharging their fiduciary obligations. Where directors fail to act in the face of a known duty to act, thereby demonstrating a conscious disregard for their responsibilities, they breach their duty of loyalty by failing to discharge that fiduciary obligation in good faith. *Stone v. Ritter, 911 A.2d 362, 2006 Del. LEXIS 597 (Nov. 6, 2006).*

Deepening insolvency doctrine rejected. — If the board of an insolvent corporation, acting with due diligence and good faith, pursues a business strategy that it believes will increase the corporation's value, but that also involves the incurrence of additional debt, it does not become a guarantor of that strategy's success. That the strategy results in continued insolvency and an even more insolvent entity does not in itself give rise to a cause of action. Rather, in such a scenario the directors are protected by the business judgment rule. To conclude otherwise would fundamentally transform Delaware law. *Trenwick Am. Litig. Trust v. Ernst & Young, L.L.P., 906 A.2d 168, 2006 Del. Ch. LEXIS 139 (Aug. 10, 2006).*

The rejection of an independent cause of action for deepening insolvency does not absolve directors

of insolvent corporations of responsibility. Rather, it remits plaintiffs to the contents of their traditional toolkit, which contains, among other things, causes of action for breach of fiduciary duty and for fraud. The contours of these causes of action have been carefully shaped by generations of experience, in order to balance the societal interests in protecting investors and creditors against exploitation by directors and in providing directors with sufficient insulation so that they can seek to create wealth through the good faith pursuit of business strategies that involve a risk of failure. If a plaintiff cannot state a claim that the directors of an insolvent corporation acted disloyally or without due care in implementing a business strategy, it may not cure that deficiency simply by alleging that the corporation became more insolvent as a result of the failed strategy. *Trenwick Am. Litig. Trust v. Ernst & Young, L.L.P., 906 A.2d 168, 2006 Del. Ch. LEXIS 139 (Aug. 10, 2006).*

Application of business judgment rule, of necessity, depends upon a showing that informed directors did, in fact, make a business judgment authorizing the transaction under review. *Gimbel v. Signal Cos., 316 A.2d 599 (Del. Ch.), aff'd, 316 A.2d 619 (Del. 1974).*

Where there is no conscious decision by directors to act or refrain from acting, the business judgment rule has no application. *Rales v. Blasband, 634 A.2d 927 (Del. 1993).*

Business judgment rule does not irrevocably shield decisions of corporate directors from challenge. *Gimbel v. Signal Cos., 316 A.2d 599 (Del. Ch.), aff'd, 316 A.2d 619 (Del. 1974).*

And rule provides shield with which directors may oppose stockholders' attacks on the decisions made by them. *Maldonado v. Flynn, 413 A.2d 1251 (Del. Ch. 1980), rev'd on other grounds, 430 A.2d 779 (Del. 1981).*

But rule does not protect fraudulent, illegal or reckless decisions by directors. *Maldonado v. Flynn, 413 A.2d 1251 (Del. Ch. 1980), rev'd on other grounds, 430 A.2d 779 (Del. 1981).*

Deliberate indifference. — Shareholder's pleading is sufficient to withstand a motion to dismiss where the shareholders' claims are based on an alleged knowing and deliberate indifference to a potential risk of harm to the corporation; where a director consciously ignores duties to the corporation, thereby causing economic injury to its stockholders, the director's actions are either not in good faith or involve intentional misconduct. *In re Walt Disney Co. Derivative Litig., 825 A.2d 275 (Del. Ch. 2003).*

The business judgment rule has no application where the directors have profited at the expense of the corporation. *Maldonado v. Flynn, 413 A.2d 1251 (Del. Ch. 1980), rev'd on other grounds, 430 A.2d 779 (Del. 1981).*

Presumption of sound business judgment reposed in directors will not be disturbed if any rational business purpose can be attributed to its decision. *Kaplan v. Goldsamt, 380 A.2d 556 (Del. Ch. 1977).*

In order to overcome presumption that decision of directors is proper under the business judgment rule and successfully assail the directors' decision, a derivative plaintiff must first show facts which, if true, would remove the directors' decision from the protection of

the rule. *Maldonado v. Flynn, 413 A.2d 1251 (Del. Ch. 1980), rev'd on other grounds, 430 A.2d 779 (Del. 1981).*

When the business judgment rule is applied to defend directors against personal liability, as in a derivative suit, the plaintiff has the initial burden of proof and the ultimate burden of persuasion. *Unitrin, Inc. v. American Gen. Corp., 651 A.2d 1361 (Del. 1995).*

In order to rebut the protection of the business judgment rule, the burden on the plaintiffs will be to demonstrate, by a preponderance of the evidence, that the directors' decisions were primarily based on (1) perpetuating themselves in office or (2) some other breach of fiduciary duty such as fraud, overreaching, lack of good faith, or (3) being uninformed. *Unitrin, Inc. v. American Gen. Corp., 651 A.2d 1361 (Del. 1995).*

Sale of stock to employee stock ownership plan. — Where company adopted plan to sell repurchased stock to newly formed employee stock ownership plan as defensive measure, a proper corporate purpose was served by the defensive measure but action was not reasonable in relation to the threat posed. *AC Acquisitions Corp. v. Anderson, Clayton & Co., 519 A.2d 103 (Del. Ch. 1986).*

In responding to a takeover threat, neither a board's failure to become adequately informed nor its failure to apply the analysis of *Unocal Corp. v. Mesa Petroleum Co., Del. Supr., 493 A.2d 946 (1985)* where such an approach is required, will automatically invalidate a corporate transaction; under either circumstance, the business judgment rule will not be applied and the transaction at issue will be scrutinized to determine whether it is entirely fair. *Shamrock Holdings, Inc. v. Polaroid Corp., 559 A.2d 257 (Del. Ch. 1989).*

The business judgment rule applies to the conduct of directors in the context of a takeover. *Unitrin, Inc. v. American Gen. Corp., 651 A.2d 1361 (Del. 1995).*

Duty to inform shareholders. — The question whether shareholders have been provided with appropriate information upon which an informed choice on a matter of fundamental corporate importance may be made, is not a decision concerning the management of business and affairs of the enterprise of the kind the business judgment rule is intended to protect; it is rather a matter relating to the directors' duty to shareholders. *Bear, Stearns & Co. v. Anderson, Clayton & Co., 519 A.2d 669 (Del. Ch. 1986).*

Duty to provide materially complete information. — Once a board broaches a topic in its disclosures, a duty attaches to provide information that is materially complete and unbiased by the omission of material facts. For this reason, when a banker's endorsement of the fairness of a transaction is touted to shareholders, the valuation methods used to arrive at that opinion as well as the key inputs and range of ultimate values generated by those analyses must also be fairly disclosed. Only providing some of that information is insufficient to fulfill the duty of providing a fair summary of the substantive work performed by the investment bankers upon whose advice the recommendations of the board as to how to vote rely. *In re Netsmart Techs., Inc. S'holders Litig., 924 A.2d 171; 2007 Del. Ch. LEXIS 35 (March 14, 2007).*

Corporations

Disclosure of past interlocking board service. — In view of the tightened definitions of independence that now prevail, the chancery court is chary about adding a judicially-imposed disclosure requirement that past interlocking board service involving a target's CEO and another independent director must always be disclosed. This area of disclosure — i.e., the description of factors bearing on independence — is already well-covered, some might even say smothered. *In re Netsmart Techs., Inc. S'holders Litig, 924 A.2d 171; 2007 Del. Ch. LEXIS 35 (March 14, 2007).*

Disclosure harm not encompassing risk of investigation. — Plaintiffs seem to believe that any or all alleged malfeasance by the defendants may somehow be shoehorned into a disclosure claim because anything that defendants failed to disclose exposed defendants to SEC scrutiny. Disclosure claims do not allow so broad a target. For a disclosure claim to be viable, it must demonstrate damages that flow from the failure to adequately disclose information, not that the information disclosed concerned matters for which damages are appropriate. Plaintiffs must at the very least allege some connection between the lack of disclosure and an actual harm. Exposure to risk of investigation does not suffice. Attempting to expand the concept of harm to include the risk of investigation represents a triumph of imagination, but little else. *In re Tyson Foods, Inc. Consol. S'holder Litig., 919 A.2d 563; 2007 Del. Ch. LEXIS 19 (February 6, 2007).*

Standard of review for business judgment rule. — Because the effect of the proper invocation of the business judgment rule is so powerful and the standard of entire fairness so exacting, the determination of the appropriate standard of judicial review frequently is determinative of the outcome of derivative litigation; thus where a board takes action designed to defeat a threatened change in control of a company, a flexible, intermediate form of judicial review is appropriate. First, there must be shown some basis for the board to have concluded that a proper corporate purpose was served by implementation of the defensive measure and, second, that measure must be found reasonable in relation to the threat posed by the change in control that instigates the action. *AC Acquisitions Corp. v. Anderson, Clayton & Co., 519 A.2d 103 (Del. Ch. 1986).*

When business judgment rule is rebutted. — The entire fairness standard applies only if the presumption of the business judgment rule is defeated, and requires judicial scrutiny regarding both "fair dealing" and "fair price." *Unitrin, Inc. v. American Gen. Corp., 651 A.2d 1361 (Del. 1995).*

Directorial self-compensation decisions. — Directorial self-compensation decisions lie outside the business judgment rule's presumptive protection, so that, where properly challenged, the receipt of self-determined benefits is subject to an affirmative showing that the compensation arrangements are fair to the corporation. *In re Walt Disney Co. Derivative Litig., 825 A.2d 275 (Del. Ch. 2003).*

Directors' failure to carry their initial burden under *Unocal Corp. v. Mesa Petro. Co., Del. Supr., 493 A.2d 946 (1995)* does not, ipso facto, invalidate the board's actions; instead, once the Court of Chancery finds the business judgment rule does not apply, the burden remains on the directors to prove "entire fairness." *Unitrin, Inc. v. American Gen. Corp., 651 A.2d 1361 (Del. 1995).*

Directors' powers do not include power to give away corporate property; they cannot make gifts except as authorized by *8 Del. C. § 122. Taussig v. Wellington Fund, Inc., 187 F. Supp. 179 (D. Del. 1960),* aff'd, *313 F.2d 472 (3d Cir.), cert. denied, 374 U.S. 806, 83 S. Ct. 1693, 10 L. Ed. 2d 1031 (1963).*

Power to oust members of foundation. — Where members were responsible for the foundation's creation and continued endowment and electing its directors, the members' power was intended to resemble that of stockholders, and as a result, the foundation's members could not be ousted by the very directors whom they had elected, for any other interpretation would render the foundation's corporate structure fundamentally unstable. *Oberly v. Kirby, 592 A.2d 445 (Del. 1991).*

Wrongdoing by employees is not required to be anticipated as a general proposition, and it is only where the facts and circumstances of an employee's wrongdoing clearly throw the onus for the ensuing results on inattentive or supine directors that the law shoulders them with the responsibility. *Graham v. Allis-Chalmers Mfg. Co., 40 Del. Ch. 335, 182 A.2d 328 (1962),* aff'd, *41 Del. Ch. 78, 188 A.2d 125 (1963).*

Especially in large corporation. — Though corporate directors, particularly of a small corporation, may cause themselves to become personally liable when they foolishly or recklessly repose confidence in an untrustworthy officer or agent and in effect turn away when corporate corruption could be readily spotted and eliminated, such principle is hardly applicable to a large corporation, whose operation is hedged about with numerous and sometimes conflicting federal and state controls. *Graham v. Allis-Chalmers Mfg. Co., 40 Del. Ch. 335, 182 A.2d 328 (1962),* aff'd, *41 Del. Ch. 78, 188 A.2d 125 (1963).*

But each case must be factually considered. — The degree of care required of corporate directors in the selection and supervision of employees is that each case of alleged negligence must be considered on its own facts, giving regard to the nature of the business, its size, the extent, method and reasonableness of delegation of executive authority, and the existence or nonexistence of zeal and honesty of purpose in the directors' performance of their duties. *Graham v. Allis-Chalmers Mfg. Co., 40 Del. Ch. 335, 182 A.2d 328 (1962),* aff'd, *41 Del. Ch. 78, 188 A.2d 125 (1963).*

No authority to cause corporation to become a rogue. — By consciously causing the corporation to violate the law, a director would be disloyal to the corporation and could be forced to answer for the harm he has caused. Although directors have wide authority to take lawful action on behalf of the corporation, they have no authority knowingly to cause the corporation to become a rogue, exposing the corporation to penalties from criminal and civil regulators. Delaware corporate law has long been clear on this rather obvious notion; namely, that it is utterly inconsistent with one's duty of fidelity to the corporation to consciously cause the corporation to act unlawfully. The knowing use of illegal means to pursue profit for the corporation is director misconduct. *Desimone v. Barrows, 924 A.2d 908; 2007 Del. Ch. LEXIS 75 (June 7, 2007).*

Directors giving themselves stock to retain control. — Where the directors in whose control the company's stock was vested as its trustees, gave it to themselves for nothing in pursuance of a deliberate plan to retain control over its affairs, there was a clear breach of trust. *Bowen v. Imperial Theatres, Inc., 13 Del. Ch. 120, 115 A. 918 (1922).*

Overvaluation of stock. — In a shareholders' derivative action, once the shareholders had made a showing that the corporation's former chief executive officer (CEO) had used stock (the inflated price of which was due entirely to inaccurate financial information that the CEO had signed) to pay back a loan from the corporation, the burden of production shifted to the CEO (whose arguments that the board, which was entitled to rely on information supplied by officers, was somehow in pari delicto or that the CEO was the victim of subordinates' misrepresentations), were entirely inadequate; the court therefore entered summary judgment rescinding the stock buyback agreement. *In re HealthSouth Corp. S'holders Litig., 845 A.2d 1096 (Del. Ch. 2003).*

Option grant analysis. — If allegations that a company disclosed material information affecting its stock price in proximity to an automatic, regularly-scheduled option grant are to support a breach of fiduciary duty claim based on the theory accepted in *Tyson*, they must involve allegations that the company deviated from a regular disclosure pattern in a deceptive, non-candid effort to influence the exercise price of options and circumvent the intended functioning of the stockholder-approved option plan. But when, as here, the complaint simply alleges that the directors took the good and the bad that came with a non-discretionary plan, by receiving their options annually on the specified date regardless of the positive or negative nature of the regularly-issued quarterly report preceding the grants, no breach of fiduciary duty claim is stated. *Desimone v. Barrows, 924 A.2d 908; 2007 Del. Ch. LEXIS 75 (June 7, 2007).*

A director who approves the backdating of options faces at the very least a substantial likelihood of liability, if only because it is difficult to conceive of a context in which a director may simultaneously lie to his shareholders (regarding his violations of a shareholder-approved plan, no less) and yet satisfy his duty of loyalty. Ryan v. Gifford, 918 A.2d 341; 2007 Del. Ch. LEXIS 22 (February 6, 2007).

Violation of a shareholder approved stock option plan, coupled with fraudulent disclosures regarding the directors' purported compliance with that plan, constitute conduct that is disloyal to the corporation and is therefore an act in bad faith. Ryan v. Gifford, 918 A.2d 341; 2007 Del. Ch. LEXIS 22 (February 6, 2007).

Stay denied. — The allegations in the instant case involve backdating option grants and whether such practice violates one or more of Delaware's common law fiduciary duties. Delaware courts have not as yet addressed these fundamental issues. Nevertheless, Delaware law directly controls and affects many of the option backdating cases. An answer regarding the legality of these practices pursuant to Delaware law plainly will affect not only the parties to this action, but also parties in other civil and criminal proceedings where Delaware law controls or applies. By directly stating the fiduciary principles applicable in this context, Delaware courts may remove doubt regarding Delaware law and avoid inconsistencies that might arise in the event other state or federal courts, in applying Delaware law, reach differing conclusions. Because Delaware has an overwhelming interest in resolving questions of first impression under Delaware law, defendants' McWane-based stay request is denied. Ryan v. Gifford, 918 A.2d 341; 2007 Del. Ch. LEXIS 22 (February 6, 2007).

Granting spring-loaded options, without explicit authorization from shareholders, clearly involves an indirect deception. A director's duty of loyalty includes the duty to deal fairly and honestly with the shareholders for whom he is a fiduciary. It is inconsistent with such a duty for a board of directors to ask for shareholder approval of an incentive stock option plan and then later to distribute shares to managers in such a way as to undermine the very objectives approved by shareholders. This remains true even if the board complies with the strict letter of a shareholder-approved plan as it relates to strike prices or issue dates. In re Tyson Foods, Inc. Consol. S'holder Litig., 919 A.2d 563; 2007 Del. Ch. LEXIS 19 (February 6, 2007).

In order to show that a spring-loaded option issued by a disinterested and independent board is nevertheless beyond the bounds of business judgment, a plaintiff must first allege that options were issued according to a shareholder-approved employee compensation plan. Second, a plaintiff must allege that the directors that approved spring-loaded (or bullet-dodging) options (a) possessed material non-public information soon to be released that would impact the company's share price, and (b) issued those options with the intent to circumvent otherwise valid shareholder-approved restrictions upon the exercise price of the options. Such allegations would satisfy a plaintiff's requirement to show adequately at the pleading stage that a director acted disloyally and in bad faith and is therefore unable to claim the protection of the business judgment rule. In re Tyson Foods, Inc. Consol. S'holder Litig., 919 A.2d 563; 2007 Del. Ch. LEXIS 19 (February 6, 2007).

Use of corporate funds to acquire shares of dissident stockholder faction is proper exercise of business judgment where it is done to eliminate what appears to be a clear threat to the future business or the existing, successful business policy of a company and is not accomplished for the sole or primary purpose of perpetuating the control of management. *Kaplan v. Goldsamt, 380 A.2d 556 (Del. Ch. 1977).*

Takeover bids. — When a board considers a takeover bid, it is obliged to determine whether the offer is in the best interests of the corporation and its shareholders and, if the board gives a negative answer to that inquiry, a Delaware court will not substitute its judgment for that of the board, provided that the answer the board gave can be attributed to any rational business purpose. *Grand Metro. Pub. Ltd. v. Pillsbury Co., 558 A.2d 1049 (Del. Ch. 1988).*

Evidence sufficient to find that actions of board of directors in response to takeover bid were entitled to protection of business judgment rule and that the actions were proper and in fulfillment of the board's fiduciary duties to the corporation and all its shareholders. *Gilbert v. El Paso Co., 575 A.2d 1131 (Del. 1990).*

Directors of corporation acted in good faith and with due care in recommending one takeover offer over another, accordingly, the board's decision was entitled to the presumption of the business judgment rule. *Citron v. Fairchild Camera & Instrument Corp., 569 A.2d 53 (Del. 1989).*

Delayed redemption provision was invalid since it would have prevented a new board of directors from managing the corporation by redeeming a rights plan to facilitate a transaction that would have served the stockholders' best interests, even under circumstances where the board would have been required to do so because of its fiduciary duties to stockholders. *Quickturn Design Sys. v. Shapiro, 721 A.2d 1281 (Del. 1998).*

Lock-ups (options to purchase assets of corporation) and related agreements are permitted under Delaware law where their adoption is untainted by director interest or other breaches of fiduciary duty. *Revlon, Inc. v. MacAndrews & Forbes Holdings, Inc., 506 A.2d 173 (Del. 1985).*

Adoption of "poison pill" plan, by which shareholders receive the right to be bought out by the corporation at a substantial premium on the occurrence of a stated triggering event, was consistent with the directors' fiduciary duty in facing a takeover threat perceived as detrimental to corporate interests. *Revlon, Inc. v. MacAndrews & Forbes Holdings, Inc., 506 A.2d 173 (Del. 1985).*

The adoption of the poison pill and the limited repurchase of stock program were not coercive. *Unitrin, Inc. v. American Gen. Corp., 651 A.2d 1361 (Del. 1995).*

Violations stated in challenge to validity of rights plan. — Complaint challenging the validity of a "dead hand" provision in a poison pill rights plan stated violations of subsections (b) and (d) because the plan conferred the right to redeem the pill only upon some, but not all, directors; vested the pill redemption power exclusively in continuing directors which transgressed the shareholders' right to elect directors who would be so empowered; and impermissibly interfered with the directors' statutory powers to manage the business and affairs of the corporation. *Carmody v. Toll Bros., 723 A.2d 1180 (Del. Ch. 1998).*

Preferred share purchase rights plan giving shareholders one right per common share upon announcement of tender offer for 30% of corporation's shares or acquisition of 20% of corporation's shares by any single entity or group was authorized by this section and constituted a legitimate exercise of business judgment by directors concerned over takeovers. *Moran v. Household Int'l, 500 A.2d 1346 (Del. 1985).*

Showing sufficient to support board's decision to buy out threatening stockholders. — The presence of 10 outside directors out of 13 on the board of a corporation, coupled with the advice rendered by an investment banker and legal counsel that the stock held by certain investors posed a threat to the corporation, constituted a prima facie showing of good faith and reasonable investigation supporting the board's decision to buy out the investors at a premium. *Polk v. Good, 507 A.2d 531 (Del. 1986).*

Board of directors approval of merger reasonable. — Finally adopted merger agreement that contained four deal protection measures ((1) a fixed termination fee of $247.5 million, equal to 3.75% of equity value or 3.25% of enterprise value — payable for the most part only if the acquired corporation terminated the merger agreement in order to sign up another acquisition proposal within a year; (2) an agreement to pay up to $30 million in documented expenses after a naked no vote; (3) a relatively non-restrictive no-shop clause that permitted the consideration of unsolicited bids; and (4) a temporally-limited 3-day match right) was considered to be reasonable to secure a superior merger proposal and allowed a subsequent bidder room to make a bid that was within the range of estimated values for the corporation that would still net the corporation more money after paying the termination fee; a 50% "trigger" to allow the board to consider a superior offer did not preclude the board from changing its recommendation if such a bid was received, although that decision would also have triggered the payment of a termination fee. *In re Toys "R" Us, Inc., Shareholder Litig., 877 A.2d 975 (Del. Ch. 2005).*

Adding a control premium on top of a discounted cash flow (DCF) is not intuitively or theoretically logical; indeed, because a Gordon growth model DCF is not infected by a minority discount, it is the model most consistent with what a company's stockholders would receive in an appraisal (their pro rata share of the company's value) which is precisely the kind of information the Delaware Supreme Court has said it should have. *In re Toys "R" Us, Inc., Shareholder Litig., 877 A.2d 975 (Del. Ch. 2005).*

Second-guessing the board's decision not to insist on a smaller termination fee, more like 2.5% or 3.0%, and the abandonment of the matching right, was precisely the sort of quibble that did not suffice to prove a *Revlon, Inc. v. MacAndrews & Forbes Holdings, Inc., 506 A.2d 173 (Del. 1985)* claim. *In re Toys "R" Us, Inc., Shareholder Litig., 877 A.2d 975 (Del. Ch. 2005).*

Argument that financial buyers for the corporation were typically more deterred by termination fees than strategic buyers (because financial buyers could not reap the gains from operational synergies) was rejected because those were exactly the same universe of buyers that had already been broadly solicited at the commencement of the strategic review, and were therefore least likely to have missed out on the opportunity to bid on the company; the unknown, synergistic strategic bidder that the plaintiff shareholders hoped was waiting in the wings was precisely the least likely buyer to be deterred by existing deal protections. *In re Toys "R" Us, Inc., Shareholder Litig.*, 877 A.2d 975 (Del. Ch. 2005).

It was reasonable for board not to consider selling the company's most marginally profitable and fastest growing retail business, while retaining the more mature business, based, in part, on the profound adverse tax implications of such a strategy. *In re Toys "R" Us, Inc., Shareholder Litig.*, 877 A.2d 975 (Del. Ch. 2005).

Board's procedure to conduct as independent a search for merger proposal bidders as it could included a requirement that the its investment banker not discuss financing with any bidders before the merger was finalized; the investment banker's request to the board to finance the high bidder (made 2 months after the merger was finalized, but before the shareholder vote to approve the merger) created the appearance of impropriety, playing into already heightened suspicions about the ethics of investment banking firms, but was not considered to be causally related to the board's merger decisions. *In re Toys "R" Us, Inc., Shareholder Litig.*, 877 A.2d 975 (Del. Ch. 2005).

Board was not found to have considered an unreasonably low value for the entire company, where it excluded a 25% control premium that it might have been able to later obtain (if it retained 1 of its divisions), because, associated with retention of just that 1 division, there were: (1) increased expenses; (2) complications related to ongoing operations that interfered with the sale of the other divisions, because of the divisions' interrelated facilities and services; (3) no assurances the control premium could be obtained; and (4) no assurances the projected basic value could be obtained,because the potential buyers would primarily include the buyer who successfully bought the other divisions and would likely bid a lower amount because of the interrelationships. *In re Toys "R" Us, Inc., Shareholder Litig.*, 877 A.2d 975 (Del. Ch. 2005).

Board was not to be faulted for considering a value for the entire company that included the investment banker's discounted cash flow value (DCF) for 1 division at the value that division had if it was retained by the company (which DCF did not include a control premium, because the shares would have traded on a minority basis in the marketplace), because that had been value the investment banker derived under the company's strategic plan to retain that division until it was presented with whole-company sale proposals; the DCF the board received was consistent with what the Delaware Supreme Court required. *In re Toys "R" Us, Inc., Shareholder Litig.*, 877 A.2d 975 (Del. Ch. 2005).

Board of directors of corporation is entitled to rely on summaries, reports and corporate records in making broad policy decisions. *Graham v. Allis-Chalmers Mfg. Co.*, 41 Del. Ch. 78, 188 A.2d 125 (1963).

Subsection (e) of this section "protects" directors relying in good faith upon certain reports made to the corporation. *David J. Greene & Co. v. Dunhill Int'l, Inc.*, 249 A.2d 427 (Del. Ch. 1968).

Subsection (e) of this section fully protects directors of a corporation where they rely in good faith on books of account and reports made by any of its officials, or by an independent certified public accountant. *Prince v. Bensinger*, 244 A.2d 89 (Del. Ch. 1968).

While a board of directors may rely in good faith upon "information, opinions, reports or statements presented" by corporate officers, employees and experts "selected with reasonable care," pursuant to subsection (e), it may not avoid its active and direct duty of oversight in a matter as significant as the sale of corporate control, particularly where insiders are among the bidders. *Mills Acquisition Co. v. Macmillan, Inc.*, 559 A.2d 1261 (Del. 1988).

Reliance on counsel. — Reasonable reliance upon expert counsel is a pertinent factor in evaluating whether corporate directors have met a standard of fairness in their dealings with respect to corporate powers. *Cinerama, Inc. v. Technicolor, Inc.*, 663 A.2d 1134 (Del. Ch. 1994), aff'd, 663 A.2d 1156 (Del. 1995).

Under subsection (e), report must be pertinent to the subject matter upon which a board is called to act, and be entitled to good faith, not blind reliance. *Smith v. Van Gorkom*, 488 A.2d 858 (Del. 1985).

Incumbent board speaks for corporation. — The incumbent board of directors, so long as they maintain that status, are alone entitled to speak for or to authorize others to speak for the corporation. *Empire S. Gas Co. v. Gray*, 29 Del. Ch. 95, 46 A.2d 741 (1946).

The actions of the board of directors, speaking through the majority of its members, must be recognized no matter which particular faction may be in control. *Empire S. Gas Co. v. Gray*, 29 Del. Ch. 95, 46 A.2d 741 (1946).

And right to speak for board may be given or withheld. — The right to speak for the board of directors may be given or withheld by those in control of the board as they see fit, and if one purports to speak on its behalf without authority, the board acting through the corporate entity should be able to and can prevent it, whether it be in a proxy contest or otherwise. *Empire S. Gas Co. v. Gray*, 29 Del. Ch. 95, 46 A.2d 741 (1946).

Director who misrepresents action of board of directors is thereby misrepresenting action of corporation, because under this section the directors are authorized to manage the business of the corporation. *Empire S. Gas Co. v. Gray*, 29 Del. Ch. 95, 46 A.2d 741 (1946).

Majority of stock cannot be substituted for quorum requirements. — The fact that directors owning a majority of the stock vote in favor of certain corporate action cannot be substituted for the quorum requirements imposed by law concerning meetings of the board of directors. *Belle Isle Corp. v. MacBean*, 29 Del. Ch. 261, 49 A.2d 5, aff'd sub nom. *Belle Isle Corp. v. Corcoran*, 29 Del. Ch. 554, 49 A.2d 1 (1946).

Each director has single vote. — In the absence of certificate provisions providing otherwise, directors, including those designated by a special class of stock, are elected annually pursuant to *8 Del. C. § 211* and each director has a single vote on each matter that occasions board action pursuant to subsection (b). *Insituform of N. Am., Inc. v. Chandler*, 534 A.2d 257 (Del. Ch. 1987).

Action taken without required quorum is void. — Where the bylaws of a corporation required specific number to constitute a quorum of directors, an action by the directors with less than that number present is unauthorized. *Drob v. National Mem. Park, 28 Del. Ch. 254, 41 A.2d 589 (1945).*

Approval of minutes of meeting is not approval of unauthorized act. — When a board of directors approves an act which is void because the meeting of the board was illegal for lack of a quorum, the approval of the minutes of such meeting at a subsequent meeting is not an approval of such an unauthorized act. *Belle Isle Corp. v. MacBean, 29 Del. Ch. 261, 49 A.2d 5,* aff'd sub nom. *Belle Isle Corp. v. Corcoran, 29 Del. Ch. 554, 49 A.2d 1 (1946).*

And approval of minutes of preceding directors' meeting is simply assertion that secretary had properly recorded them and is not a legalizing of invalid acts recorded therein. *In re Chelsea Exch. Corp., 18 Del. Ch. 287, 159 A. 432 (1932).*

Minutes of meetings of corporate directors are prima facie correct. *Young v. Janas, 34 Del. Ch. 287, 103 A.2d 299 (1954).*

Where the oral testimony of corporate directors is in conflict as to the results of an election to fill a vacancy, the court will accept the minutes of the directors' meeting as depicting what occurred. *Young v. Janas, 34 Del. Ch. 287, 103 A.2d 299 (1954).*

Adjournment of meeting by legally elected directors. — Where motion to adjourn a meeting of corporate directors appears to be defeated, but was actually approved by a majority of the legally elected directors, the meeting was legally adjourned, and subsequent action of the meeting was void. *Young v. Janas, 34 Del. Ch. 287, 103 A.2d 299 (1954).*

Stockholders may ratify voidable acts of directors. — Stockholders' ratification of voidable acts of directors is effective for all purposes unless the action of the directors constituted a gift of corporate assets to themselves or was ultra vires, illegal or fraudulent. *Kerbs v. California E. Airways, Inc., 33 Del. Ch. 69, 90 A.2d 652 (1952).*

Courts generally look with apprehension upon ratification of previous corporate acts after action has been instituted questioning validity of such acts. However, in the absence of fraud subsequent action by the board within director authority will be held to be valid. *Blish v. Thompson Automatic Arms Corp., 30 Del. Ch. 538, 64 A.2d 581 (1948).*

Overcoming presumption requires particularized pleading. — Stockholder derivative complaint was subject to dismissal for failure to set forth particularized facts creating a reasonable doubt that the director defendants were disinterested and independent or that their conduct was protected by the business judgment rule. *Brehm v. Eisner, 746 A.2d 244 (Del. 2000).*

Plaintiffs failed to overcome presumption. — Plaintiffs were required to rebut the presumption that the directors properly exercised their business judgment, including their good faith reliance on expert's advice, but what expert believed in hindsight that he and the Board should have done in the past does not provide that rebuttal. *Brehm v. Eisner, 746 A.2d 244 (Del. 2000).*

To survive a rule 23.1 motion to dismiss in a due care case where an expert has advised the board in its decision-making process, the complaint must allege particularized facts, not conclusions. *Brehm v. Eisner, 746 A.2d 244 (Del. 2000).*

Shifting the burden to prove entire fairness. — As the majority of the board can be considered interested at all relevant times, transactions not sterilized by independent review receive no protection from the business judgment rule, and plaintiffs must only allege that the transactions were in some way unfair to shift the burden upon the defendants to prove their entire fairness. *In re Tyson Foods, Inc. Consol. S'holder Litig., 919 A.2d 563; 2007 Del. Ch. LEXIS 19 (February 6, 2007).*

Although reasonable reliance on expert counsel is a pertinent factor in evaluating whether corporate directors have met a standard of fairness in their dealings with respect to corporate powers, its existence is not outcome determinative of entire fairness. To hold otherwise would replace this court's role in determining entire fairness under 8 Del. C. § 144 with that of various experts hired to give advice to the directors in connection with the challenged transaction, creating a conflict between sections 141(e) and 144 of the Delaware General Corporation Law. *Valeant Pharms. Int'l v. Jerney, 921 A.2d 732; 2007 Del. Ch. LEXIS 31 (March 1, 2007).*

Disgorgement of bonus. — Because defendant has failed to show that the transaction was entirely fair, it is clear that he has no right to retain any of the $ 3 million bonus he received. As between defendant and the company, that payment must be rescinded, requiring him to disgorge the full amount. His liability in this regard will not be limited to the excess of what the court might conclude was a fair bonus. There is also no suggestion that the corporation has been made whole as a result of its settlements with the other defendants or that it would be unjustly enriched by return of his bonus. Thus, there is no inequity in requiring defendant to disgorge the payment he received. Nor will the court apportion responsibility to account for the fact that several of the settling directors signed joint tortfeasor releases since his disgorgement obligation stems from his receipt of the company's money, not from his participation in the decision to authorize the payment. *Valeant Pharms. Int'l v. Jerney, 921 A.2d 732; 2007 Del. Ch. LEXIS 31 (March 1, 2007).*

Votes of interested directors cannot be counted to make up majority of the board and if a majority of the directors are adversely interested, any transaction between themselves and the corporation as represented by its board is a case of officers dealing with themselves. *Italo-Petro. Corp. of Am. v. Hannigan, 40 Del. 534, 14 A.2d 401 (1940).*

Director present but not voting counted in negative as to majority vote. — Where a statute requires a vote of a majority of directors present to pass a resolution, a director who is present and does not vote at all on the resolution is counted in the negative for the purpose of determining whether the resolution has been carried by a majority vote. *Dillon v. Berg, 326 F. Supp. 1214 (D. Del.), aff'd, 453 F.2d 876 (3d Cir. 1971).*

Evidence supports breach of fiduciary duty. — See *Smith v. Van Gorkom, 488 A.2d 858 (Del. 1985).*

C. ELECTION.

Nomination of directors — In shareholder's suit against casino corporation in which it owned 49 percent of shares, shareholder was awarded right to nominate 2 directors (instead of 1); the charter's and bylaws' ambiguities, under contract construction principles, were resolved in favor of the right of a shareholder to participate in the board electoral process, restrictions of which (including consideration of external evidence) were enforceable only if they were clear and convincing. *Harrah's Entm't, Inc. v. JCC Holding Co., 802 A.2d 294 (Del. Ch. 2002).*

Directors shall be elected at annual meeting of stockholders, and it is the duty of those holding proxies to attend the meeting as well as vote the stock they represent and the election should not be prevented by objections of a purely technical character interposed by stockholders who are disappointed or dissatisfied because of their inability to control the meeting. *Duffy v. Loft, Inc., 17 Del. Ch. 376, 152 A. 849 (1930).*

Directors' right to hold office. — Directors of Delaware corporations have no vested right to hold office in defiance of a properly expressed will of the majority of stockholders. *Roven v. Cotter, 547 A.2d 603 (Del. Ch. 1988).*

Stockholders, under Delaware law, do not have a fundamental right to be directors. *Stroud v. Milliken Enters., Inc., 585 A.2d 1306 (Del. Ch. 1988),* appeal dismissed, *552 A.2d 476 (Del. 1989).*

Director qualifications. — The certificate of incorporation can provide for reasonable director qualifications. *Stroud v. Milliken Enters., Inc., 585 A.2d 1306 (Del. Ch. 1988),* appeal dismissed, *552 A.2d 476 (Del. 1989).*

Acceptance on newly elected director's part is necessary and by reason of his refusal to serve on the board of directors he did not become a director and no notice of directors' meeting should have been given to him, and any action taken by the board without notice to him was valid. *Blish v. Thompson Automatic Arms Corp., 30 Del. Ch. 538, 64 A.2d 581 (1948).*

Director need not be stockholder at time of election. — In the absence of express statutory provision, a director need not be a holder of any shares at the time of his or her election, but it will be sufficient if the director qualifies himself or herself by becoming a holder of the requisite number of shares before he or she enters upon the office of director. *Triplex Shoe Co. v. Rice & Hutchins, Inc., 17 Del. Ch. 356, 152 A. 342 (1930).*

Corporation need not provide in its certificate for staggered terms for its directors; this section is permissive. *Essential Enters. Corp. v. Automatic Steel Prods., Inc., 39 Del. Ch. 93, 159 A.2d 288 (1960).*

Actual written notice of resignation required. — The phrase "written notice to the corporation," used in subsection (b) of this section in connection with the resignation of a director, means actual written notice to each and every member of the board of directors or actual written notice to an agent of the corporation, such as its chairperson of the board, president or secretary. *Dillon v. Berg, 326 F. Supp. 1214 (D. Del.),* aff'd, *453 F.2d 876 (3d Cir. 1971).*

When notice to agent of corporation sufficient. — Giving actual written notice to an agent of the corporation would, in the normal case, meet the requirements of this section, but not where the corporate agent's relation to the subject matter is substantially adverse to the corporation. *Dillon v. Berg, 326 F. Supp. 1214 (D. Del.),* aff'd, *453 F.2d 876 (3d Cir. 1971).*

Number of directors may be fixed by board. — Delaware law allows the board to fix the number of directors within the restrictions imposed by the certificate of incorporation. *Stroud v. Milliken Enters., Inc., 585 A.2d 1306 (Del. Ch. 1988),* appeal dismissed, *552 A.2d 476 (Del. 1989).*

Bylaws to prescribe number of directors. — Reasonably construed, this section explicitly authorizes the adoption of a bylaw provision which fixes a method of determining the number of directors to be elected. *Ellin v. Consolidated Caribou Silver Mines, Inc., 31 Del. Ch. 149, 67 A.2d 416 (1949).*

"Withhold authority" proxy cards were required to be counted. — Where the corporation's nominees were not re-elected because the "withhold authority" proxy cards were required to be counted, the nominees continued to be in office as holdovers and had a right to remain in office only until their successors were elected and qualified. *North Fork Bancorporation, Inc. v. Toal, 825 A.2d 860 (Del. Ch. 2000),* aff'd, *781 A.2d 693 (Del. 2001).*

Board's actions entitled to protection of business judgment rule. — The plaintiffs failed to produce evidence creating a genuine issue of material fact regarding whether the board's actions were entitled to the protection of the business judgment rule where they produced no evidence; (1) that the independence or disinterestedness of the corporate directors was compromised, (2) that the board acted without due care or for improper purposes, or (3) that the defensive measures did not have a rational business purpose. *In re Gaylord Container Corp. Shareholders Litig., 753 A.2d 462 (Del. Ch. 2000).*

D. REMOVAL.

And may authorize method of director removal. — Where plaintiff stockholder has been properly removed as a director of defendant corporation under a bylaw adopted by defendant's incorporators and approved by defendant's directors, which is consistent with this section, she is in no position to attack its application to her. *Everett v. Transnation Dev. Corp., 267 A.2d 627 (Del. Ch. 1970).*

Automatic termination of directors upon failure to remain qualified. — Certificate of incorporation could provide for automatic termination of directors upon a predetermined occurrence, where only the failure to remain qualified would cause a director to be removed. *Stroud v. Milliken Enters., Inc., 585 A.2d 1306 (Del. Ch. 1988),* appeal dismissed, *552 A.2d 476 (Del. 1989).*

Corporations

Stockholder's right to remove directors for cause did not preclude the automatic termination of a director upon failure to be qualified under the categories set forth in proposed certificate of incorporation. *Stroud v. Milliken Enters., Inc., 585 A.2d 1306 (Del. Ch. 1988)*, appeal dismissed, *552 A.2d 476 (Del. 1989)*.

The stockholders have power to remove directors for cause. *Campbell v. Loew's, Inc., 36 Del. Ch. 563, 134 A.2d 852 (1957); Dillon v. Berg, 326 F. Supp. 1214 (D. Del.)*, aff'd, *453 F.2d 876 (3d Cir. 1971)*.

The stockholders have the power to remove a director for cause even where there is a provision for cumulative voting. *Campbell v. Loew's, Inc., 36 Del. Ch. 563, 134 A.2d 852 (1957)*.

Shareholders may be given power to remove without cause. — Corporate bylaws may provide for removal of a director without cause by the shareholders. *Dillon v. Berg, 326 F. Supp. 1214 (D. Del.)*, aff'd, *453 F.2d 876 (3d Cir. 1971)*.

Shareholders are permitted to amend a certificate of incorporation, thereby eliminating a bylaw establishing a classified board of directors, so that the stockholders can then remove a director without cause. *Roven v. Cotter, 547 A.2d 603 (Del. Ch. 1988)*.

Director/member's ousting of his siblings could be viewed as exhibiting a lack of familial regard, but in his capacity as member and director of the foundation, he owed no fiduciary duties to other directors, only to the foundation, and as long as director's actions posed no threat to the foundation, director's status as member gave director the power to oust the siblings for any reason or even for no reason at all. *Oberly v. Kirby, 592 A.2d 445 (Del. 1991)*.

But allowing board to remove without cause violates shareholder rights. — To allow the board to remove 1 of its own members at any time without cause would seem to be completely violative of shareholder rights. *Dillon v. Berg, 326 F. Supp. 1214 (D. Del.)*, aff'd, *453 F.2d 876 (3d Cir. 1971)*.

Boards subject to removal for cause only. — The phrase "classified as provided in subsection (d)", which is used in subsection (k)(1) but not in the last sentence of subsection (k), was meant to refer only to staggered boards (pursuant to the first sentence of subsection (d)) and not to specially designated directorships. *Insituform of N. Am., Inc. v. Chandler, 534 A.2d 257 (Del. Ch. 1987)*.

III. SALE OR PURCHASE OF ASSETS OR CONTROL.

Reimbursement by corporation for proxy solicitation expenses. — The incumbent board of directors of a corporation may look to the corporation for payment of expenses incurred by them in soliciting proxies where a question of policy is involved. *Empire S. Gas Co. v. Gray, 29 Del. Ch. 95, 46 A.2d 741 (1946)*.

Business judgment rule weighs in favor of directors' decision to sell assets unless the complaining shareholders can prove fraud or a clearly inadequate sale price. *Gimbel v. Signal Cos., 316 A.2d 599 (Del. Ch.)*, aff'd, *316 A.2d 619 (Del. 1974)*.

Unless shareholders can prove fraud. — It is incumbent on the shareholders to prove that the directors against whom relief is sought were either guilty of actual fraud or that the price fixed for the sale of assets was so clearly inadequate as constructively to carry the badge of fraud. *Gimbel v. Signal Cos., 316 A.2d 599 (Del. Ch.)*, aff'd, *316 A.2d 619 (Del. 1974)*.

The burden is on the shareholders to establish some fraud, or what amounts to fraud, on the part of the corporation in order to prevail. *Muschel v. Western Union Corp., 310 A.2d 904 (Del. Ch. 1973)*.

Actual fraud is not necessary. — Actual fraud, whether resulting from self-dealing or otherwise, is not necessary to challenge a sale of assets. *Gimbel v. Signal Cos., 316 A.2d 599 (Del. Ch.)*, aff'd, *316 A.2d 619 (Del. 1974)*.

There are limits on business judgment rule which fall short of intentional or inferred fraudulent misconduct and which are based simply on gross inadequacy of price in the sale of assets. *Gimbel v. Signal Cos., 316 A.2d 599 (Del. Ch.)*, aff'd, *316 A.2d 619 (Del. 1974)*.

Showing necessary to prove fraudulent valuation of corporate assets. — In order to enjoin a proposed merger on the theory of constructive fraud based on a claimed discriminatory undervaluation or overvaluation of corporate assets, it must be plainly demonstrated that the overvaluation or undervaluation, as the case may be, is such as to show a conscious abuse of discretion before fraud at law can be made out. *Muschel v. Western Union Corp., 310 A.2d 904 (Del. Ch. 1973)*.

Mere inadequacy of price will not reveal fraud, but rather the disparity must be so gross as to lead the court to conclude that it was not due to an honest error of judgment, but rather to bad faith, or to reckless indifference to the rights of others interested. *Muschel v. Western Union Corp., 310 A.2d 904 (Del. Ch. 1973)*.

Directors entitled to presumption. — Where the evidence did not establish that the board of directors of the acquiring corporation failed to make an informed judgment when the merger plan was presented, they were entitled to the presumption of having made an informed judgment in good faith which could be attributed to a rational business purpose. *Muschel v. Western Union Corp., 310 A.2d 904 (Del. Ch. 1973)*.

Controlling shareholders have no inalienable right to usurp the asset sales authority of boards of directors that they elect, since a central premise of the *8 Del. C. § 141* vests most managerial power over the corporation in the board (and not in the stockholders); that the majority of a company's voting power is concentrated in one stockholder does not mean that that stockholder must be given a veto over board decisions when such a veto would not also be afforded to dispersed stockholders who collectively own a majority of the votes. *Hollinger Inc. v. Hollinger Int'l, Inc., 858 A.2d 342 (Del. Ch. 2004)*.

The responsibility of the directors in a sale of corporate control is to get the highest value reasonably attainable for the shareholders. *Mills Acquisition Co. v. Macmillan, Inc., 559 A.2d 1261 (Del. 1988)*.

Tender offer and sale of corporate assets held protected by business judgment rule. — See *Thompson v. Enstar Corp.*, 509 A.2d 578 (Del. Ch. 1984).

Decision regarding poison pill not protected by business judgment rule. — Board's decision to keep the poison pill in place was not reasonable in relationship to any threat posed and, therefore, the board's decision is not protected by the business judgment rule. *Grand Metro. Pub. Ltd. v. Pillsbury Co.*, 558 A.2d 1049 (Del. Ch. 1988).

Postponement of annual meeting. — A board's decision to defer the annual meeting to a later time in conformity with the company's bylaws and this section is not a decision that threatens the legitimacy of the electoral process and the propriety of such decision is to be measured by the permissive business judgment form of review. *Stahl v. Apple Bancorp, Inc.*, 579 A.2d 1115 (Del. Ch. 1990).

Weight given to private equity bids. — Simply because many deals in the large-cap arena seem to be going the private equity buyers' way these days does not mean that a board can lightly forsake any exploration of interest by strategic bidders. *In re Netsmart Techs., Inc. S'holders Litig*, 924 A.2d 171; 2007 Del. Ch. LEXIS 35 (March 14, 2007).

Failure to examine universe of possible buyers found. — Plaintiffs have demonstrated a reasonable probability that they will later prove that the board's failure to engage in any logical efforts to examine the universe of possible strategic buyers and to identify a select group for targeted sales overtures was unreasonable and a breach of their Revlon duties. In re Netsmart Techs., Inc. S'holders Litig, 924 A.2d 171; 2007 Del. Ch. LEXIS 35 (March 14, 2007).

IV. STOCKHOLDERS.

Procedure for redress of perceived wrong against corporation. — In the usual case, a shareholder's remedy for a perceived wrong against the corporation is limited to a demand upon the board that the corporation pursue redress. The board, in the exercise of its statutorily conferred managerial powers, then makes the ultimate decision of whether or not to prosecute the claim. *Heineman v. Datapoint Corp.*, 611 A.2d 950 (Del. 1992).

Stockholders' recourse is to bring derivative suit. — When stockholders are dissatisfied with a decision of the directors with respect to the corporation, their recourse is to bring a stockholder's derivative suit. *Maldonado v. Flynn*, 413 A.2d 1251 (Del. Ch. 1980), rev'd on other grounds, 430 A.2d 779 (Del. 1981).

Stockholder's individual right to bring derivative action does not ripen until the stockholder has made a demand on the corporation which has been met with a refusal by the corporation to assert its cause of action or unless the stockholder can show a demand to be futile. *Maldonado v. Flynn*, 413 A.2d 1251 (Del. Ch. 1980), rev'd on other grounds, 430 A.2d 779 (Del. 1981).

Review upon refusal of stockholder demand. — Stockholders who make a demand upon the board of directors which is refused, subject the board's decision to judicial review according to the traditional business judgment rule. *Spiegel v. Buntrock*, 571 A.2d 767 (Del. 1990).

Director response to stockholder demand. — The task of a board of directors in responding to a stockholder demand letter is a 2-step process: First, the directors must determine the best method to inform themselves of the facts relating to the alleged wrongdoing and the considerations, both legal and financial, bearing on a response to the demand; second, the board must weigh the alternatives available to it, including the advisability of implementing internal corrective action and commencing legal proceedings. *Rales v. Blasband*, 634 A.2d 927 (Del. 1993).

Where demand would be futile. — A court should not apply the *Aronson v. Lewis*, Del. Supr., 473 A.2d 805, 814 (1984) test for demand futility where the board that would be considering the demand did not make a business decision which is being challenged in the derivative suit; this situation would arise in three principal scenarios: (1) Where a business decision was made by the board of a company, but a majority of the directors making the decision have been replaced; (2) where the subject of the derivative suit is not a business decision of the board; and (3) where the decision being challenged was made by the board of a different corporation. *Rales v. Blasband*, 634 A.2d 927 (Del. 1993).

Demand futility in a double derivative suit. — A plaintiff in a double derivative suit is still required to satisfy the *Aronson v. Lewis*, Del. Supr., 473 A.2d 805, 814 (1984) test in order to establish that demand on the subsidiary's board is futile. *Rales v. Blasband*, 634 A.2d 927 (Del. 1993).

The *Aronson v. Lewis*, Del. Supr., 473 A.2d 805, 814 (1984) test does not apply in the context of a double derivative suit where the board was not involved in the challenged transaction. *Rales v. Blasband*, 634 A.2d 927 (Del. 1993).

Shareholders' burden in derivative suit challenging executive stock option plan. — Shareholders in a derivative suit alleging that allowance and acceptance of payments under executive stock option compensation plan were breaches of fiduciary duty had the burden of demonstrating that the compensation plan itself, having been added by a majority of disinterested directors and later ratified by shareholders with no allegation of inadequate disclosure in proxy materials, was so devoid of legitimate corporate purpose as to be a waste of assets. *Pogostin v. Rice*, 480 A.2d 619 (Del. 1984).

Stockholder ratification in self-interested deals. — Where management seeks and receives approval of a self-interested transaction from a majority of disinterested stockholders, the Chancery Court will defer to the stockholders' endorsement. *In re Walt Disney Co. Derivative Litig.*, 731 A.2d 342 (Del. Ch. 1998). But see *Brehm v. Eisner*, 746 A.2d 244 (Del. 2000).

Directors cannot compel dismissal of pending stockholder's derivative suit which seeks redress for an apparent breach of fiduciary duty by merely reviewing the suit and making a business judgment that it is not in the best interests of the corporation. *Maldonado v. Flynn*,

Corporations

413 A.2d 1251 (Del. Ch. 1980), rev'd on other grounds, 430 A.2d 779 (Del. 1981).

Motion by special litigation committee to dismiss derivative suit. — For case discussing motion generated by special litigation committee to dismiss stockholders' derivative suit under the authority of *Zapata Corp. v. Maldonado, 430 A.2d 779 (Del. 1981),* see *Kaplan v. Wyatt, 484 A.2d 501 (Del. Ch. 1984),* aff'd, *499 A.2d 1184 (Del. 1985).*

Special litigation committee powers to oppose suit dismissal. — Voluntary dismissal of an action by derivative plaintiff stockholders was denied where the corporation appointed a special litigation committee, as dismissal of the action would impinge on the committee's range of action, and would usurp its function. *In re Oracle Corp. Derivative Litig., 808 A.2d 1206 (Del. Ch. 2002).*

Mismanagement depressing stock value must be remedied through derivative action. — Mismanagement which depresses the value of stock is a wrong to the corporation, and therefore to the stockholders collectively, and thus is one which must be remedied through a derivative action. *Reeves v. Transport Data Communications, Inc., 318 A.2d 147 (Del. Ch. 1974).*

DELAWARE CASE NOTES — UNREPORTED

Demand for jury trial stricken. — When the long history of treating breach of fiduciary duty claims as equitable is considered and balanced with the mixed equitable and legal remedies sought in the instant case, the scales tip in favor of plaintiffs' claims being judged equitable. To weigh the factors differently would effectively ignore the historical factor, contrary both to the Seventh Amendment's purpose to preserve the right to jury trial as it existed in 1791, and to the express holding of *Granfinanciera,* that history is to be accorded weight in the balancing. Therefore, plaintiffs' demand for a jury trial of their claims is stricken. *Cantor v. Perelman, 2006 U.S. Dist. LEXIS 5210 (D. Del. Feb. 10, 2006).*

Federal fiduciary duty pleading standard. — Given that the Third Circuit has emphasized the view that the Federal Rules of Civil Procedure do not require a plaintiff to plead detailed facts to make out a claim for breach of fiduciary duties under Delaware law, district court is bound to hold that the plaintiff's allegations are sufficient in instance case. *IT Group, Inc. v. D'Aniello, 2005 U.S. Dist. LEXIS 27869 (D. Del. Nov. 15, 2005).*

Commitment to private ordering by charter. — Delaware's corporate statute is widely regarded as the most flexible in the nation because it leaves the parties to the corporate contract (managers and stockholders) with great leeway to structure their relations, subject to relatively loose statutory constraints and to the policing of director misconduct through equitable review. Subdivision (b)(1) of Section 102 and subsection (a) of this section are therefore logically read as important provisions that embody Delaware's commitment to private ordering in the charter. By their plain terms, they are sections of broad effect, which apply to a myriad of issues involving the exercise of corporate power. *Jones Apparel Group v. Maxwell Shoe Co., 2004 Del. Ch. LEXIS 74, No. 365-N (May 27, 2004).*

Classified boards. — Because the classified board provision clearly and unambiguously provides that the board will become classified and staggered at the 2006 annual meeting, and because defendant corporation's claims for reformation fail as a matter of law, defendant corporation does not presently have a classified board and all six of its board members must stand for election at the 2006 annual meeting. To rely on equitable powers to declare that defendant's board was classified as of the 2005 meeting would circumvent the explicit statutory requirements of subsection (d) of this section. Defendant corporation cites no authority to support the proposition that equity may properly be invoked to rescue a corporate act that violates a statutory command and furthermore, the Supreme Court has made it clear that equitable principles cannot be employed to change the terms of authoritatively binding corporate documents. *Lions Gate Entm't Corp. v. Image Entm't, Inc., 2006 Del. Ch. LEXIS 108 (Del. June 5, 2006).*

What constitutes a meeting. — Although the corporation law does not prescribe in detail formal requirements for board meetings, the meetings do have to take place. The evidence presented at trial leaves many doubts about whether the confrontation between the independent directors and CEO on the morning of June 29 constitutes a meeting. The mere fact that directors are gathered together does not a meeting make. There was no formal call to the meeting, and there was no vote whatsoever. The independent directors caucused on their own in what they admit was not a meeting and informally decided among themselves how they would proceed. Simply polling board members does not constitute a valid meeting or effective corporate action. *Fogel v. U.S. Energy Sys., 2007 Del. Ch. LEXIS 178 (December 13, 2007).*

Meetings represent more than a mere technicality; they are a substantive protection. A proper meeting should be informative and should encourage the free exchange of ideas so that a corporation's directors—through their active, meaningful participation—may keep themselves fully informed and in compliance with their fiduciary duty of care. The exchange on the morning of June 29—there was no discussion of the termination of the CEO issue and no vote of the board members—was unidirectional and was insufficient to constitute a meeting under Delaware law. *Fogel v. U.S. Energy Sys., 2007 Del. Ch. LEXIS 178 (December 13, 2007).*

Unanimity of entire board. — Action by written consent under subsection (f) of this section requires unanimity of the entire board, not just the unanimity of the disinterested directors. There is no exception to this rule, even if a director has an interest in the transaction at issue. *Solstice Capital II, Ltd. P'shp v. Ritz, 2004 Del. Ch. LEXIS 39 , No. 278-N (April 6, 2004).*

Determination of executive compensation. — The Delaware General Corporation Law (DGCL) expressly empowers a board of directors to appoint committees and to delegate to them a broad range of responsibilities, which may include setting executive compensation. Nothing in the DGCL mandates that the entire board must make those decisions. At Disney, the responsibility to consider and approve executive compensation was allocated to the compensation committee, as distinguished from the full board. The Chancellor's ruling — that executive compensation was to be fixed by the compensation committee — was legally correct. *Brehm v. Eisner (In re Walt Disney Co. Derivative Litig.), 2006 Del. LEXIS 307 (Del. June 8, 2006).*

Third-party contracts. — The Delaware General Corporation Law does not contain provisions that prevent directors from entering into contracts with third-parties for legitimate reasons simply because those contracts necessarily impinge on the directors' future freedom to act. If the judiciary invented such a per se rule, directors would be rendered unable to manage, because they would not have the requisite authority to cause the corporation to enter into credible commitments with other actors in commerce. *Sample v. Morgan, 2007 Del. Ch. LEXIS 16 (Jan. 23, 2007).*

Waste. — The Delaware Supreme Court has implicitly held that committing waste is an act of bad faith. It is not necessarily true, however, that every act of bad faith by a director constitutes waste. For example, if a director acts in bad faith (for whatever reason), but the transaction is one in which a businessperson of ordinary, sound judgment concludes that the corporation received adequate consideration, the transaction would not constitute waste. *In re Walt Disney Co. Derivative Litig., 2005 Del. Ch. LEXIS 113, No. 15452 (Aug. 9, 2005).*

The fiduciary duty of due care requires that directors of a Delaware corporation "use that amount of care which ordinarily careful and prudent men would use in similar circumstances," and — "consider all material information reasonably available" in making business decisions, and that deficiencies in the directors' process are actionable only if the directors' actions are grossly negligent. *In re Walt Disney Co. Derivative Litig., 2005 Del. Ch. LEXIS 113, No. 15452 (Aug. 9, 2005).*

Bad/Good faith. — Decisions from the Delaware Supreme Court and the Court of Chancery are far from clear with respect to whether there is a separate fiduciary duty of good faith. Good faith has been said to require an "honesty of purpose," and a genuine care for the fiduciary's constituents, but, at least in the corporate fiduciary context, it is probably easier to define bad faith rather than good faith. This may be so because Delaware law presumes that directors act in good faith when making business judgments. Bad faith has been defined as authorizing a transaction "for some purpose other than a genuine attempt to advance corporate welfare or [when the transaction] is known to constitute a violation of applicable positive law." In other words, an action taken with the intent to harm the corporation is a disloyal act in bad faith. *In re Walt Disney Co. Derivative Litig., 2005 Del. Ch. LEXIS 113, No. 15452 (Aug. 9, 2005).*

Good faith standard. — Upon long and careful consideration, the chancery court is of the opinion that the concept of intentional dereliction of duty, a conscious disregard for one's responsibilities, is an appropriate (although not the only) standard for determining whether fiduciaries have acted in good faith. Deliberate indifference and inaction in the face of a duty to act is conduct that is clearly disloyal to the corporation. It is the epitome of faithless conduct. *In re Walt Disney Co. Derivative Litig., 2005 Del. Ch. LEXIS 113, No. 15452 (Aug. 9, 2005).*

The universe of fiduciary misconduct is not limited to either disloyalty in the classic sense (*i.e.*, preferring the adverse self-interest of the fiduciary or of a related person to the interest of the corporation) or gross negligence. Cases have arisen where corporate directors have no conflicting self-interest in a decision, yet engage in misconduct that is more culpable than simple inattention or failure to be informed of all facts material to the decision. To protect the interests of the corporation and its shareholders, fiduciary conduct of this kind, which does not involve disloyalty (as traditionally defined) but is qualitatively more culpable than gross negligence, should be proscribed. A vehicle is needed to address such violations doctrinally, and that doctrinal vehicle is the duty to act in good faith. *Brehm v. Eisner (In re Walt Disney Co. Derivative Litig.), 2006 Del. LEXIS 307 (Del. June 8, 2006).*

Grossly negligent conduct, without more, does not and cannot constitute a breach of the fiduciary duty to act in good faith. The conduct that is the subject of due care may overlap with the conduct that comes within the rubric of good faith in a psychological sense, but from a legal standpoint those duties are and must remain quite distinct. Both legislative history and common law jurisprudence distinguish sharply between the duties to exercise due care and to act in good faith, and highly significant consequences flow from that distinction. *Brehm v. Eisner (In re Walt Disney Co. Derivative Litig.), 2006 Del. LEXIS 307 (Del. June 8, 2006).*

Inapplicability of business judgment rule protections. — Even if the directors have exercised their business judgment, the protections of the business judgment rule will not apply if the directors have made an "unintelligent or unadvised judgment." Furthermore, in instances where directors have not exercised business judgment, that is, in the event of director inaction, the protections of the business judgment rule do not apply. Under those circumstances, the appropriate standard for determining liability is widely believed to be gross negligence, but a single Delaware case has held that ordinary negligence would be the appropriate standard. *In re Walt Disney Co. Derivative Litig., 2005 Del. Ch. LEXIS 113, No. 15452 (Aug. 9, 2005).*

Construction with foreign laws. — Maryland statutory enactments that would mandate changes in the number and qualifications of directors of a health care service holding company with which a Delaware health care service corporation was affiliated necessarily affected the protections of the Delaware corporation and its subscribers by changing provisions contained in the bylaws; this fact was an important component in a reviewing court's determination that substantial evidence supported Delaware's Insurance Commissioner's decision to withdraw the approval previously given to the affiliation. *In re Proposed Affiliation of BCBSD, Inc. with CareFirst, Inc., 2004 Del. Super. LEXIS 333 (Oct. 4, 2004).*

Amendment to voting trust. — Shareholder agreement amended a voting trust agreement by obligating the voting trustees to vote their shares in a specific manner that would guarantee that the 4 shareholder groups subject to the shareholder agreement: (1) had equal director representation on the corporation's board; (2) had combined director representation that would constitute a majority of the corporation's board; and (3) had a veto fixing the number of directors at 6, unless each of the 4 shareholder groups consented; these rights and obligations had the effect of altering the original terms of the voting trust, and therefore the shareholder agreement was considered an amendment to the voting trust agreement. *President & Fellows of Harvard Coll. v. Glancy, 2003 Del. Ch. LEXIS 25 (Mar. 21, 2003).*

Court dismissed (for failure to adequately state a claim upon which relief could be granted) a 35 percent shareholder's claim that a 45 percent shareholder/director/officer (SDO) breached the SDO's fiduciary duty, by not including an alleged 15 percent permissible profit margin in the corporation's government contract bids, based on insufficient showings: (1) that the SDO's and the corporation's interests differed; and (2) of the negative effect, factually, on the corporation. *Ronsdorf v. Jacobson, 2004 Del. Ch. LEXIS 137 (Sept. 16, 2004).*

Voting trustee removal. — Although voting trustees may have extremely broad discretion in the management of the trust, where they have given preferential consideration to the interests of certain beneficiaries without considering the interest of the disfavored beneficiary, then these alleged facts give rise to an inference that the voting trustees have acted in such a manner as to have negligently discharged their duties, which can be grounds for removing a voting trustee. *President & Fellows of Harvard Coll. v. Glancy, 2003 Del. Ch. LEXIS 25 (Mar. 21, 2003).*

Secretly obtained consent to remove. — Although 2 directors of a family corporation secretly obtained 8 Del. C. § 228 written stockholder consents and utilized them to remove a third director and his sons as officers under 8 Del. C. §§ 141(k), 142(b), the consents were deemed valid where they conformed to the strict requirements of 8 Del. C. § 228 and were made by consenting shareholders who had received adequate disclosures; it was unreasonable for insiders of a private family corporation, when faced with removal by written consents under 8 Del. C. § 228, to insist that those seeking their removal under 8 Del. C. § 141(k) were required to meet a higher disclosure standard that was more akin to that of a public company. *Unanue v. Unanue, 2004 Del. Ch. LEXIS 153 (Nov. 3, 2004).*

Allegations of bad faith make recovery for deepening insolvency possible under Delaware law. Buckley v. O'Hanlon, 2007 U.S. Dist. LEXIS 22211 (D. Del. March 28, 2007).

Improper procedure for removal of CEO. — CEO's' motion for partial summary judgment was granted in an action pursuant to 8 Del. C. § 225, and it was determined that CEO retained the position; directors' attempt to remove the CEO failed as the board of directors did not unanimously consent to the action in writing, as required by subsection (f) of this section. *Solstice Capital II, Ltd. P'ship v. Ritz, 2004 Del. Ch. LEXIS 39 (Apr. 6, 2004).*

Repricing inference not shown. — Shareholder's allegations of ownership and repricing of stock options did not provide a basis to support an inference that there was a repricing scheme or conspiracy; the award of options was a form of director compensation authorized under subsection (h) of this section. *Cal. Pub. Employees Ret. Sys. v. Coulter, 2002 Del. Ch. LEXIS 144 (Dec. 18, 2002).*

Charter provision was valid and its plain terms established the record date for consent solicitation. Both subdivision (b)(1) of Section 102 and subsection (a) of this section of the Delaware General Corporation Law ("DGCL") provide authority for charter provisions to restrict the authority that directors have to manage firms, unless those restrictions are "contrary to the laws of this State." The charter provision is a valid exercise of authority under those sections and is not contrary to law, in the sense that our courts have interpreted that phrase. A consideration of subsection (b) of Section 213's terms and legislative history, as well as of the related statutory section governing consent solicitations, Section 228, reveals that no public policy set forth in the DGCL (or in Delaware's common law of corporations) is contravened by the charter provision at issue. Given the absence of any conflict with a mandatory aspect of Delaware corporate law, the charter provision's restriction on the board's authority to set a record date was valid. *Jones Apparel Group v. Maxwell Shoe Co., 2004 Del. Ch. LEXIS 74, No. 365-N (May 27, 2004).*

Appointment of new president. — Minority shareholder's claim that board breached its fiduciary duty when it appointed a new president was not dismissed since that claim was a shareholder claim and it was pleaded with sufficient particularity as to why the appointment by the board breached a fiduciary duty to the shareholder; the shareholder alleged that the new president was not qualified and was appointed primarily because of being related to the controlling shareholder. *Dweck v. Albert Nassar & Kids Int'l Corp., 2005 Del. Ch. LEXIS 183 (Del. Ch. Nov. 23, 2005).*

Dismissal of officer. — Minority shareholder's claim that board breached its fiduciary duty when it terminated employment as president was dismissed since that claim was a personal claim, not a shareholder claim, and since it was otherwise not pleaded with sufficient particularity as to why the termination by the board breached a duty to the minority shareholder. *Dweck v. Albert Nassar & Kids Int'l Corp., 2005 Del. Ch. LEXIS 183 (Del. Ch. Nov. 23, 2005).*

Creation of legal right. — Court's rejection of a litigant's argument that a contract is "legally unenforceable" because of a statute, this section, or because of certain judicial precedents establishes a legal right. *Unisuper Ltd. v. News Corp., 2006 Del. Ch. LEXIS 11 (Del. Ch. Jan. 19, 2006).*

When board must give way. — Delaware's corporation law vests managerial power in the board of directors because it is not feasible for shareholders, the owners of the corporation, to exercise day-to-day power over the company's business and affairs. Nonetheless, when shareholders exercise their right to vote in order to assert control over the business and affairs of the corporation the board must give way. This is because the board's power-which is that of an agent's with regard to its principal-derives from the shareholders, who are the ultimate holders of power under Delaware law. *Unisuper Ltd. v. News Corp., 2005 Del. Ch. LEXIS 205 (Del. Ch. Dec. 20, 2005).*

Nature and purpose of fiduciary duties misconstrued. — To the extent defendants argue that the board's fiduciary duties would be disabled after a hypothetical shareholder vote, this argument also misconceives the nature and purpose of fiduciary duties. Once the corporate contract is made explicit on a particular issue, the directors must act in accordance with the amended corporate contract. There is no more need for the gap-filling role performed by fiduciary duty analysis. *Unisuper Ltd. v. News Corp., 2005 Del. Ch. LEXIS 205 (Del. Ch. Dec. 20, 2005).*

Former service as outside directors. — Under certain circumstances, professional, financial, and personal relationships of directors may preclude a finding of independence. However, the plaintiff's factual allegations do not meet the relevant standard. The plaintiff does not allege that these former business relationships were material to the directors or that majority shareholder has or ever had an ability to influence or exert any control over these directors. Our cases have determined that personal friendships, without more; outside business relationships, without more are each insufficient to raise a reasonable doubt of a director's ability to exercise independent business judgment. Thus, the court cannot infer that majority shareholder had the ability to influence and impair the business judgment of these directors because they formerly served as outside directors for companies in which shareholder held an equity interest. *In re CompuCom Sys. Stockholders Litig., 2005 Del. Ch. LEXIS 145 (Del. Ch. Sept. 29, 2005).*

Delaware case law recognizes that a director breaches her fiduciary duty to creditors if she fails to comply with the dissolution procedures set forth in 8 Del. C. §§ 280-282. *Akande v. Transamerica Airlines, Inc. (In re Transamerica Airlines, Inc.), 2006 Del. Ch. LEXIS 47 (Del. Ch. Feb. 28, 2006).*

The fact that the alleged contract in this case gives power to the shareholders saves it from invalidation under Section 141(a). The alleged contract did not cede power over poison pills to an outside group; rather, it ceded that power to shareholders. *Unisuper Ltd. v. News Corp., 2005 Del. Ch. LEXIS 205 (Del. Ch. Dec. 20, 2005).*

Failure to allege facts with particularity. — Motion to dismiss a stockholder's complaint in a derivative action was granted under Ch. Ct. R. 23.1, because demand should have been made before pursuing the action; the stockholder failed to allege facts with particularity indicating that the corporations' directors either lacked independence or took action to create a reasonable doubt that the challenged transactions were other than the product of a valid exercise of business judgment under 8 Del. C. § 141(a). *Highland Legacy Ltd. v. Singer, 2006 Del. Ch. LEXIS 55 (Del. Ch. Mar. 17, 2006).*

When group pleading is utilized by a plaintiff, the identification of the individual sources of statements is unnecessary when the fraud allegations arise from the misstatements or omissions in group-published documents, such as annual reports, prospectuses, registration statements, press releases or other group-published information that presumably constitute the collective actions of those individuals involved in the day-to-day affairs of the corporation. *Buckley v. O'Hanlon, 2007 U.S. Dist. LEXIS 22211 (D. Del. March 28, 2007).*

Controlling stockholder requirement. — While corporate directors as a group were charged by *8 Del. C. § 141(a)* with a duty to manage the business and affairs of the corporation they served, a court could not aggregate the stockholdings of the corporation's directors to satisfy the controlling stockholder requirement for a cofounder of the corporation to maintain a direct claim for equity dilution. *Feldman v. Cutaia, 2007 Del. Ch. LEXIS 111 (Del. Ch. Aug. 1, 2007).*

Where demand would be futile. — Ch. Ct. R. 23.1 did not bar a stockholder's derivative action for breach of fiduciary duty regarding the alleged backdating of stock options because the complaint adequately alleged demand futility as 2 of the corporation's 10 directors allegedly received backdated options, and 3 of the remaining directors served on the compensation committee which authorized the option grants. *Conrad v. Blank, 2007 Del. Ch. LEXIS 130 (Del. Ch. Sept. 7, 2007).*

Demand futility shown. — Although 8 Del. C. § 141(a) provided that the business and affairs of a corporation were to be managed by or under the discretion of the corporation's board of directors, a shareholder was not required under Ch. Ct. R. 23.1 to have made a pre-suit demand of the corporation's directors before bringing a derivative action on behalf of the corporation because the shareholder showed that the demand would have been futile. *Feldman v. Cutaia, 2006 Del. Ch. LEXIS 70 (Del. Ch. Apr. 5, 2006).*

It is no safe harbor to claim that one was a paid stooge for a controlling stockholder. The two individuals voluntarily assumed the fiduciary roles of directors of the Delaware holding company. For them to say that they never bothered to check whether the Delaware holding company retained its primary assets and never took any steps to recover the LBC operating companies once they realized that those assets were gone is not a defense. To the contrary, it is a confession that they consciously abandoned any attempt to perform their duties independently and impartially, as they were required to do by law. Their behavior was not the product of a lapse in attention or judgment; it was the product of a willingness to serve the needs of their employer, even when that meant intentionally abandoning the important obligations they had taken on to the Delaware holding company and its minority stockholder. ATR-Kim Eng Fin. Corp. v. Araneta, 2006 Del. Ch. LEXIS 215 (Dec. 21, 2006).

Individual creditors of a Delaware corporation that is either insolvent or in the zone of insolvency have no right to assert direct claims for breach of fiduciary duty against corporate directors. Creditors may nonetheless protect their interest by bringing derivative claims on behalf of the insolvent corporation or any other direct nonfiduciary claim that may be available for individual creditors. *N. Am. Catholic Educ. Programming Found., Inc. v. Gheewalla, 2007 Del. LEXIS 227 (May 18,. 2007).*

CEO's material economic motivations. — Because the CEO might rationally have expected a going private transaction to provide him with a unique means to achieve his personal objectives, and because the merger in fact secured for the CEO the joint benefits of immediate liquidity and continued employment that he sought just before negotiating that merger, the stockholders are entitled to know that the CEO harbored material economic motivations that differed from their own that could have influenced his negotiating posture. Given that the special committee delegated to the CEO the sole authority to conduct the merger negotiations, this concern is magnified. As such, an injunction will issue preventing the vote on the merger vote until such time as the shareholders are apprised of the CEO's overtures to the board concerning his retirement benefits. In re Lear Corp. S'holder Litig., 2007 Del. Ch. LEXIS 88 (June 15, 2007).

Match rights are hardly novel and have been upheld by this court when coupled with termination fees despite the additional obstacle they are present. And, in this case, the match right was actually a limited one that encouraged bidders to top the original bidder in a material way. As described, a bidder whose initial topping move was over $ 37 could limit the original bidder to only one chance to match. Therefore, a bidder who was truly willing to make a materially greater bid had it within its means to short-circuit the match right process. Given all those factors, and the undisputed reality that second bidders have been able to succeed in the face of a termination fee/matching right combination of this potency, the chancery court is skeptical that a trial record would convince it that the board acted unreasonably in assenting to the termination fee and match right provisions in the merger agreement. In re Lear Corp. S'holder Litig., 2007 Del. Ch. LEXIS 88 (June 15, 2007).

Standstill agreement. — What competing bidder is asking for is release from the prior restraint on it, a prior restraint that prevents defendants' stockholders from choosing another higher-priced deal. Given that the board has decided to sell the company, and is not using the standstill agreement for any apparent legitimate purpose, its refusal to release competing bidder justifies an injunction. Otherwise, the defendant's stockholders may be foreclosed from ever considering competing offer, a result that, under precedent, threatens irreparable injury. Upper Deck. Co. v. Topps Co. (In re Topps Co. S'holders Litig.), 2007 Del. Ch. LEXIS 82 (June 14, 2007).

Private equity topping bids. — It is, of course, a reality that there is not a culture of rampant topping among the larger private equity players, who have relationships with each other that might inhibit such behavior. But the plaintiffs have not done anything to show that such a culture, if it exists and if it can persist given the powerful countervailing economic incentives at work, inhibited a topping bid against the original bidder. Even less have they shown that there was a perception that management was particularly enamored of original bidder, or that it would not work for another reputable financial buyer. In re Lear Corp. S'holder Litig., 2007 Del. Ch. LEXIS 88 (June 15, 2007).

Firing of CEO ineffective. — The mere congregation of a corporation's directors in the same room does not necessarily result in a board meeting, and the mere fact that three out of four directors determined how they wished to proceed does not obviate the need for adherence to bylaws and the general corporation law. The independent directors polled one another and informally decided that they should fire the company's CEO. They communicated this predetermined conclusion to him by ambush on June 29. Either because there was no proper meeting of the board or because CEO's attendance at the meeting was procured by deceit, the board's action is void ab initio. Therefore, CEO was still employed and was still authorized to call for a special election of stockholders. *Fogel v. U.S. Energy Sys., 2007 Del. Ch. LEXIS 178 (December 13, 2007).*

CASE NOTES — OTHER STATES

California

A hallmark of the business judgment rule is that a court will not substitute its judgment for that of the board if the latter's decision can be "attributed to any rational business purpose." *Katz v. Chevron Corporation, 22 Cal. App. 4th 1352, 27 Cal. Rptr. 2d 681 (1994).*

Reasonable grounds for defensive measures. — When corporate directors adopt defensive measures the possibility that they might be acting to protect their own interests rather than those of the corporation and shareholders creates an enhanced duty which calls for judicial examination at the threshold before the protections of the business judgment rule may be conferred. Accordingly, the directors must show that they had reasonable grounds for believing that a danger to corporate policy and effectiveness existed because of another person's stock ownership and that the defensive measure taken was reasonable in relation to the threat posed. The directors' burden of showing reasonable grounds for believing a threat to corporate policy and effectiveness exists may be satisfied by showing good faith and reasonable investigation. *Katz v. Chevron Corporation, 22 Cal. App. 4th 1352, 27 Cal. Rptr. 2d 681 (1994).*

Proof of good faith and reasonable investigation is materially enhanced by the approval of a board comprised of a majority of outside independent directors. *Katz v. Chevron Corporation, 22 Cal. App. 4th 1352, 27 Cal. Rptr. 2d 681 (1994).*

Lack of independence. — A director's association with a company that does business with the corporation does not in and of itself establish a lack of independence. *Katz v. Chevron Corporation, 22 Cal. App. 4th 1352, 27 Cal. Rptr. 2d 681 (1994).*

Obligation to bondholders. — The relationship between a corporation and the holders of its debt securities, even convertible debt securities, is contractual in nature. Arrangements among a corporation, the underwriters of its debt, trustees under its indentures and sometimes ultimate investors are typically thoroughly negotiated and massively documented. The rights and obligations of the various parties are or should be spelled out in that documentation. The terms of the contractual relationship agreed to and not broad concepts such as fairness define the corporation's obligation to its bondholders. *Pittelman v. Pearce, 6 Cal. App. 4th 1436, 8 Cal. Rptr. 2d 359 (1992).*

The policy underlying the Delaware participation requirement is that all trustees or board members should be able to hear and see each other and be able to exchange views before voting. The Delaware rule rests upon the premise that the board of directors should act as a board and speak as a board, and board decisions should be made only after conscientious, joint consideration of every proposition before them. *Professional Hockey Corp. v. World Hockey Assn., 143 Cal. App. 3d 410, 191 Cal. Rptr. 773 (1983).*

That directors breached their duty of due care is among the most difficult type of fiduciary duty claims on which to prevail. Such claims are at least subject to a gross negligence standard, which is a very high hurdle. *Robbins v. Alibrandi, 2005 Cal. App. Unpub. LEXIS 1019 (2005).*

A shareholder stating a claim for corporate waste must allege facts demonstrating that the directors authorized a transaction that was so one sided that no business person of ordinary, sound judgment could conclude that the corporation has received adequate consideration. The transaction must either serve no corporate purpose or be so completely devoid of consideration that it is in effect a gift. *Shaev v. Claflin, 2004 Cal. App. Unpub. LEXIS 5840 (2004).*

Colorado

Rescissory damages. — Where fraud, misrepresentation, self-dealing, deliberate waste of corporate assets, or gross and palpable overreaching are involved, a dissenting shareholder may bring an equitable action. In Delaware, a dissenting shareholder may receive rescissory damages in an equitable action. In this situation, the court awards rescissory damages when a traditional form of equitable relief, like rescission, is not feasible. *Szaloczi v. John R. Behrmann Revocable Trust, 90 P.3d 835 (Colo 2002).*

The business judgment rule is the offspring of the fundamental principle that the business and affairs of a corporation are managed by or under its board of directors. In carrying out their managerial roles, directors are charged with a fiduciary duty to the corporation and its shareholders. The business judgment rule exists to protect and promote the full and free exercise of the managerial power granted to directors. The rule establishes a presumption that in making a business decision, the directors of a corporation acted on an informed basis, in good faith, and in the honest belief that the action taken was in the best interests of the company. *Ajay Sports, Inc. v. Casazza, 1 P.3d 267 (Colo. App. 2000).*

The protections of the business judgment rule can only be claimed by disinterested directors whose conduct otherwise meets the tests of business judgment. Directors can neither appear on both sides of a transaction nor expect to derive any personal financial benefit from it in the sense of self-dealing, as opposed to a benefit which devolves upon the corporation or all stockholders generally. To invoke the protection of the business judgment rule, directors have a duty to inform themselves, before making a business decision, of all material information reasonably available to them. They must then act with requisite care in the discharge of their duties. While the Delaware cases use a variety of terms to describe the applicable standard of care, under the business judgment rule director liability is predicated upon concepts of gross negligence. *Ajay Sports, Inc. v. Casazza, 1 P.3d 267 (Colo. App. 2000).*

Connecticut

In performing their duties, the directors owe fundamental fiduciary duties of loyalty and care to the corporation and its shareholders. Subject to certain well-defined limitations, a board enjoys the protection of the business judgment rule discharging its responsibilities. The rule creates a presumption that in making a business decision the directors of a corporation acted on an informed basis, in good faith, and in the honest belief that the action taken was in the best interests of the corporation. *Hedberg v. Pantepec Iinternational Inc., 35 Conn. App. 19, 645 A.2d 543 (1994).*

The business judgment rule is available to directors even where they are responding to a takeover threat. In those circumstances, however, there is an omnipresent specter that a board may be acting primarily in its own interest. As a result, before the business judgment rule will be applied in this context, the directors must establish "reasonable grounds for believing that a danger to corporate policy and effectiveness existed" and the defensive measure chosen by the board must be "reasonable in relation to the threat posed." Once the directors make the above showings, the burden shifts back to the defendants who have the ultimate burden of persuasion to show a breach of the directors' fiduciary duties. *Hedberg v. Pantepec International, Inc., 35 Conn. App. 19; 645 A.2d 543 (1994).*

Duty to maximize assets. — Under Delaware law, the only fiduciary duty that is owed by corporate officers and directors to the creditors of an insolvent or nearly insolvent Delaware corporation is to maximize the assets of the corporation for the common benefit of all creditors,

Corporations

for whom those assets, in times of insolvency or near insolvency, are held in constructive trust. *Bennett Restructuring Fund, L.P. v. Hamburg, 2003 Conn. Super. LEXIS 61 (2003).*

The underlying duty to maximize corporate assets, upon whose breach the claim is based, is owed directly to corporation itself, and only indirectly to individual creditors as members of the broader community of interests that comprise the corporation. Therefore, such a claim is a classic derivative claim that can only be asserted either by or on behalf of the corporation, if it is not in bankruptcy, or by the bankruptcy trustee if bankruptcy proceedings have begun. *Bennett Restructuring Fund, L.P. v. Hamburg, 2003 Conn. Super. LEXIS 61 (2003).*

Extra duties to special creditors. — In Delaware, although the officers and directors of a corporation generally owe no duties to the creditors of their corporation apart from those arising under the creditors' contracts with the corporation, they owe certain "extra duties" to corporate creditors when there are special circumstances which affect their rights as creditors of the corporation, e.g. fraud, insolvency, or a violation of a statute. *Bennett Restructuring Fund, L.P. v. Hamburg, 2003 Conn. Super. LEXIS 61 (2003).*

With respect to a claim that a corporate officer or director of a Delaware corporation owes a fiduciary duty to any creditor of the corporation whom he or she defrauds, the courts of Delaware have long rejected that claim. With respect to whether under the "special circumstances rule" the extra duties imposed upon corporate officers and directors who defraud corporate creditors are fiduciary duties, for breach of which defrauded creditors can sue offending officers and directors both for fraud and for breach of fiduciary duty, Delaware courts conclude that such "extra duties" are not fiduciary in nature, and have dismissed a plaintiff's breach-of-fiduciary-duty claim while permitting its parallel fraud claim to proceed. *Bennett Restructuring Fund, L.P. v. Hamburg, 2003 Conn. Super. LEXIS 61 (2003).*

Constructive trust. — When a corporation becomes insolvent or nearly insolvent, the Delaware courts have recognized that the interests of creditors in the assets of the corporation become senior to those of the corporation's shareholders, for it is from those assets that the corporation's debt to its creditors must be paid. The law thus imposes a constructive trust upon those assets for the benefit of all creditors, and a fiduciary duty upon the corporation's officers and directors to preserve those assets for the benefit of creditors. *Bennett Restructuring Fund, L.P. v. Hamburg, 2003 Conn. Super. LEXIS 61 (2003).*

Reasonable grounds for defensive measures. — Under Delaware law, corporate directors, who owe the corporation a fiduciary duty, are presumed to act in good faith under the "business judgment rule," by which courts refuse to substitute their judgment for the judgment of directors as to business decisions made in good faith. Though the business judgment rule has been held to be applicable in the context of a takeover, in that context the presumption of valid exercise of business judgment is subject to inquiry when the business judgment at issue is the board's adoption of a defensive mechanism. In such a situation it must be established by the party seeking to uphold the validity of the directors' actions that (1) they had reasonable grounds to believe that the defensive mechanism was justified by a danger to corporate policy and effectiveness, and (2) that the defense mechanism adopted was reasonable in relation to the threat posed. While directors have a fiduciary duty to protect the corporation and owners from perceived harm, the defensive measures they take in the face of a potential change in control must be shown to be motivated by a good-faith concern for the welfare of the corporation and its stockholders and must be reasonable in relation to the threat posed. *Hedberg v. Pantepec Iinternational Inc., 1993 Conn. Super. LEXIS 529 (1993).*

The fact that a board enters into obligations with employees that may affect the options of subsequent boards and act as a defensive mechanism, does not, alone, make the obligations unfair. Even if a compensation plan is initiated as a defensive mechanism, it is valid if it benefits the company and is fair. *Hedberg v. Pantepec International, Inc., 1993 Conn. Super. LEXIS 529 (1993).*

Refraining from acting. — The business judgment rule operates only in the context of director action. Technically speaking, it has no role where directors have either abdicated their functions, or absent a conscious decision, have failed to act. But it also follows that under applicable principles, a conscious decision to refrain from acting may nonetheless be a valid exercise of business judgment and enjoy the protection of the rule. *Noble v. Baum, 1991 Conn. Super. LEXIS 1231 (1991).*

The business judgment rule provides that directors or officers will not be held liable for breach of fiduciary duty to a corporation or its stockholders for mistakes of fact or law that cause harm to the corporation or its stockholders, if the directors acted in good faith. Under the business judgment doctrine, acts of directors, within the powers of a corporation, in furtherance of its business, made in good faith and in the exercise of honest judgment, are valid and conclude the corporation and its stockholders; questions of management policy, contract expediency, and adequate consideration are left to the directors honest and unselfish decision, judgment and discretion and may not be interfered with or restrained. *Noble v.Baum, 1991 Conn. Super. LEXIS 1231 (1991).*

Waiver of business judgment rule. — In rare cases a transaction may be so egregious on its face that board approval cannot meet the test of business judgment, and a substantial likelihood of director liability therefore exists. Absent particularized facts, however, the protections of the business judgment rule are waived only in the case of improperly motivated corporate decisions, not in the case of poor ones. *Noble v. Baum, 1991 Conn. Super. LEXIS 1231 (1991).*

Board decisions carry a strong presumption of good faith and validity. This good-faith presumption can only be overcome by facts pleaded with particularity. *Noble v. Baum, 1991 Conn. Super. LEXIS 1231 (1991).*

The business judgment rule does not apply when the corporate decision lacks a business purpose, is tainted by a conflict of interest, is so egregious as to amount to a no-win decision, or results from an obvious or prolonged failure to exercise oversight or supervision. *Noble v. Baum, 1991 Conn. Super. LEXIS 1231 (1991)*.

District of Columbia

"Appropriate." — Under Delaware law, the court looks first to the bylaws to determine the validity of the board's actions. In interpreting bylaws which required the board's actions to be lawful and appropriate, in the context of the cooperative contract and bylaws, "appropriate" means "reasonable" and accordingly, the court reviews a surcharge imposed on rentals to determine whether it is reasonable. *Burgess v. Pelkey, 738 A.2d 783 (D.C. App. 1999)*.

Illinois

Self-dealing. — A majority shareholder, or a group of shareholders who combine to form a majority, has a fiduciary duty to the corporation and to its minority shareholders if the majority shareholder dominates the board of directors and controls the corporation. The circumstances of the challenged action or inaction dictate the scope of the fiduciary duty. If a shareholder plaintiff can prove that the majority shareholder has used his or her control over the corporation's board of directors to engage in self-dealing, Delaware law requires judgment of the self-dealing action of the dominated board by the entire fairness test. Self-dealing occurs when the majority shareholders cause the dominated corporation to act in such a way that the majority shareholders receive something from the corporation to the exclusion and detriment of the minority shareholders. The entire fairness test remains applicable even when an independent committee is utilized because the underlying factors that raise the specter of impropriety can never be eradicated completely and still require careful judicial scrutiny. This rule reflects the reality that in a transaction such as the sale of interest in a corporation, the controlling shareholder will continue to dominate the company regardless of the outcome of the transaction. *Feldheim v. Soms, 344 Ill. App. 3d 135, 800 N.E.2d 410, 279 Ill. Dec. 342 (2003)*.

The general rule is that directors do not owe creditors duties beyond the relevant contractual terms. However, in special circumstances, e.g., fraud, insolvency, or a violation of a statute, directors do owe a duty. *Prime Leasing, Inc. v. Kendig, 332 Ill. App. 3d 300, 773 N.E.2d 84; 200, 265 Ill. Dec. 722 (2002)*.

Duty of disclosure. — Delaware courts address the duty of disclosure by corporate directors only with respect to the following five scenarios: mergers, proxy solicitations, tender offers, self-tender offers, and stockholder votes. *Sims v. Tezak, 296 Ill. App. 3d 503, 694 N.E.2d 1015, 230 Ill. Dec. 737.Dec. 737 (1998)*.

Duty of candor. — Corporate directors of a closely held corporation do not owe minority shareholders a fiduciary duty of candor with respect to a repurchase of the minority shareholders' shares. *Sims v. Tezak, 296 Ill. App. 3d 503, 694 N.E.2d 1015, 230 Ill. Dec. 737 (1998)*.

Essentially, the duty of loyalty mandates that the best interest of the corporation and its shareholders takes precedence over any interest possessed by a director, officer or controlling shareholder and not shared by the stockholders generally. *Shaper v. Bryan, 371 Ill. App. 3d 1079; 864 N.E.2d 876; 2007 Ill. App. LEXIS 195; 309 Ill. Dec. 635 (March 8, 2007)*.

Fairness burden. — A person standing on both sides of the transaction (i.e., as majority shareholder voting to sell the shares and as employee wishing to purchase such shares) has the burden of proving the fairness of such a transaction. *Regnery v. Regnery, 287 Ill. App. 3d 354, 679 N.E.2d 74, 223 Ill. Dec. 130 (1997)*.

Payment of proxy expenses. — The Delaware Supreme Court has held that an incumbent board of directors may look to the corporation for payment of expenses incurred in soliciting proxies on a question of corporate policy. However, the Delaware court noted in its decision that there was a board resolution which committed the corporation to pay the proxy expenses of any person running for election on the management slate. *Foley v. Santa Fe Pacific Corporation, 267 Ill. App. 3d 555, 641 N.E.2d 992, 204 Ill. Dec. 562 (1994)*.

Removal of directors. — Under Delaware law, the shareholders may remove a director at any time without cause. *International Games, Inc. v. Sims, 111 Ill. App. 3d 922, 444 N.E.2d 736, 67 Ill. Dec. 500 (1982)*.

Under Delaware law, only the shareholders can remove a director without cause. *International Games, Inc. v. Sims, 111 Ill. App. 3d 922, 444 N.E.2d 736, 67 Ill. Dec. 500 (1982)*.

Del. Corp. Law Ann. § 141(k) (1981) provides for an exception to the general rule that directors may be removed without cause and also places cumulative voting restrictions on the removal of the directors. *International Games, Inc. v. Sims, 111 Ill. App. 3d 922, 444 N.E.2d 736, 67 Ill. Dec. 500 (1982)*.

The corporate opportunity doctrine is but one of the manifestations of the general equitable rule which demands of an officer or director of a corporation the utmost good faith and loyalty in his or her relations to the principal which he or she represents, and requires an undivided and unselfish loyalty to the corporate principal without conflict between this duty and the self-interest anticipated of human nature. The rule, described as inveterate and uncompromising in its rigidity, rests upon the broad foundation of a wise public policy that, for the purpose of removing all temptation, extinguishes all possibility of profit flowing from a breach of the confidence imposed by the fiduciary relation. *Paulman v. Kritzer, 74 Ill. App. 2d 284, 219 N.E.2d 541 (1966)*.

In this case, plaintiffs have failed to allege sufficient facts to show that CEO was self-interested in the merger. There was no evidence that he appeared on both sides of the merger or that he received a personal benefit not shared by shareholders. While plaintiffs alleged that his negotiations to retain his CEO position at the newly formed company constituted self-dealing,

Delaware law has routinely rejected the notion that a director's interest in maintaining his office is a debilitating factor. In addition, the record shows that the terms of the merger agreement were disclosed in the joint proxy statement. The merger agreement, which was approved by the Board and shareholders, disclosed the pay pledge that Dimon was to receive and his succession to become CEO. *Shaper v. Bryan, 371 Ill. App. 3d 1079; 864 N.E.2d 876; 2007 Ill. App. LEXIS 195; 309 Ill. Dec. 635 (March 8, 2007).*

Louisiana

Subdivision (k)(2) is a substantive provision that spells out the requirements for removing a director of a corporation having cumulative voting. *Crutcher v. Tufts, 898 So. 2d 529 (La. App. 4 Cir. 1995).*

The general rule allowing majority shareholders the power to remove directors elected by minority shareholders creates obvious possibilities of getting rid of directors who have been elected by cumulative voting. Because of this possibility, state legislatures early on began enacting statutes similar to Del. Code Ann. tit. 8, § 141(k)(2). *Crutcher v. Tufts, 898 So. 2d 529 (La. App. 4 Cir. 1995).*

Maryland

Disclosure obligations. — Under Delaware corporate law, the members of the board of directors of a Delaware corporation are corporate fiduciaries who owe a triad of duties to the corporation's shareholders: the duties of care, loyalty, and good faith. These fiduciary duties give rise to certain disclosure obligations. Often, the obligation to disclose will arise in the context of a communication being made by the directors to the shareholders about stockholder action that is being considered or solicited. *Paskowitz v. Wohlstadter, 151 Md. App. 1, 822 A.2d 1272 (2003).*

Under Delaware law, corporate fiduciaries are not required to engage in self-flagellation, as their duty of disclosure does not oblige them to characterize their conduct in such a way as to admit wrongdoing. *Paskowitz v. Wohlstadter, 151 Md. App. 1, 822 A.2d 1272 (2003).*

The Delaware law of the fiduciary duties of directors, as developed in judicial decisions, establishes a general duty of directors to disclose to stockholders all material information reasonably available when seeking stockholder action. Whether or not a failure to fulfill that duty will result in personal liability for damages against directors depends upon the nature of the stockholder action that was the object of the solicitation of stockholder votes and the misstated or omitted disclosures in connection with that solicitation. The mere fact that a director breaches his duty to disclose material information when seeking stockholder action, i.e., votes, does not necessarily result in personal liability on the director's part. Whether the stockholder has suffered an injury depends on the nature of the stockholder action that was the object of the solicitation of votes. *Paskowitz v. Wohlstadter, 151 Md. App. 1, 822 A.2d 1272 (2003).*

Under Delaware law, there is no per se rule that would allow damages for all director breaches of the fiduciary duty of disclosure. *Paskowitz v. Wohlstadter, 151 Md. App. 1, 822 A.2d 1272 (2003).*

Under corporate case law in Delaware, director disclosure violations that negatively impact voting or economic rights support a direct shareholder claim, and require proof of actual damages; disclosure violations that do not negatively impact voting or economic rights may be dismissed for failure to state a claim. *Paskowitz v. Wohlstadter, 151 Md. App. 1, 822 A.2d 1272 (2003).*

Under both Maryland and Delaware law, the director may find "safe harbor" by disclosing to the corporation the conflict of interest and pertinent facts surrounding the conflict so that a majority of the remaining disinterested shareholders or directors may ratify the transaction or, as the case may be, otherwise take action to protect the corporation's financial interests. *Storetrax.com, Inc. v. Gurland, 397 Md. 37; 915 A.2d 991; 2007 Md. LEXIS 68 (February 6, 2007).*

Applicability of Delaware law. — Because director was alleged to have breached his fiduciary duty to his corporation, a matter peculiar to the relationships among and between the corporation and its directors, pursuant to the internal affairs doctrine, Delaware law more appropriately applied to the present dispute. *Storetrax.com, Inc. v. Gurland, 168 Md. App. 50, 2006 Md. App. LEXIS 39 (Mar. 31, 2006).*

Breach of contract complaint. — Director did not violate, as a matter of law, his fiduciary duties to corporation by filing a complaint for breach of contract after he provided the corporation with written notice of his complaint. *Storetrax.com, Inc. v. Gurland, 168 Md. App. 50, 2006 Md. App. LEXIS 39 (Mar. 31, 2006).*

Declining to lift garnishment. — When director became a creditor of the corporation, he had the same rights to collect as any other judgment creditor. To adopt corporation's argument that director had a continuing fiduciary obligation to lift the garnishment upon its request would put director in the illogical and unjust position of being able to collect on the judgment only with the corporation's consent. Thus, declining to lift the garnishment was not a continuing breach of director's fiduciary duty. *Storetrax.com, Inc. v. Gurland, 168 Md. App. 50, 2006 Md. App. LEXIS 39 (Mar. 31, 2006).*

Overall demand committee procedure was reasonable under Delaware law. The committee hired independent counsel and worked together with counsel in the investigation and report writing. The demand committee directors, and not legal counsel made the decision to forego pursuit of the demand. The demand committee produced a report in writing that was sixty-one pages in length, contained one hundred and eighty-four exhibits, and detailed the process utilized in the demand committee's investigation. The committee properly identified the issues raised by appellants in their demand letter and responded to those issues in their written report. The committee interviewed eleven witnesses and requested interviews with appellants, but received no response. The committee also reviewed hundreds of documents in reference to appellants' claims, including corporate records, contracts, financial records, correspondence, and partnership and joint venture documents, among others. *Bender v. Schwartz, 172 Md. App. 648; 917 A.2d 142; 2007 Md. App. LEXIS 20 (March 1, 2007).*

Massachusetts

The business judgment rule, as expressed by the Delaware courts, protects the actions of directors. The business judgment rule is a presumption that in making a business decision the directors of a corporation acted on an informed basis, in good faith, and in the honest belief that the action taken was in the best interest of the company. *Kroutik v. Momentix, Inc., 2003 Mass. Super. LEXIS 112 (2003).*

Internal management. — The rule in Delaware is that in the absence of fraud, either express or implied, the action of the governing body of a corporation, in matters of internal management . . . will not be disturbed by a court of equity. *Beacon Wool Corporation v. Johnson, 331 Mass. 274, 119 N.E.2d 195 (1954).*

Freezeout. — In Delaware, in cases where the controlling shareholders stood personally to benefit by the actions alleged to constitute the freezeout, the entire fairness test, correctly applied and articulated, is the proper judicial approach. Indeed, majority stockholders may well owe fiduciary duties where a plaintiff's termination might amount to a wrongful freezeout of his or her stock interest. *Clemmer v. Cullinane, 62 Mass. App. Ct. 904, 815 N.E.2d 651 (2004).*

Delaware law may permit a claim for negligent misrepresentation against a corporate fiduciary, even where the allegedly false statement was made in connection with a stock offering rather than a request for shareholder action. *Venture Inv. Partners, LLC v. JT Venture Partners, LLC, 23 Mass. L. Rep. 304, 2007 Mass. Super. LEXIS 461 (October 25, 2007).*

Derivative action. — A cardinal precept of the General Corporation Law of the State of Delaware is that directors, rather than shareholders, manage the business and affairs of the corporation. The existence and exercise of this power carries with it certain fundamental fiduciary obligations to the corporation and its shareholders. Moreover, a stockholder is not powerless to challenge director action which results in harm to the corporation. The machinery of corporate democracy and the derivative suit are potent tools to redress the conduct of a torpid or unfaithful management. The derivative action developed in equity to enable shareholders to sue in the corporation's name where those in control of the company refused to assert a claim belonging to it. The nature of the action is two-fold. First, it is the equivalent of a suit by the shareholders to compel the corporation to sue. Second, it is a suit by the corporation, asserted by the shareholders on its behalf, against those liable to it. *South Shore Gastroninterology UA v. Richard F. Selden, 17 Mass. L. Rep. 673 (Super. 2004).*

By its very nature the derivative action impinges on the managerial freedom of directors. Hence, the demand requirement of Del. Ch. Ct. R. 23.1 exists at the threshold, first to insure that a stockholder exhausts his or her intracorporate remedies, and then to provide a safeguard against strike suits. Thus, by promoting this form of alternate dispute resolution, rather than immediate recourse to litigation, the demand requirement is a recognition of the fundamental precept that directors manage the business and affairs of corporations. In determining demand futility the court must make two inquiries, one into the independence and disinterestedness of the directors and the other into the substantive nature of the challenged transaction and the board's approval thereof. *South Shore Gastroninterology UA v. Richard F. Selden, 17 Mass. L. Rep. 673 (Super. 2004).*

Under Delaware law, a corporate entity does not owe a fiduciary duty to shareholders. *Gerzof v. Cignal Global Communications, Inc., 13 Mass. L. Rep. 429 (Super 2001).*

Delaware law does not impose broad fiduciary duties on stockholders of a closely held corporation. *Olsen v. Seifert, 9 Mass. L. Rep. 268 (Super. 1998).*

Entire fairness test. — Delaware law protects minority shareholders by reviewing those transactions where a controlling shareholder benefits from a transaction in a way that goes beyond the benefits accorded to other stockholders. This analysis, referred to as the "entire fairness test," requires the controlling shareholder(s) to prove the "entire fairness" of such a transaction. The "entire fairness" doctrine is designed to deal with those situations where a controlling shareholder has his or her own interest in the outcome of a transaction that might cloud his or her otherwise objective business judgment. *Olsen v. Seifert, 9 Mass. L. Rep. 268 (Super. 1998).*

Advice of Counsel. — Delaware law does not require a fairness opinion or an outside valuation before a board of directors can act on a merger proposal. However, unless the directors had before them adequate information regarding the intrinsic value of the Company, upon which a proper exercise of business judgment could be made, mere [advice of counsel that a fairness opinion is not required is meaningless. *Galvin v. The Gillette Co., 19 Mass. L. Rep. 291 (Super. 2005).*

Michigan

Determination of corporate opportunity. — A court, when determining whether a business opportunity is a corporate opportunity, must first ascertain whether the opportunity was presented to a corporate officer in the officer's individual or representative capacity. Second, after determining the manner in which the opportunity was presented, the court must determine the nature of the opportunity. Third, the nature of the opportunity is analyzed differently, depending on whether the opportunity is presented to a corporate official in the official's individual or corporate representative capacity. *Rapistan Corporation v. Michaels, 203 Mich. App. 301, 511 N.W.2d 918 (1994).*

Even though a business opportunity may not constitute a corporate opportunity under the conventional tests employed in determining whether a corporate opportunity exists, a corporate representative will be estopped nevertheless from denying that the business opportunity was a corporate opportunity if the representative wrongfully embarked the corporation's assets in the

Corporations

development or acquisition of the business opportunity. *Rapistan Corporation v. Michaels, 203 Mich. App. 301, 511 N.W.2d 918 (1994).*

When a corporation's fiduciary uses corporate assets to develop a business opportunity, the fiduciary is estopped from denying that the resulting opportunity belongs to the corporation whose assets were misappropriated, even if it was not feasible for the corporation to pursue the opportunity or it had no expectancy in the project. *Rapistan Corporation v. Michaels, 203 Mich. App. 301, 511 N.W.2d 918 (1994)*

The proscription against appropriation of corporate property for private gain is of broader application than the corporate opportunity rule. The latter is but a specialized application of the former. It essentially treats a corporation's expectations regarding certain business opportunities which are in the corporation's line of business and of practical advantage to it as corporate property which may not be appropriated for personal gain. On the other hand, the general proscription against misapplication of corporate funds applies equally to business opportunities outside the corporation's line of business. Thus, a business opportunity falling outside a corporation's line of business and which would not otherwise be considered a corporate opportunity, nevertheless will be deemed a corporate opportunity if developed or financed with corporate funds. *Rapistan Corporation v. Michaels, 203 Mich. App. 301, 511 N.W.2d 918 (1994).*

Minnesota

Directors may take action by unanimous written consent in lieu of a meeting in the absence of limiting language in the certificate of incorporation and the bylaws. *Erickson v. Horing, 2002 Minn. App. LEXIS 1137 (2002).*

Attribution of fiduciary duties. — Under Delaware law, a director owes a fiduciary duty to disclose fully and fairly all material information within the board's control when it seeks shareholder action. A minority shareholder who exercises actual control of corporate conduct will be attributed fiduciary duties. *Erickson v. Horing, 2002 Minn. App. LEXIS 1137 (2002).*

Disclosure of facts. — To establish a breach of fiduciary duty, a plaintiff must present evidence that a defendant made materially false statements, omitted material facts, or made partial or misleading facts. A fact is material if there is a substantial likelihood that a reasonable shareholder would consider it important in deciding how to vote. But there is no duty to disclose facts that are reasonably available to the stockholders. *Erickson v. Horing, 2002 Minn. App. LEXIS 1137 (2002).*

The demand requirement protects the corporate structure by recognizing that the directors of a corporation, and not the shareholders, have the power to manage the business and affairs of the corporation. Thus, a shareholder may not bring a cause of action to enforce the rights of the corporation unless the shareholder demands that the directors pursue the claim and the directors wrongfully refuse to do so or the shareholder shows that demand is excused because the directors

cannot make an impartial decision. *Professional Management. Associates. v. Coss, 2001 Minn. App. LEXIS 800 (2001).*

Reasonable doubt of directors' independence. — The directors' ability to affect the continued employment and remuneration of other directors as corporate officers raises a reasonable doubt that those directors could act independently. *Professional Management Associates v. Coss, 574 N.W.2d 107 (Minn. App. 1999).*

Burden of proof. — The business judgment rule posits a powerful presumption that a court will not interfere with decisions made by a loyal and informed board. It is the claimant's burden to rebut the presumption with evidence that directors, in reaching their challenged decision, breached any one of the triads of their fiduciary duty—good faith, loyalty, or due care. If the plaintiffs meet their burden, then the business judgment rule will not apply, and the directors will have to show the "entire fairness" of the challenged transaction to the shareholder-creditor plaintiffs. If the rule does apply, if the decision is found to have been made by a loyal and informed board, then the decision will not be overturned by the courts unless it cannot be attributed to any rational business purpose. *Potter v. Pohlad, 560 N.W.2d 389 (Minn. App. 1997).*

Duty to inform themselves. — As part of their fiduciary duties, corporate officers have a duty to inform themselves, prior to making a business decision, of all material information reasonably available to them. Having become so informed, they must then act with requisite care in the discharge of their duties. The duty of care is judged under a gross negligence standard. The court's role in evaluating the duty is to provide an objective review of the process by which the officers reached the decision under review. *Potter v. Pohlad, 560 N.W.2d 389 (Minn. App. 1997).*

Gross negligence for breach of a fiduciary duty is defined as reckless indifference to or a deliberate disregard of the whole body of stockholders or actions that are without the bounds of reason. *Potter v. Pohlad, 560 N.W.2d 389 (Minn. App. 1997).*

An informed decision to delegate a task is as much an exercise of business judgment as any other. The amount of information that it is prudent to have before a decision is made is itself a business judgment. *Potter v. Pohlad, 560 N.W.2d 389 (Minn. App. 1997).*

Bad faith. — A showing that the directors of a corporation acted in bad faith will rebut the presumption of the business judgment rule. Courts analyzing claims of bad faith generally inquire into the motives of the board members. *Potter v. Pohlad, 560 N.W.2d 389 (Minn. App. 1997).*

Duty of candor. — To the extent that a duty of candor exists separate from the duties of care and good faith, it entails the obligation to disclose all material information to shareholders when seeking shareholder approval. *Potter v. Pohlad, 560 N.W.2d 389 (Minn. App. 1997).*

The duty of candor, the obligation to disclose material information, is implied in an officer's relationship to the board which is charged with making informed decisions. *Potter v. Pohlad, 560 N.W.2d 389 (Minn. App. 1997).*

No close corporation exception for corporate fiduciary duty. — District court's conclusion that corporation owed no fiduciary duty to its shareholders and, thus, cannot breach duties of care, loyalty, or good faith was upheld by the appellate court. The district court's conclusion is rooted firmly in existing Delaware law. Appellants' argument that the appellate court should create an exception in Delaware law, imposing a fiduciary duty on close corporations to shareholders because (a) like partnerships, there is little division between the majority stockholders and the directors and (b) minority shareholders in close corporations cannot easily liquidate their investment if dissatisfied with the direction of the corporation was similarly unpersuasive. Appellants cite to no Delaware authority either approving an exception for close corporations or even entertaining the prospect of any exception to the general rule that corporations do not owe a fiduciary duty to shareholders. Accordingly, the district court did not err in refusing to interpret Delaware law contrary to Delaware courts. *Ahlberg v. Timm Med. Techs., Inc., 2006 Minn. App. Unpub. LEXIS 71 (Jan. 17, 2006)*

To establish that a director's independence was compromised by a financial interest, appellants had to demonstrate that the interest was of sufficiently material importance, in the context of the director's economic circumstances, as to have made it improbable that the director could not perform her fiduciary duties without undue influence. Appellants' allegations of self-interest in the instant case do not meet the threshold necessary to rebut the presumption of the business-judgment rule. First, appellants failed to produce any evidence to suggest that respondents' actions were motivated by improper or selfish interests. And appellants had the initial burden of establishing some credible and direct evidence to support their essential allegations in order to survive summary judgment. Appellants showed that two board members had a financial interest in the plan as shareholders, but failed to demonstrate how that interest was material and debilitating. Further, appellants' assertion that directors were incapable of exercising their duties independently lacks credible evidentiary support. *Ahlberg v. Timm, 2006 Minn. App. Unpub. LEXIS 641, (June 20, 2006).*

To establish a fraud claim under Delaware or Minnesota law, appellants must plead with sufficient particularity (1) a material misrepresentation, (2) made with knowledge or belief that the representation was false, or with reckless indifference to the truth, (3) with intent to induce appellants' action or inaction, (4) appellants' reliance, and (5) resulting damage. Appellants' fraud claim in the instant case lacks merit. Assuming the letter contained material misrepresentations intending to induce reliance, appellants fail to demonstrate how their reliance caused them to bring an action against the corporation as opposed to against the individual directors. *Ahlberg v. Timm, 2006 Minn. App. Unpub. LEXIS 641, (June 20, 2006).*

Nebraska

Merger. — A corporate director must act in the best interests of shareholders and is obligated to the duties of fidelity, good faith, and prudence with respect to the interests of security holders, as well as the duty to exercise independent judgment with respect to matters committed to the discretion of the board of directors and lying at the heart of the management of the corporation. These duties are applicable to a director's acts in recommending a proposed merger. In the context of a proposed merger, a director has a duty to act in an informed and deliberate manner. *ConAgra, Inc. v. Cargill, Inc., 222 Neb. 136, 382 N.W.2d 576 (1986).*

After a merger agreement is signed a board may not, consistent with its fiduciary obligations to its shareholders, withhold information regarding a potentially more attractive competing offer. *ConAgra, Inc. v. Cargill, Inc., 222 Neb. 136, 382 N.W.2d 576 (1986).*

Informing themselves. — A director's duty to inform himself or herself in preparation for a decision derives from the fiduciary capacity in which he or she serves the corporation and its shareholders. Because a director is vested with the responsibility for the management of the affairs of the corporation, he or she must execute that duty with the recognition that he or she acts on behalf of others. Such obligation does not tolerate faithlessness or self-dealing. Even if the board of directors enters into a contract containing a lockup provision, the agreement must not infringe on the voting rights of shareholders or chill the bidding process. *ConAgra, Inc. v. Cargill, Inc., 222 Neb. 136, 382 N.W.2d 576 (1986).*

New Jersey

In order to be protected by the business judgment rule, the directors making a business decision must have become fully informed and acted in good faith and in the honest belief that their actions are in the corporation's best interest. The court must determine whether the directors made a fully informed judgment when they rejected the shareholder's demand and that the rejection was in the best interests of the corporation. *In re PSE & G Shareholder Litigation, 315 N.J. Super. 323, 801 A.2d 295 (2002).*

The business judgment rule operates only in the context of director action. Technically speaking, it has no role where directors have either abdicated their functions or, absent a conscious decision, failed to act. *In re Prudential Insurance Company Derivative Litigation, 282 N.J. Super. 256, 659 A.2d 961 (1995).*

Demand. — Where directors are sued derivatively because they have failed to do something, such as a failure to oversee subordinates, demand should not be excused automatically in the absence of allegations demonstrating why the board is in incapable of considering a demand. Indeed, requiring demand in such circumstances is consistent with the board's managerial prerogatives because it permits the board to have the opportunity to take action where it has not previously considered doing so. *In re Prudential Insurance Company Derivative Litigation, 282 N.J. Super. 256, 659 A.2d 961 (1995).*

Corporations

New York

In general. — Under Delaware law, corporate officers, directors, and controlling shareholders owe their corporation and its minority shareholders a fiduciary obligation of honesty, loyalty, good faith, and fairness. Delaware law imposes a duty upon corporations to disclose all available material information when obtaining shareholder approval. Only damages caused by the breach of fiduciary duty are compensable. *Lama Holding Company v. Smith Barney Inc., 88 N.Y.2d 413, 668 N.E.2d 1370, 646 N.Y.S.2d 76 (1996).*

Management functions. — The business and affairs of a corporation organized under the Delaware corporation laws is to be managed by a board of directors, except as may be otherwise provided in this chapter or in its certificate of incorporation. *Zion v. Kurtz, 50 N.Y.2d 92, 405 N.E.2d 681, 428 N.Y.S.2d 199 (1980).*

The public policy of Delaware does not proscribe a provision contained in a shareholders' agreement even though it takes all management functions away from the directors. Although some decisions outside Delaware have sustained reasonable restrictions upon director discretion contained in stockholder agreements, the theory of Del. Corp. Laws § 350 is to declare unequivocally, as a matter of public policy, that stockholder agreements of this character are not invalid, that § 351 recognizes a special subclass of close corporations which operate by direct stockholder management, and with respect to § 354 that it should be liberally construed to authorize all sorts of internal agreements and arrangements which are not affirmatively improper or, more particularly, injurious to third parties. *Zion v. Kurtz, 50 N.Y.2d 92, 405 N.E.2d 681, 428 N.Y.S.2d 199 (1980).*

A written agreement between the holders of a majority of a corporation's stock is not invalid, as between the parties to the agreement, on the ground that it so relates to the conduct of the business and affairs of the corporation as to restrict or interfere with the discretion or powers of the board of directors or on the ground that it is an attempt by the parties to the agreement or by the stockholders of the corporation to treat the corporation as if it were a partnership. *Zion v. Kurtz, 50 N.Y.2d 92, 405 N.E.2d 681, 428 N.Y.S.2d 199 (1980).*

Proof of misappropriation of corporate opportunity. — Governing Delaware law does not necessarily require proof that a director have personally obtained a tangible benefit for purposes of a derivative claim for misappropriation of corporate opportunity, but only that he or she acquiesced in approving a wrongful transaction or failed to protect the interests of the corporation and the minority shareholders. *Brinckerhoff v. JAC Holding Corp., 10 A.D.3d 520, 782 N.Y.S.2d 58 (2004).*

Pre-suit demand. — Delaware law requires, generally, that as a condition precedent to a plaintiff bringing a shareholder derivative lawsuit, said plaintiff must make a pre-suit demand upon the board of directors to prosecute the contemplated action. A plaintiff need not meet this requirement if he or she sets forth in the complaint particularized factual allegations sufficient to create a reasonable doubt either as to whether the directors are disinterested and independent or whether the transaction at issue resulted from a valid exercise of business judgment. Where a derivative claim complains of the board's nonfeasance, as opposed to a business decision, a court need only determine whether or not the particularized factual allegations create a reasonable doubt that the board of directors could have properly exercised its independent and disinterested business judgment in responding to a demand. *Simon v. Becherer, 7 A.D.3d 66, 775 N.Y.S.2d 313 (2004).*

By-laws are unenforceable as contravening applicable Delaware law which precludes trustees of a not-for-profit corporation from binding themselves in advance to elect a particular individual to the board because the trustees have a duty to use their best judgment in filling a vacancy on the board of trustees as of the time the need arises. *Nesbeda v. Edna McConnell Clark Foundation, 266 A.D.2d 72; 698 N.Y.S.2d 627 (1999).*

Futility standard. — Where the wrong alleged is the inaction of the board of directors rather than a conscious decision approving some action taken by the corporation, the business judgment rule is inapplicable. The standard by which futility is assessed involves deciding what board members would have done had they been presented with a demand to investigate the alleged wrongdoing at the time the complaint was filed. In response to the demand, it is expected that the directors will determine the best method of informing themselves about the alleged misconduct and weigh available alternatives, including "internal corrective action and commencing legal proceedings." A director is considered disqualified from being able to make an independent decision in response to the demand if "interested" in its subject matter. Director interest is defined as the receipt of a "personal financial benefit from a transaction that is not equally shared by the stockholders." Alternatively, "interest also exists where a corporate decision will have a materially detrimental impact on a director, but not on the corporation and the stockholders." *Miller v. Schreyer, 257 A.D.2d 358, 683 N.Y.S.2d 51 (1999).*

Where inaction, rather than action, by a board is charged and directors are sued derivatively because they have failed to do something (such as a failure to oversee subordinates), demand should not be excused automatically in the absence of allegations demonstrating why the board is incapable of considering a demand. Indeed, requiring demand in such circumstances is consistent with the board's managerial prerogatives because it permits the board to have the opportunity to take action where it has not previously considered doing so. In such a case, it is appropriate to examine whether the board that would be addressing the demand can impartially consider its merits without being influenced by improper considerations. A court must determine whether or not the particularized factual allegations of a derivative stockholder complaint create a reasonable doubt that, as of the time the complaint is filed, the board of directors could have properly exercised its independent and disinterested business judgment in responding to a demand. *Wilson v. Tully, 243 A.D.2d 229, 676 N.Y.S.2d 531 (1998)*.

The entire review is factual in nature and, in determining demand futility, a court in the proper exercise of its discretion must decide whether, under the particularized facts alleged, a reasonable doubt is created that: (1) the directors are disinterested and independent and (2) the challenged transaction was otherwise the product of a valid exercise of business judgment. Similarly, a court should not apply the test for demand futility where the board that would be considering the demand did not make the business decision that is being challenged. *Wilson v. Tully, 243 A.D.2d 229, 676 N.Y.S.2d 531 (1998)*.

Although no demand upon directors of a corporation to pursue a derivative complaint will be required where it would be futile, the Delaware Supreme Court has held that the entire question of demand futility is inextricably bound to issues of business judgment and the standards of that doctrine's applicability. The business judgment rule is an acknowledgement of the managerial prerogatives of Delaware directors and is a presumption that in making a business decision the directors of a corporation acted on an informed basis, in good faith, and in the honest belief that the action taken was in the best interests of the company. Proper business judgment includes both substantive due care (the terms of the transaction) and procedural due care (an informed decision). *Wilson v. Tully, 243 A.D.2d 229, 676 N.Y.S.2d 531 (1998)*.

Insufficient evidence to challenge directors. — Where there is no claim that a majority of defendant directors are not disinterested and independent, the mere threat of personal liability for approving a questioned transaction, standing alone, is insufficient to challenge either the independence or disinterestedness of directors, although in rare cases a transaction may be so egregious on its face that board approval cannot meet the test of business judgment, and a substantial likelihood of director liability therefore exists. *Wilson v. Tully, 243 A.D.2d 229, 676 N.Y.S.2d 531 (1998)*.

Gross negligence, in the corporate context, means reckless indifference to or a deliberate disregard of the whole body of stockholders' or actions which are without the bounds of reason. *Wilson v. Tully, 243 A.D.2d 229, 676 N.Y.S.2d 531 (1998)*.

The gravamen of a director's fiduciary duty is the obligation of loyalty to the corporation. *Wilson v. Tully, 243 A.D.2d 229, 676 N.Y.S.2d 531 (1998)*.

Stock purchases. — Delaware law authorizes an officer or director to purchase the stock of the corporation with which he or she is associated except where the company involved has a policy of reacquiring its own stock, the director or officer takes advantage of superior or insider information or wrongly applies corporate resources to facilitate the purchase. *Ault v. Soutter, 167 A.D.2d 38, 570 N.Y.S.2d 280 (1991)*.

Special litigation committee. — The burden is upon the movant to prove the independence of the special litigation committee, and that it conducted a reasonable investigation of the matters alleged in the complaint in good faith. *Weiser v.Grace, 179 Misc. 2d 116, 683 N.Y.S.2d 781 (1998)*.

Executive committee. — Section 9 of the General Corporation Law of Delaware provides: The board of directors may designate two or more of their number to constitute an executive committee, who, to the extent provided in the said resolution or in the bylaws of the company, shall have and exercise the powers of the board of directors in the management of the business and affairs of the company. *Fensterer v. Pressure Lighting Co., 85 Misc. 621, 149 N.Y.S. 49 (Sup. 1914)*.

Independence of compensation committee. — Plaintiff's conclusory allegation that the committee was a "rubberstamp" for defendants' two eponymous controlling shareholders does not warrant a different result. Under Delaware law, the committee is presumed independent. The fact that individual committee members were selected and can be removed by these two shareholders by reason of their controlling interest is insufficient to rebut that presumption. The committee's minutes, and defendants' report to the committee, were properly considered on this pre-answer motion to dismiss, as they conclusively demonstrate that the committee examined all of the relevant evidence, considered the relevant contractual provisions and made a rational determination. *Brooks v. Cohen & Steers, Inc., 2006 NY Slip Op 4754, 817 N.Y.S.2d 235, 2006 N.Y. App. Div. LEXIS 7864 (June 13, 2006)*.

Reality, not injury, shown. — The board in the present case rejected plaintiff's offer of a bridge loan, and instead pursued other offerings, after consulting its advisors. That is not an injury. It is a reality flowing from a proper turning of the wheels of corporate democracy. Consequently, the motion to dismiss the causes of action for breach of fiduciary duty is granted. *Zoo Holdings, LLC v. Clinton, 2006 NY Slip Op 50167U, 2006 N.Y. Misc. LEXIS 225. (Jan. 24, 2006)*.

Delisting. — Delaware law recognizes the power of the issuing corporation's directors, in a proper exercise of their business judgment, to cause the corporation to delist even if, as an incidental matter, the delisting and deregistration might adversely impact the market for the corporation's securities. However, a plaintiff may state a valid claim under Delaware law for breach of fiduciary duty by alleging particular facts showing the decision to delist was for self-interested reasons rather than to avoid the continuing expense of complying with the reporting requirements of the Securities Exchange Act. Delisting a corporation's stock, even where legally permissible, will be proscribed if taken for an inequitable purpose. *Berger v. Scharf, 2005 NY Slip Op 51752U, 9 Misc. 3d 1122A, 2005 N.Y. Misc. LEXIS 2397 (Oct. 24, 2005)*.

Alllegations that (1) corporation delisted pursuant to a decision of the board of directors as dominated by defendant; (2) insiders like defendant can benefit from a company going dark because they have information the public shareholders do not, and can engage in transactions and receive compensation without revealing the details the SEC would require; (3) at the time that the board decided to delist, the company's finances were improving; (4) after delisting, corporation executed a high ratio reverse split, causing plaintiff and other members of the class to be cashed out of their positions; and (5) after the reverse split, the company executed a forward split in the same ratio as the reverse split, supported argument that defendants suggested motivation for delisting, to eliminate the cost of reporting, was pretextual. *Berger v. Scharf, 2005 NY Slip Op 51752U; 9 Misc. 3d 1122A, 2005 N.Y. Misc. LEXIS 2397 (Oct. 24, 2005).*

A plaintiff states a valid claim under Delaware law for breach of fiduciary duty by alleging particular facts showing that the directors decided to delist for self-interested reasons rather than to avoid the continuing expense of complying with the reporting requirements of the Securities Exchange Act. *Berger v. Scharf, 2006 NY Slip Op 50519U, 11 Misc. 3d 1072A; 816 N.Y.S.2d 693; 2006 N.Y. Misc. LEXIS 674 (Mar. 29, 2006).*

Share price. — Defendants' argument that plaintiff failed to show self-interest on the part of board chair and the individual defendants because any decrease in share price would equally affect both the individual defendants' stake in the company and plaintiff's interest was unpersuasive. The negative impact on the share price affects the defendant shareholders differently. Even though board chair's shares suffered the same drop in price as plaintiff's, board chair, as a director who dominates the board, now had sufficient control over corporation to structure any sale so that he receives an unfair amount of compensation. Plaintiff's allegations were sufficiently particular to show that board chair improperly used the corporation machinery to acquire the ability to engage in such transactions or to otherwise cause corporation to award himself an unfair amount of compensation. *Berger v. Scharf, 2006 NY Slip Op 50519U, 11 Misc. 3d 1072A; 816 N.Y.S.2d 693; 2006 N.Y. Misc. LEXIS 674 (Mar. 29, 2006).*

Insolvency. — Delaware law does not recognize a general fiduciary duty owed by corporate directors and officers toward creditors. However, Delaware law has long recognized that fiduciary duties may arise in favor of creditors over shareholders when a corporation is insolvent, or in the zone of insolvency. *Kensington Int'l v. Hiner, 2006 N.Y. Misc. LEXIS 2321, 236 N.Y.L.J. 40 (Aug. 22, 2006).*

Under Delaware law, directors of insolvent corporations may prefer one creditor, over another and may dispose of its assets so as to prefer favorite creditors, although the result may be to leave nothing for others who stand on a footing equally meritorious. Indeed, the mere fact that directors of an insolvent firm favor certain creditors over others of similar priority does not constitute a breach of fiduciary duty, absent self-dealing. Thus, any alleged—or proven—preference by the defendants to the assignors, by itself, does not constitute self dealing. Rather, the plaintiffs must plead other facts that, if true, would constitute self-dealing. This they have failed to do. Kensington Int'l v. Hiner, 2006 N.Y. Misc. LEXIS 2321, 236 N.Y.L.J. 40 (Aug. 22, 2006).

Negligence. — Plaintiffs negligence claim should be dismissed because, under Delaware law, such a claim is not actionable and, only where a director fails to act as a result of ignorance, can a claim for negligence be brought against a fiduciary. *Oppman v. IRMC Holdings, Inc., 2007 NY Slip Op 50093U, 2007 N.Y. Misc. LEXIS 117 (Jan. 23, 2007).*

Ohio

Transactional justification. — The business judgment rule is a tool of judicial review, not a standard of conduct. When the director's personal liability in damages is at issue, liability is predicated upon concepts of gross negligence. However, when the justification of a particular transaction is at issue, the court adopts a standard of judicial review whereby it must weigh the objective reasonableness of the business decision. Where the elements of the rule are satisfied in a transactional justification case, that decisions of disinterested directors will not be disturbed if they can be attributed to any rational business purpose. *Gries Sports Enterprises, Inc. v. Cleveland Browns Football Co., Inc., 26 Ohio St. 3d 15, 496 N.E.2d 959 (1986).*

A transaction not given protection by the business judgment rule is subject to strict scrutiny, and the directors have the burden of showing the transaction was fair. *Gries Sports Enterprises, Inc. v. Cleveland Browns Football Co., Inc., 26 Ohio St. 3d 15, 496 N.E.2d 959 (1986).*

Breach of fiduciary duty pleadings. — Under Delaware law, directors cannot be accused of a breach of fiduciary duty in the absence of allegations that the business judgment rule does not protect a board's decisionmaking. Such allegations must rise above the assertion that a corporate board acted against the interests of the corporation or engaged in bad decision-making and include, for example, allegations that the board was self-interested or that the board failed to exert any deliberative effort in making its decision. *NCS Healthcare, Inc., Plaintiff-Appellant v. Candlewood Partners, LLC, 160 Ohio App. 3d 421, 2005 Ohio 1669, 827 N.E.2d 797 (2005).*

Sale of all assets. — Generally, the management of the business and affairs of a Delaware corporation is entrusted to its directors, who are the duly elected and authorized representatives of the stockholders. Under normal circumstances, the business judgment rule mandates deference to directors' decisions, presuming that in making a business decision the directors of a corporation acted on an informed basis, in good faith, and in the honest belief that the action taken was in the best interests of the company. However, a sale of all assets is considered an extraordinary transaction, and subjects the directors' conduct to enhanced scrutiny to ensure that it is reasonable. *Huang v. Landixe Thermocomposites, Inc., 144 Ohio App. 3d 289, 760 N.E.2d 14 (2001).*

Interested directors. — Actions of interested directors are evaluated according to a higher standard than are those of disinterested directors. As defined by Delaware law, an interested director is one who either appears on both sides of a transaction or, through the transaction, acquires a personal financial benefit not equally received by the corporation or its stockholders. *Huang v. Landixe*

Thermocomposites, Inc., 144 Ohio App. 3d 289, 760 N.E.2d 14 (2001).

Fiduciary obligation does not require self-sacrifice. More particularly, it does not necessarily impress its special limitation on legal powers held by one otherwise under a fiduciary duty, when such collateral legal powers do not derive from the circumstances or conditions giving rise to the fiduciary obligation in the first instance. *Huang v. Landixe Thermocomposites, Inc., 144 Ohio App. 3d 289, 760 N.E.2d 14 (2001).*

Creditor and fiduciary. — One who may be both a creditor and a fiduciary (e.g., a director or controlling shareholder) does not by reason of that status alone have special limitations imposed upon the exercise of his or her creditors' rights. *Huang v. Landixe Thermocomposites, Inc., 144 Ohio App. 3d 289, 760 N.E.2d 14 (2001).*

Requesting board to sue itself. — Courts have expressed concern that the acceptance of the argument that it is futile for a shareholder to request a board of directors to sue itself would abrogate Rule 23.1 and weaken the managerial powers of directors. *Drage v. Procter & Gamble, 119 Ohio App. 3d 19, 694 N.E.2d 479 (1997).*

The business judgment rule is a presumption that in making a business decision the directors of a corporation acted on an informed basis, in good faith and in the honest belief that the action taken was in the best interests of the company. *Drage v. Ameritrust Corp., 1988 Ohio App. LEXIS 3972.*

In order to utilize the business judgment rule as a defense, the directors of a corporation must initially make several showings at trial. The directors must show that they had reasonable grounds for believing that a danger to corporate policy and effectiveness existed. They satisfy the burden by showing good faith, and reasonable investigation. In addition, the directors must show that the defensive mechanism was reasonable in relation to the threat posed. Moreover, that proof is materially enhanced where a majority of the board favoring the proposal consisted of outside independent directors who have acted in accordance with the foregoing standards. *Drage v. Ameritrust Corp., 1988 Ohio App. LEXIS 3972 (1988).*

Business judgment rule applicable. — The law of Delaware is well established that in the absence of evidence of fraud or unfairness, a corporation's repurchase of its capital stock, at a premium over market from a dissident shareholder is entitled to the protection of the business judgment rule. *Drage v. Ameritrust Corp., 1988 Ohio App. LEXIS 3972 (1988).*

Modified business judgment rule applicable. — When decisions are made by directors in actual or threatened take-over situations the modified business judgment rule applies. *Drage v. Ameritrust Corp., 1988 Ohio App. LEXIS 3972 (1988).*

Delaware courts have expressly held that directors have no duty to submit to shareholders acquisition proposals or takeover bids. *Abrahamson v. Waddell, 63 Ohio Misc. 2d 270, 624 N.E.2d 1118 (CP Ham. 1992).*

Oklahoma

Stock purchases. — Under Delaware laws, the purchase of shares of stock in a corporation by a director is entirely legal and proper. *Adams v. Mid-West Chevrolet Corp., 198 Okla. 461, 179 P.2d 147 (1946).*

Pennsylvania

Application of court's own business judgment. — Delaware law permits a court in some cases ("demand excused" cases) to apply its own business judgment in the review process when deciding to honor the directors' decision to terminate derivative litigation. *Cuker v. Mikalauskas, 547 Pa. 600, 692 A.2d 1042 (1997).*

Fiduciary duty violation. — Tinkering with corporate elections to interfere with shareholders' electoral rights violates a director's fiduciary duty to shareholders and is enjoinable. *Jewelcor Management, Inc. v. Thistle Group Holdings, Co., 2002 Phila. Ct. Com. Pl. LEXIS 79 (2004).*

Inequitable action does not become permissible simply because it is legally possible. *Jewelcor Management, Inc. v. Thistle Group Holdings, Co., 2002 Phila. Ct. Com. Pl. LEXIS 79 (2002).*

Under Delaware law, the standard for disclosure in a tender offer is that a corporate director or majority shareholder owes a fiduciary duty to their stockholders to disclose all facts material to the transaction in an atmosphere of entire candor. Similar standards have been applied in the context of limited partnerships. In extending an offer to the limited partners to buy their limited partnership units, the general partner owes a duty of full disclosure of material information respecting the business and value of the partnership which is in its possession. *Wurtzel. v. Park Towne Place Associates Limited Partnership, 2002 Phila. Ct. Com. Pl. LEXIS 29.*

Corporate directors owe a fiduciary duty to their shareholders to disclose fully all facts material to the transaction in an atmosphere of entire fairness. A fact is material if the plaintiff shows a substantial likelihood that under all circumstances, the omitted fact would have assumed actual significance in the deliberations of the reasonable shareholder. A corporate general partner owes a fiduciary duty to limited partners of the limited partnership of which it is a general partner. Because the relationship between general partners and limited partners is similar to the relationship between directors and shareholders, general fiduciary principles for directors apply to general partners. Thus, a general partner has a like duty of full and fair disclosure. *Alan Wurtzel Commerce Program v. Park Towne Place Apartments Limited Partnership, 2001 Phila. Ct. Com. Pl. LEXIS 79 (2001).*

Rhode Island

Applicability of business judgment rule. — The business judgment rule is a presumption that in making a business decision the directors of a corporation acted on an informed basis, in good faith and in the honest belief that the action taken was in the best interests of the company. This presumption, which protects a board-approved transaction, can only be claimed by disinterested directors, meaning that directors can neither appear on both sides of a transaction nor expect to derive any personal financial benefit from it in the sense of self-dealing, as opposed to a benefit which devolves upon the corporation or all stockholders generally. If the transaction at issue is an "interested" director transaction, the business judgment rule will be rendered inapplicable. When, however, the business judgment rule does apply, directors will be protected from liability, and the party challenging the transaction has the burden of rebutting the presumption. *Lynch v. John W. Kennedy Co., 2005 R.I. Super. LEXIS 103 (2005).*

In essence, the business judgment rule creates a rebuttable presumption that directors have acted properly. *Heritage Healthcare Services, Inc. v. The Beacon Mutual Insurance Company, 2004 R.I. Super. LEXIS 29 (2004).*

Tennessee

Capital assets may be revalued by the officers of a corporation from time to time as the actual value may increase or decrease. *Titus et al. v. Piggly Wiggly Corporation, 2 Tenn. App. 184 (1925).*

Texas

Change-in-control benefits. — Simply because a director stands to gain financially through change-in-control benefits does not mean the director has a financial interest in the merger so that the board may not delegate negotiating authority to that director. *Elloway v. Pate, 238 S.W.3d 882, 2007 Tex. App. LEXIS 8832 (November 1, 2007).*

Virginia

Legal responsibility. — The board of directors of a Delaware corporation has the legal responsibility to manage its business for the benefit of the corporation and its shareholders with due care, good faith, and loyalty. The board of directors of a Delaware corporation has the legal responsibility to manage its business for the benefit of the corporation and its shareholders with due care, good faith, and loyalty. *Stockbridge v. Gemini Air Cargo Inc., 269 Va. 609, 611 S.E.2d 600 (2005).*

Washington

Before bringing a shareholders' derivative action, shareholders must present their claims to the corporation and give the corporation an opportunity to pursue the case. Under Delaware law, the corporation has a variety of options, one of which is to form a special litigation committee (SLC) to evaluate the shareholders' claims. If the SLC concludes that the suit is in the corporation's best interest, the corporation may assume the shareholders' place and pursue the suit on its own. However, if the SLC concludes the action is not in the corporation's best interest, the corporation may bring a motion to terminate the suit. If the court does not grant the motion, the court may permit the shareholders to prosecute the suit on the corporation's behalf. *Dreiling v. Jain, 151 Wash.2d 900, 93 P.3d 861 (2004).*

Wisconsin

Merger proposal. — There is no duty under Delaware law to get an independent appraisal of a subsidiary before a merger. *Stauffacher v. Checota, 149 Wis. 2d 762, 441 N.W.2d 755 (Wis. App. 1979).*

CASE NOTES — FEDERAL

First Circuit

Fiduciary duties generally. — The directors of a Delaware corporation owe fiduciary duties to the corporation and its shareholders. To state a claim for breach of fiduciary duty, a complaint must allege facts from which one could reasonably conclude that directors, in reaching their challenged decision, breached any one of the triads of their fiduciary duty-good faith, loyalty, or due care. *Growe v. Bedard, 2004 U.S. Dist. LEXIS 23746 (D.Me. 2004).*

The duty of loyalty is transgressed when a corporate fiduciary, whether director, officer, or controlling shareholder, uses his or her corporate office or, in the case of a controlling shareholder, control over corporate machinery, to promote, advance or effectuate a transaction between the corporation and such person (or an entity in which the fiduciary has a substantial economic interest, directly or indirectly) and that transaction is not substantively fair to the corporation. Essentially, the duty of loyalty mandates that the best interest of the corporation and its shareholders takes precedence over any interest possessed by a director, officer, or controlling shareholder. *Growe v. Bedard, 2004 U.S. Dist. LEXIS 23746 (D.Me. 2004).*

To establish a breach of the duty of due care, a plaintiff must ordinarily establish gross negligence on the part of corporate directors. *Growe v. Bedard, 2004 U.S. Dist. LEXIS 23746 (D.Me. 2004).*

Under Delaware law, director liability for a breach of the duty to exercise appropriate attention may, in theory, arise from an unconsidered failure of the board to act in circumstances in which due attention would, arguably, have prevented the loss. A failure to act that leads to harm does not, however, automatically rise to the level of director negligence, or a breach of due care, because most of the decisions that a corporation, acting through its human agents, makes are not the subject of director attention. Legally, the board itself will be required only to authorize the most significant corporate acts or transactions: mergers, changes in capital structure, fundamental changes in business, appointment and compensation of the CEO, etc. *Growe v. Bedard, 2004 U.S. Dist. LEXIS 23746 (D.Me. 2004).*

Although a Del. Code Ann. tit. 8, § 102(b)(7), provision does not operate to defeat the validity of a plaintiff's claim on the merits, it can operate to defeat the plaintiff's ability to recover monetary damages. Accordingly, if the shareholder complaint only alleges a duty of care violation, the entry of a monetary judgment following a finding of unfairness would be uncollectable. Consequently, a trial pursuant to the entire fairness standard of review would serve no useful purpose. Thus, under those specific circumstances, when the presumption of the business judgment rule has been rebutted in the shareholder complaint solely by successfully alleging a duty of care violation, the director defendants do not have to prove entire fairness to the trier of fact, because of the exculpation afforded to the directors by the § 102(b)(7) provision inserted by the shareholders into the corporation's charter. *Growe v. Bedard, 2004 U.S. Dist. LEXIS 23746 (D.Me. 2004).*

Directors of Delaware corporations are fiduciaries who owe duties of due care, good faith, and loyalty to the company and its stockholders. *CCBN.com, Inc. v. Thomson Financial, Inc., 270 F. Supp. 2d 146 (D.Mass. 2003).*

To establish gross negligence under Delaware law, plaintiffs must demonstrate that defendant acted with reckless indifference to or a deliberate disregard of its obligations. A finding of bad faith requires even more: a person is said to act in bad faith where he or she consciously does wrong for a dishonest or deceptive purpose. *Brandt v. Hicks, Muse & Co., 213 B.R. 784 (D.Mass. 1997).*

Application of business judgment rule. — The business judgment rule posits a powerful presumption in favor of actions taken by the directors in that a decision made by a loyal and informed board will not be overturned by the courts unless it cannot be attributed to any rational business purpose. To rebut the rule, a plaintiff must provide evidence that the directors, in reaching a challenged decision, breached their fiduciary duties to the corporation or its shareholders. Among the kind of evidence that may suffice to rebut the business judgment rule is evidence that the defendant directors abdicated their duties. Unless the rule is rebutted, it is inappropriate for the court to second-guess the directors' decision. However, if the rule is rebutted, the burden shifts to the defendant directors, the proponents of the challenged transaction, to prove by a preponderance of the evidence to the trier of fact the entire fairness of the transaction. *Growe v. Bedard, 2004 U.S. Dist. LEXIS 23746 (D.Me. 2004).*

The entire fairness doctrine is a procedural rule that Delaware courts apply to place the initial burden of proof on defendant directors at trial when a case raises legitimate issues regarding the director defendants' breach of the fiduciary duties of good faith and loyalty to the corporation and its shareholders. *Growe v. Bedard, 2004 U.S. Dist. LEXIS 23746 (D.Me. 2004).*

Limitation on reach of exculpatory provision. — Unless a breach of good faith or loyalty is made out on the part of a director, an exculpatory provision in the articles will prevent a plaintiff from recovering money damages from that director and, by extension, obviates the need for said director to prove entire fairness to the trier of fact, even if a breach of the duty of care is made out. However, where a question is raised with regard to loyalty, an exculpatory provision will not justify a summary disposi-

tion. *Growe v. Bedard, 2004 U.S. Dist. LEXIS 23746 (D.Me. 2004).*

When entire fairness is the applicable standard of judicial review, injury or damages becomes a proper focus only after a transaction is determined not to be entirely fair. A fortiori, the exculpatory effect of a Del. Code Ann. tit. 8, § 102(b)(7) provision only becomes a proper focus of judicial scrutiny after the directors' potential personal liability for the payment of monetary damages has been established. Accordingly, although a § 102(b)(7) charter provision may provide exculpation for directors against the payment of monetary damages that is attributed exclusively to violating the duty of care, even in a transaction that requires the entire fairness review standard ab initio, it cannot eliminate an entire fairness analysis by the court. *Growe v. Bedard, 2004 U.S. Dist. LEXIS 23746 (D.Me. 2004).*

Duty of loyalty implicated. — Under Delaware law, directorial abdication of duty is sufficiently serious to implicate directors' duty of loyalty, not merely their duty of care. *Growe v. Bedard, 2004 U.S. Dist. LEXIS 23746 (D.Me. 2004).*

Waste. — The legal standard a plaintiff must meet to establish waste is onerous. Waste entails an exchange of corporate assets for consideration so disproportionately small as to lie beyond the range at which any reasonable person might be willing to trade. Most often the claim is associated with a transfer of corporate assets that serves no corporate purpose; or for which no consideration at all is received. Such a transfer is in effect a gift. Thus, waste is confined to unconscionable cases where directors irrationally squander or give away corporate assets. *Growe v. Bedard, 2004 U.S. Dist. LEXIS 23746 (D.Me. 2004).*

Under Delaware law transactions in which what the corporation has received is so inadequate in value that no person of ordinary, sound business judgment would deem it worth that which the corporation has paid constitute corporate waste. *Nault v. XTRA Corp., 1992 U.S. Dist. LEXIS 10512 (D.Mass. 1992).*

Golden parachute agreements. — Just as a board of directors may legitimately attempt to retain key executives during a hostile tender offer in order to secure their advice, the board may legitimately do the same regarding a disputed election for control of the company. A golden parachute agreement adopted in the face of a tender offer is a legitimate means to retain key employees. *Nault v. XTRA Corp., 1992 U.S. Dist. LEXIS 10512 (D.Mass. 1992).*

To show directorial liability where there was a reporting and information system in place, the plaintiffs would need to show that the directors knew of the inadequacies and failed to act. In other words, if the plaintiffs had pleaded that something like the internal investigation report in this case had been presented to the directors *before* the period in question, not after it, and that the directors had failed to address the problems revealed in the report, then the complaint would have met the standards for futility of a demand on that board. However, allegations that the directors became aware of problems and promptly conducted an investigation rooting out the causes for failure does not constitute a showing of conscious neglect and misfeasance, yet those are precisely the sort of allegations the plaintiffs contend would have saved the state complaint. *Pisnoy v. Ahmed (In re Sonus Networks, Inc.), 499 F.3d 47, 2007 U.S. App. LEXIS 19471 (1st Cir., Mass., August 16, 2007).*

Discrimination. — The Delaware courts distinguish between discrimination among shareholders and discrimination among shares, finding the former permissible; in the final analysis, these restrictions are limitations upon the voting rights of the stockholder not variations in the voting powers of the stock per se. The voting power of the stock in the hands of a large stockholder is not differentiated from all others in its class; it is the personal right of the stockholder to exercise that power that is altered by the size of his or her holding. Moreover, dicta in Delaware case law finds statutory authority for a discriminatory note purchase rights plan. *Georgia-Pacific Corp. v. Great Northern Nekoosa Corp., 728 F. Supp. 807 (D.Me. 1990).*

Demand futility. — Under Delaware law, *Aronson v. Lewis*, remains the seminal precedent on the circumstances for demand futility when a shareholder challenges a decision by the board of the corporation as a whole. *Aronson* and its progeny provide that demand futility is established if, accepting the well-pleaded facts of the complaint as true, the alleged particularized facts raise a reasonable doubt that either (1) the directors are disinterested or independent with respect to the challenged transaction or (2) the challenged transaction was the product of a valid exercise of the directors' business judgment. *Landy v. D'Alessandro, 316 F. Supp. 2d 49 (D.Mass. 2004).*

Aronson applies only to challenged transactions that were made by the board as a whole. For transactions made by individual directors or subsets of the board, Delaware law turns to the *Rales* test. *Landy v. D'Alessandro, 316 F. Supp. 2d 49 (D.Mass. 2004).*

Under *Rales*, a court must determine whether or not the particularized factual allegations of a derivative stockholder complaint create a reasonable doubt that, as of the time the complaint is filed, the board of directors could have properly exercised its independent and disinterested business judgment in responding to a demand. If the derivative plaintiff satisfies this burden, then demand will be excused as futile. *Landy v. D'Alessandro, 316 F. Supp. 2d 49 (D.Mass. 2004).*

The court in *Aronson* has explained the second prong of the test for demand futility in the following way: in determining demand futility, the court in the proper exercise of its discretion must decide whether, under the particularized facts alleged, a reasonable doubt is created that the challenged transaction was otherwise the product of a valid exercise of business judgment. The court makes an inquiry into the substantive nature of the challenged transaction and the board's approval thereof. Under Delaware law this is a heavy burden. *Landy v. D'Alessandro, 316 F. Supp. 2d 49 (D.Mass. 2004).*

The *Aronson* standard of reasonable doubt is not meant to alter or affect the definition of business judgment. The question in *Aronson* is whether the facts create an objective, reasonable doubt that the board exercised business judgment. *Landy v. D'Alessandro, 316 F. Supp. 2d 49 (D.Mass. 2004).*

The court in *Aronson* has articulated the basic principle of board interest: from the standpoint of interest, this means that directors can neither appear on both sides of a transaction nor expect to derive any personal financial benefit from it in the sense of self-dealing, as opposed to a benefit which devolves upon the corporation or all stockholders generally. *Landy v. D'Alessandro, 316 F. Supp. 2d 49 (D.Mass. 2004).*

A court employs a standard other than *Aronson* when determining whether plaintiff should have made demand on the board before bringing a derivative suit with respect to these types of decisions or transactions. Under *Rales*, a court must determine whether or not the particularized factual allegations of a derivative stockholder complaint create a reasonable doubt that, as of the time the complaint is filed, the board of directors could have properly exercised its independent and disinterested business judgment in responding to a demand. If the derivative plaintiff satisfies this burden, then demand will be excused as futile. *Landy v. D'Alessandro, 316 F. Supp. 2d 49 (D.Mass. 2004).*

If an action is derivative in nature, the shareholders must first make a demand on the corporate officers or directors to bring the suit on behalf of the corporation. This demand requirement can only be excused where facts are alleged with particularity which create a reasonable doubt that the directors' action was entitled to the protections of the business judgment rule. The business judgment rule is a presumption that in making a business decision the directors of a corporation acted on an informed basis, in good faith, and in the honest belief that the action taken was in the best interests of the company. Absent an abuse of discretion, that judgment will be respected by the courts. The burden is on the party challenging the decision to establish facts rebutting the presumption. *Niehoff v. Maynard, 2000 U.S. Dist. LEXIS 22009 (D.R.I. 2000).*

Judicial review. — When directors are subjected to litigation for breach of the duties owed a corporation or, by virtue of insolvency, its creditors, generally one of three standards of judicial review is applied: the traditional business judgment rule, an intermediate standard of enhanced judicial scrutiny, or the entire fairness analysis. The default standard is set by the business judgment rule. *Growe v. Bedard, 2004 U.S. Dist. LEXIS 23746 (D.Me. 2004).*

The business judgment rule can insulate unlawful conduct. As the Delaware Supreme Court has explained in *Aronson*, the business judgment rule is a presumption that in making a business decision the directors of a corporation acted on an informed basis, in good faith, and in the honest belief that the action taken was in the best interests of the company. One can reasonably conceive of numerous situations in which directors might act on an informed basis, in good faith, and in the honest belief that an action taken is in the best interests of the company and yet approve a transaction that, in the end, proves to be unlawful. *Landy v. D'Alessandro, 316 F. Supp. 2d 49 (D.Mass. 2004).*

Shareholders may bring direct and derivative actions simultaneously. *Niehoff v. Maynard, 2000 U.S. Dist. LEXIS 22009 (D.R.I. 2000).*

The following activities give rise to derivative actions: actions against directors or officers for breach of fiduciary duty to the corporation (e.g., waste of corporate assets, self-dealing, mismanagement of corporate business, misappropriation of corporate assets or business opportunities) and actions to recover damages for a consummated ultra vires act. *Niehoff v. Maynard, 2000 U.S. Dist. LEXIS 22009 (D.R.I. 2000).*

The following activities give rise to direct actions: fraudulent statements which directly affect the value of securities held by the shareholder; a suit brought to inspect corporate books and records; a suit against directors for fraud in the sale or purchase of the individual shareholder's stock; actions to compel payment of dividends; actions to preserve shareholders' rights to vote; a claim that a transaction improperly dilutes a shareholder's ownership interest or infringes the shareholder's preemptive rights; a claim that a proposed merger, recapitalization, or similar transaction unfairly affects minority shareholders; and a claim that a proposed corporate action should be enjoined as ultra vires, fraudulent, or designed to harm a specific shareholder illegitimately. *Niehoff v. Maynard, 2000 U.S. Dist. LEXIS 22009 (D.R.I. 2000).*

Second Circuit

Business judgment rule generally. — The business judgment rule is a presumption which states that in making a business decision the directors of a corporation have acted on an informed basis, in good faith and in the honest belief that the action taken was in the best interests of the company. The burden of rebutting this presumption is usually on the party challenging the board's decision. However, if a party challenging the transaction is able to demonstrate that a majority of the voting members of the board of directors had a personal financial interest in the merger, the directors cannot be shielded by the business judgment rule and the burden of proving the fairness of the transaction shifts to the directors. *Caruso v. Metex Corp., 1992 U.S. Dist. LEXIS 14556 (E.D.N.Y. 1992).*

Under the business judgment rule, where a board of directors is found to have acted in good faith, a court will not try to substitute its judgment for that of the board, and will uphold the board's decisions as long as they are attributable to any rational business purpose. *CRTF Corp. v. Federated Department Stores, Inc., 683 F. Supp. 422 (S.D.N.Y. 1988).*

The business judgment rule applies even where a majority of a board of directors has a financial interest in a transaction, providing that such transaction was approved by the fully informed disinterested directors. *Caruso v. Metex Corp., 1992 U.S. Dist. LEXIS 14556 (E.D.N.Y. 1992).*

Overcoming the powerful presumptions of the business judgment rule presents a heavy burden of establishing that: (1) the directors were not disinterested and independent; and that (2) the challenged transaction was not the product of a valid exercise of business judgment. Moreover, the defendants can be held personally liable only if there is evidence of their bad faith, intentional misconduct, or knowing violation of the law. *Yeung Chan v. Diamond, 2005 U.S. Dist. LEXIS 6939 (S.D.N.Y. 2005).*

Proper business judgment involves both a substantive element — related to the actual terms of the transaction — and a procedural element — related to making an informed decision. *Halpert Enters. v. Harrison, 362 F. Supp. 2d 426 (S.D.N.Y. 2005).*

Board members enjoy the benefit of the business judgment rule, a presumption that in making a business decision the directors of a corporation acted on an informed basis, in good faith and in the honest belief that the action was taken in the best interests of the company. *Halpert Enters. v. Harrison, 362 F. Supp. 2d 426 (S.D.N.Y. 2005).*

Under Delaware law, to establish a breach of fiduciary duty, a plaintiff first must prove facts sufficient to overcome the presumption inherent in the business judgment rule. The business judgment rule is a presumption that in making a business decision the directors of a corporation acted on an informed basis, in good faith and in honest belief that the action taken was in the best interests of the company. Four elements define the business judgment rule presumption: (1) a business decision; (2) disinterestedness and independence; (3) due care; and (4) good faith. The presumption of the business judgment rule is rebutted in those rare cases where a plaintiff establishes facts to show that any of the four elements was not present. *Roselink Investors, L.L.C. v. Shenkman, 2004 U.S. Dist. LEXIS 6905 (S.D.N.Y. 2004).*

While the Delaware cases use a variety of terms to describe the applicable standard of care, under the business judgment rule director liability is predicated upon concepts of gross negligence. Under Delaware law, a court should reach conclusions as to the sufficiency of allegations regarding interest and independence only after considering all the facts alleged on a case-by-case basis. *Roselink Investors, L.L.C. v. Shenkman, 2004 U.S. Dist. LEXIS 6905 (S.D.N.Y. 2004).*

The duty of the directors of a company to act on an informed basis forms the duty-of-care element of the business judgment rule. To invoke the rule's protection directors have a duty to inform themselves, prior to making a business decision, of all material information reasonably available to them. The standard for judging the informational component of the directors' decisionmaking does not mean that the board must be informed of every fact. The board is responsible for considering only material facts that are reasonably available, not those that are immaterial or out of the board's reasonable reach. The concept of gross negligence is the proper standard for determining whether a business judgment reached by a board of directors was an informed one. *Roselink Investors,*

L.L.C. v. Shenkman, 2004 U.S. Dist. LEXIS 6905 (S.D.N.Y. 2004).

Under the business judgment rule, courts do not examine the wisdom of the decision itself. The court gives great deference to the substance of the directors' decision and will not invalidate the decision, will not examine its reasonableness, and will not substitute its view for those of the board if the latter's decision can be attributed to any rational business purpose. Roselink Investors, L.L.C. v. Shenkman, 2004 U.S. Dist. LEXIS 6905 (S.D.N.Y. 2004).

Derivative actions generally. — Derivative actions, which are an extremely useful check on directors' faithful performance of their duties, are justified in the face of directors' inaction, whether a failure to act diligently or an unjustified refusal to act. Action by the directors may be prompted by a demand, thereby vitiating the need for a lawsuit. Refusal to act can then be overcome, in protection of the corporation and its shareholders, by the derivative lawsuit. Nonetheless, the board should have the initial opportunity to make the decision. Excusing a demand will not provide the directors an opportunity to seek to impose responsibility on the actual wrongdoers. Faced with a demand, no action may be taken, but the directors should not be denied the opportunity. Citron v. Daniell, 796 F. Supp. 649 (D.Conn. 1992).

As the mere threat of personal liability is insufficient to challenge either the independence or disinterestedness of directors, a plaintiff in a derivative suit must allege particular facts giving rise to a substantial likelihood of director liability. Halpert Enters. v. Harrison, 362 F. Supp. 2d 426 (S.D.N.Y. 2005).

Since claims asserted in a shareholder derivative suit belong to the corporation, it is incumbent upon the shareholder plaintiff to make a demand upon the corporation's board of directors prior to commencing the action. This requirement stems from the well-settled principle that directors, rather than shareholders, manage the affairs of the corporation and the decision to bring or not to bring a lawsuit on behalf of a corporation is a decision concerning the management of the corporation. Therefore, a motion to dismiss for failure to make a demand is not intended to test the legal sufficiency of the plaintiff's substantive claim. Rather, its purpose is to determine who is entitled, as between the corporation and its shareholders, to assert the plaintiff's underlying substantive claim on the corporation's behalf. In re Trump Hotels Shareholder Derivative Litig., 2000 U.S. Dist. LEXIS 13550 (S.D.N.Y. 2000).

Under Delaware law, a complaint in a shareholder derivative suit must allege with particularity the efforts, if any, made by a plaintiff to obtain the action the plaintiff desires from the directors or comparable authority and the reasons for the plaintiff's failure to obtain the action or for not making the effort. The purpose of the pre-suit demand is to assure that the stockholder affords the corporation the opportunity to address an alleged wrong without litigation, to decide whether to invest the resources of the corporation in litigation, and to control any litigation which does occur. This requirement is a recognition of the important principle that directors manage the business

and affairs of corporations. Nemazee v. Premier, Inc., 232 F. Supp. 2d 172 (S.D.N.Y. 2002).

Under Del. Ch. Ct. R. 23.1 and the cases interpreting it, a plaintiff who wishes to file a derivative suit must either make a demand on the company's board (and argue wrongful refusal if and when the board refuses the demand) or argue that demand need not be made because it would be futile. Under Delaware law, a plaintiff may not both make a demand on the board of directors and simultaneously argue that making such a demand would be futile. A stockholder who asserts a derivative claim cannot stand neutral, in effect, with respect to the board of directors' ability to respond to a request to take action, by simultaneously making a demand for such action and continuing to argue that demand is excused. Moreover, once a plaintiff makes a demand on the board, even a post-suit demand, the original argument that making a demand would be futile, is moot. While this approach has been criticized in other jurisdictions as being "arbitrary," "too restrictive," and having "no logical basis," the Spiegel rule is well-established in Delaware. Nemazee v. Premier, Inc., 232 F. Supp. 2d 172 (S.D.N.Y. 2002).

It is generally recognized that a stockholder who has acquiesced or participated in the acts giving rise to his or her claim has no standing to vindicate the rights of the corporation in a derivative action. The rule is designed, among other things, to prevent speculation by the stockholder on the results of corporate transactions, with the object of accepting the advantages if they turn out well or challenging them if they are not beneficial. In other words, it prevents a shareholder from eating his or her cake and having it too. Rosenfeld v. Schwitzer Corp., 251 F. Supp. 758 (S.D.N.Y. 1966).

Fiduciary duties generally. — Under Delaware law, directors and officers of a corporation owe a fiduciary duty to the corporation to manage it honestly, impartially, and on behalf of the corporation, and cannot use the position to further their personal interests. Cohen v. Bloch, 539 F. Supp. 760 (S.D.N.Y. 1981).

If an officer or director of a corporation, in violation of his or her fiduciary duty, acquires gain or advantage for himself or herself, the law charges the interest so acquired with a trust for the benefit of the corporation, at its election, which it denies to the betrayer all benefit and profit. Cohen v. Bloch, 539 F. Supp. 760 (S.D.N.Y. 1981).

Under Delaware law, a common-law claim for breach of fiduciary duty by a corporate director or officer can only be asserted (a) by the corporation or on the corporation's behalf in a derivative action or (b) by individual shareholders when a special injury has occurred. Zimmerman v. Prime Medical Services, Inc., 729 F. Supp. 23 (S.D.N.Y. 1990).

Corporate directors have fiduciary duties of loyalty to the corporation, and of due care in the administration of corporate affairs. CRTF Corp. v. Federated Department Stores, Inc., 683 F. Supp. 422 (S.D.N.Y. 1988).

Directors are bound to protect the interests of the corporation through exercise of the duties of due care, good faith, and loyalty. This obligation has been described as a duty not only affirmatively to protect the interests of the corporation committed to an officer's charge, but also to refrain from doing anything that would work injury to the corporation. *In re Trump Hotels Shareholder Derivative Litig., 2000 U.S. Dist. LEXIS 13550 (S.D.N.Y. 2000).*

As authorized by Delaware corporate law, a certificate of incorporation can eliminate directors' personal liability for breaches of their fiduciary duties. To overcome this protection, plaintiff must demonstrate that his claim against the director defendants falls outside of § 102(b)(7) by showing bad faith, intentional misconduct, or a knowing violation of the law on the part of the defendants. *Karpus v. Borelli, 2004 U.S. Dist. LEXIS 21429 (S.D.N.Y. 2004).*

To state a claim for breach of fiduciary duty under Delaware law, a plaintiff must satisfy a three-pronged test. The plaintiff must allege: (1) the existence of a fiduciary duty; (2) a breach of that duty; (3) knowing participation in the breach by the defendants. *Aquilio v. Manaker, 1991 U.S. Dist. LEXIS 14592 (N.D.N.Y. 1991).*

Delaware law does not seem to impose a duty of care on controlling shareholders in cases in which there is no breach of the duty of loyalty. The board of directors owes a "triad" of fiduciary duties to the corporation: loyalty, due care, and good faith. An independent duty of care has been recognized in certain contexts. *Official Committee of the Unsecured Creditors v. Investcorp, S.A., 137 F. Supp. 2d 502 (S.D.N.Y 2001).*

Under Delaware law, whenever directors communicate publicly or directly with shareholders about the corporation's affairs, they have a fiduciary duty to exercise due care, good faith, and loyalty, which is breached when they knowingly disseminate false or misleading information about the financial condition of the company. *Benjamin v. Kim, 1999 U.S. Dist. LEXIS 6089 (S.D.N.Y. 1999).*

"Bad faith". — The Delaware Supreme Court has defined "bad faith" as not simply bad judgment or negligence, but, rather, it implies the conscious doing of a wrong because of dishonest purpose or moral obliquity; it is different from the negative idea of negligence in that it contemplates a state of mind affirmatively operating with furtive design or ill will. The absence of significant financial adverse interest creates a presumption of good faith, although the good-faith requirement further demands an ad hoc determination of the board's motives in making the business decision. Bad faith may be found where a business decision is so far beyond the bounds of reasonable judgment that it seems essentially inexplicable on any ground other than bad faith.*Roselink Investors, L.L.C. v. Shenkman, 2004 U.S. Dist. LEXIS 6905 (S.D.N.Y. 2004).*

"Independent". — The Delaware Supreme Court has defined "independent" under a business judgment rule analysis as meaning that a director's decision is based on the corporate merits of the subject before the board rather than extraneous considerations or influences. In assessing director independence, Delaware courts apply a subjective "actual person" standard to determine whether a given director was likely to be affected in the same or similar circumstances. There must be coupled with the allegations of control such facts as would demonstrate that through

personal or other relationships the directors are beholden to the controlling person. To be disqualifying, the nature of the director interest must be substantial and not merely incidental. If a plaintiff successfully demonstrates facts sufficient to rebut the business judgment rule presumption, then the burden of proof shifts to the defendant directors to establish the entire fairness of the challenged transaction. *Roselink Investors, L.L.C. v. Shenkman, 2004 U.S. Dist. LEXIS 6905 (S.D.N.Y. 2004).*

To establish lack of independence, a plaintiff meets his or her burden by showing that the directors are either beholden to the controlling shareholder or so under its influence that their discretion is sterilized. *In re Trump Hotels Shareholder Derivative Litig., 2000 U.S. Dist. LEXIS 13550 (S.D.N.Y. 2000).*

The question of independence flows from an analysis of the factual allegations pertaining to the influences upon corporate directors' performance of their duties generally, and more specifically in respect to the challenged transaction. *In re Trump Hotels Shareholder Derivative Litig., 2000 U.S. Dist. LEXIS 13550 (S.D.N.Y. 2000).*

"Insolvency". — The Delaware Supreme Court has defined "interest" under a business judgment rule analysis as meaning that directors can neither appear on both sides of a transaction nor expect to derive any personal financial benefit from it in the sense of self-dealing, as opposed to a benefit which devolves upon the corporation or all stockholders generally. Further, the benefit to a director must be material, which means that it must be significant enough, in the context of the director's economic circumstances, as to have made it improbable that the director could perform his or her fiduciary duties to the shareholders without being influenced by his or her overriding personal interest. *Roselink Investors, L.L.C. v. Shenkman, 2004 U.S. Dist. LEXIS 6905 (S.D.N.Y. 2004).*

"Special injury". — Under Delaware law, if a claim alleges a breach of fiduciary duty resulting in a loss of stock value to a company, the alleged wrongdoing harms the corporation and therefore — because they own the corporation — the shareholders derivatively. In order to assert a direct action, a shareholder must allege "special injury." Special injury has evolved into a two-prong test. The plaintiff must either allege (1) an injury which is separate and distinct from that suffered by other shareholders, or (2) a wrong involving a contractual right of a shareholder, which exists independent of any right of the corporation. *Clifton v. Vista Computer Servs., 2002 U.S. Dist. LEXIS 12977 (S.D.N.Y. 2002).*

Under Delaware law, the duty of fairness has two components, fair dealing and fair price. Fair dealing focuses upon the actual conduct of corporate fiduciaries in effecting a transaction, such as its initiation, structure, and negotiation. Included within the concept of fair dealing is the duty to fully disclose all material information that would have a significant effect on a shareholder's vote. The element of fair price mandates that directors commit themselves, inexorably, to obtaining the highest value reasonably available to the shareholders. *Caruso v. Metex Corp., 1992 U.S. Dist. LEXIS 14556 (E.D.N.Y. 1992).*

Corporations

Delaware law does not recognize an independent duty of good faith. Under Delaware law, although corporate directors are unquestionably obligated to act in good faith, doctrinally that obligation does not exist separate and apart from the fiduciary duty of loyalty. Rather, it is a subset or subsidiary requirement that is subsumed within the duty of loyalty, as distinguished from being a compartmentally distinct fiduciary duty of equal dignity with the two bedrock fiduciary duties of loyalty and due care. Good faith is also subsumed within the duty of due care. *Roselink Investors, L.L.C. v. Shenkman, 2004 U.S. Dist. LEXIS 6905 (S.D.N.Y. 2004).*

Disclosure. — Delaware law imposes upon a board of directors the fiduciary duty to disclose fully and fairly all material facts within its control that would have a significant effect upon a stockholder vote. The board of directors also has a duty of full disclosure in assessing the adequacy of proxy material under state law. Delaware requires proxy voters to have all material information reasonably available before casting their votes to insure that directors do not use their special knowledge to their own advantage and to the detriment of the stockholders. To determine whether a director has satisfied the fiduciary duty of disclosure, the question is one of materiality. *Caruso v. Metex Corp., 1992 U.S. Dist. LEXIS 14556 (E.D.N.Y. 1992).*

Delaware does not prohibit a provision in the corporation's charter stating that interested directors did not have to disclose their interest or refrain from participation in settlement negotiations and agreements. *Piccard v. Sperry Corp., 48 F. Supp. 465 (S.D.N.Y. 1943).*

The question whether shareholders have, under the circumstances, been provided with appropriate information upon which an informed choice on a matter of fundamental corporate importance may be made, is not a decision concerning the management of business and affairs of the enterprise of the kind the business judgment rule is intended to protect; it is rather a matter relating to the directors' duty to shareholders who are technically outside of the corporation. Less technically, decisions dealing with the quality of, and the circumstances surrounding, disclosures are not inherently of the kind which courts are ill suited to treat on their merits. *Vides v. Amelio, 265 F. Supp. 2d 273 (S.D.N.Y. 2003).*

The "duty of candor" is the well-recognized proposition that directors of Delaware corporations are under a fiduciary duty to disclose fully and fairly all material information within the board's control when it seeks shareholder action. This duty of disclosure is based on the materiality standard advanced by the court in *TSC Industries*: directors must disclose all facts which, under all the circumstances, would have assumed actual significance in the deliberations of the reasonable shareholder. *In re Trump Hotels Shareholder Derivative Litig., 2000 U.S. Dist. LEXIS 13550 (S.D.N.Y. 2000).*

Waste. — Allegations which raise a reasonable doubt as to whether a transaction constitutes a waste of corporate assets in turn create a reasonable doubt that the transaction was the product of a valid exercise of business judgment. *In re Trump Hotels Shareholder Derivative Litig., 2000 U.S. Dist. LEXIS 13550 (S.D.N.Y. 2000).*

The judicial standard for determination of corporate waste entails an exchange of corporate asset for consideration so disproportionately small as to lie beyond the range at which any reasonable person might be willing to trade. If, however, there is any substantial consideration received by the corporation, and if there is a good faith judgment that in the circumstances the transaction is worthwhile, there should be no finding of waste, even if the fact finder would conclude ex post that the transaction was unreasonably risky. *In re Trump Hotels Shareholder Derivative Litig., 2000 U.S. Dist. LEXIS 13550 (S.D.N.Y. 2000).*

Waste versus gift. — A waste or gift of corporate assets may arise anytime an asset of a corporation is transferred, lost or destroyed. The essence of a claim of gift is lack of consideration; the essence of waste is the diversion of corporate assets for improper or unnecessary purposes. *Oye v. Schwartz, 762 F. Supp. 510 (E.D.N.Y. 1991).*

Indemnification. — Del. Code Ann. tit. 8, § 145 provides for indemnification of expenses, including attorney's fees, reasonably incurred in connection with the defense of litigation. Del. Code Ann. tit. 8, § 145(b), (c). Del. Code Ann. tit. 8, § 145(c) is a mandatory provision that applies to all Delaware corporations and grants an absolute right of indemnification in such situations. *Kaslof v. Global Health Alternatives, Inc., 2000 U.S. Dist. LEXIS 21053 (E.D.N.Y. 2000).*

A dismissal without prejudice solely because the same charge is being litigated in other presently pending actions does not fall within the underlying purpose of the indemnification statute. *Kaslof v. Global Health Alternatives, Inc., 2000 U.S. Dist. LEXIS 21053 (E.D.N.Y. 2000).*

When a case is dismissed without prejudice so that the same issue may be litigated in another pending case, an indemnification award would be premature and contrary to the spirit of the statute. *Kaslof v. Global Health Alternatives, Inc., 2000 U.S. Dist. LEXIS 21053 (E.D.N.Y. 2000).*

Del Code Ann. tit. 8, § 102(b)(7) allows a corporation to limit or eliminate directors' liability for monetary damages for breach of fiduciary duty by including an exculpatory provision in its certificate of incorporation. However, the statute is strictly limited, prohibiting indemnification for any breach of the director's duty of loyalty to the corporation or its stockholders, for acts or omissions not in good faith or involving intentional misconduct or for any transaction for which the director derived an improper personal benefit. *In re Trump Hotels Shareholder Derivative Litig., 2000 U.S. Dist. LEXIS 13550 (S.D.N.Y. 2000).*

Demand futility. — Under Delaware law, demand is excused by demonstrating futility under the following standard: the particularized allegations of the complaint must raise a reasonable doubt as to (i) director disinterest or independence or (ii) whether the directors exercised proper business judgment in approving the challenged transaction. The entire review is factual in nature and is within the sound discretion of the court. *Oye v. Schwartz, 762 F. Supp. 510 (E.D.N.Y. 1991).*

A demand against the directors of a corporation is futile only where, under the particularized facts alleged, a reasonable doubt is created that: (1) the directors are disinterested and independent and (2) the challenged transaction was otherwise the product of a valid exercise of business judgment. Further, it is plaintiff's burden to allege with particularity that the improper motive in a given set of circumstances was the sole or primary purpose of the wrongdoer's conduct. *Brickman v. Tyco Toys, Inc., 722 F. Supp. 1054 (S.D.N.Y.1989).*

Acts of self-dealing which involve a majority of the directors will generally support the excusing of demand. *Oye v. Schwartz, 762 F. Supp. 510 (E.D.N.Y. 1991).*

Under Delaware law, failure to make a demand upon the board will be excused only if such a demand would be futile. To plead demand futility adequately, a plaintiff must allege with particularity facts creating a reasonable doubt that: (1) the directors are disinterested and independent or (2) the challenged transaction was otherwise the product of a valid exercise of business judgment. *Ryan v. Aetna Life Ins. Co., 765 F. Supp. 133 (S.D.N.Y. 1991).*

As to the first *Aronson* inquiry, the Court reviews the factual allegations of the complaint to determine whether they create a reasonable doubt as to the disinterestedness and independence of the directors at the time the complaint was filed. In order to raise a reasonable doubt in this respect, plaintiff must allege that the directors expected a personal benefit from the challenged transaction or appeared on both sides of the transaction, showing divided loyalties. *Ryan v. Aetna Life Ins. Co., 765 F. Supp. 133 (S.D.N.Y. 1991).*

Delaware law holds that demand must be made upon the board if the disputed transaction has been approved by a majority consisting of the disinterested directors. *Ryan v. Aetna Life Ins. Co., 765 F. Supp. 133 (S.D.N.Y. 1991).*

Under the second prong of the *Aronson* test, the Court must look to the allegations of impropriety in the exercise of both substantive due care (purchase terms), and procedural due care (an informed decision). On the issue of substantive due care, Delaware courts focus on whether the transaction represents a fair exchange. *Ryan v. Aetna Life Ins. Co., 765 F. Supp. 133 (S.D.N.Y. 1991).*

The decision to bring a lawsuit on behalf of a corporation is ordinarily at the discretion of a board of directors because that body is charged with the management of the affairs of a corporation. Therefore, a plaintiff must make a demand of the board — unless to do so would be futile — before pursuing litigation in the name of the corporation. *Halpert Enters. v. Harrison, 362 F. Supp. 2d 426 (S.D.N.Y. 2005).*

The demand rule is meant to give a derivative corporation itself the opportunity to take over a suit which was brought on its behalf in the first place, and thus to allow the directors the chance to occupy their normal status as conductors of the corporation's affairs. *Halpert Enters. v. Harrison, 362 F. Supp. 2d 426 (S.D.N.Y. 2005).*

In determining whether making a demand on a board of directors would be futile, a court must determine whether, under the particularized facts alleged, a reasonable doubt is created that: (1) the directors are disinterested and independent or (2) the challenged transaction was otherwise the product of a valid exercise of business judgment. The test is disjunctive, offering alternative avenues for pleading that it would be futile to make a demand on the board that the corporation bring the action itself. *Halpert Enters. v. Harrison, 362 F. Supp. 2d 426 (S.D.N.Y. 2005).*

The second alternative available to plaintiffs alleging demand futility is to plead particularized facts that raise a reasonable doubt that the directors exercised proper business judgment in a transaction. *Halpert Enters. v. Harrison, 362 F. Supp. 2d 426 (S.D.N.Y. 2005).*

Under the well-settled rule, demand will be excused if a reasonable doubt is created that: (1) the directors were disinterested and independent or; (2) the challenged transaction was otherwise the product of a valid exercise of business judgment. *In re Trump Hotels Shareholder Derivative Litig., 2000 U.S. Dist. LEXIS 13550 (S.D.N.Y. 2000).*

The machinery of corporate democracy and the derivative suit are potent tools to redress the conduct of a torpid and unfaithful management. In such instances, stockholders often do not make a demand on the board of directors, and instead file suit claiming that demand is excused. Demand as a precondition to suit is required, unless excused for extraordinary conditions. *In re Oxford Health Plans, Inc. Sec. Litig., 192 F.R.D. 111 (S.D.N.Y. 2000).*

The issues of pre-suit demand futility rest upon the allegations of the complaint and the test of futility has long been recognized as whether the board of directors, at the time of the filing of the suit, could have impartially considered and acted upon the demand. To establish demand futility in a case involving action, the plaintiff need not allege that the challenged transaction could never be deemed a product of business judgment. *In re Oxford Health Plans, Inc. Sec. Litig., 192 F.R.D. 111 (S.D.N.Y. 2000).*

Where board of director interest, approval, or acquiescence in the wrongdoing exists, the pre-suit demand is excused as futile, and where officers and directors are under an influence which sterilizes their discretion, they cannot be considered proper persons to conduct litigation on behalf of the corporation, and here again pre-suit demand would be futile. *In re Oxford Health Plans, Inc. Sec. Litig., 192 F.R.D. 111 (S.D.N.Y. 2000).*

In determining pre-suit demand futility, the court in the proper exercise of its discretion must decide whether under the particularized facts alleged a reasonable doubt is created that: (1) the board of directors are disinterested and independent; and (2) the challenged transaction was otherwise the product of a valid exercise of business judgment. *In re Oxford Health Plans, Inc. Sec. Litig., 192 F.R.D. 111 (S.D.N.Y. 2000).*

Under Delaware law, the demand requirement is predicated upon the presumption that directors manage the corporation with the good-faith belief that their actions are in the best interest of the company. Demand is excused only when the facts cast doubt on this presumption such that the conduct at issue was not approved by a majority consisting of the disinterested directors. *Langner v. Brown, 913 F. Supp. 260 (S.D.N.Y. 1996)*.

In determining the sufficiency of a demand futility claim, the trial court considers: (1) whether threshold presumptions of director disinterest or independence are rebutted by well-pleaded facts; and if not, (2) whether the complaint pleads particularized facts sufficient to create a reasonable doubt that the challenged transaction was the product of a valid exercise of business judgment. Mere director approval of a transaction, without particularized facts establishing a breach of fiduciary duty claim or a lack of independence or disinterestedness of a majority of the directors, is insufficient to excuse demand. The burden is on the plaintiff to show particularized facts demonstrating a reasonable doubt of business judgment protection. It is only when the alleged facts, considered as true, would demonstrate that a majority of the directors who would have received the demand letter are "interested" in the challenged transaction or "lack independence" because of domination by an interested party or otherwise, that demand is excused. *Langner v. Brown, 913 F. Supp. 260 (S.D.N.Y. 1996)*.

To rebut a demand futility claim, a plaintiff must allege with particularity that a majority of the directors were dominated or otherwise controlled by an individual or entity interested in the transaction. The plaintiff also has the burden of supplying facts which if considered true would show that the directors failed to fulfill their duty of procedural due care, by becoming fully informed, and their duty of substantive due care, by not engaging in, e.g., a waste of corporate assets. *Langner v. Brown, 913 F. Supp. 260 (S.D.N.Y. 1996)*.

The receipt of directors' fees does not constitute a disqualifying interest for the purposes of the demand requirement. *Langner v. Brown, 913 F. Supp. 260 (S.D.N.Y. 1996)*.

Where the subject of the derivative suit concerns breach by a third party, it is appropriate to examine whether the board can impartially consider the merits of the demand without being influenced by improper considerations; whether the board could properly exercise its independent and disinterested business judgment in responding to the demand. *In re Trump Hotels Shareholder Derivative Litig., 2000 U.S. Dist. LEXIS 13550 (S.D.N.Y. 2000)*.

The province of a court, in reviewing a challenge to a decision by the directors not to bring a lawsuit demanded by one or more stockholders, is to review the good faith and reasonableness of the board's investigation, for the challenge under Delaware law must be not to the underlying transaction, but to the board's decision not to bring the lawsuit. *In re Boston Sci. Corp. S'holders Litig., 2007 U.S. Dist. LEXIS 42540 (D.N.Y. June 13, 2007)*.

Board's litigation powers. — The power of the board to manage the corporation without improper judicial or shareholder interference includes within its scope the power to conduct the corporation's litigation for example, whether to institute litigation in the first instance,

abandon the litigation, or settle the action. *Abramowitz v. Posner, 513 F. Supp. 120 (S.D.N.Y. 1981)*.

A stockholder cannot sue on a corporation's behalf when the managing body of the corporation refuses. Moreover, a decision such as whether to proceed with a derivative action may be approved in the exercise of independent business judgment by the independent directors. Whether or not a corporation shall seek to enforce in the courts a cause of action for damage is, like other business questions, ordinarily a matter of internal management, and is left to the discretion of the directors, in the absence of instruction by vote of the stockholders. *Seigal v. Merrick, 1979 U.S. Dist. LEXIS 7851 (S.D.N.Y. 1979)*.

Because Delaware law empowers a board of directors to delegate all of its authority to a committee, a properly authorized independent committee has the authority, to the extent provided in the board's resolution, to seek the termination of litigation charging fellow directors with wrongdoing. Moreover, even if a majority of directors are interested in the transactions at issue, a board can still delegate its authority to a committee of disinterested directors. *Stein v. Bailey, 531 F. Supp. 684 (S.D.N.Y. 1982)*.

Delaware law authorizes a corporation's outside directors to terminate a stockholder's derivative action. The procedure followed by the corporation's board of directors in delegating its decision-making authority to a special committee is an appropriate method of insulating the corporation from shareholder interference by meeting the requirements of the business judgment rule. A corporation is specifically authorized to establish an independent committee of outside directors. Thus, under the business judgment rule, as followed by the courts of Delaware, a special review committee of outside directors is authorized to terminate a stockholder's derivative action. *Seigal v. Merrick, 1979 U.S. Dist. LEXIS 7851 (S.D.N.Y. 1979)*.

Under Delaware law, a corporation may appoint a special review committee of disinterested, independent directors with authority to refuse a stockholder's demand or to terminate a stockholders' derivative suit. *Seigal v. Merrick, 1979 U.S. Dist. LEXIS 7851 (S.D.N.Y. 1979)*.

Under Delaware law, a decision such as whether to proceed with a derivative action may be approved in the exercise of independent business judgment by the independent directors. The corporation may choose to establish an independent committee to determine whether to prosecute a derivative action. *Siegal v. Merrick, 84 F.R.D. 106 (S.D.N.Y. 1979)*.

The refusal of the board of directors to take up a derivative suit is wrongful if its investigation was not reasonable or if the decision was made in bad faith. A shareholder plaintiff must allege with particularity facts that create a reasonable basis for inferring that the board's refusal was wrongful. Allegations as to the self-interest of one or more directors are insufficient absent particularized allegations that such directors controlled, dominated, or otherwise influenced a sufficient number of the other directors. *Sterling v. Mulholland, 1998 U.S. Dist. LEXIS 19550 (S.D.N.Y. 1998)*.

A committee of disinterested and independent directors may move to terminate a derivative action which the committee determines in good faith to be contrary to the corporation's best interests. *Strougo ex rel. Brazil Fund v. Padegs, 1 F. Supp. 2d 276 (S.D.N.Y. 1998).*

When a special litigation committee attempts to discontinue a derivative suit, the burden of proof is on the corporation. If the court determines that the committee is independent, acted in good faith, and had reasonable bases for its conclusion, then the court proceeds with a second step. It must then determine whether the motion should be granted. *Strougo ex rel. Brazil Fund v. Padegs, 1 F. Supp. 2d 276 (S.D.N.Y. 1998).*

A board of directors has the inherent authority to rid itself of litigation it deems detrimental to the corporation, even after a derivative suit is properly commenced. *Sterling v. Mulholland, 1998 U.S. Dist. LEXIS 19550 (S.D.N.Y. 1998).*

Intentional interference with business opportunities. — To state a claim for intentional interference with business opportunities under Delaware law, the plaintiff would have to allege facts indicating that (1) the plaintiff had a reasonable probability of a business opportunity, (2) defendant intentionally interfered with that opportunity, (3) proximate causation, and (4) damages. The New York standard is more stringent because it requires the plaintiff to allege each of these elements plus improper motive on the part of the defendant. *Aquilio v. Manaker, 1991 U.S. Dist. LEXIS 14592 (N.D.N.Y. 1991).*

Fiduciary relationship with individual stockholders. Delaware corporations law provides that although directors generally do not occupy a fiduciary position with respect to stockholders in direct personal dealing as opposed to dealings with stockholders as a class, Delaware does create a duty in special circumstances where advantage is taken of inside information by a corporate insider who deliberately misleads an ignorant stockholder, when the latter relies on the misrepresentation or omission. *Aquilio v. Manaker, 1991 U.S. Dist. LEXIS 14592 (N.D.N.Y. 1991).*

Delaware corporations law provides that although directors generally do not occupy a fiduciary position with respect to stockholders in direct personal dealing as opposed to dealings with stockholders as a class, Delaware does create such a duty in special circumstances where advantage is taken of inside information by a corporate insider who deliberately misleads an ignorant stockholder, when the latter relies on the misrepresentation or omission. *Caballero v. Anselmo, 720 F. Supp. 1088 (S.D.N.Y. 1989).*

Delegation of authority. — Because Delaware law empowers a board of directors to delegate all of its authority to a committee, a properly authorized independent committee has the authority, to the extent provided in the board's resolution, to seek the termination of litigation charging fellow directors with wrongdoing. Moreover, even if a majority of directors are interested in the transactions at issue, a board can still delegate its authority to a committee of disinterested directors. *Stein v. Bailey, 531 F. Supp. 684 (S.D.N.Y. 1982).*

Holders of convertible debentures. — Under Delaware law, convertible debenture holders do not possess all the rights of shareholders with respect to actions taken by corporate directors or majority shareholders. In certain circumstances, a holder of a convertible debenture is entitled to different treatment from a mere creditor of a corporation, and a cause of action for breach of fiduciary duty may lie under Delaware law apart from the express terms of an indenture agreement. *Green v. Hamilton International Corp., 1981 U.S. Dist. LEXIS 13439 (S.D.N.Y. 1981).*

A convertible debenture has the qualities of a debt and an equity security. If the wrongs alleged in a derivative action against a corporation impact upon the securities so as to undermine the debtor-creditor relationship, a contract analysis is appropriate, and plaintiffs, as creditors of the corporation, are owed no special duty outside the bounds of the contract. If the wrongs alleged impinge upon the equity aspects, then the analysis more properly treats plaintiffs like shareholders to whom the majority shareholders and directors of a corporation owe a duty of honesty, loyalty, good faith, and fairness. *Green v. Hamilton International Corp., 1981 U.S. Dist. LEXIS 13439 (S.D.N.Y. 1981).*

A Delaware court would interpret the state's corporate law to recognize a fiduciary obligation owed by a corporation to a holder of a convertible debenture where (1) the corporation is self-dealing, (2) misleading public statements are made that are material to plaintiffs' redemption decision, (3) material nondisclosures are not corrected, and (4) several officers of the corporation deal in the corporation's securities prior to the announcement of a merger. *Green v. Hamilton International Corp., 1981 U.S. Dist. LEXIS 13439 (S.D.N.Y. 1981).*

Under Delaware law, absent fraud or other special circumstances, a convertible debenture holder lacks standing to bring a claim for breach of fiduciary duty. Because a convertible debenture represents a contractual entitlement to the repayment of a debt and does not represent an equitable interest in the issuing corporation necessary for the imposition of a trust relationship with concomitant fiduciary duties, the holder of such an instrument may not assert a claim for breach of fiduciary duty unless the debenture is converted into stock. Nor is any duty owed to the creditors of a corporation, unless the corporation is insolvent. *Benjamin v. Kim, 1999 U.S. Dist. LEXIS 6089 (S.D.N.Y. 1999).*

Expenditures from corporate treasury. — Where a controversy is concerned with a question of policy as distinguished from personnel of management and the stockholders are called upon to decide it, the incumbent directors may with perfect propriety make such expenditures from the corporate treasury as are reasonably necessary to inform the stockholders of the considerations which the directors deem sufficient to support the wisdom of the policy advocated by them and under attack; also, in the same communications which the directors address to the stockholders in support of their policy they may solicit proxies in its favor. *Steinberg v. Adams, 90 F. Supp. 604 (S.D.N.Y. 1950).*

Repurchase of shares. — Neither federal nor Delaware law imposes on a corporation any obligation to repurchase its outstanding shares on an equal basis from all of its shareholders. The Delaware Corporations statute specifically authorizes a corporation to purchase its own securities, and the Delaware courts have upheld selective repurchase transactions in the absence of self-dealing on the part of corporate officers or directors. *Heine v. Signal Cos., 1977 U.S. Dist. LEXIS 17071 (S.D.N.Y. 1977).*

Under Delaware law, a plaintiff asserting proxy claims need not comply with the federal demand requirement. False proxy claims are not subject to the demand requirement of Del. Ch. Ct. R. 23.1. *Katz v. Pels, 774 F. Supp. 121 (S.D.N.Y. 1991).*

Procedural due care. — Approval of a transaction by a majority of independent, disinterested directors almost always bolsters a presumption that the business judgment rule attaches to transactions approved by a board of directors that are later attacked on grounds of procedural due care. In such cases, a heavy burden falls on a plaintiff to avoid presuit demand. *Ryan v. Aetna Life Ins. Co., 765 F. Supp. 133 (S.D.N.Y. 1991).*

Representation by independent counsel. — Both New York and Delaware law contemplate that a special litigation committee be represented by independent counsel. In re Par Pharmaceutical, Inc. Derivative Litigation, 750 F. Supp. 641 (S.D.N.Y. 1990).

Applicability of Section 350. — Where a corporation would be eligible for close corporation status, there are no intervening rights of third parties, nothing in the shareholders agreement is forbidden by statute, and all of the shareholders have subscribed to the agreement, § 350 governs even if the corporation has not formally elected close corporation treatment under § 344. *Davis v. Rondina, 741 F. Supp. 1115 (S.D.N.Y. 1990).*

Familial and financial relationships. — In order to rebut the presumption of director independence on familial and financial relationships grounds, there must be coupled with the allegation of control such facts as would demonstrate that through personal or other relationships the directors are beholden to the controlling person. *Brickman v. Tyco Toys, Inc., 722 F. Supp. 1054 (S.D.N.Y.1989).*

Merger. — When a corporate board of directors authorizes management to engage in merger negotiations, the board has a fiduciary duty to maximize the value of the corporation for the stockholders' benefit. *Caruso v. Metex Corp., 1992 U.S. Dist. LEXIS 14556 (E.D.N.Y. 1992).*

A board of directors of a corporation, to fulfill their fiduciary responsibilities, must actively and directly oversee matters relating to the sale or merger of the corporation. *Caruso v. Metex Corp., 1992 U.S. Dist. LEXIS 14556 (E.D.N.Y. 1992).*

Takeovers. — The business judgment rule is a presumption that in making a business decision the directors of a corporation acted on an informed basis, in good faith and in the honest belief that the action taken was in the best interests of the company. This rule applies in the context of takeovers under Delaware law. *CRTF Corp. v. Federated Department Stores, Inc., 683 F. Supp. 422 (S.D.N.Y. 1988).*

To determine whether a board of directors has violated its fiduciary duty to its shareholders in enacting or taking actions under a challenged "Poison Pill" Rights Plan, a court must examine the motivations of the board as it made its decisions, from the initiation of the plan through any actions taken under it; it must consider whether the board made an informed decision based on reasonable investigation, considered under a standard of gross negligence; or perhaps of reasonable diligence; and it must evaluate the reasonableness of the board's actions as a response to any given threats it perceives to the company. *CRTF Corp. v. Federated Department Stores, Inc., 683 F. Supp. 422 (S.D.N.Y. 1988).*

The approval of any defensive measures by a board composed of a majority of outside independent directors acting in good faith and upon reasonable investigation materially enhances the proof that the board has acted reasonably in response to the threat posed. If the directors succeed in making this showing, the burden shifts back to the plaintiffs, who have the ultimate burden of persuasion to show a breach of the directors' fiduciary duties. *CRTF Corp. v. Federated Department Stores, Inc., 683 F. Supp. 422 (S.D.N.Y. 1988).*

Corporate directors have fiduciary duties of loyalty to the corporation and of due care in the administration of corporate affairs. Under the business judgment rule, where a board of directors is found to have acted in good faith, a court will not try to substitute its judgment for that of the board and will uphold the board's decision so long as they are attributable to any rational business purpose. Under Delaware law, the business judgment rule, a presumption that in making a business decision the directors of a corporation acted on an informed basis, in good faith, and on the honest belief that the action taken was in the best interests of the company, applies in the context of takeovers. This is true despite the inherent potential conflict of interest that exists when a board is in the position of deciding whether and how to defend against a takeover attempt. To deal with this potential conflict, the Delaware Supreme Court has announced an enhanced duty on the part of directors in this position. The directors carry this burden by showing good faith and reasonable investigation, and that the defensive mechanism was reasonable in relation to the threat posed. *CRTF Corp. v. Federated Dep't Stores, 1988 U.S. Dist. LEXIS 2775 (S.D.N.Y. 1988).*

To determine whether a board of directors has violated its fiduciary duty to its shareholders in enacting or taking actions under a challenged rights plan, the court must examine the motivations of the board as it made its decisions, from the initiation of the plan to any actions taken under it. It must consider whether the board made an informed decision based on reasonable investigation, considered on a standard of gross negligence, or perhaps of reasonable diligence. Also, it must evaluate the reasonableness of the board's actions as a response to any given threats it perceives to the company. The approval of any defensive measures by a board composed of a majority of outside independent directors acting on good faith and upon reasonable investigation, materially enhances the proof that the board has acted reasonably in response to the threat posed. If the directors succeed in making this showing, the burden shifts back to the plaintiffs, who have the ultimate burden of persuasion to show a breach of the directors' fiduciary duties. *CRTF Corp. v. Federated Dep't Stores, 1988 U.S. Dist. LEXIS 2775 (S.D.N.Y. 1988).*

Under Delaware law, a board of directors need not be a passive observer to a sale. According to the Delaware Supreme Court, concerns that may give rise to reasonable defensive responses include inadequacy of the price offered, nature and timing of the offer, questions of illegality, the impact on constituencies other than shareholders, the risk of non-consummation, and the quality of securities being offered in the exchange. *CRTF Corp. v. Federated Dep't Stores, 1988 U.S. Dist. LEXIS 2775 (S.D.N.Y. 1988).*

In discharging its function of managing a corporation, a board of directors owes a duty of care to act in the best interests of the shareholders. This duty of care also requires the board to protect the corporate enterprise from harm, reasonably perceived, irrespective of its source. Such a threat includes a hostile takeover at a price below a company's value. *Samjens Partners I v. Burlington Industries, Inc., 663 F. Supp. 614 (S.D.N.Y. 1987).*

The business judgment rule protects the decisions of the board in carrying out its duty of care if certain requirements are met. Both the duty of care and the business judgment rule apply when the board is responding to a hostile tender offer. The board's decisions, however, are subject to closer scrutiny in such a context. There is an enhanced duty that calls for judicial examination at the threshold before the protection of the business judgment rule may be conferred. Directors must show that they had reasonable grounds for believing that a danger to corporate policy and effectiveness existed because of another person's stock ownership. The board can satisfy this burden by showing good faith and reasonable investigation, and such proof is enhanced when a board is comprised of a majority of outside directors. *Samjens Partners I v. Burlington Industries, Inc., 663 F. Supp. 614 (S.D.N.Y. 1987).*

In the midst of a takeover battle, when it becomes obvious that a company is for sale — when, for example, the board authorizes management to negotiate a merger or buyout with a third-party — the duty of the board shifts. The directors' role changes from defenders of the corporate bastion to auctioneers charged with getting the best price for the stockholders at a sale of the company. *Samjens Partners I v. Burlington Industries, Inc., 663 F. Supp. 614 (S.D.N.Y. 1987).*

Defensive measures enacted by a board of directors in response to a hostile tender offer must meet a two-part test: there must be a basis for the board to have concluded that the defensive measure served a proper corporate purpose and the measure must be reasonable in light of the threat posed. *Samjens Partners I v. Burlington Industries, Inc., 663 F. Supp. 614 (S.D.N.Y. 1987).*

Auctions. — In an auction situation, the directors' role remains an active one, changed only in the respect that they are charged with the duty of selling the company at the highest price attainable for the stockholders' benefit. The directors' responsibility in carrying out their fiduciary duty becomes the maximization of the company's value at a sale for the stockholders' benefit. *CRTF Corp. v. Federated Department Stores, Inc., 683 F. Supp. 422 (S.D.N.Y. 1988).*

In coordinating the bidding process, the board can institute strategies, such as granting a "lock-up" agreement, a break-up fee, or a no-shop agreement to a "white knight," but only if their strategies enhance the bidding. Such arrangements may also be legitimately necessary to convince a "white knight" to enter the bidding by providing some form of compensation for the risks it is undertaking. Arrangements that effectively end the auction, however, are generally detrimental to shareholders' interests and not protected by the business judgment rule. *Samjens Partners I v. Burlington Industries, Inc., 663 F. Supp. 614 (S.D.N.Y. 1987).*

Not shielded by business judgment rule. — Under Delaware law, action of the board which is calculated to alter the structure of the corporation and results in a fundamental transfer of power from one corporate constituency to another, is not shielded by the business judgment rule. *Unilever Acquisition Corp. v. Richardson-Vicks, Inc., 618 F. Supp. 407 (S.D.N.Y. 1985).*

The business judgment rule does not apply to allegations regarding misrepresentations or omissions in a proxy statement. *Vides v. Amelio, 265 F. Supp. 2d 273 (S.D.N.Y. 2003).*

Operating in vicinity of insolvency. — Under Delaware law, when one company wholly owns another, the directors of the parent and the subsidiary are obligated to manage the affairs of the subsidiary in the best interests only of the parent and its shareholders. However, where a corporation is operating in the vicinity of insolvency, a board of directors is not merely the agent of the residue risk bearers, but owes its duty to the corporate enterprise. *Roselink Investors, L.L.C. v. Shenkman, 2004 U.S. Dist. LEXIS 6905 (S.D.N.Y. 2004).*

Delaware law requires that directors recognize that in managing the business affairs of a solvent corporation in the vicinity of insolvency, circumstances may arise when the right (both the efficient and the fair) course to follow for the corporation may diverge from the choice that the stockholders (or the creditors, or the employees, or any single group interested in the corporation) would make if given the opportunity to act. Once a corporation enters "the zone of insolvency," the directors owe fiduciary duties not only to the corporation's shareholders but to its creditors as well. This means that directors of a wholly owned subsidiary, who otherwise would owe fiduciary duties only to the parent, also owe fiduciary duties to creditors of the subsidiary when the subsidiary enters the zone of insolvency. *Roselink Investors, L.L.C. v. Shenkman, 2004 U.S. Dist. LEXIS 6905 (S.D.N.Y. 2004).*

In Delaware, directors of a corporation in the vicinity of insolvency owe a fiduciary duty to the enterprise, including creditors as well as to shareholders. *Management Techs. v. Morris, 961 F. Supp. 640 (S.D.N.Y. 1997).*

Presence on both sides of the transaction does not automatically rebut the business judgment rule presumption. *Roselink Investors, L.L.C. v. Shenkman, 2004 U.S. Dist. LEXIS 6905 (S.D.N.Y. 2004).*

Certainly simultaneous service on a board of an entity that does business with another entity alone does not rise to the level of egregious behavior contemplated by case law. *In re Xethanol Corp. Derivative Litig., 2007 U.S. Dist. LEXIS 60082 (D.N.Y. August 16, 2007).*

Wholly owned subsidiary. — Under Delaware law, in a parent and wholly owned subsidiary context, the directors of the subsidiary are obligated only to manage the affairs of the subsidiary in the best interests of the parent and its shareholders. *Roselink Investors, L.L.C. v. Shenkman, 2004 U.S. Dist. LEXIS 6905 (S.D.N.Y. 2004).*

Where there are shareholders in addition to the parent company, both the directors of the subsidiary and the parent company, as controlling shareholder, have a duty to consider the interests of the minority shareholders. However, where the subsidiary is wholly owned by the parent, the directors of the subsidiary owe the parent a fiduciary duty to manage the subsidiary in the best interests of the parent. *Roselink Investors, L.L.C. v. Shenkman, 2004 U.S. Dist. LEXIS 6905 (S.D.N.Y. 2004).*

Inapplicability of proxy disclosure claims to demand rule. — The purpose of requiring a demand upon the board of directors before proceeding with derivative litigation is to obtain the business judgment of the board on whether the litigation is in the best interests of the corporation and its shareholders. The requirement is appropriate, for example, where the litigation involves a transaction presenting questions of business judgment, where a court should be reluctant to substitute its judgment for that of the corporation's legitimate management. That purpose has little bearing on a claim that a proxy statement makes a false assertion or an insufficient disclosure. Such questions are normally determined without particular need for business judgment, and the courts decide them as a matter of course. Whether a proxy statement properly omitted an item is regarded as a question of materiality, not one protected by the business judgment rule. Thus, subjecting proxy disclosure claims to a demand requirement would be inconsistent with Delaware case law holding that the business judgment rule does not apply to the question whether shareholders have, under the circumstances, been provided with appropriate information upon which an informed choice on a matter of fundamental corporate importance may be made. *Vides v. Amelio, 265 F. Supp. 2d 273 (S.D.N.Y. 2003).*

Directors' decisions will be respected by courts unless the directors are interested or lack independence relative to the decision, do not act in good faith, act in a manner that cannot be attributed to a rational business purpose or reach their decision by a grossly negligent process that includes the failure to consider all material facts reasonably available. *Kidd v. Swink, 2002 U.S. Dist. LEXIS 20287 (S.D.N.Y. 2002).*

"Entire fairness". — Where a controlling shareholder stands on both sides of a transaction, the standard ordinarily is that the controlling shareholder (and the directors who are subject to that control) will bear the burden of proving the entire fairness of the transaction. The concept of "entire fairness" encompasses fair dealing and fair price. *Official Committee of the Unsecured Creditors v. Investcorp, S.A., 137 F. Supp. 2d 502 (S.D.N.Y 2001).*

Delaware courts have applied the "entire fairness" test only to transactions between a corporation and its controlling shareholder. *Ibar v. Field, 2000 U.S. App. LEXIS 11020 (2d Cir. 2000).*

To show self-dealing, a plaintiff must show that the shareholder defendants received something to the exclusion of, and detriment to, the minority stockholders. *Official Committee of the Unsecured Creditors v. Investcorp, S.A., 137 F. Supp. 2d 502 (S.D.N.Y 2001).*

Preference for interests of common stock. —Generally it will be the duty of the board, where discretionary judgment is to be exercised, to prefer the interests of common stock — as the good-faith judgment of the board sees them to be — to the interests created by the special rights preferences, etc., of preferred stock where there is a conflict. Thus, while a board is required to respect the contractual rights and protections conferred on the preferred shareholders by their stock certificate, the imposition by the board of economic risks upon the preferred stock which the holders of the preferred did not want by virtue of a board decision taken for the benefit largely of the common stock, does not constitute a breach of duty. *Official Committee of the Unsecured Creditors v. Investcorp, S.A., 137 F. Supp. 2d 502 (S.D.N.Y 2001).*

A breach-of-loyalty claim against a director cannot succeed without proof that a majority of the board had a material interest in, or lacked independence with respect to, the challenged transaction. *Official Committee of the Unsecured Creditors v. Investcorp, S.A., 137 F. Supp. 2d 502 (S.D.N.Y 2001).*

Control of the board. — From a practical perspective, the confluence of voting control with directorial and official decision making authority is itself quite consistent with control of the board. Delaware courts have found substantial minority interests, ranging from 20% to 40% sufficient to grant the holder working control. *In re Trump Hotels Shareholder Derivative Litig., 2000 U.S. Dist. LEXIS 13550 (S.D.N.Y. 2000).*

Pre-suit demand is essential where the acts of third parties are at issue because the demand requirement draws the attention of the board to its managerial duties where it may not have previously considered action. *In re Trump Hotels Shareholder Derivative Litig., 2000 U.S. Dist. LEXIS 13550 (S.D.N.Y. 2000).*

De facto director. — Under Delaware law, a director who assumes office pursuant to an irregular election achieves only de facto status which may be successfully attacked by the stockholders. Where stockholders challenge officer conduct not primarily involving third parties, courts may void those actions. *In re Trump Hotels*

Shareholder Derivative Litig., 2000 U.S. Dist. LEXIS 13550 (S.D.N.Y. 2000).

The protections of the business judgment rule can only be claimed by disinterested directors whose conduct otherwise meets the test of business judgment and that the directors thus cannot appear on both sides of the transaction nor expect to derive any personal financial benefit from it. Essentially, the liability is based upon concepts of gross negligence, and the business judgment rule technically speaking has no role where directors have either abdicated their functions, or absent a conscience decision, failed to act. *In re Oxford Health Plans, Inc. Sec. Litig., 192 F.R.D. 111 (S.D.N.Y. 2000).*

Violations of the law concerning the dissemination of false and misleading financial statements cannot be deemed to be the product of a valid exercise of business judgment, and therefore protected from a pre-suit demand futility allegation. *In re Oxford Health Plans, Inc. Sec. Litig., 192 F.R.D. 111 (S.D.N.Y. 2000).*

A violation of fiduciary duty exists if the directors either lack good faith in the exercise of their monitoring responsibilities or permitted a known violation of law by the corporation to occur. *In re Oxford Health Plans, Inc. Sec. Litig., 192 F.R.D. 111 (S.D.N.Y. 2000).*

Reasonable oversight. — While it is true that a director is not under a duty to install and operate a corporate system of espionage to ferret out wrongdoing which they have no reason to suspect exists, a director does have a duty to be reasonably informed about the company and must make sure that appropriate information and reporting systems are in place so that the board receives relevant and timely information necessary to satisfy its supervisory and monitoring role. Thus, a claim of directorial liability predicated upon ignorance of liability creating activities within the corporation will lie where the plaintiff shows a sustained or systematic failure of a director to exercise reasonable oversight. *Benjamin v. Kim, 1999 U.S. Dist. LEXIS 6089 (S.D.N.Y. 1999).*

Diverting corporate opportunity. — A claim that a director has breached his or her fiduciary duties by diverting a corporate opportunity generally alleges injury to the corporation itself and is therefore properly brought as a derivative rather than a direct claim. *Benjamin v. Kim, 1999 U.S. Dist. LEXIS 6089 (S.D.N.Y. 1999).*

No fiduciary duties are owed to option holders under Delaware law. *Powers v. British Vita, P.L.C., 969 F. Supp. 4 (S.D.N.Y. 1997).*

Interest for the benefit of corporation. — If an officer or director of a corporation, in violation of his or her fiduciary duty, acquires gain or advantage for himself or herself, the law charges the interest so acquired with a trust for the benefit of the corporation, at its election, which it denies to the betrayer all benefit and profit. *Cohen v. Bloch, 539 F. Supp. 760 (S.D.N.Y. 1981).*

Impairment of capital. — The board of directors may declare a dividend out of net assets in excess of the company's capital, but may not impair its capital. *In re Schenker, 1963 U.S. Dist. LEXIS 9993 (S.D.N.Y. 1963).*

Proscribed fourth class. — Delaware General Corporation Law makes clear that directors elected pursuant to a special provision in the charter by the holders of a class or series of stock will not constitute a proscribed fourth class whether or not their terms coincide with that of an existing class. *Lacos Land Co. v. Lone Star Industries, Inc., 141 B.R. 815 (Bankr. S.D.N.Y. 1992).*

Standing for direction of meeting action. — That the equity committee is neither a "stockholder" nor a "director" within the meaning of Delaware General Corporation Law tit. 8, § 211(c) does not detract from its standing in this court for an order directing the debtor to conduct an annual shareholders' meeting in accordance with its corporate bylaws. *Official Committee of Equity Sec. Holders of Lone Star Industries, Inc., v. Lone Star Industries, Inc., 138 B.R. 420 (Bankr. S.D.N.Y. 1992).*

Repurchase of shares. — Stock Neither federal nor Delaware law imposes on a corporation any obligation to repurchase its outstanding shares on an equal basis from all of its shareholders. The Delaware Corporations statute specifically authorizes a corporation to purchase its own securities, and the Delaware courts have upheld selective repurchase transactions in the absence of self-dealing on the part of corporate officers or directors. *Heine v. Signal Cos., 1977 U.S. Dist. LEXIS 17071 (S.D.N.Y. 1977).*

Appointment of president. — Incorporators have no power to appoint a president and fix his or her salary before a board of directors is appointed. *Kenyon v. Holbrook Microfilming Service, Inc., 155 F.2d 913 (2d Cir. 1946).*

Rights of bankruptcy trustee. — Although corporate officers and directors owe fiduciary duties to creditors when a corporation is insolvent in fact, those duties do not expand the circumscribed rights of a bankruptcy trustee, who may only assert claims of the bankrupt corporation, not its creditors. *Pereira v. Farace, 413 F.3d 330 (2d Cir. 2005).*

Third Circuit

Business judgment generally. — The business judgment rule is a presumption that in making a business decision the directors of a corporation acted on an informed basis, in good faith, and in the honest belief that the action taken was in the best interests of the company. *In re Cendant Corp. Derivative Action Litigation, 189 F.R.D. 117 (D.N.J. 1999).*

The business judgment rule is primarily a tool of judicial review. The strength of the presumption may vary from situation to situation and it may vary depending on the procedural context in which it is raised. *Asarco, Inc. v. Court, 611 F. Supp. 468 (D.N.J. 1985).*

If a board satisfies its burden of proof under both prongs of a threshold judicial analysis, the presumption of the business judgment rule takes effect, and the burden of proof shifts to the plaintiff to rebut the presumption by showing by a preponderance of the evidence that the directors' decisions were: (1) motivated by a lack of good faith, (2) made without adequate information, (3) primarily based on perpetuating themselves in office, or (4) either fraudulent or characterized by overreaching. Absent such a showing, a court will not substitute its judgment for that of the board. *Gregory v. Correction*

Corporations

Connection, Inc., 1991 U.S. Dist. LEXIS 3659 (E.D.Pa. 1991).

If a board has not satisfied its burden of proof under both prongs of the threshold judicial analysis, however, the board has breached its duty of loyalty, the intrinsic fairness test will apply, and the burdens of production and of persuasion will remain with the board to prove by a preponderance of the evidence that all aspects of its challenged action were entirely fair. *Gregory v. Correction Connection, Inc., 1991 U.S. Dist. LEXIS 3659 (E.D.Pa. 1991).*

The issue of reasonableness implicates the business judgment rule's requirement of procedural due care, i.e., whether the board acted on an informed basis in refusing the demand. *Abrams v. Koether, 1992 U.S. Dist. LEXIS 16295 (D.N.J. 1992).*

Under Delaware law, the independence of the majority of the board must be challenged to strip the individual directors of the business judgment presumption. *In re Cendant Corp. Derivative Action Litigation, 189 F.R.D. 117 (D.N.J. 1999).*

Delaware law does not authorize the automatic removal of the business judgment presumption from every considered decision of a company owned by a controlling shareholder. The presumption is removed only when the corporation affirmatively deals with the controlling shareholder or one of its controlled entities. *In re Cendant Corp. Derivative Action Litigation, 189 F.R.D. 117 (D.N.J. 1999).*

To rebut the business judgment rule's presumption, a plaintiff has the burden of coming forward with evidence sufficient to show that the board breached its duty of care, breached its duty of loyalty, or abused its discretion. That burden of production is difficult to carry; a court will not substitute its judgment for that of a board if the latter's decision can be attributed to any rational business purpose. *Gregory v. Correction Connection, Inc., 1991 U.S. Dist. LEXIS 3659 (E.D.Pa. 1991).*

Duty of care. — A Delaware board of directors derives its inherent power to manage the business and affairs of a corporation from Del. Code Ann. tit. 8, § 141(a). In exercising that power, a board is charged with fiduciary obligations of care and loyalty. To fulfill their duty of care, directors must inform themselves, prior to making a business or distributional decision, of all material information reasonably available to them. *Gregory v. Correction Connection, Inc., 1991 U.S. Dist. LEXIS 3659 (E.D.Pa. 1991).*

Duty of loyalty. — The duty of loyalty demands of a director, the most scrupulous observance of his duty, not only affirmatively to protect the interests of the corporation committed to his charge, but also to refrain from doing anything that would work injury to the corporation, or deprive it of profit or advantage which his skill and ability might properly bring to it, or to enable it to make in the reasonable and lawful exercise of its powers. The rule that requires an undivided and unselfish loyalty to the corporation demands that there shall be no conflict between duty and self-interest. *Gregory v. Correction*

Connection, Inc., 1991 U.S. Dist. LEXIS 3659 (E.D.Pa. 1991).

Directors of a corporation do not breach their fiduciary duty to the corporation by taking action which was taken at the behest of all the shareholders of the corporation. *In re REA Express, Inc., 412 F. Supp. 1239 (E.D. Pa. 1976).*

Derivative suit right. — The right of a stockholder of a Delaware corporation to maintain a derivative suit on behalf of the corporation is based upon a breach of fiduciary duty by the directors or officers of the corporation. The officers and directors of a Delaware corporation are trustees for its stockholders. *Beneficial Industrial Loan Corp. v. Smith, 170 F.2d 44 (3d Cir. 1948).*

Demand and the business judgment rule. — A shareholder lacks standing to bring a shareholder derivative action unless he or she pleads with particularity that demand was made (termed "demand refusal" cases) or that demand would have been futile (termed "demand excused" cases). Where demand is made on the board, its refusal to investigate the allegations is deemed an exercise of reasonable business judgment, unless the plaintiff pleads facts with particularity to create a reasonable doubt that the refusal is protected by the business judgment rule, i.e., sufficient facts to support an inference of wrongful refusal. The business judgment rule is a presumption that in making a decision not involving self-interest, the directors of a corporation acted on an informed basis in good faith and in the honest belief that the action taken was in the best interests of the company. The burden is on the plaintiff to establish facts rebutting this presumption. The business judgment rule may not be invoked where there is an absence of good faith or evidence of self-dealing. *Abrams v. Koether, 1992 U.S. Dist. LEXIS 16295 (D.N.J. 1992).*

Demand-refused. — By electing to make a demand, a shareholder plaintiff tacitly concedes the independence of a majority of the board to respond. Therefore, when a board refuses a demand, the only issues to be examined are the good faith and reasonableness of its investigation. Absent an abuse of discretion, if the requirements of the traditional business judgment rule are met, the board of directors' decision not to pursue the derivative claim will be respected by the courts. In such cases, a board of directors' motion to dismiss an action filed by a shareholder, whose demand has been rejected, must be granted. Thus, for demand-refused cases the sole question for the court is whether the complaint contains sufficient facts to create a doubt as to the good faith of the directors or the reasonableness of their investigation. By conceding independence when demand is made, the plaintiff cannot raise issues of non-independence in demand-refused cases. *Abrams v. Koether, 1992 U.S. Dist. LEXIS 16295 (D.N.J. 1992).*

Demand-excused. — In a demand-excused case, the plaintiff-shareholder must plead with particularity facts to create a reasonable doubt as to the directors' disinterestedness or independence, or whether the directors exercised proper business judgment. A reasonable doubt as to the directors' independence may be created by alleging facts demonstrating that the directors are dominated or otherwise controlled by one interested in the transaction, or that the board is "so under his influence that its discretion is sterilized." The directors must be disinterested to gain protection of the business judgment rule, i.e., they cannot appear on both sides of a transaction or expect to derive any personal financial benefit from it. *Abrams v. Koether, 1992 U.S. Dist. LEXIS 16295 (D.N.J. 1992).*

Demand is also excused where the plaintiff pleads with particularity that the directors failed to exercise proper business judgment. Proper business judgment is the exercise of substantive due care (fairness in the terms of the transaction) and procedural due care (making an informed decision). Due care is absent where the directors make an uninformed or undeliberated decision, or where the directors reach a decision in which the terms are so inadequate that no person of ordinary business judgment would assent to them (such as corporate waste). *Abrams v. Koether, 1992 U.S. Dist. LEXIS 16295 (D.N.J. 1992).*

Delaware law excuses demand as futile where facts are pleaded with sufficient particularity to create a reasonable doubt that the directors are disinterested and independent, or that the challenged transaction was otherwise the product of a valid exercise of business judgment. Where the allegations of a complaint raise a reasonable doubt as to the disinterestedness of the directors, demand is excused and the court does not proceed to the second part of the test. *Abrams v. Koether, 1992 U.S. Dist. LEXIS 16295 (D.N.J. 1992).*

Under Delaware law, the decision to bring a lawsuit or to refrain from litigating a claim on behalf of the corporation is a decision concerning the management of the corporation and consequently is the responsibility of the directors. Because the derivative action impinges on the managerial freedom of directors, the demand requirement exists at the threshold, first to insure that a stockholder exhausts his or her intracorporate remedies, and then to provide a safeguard against strike suits. Demand may be excused if futile. *In re Cendant Corp. Derivative Action Litigation, 96 F. Supp. 2d 394 (D.N.J. 2000).*

In determining the sufficiency of a complaint to withstand demand futility, the trial court is confronted with two questions: whether threshold presumptions of director disinterest or independence are rebutted by well-pleaded facts; and, if not, whether the complaint pleads particularized facts sufficient to create a reasonable doubt that the challenged transaction was the product of a valid exercise of business judgment. The entire review is factual in nature, and in order for demand to be excused, the trial court must be satisfied that a plaintiff has alleged facts with particularity which, taken as true, support a reasonable doubt as to a director's interest or independence or that the challenged transaction was the product of a valid exercise of business judgment. In its determination, the trial court must not rely on any one factor but must examine the totality of the circumstances and consider all of the relevant factors. *In re Cendant Corp. Derivative Action Litigation, 189 F.R.D. 117 (D.N.J. 1999).*

Pertaining to a shareholder derivative suit brought under Delaware law, there is a two-part test for evaluating a claim of demand futility: in determining the sufficiency of a complaint to withstand demand futility, the controlling legal standard is well established. The trial court is confronted with two related but distinct questions: (1) whether threshold presumptions of director disinterest or independence are rebutted by well-pleaded facts; and, if not, (2) whether the complaint pleads particularized facts sufficient to create a reasonable doubt that the challenged transaction was the product of a valid exercise of judgment. *Coyer v. Hemmer, 901 F. Supp. 872 (D.N.J. 1995).*

Pertaining to a shareholder derivative suit brought under Delaware law, the two parts of the demand futility test are two alternative hurdles, either of which a derivative shareholder complaint must overcome to successfully withstand a Fed. R. Civ. P. 23.1 motion. Under the first part of the test, the court reviews the factual allegations of the complaint to determine whether they create a reasonable doubt as to the disinterestedness and independence of the directors at the time the complaint was filed. Directoral interest exists whenever divided loyalties are present, or where the director stands to receive a personal financial benefit from the transaction not equally shared by the shareholders. Directoral independence means that a director's decision is based on the corporate merits of the subject before the board rather than extraneous considerations or influences. *Coyer v. Hemmer, 901 F. Supp. 872 (D.N.J. 1995).*

Pertaining to a shareholder derivative suit brought under Delaware law, it is not sufficient to simply allege domination and control of the directors by another person. Nor is it sufficient to allege that a director a had a financial interest in the transaction. Rather, in order to establish demand futility under the first part of the applicable test: the stockholder must show, through the pleading of particularized facts, that a majority of the board have a financial interest in the transaction or are so dominated by the proponent of the transaction that their discretion is sterilized. *Coyer v. Hemmer, 901 F. Supp. 872 (D.N.J. 1995).*

Pertaining to Delaware's demand futility test, control will not be presumed merely because one is a majority shareholder. It is not enough to charge that a director was nominated by or elected at the behest of those controlling the outcome of a corporate election. It is the care, attention, and sense of individual responsibility to the performance of one's duties, not the method of election, that generally touches upon independence. *Coyer v. Hemmer, 901 F. Supp. 872 (D.N.J. 1995).*

Under Delaware law, derivative plaintiffs must satisfy one of two tests to establish that demand is excused. When a plaintiff's claims arise from an affirmative business decision made by a corporation's board of directors, courts apply the two-prong *Aronson* test laid. Under the *Aronson* test, courts will excuse pre-suit demand if the complaint alleges, with particularity, sufficient facts to create a reasonable doubt that (1) the majority of the directors are disinterested and independent, or (2) the challenged transaction is otherwise the product of the directors' valid exercise of business judgment. If either prong is satisfied, demand is excused. *Amalgamated Bank v. Yost, 2005 U.S. Dist. LEXIS 1280 (E.D.Pa. 2005).*

Under the first prong of Delaware's *Aronson*'s test, a derivative plaintiff seeking to excuse demand must use particularized facts to create a reasonable doubt that the directors are disinterested and independent. To satisfy its burden, a plaintiff must show that at least half of the board was either interested or not independent. Directors are interested when they appear on both sides of a challenged transaction or expect to derive a personal financial benefit from a transaction that is not shared by stockholders generally. *Amalgamated Bank v. Yost, 2005 U.S. Dist. LEXIS 1280 (E.D.Pa. 2005).*

Even if a plaintiff fails to create a reasonable doubt about the board's independence, a court will excuse the demand requirement if a plaintiff raises a reasonable doubt that the directors exercised proper business judgment in the transaction. Even if directors appear disinterested and independent, if they acted illegally in approving a transaction, their interest in avoiding personal liability automatically and absolutely disqualifies them from passing on a shareholder's demand. *Amalgamated Bank v. Yost, 2005 U.S. Dist. LEXIS 1280 (E.D.Pa. 2005).*

When a derivative plaintiff does not challenge an affirmative business decision, Delaware courts employ the modified *Rales* test. Under the *Rales* test, courts will excuse pre-suit demand if the complaint makes particularized factual allegations that create a reasonable doubt that the board of directors could have properly exercised its independent and disinterested business judgment in response to a demand. *Amalgamated Bank v. Yost, 2005 U.S. Dist. LEXIS 1280 (E.D.Pa. 2005).*

Under Delaware's *Rales* test, a court must determine whether the complaint creates a reasonable doubt that the board of directors could have properly exercised its independent and disinterested business judgment in responding to a demand. The mere threat of personal liability is insufficient to challenge the independence or disinterestedness of directors. Rather, plaintiff must show that directors face a sufficiently substantial threat of personal liability to compromise their ability to act impartially on a demand. *Amalgamated Bank v. Yost, 2005 U.S. Dist. LEXIS 1280 (E.D.Pa. 2005).*

Under Delaware law, in the context of a shareholder's derivative lawsuit, a demand on a board of directors is excused where half of the members of an even numbered board are alleged to be interested or lack independence. *Shaev v. Saper, 320 F.3d 373 (3d Cir. 2003).*

Directorial interest. — With regard to demand futility in a shareholder's derivative action, the court reviews the factual allegations of the complaint to determine whether they create a reasonable doubt as to the disinterestedness and independence of the directors at the time the complaint was filed. If the transaction at issue is an "interested" director transaction, such that the business judgment rule is inapplicable to the board majority approving the transaction, then the inquiry ceases. Directorial interest exists whenever divided loyalties are present, or where the director stands to receive a personal benefit from the transaction not equally shared by the shareholders. A director is also interested when a corporate decision will have a materially detrimental impact on a director. Directorial independence requires a director's decision to be based on the corporate merits of the subject before the board rather than extraneous considerations or influences. *In re Cendant Corp. Derivative Action Litigation, 189 F.R.D. 117 (D.N.J. 1999).*

Legal action authority. — Under Delaware law, directors of a corporation are granted the authority to manage the business and affairs of the corporation. This authority is tempered by fundamental fiduciary obligations owed by the directors to the corporation and its shareholders. Included in their responsibilities is the decision whether or not to bring suit on behalf of the corporation concerning the management of the corporation. *Abrams v. Koether, 1992 U.S. Dist. LEXIS 16295 (D.N.J. 1992).*

Ratification. — Delaware law holds that shareholder or director ratification will not be effective if the directors or majority shareholders breached their fiduciary duties. *Abrams v. Koether, 1992 U.S. Dist. LEXIS 16295 (D.N.J. 1992).*

Neutral decision making body. — When an action by a board of directors of a Delaware corporation is challenged, the courts determine whether a conflict of interest of board members has deprived stockholders of a neutral decisionmaking body. The focus is on whether a majority of the corporation's board of directors was neutral and independent in passing on the proposed corporate action. *In re Cendant Corp. Derivative Action Litigation, 189 F.R.D. 117 (D.N.J. 1999).*

Presumption of regularity and respect. — Under the *Cinerama* formulation for determining if the interest of one or more directors was material to the independence of the entire board, a complaint fails to rebut the business judgment rule unless it alleges facts from which one could infer that the director defendants, through their dominance over the other board members, so infected or affected the deliberative process of the board as to disarm the board of its presumption of regularity and respect. *In re Cendant Corp. Derivative Action Litigation, 189 F.R.D. 117 (D.N.J. 1999).*

Insider trading. — Both Delaware and New Jersey recognize a common-law cause of action for a derivative plaintiff against a corporate officer who has traded stock of the corporation on the basis of inside information. Under the laws of both states, directors who trade stock on the basis of inside information violate their fiduciary obligations to the corporation. To state a claim for breach of fiduciary duty, a plaintiff must show a duty, a breach of that duty, an injury and causation. *In re Cendant Corp. Derivative Action Litigation, 189 F.R.D. 117 (D.N.J. 1999).*

Waste. — In Delaware, a shareholder's allegations that a board of directors committed waste by authorizing the issuance of stock for inadequate consideration are derivative in nature. Waste of corporate assets injures the corporation itself. On the other hand, when it is alleged that a board issued stock with the primary and wrongful intent of entrenching itself, and when the consideration paid for such stock is not the basis for allegations of waste, an individual action lies to the extent that the alleged entrenching activity directly impairs some right the plaintiff possesses as a shareholder. *Gregory v. Correction Connection, Inc., 1991 U.S. Dist. LEXIS 3659 (E.D.Pa. 1991).*

Delaware courts have defined "waste" to mean an exchange of corporate assets for consideration so disproportionately small as to lie beyond the range at which any reasonable person might be willing to trade. If there is any substantial consideration received by the corporation, and if there is a good-faith judgment that in the circumstances the transaction is worthwhile, there should be no finding of waste. *Amalgamated Bank v. Yost, 2005 U.S. Dist. LEXIS 1280 (E.D.Pa. 2005).*

A claim for corporate waste is based upon the diversion of corporate assets for improper or unnecessary purposes. A waste entails an exchange of corporate assets for consideration so disproportionately small as to lie beyond the range at which any reasonable person might be willing to trade. Directors are bound to act out of fidelity and honesty in their roles as fiduciaries and not commit acts of waste. Directors may not, simply because of their position, by way of excessive salaries and other devices, oust the minority of a fair return upon its investment. *Delta Star, Inc. v. Patton, 76 F. Supp. 2d 617 (W.D.Pa. 1999).*

Defensive tactics—Tender offers. — In cases that involve tender offer defensive tactics, when a board acts in a defensive posture, it is inappropriate initially to presume that the board has fulfilled its duty of loyalty. *Gregory v. Correction Connection, Inc., 1991 U.S. Dist. LEXIS 3659 (E.D.Pa. 1991).*

When addressing a pending takeover bid, a board has an enhanced duty of loyalty that calls for judicial examination at the threshold before the protections of the business judgment rule may be conferred. *Gregory v. Correction Connection, Inc., 1991 U.S. Dist. LEXIS 3659 (E.D.Pa. 1991).*

Defensive tactics—Threats to policy and effectiveness. — An enhanced duty of loyalty and a threshold judicial examination are invoked not only when a board is faced with a pending takeover bid but also when a board employs any defensive measures taken in response to some threat to corporate policy and effectiveness which touch upon issues of control. *Gregory v. Correction Connection, Inc., 1991 U.S. Dist. LEXIS 3659 (E.D.Pa. 1991).*

The first prong of the threshold judicial inquiry requires directors to show that, when they acted, they had reasonable grounds for believing that a threat to corporate policy and effectiveness existed. It is the reasonableness of a board's perception of a threat to corporate policy and effectiveness, rather than the actual existence of such a threat, that a court is to determine. Among the reasonably perceived threats to corporations that Delaware courts have recognized has been an internal threat from a shareholder. *Gregory v. Correction Connection, Inc., 1991 U.S. Dist. LEXIS 3659 (E.D.Pa. 1991).*

A threat to corporate policy and effectiveness is reasonably perceived if it is perceived in good faith and after reasonable investigation. The requirement that directors act in good faith involves the directors' duty of loyalty and simply requires the directors to demonstrate why they believe that the threat will affect the corporation negatively. The requirement that directors conduct a reasonable investigation is, on the other hand, an admonition to directors to fulfill their duty of care. That duty requires directors to inform themselves of all material information reasonably available to them; directors can fulfill the duty by recording the time, attention, and information they gathered and received before making a decision. Proof of good faith and of a reasonable investigation is materially enhanced by the approval of a board comprised of a majority of outside, independent directors. *Gregory v. Correction Connection, Inc., 1991 U.S. Dist. LEXIS 3659 (E.D.Pa. 1991).*

The second prong of the threshold judicial inquiry is designed to ensure that once a threat to corporate policy and effectiveness is reasonably perceived to exist, a board's defensive response is animated primarily by a desire to eliminate the threat, rather than by a desire to perpetuate control. Moreover, the second prong requires a balanced, rather than a draconian, response. Stated broadly, a defensive measure must be reasonable in relation to the threat posed. Parsing that requirement into its two component parts, (1) a board must have reasonably determined that its defensive measure was logically related to the threat posed, and (2) a court must conclude that the defensive measure was, as eventually employed, proportionate to the threat. *Gregory v. Correction Connection, Inc., 1991 U.S. Dist. LEXIS 3659 (E.D.Pa. 1991).*

In evaluating whether a board properly concluded that a defensive response was logically related to a threat to corporate policy and effectiveness, a court must carefully assess the reasonableness of the defensive measures employed and the results achieved. To show that the defensive measures that they employed and the results that they achieved were reasonable, directors must demonstrate good faith and reasonable investigation. Specifically, directors must show that they engaged in an analysis of both the threat and the appropriate response that included the following: a clear identification of the nature of the threat; an evaluation of the importance of the corporate objective threatened; a discussion of alternate methods of protecting the corporate objective; and consideration of the impact of the defensive measures eventually undertaken. *Gregory v. Correction Connection, Inc., 1991 U.S. Dist. LEXIS 3659 (E.D.Pa. 1991).*

Interference with exercise of shareholder voting rights. — Board action designed principally to interfere with the exercise of shareholder voting rights inherently involves a conflict of interest between the board and the shareholder majority. *Gregory v. Correction Connection, Inc., 1991 U.S. Dist. LEXIS 3659 (E.D.Pa. 1991).*

Break-up of corporation. — When the break-up of a corporation is inevitable, the duty of the board of directors changes from preserving the corporation to an immediate maximizing of the corporation's value at a sale for the benefit of stockholders. *Gregory v. Correction Connection, Inc., 1991 U.S. Dist. LEXIS 3659 (E.D.Pa. 1991).*

There are two specific ways in which a board of directors' duties may arise. The first, and clearer one, is when a corporation initiates an active bidding process seeking to sell itself or to effect a business reorganization involving a clear break-up of the company. The second is where, in response to a bidder's offer, a target abandons its long-term strategy and seeks an alternative transaction involving the break-up of the company. *Gregory v. Correction Connection, Inc., 1991 U.S. Dist. LEXIS 3659 (E.D.Pa. 1991).*

Fairness. — The concept of fairness has two basic aspects: fair dealing and fair price. The former embraces questions of when the transaction was timed, how it was initiated, structured, and disclosed to the directors, and how the approvals of the directors and the stockholders were obtained. The latter aspect of fairness relates to the economic and financial considerations of the proposed merger, including all relevant factors: assets, market value, earnings, future prospects, and any other elements that affect the intrinsic or inherent value of a company's stock. However, the test for fairness is not a bifurcated one as between fair dealing and fair price. All aspects of the issue must be examined as a whole since the question is one of entire fairness. *Gregory v. Correction Connection, Inc., 1991 U.S. Dist. LEXIS 3659 (E.D.Pa. 1991).*

Named parties. — Where a wrong is committed against a corporation, redress of that wrong can be sought only by the corporation. Therefore, a cause of action against a director or officer for mismanagement of a corporation may be asserted only in the name of the corporation. *Penguin Industries v. Kuc, 1986 U.S. Dist. LEXIS 22328 (E.D.Pa 1986).*

Exemption of director liability. — Under Delaware law, when a certificate of incorporation exempts directors from liability, the risk of liability does not disable them from considering a demand fairly unless particularized pleading permits the court to conclude that there is a substantial likelihood that their conduct falls outside the exemption. *Amalgamated Bank v. Yost, 2005 U.S. Dist. LEXIS 1280 (E.D.Pa. 2005).*

Liability for oversight. — A failure to oversee theory is possibly the most difficult theory in corporation law upon which a plaintiff might hope to win a judgment. To establish liability for oversight, a plaintiff must prove a sustained or systematic failure of the board to exercise oversight. Often, this necessitates that plaintiffs plead with particularity that the directors ignored obvious danger signs of employee wrongdoing. *Amalgamated Bank v. Yost, 2005 U.S. Dist. LEXIS 1280 (E.D.Pa. 2005).*

Outside director. — Under Delaware law, an outside director is a nonemployee and nonmanagement director. *Franklin v. SKF USA, Inc., 126 F. Supp. 2d 911 (E.D.Pa. 2001).*

The business and affairs of a corporation are managed by or under the direction of its board of directors. The existence and exercise of this power carries with it certain fundamental fiduciary obligations to the corporation and its shareholders. Directors have a duty to inform themselves, prior to making a business decision, of all material information reasonably available to them. Having become so informed, they must then act with requisite care in the discharge of their duties. Directors have an unyielding duty to protect the interests of the corporation and to act in the best interests of its shareholders. Directors have a duty to place the best interest of the corporation and its shareholders over any interest possessed by a director and not shared by the stockholders generally. Directors have a duty not to use the position of trust and confidence that they hold with the company to further their private interests. *Delta Star, Inc. v. Patton, 76 F. Supp. 2d 617 (W.D.Pa. 1999).*

Interested directors. — The rule that requires a director's undivided and unselfish loyalty toward the corporation and its shareholders demands that there be no conflict between the director's duties and self-interest. A director must act independently and without self-interest. A director acts independently and without self-interest only when the director's decision is based entirely on the corporate merits of a transaction and is not influenced by personal or extraneous considerations. A director who receives a substantial benefit from supporting a transaction cannot be objectively viewed as disinterested or independent. Without the guidance of a truly independent judgment, self-interested directors cannot with confidence know the right course in order to pursue it. In all events, the law will accord scant weight to the subjective judgment of an interested director concerning the fairness of transactions that benefit him. *Delta Star, Inc. v. Patton, 76 F. Supp. 2d 617 (W.D.Pa. 1999).*

Self-dealing. — Self-dealing transactions by corporate officers or directors are not strictly prohibited by Delaware law. Instead, Delaware law provides specific procedures that may be employed by a corporate officer or director to remove the taint that any such transaction may possess solely by reason of its self-interested character. To remove the taint of a self-dealing transaction, a corporate officer or director must establish to an independent body, whether it be a court in litigation, an independent committee of the board of directors, or a group of disinterested ratifying shareholders on full and complete information, that the transaction is fully fair. *Delta Star, Inc. v. Patton, 76 F. Supp. 2d 617 (W.D.Pa. 1999).*

A self-dealing fiduciary may be required to respond in damages or with any other appropriate remedy if a transaction is found to be not an entirely fair one to the corporation or its shareholders. Delaware courts now recognize a right to recover under a theory of quantum meruit where an officer or director has fixed his own compensation. The burden of establishing the reasonableness of the compensation received in connection with a self-dealing transaction, and thus the entitlement to a recovery under the doctrine of quantum meruit, is on the recipient. *Delta Star, Inc. v. Patton, 76 F. Supp. 2d 617 (W.D.Pa. 1999).*

Stock price action. — Since any devaluation of stock is shared collectively by all the shareholders, rather than independently by any individual shareholder, an injury centered around the price at which stock was sold will not suffice to maintain a direct suit. *Furst v. Feinberg, 2002 U.S. App. LEXIS 26174 (3d Cir. 2002).*

The board retains the ultimate freedom to direct the strategy and affairs of a company. *Schoonejongen v. Curtiss-Wright Corp., 143 F.3d 120 (3d Cir. 1998).*

Authorized corporate agents. — Beyond the board of directors, a corporation may validly act through its directors and officers as authorized corporate agents. In general, an officer's powers stem from the organic law of the corporation, or a board delegation of authority, which may be express or implied. Express authority to act on behalf of the corporation is usually manifested through a statute, the certificate of corporation, the bylaws, or a board or shareholder action. Implied actual authority, which is express authority circumstantially proved, may be found through evidence as to the manner in which the business has operated in the past, the facts attending the transaction in question, circumstantial evidence of board declarations surrounding the given transaction, or the habitual usage or course of dealing common to the company. Similarly, authority will be implied when it is reasonably necessary and proper to effectuate the purpose of the office or the main authority conferred. *Schoonejongen v. Curtiss-Wright Corp., 143 F.3d 120 (3d Cir. 1998).*

An officer broadly charged with managing the affairs of a corporation impliedly possesses the authority to appoint subordinate agents under his control to act on behalf of the corporation. Nevertheless, the power of delegation is not without limits, and in determining such limits, the focus is on whether the delegated authority involves ministerial functions or acts that require the exercise of discretion by the sub-agent. As the very term management connotes, however, corporate officers and subordinate agents must be afforded some level of discretion when faced with the demands of supervising a modern corporation. Thus, given the necessities of the case and usage, corporate law recognizes that many discretionary acts will be carried out by officers and other subordinates. The critical factors are often the complexity of the corporation, the intent of the board, and the corporation's implied course of conduct. *Schoonejongen v. Curtiss-Wright Corp., 143 F.3d 120 (3d Cir. 1998).*

The business decision of appointing a corporate officer to manage retirement health benefits for the corporation does not have the effect of removing from directors in a very substantial way their duty to use their own best judgment on management matters. *Schoonejongen v. Curtiss-Wright Corp., 143 F.3d 120 (3d Cir. 1998).*

Fourth Circuit

The business judgment rule is only available when the directors neither appear on both sides of a transaction nor expect to derive any personal financial benefit from it in the sense of self-dealing, as opposed to a benefit which devolves upon the corporation or all stockholders generally. *Williams v. 5300 Columbia Pike Corp., 901 F. Supp. 208 (E.D.Va. 1995).*

Fiduciary duty traditionally encompasses both the duty of care and the duty of loyalty. *Bank of America v. Musselman, 222 F. Supp. 2d 792 (E.D.Va. 2002).*

Limitation on duties. — With respect to officers of a corporation, one court applying Delaware law has noted an important limitation: no fiduciary duty governing the management of a corporation's affairs can be imposed on persons who have no authority to manage those affairs. In the absence of allegations that an officer has such authority under the certificate of incorporation, that officer has no fiduciary duty. *Bank of America v. Musselman, 222 F. Supp. 2d 792 (E.D.Va. 2002).*

Strict demand requirements. — It is a cardinal precept of the Delaware General Corporation Law that directors, rather than shareholders, manage the business and affairs of the corporation. Because by its very nature the derivative action impinges upon the managerial freedom of directors, strict demand requirements are imposed. In situations where derivative plaintiffs are attacking an affirmative business decision made by the board, a court of chancery in the proper exercise of its discretion must decide whether, under the particularized facts alleged, a reasonable doubt is created that: (1) the directors are disinterested and independent and (2) the challenged transaction was otherwise the product of a valid exercise of business judgment. Further, a derivative plaintiff must establish that a majority of the board is interested or lacks independence in order to excuse demand on that ground. *In re Mut. Funds Investent Litigation, 2005 U.S. Dist. LEXIS 18082 (D.Md. 2005).*

Disjunctive demand test. — The test for determining whether demand is excused in a derivative action is disjunctive, because demand is excused if a plaintiff has pleaded facts raising a reasonable doubt either that a majority of the members of the board are not disinterested or independent, or that the challenged decision was not otherwise a product of a valid exercise of business judgment. *In re Mut. Funds Investent Litigation, 2005 U.S. Dist. LEXIS 18082 (D.Md. 2005).*

Modified demand test. — In cases where derivative plaintiffs are not challenging an affirmative decision made by the present board, a modified test for whether demand is excused applies to cases in which the board is charged with a failure of oversight. Under the modified test, a court is to determine (in addition to making an appropriate inquiry under the first prong of the test) whether or not the particularized factual allegations of a derivative stockholder complaint create a reasonable doubt that, as of the time the complaint is filed, the board of directors could have properly exercised its independent and disinterested business judgment in responding to a demand. *In re Mut. Funds Investent Litigation, 2005 U.S. Dist. LEXIS 18082 (D.Md. 2005).*

Construction with other laws. — Delaware statute expressly declares that any investment company trustee who is not to be considered an interested trustee under the Investment Company Act, 15 U.S.C.S. § 80a-1 et seq., is deemed to be independent and disinterested for all purposes. Del. Code Ann. tit. 12, § 3801(h) (1998). This statutes are substantively identical to the Maryland

Corporations

statute, Md. Code Ann., Corp. & Ass'ns § 2-405.3(b) (1998), which was enacted in response to a court decision holding that service on multiple fund boards at a high salary could render a trustee interested and undermine his independence in considering a demand for suit from a derivative plaintiff. Thus, there can be no question that the statutes apply in the demand futility context. *In re Mut. Funds Investent Litigation, 2005 U.S. Dist. LEXIS 18082 (D.Md. 2005).*

Duties during insolvency. — Directors do not breach their fiduciary duties when they enable a secured creditor to foreclose on corporate assets, eliminating shareholder equity. Under Delaware law, when a corporation is insolvent, the fiduciary duties of officers and directors shift, so that a duty to creditors trumps the duty to shareholders. *Galaxy CSI, LLC v. Galaxy Computer Servs., Inc., 2004 U.S. Dist. LEXIS 28162 (E.D.Va. 2004).*

Fairness of stock purchase price. — Delaware law provides that in general the plaintiff bears the burden of proof as to the fairness or unfairness of the purchase price of stock shares and must overcome the "business judgment" rule, a rule that mandates substantial judicial deference to the decisions of a board of directors. But the burden shifts to the defendant directors where the plaintiff establishes that there is a conflict of interest between the directors and the shareholders. More specifically, a conflict of interest between the directors and the shareholders serves to shift to the defendant directors the burden of establishing the "intrinsic fairness" of the transaction, including the fairness of the price. *Williams v. 5300 Columbia Pike Corp., 901 F. Supp. 208 (E.D.Va. 1995).*

Under the business judgment rule, director liability is predicated upon concepts of gross negligence. Specifically, in the area of valuation, wide discretion is allowed to directors, and as long as they appear to act in good faith, with honest motives, and for honest ends, the exercise of their discretion will not be interfered with by the courts. *Williams v. 5300 Columbia Pike Corp., 901 F. Supp. 208 (E.D.Va. 1995).*

Sale of assets. — A corporation may sell all or substantially all of its assets, but the directors have a fiduciary duty to obtain a fair price. A fair price is one to which a reasonable and willing seller and a reasonable and willing buyer, under all circumstances, would agree. Ordinarily, determination of assets' fair value is within the directors' business judgment and discretion, and the burden of proof is on a dissenting shareholder to demonstrate unfairness. But where directors and shareholders who approved a sale have an interest in the transaction, the burden shifts to the proponents of a sale to show the directors' utmost good faith and the transaction's scrupulous fairness. *Williams v. 5300 Columbia Pike Corp., 891 F. Supp. 1169 (E.D.Va. 1995).*

Material omitted fact. — Delaware law defines an omitted fact as material if there is a substantial likelihood that a reasonable shareholder would consider it important in deciding how to vote or if disclosure of the omitted fact would have been viewed by a reasonable investor as having significantly altered the total mix of information made available. *Williams v. 5300 Columbia Pike Corp., 1996 U.S. App. LEXIS 31004 (4th Cir. 1996).*

Fifth Circuit

Fiduciary duties generally. — The directors of a Delaware corporation stand in a fiduciary relationship not only to the stockholders but also to the corporations upon whose boards they serve. The directors' fiduciary duties have been characterized as a triad: due care, good faith, and loyalty. *H.I.G. P-Xi Holding, Inc., 2001 U.S. Dist. LEXIS 5074 (E.D.La. 2001).*

Under Delaware law, a director is required not only affirmatively to protect the interests of the corporation committed to an officer's charge, but also to refrain from doing anything that would work injury to the corporation. *Cohn v. Nelson, 375 F. Supp. 2d 844 (E.D.Miss. 2005).*

Delaware places a high fiduciary duty upon interlocking directorates regarding transactions between the corporations. Delaware imposes no fiduciary duty on the part of officers or directors or majority stockholders in buying stock from the minority or individual stockholders. *Mansfield Hardwood Lumber Co. v. Johnson, 268 F.2d 317 (5th Cir. 1959).*

Duties of loyalty and care. — Under Delaware law, corporate directors have a trustee's duty of loyalty and care. The duty of care obliges directors to make informed decisions, and the duty of loyalty obliges them to act in good faith to the owners, without self interest. *Southdown, Inc. v. Moore McCormack Resources, Inc., 686 F. Supp. 595 (S.D.Tex. 1988).*

Under state law, a director owes a duty of care and loyalty. The duty of care requires a director to exercise that degree of care that an ordinarily careful and prudent person would exercise under the same or similar circumstances. *National Convenience Stores v. Shields (In re Schepps Food Stores), 160 B.R. 792 (Bankr. S.D.Tex. 1993).*

Business judgment rule generally. — Under the business judgment rule, when a board acts in good faith, a court will not substitute its judgment for that of the board as long as the decisions are attributable to any rational business purpose of the owners. *Southdown, Inc. v. Moore McCormack Resources, Inc., 686 F. Supp. 595 (S.D.Tex. 1988).*

Ordinarily, the business judgment rule provides a presumption that in making a business decision the directors of a corporation acted only after they were appropriately informed and after they had honestly determined that the action taken was in the best interests of the company. Because contests for control have an omnipresent specter that a board may be acting primarily in its own interests, the directors have an enhanced duty to prove that they had reasonable grounds for believing that a danger to corporate policy and effectiveness existed because of another person's stock ownership. *Southdown, Inc. v. Moore McCormack Resources, Inc., 686 F. Supp. 595 (S.D.Tex. 1988).*

In a derivative action, Delaware courts often apply the business judgment rule, a rebuttable presumption that directors do not breach their duty of care. Only a

Corporations

disinterested corporate director can assert the business judgment rule as a defense to a derivative action. A disinterested director is a director who has not appeared on both sides of a business transaction and who has not received a personal financial benefit from the transaction. *H.I.G. P-Xi Holding, Inc., 2001 U.S. Dist. LEXIS 5074 (E.D.La. 2001).*

Director suits. — Unfair actions or breaches of corporate duties are usually challenged by shareholders in derivative actions because the directors who abused their positions are unlikely to sue themselves. Under Delaware law, a corporation can, however, sue its directors for breaches of corporate duties. *H.I.G. P-Xi Holding, Inc., 2001 U.S. Dist. LEXIS 5074 (E.D.La. 2001).*

Derivative actions. — Under the business judgment rule, plaintiffs in a derivative action have the burden of showing that the defendants acted without the requisite due care or in bad faith or disloyally, failing to exercise reasonable business judgment. It is a very difficult standard. *Cohn v. Nelson, 375 F. Supp. 2d 844 (E.D.Miss. 2005).*

Delaware courts characterize suits alleging mismanagement that depresses the value of stock as a wrong to the corporation or stockholders collectively that should be enforced by a derivative action. Any devaluation of the stock is shared collectively by the shareholders, rather than independently by the plaintiff or other individual shareholder. Thus the wrong alleged is entirely derivative in nature. *King v. Douglass, 973 F. Supp. 707 (S.D.Tex. 1996).*

A plaintiff-shareholder must overcome the presumptions of the business judgment rule, when it is asserted by a defendant, before they will be permitted to pursue derivative claims. The business judgment rule requires the trial court to presume that directors have acted in good faith and in the honest belief that their actions served the corporation's best interest. *King v. Douglass, 973 F. Supp. 707 (S.D.Tex. 1996).*

To prove a violation of the "duty to monitor" in a derivative action, a plaintiff must plead and prove facts that demonstrate a sustained or systematic failure of the board to exercise oversight — such an utter failure to attempt to assure a reasonable information and reporting system exists. Liability is premised on a showing that the directors were conscious of the fact that they were not doing their jobs. This is a difficult standard to allege, let alone prove on summary judgment or at trial. *Cohn v. Nelson, 375 F. Supp. 2d 844 (E.D.Miss. 2005).*

Demand requirement. — Delaware law requires a stockholder to make a demand on the board of directors to pursue the corporate claim because directors are empowered to manage, or direct the management of, the business and affairs of the corporation. *Kaltman v. Sidhu, 2004 U.S. Dist. LEXIS 2818 (N.D. Tex. 2004).*

In deciding whether demand on the board of directors prior to filing a derivative suit is futile, the trial court must determine whether the particularized factual allegations of a derivative stockholder complaint create a reasonable doubt that, as of the time the complaint is filed, the board of directors could have properly exercised its independent and disinterested business judgment in responding to a demand. To create a doubt that the board of directors could exercise its independent and disinterested business judgment, plaintiff must allege with particularity facts that create a reasonable doubt that the board is capable of acting free from personal financial interest and improper extraneous influences. The test is employed where directors are sued because they have failed to do something. Demand should not be excused automatically in the absence of allegations demonstrating why the board is incapable of considering a demand. *Kaltman v. Sidhu, 2004 U.S. Dist. LEXIS 2818 (N.D. Tex. 2004).*

In the context of Fed. R. Civ. P. 23.1, under Delaware law, the *Rales* test is employed where directors are sued because they have failed to do something; demand should not be excused automatically in the absence of allegations demonstrating why the board is incapable of considering a demand. The court must consider whether the particularized factual allegations of a derivative stockholder complaint create a reasonable doubt that, as of the time the complaint is filed, the board of directors could have properly exercised its independent and disinterested business judgment in responding to a demand. To create a doubt that the board of directors could exercise its independent and disinterested business judgment, the plaintiff would need to allege with particularity facts that create a reasonable doubt that the board is capable of acting free from personal financial interest and improper extraneous influences. *Spector v. Sidhu, 2004 U.S. Dist. LEXIS 876 (N.D.Tex. 2004).*

Interested director. — A director is considered interested where he or she will receive a personal financial benefit from a transaction that is not equally shared by the stockholders, or where a corporate decision will have a materially detrimental impact on a director, but not on the corporation and the stockholders. To establish lack of independence, plaintiff must show that the directors are beholden to the interested director or so under his influence that their discretion would be sterilized. *Kaltman v. Sidhu, 2004 U.S. Dist. LEXIS 2818 (N.D. Tex. 2004).*

The mere threat of personal liability for approving a questioned transaction, standing alone, is insufficient to challenge either the independence or disinterestedness of directors. Only when the potential for liability rises from a mere threat of personal liability to a substantial likelihood of personal liability will directors be considered interested. *Kaltman v. Sidhu, 2004 U.S. Dist. LEXIS 2818 (N.D. Tex. 2004).*

The mere fact that the board has elected not to sue before the derivative action was filed should not of itself indicate interestedness. It is the board's inaction in most every case which is the raison d'etre for Fed. R. Civ. P. 23.1. *Kaltman v. Sidhu, 2004 U.S. Dist. LEXIS 2818 (N.D. Tex. 2004).*

Under Delaware law, a director is considered interested where he or she will receive a personal financial benefit from a transaction that is not equally shared by the stockholders, or where a corporate decision will have a materially detrimental impact on a director, but not on the corporation and the stockholders. To establish lack of independence, plaintiff must show that the directors are "beholden" to the interested director or so under their influence that their discretion would be sterilized. *Spector v. Sidhu, 2004 U.S. Dist. LEXIS 876 (N.D.Tex. 2004).*

Potential investor owed no duties. — Under Delaware law, directors of corporations are fiduciaries who owe duties of due care, good faith and loyalty to the company and its stockholders. However, no fiduciary duties are owed to a potential investor. *Kunzweiler v. Zero.net, Inc., 2002 U.S. Dist. LEXIS 12080 (N.D.Tex. 2002).*

Standing of charitable entity. — Delaware courts have allowed for standing by one director of a charitable corporation against the corporation in situations where warring factions of the board dispute the actions of a corporate board. Directors of charitable corporations have standing to maintain an action on behalf of the corporation for breach of fiduciary duty. As a fiduciary, the trustee of a charitable trust or director of a charitable corporation has a sufficiently concrete interest in the outcome of litigation involving a breach of fiduciary duty to the charitable entity that he has standing. *Hand of Help USA v. Hand of Help Romania, 2002 U.S. Dist. LEXIS 3828 (N.D.Tex 2002).*

Protection of assets of insolvent corporation. — Delaware law recognizes that when a corporation becomes insolvent, the assets of the corporation become a trust for the benefit of the corporation's creditors. The corporate directors then hold a fiduciary duty as trustees to protect the assets for the creditors. The breach of that duty gives rise to a claim that can be pursued by the creditors. *Jewel Recovery, L.P. v. Gordon, 196 B.R. 348 (N.D.Tex. 1996).*

The business judgment rule is a purely defensive rule, and not a basis for granting a motion to dismiss a stockholders' derivative suit against a corporation and its directors alleging a breach of fiduciary duty when the corporate directors, or a committee thereof, in their collective business judgment, determined that the suit was not in the best interests of the corporation. *Maher v. Zapata Corp., 490 F. Supp. 348 (S.D. Tex. 1980).*

Approval of defensive acts. — The duty of restraining management to proportionate responses requires that the directors approve only those defensive acts that are reasonable in relation to the threat posed; the duty of proportion entails that the directors understand both whom the threat endangers and whom the defensive reaction will ultimately harm. *Southdown, Inc. v. Moore McCormack Resources, Inc., 686 F. Supp. 595 (S.D.Tex. 1988).*

Under Delaware law, a minority of a corporation's board has no power. *Halliburton Company Benefits Comm. v. Graves, 2004 U.S. Dist. LEXIS 25684 (S.D.Tex. 2004).*

Directors do not owe creditors duties beyond the relevant contractual terms absent special circumstances, e.g., fraud, insolvency, or a violation of a statute. *Weaver v. Kellogg, 216 B.R. 563 (S.D.Tex. 1997).*

Good faith action. — Under the business judgment rule, corporate decisionmakers are not liable for business decisions made on an informed basis, in good faith, and in the exercise of honest judgment in the lawful and legitimate furtherance of corporate purposes. A corporate decisionmaker acts in good faith if his or her conduct is genuinely motivated by an honest desire to benefit the business' shareholders and not by some other purpose such as personal gain. *King v. Douglass, 973 F. Supp. 707 (S.D.Tex. 1996).*

Fairness test. — Under Delaware law, when the presumption of the business judgment rule has been rebutted, the burden shifts to the defendants to demonstrate the unfairness of the board's action. The concept of fairness has two basic aspects: fair dealing and fair price. The former embraces questions of when the transaction was timed, how it was initiated, structured, negotiated, disclosed to the directors, and how the approvals of the directors and the stockholders were obtained. The latter aspect of fairness relates to the economic and financial considerations of the proposed transaction, including all relevant factors. The test for fairness is not a bifurcated one as between fair dealing and price. All aspects of the issue must be examined as a whole since the question is one of entire fairness. *King v. Douglass, 973 F. Supp. 707 (S.D.Tex. 1996).*

Scope of corporate indemnification. — The scope of corporate indemnification under Delaware law, while justly broad, cannot cover individual conduct by a person that is wholly outside and indeed prior to his corporate employment. *West v. Balfour Beatty Construction, Inc., 290 F.3d 263 (5th Cir. 2002).*

Creditor claims. — In the absence of an authoritative and comprehensive discussion of the issues, the best developed and most analogous case law suggests that Delaware's courts evaluate claims by creditors against directors under the trust fund doctrine and classify the insolvency exception as a defense to suits against directors. *Floyd v. Hefner, 2006 U.S. Dist. LEXIS 70922 (D. Tex. Sept. 29, 2006).*

Sixth Circuit

Powerful presumptions of business judgment rule. — A basic premise of corporate governance under Delaware law is that the directors, rather than the shareholders, manage the business and affairs of the corporation. Shareholders, thus, are permitted to challenge the propriety of decisions made by directors under their authority, only by overcoming the powerful presumptions of the business judgment rule. The specific requirements for overcoming these presumptions vary somewhat depending upon the precise nature of the challenged action. *Salsitz v. Nasser, 208 F.R.D. 589 (E.D. Mich. 2002).*

Generally, when reviewing the action of directors, Delaware courts have applied the business judgment rule which presumes that the directors of a corporation acted on an informed basis, in good faith and in the honest belief that the action taken was in the best interest of the company. *Buckhorn, Inc. v. Ropak Corp., 656 F. Supp. 209 (S.D.Ohio 1987).*

Because derivative suits challenge the propriety of decisions made by directors under their authority, stockholder plaintiffs must overcome the powerful presumptions of the business judgment rule before they will be permitted to pursue the derivative claim. *McCall v. Scott, 239 F.3d 808 (6th Cir. 2001).*

In Delaware, a plaintiff must show that the majority of the board acted in a manner that rises to the level of gross negligence before a court may second guess its business judgment. *Campbell v. Potash Corp. of Saskatchewan, Inc., 238 F.3d 792 (6th Cir. 2001).*

Duty of care. — Under Delaware law, the directors of a corporation owe unyielding fiduciary duties of care and loyalty to the corporation and its shareholders. The fiduciary duty of care requires a director to exercise an informed business judgment and to consider all material information reasonably available before making a business judgment. *Buckhorn, Inc. v. Ropak Corp., 656 F. Supp. 209 (S.D.Ohio 1987).*

Duty of loyalty. — With respect to the duty of loyalty, directors must act in the interests of the corporation and shareholders, and not in a manner which personally enriches any director at the expense of the corporation. *Buckhorn, Inc. v. Ropak Corp., 656 F. Supp. 209 (S.D.Ohio 1987).*

The duty of loyalty requires that the best interests of the corporation and its shareholders take precedence over any self-interest of a director, officer, or controlling shareholder that is not shared by the stockholders generally. *McCall v. Scott, 239 F.3d 808 (6th Cir. 2001).*

Under Delaware law, the duty of good faith is violated where a corporate director consciously disregards his or her duties to the corporation. Mere sustained inattention is insufficient. *Salsitz v. Nasser, 208 F.R.D. 589 (E.D. Mich. 2002).*

Under Delaware law, the duty of good faith may be breached where a director consciously disregards his or her duties to the corporation, thereby causing its stockholders to suffer. *McCall v. Scott, 250 F.3d 997 (6th Cir. 2001).*

Duty standard. — In evaluating whether directors have breached a fiduciary duty, Delaware courts predicate liability upon "concepts of gross negligence." *Buckhorn, Inc. v. Ropak Corp., 656 F. Supp. 209 (S.D.Ohio 1987).*

Gross negligence is the standard for measuring a director's liability for a breach of the duty of care. *McCall v. Scott, 239 F.3d 808 (6th Cir. 2001).*

Demand futility. — Under Delaware law, a basic premise of corporate governance is that the board of directors manages the affairs of the corporation, not the shareholders. Frequently, derivative suits have challenged the propriety of decisions made by directors pursuant to their managerial authority. In such situations, a shareholder seeking to demonstrate demand futility must either: (1) create a reasonable doubt as to the disinterest and independence of the directors or (2) create a reasonable doubt as to whether the challenged decision was the product of a valid exercise of the business judgment rule. *In re Concord EFS, Inc. Derivative Litigations., 2004 U.S. Dist. LEXIS 25569 (W.D.Tenn. 2004).*

Where there is no conscious decision by corporate directors to act or refrain from acting, the demand requirement for bringing a shareholder derivative action is excused when the particularized facts create a reasonable doubt that, as of the time the complaint is filed, a majority of the board of directors could have properly exercised its independent and disinterested business judgment in responding to the demand. Under this standard, corporate boards cannot be charged with wrongdoing simply for assuming the integrity of employees and the honesty of their dealings on the company's behalf. Rather, the rule recognizes the balance between two potentially conflicting principles of corporate governance. On one side is the principle that most of the decisions that a corporation, acting through its human agents, makes are not the subject of director attention. Legally, the board itself is required only to authorize the most significant corporate acts or transactions: mergers, changes in capital structure. Nonetheless, ordinary business decisions made by officers and employees deeper in the interior of the organization can vitally affect the welfare of the corporation and its ability to achieve its various strategic and financial goals. *Salsitz v. Nasser, 208 F.R.D. 589 (E.D. Mich. 2002).*

Under the *Rales* test, the court must determine whether or not the particularized factual allegations create a reasonable doubt that, as of the time the complaint was filed, a majority of the board of directors could have properly exercised its independent and disinterested business judgment in responding to a demand. To establish a reasonable doubt, plaintiffs are not required to plead facts that would be sufficient to support a judicial finding of demand futility. Nor must plaintiffs demonstrate a reasonable probability of success on the merits. Whether plaintiffs have alleged facts sufficient to create a reasonable doubt concerning the disinterestedness and independence of a majority of the board must be determined from the accumulation of all the facts taken together. *McCall v. Scott, 239 F.3d 808 (6th Cir. 2001).*

Inaction by the board will not excuse the failure to make a demand because it would deprive the board of the opportunity to be "prodded" into action, which is a fundamental goal of the demand requirement. *McCall v. Scott, 239 F.3d 808 (6th Cir. 2001).*

Director independence. — Where a conscious decision by corporate directors to act or refrain from acting is made, the demand requirement for a shareholder to bring a derivative action is excused when under the particularized facts alleged, a reasonable doubt is created that: (1) a majority of the directors are disinterested and independent; or (2) the challenged transaction was otherwise the product of a valid exercise of business judgment. Under the first prong, independence requires that a director's decision be based on the corporate merits of the subject before the board rather than extraneous considerations or influences. This standard is satisfied if a majority of the board that was in office at the time of filing was free from personal interest or domination and control, and thus capable of objectively evaluating a demand and, if necessary, remedying the alleged injury. It is no answer to say that demand is necessarily futile because: (a) the directors would have to sue themselves, thereby placing the conduct of the litigation in hostile hands; or (b) that they approved the underlying transaction. *Salsitz v. Nasser, 208 F.R.D. 589 (E.D. Mich. 2002).*

Good faith/rationality of process used. — Where a conscious decision by corporate directors to act or refrain from acting is made, the demand requirement for a shareholder to bring a derivative action is excused when under the particularized facts alleged, a reasonable doubt is created that: (1) a majority of the directors are disinterested and independent; or (2) the challenged transaction was otherwise the product of a valid exercise of business judgment. Under the second prong, the business judgment rule provides that whether a judge or jury considering a business decision after the fact, believes a decision substantively wrong, or degrees of wrong extending through stupid to egregious or irrational, provides no ground for director liability, so long as the court determines that the process employed was either rational or employed in a good faith effort to advance corporate interests. Thus, a court may not consider the content of the board decision that leads to corporate loss, apart from consideration of the good faith or rationality of the process employed. *Salsitz v. Nasser, 208 F.R.D. 589 (E.D. Mich. 2002).*

When corporate director liability is predicated upon ignorance of liability-creating activities, only a sustained or systematic failure of the board to exercise oversight — such as an utter failure to attempt to assure a reasonable information reporting system exists — will establish the lack of good faith that is a necessary condition to liability. As long as a reasonable information system exists, the level of detail that is appropriate is a question of business judgment. *Salsitz v. Nasser, 208 F.R.D. 589 (E.D. Mich. 2002).*

Where plaintiff shareholders allege ignorance of liability-creating activities by individual corporate management defendants, only a sustained or systematic failure of the board to exercise oversight, such as an utter failure to attempt to assure a reasonable information and reporting system exists, will establish the lack of good faith that is a necessary condition to liability. Only through gross negligence may a director be found to have breached the duty of care. *In re Concord EFS, Inc. Derivative Litigations., 2004 U.S. Dist. LEXIS 25569 (W.D.Tenn. 2004).*

Waiver-of-liability provisions contained in a corporate charter are authorized pursuant to Del. Code Ann. tit. 8, § 102(b)(7). *Salsitz v. Nasser, 208 F.R.D. 589 (E.D. Mich. 2002).*

Del. Code Ann. tit. 8, § 102(b)(7)(ii) exempts acts or omissions not in good faith or which involve intentional misconduct from the protection of the waiver of directors' liability. *McCall v. Scott, 250 F.3d 997 (6th Cir. 2001).*

When the validity of a waiver of liability provision is not contested and the factual basis for the claims implicates only a breach of the duty of care, the waiver may properly be considered and applied in deciding a motion to dismiss for failure to make a pre-suit demand. *McCall v. Scott, 239 F.3d 808 (6th Cir. 2001).*

"Entire fairness". — Under Delaware law, where corporate directors stand on both sides of a transaction, they have the burden of demonstrating the "entire fairness" of the transaction, which has two aspects: fair dealing (or procedural fairness) and fair price. The fair dealing prong embraces questions of when the transaction was timed, how it was initiated, structured, negotiated, disclosed to the directors, and how the approvals of the directors and stockholders were obtained. Fair price relates to the economic and financial considerations of the proposed merger, including all relevant factors: assets, market value, earnings, future prospects, and any other elements that affect the intrinsic or inherent value of a company's stock. The use of cash-out mergers is sanctioned as a means of eliminating minority interests. *Krieger v. Gast, 179 F. Supp. 2d 762 (W.D.Mich. 2001).*

A director's disclosure violation may implicate either the duty of loyalty or the duty of care. A claim for breach of the fiduciary duty of disclosure implicates only the duty of care when the factual basis for the alleged violation suggests that the violation was made as a result of a good faith, but, nevertheless, erroneous judgment about the proper scope or content of the required disclosure. However, where a complaint alleges or pleads facts sufficient to support the inference that the disclosure violation was made in bad faith, knowingly, or intentionally, the alleged violation implicates the duty of loyalty. *Krieger v. Gast, 179 F. Supp. 2d 762 (W.D.Mich. 2001).*

Threat to control. — Recognizing the inherent danger in the purchase of shares with corporate funds to remove a threat to corporate policy when a threat to control is involved, Delaware courts now require directors, when faced with such a conflict to show that they had reasonable grounds for believing that a danger to corporate policy and effectiveness existed because of another person's stock ownership. A board of directors satisfies their burden by showing good faith and reasonable investigation. *Buckhorn, Inc. v. Ropak Corp., 656 F. Supp. 209 (S.D.Ohio 1987).*

Under Delaware law, reasonable investigation requires that the directors inform themselves prior to making a business decision, of all material information reasonably available to them. The directors' proof is materially enhanced if they show that defensive measures were approved by a board comprised of a majority of outside independent directors who have acted in accordance with the foregoing standards. In addition to demonstrating good faith and reasonable investigation, the directors must also show that the defensive measure taken is reasonable in relation to the threat posed. This entails an analysis by the directors of the nature of the takeover bid and its effect on the corporate enterprise. *Buckhorn, Inc. v. Ropak Corp., 656 F. Supp. 209 (S.D.Ohio 1987).*

Defensive measures. — Where defensive measure are adopted by the directors, the directors have the burden under Delaware law of proving that: (1) the defensive measures were adopted as a result of an informed business judgment based on an evaluation of all material information; (2) they had reasonable grounds to perceive the take over offer as a danger to corporate policy and effectiveness; and (3) the defensive measures adopted were a reasonable response to the threat posed by a takeover offer. *Buckhorn, Inc. v. Ropak Corp., 656 F. Supp. 209 (S.D.Ohio 1987)*.

Courts have repeatedly held that adoption of a poison pill is a reasonable response by directors when they believe that the price offered is inadequate and threatens the interests of shareholders. *Buckhorn, Inc. v. Ropak Corp., 656 F. Supp. 209 (S.D.Ohio 1987)*.

It is critical that the directors demonstrate that they used due care in arriving at their decision in adopting the poison pill. Under Delaware law, this means that the directors must show that they informed themselves prior to making a business judgment decision, of all material information reasonably available to them. *Buckhorn, Inc. v. Ropak Corp., 656 F. Supp. 209 (S.D.Ohio 1987)*.

While it is certainly permissible for the directors to adopt measures for the benefit of its employees during the midst of a corporate control struggle, the directors must show that there are rationally related benefits accruing to the stockholders from adopting such measures. Furthermore, it is appropriate to look at such factors as the timing of the employee stock ownership plan (ESOP) establishment, the financial impact upon the company, the identity of the trustees and the voting control of the ESOP shares in determining whether the ESOP was created to benefit the employees and not simply to further entrench management. *Buckhorn, Inc. v. Ropak Corp., 656 F. Supp. 209 (S.D.Ohio 1987)*.

Void or voidable transaction. — A contract or transaction between a Delaware corporation and one or more of its directors or officers in which the officer or director has a financial interest may be void or voidable unless one of three tests are met: (1). the contract or transaction was approved by a majority of disinterested directors, even if less than a quorum, after full disclosure is made; (2). the contract or transaction was specifically approved by shareholders after full disclosure; or (3). the contract or transaction was fair to the corporation at the time it was approved or ratified. *In re Revco D.S., Inc., 1990 Bankr. LEXIS 2966 (Bankr. N.D.Ohio 1990)*.

Participation in material misstatements. — Under Delaware law, shareholder plaintiffs cannot merely posit, without any particularized facts, that individual corporate management defendants knew of, or directly participated in, the allegedly material misstatements. *In re Concord EFS, Inc. Derivative Litigations., 2004 U.S. Dist. LEXIS 25569 (W.D.Tenn. 2004)*.

Business judgment rule inapplicable. — Infrequently, a derivative suit will be filed where there is no conscious decision by the directors to act or refrain from acting. Such lack of decision by the board makes it impossible to apply the business judgment rule. In these situations, it is appropriate to examine whether the board that would be addressing the demand can impartially consider its merits without being influenced by improper considerations. *In re Concord EFS, Inc. Derivative Litigations., 2004 U.S. Dist. LEXIS 25569 (W.D.Tenn. 2004)*.

Demanding extra compensation to support merger. — Although Delaware courts require an extra showing of unfairness in order to sustain a collateral attack on a stock merger deal where a director or officer has breached his fiduciary duties by demanding extra compensation to support the deal, this does not mean that the demand for such payment does not, in every case, constitute a breach of the director or officer's fiduciary duties. It does. *Roberts v. Fin. Tech. Ventures, L.P., 2007 U.S. Dist. LEXIS 78448 (MD Tenn., October 23, 2007)*.

Trading in corporation's stock. — Insider trading constitutes a breach of the duty of loyalty. In general, however, directors may trade in a corporation's stock without liability to the corporation. As a matter of course, corporate insiders may be expected sell company stock during their tenure. To recover insider profits for a breach of the duty of loyalty, it must be shown that each sale by each individual defendant was entered into and completed on the basis of, and because of, adverse material nonpublic information. Fraudulent intent may be inferred from the timing and quantities of the trades. *In re Concord EFS, Inc. Derivative Litigations., 2004 U.S. Dist. LEXIS 25569 (W.D.Tenn. 2004)*.

Under Delaware common law, a fiduciary of a corporation who trades for his or her own benefit on the basis of confidential information acquired through his or her fiduciary position breaches his or her duty to the corporation and may be held accountable to that corporation for any gains without regard to whether the corporation suffered damages. *McCall v. Scott, 239 F.3d 808 (6th Cir. 2001)*.

The mere fact that stocks were traded by an officer or director does not establish a breach of the duty of loyalty. A director is free to trade in the corporation's stock without liability to the corporation. In fact, when directors and officers own stock or receive compensation in stock, they should be expected to trade those securities in the normal course of events. *McCall v. Scott, 239 F.3d 808 (6th Cir. 2001)*.

To recover insider profits for a breach of the duty of loyalty, it must be shown that each sale by each individual defendant was entered into and completed on the basis of, and because of, adverse material non-public information. Fraudulent intent may be inferred from the timing and quantities of the trades. *McCall v. Scott, 239 F.3d 808 (6th Cir. 2001)*.

Waste. — To excuse demand on grounds of corporate waste, shareholder plaintiffs must allege particularized facts that the consideration received by the corporation was so inadequate that no person of ordinary sound business judgment would deem it worth that which the corporation has paid. *In re Concord EFS, Inc. Derivative Litigations., 2004 U.S. Dist. LEXIS 25569 (W.D.Tenn. 2004)*.

Failure to exercise appropriate attention. — Director liability for breach of the duty to exercise appropriate attention to potentially illegal corporate activities may arise (1) from a board decision that resulted in a loss because the decision was ill-advised, or (2) from an unconsidered failure of the board to act in circumstances in which due attention would, arguably, have prevented the loss. *McCall v. Scott, 250 F.3d 997 (6th Cir. 2001).*

When director liability is predicated upon ignorance of liability-creating activities, only a sustained or systematic failure of the board to exercise oversight, such as an utter failure to attempt to assure a reasonable information and reporting system exists, will establish the lack of good faith that is a necessary condition to liability. *McCall v. Scott, 250 F.3d 997 (6th Cir. 2001).*

Unconsidered inaction can be the basis for director liability because, even though most corporate decisions are not subject to director attention, ordinary business decisions of officers and employees deeper in the corporation can significantly injure the corporation and make it subject to criminal sanctions. The question of whether a corporate director has become liable for losses to the corporation through neglect of duty is determined by the circumstances. If he or she has recklessly reposed confidence in an obviously untrustworthy employee, has refused or neglected cavalierly to perform his or her duty as a director, or has ignored either willfully or through inattention obvious danger signs of employee wrongdoing, the law will cast the burden of liability upon him or her. Gross negligence is the standard for measuring a director's liability for a breach of the duty of care. *McCall v. Scott, 250 F.3d 997 (6th Cir. 2001).*

Consideration of liability waiver. — Del. Code Ann. tit. 8, § 102(b)(7) allows a corporation to amend its certificate of incorporation to protect its directors against claims for gross negligence. When the validity of such a provision is not contested and the factual basis for the claims implicates only a breach of the duty of care, the waiver may properly be considered and applied in deciding a motion to dismiss for failure to make a pre-suit demand. *McCall v. Scott, 250 F.3d 997 (6th Cir. 2001).*

Plaintiff's contract was illegal under Delaware law, constituting a blatant violation of his fiduciary duty of loyalty to corporation. Under his own admissions, the plaintiff extracted a payment from another shareholder in exchange for supporting, as CEO, an action that he otherwise did not think was in the best interest of the shareholders. If the court were to find that the action was, in fact, in the best interest of the shareholders, that would mean that the plaintiff extracted a payment from another shareholder by threatening not to support an advantageous corporate action. In either event, the plaintiff breached his duty of loyalty by entering into this agreement. *Roberts v. Fin. Tech. Ventures, L.P., 2007 U.S. Dist. LEXIS 78448 (MD Tenn., October 23, 2007).*

Seventh Circuit

Under Delaware law, the board of directors has the ultimate responsibility for managing the business affairs of a corporation. *Steinberg v. Kendig, 2000 U.S. Dist. LEXIS 276 (N.D.Ill. 2000).*

Under Delaware law, the board of directors has the ultimate responsibility for managing the business affairs of a corporation. *Jackson Nat'l Life Ins. Co. v. Kendig, 1999 U.S. Dist. LEXIS 16645 (N.D.Ill. 1999).*

Delaware law imposes management responsibility to directors, but not to officers. The exception to this rule is that the business and affairs of every corporation shall be managed by or under the direction of a board of directors, except as may be otherwise provided in its certificate of incorporation. *Jackson Nat'l Life Ins. Co. v. Kendig, 1999 U.S. Dist. LEXIS 16645 (N.D.Ill. 1999).*

No fiduciary duty governing the management of a corporation's affairs can be imposed on persons who have no authority to manage those affairs. *Jackson Nat'l Life Ins. Co. v. Kendig, 1999 U.S. Dist. LEXIS 16645 (N.D.Ill. 1999).*

Fiduciary duties generally. — The ultimate responsibility for managing the business and affairs of the corporation belongs to the board of directors. In fulfilling this responsibility the directors have a fiduciary duty to act in the best interest of the corporation and its shareholders. This duty includes protecting the corporate enterprise and the shareholders from harm reasonably perceived, irrespective of its source. *Newell Co. v. Vermont American Corp., 725 F. Supp. 351 (N.D.Ill. 1989).*

The ultimate responsibility for managing the business and affairs of the corporation lies with the board of directors, but the board's authority is not without limits, the directors have a fundamental duty to protect the corporate enterprise from harm reasonably perceived, irrespective of its source. Specifically, the board of directors is charged with the fiduciary obligations of care and loyalty to the corporation and its shareholders. *Air Line Pilots Association, International v. UAL Corp., 717 F. Supp. 575 (N.D.Ill. 1989).*

A board of directors is ultimately responsible for managing the affairs of a corporation, and in so doing the directors owe fiduciary duties of care and loyalty to the corporation and its shareholders. These responsibilities require directors to take an active role in responding to a pending takeover bid. *Desert Partners, L.P. v. USG Corp., 686 F. Supp. 1289 (N.D.Ill. 1988).*

Directors and officers of a Delaware corporation are fiduciaries to the corporation and its stockholders. *Dasho v. Susquehanna Corp., 1970 U.S. Dist. LEXIS 12923 (N.D. Ill. 1970).*

Directors stand in a fiduciary relation to the corporation and its shareholders, and that their primary duty is to deal fairly and justly. It is a breach of this duty for directors to make use of the issuance of shares to accomplish an improper purpose, such as to enable a particular person or group to maintain or obtain voting control, against the objection of shareholders from whom control is thereby wrested. *Calumet Industries, Inc. v. MacClure, 464 F. Supp. 19 (N.D. Ill. 1978).*

Under Delaware law, directors owe a fiduciary duty of fairness to a class of minority shareholders. Fairness requires fair dealing and fair price. Fair dealing involves the duty of candor and the duty to conduct the merger in a way that protects the interests of minority shareholders. The state of incorporation determines the fiduciary obligations owed by directors to their shareholders. The duty of candor or disclosure is defined in terms almost identical to those used under federal securities laws: the limited function of a court is to determine whether defendants disclosed all information in their "possession" germane to the transaction in issue. Germane means information such as a reasonable shareholder would consider important in deciding whether to sell or retain stock. *Eliasen v. Hamilton, 1987 U.S. Dist. LEXIS 1826 (N.D.Ill. 1987).*

Under Delaware law, key managerial personnel owe their employer duties of loyalty and due care. *Anic v. DVI, Inc., 2002 U.S. Dist. LEXIS 23943 (N.D.Ill. 2002).*

Directors and officers of a Delaware corporation are fiduciaries to the corporation and its stockholders. *Dasho v. Susquehanna Corp., 1970 U.S. Dist. LEXIS 12923 (N.D. Ill. 1970).*

Directors do not breach their fiduciary duty to their stockholders or the common law, where, as the result of the exercise of an informed business judgment, and in the absence of bad faith, a corporate asset was exchanged on a market-to-market basis for shares of their corporation held by dissident stockholders. *Dasho v. Susquehanna Corp., 1970 U.S. Dist. LEXIS 12923 (N.D. Ill. 1970).*

Directors do not owe duties to creditors beyond the relevant contractual terms absent special circumstances. Special circumstances may arise in the case of fraud, insolvency, or a violation of a statute. When the insolvency exception does arise, it creates fiduciary duties for directors for the benefit of creditors. *Jackson Nat'l Life Ins. Co. v. Kendig, 1999 U.S. Dist. LEXIS 16645 (N.D.Ill. 1999).*

Generally, directors do not owe duties to creditors beyond the relevant contractual terms absent special circumstances, which may arise in the case of fraud, insolvency, or a violation of a statute. *Steinberg v. Kendig, 2000 U.S. Dist. LEXIS 276 (N.D.Ill. 2000).*

Under Delaware law, officers and directors of a corporation owe a fiduciary duty to the shareholders of that corporation. However, that duty does not emerge until there is an actual director-shareholder relationship. *Premier Capital Management., L.L.C. v. Cohen, 2004 U.S. Dist. LEXIS 24981 (N.D.Ill. 2004).*

The most that Delaware law requires of corporate directors, though they are fiduciaries, is that the not be grossly negligent. *Niki Development Corp. v. HOB Hotel Chicago Partners, L.P., 2003 U.S. Dist. LEXIS 4949 (N.D.Ill. 2003).*

Individual versus derivative claims. — Under Delaware law, the issue of whether claims are individual or derivative is determined by viewing the complaint taken as a whole. Characterizations made in the pleadings are not controlling. A single complaint may contain both derivative and individual claims if there are sufficient allegations to support both claims. Generally, claims are considered to be derivative where all stockholders are affected equally. There are two exceptions which give rise to individual claims. A stockholder may have an individual claim if he or she has suffered a special injury which is distinct from the harm to the corporation. A stockholder may also have an individual claim if he or she is deprived of a contractual right. Allegations of mismanagement which depress the value of stock, as those alleged here,

represent wrongs against the corporation, not an individual. As to right of alienability, plaintiff must allege a direct restriction of transferability in order to state an individual claim. *Seidel v. Allegis Corp., 702 F. Supp. 1409 (N.D.Ill. 1989).*

In a derivative suit, the recovery, if any, must go to the corporation. That is in contrast with a direct suit by a shareholder. Such a claim an individual suit is distinct from an injury caused to the corporation alone. In such individual suits, the recovery or other relief flows directly to the stockholders, not to the corporation. *Weinstein v. Schwartz, 2005 U.S. App. LEXIS 18976 (7th Cir. 2005).*

The analysis for determining whether an action should be classified as direct or derivative must be based solely on the following questions: Who suffered the alleged harm — the corporation or the suing stockholder individually — and who would receive the benefit of the recovery or other remedy? *Weinstein v. Schwartz, 2005 U.S. App. LEXIS 18976 (7th Cir. 2005).*

Derivative actions. — Stockholder actions charging mismanagement which depresses the value of stock allege a wrong to the corporation, i.e., the stockholders collectively, to be enforced by a derivative action. *Lynch v. Marklin of America, Inc., 724 F. Supp. 595 (N.D.Ill. 1989).*

Under Delaware law, a shareholder's power to bring a derivative action on behalf of the corporation is terminated once a presuit demand has been made and rejected. Thus, just as a corporate board's decisions regarding the routine business transactions of the corporation are accorded great deference under the business judgment rule, its decision not to pursue legal recourse pursuant to a shareholder's complaint is given the same treatment. Following a refused demand, a shareholder can only maintain a derivative action if he or she can demonstrate that the board's decision not to sue was improperly motivated or tainted with self-interest such that the directors were not acting in the best interests of the corporation. *Lewis v. Hilton, 648 F. Supp. 725 (N.D.Ill. 1986).*

Investigation of derivative claims. — Under Delaware law, a corporation itself has the initial, preemptive opportunity to investigate derivative claims, and to determine whether the corporation should pursue them. The directors of a Delaware corporation may make this determination by appointing a committee. The directors may delegate to this committee the power both to investigate and to terminate derivative litigation. A dissatisfied shareholder may attack the committee's conclusion only after the corporation adopts it. *Grafman v. Century Broadcasting Corp., 743 F. Supp. 544 (N.D.Ill. 1990).*

Demand requirements. — The animating principle of the demand futility doctrine is that the directors can not faithfully decide whether proceeding with the corporation's litigation is in the corporation's best interest when the complaint seeks redress for the conduct that gives rise to the personal financial benefit for which the directors alone have received. The case law makes it clear that the personal benefit must arise from the challenged transaction. *In re General Instrument Corp., 23 F. Supp. 2d 867 (N.D.Ill. 1998).*

According to Delaware law, the demand requirements are predicated upon and inextricably bound to issues of business judgment. *Miller v. Loucks, 1992 U.S. Dist. LEXIS 16966 (N.D.Ill. 1992).*

To excuse demand, plaintiffs must offer a particularized, legally recognized reason for the board of directors' inability to consider objectively a demand to pursue the derivative claims directly. *Miller v. Loucks, 1992 U.S. Dist. LEXIS 16966 (N.D.Ill. 1992).*

Under Delaware law, the sufficiency of a complaint pleading demand futility is tested by making two determinations: (1) whether the well-pleaded facts rebut the threshold presumptions of director disinterest or independence; and, if not, (2) whether the well-pleaded facts create a reasonable doubt that the challenged transaction was the product of a valid exercise of business judgment. *Miller v. Loucks, 1992 U.S. Dist. LEXIS 16966 (N.D.Ill. 1992).*

Under Delaware law, the rule that a shareholder must make a demand upon a corporation's directors before initiating a derivative suit, unless such demand would be futile, is more than a mere pleading requirement; it is a substantive right. The standard for determining whether a complaint adequately alleges demand futility is: whether taking the well-pleaded facts as true, the allegations raise a reasonable doubt as to (i) director disinterest or independence or (ii) whether the directors exercised proper business judgment in approving the challenged transaction. Moreover, conclusory allegations of fact or law contained in the complaint need not be considered true in determining demand futility unless they are supported by specific facts. *Shields v. Erikson, 1989 U.S. Dist. LEXIS 10079 (N.D.Ill. 1989).*

Delaware law, like federal law, recognizes the demand requirement in Fed. R. Civ. P. 23.1 as based on the fundamental precept that directors manage the corporation, not shareholders. Demand is excused if the complaint demonstrates that the directors are not disinterested. However, the mere fact that the lawsuit will subject the directors to liability is insufficient to show interest. Nor is there interest merely because the board receives payment for its services. Vague allegations of control or domination of the board of directors will not suffice to excuse demand. Allegations that the entire board participates in the wrongs or approves of them is also insufficient. *Shields on behalf of Sundstrand Corp. v. Erickson, 710 F. Supp. 68 (N.D.Ill. 1989).*

The Delaware Supreme Court establishes the standards for excusing the demand requirement in derivative suits against Delaware corporations. The court notes that the derivative nature of shareholder suits extends from the primary right of a corporation to pursue its own legal interests. Hence, under ordinary circumstances, a corporation through its board of directors, should be able to make the decision whether to pursue legal remedies for injuries to the corporate entity. As with other corporate decisionmaking processes, the decision of whether to sue is accorded great deference by the courts under the business

judgment rule. *Cottle v. Hilton Hotels Corp., 635 F. Supp. 1094 (N.D.Ill. 1986).*

In paring considerations down to a test for determining the futility of the shareholder demand requirement, the Delaware Supreme Court requires that a trial court must decide whether, under the particularized facts alleged, a reasonable doubt is created that: (1) the directors are disinterested and independent and (2) the challenged transaction was otherwise the product of a valid exercise of business judgment. Hence, the court must make two inquiries, one into the independence and disinterestedness of the directors and the other into the substantive nature of the challenged transaction and the board's approval thereof. If a reasonable doubt has been raised with respect to either the directors' disinterestedness and independence or whether the decision was otherwise a valid business judgment, the demand requirement will be excused and the shareholder permitted to pursue the derivative action. *Cottle v. Hilton Hotels Corp., 635 F. Supp. 1094 (N.D.Ill. 1986).*

The mere fact that directors participated in and authorized the disputed transactions underlying the derivative suit is not enough by itself to excuse demand. If this were the only prerequisite to excusing demand, the demand requirement would be effectively repealed since, by definition, the directors have a hand in all corporate transactions of any consequence. *Cottle v. Hilton Hotels Corp., 635 F. Supp. 1094 (N.D.Ill. 1986).*

As the first part of the *Aronson* test suggests, the allegations must create a reasonable doubt that the underlying corporate transactions were made by disinterested and independent directors. *Cottle v. Hilton Hotels Corp., 635 F. Supp. 1094 (N.D.Ill. 1986).*

A plaintiff-shareholder can also be excused from demand under *Aronson* if he or she can allege particularized facts which create a reasonable doubt that the challenged transaction was the product of a valid business judgment notwithstanding the directors' disinterestedness and independence. This aspect of the test has not been examined as thoroughly by the courts, though the *Aronson* court alluded to the narrowness of this exception when it noted that in rare cases a transaction may be so egregious on its face that board approval cannot meet the test of business judgment, and a substantial likelihood of director liability therefore exists. *Cottle v. Hilton Hotels Corp., 635 F. Supp. 1094 (N.D.Ill. 1986).*

The *Rales* court found that the "essential predicate" for applying the *Aronson* test was that a decision of the board of directors is being challenged in the derivative suit. The court in *Rales* stated that where the board that would be considering the demand did not make a business decision which is being challenged in the derivative suit, there are three scenarios in which the *Aronson* test would not apply: (1) where a business decision was made by the board of a company, but a majority of the directors making the decision have been replaced, (2) where the subject of the derivative suit is not a business decision of the board, and (3) where the decision being challenged was made by the board of a different corporation. *In re Abbott Labs.*

Derivative Shareholders Litigation, 325 F.3d 795 (7th Cir. 2003).

While a claim that directors have acted with the sole or primary motive of perpetuating themselves in office would be sufficient to excuse demand, the plaintiff must allege particularized facts to sustain such a claim. *Cottle v. Hilton Hotels Corp., 635 F. Supp. 1094 (N.D.Ill. 1986).*

In determining whether a demand would be futile, the court must consider whether the particularized factual allegations of a derivative stockholder complaint create a reasonable doubt that, as of the time the complaint is filed, the board of directors could have properly exercised its independent and disinterested business judgment in responding to a demand. If the derivative plaintiff satisfies this burden, then demand will be excused as futile. To establish a reasonable doubt, plaintiffs are not required to plead facts that would be sufficient to support a judicial finding of demand futility nor must plaintiffs demonstrate a reasonable probability of success on the merits. *Dollens v. Zionts, 2002 U.S. Dist. LEXIS 13511 (N.D.Ill. 2002).*

Challenging disinterestedness or independence of directors. — Under Delaware law, the mere threat of personal liability for approving a questioned transaction, standing alone, is insufficient to challenge either the independence or disinterestedness of directors, although in rare cases a transaction may be so egregious on its face that board approval cannot meet the test of business judgment, and a substantial likelihood of director liability therefore exists. *Miller v. Loucks, 1992 U.S. Dist. LEXIS 16966 (N.D.Ill. 1992).*

Whether the plaintiffs in a derivative stockholder complaint have alleged facts sufficient to create a reasonable doubt concerning the disinterestedness and independence of a majority of the board of directors must be determined from the accumulation of all the facts taken together. A director is interested when he or she will receive a personal financial benefit from a transaction that is not equally shared by the stockholders, or when a corporate decision will have a materially detrimental impact on a director but not the corporation or its stockholders. However, the mere threat of personal liability in the derivative action does not render a director interested. Rather, reasonable doubt as to the disinterestedness of a director is created when the particularized allegations in the complaint present a substantial likelihood of liability on the part of a director. Moreover, even if a director has no personal interest in a decision, his or her discretion must also be free from the influence of other interested persons. A director is independent if he or she can make a decision based on the corporate merits of the subject before the board rather than extraneous considerations or influences. *Dollens v. Zionts, 2002 U.S. Dist. LEXIS 13511 (N.D.Ill. 2002).*

A director is independent when he or she is able to reach his or her decision solely on the merits without being governed by outside influences or considerations. To show a lack of independence, the plaintiff must demonstrate that outside considerations influenced the decisions of the committee. *Grafman v. Century Broadcasting Corp., 762 F. Supp. 215 (N.D.Ill. 1991).*

The business judgment rule is a presumption that in making a business decision, the directors of a corporation acted on an informed basis, in good faith, and in the honest belief that the action taken was in the best interests of the company. To determine whether a complaint raises a reasonable doubt that the directors exercised proper business judgment, the second prong of the *Aronson* test requires a court to look at both the substantive due care (substance of the transaction) as well as the procedural due care (an informed decision) used by the directors. The mere threat of personal liability for approving a questioned transaction, standing alone, is insufficient to challenge either the independence or disinterestedness of directors. However, demand may be excused if in rare cases a transaction may be so egregious on its face that board approval cannot meet the test of business judgment, resulting in a substantial likelihood of director liability, or if the directors exhibited gross negligence in breaching their duty of care. *In re Abbott Labs. Derivative Shareholders Litigation, 325 F.3d 795 (7th Cir. 2003).*

Independence exists when a director's decision is based on the corporate merits of the subject before the board rather than extraneous considerations or influences. *In re Abbott Labs. Derivative Shareholders Litigation, 325 F.3d 795 (7th Cir. 2003).*

Share issuance for improper purpose. — Directors stand in a fiduciary relation to the corporation and its shareholders, and that their primary duty is to deal fairly and justly. It is a breach of this duty for directors to make use of the issuance of shares to accomplish an improper purpose, such as to enable a particular person or group to maintain or obtain voting control, against the objection of shareholders from whom control is thereby wrested. *Calumet Industries, Inc. v. MacClure, 464 F. Supp. 19 (N.D. Ill. 1978).*

Non-interference with business judgment. — In the absence of a showing of bad faith on the part of the directors or of a gross abuse of discretion, the business judgment of the directors will not be interfered with by the courts. *Dasho v. Susquehanna Corp., 1970 U.S. Dist. LEXIS 12923 (N.D. Ill. 1970).*

Exchange of corporate asset. — Directors do not breach their fiduciary duty to their stockholders or the common law, where, as the result of the exercise of an informed business judgment, and in the absence of bad faith, a corporate asset was exchanged on a market-to-market basis for shares of their corporation held by dissident stockholders. *Dasho v. Susquehanna Corp., 1970 U.S. Dist. LEXIS 12923 (N.D. Ill. 1970).*

Good faith reliance protections. — Delaware General Corporation Law § 141(e) states that a member of the board of directors, or a member of any committee designated by the board of directors, shall, in the performance of his or her duties, be fully protected in relying in good faith upon the records of the corporation and upon such information, opinions, reports or statements presented to the corporation by any of the corpora-

Corporations

tion's officers or employees, or committees of the board of directors, or by any other person as to matters that member reasonably believes are within such other person's professional or expert competence and who has been selected with reasonable care by or on behalf of the corporation. *Holland v. Stenhouse, 1991 U.S. Dist. LEXIS 2518 (N.D.Ill. 1991).*

Under Delaware General Corporation Law § 141(e), reliance must be reasonable, and blind reliance is not protected. Under the business judgment rule there is no protection for unadvised or unintelligent judgment. In addition, a director's reliance may not be unfounded and must end when a director is put on notice that something is wrong. *Holland v. Stenhouse, 1991 U.S. Dist. LEXIS 2518 (N.D.Ill. 1991).*

The standard of judicial review applied to a board of directors' business decisions may depend on the context of the transaction and the potential for directorial misconduct. A reviewing court will ordinarily apply the business judgment rule to a disinterested board's corporate decision, if their business decision can be attributed to any rational business purpose. *Air Line Pilots Association, International v. UAL Corp., 717 F. Supp. 575 (N.D.Ill. 1989).*

To overcome directors' protection under the business judgment rule, a plaintiff must show that the directors acted solely or primarily to perpetuate themselves in office. *Desert Partners, L.P. v. USG Corp., 686 F. Supp. 1289 (N.D.Ill. 1988).*

The business judgment rule posits a powerful presumption in favor of actions taken by the directors. In the absence of any evidence of fraud, bad faith, or self-dealing in the usual sense of personal profit or betterment, a decision made by a loyal and informed board will not be overturned by the courts unless the decision cannot be attributed to any rational business purpose. *Gunter v. Novopharm USA, Inc., 2001 U.S. Dist. LEXIS 2117 (N.D.Ill. 2001).*

A litigant challenging a decision by a corporate officer has the burden at the outset to rebut the rule's presumption by providing evidence that the officer, in reaching their challenged decision, breached any one of the triads of their fiduciary duty — good faith, loyalty, or due care. If a litigant fails to meet this evidentiary burden, the business judgment rule attaches to protect corporate officers and directors and the decisions that they make. The courts will not second-guess these business judgments. If the presumption of the rule is rebutted, however, the burden shifts to the corporate officer, the proponent of the challenged transaction, to prove to the trier of fact the "entire fairness" of the transaction. Under the "entire fairness" standard of judicial review, the corporate officers must establish to the court's satisfaction that the transaction was the product of both fair dealing and fair price. *Gunter v. Novopharm USA, Inc., 2001 U.S. Dist. LEXIS 2117 (N.D.Ill. 2001).*

The business judgment rule requires courts to defer to the decisions of corporate directors made in the good-faith exercise of business judgment so long as the directors act for what is arguably a rational business purpose. The business judgment rule also creates a presumption that in making a business decision the directors of a corporation acted on an informed basis, in good faith, and in the honest belief that the action taken was in the best interests of the company. This presumption is particularly strong where the decision is made by outside directors. A court applying the business judgment rule will not substitute its own business judgment for that of a board of directors, nor will a court act as a super-board of directors. *Rosenfield v. Becor Western, Inc., 1987 U.S. Dist. LEXIS 14276 (E.D.Wis. 1987).*

Inapplicability of presumptions of good faith. — Notwithstanding the benefits of the business judgment rule, there are some circumstances where the presumption of the board's good faith cannot be applied as readily. The strictest standard of scrutiny is applied if the conduct at issue arises in a context where the corporate fiduciaries may have stood on both sides of the transaction when the terms were agreed upon. Thus, fiduciaries are required to demonstrate to the court the intrinsic fairness of the transaction vis-a-vis the shareholders before the protections of the business judgment rule are applied to the directors' conduct. *Air Line Pilots Association, International v. UAL Corp., 717 F. Supp. 575 (N.D.Ill. 1989).*

The plaintiff shareholder must plead particular facts suggesting that the corporate directors are not entitled to hide within the impenetrable fortress of the business judgment rule with respect to their participation in the transactions for which legal remedies are sought by the shareholder. The same circumstances which remove the business judgment rule's protections in other contexts will negate its applicability to the shareholder demand requirement. Thus, directors cannot raise the business judgment rule where they are personally interested in the questioned transactions such as where they sit on both sides of a corporate transaction or engage in self-dealing. Furthermore, their judgment must follow the consideration of all material information reasonably available of which they have a duty to inform themselves. *Cottle v. Hilton Hotels Corp., 635 F. Supp. 1094 (N.D.Ill. 1986).*

The business judgment rule is a presumption that in making a business decisions the directors of a corporation acted on an informed basis, in good faith, and in the honest belief that the action taken was in the best interests of the company. The presumption, however, attaches only to the decisions of directors who are fully independent and wholly disinterested. When the business judgment rule applies, it insulates directors from liability, and imposes upon the party challenging the decision the burden of rebutting the presumption. A hallmark of the business judgment, rule is that a court will not substitute its judgment for that of a board if the latter's decision can be attributed to any rational business purpose. *Niki Development Corp. v. HOB Hotel Chicago Partners, L.P., 2003 U.S. Dist. LEXIS 4949 (N.D.Ill. 2003).*

A board of directors has a legal right, and at times a duty, to defend the corporation from real threats. *Newell Co. v. Vermont American Corp., 725 F. Supp. 351 (N.D.Ill. 1989).*

Review of defensive actions. — The standard by which a court will review a board of directors' business decisions may depend on the context of the transaction and the potential for directorial misconduct. Ordinarily the court will apply the business judgment rule to a business decision and refrain from any substantive review of the board action. But when actions are taken by the board because of a threat to the control of the corporation and the board's actions are defensive in character, because of the omnipresent specter that a board may be acting primarily in its own interests, rather than those of the corporation and its shareholders, a heightened test must be applied to determine whether a board is entitled to the protection of the business judgment rule. *Newell Co. v. Vermont American Corp., 725 F. Supp. 351 (N.D.Ill. 1989).*

The *Unocal* analysis requires a two-tier proportionality test, which shifts the burden to the directors. The directors must first show that they had reasonable grounds for supposing that there was a danger to corporate policy or effectiveness. Second, the board must demonstrate that the measures they adopted in response to threat were reasonable in relation to the threat posed. These burdens can be satisfied by showing good faith and reasonable investigation. This requires an analysis by the directors of the nature of the takeover bid and its effect on the corporate enterprise. If the board can satisfy these prerequisites the business judgment rule will apply to the board's action and the burden will shift back to plaintiff to overcome the business judgment rule's presumption of directorial propriety. *Newell Co. v. Vermont American Corp., 725 F. Supp. 351 (N.D.Ill. 1989).*

A board of directors may be equally justified in defending against a non-coercive offer as it would a perceived coercive offer. *Newell Co. v. Vermont American Corp., 725 F. Supp. 351 (N.D.Ill. 1989).*

Where the directors take appropriate steps to inform themselves and in good faith, on the basis of information they obtain, determine that there exists a threat to the corporation and the shareholders, the directors may respond to the threat in a reasonable manner. *Newell Co. v. Vermont American Corp., 725 F. Supp. 351 (N.D.Ill. 1989).*

The directors may in good faith and on an informed basis pursue long-term interests at the expense of immediate value maximization when responding to a take-over bid. *Newell Co. v. Vermont American Corp., 725 F. Supp. 351 (N.D.Ill. 1989).*

The role of the reviewing court is not to determine, in hindsight, if a company was actually a threat, but whether the target board after proper investigation was reasonable in its inclination to protect the company. This review must be done in the context of the particular circumstances of the target board. *Newell Co. v. Vermont American Corp., 725 F. Supp. 351 (N.D.Ill. 1989).*

When a board addresses a takeover situation its obligation to determine if the offer is in the best interest of the shareholders is no different from the board's responsibility in other contexts, and its business decisions should be no less entitled to deference than in other realms of business

judgment. *Air Line Pilots Association, International v. UAL Corp., 717 F. Supp. 575 (N.D.Ill. 1989).*

When directors face threat to their control of the corporation, the *Unocal* court introduced a two-tier proportionality test which shifts the burden to the directors. The directors must first show that they had reasonable grounds for supposing that there was a danger to corporate policy or effectiveness. This burden will be satisfied by a showing of good faith and reasonable investigation. Second, the board must establish that the measures they adopted in response to the threat were reasonable in relation to the threat posed. *Air Line Pilots Association, International v. UAL Corp., 717 F. Supp. 575 (N.D.Ill. 1989).*

The business judgment rule applies when a board of directors adopts defensive mechanisms to thwart potential takeovers. Under Delaware's business judgment rule, courts presume that directors have made their business decisions on an informed basis, in good faith, and with the honest belief that they acted in the best interests of the company. A court should not substitute its judgment for that of the board if the latter's decision can be attributed to any rational business purpose. *Desert Partners, L.P. v. USG Corp., 686 F. Supp. 1289 (N.D.Ill. 1988).*

A conflict of interest confronts directors who are faced with a threat to their control of a corporation. Because of the threat that the directors may be more concerned about their own interests than the interests of the corporation and its shareholders, there is an enhanced duty which calls for judicial examination at the threshold before the protections of the business judgment rule may be conferred. *Desert Partners, L.P. v. USG Corp., 686 F. Supp. 1289 (N.D.Ill. 1988).*

In evaluating the directors' actions in defending against the threat of a takeover, the courts place upon the directors the burden of proving (1) that the threatened takeover posed a danger to corporate policy and effectiveness, and (2) that they adopted defensive measures which were reasonable in relation to the threat posed. The directors satisfy this burden by showing that they acted in good faith and after reasonable investigation. To overcome the presumption enjoyed by the directors by virtue of the business judgment rule, the plaintiff has the burden of persuasion to show a breach of the directors' fiduciary duties. The plaintiff may show this by demonstrating that the directors acted solely or primarily out of a desire to perpetuate themselves in office. *Desert Partners, L.P. v. USG Corp., 686 F. Supp. 1289 (N.D.Ill. 1988).*

Stock repurchase programs as alternative to hostile offer. — Stock repurchase programs funded by corporate monies, which give stockholders an alternative to a hostile offer, have been expressly endorsed by Delaware courts as an appropriate response to an unsolicited tender offer found to be inadequate. *Newell Co. v. Vermont American Corp., 725 F. Supp. 351 (N.D.Ill. 1989).*

Delaware law does not prohibit a board from issuing voting stock to friendly third parties, so long as the placement can be justified by a valid corporate purpose, such as deterring an inadequate or coercive bid,

Corporations

which the board finds, is not in the corporation's best interest. *Newell Co. v. Vermont American Corp., 725 F. Supp. 351 (N.D.Ill. 1989).*

Revising corporate transaction. — A board of director's decision to revise a corporate transaction in reaction to a hostile acquisition has been upheld in Delaware courts, where (1) the corporate transaction originated for bona fide business purposes and (2) the structure of the transaction was not primarily motivated by the desire to entrench. *Newell Co. v. Vermont American Corp., 725 F. Supp. 351 (N.D.Ill. 1989).*

In reviewing a report by an independent committee, the court should first look at the independence of the committee, whether its recommendations were made in good faith, and whether the committee made a reasonable investigation. The court can then, in its own discretion, move to a second step and apply its own business judgment to determine whether the suit should be pursued. *Grafman v. Century Broadcasting Corp., 762 F. Supp. 215 (N.D.Ill. 1991).*

Poison-pill plans. — Delaware law clearly authorizes corporate directors to adopt poison-pill plans to protect their corporation against unfair and hostile takeovers. However, poison-pill plans are neither per se valid nor per se invalid; each must be evaluated individually in light of the circumstances surrounding its implementation. *Desert Partners, L.P. v. USG Corp., 686 F. Supp. 1289 (N.D.Ill. 1988).*

In concluding whether the directors of a corporation acted reasonably in adopting a poison plan, the court may consider three factors: (1) whether the poison pill plan precludes or otherwise affects a proxy contest for control of the corporation; (2) whether the plan is adopted pursuant to the directors' informed business judgment; (3) whether the plan precludes all hostile takeovers, or only those which are inadequate or unfair to shareholders. *Desert Partners, L.P. v. USG Corp., 686 F. Supp. 1289 (N.D.Ill. 1988).*

Two-tiered tender offers tend to coerce shareholders into tendering their shares in order to avoid a disadvantageous second-tier transaction. It is now well recognized that two-tiered offers are a classic coercive measure designed to stampede shareholders into tendering at the first tier, even if the price is inadequate, out of fear of what they will receive at the back end of the transaction. *Desert Partners, L.P. v. USG Corp., 686 F. Supp. 1289 (N.D.Ill. 1988).*

Insider trading. — Delaware law provides a claim of breach of fiduciary duty based on insider trading. It is an act of disloyalty for a fiduciary to profit personally from the use of information secured in a confidential relationship, even if such a profit or advantage is not gained at the expense of the fiduciary. *Dollens v. Zionts, 2002 U.S. Dist. LEXIS 13511 (N.D.Ill. 2002).*

Delaware law has long recognized the availability of a stockholder derivative action to recover profits obtained by corporate insiders through breach of their fiduciary duties. *Dollens v. Zionts, 2002 U.S. Dist. LEXIS 13511 (N.D.Ill. 2002).*

Self-dealing in a corporate context occurs when a corporate director or officer appears on both sides of a transaction. *Howington v. Ghourdjian, 2002 U.S. Dist. LEXIS 400 (N.D.Ill. 2002).*

Under Del. Code Ann. tit. 8, § 144(a)(2), a self-dealing transaction is not void or voidable solely because of the interest of a director, if the material facts as to the director's or officer's relationship or interest and as to the contract or transaction are disclosed or are known to the shareholders entitled to vote thereon, and the contract or transaction is specifically approved in good faith by vote of the shareholders. *Howington v. Ghourdjian, 2002 U.S. Dist. LEXIS 400 (N.D.Ill. 2002).*

Under Delaware law, a self-dealing transaction by corporate officer or director is not strictly prohibited. Instead, Delaware law provides specific procedures that may be employed by a corporate officer or director to remove the taint that any such transaction may possess. To remove the taint of a self-dealing transaction, a corporate officer or director must establish to an independent body, whether it be a court in litigation, an independent committee of the board of directors, or a group of disinterested ratifying shareholders on full and complete information, that the transaction in question was fully fair and in the best interests of the corporation as a whole. *Gunter v. Novopharm USA, Inc., 2001 U.S. Dist. LEXIS 2117 (N.D.Ill. 2001).*

In a self-dealing transaction, Delaware corporate and fiduciary law gives no deference to "business judgment" and judicial scrutiny is applied regarding both "fair dealing" and "fair price." Fair dealing focuses on the procedures used in seeking a buyer and fair price on whether the directors obtained the highest value reasonably available. *Montgomery v. Aetna Plywood, Inc., 39 F. Supp. 2d 915 (N.D.Ill. 1998).*

A disinterested director can neither appear on both sides of a transaction nor expect to derive any personal financial benefit from the challenged transaction in the sense of self-dealing, as opposed to a benefit which devolves upon the corporation or all stockholders generally. *In re Abbott Labs. Derivative Shareholders Litigation, 325 F.3d 795 (7th Cir. 2003).*

Fairness of the bargain. — When directors of a Delaware corporation are on both sides of a transaction, they are required to demonstrate their utmost good faith and the most scrupulous fairness of the bargain. The requirement of fairness is unflinching in its demand that were one stands on both sides of a transaction, he or she has the burden of establishing its entire fairness. *Howington v. Ghourdjian, 2002 U.S. Dist. LEXIS 400 (N.D.Ill. 2002).*

Delaware law requires that the conduct of majority shareholders of a corporation toward minority shareholders be tested by the same standards of fiduciary duty which directors observe toward all their shareholders. *In re Transocean Tender Offer Securities Litigation, 427 F. Supp. 1211 (N.D. Ill. 1997).*

Oppressive conduct by majority stockholder. — Delaware recognizes two alternate definitions of oppressive conduct by a majority stockholder: (1) a reasonable expectations standard, i.e., the spoken or unspoken understandings on which the founders of a venture rely when commencing a venture; and (2) burdensome, harsh, and wrongful conduct; a lack of probity and fair dealing in the affairs of a company to the prejudice to some of its members; or visible departure from the standards of fair dealing, and a violation of fair play on which every shareholder who entrusts his money to a company is entitled to rely. *Minor v. Albright, 2001 U.S. Dist. LEXIS 19436 (N.D.Ill. 2001).*

Individual standing. — Under Delaware law, an individual has standing to challenge corporate mismanagement only if he or she can allege some "special injury" distinct from that suffered by the corporation and other shareholders. *Miller v. Loucks, 1992 U.S. Dist. LEXIS 16966 (N.D.Ill. 1992).*

Waste and misappropriation of corporate assets are harms against the corporation and must be brought derivatively. Delaware law, however, also recognizes the special injury exception to this rule, permitting a shareholder to litigate individually if the wrong to the corporation inflicts a distinct and disproportionate injury on the investor. *Minor v. Albright, 2001 U.S. Dist. LEXIS 19436 (N.D.Ill. 2001).*

Delaware's safe harbor provision protects contracts between directors and corporations where full disclosure is made to the board of directors and a majority of the disinterested directors in good faith approve the contract, Del. Code Ann. tit. 8, § 144(1), or where the contract or transaction is fair as to the corporation as of the time it is authorized, approved or ratified by the board, Del. Code Ann. tit. 8, § 144(3). The fairness referred to in subsection (3) is a question of fact. *Pentz v. Truserv Corp., 2001 U.S. Dist. LEXIS 11094 (N.D.Ill. 2001).*

Vicinity of insolvency. — Where a corporation is operating in the vicinity of insolvency, a board of directors is not merely the agent of the residue risk bearers but owes its duty to the corporate enterprise. *Steinberg v. Kendig, 2000 U.S. Dist. LEXIS 276 (N.D.Ill. 2000).*

When insolvency arises, it creates fiduciary duties for directors for the benefit of creditors. It is the fact of insolvency and not the institution of statutory proceeding which causes fiduciary duties to creditors to arise. *Steinberg v. Kendig, 2000 U.S. Dist. LEXIS 276 (N.D.Ill. 2000).*

It is the fact of insolvency and not the institution of statutory proceeding which causes a director's fiduciary duties to creditors to arise. *Jackson Nat'l Life Ins. Co. v. Kendig, 1999 U.S. Dist. LEXIS 16645 (N.D.Ill. 1999).*

Where a corporation is operating in the vicinity of insolvency, a board of directors is not merely the agent of the residue risk bearers, but owes its duty to the corporate enterprise. *Jackson Nat'l Life Ins. Co. v. Kendig, 1999 U.S. Dist. LEXIS 16645 (N.D.Ill. 1999).*

Directors who conceive of their corporations as legal and economic entities will recognize that in managing the business affairs of a solvent corporation in the vicinity of insolvency, circumstances may arise when the right, both the efficient and the fair, course to follow for the corporation may diverge from the choice that the stockholders, or the creditors, or the employees, or any single group interested in the corporation, would make if given the opportunity to act. *Jackson Nat'l Life Ins. Co. v. Kendig, 1999 U.S. Dist. LEXIS 16645 (N.D.Ill. 1999).*

The fiduciary duties at the moment of insolvency may cause directors to choose a course of action that best serves the entire corporate enterprise rather than any single group interested in the corporation at a point in time when shareholders' wishes should not be the directors only concern. *Jackson Nat'l Life Ins. Co. v. Kendig, 1999 U.S. Dist. LEXIS 16645 (N.D.Ill. 1999).*

Under Delaware law, in a "change of control" transaction, the directors have a heightened obligation to the shareholders to inform themselves fully of the value of a company's shares; maximize value recoverable for all shareholders; and obtain full fair market value on any sale of shares. Decisions under the Delaware *Revlon* doctrine hold that, once the directors have determined to enter the corporation into a "change of control" transaction, the directors owe a duty to obtain the maximum possible price for the selling shareholders. *Montgomery v. Aetna Plywood, Inc., 39 F. Supp. 2d 915 (N.D.Ill. 1998).*

Duty to exercise appropriate attention. — Where there is no conflict of interest or no facts suggesting suspect motivation, it is difficult to charge directors with responsibility for corporate losses for an alleged breach of care. In determining the directors' alleged breach of the duty of care, liability may arise from two possible situations — liability for decisions made by the directors or liability for the directors' failure to monitor the actions of the corporation. Director liability for a breach of the duty to exercise appropriate attention may, in theory, arise in two distinct contexts. First, such liability may be said to follow from a board decision that results in a loss because that decision was ill-advised or negligent. Second, liability to the corporation for a loss may be said to arise from an unconsidered failure of the board to act in circumstances in which due attention would, arguably, have prevented the loss. The first setting for liability is subject to review under the business judgment rule, assuming the decision was the product of a process that was either deliberately considered in good faith or was otherwise rational. The second approach has been labeled as "unconsidered" failure to act. *In re Abbott Labs. Derivative Shareholders Litigation, 325 F.3d 795 (7th Cir. 2003).*

Delaware law states that director liability may arise for the breach of the duty to exercise appropriate attention to potentially illegal corporate activities from an unconsidered failure of the board to act in circumstances in which due attention would, arguably, have prevented the loss. A sustained or systematic failure of the board to exercise oversight will establish the lack of good faith that is a necessary condition to director liability. *In re Abbott Labs. Derivative Shareholders Litigation, 325 F.3d 795 (7th Cir. 2003).*

The totality of the allegations in a complaint based on demand futility for directors' conscious inaction need only support a reasonable doubt of business judgment protection, not a judicial finding that the directors' actions are not protected by the business judgment rule. *In re Abbott Labs. Derivative Shareholders Litigation, 325 F.3d 795 (7th Cir. 2003).*

Eighth Circuit

Director liability. — For the purpose of removing temptation to profit from a breach of his or her confidential relationship, an officer or director of a corporation who, in violation of his or her duty as such, acquires gain or advantage for himself or herself, is liable to the corporation for the benefit or profit so acquired. *Polin v. Conductron Corp., 411 F. Supp. 698 (E.D. Mo. 1976).*

Implementation of voting trust. — The accomplishment of some definite plan or policy to benefit the company, to assure stability and continuity of management for this purpose and to prevent rival concerns or competitors from gaining control are legitimate bases for implementation of a voting trust. If, however, the only object or purpose of a voting trust is to corner the majority stockholders' right to vote in an arrangement from which they cannot escape and to secure permanency of management and office holding for a scheming group, this would seem clearly contrary to the policy of the law. *Watts v. Des Moines Register & Tribune, 525 F. Supp. 1311 (S.D. Iowa 1981).*

In exercising its own business judgment, the court should carefully consider and weigh the strength of the corporate interest in dismissal when faced with a nonfrivolous lawsuit and, when appropriate, give special consideration to matters of law and public policy in addition to the corporation's best interests. Ethical, commercial, promotional, public and employee relations, and fiscal, as well as legal factors should be considered in analyzing the committee's decision to terminate a particular lawsuit, and in exercising the court's own business judgment. *Watts v. Des Moines Register & Tribune, 525 F. Supp. 1311 (S.D. Iowa 1981).*

The four-pronged analysis to be applied in evaluating a dismissal motion premised upon an independent litigation committee's exercise of business judgment requires a judicial assessment of: (1) the procedural propriety of a complaining shareholder's initiation of suit; (2) whether the board committee is endowed with the requisite corporate power to seek dismissal of a derivative suit; (3) whether the movants have adequately demonstrated the disinterest, independence and good faith of committee members, the bases for the conclusions of such members and the appropriateness and sufficiency of their investigative techniques; and (4) whether, in the court's exercise of its own independent business judgment, dismissal of derivative counts is warranted. *Watts v. Des Moines Register & Tribune, 525 F. Supp. 1311 (S.D. Iowa 1981).*

Demand futility. — Under Delaware law, a shareholder must satisfy a stringent pleading standard and allege particularized facts justifying any failure to make a demand. In a derivative action brought by one or more shareholders the complaint shall also allege with particularity the efforts, if any, made by the plaintiff to obtain the action desired from the directors or the reasons for the plaintiff's failure to make such efforts. A demand is considered futile and may be excused only if the particularized facts alleged in the complaint create a reasonable doubt that: (1) the directors are disinterested and independent; or (2) the challenged transaction was otherwise the product of a valid exercise of business judgment. *Wesenberg v. Zimmerman, 2002 U.S. Dist. LEXIS 11868 (D.Minn. 2002).*

Under Delaware law, it is clear that a plaintiff may only establish futility and therefore excuse a demand by creating a reasonable doubt that either: (1) the directors are independent or disinterested for the purposes of responding to the demand; or (2) the underlying transaction is protected by the business judgment rule. These prongs are in the disjunctive. *Wesenberg v. Zimmerman, 2002 U.S. Dist. LEXIS 11868 (D.Minn. 2002).*

Allegations of directors' perpetuating themselves in office is sufficient to satisfy the *Aronson* test. *Reimel v. MacFarlane, 9 F. Supp. 2d 1062 (D.Minn. 1998).*

Ninth Circuit

Under this section, director and other board members are allowed to rely on corporate records in good faith. Unless he had reason to know that corporation's prior statements were false, he could rely on them. Plaintiffs have not pleaded facts that would indicate that such reliance was not in good faith. They only plead that backdating happened at some time, therefore, all of the directors at all times in a ten-year period must have known about it. This simply does not meet the standard for pleading facts with particularity that director knew or should have known of the alleged backdated options. *In re CNET Networks, Inc, 483 F. Supp. 2d 947; 2007 U.S. Dist. LEXIS 29780 (N.D. Cal. April 11, 2007).*

Fiduciary duties generally. — Under Delaware law, directors owe a company and its shareholders fiduciary duties of care, loyalty, and good faith, and may not waste the company's assets. The duty of care is one of procedural due care, not substantive due care, which, in the decisionmaking context, is foreign to the business judgment rule. The standard for finding a breach of procedural due care is gross negligence. A fiduciary's decision is considered wasteful only if it egregiously served no corporate purpose: if there is any substantial consideration received by the corporation, and if there is good-faith judgment that in the circumstances the transaction is worthwhile, there should be no finding of waste, even if the fact finder would conclude ex post that the transaction was unreasonably risky. A director breaches the duty of loyalty when the director uses a position of trust and confidence to further the director's own interests to the detriment of the company. *Official Committee of Bond Holders v. Official Committee of Trade Creditors, 2004 U.S. Dist. LEXIS 19497 (N.D.Cal. 2004).*

The directors and officers of a corporation have fiduciary duties of care to the corporation and its shareholders to (a) discharge their duties with the care an ordinary prudent person in a like position would exercise under similar circumstances; (b) discharge their duties with a critical eye to assessing information, performing actions carefully, thoroughly, thoughtfully, and in an informed manner; (c) seek all relevant material information before making decisions on behalf of the corporation; and (d) avoid and prevent corporate waste and unnecessary expense. They also have affirmative duties to protect the corporation and its shareholders' interests and to be aware of the corporation's affairs. In addition, they owe fiduciary duties of loyalty to the corporation and its shareholders, which require that each discharge his or her duties in good faith. Finally, they owe undivided loyalty to the corporation and its shareholders to ensure that neither they, nor any other officer or director, obtain any profit or advantage at the expense of the corporation. *Grassmueck v. Barnett, 281 F. Supp. 2d 1227 (W.D.Wash. 2003)*.

Officers and directors of a corporation owe a fiduciary duty to the corporation and its shareholders. However, directors and officers cannot be held liable for mere negligence in the conduct of their obligations. Under Delaware law, they are presumed to act in good faith and in the honest belief that their actions are in the best interests of the company. *In re Sagent Technology, Inc, 278 F. Supp. 2d 1079 (N.D.Cal 2003)*.

"Breach of fiduciary duty" is a state law claim. Corporations, in general, are governed by state corporations law. *Grassmueck v. Barnett, 281 F. Supp. 2d 1227 (W.D.Wash. 2003)*.

In general, fiduciary duty comprises three sub-duties: the duty of loyalty, the duty of care, and the duty to act in good faith. *Grassmueck v. Barnett, 281 F. Supp. 2d 1227 (W.D.Wash. 2003)*.

Directors are protected against general claims for breach of the duty of care when pursuant to state law a corporation adopts a director protection provision into its articles of incorporation. However, if directors breach the duty of care intentionally, knowingly, or in bad faith, the director protection statutes will not shield them from personal liability. Furthermore, when directors breach the duty of loyalty or act in bad faith they are not shielded by the director protection statutes. Therefore, to successfully plead breach of fiduciary duty against the directors of a corporation, a plaintiff must sufficiently plead breach of the duty of loyalty, bad-faith performance of duties, or intentional or knowing breach of the duty of care. *Grassmueck v. Barnett, 281 F. Supp. 2d 1227 (W.D.Wash. 2003)*.

In Delaware, a plaintiff may bring a general claim of breach of fiduciary duty against a director as long as he or she claims that the director's acts or omissions involved (i) a breach of the director's duty of loyalty to the corporation or its stockholders; (ii) acts or omissions not in good faith or which involve intentional misconduct or a knowing violation of law; (iii) under Del. Code Ann. tit. 8, § 174 (which includes willful or negligent violation of Del. Code Ann. tit. 8, §§ 160 or 173 regarding voting and trading); or (iv) any transaction from which the director derived an improper personal benefit. *Grassmueck v. Barnett, 281 F. Supp. 2d 1227 (W.D.Wash. 2003)*.

Under Delaware law, a director owes a fiduciary duty to the corporation and its shareholders, and can be held liable for the breach of such duty. *Frankston v. Aura Systems, 1998 U.S. App. LEXIS 20531 (9th Cir. 1998)*.

Typically, directors do not owe fiduciary duties to creditors because the relationship between debtor and creditor is contractual in nature. At the moment a corporation becomes insolvent, however, the insolvency triggers fiduciary duties for directors for the benefit of creditors. Such duties exist when a company becomes "insolvent in fact," that is, when it is within the "zone" or "vicinity" of insolvency, a poorly defined state that may exist when the corporation cannot generate and/or obtain enough cash to pay for its projected obligations and fund its business requirements for working capital and capital expenditures with a reasonable cushion to cover the variability of its business needs over time. Creditors have a right to expect that directors will not divert, dissipate, or unduly risk assets necessary to satisfy their claims. Notably, in insolvency the duty runs not directly to the creditors but to the "community of interest." Thus, while this duty does not necessarily place creditor interests ahead of the interests of stockholders, it requires the board to maximize the corporation's long-term wealth-creating capacity. *Official Committee of Bond Holders v. Official Committee of Trade Creditors, 2004 U.S. Dist. LEXIS 19497 (N.D.Cal. 2004)*.

The duty of loyalty mandates that the best interest of the corporation and its shareholders takes precedence over any interest possessed by a director. *McMichael v. United States Filter Corp., 2001 U.S. Dist. LEXIS 3918 (C.D.Cal. 2001)*.

A breach of loyalty claim is not dependent upon a showing of self-dealing or a showing that a fiduciary "received a personal benefit not shared by all shareholders. *Disney* leaves no room for doubt; it is possible under Delaware law to find a lack of good faith, and in turn a violation of the duty of loyalty, even outside the "classic" breach of loyalty situations just described. *Mann v. GTCR Golder Rauner, L.L.C., 483 F. Supp. 2d 884; 2007 U.S. Dist. LEXIS 54998 (D. Ariz. March 30, 2007)*.

Exculpatory clauses authorized. — Under Delaware law, corporations are authorized to adopt exculpatory clauses regarding directors' duty of care. *In re McKesson HBOC, Inc. Securities Litigation, 126 F. Supp. 2d 1248 (N.D.Cal. 2000)*.

Classification of action. — Absent a "special injury" affecting only certain shareholders, a claim for breach of the fiduciary duty of care must be brought derivatively on behalf of the corporation. *In re McKesson HBOC, Inc. Securities Litigation, 126 F. Supp. 2d 1248 (N.D.Cal. 2000)*.

Business judgment rule generally. — When assessing whether fiduciary duties have been breached, a court applies the business judgment rule, which is a presumption that in making a business decision the directors of a corporation acted on an informed basis, in good faith, and in the honest belief that the action taken was in the best interests of the company. The burden is on the party challenging the decision to establish facts rebutting the presumption. Whether a judge or jury considering the matter after the fact, believes a decision substantively wrong, or degrees of wrong extending through "stupid" to "egregious" or "irrational," provides no ground for director liability, so long as the court determines that the process employed was either rational or employed in a good-faith effort to advance corporate interests. *Official Committee of Bond Holders v. Official Committee of Trade Creditors, 2004 U.S. Dist. LEXIS 19497 (N.D.Cal. 2004).*

The business judgment rule sets up a presumption that directors' decisions are made in good faith and are based upon sound and informed business judgment. *McMichael v. United States Filter Corp., 2001 U.S. Dist. LEXIS 3918 (C.D.Cal. 2001).*

The business judgment rule reflects the principle that the business and affairs of a corporation are managed by or under the corporation's board of directors. In exercising their managerial powers, directors are charged with an unyielding fiduciary duty to protect the interests of the corporation and to act in the best interests of its shareholders. *McMichael v. United States Filter Corp., 2001 U.S. Dist. LEXIS 3918 (C.D.Cal. 2001).*

The business judgment rule is a presumption that in making a business decision the directors of a corporation acted on an informed basis, in good faith, and in the honest belief that the action taken was in the best interests of the company. The presumption, however, attaches only to the decisions of directors who are fully independent and wholly disinterested. When the business judgment rule applies, it insulates directors from liability, and imposes upon the party challenging the decision the burden of rebutting the presumption. A hallmark of the business judgment rule is that a court will not substitute its judgment for that of the board if the latter's decision can be attributed to any rational business purpose. *Navellier v. Sletten, 262 F.3d 923 (9th Cir. 2001).*

The business judgment rule can only protect disinterested directors. A director involved in a proxy contest cannot claim the presumption of good faith afforded by the business judgment rule if he or she has a personal interest in the outcome of the election even if the interest is not financial and he or she seeks to serve from the best of motives. *NL Indusustries, Inc. v. Lockheed Corp., 1992 U.S. Dist. LEXIS 22652 (C.D.Cal. 1992).*

To rebut the presumption of the business judgment rule, a shareholder plaintiff assumes the burden of providing evidence that a board of directors, in reaching its challenged decision, breached any one of its triad of fiduciary duties: good faith, loyalty, or due care. Thus, the plaintiff must plead facts supporting the conclusion either that a majority of directors of the proposed transaction. *Official Committee of Bond Holders v. Official Committee of Trade Creditors, 2004 U.S. Dist. LEXIS 19497 (N.D.Cal. 2004).*

The business judgment rule posits a powerful presumption in favor of actions taken by the directors in that a decision made by a loyal and informed board will not be overturned by the courts unless it cannot be attributed to any rational business purpose. To rebut the rule, plaintiff must provide evidence that directors, in reaching their challenged decision, breached any one of the triads of their fiduciary duty — good faith, loyalty, or due care. If the

plaintiff cannot overcome the presumption, the business judgment rule attaches to protect corporate officers and directors and the decisions they make, and courts hesitate to second-guess such decisions. Should a plaintiff rebut the rule, the burden shifts to the defendant directors to prove the "entire fairness" of the transaction. *McMichael v. United States Filter Corp., 2001 U.S. Dist. LEXIS 3918 (C.D.Cal. 2001).*

Takeover threats. — The business judgment rule may protect directors of a corporation when they are responding to a takeover threat. However, in such circumstances there is an omnipresent specter that a board may be acting primarily in its own interests. Before the business judgment rule will be applied in such a context, it must be established that: (1) there were reasonable grounds for believing that corporate policy and effectiveness were endangered; after which, (2) the defensive measure chosen must be reasonable in relation to the threat posed. The directors may satisfy this burden by showing good faith and reasonable investigation. This is called the *Unocal* analysis. If a defensive mechanism is intended to act primarily as an anti-takeover device, the *Unocal* analysis will apply in determining the propriety of the mechanism. If it has some other purpose, and only incidentally acts as an anti-takeover device, then the business judgment rule applies. *NL Indusustries, Inc. v. Lockheed Corp., 1992 U.S. Dist. LEXIS 22652 (C.D.Cal. 1992).*

Management committees. — The General Corporation Law of Delaware § 9, Del. Rev. Code § 2041 (1935), permits the designation of committees to exercise the powers of the board of directors in the management of the business and affairs of the corporation. *Wingate v. Bercut, 146 F.2d 725 (9th Cir. 1945).*

Special litigation committees. — Delaware law endows a corporation in a derivative suit with the power to form a special litigation committee (SLC) of the board of directors, and to either terminate or assume prosecution of the suit based upon the SLC's review and recommendation. *Johnson v. Hui, 811 F. Supp. 479 (N.D.Cal. 1991).*

A special litigation committee has the power to terminate a derivative action to the extent allowed by the law of the state of incorporation. Under Delaware law, a special litigation committee has the power to terminate a derivative action under certain circumstances. *Johnson v. Hui, 811 F. Supp. 479 (N.D.Cal. 1991).*

A special litigation committee may terminate a derivative action with leave of the court following an appropriate motion to terminate by the affected corporation. *Johnson v. Hui, 811 F. Supp. 479 (N.D.Cal. 1991).*

Failure to exercise proper oversight. — As Delaware courts note, a claim for failure to exercise proper oversight is a very difficult theory upon which to prevail. In such a case, plaintiffs generally have to demonstrate that directors were grossly negligent in failing to supervise. *Mitzner v. Hastings, 2005 U.S. Dist. LEXIS 835 (N.D.Cal. 2005).*

Void meeting action. — Under Delaware law, when a special board meeting takes place where notice has not been given to a director, the action taken at that meeting is void. *In re Sagent Technology, Inc, 278 F. Supp. 2d 1079 (N.D.Cal 2003).*

The trading of stock by a corporate officer or director is not in itself improper under Delaware law. *In re Sagent Technology, Inc, 278 F. Supp. 2d 1079 (N.D.Cal 2003).*

Waste. — The essence of a claim of waste of corporate assets is the diversion of corporate assets for improper or unnecessary purposes. Corporate waste entails an exchange of corporate assets for consideration so disproportionately small as to lie beyond the range at which any reasonable person might be willing to trade. Most often the claim is based on a transfer of corporate assets that serves no purpose for the corporation or for which no consideration is received. A cause of action for corporate waste must be asserted in a derivative action, because a cause of action for impairment or destruction of the corporation's business vests in the corporation rather than in the individual shareholders. *In re Sagent Technology, Inc, 278 F. Supp. 2d 1079 (N.D.Cal 2003).*

Merger or sale. — In the context of a merger or a sale, directors are charged with the duty of informing themselves of all material information reasonably available to them before voting on a proposed plan. The duty of care, therefore, is a duty to act on an informed basis. Under the business judgment rule's presumption, a court will not find the directors to have breached their duty of care unless they individually and the board collectively have failed to inform themselves fully and in a deliberate manner before voting. *McMichael v. United States Filter Corp., 2001 U.S. Dist. LEXIS 3918 (C.D.Cal. 2001).*

Courts are hesitant to challenge a board's decision to recommend an offer where there is no evidence of a competing offer. *McMichael v. United States Filter Corp., 2001 U.S. Dist. LEXIS 3918 (C.D.Cal. 2001).*

Enhanced scrutiny. — When a transaction results in a change in control of the company, the transaction is subject to enhanced scrutiny and defendants have the burden to show they were informed adequately and acted reasonably. *McMichael v. United States Filter Corp., 2001 U.S. Dist. LEXIS 3918 (C.D.Cal. 2001).*

Interested directors. — Under Delaware law, directors are interested if they are on both sides of a transaction, or if they benefit financially from a transaction. One director's interest in a challenged transaction is insufficient, without more, to deprive the board of protection under the business judgment rule. *In re Silicon Graphics, Inc., 1996 U.S. Dist. LEXIS 16989 (N.D.Cal. 1996).*

Legally cognizable issues. — Inadequacy of an offer to purchase is a legally cognizable threat to the corporation. *Hilton Hotels Corp. v. ITT Corp., 978 F. Supp. 1342 (D.Nev. 1997).*

A bare claim that if demand were to be made the director defendants would be asked to bring an action against themselves raises no legally cognizable issue under Delaware corporate law. *In re Silicon Graphics, Inc., 1996 U.S. Dist. LEXIS 16989 (N.D.Cal. 1996).*

Board power not unbridled. — A board has power over the management and assets of a corporation, but that power is not unbridled. That power is limited by the right of shareholders to vote for the members of the board. This right underlies the concept of corporate democracy. *Hilton Hotels Corp. v. ITT Corp., 978 F. Supp. 1342 (D.Nev. 1997).*

Analysis of defensive measures. — The *Unocal* test requires the court to consider the following two questions: (1) Does the board have reasonable grounds for believing a danger to corporate policy and effectiveness exists? (2) Is the response reasonable in relation to the threat? If it is a defensive measure touching on issues of control, the court must examine whether the board purposefully disenfranchised its shareholders, an action that cannot be sustained without a compelling justification. *Hilton Hotels Corp. v. ITT Corp., 978 F. Supp. 1342 (D.Nev. 1997).*

A board cannot "cram down" on shareholders a management sponsored alternative to an offer to purchase the corporation. *Hilton Hotels Corp. v. ITT Corp., 978 F. Supp. 1342 (D.Nev. 1997).*

To show futility under Delaware law, a plaintiff must allege particularized facts creating a reasonable doubt that (1) the directors are disinterested and independent, or (2) the challenged transaction was otherwise the product of a valid exercise of business judgment. *Janas v. McCracken, 183 F.3d 970 (9th Cir. 1999).*

Tenth Circuit

Duty of loyalty. — Individuals who hold dual or multiple directorships, as in the parent-subsidiary context, owe each corporation and each set of shareholders an "uncompromising duty of loyalty." A director may breach his or her duty of loyalty by failing to disclose material information under circumstances in which full disclosure was obviously expected. A good-faith erroneous judgment as to the proper scope or content of the required disclosure, however, implicates only the duty of care and does not give rise to a separate claim for breach of the duty of loyalty. *Waddell & Reed Fin., Inc. v. Torchmark Corp., 337 F. Supp. 2d 1243 (D.Kan. 2004).*

Duty to disclose. — A director does not have a fiduciary duty to disclose information where the complaining party already knows such information. *Waddell & Reed Fin., Inc. v. Torchmark Corp., 337 F. Supp. 2d 1243 (D.Kan. 2004).*

Duty to shareholders. — Although directors generally do not occupy a fiduciary position with respect to stockholders in face-to-face dealings, Delaware law does create such a duty in special circumstances where advantage is taken of inside information by a corporate insider who deliberately misleads an ignorant stockholder. Therefore, under Delaware law, directors who possess inside information regarding the value of stock owe a fiduciary duty when reacquiring outstanding corporate stock not only to the corporation and to the shareholders collectively, but also to the minority shareholders from whom the stock is being reacquired. *Alta Health Strategies, Inc. v. Kennedy, 790 F. Supp. 1085 (D.Utah 1992).*

Delaware law makes it clear that the business judgment rules presupposes that the directors act on an informed basis and in the honest belief they acted in the best interest of the corporation. *Carson v. Lynch Multimedia Corp., 123 F. Supp. 2d 1254 (D.Kan. 2000)*.

Inapplicability of business judgment rule. — Even ostensibly independent directors cannot invoke the business judgment rule where they have either abdicated their functions, or absent a conscious decision, failed to act. *Geer v. Cox, 242 F. Supp. 2d 1009 (D.Kan 2003)*.

Demand futility. — Demand on the board of directors is excused as futile where, taking the well-pled facts as true, the allegations raise a reasonable doubt as to the directors' disinterest or whether the directors exercised proper business judgment in approving the challenged transaction. *In re Storage Technology Corp. Securities Litigation, 804 F. Supp. 1368 (D.Colo. 1992)*.

When a plaintiff advances numerous reasons supporting his or her claim that demand would be futile, none of which standing alone is sufficient to excuse demand, the court must consider whether the totality of these reasons raises a reasonable doubt as to the directors' disinterest or independence. *In re Storage Technology Corp. Securities Litigation, 804 F. Supp. 1368 (D.Colo. 1992)*.

To excuse demand on a corporation's board under Delaware law, plaintiff must allege facts which create a reasonable doubt that (1) the directors are disinterested and independent or (2) the challenged transaction was otherwise the product of a valid exercise of business judgment. To satisfy the first prong under the federal pleading standard, plaintiff must plead particularized facts demonstrating either a financial interest or entrenchment on the part of the directors. To satisfy the second prong, plaintiff must plead particularized facts which raise a reasonable doubt that the directors exercised proper business judgment in the transaction. *Grogan v. O'Neil, 307 F. Supp. 2d 1181 (D.Kan. 2004)*.

Under Delaware law, demand on a corporation's board of directors will be excused only if under the particularized facts alleged, a reasonable doubt is created that: (1) the directors are disinterested and independent or (2) the challenged transaction was otherwise the product of a valid exercise of business judgment. The test is disjunctive. In order to satisfy the first prong of the *Aronson* test, a plaintiff must plead particularized facts demonstrating either a financial interest or entrenchment on the part of the directors. In order to satisfy the second prong of the *Aronson* test, the plaintiff must plead particularized facts, which raise a reasonable doubt that the directors exercised proper business judgment in the transaction. Proper business judgment means both substantive due care (terms of the transaction) and procedural due care (an informed decision). *Geer v. Cox, 242 F. Supp. 2d 1009 (D.Kan 2003)*.

In a derivative action against a corporation, to satisfy the first prong of *Aronson* under the federal pleading standard, a plaintiff must plead particularized facts demonstrating either a financial interest or entrenchment on the part of the directors. To satisfy the second prong of *Aronson*, the plaintiff must plead particularized facts which raise a reasonable doubt that the directors exercised proper business judgment in the transaction. *Grogan v. O'Neil, 292 F. Supp. 2d 1282 (D.Kan. 2003)*.

Waste. — A corporate waste claim ordinarily involves board approval of an exchange of corporate assets for consideration so disproportionately small as to lie beyond the range at which any reasonable person might be willing to trade. *Grogan v. O'Neil, 292 F. Supp. 2d 1282 (D.Kan. 2003)*.

As a practical matter on a corporate waste claim, a stockholder plaintiff must generally show that the board irrationally squandered corporate assets, for example, where the challenged transaction served no corporate purpose or where the corporation received no consideration at all. *Grogan v. O'Neil, 292 F. Supp. 2d 1282 (D.Kan. 2003)*.

A corporate waste claim must fail if there is any substantial consideration received by the corporation, and there is a good-faith judgment that in the circumstances the transaction is worthwhile. Courts are ill-fitted to weigh the adequacy of consideration or after the fact, to judge appropriate degrees of business risk. Absent some reasonable doubt that the board proceeded based on a good-faith assessment of the corporation's best interests, the board's decisions are entitled to deference under the business judgment rule. *Grogan v. O'Neil, 292 F. Supp. 2d 1282 (D.Kan. 2003)*.

Delaware courts have taken judicial notice of a corporate exculpatory charter provision where the defendant has presented a certified copy of such a provision on file with the secretary of state. *Grogan v. O'Neil, 292 F. Supp. 2d 1282 (D.Kan. 2003)*.

Violation of Del. Code Ann. tit. 8, § 271 would be gross negligence if the board completely failed to even attempt to comply with its statutory obligation. *Geer v. Cox, 242 F. Supp. 2d 1009 (D.Kan 2003)*.

Eleventh Circuit

Business judgment presumption. — Where the directors neither act in their own self interest or otherwise breach their fiduciary duties, state law mandates the court defer to their judgment, and the presumption arises that the directors exercised their business judgment in good faith. Under the business judgment rule, directors will be held liable only if they are grossly negligent. *Hastings-Murtagh v. Texas Air Corp., 649 F. Supp. 479 (S.D.Fla. 1986)*.

Direct relief. — Delaware law allows an individual shareholder to prevail against officers or directors of a corporation only when alleging direct and not derivative injury. A shareholder seeking direct relief must allege "special injury." The Delaware courts have developed a two-prong test for distinguishing direct and derivative claims. A plaintiff seeking individual relief must allege either "an injury which is separate and distinct from that suffered by other shareholders" or a wrong involving a contractual right of a shareholder, such as the right to vote, or to assert majority control, which exists independently of any right of the corporation." *Chalk Line Mfg. v. Frontenac Venture V, Ltd., 1994 Bankr. LEXIS 1087 (Bankr N.D.Ala. 1994)*

Lock-up and no-shop provisions are not void per se. Rather, such provisions are impermissible only if they are adopted in a situation where there is a live auction with competing bidders. Where lock-up and no-shop provisions are used to encourage a bidder to submit an offer, as distinguished from precluding bidders in an active auction, they are upheld. *Hastings-Murtagh v. Texas Air Corp., 649 F. Supp. 479 (S.D.Fla. 1986).*

District of Columbia Circuit

When board not needed. — Section 141(a) explicitly recognizes two situations in which a board of directors is not needed: when "otherwise provided [i] in this Chapter or [ii] in its certificate of incorporation." *In re United Press International, Inc., 60 B.R. 265 (Bankr. D..C. 1986).*

Voidable versus void acts. — The law of Delaware distinguishes between those improper acts of a corporate board which are "void" and those which are merely "voidable." As the Delaware courts have explained, the essential distinction between voidable and void acts are that those acts which the corporation could accomplish lawfully but which it has undertaken to accomplish in an inappropriate manner are voidable. Acts which the corporation could not accomplish lawfully, no matter how undertaken, are void and cannot be cured. *CarrAmerica Realty Corp. v. Kaidanow, 321 F.3d 165 (D.C. Cir. 2003).*

Under Delaware corporation law, a void result occurs when a corporate board acts without authorization, while the result of an authorized act improperly accomplished may be merely voidable. *CarrAmerica Realty Corp. v. Kaidanow, 321 F.3d 165 (D.C. Cir. 2003).*

Derivative suits. — When the corporation is injured by a third party, the corporation's directors are left to exercise their business judgment in deciding whether bringing suit is in the best interests of the corporation, and that the individual stockholders must rely on their directors to manage the firm. Only in "exceptional situations," where a corporate concern may not be resolved through the processes of business judgment is a shareholder derivative suit on behalf of the corporation permitted. A derivative action is disfavored because it is an encroachment upon the prerogative of the board of directors to manage the corporation. *Labovitz v. Washington Times Corp., 900 F. Supp. 500 (D.D.C. 1995).*

Demand requirement. — Under Delaware law, a shareholder must first make a demand of the corporation's board of directors before bringing a derivative action on behalf of the corporation. The demand requirement is a recognition of the fundamental precept that directors manage the business and affairs of corporations and its principal goal is to give the board of directors an opportunity to address the grievance themselves, to alert it to problems of which it may be unaware, and to give it the opportunity to use the corporation's own resources in championing causes of action the board deems meritorious. *Washington Bancorporation v. Washington, 1989 U.S. Dist. LEXIS 11437 (D.D.C Cir. 1989).*

The requirement of a demand, however, may be excused as futile when the presumption that the directors would exercise good business judgment in evaluating the demand is overcome. Because it is presumed that in making a business decision the directors of a corporation act on an informed basis, in good faith, and in the honest belief that the action is in the best interests of the corporation, the party challenging the decision has the burden of rebutting that presumption. *Washington Bancorporation v. Washington, 1989 U.S. Dist. LEXIS 11437 (D.D.C. Cir. 1989).*

In determining whether failure to make a demand is excused in a particular case, the court in the proper exercise of its discretion, must decide whether, under the particularized facts alleged, a reasonable doubt is created that the directors are disinterested and independent and the challenged transaction was otherwise the product of a valid exercise of business judgment. If the court in the exercise of its sound discretion is satisfied that a plaintiff has alleged facts which support a reasonable doubt, the futility of demand is established and the court's inquiry ends. *Washington Bancorporation v. Washington, 1989 U.S. Dist. LEXIS 11437 (D.D.C. Cir. 1989).*

In order to show lack of independence, it is not sufficient to show that the director merely approved the challenged transaction. Instead, there must be coupled with the allegation of control such facts as would demonstrate that through personal or other relationships the directors are beholden to the controlling person. *Washington Bancorporation v. Washington, 1989 U.S. Dist. LEXIS 11437 (D.D.C. Cir. 1989).*

Effect of voting trust on shareholders rights. — Directors and officers of a corporation manage the company for the benefit of its shareholders and they owe those shareholders fiduciary duties to manage the company in an acceptable manner. A voting trust adds nothing to shareholders' rights in this regard, but rather takes away from them the right to vote their stock on certain issues. *Foltz v. U.S. News & World Report, Inc., 663 F. Supp. 1494 (D.D.C.. 1987).*

Duty to minority shareholders. — Under Delaware law, a majority shareholder, to the extent that it can make its power felt, is under a duty not to act to the detriment of minority shareholders. Similarly, under the Employee Retirement Income Security Act of 1974, 29 U.S.C.S. §§ 1001 et seq., a plan fiduciary who is also a director or majority stockholder owes fiduciary duties as well to non-plan shareholders. *Foltz v. U.S. News & World Report, Inc., 663 F. Supp. 1494 (D.D.C. 1987).*

Director stock purchases. — Under the laws of Delaware, the purchase of the shares of stock in a corporation by a director is entirely legal and proper. This is also the rule in practically all of the other states. The great weight of authority is that a director is not the trustee of stockholders in dealing with one of them for the purchase of his stock, as the term "trustee" is ordinarily used. At most, the relationship is a circumstance which may enter into the question of actionable fraud or deceit. *Chenery Corp. v. Securities & Exchange Commission, 128 F.2d 303 (U.S.App. D.C. 1942).*

Dividends. — The declaration and payment of a dividend rests in the discretion of a corporation's board of directors in the exercise of its business judgment. *Mann-Paller Foundation, Inc. v. Econometric Research, Inc., 644 F. Supp. 92 (D.D.C. 1986).*

Corporations

Under Delaware law, the alter ego theory of liability does not require any showing of fraud. *In re Vitamins Antitrust Litigation, 2002 U.S. Dist. LEXIS 25788 (D.D.C. 2002).*

Retroactive ratification. — Under Delaware corporation law, where board authorization of a corporate action that falls within the board's de jure authority is defective, the defect in authority can be cured retroactively by board ratification. Directors may ratify a corporate action either expressly or impliedly. Ratification may be implied if the corporation, represented by the board of directors, who have knowledge of the facts, accepts and retains the benefits of the contract or act, or recognizes it as binding, or acquiesces in it. *CarrAmerica Realty Corp. v. Kaidanow, 321 F.3d 165 (D.C. Cir. 2003).*

Federal Claims Court

Wind-up period. — The statute does not permit the three-year winding up period to be further extended by actions of either the corporation or by outside creditors after the period has expired. It provides a continuation of corporate existence until judgment only for actions, suits, and proceedings that were commenced prior to the expiration of the three-year period. It does not prolong the capacity of the corporation to sue or be sued for actions, suits or proceedings that were commenced after the three-year period. *BLH, Inc. v. United States, 2 Cl. Ct. 463 (Cl. Ct. 1983).*

Delaware provides an orderly process for the fixing of a finite time at which a corporation is terminated. The legal capacity of a dissolved corporation is controlled exclusively by Del. Code Ann. tit. 8, § 278. To allow the dissolved corporation or its creditors to extend the three-year period would destroy the statutory scheme for finality in a dissolution, and render a major part of the statute meaningless. *BLH, Inc. v. United States, 2 Cl. Ct. 463 (Cl. Ct. 1983).*

Proceedings under Section 278. — Activities incident to the administration of a contract by the contracting officer, including activities involving the changes and dispute clauses, do not ripen into an administrative suit or action, for the purposes of Del. Code Ann. tit. 8, § 278, until the contracting officer has rendered a decision, and that decision is appealed. A first principle of contract administration, from the initial submission of a claim for an equitable adjustment and until the final decision of the contracting officer pursuant to the Disputes Clause, is that the posture of the parties is one of negotiation and compromise. The administration of the contract during this period is not an adversary proceeding, and until the government's position is embodied in a final decision, no dispute exists. Procedures pursuant to the disputes clause become a proceeding within the meaning of § 278, when the dispute is presented to a board of contract appeals under the contract or to a court pursuant to the Contract Disputes Act. In such proceedings both the board and the court proceed de novo, and neither is bound by the findings and conclusions of the contracting officer. *BLH, Inc. v. United States, 2 Cl. Ct. 463 (Cl. Ct. 1983).*

Tax Court

Priority of director interests. — Under Delaware law, corporate directors and shareholders generally are required to put the interests of the corporation before their personal interests as shareholders. *Daniels v. Commissioner, T.C. Memo 1994-591 (Tax Ct. 1994).*

Business judgment standard of review. — Absent some showing of abuse of discretion or evidence that the board of directors failed to select a reasonable course of action, a court will not substitute its own judgment of what is or is not sound business judgment. *Daniels v. Commissioner, T.C. Memo 1994-591 (Tax Ct. 1994).*

§ 142. Officers; titles, duties, selection, term; failure to elect; vacancies

DELAWARE CASE NOTES — REPORTED

Corporate officers may acquire apparent authority. — Apparent authority may result from (1) the general manner by which the corporation holds out an officer or agent as having power to act or (2) the acquiescence in an officer or agent's acts of a particular nature, with actual or constructive knowledge thereof. *Colish v. Brandywine Raceway Ass'n, 49 Del. 493, 119 A.2d 887 (1955).*

Fiduciary relationship to corporation and stockholders. — Corporate officers and directors are not permitted to use their position of trust and confidence to further their private interests and while technically not trustees, they stand in a fiduciary relation to the corporation and its stockholders. *Gottlieb v. McKee, 34 Del. Ch. 537, 107 A.2d 240 (1954).*

If an officer or a director of a corporation, in violation of his or her duty as such, acquires gain or advantage for himself or herself, the law charges the interest so acquired with a trust for the benefit of the corporation and its directors while it denies to the betrayer all benefit and

profit. *Gottlieb v. McKee, 34 Del. Ch. 537, 107 A.2d 240 (1954).*

Officers as corporate employees. — A corporate officer is not, as a matter of law, also a corporate employee merely by virtue of his office; whether a corporate officer is also an employee depends on the incidents of his or her relationship to the corporation. *Haft v. Dart Group Corp., 841 F. Supp. 549 (D. Del. 1993).*

Office of president of corporation carries with it certain implied powers of agency and the president is usually either expressly or by implied consent made the chief executive officer and without special authority or explicitly delegated power he or she may perform all acts of an ordinary nature which by usage or necessity are incident to his or her office. *Joseph Greenspon's Sons Iron & Steel Co. v. Pecos Valley Gas Co., 34 Del. 567, 156 A. 350 (1931).*

The president of a private corporation is presumed to have, by virtue of his or her office, certain more or less limited powers in the transaction of the usual and ordinary business of the corporation. *Italo-Petro. Corp. of Am. v. Hannigan, 40 Del. 534, 14 A.2d 401 (1940).*

President has power to transfer and execute negotiable paper. — The president has the authority to bind the corporation by executing and transferring negotiable paper to pay the debts of the corporation; and the president has the authority to bind the corporation by the execution and transfer of negotiable paper in the ordinary course of the corporation's business. *Italo-Petro. Corp. of Am. v. Hannigan, 40 Del. 534, 14 A.2d 401 (1940).*

In an action on notes executed on behalf of a corporation by its president, the question whether its president had authority to bind the corporation by executing the notes was for the jury if evidence to overcome the presumption of the execution by the corporate seal was, in fact, introduced. *Italo-Petro. Corp. of Am. v. Hannigan, 40 Del. 534, 14 A.2d 401 (1940).*

But has no limited implied powers outside of regular course of business. — The rule that the president of a private corporation is presumed to have, by virtue of his or her office, certain more or less limited powers in the transaction of the usual and ordinary business of the corporation, is not applicable where the particular transaction was not in the ordinary course of defendant's business. *Colish v. Brandywine Raceway Ass'n, 49 Del. 493, 119 A.2d 887 (1955).*

Unless they are specifically granted to him or her. — The powers of a president of a corporation, in excess of power over the ordinary and usual business of the corporation, must be specifically given. *Joseph Greenspon's Sons Iron & Steel Co. v. Pecos Valley Gas Co., 34 Del. 567, 156 A. 350 (1931).*

Unauthorized act of president can subsequently be ratified. — If a president of a corporation exceeds his or her power by doing an act and that act is subsequently ratified by those who could ratify such an act, then such ratification would have the same effect as an original approval. *Joseph Greenspon's Sons Iron & Steel Co. v. Pecos Valley Gas Co., 34 Del. 567, 156 A. 350 (1931).*

Unusual powers of president can be implied from previous conduct. — The most usual source of the grant of the unusual or extraordinary powers of a president arises by implication of law from a course of conduct on the part of both the president and the corporation showing that the president had been in the habit of acting in similar matters on behalf of the company and that the company had authorized him so to act and had recognized, approved and ratified his former and similar actions. *Joseph Greenspon's Sons Iron & Steel Co. v. Pecos Valley Gas Co., 34 Del. 567, 156 A. 350 (1931).*

No written authorization to enter into a personal services contract is required for the president of a small, closely held corporation which has habitually operated its business without any formal authorization to its president. *Hessler, Inc. v. Farrell, 226 A.2d 708 (Del. 1967).*

As may any corporate officer acquire implied powers. — When, in the usual course of the business of a corporation, an officer or agent has been allowed to manage certain of its affairs, and when this is known to the other party to the contract, the authority of the officer to act for the corporation is implied from the past conduct never challenged by the corporate officials. *Hessler, Inc. v. Farrell, 226 A.2d 708 (Del. 1967).*

President cannot bind corporation by contract of guaranty. — In most cases the president of the ordinary business corporation has no implied or presumed authority to bind the corporation by a mere contract of guaranty, in which it has no apparent interest. *Atlantic Ref. Co. v. Ingalls & Co., 37 Del. 503, 185 A. 885 (1936).*

But if president is sole stockholder his or her contracting power is not limited by bylaw. — When a corporate president signed a contract on behalf of the corporation of which he was the sole stockholder, he was unhampered by either the absence of authorizing bylaw or by the restraining force of any existent bylaw. *Community Stores, Inc. v. Dean, 40 Del. 566, 14 A.2d 633 (1940).*

Where by contract the president and sole stockholder of a corporation agreed to turn over the entire management of the company and to become a minority stockholder, and where it was agreed that while he was employed by the company he was to receive $35 per week, the contract needed no ratification and the relation of the president to the company could subsequently be severed. *Community Stores, Inc. v. Dean, 40 Del. 566, 14 A.2d 633 (1940).*

Authority cannot be found in implied powers of treasurer and director or of vice-president and director for the employment of a final architect where the employment was not an act of an ordinary nature which by usage or necessity was incidental to the office of either of them. *Colish v. Brandywine Raceway Ass'n, 49 Del. 493, 119 A.2d 887 (1955).*

Corporate officer or director is entirely free to engage in independent competitive business, so long as the officer or director violates no legal or moral duty with respect to the fiduciary relation that exists between the corporation and himself or herself. *Craig v. Graphic Arts Studio, Inc., 39 Del. Ch. 447, 166 A.2d 444 (1960).*

When a business opportunity comes to a corporate officer or director in his or her individual capacity rather than his or her official capacity, and the opportunity is one which, because of the nature of the enterprise, is not essential to his or her corporation, and is one in which it has no interest or expectation, the officer or director is entitled to treat the opportunity as his or her own, and the corporation has no interest in it, if, of course, the officer or director has not wrongfully embarked the corporation's resources therein. *Gottlieb v. McKee, 34 Del. Ch. 537, 107 A.2d 240 (1954).*

The test of an officer's or director's capacity at the time of a business opportunity seems to be whether there was a specific duty on the part of the officer or director sought to be held liable to act or contract in the particular matter as the representative of the corporation. *Gottlieb v. McKee, 34 Del. Ch. 537, 107 A.2d 240 (1954).*

Actions of de facto officers are only binding on corporation so far as third persons are concerned. *Drob v. National Mem. Park, 28 Del. Ch. 254, 41 A.2d 589 (1945).*

General manager, manager for all general purposes of corporation, has implied authority to do anything that the corporation could do in the general scope and operation of its business. *Phoenix Fin. Corp. v. Iowa-Wisconsin Bridge Co., 41 Del. 130, 16 A.2d 789 (1940).*

Ratification of acts of general manager. — The sale of tickets by the general manager of a corporation and discussed by the board of directors, and not disavowed by them, was binding on the corporation when the corporation retained and used the full consideration of the tickets.

Phoenix Fin. Corp. v. Iowa-Wisconsin Bridge Co., 41 Del. 130, 16 A.2d 789 (1940).

Offices of corporation are subject to writ of quo warranto. — Offices of a corporation created by special act of the General Assembly or under the general corporation law of this State, are offices of a public character within the meaning that the remedy by information in the nature of a writ of quo warranto lies against one who usurps such an office. *Brooks v. State ex rel. Richards, 26 Del. 1, 79 A. 790 (1911).*

DELAWARE CASE NOTES — UNREPORTED

Removal of officers via secretly obtained consent. — Although two directors of a family corporation secretly obtained 8 Del. C. § 228 written stockholder consents and utilized them to remove a third director and his sons as officers under 8 Del. C. §§ 141(k), 142(b), the consents were deemed valid where they conformed to the strict requirements of 8 Del. C. § 228 and were made by consenting shareholders who had received adequate disclosures; it was unreasonable for insiders of a private family corporation, when faced with removal by written consents under 8 Del. C. § 228, to insist that those seeking their removal under 8 Del. C. § 141(k) were required to

meet a higher disclosure standard that was more akin to that of a public company. *Unanue v. Unanue, 2004 Del. Ch. LEXIS 153 (Del. Ch. Nov. 3, 2004).*

Office of president not generally regarded as permanent. — Chairman and vice president of a corporation did not violate a shareholder agreement by removing the president of the coroporation from office; although the shareholder's agreement stated that the party would be the president of the corporation, the agreement did guarantee a permanent position as president of the corporation. *Carlson v. Hallinan, 2006 Del. Ch. LEXIS 58 (Del. Ch. Mar. 21, 2006).*

CASE NOTES — OTHER STATES

Illinois

Affirmative protection of corporate interests. — A corporate officer is held to scrupulous observance of his or her duty to both affirmatively protect the interests of the corporation committed to his charge and to refrain from doing anything that would work injury to the corporation. Its officers and directors owe the corporation a fiduciary obligation of honesty, loyalty, good faith, and fairness. *Pros v. Mid-America Computer Corporation, 142 Ill. App. 3d 453, 491 N.E.2d 851, 96 Ill. Dec. 572 (1986).*

Opportunity test. — Where a business opportunity is presented to an officer in his or her individual capacity, rather than in his or her official capacity as an officer or director, and the opportunity is one not essential to the corporation nor in which the corporation has any interest or expectancy, the opportunity is that of the officer and not of the corporation. The test of whether a particular opportunity is an individual or corporate one seems to be whether there is a specific duty, on the part of the officer sought to be held liable, to act or contract in regard to the particular matter as the representative of the corporation, all of which is largely a question of fact. Whether a corporate officer seizes a corporate opportunity for his or her own depends not on any single factor nor is it determined by any fixed standard. Numerous factors are to be weighed, including the manner in which the offer is communicated to the officer, the good faith of the officer, the use of corporate assets to acquire the opportunity, the financial ability of the corporation to acquire the opportunity, the degree of disclosure made to the corporation, the action taken by the corporation with reference thereto, and the need or interest of the corporation in the

opportunity. The presence or absence of any single factor is not determinative of the issue of corporate opportunity. *Paulman v. Kritzer, 74 Ill. App. 2d 284, 219 N.E.2d 541 (1966).*

Massachusetts

Compensation. — The rule in Delaware is that directors have no right to compensation for services rendered outside their duties as directors unless there is an express contract to pay for such services, or, as some cases hold, unless the services were clearly outside their duties as directors and performed under circumstances sufficient to show that it was understood by the proper officers, as well as by the directors claiming compensation, that the services were to be paid for by the corporation. A contract to pay compensation for such services must be made with directors, or other proper corporate officers who have no personal interest, directly or indirectly, in the contract, and who are competent to represent the company in the transaction. *Beacon Wool Corporation v. Johnson, 331 Mass. 274, 119 N.E.2d 195 (1954).*

Michigan

Opportunity test. — A court, when determining whether a business opportunity is a corporate opportunity, must first ascertain whether the opportunity was presented to a corporate officer in the officer's individual or representative capacity. Second, after determining the manner in which the opportunity was presented, the court must determine the nature of the opportunity. Third, the nature of the opportunity is analyzed differently, depending on whether the opportunity is presented to a corporate official in the official's individual or corporate representative capacity. *Rapistan Corporation v. Michaels, 203 Mich. App. 301, 511 N.W.2d 918 (1994).*

Even though a business opportunity may not constitute a corporate opportunity under the conventional tests employed in determining whether a corporate opportunity exists, a corporate representative will be estopped nevertheless from denying that the business opportunity was a corporate opportunity if the representative wrongfully embarked the corporation's assets in the development or acquisition of the business opportunity. *Rapistan Corporation v. Michaels, 203 Mich. App. 301, 511 N.W.2d 918 (1994).*

When a corporation's fiduciary uses corporate assets to develop a business opportunity, the fiduciary is estopped from denying that the resulting opportunity belongs to the corporation whose assets were misappropriated, even if it was not feasible for the corporation to pursue the opportunity or it had no expectancy in the project. *Rapistan Corporation v. Michaels, 203 Mich. App. 301, 511 N.W.2d 918 (1994).*

Misapplication of corporate funds. — The proscription against appropriation of corporate property for private gain is of broader application than the corporate opportunity rule. The latter is but a specialized application of the former. It essentially treats a corporation's expectations regarding certain business opportunities which are in the corporation's line of business and of practical advantage to it as corporate property which may not be appropriated for personal gain. On the other hand, the general proscription against misapplication of corporate funds applies equally to business opportunities outside the corporation's line of business. Thus, a business opportunity falling outside a corporation's line of business and which would not otherwise be considered a corporate opportunity, nevertheless will be deemed a corporate opportunity if developed or financed with corporate funds. *Rapistan Corporation v. Michaels, 203 Mich. App. 30, 511 N.W.2d 918 (1994).*

Minnesota

Reasonable doubt of directors' independence. — The directors' ability to affect the continued employment and remuneration of other directors as corporate officers raises a reasonable doubt that those directors could act independently. *Professional Management Associates v. Coss, 574 N.W.2d 107 (Minn. App. 1999).*

The duty of candor, the obligation to disclose material information, is implied in an officer's relationship to the board which is charged with making informed decisions. *Potter v. Pohlad, 560 N.W.2d 389 (Minn. App. 1997).*

New York

In general. — Under Delaware law, corporate officers, directors, and controlling shareholders owe their corporation and its minority shareholders a fiduciary obligation of honesty, loyalty, good faith, and fairness. Delaware law imposes a duty upon corporations to disclose all available material information when obtaining shareholder approval. Only damages caused by the breach of fiduciary duty are compensable. *Lama Holding Company v. Smith Barney Inc., 88 N.Y.2d 413, 668 N.E.2d 1370, 646 N.Y.S.2d 76 (1996).*

Prohibited individual opportunity. — When there is presented to a corporate officer a business opportunity which the corporation is financially able to undertake, and which, by its nature, falls into the line of the corporation's business and is of practical advantage to it, or is an opportunity in which the corporation has an actual or expectant interest, the officer is prohibited from permitting his or her self-interest to be brought into conflict with the corporation's interest and may not take the opportunity for him- or herself. *Ault v. Soutter, 167 A.D.2d 38, 570 N.Y.S.2d 280 (1991).*

Ohio

Officers of a corporation owe fiduciary duties of due care and loyalty to the shareholder. *Allied Paper Inc. v. H.M. Holdings, Inc., 86 Ohio App. 3d 8, 619 N.E.2d 1121 (1993).*

CASE NOTES — FEDERAL

First Circuit

Duty of loyalty. — The duty of loyalty is transgressed when a corporate fiduciary, whether director, officer, or controlling shareholder, uses his or her corporate office or, in the case of a controlling shareholder, control over corporate machinery, to promote, advance or effectuate a transaction between the corporation and such person (or an entity in which the fiduciary has a substantial economic interest, directly or indirectly) and that transaction is not substantively fair to the corporation. Essentially, the duty of loyalty mandates that the best interest of the corporation and its shareholders takes precedence over any interest possessed by a director, officer, or controlling shareholder. *Growe v. Bedard, 2004 U.S. Dist. LEXIS 23746 (D.Me. 2004).*

Derivative actions. — The following activities give rise to derivative actions: actions against directors or

officers for breach of fiduciary duty to the corporation (e.g., waste of corporate assets, self-dealing, mismanagement of corporate business, misappropriation of corporate assets or business opportunities) and actions to recover damages for a consummated ultra vires act. *Niehoff v. Maynard, 2000 U.S. Dist. LEXIS 22009 (D.R.I. 2000).*

Direct actions. — The following activities give rise to direct actions: fraudulent statements which directly affect the value of securities held by the shareholder; a suit brought to inspect corporate books and records; a suit against directors for fraud in the sale or purchase of the individual shareholder's stock; actions to compel payment of dividends; actions to preserve shareholders' rights to vote; a claim that a transaction improperly dilutes a shareholder's ownership interest or infringes the shareholder's preemptive rights; a claim that a proposed merger, recapitalization, or similar transaction unfairly

Corporations

affects minority shareholders; and a claim that a proposed corporate action should be enjoined as ultra vires, fraudulent, or designed to harm a specific shareholder illegitimately. *Niehoff v. Maynard, 2000 U.S. Dist. LEXIS 22009 (D.R.I. 2000).*

Second Circuit

Corporation fiduciary duties. — Under Delaware law, a corporation does not owe a fiduciary duty to its shareholders nor may it be held vicariously liable for breaches of fiduciary duty that are committed by its officers. *Onex Food Servs. v. Grieser, 1996 U.S. Dist. LEXIS 2797 (S.D.N.Y. 1996).*

Director/officer fiduciary duties. — Under Delaware law, directors and officers of a corporation owe a fiduciary duty to the corporation to manage it honestly, impartially, and on behalf of the corporation, and cannot use the position to further their personal interests. *Cohen v. Bloch, 539 F. Supp. 760 (S.D.N.Y. 1981).*

Standing for breach of duty claim. — Under Delaware law, a common-law claim for breach of fiduciary duty by a corporate director or officer can only be asserted (a) by the corporation or on the corporation's behalf in a derivative action or (b) by individual shareholders when a special injury has occurred. *Zimmerman v. Prime Medical Services, Inc., 729 F. Supp. 23 (S.D.N.Y. 1990)*

Trust for benefit of corporation. — If an officer or director of a corporation, in violation of his or her fiduciary duty, acquires gain or advantage for himself or herself, the law charges the interest so acquired with a trust for the benefit of the corporation, at its election, which it denies to the betrayer all benefit and profit. *Cohen v. Bloch, 539 F. Supp. 760 (S.D.N.Y. 1981).*

Demand futility. — Where board of director interest, approval or acquiescence in the wrongdoing exists, the pre-suit demand is excused as futile, and where officers and directors are under an influence which sterilizes their discretion, they cannot be considered proper persons to conduct litigation on behalf of the corporation, and here again pre-suit demand would be futile. *In re Oxford Health Plans, Inc. Sec. Litig., 192 F.R.D. 111 (S.D.N.Y. 2000).*

To show self-dealing, a plaintiff must show that the shareholder defendants received something to the exclusion of, and detriment to, the minority stockholders. *Official Committee of the Unsecured Creditors v. Investcorp, S.A., 137 F. Supp. 2d 502 (S.D.N.Y 2001).*

Ratification of unauthorized act. — If a corporate officer performs an act without being authorized so to do, but which could have been authorized in the first instance by the board of directors such transaction may nevertheless become binding on the company if ratified expressly or by implication. Ratification is a concept deriving from the law of agency which contemplates the ex post conferring upon or confirming of the legal authority of an agent in circumstances in which the agent had no authority or arguably had no authority. One way of conceptualizing its effect is that it provides, after the fact, the grant of authority that may have been wanting at the time of the agent's act. In order to be effective, the agent must fully disclose all relevant circumstances with respect to the transaction to the principal prior to the ratification. *Bradbury v. PTN Publishing Co., 1998 U.S. Dist. LEXIS 10185 (E.D.N.Y. 1998).*

Binding corporation. — Under Delaware law, a corporation's principal executive officers do not need express written authority to bind their corporation. *Lehman Bros. Commer. Corp. v. Minmetals International Non-Ferrous Metals Trading Co., 1996 U.S. Dist. LEXIS 8842 (S.D.N.Y. 1996).*

Rights of bankruptcy trustee. — Although corporate officers and directors owe fiduciary duties to creditors when a corporation is insolvent in fact, those duties do not expand the circumscribed rights of a bankruptcy trustee, who may only assert claims of the bankrupt corporation, not its creditors. *Pereira v. Farace, 413 F.3d 330 (2d Cir. 2005).*

Appointment of president. — Incorporators have no power to appoint a president and fix his or her salary before a board of directors is appointed. *Kenyon v. Holbrook Microfilming Service, Inc., 155 F.2d 913 (2d Cir. 1946).*

The directors or shareholders are to elect the president. *Kenyon v. Holbrook Microfilming Service, Inc., 155 F.2d 913 (2d Cir. 1946).*

Auto dealer lacked standing for fiduciary duty action. — Auto dealer's breach of fiduciary duty claim would arguably be derivative rather than direct, given the Delaware Supreme Court's recent holding that for a breach of fiduciary duty claim to be direct, the stockholder's claimed direct injury must be independent of any alleged injury to the corporation. The stockholder must demonstrate that the duty breached was owed to the stockholder and that he or she can prevail without showing an injury to the corporation. As the district court ruled in its earlier order, because plaintiff shareholder did not maintain an equity interest in the dealership corporation throughout the pendency of the litigation, he lacked standing to bring a derivative claim. *Adkins v. GMC, 2006 U.S. App. LEXIS 5688 (2d Cir. Mar. 3, 2006).*

Third Circuit

Authorized corporate agents. — Beyond the board of directors, a corporation may validly act through its directors and officers as authorized corporate agents. In general, an officer's powers stem from the organic law of the corporation, or a board delegation of authority, which may be express or implied. Express authority to act on behalf of the corporation is usually manifested through a statute, the certificate of corporation, the bylaws, or a board or shareholder action. Implied actual authority, which is express authority circumstantially proved, may be found through evidence as to the manner in which the business has operated in the past, the facts attending the transaction in question, circumstantial evidence of board declarations surrounding the given transaction, or the habitual usage or course of dealing common to the company. Similarly, authority will be implied when it is reasonably necessary and proper to effectuate the purpose of the office or the main authority conferred. *Schoonejongen v. Curtiss-Wright Corp., 143 F.3d 120 (3d Cir. 1998).*

Named plaintiff. — Where a wrong is committed against a corporation, redress of that wrong can be sought only by the corporation. Therefore, a cause of action against a director or officer for mismanagement of a corporation may be asserted only in the name of the corporation. *Penguin Industries v. Kuc, 1986 U.S. Dist. LEXIS 22328 (E.D.Pa 1986).*

Right to maintain derivative suit. — The right of a stockholder of a Delaware corporation to maintain a derivative suit on behalf of the corporation is based upon a breach of fiduciary duty by the directors or officers of the corporation. The officers and directors of a Delaware corporation are trustees for its stockholders. *Beneficial Industrial Loan Corp. v. Smith, 170 F.2d 44 (3d Cir. 1948).*

Insider trading. — Both Delaware and New Jersey recognize a common-law cause of action for a derivative plaintiff against a corporate officer who has traded stock of the corporation on the basis of inside information. Under the laws of both states, directors who trade stock on the basis of inside information violate their fiduciary obligations to the corporation. To state a claim for breach of fiduciary duty, a plaintiff must show a duty, a breach of that duty, an injury and causation. *In re Cendant Corp. Derivative Action Litigation, 189 F.R.D. 117 (D.N.J. 1999).*

Management of retirement health benefits. — The business decision of appointing a corporate officer to manage retirement health benefits for the corporation does not have the effect of removing from directors in a very substantial way their duty to use their own best judgment on management matters. *Schoonejongen v. Curtiss-Wright Corp., 143 F.3d 120 (3d Cir. 1998).*

Powers of general manager. — The president as general manager commands the power to do anything the corporation could do in the general scope and operation of its business. *Schoonejongen v. Curtiss-Wright Corp., 143 F.3d 120 (3d Cir. 1998).*

A general manager's action on behalf of the corporation is generally upheld unless it is unusual or extraordinary. *Schoonejongen v. Curtiss-Wright Corp., 143 F.3d 120 (3d Cir. 1998).*

Fourth Circuit

In general. — Under Delaware law, corporate officers and directors owe their corporation the fiduciary duties of due care, good faith, and loyalty. The duty of care requires that corporate officers and directors exercise an informed business judgment to make decisions reasonably determined to be in the best interests of the corporation and its shareholders. Officers and directors are protected from liability for their decisions under the rebuttable presumption of the business judgment rule, that is, that in making a business decision the directors of a corporation acted on an informed basis, in good faith and in the honest belief that the action taken was in the best interests of the company. The business judgment rule focuses on the process by which directors and officers make informed decisions, not on the substance of the decision itself. *Miller v. U.S. Foodservice, Inc., 361 F. Supp. 2d 470 (D.Md. 2005).*

Fiduciary duty traditionally encompasses both the duty of care and the duty of loyalty. *Bank of America v. Musselman, 222 F. Supp. 2d 792 (E.D.Va. 2002).*

Prerequisite to officer fiduciary duty. — With respect to officers of a corporation, one court applying Delaware law has noted an important limitation: no fiduciary duty governing the management of a corporation's affairs can be imposed on persons who have no authority to manage those affairs. In the absence of allegations that an officer has such authority under the certificate of incorporation, that officer has no fiduciary duty. *Bank of America v. Musselman, 222 F. Supp. 2d 792 (E.D.Va. 2002).*

Standard of review for consideration disputes. — Directors are only liable for corporate waste claims when they authorize an exchange that is so one sided that no business person of ordinary, sound judgment could conclude that the corporation has received adequate consideration. Generally, courts grant broad discretion to directors in matters of executive compensation. Accordingly, if reasonable, informed minds might disagree on the question, then in order to preserve the wide domain over which knowledgeable business judgment may safely act, a reviewing court will not attempt to itself evaluate the wisdom of the bargain or the adequacy of the consideration. *Miller v. U.S. Foodservice, Inc., 361 F. Supp. 2d 470 (D.Md. 2005).*

Fifth Circuit

Stock purchases. — Delaware imposes no fiduciary duty on the part of officers or directors or majority stockholders in buying stock from the minority or individual stockholders. *Mansfield Hardwood Lumber Co. v. Johnson, 268 F.2d 317 (5th Cir. 1959).*

Injury to corporation itself. — When a corporation, through its officers, misstates its financial condition, thereby causing a decline in the company's share price when the truth is revealed, the corporation itself has been injured. *Smith v. Waste Management Inc., 407 F.3d 381 (5th Cir. 2005).*

Seventh Circuit

Under Delaware law, a corporate officer owes the corporation a duty of good faith, loyalty, and fair dealing. *Claire's Stores, Inc. v. Abrams, 1989 U.S. Dist. LEXIS 12224 (N.D.Ill. 1989).*

Directors and officers of a Delaware corporation are fiduciaries to the corporation and its stockholders. *Dasho v. Susquehanna Corp., 1970 U.S. Dist. LEXIS 12923 (N.D. Ill. 1970).*

When duty emerges. — Under Delaware law, officers and directors of a corporation owe a fiduciary duty to the shareholders of that corporation. However, that duty does not emerge until there is an actual director-shareholder. *Premier Capital Management., L.L.C. v. Cohen, 2004 U.S. Dist. LEXIS 24981 (N.D.Ill. 2004).*

Self-dealing. — Although Delaware courts have found that officers owe fiduciary duties to the corporation, the only instances where such a duty is found are where the circumstances involved self-dealing. *Jackson Nat'l Life*

Corporations

Ins. Co. v. Kendig, 1999 U.S. Dist. LEXIS 16645 (N.D.Ill. 1999).

Management responsibility of officers. — Delaware law imposes management responsibility to directors, but not to officers. The exception to this rule is that the business and affairs of every corporation shall be managed by or under the direction of a board of directors, except as may be otherwise provided in its certificate of incorporation. *Jackson Nat'l Life Ins. Co. v. Kendig, 1999 U.S. Dist. LEXIS 16645 (N.D.Ill. 1999).*

Under Delaware law, key managerial personnel owe their employer duties of loyalty and due care. *Anic v. DVI, Inc., 2002 U.S. Dist. LEXIS 23943 (N.D.Ill. 2002).*

An act taken after a manager's resignation cannot be a basis for a breach of fiduciary duty action. *Anic v. DVI, Inc., 2002 U.S. Dist. LEXIS 23943 (N.D.Ill. 2002).*

Standard of business judgment review. — A litigant challenging a decision by a corporate officer has the burden at the outset to rebut the business judgment rule's presumption by providing evidence that the officer, in reaching their challenged decision, breached any one of the triads of their fiduciary duty — good faith, loyalty, or due care. If a litigant fails to meet this evidentiary burden, the business judgment rule attaches to protect corporate officers and directors and the decisions that they make. The courts will not second-guess these business judgments. If the presumption of the rule is rebutted, however, the burden shifts to the corporate officer, the proponent of the challenged transaction, to prove to the trier of fact the "entire fairness" of the transaction. Under the "entire fairness" standard of judicial review, the corporate officers must establish to the court's satisfaction that the transaction was the product of both fair dealing and fair price. *Gunter v. Novopharm USA, Inc., 2001 U.S. Dist. LEXIS 2117 (N.D.Ill. 2001).*

Individual standing. — Under Delaware law, an individual has standing to challenge corporate mismanagement only if he or she can allege some "special injury" distinct from that suffered by the corporation and other shareholders. *Miller v. Loucks, 1992 U.S. Dist. LEXIS 16966 (N.D.Ill. 1992).*

Depression of stock value. — Stockholder actions charging mismanagement which depresses the value of stock allege a wrong to the corporation, i.e., the stockholders collectively, to be enforced by a derivative action. *Lynch v. Marklin of America, Inc., 724 F. Supp. 595 (N.D.Ill. 1989).*

Eighth Circuit

Liability for profit acquired. — For the purpose of removing temptation to profit from a breach of his or her confidential relationship, an officer or director of a corporation who, in violation of his or her duty as such, acquires gain or advantage for himself or herself, is liable to the corporation for the benefit or profit so acquired. *Polin v. Conductron Corp., 411 F. Supp. 698 (E.D. Mo. 1976).*

Ninth Circuit

The business judgment rule posits a powerful presumption in favor of actions taken by the directors in that a decision made by a loyal and informed board will not be overturned by the courts unless it cannot be attributed to any rational business purpose. To rebut the rule, plaintiff must provide evidence that directors, in reaching their challenged decision, breached any one of the triads of their fiduciary duty — good faith, loyalty, or due care. If the plaintiff cannot overcome the presumption, the business judgment rule attaches to protect corporate officers and directors and the decisions they make, and courts hesitate to second-guess such decisions. Should a plaintiff rebut the rule, the burden shifts to the defendant directors to prove the "entire fairness" of the transaction. *McMichael v. United States Filter Corp., 2001 U.S. Dist. LEXIS 3918 (C.D.Cal. 2001).*

Eleventh Circuit

Removal of president. — The Delaware law provides that a president cannot be removed until his or her office has expired except for cause, and that cause must be established in a suit at law brought in behalf of the board of directors. *Ingalls v. Patterson, 158 F. Supp. 627 (N.D. Ala. 1958).*

District of Columbia Circuit

An officer who has no express contract with the corporation cannot sue in quantum meruit for the value of his or her services. *Air Traffic & Service Corp. v. Fay, 196 F.2d 40 (D.C. Cir. 1952).*

§ 143. Loans to employees and officers; guaranty of obligations of employees and officers

DELAWARE CASE NOTES — REPORTED

Officers as corporate employees. — A corporate officer is not, as a matter of law, also a corporate employee merely by virtue of office; whether a corporate officer is also an employee depends on the incidents of the relationship to the corporation. *Haft v. Dart Group Corp., 841 F. Supp. 549 (D. Del. 1993).*

§ 144. Interested directors; quorum

DELAWARE CASE NOTES — REPORTED

Purpose of section. — This section merely removes an "interested director" cloud when its terms are met and provides against invalidation of an agreement "solely" because such a director or officer is involved. *Fliegler v. Lawrence, 361 A.2d 218 (Del. 1976).*

Corporations

Legislative intent of subsection (a)(1). — Subsection (a)(1) appears to be a legislative mandate that an approving vote of a majority of informed and disinterested directors shall remove any taint of director or directors' self-interest in a transaction. *Cede & Co. v. Technicolor, Inc., 634 A.2d 345 (Del. 1993).*

Limitation of stockholder's power to nullify transactions. — The enactment of this section limited the stockholders' power to nullify an interested transaction in two ways: First, a committee of disinterested directors may approve a transaction and bring it within the scope of the business judgment rule; and second, where an independent committee is not available, the stockholders may either ratify the transaction or challenge its fairness in a judicial forum, but they lack the power automatically to nullify it. *Oberly v. Kirby, 592 A.2d 445 (Del. 1991).*

Exclusiveness of validation provisions. — This section is not exclusive means by which interested director contract can be validated. *Robert A. Wachsler, Inc. v. Florafax Int'l, Inc., 778 F.2d 547 (10th Cir. 1985).*

Nothing in this section sanctions unfairness to corporation or removes transaction from judicial scrutiny. *Fliegler v. Lawrence, 361 A.2d 218 (Del. 1976).*

Business opportunities of no interest to corporation may be utilized by director or officer. — When a business opportunity comes to a corporate officer or director in his or her individual capacity rather than in his or her official capacity, and the opportunity is one which, because of the nature of the enterprise, is not essential to his or her corporation, and is one in which it has no interest or expectancy, the officer or director is entitled to treat the opportunity as his or her own, and the corporation has no interest in it, if, of course, the officer or director has not wrongfully embarked the corporation's resources therein. *Guth v. Loft, Inc., 23 Del. Ch. 255, 5 A.2d 503 (1939), aff'd, 25 Del. Ch. 363, 19 A.2d 721 (1941); Gottlieb v. McKee, 34 Del. Ch. 537, 107 A.2d 240 (1954); Johnston v. Greene, 35 Del. Ch. 479, 121 A.2d 919 (1956).*

If a business opportunity comes to a corporate director in his or her individual capacity, and if the opportunity is not essential to his or her corporation and in which his or her corporation has no interest, and if the corporate resources have not been wrongfully embarked therein, the corporate director is free to treat the opportunity as his or her own. *Kaplan v. Fenton, 278 A.2d 834 (Del. 1971).*

Better employment not an interest under this section. — The alleged hope of better employment opportunities does not constitute the kind of interest covered by this section. *Cinerama, Inc. v. Technicolor, Inc., 663 A.2d 1134 (Del. Ch. 1994), aff'd, 663 A.2d 1156 (Del. 1995).*

But opportunities of interest must not be accepted. — If there is presented to a corporate officer or director a business opportunity which the corporation is financially able to undertake, is, from its nature, in the line of the corporation's business and is of practical advantage to it, is one in which the corporation has an interest or a reasonable expectancy, and, by embracing the opportunity, the self-interest of the officer or director will be brought into conflict with that of his or her corporation, the law will not permit him or her to seize the opportunity for himself or herself. *Guth v. Loft, Inc., 23 Del. Ch. 255, 5 A.2d 503 (1939), aff'd, 25 Del. Ch. 363, 19 A.2d 721 (1941); Johnston v. Greene, 35 Del. Ch. 479, 121 A.2d 919 (1956); Equity Corp. v. Milton, 43 Del. Ch. 160, 221 A.2d 494 (1966); David J. Greene & Co. v. Dunhill Int'l, Inc., 249 A.2d 427 (Del. Ch. 1968); Kaplan v. Fenton, 278 A.2d 834 (Del. 1971).*

If the essential of a corporate opportunity is reasonably within the scope of a corporation's activities, latitude should be allowed for development and expansion. *Guth v. Loft, Inc., 23 Del. Ch. 255, 5 A.2d 503 (1939), aff'd, 25 Del. Ch. 363, 19 A.2d 721 (1941).*

Or director will have breached his or her fiduciary obligation. — Where directors of a corporation are required to answer for wrongful acts of commission by which they have enriched themselves to the injury of the corporation, a court of conscience will not regard such acts as mere torts, but as serious breaches of trust, and will point out the moral and make clear the principle that corporate officers and directors, while not in strictness trustees, will, in such case, be treated as though they were in fact trustees of an express and subsisting trust, and without the protection of the statute of limitations. *Bovay v. H.M. Byllesby & Co., 27 Del. Ch. 381, 38 A.2d 808 (1944).*

Test of officer's or director's capacity at time of business opportunity seems to be whether there was a specific duty on the part of the officer or director sought to be held liable to act or contract in the particular matter as the representative of the corporation. *Gottlieb v. McKee, 34 Del. Ch. 537, 107 A.2d 240 (1954).*

Effect of corporation's rejection of corporate opportunity. — Evidence indicated that the chance to acquire certain claims was a corporate opportunity which should have been and was offered to the corporation. Because the corporation was not in a position, either financially or legally, to accept the opportunity at that time, the president of the corporation and other persons associated with the corporation were entitled to acquire it for themselves after the corporation rejected it. *Fliegler v. Lawrence, 361 A.2d 218 (Del. 1976).*

Profits from breach of trust belong to corporation. — If an officer or a director of a corporation, in violation of his or her duty as such, acquires gain or advantage for himself or herself, the law charges the interest so acquired with a trust for the benefit of the corporation and its directors while it denies to the betrayer all benefit and profit. *Guth v. Loft, Inc., 23 Del. Ch. 255, 5 A.2d 503 (1939), aff'd, 25 Del. Ch. 363, 19 A.2d 721 (1941); Gottlieb v. McKee, 34 Del. Ch. 537, 107 A.2d 240 (1954).*

Or receiver of insolvent corporation. — Where a director received fraudulently issued stock and was paid a dividend thereon and then sold the stock to an innocent purchaser, who also received dividends, the director was liable to the receiver of the insolvent company for the dividends both he and the innocent purchaser had received. *Cahall v. Burbage, 14 Del. Ch. 55, 121 A. 646 (1923).*

Whether or not director has appropriated corporate opportunity is factual question. — Whether or not the director has appropriated for himself or herself something that in fairness should belong to his or her corporation is a factual question to be decided by reasonable inference from objective facts. *Johnston v. Greene, 35 Del. Ch. 479, 121 A.2d 919 (1956).*

Where a corporation is engaged in a certain business, and an opportunity is presented to it embracing an activity as to which it has fundamental knowledge, practical experience and ability to pursue, which, logically and naturally, is adaptable to its business having regard for its financial position, and is one that is consonant with its reasonable needs and aspirations for expansion, it may be properly said that the opportunity is in the line of the corporation's business. *Guth v. Loft, Inc., 23 Del. Ch. 255, 5 A.2d 503 (1939),* aff'd, *25 Del. Ch. 363, 19 A.2d 721 (1941).*

And burden of proof is on director. — It is incumbent upon a director to show that his or her every act in dealing with a corporate opportunity presented was in the exercise of the utmost good faith to his or her corporation; and the burden cast upon him or her satisfactorily to prove that the offer was made to him or her individually. *Guth v. Loft, Inc., 23 Del. Ch. 255, 5 A.2d 503 (1939),* aff'd, *25 Del. Ch. 363, 19 A.2d 721 (1941).*

Where directors deal with another corporation of which they are sole directors and officers, they assume the burden of showing the entire fairness of the transaction. *Keenan v. Eshleman, 23 Del. Ch. 234, 2 A.2d 904 (1938).*

Paragraph (2) of subsection (a) of this section does not remove from certain corporate officers the burden of proving that a transaction in which the corporation acquired a second corporation in which they held a significant interest was intrinsically fair. *Fliegler v. Lawrence, 361 A.2d 218 (Del. 1976).*

Directors are required to demonstrate both their utmost good faith and the most scrupulous inherent fairness of transactions in which they possess a financial, business or other personal interest which does not devolve upon the corporation or all stockholders generally. *Mills Acquisition Co. v. Macmillan, Inc., 559 A.2d 1261 (Del. 1988).*

Ratification by shareholders. — Where a majority of the shares of a corporation voted in favor of exercising an option to purchase a second corporation were voted by persons alleged to have acted detrimentally to the first corporation for purposes of personal gain, ratification of the option by the shareholders did not affect the burden of showing the intrinsic fairness of the transaction. *Fliegler v. Lawrence, 361 A.2d 218 (Del. 1976).*

In no case has the court held that stockholder ratification automatically extinguishes a claim for breach of the directors' duty of loyalty. Rather, the operative effect of shareholder ratification in duty of loyalty cases has been either to change the standard of review to the business judgment rule, with the burden of proof resting upon the plaintiff, or to leave "entire fairness" as the review standard, but shift the burden of proof to the plaintiff. *In re Wheelabrator Technologies, Inc. Shareholders Litig., 663 A.2d 1194 (Del. Ch. 1995).*

Stockholder ratification in self-interested deals. — Because of subsection (a)(2), where an interested transaction is between the corporation and a director or the director's affiliates, rather than the majority stockholder, stockholder ratification does not shift the burden of persuasion to the plaintiff under entire fairness. *In re Walt Disney Co. Derivative Litig., 731 A.2d 342 (Del. Ch. 1998).* But see *Brehm v. Eisner, 746 A.2d 244 (Del. 2000).*

Prerequisites for finding self-interest. — At the very least, subsection (a) protects corporate actions from invalidation on grounds of director self-interest if such self-interest is: (1) disclosed to and approved by a majority of disinterested directors; (2) disclosed to and approved by the shareholders; or (3) the contract or transaction is found to be fair as to the corporation. *Cede & Co. v. Technicolor, Inc., 634 A.2d 345 (Del. 1993).*

One director's self-interest may not be problematic. — One director's colorable interest in a challenged transaction is not sufficient, without more, to deprive a board of the protection of the business judgment rule presumption of loyalty. *Cede & Co. v. Technicolor, Inc., 634 A.2d 345 (Del. 1993).*

Interested transactions by charitable corporations. — The fact that a corporation is to be managed on behalf of charitable beneficiaries rather than stockholders, does not alter the basic premise that interested transactions are not inherently wrong. *Oberly v. Kirby, 592 A.2d 445 (Del. 1991).*

There is no reason why independent directors and courts should not also have the power to evaluate the fairness of an interested transaction undertaken by a charitable corporation. *Oberly v. Kirby, 592 A.2d 445 (Del. 1991).*

The Attorney General holds the power and bears the duty of invoking the jurisdiction of the courts to evaluate the fairness of any interested transaction that has not been approved by an independent committee and that the Attorney General feels is detrimental to a charitable corporation. *Oberly v. Kirby, 592 A.2d 445 (Del. 1991).*

By failing to challenge a given transaction of a charitable corporation, the Attorney General would effectively ratify it on behalf of the beneficiaries, for he represents their interests. *Oberly v. Kirby, 592 A.2d 445 (Del. 1991).*

This section is not applicable where the approval of the transaction did not take place at a formal board meeting or necessarily after full disclosure of all material facts. *Lewis v. Fuqua, 502 A.2d 962 (Del. Ch. 1985).*

Responsibility of controlling shareholder setting terms of self-dealing transaction. — Whenever a controlling shareholder sets out to exercise his or her power to set the terms of a self-dealing transaction and compel its effectuation, such shareholder assumes a new and significant responsibility of establishing to an independent body, whether a court in litigation, an independent committee of the board under subsection (a)(1) of this section, or disinterested ratifying shareholders on full and complete information, that the transaction is fully fair. Should a reviewing court be required to pass upon the fairness of such a transaction, the self-dealing fiduciary may be required to respond in damages or with another appropriate remedy if the transaction, despite any good faith on the fiduciary's part, is found to be not an entirely fair one to the corporation or to minority shareholders. *Merritt v. Colonial Foods, Inc., 505 A.2d 757 (Del. Ch. 1986).*

Dealings with corporation to be viewed with reasonable strictness. — Sound public policy requires the acts of corporate officers and directors in dealing with the corporation to be viewed with a reasonable strictness. *Bovay v. H.M. Byllesby & Co., 27 Del. Ch. 381, 38 A.2d 808 (1944).*

A transaction between the dominating director and his or her corporation is subject to strict scrutiny, and the director has the burden of showing that it was fair. *Johnston v. Greene, 35 Del. Ch. 479, 121 A.2d 919 (1956).*

Judicial scrutiny of transaction on basis of subsection (a)(1) not precluded. — Where disinterested director did not participate at board meeting in which it was resolved to exercise option in which the corporation would purchase assets of a second corporation in which many of the acquiring corporation's shareholders and officers held an interest, fact that the director was not interested in the transaction and approved of the acquisition of the option did not preclude judicial scrutiny of the transaction on the basis of paragraph (1) of subsection (a) of this section. *Fliegler v. Lawrence, 361 A.2d 218 (Del. 1976).*

Compliance with section shifts burden to plaintiff. — Compliance with the terms of this section does not restore to the board the presumption of the business judgment rule; it simply shifts the burden to plaintiff to prove unfairness. *Cinerama, Inc. v. Technicolor, Inc., 663 A.2d 1134 (Del. Ch. 1994), aff'd, 663 A.2d 1156 (Del. 1995).*

In determining the intrinsic fairness of 1 corporation's option to acquire a second corporation in view of the fact that certain persons owned stock and held positions in both corporations, the transaction would be examined as of the date on which shareholder approval was given. *Fliegler v. Lawrence, 361 A.2d 218 (Del. 1976).*

Standard of review of parent-subsidiary merger is entire fairness. — In a parent-subsidiary merger context, shareholder ratification operates only to shift the burden of persuasion, not to change the substantive standard of review which should be entire fairness; nor does the fact that the merger was negotiated by a committee of independent, disinterested directors alter the review standard. *Citron v. E.I. Du Pont de Nemours & Co., 584 A.2d 490 (Del. Ch. 1990).*

Business judgment rule applied over the entire fairness rule. — The shareholder pled facts from which it was reasonable to question the independence and disinterest, to overcome initially the business judgment rule presumption, of a majority of the 11-member corporate board; the entire fairness rule did not apply since the control group (comprising 2/3 of the majority voters) did not stand on both sides of the transaction. *Orman v. Cullman, 794 A.2d 5 (Del. Ch. 2002).*

The directors' responsibility in a sale of corporate control is to get the highest value reasonably attainable for the shareholders. *Mills Acquisition Co. v. Macmillan, Inc., 559 A.2d 1261 (Del. 1988).*

Merger not unfair. — Where the merger-targeted corporation was well-equipped to defend itself against any hostile effort to gain control over it, and the corporation selecting merger was an independent third party with no power to force the initiation of a deal, there was no basis for a finding that the transaction was unfairly initiated. *Cinerama, Inc. v. Technicolor, Inc., 663 A.2d 1156 (Del. 1995), aff'd, 663 A.2d 1156 (Del. 1995).*

Although reasonable reliance on expert counsel is a pertinent factor in evaluating whether corporate directors have met a standard of fairness in their dealings with respect to corporate powers, its existence is not outcome determinative of entire fairness. To hold otherwise would replace this court's role in determining entire fairness under 8 Del. C. § 144 with that of various experts hired to give advice to the directors in connection with the challenged transaction, creating a conflict between sections 141(e) and 144 of the Delaware General Corporation Law. *Valeant Pharms. Int'l v. Jerney, 921 A.2d 732; 2007 Del. Ch. LEXIS 31 (March 1, 2007).*

Disgorgement of bonus. — Because defendant has failed to show that the transaction was entirely fair, it is clear that he has no right to retain any of the $ 3 million bonus he received. As between defendant and the company, that payment must be rescinded, requiring him to disgorge the full amount. His liability in this regard will not be limited to the excess of what the court might conclude was a fair bonus. There is also no suggestion that the corporation has been made whole as a result of its settlements with the other defendants or that it would be unjustly enriched by return of his bonus. Thus, there is no inequity in requiring defendant to disgorge the payment he received. Nor will the court apportion responsibility to account for the fact that several of the settling directors signed joint tortfeasor releases since his disgorgement obligation stems from his receipt of the company's money, not from his participation in the decision to authorize the payment. Valeant Pharms. Int'l v. Jerney, 921 A.2d 732; 2007 Del. Ch. LEXIS 31 (March 1, 2007).

Corporations

DELAWARE CASE NOTES — UNREPORTED

The Delaware doctrine of ratification does not embrace a "blank check" theory. When uncoerced, fully informed, and disinterested stockholders approve a specific corporate action, the doctrine of ratification, in most situations, precludes claims for breach of fiduciary duty attacking that action. But the mere approval by stockholders of a request by directors for the authority to take action within broad parameters does not insulate all future action by the directors within those parameters from attack. Although the fact of stockholder approval might have some bearing on consideration of a fiduciary duty claim in that context, it does not, by itself, preclude such a claim. *Sample v. Morgan, 2007 Del. Ch. LEXIS 16 (Jan. 23, 2007).*

Good faith.—Under subsection (a) a transaction between a corporation and its directors or officers will be deemed valid if approved by a majority of the independent directors, assuming three criteria are met: 1) the approving directors were aware of the conflict inherent in the transaction; 2) the approving directors were aware of all facts material to the transaction; and 3) the approving directors acted in good faith. In other words, the inside transaction is valid where the independent and disinterested (loyal) directors understood that the transaction would benefit a colleague (factor 1), but they considered the transaction in light of the material facts (factor 2 — due care) mindful of their duty to act in the interests of the corporation, unswayed by loyalty to the interests of their colleagues or cronies (factor 3 — good faith). On the other hand, where the evidence shows that a majority of the independent directors were aware of the conflict and all material facts, in satisfaction of factors 1 and 2 (as well as the duties of loyalty and care), but acted to reward a colleague rather than for the benefit of the shareholders, the Court will find that the directors failed to act in good faith and, thus, that the transaction is voidable. In such a case, the duties of care and loyalty, as traditionally defined, might be insufficient to protect the equitable interests of the shareholders, and the matter would turn on the good faith of the directors. *In re Walt Disney Co. Derivative Litig., 2005 Del. Ch. LEXIS 113, No. 15452 (Aug. 9, 2005).*

Summary judgment was denied to a corporation seeking to rescind a sale of its subsidiary's stock in a transaction involving self-dealing by a principal of the seller and buyer, where there were several unresolved fact issues regarding the fairness of the transaction: (1) the effect of the principal's attempts to market the subsidiary and develop a corporate restructuring plan; (2) the sale price's exceeding an independent valuation of the subsidiary; and (3) several questions affecting the fairness of the price. *Summit Metals, Inc. v. Gray, 2002 U.S. Dist. LEXIS 15599 (Aug. 20, 2002).*

Equity financing. —Majority of the disinterested and independent directors of a corporation approved issuing stock, and acted with a good faith belief that equity financing represented the best method to finance a renovation plan; consequently, the board members validly exercised their business judgment in approving the transaction, did not breach any fiduciary duty to the operator or its stockholders, and met the requirements of 8

Del. C. § 144(a)(1). *Benihana of Tokyo, Inc. v. Benihana, Inc., 2005 Del. Ch. LEXIS 191 (Del. Ch. Dec. 8, 2005).*

Failure of ratification argument. — An essential aspect of our form of corporate law is the balance between law (in the form of statute and contract, including the contracts governing the internal affairs of corporations, such as charters and bylaws) and equity (in the form of concepts of fiduciary duty). Stockholders can entrust directors with broad legal authority precisely because they know that that authority must be exercised consistently with equitable principles of fiduciary duty. Therefore, the entrustment to the compensation committee of the authority to issue up to 200,000 shares to key employees under discretionary terms and conditions cannot reasonably be interpreted as a license for the committee and other directors making proposals to it to do whatever they wished, unconstrained by equity. Rather, it is best understood as a decision by the stockholders to give the directors broad legal authority and to rely upon the policing of equity to ensure that that authority would be utilized properly. For this reason alone, the directors' ratification argument fails. *Sample v. Morgan, 2007 Del. Ch. LEXIS 16 (Jan. 23, 2007).*

Another reason that the directors' ratification argument fails is that they have failed to demonstrate that they disclosed all the material facts relevant to the stockholders' consideration of the charter amendment and the incentive plan. As to this issue, the directors' ratification defense and the complaint's disclosure count intersect. One way that a defendant may obtain dismissal of a breach of fiduciary duty claim is by demonstrating that, even after giving the plaintiff all reasonable pleading-stage inferences, the complaint does not plead facts supporting an inference that the directors failed to disclose a material fact or otherwise misled the stockholders. In other words, in order for directors to access the safe harbor of ratification, they must meet an affirmative burden of demonstrating full and fair disclosure. One way of meeting that burden is to take on the onerous task of showing that a plaintiff's claim of a disclosure violation cannot withstand challenge in the plaintiff-friendly environment of a Rule 12(b)(6) motion. *Sample v. Morgan, 2007 Del. Ch. LEXIS 16 (Jan. 23, 2007).*

CASE NOTES — OTHER STATES

Colorado

The protections of the business judgment rule can only be claimed by disinterested directors whose conduct otherwise meets the tests of business judgment. Directors can neither appear on both sides of a transaction nor expect to derive any personal financial benefit from it in the sense of self-dealing, as opposed to a benefit which devolves upon the corporation or all stockholders generally. To invoke the protection of the business judgment rule, directors have a duty to inform themselves, before making a business decision, of all material information reasonably available to them. They must then act with requisite care in the discharge of their duties.

While the Delaware cases use a variety of terms to describe the applicable standard of care, under the business judgment rule director liability is predicated upon concepts of gross negligence. *Ajay Sports, Inc. v. Casazza, 1 P.3d 267 Colo. App. 2000).*

Illinois

Fairness test. — A majority shareholder, or a group of shareholders who combine to form a majority, has a fiduciary duty to the corporation and to its minority shareholders if the majority shareholder dominates the board of directors and controls the corporation. The circumstances of the challenged action or inaction dictate the scope of the fiduciary duty. If a shareholder plaintiff can prove that the majority shareholder has used his or her control over the corporation's board of directors to engage in self-dealing, Delaware law requires judgment of the self-dealing action of the dominated board by the entire fairness test. Self-dealing occurs when the majority shareholders cause the dominated corporation to act in such a way that the majority shareholders receive something from the corporation to the exclusion and detriment of the minority shareholders. The entire fairness test remains applicable even when an independent committee is utilized because the underlying factors that raise the specter of impropriety can never be eradicated completely and still require careful judicial scrutiny. This rule reflects the reality that in a transaction such as the sale of interest in a corporation, the controlling shareholder will continue to dominate the company regardless of the outcome of the transaction. *Feldheim v. Sims, 344 Ill. App. 3d 135, 800 N.E.2d 410, 279 Ill. Dec. 342 (2003).*

Any transaction between a corporation and one of its directors apparently need not be fully disclosed in order for it to be valid; however, the fairness of any such transaction to the corporation at the time of its approval must be affirmatively shown by the individual attempting to enforce the contract. The burden of proof rests on the interested parties when "fairness" alone can sustain the transaction. *Harris Trust & Savings Bank v. Joanna-Western Mills Company, 53 Ill. App. 3d 542, 368 N.E.2d 629, 11 Ill. Dec. 78 (1977).*

Ratification by silence. — Knowledge of the allegedly unauthorized agreement is a requisite before any ratification by silence may be inferred. *Harris Trust & Savings Bank v. Joanna-Western Mills Company, 53 Ill. App. 3d 542, 368 N.E.2d 629, 11 Ill. Dec. 78 (1977).*

Implied ratification of a previously unauthorized act may result from (1) accepting and retaining the benefits of the act or contract, (2) silence or acquiescence, or (3) other affirmative acts showing an adoption of the act or contract. *Harris Trust & Savings Bank v. Joanna-Western Mills Company, 53 Ill. App. 3d 542, 368 N.E.2d 629, 11 Ill. Dec. 78 (1977).*

Ratification may not be inferred from acts readily explainable without being accompanied by an intention to ratify. *Harris Trust & Savings Bank v. Joanna-Western Mills Company, 53 Ill. App. 3d 542, 368 N.E.2d 629, 11 Ill. Dec. 78 (1977).*

Massachusetts

Directors are not interested or lacking in independence merely because they share outside professional associations or relationships. *In re Sonus Networks, Inc., 18 Mass. L. Rep. 295 (Super. 2004).*

The purpose of the distinction between interested and disinterested directors is to ensure that the directors voting on a plaintiff's demand can exercise their business judgment in the best interests of the corporation, free from significant contrary personal interests and apart from the domination and control of those who are alleged to have participated in wrongdoing. *In re PolyMedica Corp. Shareholder Derivative Litigation, 15 Mass. L. Rep. 115, 2002 Mass. Super. LEXIS 271 (2002).*

Entire fairness test. — Delaware law protects minority shareholders by reviewing those transactions where a controlling shareholder benefits from a transaction in a way that goes beyond the benefits accorded to other stockholders. This analysis, referred to as the "entire fairness test," requires the controlling shareholder(s) to prove the "entire fairness" of such a transaction. The "entire fairness" doctrine is designed to deal with those situations where a controlling shareholder has his or her own interest in the outcome of a transaction that might cloud his or her otherwise objective business judgment. *Olsen v. Seifert, 9 Mass. L. Rep. 268 (Super. 1998).*

New York

A director is considered interested where he or she will receive a personal financial benefit from a transaction that is not equally shared by the stockholders. Directorial interest also exists where a corporate decision will have a materially detrimental impact on a director, but not on the corporation and the stockholders. In such circumstances, a director cannot be expected to exercise his or her independent business judgment without being influenced by the adverse personal consequences resulting from the decision. Directors who are sued for failure to oversee subordinates have a disabling interest when the potential for liability is not a mere threat but instead may rise to a substantial likelihood. *Simon v. Becherer, 7 A.D.3d 66, 775 N.Y.S.2d 313 (2004).*

Presumption of business judgment rule applicability. — Approval of a transaction by a majority of independent, disinterested directors almost always bolsters a presumption that the business judgment rule attaches to transactions approved by a board of directors that are later attacked on grounds of lack of due care. In such cases, a heavy burden falls on a plaintiff to avoid presuit demand upon directors of a corporation to pursue a derivative complaint. *Wilson v. Tully, 243 A.D.2d 229, 676 N.Y.S.2d 531 (1998).*

A director is independent if that director is capable of making decisions for the corporation based on the merits of the subject rather than extraneous considerations or influences. *Wilson v. Tully, 243 A.D.2d 229, 676 N.Y.S.2d 531 (1998).*

Ohio

Interested, independent, informed standards. — Under Delaware law, a director is interested if he or she appears on both sides of a transaction or he or she has or expects to derive personal financial benefit not equally received by the stockholders. A director is independent if his or her decision is based on the corporate merits of the subject before the board rather than extraneous considerations or influences. A director is not independent when he or she is dominated by or beholden to another person through personal or other relationships. A director is informed if he or she makes a reasonable effort to become familiar with the relevant and reasonably available facts prior to making a business judgment. *Gries Sports*

Enterprises, Inc. v. Cleveland Browns Football Co., Inc., 26 Ohio St. 3d 15, 496 N.E.2d 959 (1986).

Duty of fair dealing. — Under Delaware law, which governs the conduct of officers of corporations incorporated in Delaware, the duty of fair dealing requires that officers disclose all material information relevant to corporate decisions from which they may derive a personal benefit. Liability attaches for a breach of fiduciary duty regardless of any actual intent to defraud as long as the officer puts him- or herself in a position of conflicting loyalties. *Allied Paper Inc. v. H.M. Holdings, Inc., 86 Ohio App. 3d 8, 619 N.E.2d 1121 (1993).*

Tennessee

Delaware courts distinguish between derivative and direct suits on the basis of injury rather than duty.

A shareholder can maintain a direct action only when he or she sustains a "special injury." That is, an injury distinct from that suffered by other shareholders or a wrong involving a contractual right of a shareholder. Wrongs involving contractual rights of a shareholder are such rights as the right to vote or the right of the majority shareholder to exert control over rights which exists independent of corporation rights. Mismanagement which depresses the value of stock is a wrong to the corporation, i.e., the stockholders collectively, to be enforced by a derivative action. *Bayberry Associates v. Jones, 783 S.W.2d 553 (Tenn. 1990).*

CASE NOTES — FEDERAL

First Circuit

A director is interested if he or she will be materially affected, either to his or her benefit or detriment, by a decision of the board, in a manner not shared by the corporation and the stockholders. In such circumstances, a director cannot be expected to exercise his or her independent business judgment without being influenced by the adverse personal consequences resulting from the decision. The "mere threat" of personal liability is insufficient to challenge the disinterestedness of a director. A plaintiff must articulate particularized facts showing that a director faces "a substantial likelihood" of liability. *Caviness v. Evans, 2005 U.S. Dist. LEXIS 17350 (D.Mass. 2005).*

Independence means that a director's decision is based on the corporate merits of the subject before the board rather than extraneous considerations or influences. Allegations of mere personal friendship or a mere outside business relationship, standing alone, are insufficient to raise a reasonable doubt about a director's independence. *Caviness v. Evans, 2005 U.S. Dist. LEXIS 17350 (D.Mass. 2005).*

Demand futility. — If an action is derivative in nature, the shareholders must first make a demand on the corporate officers or directors to bring the suit on behalf of the corporation. This demand requirement can only be excused where facts are alleged with particularity which create a reasonable doubt that the directors' action was entitled to the protections of the business judgment rule. The business judgment rule is a presumption that in making a business decision the directors of a corporation acted on an informed basis, in good faith, and in the honest belief that the action taken was in the best interests of the company. Absent an abuse of discretion, that judgment will be respected by the courts. The burden is on the party challenging the decision to establish facts rebutting the presumption. *Niehoff v. Maynard, 2000 U.S. Dist. LEXIS 22009 (D.R.I. 2000).*

Under *Aronson*, the question of independence flows from an analysis of the factual allegations pertaining to the influences upon the directors' performance of their duties generally, and more specifically in respect to the challenged transaction. In other words, is the board incapable, due to domination or control, of objectively evaluating a demand, if made, that the board assert the corporation's claims that are raised by plaintiffs? A majority of the board must be dependent to excuse demand as futile. *Landy v. D'Alessandro, 316 F. Supp. 2d 49 (D.Mass. 2004).*

A court employs a standard other than *Aronson* when determining whether plaintiff should have made demand on the board before bringing a derivative suit with respect to these types of decisions or transactions. Under *Rales*, a court must determine whether or not the particularized factual allegations of a derivative stockholder complaint create a reasonable doubt that, as of the time the complaint is filed, the board of directors could have properly exercised its independent and disinterested business judgment in responding to a demand. If the derivative plaintiff satisfies this burden, then demand will be excused as futile. *Landy v. D'Alessandro, 316 F. Supp. 2d 49 (D.Mass. 2004).*

The court in *Aronson* has articulated the basic principle of board interest: from the standpoint of interest, this means that directors can neither appear on both sides of a transaction nor expect to derive any personal financial benefit from it in the sense of self-dealing, as opposed to a benefit which devolves upon the corporation or all stockholders generally. *Landy v. D'Alessandro, 316 F. Supp. 2d 49 (D.Mass. 2004).*

Self-compensation. — Delaware courts have stated explicitly that a director is interested when the challenged transaction involves self-compensation. The Delaware Supreme Court recently concluded the following: like any other interested transaction, directorial self-compensation decisions lie outside the business judgment rule's presumptive protection. *Landy v. D'Alessandro, 316 F. Supp. 2d 49 (D.Mass. 2004).*

A self-dealing transaction may be approved by the consent of a majority of fully informed and disinterested directors, by the consent of fully informed shareholders, or by a showing that the contract or transaction is fair to the corporation as of the time it is authorized, approved, or ratified, by the board of directors, a committee or the shareholders. *Liston v. Gottsegen, 348 F.3d 294 (1st Cir. 2003).*

Second Circuit

In general. — Delaware law does not require the approval of disinterested directors before the full board of directors takes action on behalf of a corporation. Del. Code Ann. tit. 8, § 144(a) provides that a corporate act taken by a board which includes interested directors is valid if the transaction is fair as to the corporation as of the time it is authorized. *THC Holdings Corp. v. Tishman, 1996 U.S. Dist. LEXIS 7562 (S.D.N.Y. 1996).*

Interest analysis. — The Delaware Supreme Court has defined "interest" under a business judgment rule analysis as meaning that directors can neither appear on both sides of a transaction nor expect to derive any personal financial benefit from it in the sense of self-dealing, as opposed to a benefit which devolves upon the corporation or all stockholders generally. Further, the benefit to a director must be material, which means that it must be significant enough, in the context of the director's economic circumstances, as to have made it improbable that the director could perform his or her fiduciary duties to the shareholders without being influenced by his or her overriding personal interest. *Roselink Investors, L.L.C. v. Shenkman, 2004 U.S. Dist. LEXIS 6905 (S.D.N.Y. 2004).*

A director is interested whenever divided loyalties are present, or where the director stands to receive a personal benefit from the transaction not equally shared by the shareholders. *Halpert Enters. v. Harrison, 362 F. Supp. 2d 426 (S.D.N.Y. 2005).*

Independence analysis. — The Delaware Supreme Court has defined "independent" under a business judgment rule analysis as meaning that a director's decision is based on the corporate merits of the subject before the board rather than extraneous considerations or influences. In assessing director independence, Delaware courts apply a subjective "actual person" standard to determine whether a given director was likely to be affected in the same or similar circumstances. There must be coupled with the allegations of control such facts as would demonstrate that through personal or other relationships the directors are beholden to the controlling person. To be disqualifying, the nature of the director interest must be substantial and not merely incidental. If a plaintiff successfully demonstrates facts sufficient to rebut the business judgment rule presumption, then the burden of proof shifts to the defendant directors to establish the entire fairness of the challenged transaction. *Roselink Investors, L.L.C. v. Shenkman, 2004 U.S. Dist. LEXIS 6905 (S.D.N.Y. 2004).*

A director is independent when his decision is based on the corporate merits of the subject before the board rather than extraneous considerations or influences. *Halpert Enters. v. Harrison, 362 F. Supp. 2d 426 (S.D.N.Y. 2005).*

Independence means that a director's decision is based on the corporate merits of the subject before the board rather than extraneous considerations or influences. *Official Committee of the Unsecured Creditors v. Investcorp, S.A., 137 F. Supp. 2d 502 (S.D.N.Y 2001).*

As to the first *Aronson* inquiry, the Court reviews the factual allegations of the complaint to determine whether they create a reasonable doubt as to the disinterestedness and independence of the directors at the time the complaint was filed. In order to raise a reasonable doubt in this respect, plaintiff must allege that the directors expected a personal benefit from the challenged transaction or appeared on both sides of the transaction, showing divided loyalties. *Ryan v. Aetna Life Ins. Co., 765 F. Supp. 133 (S.D.N.Y. 1991).*

To establish lack of independence, a plaintiff meets his or her burden by showing that the directors are either beholden to the controlling shareholder or so under its influence that their discretion is sterilized. *In re Trump Hotels Shareholder Derivative Litig., 2000 U.S. Dist. LEXIS 13550 (S.D.N.Y. 2000).*

The question of independence flows from an analysis of the factual allegations pertaining to the influences upon corporate directors' performance of their duties generally, and more specifically in respect to the challenged transaction. *In re Trump Hotels Shareholder Derivative Litig., 2000 U.S. Dist. LEXIS 13550 (S.D.N.Y. 2000).*

Independence means that a director's decision is based on the corporate merits of the subject before the board rather than extraneous considerations or influences. *In re Trump Hotels Shareholder Derivative Litig., 2000 U.S. Dist. LEXIS 13550 (S.D.N.Y. 2000).*

The business judgment rule applies even where a majority of a board of directors has a financial interest in a transaction, providing that such transaction was approved by the fully informed disinterested directors. *Caruso v. Metex Corp., 1992 U.S. Dist. LEXIS 14556 (E.D.N.Y. 1992).*

The protections of the business judgment rule can only be claimed by disinterested directors whose conduct otherwise meets the test of business judgment and that the directors thus cannot appear on both sides of the transaction nor expect to derive any personal financial benefit from it. Essentially, the liability is based upon concepts of gross negligence, and the business judgment rule technically speaking has no role where directors have either abdicated their functions, or absent a conscience decision, failed to act. *In re Oxford Health Plans, Inc. Sec. Litig., 192 F.R.D. 111 (S.D.N.Y. 2000).*

Bolstering presumption of attachment of business judgment rule to transaction. — Approval of a transaction by a majority of independent, disinterested directors almost always bolsters a presumption that the business judgment rule attaches to transactions approved by a board of directors that are later attacked on grounds of procedural due care. In such cases, a heavy burden falls on a plaintiff to avoid presuit demand. *Ryan v. Aetna Life Ins. Co., 765 F. Supp. 133 (S.D.N.Y. 1991).*

Overcoming the powerful presumptions of the business judgment rule presents a heavy burden of establishing that: (1) the directors were not disinterested and independent; and that (2) the challenged transaction was not the product of a valid exercise of business judgment. Moreover, the defendants can be held personally liable only if there is evidence of their bad faith, intentional misconduct, or knowing violation of the law. *Yeung Chan v. Diamond, 2005 U.S. Dist. LEXIS 6939 (S.D.N.Y. 2005).*

Demand requirement. — Delaware law holds that demand must be made upon the board if the disputed transaction has been approved by a majority consisting of the disinterested directors. *Ryan v. Aetna Life Ins. Co., 765 F. Supp. 133 (S.D.N.Y. 1991).*

Under Delaware law, failure to make a demand upon the board will be excused only if such a demand would be futile. To plead demand futility adequately, a plaintiff must allege with particularity facts creating a reasonable doubt that: (1) the directors are disinterested and independent or (2) the challenged transaction was otherwise the product of a valid exercise of business judgment. *Ryan v. Aetna Life Ins. Co., 765 F. Supp. 133 (S.D.N.Y. 1991).*

In determining whether making a demand on a board of directors would be futile, a court must determine whether, under the particularized facts alleged, a reasonable doubt is created that: (1) the directors are disinterested and independent or (2) the challenged transaction was otherwise the product of a valid exercise of business judgment. The test is disjunctive, offering alternative avenues for pleading that it would be futile to make a demand on the board that the corporation bring the action itself. *Halpert Enters. v. Harrison, 362 F. Supp. 2d 426 (S.D.N.Y. 2005).*

Under the well-settled rule, demand will be excused if a reasonable doubt is created that: (1) the directors were disinterested and independent or; (2) the challenged transaction was otherwise the product of a valid exercise of business judgment. *In re Trump Hotels Shareholder Derivative Litig., 2000 U.S. Dist. LEXIS 13550 (S.D.N.Y. 2000).*

To establish demand futility based on lack of independence, plaintiffs must raise a reasonable doubt that a majority of the directors were interested or controlled. *In re Trump Hotels Shareholder Derivative Litig., 2000 U.S. Dist. LEXIS 13550 (S.D.N.Y. 2000).*

The issues of pre-suit demand futility rest upon the allegations of the complaint and the test of futility has long been recognized as whether the board of directors, at the time of the filing of the suit, could have impartially considered and acted upon the demand. To establish demand futility in a case involving action, the plaintiff need not allege that the challenged transaction could never be deemed a product of business judgment. *In re Oxford Health Plans, Inc. Sec. Litig., 192 F.R.D. 111 (S.D.N.Y. 2000).*

Where board of director interest, approval or acquiescence in the wrongdoing exists, the pre-suit demand is excused as futile, and where officers and directors are under an influence which sterilizes their discretion, they cannot be considered proper persons to conduct litigation on behalf of the corporation, and here again pre-suit demand would be futile. *In re Oxford Health Plans, Inc. Sec. Litig., 192 F.R.D. 111 (S.D.N.Y. 2000).*

In determining pre-suit demand futility, the court in the proper exercise of its discretion must decide whether under the particularized facts alleged a reasonable doubt is created that: (1) the board of directors are disinterested and independent; and (2) the challenged transaction was otherwise the product of a valid exercise of business judgment. *In re Oxford Health Plans, Inc. Sec. Litig., 192 F.R.D. 111 (S.D.N.Y. 2000).*

Under Delaware law, the demand requirement is predicated upon the presumption that directors manage the corporation with the good-faith belief that their actions are in the best interest of the company. Demand is excused only when the facts cast doubt on this presumption such that the conduct at issue was not approved by a majority consisting of the disinterested directors. *Langner v. Brown, 913 F. Supp. 260 (S.D.N.Y. 1996).*

In determining the sufficiency of a demand futility claim, the trial court considers: (1) whether threshold presumptions of director disinterest or independence are rebutted by well-pleaded facts; and if not, (2) whether the complaint pleads particularized facts sufficient to create a reasonable doubt that the challenged transaction was the product of a valid exercise of business judgment. Mere director approval of a transaction, without particularized facts establishing a breach of fiduciary duty claim or a lack of independence or disinterestedness of a majority of the directors, is insufficient to excuse demand. The burden is on the plaintiff to show particularized facts demonstrating a reasonable doubt of business judgment protection. It is only when the alleged facts, considered as true, would demonstrate that a majority of the directors who would have received the demand letter are "interested" in the challenged transaction or "lack independence" because of domination by an interested party or otherwise, that demand is excused. *Langner v. Brown, 913 F. Supp. 260 (S.D.N.Y. 1996).*

Authority of independent committee. — Because Delaware law empowers a board of directors to delegate all of its authority to a committee, a properly authorized independent committee has the authority, to the extent provided in the board's resolution, to seek the termination of litigation charging fellow directors with wrongdoing. Moreover, even if a majority of directors are interested in the transactions at issue, a board can still delegate its authority to a committee of disinterested directors. *Stein v. Bailey, 531 F. Supp. 684 (S.D.N.Y. 1982).*

Under Delaware law, a decision such as whether to proceed with a derivative action may be approved in the exercise of independent business judgment by the independent directors. The corporation may choose to establish an independent committee to determine whether to prosecute a derivative action. *Siegal v. Merrick, 84 F.R.D. 106 (S.D.N.Y. 1979).*

Nondisclosure charter provision not prohibited. — Delaware does not prohibit a provision in the corporation's charter stated that interested directors did not have to disclose their interest or refrain from participation in settlement negotiations and agreements. *Piccard v. Sperry Corp., 48 F. Supp. 465 (S.D.N.Y. 1943).*

Reasonable response to threat. — To determine whether a board of directors has violated its fiduciary duty to its shareholders in enacting or taking actions under a challenged rights plan, the court must examine the motivations of the board as it made its decisions, from the initiation of the plan to any actions taken under it. It must consider whether the board made an informed decision based on reasonable investigation, considered on a standard of gross negligence, or perhaps of reasonable diligence. Also, it must evaluate the reasonableness of the board's actions as a response to any given threats it perceives to the company. The approval of any defensive measures by a board composed of a majority of outside independent directors acting on good faith and upon reasonable investigation, materially enhances the proof that the board has acted reasonably in response to the threat posed. If the directors succeed in making this showing, the burden shifts back to the plaintiffs, who have the ultimate burden of persuasion to show a breach of the directors' fiduciary duties. *CRTF Corp. v. Federated Dep't Stores, 1988 U.S. Dist. LEXIS 2775 (S.D.N.Y. 1988).*

Derivative suit pleading requirements. — As the mere threat of personal liability is insufficient to challenge either the independence or disinterestedness of directors, a plaintiff in a derivative suit must allege particular facts giving rise to a substantial likelihood of director liability. *Halpert Enters. v. Harrison, 362 F. Supp. 2d 426 (S.D.N.Y. 2005).*

Directors' decisions will be respected by courts unless the directors are interested or lack independence relative to the decision, do not act in good faith, act in a manner that cannot be attributed to a rational business purpose or reach their decision by a grossly negligent process that includes the failure to consider all material facts reasonably available. *Kidd v. Swink, 2002 U.S. Dist. LEXIS 20287 (S.D.N.Y. 2002).*

Working control. — From a practical perspective, the confluence of voting control with directorial and official decision making authority is itself quite consistent with control of the board. Delaware courts have found substantial minority interests, ranging from 20% to 40% sufficient to grant the holder working control. *In re Trump Hotels Shareholder Derivative Litig., 2000 U.S. Dist. LEXIS 13550 (S.D.N.Y. 2000).*

The ability of controlling officers to affect the compensation or influence of a director is one factor that may support a finding of reasonable doubt. *In re Trump Hotels Shareholder Derivative Litig., 2000 U.S. Dist. LEXIS 13550 (S.D.N.Y. 2000).*

Extinguishment of claim. — A vote by the fully informed shareholders ratifies a challenged transaction and extinguishes any claim that a disinterested director breached his or her duty of care in connection with it. *In re Trump Hotels Shareholder Derivative Litig., 2000 U.S. Dist. LEXIS 13550 (S.D.N.Y. 2000).*

The receipt of directors' fees does not constitute a disqualifying interest for the purposes of the demand requirement. *Langner v. Brown, 913 F. Supp. 260 (S.D.N.Y. 1996).*

Third Circuit

Interested. — In the context of a shareholder's derivative lawsuit and whether a demand on a board of directors is excused, an interested director is one who receives a financial benefit from a corporate transaction. *Shaev v. Saper, 320 F.3d 373 (3d Cir. 2003).*

Independent and without self-interest. — The rule that requires a director's undivided and unselfish loyalty toward the corporation and its shareholders demands that there be no conflict between the director's duties and self-interest. A director must act independently and without self-interest. A director acts independently and without self-interest only when the director's decision is based entirely on the corporate merits of a transaction and is not influenced by personal or extraneous considerations. A director who receives a substantial benefit from supporting a transaction cannot be objectively viewed as disinterested or independent. Without the guidance of a truly independent judgment, self-interested directors cannot with confidence know the right course in order to pursue it. In all events, the law will accord scant weight to the subjective judgment of an interested director concerning the fairness of transactions that benefit him. *Delta Star, Inc. v. Patton, 76 F. Supp. 2d 617 (W.D.Pa. 1999).*

Reasonable doubt of director's independence. — In Delaware, neither mere personal friendships alone, nor mere outside business relationships alone, are sufficient to raise a reasonable doubt regarding a director's independence for purposes of excusing pre-suit demand in a derivative action. *Amalgamated Bank v. Yost, 2005 U.S. Dist. LEXIS 1280 (E.D.Pa. 2005).*

Transaction analysis. — A majority of the board must be "interested", i.e., on both sides of a transaction or receiving personal financial benefit from the transaction which did not devolve on the shareholders generally. In addition, the board is not disinterested where it has divided loyalties. Conclusory allegations are insufficient to create the requisite reasonable doubt. Nor can a plaintiff employ a "bootstrap" argument that demand is excused by alleging that the directors would otherwise have to sue themselves to create the requisite reasonable doubt. Moreover, mere approval of the allegedly injurious transaction does not incapacitate a board for purposes of considering a demand under demand futility analysis. *Abrams v. Koether, 1992 U.S. Dist. LEXIS 16295 (D.N.J. 1992).*

When an action by a board of directors of a Delaware corporation is challenged, the courts determine whether a conflict of interest of board members has deprived stockholders of a neutral decisionmaking body. The focus is on whether a majority of the corporation's board of directors was neutral and independent in passing on the proposed corporate action. *In re Cendant Corp. Derivative Action Litigation, 189 F.R.D. 117 (D.N.J. 1999).*

Under the *Cinerama* formulation for determining if the interest of one or more directors was material to the independence of the entire board, a complaint fails to rebut the business judgment rule unless it alleges facts from which one could infer that the director defendants, through their dominance over the other board members, so infected or affected the deliberative process of the board as to disarm the board of its presumption of regularity and

Corporations

respect. *In re Cendant Corp. Derivative Action Litigation, 189 F.R.D. 117 (D.N.J. 1999).*

Under Delaware law, the independence of the majority of the board must be challenged to strip the individual directors of the business judgment presumption. *In re Cendant Corp. Derivative Action Litigation, 189 F.R.D. 117 (D.N.J. 1999).*

Demand futility analysis. — In determining the sufficiency of a complaint to withstand demand futility, the trial court is confronted with two questions: whether threshold presumptions of director disinterest or independence are rebutted by well-pleaded facts; and, if not, whether the complaint pleads particularized facts sufficient to create a reasonable doubt that the challenged transaction was the product of a valid exercise of business judgment. The entire review is factual in nature, and in order for demand to be excused, the trial court must be satisfied that a plaintiff has alleged facts with particularity which, taken as true, support a reasonable doubt as to a director's interest or independence or that the challenged transaction was the product of a valid exercise of business judgment. In its determination, the trial court must not rely on any one factor but must examine the totality of the circumstances and consider all of the relevant factors. *In re Cendant Corp. Derivative Action Litigation, 189 F.R.D. 117 (D.N.J. 1999).*

With regard to demand futility in a shareholder's derivative action, the court reviews the factual allegations of the complaint to determine whether they create a reasonable doubt as to the disinterestedness and independence of the directors at the time the complaint was filed. If the transaction at issue is an "interested" director transaction, such that the business judgment rule is inapplicable to the board majority approving the transaction, then the inquiry ceases. Directorial interest exists whenever divided loyalties are present, or where the director stands to receive a personal benefit from the transaction not equally shared by the shareholders. A director is also interested when a corporate decision will have a materially detrimental impact on a director. Directorial independence requires a director's decision to be based on the corporate merits of the subject before the board rather than extraneous considerations or influences. *In re Cendant Corp. Derivative Action Litigation, 189 F.R.D. 117 (D.N.J. 1999).*

Pertaining to a shareholder derivative suit brought under Delaware law, the two parts of the demand futility test are two alternative hurdles, either of which a derivative shareholder complaint must overcome to successfully withstand a Fed. R. Civ. P. 23.1 motion. Under the first part of the test, the court reviews the factual allegations of the complaint to determine whether they create a reasonable doubt as to the disinterestedness and independence of the directors at the time the complaint was filed. Directoral interest exists whenever divided loyalties are present, or where the director stands to receive a personal financial benefit from the transaction not equally shared by the shareholders. Directoral independence means that a director's decision is based on the corporate merits of the subject before the board rather

than extraneous considerations or influences. *Coyer v. Hemmer, 901 F. Supp. 872 (D.N.J. 1995).*

Pertaining to a shareholder derivative suit brought under Delaware law, it is not sufficient to simply allege domination and control of the directors by another person. Nor is it sufficient to allege that a director a had a financial interest in the transaction. Rather, in order to establish demand futility under the first part of the applicable test: the stockholder must show, through the pleading of particularized facts, that a majority of the board have a financial interest in the transaction or are so dominated by the proponent of the transaction that their discretion is sterilized. *Coyer v. Hemmer, 901 F. Supp. 872 (D.N.J. 1995).*

Under Delaware law, derivative plaintiffs must satisfy one of two tests to establish that demand is excused. When a plaintiff's claims arise from an affirmative business decision made by a corporation's board of directors, courts apply the two-prong *Aronson* test laid. Under the *Aronson* test, courts will excuse pre-suit demand if the complaint alleges, with particularity, sufficient facts to create a reasonable doubt that (1) the majority of the directors are disinterested and independent, or (2) the challenged transaction is otherwise the product of the directors' valid exercise of business judgment. If either prong is satisfied, demand is excused. *Amalgamated Bank v. Yost, 2005 U.S. Dist. LEXIS 1280 (E.D.Pa. 2005).*

Under the first prong of Delaware's *Aronson*'s test, a derivative plaintiff seeking to excuse demand must use particularized facts to create a reasonable doubt that the directors are disinterested and independent. To satisfy its burden, a plaintiff must show that at least half of the board was either interested or not independent. Directors are interested when they appear on both sides of a challenged transaction or expect to derive a personal financial benefit from a transaction that is not shared by stockholders generally. *Amalgamated Bank v. Yost, 2005 U.S. Dist. LEXIS 1280 (E.D.Pa. 2005).*

When a derivative plaintiff does not challenge an affirmative business decision, Delaware courts employ the modified *Rales* test. Under the *Rales* test, courts will excuse pre-suit demand if the complaint makes particularized factual allegations that create a reasonable doubt that the board of directors could have properly exercised its independent and disinterested business judgment in response to a demand. *Amalgamated Bank v. Yost, 2005 U.S. Dist. LEXIS 1280 (E.D.Pa. 2005).*

Under Delaware's *Rales* test, a court must determine whether the complaint creates a reasonable doubt that the board of directors could have properly exercised its independent and disinterested business judgment in responding to a demand. The mere threat of personal liability is insufficient to challenge the independence or disinterestedness of directors. Rather, plaintiff must show that directors face a sufficiently substantial threat of personal liability to compromise their ability to act impartially on a demand. *Amalgamated Bank v. Yost, 2005 U.S. Dist. LEXIS 1280 (E.D.Pa. 2005).*

Under Delaware law, in the context of a shareholder's derivative lawsuit, a demand on a board of directors is excused where half of the members of an even numbered board are alleged to be interested or lack independence. *Shaev v. Saper, 320 F.3d 373 (3d Cir. 2003).*

Presumption of control. — Pertaining to Delaware's demand futility test, control will not be presumed merely because one is a majority shareholder. It is not enough to charge that a director was nominated by or elected at the behest of those controlling the outcome of a corporate election. It is the care, attention, and sense of individual responsibility to the performance of one's duties, not the method of election, that generally touches upon independence. *Coyer v. Hemmer, 901 F. Supp. 872 (D.N.J. 1995).*

Removing taint of self-dealing. — Self-dealing transactions by corporate officers or directors are not strictly prohibited by Delaware law. Instead, Delaware law provides specific procedures that may be employed by a corporate officer or director to remove the taint that any such transaction may possess solely by reason of its self-interested character. To remove the taint of a self-dealing transaction, a corporate officer or director must establish to an independent body, whether it be a court in litigation, an independent committee of the board of directors, or a group of disinterested ratifying shareholders on full and complete information, that the transaction is fully fair. *Delta Star, Inc. v. Patton, 76 F. Supp. 2d 617 (W.D.Pa. 1999).*

Remedies in self-dealing actions. — EcovA self-dealing fiduciary may be required to respond in damages or with any other appropriate remedy if a transaction is found to be not an entirely fair one to the corporation or its shareholders. Delaware courts now recognize a right to recover under a theory of quantum meruit where an officer or director has fixed his own compensation. The burden of establishing the reasonableness of the compensation received in connection with a self-dealing transaction, and thus the entitlement to a recovery under the doctrine of quantum meruit, is on the recipient. *Delta Star, Inc. v. Patton, 76 F. Supp. 2d 617 (W.D.Pa. 1999).*

Fourth Circuit

An individual is "interested" in a sale transaction if he or she serves as a director, or shareholder, of both the selling and purchasing corporations. *Williams v. 5300 Columbia Pike Corp., 891 F. Supp. 1169 (E.D.Va. 1995).*

The business judgment rule is only available when the directors neither appear on both sides of a transaction nor expect to derive any personal financial benefit from it in the sense of self-dealing, as opposed to a benefit which devolves upon the corporation or all stockholders generally. *Williams v. 5300 Columbia Pike Corp., 901 F. Supp. 208 (E.D.Va. 1995).*

Demand excused tests. — It is a cardinal precept of the Delaware General Corporation Law that directors, rather than shareholders, manage the business and affairs of the corporation. Because by its very nature the derivative action impinges upon the managerial freedom of directors, strict demand requirements are imposed. In situations where derivative plaintiffs are attacking an affirmative business decision made by the board, a court of chancery in the proper exercise of its discretion must decide whether, under the particularized facts alleged, a reasonable doubt is created that: (1) the directors are disinterested and independent and (2) the challenged transaction was otherwise the product of a valid exercise of business judgment. Further, a derivative plaintiff must establish that a majority of the board is interested or lacks independence in order to excuse demand on that ground. *In re Mut. Funds Investent Litigation, 2005 U.S. Dist. LEXIS 18082 (D.Md. 2005).*

The test for determining whether demand is excused in a derivative action is disjunctive, because demand is excused if a plaintiff has pleaded facts raising a reasonable doubt either that a majority of the members of the board are not disinterested or independent, or that the challenged decision was not otherwise a product of a valid exercise of business judgment. *In re Mut. Funds Investent Litigation, 2005 U.S. Dist. LEXIS 18082 (D.Md. 2005).*

In cases where derivative plaintiffs are not challenging an affirmative decision made by the present board, a modified test for whether demand is excused applies to cases in which the board is charged with a failure of oversight. Under the modified test, a court is to determine (in addition to making an appropriate inquiry under the first prong of the test) whether or not the particularized factual allegations of a derivative stockholder complaint create a reasonable doubt that, as of the time the complaint is filed, the board of directors could have properly exercised its independent and disinterested business judgment in responding to a demand. *In re Mut. Funds Investent Litigation, 2005 U.S. Dist. LEXIS 18082 (D.Md. 2005).*

Fairness of stock purchase price. — Delaware law provides that in general the plaintiff bears the burden of proof as to the fairness or unfairness of the purchase price of stock shares and must overcome the "business judgment" rule, a rule that mandates substantial judicial deference to the decisions of a board of directors. But the burden shifts to the defendant directors where the plaintiff establishes that there is a conflict of interest between the directors and the shareholders. More specifically, a conflict of interest between the directors and the shareholders serves to shift to the defendant directors the burden of establishing the "intrinsic fairness" of the transaction, including the fairness of the price. *Williams v. 5300 Columbia Pike Corp., 901 F. Supp. 208 (E.D.Va. 1995).*

Fifth Circuit

A director is "interested" in a transaction if either that transaction will provide the director with a personal financial benefit not equally shared by other shareholders or that the director stands on both sides of the transaction. *King v. Douglass, 973 F. Supp. 707 (S.D.Tex. 1996).*

A director is "independent" if he or she is capable of making decisions based on the merits of the subject rather than the extraneous considerations or influences. *King v. Douglass, 973 F. Supp. 707 (S.D.Tex. 1996).*

Disinterested director. — In a derivative action, Delaware courts often apply the business judgment rule, a rebuttable presumption that directors do not breach their duty of care. Only a disinterested corporate director can assert the business judgment rule as a defense to a derivative action. A disinterested director is a director who has not appeared on both sides of a business transaction and who has not received a personal financial benefit from the transaction. *H.I.G. P-Xi Holding, Inc., 2001 U.S. Dist. LEXIS 5074 (E.D.La. 2001).*

Failure to act. — In the context of Fed. R. Civ. P. 23.1, under Delaware law, the *Rales* test is employed where directors are sued because they have failed to do something; demand should not be excused automatically in the absence of allegations demonstrating why the board is incapable of considering a demand. The court must consider whether the particularized factual allegations of a derivative stockholder complaint create a reasonable doubt that, as of the time the complaint is filed, the board of directors could have properly exercised its independent and disinterested business judgment in responding to a demand. To create a doubt that the board of directors could exercise its independent and disinterested business judgment, the plaintiff would need to allege with particularity facts that create a reasonable doubt that the board is capable of acting free from personal financial interest and improper extraneous influences. *Spector v. Sidhu, 2004 U.S. Dist. LEXIS 876 (N.D.Tex. 2004).*

Enhanced duty in control contests. — Ordinarily, the business judgment rule provides a presumption that in making a business decision the directors of a corporation acted only after they were appropriately informed and after they had honestly determined that the action taken was in the best interests of the company. Because contests for control have an omnipresent specter that a board may be acting primarily in its own interests, the directors have an enhanced duty to prove that they had reasonable grounds for believing that a danger to corporate policy and effectiveness existed because of another person's stock ownership. *Southdown, Inc. v. Moore McCormack Resources, Inc., 686 F. Supp. 595 (S.D.Tex. 1988).*

Sixth Circuit

A director is considered interested when, for example, he or she will receive a personal financial benefit from a transaction that is not equally shared by the stockholders, or when a corporate decision will have a materially detrimental impact on a director but not the corporation or its stockholders. While the mere threat of personal liability is not sufficient, reasonable doubt as to the disinterestedness of a director is created when the particularized allegations in the complaint present "a substantial likelihood" of liability on the part of a director. *McCall v. Scott, 239 F.3d 808 (6th Cir. 2001).*

The duty of loyalty requires that the best interests of the corporation and its shareholders take precedence over any self-interest of a director, officer, or controlling shareholder that is not shared by the stockholders generally. *McCall v. Scott, 239 F.3d 808 (6th Cir. 2001).*

Entire fairness of transaction. — Under Delaware law, where corporate directors stand on both sides of a transaction, they have the burden of demonstrating the "entire fairness" of the transaction, which has two aspects: fair dealing (or procedural fairness) and fair price. The fair dealing prong embraces questions of when the transaction was timed, how it was initiated, structured, negotiated, disclosed to the directors, and how the approvals of the directors and stockholders were obtained. Fair price relates to the economic and financial considerations of the proposed merger, including all relevant factors: assets, market value, earnings, future prospects, and any other elements that affect the intrinsic or inherent value of a company's stock. The use of cash-out mergers is sanctioned as a means of eliminating minority interests. *Krieger v. Gast, 179 F. Supp. 2d 762 (W.D.Mich. 2001).*

Demand excused. — Where a conscious decision by corporate directors to act or refrain from acting is made, the demand requirement for a shareholder to bring a derivative action is excused when under the particularized facts alleged, a reasonable doubt is created that: (1) a majority of the directors are disinterested and independent; or (2) the challenged transaction was otherwise the product of a valid exercise of business judgment. Under the first prong, independence requires that a director's decision be based on the corporate merits of the subject before the board rather than extraneous considerations or influences. This standard is satisfied if a majority of the board that was in office at the time of filing was free from personal interest or domination and control, and thus capable of objectively evaluating a demand and, if necessary, remedying the alleged injury. It is no answer to say that demand is necessarily futile because: (a) the directors would have to sue themselves, thereby placing the conduct of the litigation in hostile hands; or (b) that they approved the underlying transaction. *Salsitz v. Nasser, 208 F.R.D. 589 (E.D. Mich. 2002).*

Where a conscious decision by corporate directors to act or refrain from acting is made, the demand requirement for a shareholder to bring a derivative action is excused when under the particularized facts alleged, a reasonable doubt is created that: (1) a majority of the directors are disinterested and independent; or (2) the challenged transaction was otherwise the product of a valid exercise of business judgment. Under the second prong, the business judgment rule provides that whether a judge or jury considering a business decision after the fact, believes a decision substantively wrong, or degrees of wrong extending through stupid to egregious or irrational, provides no ground for director liability, so long as the court determines that the process employed was either rational or employed in a good faith effort to advance corporate interests. Thus, a court may not consider the content of the board decision that leads to corporate loss, apart from consideration of the good faith or rationality of the process employed. *Salsitz v. Nasser, 208 F.R.D. 589 (E.D. Mich. 2002).*

Under Delaware law, a basic premise of corporate governance is that the board of directors manages the affairs of the corporation, not the shareholders. Frequently, derivative suits have challenged the propriety of decisions made by directors pursuant to their managerial authority. In such situations, a shareholder seeking to demonstrate demand futility must either: (1) create a reasonable doubt as to the disinterest and independence of the directors or (2) create a reasonable doubt as to whether the challenged decision was the product of a valid exercise of the business judgment rule. *In re Concord EFS, Inc. Derivative Litigations., 2004 U.S. Dist. LEXIS 25569 (W.D.Tenn. 2004).*

Under the *Rales* test, the court must determine whether or not the particularized factual allegations create a reasonable doubt that, as of the time the complaint was filed, a majority of the board of directors could have properly exercised its independent and disinterested business judgment in responding to a demand. To establish a reasonable doubt, plaintiffs are not required to plead facts that would be sufficient to support a judicial finding of demand futility. Nor must plaintiffs demonstrate a reasonable probability of success on the merits. Whether plaintiffs have alleged facts sufficient to create a reasonable doubt concerning the disinterestedness and independence of a majority of the board must be determined from the accumulation of all the facts taken together. *McCall v. Scott, 239 F.3d 808 (6th Cir. 2001).*

Establishment of employee stock ownership plans. — While it is certainly permissible for the directors to adopt measures for the benefit of its employees during the midst of a corporate control struggle, the directors must show that there are rationally related benefits accruing to the stockholders from adopting such measures. Furthermore, it is appropriate to look at such factors as the timing of the employee stock ownership plan (ESOP) establishment, the financial impact upon the company, the identity of the trustees and the voting control of the ESOP shares in determining whether the ESOP was created to benefit the employees and not simply to further entrench management. *Buckhorn, Inc. v. Ropak Corp., 656 F. Supp. 209 (S.D.Ohio 1987).*

Void or voidable tests. — A contract or transaction between a Delaware corporation and one or more of its directors or officers in which the officer or director has a financial interest may be void or voidable unless one of three tests are met: (1). the contract or transaction was approved by a majority of disinterested directors, even if less than a quorum, after full disclosure is made; (2). the contract or transaction was specifically approved by shareholders after full disclosure; or (3). the contract or transaction was fair to the corporation at the time it was approved or ratified. *In re Revco D.S., Inc., 1990 Bankr. LEXIS 2966 (Bankr. N.D.Ohio 1990).*

Trading in corporation's stock. — The mere fact that stocks were traded by an officer or director does not establish a breach of the duty of loyalty. A director is free to trade in the corporation's stock without liability to the corporation. In fact, when directors and officers own stock or receive compensation in stock, they should be expected to trade those securities in the normal course of events. *McCall v. Scott, 239 F.3d 808 (6th Cir. 2001).*

To recover insider profits for a breach of the duty of loyalty, it must be shown that each sale by each individual defendant was entered into and completed on the basis of, and because of, adverse material non-public information.

Fraudulent intent may be inferred from the timing and quantities of the trades. *McCall v. Scott, 239 F.3d 808 (6th Cir. 2001).*

Accountability for gains. — Under Delaware common law, a fiduciary of a corporation who trades for his or her own benefit on the basis of confidential information acquired through his or her fiduciary position breaches his or her duty to the corporation and may be held accountable to that corporation for any gains without regard to whether the corporation suffered damages. *McCall v. Scott, 239 F.3d 808 (6th Cir. 2001).*

Seventh Circuit

Interested versus independent director. — Whether the plaintiffs in a derivative stockholder complaint have alleged facts sufficient to create a reasonable doubt concerning the disinterestedness and independence of a majority of the board of directors must be determined from the accumulation of all the facts taken together. A director is interested when he or she will receive a personal financial benefit from a transaction that is not equally shared by the stockholders, or when a corporate decision will have a materially detrimental impact on a director but not the corporation or its stockholders. However, the mere threat of personal liability in the derivative action does not render a director interested. Rather, reasonable doubt as to the disinterestedness of a director is created when the particularized allegations in the complaint present a substantial likelihood of liability on the part of a director. Moreover, even if a director has no personal interest in a decision, his or her discretion must also be free from the influence of other interested persons. A director is independent if he or she can make a decision based on the corporate merits of the subject before the board rather than extraneous considerations or influences. *Dollens v. Zionts, 2002 U.S. Dist. LEXIS 13511 (N.D.Ill. 2002).*

An **"interested" director is one who** receives a personal financial benefit from the challenged transaction which is not equally shared by the stockholders. *In re General Instrument Corp., 23 F. Supp. 2d 867 (N.D.Ill. 1998).*

A director is independent when he or she is able to reach his or her decision solely on the merits without being governed by outside influences or considerations. To show a lack of independence, the plaintiff must demonstrate that outside considerations influenced the decisions of the committee. *Grafman v. Century Broadcasting Corp., 762 F. Supp. 215 (N.D.Ill. 1991).*

Independence exists when a director's decision is based on the corporate merits of the subject before the board rather than extraneous considerations or influences. *In re Abbott Labs. Derivative Shareholders Litigation, 325 F.3d 795 (7th Cir. 2003).*

A disinterested director can neither appear on both sides of a transaction nor expect to derive any personal financial benefit from the challenged transaction in the sense of self-dealing, as opposed to a benefit which devolves upon the corporation or all stockholders generally. *In re Abbott Labs. Derivative Shareholders Litigation, 325 F.3d 795 (7th Cir. 2003).*

Standard of business decisions review. — The standard by which a court will review a board of directors' business decisions may depend on the context of the transaction and the potential for directorial misconduct. Ordinarily the court will apply the business judgment rule to a business decision and refrain from any substantive review of the board action. But when actions are taken by the board because of a threat to the control of the corporation and the board's actions are defensive in character, because of the omnipresent specter that a board may be acting primarily in its own interests, rather than those of the corporation and its shareholders, a heightened test must be applied to determine whether a board is entitled to the protection of the business judgment rule. *Newell Co. v. Vermont American Corp., 725 F. Supp. 351 (N.D.Ill. 1989).*

The business judgment rule is a presumption that in making a business decisions the directors of a corporation acted on an informed basis, in good faith, and in the honest belief that the action taken was in the best interests of the company. The presumption, however, attaches only to the decisions of directors who are fully independent and wholly disinterested. When the business judgment rule applies, it insulates directors from liability, and imposes upon the party challenging the decision the burden of rebutting the presumption. A hallmark of the business judgment, rule is that a court will not substitute its judgment for that of a board if the latter's decision can be attributed to any rational business purpose. *Niki Development Corp. v. HOB Hotel Chicago Partners, L.P., 2003 U.S. Dist. LEXIS 4949 (N.D.Ill. 2003).*

The business judgment rule requires courts to defer to the decisions of corporate directors made in the good-faith exercise of business judgment so long as the directors act for what is arguably a rational business purpose. The business judgment rule also creates a presumption that in making a business decision the directors of a corporation acted on an informed basis, in good faith, and in the honest belief that the action taken was in the best interests of the company. This presumption is particularly strong where the decision is made by outside directors. A court applying the business judgment rule will not substitute its own business judgment for that of a board of directors, nor will a court act as a super-board of directors. *Rosenfield v. Becor Western, Inc., 1987 U.S. Dist. LEXIS 14276 (E.D.Wis. 1987).*

Directors not entitled to hide behind business judgment rule. — The plaintiff shareholder must plead particular facts suggesting that the corporate directors are not entitled to hide within the impenetrable fortress of the business judgment rule with respect to their participation in the transactions for which legal remedies are sought by the shareholder. The same circumstances which remove the business judgment rule's protections in other contexts will negate its applicability to the shareholder demand requirement. Thus, directors cannot raise the business judgment rule where they are personally interested in the questioned transactions such as where they sit on both sides of a corporate transaction or engage in self-dealing. Furthermore, their judgment must follow the consideration of all material information reasonably available of which they have a duty to inform themselves. *Cottle v. Hilton Hotels Corp., 635 F. Supp. 1094 (N.D.Ill. 1986).*

Self-dealing in a corporate context occurs when a corporate director or officer appears on both sides of a transaction. *Howington v. Ghourdjian, 2002 U.S. Dist. LEXIS 400 (N.D.Ill. 2002).*

When directors of a Delaware corporation are on both sides of a transaction, they are required to demonstrate their utmost good faith and the most scrupulous fairness of the bargain. The requirement of fairness is unflinching in its demand that were one stands on both sides of a transaction, he or she has the burden of establishing its entire fairness. *Howington v. Ghourdjian, 2002 U.S. Dist. LEXIS 400 (N.D.Ill. 2002).*

In a self-dealing transaction, Delaware corporate and fiduciary law gives no deference to "business judgment" and judicial scrutiny is applied regarding both "fair dealing" and "fair price." Fair dealing focuses on the procedures used in seeking a buyer and fair price on whether the directors obtained the highest value reasonably available. *Montgomery v. Aetna Plywood, Inc., 39 F. Supp. 2d 915 (N.D.Ill. 1998).*

Under Del. Code Ann. tit. 8, § 144(a)(2), a self-dealing transaction is not void or voidable solely because of the interest of a director, if the material facts as to the director's or officer's relationship or interest and as to the contract or transaction are disclosed or are known to the shareholders entitled to vote thereon, and the contract or transaction is specifically approved in good faith by vote of the shareholders. *Howington v. Ghourdjian, 2002 U.S. Dist. LEXIS 400 (N.D.Ill. 2002).*

Demand futility. — The animating principle of the demand futility doctrine is that the directors can not faithfully decide whether proceeding with the corporation's litigation is in the corporation's best interest when the complaint seeks redress for the conduct that gives rise to the personal financial benefit for which the directors alone have received. The case law makes it clear that the personal benefit must arise from the challenged transaction. *In re General Instrument Corp., 23 F. Supp. 2d 867 (N.D.Ill. 1998).*

Under Delaware law, the rule that a shareholder must make a demand upon a corporation's directors before initiating a derivative suit, unless such demand would be futile, is more than a mere pleading requirement; it is a substantive right. The standard for determining whether a complaint adequately alleges demand futility is: whether taking the well-pleaded facts as true, the allegations raise a reasonable doubt as to (i) director disinterest or independence or (ii) whether the directors exercised proper business judgment in approving the challenged transaction. Moreover, conclusory allegations of fact or law contained in the complaint need not be considered true in determining demand futility unless they are supported by specific facts. *Shields v. Erikson, 1989 U.S. Dist. LEXIS 10079 (N.D.Ill. 1989).*

In paring considerations down to a test for determining the futility of the shareholder demand requirement, the Delaware Supreme Court requires that a trial court must decide whether, under the particularized facts alleged, a reasonable doubt is created that: (1) the directors are disinterested and independent and (2) the challenged transaction was otherwise the product of a valid exercise of business judgment. Hence, the court must make two inquiries, one into the independence and disinterestedness of the directors and the other into the substantive nature of the challenged transaction and the board's approval thereof. If a reasonable doubt has been raised with respect to either the directors' disinterestedness and independence or whether the decision was otherwise a valid business judgment, the demand requirement will be excused and the shareholder permitted to pursue the derivative action. *Cottle v. Hilton Hotels Corp., 635 F. Supp. 1094 (N.D.Ill. 1986).*

A plaintiff-shareholder can also be excused from demand under *Aronson* if he or she can allege particularized facts which create a reasonable doubt that the challenged transaction was the product of a valid business judgment notwithstanding the directors' disinterestedness and independence. This aspect of the test has not been examined as thoroughly by the courts, though the *Aronson* court alluded to the narrowness of this exception when it noted that in rare cases a transaction may be so egregious on its face that board approval cannot meet the test of business judgment, and a substantial likelihood of director liability therefore exists. *Cottle v. Hilton Hotels Corp., 635 F. Supp. 1094 (N.D.Ill. 1986).*

As the first part of the *Aronson* test suggests, the allegations must create a reasonable doubt that the underlying corporate transactions were made by disinterested and independent directors. *Cottle v. Hilton Hotels Corp., 635 F. Supp. 1094 (N.D.Ill. 1986).*

The business judgment rule is a presumption that in making a business decision, the directors of a corporation acted on an informed basis, in good faith and in the honest belief that the action taken was in the best interests of the company. To determine whether a complaint raises a reasonable doubt that the directors exercised proper business judgment, the second prong of the *Aronson* test requires a court to look at both the substantive due care (substance of the transaction) as well as the procedural due care (an informed decision) used by the directors. The mere threat of personal liability for approving a questioned transaction, standing alone, is insufficient to challenge either the independence or disinterestedness of directors. However, demand may be excused if in rare cases a transaction may be so egregious on its face that board approval cannot meet the test of business judgment, resulting in a substantial likelihood of director liability, or if the directors exhibited gross negligence in breaching their duty of care. *In re Abbott Labs. Derivative Shareholders Litigation, 325 F.3d 795 (7th Cir. 2003).*

In determining whether a demand would be futile, the court must consider whether the particularized factual allegations of a derivative stockholder complaint create a reasonable doubt that, as of the time the complaint is filed, the board of directors could have properly exercised its independent and disinterested business judgment in responding to a demand. If the derivative plaintiff satisfies this burden, then demand will be excused as futile. To establish a reasonable doubt, plaintiffs are not required to plead facts that would be sufficient to support a judicial finding of demand futility nor must plaintiffs demonstrate a reasonable probability of success on the merits. *Dollens v. Zionts, 2002 U.S. Dist. LEXIS 13511 (N.D.Ill. 2002).*

Enhanced duty in control contest. — A conflict of interest confronts directors who are faced with a threat to their control of a corporation. Because of the threat that the directors may be more concerned about their own interests than the interests of the corporation and its shareholders, there is an enhanced duty which calls for judicial examination at the threshold before the protections of the business judgment rule may be conferred. *Desert Partners, L.P. v. USG Corp., 686 F. Supp. 1289 (N.D.Ill. 1988).*

In evaluating the directors' actions in defending against the threat of a takeover, the courts place upon the directors the burden of proving (1) that the threatened takeover posed a danger to corporate policy and effectiveness, and (2) that they adopted defensive measures which were reasonable in relation to the threat posed. The directors satisfy this burden by showing that they acted in good faith and after reasonable investigation. To overcome the presumption enjoyed by the directors by virtue of the business judgment rule, the plaintiff has the burden of persuasion to show a breach of the directors' fiduciary duties. The plaintiff may show this by demonstrating that the directors acted solely or primarily out of a desire to perpetuate themselves in office. *Desert Partners, L.P. v. USG Corp., 686 F. Supp. 1289 (N.D.Ill. 1988).*

Maintenance of action following refused demand. — Under Delaware law, a shareholder's power to bring a derivative action on behalf of the corporation is terminated once a presuit demand has been made and rejected. Thus, just as a corporate board's decisions regarding the routine business transactions of the corporation are accorded great deference under the business judgment rule, its decision not to pursue legal recourse pursuant to a shareholder's complaint is given the same treatment. Following a refused demand, a shareholder can only maintain a derivative action if he or she can demonstrate that the board's decision not to sue was improperly motivated or tainted with self-interest such that the directors were not acting in the best interests of the corporation. *Lewis v. Hilton, 648 F. Supp. 725 (N.D.Ill. 1986).*

Pleading specificity for perpetuation in office claims. — While a claim that directors have acted with the sole or primary motive of perpetuating themselves in office would be sufficient to excuse demand, the plaintiff must allege particularized facts to sustain such a claim. *Cottle v. Hilton Hotels Corp., 635 F. Supp. 1094 (N.D.Ill. 1986).*

Inapplicability of liability waiver. — Directors' fiduciary duties include not only the duty of care but also the duties of loyalty and good faith; although duty-of-care claims alleging only grossly negligent conduct are precluded by the Del. Code. Ann. tit. 8, § 102(b)(7) waiver provision, duty-of-care claims based on reckless or intentional misconduct are not. To the extent that recklessness involves a conscious disregard of a known risk, it could be argued that such an approach is not one taken in good faith and thus could not be liability exempted under the statute. Under Delaware law, the duty of good faith may be breached where a director consciously disregards his duties to the corporation, thereby causing its stockholders to suffer. A certificate of incorporation which exempts the directors from personal liability, a conscious disregard of known risks, which conduct, if proven, cannot have been undertaken in good faith; thus, claims are not precluded by the company's § 102(b)(7) waiver provision. *In re Abbott Labs. Derivative Shareholders Litigation, 325 F.3d 795 (7th Cir. 2003).*

Eighth Circuit

The mere threat of personal liability for approving a questioned transaction, standing alone, is insufficient to challenge either the independence or disinterestedness of directors. To succeed with such an argument, the shareholder would need to show that there is a "substantial likelihood" that the directors will have to pay damages to the company. *Wesenberg v. Zimmerman, 2002 U.S. Dist. LEXIS 11868 (D.Minn. 2002).*

Review of action of independent litigation committee. — The four-pronged analysis to be applied in evaluating a dismissal motion premised upon an independent litigation committee's exercise of business judgment requires a judicial assessment of: (1) the procedural propriety of a complaining shareholder's initiation of suit; (2) whether the board committee is endowed with the requisite corporate power to seek dismissal of a derivative suit; (3) whether the movants have adequately demonstrated the disinterest, independence and good faith of committee members, the bases for the conclusions of such members and the appropriateness and sufficiency of their investigative techniques; and (4) whether, in the court's exercise of its own independent business judgment, dismissal of derivative counts is warranted. *Watts v. Des Moines Register & Tribune, 525 F. Supp. 1311 (S.D. Iowa 1981).*

Demand futility. — Under Delaware law, a shareholder must satisfy a stringent pleading standard and allege particularized facts justifying any failure to make a demand. In a derivative action brought by one or more shareholders the complaint shall also allege with particularity the efforts, if any, made by the plaintiff to obtain the action desired from the directors or the reasons for the plaintiff's failure to make such efforts. A demand is considered futile and may be excused only if the particularized facts alleged in the complaint create a reasonable doubt that: (1) the directors are disinterested and independent; or (2) the challenged transaction was otherwise the product of a valid exercise of business judgment. *Wesenberg v. Zimmerman, 2002 U.S. Dist. LEXIS 11868 (D.Minn. 2002).*

Under Delaware law, it is clear that a plaintiff may only establish futility and therefore excuse a demand by creating a reasonable doubt that either: (1) the directors are independent or disinterested for the purposes of responding to the demand; or (2) the underlying transaction is protected by the business judgment rule. These prongs are in the disjunctive. *Wesenberg v. Zimmerman, 2002 U.S. Dist. LEXIS 11868 (D.Minn. 2002).*

Ninth Circuit

Under Delaware law, directors are interested if they are on both sides of a transaction, or if they benefit financially from a transaction. One director's interest in a challenged transaction is insufficient, without more, to deprive the board of protection under the business judgment rule. *In re Silicon Graphics, Inc., 1996 U.S. Dist. LEXIS 16989 (N.D.Cal. 1996).*

A director is independent if he or she can base his or her decision on the corporate merits of the subject before the board rather than extraneous considerations or influences. To raise a question concerning the independence of a particular board member, a plaintiff asserting the control of one or more directors must allege particularized facts manifesting a direction of corporate conduct in such a way as to comport with the wishes or interests of the corporation (or persons) doing the controlling. *Mitzner v. Hastings, 2005 U.S. Dist. LEXIS 835 (N.D.Cal. 2005).*

The business judgment rule can only protect disinterested directors. A director involved in a proxy contest cannot claim the presumption of good faith afforded by the business judgment rule if he or she has a personal interest in the outcome of the election even if the interest is not financial and he or she seeks to serve from the best of motives. *NL Indusustries, Inc. v. Lockheed Corp., 1992 U.S. Dist. LEXIS 22652 (C.D.Cal. 1992).*

Delaware law is well-settled on the point that a previous business relationship is not enough to overcome the presumption of a director's independence. *Mitzner v. Hastings, 2005 U.S. Dist. LEXIS 835 (N.D.Cal. 2005).*

The duty of loyalty mandates that the best interest of the corporation and its shareholders takes precedence over any interest possessed by a director. *McMichael v. United States Filter Corp., 2001 U.S. Dist. LEXIS 3918 (C.D.Cal. 2001).*

The trading of stock by a corporate officer or director is not in itself improper under Delaware law. *In re Sagent Technology, Inc, 278 F. Supp. 2d 1079 (N.D.Cal 2003).*

Mere negligence not grounds for liability. — Officers and directors of a corporation owe a fiduciary duty to the corporation and its shareholders. However, directors and officers cannot be held liable for mere negligence in the conduct of their obligations. Under Delaware law, they are presumed to act in good faith and in the honest belief that their actions are in the best interests of the company. *In re Sagent Technology, Inc, 278 F. Supp. 2d 1079 (N.D.Cal 2003).*

The business judgment rule is a presumption that in making a business decision the directors of a corporation acted on an informed basis, in good faith, and in the honest belief that the action taken was in the best interests of the company. The presumption, however, attaches only to the decisions of directors who are fully independent and wholly disinterested. When the business judgment rule applies, it insulates directors from liability, and imposes upon the party challenging the decision the burden of rebutting the presumption. A hallmark of the business judgment rule is that a court will not substitute its judgment for that of the board if the latter's decision can be attributed to any rational business purpose. *Navellier v. Sletten, 262 F.3d 923 (9th Cir. 2001).*

Rebuttal of business judgment rule presumption. — The business judgment rule posits a powerful presumption in favor of actions taken by the directors in that a decision made by a loyal and informed board will not be overturned by the courts unless it cannot be attributed to any rational business purpose. To rebut the rule, plaintiff must provide evidence that directors, in reaching their challenged decision, breached any one of the triads of their fiduciary duty — good faith, loyalty, or due care. If the plaintiff cannot overcome the presumption, the business judgment rule attaches to protect corporate officers and directors and the decisions they make, and courts hesitate to second-guess such decisions. Should a plaintiff rebut the rule, the burden shifts to the defendant directors to prove the "entire fairness" of the transaction. *McMichael v. United States Filter Corp., 2001 U.S. Dist. LEXIS 3918 (C.D.Cal. 2001).*

To show futility under Delaware law, a plaintiff must allege particularized facts creating a reasonable doubt that (1) the directors are disinterested and independent, or (2) the challenged transaction was otherwise the product of a valid exercise of business judgment. *Janas v. McCracken, 183 F.3d 970 (9th Cir. 1999).*

Tenth Circuit

Even ostensibly independent directors cannot invoke the business judgment rule where they have either abdicated their functions, or absent a conscious decision, failed to act. *Geer v. Cox, 242 F. Supp. 2d 1009 (D.Kan 2003).*

Under Delaware law, demand on a corporation's board of directors will be excused only if under the particularized facts alleged, a reasonable doubt is created that: (1) the directors are disinterested and independent or (2) the challenged transaction was otherwise the product of a valid exercise of business judgment. The test is disjunctive. In order to satisfy the first prong of the *Aronson* test, a plaintiff must plead particularized facts demonstrating either a financial interest or entrenchment on the part of the directors. In order to satisfy the second prong of the *Aronson* test, the plaintiff must plead particularized facts, which raise a reasonable doubt that the directors exercised proper business judgment in the transaction. Proper business judgment means both substantive due care (terms of the transaction) and procedural due care (an informed decision). *Geer v. Cox, 242 F. Supp. 2d 1009 (D.Kan 2003).*

Eleventh Circuit

Independence analysis factors. — The independence of directors is measured not just by financial ties, but by other considerations, including psychological or friendship pressures that may bear on the decision to be made by a committee of independent directors. *Klein v. FPL Group, Inc., 2003 U.S. Dist. LEXIS 19979 (S.D.Fla. 2003).*

Deference to directors' judgment. — Where the directors neither act in their own self interest or otherwise breach their fiduciary duties, state law mandates the court defer to their judgment, and the presumption arises that the directors exercised their business judgment in good faith. Under the business judgment rule, directors will be held liable only if they are grossly negligent. *Hastings-Murtagh v. Texas Air Corp., 649 F. Supp. 479 (S.D.Fla. 1986).*

§ 145. Indemnification of officers, directors, employees and agents; insurance

DELAWARE CASE NOTES — REPORTED

Purpose of indemnification statutes. — Indemnification statutes were enacted in this State, and elsewhere, to induce capable and responsible businesspersons to accept positions in corporate management. *Merritt-Chapman & Scott Corp. v. Wolfson, 264 A.2d 358 (Del. Super. Ct. 1970).*

Purpose of section. — This section is a new statute, enacted to clarify its predecessor, and to give vindicated directors and others involved in corporate affairs a judicially enforceable right to indemnification. *Galdi v. Berg, 359 F. Supp. 698 (D. Del. 1973).*

The purpose of this section is not to encourage litigation or to deter the losing party in the underlying action from prescribed categories of conduct; rather, its purpose is to encourage capable persons to serve as officers, directors, employees or agents of Delaware corporations, by assuring that their reasonable legal expenses will be paid. *Mayer v. Executive Telecard, Ltd., 705 A.2d 220 (Del. Ch. 1997).*

The function of a subsection (k) advancement case under this section is not to inject a trial court as a monthly monitor of the precision and integrity of advancement requests, so, unless some gross problem arises, a balance of fairness and efficiency concerns would seem to counsel deferring fights about details until a final indemnification proceeding, by which time the details may not even matter as an agent may be obligated to repay all of the funds. *Fasciana v. Elec. Data Sys. Corp., 829 A.2d 160 (Del. Ch. 2003).*

Agent defined. — Trial court looked to the purpose of this section and indemnification law, to assist corporation's to hire qualified agents by protecting them from litigation, to conclude that this section embraced the more restrictive common law definition of agent, which generally applied only when a person (the agent) acted on behalf of another (the principal) in relations with third parties; the coverage of agents logically extended to only those situations when an outside contractor — such as an attorney — could be said to be acting as an arm of the corporation vis-a-vis the outside world. *Fasciana v. Elec. Data Sys. Corp., 829 A.2d 160 (Del. Ch. 2003).*

Outside attorneys not agents. — Although it was true that attorneys were often described as agents of their clients, this loose general usage was not a helpful or sensible ascription to use in implementing this section otherwise, outside attorneys retained by corporations would be able to seek advancement whenever they were accused of malpractice so long as their employing corporations had adopted a maximal bylaw extending coverage to the limits of this section. *Fasciana v. Elec. Data Sys. Corp., 829 A.2d 160 (Del. Ch. 2003).*

Outside attorneys as agents. — An outside attorney can be covered by this section, but only if that attorney actually falls within the rubric of "agent;" if corporations wish to hire outside attorneys on the contractual promise that the outside attorneys will have their litigation costs fronted by the corporation in a malpractice dispute, they can forge that result by a specific contract. *Fasciana v. Elec. Data Sys. Corp., 829 A.2d 160 (Del. Ch. 2003).*

Who is entitled to indemnification. — Chairperson of the board and president of wholly owned subsidiary of parent corporation entitled to benefit of this section. *Merritt-Chapman & Scott Corp. v. Wolfson, 321 A.2d 138 (Del. Super. Ct. 1974).*

Where the president and chairperson of the board of a subsidiary corporation participated in the fraudulent stock repurchase plan, shared the inside information, and was prosecuted because of his employment or agency relationship, he is entitled to indemnification. *Merritt-Chapman & Scott Corp. v. Wolfson, 321 A.2d 138 (Del. Super. Ct. 1974).*

Subsection (a) of this section does not oblige Delaware corporations to indemnify those who serve other enterprises at their request; if a corporation wishes not to extend indemnification rights to those who serve elsewhere at its request, it can say so in its bylaws, or it can say nothing at all, thereby achieving the same result. *VonFeldt v. Stifel Fin. Corp., 714 A.2d 79 (Del. 1998).*

The director of a subsidiary corporation who was successful in defending a derivative action against the subsidiary could not recover attorney fees in an indemnification suit against the parent corporation which was not a successor in interest to the subsidiary. *Chamison v. Healthtrust, Inc., 735 A.2d 912 (Del. Ch. 1999),* aff'd, *748 A.2d 407 (Del. 2000).*

Must be a covered proceeding. — First requirement for indemnification under this section is that the expenses in question be incurred in connection with a covered proceeding as described in subsection (a) or (b) of this section. *Shearin v. E.F. Hutton Group, Inc., 652 A.2d 578 (Del. Ch. 1994).*

The provisions at issue in both *Cochran* **and** *Fasciana* **required indemnification to the fullest extent authorized by** Delaware law. A contractual agreement for indemnification of fees on fees, then, cannot overstep this bright-line legal boundary. A party must succeed (at least to some extent) on its underlying indemnification action to have a legally cognizable claim for monies expended in forcing its indemnitor to make it whole. Because a Delaware corporation cannot take actions which our law does not countenance, a contract provision which mandates indemnification for fees on fees in unsuccessful litigation is invalid since it flouts the lucid precepts of *Cochran* and *Fasciana. Levy v. HLI Operating Co., 924 A.2d 210; 2007 Del. Ch. LEXIS 66 (May 16, 2007).*

Judicial determination of indemnitee's corporate position not required. — Subsections (a) and (b) of this section do not require a prior judicial determination of the validity of the indemnitee's position as to the proceeding for which indemnification is sought. *Green v. Westcap Corp., 492 A.2d 260 (Del. Super. Ct. 1985).*

Parent and subsidiary. — Where a 100 percent stockholder elects a director to the board of a subsidiary, that director thereafter serves the subsidiary "at the request of" the stockholder, within the meaning of subsection (a) of this section. *VonFeldt v. Stifel Fin. Corp., 714 A.2d 79 (Del. 1998).*

Language "in subsections (a) and (b)," referred to in subsection (c), incorporates those portions of subsections (a) and (b) of this section which define the type of action, suit or proceeding but does not incorporate the subsequent qualifications required for indemnification. *Green v. Westcap Corp., 492 A.2d 260 (Del. Super. Ct. 1985).*

Subsection (c) is mandatory. — Subsection (c) is a mandatory provision that applies to all Delaware corporations and grants an absolute right of indemnification. *Witco Corp. v. Beekhuis, 38 F.3d 682 (3d Cir. 1994).*

Indemnity not restricted to those standing as defendants in main action. — By the language of subsections (a) and (b) of this section, indemnity is not limited to only those who stand as defendants in the main action. *Hibbert v. Hollywood Park, Inc., 457 A.2d 339 (Del. 1983).*

Claimant assumes risk of not being indemnified. — Where indemnification is sought, the claimant will have usually assumed the risk of not being indemnified. *Merritt-Chapman & Scott Corp. v. Wolfson, 321 A.2d 138 (Del. Super. Ct. 1974).*

Corporation can also grant indemnification rights beyond those provided by statute. *Hibbert v. Hollywood Park, Inc., 457 A.2d 339 (Del. 1983).*

Under subsection (c), to the extent a claimant has not been successful "on the merits or otherwise," the claimant may still be entitled to indemnification of expense incurred in a covered proceeding, if a disinterested quorum of the board, or legal counsel at the request of the board, or the shareholders, specifically determines: (1) if the indemnification is sought in respect to a civil matter; (2) that the proceeding was a covered proceeding; and (3) that the claimant acted in good faith and in a manner the claimant reasonably believed to be in or not opposed to the best interest of the corporation. *Shearin v. E.F. Hutton Group, Inc., 652 A.2d 578 (Del. Ch. 1994).*

Authority mandated by bylaws. — While permissive authority to indemnify its directors, officers, etc., may be exercised by a corporation's board of directors on a case-by-case basis, most corporations and virtually all public corporations have by bylaw exercised the authority recognized by this section so as to mandate the extension of indemnification rights in circumstances in which indemnification would be permissible under this section. *Advanced Mining Sys. v. Fricke, 623 A.2d 82 (Del. Ch. 1992)*.

Chancery court jurisdiction. — Court of Chancery of Delaware has jurisdiction over advancement actions pursuant to subsection (k) of this section and may, pursuant to subsection (k), summarily determine a corporation's obligation to advance expenses, including attorneys' fees. *Fasciana v. Elec. Data Sys. Corp., 829 A.2d 160 (Del. Ch. 2003)*.

Exclusive jurisdiction. — While this sectiondoes not specifically speak to contribution actions brought by a co-indemnitor, the fact that such an action is singularly predicated on concurrent indemnification obligations existing in the first instance likely means the legislature intended for the Court of Chancery to have exclusive jurisdiction over these types of contribution suits as well. *Levy v. HLI Operating Co., 924 A.2d 210; 2007 Del. Ch. LEXIS 66 (May 16, 2007)*.

This section does not require complete success but provides for indemnification to the extent of success "in defense of any claim, issue or matter" in an action. *Merritt-Chapman & Scott Corp. v. Wolfson, 321 A.2d 138 (Del. Super. Ct. 1974)*.

Fees on fees award for former outside counsel were assessed only so far as prosecutions and lawsuits arose from situations in which counsel could have been said to have acted as the corporation's agent; since this amounted to less than half of the charges and claims against counsel, counsel was entitled to indemnification for about one-third of the fees incurred in the *8 Del. C. § 145* indemnification action. *Fasciana v. Elec. Data Sys. Corp., 829 A.2d 178 (Del. Ch. 2003)*.

Where a former officer and director prevailed against the corporation as to only certain issues, it did not matter that the attorneys' records did not show with exact precision which issues were worked on at which times, since it was possible to come up with a fair estimate of what proportions of the attorneys' time was attributable to various issues. *May v. Bigmar, Inc., 838 A.2d 285 (Del. Ch. Dec. 10, 2003)*.

A mandate to indemnify does not include an obligation to advance expenses prior to a determination of whether indemnification is permitted or required. *Advanced Mining Sys. v. Fricke, 623 A.2d 82 (Del. Ch. 1992)*.

Inherent in the very nature of a subsection (k) "summary" advancement action under this section is the necessity for a trial court to act in the face of some factual uncertainty, so, the key question is whether the party seeking advancement is facing claims that are subject to an advancement right, a determination that can, in most cases, be made based on a review of the pleadings against the party in the actions for which advancement is sought. *Fasciana v. Elec. Data Sys. Corp., 829 A.2d 160 (Del. Ch. 2003)*.

Advancement of expenses. — Subsection (e) leaves to the business judgment of the board the task of determining whether the undertaking proffered in all of the circumstances is sufficient to protect the corporation's interest in repayment and whether, ultimately, advancement of expenses would on balance be likely to promote the corporation's interests. *Advanced Mining Sys. v. Fricke, 623 A.2d 82 (Del. Ch. 1992)*.

This section does not afford a director a right to advancement of his or her litigation expenses. *VonFeldt v. Stifel Fin. Corp., 714 A.2d 79 (Del. 1998)*.

The Business Trust Act does not prohibit a business trust from advancing litigation expenses to trustees. *Nakahara v. NS 1991 Am. Trust, 739 A.2d 770 (Del. Ch. 1998)*.

Company director was not entitled to advance for costs of litigation where language of company's bylaws precluded mandatory advancement whenever the director acted as a plaintiff in commencing litigation against the company; the trial court's ruling that there was no ambiguity in the company's bylaws, which mandated advancement only where a director was a named defendant or respondent in litigation, was supported by the record. *Gentile v. SinglePoint Fin., Inc., 788 A.2d 111 (Del. 2001)*.

Subsection (b) is not grant of absolute immunity. — Subsection (b) of this section does not necessarily preclude personal liability of directors because it is not a grant of absolute immunity. *Bergstein v. Texas Int'l Co., 453 A.2d 467 (Del. Ch. 1982)*.

In criminal action, any result other than conviction must be considered success. *Merritt-Chapman & Scott Corp. v. Wolfson, 321 A.2d 138 (Del. Super. Ct. 1974)*.

Claimants are entitled to partial indemnification if successful on a count of an indictment, which is an independent criminal charge, even if unsuccessful on another related count. *Merritt-Chapman & Scott Corp. v. Wolfson, 321 A.2d 138 (Del. Super. Ct. 1974)*.

Finding or inference of wrongdoing has generally precluded indemnification under this section. *McLean v. Alexander, 449 F. Supp. 1251 (D. Del. 1978)*, rev'd on other grounds, *599 F.2d 1190 (3d Cir. 1979)*.

What constitutes judgment of conviction. — Although a plea of nolo contendere may not be used as an admission in another action, upon acceptance by the court and imposition of sentence there is a judgment of conviction against the claimant. *Merritt-Chapman & Scott Corp. v. Wolfson, 321 A.2d 138 (Del. Super. Ct. 1974)*.

Conviction after 1 allegation of criminal indictment removed. — Where an alleged violation under a count of a criminal indictment was removed, but defendant was still convicted under the count for other violations, defendant had not been "successful" on the merits or otherwise. *Merritt-Chapman & Scott Corp. v. Wolfson, 264 A.2d 358 (Del. Super. Ct. 1970)*.

When case is dismissed without prejudice so that same issue may be litigated in another pending

Corporations

case, an indemnification award would be premature and contrary to the spirit of the statute. *Galdi v. Berg, 359 F. Supp. 698 (D. Del. 1973).*

Standard of review. — The reviewing court must treat the Court of Chancery's findings under subsection (b) with substantial deference. *Yiannatsis v. Stephanis ex rel. Sterianou, 653 A.2d 275 (Del. 1995).*

Court which finally resolves issue has authority to award indemnification, if justified under subsection (b) of this section. *Galdi v. Berg, 359 F. Supp. 698 (D. Del. 1973).*

And such award could include reasonable fees and expenses incurred in defense. *Galdi v. Berg, 359 F. Supp. 698 (D. Del. 1973).*

Standards used in determining whether fees have been "reasonably incurred" for purposes of this section are similar to standards used by courts in awarding fees. *Merritt-Chapman & Scott Corp. v. Wolfson, 321 A.2d 138 (Del. Super. Ct. 1974).*

Charging flat fee for each trial is not inherently unreasonable for indemnification under this section. *Merritt-Chapman & Scott Corp. v. Wolfson, 321 A.2d 138 (Del. Super. Ct. 1974).*

Fees deducted from award. — Where the initial purchase of stock represented usurpation of a corporate opportunity, the Court of Chancery properly deducted attorney's fees and past payments from the amounts to be paid to a corporate shareholder for the repurchase of the stock. *Yiannatsis v. Stephanis ex rel. Sterianou, 653 A.2d 275 (Del. 1995).*

Recovery of expenses of proxy contest, couched in terms of board election, involving substantive differences about corporate policy. — Where a proxy contest, though couched in terms of election to the board, was actually one involving substantive differences about corporation policy, former corporate directors, determined to be the management group for the purposes of reelection to the board and, therefore, entitled to use corporate funds to present its position, had an equitable and legal right to recover from the corporation their reasonable expenses resulting from the proxy contest. *Hibbert v. Hollywood Park, Inc., 457 A.2d 339 (Del. 1983).*

Expenses incurred in establishing entitlement to indemnification. — This section allows for indemnification of legal fees only in the underlying action against an officer or director, and does not allow for recovery of legal fees and expenses incurred in a proceeding to establish an entitlement to such indemnification. *Mayer v. Executive Telecard, Ltd., 705 A.2d 220 (Del. Ch. 1997).*

Officers as corporate employees. — A corporate officer is not, as a matter of law, also a corporate employee merely by virtue of office; whether a corporate officer is also an employee depends on the incidents of the relationship to the corporation. *Haft v. Dart Group Corp., 841 F. Supp. 549 (D. Del. 1993).*

Former directors held entitled to indemnification for legal fees relative to unsuccessful reelection bid. — Former corporate directors were entitled to indemnification for legal fees and related costs incurred with respect to suits filed by them in their unsuccessful bid for reelection to the corporation's board where the pertinent corporation bylaw contained no limitation on the type of action for which an individual, otherwise qualified under the bylaw, must be indemnified and where indemnification would be consistent with subsections (a) and (b) of this section. *Hibbert v. Hollywood Park, Inc., 457 A.2d 339 (Del. 1983).*

In the absence of a statutory requirement, a demand on the board for indemnification was not a prerequisite to indemnification of a former employee and director whose conviction of offenses arising out of employment had been reversed; recovery of attorneys' fees incurred in the employee's action seeking indemnification was authorized. *Stifel Fin. Corp. v. Cochran, 809 A.2d 555 (Del. 2002).*

Without interest on expenses actually paid, indemnification would be incomplete. Merritt-Chapman & Scott Corp. v. Wolfson, 321 A.2d 138 (Del. Super. Ct. 1974).

There are several factors to be considered in indemnification for attorneys' fees: (a) The time and labor required, the novelty and difficulty of the questions involved, and the skill requisite to perform the legal service competently, (b) the likelihood that a particular retainer will preclude other employment by the attorney, (c) the fee customarily charged in the community for similar services, (d) the amount involved in the litigation and the results obtained, (e) the time limitations imposed by the litigation, (f) the nature and length of professional relationship with the client, (g) the experience, reputation and ability of the lawyer performing the services, and (h) a consideration whether the fee is fixed or contingent. *Galdi v. Berg, 359 F. Supp. 698 (D. Del. 1973).*

Proper remedy. — When an indemnitor, pursuant to this section, fully satisfies a joint indemnification obligation it shares with a co-indemnitor covering the same indemnitee and the same challenged activity, the indemnitor must sue the co-indemnitor on a theory of contribution. The facts presented here fit squarely within this framework, and proper resolution of this case, then, also rests on contribution. *Levy v. HLI Operating Co., 924 A.2d 210; 2007 Del. Ch. LEXIS 66 (May 16, 2007).*

DELAWARE CASE NOTES — UNREPORTED

In general. — Under Delaware statutory law a director or officer of a corporation can be indemnified for liability (and litigation expenses) incurred by reason of a violation of the duty of care, but not for a violation of the duty to act in good faith. *Brehm v. Eisner (In re Walt Disney Co. Derivative Litig.), 2006 Del. LEXIS 307 (Del. June 8, 2006).*

"By".—The language of subsection (b) is plain and clearly applies to all actions "by or in the right of the corporation." The legislature's use of the word "by" reflects the legislature's intent to provide indemnification in situations where a director has successfully defended himself against an action brought directly by the corporation. *MCI Telecommunications Corp. v. Wanzer, 1990 Del. Super. LEXIS 222 (1990).*

"By reason of the fact". — When this court has construed the "by reason of the fact" requirement of this section in the indemnification context, it has done so broadly and in favor of indemnification. Thus, for instance, a corporate officer was found entitled to indemnification after an unsuccessful criminal prosecution for, among other things, investing beyond his authority and directing that corporate funds be applied for his personal benefit. However, "by reason of the fact" is not construed so broadly as to encompass every suit brought against an officer and director. For example, claims brought by a corporation against an officer for excessive compensation paid or breaches of a non-competition agreement are quintessential examples of a dispute between an employer and an employee and are not brought "by reason of the fact" of the director's position with the corporation. *Weaver v. ZeniMax Media, Inc., 2004 Del. Ch. LEXIS 10, No. 20439-NC (January 30, 2004).*

In order for one to be deemed a party to a proceeding contemplated by 8 Del. C. § 145(e), by reason of the fact of one's corporate position, there must be a causal connection or nexus between the underlying proceeding and the corporate function or official corporate capacity. *Homestore, Inc. v. Tafeen, 2005 Del. LEXIS 462 (Del. Nov. 17, 2005).*

Stay of proceedings. — Company's motion to stay an indemnification action by former directors of the company, who made payments to settle class actions against the company based upon materially misleading information in the company's financial statements, was denied because under the former directors' indemnification agreements the indemnification claims could not be stayed under this section pending the conclusion of an investigation by the Securities and Exchange Commission regarding the underlying accounting regularities; the indemnification claims became due and payable upon payment by the former directors to settle the underlying financial irregularities claims. *Levy v. Hayes Lemmerz Int'l, Inc., 2006 Del. Ch. LEXIS 68 (Del. Ch. Apr. 5, 2006).*

Judgment of advancement upheld. — Judgment regarding the reasonableness of a former officer's advancement request and that ordered such advancement was upheld because the former officer incurred substantial expenses due to several investigations, civil actions, and a criminal indictment; the allegations that the former officer had unclean hands by hiding assets or purposefully wasted assets to hide from creditors by purchasing an expensive home in Florida were found without merit. *Homestore, Inc. v. Tafeen, 2005 Del. LEXIS 462 (Del. Nov. 17, 2005).*

When right to advancement attaches most strongly. — Corporations that voluntarily extend to their officers and directors the right to indemnification and advancement under 8 *Del. C.* § 145 have a duty to fulfill their obligations under such provisions with good faith and dispatch. It is no answer to an advancement action, as either a legal or logical matter, to say that the corporation now believes the fiduciary to have been unfaithful. Indeed, it is in those very cases that the right to advancement attaches most strongly. *Radiancy, Inc. v. Azar, 2006 Del. Ch. LEXIS 13 (Del. Ch. Jan. 23, 2006).*

Effect of conversion. — Corporation's bylaws providing a mandatory right of advancement to its officers and directors should not be read to apply equally to the former managers of the limited liability company (LLC), even where the LLC's operating agreement provided for indemnification but not for mandatory advancement. The right to indemnification or advancement for claims that arose during the life of the LLC continues to be governed by the terms of the old operating agreement. *Bernstein v. Tractmanager, Inc., 2007 Del. Ch. LEXIS 172 (November 20, 2007). [For the full text of this case opinion, please see the Appendix at the end of this Volume.]*

Limited liability companies and corporations differ in important ways, most pertinently in regard to indemnification: mandating it in the case of corporate directors and officers who successfully defend themselves, but leaving the indemnification of managers or officers of limited liability companies to private contract. While the business of the LLC continued on in the corporate form following the 2003 conversion, there is no reason to infer that the directors who approved the new certificate of incorporation and bylaws intended to change, adjust, or expand any of the existing rights or duties governing the LLC. *Bernstein v. Tractmanager, Inc., 2007 Del. Ch. LEXIS 172 (November 20, 2007). [For the full text of this case opinion, please see the Appendix at the end of this Volume.]*

Entitlement. — The clear language of subsection (c) supports the conclusion that a director who has been partially successful in defending three out of four counts of a civil complaint is entitled to mandatory indemnification. *MCI Telecommunications Corp. v. Wanzer, 1990 Del. Super. LEXIS 222 (1990).*

Equitable relief. — Advancement is merely a contractual right that parties can agree to in the instruments that govern their relationship. This court's statutory authority under subsection (k) of this section to make determinations regarding advancement does not turn an advancement claim into a claim for equitable relief. *Yuen v. Gemstar-TV Guide Int'l, Inc., 2004 Del. Ch. LEXIS 96, No. 398-N (June 30, 2004].*

Mandatory expense advancement language permissible. - -This section is designed to ensure that qualified men and women serve corporations as officers or directors and provide leadership and experience, without unjust fear of personal liability. This also provides that a corporation may provide for the advancement of expenses, including legal fees. The corporation can agree to make such advancements mandatory, as they have done here. *Kapoor v. Fujisawa Pharm. Co., 1994 Del. Super. LEXIS 233 (1994).*

Construction of mandatory advancement agreement. — Delaware courts have broadly construed mandatory advancement provisions to provide corporate officials with immediate interim relief from the personal out-of-pocket financial burden of paying the significant expenses often involved in legal proceedings. In the instant case, the indemnification agreement and the company's bylaws state that the company shall advance expenses "to the fullest extent permitted by law." Therefore, the plain terms of the indemnification agreement and the company's bylaws provide for mandatory advancement to the broadest extent possible under Delaware law. *Brown v. LiveOps, Inc., 2006 Del. Ch. LEXIS 113 (Del. Ch. June 12, 2006).*

Financial hardship exemption. — This court has historically given great deference to informed decisions of a board of directors. Whether ultimately proven to be a fiscally advantageous or disadvantageous decision, this court will not interfere with informed and loyal decisions of an independent board. The same is to be said of the drafters of a company's bylaws. Defendant's bylaws may ultimately prove to be disadvantageous; indeed here they may significantly lower their chances for future operations and related recovery. But there is no case precedent, nor good reason, to interfere with the decision of the bylaw drafters simply because the bylaws might cause the company financial hardship. Indeed, to allow a financial hardship exemption, without more, would be to undermine the salutary purpose of allowing advancement. Advancement would be less of an inducement to becoming a director or officer of a company if the company could simply avoid its advancement obligation when times are difficult. *Tafeen v. Homestore, Inc., 2004 Del. Ch. LEXIS 38, No. 023-N (March 22, 2004).*

Unclean hands. — The Court acknowledges the strong Delaware policy of encouraging able persons to become directors and officers that is embodied in subsection (e) of this section. Since subsection (e) represents this strong public policy, the policy underlying the doctrine of unclean hands must be balanced against the statute. Where, as here, the allegations underlying the unclean hands defense involve conduct that, if true, would undermine the spirit of the statute, the balance is clearly in favor of not rewarding the alleged inequitable conduct. *Tafeen v. Homestore, Inc., 2004 Del. Ch. LEXIS 38, No. 023-N (March 22, 2004).*

The provisions for indemnification and advancement of expenses set forth in this section are not the director's exclusive remedy. The corporation may provide greater protection than that granted by the statute. Entitlement to advancement of expenses may be conferred on the director, inter alia, by the corporate bylaws or a separate agreement. *Salaman v. National Media Corp., 1992 Del. Super. LEXIS 564 (1992).*

Right to advancement of legal fees independent of right to indemnification. — Delaware courts have historically held that a right to advancement of legal fees is independent from an ultimate right to indemnification for legal fees, even if repayment of advanced expenses may ultimately turn on a right to indemnification; thus, former officer's promise to pay back expenses if indemnification was found not to exist did not entitle the officer to summary judgment on an advancement claim, nor did it entitle the corporation to summary judgment on that claim. *Tafeen v. Homestore, Inc., 2004 Del. Ch. LEXIS 38 (Mar. 16, 2004).*

It would be premature for a court to attempt to address corporate director indemnification issues before the questions of liability are determined; apart from the issue of advancement of legal fees to a director pursuant to 8 Del. C. § 145(c), courts tend to defer deciding whether a party is entitled to indemnification until after the merits of the underlying dispute have been resolved. *Brooks-McCollum v. Emerald Ridge Serv. Corp., 2004 Del. Ch. LEXIS 105 (July 29, 2004).*

Former employee (who was alleged to have participated in a conspiracy to manipulate the price of natural gas and to commit wire fraud) was not entitled to an unconditional, unsecured advancement of legal expenses from the employer corporation, because the advancement bylaw of the corporation vested the corporation's board directors with the ability to place reasonable conditions on any credit advanced to the employee; furthermore, the board of directors used its contractual discretion rationally and in good faith in resolving to grant any advancement to the employee on the condition that the employee execute a fully-secured undertaking. *Thompson v. The Williams Cos., 2007 Del. Ch. LEXIS 112 (Del. Ch. July 31, 2007).*

Subsection (b) not grant of absolute immunity. — Chairman and vice president of a corporation were required to pay to a corporation funds that the corporation expended in defense of a breach of fiduciary duty action against them; subsection (b) of this section prohibited indemnification of directors and officers, if such persons were adjudged to be liable to the corporation. *Carlson v. Hallinan, 2006 Del. Ch. LEXIS 58 (Del. Ch. Mar. 21, 2006).*

Limitation of subsection (f). — Subsection (f) of this section does not speak in terms of corporate power, and therefore cannot be read to free a corporation from the limitations explicitly imposed in subsections (a) and (b). *Kapoor v. Fujisawa Pharm. Co., 1997 Del. Super. LEXIS 386 (1997).*

Supervisory functions. — The ubiquitous Blackberry has changed the way business is run, enabling managers to remain involved in the day-to-day affairs of their business from afar. Plaintiff's physical absence from New York in no way makes it hard to imagine how he nonetheless performed management supervisory functions over his team of brokers. *Sassano v. CIBC World Mkts. Corp., 2008 Del. Ch. LEXIS 5 (November 29, 2007).*

Nominal officers. — Bylaws provide mandatory advancement to employees of corporation who hold officer titles (not necessarily with corporation or through appointment by the President), and have management-level supervisory duties. Nominal officer plaintiff is such an employee. *Sassano v. CIBC World Mkts. Corp., 2008 Del. Ch. LEXIS 5 (November 29, 2007).*

Expediting cases. — This Court has the ability to expedite cases and will do so in order to balance the salutary policy underlying subsection (e) of this section against the need to protect corporations and their stockholders from the type of conduct alleged here. *Tafeen v. Homestore, Inc., 2004 Del. Ch. LEXIS 38, No. 023-N (March 22, 2004).*

Superfluous motions. — A motion to expedite proceedings under subsection (k) of this section is superfluous. The text of the subsection dictates that a proceeding under that provision is "summary." In order to receive summary adjudication of a claim for advancement it is not necessary to file a motion to expedite. If a plaintiff files a motion to expedite it is, in effect, a request to expedite a summary proceeding. Only when unique circumstances are present, e.g., insolvency of the putative indemnitee or inability to retain counsel without advancement, will the chancery court entertain a request to "expedite" a proceeding that is already summary in nature. In the opinion of the chancery court, this reasoning extends to other summary proceedings, such as those brought under Sections 220 and 225 of the General Corporation Law. *Brown v. Rite Aid Corp., 2004 Del. Ch. LEXIS 29, No. 094-N (May 29, 2004).*

Construction with other law. — Although (unlike the Delaware General Corporation Law in 8 Del. C. § 145(e)) the Limited Liability Company Act (LLCA) is entirely mute on the subject of advancement, 6 Del. C. § 18-108 of the LLCA gives broad authority to members of LLCs to set the terms for indemnification in their operating agreements; given that the broad freedom of members of LLCs to define their obligations inter sese by contract is germane to the formation and interpretation of LLC agreements, persons forming LLCs clearly have the authority to require a written undertaking as a condition to advancement. *Senior Tour Players 207 Mgmt. Co. LLC v. Golftown 207 Holding Co. LLC, 2004 Del. Ch. LEXIS 22 (Mar. 10, 2004).*

Governing statutory scheme for limited liability companies, including 8 Del. C. § 145 and 6 Del. C. § 18-108, does not support the implication that any party receiving an advancement would be obligated to execute a written undertaking to repay; therefore, because the operating agreement of a limited liability company was silent on the issue of a written undertaking, the court would not read such a requirement into the contract. *Senior Tour Players 207 Mgmt. Co. LLC v. Golftown 207 Holding Co. LLC, 2004 Del. Ch. LEXIS 22 (Del. Ch. Mar. 10, 2004).*

Trial court had to deny the former corporate employer's counterclaim for repayment of funds it advanced to the former chief financial officer after numerous proceedings arose regarding the former corporate employer's accounting practices, as its counterclaim that the chief financial officer's guilty plea to a charge of criminal conspiracy to defraud the former corporate employer terminated any right the officer had to advancement or indemnification had to be rejected because the guilty plea was not a final disposition; thus, its counterclaim was not ripe for adjudication. *Bergonzi v. Rite Aid Corp., 2003 Del. Ch. LEXIS 117 (Oct. 20, 2003).*

Final adjudication on merits found. — Where a party voluntarily dismissed an action, which was then dismissed by the court with prejudice pursuant to Del. Ch. Ct. R. 41, it was considered a final adjudication on the merits which was favorable to a litigant in a claim for indemnification for legal fees and expenses incurred in other actions, and accordingly, summary judgment

pursuant to Del. Ch. Ct. R. 56 was granted to the litigant on the claim; it was determined that the claims were made within the applicable limitations period pursuant to this section, as the limitations period accrued when the appellate courts issued their opinions. *Salovaara v. SSP Advisors, L.P., 2003 Del. Ch. LEXIS 142 (Dec. 22, 2003).*

Corporate officer satisfied the elements of subsection (c) of this section for the purposes of establishing a claim for indemnification by the corporation of attorneys fees and expenses incurred as a result of an investigation by the Securities and Exchange Commission, which targeted the officer as the source of material, nonpublic information that had been used for illicit trading of the corporate stock, where the investigation was "done in officer's capacity" as a corporate officer; the officer also satisfied the indemnification provisions of a merger agreement and of the corporate bylaws. *Scharf v. Edgcomb Corp., 2004 Del. Ch. LEXIS 34 (Mar. 24, 2004).*

Debtor's motion to dismiss the former chief executive officer's (CEO) counterclaim for indemnification was denied; if the CEO was successful in defending against the debtor's claims then the CEO would have a later opportunity to be able to prove sufficient facts to support his request for indemnification under 8 Del. C. § 145(c). *Protarga, Inc. v. Webb (In re Protarga, Inc.), 2004 Bankr. LEXIS 1255 (Bankr. D. Del. Aug. 25, 2004).*

Defense of action in personal capacity. — Summary judgment was denied in a former director's indemnification action, wherein the director sought recovery of costs incurred in successfully defending a libel and slander action, because a factual issue existed as to whether the director had made the statements and whether the director was sued by reason of the fact of being a director, or whether the director had acted for personal gain. *Westphal v. U.S. Eagle Corp., 2002 Del. Ch. LEXIS 149 (Nov. 27, 2002).*

Trial court granted summary judgment pursuant to Del. Ch. Ct. R. 56 to a corporation in an executive's claim for advancement of fees and costs pursuant to 8 Del. C. § 145 incurred in defending against a counterclaim asserted by the corporation (alleging breach of the executive's employment agreement), as the claim involved the executive's functioning as an employee in a personal capacity rather than it having arisen "by reason of the fact" that the executive was an officer or director; accordingly, as the corporate bylaws only made reference to permissive advancement of costs to employees, the corporation was not required to do so. *Weaver v. ZeniMax Media, Inc., 2004 Del. Ch. LEXIS 10 (Jan. 30, 2004).*

Former employee was entitled to advancement of litigation expenses from former employer (including attorney's fees) in both a criminal prosecution and a civil action filed by the former employer alleging fraudulent activities while an executive employee of the employer, without executing an undertaking to repay those expenses, but was liable to repay those expenses if former employer was eventually found not to be entitled to indemnification. *Reddy v. Electronic Data Sys. Corp., 2002 Del. Ch. LEXIS 69 (June 18, 2002).*

Trial court granted company's motion to dismiss an advancement of legal fees action brought by former company executives, pursuant to Del. Ch. Ct. R. 12, where the agreements between the parties dictated that the matter be arbitrated; although the court had subject matter jurisdiction over such a proceeding pursuant to subsection (k) of this section, the claim was not one for equitable relief pursuant to 10 Del. C. § 342 and, accordingly, it was not within the "equitable relief" carve-out of the arbitration provision. *Yuen v. Gemstar-TV Guide Int'l, Inc., 2004 Del. Ch. LEXIS 96 (June 30, 2004).*

Where a former corporate officer, that officer's counsel, and a purported consultant all acted in bad faith to prolong what should have been a summary advancement proceeding, and where there was no showing that the fees sought were reasonable, the chancery court not only denied any future recovery of fees and expenses and authorized the corporation to recover any overpayments made earlier, but also awarded the corporation its own fees and expenses in defending the proceeding. *Kaung v. Cole Nat'l Corp., 2004 Del. Ch. LEXIS 126 (Aug. 27, 2004).*

Advancement of expenses. — Former corporate officer was entitled to advancement of legal fees and costs, as well as indemnification, with regard to a host of lawsuits and investigations arising from financial improprieties in a corporation's according practices and financial statements, where the corporation failed to meet its burden of establishing its claimed unclean hands defense in that the former officer did not engage in any deliberate efforts to waste corporate assets. *Tafeen v. Homestore, Inc., 2004 Del. Ch. LEXIS 156 (Oct. 27, 2004).*

Directors of entity winding up. — Indemnification rights of former officers and directors fall within 8 Del. C. § 281(b)(i), as opposed to § 281(b)(iii); no provision for future indemnification claims is reasonable. *In re Delta Holdings, Inc., 2004 Del. Ch. LEXIS 104 (Del. Ch. July 26, 2004).*

Claimant assumes risk of not being indemnified. — Corporation's payment of the chairman's and the vice president's expenses for the defense of an action was ultra vires, as the chairman and the vice president never even considered an undertaking to repay the corporation if they were not entitled to indemnification by the corporation and made no decision to accept an implicit one; therefore, the presumptions and protection of the business judgment rule did not attach. *Carlson v. Hallinan, 2006 Del. Ch. LEXIS 58 (Del. Ch. Mar. 21, 2006).*

Advancement of expenses for former directors. — Former directors of investment funds established their entitlement to advancement of fees and costs incurred in defending claims against them by their former employer's entities after their abrupt departure, since the plain language of the entity operating agreement did not limit indemnification rights only to current persons who fell into the definition of indemnified persons. *Weinstock v. Lazard Debt Recovery GP, LLC, 2003 Del. Ch. LEXIS 83 (Aug. 1, 2003).*

Indemnification of legal fees in suit for indemnification. — Court determined the officer was entitled to indemnification in defense of criminal embezzlement action officer he was "successful on the merits or otherwise," as subsection (c) of this section required, and the criminal prosecution occurred "by reason of the fact that defendant was an officer" as required by subsection (a) of this section whether or not officer acted in good faith or in the best interests of the corporation in oil futures trading which commingled officer's funds with corporation's funds; but, the court did not award legal fees for bringing this action since the corporation's broad bylaws could have, but did not, specifically authorize or require the payment of fees for fees. *Perconti v. Thornton Oil Corp., 2002 Del. Ch. LEXIS 51 (May 3, 2002).*

Corporate executive was entitled to advancement of costs and fees for advancement action, pursuant to 8 Del. C. § 145, as the corporation was obligated to pay "fees on fees" unless it specifically included language which excluded such advancement, and such holding furthered the policies of advancement; an award of fees on fees was to be proportionate to the success achieved by a plaintiff, and could be based upon submission by the prevailing plaintiff of a good faith estimate of expenses incurred, as well as an attorney's affidavit certifying a good faith and informed belief that the litigation expenses identified related solely to defense activity related to the advancement claim. *Weaver v. ZeniMax Media, Inc., 2004 Del. Ch. LEXIS 10 (Jan. 30, 2004).*

Attorney fees barred by statute of limitations. — Corporate officer's claim for indemnification of his attorneys fees and expenses was barred by the three-year limitations period of 10 Del. C. § 8106 where a letter from the Securities and Exchange Commission (SEC), which was investigating the officer's conduct with respect to possible disclosure of information that led to illicit trading, had indicated that the officer was no longer the subject of an investigation and, shortly thereafter, the SEC filed a lawsuit against a number of participants in the trading scheme which did not include the officer; the corporation did not engage in inequitable conduct that prohibited it from asserting the defense, nor did language in its bylaws that it would indemnify the officer to the "fullest extent of the law" require the corporation not to assert the defense of the limitations bar. *Scharf v. Edgcomb Corp., 2004 Del. Ch. LEXIS 34 (Mar. 24, 2004).*

Insurance for director liability. — Summary judgment in directors and officers' (D&O) declaratory judgment action against corporation's D&O insurer required insurer to defend and indemnify D&O in corporation's creditors' committee's underlying action that was derived from the corporation's bankruptcy trustee's authorization under 11 U.S.C. §§ 105, 1103(c)(5), 1109(b) (and not the corporation as the debtor in possession); the D&O policy's "insured versus insured" (one insured being the D&O and the other insured being the corporation) clause did not exclude coverage when the underlying action was derivatively brought on behalf of the bankruptcy estate (indirectly for the creditors and corporation) in reliance on the trustee's power to bring the suit and the bankruptcy court's authority under 11 U.S.C. § 105(a) to craft flexible remedies. *Cirka v. Nat'l Union Fire Ins. Co., 2004 Del. Ch. LEXIS 118 (Aug. 6, 2004).*

Corporations

Summary judgment in directors and officers' (D&O) declaratory judgment action against corporation's D&O insurer required insurer to defend and indemnify D&O; for a particular director, even though by agreement with the plaintiffs (the corporation's bankruptcy trustee acting through the corporation's creditors' committee), that director loss was limited to that director's insurance coverage under the policy, the director was still considered to be at risk. *Cirka v. Nat'l Union Fire Ins. Co., 2004 Del. Ch. LEXIS 118 (Aug. 6, 2004).*

Person seeking indemnification need not personally pay fees. — Where the former employee sought advancement of legal fees related to underlying litigation (but said fees in the underlying action were being paid by the newly formed entity that the former employee owned), the argument that advancement of legal fees to the former employee was improper (since the former employee was not paying the legal fees) was inconsistent with the policy stated in this section; that section's purpose is to encourage corporate officers to resist what they considered to be unjustifiable suits and claims. *DeLucca v. KKAT Mgmt., 2006 Del. Ch. LEXIS 19 (Del. Ch. Jan. 23, 2006).*

Timing of director's actions. — Where the facts alleged and the claims asserted in the California action were directly related to plaintiff's status as cofounder, officer, and director of the company and the complaint explicitly alleged that plaintiff wrongly retained and copied the proprietary information while he was at the company, the court could not reasonably conclude that the allegations were strictly confined to his actions after his termination as a director and officer of the company. *Brown v. LiveOps, Inc., 2006 Del. Ch. LEXIS 113 (Del. Ch. June 12, 2006).*

Indemnification denied. — In the specific context of this case, construing the statute to exclude a person, like individual seeking indemnification here, who was not a director but claimed entitlement to hold that position based on a contractual right granted to a preferred stockholder by the corporation would not disserve the policies motivating indemnification. No action of his taken in the capacity of a director of the defendant company is at issue in this case. *FGC Holdings Ltd. v. Teltronics, Inc., 2007 Del. Ch. LEXIS 14 (Jan. 22, 2007).*

CASE NOTES — OTHER STATES

Colorado

Eligibility. — A corporation has the power to indemnify, against expenses and judgments, a person who is sued by reason of the fact that he or she was a director or agent of the corporation if the person acted in good faith and in a manner the person reasonably believed to be in or not opposed to the best interests of the corporation. The termination of any action, suit, or proceeding by judgment does not, of itself, create a presumption that the person did not act in good faith and in a manner which the person reasonably believed to be in or not opposed to the best interests of the corporation. *Equitex, Inc. v. Ungar, 60 P.3d 746 (Colo. App. 2002).*

Mandatory and permissive. — The statute provides for mandatory and permissive indemnification. If a director or agent is successful on the merits in an action, indemnification is mandatory. If, however, the director or agent is not successful on the merits, then indemnification is permissive, and the corporation may provide indemnity only if the director or agent acted in good faith and in the best interests of the corporation. The good-faith requirement is related to the duty of loyalty a director or agent owes to the corporation. Thus, good faith toward the corporation is the determinative issue. *Equitex, Inc. v. Ungar, 60 P.3d 746 (Colo. App. 2002).*

Illinois

Eligibility. — Absent approval by a majority of the board of directors, none of which shall be defendants, indemnity of officers or directors is available only to those officers and directors whose actions comport with a prescribed manner of conduct, and therefore is only to occur upon a final adjudication with respect to the alleged acts or omissions. *Greenspan v. Mesirow, 138 Ill. App. 3d 294, 485 N.E.2d 1196, 92 Ill. Dec. 953 (1985).*

Massachusetts

Survival into enforceability. — It is generally accepted that an agreement to indemnify within § 145(f) of the Delaware General Corporation Law to survive into enforceability, must be able to withstand an attack on grounds of policy or basic equity, that is, a defense amounting to illegality. *Galvin v. The Gillette Co., 19 Mass. L. Rep. 291 (Super. 2005).*

Minnesota

Applicability of 1997 amendment. — The Delaware legislature amended Del. Code Ann. tit. 8, § 145(c) in 1997 to remove the right of employees or agents of the corporation to obtain mandatory indemnification. 71 Del. Laws ch. 120, § 5 (1997). But the revisor's note explicitly provides that the section would become effective with respect to indemnification of expenses (including attorney's fees) for acts or omissions occurring on or after July 1, 1997. Where acts or omissions occurred before this date, the earlier version applies. *Rudebeck v. Paulson, 612 N.W.2d 450 (Minn. App. 2000).*

The statute provides mandatory indemnification for any person who is a party to a lawsuit by reason of the fact that he is or was a director, officer, employee, or agent of the corporation, to the extent the person succeeds on the merits or in defense of any action. This is a mandatory provision that applies to all Delaware corporations and grants an absolute right of indemnification in such situations. It has been broadly interpreted. *Rudebeck v. Paulson, 612 N.W.2d 450 (Minn. App. 2000).*

The statute applies where one eligible for indemnification under the statute successfully defends against claims of personal liability that arise from or have a nexus to his or her corporate position. *Rudebeck v. Paulson, 612 N.W.2d 450 (Minn. App. 2000).*

New Jersey

"Reason of the fact". — In addition to including suits against directors or officers in their official capacity, Delaware's "by reason of the fact" statutory language encompasses suits against directors and officers that arise indirectly from their status, position, or role as a director or officer. *Vergopia v. Shaker, 191 N.J. 217; 922 A.2d 1238; 2007 N.J. LEXIS 687 (June 11, 2007).*

Expansive construction. — Trial court erred when it proceeded from the basis that this section should be given a narrow construction. Rather, as one commentator has noted, a survey of the history of corporate indemnification law in the state of Delaware reveals the General Assembly's intent to expand, rather than limit, the availability of indemnification to corporate actors. *Vergopia v. Shaker, 2006 N.J. Super. LEXIS 39 (Feb. 16, 2006).*

Termination decision. — That plaintiffs may have contended that defendant was personally involved in the decision to terminate them is, however, immaterial to whether defendant was joined as a defendant to this action by reason of the fact that he was an officer of corporation. He need not have been an officer of corporation to have participated in that decision-making process, if indeed he did so. His status as a defendant in this litigation was, in consequence, unrelated to his status as assistant secretary of corporation. The claims of the plaintiffs against defendant were not made by reason of the fact that defendant was an officer of corporation. Thus, the trial court correctly concluded that defendant's status as an officer of corporation did not entitle him to indemnification in the context of this case. *Vergopia v. Shaker, 2006 N.J. Super. LEXIS 39 (Feb. 16, 2006).*

Agent of corporation. — A close analysis of the allegations presented against defendant in the course of the litigation supports a conclusion that defendant's role extended to and impacted upon third parties. Thus, he may be deemed an agent of corporation and entitled to indemnification for the legal expenses he incurred. *Vergopia v. Shaker, 2006 N.J. Super. LEXIS 39 (Feb. 16, 2006).*

Entitlement to indemnification found. — When respondent was added as a party to the suit, he was serving as an assistant secretary of the corporation. Although the claims against respondent were not related directly to his official duties as an assistant secretary of the corporation, as defined by corporation's bylaws, he nevertheless was sued while serving as an officer of the corporation for actions he took in furtherance of the corporation's business interests. As such, he was entitled to indemnification under the terms of the corporation's certificate of incorporation. *Vergopia v. Shaker, 191 N.J. 217; 922 A.2d 1238; 2007 N.J. LEXIS 687 (June 11, 2007).*

New York

Interim indemnification. — Delaware's law provides for interim indemnification at the corporation's discretion upon the posting of an undertaking by the person indemnified to repay such amount if it is ultimately determined that he is not entitled to indemnification, but contains no provision for court-ordered interim indemnification analogous to N.Y. Bus. Corp. Law § 724 (c). Delaware case law reads the statute as providing that, absent contractual agreement, the question of interim indemnification lies solely within the corporation's discretion. *Bear, Stearns & Co., Inc. v. D. F. King & Co., Inc., 243 A.D.2d 252, 663 N.Y.S.2d 12 (1997).*

The larger purpose of this section is to encourage capable men to serve as corporate directors, secure in the knowledge that expenses incurred by them in upholding their honesty and integrity as directors will be borne by the corporation they serve. *Stewart v. Continental Copper and Steel Industries, Inc., 67 A.D.2d 293, 414 N.Y.S.2d 910 (1979).*

A grand jury investigation is covered under Del. Code Ann. tit. 8, § 145(a) as an "investigative proceeding." *Stewart v. Continental Copper and Steel Industries, Inc., 67 A.D.2d 293, 414 N.Y.S.2d 910 (1979).*

Broad indemnifications are permitted under Delaware law. Indeed, the language in this portion of the clause clearly parallels the language of 8 Del C § 145, On the indemnification of officers and directors, etc. Delaware courts have long upheld a broad interpretation of such indemnification clauses. In fact, where the "bylaw contains no limitation on the type of action for which an individual, otherwise qualified under the bylaw, must be indemnified" then the indemnification must be interpreted based on the language used. Thus, there is no question that under Delaware law, a corporation can also grant indemnification rights beyond those provided for by the statute. *Kensington Int'l v. Hiner, 2006 N.Y. Misc. LEXIS 2321, 236 N.Y.L.J. 40 (Aug. 22, 2006).*

Pennsylvania

The statute permits a corporation to advance defense costs where there has been no judicial determination that the officers did not act in good faith or that they engaged in willful misconduct or recklessness. *Neal v. Neumann Medical Center, 667 A.2d 479 (Pa. Commwlth 1995).*

Not entitled to indemnification. — Appellant was not using his entrusted corporate powers and was not performing his employment responsibilities when he handed appellee the fraudulent document for severance pay. Likewise, he did not exercise corporate authority or discharge employment duties when he benefited from the manipulation of the corporate records. Therefore, the acts alleged in the complaint were performed in a personal capacity and solely for personal gain and the trial court herein correctly concluded that appellant is not entitled to indemnification. *Souder v. Rite Aid Corp., 2006 PA Super 292, 911 A.2d 506, 2006 Pa. Super. LEXIS 3450 (Oct. 13, 2006).*

Tennessee

The final requisite for indemnification from a corporation is whether the plaintiff was made a party to the lawsuit because he or she is or was a director, officer or employee, of the corporation. In order to be entitled to mandatory indemnification, the plaintiff must show that he or she was sued by the defendant because he or she is or was a director, officer or employee, of the corporation.

Sherman v. American Water Heater Co., 50 S.W.3d 455 (Tenn. App. 2001).

Texas

Eligibility. — A corporation may indemnify any person who was or is a party or is threatened to be made a party to any threatened, pending, or completed action, suit or proceeding, whether civil, criminal, administrative, or investigative by reason of the fact that he or she is or was a director, officer, employee or agent of the corporation. If such officer, director, employee, or agent is successful on the merits of the underlying case, then the indemnification becomes mandatory. *Grove v. Daniel Valve Co., 874 S.W.2d 150 (Tex. App. 1994).*

Employees. — The corporate employer is also liable when the employee's negligence occurs pursuant to the employee's good-faith execution of his job description. The indemnification statute, however, expressly provides that if an employee's job exposes him or her to liability, then the corporation must indemnify him or her if the employee is successful on the merits of the suit. The policy behind indemnifying employees parallels that for officers and directors that policy being to encourage employees to accept positions of responsibility and to make good-faith decisions without fear of penalty. The corporate employer is also liable when the employee's negligence occurs pursuant to the employee's good-faith execution of his or her job description. The indemnification statute, however, expressly provides that if an employee's job exposes him or her to liability, then the corporation must indemnify him or her if the employee is successful on the merits of the suit. The policy behind indemnifying employees parallels that for officers and directors that policy being to encourage employees to accept positions of responsibility and to make good-faith decisions without fear of penalty. *Grove v. Daniel Valve Co., 874 S.W.2d 150 (Tex. App. 1994).*

CASE NOTES — FEDERAL

First Circuit

Insider trading. — Even under Delaware law, it is debatable whether an insider-trading violation can ever be "not opposed to" the best interests of the company. There is respectable commentary that Delaware law permits indemnification for at least some violations of this type; but one could also argue that insider trading inherently damages a company by poisoning relations with current and prospective shareholders who supply the capital. *Happ v. Corning, Inc., 466 F.3d 41, 2006 U.S. App. LEXIS 26027 (Oct. 20, 2006).*

As it happens, plaintiff's claim to indemnification would probably fail even if the undertaking were phrased solely in the language of section 145. This is so because, given the jury verdict in the enforcement action, plaintiff could not easily meet either of the two requirements of Delaware law—namely, that the conduct to be indemnified has been (1) in good faith and (2) not opposed to the best interests of the company. It is hard to see how the good faith test could be satisfied if plaintiff knowingly violated a federal regulatory statute aimed at protecting the public. Plaintiff does not claim to have been ignorant of insider-trading restrictions; rather, he argued in the enforcement case that his sale of shares was not prompted by inside knowledge but rather by a need for cash. It is apparent from the jury's verdict that it did not agree. Similarly, even if an act of insider trading might occur without being adverse to the interests of the company, that would not appear to help plaintiff: the jury's special verdict in this case found that he had violated a duty of trust and confidence owed to the company and its stockholders. Either a finding of bad faith or of opposition to company interests would bar his claim under Delaware law. Here the jury appears to have made both. *Happ v. Corning, Inc., 466 F.3d 41, 2006 U.S. App. LEXIS 26027 (Oct. 20, 2006).*

Second Circuit

The Delaware indemnification statute was enacted primarily to permit corporate executives to be indemnified in situations where the propriety of their actions as corporate executives is brought under attack. The fact that substantial discretion was vested in management in making those recommendations does not negate agency as defined in the statute. *Cambridge Fund, Inc. v. Abella, 501 F. Supp. 598 (S.D.N.Y. 1980).*

Discretionary authority may be found either in a vote of independent directors referred to in § 145(f) of the Delaware indemnification statute, or in a bylaw of the corporation if there is no conflicting charter provision. *Cambridge Fund, Inc. v. Abella, 501 F. Supp. 598 (S.D.N.Y. 1980).*

Mandatory indemnification. — Under Delaware law, while a board of directors may vote to indemnify its directors on a case-by-case basis, the board may also make mandatory the permissible indemnification rights of the Del. Code Ann. tit. 8, § 145 by means of a corporate bylaw. *Anselmo v. Univision Station Group, Inc., 1993 U.S. Dist. LEXIS 428 (S.D.N.Y. 1993).*

Determination of eligibility. — Del. Code Ann. tit. 8, § 145(d) outlines the specific procedure by which a corporation determines the eligibility of directors of officers for indemnification. The determination shall be made (1) by the board of directors by a majority vote of a quorum consisting of directors who were not parties to such action, suit or proceeding, or (2) if such quorum is not obtainable, or, even if obtainable a quorum of disinterested directors so directs, by independent legal counsel in a written opinion, or (3) by the stockholders. *MacMillan, Inc. v. Federal Ins. Co., 741 F. Supp. 1079 (S.D.N.Y 1990).*

When a company indemnifies pursuant to § 145(a), (b), the procedure of § 145(d) applies. *MacMillan, Inc. v. Federal Ins. Co., 741 F. Supp. 1079 (S.D.N.Y 1990).*

Subsections (a) and (b). — Del. Code Ann. tit. 8, § 145(a) governs indemnification of directors and officers sued in third party actions, and Del. Code Ann. tit. 8, § 145(b) governs their indemnification in actions brought by or in the right of the corporation. Del. Code Ann. tit. 8, § 145(a) permits a corporation to indemnify its officers and directors for attorneys' fees and other litigation expenses, as well as for judgments or settlement payments made in civil cases. In contrast, § 145(b) permits indemnification only for expenses and does not authorize indemnification for amounts paid in settlement in derivative suits. *TLC Beatrice International Holdings, Inc. v. CIGNA Insurance Co., 1999 U.S. Dist. LEXIS 605 (S.D.N.Y. 1999).*

Del. Code Ann. tit. 8, § 145(a)-(b) (1991) expressly grant a corporation the power to indemnify directors, officers, and others, if they "acted in good faith and in a manner reasonably believed to be in or not opposed to the best interest of the corporation." These provisions thus limit the scope of the power that they confer. They are permissive in the sense that a corporation may exercise less than its full power to grant the indemnification rights set out in these provisions. *Waltuch v. Conticommodity Services, Inc., 88 F.3d 87 (2d Cir. 1996).*

"Success is vindication" insofar as it relates to Del. Code Ann. tit. 8, § 145(c). Although vindication, when used as a synonym for "success" under § 145(c), does not mean moral exoneration, there must be a showing that a party escaped from an adverse judgment or other detriment, for whatever reason. Thus, where a director has asserted "a technical defense" to his or her adversary's claim and, as a consequence, the case is dismissed, he or she is considered "successful" in the palpable sense that he or she has won whether or not the victory is deserved in merits terms. *Kaslof v. Global Health Alternatives, Inc., 2000 U.S. Dist. LEXIS 21053 (E.D.N.Y. 2000).*

Consistency rule. — A corporation's indemnification powers cannot be inconsistent with the substantive statutory provisions of Del. Code Ann. tit. 8, § 145, notwithstanding the broader grant of powers under Del. Code Ann. tit. 8, § 145(f). The consistency rule provides that the indemnification rights provided by contract may not exceed the scope of a corporation's indemnification powers as set out by the statute. *TLC Beatrice International Holdings, Inc. v. CIGNA Insurance Co., 1999 U.S. Dist. LEXIS 605 (S.D.N.Y. 1999).*

Indemnification rights granted by a corporation may be broader than those set out in Del. Code Ann. tit. 8, § 145(a) (1991), but they cannot be inconsistent with the scope of the corporation's power to indemnify, as delineated in the statute's substantive provisions. *Waltuch v. Conticommodity Services, Inc., 88 F.3d 87 (2d Cir. 1996).*

Del. Code Ann. tit. 8, § 145(f) (1991) merely acknowledges that one seeking indemnification may be entitled to "other rights" of indemnification or otherwise; it does not speak in terms of corporate power, and therefore cannot be read to free a corporation from the "good faith" limit explicitly imposed in Del. Code Ann. tit. 8, § 145(a)-(b) (1991). *Waltuch v. Conticommodity Services, Inc., 88 F.3d 87 (2d Cir. 1996).*

Circumvention of good faith clause. — Del. Code Ann. tit. 8, § 145(g) (1991) explicitly allows a corporation to circumvent the "good faith" clause of § 145(a) by purchasing a directors and officers liability insurance policy. *Waltuch v. Conticommodity Services, Inc., 88 F.3d 87 (2d Cir. 1996).*

Derivative indemnification not empowered. — Delaware law does not empower a corporation to indemnify directors for sums paid in settlement of a derivative suit. Any provision in a corporation's bylaws to the contrary is inconsistent with the law. *TLC Beatrice International Holdings, Inc. v. CIGNA Insurance Co., 1999 U.S. Dist. LEXIS 605 (S.D.N.Y. 1999).*

Expectation of payment of legal expenses. — The statute that governed partnership gives it the authority to indemnify and hold harmless any partner or other person from and against any and all claims and demands whatsoever. This includes the authority to advance defense costs prior to final judgment. Company had an unbroken track record of paying the legal expenses of its partners and employees incurred as a result of their jobs, without regard to cost. All of the defendants therefore had, at a minimum, every reason to expect that company would pay their legal expenses in connection with the government's investigation and, if they were indicted, defending against any charges that arose out of their employment by the company. *United States v. Stein, 2006 U.S. Dist. LEXIS 42915 (D. N.Y. June 26, 2006).*

Government interference. — The fact that advancement of legal fees occasionally might be part of an obstruction scheme or indicate a lack of full cooperation by a prospective defendant is insufficient to justify the government's interference with the right of individual criminal defendants to obtain resources lawfully available to them in order to defend themselves, regardless of the legal standard of scrutiny applied. *United States v. Stein, 2006 U.S. Dist. LEXIS 42915 (D. N.Y. June 26, 2006).*

Violation of 5th and 6th Amendment found. — So much of the memorandum and the activities of the prosecution as threatened to take into account, in deciding whether to indict partnership, whether partners would advance attorneys' fees to present or former employees in the event they were indicted for activities undertaken in the course of their employment interfered with the rights of such employees to a fair trial and to the effective assistance of counsel and therefore violated the Fifth and Sixth Amendments to the Constitution. *United States v. Stein, 2006 U.S. Dist. LEXIS 42915 (D. N.Y. June 26, 2006).*

Applicability of EAJA. — The cases that have disallowed awards under the Equal Access to Justice Act (EAJA) where the prevailing party had the right to indemnification from a third party have all contemplated a solvent third party, financially capable of honoring its indemnification obligation. Thus, the existence of a contractual or legal obligation to indemnify alone is not sufficient; where an indemnitor is insolvent or financially incapable of making good on its obligation, the party has, in reality, "incurred" litigation expenses and an award of attorneys' fees and costs under the EAJA is appropriate. Thus, in the instant case, where only part of the former defendant's legal bill has been paid, it is clear that the default on the balance is due to the inability of entity to make the remaining payment, and under the terms of his retainer agreement, former defendant will therefore remain liable for this outstanding balance, former defendant has incurred his attorneys' fees and expenses within the meaning of the EAJA. *SEC v. Cedric Kushner Promotions, Inc., 2006 U.S. Dist. LEXIS 32846 (D.N.Y. May 23, 2006).*

Third Circuit

In general. — Delaware law permits Delaware corporations to provide for the indemnification of its officers and director. Delaware confers this power onto corporations whether or not the suit was initiated by a third party or by the corporation itself. The power to provide indemnification is generally within the discretion of the shareholders or other disinterested directors. Delaware law permits indemnification only if the director or officer acted in good faith and in a manner that he reasonably believed to be in the best interests of the corporation. Del. Code Ann. tit. 8, § 145(e) also provides for the advancement of expenses, including attorney's fees. *Pearson v. Exide Corp., 157 F. Supp. 2d 429 (E.D.Pa. 2001).*

A corporation may advance monies to the directors for their litigation expenses upon a resolution of the Board of Directors and receipt of an undertaking. A director is required to repay such expenses in the event that he or she is ultimately adjudged to have been liable for negligence or misconduct in the performance of his or her duty to the corporation. *Messing v. FDI, Inc., 439 F. Supp. 776 (D.N.J. 1977).*

Corporation may bind itself in advance. — Whereas Delaware law specifically states that indemnification is permissible only as authorized in the specific case by disinterested directors or shareholders, Del. Code Ann. tit. 8, § 145(d), there is no such requirement for advances of expenses under Del. Code Ann. tit. 8, § 145(e). In interpreting § 145(e), Delaware courts have consistently found that a corporation may bind itself in advance, through its bylaws or by contract, to advance the costs of litigation incurred by present or former directors or officers. *Pearson v. Exide Corp., 157 F. Supp. 2d 429 (E.D.Pa. 2001).*

"In defending". — The Delaware Supreme Court has broadly interpreted the words "in defending" as used in a contract provision concerning the advancements of litigation expenses to a corporate officer or director by a corporation. Any compulsory counterclaims asserted by a plaintiff are necessarily part of the same dispute and are advanced to defeat, or offset, the corporation's claim against him or her. *Pearson v. Exide Corp., 157 F. Supp. 2d 429 (E.D.Pa. 2001).*

A defendant's right to indemnification cannot be determined until the underlying case is resolved on the merits. *Stainless Broadcasting Co. v. Guzewicz, 1997 U.S. Dist. LEXIS 9205 (E.D.Pa. 1997).*

Irrelevancy of merits of claim. — Under Delaware law, the right to receive the costs of defense in advance does not depend upon the merits of the claims asserted against them, and is separate and distinct from any right of indemnification they may later be able to establish. Indeed, § 145(e) of the Delaware corporation law, conditioning the obligation to advance defense costs upon an undertaking to repay such amount if it shall ultimately

be determined that the officer is not entitled to be indemnified by the corporation leaves no room for argument on that score. *Ridder v. Cityfed Fin. Corp., 47 F.3d 85 (3d Cir. 1995).*

Fourth Circuit

Under Delaware law, officers and directors cannot be indemnified if it is found they violated duties of good faith and loyalty. *Miller v. U.S. Foodservice, Inc., 361 F. Supp. 2d 470 (D.Md. 2005).*

Mandatory indemnification does not apply to claims which arise out of the officer or employee's actions prior to or concurrent with the accepting employment and not out of a position with the indemnitor. *Schroeder v. Tenneco Packaging, Inc., 1997 U.S. Dist. LEXIS 15850 (E.D.Va. 1997).*

Obligation to pay legal fees and expenses. — Nothing in this section or cited court decisions would eliminate defendant's obligation to pay as incurred former employee's legal fees and expenses. As subsection (e) makes clear, a corporation may advance legal fees and expenses to an officer if the officer promises to repay the legal fees and expenses if the court ultimately does not find that he met the good faith requirement. Hence, while defendant may later be entitled to a refund from former employee, nothing in the Delaware statute absolves defendant from fulfilling its contractual obligation to pay former employee's reasonable legal fees and expenses as incurred. Accordingly, the employment agreement did not violate Delaware public policy. *Miller v. United States Foodservice, Inc., 405 F. Supp. 2d 607, 2005 U.S. Dist. LEXIS 33672 (D. Md. 2005).*

Court will not allow defendant's recoupment and setoff claims to delay the payment of attorney's fees to former employee. A proceeding of this kind must be summary in character, because if advance indemnification is to have any utility or meaning, a claimant's entitlement to it must be decided relatively promptly. If a corporation can circumvent its obligation to pay an officer's legal fees simply by filing a counterclaim against the officer, then advance indemnification provisions will be rendered virtually null whenever a corporation wishes to avoid that obligation. As with the possible reimbursement of fees, recoupment and setoff can be addressed at the conclusion of the case. *Miller v. United States Foodservice, Inc., 405 F. Supp. 2d 607, 2005 U.S. Dist. LEXIS 33672 (D. Md. 2005).*

Choice of law. — The law of a corporation's state of incorporation applies to claims arising from the company's internal affairs. Indemnification, as an internal corporate affair, is governed by the law of the state of incorporation. Defendant is a Delaware corporation. Accordingly, Delaware law, not Maryland law, should control the extent of the indemnification provisions in the employment agreement. *Miller v. United States Foodservice, Inc., 405 F. Supp. 2d 607, 2005 U.S. Dist. LEXIS 33672 (D. Md. 2005).*

Fifth Circuit

"By reason of the fact". — Delaware intended to encourage capable people to serve as corporate employees,

Corporations

officers, and directors by permitting corporations to shield them from liability for their official activities. Indemnification also ensures that corporate officials will and can defend themselves against unjustified suits and claims. The cases thus broadly interpret the "by reason of the fact" language in Del. Code Ann. tit. 8, § 145(a) to require no more than a nexus between a corporate officer's or director's official activity and the matter for which indemnification is sought. Further, whether a nexus exists is a question of fact to be determined by a trial court considering all the circumstances surrounding the proposed indemnification. *West v. Balfour Beatty Construction, Inc., 290 F.3d 263 (5th Cir. 2002).*

The right to corporate indemnification is necessarily judged case-by-case. *West v. Balfour Beatty Construction, Inc., 290 F.3d 263 (5th Cir. 2002).*

Conduct before employment not basis. — Conduct that occurs prior to employment cannot, by definition, be related to an employee's corporate duties and therefore cannot be a basis for indemnity. *West v. Balfour Beatty Construction, Inc., 290 F.3d 263 (5th Cir. 2002).*

Sixth Circuit

Bylaws modification. — Del. Code Ann. tit. 8, § 145(f) defines a basic structure that can be modified, within limits, by the adoption of bylaws. The basic structure has two types of indemnification, mandatory and permissive. Mandatory indemnification for defense expenses occurs when the director is successful on the merits or otherwise in defense of the action brought against him or her. Permissive indemnification may occur, if the corporation so chooses, for the costs imposed on directors who have been determined to have acted in good faith. The requirement of good faith on the part of the directors indemnified under § 145(a), (b), however, is statutory, and cannot be waived by attempting to extend indemnification even further. A default method for the determination of good faith by the corporation is described by Del. Code Ann. tit. 8, § 145(d). *Corning v. National Union Fire Insurance Co., 257 F.3d 484 (6th Cir. 2001).*

Inapplicability of subsection (c) to settlements. — The provisions in Del. Code Ann. tit. 8, § 145(a), (b) are much more clearly designed for situations where settlements are paid out. Both § 145(a), (b) explicitly mention settlement, whereas Del. Code Ann. tit. 8, § 145(c) does not, limiting itself to costs and attorney's fees. This provides a strong indication that § 145(c), unlike Del. Code Ann. tit. 8, § 145(a), (b), is not intended to be ordinarily applicable to settlements. *Corning v. National Union Fire Insurance Co., 257 F.3d 484 (6th Cir. 2001).*

Rebuttable presumption of good faith. - Corporations do have significant flexibility regarding their procedures, as long as they remain consistent with public policy and the controlling corporate law. It is not impermissible for a Delaware corporation to accord a director seeking indemnification a rebuttable presumption of good faith. Therefore, where a corporation has extended indemnification to the maximum permissible extent, such a presumption may be applied. *Corning v. National Union Fire Insurance Co., 257 F.3d 484 (6th Cir. 2001).*

Determinations under subsection (d) not necessarily mandatory. — The powers of a corporation include provision of accelerated procedures for the determination required by Del. Code Ann. tit. 8, § 145(d) or procedures under which a favorable determination will be deemed to have been made under circumstances where the board fails or refused to act. Thus, the specific provisions of § 145(d) are not mandatory in such circumstances with regard to indemnification under Del. Code Ann. tit. 8, § 145(a), (b). *Corning v. National Union Fire Insurance Co., 257 F.3d 484 (6th Cir. 2001).*

Seventh Circuit

The indemnification rights provided by statutory grant co-exist with the rights conferred by corporate bylaws. *Heffernan v. Pacific Dunlop GNB Corp., 1993 U.S. Dist. LEXIS 5 (N.D.Ill. 1993).*

"To incur". — Fees and expenses must be actually and reasonably incurred. To incur means to "become liable or subject to;" it does not require that the fees actually have been paid. *Truck Components v. Beatrice Co., 1996 U.S. Dist. LEXIS 3249 (N.D.Ill. 1996).*

Effect of subsequent purchase or takeover. — There is no basis to disregard a former director's right to indemnification simply because his or her former corporation had been purchased or taken over by another corporation. *Heffernan v. Pacific Dunlop GNB Corp., 1993 U.S. Dist. LEXIS 5 (N.D.Ill. 1993).*

Indemnification rights and advancement rights stand apart as two distinct types of legal rights. More importantly, as a matter of law, that a bylaw provision that requires the corporation to indemnify its corporate directors to the extent permitted under Delaware law did not wrest from a corporation the ability, granted by Del. Code Ann. tit. 8, § 145(e) (1990), to refuse advance payments. *Heffernan v. Pacific Dunlop GNB Corp., 1992 U.S. Dist. LEXIS 14809 (N.D.Ill. 1992).*

Violation of securities laws. — Allowable indemnification under Delaware law in the context of civil penalties for violating securities laws is narrowed to instances when an individual is not actually found to have violated federal securities laws. *CFTC v. Richards, 1996 U.S. Dist. LEXIS 5359 (N.D.Ill. 1996).*

Eighth Circuit

Defendant has not met the standard of conduct necessary to qualify for indemnification under subsection (a). In his plea agreement, defendant admitted that he, "did knowingly and willfully participate in a scheme to defraud Charter's stockholders." In addition, defendant stated that he "knew that the purpose of [the managed disconnect process]. . . . was to inflate Charter's quarterly growth in subscriber numbers that were intended to be reported to the public." Given these admissions, defendant cannot now assert that he had no reasonable cause to believe his conduct was unlawful. *Charter Communs., Inc. v. McCall, 2005 U.S. Dist. LEXIS 30970 (E.D. Mo. Nov. 18, 2005).*

"Successful". — Delaware law would not consider a defendant who pled guilty to the only count of a criminal indictment under which he was charged, successful, and thus entitled to mandatory indemnification under subsection (c) by his corporate employer. *Charter Communs., Inc. v. McCall, 2005 U.S. Dist. LEXIS 30970 (E.D. Mo. Nov. 18, 2005).*

Under Delaware law, if a defendant pleads nolo contendere to one criminal charge, he is successful on the merits and entitled to indemnification for expenses incurred in defending the dropped charges. Because subsection (c)

does not authorize "going behind the result," the Court sees no distinction between a nolo contendere plea and a guilty plea. Delaware law requires that a defendant who is partially successful on a claim be indemnified for the costs incurred. Defendant successfully defended seven counts of wire fraud on the merits or otherwise. *Charter Communs. v. Smith, 2005 U.S. Dist. LEXIS 24903 (E.D. Mo. Oct. 25, 2005).*

§ 146. Submission of matters for stockholder vote

CASE NOTES — OTHER STATES

Maryland

Self-flagellation not required. — Under Delaware law, corporate fiduciaries are not required to engage in self-flagellation, as their duty of disclosure does not oblige them to characterize their conduct in such a way as to admit wrongdoing. *Paskowitz v. Wohlstadter, 151 Md. App. 1, 822 A.2d 1272 (2003).*

Liability of directors. — The Delaware law of the fiduciary duties of directors, as developed in judicial decisions, establishes a general duty of directors to disclose to stockholders all material information reasonably available when seeking stockholder action. Whether or not a failure to fulfill that duty will result in personal liability for damages against directors depends upon the nature of the stockholder action that was the object of the solicitation of stockholder votes and the misstated or omitted disclosures in connection with that solicitation. The mere fact that a director breaches his duty to disclose material information when seeking stockholder action, i.e., votes, does not necessarily result in personal liability on the director's part. Whether the stockholder has suffered an injury depends on the nature of the stockholder action that was the object of the solicitation of votes. *Paskowitz v. Wohlstadter, 151 Md. App. 1, 822 A.2d 1272 (2003).*

Under Delaware law there is no per se rule that would allow damages for all director breaches of the fiduciary duty of disclosure. *Paskowitz v. Wohlstadter, 151 Md. App. 1, 822 A.2d 1272 (2003).*

Under corporate case law in Delaware, director disclosure violations that negatively impact voting or economic rights support a direct shareholder claim, and require proof of actual damages; disclosure violations that do not negatively impact voting or economic rights may be dismissed for failure to state a claim. *Paskowitz v. Wohlstadter, 151 Md. App. 1, 822 A.2d 1272 (2003).*

Massachusetts

Entire fairness test. — Delaware law protects minority shareholders by reviewing those transactions where a controlling shareholder benefits from a transaction in a way that goes beyond the benefits accorded to other stockholders. This analysis, referred to as the "entire

fairness test," requires the controlling shareholder(s) to prove the "entire fairness" of such a transaction. The "entire fairness" doctrine is designed to deal with those situations where a controlling shareholder has his or her own interest in the outcome of a transaction that might cloud his or her otherwise objective business judgment. *Olsen v. Seifert, 9 Mass. L. Rep. 268 (Super. 1998).*

Minnesota

Attribution of fiduciary duties. — Under Delaware law, a director owes a fiduciary duty to disclose fully and fairly all material information within the board's control when it seeks shareholder action. A minority shareholder who exercises actual control of corporate conduct will be attributed fiduciary duties. *Erickson v. Horing, 2002 Minn. App. LEXIS 1137 (2002).*

To establish a breach of fiduciary duty, a plaintiff must present evidence that a defendant made materially false statements, omitted material facts, or made partial or misleading facts. A fact is material if there is a substantial likelihood that a reasonable shareholder would consider it important in deciding how to vote. But there is no duty to disclose facts that are reasonably available to the stockholders. *Erickson v. Horing, 2002 Minn. App. LEXIS 1137 (2002).*

Duty of candor. — To the extent that a duty of candor exists separate from the duties of care and good faith, it entails the obligation to disclose all material information to shareholders when seeking shareholder approval. *Potter v. Pohlad, 560 N.W.2d 389 (Minn. App. 1997).*

New York

Compensable damages. — Under Delaware law, corporate officers, directors, and controlling shareholders owe their corporation and its minority shareholders a fiduciary obligation of honesty, loyalty, good faith, and fairness. Delaware law imposes a duty upon corporations to disclose all available material information when obtaining shareholder approval. Only damages caused by the breach of fiduciary duty are compensable. *Lama Holding Company v. Smith Barney Inc., 88 N.Y.2d 413, 668 N.E.2d 1370, 646 N.Y.S.2d 76 (1996).*

CASE NOTES — FEDERAL

Second Circuit

Effect of vote. — A vote by the fully informed shareholders ratifies a challenged transaction and extinguishes

any claim that a disinterested director breached his or her duty of care in connection with it. *In re Trump Hotels*

Shareholder Derivative Litig., 2000 U.S. Dist. LEXIS 13550 (S.D.N.Y. 2000).

Director communications prior to vote. — Where a controversy is concerned with a question of policy as distinguished from personnel of management and the stockholders are called upon to decide it, the incumbent directors may with perfect propriety make such expenditures from the corporate treasury as are reasonably necessary to inform the stockholders of the considerations which the directors deem sufficient to support the wisdom of the policy advocated by them and under attack; also, in the same communications which the directors address to the stockholders in support of their policy they may solicit proxies in its favor. *Steinberg v. Adams, 90 F. Supp. 604 (S.D.N.Y. 1950).*

Third Circuit

Delaware law holds that shareholder or director ratification will not be effective if the directors or majority shareholders breached their fiduciary duties. *Abrams v. Koether, 1992 U.S. Dist. LEXIS 16295 (D.N.J. 1992).*

Under Delaware corporate law a ratification cannot relate back so as to defeat intervening rights of strangers to the transactions. *Schoonejongen v. Curtiss-Wright Corp., 143 F.3d 120 (3d Cir. 1998).*

Seventh Circuit

Validity of ratification. — Under Delaware law, a validly accomplished shareholder ratification relates back to cure otherwise unauthorized acts of officers and directors. To be valid, a ratification must, in most circumstances, be made by a majority of the shareholders who have been adequately informed of the consequences of their acts and the reasons therefor. *Munson Transportation, Inc. v. Hajjar, 148 F.3d 711 (7th Cir. 1998).*

Subchapter V.
Stock and Dividends

§ 151. Classes and series of stock; redemption; rights

DELAWARE CASE NOTES — REPORTED

Stock may have only voting rights or property rights. — Subsection (a) of this section permits the creation of stock having voting rights only, as well as stock having property rights only. *Lehrman v. Cohen, 43 Del. Ch. 222, 222 A.2d 800 (1966).*

Power to issue stock must rest upon authority conferred by law of corporation's existence. *Rice & Hutchins, Inc. v. Triplex Shoe Co., 16 Del. Ch. 298, 147 A. 317 (1929), aff'd, 17 Del. Ch. 356, 152 A. 342 (1930).*

Board of directors has exclusive authority to issue stock. — This section and §§ 152, 153, 157, 161 and 166 of this title, taken together, confirm the board's exclusive authority to issue stock and regulate a corporation's capital structure; to ensure certainty, these provisions contemplate board approval and a written instrument evidencing the relevant transactions affecting issuance of stock and the corporation's capital structure. *Grimes v. Alteon Inc., 804 A.2d 256 (Del. 2002).*

Attempt of a corporate board of directors to retroactively allow the issuance of preferred stock it had previously authorized by filing a certificate of designations was ineffective, as it did not approve that certificate by resolution, as required by subsection (g) of this section. *Liebermann v. Frangiosa, 844 A.2d 992 (Del. Ch. 2002).*

Common stock received through exercise of conversion options attached to invalid preferred shares deemed void. — Where former president/CEO and his wife received common stock through the exercise of their conversion options attached to preferred shares, and the preferred shares were invalid, the trial court had no basis to ignore established principals of Delaware corporate law and should not have invoked equitable remedies to resuscitate plainly void stock. *STAAR Surgical Co. v. Waggoner, 588 A.2d 1130 (Del. 1991).*

Rights of stockholders are contract rights. *Gaskill v. Gladys Belle Oil Co., 16 Del. Ch. 289, 146 A. 337 (1929).*

The rights of stockholders are contract rights and it is necessary to look to the certificate of incorporation to ascertain what those rights are. *Ellingwood v. Wolf's Head Oil Ref. Co., 27 Del. Ch. 356, 38 A.2d 743 (1944).*

The rights of stockholders are contract rights, and in interpreting charter provisions with regard to stock preferences, the same method is applied as that which is followed in interpreting written contracts generally. *Shanghai Power Co. v. Delaware Trust Co., 316 A.2d 589 (Del. Ch. 1974), aff'd in part and rev'd in part, 378 A.2d 624 (Del. 1977).*

Owner of shares of stock in company is not owner of corporation's property, but has the right to share in the earnings of the corporation, as they may be declared in dividends, arising from the use of all its property, and in the dissolution of the corporation may take proportionate share in what is left, after the debts of the corporation have been paid and the assets are divided. *Bird v. Wilmington Soc'y of Fine Arts, 28 Del. Ch. 449, 43 A.2d 476 (1945).*

Thus, fact that 1 person owns all stock of corporation does not make such person and corporation 1 and same person. *Bird v. Wilmington Soc'y of Fine Arts, 28 Del. Ch. 449, 43 A.2d 476 (1945).*

Term "stockholder" ordinarily is taken to apply to holder of legal title to shares of stock and registration, or its equivalent, is essential to pass the legal title as against the corporation; and the unregistered transferee is not entitled to the rights and privileges of a stockholder in the stockholder's relations with the corporation. *Salt Dome Oil Corp. v. Schenck, 28 Del. Ch. 433, 41 A.2d 583 (1945).*

The record owner may be but the nominal owner, and, technically, a trustee for the holder of the certificate, but legally he or she is still a stockholder, and may be treated as the owner by the corporation. *Salt Dome* Oil *Corp. v. Schenck, 28 Del. Ch. 433, 41 A.2d 583 (1945).*

Whatever may be the equitable rights that may arise by a delivery of the stock certificate accompanied with a power of attorney for its transfer, the legal title and legal rights and liabilities of the stockholder of record remain unchanged until the transfer is actually accomplished. *Salt Dome Oil Corp. v. Schenck, 28 Del. Ch. 433, 41 A.2d 583 (1945).*

Authority of Delaware corporation to issue special kinds of stock must be express authority in charter. *Standard Scale & Supply Corp. v. Chappel, 16 Del. Ch. 331, 141 A. 191 (1928).*

If the stockholders wish to confer special rights upon a given class of stock they must express their wish in the instrument which this section designates as the place for its recordation; that place is the certificate of incorporation. *Gaskill v. Gladys Belle Oil Co., 16 Del. Ch. 289, 146 A. 337 (1929).*

As long as special provisions do not offend public policy. — A certificate of incorporation may contain any provision with respect to the stock to be issued by the corporation, and the voting rights to be exercised by said stock, that is agreed upon by the stockholders, provided that the provision agreed to is not against public policy. *Ellingwood v. Wolf's Head Oil Ref. Co., 27 Del. Ch. 356, 38 A.2d 743 (1944).*

Charter restrictions on voting. — In the absence of any express provision in subsection (a) of this section, or elsewhere in the law, prohibiting charter restrictions on voting, the provisions of subsection (a) of § 212 of this title control in determining the validity of those restrictions. *Providence & Worcester Co. v. Baker, 378 A.2d 121 (Del. 1977).*

The absence in subsection (a) of § 212 of this title of a cross reference to subsection (a) of this section is indicative of the absence of any legislative intent to prohibit, by subsection (a) of this section, charter restrictions upon stockholders' voting rights. *Providence & Worcester Co. v. Baker, 378 A.2d 121 (Del. 1977).*

Distinguishing characteristic of preferred or special stock speaks of rights or favors in relation to other stock. *Starring v.* American *Hair & Felt Co., 21 Del. Ch. 380, 191 A. 887 (1937),* aff'd, *2 A.2d 249 (Del. Ch. 1938).*

Preferred stock is defined as a stock which in relation to other classes enjoys certain defined rights and privileges and these rights and privileges are generally associated with specified dividend and liquidation priorities. *In re Louisville Gas & Elec. Co., 77 F. Supp. 176 (D. Del. 1948).*

Preferences which are claimed for stock should be clearly expressed and if those preferences are stated in terms that are irreconcilable in their repugnancy, the claimed preferences have not been demonstrated with sufficient clearness. *Holland v. National Automotive Fibres, Inc., 22 Del. Ch. 99, 194 A. 124 (1937).*

As preferences attaching to stock are the exception, nothing should be presumed in their favor; they ought to be clearly expressed, if not by words of explicit import, at least by necessary implication. *Holland v. National Automotive Fibres, Inc., 22 Del. Ch. 99, 194 A. 124 (1937).*

Nothing is to be presumed in favor of preferences attached to stock, but rather they must be expressed in clear language. *Shanghai Power Co. v. Delaware Trust Co., 316 A.2d 589 (Del. Ch. 1974),* aff'd in part and rev'd in part, *378 A.2d 624 (Del. 1977).*

"Clearly and expressly set forth" required. — Any rights, preferences, and limitations of preferred stock that distinguish that stock from common stock must be expressly and clearly stated, as provided by subsection (a) of this section; these rights, preferences, and limitations will not be presumed or implied. *Elliott Assocs. v. Avatex Corp., 715 A.2d 843 (Del. 1998).*

But mere word "preferred," unless it is supplemented by definition of its significance, conveys no special meaning and the holder of preferred stock must refer to the appropriate language of the corporate contract for the ascertainment of his or her rights. *Gaskill v. Gladys Belle Oil Co., 16 Del. Ch. 289, 146 A. 337 (1929).*

Where in the original certificate of incorporation 2 classes of stock were created, a preferred with a par value and a common with no par value, but the preferred was simply called such and any description of preferences was omitted, the word "preferred" meant nothing. *Rice & Hutchins, Inc. v. Triplex Shoe Co., 16 Del. Ch. 298, 147 A. 317 (1929),* aff'd, *17 Del. Ch. 356, 152 A. 342 (1930).*

The term "preferred stock" is not a term of art, and the nature of the security must be determined from its rights and character and not its name. *In re Louisville Gas & Elec. Co., 77 F. Supp. 176 (D. Del. 1948).*

Thus entire certificate to be construed as whole. — In ascertaining the meaning of the certificate of incorporation in the matter of the respective rights and privileges of classes of stock, the entire instrument is to be considered and its language construed as a whole. In this respect the rule of interpretation is no different from that which appertains to written contracts generally. *Holland v. National Automotive Fibres, Inc., 22 Del. Ch. 99, 194 A. 124 (1937).*

Ambiguity construed in favor of preferred shareholders. — Where the stock certificate was ambiguous on preferred shareholders' rights regarding a reclassification of common stock into two new classes of stock, the court construed the language of the certificate in favor of the preferred stockholders so as to adhere to the reasonable expectations of the investors who purchased the security and thereby subjected themselves to its terms. *Kaiser Aluminum Corp. v. Matheson, 681 A.2d 392 (Del. 1996).*

Preferred stock voting rights exist unless denied in certificate. — A corporation may deny to preferred stock a right to vote at stockholders' meetings, but such right, unless expressly denied in the certificate of incorporation, is to be regarded as existing. *Morris v. American Pub. Util. Co., 14 Del. Ch. 136, 122 A. 696 (1923).*

Corporations

Unless a preferred stock is denied the right to vote in the certificate of incorporation, it has such right. *Rice & Hutchins, Inc. v. Triplex Shoe Co., 16 Del. Ch. 298, 147 A. 317 (1929),* aff'd, *17 Del. Ch. 356, 152 A. 342 (1930).*

Reformation of certificate to delineate voting rights. — The failure to delineate the voting rights of the class A and class B stock in the certificate of incorporation resulted in an instrument which in its legal effect does not truly express the intentions of the parties; this situation, which amounts to mutual mistake, provides a legally sufficient basis for causing the certificate to be reformed so as to reflect their intentions. *In re Farm Indus., Inc., 41 Del. Ch. 379, 196 A.2d 582 (1963).*

No corporation can create preferred stock by bylaw provision. *Gaskill v. Gladys Belle Oil Co., 16 Del. Ch. 289, 146 A. 337 (1929).*

Straight voting right for directors is not special right. — The right of the majority to elect directors by the system of straight voting is just as much a right while it continues as is the right to elect by cumulative voting; but the ordinary right of straight voting is not a special right. *Hartford Accident & Indem. Co. v. W.S. Dickey Clay Mfg. Co., 26 Del. Ch. 411, 24 A.2d 315 (1942).*

Nor is a favored voting position. — A favored voting position which the charter gives to a stock is not such a preference or relative or special right as this section contemplates. *Starring v. American Hair & Felt Co., 21 Del. Ch. 380, 191 A. 887 (1937),* aff'd, *2 A.2d 249 (Del. Ch. 1938).*

Special powers with respect to voting are not to be catalogued with "preferences and relative, participating, optional or other special rights," which this section says may be attached to preferred or special stock. *Starring v. American Hair & Felt Co., 21 Del. Ch. 380, 191 A. 887 (1937),* aff'd, *2 A.2d 249 (Del. Ch. 1938).*

Right of veto of election. — If the extraordinary power of the right of veto in the election of directors conferred on a particular class of stock is to be upheld, some provision of the law must be found which, either by express words or necessary intendment, authorizes the creation of the power, and it is sufficient to say that the right conferred on the special class of stock, in the guise of a voting right, is not within the intendment of the law. *Aldridge v. Franco Wyo. Oil Co., 24 Del. Ch. 349, 14 A.2d 380 (1940).*

Position of class of shares is not special right. — A position of a class of shares, as related to other shares in the capital structure, is not a relative and, therefore, a special right of the shares. *Hartford Accident & Indem. Co. v. W.S. Dickey Clay Mfg. Co., 26 Del. Ch. 411, 24 A.2d 315 (1942).*

Restrictions on redemption valid. — Nonredemption provision in corporation's certificate of incorporation, prohibiting corporation from redeeming junior preferred stock if such redemption would violate any covenant contained in any contract, agreement, obligation, or guarantee of corporation, was valid under subsection (a). *In re Bicoastal Corp., 600 A.2d 343 (Del. 1991).*

Directors determine when to redeem and at what price. — The directors are the ones upon whom certificate of incorporation casts the duty of determining when and the price at which redemption shall take place. *Corbett v. McClintic-Marshall Corp., 17 Del. Ch. 165, 151 A. 218 (1930).*

Price must be considered before directors redeem. — Simply because directors resolve to redeem at a given price, does not lend any countenance to the idea that redemption and price are so unrelated to each other that the directors intend the former to proceed regardless of their view with respect to the latter. *Corbett v. McClintic-Marshall Corp., 17 Del. Ch. 165, 151 A. 218 (1930).*

If stock is undervalued directors must write-up before redemption. — Directors, before effecting a redemption of preferred stock, are bound to go back into the books and order a write-up of the values therein given to the assets so as to bring them in line with present worth, if it appears that the undervaluations are not consistent with and justified by sound principles of corporate accounting. *Corbett v. McClintic-Marshall Corp., 17 Del. Ch. 165, 151 A. 218 (1930).*

DELAWARE CASE NOTES — UNREPORTED

Subsection (a) of this section affords Delaware corporations the ability to provide for the flexible financing that is necessary to meet the unique funding needs of the enterprise and the requirements of diverse investors in today's competitive global capital markets. *Matulich v. Aegis Commns. Essar Invs., Ltd., 2008 Del. LEXIS 20 (January 15, 2008).*

Dividend rights.—The Legislature did not intend to mandate that all preferred stock include dividend rights. *Shintom Co., Ltd. v. Audiovox Corp., 2005 Del. Ch. LEXIS 63, No. 693-N (May 4, 2005).*

It was not mandated by 8 Del. C. § 151(c) that all preferred stock confer a right to payment of dividends, but preferred stock was required to have some bona fide preference over other stock; a liquidation preference of preferred stock, without more, was sufficient to create a preferred stock, and the stock was lawfully issued. *Shintom Co. v. Audiovox Corp., 2005 Del. LEXIS 421 (Del. Oct. 31, 2005).*

What this section establishes is that the rights that a preferred stockholder holds against the corporation are formed via contract, and the stockholder can only claim those rights enunciated in the certificate. The entirety of this section must be viewed as though it is discussing rights that exist between the corporation and preferred stockholders, rights that are found in the certificate of incorporation and are enumerated on the stock certificate. *Shintom Co., Ltd. v. Audiovox Corp., 2005 Del. Ch. LEXIS 63, No. 693-N (May 4, 2005).*

The rules of construction which are used to interpret contracts and other written instruments are applicable when construing corporate charters and certificates of designation. *Matulich v. Aegis Commns. Essar Invs., Ltd., 2008 Del. LEXIS 20 (January 15, 2008).*

Corporations

Contractual, statutory rights distinguished. — Series B shareholders' contractual right to consent and approve does not constitute a statutory right to vote on the merger. Therefore, the court of chancery properly concluded that the contractual rights of the Series B Preferred Shareholders were irrelevant in calculating whether company Focus had the statutory voting power necessary to execute a short-form merger. Consequently, as a matter of law, plaintiff's challenge to the merger is without merit. *Matulich v. Aegis Communs. Essar Invs., Ltd., 2008 Del. LEXIS 20 (January 15, 2008).*

Certificate filing is necessary act. — Filing of a Certificate of Designation of Rights and Preferences is a necessary act to the complete the issuance of preferred shares; the composition of a corporation's board and the status of certain corporate offices is intimately bound up with whether that filing and the preferred stock are valid. *Chandler v. Ciccoricco, 2003 Del. Ch. LEXIS 47 (May 5, 2003).*

Personal jurisdiction under a conspiracy theory was upheld in a declaratory judgment action where the plaintiff alleged concerted activity to entrench certain conspirators, namely the directors of a franchise in an office at a Delaware corporation, through an improper stock issuance, which satisfied the plaintiff's prima facie burden to show a conspiracy to defraud; as a result, defendants' motion to dismiss for lack of personal jurisdiction was denied. *Benihana of Tokyo, Inc. v. Benihana, Inc., 2005 Del. Ch. LEXIS 19 (Feb. 4, 2005).*

Corporation's board had the authority to issue preferred stock with preemptive rights under its certificate of incorporation (COI) and the applicable provisions of the Delaware General Corporation Law; 8 Del. C. § 151(a) did not invalidate the transaction, where the blank check provision in the corporation's COI suggested that the certificate was never intended to limit the corporation's ability to issue preemptive rights by contract to purchasers of preferred stock. *Benihana of Tokyo, Inc. v. Benihana, Inc., 2005 Del. Ch. LEXIS 191 (Del. Ch. Dec. 8, 2005).*

CASE NOTES — OTHER STATES

Minnesota

In general. — Section 27 of the Delaware Corporation Law authorizes the issue of preferred stock, and redemption or purchase thereof, subject to the provisions of its certificate of incorporation. *Peterson v. New England Furniture & Carpet Company, 210 Minn. 449, 299 N.W. 208 (1941).*

Nebraska

Merger. — A corporate director must act in the best interests of shareholders and is obligated to the duties of fidelity, good faith, and prudence with respect to the interests of security holders, as well as the duty to exercise independent judgment with respect to matters committed to the discretion of the board of directors and lying at the heart of the management of the corporation. These duties are applicable to a director's acts in recommending a proposed merger. In the context of a proposed merger, a director has a duty to act in an informed and deliberate manner. *ConAgra, Inc. v. Cargill, Inc., 222 Neb. 136, 382 N.W.2d 576 (1986).*

After a merger agreement is signed a board may not, consistent with its fiduciary obligations to its shareholders, withhold information regarding a potentially more attractive competing offer. *ConAgra, Inc. v. Cargill, Inc., 222 Neb. 136, 382 N.W.2d 576 (1986).*

Lock-up provisions. — A director's duty to inform him- or herself in preparation for a decision derives from the fiduciary capacity in which he or she serves the corporation and its shareholders. Because a director is vested with the responsibility for the management of the affairs of the corporation, he or she must execute that duty with the recognition that he or she acts on behalf of others. Such obligation does not tolerate faithlessness or self-dealing. Even if the board of directors enters into a contract containing a lockup provision, the agreement must not infringe on the voting rights of shareholders or chill the bidding process. *ConAgra, Inc. v. Cargill, Inc., 222 Neb. 136, 382 N.W.2d 576 (1986).*

New Jersey

The laws of Delaware permit a corporation to purchase its own stock, provided that no impairment of capital is thereby caused. *Mayer v. Oxidation Productss Co., 110 N.J. Eq. 141, 159 A. 377 (1932).*

New York

Delaware law authorizes an officer or director to purchase the stock of the corporation with which he or she is associated except where the company involved has a policy of reacquiring its own stock, the director or officer takes advantage of superior or insider information or wrongly applies corporate resources to facilitate the purchase. *Ault v. Soutter, 167 A.D.2d 38, 570 N.Y.S.2d 280 (1991).*

Pennsylvania

Delaware law does not require a corporation's certificate of incorporation to authorize a corporation to repurchase shares of its own stock. *Wyatt v. Phillips, 2004 Phila. Ct. Com. Pl. LEXIS 89 (2004).*

Wisconsin

"Impairment of the 'capital'" of a company means the reduction of the amount of the assets of the company below the amount represented by the aggregate outstanding shares of the capital stock of the company. In other words, a corporation may use only its surplus for the purchase of shares of its own capital stock. *Turner v. Goetz, 184 Wis. 508, 199 N.W. 155 (1924).*

CASE NOTES — FEDERAL

First Circuit

Past consideration is insufficient to render a later stock option valid. *Feldman v. Detarando, 1980 U.S. Dist. LEXIS 14272 (D.Mass 1980).*

Option rights granted for personal services terminate upon the death of the holder because performance, consideration for the option, then becomes impossible. *Feldman v. Detarando, 1980 U.S. Dist. LEXIS 14272 (D.Mass 1980).*

When offer must be kept open. — An irreversible offer to sell stock at a given price for a fixed period of time, if given for present consideration, commits the corporation to keep the offer open. *Feldman v. Detarando, 1980 U.S. Dist. LEXIS 14272 (D.Mass 1980).*

Second Circuit

The Delaware Constitution mandates that a corporation may not issue stock except for money actually paid. *Elfenbein v. American Financial Corp., 487 F. Supp. 619 (S.D.N.Y. 1980).*

Empowerment to issue stock without shareholder approval. — The board is empowered to authorize by resolution, without shareholder approval, the issuance of new stock not authorized in the certificate of incorporation if it is explicitly authorized to do so by the provisions of the certificate of incorporation and it files a certificate meeting certain requirements with the Secretary of State. *Unilever Acquisition Corp. v. Richardson-Vicks, Inc., 618 F. Supp. 407 (S.D.N.Y. 1985).*

A stock split, by definition, divides the outstanding shares of a corporation without altering any shareholder's interest. *Satterfield v. Monsanto Co., 88 F. Supp. 2d 288 (S.D.N.Y. 2000).*

Option plan consideration requirement. — A corporation which issues employee stock options must make arrangements to assure that the employees involved will render some consideration to the issuing company in exchange for those valuable rights. Delaware law requires that any option plan must contain consideration passing to the corporation which could take variable forms, such as the retention of services of a valued employee or the gaining of services of a new employee. The plan, itself, or the surrounding circumstances, must be such as to insure that this consideration will in all reasonable probability be received by the corporation. One method of meeting this consideration requirement is for the issuing corporation to require that the optionee/employee remain in the employ of the corporation for some fixed period before the options involved will be exercisable. The mere existence of stock options, standing alone, does not alter the employment relationship between the parties. A stock option, in and of itself, only engenders a duty of the employer to deal in good faith, that is, to refrain from directly frustrating the exercise of the option. *Liebler v. Morton-Norwich Products, Inc., 1978 U.S. Dist. LEXIS 15220 (S.D.N.Y. 1978).*

Construction of certificate of incorporation. — The interpretation of language in a certificate of incorporation of a Delaware corporation is viewed as a contract among shareholders, so that the general rules of contract interpretation should apply to its terms. In interpreting the rights accorded to preferred shareholders, the courts must apply a strict construction, without presuming in favor of the preferred shares because preferences are regarded by Delaware courts as in derogation of the common law. The certificate of incorporation should be construed in its entirety, and all of the language reviewed together in order to reconcile all of the certificate's provisions so as to determine the meaning intended to be given to any portion of it. *Lacos Land Co. v. Lone Star Industries, Inc., 141 B.R. 815 (Bankr. S.D.N.Y. 1992).*

Merger. — Because mergers are permitted under Delaware law, and the accomplishment of a merger necessarily involves adjusting the rights of shareholders, a shareholder's preferential rights are subject to defeasance. Stockholders are charged with knowledge of this possibility at the time they acquire their shares. Moreover, Delaware provides specific protection to shareholders who believe that they have received insufficient value for their stock as the result of a merger: they may obtain an appraisal under § 262. Furthermore, the decision to merge with another company does not relieve the corporation or its directors of the duty to accord to the minority fair and equitable terms of conversion. The measure of fair value, however, is the amount equal to the corporation, not the stated redemption or liquidation value of the shares. *Rauch v. RCA Corp., 1987 U.S. Dist. LEXIS 3323 (S.D.N.Y. 1987).*

Under Delaware law, minority stock interests may be eliminated by merger. Also, where a merger of corporations is permitted by law, a shareholder's preferential rights are subject to defeasance. Stockholders are charged with knowledge of this possibility at the time they acquire their shares. *Satterfield v. Monsanto Co., 88 F. Supp. 2d 288 (S.D.N.Y. 2000).*

Third Circuit

Merger. — It is elementary that the substantial elements of the merger and consolidation provisions of the General Corporation Law are written into every corporate charter. The shareholder has notice that the corporation whose shares he or she has acquired may be merged with another corporation if the required majority of the shareholders agree. He or she is informed that the merger agreement may prescribe the terms and conditions of the merger, the mode of carrying it into effect, and the manner of converting the shares of the constituent corporations into the shares of the resulting corporation. A well-understood meaning of the word "convert" is to alter in form, substance, or quality. Substantial rights of shareholders, as is well known, may include rights in respect of voting, options, preferences, and dividends. The average intelligent mind must be held to know that dividends may accumulate on preferred stock, and that in the event of a merger of the corporation issuing the stock with another corporation, the various rights of shareholders, including the right to dividends on preference stock accrued but unpaid, may, and perhaps must, be the subject of reconcilement and adjustment. *Langfelder v. Universal Laboratories, Inc., 163 F.2d 804 (3d Cir. 1947).*

Fourth Circuit

Unequal treatment of shareholders. — Delaware courts recognize that in some circumstances Delaware law permits shareholders (as distinguished from shares) to be treated unequally. *Williams v. 5300 Columbia Pike Corp., 891 F. Supp. 1169 (E.D.Va. 1995).*

Sixth Circuit

Transferability of the preferred stock did not require the subsequent transferee assume the indemnification obligations contained in the purchase agreement. If that were the intent of the parties, they were required under Delaware law to be clearly referenced on the certificate of designations and the stock certificate itself. It is undisputed no such restrictions or obligations are found on the certificate of designations, the amended certificate of designations or the preferred stock certificate. Therefore, if no indemnification requirement followed the preferred stock, such obligation was not a part of the preferred stock transfer. *Oil States Int'l, Inc. v. LTV Corp., 2006 U.S. Dist. LEXIS 77307 (D.Ohio Oct. 24, 2006).*

Eighth Circuit

Shares may not be issued solely to preserve or to gain corporate control and corporate action, though technically correct and in compliance with Delaware Corporation Law, may not be undertaken for an inequitable purpose. *Watts v. Des Moines Register & Tribune, 525 F. Supp. 1311 (S.D.Iowa 1981).*

Eleventh Circuit

Under the Delaware Corporation Law, the holders of the preferred stock had the right as a class to vote upon and veto any proposed amendment of the charter which would alter or change the preferences, special rights, or powers of the preferred so as to affect the preferred adversely, or which would increase or decrease the amount of preferred or the par value. *Penfield v. Davis, 105 F. Supp. 292 (N.D. Ala. 1952).*

District of Columbia Circuit

Voidable shares. — Under Delaware law, shares of corporate stock that have not been initially authorized in full compliance with the requirements of the Delaware General Corporate Law, prior to ratification, are merely voidable, not void, because only voidable acts would be open to ratification. *CarrAmerica Realty Corp. v. Kaidanow, 321 F.3d 165 (D.C. Cir. 2003).*

§ 152. Issuance of stock; lawful consideration; fully paid stock

DELAWARE CASE NOTES — REPORTED

Definition of "consideration." — Delaware courts define "consideration," in general, as that which is given to induce a promise or performance in return. *Haft v. Dart Group Corp., 841 F. Supp. 549 (D. Del. 1993).*

Time for judging adequacy of consideration. — The critical time for determining whether lawful consideration exists is the date the shares were actually issued. *Haft v. Dart Group Corp., 841 F. Supp. 549 (D. Del. 1993).*

This section is part of contract, express or implied, respecting both preferred and common stock. *John W. Cooney Co. v. Arlington Hotel Co., 11 Del. Ch. 286, 101 A. 879 (1917),* modified on other grounds, *11 Del. Ch. 430, 106 A. 39 (1918).*

State law cannot be changed by incorporators or officers. — The authority of a corporation to issue stock is fixed by the law of the State which grants the authority, and neither the incorporators nor any other officers can change, modify or supplement the law in that regard. *Triplex Shoe Co. v. Rice & Hutchins, Inc., 17 Del. Ch. 356, 152 A. 342 (1930).*

Void issuance. — The modern trend of the law is that an issuance of stock without receipt by the company of valid consideration is void. *MBKS Co. v. Reddy, 924 A.2d 965; 2007 Del. Ch. LEXIS 52 (April 30, 2007).*

Void versus voidable dichotomy. – With the 2004 revisions to section 153, the legislature expanded the definition of consideration to include "any benefit to the corporation." When this broad definition is combined with the widespread use of no par stock, stock issued for no consideration of any kind — i.e. no benefit to the corporation — is one of the limited number of circumstances likely to fall under the void versus voidable dichotomy. *MBKS Co. v. Reddy, 924 A.2d 965; 2007 Del. Ch. LEXIS 52 (April 30, 2007).*

CEO attempt to set consideration. — Agreement between appellant stockholders and appellee chief executive officer was not enforceable where: it was neither approved by appellee corporation's board of directors nor set forth in a written agreement; it violated this section, as it fixed the consideration for the alleged offering; and § 157 of this title, as it created a right, which was not approved by the board. *Grimes v. Alteon Inc., 804 A.2d 256 (Del. 2002).*

Directors have right to issue stock to themselves. *Lofland v. Cahall, 13 Del. Ch. 384, 118 A. 1 (1922).*

But they cannot accept their own promissory notes for stock. — The directors of a corporation cannot issue stock to themselves, accept their own promissory notes in payment therefor, conceal the transaction from the other stockholders, and be regarded in equity as the legal holders of the stock. *Lofland v. Cahall, 13 Del. Ch. 384, 118 A. 1 (1922).*

Nor can they vote themselves stock for sale of stock in the course of their duties. — Directors of a corporation could not vote stock to themselves in consideration for having sold their company's stock under circumstances that indicated that the sales were but in the course of the directors' duty as such. *Blair v. F.H. Smith Co., 18 Del. Ch. 150, 156 A. 207 (1931)*.

Or for sales of stock past or future. — Since directors cannot vote stock to themselves in consideration for past sales, it is forbidden to them to vote stock to themselves in consideration of future sales. *Blair v. F.H. Smith Co., 18 Del. Ch. 150, 156 A. 207 (1931)*.

Grant of exclusive license to use patent is prima facie evidence of property, and is ordinarily sufficient consideration to justify the issuance of corporate stock. *West v. Sirian Lamp Co., 28 Del. Ch. 398, 44 A.2d 658 (1945)*.

And expenditure of money to protect interest does not invalidate. — The mere fact that a corporation may be required to expend money in the future to protect its interests in property rights acquired, and for which it has issued stock, does not necessarily render the consideration invalid. *West v. Sirian Lamp Co., 28 Del. Ch. 90, 37 A.2d 835 (1944)*.

Shares of stock of corporation are personal property and constitute good consideration in payment for the shares of stock of another company. *Peyton v. William C. Peyton Corp., 22 Del. Ch. 187, 194 A. 106 (1937), rev'd on other grounds, 23 Del. Ch. 321, 7 A.2d 737 (1939)*.

Surrender of old stock for new stock is valid exchange. — Where new prior preference stock and new common stock were issued under a recapitalization plan in consideration of the surrender of old preference stock or common stock, the old stock was personal property within the meaning of this section. *Shanik v. White Sewing Mach. Corp., 25 Del. Ch. 371, 19 A.2d 831 (1941)*.

Release of valid claim against corporation provides adequate consideration for issuance of stock. *Blish v. Thompson Automatic Arms Corp., 30 Del. Ch. 538, 64 A.2d 581 (1948)*.

Consideration is supplied by an agreement to relinquish rights created under a prior agreement. *Equitable Trust Co. v. Gallagher, 34 Del. Ch. 76, 99 A.2d 490 (1953), modified, 34 Del. Ch. 249, 102 A.2d 538 (1954)*.

And judgment of board of directors as to amount thereof shall be conclusive. *Blish v. Thompson Automatic Arms Corp., 30 Del. Ch. 538, 64 A.2d 581 (1948)*.

Services and expenditures before incorporation. — If services are rendered and money is paid in behalf of a proposed corporation by its promoters before its actual existence, it is competent for the corporation to adopt the contract made by the promoters that payment therefor should be in stock and issue its stock in consideration of the services thus rendered and the money thus spent in its behalf in anticipation of its creation. *Shore v. Union Drug Co., 18 Del. Ch. 74, 156 A. 204 (1931)*.

Services extended for a corporation before its creation constitute good consideration for the issuance of stock of the corporation organized under *Delaware law. Blish v. Thompson Automatic Arms Corp., 30 Del. Ch. 538, 64 A.2d 581 (1948)*.

Property given by promoters. — Promoters, having given full value in the form of property for their stock, are in as good a position as they would be in if they had given cash in the full amount of the par value of the stock. *Henderson v. Plymouth Oil Co., 15 Del. Ch. 40, 131 A. 165 (1925)*.

If promoters give full value for the stock they receive, they may turn it back to the treasury to be sold for the benefit of the corporation, and purchasers thereof have no better right than the original promoter to complain in the name of the corporation against any supposed wrongs that may have attended its issuance. *Henderson v. Plymouth Oil Co., 15 Del. Ch. 40, 131 A. 165 (1925)*.

Plan of business, having no element of property, and could not in any fair sense be "acquired" by the company, was neither labor done, nor services rendered and did not constitute a valid consideration. *Scully v. Automobile Fin. Co., 12 Del. Ch. 174, 109 A. 49 (1920)*.

Promise to pay, by note or otherwise, is not payment of money within the meaning of this section. *Lofland v. Cahall, 13 Del. Ch. 384, 118 A. 1 (1922)*.

A promise to pay money does not meet the constitutional requirement for consideration for stock. *Sohland v. Baker, 15 Del. Ch. 431, 141 A. 277 (1927)*.

Even if it is promissory note. — A promissory note in a broad sense is property; but it is only a promise to pay money and, therefore, is a mere evidence of indebtedness and a promise to pay money is not money paid, and cannot be so taken, and it is not property actually acquired and, therefore, may not be taken in payment for shares where there is a prohibition such as there is in *Delaware. Cahall v. Lofland, 12 Del. Ch. 299, 114 A. 224 (1921), aff'd, 13 Del. Ch. 384, 118 A. 1 (1922); Sohland v. Baker, 15 Del. Ch. 431, 141 A. 277 (1927)*.

A promise to lend money to a corporation is not such a consideration for stock as will satisfy the requirements of this section, but a corporation may in agreeing to sell its stock stipulate as a matter of contract that in addition to paying full lawful consideration therefor the subscriber or purchaser shall also lend money to it. *Riegel v. Only Package Pie, Inc., 14 Del. Ch. 356, 128 A. 110 (1925)*.

The unsecured promissory note of a subscriber of stock of a corporation is neither "money paid" nor "property actually acquired" within the meaning of the Constitution and this section. *Baker v. Bankers Mtg. Co., 15 Del. Ch. 183, 133 A. 698 (1926)*.

But negotiable promissory note is valid consideration. — A negotiable promissory note of a subscriber for stock secured by the proper collateral may constitute property actually acquired and would be lawful consideration for the issuance of stock. *Sohland v. Baker, 15 Del. Ch. 431, 141 A. 277 (1927)*.

Continuation of relationship between 1 corporation and another is not legal consideration for stock. *In re Seminole Oil & Gas Corp., 38 Del. Ch. 246, 150 A.2d 20 (1959), appeal dismissed, 159 A.2d 276 (Del. 1960)*.

Future services to company of 1 kind and another are not lawful consideration. *Finch v. Warrior Cement Corp., 16 Del. Ch. 44, 141 A. 54 (1928)*.

When the interests of creditors are affected, "work done" should not include prospective labor as an equivalent for money in exchange for shares of stock, since "work done" does not include work to be done, or work done and to be done. *John W. Cooney Co. v. Arlington Hotel Co., 11 Del. Ch. 286, 101 A. 879 (1917)*, modified, *11 Del. Ch. 430, 106 A. 39 (1918)*.

Services to be rendered cannot be a valid consideration for the issuance of full-paid, nonassessable shares of stock, for these can be issued only for "labor done," after it has been done. *Scully v. Automobile Fin. Co., 12 Del. Ch. 174, 109 A. 49 (1920)*.

Labor to be done was not "labor done" and was not a good consideration for the issuance of stock in a Delaware corporation. *Sohland v. Baker, 15 Del. Ch. 431, 141 A. 277 (1927)*.

Where the services accepted in payment for stock were to be rendered in the future, such services were not a lawful consideration for the issuance of full-paid, nonassessable stock. *Rice & Hutchins, Inc. v. Triplex Shoe Co., 16 Del. Ch. 298, 147 A. 317 (1929)*, aff'd, *17 Del. Ch. 356, 152 A. 342 (1930)*.

This section does not authorize the issuance of full-paid stock for future services. *Maclary v. Pleasant Hills, Inc., 35 Del. Ch. 39, 109 A.2d 830 (1954)*.

Future profits are not valid consideration for the issuance of stock in a Delaware corporation. *Norton v. Digital Applications, Inc., 305 A.2d 656 (Del. Ch. 1973)*.

Directors must place value on property acquired as consideration for issuance of stock. *Field v. Carlisle Corp., 31 Del. Ch. 227, 68 A.2d 817 (1949)*.

While this section does not in terms require that the directors shall place a value on labor done and property acquired as a consideration for the issuance of stock, yet they must, because where the value of a thing is not self-evident the judgment of someone must be consulted, and the directors of the corporation are the persons upon whose judgment the corporation would naturally rely. *Bowen v. Imperial Theatres, Inc., 13 Del. Ch. 120, 115 A. 918 (1922)*.

But directors have no power to adjudge value to future services as basis for full-paid stock. *Scully v. Automobile Fin. Co., 12 Del. Ch. 174, 109 A. 49 (1920)*.

Past services as consideration. — Where plaintiff had performed some services for corporation prior to the issuance of the plaintiff's shares, the judgment of defendant's directors as to its value was conclusive in the absence of actual fraud. *Haft v. Dart Group Corp., 841 F. Supp. 549 (D. Del. 1993)*.

Restricted shares initially were issued for valid consideration in the form of labor done. *Haft v. Dart Group Corp., 841 F. Supp. 549 (D. Del. 1993)*.

Board of directors may employ nondirectors to assist them in arriving at value to be placed on the property to be received in exchange for the corporation's stock. *Field v. Carlisle Corp., 31 Del. Ch. 227, 68 A.2d 817 (1949)*.

But directors do not have the power to delegate this vitally important duty of determining consideration for stock. The importance to the corporation of the subject matter, ownership of the corporation, tends also to negative any implication that the directors might delegate it in a manner not explicitly authorized by this section. *Field v. Carlisle Corp., 31 Del. Ch. 227, 68 A.2d 817 (1949)*.

Personally interested directors may not take part in valuation. — By "directors" in this section the General Assembly meant officers who were competent to represent the company in making the valuation, and not those who were personally interested in the valuation, and, therefore, wholly incompetent to represent the company in the transaction. *Lofland v. Cahall, 13 Del. Ch. 384, 118 A. 1 (1922)*.

Valuation need not be formally recorded. — This section does not require that the judgment concerning the value of consideration be formally recorded. *Bowen v. Imperial Theatres, Inc., 13 Del. Ch. 120, 115 A. 918 (1922)*.

Judgment of directors is conclusive in absence of actual fraud. — In the absence of actual fraud in the transaction the judgment of the directors as to the value of the alleged consideration for the issuance of stock is conclusive. *Belle Isle Corp. v. MacBean, 29 Del. Ch. 261, 49 A.2d 5*, aff'd sub nom. *Belle Isle Corp. v. Corcoran, 29 Del. Ch. 554, 49 A.2d 1 (1946)*.

Under this section, one attacking the issuance of stock must show actual fraud on the part of the directors in evaluating the consideration for which the shares were issued. *Belle Isle Corp. v. MacBean, 30 Del. Ch. 373, 61 A.2d 699 (1948)*.

Stockholders may not complain of a corporate purchase made in conformity with Delaware statutory authority unless such transaction is fraudulent as having been carried out for a grossly inadequate consideration or otherwise made in bad faith. *Heilbrunn v. Sun Chem. Corp., 37 Del. Ch. 552, 146 A.2d 757 (1958)*, aff'd, *38 Del. Ch. 321, 150 A.2d 755 (1959)*.

Conscious overvaluation by directors of labor or services received would be actual fraud and would render the subscription contract unlawful. *Scully v. Automobile Fin. Co., 12 Del. Ch. 174, 109 A. 49 (1920)*.

As is stock issued for consideration never received. — The issuance of stock as full paid for a consideration never delivered to, nor acquired by, the corporation constitutes "actual fraud" within the meaning of this section. *Diamond State Brewery, Inc. v. de la Riguardiere, 25 Del. Ch. 257, 17 A.2d 313 (1941)*.

Actual fraud may be shown directly but it may also be inferred from the attendant circumstances, and inadequacy of consideration is a part of such circumstances. *Lewis v. Scotten Dillon Co., 306 A.2d 755 (Del. Ch. 1973)*.

However, excessive valuation, standing alone, is not enough unless it is so gross as to lead the court to conclude that it was due, not to an honest error of judgment but to bad faith or a reckless indifference to the rights of others. *Lewis v. Scotten Dillon Co., 306 A.2d 755 (Del. Ch. 1973)*.

Stockholder may maintain a bill for cancellation of stock of corporation where issue was unlawful. *Ellis v. Penn Beef Co., 9 Del. Ch. 213, 80 A. 666 (1911)*.

But stockholder is estopped from complaining against issuance he or she has ratified. — Stockholders who, with full knowledge, acquiesce in or ratify an illegal issue of stock, may thereafter be estopped from complaining against it. *Finch v. Warrior Cement Corp., 16 Del. Ch. 44, 141 A. 54 (1928).*

Acquiescence and participation in an issue of stock, without consideration or for an insufficient consideration, will bar the right of the assenting stockholder to complain against its issuance. *Finch v. Warrior Cement Corp., 16 Del. Ch. 44, 141 A. 54 (1928).*

However, failure to object to previous elections does not bar objection to present issuance. — The stockholder did not, by his failure to object at prior elections or meetings waive his right to object to the last meeting and election regarding the issuance of invalid stock. *Triplex Shoe Co. v. Rice & Hutchins, Inc., 17 Del. Ch. 356, 152 A. 342 (1930).*

Stockholder has burden to prove bad faith or improper motive. — In an action by stockholder to cancel stock issued by corporation on the grounds of improper purpose and inadequate consideration, the stockholder has the burden of proving bad faith or improper motive as the defendants are entitled to start with a presumption of good faith. *Bennett v. Breuil Petro. Corp., 34 Del. Ch. 6, 99 A.2d 236 (1953).*

One asserting the defense of lack of consideration bears the burden of proving that defense. *Haft v. Dart Group Corp., 841 F. Supp. 549 (D. Del. 1993).*

Merely because defendant is controlling stockholder, burden of showing good faith and proper purpose is not shifted to defendant. *Bennett v. Breuil Petro. Corp., 34 Del. Ch. 6, 99 A.2d 236 (1953).*

Presumption of valid consideration may be overcome by clear and convincing proof. — The quality of the consideration paid for stock issued by a corporation is usually the essential element in determining its validity and the presumption of validity may be overcome by clear and convincing proof. *West v. Sirian Lamp Co., 28 Del. Ch. 328, 42 A.2d 883 (1945).*

Stockholder may object to issuance for legally inadequate price. — A corporation is not permitted to sell its stock for a legally inadequate price, where there is objection by a stockholder who has a right to insist upon compliance with the law whether or not he or she cares to exercise the option to purchase the stock. However, a stockholder cannot block a sale for a fair price merely because he disagrees with the wisdom of the plan, but can insist that the sale price be fixed in accordance with legal requirements. *Bennett v. Breuil Petro. Corp., 34 Del. Ch. 6, 99 A.2d 236 (1953).*

Board of directors has exclusive authority to issue stock. — This section and §§ 151, 153, 157, 161 and 166 of this title, taken together, confirm the board's exclusive authority to issue stock and regulate a corporation's capital structure; to ensure certainty, these provisions contemplate board approval and a written instrument evidencing the relevant transactions affecting issuance of stock and the corporation's capital structure. *Grimes v. Alteon Inc., 804 A.2d 256 (Del. 2002).*

Issuing new shares of stock by majority stockholders, having as its primary purpose "freezing out" of minority interest, is actionable without regard to the fairness of the price. *Bennett v. Breuil Petro. Corp., 34 Del. Ch. 6, 99 A.2d 236 (1953).*

Stockholder has been injured where, under corporate reorganization, corporation offered additional stock at a grossly inadequate price, even where the stockholder was offered his or her pro rata share of the additional shares, as stockholder's right not to purchase is seriously impaired if the stock is worth substantially more than its issuing price, because any purchase at the price obviously dilutes his or her interest and impairs the value of his or her original holdings. *Bennett v. Breuil Petro. Corp., 34 Del. Ch. 6, 99 A.2d 236 (1953).*

While Del. Const., art. IX, § 3 and this section govern the quality of the consideration required to be paid for subscriptions to or purchases of the capital stock of a Delaware corporation, shares may not be issued for an improper purpose such as a takeover of voting control from others; neither may corporate machinery be manipulated so as to injure minority stockholders. *Condec Corp. v. Lunkenheimer Co., 43 Del. Ch. 353, 230 A.2d 769 (1967).*

If corporation receives proper consideration it may insist on any additional terms. — When the legal standard of consideration for stock, its quality and amount, is satisfied, the corporation is at liberty to insist on any additional terms by way of contract it may choose, whether such additional terms will furnish what in the first instance would be a lawful consideration or not. *Reigel v. Only Package Pie, Inc., 14 Del. Ch. 356, 128 A. 110 (1925).*

Consideration rules same for par and no-par stock. — As to the kind or quality of consideration for which stock may be issued, no-par stock is in exactly the same situation as is stock having a par value. *Bodell v. General Gas & Elec. Corp., 15 Del. Ch. 119, 132 A. 442 (1926), aff'd, 15 Del. Ch. 420, 140 A. 264 (1927).*

The introduction of stock without par value will not result in allowing a different kind of consideration to be received for it from that which had been required for par value stock. *Bodell v. General Gas & Elec. Corp., 15 Del. Ch. 119, 132 A. 442 (1926), aff'd, 15 Del. Ch. 420, 140 A. 264 (1927).*

The amount of the consideration received for no-par stock is of no moment, provided the quality of the consideration was such as to meet the constitutional requirement. *Finch v. Warrior Cement Corp., 16 Del. Ch. 44, 141 A. 54 (1928).*

Seeking of injunction not to effect jurisdiction to cancel. — Where stockholder has brought action to cancel issuance of stock due to corporate reorganization, the fact that stockholder also seeks additional relief by way of injunction against the individual nonresident defendants does not oust the court of its statutory jurisdiction. *Bennett v. Breuil Petro. Corp., 34 Del. Ch. 6, 99 A.2d 236 (1953).*

Conflict as to whether stock price is inadequate cannot be fairly resolved on motion for summary judgment. *Bennett v. Breuil Petro. Corp., 34 Del. Ch. 6, 99 A.2d 236 (1953).*

Nor can dispute as to motive of stock issuance. — Where plaintiff stockholder sets forth a legally recognized claim and the pleadings and affidavits raise a substantial factual dispute as to the legal propriety of the motives of the corporate defendant and its controlling stockholder, which can only be resolved by a hearing, summary judgment is not proper. *Bennett v. Breuil Petro. Corp., 34 Del. Ch. 6, 99 A.2d 236 (1953).*

Acceptors of illegally issued stock liable to corporate creditors for its par value. — The law of this State contemplates that stock may be issued contrary to this section, that is, without being paid for, and if it is so issued the acceptors are made liable to the creditors of the company to the extent of its par value. *John W. Cooney Co. v. Arlington Hotel Co., 11 Del. Ch. 430, 106 A. 39 (1918).*

Corporate stock shall not be issued without valid consideration, but if it is so issued, contrary to law, the acceptor will be bound to pay its par value if the debts of the company cannot be paid otherwise. *Scully v. Automobile Fin. Co., 12 Del. Ch. 174, 109 A. 49 (1920).*

Stock issued without consideration is voidable and not void. *Belle Isle Corp. v. MacBean, 30 Del. Ch. 373, 61 A.2d 699 (1948).*

"Free stock" as constituting stock supported by valid consideration. — See *Ash v. Brunswick Corp., 405 F. Supp. 234 (D. Del. 1975).*

If issuance of stock was void, cancellation is proper remedy; if merely voidable, then that form of relief is to be adopted which would seem to be most in accord with all the equities of the case. *Diamond State Brewery, Inc. v. de la Riguardiere, 25 Del. Ch. 257, 17 A.2d 313 (1941).*

Not entitled to vote. — The complexities and intricacies of the cases involving third parties, watered stock, treasury stock issued without valid consideration, and constitutionally inadequate consideration simply are not relevant where a self-interested party acting as the sole director of a 100% owned subsidiary issues himself stock without any consideration to the subsidiary as part of a plan to wrest majority control from the parent. Therefore, defendant's stock was at the least voidable, if not totally void, and was not entitled to vote as of the times corporation acted by written consent to appoint new directors and to remove defendant. *MBKS Co. v. Reddy, 924 A.2d 965; 2007 Del. Ch. LEXIS 52 (April 30, 2007).*

CASE NOTES — UNREPORTED

Consideration found. — Stock had been validly issued under 8 Del. C. § 152 and 8 Del. C. § 153, as a director's testimony indicated a belief that defendant had contributed substantial services, which would constitute valid consideration; and meeting minutes, reflecting the approval of defendant's prior acts and the election of a

board of directors with an 8-2 split between the parties, provided further evidence that both parties considered the earlier issuance of shares to be valid. *Fonds de Regulation et de Controle Cafe Cacao v. Lion Capital Mgmt., LLC, 2007 Del. Ch. LEXIS 12 (Del. Ch. Jan. 22, 2007).*

CASE NOTES — OTHER STATES

Illinois

Duty of disclosure. — Delaware courts address the duty of disclosure by corporate directors only with respect to the following five scenarios: mergers, proxy solicitations, tender offers, self-tender offers, and stockholder votes. *Sims v. Tezak, 296 Ill. App. 3d 503, 694 N.E.2d 1015, 230 Ill. Dec. 737.Dec. 737 (1998).*

Determination of value. — A board of directors' determination as to the value of the company's stock is conclusive absent a showing of fraud. *Regnery v. Regnery, 287 Ill. App. 3d 354, 679 N.E.2d 74, 223 Ill. Dec. 130 (1997).*

Proof of fairness of transaction. — A person standing on both sides of the transaction (i.e., as majority shareholder voting to sell the shares and as employee wishing to purchase such shares) has the burden of proving the fairness of such a transaction. *Regnery v. Regnery, 287 Ill. App. 3d 354, 679 N.E.2d 74, 223 Ill. Dec. 130 (1997).*

A note does not constitute valid consideration for the issuance of stock under the provisions of the Delaware statute and constitution. *Arndt v. Abbott, 308 Ill. App. 633, 32 N.E.2d 342 (1941).*

Massachusetts

Under Delaware law, the promise of future services is not valid consideration. *Biotrack, Inc. v. Muni, 12 Mass. L. Rep. 244 (Super. 2000).*

Delaware law appears to draw a distinction between a case where the issuance of a company's stock itself violates a provision of Delaware's Constitution, its corporation law, or the company's own corporate charter, and one where the company has the power and authority to issue stock but does so without receiving the required consideration. *Biotrack, Inc. v. Muni, 12 Mass. L. Rep. 244 (Super 2000).*

Michigan

No issuance of stock takes place until a certificate duly made out passed from the custody and control of the company into the possession of the stockholder, or some person as agent for him or her. *Waldorf v. KMS Industries, Inc., 25 Mich. App. 20, 181 N.W.2d 85 (1970).*

Missouri

Voidable issuance. — Delaware treats the absence of valid consideration as rendering the stock issuance voidable rather than void. Courts balance the equities to determine whether the corporation may cancel the shares or whether the party claiming entitlement to the shares may pay adequate consideration for the shares and cure the defect in consideration. *Yates v. Bridge Trading Co., 844 S.W.2d 56 (Mo. App. 1992).*

Promissory note inadequate consideration. —Under neither the law of Missouri nor the law of Delaware is a promissory note adequate consideration for shares of stock. *Yates v. Bridge Trading Co., 844 S.W.2d 56 (Mo. App. 1992).*

CASE NOTES — FEDERAL

First Circuit

Past consideration is insufficient to render a later stock option valid. *Feldman v. Detarando, 1980 U.S. Dist. LEXIS 14272 (D.Mass 1980).*

When offer must be kept open. — An irreversible offer to sell stock at a given price for a fixed period of time, if given for present consideration, commits the corporation to keep the offer open. *Feldman v. Detarando, 1980 U.S. Dist. LEXIS 14272 (D.Mass 1980).*

Extent of authority for share issuance. — Shareholders necessarily understand that a corporation may issue shares up to the maximum number authorized by its certificate of incorporation. Shareholders would be hard pressed to complain when that occurs in furtherance of legitimate corporate purposes, such as the settlement of a lawsuit representing a potential corporate liability. More specifically, under the corporate law of Delaware, the directors are authorized to distribute treasury stock and issue new stock (up to the limit authorized by the certificate of incorporation) at their discretion, for consideration determined by them. *Enterasys Networks, Inc. v. Gulf Insurance Co., 364 F. Supp. 2d 28 (D.N.Hamp. 2005).*

Second Circuit

Option plan consideration requirement. — A corporation which issues employee stock options must make arrangements to assure that the employees involved will render some consideration to the issuing company in exchange for those valuable rights. Delaware law requires that any option plan must contain consideration passing to the corporation which could take variable forms, such as the retention of services of a valued employee or the gaining of services of a new employee. The plan, itself, or the surrounding circumstances, must be such as to insure that this consideration will in all reasonable probability be received by the corporation. One method of meeting this consideration requirement is for the issuing corporation to require that the optionee/employee remain in the employ of the corporation for some fixed period before the options involved will be exercisable. The mere existence of stock options, standing alone, does not alter the employment relationship between the parties. A stock option, in and of itself, only engenders a duty of the employer to deal in good faith, that is, to refrain from directly frustrating the exercise of the option. *Liebler v. Morton-Norwich Products, Inc., 1978 U.S. Dist. LEXIS 15220 (S.D.N.Y. 1978).*

Under Delaware law, a stock split divides the outstanding shares of a corporation without altering any shareholder's interest. *Satterfield v. Pfizer, Inc., 2005 U.S. Dist. LEXIS 4180 (S.D.N.Y. 2005).*

A stock split, by definition, divides the outstanding shares of a corporation without altering any shareholder's interest. *Satterfield v. Monsanto Co., 88 F. Supp. 2d 288 (S.D.N.Y. 2000).*

With respect to Delaware law, past service to the issuer is valid consideration for the issuance of fully paid shares. Moreover in the absence of actual fraud in the transaction, the judgment of the directors as to the value of such consideration shall be conclusive. *Butler v. Phlo Corp., 2001 U.S. Dist. LEXIS 10809 (S.D.N.Y. 2001).*

"Outstanding". — Delaware law defines "outstanding" stock as that which can be voted, and therefore, is construed to mean stock in the hands of shareholders, not stock in the treasury. *Satterfield v. Monsanto Co., 88 F. Supp. 2d 288 (S.D.N.Y. 2000).*

Third Circuit

Where a shareholder participates in an issuance of stock, the assenting shareholder is barred from complaining against the validity of that issuance on the grounds that there was no consideration or for any other technical irregularities. *Regis Insurance Co. v. Di Loreto, 1989 U.S. Dist. LEXIS 6256 (E.D.Pa 1989).*

Fifth Circuit

Applicable laws. — The issuance of stock option plans by Delaware corporations involves the internal affairs of a Delaware corporation and is, therefore, controlled by the laws of Delaware. *Vannoy v. Verio Inc., 2004 U.S. Dist. LEXIS 14713 (N.D.Tex. 2004).*

Internal affairs doctrine. — As the ability of a corporation to issue stock is a matter peculiar to the relationships among or between the corporation and its officers, directors, and shareholders, the internal affairs doctrine dictates that only one state's laws should regulate such conduct. *Vannoy v. Verio Inc., 2004 U.S. Dist. LEXIS 14713 (N.D.Tex. 2004).*

Necessity of board approval. — Multiple provisions of the Delaware Code set forth the formal requirements for the issuance of capital stock, the consideration for the issuance of stock, and formalities regarding rights, options, and subscriptions relating to capital stock. Specifically, Del. Code Ann. tit. 8, § 157 states that board approval and a written instrument is required to create rights and options respecting stock. Indeed, the duty of a corporation's board of directors to approve a sale of stock is so important that the board cannot delegate it to the corporation's officers. *Vannoy v. Verio Inc., 2004 U.S. Dist. LEXIS 14713 (N.D.Tex. 2004).*

Sixth Circuit

Consideration for no par stock. — There is no requirement as to the amount of consideration which must be received in respect to an original issue of no par stock, although the quality of consideration must meet the same requirements as stock having a par value. *Louisville Trust Co. v. Glenn, 66 F. Supp. 872 (W.D.Ky. 1946).*

Seventh Circuit

Breach of director duty in share issuance. — Directors stand in a fiduciary relation to the corporation and its shareholders; their primary duty is to deal fairly and justly. It is a breach of this duty for directors to make use of the issuance of shares to accomplish an improper purpose, such as to enable a particular person or group to maintain or obtain voting control, against the objection of shareholders from whom control is thereby wrested. *Calumet Industries, Inc. v. MacClure, 464 F. Supp. 19 (N.D. Ill. 1978).*

Issuance to friendly third parties. — Delaware law does not prohibit a board from issuing voting stock to friendly third parties, so long as the placement can be justified by a valid corporate purpose, such as deterring an inadequate or coercive bid, which the board finds, is not in the corporation's best interest. *Newell Co. v. Vermont American Corp., 725 F. Supp. 351 (N.D.Ill. 1989).*

Under Delaware law, status as a shareholder does not depend on the issuance of a certificate of stock since the certificate is merely evidence of ownership. *Cabintaxi Corp. v. Commissioner, 63 F.3d 614 (7th Cir. 1995).*

Eighth Circuit

Shares may not be issued solely to preserve or to gain corporate control and corporate action, though technically correct and in compliance with Delaware Corporation Law may not be undertaken for an inequitable purpose. *Watts v. Des Moines Register & Tribune, 525 F. Supp. 1311 (S.D.Iowa 1981).*

Ninth Circuit

Conclusive consideration value judgment. — Consideration may take on other, less tangible forms, such as tax benefits, increased productivity or employee concessions. Indeed, the judgment of the directors as to the value of such consideration for the issuance of shares is conclusive. *NL Indusustries, Inc. v. Lockheed Corp., 1992 U.S. Dist. LEXIS 22652 (C.D.Cal. 1992).*

District of Columbia Circuit

The Delaware General Corporate Law requires that the board of directors of a corporation establish the consideration to be received for stock. *CarrAmerica Realty Corp. v. Kaidanow, 321 F.3d 165 (D.C. Cir. 2003).*

Voidable shares. — Under Delaware law, shares of corporate stock that have not been initially authorized in full compliance with the requirements of the Delaware General Corporate Law, prior to ratification, are merely voidable, not void, because only voidable acts would be open to ratification. *CarrAmerica Realty Corp. v. Kaidanow, 321 F.3d 165 (D.C. Cir. 2003).*

§ 153. Consideration for stock

DELAWARE CASE NOTES — REPORTED

Void versus voidable dichotomy. – With the 2004 revisions to section 153, the legislature expanded the definition of consideration to include "any benefit to the corporation." When this broad definition is combined with the widespread use of no par stock, stock issued for no consideration of any kind — i.e. no benefit to the corporation — is one of the limited number of circumstances likely to fall under the void versus voidable dichotomy. *MBKS Co. v. Reddy, 924 A.2d 965; 2007 Del. Ch. LEXIS 52 (April 30, 2007).*

Directors' discretion should not be interfered with in absence of fraud. — The discretion of a board of directors in the sale of its no-par-value stock should not be interfered with, except for fraud, actual or constructive, such as improper motive or personal gain or arbitrary action or conscious disregard of the interests of the corporation and the rights of its stockholders. *Bodell v. General Gas & Elec. Corp., 15 Del. Ch. 420, 140 A. 264 (1927).*

Or clear abuse. — The directors may from time to time issue no-par stock for any consideration they may see fit, even though the price they fix is far below its actual value. But, equity will, in accordance with the principles which prompt it to restrain an abuse of powers granted in absolute terms, lay its restraining hand upon the directors in case of an abuse of this absolute power. *Bodell v. General Gas & Elec. Corp., 15 Del. Ch. 119, 132 A. 442 (1926), aff'd, 15 Del. Ch. 420, 140 A. 264 (1927).*

In the absence of a clear abuse of discretion by the corporate board of directors, the amount of the consideration received for a no-par common stock issue is usually of no moment, provided its quality is such as to meet the constitutional requirements. *West v. Sirian Lamp Co., 28 Del. Ch. 90, 37 A.2d 835 (1944).*

Board of directors has exclusive authority to issue stock. — This section and §§ 151, 152, 157, 161 and 166 of this title, taken together, confirm the board's exclusive authority to issue stock and regulate a corporation's capital structure; to ensure certainty, these provisions contemplate board approval and a written instrument evidencing the relevant transactions affecting issuance of stock and the corporation's capital structure. *Grimes v. Alteon Inc., 804 A.2d 256 (Del. 2002).*

Price of no-par stock should be set in light of all legitimate considerations. — Managers of corporations ought to be required to market new issues of no-par stock at prices that are fair to the corporation and existing stockholders and best calculated to yield the largest possible capital. These prices should be fixed in the light of all legitimate considerations. *Bodell v. General Gas & Elec. Corp., 15 Del. Ch. 119, 132 A. 442 (1926), aff'd, 15 Del. Ch. 420, 140 A. 264 (1927).*

It need not conform to market value. — Market value cannot be accepted as a safe guide for the fixing of the sales value for unissued stock, and neither can book value, in itself, be so accepted. *Bodell v. General Gas &*

Corporations

Elec. Corp., 15 Del. Ch. 119, 132 A. 442 (1926), aff'd, *15 Del. Ch. 420, 140 A. 264 (1927).*

Or sales value. — This section makes no mention of "sales value" or of any other similar thing to which no-par stock issues must conform themselves. *Bodell v. General Gas & Elec. Corp., 15 Del. Ch. 119, 132 A. 442 (1926),* aff'd, *15 Del. Ch. 420, 140 A. 264 (1927).*

And length of interval between no-par issuances not a factor. — Prices at which no-par stock is issued cannot be made to depend for their fairness upon the immaterial circumstances of the length of time intervening between the moments of their issuance. No-par stock may be issued at any time for such consideration as may be fixed by the directors at the time the issue is authorized. *Bodell v. General Gas & Elec. Corp., 15 Del. Ch. 119, 132 A. 442 (1926),* aff'd, *15 Del. Ch. 420, 140 A. 264 (1927).*

Board of directors is not required under all circumstances to sell treasury stock for at least its par value. *Belle Isle Corp. v. MacBean, 30 Del. Ch. 373, 61 A.2d 699 (1948).*

And consideration does not have to meet standards of original issue. — The consideration for the issuance of treasury shares need not meet the standard of

that constitutionally required for an original issue. *Highlights for Children, Inc. v. Crown, 43 Del. Ch. 323, 227 A.2d 118 (1966).*

In absence of fraud courts will not interfere. — Treasury stock's price may be fixed by the board of directors in the exercise of its business judgment and in the absence of fraud the courts will not interfere with the fixing of such price by the directors. *Sandler v. Schenley Indus., Inc., 32 Del. Ch. 46, 79 A.2d 606 (1951).*

Not entitled to vote. — The complexities and intricacies of the cases involving third parties, watered stock, treasury stock issued without valid consideration, and constitutionally inadequate consideration simply are not relevant where a self-interested party acting as the sole director of a 100% owned subsidiary issues himself stock without any consideration to the subsidiary as part of a plan to wrest majority control from the parent. Therefore, defendant's stock was at the least voidable, if not totally void, and was not entitled to vote as of the times corporation acted by written consent to appoint new directors and to remove defendant. *MBKS Co. v. Reddy, 924 A.2d 965; 2007 Del. Ch. LEXIS 52 (April 30, 2007).*

CASE NOTES — UNREPORTED

Consideration found. — Stock had been validly issued under 8 Del. C. § 152 and 8 Del. C. § 153, as a director's testimony indicated a belief that defendant had contributed substantial services, which would constitute valid consideration; and meeting minutes, reflecting the approval of defendant's prior acts and the election of a

board of directors with an 8-2 split between the parties, provided further evidence that both parties considered the earlier issuance of shares to be valid. *Fonds de Regulation et de Controle Cafe Cacao v. Lion Capital Mgmt., LLC, 2007 Del. Ch. LEXIS 12 (Del. Ch. Jan. 22, 2007)..*

CASE NOTES — OTHER STATES

Massachusetts

Under Delaware law, the promise of future services is not valid consideration. *Biotrack, Inc. v. Muni, 12 Mass. L. Rep. 244 (Super. 2000).*

Delaware law appears to draw a distinction between a case where the issuance of a company's stock itself violates a provision of Delaware's Constitution, its corporation law, or the company's own corporate charter, and one where the company has the power and authority to issue stock but does so without receiving the required consideration. *Biotrack, Inc. v. Muni, 12 Mass. L. Rep. 244 (Super 2000).*

Texas

Under Delaware law, the critical time for determining whether lawful consideration exists is the

date corporation shares were actually issued. The Delaware Supreme Court has looked to the date the shares issued for determining whether valid consideration was given. *Coates v. Parnassus Systems, Inc., 2002 Tex. App. LEXIS 2545 (2002).*

In Delaware, the harshness of the allocation rule is ameliorated by two other principles of Delaware law. First, the failure of consideration renders stock voidable, not void. Second, a Delaware court may as a matter of equity allow a party to retain the shares upon payment rather than have them canceled at the time the court rules the original consideration to be invalid. *Coates v. Parnassus Systems, Inc., 2002 Tex. App. LEXIS 2545 (2002).*

CASE NOTES — FEDERAL

First Circuit

Extent of authority for share issuance. — Generally, shareholders necessarily understand that a corporation may issue shares up to the maximum number authorized by its certificate of incorporation. Shareholders would be hard pressed to complain when that occurs in furtherance of legitimate corporate purposes, such as the settlement of a lawsuit representing a potential corporate liability. More

specifically, under the corporate law of Delaware, the directors are authorized to distribute treasury stock and issue new stock (up to the limit authorized by the certificate of incorporation) at their discretion, for consideration determined by them. *Enterasys Networks, Inc. v. Gulf Insurance Co., 364 F. Supp. 2d 28 (D.N.Hamp. 2005).*

Second Circuit

Past service. — With respect to Delaware law, past service to the issuer is valid consideration for the issuance of fully paid shares. Moreover in the absence of actual fraud in the transaction, the judgment of the directors as to the value of such consideration shall be conclusive. *Butler v. Phlo Corp., 2001 U.S. Dist. LEXIS 10809 (S.D.N.Y. 2001).*

Third Circuit

Characterization of consideration-based waste action. — In Delaware, a shareholder's allegations that a board of directors committed waste by authorizing the issuance of stock for inadequate consideration are derivative in nature. Waste of corporate assets injures the corporation itself. On the other hand, when it is alleged that a board issued stock with the primary and wrongful intent of entrenching itself, and when the consideration paid for such stock is not the basis for allegations of waste, an individual action lies to the extent that the alleged entrenching activity directly impairs some right the plaintiff possesses as a shareholder. *Gregory v. Correction*

Connection, Inc., 1991 U.S. Dist. LEXIS 3659 (E.D.Pa. 1991).

Where a shareholder participates in an issuance of stock, the assenting shareholder is barred from complaining against the validity of that issuance on the grounds that there was no consideration or for any other technical irregularities. *Regis Insurance Co. v. Di Loreto, 1989 U.S. Dist. LEXIS 6256 (E.D.Pa 1989).*

Sixth Circuit

Consideration for no par stock. — There is no requirement as to the amount of consideration which must be received in respect to an original issue of no par stock, although the quality of consideration must meet the same requirements as stock having a par value. *Louisville Trust Co. v. Glenn, 66 F. Supp. 872 (W.D.Ky. 1946).*

District of Columbia Circuit

The Delaware General Corporate Law requires that the board of directors of a corporation establish the consideration to be received for stock. *CarrAmerica Realty Corp. v. Kaidanow, 321 F.3d 165 (D.C. Cir. 2003).*

§ 154. Determination of amount of capital; capital, surplus and net assets defined

DELAWARE CASE NOTES — REPORTED

Impairment of capital. — A repurchase impairs capital if the funds used in the repurchase exceed the amount of the corporation's "surplus" as defined by this section to mean the excess of net assets over the par value of the corporation's issued stock. *Klang v. Smith's Food & Drug Ctrs., 702 A.2d 150 (Del. 1997).*

In cases alleging impairment of capital under § 160 of this title, the trial court may defer to the board of director's measurement of surplus unless the plaintiff can show that the directors failed to fulfill their duty to

evaluate the assets on the basis of acceptable data and by standards that they are entitled to believe reasonably reflect present values. *Klang v. Smith's Food & Drug Ctrs., 702 A.2d 150 (Del. 1997).*

Repurchase of shares. — A corporation may not repurchase its shares if in so doing it would cause an impairment of capital, unless expressly authorized by § 160 of this title. *Klang v. Smith's Food & Drug Ctrs., 702 A.2d 150 (Del. 1997).*

CASE NOTES — UNREPORTED

Impairment of capital. — Repurchase of corporation's options and warrants impaired the corporation's capital because the funds used in the repurchase exceeded the amount of the corporation's surplus as defined in this section to mean the excess of net assets over the par value of the corporation's issued stock; according to the summary balance sheet contained in a disclosure

document, subtracting the aggregate par value of the corporation's outstanding equity from its net assets left a surplus within the meaning of this section, and therefore, the repurchase amount exceeded the corporation's surplus, resulting in an impairment of the corporation's capital in violation of 8 Del. C. § 160. *Feldman v. Cutaia, 2006 Del. Ch. LEXIS 70 (Del. Ch. Apr. 5, 2006).*

CASE NOTES — OTHER STATES

Tennessee

Revaluation. — Capital assets may be revalued by the officers of a corporation from time to time as the actual

value may increase or decrease. *Titus et al. v. Piggly Wiggly Corporation, 2 Tenn. App. 184 (1925).*

CASE NOTES — FEDERAL

Seventh Circuit

A corporation may designate an amount in excess of par value to be "capital." *Wright v. Heizer Corp., 503 F. Supp. 802 (N.D. Ill. 1980).*

"Paid-in capital" is merely a descriptive accounting term and certainly cannot be taken as a corporate designation of "capital" in excess of par value as defined by statute. *Wright v. Heizer Corp., 503 F. Supp. 802 (N.D. Ill. 1980).*

Corporations

§ 155. Fractions of shares

DELAWARE CASE NOTES — REPORTED

Unequal distribution among stockholders. — Corporation was statutorily allowed to issue fractional shares to some stockholders, but not to others in the same transaction, based upon the size of each stockholder's holdings; stockholders did not always have to be treated equally, just fairly. *Applebaum v. Avaya, Inc., 805 A.2d 209 (Del. Ch. 2002).*

Reverse/forward stock split approved. — Reverse/forward stock split intended to cash out shareholders below certain ownership level was approved because it assumed that the shares were no longer available for purchase in the same marketplace by the person whose shares were being appraised; thus, the court rejected plaintiff's argument that the market price was not "fair

value" for the purposes of payment for fractional shares. *Applebaum v. Avaya, Inc., 805 A.2d 209 (Del. Ch. 2002).*

This section permitted a corporation, as part of a reverse-forward stock split, to treat its stockholders unequally by cashing out the stockholders who owned only fractional interests while opting not to dispose of fractional interests of stockholders who held more than one share of stock after the reverse split; the use of a 10-day average stock market trading price fulfilled the fair price requirement (as a fair compromise to guard against price fluctuation risk), making an appraisal similar to that required under *8 Del. C. § 262* unnecessary since the corporation's stock was widely held and actively traded. *Applebaum v. Avaya, Inc., 812 A.2d 880 (Del. 2002).*

CASE NOTES — OTHER STATES

Kansas

Elimination of minority stockholders. — It is not necessary for a corporation to show a "valid corporate

purpose" for eliminating minority stockholders. *In re Hesstom Corporation, 254 Kan. 941, 870 P.2d 17 (1994).*

CASE NOTES — FEDERAL

Second Circuit

In general. — Corporations are creatures of statutes, and Del. Code Ann. tit. 8, § 155 (1999) not only authorizes the use of scrip, but makes clear that the scrip holder has no ownership interest in the corporation's assets cognizable upon liquidation. *Satterfield v. Monsanto Co., 88 F. Supp. 2d 288 (S.D.N.Y. 2000).*

Delaware law specifically approves an imposition of a cut-off date on the ability to convert scrip to shares or cash. *Satterfield v. Monsanto Co., 88 F. Supp. 2d 288 (S.D.N.Y. 2000).*

Under Delaware law, scrip conveys only an expectancy interest, not a vested ownership interest in a

corporation, except as set forth in the scrip certificates themselves. *Satterfield v. Monsanto Co., 238 F.3d 217 (2d Cir. 2001).*

Seventh Circuit

In general. — The law governing reverse stock split cash-outs is found at Del. Code Ann. tit. 8, § 155 which provides: In the event of a cash-out the corporation must pay in cash the fair value of fractions of a share as of the time when those entitled to receive such fractions are determined. *Connector Service Corp. v. Briggs, 1998 U.S. Dist. LEXIS 18864 (N.D.Ill. 1998).*

§ 156. Partly paid shares

CASE NOTES — FEDERAL

Seventh Circuit

In general. — A Delaware corporation may issue shares when they have been only partly paid for, and if the corporation subsequently declares a dividend the

owners of these shares receive the same fraction of the dividend as the fraction of the purchase price that they have already paid. *Cabintaxi Corp. v. Commissioner, 63 F.3d 614 (7th Cir. 1995).*

§ 157. Rights and options respecting stock

DELAWARE CASE NOTES — REPORTED

Governing law. — When a stockholder becomes the owner of corporate stock, the rights which he or she obtains by virtue thereof were rights granted to him or her under the laws of the state of corporation's origin and therefore the issuance of any stock option plan involves the internal affairs of the corporation and is controlled by

the laws of the state of its origin. *Elster v. American Airlines, 34 Del. Ch. 94, 100 A.2d 219 (1953).*

The issuance of stock option plans by Delaware corporations involves the internal affairs of a Delaware corporation and is, therefore, controlled by the laws of *Delaware. Beard v. Elster, 39 Del. Ch. 153, 160 A.2d 731 (1960).*

Board of directors has exclusive authority to issue stock — This section and §§ 151, 152, 153, 161 and 166 of this title, taken together, confirm the board's exclusive authority to issue stock and regulate a corporation's capital structure; to ensure certainty, these provisions contemplate board approval and a written instrument evidencing the relevant transactions affecting issuance of stock and the corporation's capital structure. *Grimes v. Alteon Inc., 804 A.2d 256 (Del. 2002)*.

Purpose of stock option plans. — As a general rule, stock option plans are an acceptable and necessary means by which corporations gain the services of new employees and retain the services of valued employees. *Michelson v. Duncan, 386 A.2d 1144 (Del. Ch. 1978), aff'd in part and rev'd in part, 407 A.2d 211 (Del. 1979)*.

Section is intended to protect directors' business judgment relating to consideration inuring to the corporation in exchange for creating and issuing stock options. *Michelson v. Duncan, 407 A.2d 211 (Del. 1979)*.

Every corporation may issue stock options, the terms of which must be either in the certificate of incorporation or in a resolution adopted by the board of directors. *Michelson v. Duncan, 386 A.2d 1144 (Del. Ch. 1978), aff'd in part and rev'd in part, 407 A.2d 211 (Del. 1979)*.

Every corporation may create and issue rights or options entitling the holder to purchase from a corporation shares of its stock. *Continental Airlines Corp. v. American Gen. Corp., 575 A.2d 1160 (Del.), cert. denied, 498 U.S. 953, 111 S. Ct. 376, 112 L. Ed. 2d 390 (1990)*.

Fundamental requirements for valid stock options are: (1) That the corporation may reasonably expect to receive the contemplated benefit from the grant of the options; (2) there must be a reasonable relationship between the value of the benefits passing to the corporation and the value of the options granted. *Olson Bros. v. Englehart, 245 A.2d 166 (Del. 1968)*.

The common law preemptive rights doctrine does not permit preemptive rights of minority stockholders to be of such a character as the majority of the stockholders see fit to create. *Bennett v. Breuil Petro. Corp., 34 Del. Ch. 6, 99 A.2d 236 (1953)*.

Lacking unanimous stockholder approval, corporation must receive legal consideration if a stock option plan is to be valid. *Kaufman v. Shoenberg, 33 Del. Ch. 211, 91 A.2d 786 (1952)*.

It is implicit in this section of the Delaware corporation law that options must be issued for consideration. *Frankel v. Donovan, 35 Del. Ch. 433, 120 A.2d 311 (1956)*.

Any option plan must contain consideration passing to the corporation which could take variable forms, such as the retention of services of a valued employee, or the gaining of services of a new employee. *Beard v. Elster, 39 Del. Ch. 153, 160 A.2d 731 (1960)*.

Implicit in the language of this section is the existence of some consideration. *Michelson v. Duncan, 407 A.2d 211 (Del. 1979)*.

Corporation's direct complaint against former board members survived a motion to dismiss for failure to state a claim where it alleged that the corporation could not reasonably have expected to receive any benefit from granting the challenged stock options and that there was no reasonable relationship between the value of the options granted and the value of the benefits passing to the corporation. *Telxon Corp. v. Bogomolny, 792 A.2d 964 (Del. Ch. 2001)*.

CEO attempt to set consideration. — Agreement between appellant stockholders and appellee chief executive officer was not enforceable where: it was neither approved by appellee corporation's board of directors nor set forth in a written agreement; it violated § 152 of this title, as it fixed the consideration for the alleged offering; and it violated this section, as it created a right, which was not approved by the board. *Grimes v. Alteon Inc., 804 A.2d 256 (Del. 2002)*.

And plan must insure that corporation will receive benefit. — The validity of a stock option plan under which selected personnel of a corporation may acquire a stock interest in the corporation depends directly upon the existence of consideration to the corporation and the inclusion in the plan of conditions, or the existence of circumstances, which may be expected to insure that the contemplated consideration will in fact pass to the corporation. *Kerbs v. California E. Airways, Inc., 33 Del. Ch. 69, 90 A.2d 652 (1952)*.

Stock option plans adopted by the exercise of proper business judgment and in good faith will not be interfered with by the courts if the plan, or the facts and circumstances surrounding it, are such as to reasonably insure that the contemplated benefit will inure to the corporation. *Kerbs v. California E. Airways, Inc., 33 Del. Ch. 69, 90 A.2d 652 (1952)*.

The plan or the surrounding facts and circumstances must be such as to reasonably insure that the corporation will receive the contemplated consideration. *Kaufman v. Shoenberg, 33 Del. Ch. 211, 91 A.2d 786 (1952)*.

There must be some reasonable assurance in the plan, or the circumstances of the particular case, which can reasonably be expected to make the corporation receive the contemplated benefit. *Beard v. Elster, 39 Del. Ch. 153, 160 A.2d 731 (1960)*.

All stock option plans must be tested against the requirement that they contain conditions, or the surrounding circumstances are such, that the corporation may reasonably expect to receive the contemplated benefit from the grant of the options and there must be a reasonable relationship between the value of the benefits passing to the corporation and the value of the options granted. *Beard v. Elster, 39 Del. Ch. 153, 160 A.2d 731 (1960); Olson Bros. v. Englehart, 42 Del. Ch. 348, 211 A.2d 610 (1965), aff'd, 245 A.2d 166 (Del. 1968)*.

Transfer of stock options for no consideration amounts to a gift or waste of corporate assets. *Michelson v. Duncan, 407 A.2d 211 (Del. 1979)*.

Consideration. — So long as there is any consideration for the issuance of shares or options, the sufficiency of the consideration fixed by the directors cannot be challenged in the absence of actual fraud; only where it is claimed that the issuance of shares or options was entirely without consideration will this section operate as a legal barrier to any claim for relief as to an illegal gift or waste of corporate assets in the issuance of stock options. *Zupnick v. Goizueta, 698 A.2d 384 (Del. Ch. 1997).*

Consideration must pass at time plan is put into effect. — A plan for additional compensation of executives and employees is to be held valid only if consideration passes to the corporation at the time the plan is put into effect. *Lieberman v. Becker, 38 Del. Ch. 540, 155 A.2d 596 (1959).*

Value of services must be reasonably related to option value. — While a corporation may under proper conditions grant an option to its officers to purchase its stock, the corporation must receive some consideration in return, and if that consideration is to be in the form of services, their value must bear some reasonable relation to the value of the right given. *Rosenthal v. Burry Biscuit Corp., 30 Del. Ch. 299, 60 A.2d 106 (1948).*

There must be a reasonable relation between the value of the benefit conferred by the plan upon the employee and the value to the corporation of the employee's service to it. *Lieberman v. Becker, 38 Del. Ch. 540, 155 A.2d 596 (1959).*

But decision is business judgment. — In an action by minority stockholder to enjoin a corporation from recognizing stock option agreements, the issue of whether anticipated benefits to the corporation constituted sufficient consideration for granting said options was a business judgment, and stockholders must show that such judgment was exercised unlawfully. *Gottlieb v. Heyden Chem. Corp., 34 Del. Ch. 84, 99 A.2d 507 (1953).*

And burden is on plaintiff to prove compensation unreasonable. — In an action by minority stockholder to enjoin corporation from recognizing stock option agreement, it is the stockholder's burden to prove that the total compensation of each optionee, including the value of the options, is unreasonable when compared with the compensation of executives similarly situated. *Gottlieb v. Heyden Chem. Corp., 34 Del. Ch. 84, 99 A.2d 507 (1953).*

Opportunity to invest is not consideration. — Unexplained, the desire of the directors to give an officer an opportunity to acquire a substantial interest by investment does not constitute legal consideration for the granting of an option. *Rosenthal v. Burry Biscuit Corp., 30 Del. Ch. 299, 60 A.2d 106 (1948).*

Unless it benefits corporation. — Every stock option plan has as its purpose the desire to give corporate officials an opportunity to acquire a stock interest in the corporation; the crucial question is whether the ultimate objective behind such purpose is calculated to benefit the corporation to such an extent that it constitutes legal consideration. *Gottlieb v. Heyden Chem. Corp., 32 Del. Ch. 231, 83 A.2d 595 (1951), rev'd on other grounds, 92 A.2d 594 (Del. 1952).*

Increased incentive for greater profits was valid consideration. — In an action by a minority stockholder to enjoin a corporation from recognizing stock option agreements, the objecting stockholder cannot argue that corporation will not receive anything of value in exchange for the options, where it can be shown that an increased incentive to create greater corporate profits and avoidance

of personnel problems will result. *Gottlieb v. Heyden Chem. Corp., 34 Del. Ch. 84, 99 A.2d 507 (1953).*

As was requirement of employment for number of years. — An express requirement of an option agreement that the optionee remain with the company to a fixed future date in order to avail himself or herself of the right to exercise the option constituted legal consideration. *Gottlieb v. Heyden Chem. Corp., 34 Del. Ch. 84, 99 A.2d 507 (1953).*

Consideration when directors vote themselves options. — In the case of directors voting themselves stock options and later obtaining stockholder ratification of their act, the duty of the court to examine the facts consisted solely in sufficient examination to determine whether the terms of the option plan were so unequal as to amount to waste, or whether the question was so close factually as to fall within the realm of the exercise of sound business judgment. In the former case the court will reverse the decision of the stockholders; in the latter it will not. *Beard v. Elster, 39 Del. Ch. 153, 160 A.2d 731 (1960).*

Burden of proof when directors vote themselves options. — Where board members vote themselves stock options and do not obtain stockholder ratification, they themselves have assumed the burden of clearly proving their utmost good faith and the most scrupulous inherent fairness of the bargain; where there is stockholder ratification, however, the burden of proof is shifted to the objector and in such a case the objecting stockholder must convince the court that no person of ordinarily sound business judgment would be expected to entertain the view that the consideration furnished by the individual directors is a fair exchange for the options conferred. *Gottlieb v. Heyden Chem. Corp., 33 Del. Ch. 177, 91 A.2d 57 (1952).*

Where a majority of the directors representing the corporation are conferring benefits upon themselves out of the assets of the corporation, the burden is upon the directors to prove not only that the transaction was in good faith, but also that its intrinsic fairness will withstand the most searching and objective analysis. *Gottlieb v. Heyden Chem. Corp., 33 Del. Ch. 82, 90 A.2d 660 (1952).*

Where there has been independent stockholder ratification, the burden is upon the complaining stockholder to show that no person of ordinary sound business judgment would say that the consideration received for the options was a fair exchange for the options granted. *Kaufman v. Shoenberg, 33 Del. Ch. 211, 91 A.2d 786 (1952).*

Absent independent stockholder ratification, interested directors have the burden of showing that the consideration to be received constitutes a fair exchange for the options. *Kaufman v. Shoenberg, 33 Del. Ch. 211, 91 A.2d 786 (1952).*

Shareholders' burden in derivative suit challenging executive stock option plan. — Shareholders in a derivative suit alleging that allowance and acceptance of payments under executive stock option compensation plan were breaches of fiduciary duty had the burden of demonstrating that the compensation plan itself, having been added by a majority of disinterested directors and later ratified by shareholders with no allegation of inadequate disclosure in proxy materials, was so devoid of legitimate corporate purpose as to be a waste of assets. *Pogostin v. Rice, 480 A.2d 619 (Del. 1984).*

Inside knowledge of directors and recipients. — It is possible that warrants or options might be vulnerable to attack on the ground that at the time of issuance, the directors and recipients had inside knowledge, withheld from the stockholders, which enabled them to foresee an extraordinary rise in the price of the stock. *Forman v. Chesler, 39 Del. Ch. 484, 167 A.2d 442 (1961).*

Agreement of co-owners to settle claims is consideration. — An agreement between co-owners of all the stock of a corporation containing mutual promises "to settle all of their outstanding differences" by an option agreement is legally sufficient consideration. *Vale v. Atlantic Coast & Inland Corp., 34 Del. Ch. 50, 99 A.2d 396 (1953).*

Optionee is not equitable shareholder. — A holder of an option to purchase stock was under no obligation to buy any shares from the corporation and so his status, at least prior to dissolution, was not comparable to that of a subscriber to corporate shares and he was not an equitable shareholder. *Gamble v. Penn Valley Crude Oil Corp., 34 Del. Ch. 359, 104 A.2d 257 (1954).*

Subsequent increase in value of shares. — The warrant holder or optionee may, at least under ordinary circumstances, lawfully expect to enjoy the advantages of any future increase in value of the shares, to the same extent as if he had invested in the stock itself. *Forman v. Chesler, 39 Del. Ch. 484, 167 A.2d 442 (1961).*

Option may be limited or unlimited in duration. — Where the language of an option makes it clear that under its terms it is unlimited in duration, the rule of law implying a reasonable time in the absence of a time provision has no application and it may be noted that this section explicitly authorizes options whose terms may be "unlimited in duration." *Gamble v. Penn Valley Crude Oil Corp., 34 Del. Ch. 359, 104 A.2d 257 (1954).*

This section explicitly authorizes the issuance of stock options and warrants "limited or unlimited in duration," and whether the issuance of perpetual warrants represents a sound public policy is not for courts to determine. *Forman v. Chesler, 39 Del. Ch. 484, 167 A.2d 442 (1961).*

And this section will not be construed to have implied limitation in form of reasonable time. *Gamble v. Penn Valley Crude Oil Corp., 34 Del. Ch. 359, 104 A.2d 257 (1954).*

Where consideration was given for option to purchase stock, corporation was committed to keep offer open. *Gamble v. Penn Valley Crude Oil Corp., 34 Del. Ch. 359, 104 A.2d 257 (1954).*

Failure to exercise option before dissolution does not invalidate it. — Holder of option's inaction with respect to option to purchase stock prior to the date of dissolution of the corporation did not invalidate the option. *Gamble v. Penn Valley Crude Oil Corp., 34 Del. Ch. 359, 104 A.2d 257 (1954).*

Unless corporation can prove unconscionable result. — The corporation has the burden of showing that the court's enforcement of an option to purchase stock in a dissolved corporation would cause an unconscionable result. *Gamble v. Penn Valley Crude Oil Corp., 34 Del. Ch. 359, 104 A.2d 257 (1954).*

Court will look to explanation of lapse of time and consideration received. — In determining whether to enforce an option to purchase stock which has lapsed after a reasonable time, the court is entitled to look at the facts generally, including the value received by the corporation for the option, explanations for the lapse of time, and the date of and the reason for the increase in value. *Gamble v. Penn Valley Crude Oil Corp., 34 Del. Ch. 359, 104 A.2d 257 (1954).*

Authority delegated to compensation committee to grant stock options. — Corporate directors do not breach their fiduciary duty by delegating authority to a compensation committee to grant stock options. *Michelson v. Duncan, 386 A.2d 1144 (Del. Ch. 1978),* aff'd in part and rev'd in part, *407 A.2d 211 (Del. 1979).*

Ratification by stockholders of unauthorized acts of directors in modifying stock option plans. — Where the stockholders, after receiving a full disclosure of all germane facts, overwhelmingly ratified the unauthorized acts of the board of directors in modifying certain stock option plans and there has been no allegation or showing of any gift or waste of corporate assets, the ratification of the stockholders is binding. *Michelson v. Duncan, 386 A.2d 1144 (Del. Ch. 1978),* aff'd in part and rev'd in part, *407 A.2d 211 (Del. 1979).*

Nonunanimous shareholder approval cannot cure an act of waste of corporate assets in the issuance of stock options. *Michelson v. Duncan, 407 A.2d 211 (Del. 1979).*

Shareholder ratification of a stock option plan is valid only where the stockholders are adequately informed of the consequences of their acts and the reasons therefor. *Michelson v. Duncan, 407 A.2d 211 (Del. 1979).*

Notice afforded stockholder. — Where all facts pertinent to the corporate option plans had been placed upon the public records of the New York Stock Exchange and had been forwarded to every stockholder of record, as required by the regulations of the Securities and Exchange Commission, said stockholder had ample notice of all pertinent facts surrounding the adoption of the option plans and had no standing to contest the plans. *Elster v. American Airlines, 34 Del. Ch. 94, 100 A.2d 219 (1953).*

Optionee must be party to suit contesting option. — A determination of the rights of the optionees in a stockholder's action to enjoin the carrying out of a stock option without making them parties thereto would be contrary to the principles of equity and good conscience. *Elster v. American Airlines, 34 Del. Ch. 500, 106 A.2d 202 (1954).*

Burden of proof of inadequacy of consideration shifted by shareholder ratification. — Where shareholders ratified a director-initiated stock-option plan, the burden of proof of want or inadequacy of consideration for the grant of the options shifted from directors to shareholders. *Michelson v. Duncan, 407 A.2d 211 (Del. 1979).*

Adoption of "poison pill" plan, by which shareholders receive the right to be bought out by the corporation at a substantial premium on the occurrence of a stated triggering event, was consistent with the directors' fiduciary duty in facing a takeover threat perceived as detrimental to corporate interests. *Revlon, Inc. v. MacAndrews & Forbes Holdings, Inc., 506 A.2d 173 (Del. 1985).*

Preferred share purchase rights plan giving shareholders one right per common share upon announcement of tender offer for 30% of corporation's shares or acquisition of 20% of corporation's shares by any single entity or group was authorized by this section and constituted a legitimate exercise of business judgment by directors concerned over takeovers. *Moran v. Household Int'l, 500 A.2d 1346 (Del. 1985).*

Preemptive rights. — The right of shareholders to subscribe for new shares issued by a corporation as an increase of its capital stock in preference to outsiders is well established, and is called a shareholder's preemptive right. *Kingston v. Home Life Ins. Co. of Am., 11 Del. Ch. 258, 101 A. 898 (1917), aff'd, 104 A. 25 (Del. Ch. 1918).*

One who acquires shares of stock of a corporation after the corporation, by action of its officers, directors and stockholders, has given to a stranger an exclusive right to take and pay for at par all of the unissued shares of the company, cannot assert as against the company, or the holder of the option, the general preemptive right of shareholders of a corporation. *Kingston v. Home Life Ins. Co. of Am., 11 Del. Ch. 258, 101 A. 898 (1917), aff'd, 104 A. 25 (Del. Ch. 1918).*

Decreasing price of stock options is not ipso facto waste of corporate assets. *Michelson v. Duncan, 386 A.2d 1144 (Del. Ch. 1978), aff'd in part and rev'd in part, 407 A.2d 211 (Del. 1979).*

Section not bar does claim of absolute failure of consideration. — This section was not intended to erect a legal barrier to any claim for relief as to an alleged gift or waste of corporate assets in the issuance of stock options where the claim asserted is one of absolute failure of consideration. *Michelson v. Duncan, 407 A.2d 211 (Del. 1979).*

Assertion of a claim of lack of consideration for grant of options is sufficient to put an opposing party on notice of the probable assertion of a claim of gift or waste. *Michelson v. Duncan, 407 A.2d 211 (Del. 1979).*

Claim that options were granted for "no consideration" is tantamount to allegation of waste. — Where the complaint did not use the words "gift or waste" but averred that options were granted for "no consideration," this was tantamount to an allegation of gift or waste of assets. *Michelson v. Duncan, 407 A.2d 211 (Del. 1979).*

Claims of gift or waste of corporate assets are seldom subject to disposition by summary judgment; and when there are genuine issues of fact as to the existence of consideration for the issuance of stock options, a full hearing is required regardless of shareholder ratification. *Michelson v. Duncan, 407 A.2d 211 (Del. 1979).*

While each case must be determined on its own facts, there is a strong disfavor for summary judgment in stock option claims where waste of corporate assets is alleged. *Michelson v. Duncan, 407 A.2d 211 (Del. 1979).*

There is no difference between deferred compensation unit plan and ordinary stock option plan; both types of plans are designed to retain the services of valued employees, and whether or not a corporation should embark upon such a method of compensating its employees is to be decided by the board of directors by the exercise of their business judgment. When a corporate decision is made in the light of the best business judgment of its management, absent fraud or bad faith, the courts do not interfere. *Lieberman v. Becker, 38 Del. Ch. 540, 155 A.2d 596 (1959).*

The deferred compensation unit plan is no more liable to attack upon the ground of no existing reasonable relation between the amount of compensation and the value of services than is the ordinary stock option plan. *Lieberman v. Becker, 38 Del. Ch. 540, 155 A.2d 596 (1959).*

Grant of stock options held not to be waste. — Board of directors' grant of stock options to a corporate officer as a form of executive compensation did not constitute waste where the directors concluded that the officer's past services were extraordinary and unusual in character and had led to great gains and profits on behalf of the corporation. *Zupnick v. Goizueta, 698 A.2d 384 (Del. Ch. 1997).*

DELAWARE CASE NOTES — UNREPORTED

Notice afforded stockholder. — While airtight written documentation of a resolution granting options was a prudent course of action for directors who wished to avoid future legal challenges, *8 Del. C. § 157(b)* did not expressly require that the resolution be included in the minutes of a board meeting at which it was adopted or that the resolution be in writing; therefore, given the representation and warranty the corporation provided to a partnership in a merger agreement that the company was required to honor the options, the partnership could have believed that alternative documentation provided during due diligence (such as options agreements and written board minutes showing director approval of the employee stock option plan itself) was sufficient under the statute. *Feldman v. Cutaia, 2007 Del. Ch. LEXIS 111 (Del. Ch. Aug. 1, 2007).*

CASE NOTES — FEDERAL

First Circuit

In general. — Del. Code. Ann. tit. 8, § 157 (1998) provides that the terms of options, including the time for exercise, shall be determined (if not in the certificate of incorporation itself) by the board of directors. *Ostler v. Codman Research Group, Inc., 241 F.3d 91 (1st Cir. 2001).*

Past consideration is insufficient to render a later stock option valid. *Feldman v. Detarando, 1980 U.S. Dist. LEXIS 14272 (D.Mass 1980).*

Option rights granted for personal services terminate upon the death of the holder because performance, consideration for the option, then becomes impossible. *Feldman v. Detarando, 1980 U.S. Dist. LEXIS 14272 (D.Mass 1980).*

Authority of board. — This section, relating to rights and options respecting stock, requires board approval and a written instrument to create such rights or options. The board of directors has the exclusive authority to issue stock and regulate a corporation's capital structure. *First Marblehead Corp. v. House, 401 F. Supp. 2d 152, 2005 U.S. Dist. LEXIS 28709, 36 Employee Benefits Cas. (BNA) 2055 (D. Mass. 2005).*

Delaware law mandates strict conformity with the statutory requirements for the issuance and sale of stock even in situations which might generate an inequitable result. *First Marblehead Corp. v. House, 401 F. Supp. 2d 152, 2005 U.S. Dist. LEXIS 28709, 36 Employee Benefits Cas. (BNA) 2055 (D. Mass. 2005).*

Requested extension too lengthy. — Rather than a 48-hour extension, appellant seeks to extend his options years beyond the expiration period set by the board. While a two-day extension arguably would not frustrate management's ability to make capital decisions with certainty, a delay of years could have a significant impact. We agree with the district court that Delaware law does not allow the relief appellant seeks under these circumstances. *First Marblehead Corp. v. House, 473 F.3d 1, 2006 U.S. App. LEXIS 31510 (Dec. 22, 2006).*

Second Circuit

Entitlement of warrant holders. — Under Delaware law, warrant holders under the warrant agreement at issue in that case were entitled to receive the same consideration that any other corporate shareholder had received in a merger. *R.A. Mackie & Co., L.P. v. Petrocorp Inc., 244 F. Supp. 2d 279 (S.D.N.Y. 2003).*

No fiduciary duties are owed to option holders under Delaware law. *Powers v. British Vita, P.L.C., 969 F. Supp. 4 (S.D.N.Y. 1997).*

Option plan consideration requirement. — A corporation which issues employee stock options must make arrangements to assure that the employees involved will render some consideration to the issuing company in exchange for those valuable rights. Delaware law requires that any option plan must contain consideration passing to the corporation which could take variable forms, such as the retention of services of a valued employee or the gaining of services of a new employee. The plan, itself, or the surrounding circumstances, must be such as to insure that this consideration will in all reasonable probability be received by the corporation. One method of meeting this consideration requirement is for the issuing corporation to require that the optionee/employee remain in the employ of the corporation for some fixed period before the options involved will be exercisable. The mere existence of stock options, standing alone, does not alter the employment relationship between the parties. A stock option, in and of itself, only engenders a duty of the employer to deal in good faith, that is, to refrain from directly frustrating the exercise of the option. *Liebler v. Morton-Norwich Products, Inc., 1978 U.S. Dist. LEXIS 15220 (S.D.N.Y. 1978).*

Fifth Circuit

In general. — Multiple provisions of the Delaware Code set forth the formal requirements for the issuance of capital stock, the consideration for the issuance of stock, and formalities regarding rights, options, and subscriptions relating to capital stock. Specifically, Del. Code Ann. tit. 8, § 157 states that board approval and a written instrument is required to create rights and options respecting stock. Indeed, the duty of a corporation's board of directors to approve a sale of stock is so important that the board cannot delegate it to the corporation's officers. *Vannoy v. Verio Inc., 2004 U.S. Dist. LEXIS 14713 (N.D.Tex. 2004).*

Realization of stock appreciation right. — A stock appreciation right (SAR) is a contingent interest; to realize this interest, the common stock of the corporation must be sold. Holders of SARs, unlike debenture holders, may not be solely creditors, but they are creditors. When the common stock of a corporation is sold, the corporation owes and is obligated to pay SAR holders the appreciation value of the stock. Further, unlike stockholders, SAR holders can share in the wealth of a corporation without the same tax liability as a shareholder. *H.I.G. P-Xi Holding, Inc., 2001 U.S. Dist. LEXIS 5074 (E.D.La. 2001).*

Ninth Circuit

Alleged oral promise of stock options, supported by consideration though it is, is nonetheless unenforceable under Delaware law due to the lack of a writing and board approval. *Patriot Sci. Corp. v. Korodi, 2007 U.S. Dist. LEXIS 38279 (D. Cal. May 5, 2007).*

§ 158. Stock certificates; uncertificated shares

DELAWARE CASE NOTES — REPORTED

Right to a proper certificate. — This section includes the right to a proper certificate without a legend or restriction, where such a legend is no longer appropriate. That result is consistent with the common law, which recognizes the existence of a claim for wrongful refusal to issue a stock certificate. *Bender v. Memory Metals, Inc., 514 A.2d 1109 (Del. Ch. 1986).*

Certificates of stock are themselves only evidence of shares; they are not shares. *Baker v. Bankers Mtg. Co., 15 Del. Ch. 209, 135 A. 486 (1926),* aff'd, *15 Del. Ch. 431, 141 A. 277 (1927).*

Though not an essential prerequisite to the fact of ownership, a certificate of stock, like all muniments of title, is a valuable paper, the possession of which evidences in permanent form the stockholder's ownership with its incidents of rights and facilitates its sale and transfer. *Smith v. Universal Serv. Motors Co., 17 Del. Ch. 58, 147 A. 247 (1929).*

A person may be the legal owner of stock even though the person has received no certificate; therefore, the certificate is only evidence of ownership. *Haskell v. Middle States Petro. Corp., 35 Del. 380, 165 A. 562 (1933).*

But possession of certificate is not essential to ownership of stock. *Mau v. Montana Pac. Oil Co., 16 Del. Ch. 114, 141 A. 828 (1928).*

However, possession imports relation of stockholder. — In the absence of explanatory facts to the contrary, the possession of certificates of shares of stock of a company import the relation of stockholder with all of the consequences of that relation. *Cooper v. Eastern Horse & Mule Co., 12 Del. Ch. 210, 110 A. 666 (1920).*

If a corporation having power to issue stock certificates does in fact issue such a certificate, in which it affirms that a designated person is entitled to a certain number of shares of stock, it thereby holds out to persons who may deal in good faith with the person named in the certificate, that such person is an owner and has capacity to transfer the shares. *Delaware-New Jersey Ferry Co. v. Leeds, 21 Del. Ch. 279, 186 A. 913 (1936).*

Mere preparation of stock certificates by the company does not constitute the issuance of stock. *Graham v. Commercial Credit Co., 41 Del. Ch. 580, 200 A.2d 828 (1964).*

Registration of share ownership facilitates shareholder-corporation relations. — The registration of shares is highly significant in corporation-shareholder transactions, as important purposes of the registration are to provide a practical means whereby the corporation may ascertain the names of the persons with whom it may ordinarily deal as shareholders and to afford a means whereby a "real" owner may readily become entitled to notification and recognition as a shareholder. *In re Northeastern Water Co., 28 Del. Ch. 139, 38 A.2d 918 (1944).*

And corporation may deal freely with registered owner. — Failure to have shares registered so as to indicate others having an interest other than the registered holder may reasonably be deemed a manifestation of intent that the corporation should deal freely with the registered holder as the true owner without investigating his or her authority. *In re Northeastern Water Co., 28 Del. Ch. 139, 38 A.2d 918 (1944).*

A corporation may not shut its eyes when it has notice that a registered holder is about to commit a breach of duty to a real owner, or that it may give no heed to a warning of a real owner not to recognize the registered holder, but it means that knowledge that a person, registered as the absolute owner, is not the beneficial owner, should not put the corporation upon inquiry as to the authority of the registered holder to act. *In re Northeastern Water Co., 28 Del. Ch. 139, 38 A.2d 918 (1944).*

Delivery prerequisite to issuance. — Until a stock certificate not only passes from the custody and control of the corporation but also is delivered into the possession of the stockholder, or of some person as agent of him or her, it has not been issued. *Smith v. Universal Serv. Motors Co., 17 Del. Ch. 58, 147 A. 247 (1929).*

Delivery, either actual or constructive, is essential before a certificate can be said to have been issued. *Graham v. Commercial Credit Co., 41 Del. Ch. 580, 200 A.2d 828 (1964).*

Once stock actually or constructively comes into the possession of the owner, it is issued and this section has no further application because it only gives the right to have an original issue of stock. *Graham v. Commercial Credit Co., 41 Del. Ch. 580, 200 A.2d 828 (1964).*

Stockholder's maid had implied authority to accept and receipt for registered mail addressed to her employer and delivered in his absence to his home; this being so, it follows that stock certificates delivered to the maid constructively came into his possession. *Graham v. Commercial Credit Co., 41 Del. Ch. 580, 200 A.2d 828 (1964).*

CASE NOTES — OTHER STATES

Michigan

No issuance of stock takes place until a certificate duly made out passed from the custody and control of the company into the possession of the stockholder, or some person as agent for him or her. *Waldorf v. KMS Industries, Inc., 25 Mich. App. 20, 181 N.W.2d 85 (1970).*

CASE NOTES — FEDERAL

Seventh Circuit

Under Delaware law, status as a shareholder does not depend on the issuance of a certificate of stock since the certificate is merely evidence of ownership. *Cabintaxi Corp. v. Commissioner, 63 F.3d 614 (7th Cir. 1995).*

§ 159. Shares of stock; personal property, transfer and taxation

DELAWARE CASE NOTES — REPORTED

There is no distinction between gift of certificate of stock and other classes of property, and there is no doubt that a certificate of stock may be the subject of a gift, if it clearly appears that there was an intention to make the gift and sufficient delivery. *Wilmington Trust Co. v. GMC, 29 Del. Ch. 572, 51 A.2d 584 (1947).*

A certificate of stock is evidence of ownership, in the nature of a chose in action, and like any other personal property may be the subject of a valid gift inter vivos. *Equitable Trust Co. v. Gallagher, 31 Del. Ch. 88, 67 A.2d 50 (1949), aff'd, 77 A.2d 548 (Del. 1950).*

And change in corporate books is sufficient to complete gift. — Where a new stock certificate is issued in the name of a donee, and so registered on the books of the corporation, it is not necessary that the stock certificate be in possession of the donee in order to complete the gift. *Wilmington Trust Co. v. GMC, 29 Del. Ch. 572, 51 A.2d 584 (1947).*

Shares may be taken in execution or reached by attachment. — Shares of stock are personal property in the state of the residence of the corporation and could be taken in execution or reached by attachment. *Haskell v. Middle States Petro. Corp., 35 Del. 380, 165 A. 562 (1933).*

There may be conversion of shares of stock since shares of corporate stock are not only made personal property, but property that may be identified, attached and sold for the payment of the debts of the owner. *Haskell v. Middle States Petro. Corp., 35 Del. 380, 165 A. 562 (1933).*

Shares may be used to purchase shares in another corporation. — Shares of stock of a corporation are personal property and as such constitute a good consideration in payment for the shares of stock of another company. *Peyton v. William C. Peyton Corp., 22 Del. Ch. 187, 194 A. 106 (1937), rev'd on other grounds, 23 Del. Ch. 321, 7 A.2d 737 (1939).*

Bylaw may not unreasonably restrain transfer of stock. — A corporate bylaw which unreasonably restrains the power of a stockholder to transfer his or her stock will be held invalid as against public policy. *Lawson v. HFC, 17 Del. Ch. 343, 152 A. 723 (1930).*

§ 160. Corporation's powers respecting ownership, voting, etc., of its own stock; rights of stock called for redemption

DELAWARE CASE NOTES — REPORTED

Broad authority of board of directors. — The board of directors is given the statutory power to deal in its own stock along with the authority to make and amend bylaws and to manage the business of the corporation under the protection afforded by the business judgment rule. This broad authority allows a Delaware corporation to deal selectively with its stockholders, so long as the directors have not acted out of the sole or primary purpose to entrench themselves in office. *Frantz Mfg. Co. v. EAC Indus., 501 A.2d 401 (Del. 1985).*

Acquisition of its own capital stock is not ordinarily essential corporate function. *Brophy v. Cities Serv. Co., 31 Del. Ch. 241, 70 A.2d 5 (1949).*

And may not impair capital. — The funds and property of the company shall not be used for the purchase of shares of its own capital stock when the value of its assets is less than the aggregate amount of all the shares of its capital stock, for a use by a corporation of its assets to purchase shares of its own capital stock under such conditions impairs the capital of the company. *In re International Radiator Co., 10 Del. Ch. 358, 92 A. 255 (1914).*

Impairment of capital. — A repurchase impairs capital if the funds used in the repurchase exceed the amount of the corporation's "surplus" as defined by § 154 of this title to mean the excess of net assets over the par value of the corporation's issued stock. *Klang v. Smith's Food & Drug Ctrs., 702 A.2d 150 (Del. 1997).*

In cases alleging impairment of capital under this section, the trial court may defer to the board of director's measurement of surplus unless the plaintiff can show that the directors failed to fulfill their duty to evaluate the assets on the basis of acceptable data and by standards that they are entitled to believe reasonably reflect present values. *Klang v. Smith's Food & Drug Ctrs., 702 A.2d 150 (Del. 1997).*

A corporation is impaired when the value of its assets is less than the aggregate amount of all the shares of its capital stock. *In re Motels of Am., Inc., 146 Bankr. 542 (Bankr. D. Del. 1992).*

A corporation cannot purchase its own shares of stock when the purchase diminishes the ability of the company to pay its debts, or lessens the security of its creditors. *In re International Radiator Co., 10 Del. Ch. 358, 92 A. 255 (1914).*

A contract to repurchase its own shares by a corporation is illegal and void when an impairment of capital results. *Pasotti v. United States Guardian Corp., 18 Del. Ch. 1, 156 A. 255 (1931).*

A corporation may purchase its own shares provided such purchase does not impair corporate capital or constitute an improper bid for control. *Schwartz v. Greene, 39 Del. Ch. 330, 163 A.2d 614 (1960).*

This section is an authorization for a corporation to use its property for the purchase of its own capital stock if such use will not impair its capital. *Alcott v. Hyman, 42 Del. Ch. 233, 208 A.2d 501 (1965).*

Impairment of capital means its reduction below amount represented by outstanding stock. — The impairment of the capital of a company, as used in this section, means the reduction of the amount of the assets of the company below the amount represented by the aggregate outstanding shares of the capital stock of the company. *In re International Radiator Co., 10 Del. Ch. 358, 92 A. 255 (1914).*

This section designs prohibition against impairment of capital for protection of stockholders as well as of creditors. *Pasotti v. United States Guardian Corp., 18 Del. Ch. 1, 156 A. 255 (1931).*

And utmost good faith and good judgment were required of directors in the delicate field of a corporation purchasing its own assets since the purchase by a corporation of its own shares is the type of transaction in which creditors or stockholders may be prejudiced even though the purchase be made in good faith, the purchase of its own stock by a corporation notwithstanding the statute being an extraordinary act. *Propp v. Sadacca, 40 Del. Ch. 113, 175 A.2d 33 (1961),* modified, *41 Del. Ch. 14, 187 A.2d 405 (1962).*

Where a director abstained from voting in good faith because he honestly believed that if he were to become involved in consideration of purchases by the corporation of its own stock, his duties as a director would somehow come in conflict with his own self-interest because of his contemporaneous sale of the corporation's stock in a rising market, he was held not legally responsible for the transaction involving the corporation's purchases, it not being the type of corporate act for which a director may clearly be held liable unless the director positively makes known his or her opposition thereto. *Propp v. Sadacca, 40 Del. Ch. 113, 175 A.2d 33 (1961),* modified, *41 Del. Ch. 14, 187 A.2d 405 (1962).*

Each case in which purchase by corporation of its own stock is attacked must be considered on its own facts. *Propp v. Sadacca, 40 Del. Ch. 113, 175 A.2d 33 (1961),* modified, *41 Del. Ch. 14, 187 A.2d 405 (1962).*

Business judgment rule may not be relied on by directors to bar plaintiff's attack on the actions complained of where directors violate requirements of this section. *Propp v. Sadacca, 40 Del. Ch. 113, 175 A.2d 33 (1961),* modified, *41 Del. Ch. 14, 187 A.2d 405 (1962).*

But as long as purchase is for proper purpose courts will not interfere. — Absent a showing that its own shares have been caused to be purchased by a corporation for an improper purpose, courts should not normally interfere with such a transaction when carried out in compliance with the statute. *Alcott v. Hyman, 40 Del. Ch. 449, 184 A.2d 90 (1962),* aff'd, *42 Del. Ch. 233, 208 A.2d 501 (1965).*

The courts will not interfere with a stock purchase transaction provided the purchase is not for an improper purpose. *Crane Co. v. Harsco Corp., 511 F. Supp. 294 (D. Del. 1981).*

Purpose of subsection (c). — Subsection (c), which prevents a corporation from voting its own stock, is designed to prevent those in control of a corporation from using corporate resources to perpetuate themselves in office. *Insituform of N. Am., Inc. v. Chandler, 534 A.2d 257 (Del. Ch. 1987).*

A harm similar to that which subsection (c) seeks to guard against is threatened where an incumbent board may exercise its control over a corporation to cause the corporation to seek to enforce a contract such as a voting agreement which secures the tenure of the incumbent board. *Insituform of N. Am., Inc. v. Chandler, 534 A.2d 257 (Del. Ch. 1987).*

Limitations on voting rights. — Policy expressed in subsection (c) would require a very clear intent to create a right of a corporation to require its shareholders to vote for the incumbent board before a court would recognize it. *Insituform of N. Am., Inc. v. Chandler, 534 A.2d 257 (Del. Ch. 1987).*

Application of subsection (c) to the internal affairs of a foreign corporation would unfairly and unconstitutionally subject those intimately involved with the management of the corporation to the laws of Delaware and would unconstitutionally violate the interstate commerce clause. *McDermott, Inc. v. Lewis, 531 A.2d 206 (Del. 1987).*

Voting of unallocated shares of employees trust. — Where shareholder stated that the stock employee compensation trust (SECT) was established primarily to frustrate their proxy contest and that the SECT shares were (in effect) shares owned by the corporation that were not to be voted under subsection (c) of this section, the court decided not to issue a temporary injunction, after applying the Unocal standard's tests of reasonableness and proportionality to the standards for issuing temporary injunctions, since the shareholder was not threatened with imminent, irreparable harm, and the balance of hardships weighed in favor of the corporation. *Aquila, Inc. v. Quanta Servs., Inc., 805 A.2d 196 (Del. Ch. 2002).*

Stockholder at odds with management may be bought out. — A reduction of capital through the purchase of shares at private sale is not illegal as a matter of law simply because the purpose or motive of the purchase is to eliminate a substantial number of shares held by a stockholder at odds with management policy, provided of course that the transaction is clear of any fraud or unfairness. *Kors v. Carey, 39 Del. Ch. 47, 158 A.2d 136 (1960).*

The statutory power granted to corporations to purchase shares of their own stock is subject to abuse, but a thoughtful and honest decision of the board of directors to buy out a stockholder who threatens actual harm to his or her corporation may be sustained. *Propp v. Sadacca, 40 Del. Ch. 113, 175 A.2d 33 (1961),* modified, *41 Del. Ch. 14, 187 A.2d 405 (1962).*

If the purchase of its own stock by the board was motivated by a sincere belief that the buying out of the dissident stockholder was necessary to maintain what the board believed to be proper business practices, the board will not be held liable for such decision, even though hindsight indicates the decision was not the wisest course. *Cheff v. Mathes, 41 Del. Ch. 494, 199 A.2d 548 (1964).*

Where a business decision was made to purchase corporate stock with corporate funds in a sudden emergency to protect the corporation from serious injury, and in the directors' judgment it was the only thing to do, the law protects them from liability. *Bennett v. Propp, 41 Del. Ch. 14, 187 A.2d 405 (1962).*

Where the purchase of shares with corporate funds was to remove a threat to corporate policy when a threat to control was involved, the directors were of necessity confronted with a conflict of interest, and an objective decision was difficult, hence the burden should be on the directors to justify such a purchase as one primarily in the corporate interest. *Bennett v. Propp, 41 Del. Ch. 14, 187 A.2d 405 (1962).*

But purchase primarily to perpetuate board is improper. — If the board in buying its own stock has acted solely or primarily because of the desire to perpetuate themselves in office, the use of corporate funds for such purposes is improper. *Cheff v. Mathes, 41 Del. Ch. 494, 199 A.2d 548 (1964).*

Use of corporate funds to purchase corporate shares primarily to maintain management in control is improper. *Petty v. Penntech Papers, Inc., 347 A.2d 140 (Del. Ch. 1975).*

Repurchase of shares. — A corporation may not repurchase its shares if in so doing it would cause an impairment of capital, unless expressly authorized by this section. *Klang v. Smith's Food & Drug Ctrs., 702 A.2d 150 (Del. 1997).*

Since governing Delaware law did not require a hardware retailers' cooperative to redeem and retire stock of a withdrawing member store (where to do so would have further impaired the cooperative's capital), summary judgment should not have been entered in the store's favor on it counterclaim seeking redemption of its shares; since the plain language of the cooperative's bylaws, as well as a loss allocation resolution, limited the reach of the loss allocation plan to those members who were stockholders at the time the plan was adopted, however, summary judgment was properly entered in the store's favor on the issue of whether it was subject to the plan, given that it had already withdrawn from the cooperative when the plan was adopted. *TruServ Corp. v. Bess Hardware & Sports, Inc., 346 Ill. App. 3d 194, 281 Ill. Dec. 646, 804 N.E.2d 611 (2 Dist. 2004).*

Repurchase of stock warrants. — The plain language of this section relieves a corporation from an obligation to purchase its own capital stock if such a purchase would result in an impairment, or a further impairment, of the corporation's capital; it does not by its terms apply to the repurchase of stock warrants. *RFE Capital Partners, L.P. v. Weskar, Inc., 652 A.2d 1093 (Del. Super. Ct.),* appeal denied, *648 A.2d 426 (Del. 1994).*

Burden on directors to justify purchase. — Where the use of corporate funds to purchase corporate shares will maintain management in control, the burden is on the directors to justify the purchase as one primarily in the corporate interest and not their own. *Petty v. Penntech Papers, Inc., 347 A.2d 140 (Del. Ch. 1975).*

The use of corporate funds to perpetuate control of the corporation is improper, and the burden should be on the directors to justify a stock purchase as one primarily in the corporate interest. *Crane Co. v. Harsco Corp., 511 F. Supp. 294 (D. Del. 1981).*

Using corporate funds to purchase corporate stock in order to remove a threat to corporate policy is proper. *Unocal Corp. v. Mesa Petro. Co., 493 A.2d 946 (Del. 1985); Polk v. Good, 507 A.2d 531 (Del. 1986).*

Corporation may pledge its unissued shares of capital stock as collateral security for a loan made to it. *In re International Radiator Co., 10 Del. Ch. 358, 92 A. 255 (1914).*

Subsidiary should be disqualified to vote its parent's stock, and the burden is on those who assert it to show an exception to this rule. *Italo Petro. Corp. of Am. v. Producers Oil Corp. of Am., 20 Del. Ch. 283, 174 A. 276 (1934).*

In this section "indirectly" voting stock includes having stock belonging to the corporation held in some third party's name and having that third party vote the stock. *Italo Petro. Corp. of Am. v. Producers Oil Corp. of Am., 20 Del. Ch. 283, 174 A. 276 (1934).*

Voting shares held directly or indirectly. — The unconditional right of company A to convert the preferred stock that it holds in company B to a controlling interest and thus become the owner of a majority of the stock entitled to vote in an election of directors of company B constitutes indirect ownership under subsection (c). *Speiser v. Baker, 525 A.2d 1001 (Del. Ch. 1987).*

Where the capital of corporation A has been invested in corporation B and that investment, in turn, is used solely to control votes of corporation A, and the sole effect of this arrangement is to muffle the voice of the public shareholders of corporation A in the governance of corporation A as contemplated by the certificate of incorporation of corporation A, subsection (c) is violated. *Speiser v. Baker, 525 A.2d 1001 (Del. Ch. 1987).*

Shares tendered to offeror not owned or controlled by target within meaning of subsection (c). — Agreement between target company and competing tender offeror did not rise to the level of control, domination, and dictation consistent with parent-subsidiary relationship, so that shares tendered to offeror were not directly or indirectly owned or controlled by the target company within meaning of subsection (c) of this section. *Kalmanovitz v. G. Heileman Brewing Co., 595 F. Supp. 1385 (D. Del. 1984),* aff'd, *769 F.2d 152 (3d Cir. 1985).*

Showing sufficient to support board's decision to buy out threatening stockholders. — The presence of

10 outside directors out of 13 on the board of a corporation, coupled with the advice rendered by an investment banker and legal counsel that the stock held by certain investors posed a threat to the corporation, constituted a prima facie showing of good faith and reasonable investigation supporting the board's decision to buy out the investors at a premium. *Polk v. Good, 507 A.2d 531 (Del. 1986).*

Directors' actions held breach of duty of loyalty. — When a corporate board entered into an auction-ending lock-up agreement with a prospective buyer on the basis of impermissible considerations at the expense of the shareholders, the directors breached their primary duty of loyalty. *Revlon, Inc. v. MacAndrews & Forbes Holdings, Inc., 506 A.2d 173 (Del. 1985).*

Assignees. — Individual creditors did not possess claims for violations of this section because the claims were general claims which could only be brought by the corporation as debtor-in-possession. Therefore, because the creditors did not have standing to bring claims under this section, the creditors could not assign them pursuant to the liquidation plan and accordingly, the liquidating entity, in its capacity as assignee of individual creditors, did not have standing to assert claims for violations of this section. *PHP Liquidating, LLC v. Robbins, 291 B.R. 603 (D. Del. 2003).*

In an action by an assignee against a director, investment fund, and partner alleging that a corporation's stock redemption plan violated this section, and that the redemption transactions were fraudulent transfers of property under *11 U.S.C. § 548*, the motions to dismiss under *Fed. R. Civ. P. 12(b)(6)* filed by the director, investment fund, and partner were granted where (1) *8 Del. C. § 124* did not provide the assignee with a remedy for violations of this section because the assignee was not a stockholder, (2) *8 Del. C. § 174* did not provide the assignee with a cause of action against the director, investment fund, and partner because they redeemed their stock in good faith, (3) the assignee did not have an implied remedy against shareholders for the corporation's violation of under this section, (4) the assignee lacked standing under *11 U.S.C. § 544*(b) because violations of this section were general claims that accrued to all creditors, not assignees, and (5) the assignee could not show fraudulent transfer under *11 U.S.C. § 548* because the assignee failed to show that the corporation did not receive reasonably equivalent value in the stock redemption transaction, or that the corporation had actual intent to defraud investors. *PHP Liquidating, LLC v. Robbins, 291 B.R. 592 (D. Del. 2003).*

Implied remedy not found. — Delaware law does not give individual creditors an implied remedy against shareholders for a corporation's violation of this section. *PHP Liquidating, LLC v. Robbins, 291 B.R. 603 (D. Del. 2003).*

CASE NOTES — UNREPORTED

Impairment of capital. — Corporate directors' motion to dismiss a shareholder's derivative action was denied because the shareholder adequately alleged a claim that a repurchase of options and warrants would cause an impairment of the corporation's capital within the meaning of this section; according to the summary balance sheet contained in a disclosure document, subtracting the aggregate par value of the corporation's outstanding equity from its net assets left a surplus and, therefore, the repurchase amount exceeded the corporation's surplus, resulting in an impairment of the corporation's capital in violation of this section. *Feldman v. Cutaia, 2006 Del. Ch. LEXIS 70 (Del. Ch. Apr. 5, 2006).*

CASE NOTES — OTHER STATES

Illinois

A withdrawing stockholder could not compel redemption of its shares where the par value of those shares exceeded the proportionate value of the corporate assets, so that redemption would constitute an impairment of capital. *Truserv Corporation v. Bess Hardware and Sports, Inc., 346 Ill. App. 3d 194, 804 N.E.2d 611 (2004).*

Limitation on directors' disclosure duty. — A directors' fiduciary duty to disclose fully and fairly all material information within the board's control when it seeks shareholder action does not extend to repurchase by the corporation of the interests of minority shareholders. *Sims v. Tezak, 296 Ill. App. 3d 503, 694 N.E.2d 1015 (1998).*

Impairment of capital. — Under Delaware law, the fact that a corporation has positive net assets is irrelevant in determining whether a corporation's capital is impaired. Delaware law provides that a corporation may not redeem its stock if the redemption would cause an impairment of capital unless expressly authorized by section 160 of the Delaware General Corporation Law. *Truserv Corporation v. Bess Hardware and Sports, Inc., 346 Ill. App. 3d 194, 804 N.E.2d 611 (2004).*

A corporation impairs its capital unless it redeems out of "surplus." *Truserv Corporation v. Bess Hardware and Sports, Inc., 346 Ill. App. 3d 194, 804 N.E.2d 611 (2004).*

The term "surplus" is defined as the excess of net assets over the par value of the corporation's issued stock. *Truserv Corporation v. Bess Hardware and Sports, Inc., 346 Ill. App. 3d 194, 804 N.E.2d 611 (2004).*

Voting stock of parent corporation. — Under Delaware caselaw precedent, where a subsidiary owns stock in the parent, and the parent corporation completely dominates the subsidiary, the latter should not be allowed to vote the stock of the parent. If there are cases where the subsidiary should be allowed to vote its parent's stock, those cases should rest on an exceptional state of facts. *Continental-Midwest Corporation v. Hotel Sherman, Inc., 13 Ill. App. 2d 188, 141 N.E.2d 400 (1957).*

Iowa

A corporation was forbidden to repurchase its own stock to the impairment of its capital. *Phoenix Finance Corporation v. Iowa-Wisconsin Bridge Company, 237 Iowa 165, 20 N.W.2d 457 (1945).*

New York

Timing of impairment analysis. — The relevant time at which to evaluate whether a corporation's capital has been impaired is the time at which the challenged obligation was entered into. *International Consolidated Industries, Inc., v. Norton & Co., Inc., 132 Misc. 2d 606, 504 N.Y.S.2d 967 (1986).*

Rights to purchase. — Corporations incorporated in Delaware may create and issue rights or options entitling the holders thereof to purchase from the corporation any shares of its capital stock such rights or options to be evidenced by or in such instrument or instruments as shall be approved by the board of directors. *Scarpinato v. National Patent Development Corp., 75 Misc. 2d 94, 347 N.Y.S.2d 623 (1973).*

Ohio

Protection of business judgment rule. — The law of Delaware is well established that in the absence of evidence of fraud or unfairness, a corporation's repurchase of its capital stock, at a premium over market from a dissident shareholder is entitled to the protection of the business judgment rule. *Drage v. Ameritrust Corp., 1988 Ohio App. LEXIS 3972 (1988).*

Pennsylvania

Authorization for repurchase. — Delaware law does not require a corporation's certificate of incorporation to authorize a corporation to repurchase shares of its own stock. *Wyatt v. Phillips, 2004 Phila. Ct. Com. Pl. LEXIS 89 (2004).*

Common law purchase restriction. — Delaware common law imposes a third restriction on a corporation's purchase of shares of its own stock, namely, a purchase will not be permitted if the purchase is not in good faith or is achieved for an improper motive or purpose. *Wyatt v. Phillips, 2004 Phila. Ct. Com. Pl. LEXIS 89 (2004).*

Virginia

Statements of financial condition. — The Delaware courts hold that the books of a corporation may not accurately reflect the corporation's true financial condition. Unrealized appreciation or depreciation may readily render book numbers inaccurate. Further, it is clear that an adverse party has the right to question whether the corporation's statement of its financial condition was made in good faith. An allegation of fraud or bad faith in a corporation's representations of its financial condition presents an issue of fact, not a question of law. *Stockbridge v. Gemini Air Ccargo Inc., 269 Va. 609, 611 S.E.2d 600 (2005).*

Purpose. — The general assembly enacted Del. Code tit. 8, § 160 to prevent boards from draining corporations of assets to the detriment of creditors and the long-term health of the corporation. *Stockbridge v. Gemini Air Ccargo Inc., 269 Va. 609, 611 S.E.2d 600 (2005).*

Avoidance of stock repurchase. — An inflexible rule that a corporation may not in any circumstances assert Del. Code tit. 8, § 160, or similar laws, to avoid a stock repurchase while its capital is impaired is not adopted. Directors have a fiduciary duty to manage the corporation's affairs with the utmost good faith in the best interests of all its shareholders and of the long-term health of the corporation itself. Whether they have done so in a particular case is a question of fact. *Stockbridge v. Gemini Air Cargo Inc., 269 Va. 609, 611 S.E.2d 600 (2005).*

A defense to an action for breach of a contract requiring a corporation to repurchase its shares that may be afforded by Del. Code tit. 8, § 160 is created by operation of law, is independent of the terms of the contract between the parties, and cannot be waived. *Stockbridge v. Gemini Air Ccargo Inc., 269 Va. 609, 611 S.E.2d 600 (2005).*

Wisconsin

In general. — Under Delaware law, a corporation may not purchase or redeem its own stock when the capital of the corporation is impaired or when such purchase or redemption would cause any impairment of the capital of the corporation. *Eldridge v. Stark Candy Co., 188 Wis. 2d 603, 526 N.W.2d 279 (Wis. App. 1994).*

"Capital impairment" means the reduction of the amount of the assets of the company below the amount represented by the aggregate outstanding shares of the capital stock of the company. In other words a corporation under the Delaware statute may only use its surplus for the purchase of shares of its capital stock. *Eldridge v. Stark Candy Co., 188 Wis. 2d 603, 526 N.W.2d 279 (Wis. App. 1994).*

CASE NOTES — FEDERAL

First Circuit

In general. — Under Delaware law, shares of its own capital stock belonging to the corporation shall neither be entitled to vote nor be counted for quorum purposes. *Enterasys Networks, Inc. v. Gulf Insurance Co., 364 F. Supp. 2d 28 (D.N.Hamp. 2005).*

Second Circuit

The purpose of subdivision (a)(1) of this section is to protect creditors from fraud. One way the statute protects a creditor from fraud is by its provision that when a corporation issues a note, debenture, or obligation, the corporation may not *later* claim that it is impaired as a way to avoid its obligations to holders of such instruments. *Azar v. 1-800 Doctors, Inc., 2007 U.S. Dist. LEXIS 68395 (SD NY, September 17, 2007).*

Under Delaware law, the point at which to measure impairment is the date upon which plaintiff requested redemption. *Azar v. 1-800 Doctors, Inc., 2007 U.S. Dist. LEXIS 68395 (SD NY, September 17, 2007).*

Under Delaware Law, the financial status of a corporation serves as the benchmark in deciding when certain duties arise and whether questioned transactions, such as the issuance of dividends and stock redemptions, are improper. *Pereira v. Farace, 413 F.3d 330 (2d Cir. 2005).*

Under Delaware law, the repurchasing of stock and payment of dividends is not permitted where a corporation's capital would become impaired. Precluding the repurchase of stock under such a situation is designed to protect the shareholders and creditors. The prohibition on payment of dividends was intended to protect creditors. *UCAR Internatonal, Inc v. Union Carbide Corp., 2004 U.S. Dist. LEXIS 914 (S.D.N.Y. 2004).*

Prohibitions on repayment of dividends. — Del. Code. Ann. tit. 8, §§ 160, 174(a) (2005), prohibit the payment of dividends while the corporation is insolvent or which will render it insolvent, or the redemption of stock when a corporation's capital is impaired or which will impair the corporate capital. *Pereira v. Farace, 413 F.3d 330 (2d Cir. 2005).*

Insolvency. — Delaware courts define insolvency in two ways. First, a company is insolvent if it is unable to pay its debts as they fall due in the usual course of business. Second, a company may be insolvent if it has liabilities in excess of a reasonable market value of assets held. *Pereira v. Farace, 413 F.3d 330 (2d Cir. 2005).*

Outstanding stock. — Delaware law defines "outstanding" stock as that which can be voted, and therefore, is construed to mean stock in the hands of shareholders, not stock in the treasury. *Satterfield v. Monsanto Co., 88 F. Supp. 2d 288 (S.D.N.Y. 2000).*

When ability to repurchase occurs. — An insolvent corporation may not repurchase its own shares of stock. Pertinent to the application of the doctrine of corporate law is the time of an actual repurchase or the obligation to make the commensurate payment. Timing questions typically arise when a repurchase agreement calls for payment by a corporation in installments and the corporation fails to make such an installment payment. Under such circumstances, there is a time differential between the date shares are actually transferred from a shareholder to a corporation and the date or dates payment for such shares is due or completed. Litigation compelling payment arises when a company first becomes insolvent or otherwise unable to repurchase the stock after the agreement has been entered into and the shares transferred, but before payments are fully made. When determining whether there is a viable obligation to pay, courts have had to determine whether the critical moment of ability to repurchase is the time a repurchase agreement is entered into and shares are transferred, or the time a particular payment is due. Courts holding that it suffices if there was an ability to repurchase at the time a repurchase agreement is entered into apply what has been nominated the "outset test," while those holding that there must be ability to repurchase at the time the payment is due apply the so-called "installment test." *Lowry v. Smith Metal Arts Co., 1991 U.S. Dist. LEXIS 13113 (W.D.N.Y. 1991).*

Third Circuit

Courts will not aid a party in the enforcement of a contract for repurchase of a corporation's stock where the payments will impair the capital of the corporation. *Davis v. Air Indies Corp., 1973 U.S. Dist. LEXIS 5200 (D.V.I. 1973).*

When issue of capital impairment arises. — Corporations are not forbidden from entering into agreements that provide for the repurchase of stock. The only requirement is that funds of the corporation not be used to purchase if their use would jeopardize the financial position of the entity. The repurchase of stock is not void at its inception; rather, it is the impairment of capital resulting from repurchase payments that is verboten. Section 160 expressly confers on a corporation the power to purchase its own stock provided it can do so without impairing capital. Therefore, in event that payments are made under the terms of the contract, it is then and only then that the issue of capital impairment would arise. If capital were impaired by payment, public policy would at that time require the intervention of the courts. This is particularly true where the parties in the agreement have made provision for the postponement of payments when it is found that such a payment would violate the statute. *Davis v. Air Indies Corp., 1973 U.S. Dist. LEXIS 5200 (D.V.I. 1973).*

Bankruptcy proceedings. — It appears that a trustee-in-bankruptcy or debtor-in-possession (or in this case, the committee through derivative standing) does acquire a right of action under § 544(b) of the Bankruptcy Code to prosecute violations of §§ 160 and 173 of the DGCL in its capacity as a putative creditor. *Official Comm. of Unsecured Creditors v. Clark (In re Nat'l Forge Co.), 344 B.R. 340 (D. Pa. June 9, 2006).*

Fourth Circuit

A Delaware corporation may use only its surplus for the purchase of its capital stock. *Cunningham v. Jaffe, 251 F. Supp. 143 (D.S.C. 1966).*

Fifth Circuit

The purpose of the statute is to protect creditors. The statute is designed to prevent a corporation from rearranging its capital structure so as to alter the assumed basis upon which creditors have extended credit. Id. In other words, the statute prevents a corporation from defrauding its creditors by redistributing assets to its shareholders. *Askanase v. Fatjo, 130 F.3d 657 (5th Cir. 1997).*

A corporation may repurchase its own shares of stock if it has a capital surplus. Capital surplus is that sum which equals the difference between the total amount of cash received for all of the corporation's outstanding shares of stock and the par value of such shares. *Georesearch, Inc. v. Morriss, 193 F. Supp. 163 (W.D. La. 1961).*

Sixth Circuit

Total rescission possible. — A literal reading of the statute suggests that a total rescission of a prohibited transaction may be possible. *In re Revco D.S., Inc., 1990 Bankr. LEXIS 2966 (Bankr. N.D. Ohio 1990).*

Seventh Circuit

In general. — A Delaware corporation is specifically authorized to purchase, redeem, or otherwise acquire shares of its own stock, provided that the corporation's capital is not impaired. *Newell Co. v. Vermont American Corp., 725 F. Supp. 351 (N.D.Ill. 1989).*

Del. Code Ann. tit. 8, § 160 provides that a corporation may not redeem its own shares when the capital of the corporation is impaired or when such purchase or redemption would cause any impairment of the capital of the corporation, except that a corporation may purchase or redeem out of capital any of its own shares which are entitled upon any distribution of its assets, whether by dividend or in liquidation, to a preference over another class or series of its stock if such shares will be retired upon their acquisition and the capital of the corporation reduced in accordance with Del. Code Ann. tit. 8, §§ 243, 244. A corporation redeeming its own shares would impair its capital within the meaning of § 160 unless it redeems shares out of surplus. *Wright v. Heizer Corp., 503 F. Supp. 802 (N.D. Ill. 1980).*

The Delaware law governing redemption is designed for the benefit of both creditors and shareholders. *Wright v. Heizer Corp., 503 F. Supp. 802 (N.D. Ill. 1980).*

The corporation may redeem preferred stock out of capital if the shares are retired and the capital reduced. *Wright v. Heizer Corp., 503 F. Supp. 802 (N.D. Ill. 1980).*

Alternative to hostile offer. — Stock repurchase programs funded by corporate monies, which give stockholders an alternative to a hostile offer, have been expressly endorsed by Delaware courts as an appropriate response to an unsolicited tender offer found to be inadequate. *Newell Co. v. Vermont American Corp., 725 F. Supp. 351 (N.D.Ill. 1989).*

Exchange of corporate asset for shares. — Directors do not breach their fiduciary duty to their stockholders or the common law, where, as the result of the exercise of an informed business judgment, and in the absence of bad faith, a corporate asset was exchanged on a market-to-market basis for shares of their corporation held by dissident stockholders. *Dasho v. Susquehanna Corp., 1970 U.S. Dist. LEXIS 12923 (N.D. Ill. 1970).*

No independent federal redemption jurisdiction. — Delaware law contains a detailed provision regarding redemption, and the issue is one which is traditionally relegated to state law. Thus, no independent federal jurisdiction exists. *Wright v. Heizer Corp., 503 F. Supp. 802 (N.D. Ill. 1980).*

Ninth Circuit

Violation grounds for breach of fiduciary duty claim. — In Delaware, a plaintiff may bring a general claim of breach of fiduciary duty against a director as long as he or she claims that the director's acts or omissions involved (i) a breach of the director's duty of loyalty to the corporation or its stockholders; (ii) acts or omissions not in good faith or which involve intentional misconduct or a knowing violation of law; (iii) under Del. Code Ann. tit. 8, § 174 (which includes willful or negligent violation of Del. Code Ann. tit. 8, §§ 160 or 173 regarding voting and trading); or (iv) any transaction from which the director derived an improper personal benefit. *Grassmueck v. Barnett, 281 F. Supp. 2d 1227 (W.D.Wash. 2003).*

§ 161. Issuance of additional stock; when and by whom

DELAWARE CASE NOTES — REPORTED

Board of directors has exclusive authority to issue stock. — This section and §§ 151, 152, 153, 157 and 166 of this title, taken together, confirm the board's exclusive authority to issue stock and regulate a corporation's capital structure; to ensure certainty, these provisions contemplate board approval and a written instrument evidencing the relevant transactions affecting issuance of stock and the corporation's capital structure. *Grimes v. Alteon Inc., 804 A.2d 256 (Del. 2002).*

CASE NOTES — FEDERAL

First Circuit

Extent of authority for share issuance. — Generally, shareholders necessarily understand that a corporation may issue shares up to the maximum number authorized by its certificate of incorporation. Shareholders would be hard pressed to complain when that occurs in furtherance of legitimate corporate purposes, such as the settlement of a lawsuit representing a potential corporate liability. More specifically, under the corporate law of Delaware, the directors are authorized to distribute treasury stock and issue new stock (up to the limit authorized by the certificate of incorporation) at their discretion, for consideration determined by them. *Enterasys Networks, Inc. v. Gulf Insurance Co., 364 F. Supp. 2d 28 (D.N.Hamp. 2005).*

§ 162. Liability of stockholder or subscriber for stock not paid in full

DELAWARE CASE NOTES — REPORTED

Corporate stock issued, outstanding and not paid for is fund for benefit of creditors, and in general all who hold stock not paid for are liable to creditors for the amount so unpaid. *John W. Cooney Co. v. Arlington Hotel Co., 11 Del. Ch. 286, 101 A. 879 (1917)*, modified, *11 Del. Ch. 430, 106 A. 39 (1918)*.

The amount due to the company for stock issued and not paid for is an asset of the company for the benefit of its creditors when it is insolvent. *Cooper v. Eastern Horse & Mule Co., 12 Del. Ch. 210, 110 A. 666 (1920)*.

If corporate debts are ascertained. — A stockholder of an insolvent corporation is liable to pay an unpaid balance of his or her subscription for the discharge of the debts of the corporation when such debts have been ascertained. *Philips v. Slocomb, 35 Del. 462, 167 A. 698 (1933)*.

The debts of the company not having been ascertained and there being no showing that the assessment or collection on the unpaid subscription is necessary either for the payment of debts of the corporation or for the purpose of equalization among the stockholders, suit cannot be maintained on a stock subscription note against a stockholder by a receiver for unpaid subscription. *Philips v. Slocomb, 35 Del. 462, 167 A. 698 (1933)*.

And assets are shown to be insufficient. — In addition to primary assets of a corporation there are other assets recoverable by a receiver; 1 kind is conditional in character, the liability of a stockholder for the unpaid par value of the stockholder's shares to pay creditors of the company when the assets of the company are insufficient for the purpose. There must be a preliminary determination by the court that there is such a deficiency and the amount thereof before particular authority to make an assessment and the amount thereof is given by the court to the receiver as well as orders or instructions as to the recovery thereof by suit. *Cahall v. Lofland, 12 Del. Ch. 162, 108 A. 752 (1920)*.

The necessary element of the establishment of a deficiency of assets to meet the claims against the company having not been shown, then this section cannot be the basis to charge a stockholder for stock not paid in full. *Philips v. Slocomb, 35 Del. 462, 167 A. 698 (1933)*.

Court makes assessments on unpaid stock. — Where a corporation is insolvent and a receiver has been appointed for it, the court through its receiver performs the duty of the directors in the matter of assessments upon unpaid stock and subscriptions when the rights of creditors require it. *Carpenter v. Griffith Mtg. Corp., 20 Del. Ch. 132, 172 A. 447 (1934)*.

An order may be entered adjudging the amount of the unpaid indebtedness of a corporation and assessing upon the subscribers to and holders of stock who have not paid in full therefor such portion of the amount due thereon as is necessary to pay the adjudicated indebtedness and the costs and expenses of administration. *Carpenter v. Griffith Mtg. Corp., 20 Del. Ch. 132, 172 A. 447 (1934)*.

Order of assessment is not judgment. — An assessment upon unpaid stock in order to put the corporation's receiver in the possession of funds necessary to pay the insolvent's debts and defray the expense incidental thereto is the equivalent of a call by the directors, had the receiver never been appointed, and the court in making such a call or assessment, takes the place and exercises the office of the directors. The order of assessment does not purport to be a judgment against anyone in particular. Nor does it undertake to determine the question of whether any particular stockholder is or is not liable in any amount. *Shaw v. Lincoln Hotel Corp., 18 Del. Ch. 87, 156 A. 199 (1931)*.

But is necessary before corporation may maintain action against stockholder. — Before a corporation can maintain an action against an alleged stockholder to recover an unpaid subscription for stock therein, or the unpaid purchase price for newly issued stock, it is incumbent upon it to show that an assessment and call has been made upon said alleged stockholder for the amount required from him or her. *Louisiana Oil Exploration Co. v. Raskob, 32 Del. 564, 127 A. 713 (1925)*.

Assessment should fall on all stockholders as equally as practicable. — While the court has power to require a resident stockholder to pay the entire assessment, the entire burden of payment should not, in the first instance, be imposed upon a single stockholder, even though there be no other found in the jurisdiction. The fair and equitable proceeding would be for the receivers to collect all the assessments, so far as practicable, and by so doing the burden would fall on all stockholders alike according to their holdings. *John W. Cooney Co. v. Arlington Hotel Co., 11 Del. Ch. 430, 106 A. 39 (1918)*.

Creditors are entitled to interest. — As against stockholders, creditors are entitled to have interest calculated on their claims. *John W. Cooney Co. v. Arlington Hotel Co., 11 Del. Ch. 286, 101 A. 879 (1917)*, modified, *11 Del. Ch. 430, 106 A. 39 (1918)*.

From time receiver asks court to assess. — Interest should commence at the time the receivers asked the court to make an assessment upon the stockholders for the payment of creditors' claims, there being nothing before which indicated that they would be expected to pay such claims. *John W. Cooney Co. v. Arlington Hotel Co., 11 Del. Ch. 430, 106 A. 39 (1918)*.

Knowledge that stock is not paid for makes it subject to assessment. — Mere knowledge that stock issued as full paid and nonassessable was not in fact paid for, should not preclude the creditor from enforcing the liability of the holder, because the creditor may also know or have good reason to believe that the holders of such stock would be legally liable for the debts of the company to the extent of the par value of their stock. *John W. Cooney Co. v. Arlington Hotel Co., 11 Del. Ch. 430, 106 A. 39 (1918)*.

Even if certificates say it is paid for. — The statement on the certificate of shares of common stock that they were full paid and nonassessable does not relieve from liability to pay therefor any holder or taker thereof, except those without notice of the fact. *John W. Cooney Co. v. Arlington Hotel Co., 11 Del. Ch. 286, 101 A. 879 (1917),* modified, *11 Del. Ch. 430, 106 A. 39 (1918).*

Enforcement of unpaid subscriptions is for benefit of creditors only. *Carpenter v. Griffith Mtg. Corp., 20 Del. Ch. 132, 172 A. 447 (1934).*

Not for benefit of other stockholders. — There is no justification in this section for the proposition that upon insolvency the court should call in all unpaid subscriptions and demand payment in full from all stockholders, not for the benefit of creditors, but for the benefit of stockholders. *Carpenter v. Griffith Mtg. Corp., 20 Del. Ch. 132, 172 A. 447 (1934).*

Once corporation is insolvent stockholder loses his setoff rights. — The right of a holder of stock not paid for to setoff a debt due him or her from the company ends when the company becomes insolvent, for the liability to pay for the stock is there for the benefit of the creditors of the company. *Cooper v. Eastern Horse & Mule Co., 12 Del. Ch. 210, 110 A. 666 (1920).*

When sued on his or her liability as the holder of stock of an insolvent corporation not paid for, a stockholder cannot set off a debt due him or her from the corporation, because to do so would give him or her a preference over other creditors to which he or she is not entitled. *Cooper v. Eastern Horse & Mule Co., 12 Del. Ch. 210, 110 A. 666 (1920).*

But once they pay their assessment they become creditors of corporation. — Stockholders who took stock with notice of the irregularities as to the issue thereof and who are also creditors of the company are not estopped from participating as creditors, after they have paid the assessment against their shares. *John W. Cooney Co. v. Arlington Hotel Co., 11 Del. Ch. 286, 101 A. 879 (1917),* modified, *11 Del. Ch. 430, 106 A. 39 (1918).*

Stock subscriptions even prior to incorporation are liable for corporate debts also. — Since subscriptions for capital stock are capital assets which are earmarked for the benefit of creditors, the time when they were received in its relation to the time of the completed formal organization of the corporation can have no possible effect in reason upon the essential nature of the liability of the subscribers as a liability incurred by them to supply the capital funds to which creditors may look for protection. *Carpenter v. Griffith Mtg. Corp., 20 Del. Ch. 132, 172 A. 447 (1934).*

Acceptor of stock without valid consideration is liable for corporate debts. — Corporate stock shall not be issued without valid consideration, but if it is so issued, contrary to law, the acceptor will be bound to pay its par value if the debts of the company cannot be paid otherwise. *Scully v. Automobile Fin. Co., 12 Del. Ch. 174, 109 A. 49 (1920).*

Holders of bonus stock are required to pay for their shares to satisfy claims of creditors. *John W. Cooney Co. v. Arlington Hotel Co., 11 Del. Ch. 286, 101 A. 879 (1917),* modified, *11 Del. Ch. 430, 106 A. 39 (1918).*

Independent of this section unpaid capital due from stockholders always was and is part of assets of company, and so belongs to the company and not to the creditors. *John W. Cooney Co. v. Arlington Hotel Co., 11 Del. Ch. 286, 101 A. 879 (1917),* modified, *11 Del. Ch. 430, 106 A. 39 (1918).*

CASE NOTES — OTHER STATES

Missouri

Voidable issuance. — Delaware treats the absence of valid consideration as rendering the stock issuance voidable rather than void. Courts balance the equities to determine whether the corporation may cancel the shares or whether the party claiming entitlement to the shares may pay adequate consideration for the shares and cure the defect in consideration. *Yates v. Bridge Trading Co., 844 S.W.2d 56 (Mo. App. 1992).*

Texas

Lawful consideration date. — Under Delaware law, the critical time for determining whether lawful consideration exists is the date corporation shares were actually issued. The Delaware Supreme Court has looked to the date the shares issued for determining whether valid consideration was given. *Coates v. Parnassus Systems, Inc., 2002 Tex. App. LEXIS 2545 (2002).*

Amelioration of allocation rule. — In Delaware, the harshness of the allocation rule is ameliorated by two other principles of Delaware law. First, the failure of consideration renders stock voidable, not void. Second, a Delaware court may as a matter of equity allow a party to retain the shares upon payment rather than have them canceled at the time the court rules the original consideration to be invalid. *Coates v. Parnassus Systems, Inc., 2002 Tex. App. LEXIS 2545 (2002).*

CASE NOTES — FEDERAL

District of Columbia Circuit

Voidable shares. — Under Delaware law, shares of corporate stock that have not been initially authorized in full compliance with the requirements of the Delaware General Corporate Law, prior to ratification, are merely voidable, not void, because only voidable acts would be open to ratification. *CarrAmerica Realty Corp. v. Kaidanow, 321 F.3d 165 (D.C. Cir. 2003).*

§ 163. Payment for stock not paid in full

CASE NOTES — OTHER STATES

Massachusetts

Under Delaware law, the promise of future services is not valid consideration. *Biotrack, Inc. v. Muni, 12 Mass. L. Rep. 244 (Super. 2000).*

Delaware law appears to draw a distinction between a case where the issuance of a company's stock itself violates a provision of Delaware's Constitution, its corporation law, or the company's own corporate charter, and one where the company has the power and authority to issue stock but does so without receiving the required consideration. *Biotrack, Inc. v. Muni, 12 Mass. L. Rep. 244 (Super. 2000).*

Missouri

Voidable issuance. — Delaware treats the absence of valid consideration as rendering the stock issuance voidable rather than void. Courts balance the equities to determine whether the corporation may cancel the shares or whether the party claiming entitlement to the shares may pay adequate consideration for the shares and cure the defect in consideration. *Yates v. Bridge Trading Co., 844 S.W.2d 56 (Mo. App. 1992).*

Texas

Lawful consideration date. — Under Delaware law, the critical time for determining whether lawful consideration exists is the date corporation shares were actually issued. The Delaware Supreme Court has looked to the date the shares issued for determining whether valid consideration was given. *Coates v. Parnassus Systems, Inc., 2002 Tex. App. LEXIS 2545 (2002).*

Amelioration of allocation rule. — In Delaware, the harshness of the allocation rule is ameliorated by two other principles of Delaware law. First, the failure of consideration renders stock voidable, not void. Second, a Delaware court may as a matter of equity allow a party to retain the shares upon payment rather than have them canceled at the time the court rules the original consideration to be invalid. *Coates v. Parnassus Systems, Inc., 2002 Tex. App. LEXIS 2545 (2002).*

§ 164. Failure to pay for stock; remedies

CASE NOTES — OTHER STATES

Massachusetts

Delaware law appears to draw a distinction between a case where the issuance of a company's stock itself violates a provision of Delaware's Constitution, its corporation law, or the company's own corporate charter, and one where the company has the power and authority to issue stock but does so without receiving the required consideration. *Biotrack, Inc. v. Muni, 12 Mass. L. Rep. 244 (Super. 2000).*

Texas

Amelioration of allocation rule. — In Delaware, the harshness of the allocation rule is ameliorated by two other principles of Delaware law. First, the failure of consideration renders stock voidable, not void. Second, a Delaware court may as a matter of equity allow a party to retain the shares upon payment rather than have them canceled at the time the court rules the original consideration to be invalid. *Coates v. Parnassus Systems, Inc., 2002 Tex. App. LEXIS 2545 (2002).*

§ 166. Formalities required of stock subscriptions

DELAWARE CASE NOTES — REPORTED

Board of directors has exclusive authority to issue stock. — This section, and §§ 151, 152, 153, 157 and 161 of this title, taken together, confirm the board's exclusive authority to issue stock and regulate a corporation's capital structure; to ensure certainty, these provisions contemplate board approval and a written instrument evidencing the relevant transactions affecting issuance of stock and the corporation's capital structure. *Grimes v. Alteon Inc., 804 A.2d 256 (Del. 2002).*

§ 167. Lost, stolen or destroyed stock certificates; issuance of new certificate or uncertificated shares

DELAWARE CASE NOTES — REPORTED

Stock certificates that have disappeared after delivery to owner's agent are "lost" within the meaning of this section. *Graham v. Commercial Credit Co., 41 Del. Ch. 355, 194 A.2d 863 (1963), aff'd, 41 Del. Ch. 580, 200 A.2d 828 (1964).*

Management may or may not require posting of bond adequate for its protection. *Mastellone v. Argo Oil Corp., 46 Del. 102, 82 A.2d 379 (1951).*

Whether or not a lost instrument bond may be required is within the discretion of management of the defendant corporation, and with this discretion the court cannot interfere. *Graham v. Commercial Credit Co., 41 Del. Ch.*

355, 194 A.2d 863 (1963), aff'd, *41 Del. Ch. 580, 200 A.2d 828 (1964).*

And courts lack power to dispense with bond requirement against corporation's will. *Mastellone v. Argo Oil Corp., 46 Del. 102, 82 A.2d 379 (1951).*

§ 168. Judicial proceedings to compel issuance of new certificate or uncertificated shares

DELAWARE CASE NOTES — REPORTED

Remedy where certificate lost, destroyed or stolen. — When a stock certificate has been lost, destroyed or stolen, the remedy is an order to issue a new certificate. *Scott v. Ametek, Inc., 277 A.2d 714 (Del. Ch. 1971).*

This section confers jurisdiction upon court of chancery to order replacement of a lost, stolen or destroyed certificate. *Scott v. Ametek, Inc., 277 A.2d 714 (Del. Ch. 1971).*

Submission of original certificates for transfer by bona fide purchaser. — The Chancery Court has subject-matter jurisdiction of a claim for delivery of new stock certificates based upon improper indorsement of the original certificates even when a bona fide purchaser has submitted the original securities for transfer, and the plaintiff in such case is not limited to an action at law for money damages. *Scott v. Ametek, Inc., 277 A.2d 714 (Del. Ch. 1971).*

Petitioner must prove ownership and loss or destruction of certificates. — The burden is upon the petitioner to establish with reasonable certainty that the certificates were owned by him and that they had become lost or destroyed. *In re Metropolitan Royalty Corp., 44 Del. 561, 62 A.2d 857 (1948); Keech v. Zenith Radio Corp., 276 A.2d 270 (Del. Ch. 1971).*

For purposes of this section, registration on the insurer's stock ledger as the owner is not critical; the substance of petitioners' claim to be the "lawful owner" of lost, stolen or destroyed certificates is. Once the mechanical test of registration is discarded, no simple or abstract test of "lawful owner" suggests itself; rather, an inquiry into the specifics of each claim is necessary. *Castro v. ITT Corp., 598 A.2d 674 (Del. Ch. 1991).*

Indemnity provisions do not lessen burden of proof. — The fact that the corporate defendant will be adequately protected by the indemnity provisions of this section in no sense lessens the burden of proof. *In re Metropolitan Royalty Corp., 44 Del. 561, 62 A.2d 857 (1948); Keech v. Zenith Radio Corp., 276 A.2d 270 (Del. Ch. 1971).*

§ 169. Situs of ownership of stock

DELAWARE CASE NOTES — REPORTED

Section constitutionally insufficient to satisfy jurisdictional requirements. — The single fact of statutory situs of stock under this section does not suffice to give Delaware sufficient contact or affiliation with a sequestration litigation to satisfy constitutional standards. *U.S. Indus., Inc. v. Gregg, 540 F.2d 142 (3d Cir. 1976),* cert. denied, *433 U.S. 908, 97 S. Ct. 2972, 53 L. Ed. 2d 1091 (1977).*

The Delaware situs statute, as construed by the Delaware courts and as applied in a nonresident stock sequestration proceeding, does not comport with the constitutional requirement that jurisdiction be predicated on minimum contacts with the forum. *U.S. Indus., Inc. v. Gregg, 540 F.2d 142 (3d Cir. 1976),* cert. denied, *433 U.S. 908, 97 S. Ct. 2972, 53 L. Ed. 2d 1091 (1977).*

The fictional situs of stock under this section alone does not pass constitutional muster as a predicate for jurisdiction under § 365 of Title 10 in an action admittedly seeking to obtain personal liability of a nonresident in connection with transactions unrelated to the forum. *U.S. Indus., Inc. v. Gregg, 540 F.2d 142 (3d Cir. 1976),* cert. denied, *433 U.S. 908, 97 S. Ct. 2972, 53 L. Ed. 2d 1091 (1977); Barber-Greene Co. v. Walco Nat'l Corp., 428 F. Supp. 567 (D. Del. 1977).*

Requisite contacts must exist or due process clause may prevent exercise of jurisdiction. — Caution must be exercised as to a fictional statutory presence of property. The requisite contacts between the defendant, the litigation and the forum state must exist. The due process clause may prevent the exercise of jurisdiction over the person's interest in the property located in the forum state, despite the existence of a strong interest by the forum state in the litigation. *Istituto Bancario Italiano SpA v. Hunter Eng'g Co., 449 A.2d 210 (Del. 1982).*

Mere ownership of stock insufficient for jurisdiction. — The mere ownership of stock that is not itself the subject matter of litigation cannot count as a contact for purposes of personal jurisdiction. *Hart Holding Co. v. Drexel Burnham Lambert Inc., 593 A.2d 535 (Del. Ch. 1991).*

This section is confirmatory of common-law principle. *Krizanek v. Smith, 32 Del. Ch. 513, 87 A.2d 871 (1952).*

Effect of former 6 del. C. § 8-317. — The amendment of former 6 Del. C. § 8-317 in 1983 was not intended to modify the effect of this situs statute or attachment mechanisms employed to bring stock into court. *Castro v. ITT Corp., 598 A.2d 674 (Del. Ch. 1991).*

No stockholder who accepts stock in Delaware corporation can be heard to deny its Delaware situs. *Bouree v. Trust Francais, 14 Del. Ch. 332, 127 A. 56 (1924).*

There is nothing novel about having situs of stock in 1 jurisdiction for 1 purpose and in another for

another purpose. *Krizanek v. Smith, 32 Del. Ch. 513, 87 A.2d 871 (1952).*

This section places vast amount of intangible property within the jurisdiction of the courts of Delaware. *TWA v. Hughes, 40 Del. Ch. 523, 185 A.2d 762 (1962).*

Reliance on unconstitutional sequestration procedure. — Even though the sequestration procedure in § 366 of Title 10, as applied to the sequestration of stock with a situs, under this section, in Delaware, was ultimately invalidated by the United States Supreme Court, a party will not be held civilly liable for reliance upon that procedure in a property seizure case, where that section had not yet been declared unconstitutional. *U.S. Indus., Inc. v. Gregg, 457 F. Supp. 1293 (D. Del. 1978),* aff'd, *605 F.2d 1199 (3d Cir. 1979),* cert. denied, *444 U.S. 1076, 100 S. Ct. 1023, 62 L. Ed. 2d 758 (1980).*

Corporation's domicile as situs of its stock without jurisdictional utility. — There is no jurisdictional utility to the fiction that the corporation's domicile — the state of incorporation — is the situs of its stock. *U.S. Indus., Inc. v. Gregg, 540 F.2d 142 (3d Cir. 1976),* cert. denied, *433 U.S. 908, 97 S. Ct. 2972, 53 L. Ed. 2d 1091 (1977).*

Corporation constitutionally protected from appearing in Delaware courts. — Where the sole connection of the defendant California corporation, its president and vice-president with Delaware is that they are the owners of corporate stock which, by statute, has its fictional and legal situs in Delaware, and where action by the plaintiff locally domiciled corporation concedes defendants' ownership of the stock in the local corporation and seeks only to determine the voting rights of such stock at an annual election of directors as such rights may or may not be affected by the California statutes on which the defendants rely, under "traditional notions of fair play and substantial justice" defendants have a constitutionally protected right to be free from appearing in the Delaware courts in such suit. *Arden-Mayfair, Inc. v. Louart Corp., 385 A.2d 3 (Del. Ch. 1978).*

This section says nothing about options or warrants to purchase stock or corporate obligations of any kind. *Baker v. Gotz, 387 F. Supp. 1381 (D. Del.),* aff'd, *523 F.2d 1050 (3d Cir. 1975).*

Negotiable instrument, other than stock, is not subject to sequestration without seizure of the instrument. This was also the intended effect of former 6 Del. C. § 8-317 in the form enacted by the *General Assembly. Baker v. Gotz, 387 F. Supp. 1381 (D. Del.),* aff'd, *523 F.2d 1050 (3d Cir. 1975).*

Seizure subjects defendants to jurisdiction to extent of interest. — Even though a case has no relation to the property attached where the property does have its situs in this State by virtue of this section and is within the jurisdiction of the Court, its seizure subjects the defendants to jurisdiction, only to the extent of their property interest. *Hibou, Inc. v. Ramsing, 324 A.2d 777 (Del. Super. Ct. 1974).*

DELAWARE CASE NOTES — UNREPORTED

This section and section 324 do not apply to shares of stock which are the subject of an appraisal proceeding under Section 262. *Ums Ptnrs v. Jackson, 1995 Del. Super. LEXIS 250 (1995).*

Jurisdiction over nonresident shareholders under property attachment theory. — This section establishes that the situs of stock in a Delaware corpora-tion is Delaware, for jurisdiction and attachment purposes; the property attachment statute, 10 Del. C. § 365, thus provides a basis to exercise jurisdiction over nonresident recipients of a Delaware corporation's preferred stock. *Chandler v. Ciccoricco, 2003 Del. Ch. LEXIS 47 (May 5, 2003).*

CASE NOTES — OTHER STATES

Maine

Determination of title. — Title to shares in corporations organized under the laws of Delaware are to be determined by the laws of Delaware, and not by the law of the state where the transfer of the certificate takes place. *Strout v. Burgess, 144 Me. 263, 68 A.2d 241 (1949).*

Minnesota

Construction with laws of other states. — Del. Code Ann. tit. 8, § 169 makes Delaware the situs of ownership of stock in Delaware corporations; the rule in the other 49 states places that situs in the state of the owner's residence. *Savchuk v. Randal Rush. State Farm Mutual Automobile Insurance Company, 311 Minn. 480, 272 N.W.2d 888 (1946).*

New York

Attachment of interest. — The law of Delaware appears to be that a stock interest in a Delaware corporation may not be attached anywhere but in Delaware, regardless of the fact that the certificates may not be in that state. *Cotnareanu v. Woods, 155 Misc. 95, 278 N.Y.S. 589 (Sup. 1935).*

Ohio

In general. — Delaware law provided that the situs of any stock in a Delaware corporation was the State of Delaware, even though the stock certificates might not be physically present in the state. *Lonigro v. Lonigro, 1988 Ohio App. LEXIS 3022 (1988).*

Texas

In general. — Delaware law characterized all shares held in a Delaware corporation, regardless of their physical location, to be in Delaware, and thus within the state's in rem jurisdiction. *Smith v. Lanier, 998 S.W.2d 324 (Tex. App. 1999).*

§ 170. Dividends; payment; wasting asset corporations

DELAWARE CASE NOTES — REPORTED

Payment to stockholders as return upon their investment is, in general, termed a dividend. *Penington v. Commonwealth Hotel Constr. Corp., 17 Del. Ch. 394, 155 A. 514 (1931).*

And dividend is sum of money or portion of divisible thing to be distributed according to some fixed scheme. *Penington v. Commonwealth Hotel Constr. Corp., 17 Del. Ch. 394, 155 A. 514 (1931).*

Stockholder does not own earnings until they are declared dividends. — The stockholder does not, and cannot, own the property of the corporation, or even the earnings, until they are declared in the form of dividends, but when they are so declared, whether in cash, or in stock purchased or newly created, they are not capital of the company, but a distribution of profits which were made by the use of the corporation's capital in the prosecution of its business. *Bryan v. Aikin, 10 Del. Ch. 446, 86 A. 674 (1913).*

And cumulative preferred stockholders are not creditors and dividends are not due them until such dividends are declared. *Treves v. Menzies, 37 Del. Ch. 330, 142 A.2d 520 (1958).*

But dividend declared creates debtor-creditor relationship. — Upon the declaration of a lawful dividend by a board of directors the relation of debtor and creditor is set up between the corporation and the stockholder, and the right of action of the stockholder is in the nature of a contract and grows out of the declaration of a lawful dividend. *Selly v. Fleming Coal Co., 37 Del. 34, 180 A. 326 (1935).*

Corporations cannot declare dividends except out of profits and the invested capital shall be kept intact. *Wittenberg v. Federal Mining & Smelting Co., 15 Del. Ch. 147, 133 A. 48 (1926), aff'd, 15 Del. Ch. 409, 138 A. 347 (1927).*

If a company is a going concern, dividends cannot be paid to the preferred stock unless there is a surplus of net earnings out of which to pay them. *Penington v. Commonwealth Hotel Constr. Corp., 17 Del. Ch. 188, 151 A. 228 (1930), modified, 17 Del. Ch. 394, 155 A. 514 (1931).*

Since dividends can only legally be paid from profits or from net assets in excess of capital, the payment or division itself, i.e., the dividend, is sometimes treated as almost synonymous and often confused with the source from which the payment or division is legally made. *Penington v. Commonwealth Hotel Constr. Corp., 17 Del. Ch. 394, 155 A. 514 (1931).*

Capital of corporation cannot be impaired by payment of dividend. — The capital of the company must not be reduced or impaired by the payment of any return or income to the stockholders on account of the money put into the company by them, but such income or return can only legally be paid from current or accumulated profits. *Penington v. Commonwealth Hotel Constr. Corp., 17 Del. Ch. 394, 155 A. 514 (1931).*

In the absence of statutory provision to the contrary, the capital of a corporation shall not be impaired by the paying out of dividends to stockholders. *Sapperstein v. Wilson & Co., 21 Del. Ch. 139, 182 A. 18 (1935).*

Corporate obligation to pay dividends with reference to preferred stock has narrowed itself down to payment as it existed at the time the stock was issued, or in such other unit of currency as may, by the time of payment, have been substituted therefor in the geographical area. *Shanghai Power Co. v. Delaware Trust Co., 316 A.2d 589 (Del. Ch. 1974), aff'd in part and rev'd in part, 378 A.2d 624 (Del. 1977).*

Cumulative payment of dividends for preferred stock. — Where the stockholders agree that the preferred dividends shall be cumulative and that no payment of dividends shall be made on the common stock unless and until all arrearage or deficiency of the dividends on the preferred stock has been paid, but there is no legal fund (surplus or profits) in the going concern from which a preferred dividend can be paid as against common stockholders, the right to this dividend is fixed and vested but the payment will be postponed until there exists a fund, from which payment can legally be made, for while the dividend cannot be paid, the claim exists and the dividend accrues and the amount accumulates awaiting the existence of a legal fund for its payment. *Penington v. Commonwealth Hotel Constr. Corp., 17 Del. Ch. 394, 155 A. 514 (1931).*

"Earnings" include current and accumulated earnings. — When dealing with preferred dividends expressly made cumulative, the natural meaning of "earnings" includes both current and accumulated earnings. *Weinberg v. Baltimore Brick Co., 35 Del. Ch. 225, 114 A.2d 812 (1955).*

And "net earnings," standing alone, has no single or fixed meaning in dividend law. *Weinberg v. Baltimore Brick Co., 35 Del. Ch. 225, 114 A.2d 812 (1955).*

But charter must be explicit to restrict dividend funds. — There is nothing to prevent the framers of a charter from expressly providing that no dividends on cumulative preferred stock shall be paid except out of a surplus of assets over capital, or except out of earned surplus, but a self-imposed restriction of that nature, that is, a restriction operative apart from the statute, will not rest in implication. *Weinberg v. Baltimore Brick Co., 35 Del. Ch. 225, 114 A.2d 812 (1955).*

Where a corporate charter provided "said first preferred stock shall entitle the holder to receive each year, out of the net earnings of the company, a fixed yearly dividend of five per centum," it was held that the term "net earnings" was not restrictive of the use of current earnings for preferred dividends. *Weinberg v. Baltimore Brick Co., 35 Del. Ch. 225, 114 A.2d 812 (1955).*

And mere incorporation in charter of language of subsection (a) is not restriction within meaning of this section; it is equivalent to a statement that dividends may be declared as provided by law. *Weinberg v. Baltimore Brick Co., 35 Del. Ch. 225, 114 A.2d 812 (1955).*

Corporations

Capital must be valued at its dollar equivalent before a dividend can be declared out of net profits for a designated period and this duty falls to the directors. *Morris v. Standard Gas & Elec. Co., 31 Del. Ch. 20, 63 A.2d 577 (1949).*

Even though formal appraisal is not required under this section, the directors are under a duty to evaluate the assets on the basis of acceptable data and by standards which they are entitled to believe reasonably reflect present "values." It is not practical to attempt to lay down a rigid rule as to what constitutes proper evidence of value for the consideration of directors in declaring a dividend under this section. The factors considered and the emphasis given will depend upon the case presented. *Morris v. Standard Gas & Elec. Co., 31 Del. Ch. 20, 63 A.2d 577 (1949).*

Factors such as future earnings and prospects of stocks owned by corporation may be considered in determining present value under this section and future prospects often constitute a most important factor where present value is sought to be determined in ascertaining if a corporation may declare dividends. *Morris v. Standard Gas & Elec. Co., 31 Del. Ch. 20, 63 A.2d 577 (1949).*

And directors must be given reasonable latitude in ascertaining value. Morris *v. Standard Gas & Elec. Co., 31 Del. Ch. 20, 63 A.2d 577 (1949).*

Compliance does not justify all dividends. — Compliance with this section may not, under all circumstances, justify all dividend payments. *Sinclair Oil Corp. v. Levien, 280 A.2d 717 (Del. 1971).*

Motive for declaration immaterial unless dividend amounts to waste. — The motives for causing the declaration of dividends are immaterial unless the plaintiff can show that the dividend payments resulted from improper motives and amounted to waste. *Sinclair Oil Corp. v. Levien, 280 A.2d 717 (Del. 1971).*

But business judgment standard applies if subsidiary's minority stockholders not excluded. — The business judgment standard, rather than the intrinsic fairness test, should be applied in the case of dividends declared by the board of directors of a subsidiary dominated by its parent corporation, where although the dividends resulted in great sums of money being transferred from the subsidiary to the parent, a proportionate share of the money was received by the subsidiary's minority shareholders, and the parent received nothing from the subsidiary to the exclusion of the minority shareholders. *Sinclair Oil Corp. v. Levien, 280 A.2d 717 (Del. 1971).*

Intrinsic fairness standard applies if dividend is self-dealing by parent. — Although a dividend declaration by the board of directors of a subsidiary dominated by its parent corporation will not inevitably demand the application of the intrinsic fairness standard, if such a dividend is in essence self-dealing by the parent, then the intrinsic fairness standard is the proper standard. *Sinclair Oil Corp. v. Levien, 280 A.2d 717 (Del. 1971).*

Directors' decision is entitled to presumption of good faith. — Whether dividends will be paid is within the sound discretion of the directors and, in the ordinary course of events, they are entitled to a presumption of good faith and inspiration by a bona fides of purpose. *Levien v. Sinclair Oil Corp., 261 A.2d 911 (Del. Ch. 1969), aff'd in part and rev'd in part, 280 A.2d 717 (Del. 1971).*

And court will not substitute its business judgment for directors. — Where the only question is one of compliance with the section and there is no suggestion that the directors have been guilty of fraud or bad faith in attempting to comply therewith, the Court of Chancery cannot substitute its concept of wisdom for that of the directors. *Morris v. Standard Gas & Elec. Co., 31 Del. Ch. 20, 63 A.2d 577 (1949); Gabelli & Co. v. Liggett Group, Inc., 444 A.2d 261 (Del. Ch. 1982), aff'd, 479 A.2d 276 (Del. 1984).*

A court will not interfere with the judgment of the board of directors in the absence of fraud or a gross abuse of discretion. *Moskowitz v. Bantrell, 41 Del. Ch. 177, 190 A.2d 749 (1963).*

Unless dividend cannot be grounded on any reasonable business objective. — If a plaintiff can meet his burden of proving that a dividend cannot be grounded on any reasonable business objective, then the courts can and will interfere with the board's decision to pay the dividend. *Sinclair Oil Corp. v. Levien, 280 A.2d 717 (Del. 1971).*

But courts have power in proper cases to compel directors to declare dividend. In such a case the court acts only after a demonstration that the corporation's affairs are in a condition justifying the declaration of the dividend as a matter of prudent business management and that the withholding of it is explicable only on the theory of an oppressive or fraudulent abuse of discretion. *Eshleman v. Keenan, 22 Del. Ch. 82, 194 A. 40 (1937), aff'd, 23 Del. Ch. 234, 2 A.2d 904 (1938).*

Declaration of dividends rests in honest discretion of directors. *Treves v. Menzies, 37 Del. Ch. 330, 142 A.2d 520 (1958).*

Shareholder-directors may vote to declare dividends. — In the absence of fraud or other unfair dealings, a director should not be disqualified from voting upon the question of a dividend declaration merely because he or she is also a stockholder. *Hannigan v. Italo Petro. Corp., 45 Del. 593, 77 A.2d 209 (1949).*

But shareholder-director cannot profit from illegally declared dividends. — Stockholder-directors who have deliberately or negligently participated in an invalid dividend declaration should not be permitted to recover them under the guise or notes given in consideration for such dividends, even though the dividends thereafter loaned to the corporation were used for proper corporate purposes and all other stockholders have been paid. *Hannigan v. Italo Petro. Corp., 45 Del. 593, 77 A.2d 209 (1949).*

And corporation may assert defense of lack of consideration. — Where dividends were improperly declared, the stockholder-directors have been deprived of nothing, because nothing was legally owed them, and the corporation should not be estopped from asserting the defense of failure of consideration even though all other stockholders have been paid their share of the dividends. *Hannigan v. Italo Petro. Corp., 45 Del. 593, 77 A.2d 209 (1949).*

If parent corporation, through its dominant position, causes its subsidiary not to declare dividend solely for former's pecuniary gain, then the transaction would not be shielded by the business judgment rule but rather should be tested for intrinsic fairness. *Gabelli & Co. v. Liggett Group, Inc., 444 A.2d 261 (Del. Ch. 1982), aff'd, 479 A.2d 276 (Del. 1984).*

Wasting asset corporations thrive by consuming their capital. *Wittenberg v. Federal Mining & Smelting Co., 15 Del. Ch. 147, 133 A. 48 (1926), aff'd, 15 Del. Ch. 409, 138 A. 347 (1927).*

Depreciation of plant must be considered. — A charge should be made against receipts in order to cover depreciation of plant before profits available for dividends can be ascertained in the case of a mining company whose plant is located at a remote mine and can be of little or no value after the mine is exhausted. *Wittenberg v. Federal Mining & Smelting Co., 15 Del. Ch. 147, 133 A. 48 (1926), aff'd, 15 Del. Ch. 409, 138 A. 347 (1927).*

Assumed risk of fluctuations in currency's value. — Parties who enter into an obligation expressed in a designated currency must assume the risk of fluctuations in its value. *Shanghai Power Co. v. Delaware Trust Co., 316 A.2d 589 (Del. Ch. 1974), aff'd in part and rev'd in part, 378 A.2d 624 (Del. 1977).*

Where suit is brought to ascertain amount due on noncommodity obligation expressed in foreign currency, values are determined in terms of United States legal tender money and the rate of exchange is that existing at the time demand is made. *Shanghai Power Co. v. Delaware Trust Co., 316 A.2d 589 (Del. Ch. 1974), aff'd in part and rev'd in part, 378 A.2d 624 (Del. 1977).*

Corporations

CASE NOTES — OTHER STATES

Connecticut

The corporation may lawfully declare dividends out of any funds it owned so long as its fixed capital was not impaired. *Wehrhane v. Peyton, 133 Conn. 478, 52 A.2d 711 (1947).*

Illinois

Delaware law does not prohibit the payment of dividends when the current liabilities of the corporation exceed the current assets. *Continental-Midwest Corporation v. Hotel Sherman, Inc., 13 Ill. App. 2d 188, 141 N.E.2d 400 (1957).*

Maryland

Liability. — In Delaware, the statutory liability of the directors does not exonerate the stockholder who has received dividends from liability to repay them for the benefit of the creditors. The statute does not transfer the liability from the stockholders to the directors, but it creates a liability on the part of the latter in favor of the corporation or the creditors in certain events. The remedy given by the statute is cumulative. *Bartlett v. Smith, 162 Md. 478, 160 A. 440 (1932).*

Massachusetts

Bonuses given as were gratuities would be improper for the defendants would have no right to distribute the profits of the company in this manner. *Beacon Wool Corporation v. Johnson, 331 Mass. 274, 119 N.E.2d 195 (1954).*

Michigan

In general. — The Delaware statute contains provisions authorizing the directors of corporations, created under that act, to declare and pay dividends either out of its net assets in excess of its capital, or, if no such excess exists, out of its net profits for the fiscal year then current and/or the preceding fiscal year. *Stratton v. Anderson, 278 Mich. 499, 270 N.W. 764 (1937).*

New York

Immaterial question. — The question of whether a dividend was paid out of net assets in excess of capital so as not to impair the capital or create a deficit is immaterial. Under the Delaware law, it was sufficient to make the payments out of profits regardless of the effect on the corporate capital. *Cowan v. Graves, 258 A.D. 699, 18 N.Y.S.2d 340 (1940).*

CASE NOTES — FEDERAL

Fourth Circuit

Unequal shareholder treatment may be permitted. — Delaware courts recognize that in some circumstances Delaware law permits shareholders (as distinguished from shares) to be treated unequally. *Williams v. 5300 Columbia Pike Corp., 891 F. Supp. 1169 (E.D.Va. 1995).*

Fifth Circuit

Realization of stock appreciation right. — A stock appreciation right (SAR) is a contingent interest; to realize this interest, the common stock of the corporation must be sold. Holders of SARs, unlike debenture holders, may not be solely creditors, but they are creditors. When the common stock of a corporation is sold, the corporation owes and is obligated to pay SAR holders the appreciation value of the stock. Further, unlike stockholders, SAR holders can share in the wealth of a corporation without the same tax liability as a shareholder. *H.I.G. P-Xi Holding, Inc., 2001 U.S. Dist. LEXIS 5074 (E.D.La. 2001).*

Sixth Circuit

In general. — Section 34 of the Delaware Corporation Law, Rev. Code 1935, § 2066, permits the payment of dividends out of surplus, or net profits for the fiscal year then current or the preceding fiscal year. However, it incorporates by reference any restrictions upon the power of the directors to declare dividends in the certificate of incorporation. *Seiberling Rubber Co. v. United States, 115 F. Supp. 798 (N.D. Ohio 1952).*

Eleventh Circuit

Authority of board of directors. — Absent contrary provision in corporate documents, under Delaware law, . the board of directors determines when and in what amount distributions will be made, subject to priorities awarded to certain classes of stock. *Alumax Inc. v. Commissioner, 165 F.3d 822 (11th Cir. 1999).*

District of Columbia Circuit

The declaration and payment of a dividend rests in the discretion of a corporation's board of directors in the exercise of its business judgment. *Mann-Paller Foundation, Inc. v. Econometric Research, Inc., 644 F. Supp. 92 (D. D.C. 1986).*

Compelled declaration. — Delaware law provides that courts may act to compel the declaration of a dividend only upon a demonstration that the withholding of it is explicable only on the theory of an oppressive or fraudulent abuse of discretion by the board of directors. *Mann-Paller Foundation, Inc. v. Econometric Research, Inc., 644 F. Supp. 92 (D.D.C. 1986).*

§ 171. Special purpose reserves

DELAWARE CASE NOTES — REPORTED

Dividend reserve when distributed is distribution of profits. — Although a corporation has the right to set apart or reserve a portion of its net earnings for a period of years, and treat them as capital, retaining them in its treasury, or expending them in the purchase of securities, or real estate for the company, yet if it subsequently divides such net earnings among the stockholders by declaring a dividend in cash, in stock, or in both, based

upon such earnings, it is a distribution of profits. *Bryan v. Aikin, 10 Del. Ch. 446, 86 A. 674 (1913).*

Corporation may permanently capitalize nondistributed earnings. — A company has the right to withhold the earnings, and to permanently capitalize them if it deemed it necessary or proper in the conduct of its business to do so. *Bryan v. Aikin, 10 Del. Ch. 446, 86 A. 674 (1913).*

§ 172. Liability of directors and committee members as to dividends or stock redemption

CASE NOTES — OTHER STATES

Maryland

In general. — In Delaware, the statutory liability of the directors does not exonerate the stockholder who has received dividends from liability to repay them for the benefit of the creditors. The statute does not transfer the

liability from the stockholders to the directors, but it creates a liability on the part of the latter in favor of the corporation or the creditors in certain events. The remedy given by the statute is cumulative. *Bartlett v. Smith, 162 Md. 478, 160 A. 440 (1932).*

§ 173. Declaration and payment of dividends

CASE NOTES — OTHER STATES

California

"Stock dividend". — .While a stock dividend is defined as a distribution of a company's own shares, the statute does not exactly define "stock dividend," however. Rather, it provides that "dividends may be paid in cash, in property, or in shares of the corporation's capital stock." This is not an exclusive list and the permissive language allows for the possibility that other forms of payment or

property could be termed dividends. *Shaev v. Claflin, 2004 Cal. App. Unpub. LEXIS 5840 (2004).*

Massachusetts

Bonuses given as were gratuities would be improper for the defendants would have no right to distribute the profits of the company in this manner. *Beacon Wool Corporation v. Johnson, 331 Mass. 274, 119 N.E.2d 195 (1954).*

CASE NOTES — FEDERAL

Second Circuit

Under Delaware law, the repurchasing of stock and payment of dividends is not permitted where a corporation's capital would become impaired. Precluding the repurchase of stock under such a situation is designed to protect the shareholders and creditors. The prohibition on payment of dividends was intended to protect creditors. *UCAR Internatonal, Inc v. Union Carbide Corp., 2004 U.S. Dist. LEXIS 914 (S.D.N.Y. 2004).*

The declaration of a dividend creates a debtor-creditor relationship between a corporation and its stockholders. *Kraft Foods Co. v. Commissioner, 232 F.2d 118 (2d Cir. 1956).*

Third Circuit

Bankruptcy proceedings. — It appears that a trustee-in-bankruptcy or debtor-in-possession (or in this case, the committee through derivative standing) does acquire a right of action under § 544(b) of the Bankruptcy

Code to prosecute violations of §§ 160 and 173 of the DGCL in its capacity as a putative creditor. *Official Comm. of Unsecured Creditors v. Clark (In re Nat'l Forge Co.), 344 B.R. 340 (D. Pa. June 9, 2006).*

Ninth Circuit

Violation grounds for breach of fiduciary duty claim. — In Delaware, a plaintiff may bring a general claim of breach of fiduciary duty against a director as long as he or she claims that the director's acts or omissions involved (i) a breach of the director's duty of loyalty to the corporation or its stockholders; (ii) acts or omissions not in good faith or which involve intentional misconduct or a knowing violation of law; (iii) under Del. Code Ann. tit. 8, § 174 (which includes willful or negligent violation of Del. Code Ann. tit. 8, §§ 160 or 173 regarding voting and trading); or (iv) any transaction from which the director derived an improper personal benefit. *Grassmueck v. Barnett, 281 F. Supp. 2d 1227 (W.D.Wash. 2003).*

§ 174. Liability of directors for unlawful payment of dividend or unlawful stock purchase or redemption; exoneration from liability; contribution among directors; subrogation

DELAWARE CASE NOTES — REPORTED

Liability not limited by 8 Del. c. § 102(b)(7). — Liability under this section is not limited or eliminated by *8 Del. C. § 102(b)(7). In re Walt Disney Co. Derivative Litig., 825 A.2d 275 (Del. Ch. 2003).*

Each director is individually liable for illegal distribution of dividends. — This section contemplates the recovery and restoration to the capital of the corporation, of the entire amount thus illegally withdrawn; and to that end each director is made individually liable for such amount. *John A. Roebling's Sons Co. ex rel. Whitley v. Mode, 17 Del. 515, 43 A. 480 (1899).*

And each creditor is entitled to his or her proportionate share from the common fund, and any action for the recovery of such illegal dividends or abstracted capital must contemplate proportionate distribution. *John A. Roebling's Sons Co. ex rel. Whitley v. Mode, 17 Del. 515, 43 A. 480 (1899).*

Therefore the plaintiff may not separately sue for and recover his or her individual claim against the defendant, because the remedy should be by proceedings in equity, where all persons interested would be made parties, and the rights and liabilities of each one could be fully considered and equitably adjusted. *John A. Roebling's Sons Co. ex rel. Whitley v. Mode, 17 Del. 515, 43 A. 480 (1899).*

Plaintiffs were not creditors and were without standing to sue. — Plaintiffs alleging that directors wrongfully approved pre-merger redemption of outstanding stock in violation of § 160 of this title did not have standing to bring suit under this section as they were not "creditors" of the pre-merger corporation when it went out of existence. *Johnston v. Wolf, 487 A.2d 1132 (Del. 1985).*

Tolling of statute of limitations. — Running of the statute of limitations for a breach of fiduciary duty action against the former directors of a corporation was tolled until the recipients of a dividend, allegedly issued after the corporation was insolvent, knew or should have known that the dividend was questionable; this could not be said to have occurred until some time after the corporation's initial bankruptcy filing, when the shareholders would have finally learned that certain creditors intended to challenge the dividend. *EBS Litig. LLC v. Barclays Global Investors, N.A., 304 F.3d 302 (3d Cir. 2002).*

Complaint alleging wrongful declaration of dividend held sufficient. — See *Harff v. Kerkorian, 347 A.2d 133 (Del. 1975).*

Purchase of capital stock. — This section imposes liability for unlawful distributions and dividend payments in addition to restricting purchase of a corporation's own shares of capital stock; company's financing of leverage buyout transactions may properly be treated as an unlawful dividend payment or distribution from company to its parent company and sole shareholder. *Official Comm. of Unsecured Creditors of Buckhead Am. Corp. v. Reliance Capital Group, Inc., 178 Bankr. 956 (D. Del. 1994).*

Purchase of parent company stock. — No amount of interpretive analysis could logically result in the determination that company purchased or redeemed "its own shares of capital stock" in supplying funds for the purchase of parent company stock. The transactions did not involve purchase or redemption of company stock; rather, the subject leverage buyout transactions involved purchase of shares of capital stock in parent corporation, with the purchases of parent company shares being made neither by parent company nor by company. *Official Comm. of Unsecured Creditors of Buckhead Am. Corp. v. Reliance Capital Group, Inc., 178 Bankr. 956 (D. Del. 1994).*

Stock sale. — Stockholders sold their stock through stockbrokers and there were no allegations that they were aware that the corporation's capital was impaired. Thus, they redeemed their stock in good faith, and this section did not provide a liquidating entity with a remedy for violations of *8 Del. C. § 160. PHP Liquidating, LLC v. Robbins, 291 B.R. 603 (D. Del. 2003).*

Assignee's action dismissed. — In an action by an assignee against a director, investment fund, and partner alleging that a corporation's stock redemption plan violated *8 Del. C. § 160*, and that the redemption transactions were fraudulent transfers of property under *11 U.S.C. § 548*, the motions to dismiss under *Fed. R. Civ. P. 12(b)(6)* filed by the director, investment fund, and partner were granted where (1) *8 Del. C. § 124* did not provide the assignee with a remedy for violations of *8 Del. C. § 160* because the assignee was not a stockholder, (2) this section did not provide the assignee with a cause of

Corporations

Corporations

action against the director, investment fund, and partner because they redeemed their stock in good faith, (3) the assignee did not have an implied remedy against shareholders for the corporation's violation of *8 Del. C. § 160*, (4) the assignee lacked standing under *11 U.S.C. § 544*(b) because violations of § 160 were general claims that accrued to all creditors, not assignees, and (5) the assignee could not show fraudulent transfer under *11 U.S.C. § 548* because the assignee failed to show that the corporation did not receive reasonably equivalent value in the stock redemption transaction, or that the corporation had actual intent to defraud investors. *PHP Liquidating, LLC v. Robbins, 291 B.R. 592 (D. Del. 2003).*

CASE NOTES — OTHER STATES

Colorado

Directors of a corporation are liable to creditors of the corporation for an illegal distribution if the directors authorize such distribution while the corporation is dissolved or insolvent. *Ajay Sports, Inc. v. Casazza, 1 P.3d 267 (Colo. App. 2000).*

Maryland

In general. — In Delaware, the statutory liability of the directors does not exonerate the stockholder who has received dividends from liability to repay them for the benefit of the creditors. The statute does not transfer the liability from the stockholders to the directors, but it creates a liability on the part of the latter in favor of the corporation or the creditors in certain events. The remedy given by the statute is cumulative. *Bartlett v. Smith, 162 Md. 478, 160 A. 440 (1932).*

Wisconsin

Dissolution or insolvency. — In the event of the dissolution or insolvency of the corporation, the directors' liability is then to the creditors, or any of them. Consequently, it is only while the corporation is solvent and undissolved that the liability in question is to the corporation, and, in the event of its dissolution or insolvency, that liability is exclusively to the creditors of the corporation, or any of them. *Morris v. Sampsell, 224 Wis. 560, 272 N.W. 53 (1937).*

CASE NOTES — FEDERAL

First Circuit

In general. — Pursuant to Del. Code Ann. tit. 8, § 174, directors of Delaware corporations are liable for unlawful payment of dividends for the amount paid as a dividend, plus interest. The purpose of § 174 is to provide a cause of action to creditors who have extended credit to a corporation based on that corporation's stated capital. Also, when the corporation impairs that capital, it depletes the creditors' trust fund and seriously jeopardizes their means to recover their debts. *Growe v. Bedard, 2004 U.S. Dist. LEXIS 23746 (D.Me. 2004).*

Construction with other law. — By its terms, Del. Code Ann. tit. 8, § 102(b)(7) insulates individual corporate directors from personal liability for money damages unless they have breached the duty of good faith and loyalty, violated Del. Code Ann. tit. 8, § 174, or authorized a transaction in which they derive improper personal benefit. *Growe v. Bedard, 2004 U.S. Dist. LEXIS 23746 (D.Me. 2004).*

Second Circuit

Del. Code. Ann. tit. 8, §§ 160, 174(a) (2005), prohibit the payment of dividends while the corporation is insolvent or which will render it insolvent, or the redemption of stock when a corporation's capital is impaired or which will impair the corporate capital. *Pereira v. Farace, 413 F.3d 330 (2d Cir. 2005).*

Under Delaware Law, the financial status of a corporation serves as the benchmark in deciding when certain duties arise and whether questioned transactions, such as the issuance of dividends and stock redemptions, are improper. *Pereira v. Farace, 413 F.3d 330 (2d Cir. 2005).*

Insolvency. — Delaware courts define insolvency in two ways. First, a company is insolvent if it is unable to pay its debts as they fall due in the usual course of business. Second, a company may be insolvent if it has liabilities in excess of a reasonable market value of assets held. *Pereira v. Farace, 413 F.3d 330 (2d Cir. 2005).*

Third Circuit

Del. Code Ann. tit. 8, § 174 holds directors, but not shareholders, liable for willfully or negligently paying dividends in violation of the general corporate law chapter of the Delaware Code. *Protocomm Corp. v. Novell Advanced Services, Inc., 171 F. Supp. 2d 459 (E.D.Pa. 2001).*

Only current creditors have standing to sue under Del. Code Ann. tit. 8, § 174. *Protocomm Corp. v. Novell Advanced Services, Inc., 171 F. Supp. 2d 459 (E.D.Pa. 2001).*

Construction with other law. — of A prior decision did not determine that Del. Code Ann. tit. 8, § 325 could be used to provide standing for a claim brought under Del Code Ann. tit. 8, § 174. Rather, the court essentially provided that the cause of action be brought under the common-law fraudulent conveyance claim. *Protocomm Corp. v. Novell Advanced Services, Inc., 171 F. Supp. 2d 459 (E.D.Pa. 2001).*

Sixth Circuit

Joint and several liability; subrogation. — In case of any willful or negligent violation of Del. Code Ann. tit. 8, § 160, the directors under whose administration the violation occurred are jointly and severally liable to the corporation's creditors for the full amount unlawfully paid for the purchase or redemption of the corporation's stock in the event of the corporation's dissolution or insolvency. A procedure exists for permitting an absent or dissenting director to exonerate himself or herself. Any director against whom such a claim is successfully asserted has a right of subrogation against the stockholders who received assets in exchange for their stock with knowledge of facts indicating that the transaction was unlawful. *In re Revco D.S., Inc., 1990 Bankr. LEXIS 2966 (Bankr. N.D.Ohio 1990).*

Seventh Circuit

Creditor standing. — Delaware law allows corporate creditors to sue directors and officers of an insolvent corporation for unlawful dividend distributions or stock purchases. This right is only given to entities who became creditors of the corporation before the unlawful distribution or stock purchase took place. *Pinellas County v. Great American Industrial Group, Inc., 1991 U.S. Dist. LEXIS 17517 (N.D.Ill. 1991).*

Subchapter VI.
Stock Transfers

§ 201. Transfer of stock, stock certificates and uncertificated stock

DELAWARE CASE NOTES — REPORTED

Common law as to stock transfers. — See *Reeves v. Transport Data Communications, Inc., 318 A.2d 147 (Del. Ch. 1974).*

DELAWARE CASE NOTES — UNREPORTED

Preliminary injunctions. — Where the payment of fees proposed to be paid was not an effort to buy off a possibly valid claim, and was not an exercise of business judgment by a corporation's board to resolve a disputed claim, a shareholders' class action was dismissed as to the named plaintiffs; therefore, the trial court properly denied the shareholders' motion for a preliminary injunction. *In re Life Techs., Inc., 2001 Del. Ch. LEXIS 164 (Apr. 16, 2001).*

CASE NOTES — OTHER STATES

Maine

Applicability of Delaware law. — Title to shares in corporations organized under the laws of Delaware are to be determined by the laws of Delaware, and not by the law of the state where the transfer of the certificate takes place. *Strout v. Burgess, 144 Me. 263, 68 A.2d 241 (1949).*

Michigan

Failure of delivery. — An attempted transfer of title to a certificate or to the shares represented thereby without delivery of the certificate shall have the effect of a promise to transfer and the obligation, if any, imposed by such promise shall be governed by the law governing the formation and performance of contracts. *Waldorf v. KMS Industries, Inc., 25 Mich. App. 20, 181 N.W.2d 85 (1970).*

New York

Tender offer. — Under Delaware law, the fiduciary duty of a majority stockholder making a tender offer is generally limited to the duty of full disclosure. *Abbey v. Montedison S.p.A. 143 Misc. 2d 72, 539 N.Y.S.2d 862 (1998).*

Under Delaware law, the limited function of a court is to determine whether majority shareholders, when making a tender offer, discloses all information in their possession germane to the transaction, i.e., information such as a reasonable shareholder would consider important in deciding whether to sell or retain stock. *Abbey v. Montedison S.p.A. 143 Misc. 2d 72, 539 N.Y.S.2d 862 (1998).*

CASE NOTES — FEDERAL

Third Circuit

Stock transfer books not reliable ownership record. — A registered holder may transfer his or her interest by mere delivery of the stock certificate, indorsed either in blank or to a specified person. Thus, it is manifest that the stock transfer books of a corporation cannot be safely relied upon to ascertain the ownership of stock. *Murdock v. Follansbee Steel Corp., 213 F.2d 570 (3d Cir. 1954).*

Sixth Circuit

Under Delaware law, a purchaser of non-publicly traded stock is entitled to specific performance of the sale agreement. *McCall v. Scott, 250 F.3d 997 (6th Cir. 2001).*

Tenth Circuit

Insider trading liability. — Although directors generally do not occupy a fiduciary position with respect to stockholders in face-to-face dealings, Delaware law does create such a duty in special circumstances where advantage is taken of inside information by a corporate insider who deliberately misleads an ignorant stockholder. Therefore, under Delaware law, directors who possess inside information regarding the value of stock owe a fiduciary duty when reacquiring outstanding corporate stock not only to the corporation and to the shareholders collectively, but also to the minority shareholders from whom the stock is being reacquired. *Alta Health Strategies, Inc. v. Kennedy, 790 F. Supp. 1085 (D.Utah 1992).*

§ 202.   Restrictions on transfer and ownership of securities

DELAWARE CASE NOTES — REPORTED

Interpretation of "security." — The term "security" is interpreted in distinct ways for purposes of subsections (a) and (b) of this section. As used in subsection (a) of this section, "security" was intended to denote some muniment of title. "Securities" as used in subsection (b) of this section was intended to mean, inter alia, a substantive ownership interest in capital stock and not the indicia of ownership represented by the stock certificate. *Joseph E. Seagram & Sons v. Conoco, Inc., 519 F. Supp. 506 (D. Del. 1981)* (decision prior to 1983 amendment).

Language of subsection (a) of this section was lifted from § 8-204 of title 6 without any consideration

to the use of the term "securities" in subsection (b) of this section. *Joseph E. Seagram & Sons v. Conoco, Inc., 519 F. Supp. 506 (D. Del. 1981)* (decision prior to 1983 amendment).

Term "securities," and not "stock," was pointedly employed in subsection (b) of this section because that provision was intended to reach a wider class of interests than mere capital shares, namely, bonds, convertible debentures, options and other forms of corporate ownership or indebtedness. *Joseph E. Seagram & Sons v. Conoco, Inc., 519 F. Supp. 506 (D. Del. 1981).*

DELAWARE CASE NOTES — UNREPORTED

Private club may expel members. — Private club may enact governance procedures allowing the expulsion of a member for cause; where the club is a corporation authorized to issue stock, and there is no linkage between expulsion and stock ownership, i.e. there is no compulsory stock transfer provision, the expulsion provision could appear in either the certificate of incorporation or the by-laws. *Capano v. Wilmington Country Club, 2001 Del. Ch. LEXIS 127 (Oct. 31, 2001).*

Enforceability of stock restriction agreement in context of equitable distribution of community property. — Under 8 Del. C. § 202, as under common law, restrictions on transfers of securities had to be shown to serve a reasonable corporate purpose to be enforceable, but a corporation challenging the right of a divorcing spouse where restricted shares had been held, with corporate permission, in a marital trust to claim a right to dividends and appreciation in value of shares otherwise subject to transfer to the other spouse (a corporate director) upon dissolution of the trust met its burden by

showing the reasonableness of a requirement that shares of the privately held corporation remain under ownership of persons involved in the corporation. *Capital Group Cos. v. Ritter, 2005 Del. Ch. LEXIS 38 (Mar. 15, 2005).*

A reasonableness inquiry is required when restrictions on the transfer of stock are contested. *Capital Group Cos. v. Armour, 2005 Del. Ch. LEXIS 38, No. 422-N (March 15, 2005).*

Standard of reasonableness inquiry. — A deferential reasonableness inquiry is required when courts are asked to invalidate a stock transfer restriction. This approach is also consistent with the general principle that Delaware corporate law is enabling, and does not impose choices on market participants. Therefore, the proper inquiry is whether the actual restrictions are reasonable to achieve a legitimate corporate purpose. *Capital Group Cos. v. Armour, 2005 Del. Ch. LEXIS 38, No. 422-N (March 15, 2005).*

CASE NOTES — OTHER STATES

Pennsylvania

Permissible restrictions. — Under Del. Code Ann. tit. 8, § 202(c)(1), (2), a restriction on the transfer of securities of a corporation is permitted, inter alia, where the corporation is given an opportunity, prior to a sale of the securities, to acquire the restricted securities, or where the corporation is obligated to purchase the securities which are the subject of an agreement restricting the purchase and sale of the restricted securities. Such a restriction need not be justified by a business purpose to be enforceable. *Estate of Hall, 1999 Pa. Super. 119, 731 A.2d 617 (1999).*

Stock price. — Under Delaware law, a valid agreement among the shareholders concerning the price of a

stock purchase will not be deemed invalid because of the disparity between actual value and book value. *Estate of Hall, 1999 Pa. Super. 119, 731 A.2d 617 (1999).*

Interpretations of charters and bylaws. — Corporate charters and bylaws are contracts among shareholders of a corporation and the general rules of contract interpretation are held to apply. *Estate of Hall, 1999 Pa. Super. 119, 731 A.2d 617 (1999).*

Section 202(a) of the Delaware General Corporation Law provides that a restriction is ineffective except against a person with actual knowledge of the restriction. *Estate of Hall, 1999 Pa. Super. 119, 731 A.2d 617 (1999).*

CASE NOTES — FEDERAL

Second Circuit

When stockholder approval required. — Under Delaware law, a change in corporate structure reducing the transferability of a stockholder's ability to vote and the value of his or her asset to such a degree, requires stockholder approval. *Unilever Acquisition Corp. v. Richardson-Vicks, Inc., 618 F. Supp. 407 (S.D.N.Y. 1985).*

Section 202(c)(1) of the Delaware Corporation Law permits a restriction on the transfer of securities if it obligates the holder of the restricted securities to offer to the corporation a prior opportunity to acquire the restricted securities. *Kerrigan v. Merrill Lynch, Pierce, Fenner & Smith, Inc., 450 F. Supp. 639 (S.D.N.Y. 1978).*

Enforceability of restriction. — Section 202(a) of the Delaware Corporation Law provides that a restriction, if noted on the shares, is enforceable against the holder or any successor including an executor, administrator, or other fiduciary entrusted with like responsibility for the person or estate of the holder. *Kerrigan v. Merrill Lynch, Pierce, Fenner & Smith, Inc., 450 F. Supp. 639 (S.D.N.Y. 1978).*

A restriction is valid if it requires the holder of restricted securities to tender them to designated persons who must act within a reasonable period of time thereafter. Such a restriction could take the form of a mere first refusal or of an option to acquire the securities. *Kerrigan v. Merrill Lynch, Pierce, Fenner & Smith, Inc., 450 F. Supp. 639 (S.D.N.Y. 1978).*

Fifth Circuit

Legislative intent. — The Delaware legislature enacted Del. Code Ann. tit.8, § 202 to eliminate the uncertainty at common law surrounding stock restrictions and to validate many common stock restrictions. *Joslin v. Shareholder Servs. Group, 948 F. Supp. 627 (S.D.Tex. 1996).*

Standard of restriction review. — Given the deference that should be granted toward a stock restriction that is expressly authorized by the Delaware Code, a reviewing court should not excessively scrutinize the reasonableness of the restriction. As long as there is no evidence that the purpose is invalid and the restriction does not appear invalid on its face, the restriction must be upheld. *Joslin v. Shareholder Servs. Group, 948 F. Supp. 627 (S.D.Tex. 1996).*

Void transfer. — No legal or equitable title was transferred when stock was pledged in violation of an endorsed stock restriction. Alternatively, even if title passed, the corporation and its shareholders retained the right to render the transfer void. The whole of the case law suggests that transfers in violation of a valid stock restriction are void and pass no interest to the recipient. *Joslin v. Shareholder Servs. Group, 948 F. Supp. 627 (S.D.Tex. 1996).*

§ 203. Business combinations with interested stockholders

DELAWARE CASE NOTES — REPORTED

Constitutionality. — Chapter harmonizes well with Commerce Clause dictates in the State takeover regulation context and is most likely constitutional under the *Commerce Clause of the United States Constitution. BNS, Inc. v. Koppers Co., 683 F. Supp. 458 (D. Del. 1988); City Capital Assocs. v. Interco, Inc., 696 F. Supp. 1551 (D. Del.), aff'd, 860 F.2d 60 (3d Cir. 1988).*

This section does not violate the Commerce Clause of the United States Constitution. *RP Acquisition Corp. v. Staley Continental, Inc., 686 F. Supp. 476 (D. Del. 1988).*

Preemption by federal legislation. — This section does not conflict with the purposes of the Williams Act, *15 U.S.C. §§ 78n (d)-(e), 78n (d)-(f) (1982),* to an impermissible degree, thus, this section is not preempted by the *Williams Act. BNS, Inc. v. Koppers Co., 683 F. Supp. 458 (D. Del. 1988); RP Acquisition Corp. v. Staley Continental, Inc., 686 F. Supp. 476 (D. Del. 1988).*

Applicability of section. — This section applies to any Delaware corporation that has not opted out of the statute's coverage. *Moore Corp. Ltd. v. Wallace Computer Servs., Inc., 907 F. Supp. 1545 (D. Del. 1995).*

Scope of state's authority. — Power of the states to regulate tender offers does not extend to complete eradication of hostile offers. *BNS, Inc. v. Koppers Co., 683 F. Supp. 458 (D. Del. 1988).*

Delegation of authority. — This section is not an improper delegation of governmental authority to private persons. *City Capital Assocs. v. Interco, Inc., 696 F. Supp. 1551 (D. Del.), aff'd, 860 F.2d 60 (3d Cir. 1988).*

"Date" defined. — The word "date" as used in subdivision (a)(1) should be construed, consistent with legislative intent, to mean "time"; thus, the words "Prior to such date" as they appear therein mean "Before the time" following the primary purpose of the section to limit abusive takeovers. *Siegman v. Columbia Pictures Entertainment, Inc., 576 A.2d 625 (Del. Ch. 1989).*

Owners. — Given an intent of this section to prevent abusive takeover tactics and the broad language used in subsection (c)(8)(iii), it is clear that the section was intended to encompass circumstances where a potential acquiror attempts to acquire an interest in more than 15% of the voting stock of a corporation without formally acquiring ownership or voting rights, otherwise the purpose of the Act could be easily subverted. *Siegman v. Columbia Pictures Entertainment, Inc., 576 A.2d 625 (Del. Ch. 1989).*

Controlling interest. — Software developer's licensing of flight reservation software to a second licensee owned by several airlines, none of which had a controlling interest, did not constitute a breach of its prior licensing agreement to a Spanish operator; Delaware statutory definitions of "a controlling interest" was not dispositive of the controlling interest issue. *Amadeus Global Travel Distrib., S.A. v. Orbitz, LLC, 302 F. Supp. 2d 329 (D. Del. 2004).*

Agreement, arrangement, etc., to acquire or hold stock. — There is nothing in subsection (c)(8)(iii) which limits the Act to noncontingent contracts. *Siegman v. Columbia Pictures Entertainment, Inc., 576 A.2d 625 (Del. Ch. 1989).*

Time of board approval of transaction. — Board approval of transaction several hours prior to the time at which acquiring corporation became an interested stockholder is sufficient to bring the transaction within the exception from the 3-year prohibition pursuant to the provisions of subsection (a)(1). *Siegman v. Columbia Pictures Entertainment, Inc., 576 A.2d 625 (Del. Ch. 1989).*

Where the only "agreement, arrangement or understanding" at the time the acquired corporation approved the merger was between a large shareholder and the acquired corporation, the agreement did not trigger the preclusive provisions of subsection (a). *Matador Capital Mgt. Corp. v. BRC Holdings, Inc., 729 A.2d 280 (Del. Ch. 1998).*

Waiver of the protections of this section. — The waiver decision needed to be analyzed under the rubric of entire fairness where all four votes to waive the protections were made by directors who not only sat on both boards, but also possessed substantial direct, personal financial interests in the proposed transaction. *In re Digex, Inc. Shareholders Litig., 789 A.2d 1176 (Del. Ch. 2000).*

CASE NOTES — OTHER STATES

New York

Sharing of control premium. — Under Delaware law, majority shareholders have no nonderivative fiduciary duty to share proportionately with minority shareholders the "control premium" received from the sale of a majority share in the corporation. *Herzog, Heine, Geduld, Inc. v. NCC Industries, Inc., 251 A.D.2d 173, 673 N.Y.S.2d 910 (1998).*

CASE NOTES — FEDERAL

First Circuit

Retention of key employees. — Just as a board of directors may legitimately attempt to retain key executives during a hostile tender offer in order to secure their advice, the board may legitimately do the same regarding a disputed election for control of the company. A golden parachute agreement adopted in the face of a tender offer is a legitimate means to retain key employees. *Nault v. XTRA Corp., 1992 U.S. Dist. LEXIS 10512 (D.Mass. 1992).*

Determination of minority shareholder's control. — Under the law of Delaware, a minority shareholder is not a fiduciary of a corporation unless it exercises actual control over the corporation. A shareholder holding less than a 50% interest is not a controlling shareholder, with the fiduciary obligations accompanying that status, unless the shareholder exercises actual control over the conduct of the corporation. The right to appoint a minority of the board members does not, without more, demonstrate a minority shareholder's control of the corporation. *CCBN.com, Inc. v. Thomson Financial, Inc., 270 F. Supp. 2d 146 (D.Mass. 2003).*

Second Circuit

Merger duties. — Under Delaware law majority shareholders have a fiduciary duty to minority shareholders in a corporate merger, and the court must scrutinize the circumstances of the merger for compliance with the rule of "entire fairness." *Richardson v. White, Weld & Co., 1979 U.S. Dist. LEXIS 12417 (S.D.N.Y. 1979).*

Takeover duties. — In discharging its function of managing a corporation, a board of directors owes a duty of care to act in the best interests of the shareholders. This duty of care also requires the board to protect the corporate enterprise from harm, reasonably perceived, irrespective of its source. Such a threat includes a hostile

takeover at a price below a company's value. *Samjens Partners I v. Burlington Industries, Inc., 663 F. Supp. 614 (S.D.N.Y. 1987).*

Assumption of fiduciary duty. — A defendant need not be a director or officer in order to owe a fiduciary duty to a corporation and its shareholders. Such a duty may arise from the exercise of control with respect to that corporation. However, it is only when a person affirmatively undertakes to dictate the destiny of the corporation that he or she assumes such a fiduciary duty. *Brickman v. Tyco Toys, Inc., 731 F. Supp. 101 (S.D.N.Y. 1990).*

Applicability of business judgment rule to takeovers. — The business judgment rule is a presumption that in making a business decision the directors of a corporation acted on an informed basis, in good faith and in the honest belief that the action taken was in the best interests of the company. This rule applies in the context of takeovers under Delaware law. *CRTF Corp. v. Federated Department Stores, Inc., 683 F. Supp. 422 (S.D.N.Y. 1988).*

Corporate directors have fiduciary duties of loyalty to the corporation and of due care in the administration of corporate affairs. Under the business judgment rule, where a board of directors is found to have acted in good faith, a court will not try to substitute its judgment for that of the board and will uphold the board's decision so long as they are attributable to any rational business purpose. Under Delaware law, the business judgment rule, a presumption that in making a business decision the directors of a corporation acted on an informed basis, in good faith, and on the honest belief that the action taken was in the best interests of the company, applies in the context of takeovers. This is true despite the inherent potential conflict of interest that exists when a board is in the position of deciding whether and how to defend against a takeover attempt. To deal with this potential conflict, the Delaware Supreme Court has announced an enhanced duty on the part of directors in this position. The directors carry this burden by showing good faith and reasonable investigation, and that the defensive mechanism was reasonable in relation to the threat posed. *CRTF Corp. v. Federated Dep't Stores, 1988 U.S. Dist. LEXIS 2775 (S.D.N.Y. 1988).*

The business judgment rule protects the decisions of the board in carrying out its duty of care if certain requirements are met. Both the duty of care and the business judgment rule apply when the board is responding to a hostile tender offer. The board's decisions, however, are subject to closer scrutiny in such a context. There is an enhanced duty that calls for judicial examination at the threshold before the protection of the business judgment rule may be conferred. Directors must show that they had reasonable grounds for believing that a danger to corporate policy and effectiveness existed because of another person's stock ownership. The board can satisfy this burden by showing good faith and reasonable investigation, and such proof is enhanced when a board is comprised of a majority of outside directors. *Samjens Partners I v. Burlington Industries, Inc., 663 F. Supp. 614 (S.D.N.Y. 1987).*

"Poison pill" analysis. — To determine whether a board of directors has violated its fiduciary duty to its shareholders in enacting or taking actions under a challenged "Poison Pill" Rights Plan, a court must examine the motivations of the board as it made its decisions, from the initiation of the plan through any actions taken under it; it must consider whether the board made an informed decision based on reasonable investigation, considered under a standard of gross negligence; or perhaps of reasonable diligence; and it must evaluate the reasonableness of the board's actions as a response to any given threats it perceives to the company. *CRTF Corp. v. Federated Department Stores, Inc., 683 F. Supp. 422 (S.D.N.Y. 1988).*

Enhanced proof of reasonable response. — The approval of any defensive measures by a board composed of a majority of outside independent directors acting in good faith and upon reasonable investigation materially enhances the proof that the board has acted reasonably in response to the threat posed. If the directors succeed in making this showing, the burden shifts back to the plaintiffs, who have the ultimate burden of persuasion to show a breach of the directors' fiduciary duties. *CRTF Corp. v. Federated Department Stores, Inc., 683 F. Supp. 422 (S.D.N.Y. 1988).*

Auctions. — In an auction situation, the directors' role remains an active one, changed only in the respect that they are charged with the duty of selling the company at the highest price attainable for the stockholders' benefit. The directors' responsibility in carrying out their fiduciary duty becomes the maximization of the company's value at a sale for the stockholders' benefit. *CRTF Corp. v. Federated Department Stores, Inc., 683 F. Supp. 422 (S.D.N.Y. 1988).*

Under Delaware law, a board of directors need not be a passive observer to a sale. According to the Delaware Supreme Court, concerns that may give rise to reasonable defensive responses include inadequacy of the price offered, nature and timing of the offer, questions of illegality, the impact on constituencies other than shareholders, the risk of non-consummation, and the quality of securities being offered in the exchange. *CRTF Corp. v. Federated Dep't Stores, 1988 U.S. Dist. LEXIS 2775 (S.D.N.Y. 1988).*

In the midst of a takeover battle, when it becomes obvious that a company is for sale — when, for example, the board authorizes management to negotiate a merger or buyout with a third-party — the duty of the board shifts. The directors' role changes from defenders of the corporate bastion to auctioneers charged with getting the best price for the stockholders at a sale of the company. *Samjens Partners I v. Burlington Industries, Inc., 663 F. Supp. 614 (S.D.N.Y. 1987).*

In coordinating the bidding process, the board can institute strategies, such as granting a "lock-up" agreement, a break-up fee, or a no-shop agreement to a "white knight," but only if their strategies enhance the bidding. Such arrangements may also be legitimately necessary to convince a "white knight" to enter the bidding by providing some form of compensation for the risks it is undertaking. Arrangements that effectively end the auction, however, are generally detrimental to shareholders' interests and not protected by the business judgment rule. *Samjens Partners I v. Burlington Industries, Inc., 663 F. Supp. 614 (S.D.N.Y. 1987).*

The board is under a further duty, when conducting the auction, to deal fairly with the bidders. It cannot deal selectively to fend off a hostile bidder. Favoritism for a white knight to the total exclusion of a hostile bidder might be justifiable when the latter's offer adversely affects shareholder interests, but when bidders make relatively similar offers, or dissolution of the company becomes inevitable, the directors cannot fulfill their enhanced duties by playing favorites with the contending factions. Market forces must be allowed to operate freely to bring the target's shareholders the best price available for their equity. *Samjens Partners I v. Burlington Industries, Inc., 663 F. Supp. 614 (S.D.N.Y. 1987).*

Defensive measures two-part test. — Defensive measures enacted by a board of directors in response to a hostile tender offer must meet a two-part test: there must be a basis for the board to have concluded that the defensive measure served a proper corporate purpose and the measure must be reasonable in light of the threat posed. *Samjens Partners I v. Burlington Industries, Inc., 663 F. Supp. 614 (S.D.N.Y. 1987).*

"Liquidation". — Under Delaware law, neither a tender offer nor a merger is a liquidation. The term "liquidation" when applied to a corporation, means the winding up of the affairs of the corporation by getting in its assets, settling with the creditors and debtors, and apportioning the amount of profit and loss. *Sedighim v. Donaldson, Lufkin & Jenrette, Inc., 167 F. Supp. 2d 639 (S.D.N.Y. 2001).*

Corporations

Fifth Circuit

Enhanced duty during contests for control. — Ordinarily, the business judgment rule provides a presumption that in making a business decision the directors of a corporation acted only after they were appropriately informed and after they had honestly determined that the action taken was in the best interests of the company. Because contests for control have an omnipresent specter that a board may be acting primarily in its own interests, the directors have an enhanced duty to prove that they had reasonable grounds for believing that a danger to corporate policy and effectiveness existed because of another person's stock ownership. *Southdown, Inc. v. Moore McCormack Resources, Inc., 686 F. Supp. 595 (S.D.Tex. 1988).*

The duty of restraining management to proportionate responses requires that the directors approve only those defensive acts that are reasonable in relation to the threat posed; the duty of proportion entails that the directors understand both whom the threat endangers and whom the defensive reaction will ultimately harm. *Southdown, Inc. v. Moore McCormack Resources, Inc., 686 F. Supp. 595 (S.D.Tex. 1988).*

Sixth Circuit

Threat to control analysis. — Recognizing the inherent danger in the purchase of shares with corporate funds to remove a threat to corporate policy when a threat to control is involved, Delaware courts now require directors, when faced with such a conflict to show that they had reasonable grounds for believing that a danger to corporate policy and effectiveness existed because of another person's stock ownership. A board of directors satisfies their burden by showing good faith and reasonable investigation. *Buckhorn, Inc. v. Ropak Corp., 656 F. Supp. 209 (S.D.Ohio 1987).*

Where defensive measure are adopted by the directors, the directors have the burden under Delaware law of proving that: (1) the defensive measures were adopted as a result of an informed business judgment based on an evaluation of all material information; (2) they had reasonable grounds to perceive the take over offer as a danger to corporate policy and effectiveness; and (3) the defensive measures adopted were a reasonable response to the threat posed by a takeover offer. *Buckhorn, Inc. v. Ropak Corp., 656 F. Supp. 209 (S.D.Ohio 1987).*

Under Delaware law, reasonable investigation requires that the directors inform themselves prior to making a business decision, of all material information reasonably available to them. The directors' proof is materially enhanced if they show that defensive measures were approved by a board comprised of a majority of outside independent directors who have acted in accordance with the foregoing standards. In addition to demonstrating good faith and reasonable investigation, the directors must also show that the defensive measure taken is reasonable in relation to the threat posed. This entails an analysis by the directors of the nature of the takeover bid and its effect on the corporate enterprise.

Buckhorn, Inc. v. Ropak Corp., 656 F. Supp. 209 (S.D.Ohio 1987).

Courts have repeatedly held that adoption of a poison pill is a reasonable response by directors when they believe that the price offered is inadequate and threatens the interests of shareholders. *Buckhorn, Inc. v. Ropak Corp., 656 F. Supp. 209 (S.D.Ohio 1987).*

It is critical that the directors demonstrate that they used due care in arriving at their decision in adopting the poison pill. Under Delaware law, this means that the directors must show that they informed themselves prior to making a business judgment decision, of all material information reasonably available to them. *Buckhorn, Inc. v. Ropak Corp., 656 F. Supp. 209 (S.D.Ohio 1987).*

Establishment of employment stock ownership plans. — While it is certainly permissible for the directors to adopt measures for the benefit of its employees during the midst of a corporate control struggle, the directors must show that there are rationally related benefits accruing to the stockholders from adopting such measures. Furthermore, it is appropriate to look at such factors as the timing of the employee stock ownership plan (ESOP) establishment, the financial impact upon the company, the identity of the trustees and the voting control of the ESOP shares in determining whether the ESOP was created to benefit the employees and not simply to further entrench management. *Buckhorn, Inc. v. Ropak Corp., 656 F. Supp. 209 (S.D.Ohio 1987).*

Treatment of golden parachute plans. — Golden parachutes that are excessive and have a gross-up feature to compensate the recipient for any tax penalty are not violative of public policy, and parachutes with such features have been upheld. *Campbell v. Potash Corp. of Saskatchewan, Inc., 238 F.3d 792 (6th Cir. 2001).*

Seventh Circuit

Constitutionality. — The Delaware Tender Offers Act clearly contravenes the purpose and spirit of the Williams Act. It upsets the carefully balanced neutrality of the federal provisions by providing, contrary to the congressional scheme, substantial advantages to incumbent management's efforts to defeat or delay a tender offer. The Delaware Tender Offers Act is inconsistent with the Williams Act and "stands as an obstacle to the accomplishment and execution of the full purposes and objectives" of the Williams Act and, accordingly, under the Supremacy Clause is unconstitutional. *Dart Industries, Inc. v. Conrad, 462 F. Supp. 1 (S.D. Ind 1978).*

A coercive offer exists where there is a perceived danger to the shareholders' freedom of choice, that is, where an offer is structured so that a choice by the shareholder not to tender shares may ultimately jeopardize the value of the shareholder's interest. *Newell Co. v. Vermont American Corp., 725 F. Supp. 351 (N.D.Ill. 1989).*

A noncoercive offer can be equally as threatening to the corporate enterprise and exists where the threat is founded on the inadequacy of the offer. That is, where the offer is unfair, ill-timed, under-priced and the target company board perceives that nonetheless, the shareholders may be enticed to accept the offer. *Newell Co. v. Vermont American Corp., 725 F. Supp. 351 (N.D.Ill. 1989).*

A board of directors may be equally justified in defending against a non-coercive offer as it would a perceived coercive offer. *Newell Co. v. Vermont American Corp., 725 F. Supp. 351 (N.D.Ill. 1989).*

Appropriate response to unsolicited tender offer. — Stock repurchase programs funded by corporate monies, which give stockholders an alternative to a hostile offer, have been expressly endorsed by Delaware courts as an appropriate response to an unsolicited tender offer found to be inadequate. *Newell Co. v. Vermont American Corp., 725 F. Supp. 351 (N.D.Ill. 1989).*

Duties of directors in takeover context. — A board of directors is ultimately responsible for managing the affairs of a corporation, and in so doing the directors owe fiduciary duties of care and loyalty to the corporation and its shareholders. These responsibilities require directors to take an active role in responding to a pending takeover bid. *Desert Partners, L.P. v. USG Corp., 686 F. Supp. 1289 (N.D.Ill. 1988).*

The business judgment rule applies when a board of directors adopts defensive mechanisms to thwart potential takeovers. Under Delaware's business judgment rule, courts presume that directors have made their business decisions on an informed basis, in good faith, and with the honest belief that they acted in the best interests of the company. A court should not substitute its judgment for that of the board if the latter's decision can be attributed to any rational business purpose. *Desert Partners, L.P. v. USG Corp., 686 F. Supp. 1289 (N.D.Ill. 1988).*

Burden on directors in defending takeover threat actions. — In evaluating the directors' actions in defending against the threat of a takeover, the courts place upon the directors the burden of proving (1) that the threatened takeover posed a danger to corporate policy and effectiveness, and (2) that they adopted defensive measures which were reasonable in relation to the threat posed. The directors satisfy this burden by showing that they acted in good faith and after reasonable investigation. To overcome the presumption enjoyed by the directors by virtue of the business judgment rule, the plaintiff has the burden of persuasion to show a breach of the directors' fiduciary duties. The plaintiff may show this by demonstrating that the directors acted solely or primarily out of a desire to perpetuate themselves in office. *Desert Partners, L.P. v. USG Corp., 686 F. Supp. 1289 (N.D.Ill. 1988).*

Poison-pill plans. — Delaware law clearly authorizes corporate directors to adopt poison-pill plans to protect their corporation against unfair and hostile takeovers. However, poison-pill plans are neither per se valid nor per se invalid; each must be evaluated individually in light of the circumstances surrounding its implementation. *Desert Partners, L.P. v. USG Corp., 686 F. Supp. 1289 (N.D.Ill. 1988).*

In concluding whether the directors of a corporation acted reasonably in adopting a poison plan, the court may consider three factors: (1) whether the poison-pill plan precludes or otherwise affects a proxy contest for control of the corporation; (2) whether the plan is adopted pursuant to the directors' informed business judgment; (3) whether the plan precludes all hostile takeovers, or only those which are inadequate or unfair to shareholders. *Desert Partners, L.P. v. USG Corp., 686 F. Supp. 1289 (N.D.Ill. 1988).*

Two-tiered tender offers tend to coerce shareholders into tendering their shares in order to avoid a disadvantageous second-tier transaction. It is now well recognized that two-tiered offers are a classic coercive measure designed to stampede shareholders into tendering at the first tier, even if the price is inadequate, out of fear of what they will receive at the back end of the transaction. *Desert Partners, L.P. v. USG Corp., 686 F. Supp. 1289 (N.D.Ill. 1988).*

Oppressive conduct by majority stockholder. — Delaware recognizes two alternate definitions of oppressive conduct by a majority stockholder: (1) a reasonable expectations standard, i.e., the spoken or unspoken understandings on which the founders of a venture rely when commencing a venture; and (2) burdensome, harsh, and wrongful conduct; a lack of probity and fair dealing in the affairs of a company to the prejudice to some of its members; or visible departure from the standards of fair dealing, and a violation of fair play on which every shareholder who entrusts his money to a company is entitled to rely. *Minor v. Albright, 2001 U.S. Dist. LEXIS 19436 (N.D.Ill. 2001).*

Delaware law requires that the conduct of majority shareholders of a corporation toward minority shareholders be tested by the same standards of fiduciary duty which directors observe toward all their shareholders. *In re Transocean Tender Offer Securities Litigation, 427 F. Supp. 1211 (N.D. Ill. 1997).*

Control potential premium. — A majority or controlling stockholder is under no duty to other stockholders to refrain from receiving a premium upon the sale of his stock which reflects merely the control potential of that stock. There is no obligation under such circumstances, to share and share alike. Control is not a corporate asset, but is rather an attribute of stock ownership. *Dasho v. Susquehanna Corp., 1970 U.S. Dist. LEXIS 12923 (N.D. Ill. 1970).*

Heightened obligation in change of control transaction. — Under Delaware law, in a "change of control" transaction, the directors have a heightened obligation to the shareholders to inform themselves fully of the value of a company's shares; maximize value recoverable for all shareholders; and obtain full fair market value on any sale of shares. Decisions under the Delaware *Revlon* doctrine hold that, once the directors have determined to enter the corporation into a "change of control" transaction, the directors owe a duty to obtain the maximum possible price for the selling shareholders. *Montgomery v. Aetna Plywood, Inc., 39 F. Supp. 2d 915 (N.D.Ill. 1998).*

Corporations

Eighth Circuit

Shares may not be issued solely to preserve or to gain corporate control and corporate action, though technically correct and in compliance with Delaware Corporation Law may not be undertaken for an inequitable purpose. *Watts v. Des Moines Register & Tribune, 525 F. Supp. 1311 (S.D.Iowa 1981).*

Voting trusts. — The accomplishment of some definite plan or policy to benefit the company, to assure stability and continuity of management for this purpose and to prevent rival concerns or competitors from gaining control are legitimate bases for implementation of a voting trust. If, however, the only object or purpose of a voting trust is to corner the majority stockholders' right to vote in an arrangement from which they cannot escape and to secure permanency of management and office holding for a scheming group, this would seem clearly contrary to the policy of the law. *Watts v. Des Moines Register & Tribune, 525 F. Supp. 1311 (S.D. Iowa 1981).*

Ninth Circuit

Prerequisites to application of business judgment rule in takeover context. — The business judgment rule may protect directors of a corporation when they are responding to a takeover threat. However, in such circumstances there is an omnipresent specter that a board may be acting primarily in its own interests. Before the business judgment rule will be applied in such a context, it must be established that: (1) there were reasonable grounds for believing that corporate policy and effectiveness were endangered; after which, (2) the defensive measure chosen must be reasonable in relation to the threat posed. The directors may satisfy this burden by showing good faith and reasonable investigation. This is called the *Unocal* analysis. If a defensive mechanism is intended to act primarily as an anti-takeover device, the *Unocal* analysis will apply in determining the propriety of the mechanism. If it has some other purpose, and only incidentally acts as an anti-takeover device, then the business judgment rule applies. *NL Indusustries, Inc. v. Lockheed Corp., 1992 U.S. Dist. LEXIS 22652 (C.D.Cal. 1992).*

Enhanced scrutiny of change in control transactions. — When a transaction results in a change in control of the company, the transaction is subject to enhanced scrutiny and defendants have the burden to show they were informed adequately and acted reasonably. *McMichael v. United States Filter Corp., 2001 U.S. Dist. LEXIS 3918 (C.D.Cal. 2001).*

The *Unocal* test requires the court to consider the following two questions: (1) Does the board have reasonable grounds for believing a danger to corporate policy and effectiveness exists? (2) Is the response reasonable in relation to the threat? If it is a defensive measure touching on issues of control, the court must examine whether the board purposefully disenfranchised its shareholders, an action that cannot be sustained without a compelling justification. *Hilton Hotels Corp. v. ITT Corp., 978 F. Supp. 1342 (D.Nev. 1997).*

Inadequacy of an offer to purchase is a legally cognizable threat to the corporation. *Hilton Hotels Corp. v. ITT Corp., 978 F. Supp. 1342 (D.Nev. 1997).*

A board cannot "cram down" on shareholders a management sponsored alternative to an offer to purchase the corporation. *Hilton Hotels Corp. v. ITT Corp., 978 F. Supp. 1342 (D.Nev. 1997).*

Tenth Circuit

Duty of director when reacquiring outstanding corporate stock. — Although directors generally do not occupy a fiduciary position with respect to stockholders in face-to-face dealings, Delaware law does create such a duty in special circumstances where advantage is taken of inside information by a corporate insider who deliberately misleads an ignorant stockholder. Therefore, under Delaware law, directors who possess inside information regarding the value of stock owe a fiduciary duty when reacquiring outstanding corporate stock not only to the corporation and to the shareholders collectively, but also to the minority shareholders from whom the stock is being reacquired. *Alta Health Strategies, Inc. v. Kennedy, 790 F. Supp. 1085 (D.Utah 1992).*

Eleventh Circuit

Under Delaware law, majority shareholders do owe minority shareholders a duty to disclose material information. Minority shareholders state a claim upon which relief can be granted against majority shareholders who provided allegedly misleading information in connection with the solicitation of votes. *Chalk Line Mfg. v. Frontenac Venture V, Ltd., 1994 Bankr. LEXIS 1087 (Bankr N.D.Ala. 1994).*

Lock-up and no-shop provisions are not void per se. Rather, such provisions are impermissible only if they are adopted in a situation where there is a live auction with competing bidders. Where lock-up and no-shop provisions are used to encourage a bidder to submit an offer, as distinguished from precluding bidders in an active auction, they are upheld. *Hastings-Murtagh v. Texas Air Corp., 649 F. Supp. 479 (S.D.Fla. 1986).*

Subchapter VII.
Meetings, Elections, Voting and Notice

§ 211. Meetings of stockholders

DELAWARE CASE NOTES — REPORTED

Delaware corporation law requires that an annual meeting of stockholders must be held for the election of directors. *Tweedy, Browne & Knapp v. Cambridge Fund, Inc., 318 A.2d 635 (Del. Ch. 1974);*

Saxon Indus., Inc. v. NKFW Partners, 488 A.2d 1298 (Del. 1984).

Mandate of subsection (b) of this section is that an annual meeting of stockholders "shall be held for the election of directors" and alternative procedures are provided to assure that there is corporate compliance therewith. *Coaxial Communications, Inc. v. CNA Fin. Corp., 367 A.2d 994 (Del. 1976).*

In the absence of certificate provisions providing otherwise, directors, including those designated by a special class of stock, must be elected annually pursuant to this section. *Insituform of N. Am., Inc. v. Chandler, 534 A.2d 257 (Del. Ch. 1987).*

Purpose of this section is to provide relief to a stockholder who makes a showing that a meeting to elect directors has not been held for more than 13 months. *Coaxial Communications, Inc. v. CNA Fin. Corp., 367 A.2d 994 (Del. 1976).*

No distinction between stockholders. — This section does not distinguish between large and small stockholders, nor between those in accord with and those in opposition to existing management. Each has the right to invoke judicial aid to compel compliance with this section. *Coaxial Communications, Inc. v. CNA Fin. Corp., 367 A.2d 994 (Del. 1976).*

No right of shareholder to insist that meeting be held at particular time. — While the right of a shareholder to compel an annual meeting under this section may be virtually absolute, a shareholder has no similar right to insist that it be held at any particular time. *Savin Bus. Machs. Corp. v. Rapifax Corp., 375 A.2d 469 (Del. Ch. 1977).*

Discretion of court. — The timing of the mandated meeting clearly falls within the discretionary authority of the court. *Savin Bus. Machs. Corp. v. Rapifax Corp., 375 A.2d 469 (Del. Ch. 1977).*

The use of the term "may summarily order" in subsection (c) of this section obviously reposes a discretion in the court to be exercised in light of the existing circumstances. *Savin Bus. Machs. Corp. v. Rapifax Corp., 375 A.2d 469 (Del. Ch. 1977)Hoschett v. TSI Int'l Software, LTD., 683 A.2d 43 (Del. Ch. 1996).*

Although satisfying the statutory elements for relief, the court refused to order an annual meeting because of the shareholders' plan to make an "end run" around federal rules and regulations governing public trading of securities. *Clabault v. Caribbean Select, Inc., 805 A.2d 913 (Del. Ch. 2002).*

Postponement of annual meeting. — The business judgment rule does not confer any presumption of propriety on the acts of the directors in postponing an annual meeting. *Aprahamian v. HBO & Co., 531 A.2d 1204 (Del. Ch. 1987).*

A board's decision to defer the annual meeting to a later time in conformity with the company's bylaws and this section is not a decision that threatens the legitimacy of the electoral process and the propriety of such decision is to be measured by the permissive business judgment form of review. *Stahl v. Apple Bancorp, Inc., 579 A.2d 1115 (Del. Ch. 1990).*

The action of deferring the company's annual meeting because of a proposed proxy contest where no meeting date has yet been set and no proxies solicited did not impair or impede the effective exercise of the corporate franchise; thus, the majority shareholder had no legal right to compel the holding of the company's annual meeting. *Stahl v. Apple Bancorp, Inc., 579 A.2d 1115 (Del. Ch. 1990).*

Acquiescence to practice of not holding meetings. — Mere acquiescence in the failure to hold earlier meetings, or indeed actual connivance to avoid earlier meetings, ought not deprive shareholders generally of the right to elect directors at an annual meeting. *Speiser v. Baker, 525 A.2d 1001 (Del. Ch. 1987).*

Written consents insufficient. — The mandatory requirement that an annual meeting of shareholders be held is not satisfied by shareholder action by written consents pursuant to § 228 of this title. *Hoschett v. TSI Int'l Software, LTD., 683 A.2d 43 (Del. Ch. 1996).*

Call for meeting issued by de facto officer is valid call, provided of course it would be if the officer were a de jure one. *Moon v. Moon Motor Car Co., 17 Del. Ch. 176, 151 A. 298 (1930).*

Special shareholder meeting. — Bylaw amendment extending from 35 to 60 the minimum time period for calling a shareholder-initiated special meeting to remove the board of directors in response to a hostile takeover threat was a reasonable response since earlier meeting could have threatened shareholders' interest in making an informed decision about a possible merger and since the response was proportionate to the threat as it only delayed but did not preclude a shareholder vote. *Kidsco Inc. v. Dinsmore, 674 A.2d 483 (Del. Ch. 1995).*

Stockholders may elect chairperson, other than the president, whenever they deem it necessary to do so. *Duffy v. Loft, Inc., 17 Del. Ch. 376, 152 A. 849 (1930).*

The presence of a corporation's president ready and willing to preside cannot be said to oust the stockholders of their right to choose a chairperson on any such theory that the president's presence makes such choice unnecessary, when the bylaws give the stockholders the right to choose a chairperson. *Duffy v. Loft, Inc., 17 Del. Ch. 140, 151 A. 223 (1930), aff'd, 17 Del. Ch. 376, 152 A. 849 (1930).*

Motion for election of chairperson may be made by stockholder. — When the corporation president refuses to put the motion to elect a chairperson for the stockholders' meeting to a vote, the stockholders can resort to a vote on the motion when put to them by one of their fellows. *Duffy v. Loft, Inc., 17 Del. Ch. 140, 151 A. 223 (1930), aff'd, 17 Del. Ch. 376, 152 A. 849 (1930).*

And choice may be made by voice vote or ballot. — When the stockholders have the right to choose a chairperson, the choice may be made by a viva voce vote rather than by a vote of shares and by ballot, if the bylaws contain a provision which so provides. *Duffy v. Loft, Inc., 17 Del. Ch. 140, 151 A. 223 (1930), aff'd, 17 Del. Ch. 376, 152 A. 849 (1930).*

Change of control. — The objection to holding a stockholders' meeting — that one person will likely be voted out of office as a director and the company will fall under the complete domination of another — would not be a reason to enjoin the meeting and cannot be a reason to excuse compliance with subsection (b). *Speiser v. Baker, 525 A.2d 1001 (Del. Ch. 1987).*

Notice need not be given as to proposed resolutions. — It was not necessary that advance notice of the proposed resolutions to be voted upon at an annual stockholders' meeting be set forth. *Gottlieb v. McKee, 34 Del. Ch. 537, 107 A.2d 240 (1954).*

Duty of court to ensure that meeting and election are prompt. — The spirit of subsection (c) of this section indicates that where more than 13 months have elapsed without a meeting of shareholders to elect directors and application is made by a shareholder for Court intervention because of this, the Court has a duty to make sure that such a meeting and election take place as promptly as possible. Normally this can only be guaranteed by the entry of an order fixing a definite date for the event to take place. *Tweedy, Browne & Knapp v. Cambridge Fund, Inc., 318 A.2d 635 (Del. Ch. 1974).*

Stockholder's request for a summary judgment compelling a company to hold an annual stockholder's meeting pursuant to this section was granted, where the company failed to take reasonable steps to hold a meeting within 13 months of the last meeting; the fact that the company set a date for the meeting within the 13 month period did not satisfy the statutory requirements, as the meeting had to actually be held within the 13 month period. *MFC Bancorp LTD v. Equidyne Corp., 844 A.2d 1015 (Del. Ch. 2003).*

Prima facie case for relief under this section was made by plaintiff because it proved that: (1) Plaintiff is a stockholder of defendant; and (2) there had not been a meeting of stockholders for election of directors during a period of more than 13 months. *Coaxial Communications, Inc. v. CNA Fin. Corp., 367 A.2d 994 (Del. 1976); Saxon Indus., Inc. v. NKFW Partners, 488 A.2d 1298 (Del. 1984).*

Not all delays in holding annual meeting are necessarily inexcusable, and certainly if there are mitigating circumstances explaining the delay or failure to act, they can be considered in fixing the time of the meeting or by such other "appropriate" order. *Tweedy, Browne & Knapp v. Cambridge Fund, Inc., 318 A.2d 635 (Del. Ch. 1974).*

Directors may convene meeting if annual meeting is not held. — If no annual meeting is held for the election of directors, the directors in office can nevertheless convene a meeting for the election. *In re Tonopah United Water Co., 16 Del. Ch. 26, 139 A. 762 (1927).*

When it becomes evident that the annual meeting cannot possibly be held in obedience to the bylaws of the company, the board of directors can proceed to call the meeting for another date, and their act in so doing does not amount to an attempted change of the annual meeting date. *In re Tonopah United Water Co., 16 Del. Ch. 26, 139 A. 762 (1927).*

Receiver for stockholder may act. — When a receiver has a valid order of appointment by the United States District Court wherein the receiver is given broad powers of management of corporate affairs, there can be no question about such receiver's authority to proceed

with an action under this section. *Prickett v. American Steel & Pump Corp., 251 A.2d 576 (Del. Ch. 1969).*

Where a receiver for a majority stockholder makes out a prima facie case both as to status under this section and as to his or her right to relief, the court cannot deny him or her relief based upon what is in its essence a collateral attack upon the receiver's authority and status as receiver. *Prickett v. American Steel & Pump Corp., 251 A.2d 576 (Del. Ch. 1969).*

Special elections for newly created director positions are not prevented. — Statutory provisions referring to an annual meeting for the purpose of electing directors pertain to regular elections and were not meant to prevent a special election for newly created positions. *Burr v. Burr Corp., 291 A.2d 409 (Del. Ch. 1972).*

Right to select directors during insolvency. — Where the corporation remains in control of its affairs while undergoing reorganization pursuant to the Bankruptcy Code, insolvency does not divest the stockholders of their right to elect directors. *Saxon Indus., Inc. v. NKFW Partners, 488 A.2d 1298 (Del. 1984).*

Courts try to sustain conclusiveness of stockholder meetings. — Where an extensive campaign has been carried on by rival groups for the votes of stockholders and the arguments pro and con have been made, the parties interested should submit to a count and let the majority prevail, so that the court should indulge in every reasonable intendment in favor of the conclusiveness of the meeting. *Duffy v. Loft, Inc., 17 Del. Ch. 140, 151 A. 223 (1930), aff'd, 17 Del. Ch. 376, 152 A. 849 (1930).*

When election has been validly held court cannot order another one. — When an election has in fact been held either on the day designated by the bylaws, or at some other day prior to the application to the Court of Chancery under this section, then the Court of Chancery has no power to order an election. *Schultz v. Commonwealth Mtg. Co., 12 Del. Ch. 104, 107 A. 774 (1919); In re Tonopah United Water Co., 16 Del. Ch. 26, 139 A. 762 (1927).*

Master to conduct meeting not appointed. — Where plaintiff stockholders have sought judgment on the pleadings, and where there was nothing alleged in the complaint which attributed any improper conduct or purpose to the present directors of defendant corporation or which would indicate futility in requiring the present management to hold the stockholders' meeting to elect directors, the Court would not appoint a master to conduct the meeting. *Tweedy, Browne & Knapp v. Cambridge Fund, Inc., 318 A.2d 635 (Del. Ch. 1974).*

Preliminary injunction enjoining holding of corporate meeting or election of directors will not be granted unless the denial thereof would cause an "irreparable injury." *Hauth v. Giant Portland Cement Co., 33 Del. Ch. 496, 96 A.2d 233 (1953).*

Shareholder's motion for a preliminary injunction to stop the corporation's annual meeting was granted because the corporation's proxy statement was false and misleading, where the corporation and its board of directors breached their fiduciary duty to disclose fully and fairly to stockholders all material information in seeking stockholder approval of the amendments to the corporation's bylaws; the threat of an uninformed stockholder vote constituted irreparable harm. *ODS Techs., L.P. v. Marshall, 832 A.2d 1254 (Del. Ch. 2003).*

Director's application for preliminary injunctive relief postponing holding of corporation's scheduled annual meeting was denied where the equities in favor of the holding of the meeting as regularly scheduled outweighed those implicit in the director's belated efforts to wage a proxy fight designed to preserve his status as a director of the corporation and to bring about the removal of the corporation's chief executive officer. *Lenahan v. National Computer Analysts Corp., 310 A.2d 661 (Del. Ch. 1973).*

Cancellation of meeting. — It is an elementary principle of corporate law that if a board has the power to adopt resolutions or policies, then it has the corresponding power to rescind them. Similarly, if bylaws authorize a board's chairman with the right to call a special meeting of stockholders, it follows that a chairman can later rescind it. *Perlegos v. Atmel Corp., 2007 Del. Ch. LEXIS 25 (February 8, 2007).*

Director defendants cannot even justify their decision to cancel meeting under a less stringent, less searching standard. The minutes of the board meeting reflect that the director defendants were concerned about the special meeting's cost and its possibility to distract management and confuse Atmel employees and shareholders. In addition, at trial, there was some testimony by the director defendants that the company could face additional governance problems and even lose its listing on NASDAQ if its independent directors were removed. None of these concerns, however, justified cancellation of the special meeting. *Perlegos v. Atmel Corp., 2007 Del. Ch. LEXIS 25 (February 8, 2007).*

DELAWARE CASE NOTES — UNREPORTED

Right to select directors during insolvency. — On remand from the state supreme court, the chancery court clarified its decision that it denied a request from shareholders who held stock in a bankrupt corporation for permission to elect directors because it thought the shareholders were involved in a scheme to evade federal securities law. *Clabault v. Caribbean Select, Inc., 2003 Del. Ch. LEXIS 93 (Aug. 28, 2003).*

Trial court properly denied relief to a corporation from a prior trial court order which required the corporation to set an annual meeting within 90 days, pursuant to 8 Del. C. § 211(c), as no meeting had been held for election of directors for 18 months, and the corporation's claim that such directive conflicted with SEC rules and statutes was erroneous because 17 C.F.R. § 14(c) served the same purpose of helping to safeguard the shareholder's foundational voting rights; no cause was shown to justify either relief from the order or the corporation's other request to stay the matter on an interim basis under Ch. Ct. R. 62(b), as the stockholder had a clear right under Delaware law to convene an annual meeting, the corporation's inability to complete its financial statements did not diminish the stockholder's right, and the matter was governed by Delaware law under the internal affairs doctrine. *Newcastle Ptnrs., L.P.*

v. Vesta Ins. Group, Inc., 2005 Del. Ch. LEXIS 174 (Del. Ch. Nov. 15, 2005).

Both the internal affairs doctrine, and the fact that the Securities and Exchange Commission had never actually indicated that holding an annual meeting and issuing proxies for it would violate the agency's rules, prompted the court to find that a corporation that had already been ordered to hold a long-overdue annual meeting had not shown newly discovered evidence or any other circumstance that would justify granting relief from that order; Delaware case law established that a properly supported application for relief under 8 Del. C. § 211 could almost never be denied, because the due process rights of stockholders were so critical. *Newcastle v. Vesta Ins. Group, 2005 Del. Ch. LEXIS 174 (Del. Ch. Nov. 15, 2005).*

Motion exceeding scope of statute. — Emergency motion to temporarily enjoin annual shareholders' meeting, or, in the alternative, amend proxy materials to include plaintiffs' specific nominee for independent director, was denied, as said motion exceeded the scope of an action filed under 8 Del. C. § 211, plaintiffs failed to cite to any other statutory authority to grant the same, and they failed to sufficiently allege the requirements for injunctive relief. *Frenz v. Gencor Indus., 2005 Del. Ch. LEXIS 141 (Del. Ch. Sept. 9, 2005).*

CASE NOTES — OTHER STATES

California

Special meetings. — The statute does not give shareholders an inherent right to call special meetings and that elimination of the right afforded by the bylaws would not inhibit a proxy contest in connection with the election of directors at annual shareholders' meetings. *Katz v. Chevron Corp., 22 Cal. App. 4th 1352, 27 Cal. Rptr. 2d 681 (1994).*

Void votes. — A proxy holder's action for his own aggrandizement will not bind the principal and votes so cast are void. *Coulter v. Junum, Inc., 2004 Cal. App. Unpub. LEXIS 6891 (2004).*

A proxy limitation deprives the proxy holder of the power to vote outside the scope of the limitation. *Coulter v. Junum, Inc., 2004 Cal. App. Unpub. LEXIS 6891 (2004).*

Illinois

Directors' duties of disclosure. — Delaware courts address the duty of disclosure by corporate directors only with respect to the following five scenarios: mergers, proxy solicitations, tender offers, self-tender offers, and stockholder votes. *Sims v. Tezak, 296 Ill. App. 3d 503, 694 N.E.2d 1015, 230 Ill. Dec. 737.Dec. 737 (1998).*

Pennsylvania

Irreparable harm. — Under Delaware law, the deprivation of a shareholder's right to vote is irreparable harm. *Alan Wurtzel Commerce Program v. Park Towne Place Apartments Limited Partnership, 2001 Phila. Ct. Com. Pl. LEXIS 79 (2001).*

Corporations

CASE NOTES — FEDERAL

Second Circuit

Quorum. — Where there are numerous shareholders it is not essential to court a quorum before voting, the question of a quorum may be determined when the votes are counted, if no statute or bylaw prohibits this procedure. Further, the courts always indulge in every reasonable intendment in favor of the conclusiveness of the meeting in passing on the question of the presence of a quorum. *Phillips v. United Corp., 1947 U.S. Dist. LEXIS 3123 (S.D.N.Y. 1947).*

Standing of equity committee. — That the equity committee is neither a "stockholder" nor a "director" within the meaning of Delaware General Corporation Law tit. 8, § 211(c) does not detract from its standing in this court for an order directing the debtor to conduct an annual shareholders' meeting in accordance with its corporate bylaws. *Official Committee of Equity Sec. Holders of Lone Star Industries, Inc., v. Lone Star Industries, Inc., 138 B.R. 420 (Bankr. S.D.N.Y. 1992).*

Eighth Circuit

Regulation of election process by another state. — An attempt by another state to regulate the solicitation and voting of proxies by a stockholder in a Delaware corporation impermissibly burdens interstate commerce in violation of the Commerce Clause. No other state has a legitimate local interest in regulating the election process of a Delaware corporation. *National City Lines, Inc. v. LLC Corp., 1981 U.S. Dist. LEXIS 16475, (W.D.Mo. 1981).*

§ 212. Voting rights of stockholders; proxies; limitations

DELAWARE CASE NOTES — REPORTED

One vote for 1 share general not special right. — The provision that each stockholder shall, at every meeting of stockholders, be entitled to 1 vote for each share of the capital stock held by him or her is declaratory of a general, not a special right. *Hartford Accident & Indem. Co. v. W.S. Dickey Clay Mfg. Co., 26 Del. Ch. 411, 24 A.2d 315 (1942).*

Who may vote at stockholders' meeting is to be determined by Delaware constitution and statutes as same are construed by its courts. *Bouree v. Trust Francais, 14 Del. Ch. 332, 127 A. 56 (1924).*

Charter restrictions on voting. — In the absence of any express provision in subsection (a) of § 151 of this title, or elsewhere in the law, prohibiting charter restrictions on voting, the provisions of subsection (a) of this section control in determining the validity of those restrictions. *Providence & Worcester Co. v. Baker, 378 A.2d 121 (Del. 1977).*

The absence in subsection (a) of this section of a cross reference to subsection (a) of § 151 of this title is indicative of the absence of any legislative intent to prohibit, by subsection (a) of § 151 of this title, charter restrictions upon stockholders' voting rights. *Providence & Worcester Co. v. Baker, 378 A.2d 121 (Del. 1977).*

Right to vote shares of corporate stock having voting powers has always been incident to its legal ownership. *In re Giant Portland Cement Co., 26 Del. Ch. 32, 21 A.2d 697 (1941); Drob v. National Mem. Park, 28 Del. Ch. 254, 41 A.2d 589 (1945); Tracy v. Brentwood Village Corp., 30 Del. Ch. 296, 59 A.2d 708 (1948).*

The right to vote shares of stock issued by a Delaware corporation is an incident of legal ownership. *Norton v. Digital Applications, Inc., 305 A.2d 656 (Del. Ch. 1973).*

Only record holders can vote shares at stockholders' meetings. *Drob v. National Mem. Park, 28 Del. Ch. 254, 41 A.2d 589 (1945).*

The real owner of corporate stock does not have the right to vote it at stockholders' meetings if it be registered on the corporate books in the name of another person.

Tracy v. Brentwood Village Corp., 30 Del. Ch. 296, 59 A.2d 708 (1948).

No one but a registered stockholder is, as a matter of right, entitled to vote and if an owner of stock chooses to register his or her shares in the name of a nominee, such stockholder takes the risks attendant upon such an arrangement, including the risk that he or she may not receive notice of corporate proceedings, or be able to obtain a proxy from his or her nominee. The corporation is entitled to recognize the exclusive right of the registered owner to vote. *American Hdwe. Corp. v. Savage Arms Corp., 37 Del. Ch. 59, 136 A.2d 690 (1957).*

Owners of preferred stock could not vote at a meeting to approve a proposed merger even though an amendment to be voted on at the meeting would give voting rights to preferred stockholders. *Mariner LDC v. Stone Container Corp., 729 A.2d 267 (Del. Ch. 1998).*

But ownership of voting stock imposes no legal duty to vote at all. *Ringling Bros. — Barnum & Bailey Combined Shows, Inc. v. Ringling, 29 Del. Ch. 610, 53 A.2d 441 (1947).*

If corporation has power to hold stock, it has incidental power to vote it notwithstanding its certificate of incorporation confers no special power to that end. *Bouree v. Trust Francais, 14 Del. Ch. 332, 127 A. 56 (1924).*

That a stock certificate was filled in with a person's name does not alone create legal ownership in such person. *Norton v. Digital Applications, Inc., 305 A.2d 656 (Del. Ch. 1973).*

Record holder could vote stock without direction and real owner. *McLain v. Lanova Corp., 28 Del. Ch. 176, 39 A.2d 209 (1944).*

And consent of unrecorded owner presumed. — The actual consent of the holder of the certificate is ordinarily not essential to the right of the record owners to vote stock standing in their names, and at any rate, in the absence of an objection consent would ordinarily be presumed. *In re Giant Portland Cement Co., 26 Del. Ch. 32, 21 A.2d 697 (1941).*

The right to vote shares of stock having voting powers is ordinarily an incident of its legal ownership, and in the absence of some peculiar inequitable circumstances affecting the rights of the real beneficial owner, the record owner can vote the stock and the beneficial owner must be taken to know this, and can protect his or her rights by demanding a proxy, or otherwise. *McLain v. Lanova Corp., 28 Del. Ch. 176, 39 A.2d 209 (1944).*

But as between transferor and transferee equities with transferee. — As between a transferor who has parted with all beneficial interest in stock and his or her transferee, the broad equities are all in favor of the latter in the matter of its voting and while the transferee may not himself or herself be qualified to vote because he or she had not caused the stock to be registered in his or her name, it does not necessarily follow that the transferor may exercise the voting right in defiance of the transferee's wishes. *In re Canal Constr. Co., 21 Del. Ch. 155, 182 A. 545 (1936).*

Transferee can protect himself or herself by having transferor give proxy. — The owners of certificates of stocks can usually protect their rights by recording the transfers and having new certificates issued; but, even though that cannot be done because the corporate transfer books are closed at the time of the assignments, they can compel the record owners to give them proxies to vote the stock standing in their names. *In re Giant Portland Cement Co., 26 Del. Ch. 32, 21 A.2d 697 (1941).*

A proxy must state that it is irrevocable, which means that the word "irrevocable," or perhaps a synonym, must appear in the proxy. *Eliason v. Englehart, 733 A.2d 944 (Del. 1999).*

Stockholder is not forbidden from voting on question of corporate policy simply because he or she is related to person who favors or opposes such policy. *Du Pont v. Du Pont, 256 F. 129 (3d Cir.), cert. denied, 250 U.S. 642, 39 S. Ct. 492, 63 L. Ed. 1185 (1919).*

Stockholder has right to vote his or her stock from whatever motive he or she may choose. *Allied Chem. & Dye Corp. v. Steel & Tube Co. of Am., 14 Del. Ch. 1, 120 A. 486 (1923).*

Stockholders have the right to exercise wide liberality of judgment in the matter of voting and may admit personal profit or even whims and caprice into the motives which determine their choice, so long as no advantage is obtained at the expense of their fellow stockholders. *Heil v. Standard Gas & Elec. Co., 17 Del. Ch. 214, 151 A. 303 (1930); Ringling Bros. — Barnum & Bailey Combined Shows, Inc. v. Ringling, 29 Del. Ch. 610, 53 A.2d 441 (1947); Beach v. KDI Corp., 336 F. Supp. 229 (D. Del. 1971).*

The motive that the stockholder may have for not attending the meeting or voting his shares is irrelevant. Even if petitioner deliberately failed to attend because he did not want to create a quorum, his reason for abstaining, if relevant, is not of a character which should preclude the relief requested. *In re Pioneer Drilling Co., 36 Del. Ch. 386, 130 A.2d 559 (1957).*

Stockholder may vote selfishly or altruisticly. — When a stockholding director is called upon to decide at a stockholders' meeting between his or her own interest as an individual and what may be his or her interest along with other stockholders in benefiting the corporation, he or she is free to exercise his or her own judgment, and to act in accordance with selfish rather than altruistic motives. *Du Pont v. Du Pont, 251 F. 937 (D. Del. 1918), aff'd, 256 F. 129 (3d Cir.), cert. denied, 250 U.S. 642, 39 S. Ct. 492, 40 S. Ct. 12, 63 L. Ed. 1185 (1919).*

And his or her motives may not be inquired into. — Where a stockholder was fully informed of the questions involved, he or she had a right to give his or her proxy to whomsoever he or she desired, and his or her motives for voting could not be inquired into. *Du Pont v. Du Pont, 251 F. 937 (D. Del. 1918), aff'd, 256 F. 129 (3d Cir.), cert. denied, 250 U.S. 642, 39 S. Ct. 492, 40 S. Ct. 12, 63 L. Ed. 1185 (1919).*

But stockholders have fiduciary duty to other stockholders. — When, in the conduct of the corporate business, a majority of the voting power in the corporation join hands in imposing their policy upon all, they are to be regarded as having placed upon themselves the same sort of fiduciary character which the law impresses upon the directors in their relation to all the stockholders. *Allied Chem. & Dye Corp. v. Steel & Tube Co. of Am., 14 Del. Ch. 1, 120 A. 486 (1923).*

Shares have not been "issued" for purposes of voting until custody and control of the certificate has passed to the stockholder. *Norton v. Digital Applications, Inc., 305 A.2d 656 (Del. Ch. 1973).*

Delivery, actual or constructive, is required to complete the transfer of the shares. *Norton v. Digital Applications, Inc., 305 A.2d 656 (Del. Ch. 1973).*

Legal ownership of escrowed shares does not pass to the stockholder until they are delivered to him or her by the bank out of escrow. *Norton v. Digital Applications, Inc., 305 A.2d 656 (Del. Ch. 1973).*

Delivery of stock or stock certificates into escrow is not a sufficient delivery for voting purposes. *Norton v. Digital Applications, Inc., 305 A.2d 656 (Del. Ch. 1973).*

This section permits stockholders to give proxies which by their terms may be irrevocable for a period. *Abercrombie v. Davies, 35 Del. Ch. 599, 123 A.2d 893 (1956), rev'd on other grounds, 36 Del. Ch. 371, 130 A.2d 338 (1957).*

Irrevocable proxy to be coupled with interest. — A proxy is revocable even though irrevocable in form, unless the Court of Chancery finds that it was coupled with an interest. *Brady v. Mexican Gulf Sulphur Co., 32 Del. Ch. 372, 88 A.2d 300 (1952).*

A proxy power must be coupled with an "interest" in order to be irrevocable. *Abercrombie v. Davies, 35 Del. Ch. 599, 123 A.2d 893 (1956), rev'd on other grounds, 36 Del. Ch. 371, 130 A.2d 338 (1957).*

Sufficiency of interest. — The interest that a seller of stock retains as the senior executive officer of that company is sufficient to render specifically enforceable an

Corporations

express contract for an irrevocable proxy. *Haft v. Haft, 671 A.2d 413 (Del. Ch. 1995)*.

In determining the validity of a claimed security interest in securities for purposes of subsection (e) of this section, one must turn first to Article 9 of the Delaware version of the *Uniform Commercial Code. Haft v. Haft, 671 A.2d 413 (Del. Ch. 1995)*.

Period of validity. — The 60-day time period for submission of written consents pursuant to § 228 of this title should not be confused with the 3-year period of validity for proxies pursuant to this section. *Viele v. Devaney, 679 A.2d 993 (Del. Ch. 1996)*.

Evidence of agency relationship. — To be accepted as valid evidence of an agency relationship, a proxy must evidence that relationship in some authentic, genuine way; proxies meeting that fundamental requirement will enjoy a presumption of validity. *Parshalle v. Roy, 567 A.2d 19 (Del. Ch. 1989)*.

Person acting as proxy for another is but latter's agent and owes to the latter the duty of acting in strict accord with those requirements of a fiduciary relationship which inhere in the conception of agency. *Rice & Hutchins, Inc. v. Triplex Shoe Co., 16 Del. Ch. 298, 147 A. 317 (1929)*, aff'd, *17 Del. Ch. 356, 152 A. 342 (1930)*.

The producing of a proxy is not the creation of the agency, only proof of it to the satisfaction of others. *Duffy v. Loft, Inc., 17 Del. Ch. 140, 151 A. 223 (1930)*, aff'd, *17 Del. Ch. 376, 152 A. 849 (1930)*.

The holder of a proxy to vote stock is an agent, and within the scope of his or her authority, has a certain fiduciary relation toward his principal. *McLain v. Lanova Corp., 28 Del. Ch. 176, 39 A.2d 209 (1944)*.

The relation between the stockholders and the holders of their proxies is that of principal and agent, and where the powers given were merely to vote the stock "as my proxy at any election." The power to act for them and in their names in calling a special stockholders meeting cannot be implied from the general authority given to vote their stock. *Josephson v. Cosmocolor Corp., 31 Del. Ch. 46, 64 A.2d 35 (1949)*.

The person designated in a proxy has a fiduciary obligation to carry out the wishes of the stockholders to the best of his or her ability. *Hauth v. Giant Portland Cement Co., 33 Del. Ch. 496, 96 A.2d 233 (1953)*.

Agent's act for own aggrandizement does not bind principal. — General proxies given to an agent cannot be used by the holder to commit the principals to acts done by the agent for his or her own aggrandizement so as to estop the principal from complaining thereat, unless the principal was advised of the proposed action in advance and expressly or impliedly approved thereof. *Blair v. F.H. Smith Co., 18 Del. Ch. 150, 156 A. 207 (1931)*.

Paper writing called proxy is nothing more than evidence of relationship; it is not the relationship. *Duffy v. Loft, Inc., 17 Del. Ch. 140, 151 A. 223 (1930)*, aff'd, *17 Del. Ch. 376, 152 A. 849 (1930)*.

Conflicting proxies. — All identical but conflicting proxies must be rejected when the conflict cannot be resolved from the face of the proxies. *Concord Fin. Group, Inc. v. Tri-State Motor Transit Co., 567 A.2d 1 (Del. Ch. 1989)*.

Later proxy revokes former proxy. — When two proxies are offered bearing the same name, the proxy that appears from the evidence to have been last executed will be accepted and counted under the theory that the latter proxy constitutes a revocation of the former although the signatures do not appear to be in the same handwriting. *Standard Power & Light Corp. v. Investment Assocs., 29 Del. Ch. 593, 51 A.2d 572 (1947)*.

Clearly a later proxy revokes an earlier one when such instructions appear on the face of the later proxy; and there is no question but that a later proxy revokes an earlier one where the total number of shares registered in the name of the person giving the proxies is included in each proxy. *Schott v. Climax Molybdenum Co., 38 Del. Ch. 450, 154 A.2d 221 (1959)*.

Where two identical proxies having differing dates, the later-dated proxy will be given effect; thus where two proxies were submitted on behalf of the same record holder, purported to vote the same number of shares, and, each proxy was regular on its face; specifically, neither bore any facial indication that the person executing the proxy was unauthorized, both proxies were entitled to a presumption of validity, but the later-dated proxy would prevail. *Parshalle v. Roy, 567 A.2d 19 (Del. Ch. 1989)*.

Later postmark determines valid proxy if all have same execution date. — If a stockholder mails a proxy to one group after he or she has mailed one to the opposing group, the later mailing must be taken to show his or her intention in the matter. *Investment Assocs. v. Standard Power & Light Corp., 29 Del. Ch. 225, 48 A.2d 501 (1946)*, aff'd, *29 Del. Ch. 593, 51 A.2d 572 (1947); Concord Fin. Group, Inc. v. Tri-State Motor Transit Co., 567 A.2d 1 (Del. Ch. 1989)*.

As to proxies without an execution date or with the same execution date given by the same person to both the management and the opposition, but containing postmarks bearing the same date but a different time of day, the inspectors should under such a state of facts recognize the postmark time as determining the later executed and therefore the valid proxy. *Investment Assocs. v. Standard Power & Light Corp., 29 Del. Ch. 225, 48 A.2d 501 (1946)*, aff'd, *29 Del. Ch. 593, 51 A.2d 572 (1947)*.

Otherwise later execution date supersedes postmark. — The later execution date presumably written by the party herself must supersede the postmark date appearing on other proxies. *Investment Assocs. v. Standard Power & Light Corp., 29 Del. Ch. 225, 48 A.2d 501 (1946)*, aff'd, *29 Del. Ch. 593, 51 A.2d 572 (1947)*.

A later postmark date on a proxy is sufficient evidence of expressed intent so as to repeal a proxy containing a later execution date but an earlier postmark date. *Investment Assocs. v. Standard Power & Light Corp., 29 Del. Ch. 225, 48 A.2d 501 (1946)*, aff'd, *29 Del. Ch. 593, 51 A.2d 572 (1947)*.

Abandonment of agency. — It cannot be held that stockholders who give proxies notwithstanding the assumption of an intent on their part that the proxies would be acted upon, by the mere entertaining of such an intent can permanently fasten the relationship of agency upon those named in the proxies so that the latter cannot refuse to act. *Duffy v. Loft, Inc., 17 Del. Ch. 140, 151 A. 223 (1930),* aff'd, *17 Del. Ch. 376, 152 A. 849 (1930).*

Proxy signed in partnership name. — The practical considerations of business suggest that if a proxy is signed in the name of a partnership which is the registered holder of the stock, and the only criticism of it is that it was neither signed by all the members of the firm nor by one who affixes his or her own name as the representative of all, it nevertheless is entitled to be taken as presumptively genuine. *Gow v. Consolidated Coppermines Corp., 19 Del. Ch. 172, 165 A. 136 (1933).*

When corporate stock is recorded in the name of a partnership, and a proxy purporting to be signed in the partnership name is sent out by the stockholder, it is prima facie evidence that the signature thereto was authorized. *McLain v. Lanova Corp., 28 Del. Ch. 176, 39 A.2d 209 (1944).*

Where names of 2 tenants by the entirety appear on proxy it is prima facie valid, and one attacking a proxy bearing the names of both tenants must be prepared to assume the burden of demonstrating to the court that the person signing the proxy, assuming 1 person signed both names, was not authorized to sign for the other or that such signature was not adopted by the other person. *Investment Assocs. v. Standard Power & Light Corp., 29 Del. Ch. 225, 48 A.2d 501 (1946),* aff'd, *29 Del. Ch. 593, 51 A.2d 572 (1947).*

Appearance of prima facie authenticity. — When a firm in whose name stock is registered sends in a proxy signed in its name, it is reasonable to say that enough appears to give it the appearance of prima facie authenticity. *Gow v. Consolidated Coppermines Corp., 19 Del. Ch. 172, 165 A. 136 (1933).*

Whatever reasonably purports to be a proxy of a shareholder entitled to vote at an election is entitled to a prima facie presumption of validity. *Standard Power & Light Corp. v. Investment Assocs., 29 Del. Ch. 593, 51 A.2d 572 (1947).*

Absence of signer's authority. — Proxy signed by person in whose name stockholder stock was registered in care of on corporation's book was valid to vote stock even though the proxy did not indicate the signor's authority to sign the proxy card. *Concord Fin. Group, Inc. v. Tri-State Motor Transit Co., 567 A.2d 1 (Del. Ch. 1989).*

Use of initial instead of spelling out of christian name did not deprive proxy of appearance of authenticity. *Atterbury v. Consolidated Coppermines Corp., 26 Del. Ch. 1, 20 A.2d 743 (1941).*

Strict proof must be presented to prove forgery. — Whenever a charge of forgery is asserted pertaining to the validity of a proxy the court should exercise due care, demanding of the accuser strict proof in support of his or her challenge. The shareholder whose signature was allegedly forged should preferably be produced, and in any event the proof should be convincing to warrant a holding that there was a forgery. Corporate elections often produce heated arguments resulting in bitter accusations, and the Court must safeguard the shareholder in this respect; otherwise, he or she might be disenfranchised without cause. *Standard Power & Light Corp. v. Investment Assocs., 29 Del. Ch. 593, 51 A.2d 572 (1947).*

Fact that signature on proxy is not in handwriting of shareholder does not invalidate proxy. *Standard Power & Light Corp. v. Investment Assocs., 29 Del. Ch. 593, 51 A.2d 572 (1947).*

Use of proxies not to be restricted so as to prohibit use. — The use of proxies in corporate elections should not be hedged about by restrictions which, because of practical considerations, are almost prohibitive. *Atterbury v. Consolidated Coppermines Corp., 26 Del. Ch. 1, 20 A.2d 743 (1941).*

And general proxies have right to vote on all matters. — When stockholders give general proxies to their representatives and place no limitations upon the extent of the power conferred thereby, it must be assumed that the proxies were authorized to vote upon all matters that might come before the meeting in the ordinary and usual course. *Gow v. Consolidated Coppermines Corp., 19 Del. Ch. 172, 165 A. 136 (1933).*

Effect of execution of limited proxy. — Unless the certificate of incorporation provides to the contrary, the legal and practical effect of executing a limited proxy is that a stockholder will contribute to the establishment of a quorum and will be bound by a majority decision of the voting power present on a proposal from which he or she has withheld the authority to vote. *Berlin v. Emerald Partners, 552 A.2d 482 (Del. 1988).*

Agent presumed to express will of stockholder. — When a stockholder gives an unrestricted proxy, naming an attorney-in-fact to act in his or her stead, it must be presumed that what the attorney does in the proper exercise of the power conferred expresses the will of the stockholder. *Hexter v. Columbia Baking Co., 16 Del. Ch. 263, 145 A. 115 (1929); Chandler v. Bellanca Aircraft Corp., 19 Del. Ch. 57, 162 A. 63 (1932).*

It will be presumed that what the attorney does in the proper exercise of the power conferred expresses the will of the stockholders. *Hauth v. Giant Portland Cement Co., 33 Del. Ch. 496, 96 A.2d 233 (1953).*

When proxies were solicited by the management and their authority was unrestricted, and it is not established that there was any misrepresentation or fraud in their solicitation, it must be assumed that the stockholders expected that their proxies would be voted in accordance with the wishes of the majority of the board of directors, since they represent the management. *Hauth v. Giant Portland Cement Co., 33 Del. Ch. 496, 96 A.2d 233 (1953).*

So stockholder cannot repudiate acts of agent. — When a meeting of stockholders has been held, and corporate action authorized by the use of general proxies permitting the exercise of unlimited discretion by the proxy holder, and that action is duly taken, the stockholder ordinarily cannot later repudiate the action of his or her agent. *Dolese Bros. Co. v. Brown, 39 Del. Ch. 1, 157 A.2d 784 (1960).*

In the absence of fraud the fact that the management failed to notify the stockholders of its intention to vote the

Corporations

proxies which it received for someone other than the plaintiff is not sufficient ground to warrant the issuance of a preliminary injunction. *Hauth v. Giant Portland Cement Co., 33 Del. Ch. 496, 96 A.2d 233 (1953).*

Unless agent uses proxy to commit fraud. — The rule that a stockholder cannot repudiate action taken under a general proxy has no application to a case in which the dominating director is charged with using the proxies to commit a fraud concealed from the stockholders whose vote is necessary to accomplish it, and in which no rights of third parties are affected. *Dolese Bros. Co. v. Brown, 39 Del. Ch. 1, 157 A.2d 784 (1960).*

But stockholder can limit proxy's power in instrument. — If a stockholder is not content to authorize his or her proxy to act generally in his or her stead upon all such matters, he or she should restrict the proxy's power by the instrument defining it. *Gow v. Consolidated Coppermines Corp., 19 Del. Ch. 172, 165 A. 136 (1933).*

Failure to submit proxies held by persons in attendance did not defeat quorum. — When it is clear that a majority of the stock of the corporation was present, either in person or by proxy, at a meeting of stockholders regularly called for the purpose of electing directors, and that an election was held, it should not be declared invalid because certain stockholders holding proxies for stock necessary to make a quorum, and in attendance at the meeting, declined to submit their proxies to the meeting. *Duffy v. Loft, Inc., 17 Del. Ch. 376, 152 A. 849 (1930).*

Board of directors was sole body empowered to make proxy solicitations on behalf of management. *Gould v. American Hawaiian S.S. Co., 351 F. Supp. 853 (D. Del. 1972).*

Corporation is proper complainant in action seeking to enjoin persons from soliciting proxies, and thereafter from voting them when such solicitations are purportedly made pursuant to the authority of the board of directors contrary to the fact. *Empire S. Gas Co. v. Gray, 29 Del. Ch. 95, 46 A.2d 741 (1946).*

Stockholder not estopped by proxy to assert certain rights. — Where stockholder had no knowledge of the fact that the resolution in question was to be presented at the annual meeting and was informed that the management of the corporation intended to present no other items of business at the meeting, he or she is not estopped from asserting any right which he or she may have had relative thereto prior to the execution of his or her proxy. *Gottlieb v. McKee, 34 Del. Ch. 537, 107 A.2d 240 (1954).*

Telecopies, facsimile copies or datagram copies of proxies. — One-sided telecopies of proxy which did not appoint anyone to vote the shares because that information was contained on the other side of the proxy card not proper and attempt to vote shares properly refused. *Concord Fin. Group, Inc. v. Tri-State Motor Transit Co., 567 A.2d 1 (Del. Ch. 1989).*

Datagram proxies lacked the fundamental indicia of authenticity and genuineness needed to accord them a presumption of validity where the datagrams lacked any written signature or signature equivalent (such as a signature stamp or facsimile), or other identifying mark or characteristic that would verifiably link the proxy to a specific shareholder of record. *Parshalle v. Roy, 567 A.2d 19 (Del. Ch. 1989).*

Proxy overvoting stock it represents. — Where a proxy overvoted the stock it represented, and that error could not be corrected by looking at the face of the proxy or the books and records of the corporation, the proxy should have been disregarded with no votes attributable to that proxy being cast for either management or the opposition board candidates. *Concord Fin. Group, Inc. v. Tri-State Motor Transit Co., 567 A.2d 1 (Del. Ch. 1989).*

DELAWARE CASE NOTES — UNREPORTED

Construction with other law. — An analysis of § 253 in the context of the entire General Corporation Law provides no reason to assume that the General Assembly wished to prevent a corporation from providing a class of shareholders with a right of collective dissent without, at the same time, preventing a majority shareholder from exercising a right to employ a short form merger. As already noted, § 212(b) contemplates the ability of a shareholder both to vote and to consent. Section 253 implicates only the right to *vote* on a merger, as opposed to a general right to assent. The difference in language allows investors to agree, *ex ante,* to order their affairs the way they wish. On the one hand, investors may agree to provide preferred shareholders with a right of refusal and, at the same time, provide minority shareholders with protection against a short-form merger. If so, the preferred stock may be granted voting rights. If, on the other hand, preferred shareholders desire a collective right to block any merger, but see no advantage in granting protection to minority shareholders, those shares may bear a right to consent, but not a right to vote on the merger itself. Although the reasons for an investor to choose one set of protections over the other is not entirely clear, the law contemplates the ability to select either structure. *Matulich v. Aegis Communs. Group, Inc., 2007 Del. Ch. LEXIS 80 (May 31, 2007).*

Subsection (b) of this section simply gives a board the power to set a record date. All the charter provision in the instant case does is eliminate that power and put in its place a rule set forth in subsection (b) itself as one of the default rules that govern when the board does not exercise that power. By its plain terms, subsection (b) does not in any way indicate that its grant of authority may not be altered by a certificate provision. And subsection (b) also enables stockholders filing consents as to subjects not requiring prior board action — such as plaintiff's consent solicitation to remove directors — to preempt the board's discretion simply by filing a one-share consent. *Jones Apparel Group v. Maxwell Shoe Co., 2004 Del. Ch. LEXIS 74, No. 365-N (May 27, 2004).*

Charter provision was valid and its plain terms established the record date for consent solicitation. Both subdivision (b)(1) of Section 102 and subsection (a) of Section 141 of the Delaware Corporation Law ("DGCL") provide authority for charter provisions to restrict the authority that directors have to manage firms, unless those restrictions are "contrary to the laws of this State." These statutory provisions are important expressions of the wide room for private ordering authorized by the DGCL, when such private ordering is reflected in the corporate charter. The charter provision is a valid exercise of authority under those sections and is not contrary to law, in the sense that our courts have interpreted that phrase. A consideration of subsection (b) of this section's terms and legislative history, as well as of the related statutory section governing consent solicitations, Section 228, reveals that no public policy set forth in the DGCL (or in Delaware's common law of corporations) is contravened by the charter provision at issue. Given the absence of any conflict with a mandatory aspect of Delaware corporate law, the charter provision's restriction on the board's authority to set a record date was valid. *Jones Apparel Group v. Maxwell Shoe Co., 2004 Del. Ch. LEXIS 74, No. 365-N (May 27, 2004).*

Unenforceable because not executed. — Since stockholder agreement, which was a voting trust, was unenforceable under 8 Del. C. § 218 because it was not executed, the court dismissed a minority shareholders' claims related to: (1) the controller's alleged breach of that agreement; (2) shareholder's alleged detrimental reliance on the voting trust when the shares were bought; and (3) since the trust was not enforceable and since there was not the voting deadlock that there could have been had the trust been enforceable, the claim for 8 Del. C. § 226 custodial relief. *Dweck v. Albert Nassar & Kids Int'l Corp., 2005 Del. Ch. LEXIS 183 (Del. Ch. Nov. 23, 2005).*

CASE NOTES — OTHER STATES

Illinois

Payment of proxy expenses. — The Delaware Supreme Court has held that an incumbent board of directors may look to the corporation for payment of expenses incurred in soliciting proxies on a question of corporate policy. However, the Delaware court noted in its decision that there was a board resolution, which committed the corporation to pay the proxy expenses of any person running for election on the management slate. *Foley v. Santa Fe Pacific Corporation, 267 Ill. App. 3d 555, 641 N.E.2d 992, 204 Ill. Dec. 562 (1994).*

Maryland

Self-flagellation not required. — Under Delaware law, corporate fiduciaries are not required to engage in self-flagellation, as their duty of disclosure does not oblige them to characterize their conduct in such a way as to admit wrongdoing. *Paskowitz v. Wohlstadter, 151 Md. App. 1, 822 A.2d 1272 (2003).*

New Jersey

Beneficial owners of stock held in a street name could assert statutory rights. *Berger v. Berger, 249 N.J. Super. 305, 592 A.2d 321 (1991).*

Pennsylvania

Enjoinable director conduct. — Tinkering with corporate elections to interfere with shareholders' electoral rights violates a director's fiduciary duty to shareholders and is enjoinable. *Jewelcor Management, Inc. v. Thistle Group Holdings, Co., 2002 Phila. Ct. Com. Pl. LEXIS 79 (2004).*

Irreparable harm. — Under Delaware law, the deprivation of a shareholder's right to vote is irreparable harm. *Alan Wurtzel Commerce Program v. Park Towne Place Apartments Limited Partnership, 2001 Phila. Ct. Com. Pl. LEXIS 79 (2001).*

CASE NOTES — FEDERAL

First Circuit

Under Delaware law, the shareholder of record is entitled to vote the stock. *In re Consolidated Auto Recyclers, Inc., 123 B.R. 130 (Bankr. D.Me. 1991).*

Discrimination among shareholders permissible. — The Delaware courts distinguish between discrimination among shareholders and discrimination among shares, finding the former permissible: in the final analysis, these restrictions are limitations upon the voting rights of the stockholder not variations in the voting powers of the stock per se. The voting power of the stock in the hands of a large stockholder is not differentiated from all others in its class; it is the personal right of the stockholder to exercise that power that is altered by the size of his or her holding. Moreover, dicta in Delaware case law finds statutory authority for a discriminatory note purchase rights plan. *Georgia-Pacific Corp. v. Great Northern Nekoosa Corp., 728 F. Supp. 807 (D.Me. 1990).*

Second Circuit

Federal demand requirement. — Under Delaware law, a plaintiff asserting proxy claims need not comply with the federal demand requirement. False proxy claims are not subject to the demand requirement of Del. Ch. Ct. R. 23.1. *Katz v. Pels, 774 F. Supp. 121 (S.D.N.Y. 1991).*

Outstanding stock. — Delaware law defines "outstanding" stock as that which can be voted, and therefore, is construed to mean stock in the hands of shareholders, not stock in the treasury. *Satterfield v. Monsanto Co., 88 F. Supp. 2d 288 (S.D.N.Y. 2000).*

Approval of merger agreement. — Under Delaware law, any merger or consolidation of domestic corporations must meet a number of statutory requirements, including that, at a special meeting for the purpose of acting on the merger agreement, a majority of the outstanding stock of the corporation entitled to vote thereon shall be voted for the adoption of the agreement. Thus, in the context of a proxy vote to approve a merger agreement under Delaware law, a majority of all outstanding shares must vote "yes" in order to approve the merger; an abstention (or any vote other than "yes") is tantamount to a "no" vote. Moreover, when two proxies are offered bearing the same name, then the proxy that appears to have been last executed will be accepted and counted under the theory that the latter — that is, more recent — proxy constitutes a revocation of the former. *Money Group, Inc. v. Highfields Capital Management, L.P., 368 F.3d 138 (2d Cir. 2004).*

Third Circuit

Inherent conflict of interest. — Board action designed principally to interfere with the exercise of shareholder voting rights inherently involves a conflict of interest between the board and the shareholder majority. *Gregory v. Correction Connection, Inc., 1991 U.S. Dist. LEXIS 3659 (E.D.Pa. 1991).*

Fourth Circuit

Unequal treatment of shareholders. — Delaware courts recognize that in some circumstances Delaware law permits shareholders (as distinguished from shares) to be treated unequally. *Williams v. 5300 Columbia Pike Corp., 891 F. Supp. 1169 (E.D.Va. 1995).*

Sixth Circuit

The contract for a post-record date sale of stock implicitly includes the transfer of voting rights for the corresponding shareholders meeting. *United Dominion Industries, Ltd. v. Commercial Intertech Corp., 943 F. Supp. 857 (S.D.Ohio 1996).*

Seventh Circuit

Interest necessary to support revocability of proxies. — Del. Code Ann. tit. 8, § 212(c) sets forth the traditional rule concerning revocability of proxies, based on the law of agency. The interest necessary in order to support irrevocability may be, for example, security for a loan, title to the stock itself, or, in more recent cases, an employee's interest in the corporation. *Calumet Industries, Inc. v. MacClure, 464 F. Supp. 19 (N.D. Ill. 1978).*

The fundamental difference between purportedly irrevocable consents and the voting agreement described in Del. Code Ann. tit. 8, § 218 is that the voting agreement is a contract whereby the shareholders

exchange promises, each in consideration of the other. The consents are given gratuitously, and thus are not part of an enforceable voting agreement. *Calumet Industries, Inc. v. MacClure, 464 F. Supp. 19 (N.D. Ill. 1978).*

Eighth Circuit

Regulation of election process by another state. — An attempt by another state to regulate the solicitation and voting of proxies by a stockholder in a Delaware corporation impermissibly burdens interstate commerce in violation of the Commerce Clause. No other state has a legitimate local interest in regulating the election process of a Delaware corporation. *National City Lines, Inc. v. LLC Corp., 1981 U.S. Dist. LEXIS 16475, (W.D.Mo. 1981).*

Ninth Circuit

Proxy solicitation is a proper purpose for the inspection of stock ledgers. *Cenergy Corp. v. Bryson Oil & Gas P.L.C., 662 F. Supp. 1144 (D.Nev. 1987).*

In order for proxy solicitation to be a proper purpose for the inspection of stock ledgers, the shareholder seeking the ledgers must have formed a bona fide intention to solicit proxies. *Cenergy Corp. v. Bryson Oil & Gas P.L.C., 662 F. Supp. 1144 (D.Nev. 1987).*

Eleventh Circuit

Duty of disclosure while soliciting votes. — Under Delaware law, majority shareholders do owe minority shareholders a duty to disclose material information. Minority shareholders state a claim upon which relief can be granted against majority shareholders who provided allegedly misleading information in connection with the solicitation of votes. *Chalk Line Mfg. v. Frontenac Venture V, Ltd., 1994 Bankr. LEXIS 1087 (Bankr N.D.Ala. 1994).*

Veto rights of holders of preferred stock. — Under the Delaware Corporation Law, the holders of the preferred stock had the right as a class to vote upon and veto any proposed amendment of the charter which would alter or change the preferences, special rights, or powers of the preferred so as to affect the preferred adversely, or which would increase or decrease the amount of preferred or the par value. *Penfield v. Davis, 105 F. Supp. 292 (N.D. Ala. 1952).*

§ 213. Fixing date for determination of stockholders of record

DELAWARE CASE NOTES — REPORTED

One purpose of this section is to permit and facilitate reasonable methods of notification. *Bryan v. Western Pac. R.R. Corp., 28 Del. Ch. 13, 35 A.2d 909 (1944).*

The underlying purpose of this section is to facilitate reasonable methods of notification by recognizing the practical necessity of dispensing with notice to persons who attempt to become registered shareholders shortly before a meeting. *Pabst Brewing Co. v. Jacobs, 549 F. Supp. 1068 (D. Del. 1982).*

Exception to strict construction. — Strict construction with provisions governing the time limits within a record date for notice of a shareholder meeting was normally required, but one-day deviation was allowed (for one time only), where corporation relied in good faith on

decisional law that appeared to calculate the sixty-day limit differently. *McKesson Corp. v. Derdiger, 793 A.2d 385 (Del. Ch. 2002).*

Corporation is entitled to rely on its stock list in determining who is entitled to vote. *Schott v. Climax Molybdenum Co., 38 Del. Ch. 450, 154 A.2d 221 (1959).*

Delaware law expressly recognizes the right of the corporation to rely upon record ownership, not beneficial ownership, in determining who is entitled to notice of and to vote at the meetings of stockholders; in dealing with its stockholders, a Delaware corporation need not look beyond the registered owners. Therefore, from the perspective of the Delaware corporation, a broker who is the stockholder of record, has the legal authority to vote in person or by

Corporations

proxy on all matters. *Berlin v. Emerald Partners, 552 A.2d 482 (Del. 1988).*

Time limits of subsection (a) balance interests of corporation and its shareholders by allowing the corporation sufficient time to determine shareholders in order to give effective notice of corporate action and assuring that the shareholders who vote have an interest in the corporation. *Pabst Brewing Co. v. Jacobs, 549 F. Supp. 1068 (D. Del. 1982).*

Consents are only valid for 60-day period set forth in subsection (a). *Pabst Brewing Co. v. Jacobs, 549 F. Supp. 1068 (D. Del. 1982).*

Subsection (b) applies whenever a record date has not been fixed by the time the first written consent is filed. *Midway Airlines v. Carlson, 628 F. Supp. 244 (D. Del. 1985).*

Former use of words "is expressed" in the statute required that the executor of a written consent who sought to impose a stockholder record date on a corporation had to clearly, explicitly, directly and unmistakeably make that known to the corporation. *Empire of Carolina, Inc. v. Deltona Corp., 501 A.2d 1252 (Del. Ch. 1985), aff'd, 505 A.2d 452 (Del. 1985).*

Setting of record date by board of directors. — Where setting of record date by corporation's board of directors was not in violation of this section, the board's action was likewise not in violation of § 228 of this title; the board of directors of a corporation is not mandated to set a record date which would give any stockholder an advantage with respect to taking action by written consent. *Empire of Carolina, Inc. v. Deltona Corp., 501 A.2d 1252 (Del. Ch. 1985), aff'd, 505 A.2d 452 (Del. 1985).*

Where stockholder has not complied with subsection (b) of this section the board of directors was authorized to set the record date under this section notwithstanding § 228 of this title. *Empire of Carolina, Inc. v. Deltona Corp., 514 A.2d 1091 (Del. 1985).*

The setting of a record date for a stockholder vote must be accomplished by a board resolution adopted before the record date, and under § 141(c)(2) of this title, a board may delegate this task to a one-person board committee, but this board committee must itself comply with subsection (a) of this section by adopting a resolution fixing a future record date. *In re Staples, Inc. Shareholders Litig., 792 A.2d 934 (Del. Ch. 2001).*

Where the drafters of a corporation charter

Statement in solicitation that consents are valid for longer period is materially misleading. — A statement in a solicitation for consents that the consents will remain in full force and effect for a period longer than the 60-day period set forth in subsection (a) of this section is materially misleading. *Pabst Brewing Co. v. Jacobs, 549 F. Supp. 1068 (D. Del. 1982).*

Change of record date after first consent filed. — The statutory language and the underlying policy considerations support the conclusion that a corporate board does not have the power to change the record date after the first consent has been filed. *Midway Airlines v. Carlson, 628 F. Supp. 244 (D. Del. 1985).*

CASE NOTES — FEDERAL

Sixth Circuit

The contract for a post-record date sale of stock implicitly includes the transfer of voting rights for the corresponding shareholders meeting. *United Dominion Industries, Ltd. v. Commercial Intertech Corp., 943 F. Supp. 857 (S.D.Ohio 1996).*

§ 214. Cumulative voting

DELAWARE CASE NOTES — REPORTED

Cumulative voting does not assure minority representation. — While the right of cumulative voting has for its purpose the affording to a minority of the voting stock an opportunity to elect 1 or more directors, the scheme does not pretend to assure to a minority a representation in any event, since the enjoyment of the right is a thing incident to each share of stock. *Maddock v. Vorclone Corp., 17 Del. Ch. 39, 147 A. 255 (1929).*

Unauthorized cumulative voting does not negate ballot. — If cumulative voting is not given in the certificate of incorporation there would be only one legal method of computation of votes, and even a clearly expressed desire to vote cumulatively would be nugatory and surplusage, but would not destroy the legal effect of the ballot where the ballot clearly expresses the names to be voted for and the number of votes cast. *Standard Scale & Supply Corp. v. Chappel, 16 Del. Ch. 331, 141 A. 191 (1928).*

But where 2 ways of voting are possible, voter, who by his or her ballot shows intent to vote cumulatively, cannot have his or her ballot counted as straight. *Chappel v. Standard Scale & Supply Corp., 15 Del. Ch. 333, 138 A. 74 (1927), rev'd on other grounds, 16 Del. Ch. 331, 141 A. 191 (1928).*

Right of cumulative voting may be given up. — Special rights, such as cumulative voting, may be resigned by the appropriate vote of the majority of those enjoying them. *Maddock v. Vorclone Corp., 17 Del. Ch. 39, 147 A. 255 (1929).*

When a majority of the shares outstanding vote to take away the right of 1 share to vote with cumulative strength, those who compose that majority take from themselves, as well as from those who compose the then minority, a right which is common to all. *Maddock v. Vorclone Corp., 17 Del. Ch. 39, 147 A. 255 (1929).*

Majority stockholders have power to remove director for cause even where there is provision for cumulative voting. *Campbell v. Loew's, Inc., 36 Del. Ch. 563, 134 A.2d 852 (1957).*

§ 215. Voting rights of members of nonstock corporations; quorum; proxies

DELAWARE CASE NOTES — UNREPORTED

Quorum requirement met. — Maintenance corporation directors were authorized to bring suit against defendants (who admitted that they placed personal property on open space in a housing development and failed to remove the property), as the directors of the corporation were elected by a quorum. *Fairthorne Maint. Corp. v. Ramunno, 2007 Del. Ch. LEXIS 107 (Del. Ch. July 20, 2007).*

CASE NOTES — OTHER STATES

New York

Compensable damages. — Under Delaware law, corporate officers, directors, and controlling shareholders owe their corporation and its minority shareholders a fiduciary obligation of honesty, loyalty, good faith, and fairness. Delaware law imposes a duty upon corporations to disclose all available material information when obtaining shareholder approval. Only damages caused by the breach of fiduciary duty are compensable. *Lama Holding Company v. Smith Barney Inc., 88 N.Y.2d 413, 668 N.E.2d 1370, 646 N.Y.S.2d 76 (1996).*

Pennsylvania

Enjoinable director conduct. — Tinkering with corporate elections to interfere with shareholders' electoral rights violates a director's fiduciary duty to shareholders and is enjoinable. *Jewelcor Management, Inc. v. Thistle Group Holdings, Co., 2002 Phila. Ct. Com. Pl. LEXIS 79 (2004).*

Irreparable harm. — Under Delaware law, the deprivation of a shareholder's right to vote is irreparable harm. *Alan Wurtzel Commerce Program v. Park Towne Place Apartments Limited Partnership, 2001 Phila. Ct. Com. Pl. LEXIS 79 (2001).*

CASE NOTES — FEDERAL

District of Columbia Circuit

The inspection rights set out in § 220 do not apply to members of nonstock corporations. *Fleisher Dev. Corp. v. Home Owners Warranty Corp., 647 F. Supp. 661 (D.D.C. 1986).*

§ 216. Quorum and required vote for stock corporations

DELAWARE CASE NOTES — REPORTED

Mere abstention from meeting of sufficient number will prevent quorum's existence, except perhaps for adjournment purposes. *Hexter v. Columbia Baking Co., 16 Del. Ch. 263, 145 A. 115 (1929).*

But failure to ascertain and announce quorum does not defeat meeting. *Atterbury v. Consolidated Coppermines Corp., 26 Del. Ch. 1, 20 A.2d 743 (1941).*

And quorum present at stockholders' meeting cannot be broken by withdrawals. *Duffy v. Loft, Inc., 17 Del. Ch. 376, 152 A. 849 (1930); Atterbury v. Consolidated Coppermines Corp., 26 Del. Ch. 1, 20 A.2d 743 (1941).*

A shareholder or proxy holder, once having attended a meeting, should be deemed present for quorum purposes in the absence of some unusual circumstances. *Atterbury v. Consolidated Coppermines Corp., 26 Del. Ch. 1, 20 A.2d 743 (1941).*

Unless there is justifiable reason for withdrawal. — When a quorum is once present, the meeting organized and transacting business however little, there must be some justifiable reason for withdrawal by anyone to break the quorum, before such withdrawal can be allowed the effect of destroying the meeting. *Hexter v. Columbia Baking Co., 16 Del. Ch. 263, 145 A. 115 (1929).*

Not mere whim, caprice or chagrin. — If withdrawing stockholders are animated by a purpose solely to destroy the meeting by breaking a quorum because of whim, caprice or chagrin, the law will consider their action as unavailing and will permit the meeting to proceed. *Hexter v. Columbia Baking Co., 16 Del. Ch. 263, 145 A. 115 (1929).*

Quorum remains through all sessions of meeting. — All sessions are but a part of the same meeting, and if there is no requirement in the corporate bylaws, or otherwise, a quorum remains continuously throughout a meeting. *Atterbury v. Consolidated Coppermines Corp., 26 Del. Ch. 1, 20 A.2d 743 (1941).*

Stock not entitled to vote cannot be counted to help make a quorum on an issue on which it cannot vote. *Italo Petro. Corp. of Am. v. Producers' Oil Corp. of Am., 20 Del. Ch. 283, 174 A. 276 (1934).*

Failure to submit proxies does not defeat quorum. — A meeting should not be declared invalid because certain stockholders holding proxies for stock necessary to make a quorum, and in attendance at the meeting, declined to submit their proxies to the meeting. *Duffy v. Loft, Inc., 17 Del. Ch. 376, 152 A. 849 (1930).*

Written evidence of authority need not be submitted to count proxies toward quorum. — When proxies were solicited on the theory that the shares represented by them would be represented at the meeting and the agents designated to represent them were in fact present, the absence or failure to show the written evidence of their authority cannot destroy the fact of its existence, so that those proxies can be counted in concluding that a quorum was present. *Duffy v. Loft, Inc., 17 Del. Ch. 140, 151 A. 223 (1930),* aff'd, *17 Del. Ch. 376, 152 A. 849 (1930).*

Stockholder who holds proxies to be counted in 2 capacities. — Where persons are authorized to appear as shareholders and also as a proxy committee for other shareholders, at a stockholders' meeting, they must be regarded as present in both capacities in determining a quorum. *Atterbury v. Consolidated Coppermines Corp., 26 Del. Ch. 1, 20 A.2d 743 (1941).*

Determination of voting power present. — A stockholder who is present by proxy for quorum purposes may not be voting power present for all purposes; voting power present is synonymous with the number of shares represented which are entitled to vote on the subject matter. *Berlin v. Emerald Partners, 552 A.2d 482 (Del. 1988).*

A stockholder who is present in person or represented at a meeting by a general proxy, is present for quorum purposes and is also voting power present on all matters; however, if the stockholder is represented by a limited proxy and does not empower its holder to vote on a particular proposal, then the shares represented by that proxy cannot be considered as part of the voting power present with respect to that proposal. *Berlin v. Emerald Partners, 552 A.2d 482 (Del. 1988).*

Majority of votes cast, provided quorum is present, is sufficient to elect. *Standard Power & Light Corp. v. Investment Assocs., 29 Del. Ch. 593, 51 A.2d 572 (1947).*

If majority rule is not to be observed, then certificate of incorporation provision must not be couched in ambiguous language, rather the language employed must be positive, explicit, clear and readily understandable and susceptible to but 1 reasonable interpretation, which would indicate beyond doubt that the rule was intended to be abrogated. *Standard Power & Light Corp. v. Investment Assocs., 29 Del. Ch. 593, 51 A.2d 572 (1947).*

Supermajority approval must be clear and unambiguous. — Although a proposed operating lease to finance expansion of a proposed pipeline project would expose the pipeline company to indebtedness, it was not indebtedness for borrowed money as specifically set forth in the pipeline company's articles of incorporation; therefore, supermajority shareholder approval was not required. *In re Explorer Pipeline Co., 781 A.2d 705 (Del. Ch. 2001).*

DELAWARE CASE NOTES — UNREPORTED

An abstention and a vote withheld because of the absence of any instruction are materially different for purposes of Delaware law, and that an abstention, whether accomplished in person or through a proxy holder following his principal's instructions, is part of the "voting power present." *Licht v. Storage Tech. Corp., 2005 Del. Ch. LEXIS 64, No. 524-N (May 13, 2005).*

Under Delaware law, there is a distinction between an abstention and the lack of authority to vote; the shares represented at the meeting by a proxy holder who has been directed to abstain are present at that meeting and entitled to vote; that they are not voted affirmatively or negatively does not change their status as constituting voting power present. *Licht v. Storage Tech. Corp., 2005 Del. Ch. LEXIS 64, No. 524-N (May 13, 2005).*

CASE NOTES — FEDERAL

First Circuit

Presumption of quorum validity. — Under Delaware law, a corporation's bylaws may specify the requisites of a quorum. Any action purportedly taken at a meeting lacking a quorum is a nullity. The court may, moreover, inquire into the underlying facts to determine the existence of a quorum despite the records of that meeting. But the parties challenging the validity of the meeting must prove the lack of quorum in the face of a presumption of validity. *Feldman v. Detarando, 1980 U.S. Dist. LEXIS 14272 (D.Mass 1980).*

Second Circuit

Presumption of quorum validity. — Where there are numerous shareholders it is not essential to court a quorum before voting, the question of a quorum may be determined when the votes are counted, if no statute or bylaw prohibits this procedure. Further, the courts always indulge in every reasonable intendment in favor of the conclusiveness of the meeting in passing on the question of the presence of a quorum. *Phillips v. United Corp., 1947 U.S. Dist. LEXIS 3123 (S.D.N.Y. 1947).*

§ 217. Voting rights of fiduciaries, pledgors and joint owners of stock

DELAWARE CASE NOTES — REPORTED

Fiduciaries may vote stock although not stockholders. — There could be no possible point in this section conferring the right upon fiduciaries to vote unless it was intended that they could exercise that right without becoming stockholders of record, for if they became such they would possess the right otherwise by reason of § 219 of this title. *Gow v. Consolidated Coppermines Corp., 19 Del. Ch. 172, 165 A. 136 (1933).*

Executor or administrator has right to vote shares registered in name of decedent. *Investment Assocs. v. Standard Power & Light Corp., 29 Del. Ch. 225, 48 A.2d 501 (1946),* aff'd, *29 Del. Ch. 593, 51 A.2d 572 (1947).*

Without short certificate. — The signature of the executor or administrator, with an appropriate indication of his or her capacity, is sufficient evidence of his or her

Corporations

authority to vote, and something more, e.g., a short certificate is not required as a matter of law. *Investment Assocs. v. Standard Power & Light Corp., 29 Del. Ch. 225, 48 A.2d 501 (1946)*, aff'd, *29 Del. Ch. 593, 51 A.2d 572 (1947)*.

Broker holding stock in margin account may vote such shares. — There is no "policy" which is frustrated by construing the statute to permit a broker holding shares in a margin account to vote such shares. This is so where the corporate books do not show that they are qualifiedly held or when the pledgor does not attempt to vote them. *Schott v. Climax Molybdenum Co., 38 Del. Ch. 450, 154 A.2d 221 (1959)*.

Clarification of voting rights between pledgors and pledgees. — This section was enacted primarily to clarify voting rights as between pledgors and pledgees and it also gives the corporation a definite rule it can follow in

conducting an election. *Schott v. Climax Molybdenum Co., 38 Del. Ch. 450, 154 A.2d 221 (1959)*.

Pledgor may vote even though he or she is no longer stockholder of record. — Under this section it is clear that a pledgor or fiduciary may vote the stock even though he or she is no longer the stockholder of record. *Gow v. Consolidated Coppermines Corp., 19 Del. Ch. 172, 165 A. 136 (1933)*.

Where names of 2 tenants by the entirety appear on proxy it is prima facie valid, and one attacking a proxy bearing the names of both tenants must be prepared to assume the burden of demonstrating to the Court that the person signing the proxy (assuming 1 person signed both names) was not authorized to sign for the other or that such signature was not adopted by the other person. *Investment Assocs. v. Standard Power & Light Corp., 29 Del. Ch. 225, 48 A.2d 501 (1946)*, aff'd, *29 Del. Ch. 593, 51 A.2d 572 (1947)*.

CASE NOTES — OTHER STATES

New Jersey

Beneficial owners of stock held in a street name could assert statutory rights. *Berger v. Berger, 249 N.J. Super. 305, 592 A.2d 321 (1991)*.

Pennsylvania

Irreparable harm. — Under Delaware law, the deprivation of a shareholder's right to vote is irreparable harm. *Alan Wurtzel Commerce Program v. Park Towne Place Apartments Limited Partnership, 2001 Phila. Ct. Com. Pl. LEXIS 79 (2001)*.

CASE NOTES — FEDERAL

First Circuit

Under Delaware law, the shareholder of record is entitled to vote the stock. *In re Consolidated Auto Recyclers, Inc., 123 B.R. 130 (Bankr. D.Me. 1991)*.

Seventh Circuit

Under Delaware law, shares pledged as collateral by a shareholder can still be voted by the shareholder. *Weinstein v. Schwartz, 2005 U.S. App. LEXIS 18976 (7th Cir. 2005)*.

§ 218. Voting trusts and other voting agreements

DELAWARE CASE NOTES — REPORTED

Delaware has discarded presumptions against voting agreements. *Schreiber v. Carney, 447 A.2d 17 (Del. Ch. 1982)*.

Effect of section is to authorize and to provide mechanics for voting trust. *Appon v. Belle Isle Corp., 29 Del. Ch. 122, 46 A.2d 749*, aff'd sub nom. *Belle Isle Corp. v. Corcoran, 29 Del. Ch. 554, 49 A.2d 1 (1946)*.

This section provides the exclusive method for creating voting trusts of stock of a Delaware corporation. *Ringling v. Ringling Bros. — Barnum & Bailey Combined Shows, Inc., 29 Del. Ch. 318, 49 A.2d 603 (1946)*, modified, *29 Del. Ch. 610, 53 A.2d 441 (1947)*.

Voting trusts derive their validity solely from this section. *Abercrombie v. Davies, 36 Del. Ch. 371, 130 A.2d 338 (1957)*.

While this section does not expressly state it is exclusive, the case law rather pointedly supports the view that this section provides the exclusive method for creating voting trusts of stock of a Delaware corporation. *Oceanic Exploration Co. v. Grynberg, 428 A.2d 1 (Del. 1981)*.

Section defines public policy of state with respect to voting trust agreements and the limitations on that

policy. *Aldridge v. Franco Wyo. Oil Co., 24 Del. Ch. 126, 7 A.2d 753 (1939)*, aff'd, *24 Del. Ch. 349, 14 A.2d 380 (1940)*; *Appon v. Belle Isle Corp., 29 Del. Ch. 122, 46 A.2d 749*, aff'd sub nom. *Belle Isle Corp. v. Corcoran, 29 Del. Ch. 554, 49 A.2d 1 (1946)*.

This section was not intended to be all inclusive in the sense that it was designed to apply to every set of facts in which voting rights are transferred to trustees incident to or as part of the assignment of other stockholder rights. *Oceanic Exploration Co. v. Grynberg, 428 A.2d 1 (Del. 1981)*.

Agreements and combinations to vote stock or control corporate action and policy are valid, if they seek without fraud to accomplish only what the parties might do as stockholders and do not attempt it by illegal proxies, trusts or other means in contravention of statutes or law. *Ringling v. Ringling Bros. — Barnum & Bailey Combined Shows, Inc., 29 Del. Ch. 318, 49 A.2d 603 (1946)*, modified, *29 Del. Ch. 610, 53 A.2d 441 (1947)*.

Voting trusts and voting trust agreements with respect to Delaware corporations derive their validity from limited statutory authorization. *Belle Isle Corp. v. Corcoran, 29 Del. Ch. 554, 49 A.2d 1 (1946).*

Provisions of section governing voting trusts are mandatory. *Perry v. Missouri-Kansas Pipe Line Co., 22 Del. Ch. 33, 191 A. 823 (1937); Smith v. Biggs Boiler Works Co., 32 Del. Ch. 147, 82 A.2d 372 (1951); Abercrombie v. Davies, 36 Del. Ch. 371, 130 A.2d 338 (1957).*

Compliance with an affirmative requirement of this section cannot be used as an excuse for failure to comply with some other affirmative and substantial requirement of the same section. *Appon v. Belle Isle Corp., 29 Del. Ch. 122, 46 A.2d 749, aff'd sub nom. Belle Isle Corp. v. Corcoran, 29 Del. Ch. 554, 49 A.2d 1 (1946).*

To establish the relationship and accomplish the purpose which this section authorizes, its requirements must be complied with. *Ringling Bros. — Barnum & Bailey Combined Shows, Inc. v. Ringling, 29 Del. Ch. 610, 53 A.2d 441 (1947).*

And courts should not be liberal in construing this section which lays down for voting trusts the law of their life. *Perry v. Missouri-Kansas Pipe Line Co., 22 Del. Ch. 33, 191 A. 823 (1937).*

The Court of Chancery is committed to the principle that this section reflects the public policy towards voting trusts, which is to require a rather strict control. *Appon v. Belle Isle Corp., 29 Del. Ch. 122, 46 A.2d 749, aff'd sub nom. Belle Isle Corp. v. Corcoran, 29 Del. Ch. 554, 49 A.2d 1 (1946).*

The broad powers granted by this section permit for a limited time the divorce of control from ownership and the persons availing themselves of such provision may expect to have it applied literally. *Adams v. Clearance Corp., 35 Del. Ch. 318, 116 A.2d 893 (1955), aff'd, 118 A.2d 924 (Del. 1956).*

The Delaware voting trust statute, being in derogation of the common law, must be strictly construed. *Adams v. Clearance Corp., 35 Del. Ch. 318, 116 A.2d 893 (1955), aff'd, 118 A.2d 924 (Del. 1956).*

Validity of agreement affecting voting rights is tested by law of incorporation. *Ringling v. Ringling Bros. — Barnum & Bailey Combined Shows, Inc., 29 Del. Ch. 318, 49 A.2d 603 (1946), modified, 29 Del. Ch. 610, 53 A.2d 441 (1947).*

Criteria of voting trust are as follows: (1) The voting rights of the stock are separated from the other attributes of ownership; (2) the voting rights granted are intended to be irrevocable for a definite period of time; and (3) the principal purpose of the grant of voting rights is to acquire voting control of the corporation. *Lehrman v. Cohen, 43 Del. Ch. 222, 222 A.2d 800 (1966).*

Not all trusts with voting rights are voting trusts. — Not all trusts of corporate stock which, either expressly or by implication, give voting rights to a trustee are voting trusts. *Oceanic Exploration Co. v. Grynberg, 428 A.2d 1 (Del. 1981).*

This section contemplates association of stockholders whether it be created by way of individual agreements or joint agreements. *Oceanic Exploration Co. v. Grynberg, 428 A.2d 1 (Del. 1981).*

Subsection (a) forbids secret voting trusts. *Abercrombie v. Davies, 36 Del. Ch. 371, 130 A.2d 338 (1957); Oceanic Exploration Co. v. Grynberg, 428 A.2d 1 (Del. 1981).*

The main purpose of this section is to avoid secret, uncontrolled combinations of stockholders formed to acquire voting control of the corporation to the possible detriment of nonparticipating shareholders. *Lehrman v. Cohen, 43 Del. Ch. 222, 222 A.2d 800 (1966).*

So as to protect stockholders, beneficiaries and corporate officers. — The provision in subsection (a) of this section respecting the filing of a copy of voting trust in the principal office in Delaware open to the inspection of any stockholder or any beneficiary of the trust is a provision obviously for the benefit of all stockholders and of all beneficiaries of the trust, who are entitled to know where voting control of a corporation resides; and the provision for transfer of the stock on the corporate books necessarily serves, though perhaps only incidentally, a similar purpose with respect to the officers and directors. *Abercrombie v. Davies, 36 Del. Ch. 371, 130 A.2d 338 (1957).*

Trustees must file agreement and surrender certificates for transfer. — This section gives rise to duties, on the part of voting trustees who have accepted the trust, to file a copy of the agreement and surrender the stock certificates for transfer and these directions become operative by force of this section alone, and not by virtue of any repetition in the agreement. *Hirschwald v. Erlebacher, Inc., 27 Del. Ch. 43, 29 A.2d 798 (1943).*

For transfer of stock on books is characteristic feature of voting trust. — Transfer of the stock on the books is not essential to effect an irrevocable transfer of voting rights to fiduciaries, divorced from the other attributes of the stock, in order to secure voting control but it is such a transfer that is the characteristic feature of a voting trust. *Abercrombie v. Davies, 36 Del. Ch. 371, 130 A.2d 338 (1957).*

And this duty enforceable by cotrustees or stockholders. — The cotrustee's duty to surrender the stock certificate for transfer, and the company's duty to issue new certificates, are enforceable by the other cotrustee as well as by a depositing stockholder, who, as a party to the agreement, is a beneficiary of the trust. *Hirschwald v. Erlebacher, Inc., 27 Del. Ch. 43, 29 A.2d 798 (1943).*

But trust may be enforced even if agreement not filed. — Although no attempt was made to comply with the statutory provisions concerning the filing of a copy of the agreement until this action was filed, there is no showing of any intention on defendants' part to abandon the agreement and intervening rights of third persons are not involved, and there has been no change of position on the part of the petitioner or the other concerned parties in reliance on any supposed abandonment, therefore the voting trust agreement should be specifically enforced. *In re Farm Indus., Inc., 41 Del. Ch. 379, 196 A.2d 582 (1963).*

Deposit of shares required. — A voting trust agreement is invalid where the mandate of subsection (a) of this section requiring a deposit of the shares with the voting trustees was not and could not be complied with. *Smith v.*

Biggs Boiler Works Co., 32 Del. Ch. 147, 82 A.2d 372 (1951).

Type of agreement determined from instrument of creation. — Whether a particular agreement constitutes a voting trust, and, therefore, what its real purpose and intent is, must ordinarily be ascertained from that instrument, when read as a whole, and the rights and powers given thereby. *Aldridge v. Franco Wyo. Oil Co., 24 Del. Ch. 126, 7 A.2d 753 (1939),* aff'd, *24 Del. Ch. 349, 14 A.2d 380 (1940).*

The provisions of the instrument determine its legal effect, and if they clearly create a voting trust, any intention of the parties to the contrary is immaterial. *Abercrombie v. Davies, 36 Del. Ch. 371, 130 A.2d 338 (1957).*

Parties may contract for terms as to both substance and mechanics. — If there is no offense against statute or public policy, parties to trust agreements are at liberty to adopt any provisions as to either substance or mechanics which they may choose to adopt. *Chandler v. Bellanca Aircraft Corp., 19 Del. Ch. 57, 162 A. 63 (1932); Scott v. Arden Farms Co., 26 Del. Ch. 283, 28 A.2d 81 (1942); Clarke Mem. College v. Monaghan Land Co., 257 A.2d 234 (Del. Ch. 1969); Winitz v. Kline, 288 A.2d 456 (Del. Ch. 1971).*

This section, in authorizing the creating of a voting trust, expressly empowers the parties thereto to state the terms and conditions of it in the agreement. *Chandler v. Bellanca Aircraft Corp., 19 Del. Ch. 57, 162 A. 63 (1932).*

The parties to a voting trust may agree upon what terms they please, so long as the purpose is not one that the law deems to be illegal. *Perry v. Missouri-Kansas Pipe Line Co., 22 Del. Ch. 33, 191 A. 823 (1937).*

And powers of voting trustees must be found in voting trust agreement itself. *Brady v. Mexican Gulf Sulphur Co., 32 Del. Ch. 372, 88 A.2d 300 (1952).*

The powers and obligations of trustees of a voting trust must be ascertained from the terms of the voting trust agreement as a whole and not from reading 1 provision to nullify another. *Clarke Mem. College v. Monaghan Land Co., 257 A.2d 234 (Del. Ch. 1969).*

Trustees determine policy and implement it by their votes. *Ringling v. Ringling Bros. — Barnum & Bailey Combined Shows, Inc., 29 Del. Ch. 318, 49 A.2d 603 (1946),* modified, *29 Del. Ch. 610, 53 A.2d 441 (1947).*

Stockholders continuing to vote own stock. — When stockholders under a voting agreement vote their own stock at all times, this is the antithesis of a voting trust, because the latter has for its chief characteristic the severance of the voting rights from the other attributes of ownership. *Ringling v. Ringling Bros. — Barnum & Bailey Combined Shows, Inc., 29 Del. Ch. 318, 49 A.2d 603 (1946),* modified, *29 Del. Ch. 610, 53 A.2d 441 (1947).*

An arrangement whereby stockholders have not divested themselves of their voting rights, although they may have diluted their voting powers, is not controlled by this section. *Lehrman v. Cohen, 43 Del. Ch. 222, 222 A.2d 800 (1966).*

Control of trustee by stockholder does not prevent formation of voting trust. — The fact that the agents of the stockholders are subject to control by their respective principals does not prevent an agreement from constituting a voting trust, where the stock is voted by the agents as a group, no 1 stockholder retains complete control over the voting of its stock, it cannot vote its own stock directly, all it can do is to direct its agent how to vote on a decision to be made by the agents as a group, the stock of any stockholder may at any time be voted against its will by the vote of the other agents, and the control of the agents rests upon provisions that they are severally chosen by the respective stockholders and each may be removed and replaced by the stockholder he or she represents. *Abercrombie v. Davies, 36 Del. Ch. 371, 130 A.2d 338 (1957).*

That each corporate stockholder participating in a voting agreement reserves the right to name and remove the fiduciary or fiduciaries representing him or her is not inconsistent with a voting trust. *Abercrombie v. Davies, 36 Del. Ch. 371, 130 A.2d 338 (1957).*

Voting trust not necessary result of recapitalization plan. — In any recapitalization involving the creation of additional voting stock, the voting power of the previously existing stock is diminished; but a voting trust is not necessarily the result. *Lehrman v. Cohen, 43 Del. Ch. 222, 222 A.2d 800 (1966).*

Voting rights divorced from ownership. — A voting trust as commonly understood is a device whereby 2 or more persons owning stock with voting powers, divorce the voting rights thereof from the ownership, retaining to all intents and purposes the latter in themselves and transferring the former to trustees in whom the voting rights of all the depositors in the trust are pooled. *Peyton v. William C. Peyton Corp., 22 Del. Ch. 187, 194 A. 106 (1937),* rev'd on other grounds, *23 Del. Ch. 321, 7 A.2d 737 (1939); Aldridge v. Franco Wyo. Oil Co., 24 Del. Ch. 126, 7 A.2d 753 (1939),* aff'd, *24 Del. Ch. 349, 14 A.2d 380 (1940); Ringling v. Ringling Bros. — Barnum & Bailey Combined Shows, Inc., 29 Del. Ch. 318, 49 A.2d 603 (1946),* modified, *29 Del. Ch. 610, 53 A.2d 441 (1947); Smith v. Biggs Boiler Works Co., 33 Del. Ch. 183, 91 A.2d 193 (1952); Abercrombie v. Davies, 36 Del. Ch. 371, 130 A.2d 338 (1957); Oceanic Exploration Co. v. Grynberg, 428 A.2d 1 (Del. 1981).*

A shareholder may effectively confer his or her voting rights upon others while retaining various other rights. *Ringling Bros. — Barnum & Bailey Combined Shows, Inc. v. Ringling, 29 Del. Ch. 610, 53 A.2d 441 (1947).*

The primary purpose behind the passage of the statute legalizing voting trusts was to authorize the separation of voting rights from the other attributes of ownership for a protracted period. *Tracey v. Franklin, 30 Del. Ch. 407, 61 A.2d 780 (1948),* aff'd, *31 Del. Ch. 477, 67 A.2d 56 (1949).*

Under a voting trust agreement the voting power of the stock is separated from the beneficial interest, the trustee or trustees holding such legal title as is necessary to separate the interest. *Smith v. Biggs Boiler Works Co., 33 Del. Ch. 183, 91 A.2d 193 (1952).*

The 1 essential feature that characterizes a voting trust is the separation of the voting rights of the stock from the other attributes of ownership. *Abercrombie v. Davies, 36 Del. Ch. 371, 130 A.2d 338 (1957)*.

What the public policy underlying the voting trust statute means to control is the separation of the vote from the stock, not from the stock ownership; thus there is nothing in this section, either expressed or implied, which requires that all stock of a Delaware corporation must have both voting rights and proprietary interests. *Lehrman v. Cohen, 43 Del. Ch. 222, 222 A.2d 800 (1966)*.

A stockholder who deposits his or her stock in a voting trust parts with his or her voting right but retains beneficial ownership of the stock; neither the depositor nor the trustee is a stockholder for all purposes. *Clarke Mem. College v. Monaghan Land Co., 257 A.2d 234 (Del. Ch. 1969)*.

In its narrowest context a voting trust is an agreement between stockholders on one side and a trustee on the other whereby rights to vote the stock are transferred to and vested in the trustee. *Clarke Mem. College v. Monaghan Land Co., 257 A.2d 234 (Del. Ch. 1969); Winitz v. Kline, 288 A.2d 456 (Del. Ch. 1971)*.

A stockholder who deposits his or her stock in a voting trust parts with his or her voting rights but retains "beneficial" ownership. *Winitz v. Kline, 288 A.2d 456 (Del. Ch. 1971)*.

By the very nature of a voting trust, all interest in deposited shares remains in the beneficiary of the trust except the right to vote them, and that is vested in the trustees. *Winitz v. Kline, 288 A.2d 456 (Del. Ch. 1971)*.

An agreement involving the transfer of stock voting rights without the transfer of ownership is not necessarily illegal and each arrangement must be examined in light of its object or purpose. *Schreiber v. Carney, 447 A.2d 17 (Del. Ch. 1982)*.

Test for determining applicability of subsections (a) and (b) of this section is whether the substance and purpose of the stock arrangement is sufficiently close to the substance and the purpose of this section to warrant its being subject to the restrictions and conditions imposed by this section. *Oceanic Exploration Co. v. Grynberg, 428 A.2d 1 (Del. 1981)*.

Holder of voting trust certificate may have rights and liabilities of shareholder. — Under certain circumstances, a holder of a voting trust certificate has the rights of a stockholder in the corporation; and, conversely, the holder has for certain purposes the liability of a stockholder. *Winitz v. Kline, 288 A.2d 456 (Del. Ch. 1971)*.

Person who accepts assignment of shares accepts trust. — Those who enter into an agreement with shareholders for the purpose of creating a "voting trust," within the meaning of this section, and who accept the assignment of shares of stock to be held under the terms of the agreement, thereby accept the trust. *Hirschwald v. Erlebacher, Inc., 27 Del. Ch. 43, 29 A.2d 798 (1943)*.

Division of voting powers among trustees sanctioned. — A division of voting power equally among voting trustees would not, of itself, create a hardship, for such division is expressly sanctioned by this section. *Hirschwald v. Erlebacher, Inc., 27 Del. Ch. 180, 33 A.2d 148 (1943), aff'd, 36 A.2d 167 (Del. 1944)*.

Shareholders bound by vote of trustee within scope of his or her authority. — Although voting trust certificate holders may, for some purposes, exercise the rights of stockholders with respect to the shares held in the voting trust, they are manifestly bound by the acts of the voting trustees, done in good faith and within the scope of their authority, in carrying out purposes of the trust. *Scott v. Arden Farms Co., 26 Del. Ch. 283, 28 A.2d 81 (1942)*.

Sole trustees. — Subsection (a) of this section contemplates in the phrase "person or persons" that an individual might be selected as a sole trustee. *Chandler v. Bellanca Aircraft Corp., 19 Del. Ch. 57, 162 A. 63 (1932)*.

Voting by proxy. — Where the agreement so provides, one trustee can appoint by proxy another one to act for him or her in the matter of reaching the decision by the trustees or a majority of them which must precede the formal casting of the vote. *Chandler v. Bellanca Aircraft Corp., 19 Del. Ch. 57, 162 A. 63 (1932)*.

This section permits voting trustees to vote by proxy. *Brady v. Mexican Gulf Sulphur Co., 32 Del. Ch. 372, 88 A.2d 300 (1952)*.

Where the voting trust instrument merely gives the trustees voting control, it does not give them powers sufficient to create a proxy coupled with an interest. *Brady v. Mexican Gulf Sulphur Co., 32 Del. Ch. 372, 88 A.2d 300 (1952)*.

Rules and regulations need not be adopted by trustees. — There is no statutory provision which makes it imperative that rules and regulations shall be adopted as a condition precedent to the exercise by the trustees of their functions. *Chandler v. Bellanca Aircraft Corp., 19 Del. Ch. 57, 162 A. 63 (1932)*.

Trustees may vote on resolution to sell substantially all corporate assets. — The trustees of a voting trust have the right to vote shares which they hold on a stockholders' resolution authorizing the sale of substantially all corporate assets. *Clarke Mem. College v. Monaghan Land Co., 257 A.2d 234 (Del. Ch. 1969)*.

To determine whether the action of trustees in voting for the sale of assets was within their powers, one must look to the agreement establishing the trust. *Clarke Mem. College v. Monaghan Land Co., 257 A.2d 234 (Del. Ch. 1969)*.

Principal object of voting trust is voting control. *Abercrombie v. Davies, 36 Del. Ch. 371, 130 A.2d 338 (1957)*.

And to insure continuity of control. — In utilizing the corporate instrumentality of the voting trust, modern business has convinced courts that this divorce of ownership from control is not without practical necessity, especially where the purpose of such voting trust is to obtain and insure continuity of control for a definite and substantial period of years and thereby, among other things, to facilitate a financial and corporate reorganization of the company and for its subsidiaries. *Hearst v. American Newspapers, Inc., 51 F. Supp. 171 (D. Del. 1943)*.

Voting trustees have continuous voting control for period of time stipulated in the agreement of

trust. *Ringling v. Ringling Bros. — Barnum & Bailey Combined Shows, Inc., 29 Del. Ch. 318, 49 A.2d 603 (1946)*, modified, *29 Del. Ch. 610, 53 A.2d 441 (1947)*.

Changes may be made in extension agreement. — Nothing in this section prevents parties from incorporating in an extension agreement certain changes in the provisions of the original voting trust agreement. *Appon v. Belle Isle Corp., 29 Del. Ch. 122, 46 A.2d 749,* aff'd sub nom. *Belle Isle Corp. v. Corcoran, 29 Del. Ch. 554, 49 A.2d 1 (1946)*.

Renewal must be within stated time period. — The provision requiring renewal within the stated period immediately preceding the termination date of the voting trust is a matter of substance and is mandatory. *Appon v. Belle Isle Corp., 29 Del. Ch. 122, 46 A.2d 749,* aff'd sub nom. *Belle Isle Corp. v. Corcoran, 29 Del. Ch. 554, 49 A.2d 1 (1946)*.

The provision of this section requiring, in effect, that an agreement of extension must be signed within the stated period prior to the expiration date of the agreement sought to be extended cannot be cast aside as unimportant. While any number of reasons may have prompted the General Assembly to incorporate this provision into the law, 1 reason was to make certain the period of the voting trust could not be extended until near the end of the trust itself, at which time it could be intelligently determined by the stockholders whether the purposes for which it was created had been defeated, altered or accomplished. *Appon v. Belle Isle Corp., 29 Del. Ch. 122, 46 A.2d 749,* aff'd sub nom. *Belle Isle Corp. v. Corcoran, 29 Del. Ch. 554, 49 A.2d 1 (1946)*.

Invalid extension invalidates election determined by votes of trustees. — Where a voting trust is invalid as an extension of the voting trust agreement, and it did not constitute a new or independent voting trust agreement, no election can be upheld where the determinative vote resulted from the votes cast by voting trustees. *Belle Isle Corp. v. Corcoran, 29 Del. Ch. 554, 49 A.2d 1 (1946)*.

Invalid restraints on alienation of beneficial interests are such an integral part of the agreement that the entire agreement should be held unenforceable. *Tracey v. Franklin, 31 Del. Ch. 477, 67 A.2d 56 (1949)*.

This section does not authorize expressly restraints on the alienation of the beneficial interests remaining in the shareholders, and such restraints are not necessary incidents of a voting trust. *Tracey v. Franklin, 31 Del. Ch. 477, 67 A.2d 56 (1949)*.

The public policy against restraints may be relaxed where the circumstances of a particular case convince the court that it is a reasonable means of accomplishing a purpose recognized as proper. But, where owners of property attempt mutually to restrain the alienation of their property for a substantial period, some purpose must appear, other than an unexplained desire to make it inalienable, in order that the restraint be enforceable. *Tracey v. Franklin, 31 Del. Ch. 477, 67 A.2d 56, 11 A.L.R. 990 (1949)*.

Voting restraints rendered unenforceable. — Application of Delaware law rendered voting restriction provisions in agreement unenforceable where they expired, pursuant to the terms of this section. *Rosenmiller v. Bordes, 607 A.2d 465 (Del. Ch. 1991)*.

Corporate stockholder may deposit its shares in voting trust. *Adams v. Clearance Corp., 35 Del. Ch. 459, 121 A.2d 302 (1956)*.

This is exception to nondelegation of duty rule. — Whenever any stock owned by a corporation is deposited in a voting trust, the directors of the depositary corporation have relinquished, to the extent of the stock deposited, their duty to vote the stock, and hence may be said to have delegated that duty and this delegation of the directors' duty to vote stock is therefore an exception to the general rule of nondelegation, carved out by the statute itself. *Adams v. Clearance Corp., 35 Del. Ch. 459, 121 A.2d 302 (1956)*.

But directors responsible for abuse of power. — The directors have the legal power to deposit in a voting trust any and all shares of stock owned by their corporation, being responsible to a court of equity for the abuse of that power. *Adams v. Clearance Corp., 35 Del. Ch. 459, 121 A.2d 302 (1956)*.

When members of charitable corporation are members only because they are trustees of the corporation, their membership status is coincidental with their fiduciary obligation to manage the affairs of the corporation in keeping with its charitable purpose to benefit deserving members of the public. As such, they are not stockholders, have no personal ownership rights which they can contract away and are not governed by this section and § 350 of this title, which recognize and enforce agreements among stockholders. *Chapin v. Benwood Found., Inc., 402 A.2d 1205 (Del. Ch.)*, aff'd, *415 A.2d 1068 (Del. 1979)*.

Voting trust is equitable trust subject to trust laws. — A voting trust is a trust in the accepted equitable sense and is subject to the principles which regulate the administration of trusts. *Chandler v. Bellanca Aircraft Corp., 19 Del. Ch. 57, 162 A. 63 (1932); Smith v. Biggs Boiler Works Co., 33 Del. Ch. 183, 91 A.2d 193 (1952)*.

Some of the principles of trust law are applicable to voting trusts. *Tracey v. Franklin, 30 Del. Ch. 407, 61 A.2d 780 (1948),* aff'd, *31 Del. Ch. 477, 67 A.2d 56 (1949)*.

A voting trust is a true trust and subject to the rules of equity in respect to trusts. *Adams v. Clearance Corp., 35 Del. Ch. 459, 121 A.2d 302 (1956)*.

Court has power to remove trustee. — The power to remove a trustee is ancillary to the duty of the Court to see that the trust is administered properly and that power will generally be exercised sparingly. *Smith v. Biggs Boiler Works Co., 33 Del. Ch. 183, 91 A.2d 193 (1952)*.

Such as when there is discord between trustee and corporation. — When discord has reached such a state that a trustee has refused to discuss matters of business of importance to the company to such extent that the welfare of the company is thereby jeopardized, then the continuance in office of that trustee would be detrimental both to the trust and to the best interests of the company. *Smith v. Biggs Boiler Works Co., 33 Del. Ch. 183, 91 A.2d 193 (1952)*.

Trust will not be continued for sole purpose of enabling trustees to earn their compensation. *H.M. Byllesby & Co. v. Doriot, 25 Del. Ch. 46, 12 A.2d 603 (1940).*

This section does not prescribe that voting trusts shall be irrevocable, nor that the principles governing the revocability of other express trusts should not apply to voting trusts. *H.M. Byllesby & Co. v. Doriot, 25 Del. Ch. 46, 12 A.2d 603 (1940).*

The mere statement in a trust instrument that it shall be irrevocable is not sufficient to prevent termination by the sole settlor who is the sole beneficiary. *H.M. Byllesby & Co. v. Doriot, 25 Del. Ch. 46, 12 A.2d 603 (1940).*

Since voting trust is sui generis it may also be a valid and enforceable contract. *Hearst v. American Newspapers, Inc., 51 F. Supp. 171 (D. Del. 1943).*

As when lender lends to corporation in reliance on voting trust. — Where banks were lending to corporation upon the faith of voting trust agreement, which could only be terminated with the consent of the lending banks, such banks could treat as nullity sole depositing shareholder's notice of termination of the agreement notwithstanding that banks may have had the right to call their loans or sue for damages and trustee could assert against shareholder such banks' right to have the trust continue. *Hearst v. American Newspapers, Inc., 51 F. Supp. 171 (D. Del. 1943).*

Where persons make loans on the basis of a voting trust agreement, the agreement cannot be terminated by the settlor without their consent, especially where the instrument of deposit contemplates such affirmative consent. *Hearst v. American Newspapers, Inc., 51 F. Supp. 171 (D. Del. 1943).*

Word "beneficiaries" in subsection (b) refers to stockholder-creators of voting trust. *Foye v. New York Univ., 269 A.2d 63 (Del. 1970).*

A "beneficiary" of a voting trust is the stockholder concerned with, and relieved of, the vote and control of the corporation for purposes that seemed good and sufficient to him or her when he or she entered into the voting trust agreement. *Foye v. New York Univ., 269 A.2d 63 (Del. 1970).*

Holding of bare legal title and custody of stock certificates do not make persons beneficiaries of trust. *H.M. Byllesby & Co. v. Doriot, 25 Del. Ch. 46, 12 A.2d 603 (1940).*

And settlor must intend to give beneficial interest. — To constitute a person a beneficiary, the settlor must manifest an intention to give him or her a beneficial interest, and unless there be such a manifestation, the fact that a person may incidentally benefit from the performance of the trust does not make him or her a beneficiary. *H.M. Byllesby & Co. v. Doriot, 25 Del. Ch. 46, 12 A.2d 603 (1940).*

Parties to alleged voting trust agreement, or outside stockholders, if injured thereby, may ordinarily attack validity of such agreement. *Aldridge v. Franco Wyo. Oil Co., 24 Del. Ch. 126, 7 A.2d 753 (1939), aff'd, 24 Del. Ch. 349, 14 A.2d 380 (1940).*

The fact that a person is a party to an illegal voting trust agreement does not preclude him or her from attacking it. *Appon v. Belle Isle Corp., 29 Del. Ch. 122, 46 A.2d 749, aff'd sub nom. Belle Isle Corp. v. Corcoran, 29 Del. Ch. 554, 49 A.2d 1 (1946).*

Clean hands not necessary to attack voting trust. — The public policy of the State would be frustrated in part if a court were to prevent a person otherwise having a proper standing to complain from asserting that a particular voting trust agreement violates this section because such person does not come into court with clean hands, or because there are facts which would otherwise justify an estoppel. While it is evident that in such a situation the court is met with 2 conflicting policies, nevertheless, the courts resolve the conflict in favor of the public policy of the State as set forth in the section and set aside an agreement in violation. *Appon v. Belle Isle Corp., 29 Del. Ch. 122, 46 A.2d 749, aff'd sub nom. Belle Isle Corp. v. Corcoran, 29 Del. Ch. 554, 49 A.2d 1 (1946).*

Settlement of suits. — In stockholders' suit to cancel a voting trust, where the directors of the corporation produced evidence that they had acted in good faith and free from disqualifying interest in settling the complaint, the suit will be defeated, and with that finding on the corporation's behalf, equity court will not inquire into the merits of the settlement. *Perrine v. Pennroad Corp., 28 Del. Ch. 342, 43 A.2d 721 (1945), aff'd, 29 Del. Ch. 531, 47 A.2d 479 (1946), cert. denied, 329 U.S. 808, 67 S. Ct. 620, 91 L. Ed. 690 (1947).*

Good faith on the part of corporate directors may be impugned by a showing that the settlement of a complaint is so unfair and grossly inadequate, from the standpoint of the corporation, as to impel the conclusion that it emanates from acts of bad faith, or a reckless indifference to the rights of others interested, rather than a reasonable exercise of business judgment. *Perrine v. Pennroad Corp., 28 Del. Ch. 342, 43 A.2d 721 (1945), aff'd, 29 Del. Ch. 531, 47 A.2d 479 (1946).*

Stock-pooling agreement is to be distinguished from voting trust; such agreements are distinct from voting trusts, and are not controlled by same principles. *Ringling v. Ringling Bros. — Barnum & Bailey Combined Shows, Inc., 29 Del. Ch. 318, 49 A.2d 603 (1946), modified on another point, 29 Del. Ch. 610, 53 A.2d 441 (1947).*

In pooling agreement owners of shares combine and vote them in accordance with agreement. *Smith v. Biggs Boiler Works Co., 32 Del. Ch. 147, 82 A.2d 372 (1951).*

There must be means of resolving differences between pool members. — By its very nature a pooling agreement admits of the possibility of differences among the stockholders and consequently, such an agreement, to be effective, must not only recognize the possibility of differences but must also provide the mechanics for resolving them in a manner which will permit collective action. *Abercrombie v. Davies, 35 Del. Ch. 599, 123 A.2d 893 (1956), rev'd on other grounds, 36 Del. Ch. 371, 130 A.2d 338 (1957).*

Not all pooling agreements are lawful. *Abercrombie v. Davies, 36 Del. Ch. 371, 130 A.2d 338 (1957).*

Corporations

If agreement occupies field of voting trust it must follow this section. — If any stockholders' agreement providing for joint or concerted voting is so drawn as in effect to occupy the field reserved for the statutory voting trust, it is illegal, whatever mechanics may be devised to attain the result. *Abercrombie v. Davies, 36 Del. Ch. 371, 130 A.2d 338 (1957)*.

As a pooling agreement in substance and purpose approaches more and more nearly the substance and purpose of subsection (a) of this section, there comes a point at which, if the subsection is not complied with, the agreement is illegal. A pooling agreement may not escape the statutory controls by calling the trustees agents and giving to the stockholders receipts instead of voting trust certificates. *Abercrombie v. Davies, 36 Del. Ch. 371, 130 A.2d 338 (1957)*.

No deposit of stock and no fiduciaries indicate pooling agreement. — Where 2 stockholders agreed to act jointly in exercising their voting rights and there was no deposit of the stock with irrevocable stock powers conferring upon a group of fiduciaries exclusive voting powers over the pooled stock, the case involved a true pooling agreement, far short of a voting trust. *Abercrombie v. Davies, 36 Del. Ch. 371, 130 A.2d 338 (1957)*.

DELAWARE CASE NOTES — UNREPORTED

Impartiality. — It is settled law in the area of trusts that where there are two or more beneficiaries of a trust, the trustee is under a duty to deal impartially with them; where voting trustees enter into a shareholder agreement, the voting trustees owe a duty to all beneficiaries, not the parties to a shareholder agreement only. *President & Fellows of Harvard Coll. v. Glancy, 2003 Del. Ch. LEXIS 25 (Mar. 21, 2003)*.

Unambiguous language. — Where the language of a voting trust agreement is unambiguous, the intent of the parties subject to it must therefore be determined from its terms. *President & Fellows of Harvard Coll. v. Glancy, 2003 Del. Ch. LEXIS 25 (Mar. 21, 2003)*.

Duty to provide basic information. — Decision about whom to elect as a director has to be considered an essential term of any voting trust agreement, and a trustee has a duty to furnish requested information to the beneficiaries of a trust about basic trust terms; moreover, a trustee may not give one beneficiary materially greater access to information and influence over the trust decisions than another beneficiary, and even in the absence of a request for information, a trustee must communicate essential facts, such as the existence of the basic terms of the trust. *President & Fellows of Harvard Coll. v. Glancy, 2003 Del. Ch. LEXIS 25 (Mar. 21, 2003)*.

Amendments. — Any agreement, oral or otherwise, that purportedly binds shareholder groups or voting trustees to act in a manner distinct from the voting trust agreement necessarily must be considered an amendment.. *President & Fellows of Harvard Coll. v. Glancy, 2003 Del. Ch. LEXIS 25 (Mar. 21, 2003)*.

With respect to any unwritten agreements granting shareholder groups the right to designate successor voting trustees and directors, to remain in compliance with this section, an amendment of this type shall be made by written agreement, a copy of which shall be filed in the registered office of the corporation in Delaware. *President & Fellows of Harvard Coll. v. Glancy, 2003 Del. Ch. LEXIS 25 (Mar. 21, 2003)*.

Shareholder agreement amended a voting trust agreement by obligating the voting trustees to vote their shares in a specific manner that would guarantee that the four shareholder groups subject to the shareholder agreement: (1) had equal director representation on the corporation's board; (2) had combined director representation that would constitute a majority of the corporation's board; and (3) had a veto fixing the number of directors at 6, unless each of the 4 shareholder groups consented; these rights and obligations had the effect of altering the original terms of the voting trust, and therefore the shareholder agreement was considered an amendment to the voting trust agreement. *President & Fellows of Harvard Coll. v. Glancy, 2003 Del. Ch. LEXIS 25 (Mar. 21, 2003)*.

Management vote buying. — Shareholder complaint to set aside a merger vote stated a cognizable cause of action upon which relief could be granted, where the allegations (if true) created a reasonable inference of improper vote-buying activity and material misrepresentations by corporate management; although shareholders were free to do whatever they wanted with their votes (including selling them to the highest bidder) management could not use corporate assets to buy votes in a hotly contested proxy contest about an extraordinary transaction that would significantly transform the corporation, unless it could be demonstrated that management's vote-buying activity did not have a deleterious effect on the corporate franchise. *Hewlett v. Hewlett-Packard Co., 2002 Del. Ch. LEXIS 44 (Del. Ch. Apr. 8, 2002)*.

Unenforceable because not executed. — Since stockholder agreement, which was a voting trust, was unenforceable under 8 Del. C. § 218 because it was not executed, the court dismissed a minority shareholders' claims related to: (1) the controller's alleged breach of that agreement; (2) shareholder's alleged detrimental reliance on the voting trust when the shares were bought; and (3) since the trust was not enforceable and since there was not the voting deadlock that there could have been had the trust been enforceable, the claim for 8 Del. C. § 226 custodial relief. *Dweck v. Albert Nassar & Kids Int'l Corp., 2005 Del. Ch. LEXIS 183 (Del. Ch. Nov. 23, 2005)*.

Since the voting agreement was not enforceable under 8 Del. C. § 218(c) because it was not signed, the court could not estop one party from denying the enforceability of that voting agreement; to have estopped that party from denying the enforcement of that agreement by promissory estoppel would have circumvented the plain requirement under 8 Del. C. § 218(c) that a stockholder voting agreement was required to be in writing and to be signed by the parties. *Dweck v. Albert Nassar & Kids Int'l Corp., 2005 Del. Ch. LEXIS 183 (Del. Ch. Nov. 23, 2005)*.

CASE NOTES — OTHER STATES

Illinois

Duration. — As of 1985, Delaware limited shareholder voting agreements to a duration of 10 years. The time limit was removed in 1994, and presently Delaware does not limit the duration of shareholder voting agreements; however, the former time limit applies to voting agreements entered into prior to July 1, 1994. *Newell Company v. Petersen, 325 Ill. App. 3d 661, 758 N.E.2d 903, 259 Ill. Dec. 495 (2001).*

New Jersey

Purpose of voting trust. — The Delaware Supreme Court has held that the principal purpose of a voting trust is to acquire voting control of a corporation. *Genway Corp. v. Director, 8 N.J. Tax 198 (1986).*

Determination of voting trust. — Whether an instrument denominated as a voting trust is in fact and law a voting trust or something else must be ascertained from the instrument read as a whole. *Genway Corp. v. Director, 8 N.J. Tax 198 (1986).*

New York

Enforceable agreement. — When all of the stockholders of a Delaware corporation agree that, except as specified in their agreement, no "business or activities" of the corporation shall be conducted without the consent of a minority stockholder, the agreement is, as between the original parties to it, enforceable even though all formal steps required by statute have not been taken. *Zion v. Kurtz, 50 N.Y.2d 92, 405 N.E.2d 681, 428 N.Y.S.2d 199 (1980).*

A written agreement between the holders of a majority of a corporation's stock is not invalid, as between the parties to the agreement, on the ground that it so relates to the conduct of the business and affairs of the corporation as to restrict or interfere with the discretion or powers of the board of directors or on the ground that it is an attempt by the parties to the agreement or by the stockholders of the corporation to treat the corporation as if it were a partnership. *Zion v. Kurtz, 50 N.Y.2d 92, 405 N.E.2d 681, 428 N.Y.S.2d 199 (1980).*

A provision of a shareholders agreement concerning corporate action is enforceable even though it was not contained, as required by the Delaware statute, in the certificate of incorporation. *Herbert H. Lehman College Foundation, Inc v. Fernandez, 292 A.D.2d 227, 739 N.Y.S.2d 375 (2002).*

Fiduciary duty. — Under Delaware law, a controlling shareholder owes a fiduciary duty to other shareholders. *Richbell Information Services, Inc. v. Jupiter Partners, L.P., 309 A.D.2d 288, 765 N.Y.S.2d 575 (2003).*

Reforming certificate of incorporation. — Delaware law does not prohibit shareholders from taking all management functions away from the directors of a close corporation, therefore, the certificate of incorporation can be ordered reformed where there are no intervening rights of third persons, and the agreement requires nothing that is not permitted by statute, and all of the stockholders of the corporation assented to it. Under such circumstances, a court may presume that the shareholders intended to perform the "ministerial" act of amending the certificate of incorporation to effectuate the provisions of the agreement. *Herbert H. Lehman College Foundation, Inc v. Fernandez, 292 A.D.2d 227, 739 N.Y.S.2d 375 (2002).*

Pennsylvania

Irreparable harm. — Under Delaware law, the deprivation of a shareholder's right to vote is irreparable harm. *Alan Wurtzel Commerce Program v. Park Towne Place Apartments Limited Partnership, 2001 Phila. Ct. Com. Pl. LEXIS 79 (2001).*

Enjoinable director conduct. — Tinkering with corporate elections to interfere with shareholders' electoral rights violates a director's fiduciary duty to shareholders and is enjoinable. *Jewelcor Management, Inc. v. Thistle Group Holdings, Co., 2002 Phila. Ct. Com. Pl. LEXIS 79 (2004).*

Virginia

In general. — Delaware law defines a voting trust as a device whereby two or more persons owning stock with voting powers, divorce the voting rights thereof from the ownership, retaining to all intents and purposes the latter in themselves and transferring the former to trustees in whom the voting rights of all the depositors in the trust are pooled. *State ex rel. Elish v. Wilson, 189 W. Va. 739, 434 S.E.2d 411 (1993).*

CASE NOTES — FEDERAL

Seventh Circuit

Irrevocable consents distinguished. — The fundamental difference between purportedly irrevocable consents and the voting agreement described in Del. Code Ann. tit. 8, § 218 is that the voting agreement is a contract whereby the shareholders exchange promises, each in consideration of the other. The consents are given gratuitously, and thus are not part of an enforceable voting agreement. *Calumet Industries, Inc. v. MacClure, 464 F. Supp. 19 (N.D. Ill. 1978).*

District of Columbia Circuit

Effect on shareholders' rights. — Directors and officers of a corporation manage the company for the benefit of its shareholders and they owe those shareholders fiduciary duties to manage the company in an acceptable manner. A voting trust adds nothing to shareholders' rights in this regard, but rather takes away from them the right to vote their stock on certain issues. *Foltz v. U.S. News & World Report, Inc., 663 F. Supp. 1494 (D.D.C. 1987).*

§ 219. List of stockholders entitled to vote; penalty for refusal to produce; stock ledger

DELAWARE CASE NOTES — REPORTED

Purposes of registration. — The purposes of the registration of shares are to provide a practical means whereby the corporation may ascertain the names of the persons with whom it may ordinarily deal as shareholders and to afford a means whereby a "real" owner may readily become entitled to notification and recognition as a shareholder. *In re Northeastern Water Co., 28 Del. Ch. 139, 38 A.2d 918 (1944).*

The list of stockholders is a continuing list for all proper purposes. State *ex rel. Healy v. Superior Oil Corp., 40 Del. 460, 13 A.2d 453 (1940).*

And voting list is designed to give stockholder information, and this must mean information that he or she may intelligently make use of at the election. *Magill v. North Am. Refractories Co., 36 Del. Ch. 185, 128 A.2d 233 (1956).*

As information requisite for conduct of meeting will be contained in voting list. *Magill v. North Am. Refractories Co., 36 Del. Ch. 185, 128 A.2d 233 (1956).*

A secondary purpose of subsection (a) of this section is to provide a convenient tool for the use of the officers or of the inspectors of election in ascertaining the presence of a quorum and in computing the vote upon all matters submitted to the meeting for decision. *Magill v. North Am. Refractories Co., 36 Del. Ch. 185, 128 A.2d 233 (1956).*

But voting list not same as stock ledger. — The list under subsection (a) of this section is a voting list, compiled as of a specific date for a specific occasion; it is not the same thing as the stock ledger, which is a continuing record of stockholdings, reflecting entries drawn from the transfer books, and including (in modern times) nonvoting as well as voting stock. *Magill v. North Am. Refractories Co., 36 Del. Ch. 185, 128 A.2d 233 (1956).*

And stock ledger is final authority as to who is entitled to vote. *Magill v. North Am. Refractories Co., 36 Del. Ch. 185, 128 A.2d 233 (1956).*

Real owner runs risk in registering stock in name of nominee. — The real owners must be taken to know that 1 of the consequences of permitting their stock to be held in the name of a nominee is that the latter will normally have the power to vote the shares without obtaining the consent of the owners, and that the corporation will recognize the registered owner as the true owner for purpose of voting the stock. *Atterbury v. Consolidated Coppermines Corp., 26 Del. Ch. 1, 20 A.2d 743 (1941).*

So far as the corporation is concerned, the record owner must be regarded as the real owner of the stock, with the consequent general right to vote it by proxy, or otherwise. *In re Giant Portland Cement Co., 26 Del. Ch. 32, 21 A.2d 697 (1941).*

The record owner may be the mere nominal owner, or, technically a trustee for the holder of the certificate, but legally he or she is still a stockholder in the corporation, and so far as the corporation is concerned, like the usual trustee, ordinarily has the right to vote the stock standing in his or her name. *In re Giant Portland Cement Co., 26 Del. Ch. 32, 21 A.2d 697 (1941).*

Where shares are so registered, as not to reveal the relationship of the real owner, the real owner necessarily runs risks that his or her interests may be prejudiced by the acts of the holder of record. *In re Northeastern Water Co., 28 Del. Ch. 139, 38 A.2d 918 (1944).*

Failure to have shares registered so as to indicate an interest in others than the registered holder may reasonably be deemed a manifestation of intent that the corporation should deal freely with the registered holder as the true owner without investigating his or her authority. *In re Northeastern Water Co., 28 Del. Ch. 139, 38 A.2d 918 (1944).*

No one but a registered stockholder is, as a matter of right, entitled to vote, and if an owner of stock chooses to register his or her shares in the name of a nominee, he or she takes the risks attendant upon such an arrangement, including the risk that he or she may not receive notice of corporate proceedings, or be able to obtain a proxy from his or her nominee. The corporation is entitled to recognize the exclusive right of the registered owner to vote. *American Hdwe. Corp. v. Savage Arms Corp., 37 Del. Ch. 59, 136 A.2d 690 (1957).*

And corporation has ordinarily discharged its obligation when it mails notice to the record owner. *American Hdwe. Corp. v. Savage Arms Corp., 37 Del. Ch. 59, 136 A.2d 690 (1957).*

Record owner has power to represent stock at meeting. *Atterbury v. Consolidated Coppermines Corp., 26 Del. Ch. 1, 20 A.2d 743 (1941).*

Unregistered stockholder is not entitled to inject himself or herself into intracorporate matters, in respect of which the corporation is entitled to rely on its stock register in dealing with its stockholders. *Coyne v. Schenley Indus., Inc., 38 Del. Ch. 535, 155 A.2d 238 (1959).*

But may record transfer of his or her shares. — A nonregistered stockholder always had it in his or her power to record the transfer of his shares, and hence is not deprived of any essential right if the corporation looks to the corporate books as sole evidence of membership. *Coyne v. Schenley Indus., Inc., 38 Del. Ch. 535, 155 A.2d 238 (1959).*

Right of fiduciaries to vote. — There could be no possible point in § 217 of this title conferring the right upon fiduciaries to vote unless it was intended that they could exercise that right without becoming stockholders of record, for if they became such they would possess the right otherwise by reason of this section. *Gow v. Consolidated Coppermines Corp., 19 Del. Ch. 172, 165 A. 136 (1933).*

Special meetings provided by bylaw. — Despite this section's 10-day posting period, a bylaw providing for a special meeting of stockholders on 5 days' notice to elect directors, can be lawfully adopted. *Moon v. Moon Motor Car. Co., 17 Del. Ch. 176, 151 A. 298 (1930).*

Subsection (c) is not origin of right to vote. — Subsection (c) of this section provides a limited but practical statutory rule of evidence whereby the persons entitled to notice of and to vote at a stockholders' meeting can be readily ascertained by an inspection of the corporate records; but it is in no sense the real origin of the stockholder's right to vote. *In re Giant Portland Cement Co., 26 Del. Ch. 32, 21 A.2d 697 (1941).*

And court not bound by showing on books. — The Court of Chancery in the exercise of its reviewing jurisdiction over elections of directors is not bound by the showing made on the books. *In re Canal Constr. Co., 21 Del. Ch. 155, 182 A. 545 (1936).*

The Chancellor, in determining the right and power of persons claiming to own stock, to vote, is not confined in his or her inquiry to a mere inspection of the stock ledger; he or she is empowered to examine all pertinent evidence with the view of reaching a determination of where justice lies. *In re Canal Constr. Co., 21 Del. Ch. 155, 182 A. 545 (1936)Viele v. Devaney, 679 A.2d 993 (Del. Ch. 1996).*

In a case contesting the validity of handwritten notations in the company's stock ledger, the court held that the stock ledger would not be regarded as exclusive, definitive evidence of the number of outstanding shares due to the lack of reliable independent evidence supporting the handwritten ledger entries, the entrenchment implications of defendant's entries, the exclusive control of the ledger by the defendant, and the fact that the integrity of the entries depended entirely on the suspect credibility of the defendant. *Viele v. Devaney, 679 A.2d 993 (Del. Ch. 1996).*

The statutorily guaranteed right to examine the stock ledger cannot be frustrated by nonfeasance. *Rainbow Nav., Inc. v. Pan Ocean Nav., Inc., 535 A.2d 1357 (Del. 1987).*

When the stock ledger is blank or nonexistent, the Court of Chancery has the power to consider other evidence to ascertain and establish stockholder status. *Rainbow Nav., Inc. v. Pan Ocean Nav., Inc., 535 A.2d 1357 (Del. 1987).*

Right to inspection. — The corporation may look to its stock ledger as the sole evidence in identifying those shareholders of record who are entitled to inspection. *Shaw v. Agri-Mark, Inc., 663 A.2d 464 (Del. 1995).*

CASE NOTES — OTHER STATES

Pennsylvania

Enjoinable director conduct. — Tinkering with corporate elections to interfere with shareholders' electoral rights violates a director's fiduciary duty to shareholders and is enjoinable. *Jewelcor Management, Inc. v. Thistle Group Holdings, Co., 2002 Phila. Ct. Com. Pl. LEXIS 79 (2004).*

CASE NOTES — FEDERAL

First Circuit

Under Delaware law, the shareholder of record is entitled to vote the stock. In re Consolidated Auto Recyclers, Inc., 123 B.R. 130 (Bankr. D.Me. 1991).

Second Circuit

The attitude of Delaware courts is to construe "stockholder" as meaning "registered holder." *Bankers National Corp. v. Barr, 7 F.R.D. 305 (S.D.N.Y. 1945).*

Right of inspection construed strictly. — Persons who supply equity capital to a corporation and directly elect its directors, but who are not stockholders of record, have no right to inspect corporate records, for Delaware has created a statutory right of inspection in favor of a stockholder. Del. Code. Ann. tit. 8 § 220(b), has defined "stockholder" to mean a stockholder of record. Del. Code Ann. tit. 8 § 220(a) has provided that the stock ledger shall be the only evidence as to who are the stockholders entitled to examine the stock ledger, the list required by this section or the books of the corporation under Del. Code Ann. tit. 8 § 219(c). The statutory right of inspection has been construed strictly, and the Delaware Supreme Court has held that establishing oneself as a stockholder of record is a mandatory condition precedent to the right to make a demand for inspection under Del. Code Ann. tit. 8 § 220. *Shaw v. Agri-Mark, Inc., 50 F.3d 117 (2d Cir. 1995).*

Third Circuit

Under the law of Delaware, the stock ledger is the only evidence as to who are the stockholders entitled to vote in person or by proxy at any meeting of stockholders. *Regis Insurance Co. v. Di Loreto, 1989 U.S. Dist. LEXIS 6256 (E.D.Pa 1989).*

Stock transfer books not reliable ownership record. — A registered holder may transfer his or her interest by mere delivery of the stock certificate, indorsed either in blank or to a specified person. Thus, it is manifest that the stock transfer books of a corporation cannot be safely relied upon to ascertain the ownership of stock. *Murdock v. Follansbee Steel Corp., 213 F.2d 570 (3d Cir. 1954).*

Fourth Circuit

Written instrument not found. — Defendants, as directors and officers of corporation, have failed to comply with Delaware law in the alleged issuing of these shares of stock of the corporation. Defendants failed to create a written instrument as evidence of the validly issued stock which supposedly removed plaintiff as majority shareholder of the corporation, as required by Delaware law. Even viewing the facts liberally, the only possible written instrument evidencing the issuance of these shares are the corporate minutes written by one of the defendants for the meeting at which the shares were purportedly issued. However, assuming these minutes were in fact genuine, they are so ambiguous as to the issuance of these particular shares that they cannot qualify as a written instrument evidencing the issuance of these shares. *Anderson v. Dobson, 2007 U.S. Dist. LEXIS 62791 (WD NC, August 24, 2007).*

§ 220. Inspection of books and records

DELAWARE CASE NOTES — REPORTED

Preemption by sec rule. — There is no express conflict with SEC Rule 14a-13(b)(2) which would merit a finding of preemption and this section represents no obstacles to the objectives of the federal law. *Shamrock Assocs. v. Texas Am. Energy Corp., 517 A.2d 658 (Del. Ch. 1986).*

Applicability of section. — While stockholders of stock corporations are entitled to enforce their inspection rights under the streamlined, summary procedures afforded by this section, members of nonstock corporations must resort to the antiquated common law procedure that was largely (but not entirely) supplanted by this section. *Scattered Corp. v. Chicago Stock Exch., Inc., 671 A.2d 874 (Del. Ch. 1994), aff'd, 676 A.2d 907 (Del. 1996).*

Application to subsidiaries. — Stockholder of a parent corporation is not entitled to inspect the subsidiary corporation's documents unless the parent corporation has actual possession and control of such records of the subsidiary; or, the parent corporation could obtain such records through the exercise of control over such subsidiary. *Weinstein Enters. v. Orloff, 870 A.2d 499 (Del. 2005).*

Shareholder of a parent corporation was not entitled to inspect the records of a subsidiary because, though the parent corporation was a 45.16% stockholder of the subsidiary, it had no actual control over the subsidiary and, therefore, had no actual possession or control of the documents the shareholder sought to have been inspected. *Weinstein Enters. v. Orloff, 870 A.2d 499 (Del. 2005).*

Even if a parent corporation can exercise actual control over the production of a subsidiary's documents, its exercise of that control is subject to two additional statutory provisos under 8 Del. C. § 220(b)(2)b.1 and b.2, namely: (1) the stockholder inspection of such books and records of the subsidiary would not constitute a breach of an agreement between the corporation or the subsidiary and a person or persons not affiliated with the corporation; and (2) the subsidiary would not have the right under the law applicable to it to deny the corporation access to such books and records upon demand by the corporation. *Weinstein Enters. v. Orloff, 870 A.2d 499 (Del. 2005).*

Common law. — Under the common law a stockholder had the right to examine the books and records of the company, and that right could not be taken away except by a statute that expressly or by necessary implication authorized it. *State ex rel. Cochran v. Penn-Beaver Oil Co., 34 Del. 81, 143 A. 257 (1926); State ex rel. Healy v. Superior Oil Corp., 40 Del. 460, 13 A.2d 453 (1940).*

Intent. — This section is intended to serve shareholders whose need for inspection is truly related to their stock

Seventh Circuit

Under Delaware law, status as a shareholder does not depend on the issuance of a certificate of stock since the certificate is merely evidence of ownership. *Cabintaxi Corp. v. Commissioner, 63 F.3d 614 (7th Cir. 1995).*

interest. *BBC Acquisition Corp. v. Durr-Fillauer Medical, Inc., 623 A.2d 85 (Del. Ch. 1992).*

There is nothing excessive about requiring a petitioner to plead the elements of the statute under which he or she petitions the court. Section 220 makes inspection available only for shareholders with a proper purpose. If a shareholder could satisfy this burden by conclusorily repeating words previously used to describe a proper purpose, the requirement would be rendered meaningless, and well settled canons of statutory construction prevent such absurd results. Second, permitting a single shareholder to hound a corporation with exclusively personal requests for books and records is a waste of corporate resources that engenders no benefit for the shareholders in general. The proper purpose requirement protects against such wealth-reducing outcomes. Finally, the "credible basis" standard is the lowest possible burden of proof in Delaware jurisprudence, and this can hardly be characterized as an excessive pleading standard. *Melzer v. CNET Networks, Inc., 934 A.2d 912, 2007 Del. Ch. LEXIS 163 (November 21, 2007). [For the full text of this case opinion, please see the Appendix at the end of this Volume.]*

Use during preparation of complaint. — Corporate books and records obtained under this section can provide the basis for the pleading of particularized facts — i.e., for the filing of a complaint that meets the legally required standard; the Delaware Supreme Court and the Delaware Chancery Court have repeatedly issued admonitions for derivative plaintiffs to proceed deliberately and to use this section's books and records device to gather the materials necessary to prepare a solid complaint. *Guttman v. Jen-Hsun Huang, 823 A.2d 492 (Del. Ch. 2003).*

Because a books and records request under this section might prevent expensive and time-consuming procedural machinations that too often occur in derivative litigation, the Supreme Court of Delaware and the Chancery Court of Delaware have repeatedly urged derivative plaintiffs to seek books and records before filing a complaint. *In re Walt Disney Co. Derivative Litig., 825 A.2d 275 (Del. Ch. 2003).*

Due to the availability of the *8 Del. C. § 220* action as a possible method of securing facts to support a demand futility claim, and the fact that the shareholder did not even attempt to use the fact-gathering tools of § 220, there was no way to know if such an effort would have been fruitless. *Beam v. Stewart, 845 A.2d 1040 (Del. 2004).*

Proceeding under this section is narrow in both purpose and scope; as to inspection of the stock ledger, it is only a "look-at-the-list" act. *Kerkorian v. Western Air Lines*, 253 A.2d 221 (Del. Ch. 1969), aff'd, *254 A.2d 240 (Del. 1969); Mite Corp. v. Heli-Coil Corp., 256 A.2d 855 (Del. Ch. 1969).*

This section has been narrowly construed. *Willard v. Harrworth Corp., 258 A.2d 914 (Del. Ch. 1969), aff'd, 267 A.2d 577 (Del. 1970).*

Inapplicable to actions brought by third parties. — This section is not a bar to discovery in actions brought by third parties outside the corporation. *In re B & F Towing & Salvage Co., 551 A.2d 45 (Del. 1988).*

Allegations or evidence necessary by person seeking inspection. — A stockholder seeking to inspect the stock ledger need allege only that he or she is a stockholder in the respondent company, a proper demand, and a failure or refusal to comply with the duty imposed by law. *Insuranshares Corp. v. Kirchner, 40 Del. 105, 5 A.2d 519 (1939).*

Plaintiff asserting right of inspection makes out a prima facie case when he or she shows that he or she is a director, he or she has demanded inspection and his or her demand has been refused. *Henshaw v. American Cement Corp., 252 A.2d 125 (Del. Ch. 1969).*

A request for an order permitting minority shareholders to inspect certain books and records of the corporation was not ripe for any sort of adjudication, where it did not appear that the minority shareholders had complied with the preliminary steps required under the terms of this section as a prerequisite to the examination of corporate books and records. *Petrick v. B-K Dynamics, Inc., 283 A.2d 696 (Del. Ch. 1971).*

Establishing oneself as a stockholder of record is a mandatory condition precedent to the right to make a demand for inspection under this section. *Rainbow Nav., Inc. v. Pan Ocean Nav., Inc., 535 A.2d 1357 (Del. 1987).*

Lowest possible burden of proof. — Although the threshold for a stockholder in a section 220 proceeding is not insubstantial, the "credible basis" standard sets the lowest possible burden of proof. The only way to reduce the burden of proof further would be to eliminate any requirement that a stockholder show some evidence of possible wrongdoing. That would be tantamount to permitting inspection based on the mere suspicion standard that plaintiff advances in this appeal. However, such a standard has been repeatedly rejected as a basis to justify the enterprise cost of an inspection. *Seinfeld v. Verizon Communs., Inc., 909 A.2d 117, 2006 Del. LEXIS 492 (Sept. 25, 2006).*

Credible basis for wrongdoing. — Should a stockholder seeking inspection under section 220 be entitled to relief without being required to show some evidence to suggest a credible basis for wrongdoing? The answer must be no. *Seinfeld v. Verizon Communs., Inc., 909 A.2d 117, 2006 Del. LEXIS 492 (Sept. 25, 2006).*

Allegations of waste and mismanagement. — While stockholders have the burden of coming forward with specific and credible allegations sufficient to warrant a suspicion of waste and mismanagement, they are not required to prove by a preponderance of the evidence that waste and mismanagement are actually occurring.

Thomas & Betts Corp. v. Leviton Mfg. Co., 681 A.2d 1026 (Del. 1996).

A party's subjective belief that waste and mismanagement were occurring was insufficient to meet the evidentiary burden required to compel inspection. *Thomas & Betts Corp. v. Leviton Mfg. Co., 681 A.2d 1026 (Del. 1996).*

Where the demanding shareholder claims waste and mismanagement as the purpose for inspection, it has a greater than normal evidentiary burden. *Thomas & Betts Corp. v. Leviton Mfg. Co., 685 A.2d 702 (Del. Ch. 1995), aff'd, 681 A.2d 1026 (Del. 1996).*

A stockholder was entitled to inspect books and records related to a merger where it alleged corporate mismanagement and where there was some evidence to support such allegation. *U.S. Die Casting & Dev. Co. v. Security First Corp., 711 A.2d 1220 (Del. Ch. 1996), aff'd as modified, 687 A.2d 563 (Del. 1997).*

An employment contract does not constitute waste simply because it continues to pay benefits to the spouse of an employee after death. A corporation entering into such a contract merely takes upon itself the cost of providing the employee with an insurance policy payable to the employee's spouse. As a matter of economics, there may be little significant difference between providing an employee with (a) an option for post-death payment of salary, (b) an equivalent life-insurance or annuity policy, or (c) a salary increase sufficient for the employee to buy such insurance on his or her own. *In re Tyson Foods, Inc. Consol. S'holder Litig., 919 A.2d 563; 2007 Del. Ch. LEXIS 19 (February 6, 2007).*

Persons entitled to examinations are to be determined from stock ledger of company. *State ex rel. Healy v. Superior Oil Corp., 40 Del. 460, 13 A.2d 453 (1940).*

The corporation may look to its stock ledger as the sole evidence in identifying those shareholders of record who are entitled to inspection. *Shaw v. Agri-Mark, Inc., 663 A.2d 464 (Del. 1995).*

A party in whose name corporate stock was registered in the stock ledger of the corporation was a "stockholder" and was entitled to examine the stock ledger under this section and to copy the list of stockholders, even though the party was merely a nominee and was not the owner of the stock registered in her name. *State ex rel. Healy v. Superior Oil Corp., 40 Del. 460, 13 A.2d 453 (1940).*

The stockholder's right to examine corporate records is a personal one in the sense that it is not transferable for the benefit of a stranger. *State ex rel. Bloch v. Sentry Safety Control Corp., 41 Del. 480, 24 A.2d 587 (1942).*

The right of inspection is personal to the stockholder and is not transferable to or for the benefit of others. *Shaw v. Agri-Mark, Inc., 663 A.2d 464 (Del. 1995).*

Scope of this section relates only to stockholder's right of inspection. *Henshaw v. American Cement Corp., 252 A.2d 125 (Del. Ch. 1969).*

Equity owner has no right to inspection. — A party who supplies equity to a stock corporation, but who is not a stockholder of record, does not have a right to inspect the corporation's books and records under common law or under this section. *Shaw v. Agri-Mark, Inc., 663 A.2d 464 (Del. 1995).*

But court has power to go beyond record title in a case under this section. *Kerkorian v. Western Air Lines, 253 A.2d 221* (Del. Ch.), aff'd, *254 A.2d 240 (Del. 1969).*

This section was not intended to deny the corporation an opportunity to show that a stockholder attained record status fraudulently, for example, or that a stockholder's title to the stock is defective. *Kerkorian v. Western Air Lines, 253 A.2d 221* (Del. Ch.), aff'd, *254 A.2d 240 (Del. 1969).*

Only if a corporation fails in its affirmative duty to maintain a stock ledger may a court look to extrinsic evidence in deciding whether a party possesses record stockholder status. *Shaw v. Agri-Mark, Inc., 663 A.2d 464 (Del. 1995).*

And stockholder may exercise his or her right through duly constituted agent. *State ex rel. Bloch v. Sentry Safety Control Corp., 41 Del. 480, 24 A.2d 587 (1942).*

A director is entitled to assistance in his or her examination of corporate records by agents of his or her own choosing. Obviously agents should be qualified to perform their duties, and they should not have any interest adverse to the corporation. *Henshaw v. American Cement Corp., 252 A.2d 125 (Del. Ch. 1969).*

But when inspection is by person other than stockholder, corporation is to be given evidence of his or her authority to so act. *Henshaw v. American Cement Corp., 252 A.2d 125 (Del. Ch. 1969).*

Qualifications of stockholder's agent. — Where the underlying reason for denying inspection was the officer's lack of confidence in the accountant selected by the stockholder to conduct the examination and the corporation never suggested another accountant, this was held not to be sufficient reason to deny stockholder his right of inspection. *State ex rel. Waldman v. Miller-Wohl Co., 42 Del. 71, 28 A.2d 147 (1942).*

Purpose of inspection must be proper one and not adverse to interests of corporation. *State ex rel. Miller v. Loft, Inc., 34 Del. 538, 156 A. 170 (1931).*

Where the motive or purpose of the examination is mere curiosity or where it is sought to be made for some indefinite, doubtful, uncertain or mere vexatious purpose, or where it has no relation to the relator's interest, as a stockholder, in the corporation, it would not be a proper purpose. *State ex rel. Miller v. Loft, Inc., 34 Del. 538, 156 A. 170 (1931).*

The right of a stockholder under this section is absolute unless the corporation is able to show that the purpose of examination is to gratify idle curiosity, or is for an improper or unlawful purpose, or for a purpose purely individual and in no way germane to the relationship of stockholder to the corporation. *State ex rel. Foster v. Standard Oil Co., 41 Del. 172, 18 A.2d 235 (1941).*

Inspection of corporate records can occur only when reason sought is found in good faith and for specific and proper purpose. *State ex rel. Waldman v. Miller-Wohl Co., 42 Del. 71, 28 A.2d 147 (1942).*

This section requires the applicant stockholder to state in its demand the substance of its intended communication sufficiently to enable the corporation, and the courts if necessary, to determine whether there was a reasonable relationship between its purpose, i.e., the intended communication, and the applicant's interest as a stockholder of the corporation. *Northwest Indus., Inc. v. B.F. Goodrich Co., 260 A.2d 428 (Del. 1969).*

The purpose required to be stated in the demand must be a "proper purpose" in order to make the demand effective; this would appear to be necessarily implied from the juxtaposition of those terms in this section. *Weisman v. Western Pac. Indus., Inc., 344 A.2d 267 (Del. Ch. 1975).*

Even though the purpose of the inspection may be proper in the sense that it is reasonably related to the person's interest as a stockholder, it must also not be adverse to the interests of the corporation. To this extent a stockholder's right of inspection is a qualified right depending upon the facts of the particular case. *Skoglund v. Ormand Indus., Inc., 372 A.2d 204 (Del. Ch. 1976).*

A qualification as to the right of inspection of books and records is that even if a proper purpose for a demand is demonstrated and such demand is shown to be reasonably related to a plaintiff's interest as a stockholder, nonetheless such demand must not be for a purpose adverse to the best interests of the corporation. *Skouras v. Admiralty Enter., Inc., 386 A.2d 674 (Del. Ch. 1978).*

Mere possibility that stockholder seeking inspection might use the information obtained to harm the corporation is not grounds for any withholding or restriction of the right of inspection. *Skouras v. Admiralty Enter., Inc., 386 A.2d 674 (Del. Ch. 1978).*

Four purposes for seeking to inspect books and records are: (1) To determine the value of its stock interest; (2) to ascertain the corporation's condition or its affairs so that petitioner can vote and otherwise exercise its rights in an informed manner; (3) to determine the reason for the nonpayment of dividends; and (4) to determine whether or not there are sufficient funds available for the payment of dividends. *Helnsman Mgt. Servs., Inc. v. A & S Consultants, Inc., 525 A.2d 160 (Del. Ch. 1987).*

Plaintiff, in stating that it seeks to communicate with the other stockholders about the economic risks of doing business in Angola, has complied with the form and manner of making a demand for a stockholder list. The burden at trial therefore was upon corporation to establish that the inspection would be for an improper purpose. *Conservative Caucus Research, Analysis & Educ. Found., Inc. v. Chevron Corp., 525 A.2d 569 (Del. Ch. 1987).*

A shareholder stated a "proper purpose" for inspection under subsection (b) of this section in seeking to solicit the participation of other shareholders in legitimate nonderivative litigation against the defendant corporation where the stockholder sought not only to seek monetary redress for their individual economic injuries, but also sought to prevent further acts of fraud or mismanagement from disrupting the fair market value of the company's stock. *Compaq Computer Corp. v. Horton, 631 A.2d 1 (Del. 1993).*

The question of a "proper purpose" under subsection (b) of this section is an issue of law and equity which this court reviews *de novo. Compaq Computer Corp. v. Horton, 631 A.2d 1 (Del. 1993).*

The threshold for a plaintiff in a § 220 case is not insubstantial. Mere curiosity or a desire for a fishing expedition will not suffice. But the threshold may be satisfied by a credible showing, through documents, logic, testimony or otherwise, that there are legitimate issues of wrongdoing. *Security First Corp. v. United States Die Casting & Dev., 687 A.2d 563 (Del. 1997).*

And must relate to status of stockholder. — Once the status of a stockholder is established, the stockholder is entitled to the stockholder list if his or her primary purpose is reasonably related to that status, regardless of the nature of any further or secondary purpose in seeking the list. *General Time Corp. v. Talley Indus., Inc., 43 Del. Ch. 531, 240 A.2d 755 (1968); Hudson v. A.C. & S. Co., 535 A.2d 1361 (Del. Super. Ct. 1987).*

Where a plaintiff complied with the provisions respecting the form and manner of making demand, and the record establishes that the inspection he or she seeks is for a proper purpose, reasonably related to his or her interest or status as a stockholder, plaintiff is entitled to an order authorizing him or her to inspect. *Henshaw v. American Cement Corp., 252 A.2d 125 (Del. Ch. 1969).*

The section requires enough substance be given to show a reasonable relationship between its purpose in making demand and its interest as a stockholder. *Mite Corp. v. Heli-Coil Corp., 256 A.2d 855 (Del. Ch. 1969).*

In order to obtain an inspection and to copy the stock list, the stockholder seeking the inspection must show a proper purpose reasonably related to such person's interest as a stockholder in the corporation, the stock list of which he or she seeks to inspect. *Willard v. Harrworth Corp., 267 A.2d 577 (Del. 1970).*

This section was enacted in order to provide speedy access to a stock list for a stockholder who has demonstrated a purpose reasonably related to his or her interest as such. *Schnell v. Chris-Craft Indus., Inc., 283 A.2d 852 (Del. 1971).*

Once the status of a stockholder is established under this section, he or she is entitled to a stockholders' list if his or her primary purpose is reasonably related to that status. *Credit Bureau of St. Paul, Inc. v. Credit Bureau Reports, Inc., 290 A.2d 689 (Del. Ch. 1972), aff'd, 290 A.2d 691 (Del. 1972).*

Such as communications relative to contest for control. — Purpose of examination was deemed proper where aim was to enable relator to communicate with other shareholders to ascertain whether they desired to effect a change in personnel of board of directors at next annual meeting of stockholders and to solicit proxies for that purpose. *State ex rel. Foster v. Standard Oil Co., 41 Del. 172, 18 A.2d 235 (1941).*

Where stockholders desire to inspect stock ledger for purpose of communicating with other stockholders, to solicit support for their slate of directors or to attempt to buy additional stock from other stockholders, or both, the purpose of inspection is one directly related to relators' status as stockholders. *E.L. Bruce Co. v. State ex rel. Gilbert, 51 Del. 252, 144 A.2d 533 (1958).*

A stockholder seeking control is not limited to communicating with stockholders through management; he or she has a right to go to stockholders directly, without procedural impediments if he or she desires to do so. *Kerkorian v. Western Air Lines, 253 A.2d 221 (Del. Ch.), aff'd, 254 A.2d 240 (Del. 1969).*

Or solicitation of proxies. — Inspection of stock ledger to solicit proxies at stockholders' meeting is proper. *E.L. Bruce Co. v. State ex rel. Gilbert, 51 Del. 252, 144 A.2d 533 (1958).*

The desire to solicit proxies for a slate of directors in opposition to management is a purpose reasonably related to the stockholder's interest as a stockholder. *General Time Corp. v. Talley Indus., Inc., 43 Del. Ch. 531, 240 A.2d 755 (1968).*

The desire to obtain a list of stockholders in order to solicit proxies for the election of a slate of directors in opposition to management constitutes a proper purpose to inspect the stock ledger. *Schnell v. Chris-Craft Indus., Inc., 283 A.2d 852 (Del. Ch. 1971).*

When a stockholder establishes his or her status as such and seeks production of a stockholders' list for a purpose germane to that status, such as a proxy solicitation, he or she is entitled to its production. *Credit Bureau of St. Paul, Inc. v. Credit Bureau Reports, Inc., 290 A.2d 689 (Del. Ch. 1972), aff'd, 290 A.2d 691 (Del. 1972).*

Where a stockholder has shown that it made a bona fide decision to solicit stockholder proxies for use at the next annual stockholders meeting, a demand under this section to inspect and copy a list of a corporation's stockholders is valid. *Hatleigh Corp. v. Lane Bryant, Inc., 428 A.2d 350 (Del. Ch. 1981).*

The claim of a corporation that a proxy solicitation has not yet received clearance from the Securities and Exchange Commission is irrelevant for purposes of a demand to inspect and copy a stockholder list. *Hatleigh Corp. v. Lane Bryant, Inc., 428 A.2d 350 (Del. Ch. 1981).*

Where brokerage firms hold stock for their customers under a central certificate depository system and the shares are listed on the books of a corporation as being held by the central depository, a stockholder demanding to inspect and copy the list of stockholders is entitled to receive a breakdown of the brokerage firms and the number of shares they hold for the purpose of soliciting proxies from the beneficial owners. *Hatleigh Corp. v. Lane Bryant, Inc., 428 A.2d 350 (Del. Ch. 1981).*

And communications with stockholders in class actions. — Where a shareholder, by a class bill, seeks relief against corporate wrongdoing and for the purpose of communicating with other shareholders tries to assert his or her statutory right of examination of the stock ledger, the purpose of the examination is one intimately connected with stock ownership. *State ex rel. Foster v. Standard Oil Co., 41 Del. 172, 18 A.2d 235 (1941).*

But this section requires more than statement of intent to communicate with other stockholders regarding forthcoming meeting. *Northwest Indus., Inc. v. B.F. Goodrich Co., 260 A.2d 428 (Del. 1969).*

As is using list for commercial purposes. — Demanding an inspection of the stock ledgers for the purpose of securing a list of the stockholders and their addresses for the purpose of commercializing the same was a highly improper purpose. *State ex rel. Theile v. Cities Serv. Co., 31 Del. 514, 115 A. 773 (1922).*

Change in accounting practices. — An action for inspection under this section cannot serve as a vehicle to force a corporation to change its accounting practices; a stockholder may not use this section as a means to invade the corporate board room. *Thomas & Betts Corp. v. Leviton Mfg. Co., 685 A.2d 702 (Del. Ch. 1995), aff'd, 681 A.2d 1026 (Del. 1996).*

Intention to purchase additional shares from other stockholders is proper purpose for inspection of stock ledger. *E. L. Bruce Co. v. State ex rel. Gilbert, 51 Del. 252, 144 A.2d 533 (1958).*

Inspection of a stock list is proper where it is sought in order to purchase additional shares of a company's stock from other stockholders. It is not made improper because the first shares were purchased as a prelude to a demand for the list. *Mite Corp. v. Heli-Coil Corp., 256 A.2d 855 (Del. Ch. 1969).*

Accepting that a desire to investigate the suitability of a director is a proper purpose does not necessarily expose corporations to greater risk of abuse.

Inspection under this section is not automatic upon a statement of a proper purpose. First, a defendant may defeat demand by proving that while stating a proper purpose, plaintiff's true or primary purpose is improper. Second, a plaintiff who states a proper purpose must also present some evidence to establish a credible basis from which the Court of Chancery could infer there are legitimate concerns regarding a director's suitability. That is, a stockholder must establish a credible basis to infer that a director is unsuitable, thereby warranting further investigation Third, a plaintiff must also prove that the information it seeks is necessary and essential to assessing whether a director is unsuitable to stand for reelection. Finally, access to board documents may be further limited by the need to protect confidential board communications. *Pershing Square, L.P. v. Ceridian Corp., 923 A.2d 810; 2007 Del. Ch. LEXIS 62 (May 11, 2007).*

Identification of existing shareholders. — The identification of existing shareholders who would be willing to purchase shares from the party seeking inspection was held to be a legitimate purpose for inspection of the stockholders list where there was no significant public market for the shares. *Thomas & Betts Corp. v. Leviton Mfg. Co., 685 A.2d 702 (Del. Ch. 1995), aff'd, 681 A.2d 1026 (Del. 1996).*

As is determination of value of stock. — Stockholder has the right to inspect and make copies of such of the books, papers, accounts and writings as are found essential and sufficient to furnish the information whereby he or she may determine the value of his or her stock. *State ex rel. Rogers v. Sherman Oil Co., 31 Del. 570, 117 A. 122 (1922).*

The valuation of one's shares is a proper purpose for the inspection of corporate books and records. *CM & M Group, Inc. v. Carroll, 453 A.2d 788 (Del. 1982).*

Because stockholders of a privately held corporation do not receive the mandated, periodic disclosures associated with a public held corporation, such shareholders may have a legitimate need to inspect the corporation's books and records to value their investment in order to decide whether to buy additional shares, sell their shares, or take other action to protect their investment. *Thomas & Betts Corp. v. Leviton Mfg. Co., 685 A.2d 702 (Del. Ch. 1995), aff'd, 681 A.2d 1026 (Del. 1996).*

That stockholders' corporation is competitor does not defeat stockholders' right of inspection. *E. L. Bruce Co. v. State ex rel. Gilbert, 51 Del. 252, 144 A.2d 533 (1958); Credit Bureau of St. Paul, Inc. v. Credit Bureau Reports, Inc., 290 A.2d 689 (Del. Ch. 1972), aff'd, 290 A.2d 691 (Del. 1972).*

The fact that a shareholder is a competitor of the corporation does not of itself defeat the right of inspection under this section. If misuse of the information obtained threatens harm to the corporation, it has a remedy in the courts in an appropriate action. *Skoglund v. Ormand Indus., Inc., 372 A.2d 204 (Del. Ch. 1976).*

And stockholder cannot be denied inspection because management insists he or she is on wrong side; a stockholder is entitled to take which side he or she prefers and to seek support from fellow stockholders and for this purpose he or she is entitled to inspection of the stock ledger. *Trans World Airlines v. State ex rel. Porterie, 54 Del. 582, 183 A.2d 174 (1962).*

An examination of books and records to ascertain the condition of corporate affairs and the propriety of certain actions is a proper purpose even though the one who seeks inspection may be hostile to management. *Henshaw v. American Cement Corp., 252 A.2d 125 (Del. Ch. 1969).*

The statutorily guaranteed right to examine the stock ledger cannot be frustrated by nonfeasance. *Rainbow Nav., Inc. v. Pan Ocean Nav., Inc., 535 A.2d 1357 (Del. 1987).*

Inspection to determine whether request was properly refused. — A stockholder who makes a serious demand and receives only a peremptory refusal has the right to use the "tools at hand" to obtain the relevant corporate records reflecting the corporate action and related information in order to determine whether or not there is a basis to assert that demand was wrongfully refused. *Grimes v. Donald, 673 A.2d 1207 (Del. 1996).*

The Court of Chancery properly denied plaintiffs' request for limited discovery in a derivative action alleging wrongful refusal of plaintiffs' pre-suit demand; plaintiffs' failure to take advantage of the opportunity to bring an action under this section to inspect minutes, reports and other books and records precluded plaintiffs from arguing that they had used the tools at hand to obtain the necessary information before filing a derivative action. *Scattered Corp. v. Chicago Stock Exch., 701 A.2d 70 (Del. 1997).*

Stockholder was entitled under this section to obtain access to corporation's books and records to determine whether there were grounds to assert that his demand to abrogate a compensation package was wrongfully refused, and if so, to assist him in meeting the pleading requirements of Chancery Court Rule 23.1. *Grimes v. DSC Communications Corp., 724 A.2d 561 (Del. Ch. 1998).*

Bad faith resistance to inspection. — Majority shareholder was not entitled to an award of legal fees incurred in prosecuting an action under this section on the grounds that the officers' and directors' opposition to the suit was in bad faith, where the case was settled without any presentation of evidence or adjudication of defenses. *Arbitrium (Cayman Islands) Handels AG v. Johnston, 705 A.2d 225 (Del. Ch. 1997).*

"Proper purpose" is defined as a purpose reasonably related to the demander's interest as a stockholder. *Weisman v. Western Pac. Indus., Inc., 344 A.2d 267 (Del. Ch. 1975).*

Burden of proving proper purpose on stockholder. — Under subsection (c) of this section, the burden of proving a proper purpose is on the stockholder, where the demand is for inspection of books and records rather than for a stock list. *Skouras v. Admiralty Enter., Inc., 386 A.2d 674 (Del. Ch. 1978).*

Subsection (c) of this section places the burden of proving proper purpose on the shareholder when he or she seeks inspection of records other than the corporation's stock ledger or list of shareholders. *CM & M Group, Inc. v. Carroll, 453 A.2d 788 (Del. 1982).*

When seeking inspection of books and records other than the corporate stock ledger or stock list, a shareholder has the burden of proving that the purpose is proper. *BBC Acquisition Corp. v. Durr-Fillauer Medical, Inc., 623 A.2d 85 (Del. Ch. 1992).*

Under this section, when a stockholder complies with the statutory requirements as to form and manner of making a demand, then the corporation bears the burden of proving that the demand is for an improper purpose; any doubt must be resolved in favor of the stockholder's right to have an inspection. *Compaq Computer Corp. v. Horton, 631 A.2d 1 (Del. 1993).*

If plaintiff establishes proper purpose then all others are irrelevant. *Mite Corp. v. Heli-Coil Corp., 256 A.2d 855 (Del. Ch. 1969).*

The desire to solicit proxies for a slate of directors in opposition to management is a purpose reasonably related to the stockholder's interest as a stockholder; any further or secondary purpose in seeking the list is irrelevant. *Credit Bureau Reports, Inc. v. Credit Bureau of St. Paul, Inc., 290 A.2d 691 (Del. 1972).*

If a proper purpose is established, it is no defense of itself that the stockholder may also have another, or secondary purpose, which may be improper. *Skoglund v. Ormand Indus., Inc., 372 A.2d 204 (Del. Ch. 1976).*

Once a proper purpose for the demand for inspection is established, it becomes irrelevant that the stockholder may have a secondary and perhaps questionable ulterior purpose behind his or her primary purpose. *Skouras v. Admiralty Enter., Inc., 386 A.2d 674 (Del. Ch. 1978).*

Once having established a proper purpose, a stockholder is entitled to the same lists and data relating to stockholders as is available to the corporation. *Hatleigh Corp. v. Lane Bryant, Inc., 428 A.2d 350 (Del. Ch. 1981).*

Once a proper purpose has been established, any secondary purpose or ulterior motive of the stockholder becomes irrelevant. *CM & M Group, Inc. v. Carroll, 453 A.2d 788 (Del. 1982).*

Since a shareholder will often have more than one purpose, the "proper purpose" requirement has been construed to mean that the shareholder's primary purpose must be proper, and any secondary purpose, whether proper or not, is irrelevant. *BBC Acquisition Corp. v. Durr-Fillauer Medical, Inc., 623 A.2d 85 (Del. Ch. 1992).*

Review of "proper purpose" determination. — The question of whether an inspection is for a proper purpose is reviewed de novo by the appellate court. *Security First Corp. v. United States Die Casting & Dev., 687 A.2d 563 (Del. 1997).*

Proper purpose not found. — Where the evidence overwhelmingly established that despite the several purposes recited in its demand, petitioner had one primary purpose for inspecting nonpublic information previously furnished: to place a value on the corporation so that petitioner could consider whether to increase its offering price and, if so, by how much; and where the other stated purposes, to the extent they had independent reality, were clearly secondary and subordinate, the primary purpose was not a "proper purpose" within the meaning of this section. *BBC Acquisition Corp. v. Durr-Fillauer Medical, Inc., 623 A.2d 85 (Del. Ch. 1992).*

Facilitation of a special type of accounting, "equity accounting," was held an insufficient reason to compel inspection, as the accounting problem was personal to the shareholder and in no way impaired the performance of the corporation. *Thomas & Betts Corp. v. Leviton Mfg. Co., 681 A.2d 1026 (Del. 1996).*

Where plaintiff testified at trial that the plaintiff had no idea what the plaintiff would do with the stockholder list, defendant met its burden of proving that the plaintiff's demand was improper. *Security First Corp. v. United States Die Casting & Dev., 687 A.2d 563 (Del. 1997).*

Stockholder's motion to lift the confidentiality designation on certain documents was denied, because the stockholder could not use confidential information received for the proper purpose of investigating and seeking to remediate wrongdoing for the purpose of being a self-appointed publisher of the corporation's proprietary information; also, there was no basis in the language of the statute to limit the proposed use of *8 Del. C. § 220* to executive compensation issues. *Disney v. Walt Disney Co., 857 A.2d 444 (Del. Ch. 2004).*

Demonstrated entitlement to inspection. — A petitioning stockholder who has complied with this statute's procedural requirements and who has satisfactorily proved a proper purpose for the requested inspection will have demonstrated his or her entitlement to inspection of the books and records needed to perform the task. *BBC Acquisition Corp. v. Durr-Fillauer Medical, Inc., 623 A.2d 85 (Del. Ch. 1992).*

Good cause for precluding application of the attorney-client privilege is determined by: (1) the number of shares owned by the stockholder and the percentage of stock they

Corporations

represent; (2) the assertion of a colorable claim; (3) the necessity of the information and its unavailability from other sources; (4) whether the stockholder has identified the information sought and is not merely fishing for information; and (5) whether the communication is advice concerning the litigation itself. *Grimes v. DSC Communications Corp., 724 A.2d 561 (Del. Ch. 1998).*

Good cause for precluding application of the work product doctrine was established where a stockholder showed that he needed access to documents that revealed the deliberative processes of a special committee of the corporation appointed to investigate a pre-suit demand of the stockholder. *Grimes v. DSC Communications Corp., 724 A.2d 561 (Del. Ch. 1998).*

Dual role of stockholder and substantial contract customer. — Where the petitioner occupies a dual relationship both as a contract partner/client and as a stockholder and the evidence shows that petitioner retained accountant to conduct the book's and record's inspection in order to further its interests both as a potential contract creditor and as a stockholder, the petitioner, even if he does have an ulterior purpose, would still not be barred from relief under this section, unless the ulterior purpose is also its primary purpose. *Helnsman Mgt. Servs., Inc. v. A & S Consultants, Inc., 525 A.2d 160 (Del. Ch. 1987).*

Communications between executives and directors. — Stockholders have a legitimate interest in monitoring how the boards of directors of Delaware corporations perform their managerial duties This includes an interest in monitoring and investigating possible breaches of fiduciary duties owed to stockholders. Although plaintiff's right to monitor the board may be served by releasing the letters from executives to directors, it seems unlikely because, as previously stated, the letters do not challenge board action or inaction. Further, testimony suggests that plaintiff has no significant interest in investigating wrongdoing but instead is primarily, if not solely, driven by a desire to publish the letters. Thus, the letters can not be released under these circumstances because the resulting harm is much greater than the purported benefit. *Pershing Square, L.P. v. Ceridian Corp., 923 A.2d 810; 2007 Del. Ch. LEXIS 62 (May 11, 2007).*

Executives may provide an invaluable source of information regarding highly relevant topics such as employee morale, employee efficiency, employee mismanagement, and a plethora of other topics. In order to keep directors well-informed in this regard, it is important as a policy matter that the court protects the confidentiality of communications. The chancery court does not suggest that any document between an executive and a board member that the company marks as confidential is automatically excluded from inspection under this section. There are circumstances where these confidential designations are overbroad, or where the benefit of disclosure outweighs the risks of harm. But, where a document indeed involves confidential business and personnel matters and where the potential benefit of disclosing the information does not outweigh the potential harm, the chancery court should exercise caution in requiring disclosure absent special circumstances. *Pershing Square, L.P. v. Ceridian Corp., 923 A.2d 810; 2007 Del. Ch. LEXIS 62 (May 11, 2007).*

Beneficial owners' list. — Where, the corporation has obtained a list identifying beneficial owners of stock (Obtained Nonobjecting Beneficial Owner list) and is or will be using it to solicit its stockholders in connection with the annual meeting, the stockholder soliciting proxies should be allowed the same channel of communication. *Shamrock Assocs. v. Texas Am. Energy Corp., 517 A.2d 658 (Del. Ch. 1986).*

Possibility of abuse does not defeat right to inspect. — Where a director asserts his right of inspection, his purpose is not improper because of the possibility that he may abuse his position as a director and make information available to persons hostile to the corporation or otherwise not entitled to it. If a director does violate his or her fiduciary duty in this regard, then the corporation has its remedy in the courts. *Henshaw v. American Cement Corp., 252 A.2d 125 (Del. Ch. 1969).*

The possibility that the stockholder if successful in an attempt to win control of the corporation may abuse that control is mere speculation, since if such control is won and abused, the minority has its remedy in the courts. *Credit Bureau of St. Paul, Inc. v. Credit Bureau Reports, Inc., 290 A.2d 689 (Del. Ch. 1972),* aff'd, *290 A.2d 691 (Del. 1972).*

Stockholders should be free from harassment, and organizations which attempt to assert positions which are only marginally related to the economic interests of a corporation must be looked upon with some suspicion; however, plaintiff has testified that it will only communicate by mail to the stockholders. In this present day, where all householders are constantly inundated with reams of mailed exhortations and appeals, the receipt of 1 more letter, no matter how useless, or bizarre, can hardly be harassment. *Conservative Caucus Research, Analysis & Educ. Found., Inc. v. Chevron Corp., 525 A.2d 569 (Del. Ch. 1987).*

Propriety of purpose determined from facts of each case. — The Court of Chancery is to determine the propriety of the purpose from the facts in each case. *CM & M Group, Inc. v. Carroll, 453 A.2d 788 (Del. 1982).*

Person may be stockholder without having in hand certificate evidencing stock ownership. *Norton v. Digital Applications, Inc., 305 A.2d 656 (Del. Ch. 1973).*

Nothing in language or history of this section limits stockholder's right of inspection to a list of that class in which the stockholder is a holder of record. *Western Pac. Indus., Inc. v. Liggett & Myers, Inc., 310 A.2d 669 (Del. Ch. 1973).*

Lack of imminence of stockholders' meeting is irrelevant to the issue of whether a stockholder has a right to inspect and copy a stockholder list if a proper purpose for the inspection exists. *Hatleigh Corp. v. Lane Bryant, Inc., 428 A.2d 350 (Del. Ch. 1981).*

Inspection of stock ledger is proper where it is sought in order to purchase additional shares of a corporation's stock from other stockholders. *Western Pac.*

Indus., Inc. v. Liggett & Myers, Inc., 310 A.2d 669 (Del. Ch. 1973).

Subsection (b) of this section expressly grants the right to inspect not only a corporation's list of present stockholders, but also the stock ledger. *Compaq Computer Corp. v. Horton, 631 A.2d 1 (Del. 1993).*

More than general statement is required in order for the Court to determine the propriety of a demand for inspection. *Skouras v. Admiralty Enter., Inc., 386 A.2d 674 (Del. Ch. 1978).*

Evidence of "proper purpose" under subsection (b). — The failure of the plaintiff's witness to articulate certain words while testifying at trial is not fatal; a court may rely on the totality of the trial record, including pleadings, briefs and other written evidence concerning the purpose for the inspection. *Security First Corp. v. United States Die Casting & Dev., 687 A.2d 563 (Del. 1997).*

Unspecific demand fails to meet requirements of section. — When an unspecific demand unrelated to an imminent stockholders' meeting or a tender offer or the like which will affect plaintiff's interest as a stockholder is made, such an unspecific demand necessarily fails to meet the strict requirement of this section. *Weisman v. Western Pac. Indus., Inc., 344 A.2d 267 (Del. Ch. 1975).*

Scope of inspection for purpose of ascertaining possible existence of corporate mismanagement and waste. — If the plaintiffs are otherwise entitled to inspection and examination of the corporate books and records for the purpose of ascertaining the possible existence of corporate mismanagement and waste, then their right should not be limited to those transactions and conditions which have been heretofore brought to their attention and which have aroused their suspicions. Rather, it should extend to the corporate minutes and financial records in general during the period into which they seek to inquire, especially where the time span is reasonably related to the specific events cited as the basis for the demand. Particularly in such a situation the right should not be limited by the decision of present management that plaintiffs may inspect some records for this purpose, but not others. *Skoglund v. Ormand Indus., Inc., 372 A.2d 204 (Del. Ch. 1976).*

Inspection not available when corporation no longer in existence. — Plaintiff's demand for a list of defendant's stockholders is for an improper purpose inasmuch as the defendant is no longer in existence as a viable corporation as opposed to one whose activities are being wound up and cannot now be revived for continuing the business for which it was organized; this is so notwithstanding the fact that the defendant corporation continues for a period of 3 years for winding-up purposes under § 278 of this title. *Willard v. Harrworth Corp., 258 A.2d 914 (Del. Ch. 1969), aff'd, 267 A.2d 577 (Del. 1970).*

When a corporation, by action of the overwhelming majority of its stockholders, has ceased to exist as a corporate entity, there are no stockholders with any legal status as stockholders of that corporation or standing to demand the inspection of a stockholder list. *Willard v. Harrworth Corp., 267 A.2d 577 (Del. 1970).*

Inspection relief should not be denied because petitioner is a business competitor; that fact alone, without more, does not defeat the statutory right of inspection. *BBC Acquisition Corp. v. Durr-Fillauer Medical, Inc., 623 A.2d 85 (Del. Ch. 1992).*

Statutory discretion to impose limitations or conditions as to inspection confirms power of court to fashion relief to ends of justice. *Kerkorian v. Western Air Lines, 253 A.2d 221 (Del. Ch.), aff'd, 254 A.2d 240 (Del. 1969).*

Scope of inspection. — In determining the scope of inspection of a corporation's books and records, the court may consider the information previously furnished by the corporation, as well as the degree of certainty of the stockholder's intent to buy or sell shares in the corporation. *Thomas & Betts Corp. v. Leviton Mfg. Co., 685 A.2d 702 (Del. Ch. 1995), aff'd, 681 A.2d 1026 (Del. 1996).*

In discharging its responsibility to narrowly tailor the inspection right to a stockholder's stated purpose, the court has wide latitude in determining the proper scope; undergirding this discretion is a recognition that the interests of the corporation must be harmonized with those of the inspecting stockholder. *Thomas & Betts Corp. v. Leviton Mfg. Co., 681 A.2d 1026 (Del. 1996).*

The scope of production in a § 220 case should be circumscribed with precision, as opposed to the more comprehensive discovery permitted under Ch. Ct. R. 34. *Security First Corp. v. United States Die Casting & Dev., 687 A.2d 563 (Del. 1997).*

Inspection of records allowed: (1) before the date the shareholder acquired shares; (2) irrespective of the source of the records; and (3) whether given to the corporation by the target before or after the merger. *Saito v. McKesson HBOC, Inc., 806 A.2d 113 (Del. 2002).*

Inspection limited to necessary and sufficient documents. — Inspection is limited to those documents that are necessary, essential, and sufficient for the shareholders' purpose. *BBC Acquisition Corp. v. Durr-Fillauer Medical, Inc., 623 A.2d 85 (Del. Ch. 1992); Thomas & Betts Corp. v. Leviton Mfg. Co., 685 A.2d 702 (Del. Ch. 1995), aff'd, 681 A.2d 1026 (Del. 1996).*

Certificate of incorporation limiting inspection is void. *Loew's Theatres, Inc. v. Commercial Credit Co., 243 A.2d 78 (Del. Ch. 1968).*

Element of refusal. — A failure to respond to a demand within the 5-day statutory period is tantamount to a refusal. In addition, even though petitioner was allowed to inspect the books and records for what it believed to be the limited purpose of determining what records would be needed to perform an audit, the corporation refused to permit a later inspection for purposes of conducting the audit itself. That also constituted a refusal. *Helnsman Mgt. Servs., Inc. v. A & S Consultants, Inc., 525 A.2d 160 (Del. Ch. 1987).*

Absence of approval by sec is irrelevant in a proceeding under this section. *Mite Corp. v. Heli-Coil Corp., 256 A.2d 855 (Del. Ch. 1969).*

Burden of proof on corporation resisting inspection. — Where an inspection of the stock ledger is sought by a stockholder, the burden is upon the corporation to show that the stockholder is attempting to exercise the statutory right for a purpose not connected with the stockholder's interest as a stockholder, or that the stockholder's purpose is otherwise improper or unlawful. *Insuranshares Corp. v. Kirchner, 40 Del. 105, 5 A.2d 519 (1939).*

Once plaintiff has complied with form and manner of making demand for inspection, then under this section the burden of proof is upon defendant to establish that the inspection sought is for an improper purpose. *Mite Corp. v. Heli-Coil Corp., 256 A.2d 855 (Del. Ch. 1969).*

The burden of proof is on corporation to establish that the inspection the stockholder seeks is for an improper purpose. *Western Pac. Indus., Inc. v. Liggett & Myers, Inc., 310 A.2d 669 (Del. Ch. 1973).*

Defenses to inspection demand. — The self-critical analysis privilege did not apply to prevent a stockholder's access to the report of a special committee of the corporation appointed to investigate a pre-suit demand of the stockholder. *Grimes v. DSC Communications Corp., 724 A.2d 561 (Del. Ch. 1998).*

Claim of inadequate disclosure of confidential financial information. — Where one challenges the validity of a shareholder vote by claiming inadequate disclosure of confidential financial information in connection with that vote, the initial burden of proving complete disclosure of material facts relevant to the vote remains with the board of directors. If the board did withhold information in these special circumstances, it would still bear the burden of proving that: (1) the withheld information was confidential; and (2) the board only withheld the material confidential information from shareholders, who having been given notice and opportunity, failed to execute a reasonable confidentiality agreement. *Stroud v. Grace, 606 A.2d 75 (Del. 1992).*

Confidentiality agreements as a prerequisite to disclosure of confidential information. — It is entirely reasonable for a court to make the execution of a confidentiality agreement a prerequisite to disclosure of confidential information to stockholders for purposes of any meeting where a vote is taken. *Stroud v. Grace, 606 A.2d 75 (Del. 1992).*

Doubts resolved in favor of stockholder. — Any doubt of a stockholder's right to inspect under this section should be resolved in favor of the statutory right of the stockholder. *State ex rel. Foster v. Standard Oil Co., 41 Del. 172, 18 A.2d 235 (1941).*

Proxy context. — The potential for abuse is very much alive when the Section 220 demand is made-as this one is-in the context of an impending or ongoing proxy contest. While a Section 220 books and records action is a summary proceeding that demands prompt attention from this court, it can be difficult to process from start to finish on a schedule that accommodates the foreshortened time frame of an ongoing proxy fight. This is especially true where the stockholder makes a broad demand and expects to be able to publicly disclose in its proxy materials otherwise confidential documents or information obtained from the corporation after trial. In that situation, the court is not only required to try and decide the case in the space of a few weeks, but also is expected to make itself available to referee the inevitable series of disputes arising from the corporation's interest in maintaining the confidentiality of its information and the stockholder's interest in using otherwise confidential information in furtherance of its proxy solicitation. In those circumstances, a stockholder must of necessity, make a narrow request calling for the production of only a small number of categories of particular documents. *Highland Select Equity Fund, L.P. v. Motient Corp., 906 A.2d 156, 2006 Del. Ch. LEXIS 127 (July 6, 2006).*

There is nothing objectionable about availing oneself of federal rights to stay discovery. But that action should not then be followed by a Section 220 that seeks what amounts to one-way discovery into the same matters. *Highland Select Equity Fund, L.P. v. Motient Corp., 906 A.2d 156, 2006 Del. Ch. LEXIS 127 (July 6, 2006).*

Prompt relief by way of summary judgment should be afforded to a stockholder who meets the terms of this section. *Loew's Theatres, Inc. v. Commercial Credit Co., 243 A.2d 78 (Del. Ch. 1968).*

This section contemplates summary proceedings and the accelerated scheduling of cases under it emphasizes prompt processing and disposition. *Mite Corp. v. Heli-Coil Corp., 256 A.2d 855 (Del. Ch. 1969).*

Motion for summary judgment before 20-day period of Del. Ch. Ct. R. 56(a) was permitted by court for plaintiff shareholder, to enforce settlement agreement of disputes underlying an *8 Del. C. § 220* action, as a part of its power to control its docket; the corporation was not prejudiced since (1) material facts were both limited and personally known by the corporation's counsel (the evidence consisting of email exchanges between opposing counsel over the course of only a few days, and (2) the § 220 action was proceeding at an expeditious pace because actions under *8 Del. C.§ 220* are summary in nature. *Loppert v. Windsortech, Inc., 865 A.2d 1282 (Del. Ch. 2004).*

Adherence to scheduling orders. — Plaintiff stockholder's request for a defendant corporation's continued adherence to the court's scheduling order in the *8 Del. C. § 220* action was not evidence that the parties positively agreed to be bound by a signed writing that contained the terms of their settlement agreement; until a dismissal, stay, or new scheduling order was submitted and approved by the court, the stockholder had every right to expect the corporation to adhere to the existing scheduling order. *Loppert v. Windsortech, Inc., 865 A.2d 1282 (Del. Ch. 2004).*

Corporation's reliance on technical defect in demand not permitted. — Where corporation has long been fully aware of the reasons behind stockholder's demand to inspect, corporation's reliance on a technical defect in the demand may not be permitted to defeat stockholder's claim. *Skouras v. Admiralty Enter., Inc., 386 A.2d 674 (Del. Ch. 1978).*

Affirmative defense based on clean hands doctrine. — Where the plaintiff is a shareholder at the time of the events as to which inspection is sought, an affirmative defense based on the clean hands doctrine is immaterial and subject to a motion to strike. *Skoglund v. Ormand Indus., Inc., 372 A.2d 204 (Del. Ch. 1976).*

Res judicata has no application to subsequent demand to inspect stockholder list if the demanding stockholder has a bona fide purpose and there has been a change of circumstances since the earlier demand was refused. *Hatleigh Corp. v. Lane Bryant, Inc., 428 A.2d 350 (Del. Ch. 1981).*

Neither the doctrine of res judicata nor the principle of the law of the case has any application to a subsequent demand to inspect the stockholder list if plaintiff has a bona fide purpose. *Security First Corp. v. United States Die Casting & Dev., 687 A.2d 563 (Del. 1997).*

When the stock ledger is blank or nonexistent, the Court of Chancery has the power to consider other evidence to ascertain and establish stockholder status. *Rainbow Nav., Inc. v. Pan Ocean Nav., Inc., 535 A.2d 1357 (Del. 1987).*

Enforcement of settlement agreements. — Specific performance of settlement agreement was ordered in a stockholder's suit against a corporation; court found money damages were not adequate to compensate the stockholder for requirements such as award of stock options, mutual non-disparagement, and a general release (including settlement of the stockholder's *8 Del. C. § 220* suit). *Loppert v. Windsortech, Inc., 865 A.2d 1282 (Del. Ch. 2004).*

Abuse of Section 220 process found. — These facts describe a remarkable confluence of events that amount to an abuse of the Section 220 process, designed for some purpose other than to exercise plaintiff's legitimate rights as a stockholder. Indeed, the facts adduced at trial clearly suggest that plaintiff's purported purpose in bringing this Section 220 action to gain information for use in its proxy fight verges on being a ruse. Highland, from the beginning of this process, intended to file a proxy contest, and had all the information it needed to take that step, whether from public filings or from long service as a director of the defendant company. Plaintiff thus appears to have maintained its books and records demand in large part because it has derived utility from the demand itself as a rhetorical platform. That is not the kind of compelling circumstance this court described in *Disney*, that would authorize the use of Section 220 as a way of publicizing concerns about mismanagement. *Highland Select Equity Fund, L.P. v. Motient Corp., 906 A.2d 156, 2006 Del. Ch. LEXIS 127 (July 6, 2006).*

Demand denied. — In these circumstances, it is not the court's responsibility to pick through the debris of a Section 220 demand in this state of disarray and to find the few documents that might be justified as necessary and essential to the plaintiff's demand. In short, Section 220 contemplates a limited, discrete investigation into possible mismanagement for a number of proper purposes. But the evidence adduced at trial shows conclusively that plaintiff's demand is broadly inconsistent with that statutory scheme. For that reason, the demand in this case must be denied. *Highland Select Equity Fund, L.P. v. Motient Corp., 906 A.2d 156, 2006 Del. Ch. LEXIS 127 (July 6, 2006).*

Advisors to Delaware corporations should realize by now that the company's books and records can serve as a "tool at hand" to defend against unfounded charges of wrongdoing. A books and records demand under 8 Del. C. § 220 can afford the company an opportunity to rebut a shareholder's complaint and actually deter the filing of litigation. *In re Tyson Foods, Inc. Consol. S'holder Litig., 919 A.2d 563; 2007 Del. Ch. LEXIS 19 (February 6, 2007).*

Reasonable inference that transactions not reviewed. — It is true that a very strong negative inference is required for the chancery court to suppose from the facts alleged that the appropriate board committees did not review the transactions at issue, yet two aspects of the complaint lead to the conclusion that a negative inference is warranted. First, plaintiffs made a § 220 request to defendants who knew the crux of plaintiffs' complaint. Even if the request was in fact narrow, defendants had the opportunity to widen the scope of documents granted in order to exculpate themselves. While they were, of course, not required to do so, it is more reasonable to infer that exculpatory documents would be provided than to believe the opposite: that such documents existed and yet were inexplicably withheld. In re Tyson Foods, Inc. Consol. S'holder Litig., 919 A.2d 563; 2007 Del. Ch. LEXIS 19 (February 6, 2007).

Plaintiffs should have access to books and records that predate their purchase of stock in order to allow them to explore a potential lapse in the good faith of the board that would excuse demand in the California derivative suit. Plaintiffs cannot effectively address the alleged problem through a derivative suit unless they can properly plead demand futility. A violation of the duty of loyalty/good faith can, in theory, excuse demand, and because plaintiffs might need older documents to establish a sustained or systematic failure, the chancery court must conclude that plaintiffs' request for the documents here is reasonably related to their proper purpose as shareholders of the board. *Melzer v. CNET Networks, Inc., 934 A.2d 912, 2007 Del. Ch. LEXIS 163 (November 21, 2007).* **[For the full text of this case opinion, please see the Appendix at the end of this Volume.]**

DELAWARE CASE NOTES — UNREPORTED

In general. — Section 220 is a summary proceeding. Historically, only record holders had standing to seek inspection rights. Proof that the plaintiff was a stockholder of record generally ended that portion of the analysis. For example, it has been held that this section does not require that a shareholder have a 'direct' economic interest in the stock she owns of record to be entitled to enforce the inspection right. In addition, record holders have inspection rights even though the possibility exists that a stockholder may later be divested of this stock in some other proceeding or be declared in some future proceeding to be holding his stock contrary to law or private agreement. *Deephaven Risk Arb Trading, LTD.*

v. UnitedGlobalCom, Inc., 2005 Del. Ch. LEXIS 107, No. 379-N (July 13, 2005).

The policy of this section allows a stockholder, even one owning a single share, access to the corporation's books and records. There is nothing in the language of this section, nor in any case cited by plaintiff, that gives a large shareholder greater access to the corporate books and records and a greater ability to share those documents with other shareholders. Nor is the chancery court convinced that allowing any one shareholder to assume the role of public scourge of management with broad rights to release the corporation's confidential documents is sound public policy. There are other avenues for bringing directors to account for their mismanagement, most notably by contesting elections and by instituting derivative litigation. Nothing suggests that plaintiff or any other stockholder needs the ability to make public disclosure of the directors' confidential, internal deliberations to successfully pursue those other avenues. *Disney v. Walt Disney Co., 2005 Del. Ch. LEXIS 94, No. 234-N (June 20, 2005).*

The public policy of the state is to encourage stockholders to utilize Section 220 before filing a derivative action, as plaintiff is attempting to do here, in order to meet the heightened pleading requirements of Court of Chancery Rule 23.1 that are applicable to such actions. The fact that others, acting independently, have chosen to file derivative actions without having first used the tools at hand should not prevent plaintiff from doing so. *Freund v. Lucent Techs., 2003 Del. Ch. LEXIS 3, No. 18893 (January 9, 2003).*

The pleading requirement set forth in our cases exists to ensure that a Section 220 plaintiff does not initiate a books and records action merely to satisfy its own curiosity or suspicion. Rather, a plaintiff must have some reason to believe that wrongdoing has taken place. *Sutherland v. Dardanelle Timber Co., 2006 Del. Ch. LEXIS 88 (Del. Ch. May 16, 2006).*

Scope of inspection. — Entitlement to inspection under this section for a stockholder demonstrating a proper purpose is not open-ended; it is restricted to inspection of the books and records needed to perform the task, so an order allowing inspection is limited to those documents reasonably required to satisfy the purpose of the demand, and, while the court has wide latitude in determining the proper scope of inspection, it is the responsibility of the trial court to tailor the inspection to the stockholder's stated purpose, but, where a plaintiff has shown evidence of wide-ranging mismanagement or waste, a more wide-ranging inspection may be justified. *Freund v. Lucent Techs, 2003 Del. Ch. LEXIS 3 (Jan. 9, 2003).*

Stockholder's right to inspect and copy a stocklist is not absolute. Rather, it is a qualified right depending on the facts presented. If a court orders inspection of books and records or stocklists, the court has wide discretion in determining the proper scope of inspection in relation to the stockholder's purpose. The scope of inspection should be circumscribed with precision and limited to those documents that are essential and sufficient to the stockholder's purpose. *Wynnefield Partners Small Cap*

Value L.P. v. Niagara Corp., 2006 Del. Ch. LEXIS 119 (Del. Ch. June 19, 2006).

To demonstrate a proper purpose when seeking to investigate possible mismanagement, a stockholder must present some credible basis from which the court can infer that waste or mismanagement may have occurred. The threshold for a plaintiff in a Section 220 case is not insubstantial. Stockholders are not required to show actual mismanagement, but they must show, by a preponderance of the evidence, that there is a credible basis to find probable corporate wrongdoing. Stockholders cannot satisfy this burden merely by expressing a suspicion of wrongdoing or a disagreement with a business decision. *Deephaven Risk Arb Trading, LTD. v. UnitedGlobalCom, Inc., 2005 Del. Ch. LEXIS 107, No. 379-N (July 13, 2005).*

Primary purpose. — Plaintiff's Section 220 action appears uniquely irrelevant to her purported ulterior motive of personal animosity. While a Section 220 claim can, as our cases have held, act as leverage where the plaintiff's real purpose is to pressure the defendant to buy its stock, or to gather information on an unrelated suit, the court finds it difficult to understand how the production plaintiff seeks could even theoretically act to address her personal grievances towards her brothers. None of the information demanded is personal, or personally embarrassing in any way other than as it relates to her potential fiduciary duty claims. Nor does any of it have anything to do with her mother, or with the trust through which one brother controls the corporations and which supposedly is at the center of plaintiff's anger. On balance, therefore, while the vehemence of her efforts might have something to do with her animosity towards two of her brothers, all the evidence supports the conclusion that her primary purpose is to gather information about a corporation in which she is a major stockholder. Plaintiff's primary purpose, thus, is precisely that for which Section 220 is designed. *Sutherland v. Dardanelle Timber Co., 2006 Del. Ch. LEXIS 88 (Del. Ch. May 16, 2006).*

Specificity of purpose. — Delaware law does not permit section 220 actions based on an ephemeral purpose, nor will this court impute a purpose absent the plaintiff stating one. Simply put, plaintiff must do more than state, in a conclusory manner, a generally accepted proper purpose. Plaintiff must state a reason for the purpose, i.e., what it will do with the information, or an end to which that investigation may lead. Here, it is clear plaintiff's sole purpose and end is to pursue a second derivative suit-an end barred by issue preclusion. West Coast Mgmt. & Capital, LLC v. Carrier Access Corp., 2006 Del. Ch. LEXIS 195 (Nov. 14, 2006).

"Under oath". — Subdivision (a)(4)'s use of "includes" authorizes use of an affirmation under penalty of perjury as an alternative to swearing an oath before a notary public in the more traditional sense. *Deephaven Risk Arb Trading Ltd. v. UnitedGlobalCom, Inc., 2004 Del. Ch. LEXIS 130, No. 379-N (Aug. 30, 2004).*

Effect of 2003 Amendment. — Before amendment, rights under this section were available only to stockholders of record, and as a result, beneficial owners whose stock was held on their behalf were required to either have shares re-issued in their names before issuing a demand letter or request that the action be prosecuted on their behalf by the record holder. The 2003 amendment to this section liberalized the statute in order to obviate such technical hurdles. *Deephaven Risk Arb Trading, LTD. v. UnitedGlobalCom, Inc., 2005 Del. Ch. LEXIS 107, No. 379-N (July 13, 2005).*

The 2003 amendment affords to beneficial holders all § 220 rights previously held by record holders. Therefore, established law that record holders need not have an economic interest in stock to have inspection rights applies with equal force to beneficial holders. *Deephaven Risk Arb Trading, LTD. v. UnitedGlobalCom, Inc., 2005 Del. Ch. LEXIS 107, No. 379-N (July 13, 2005).*

Allegations or evidence necessary by person seeking inspection. — In a suit by maintenance corporation directors brought against defendants (who admitted that they placed personal property on open space in a housing development and failed to remove the property), defendants failed to state a proper purpose for their request for the corporation's books and records. *Fairthorne Maint. Corp. v. Ramunno, 2007 Del. Ch. LEXIS 107 (Del. Ch. July 20, 2007).*

Statistical analysis performed by a shareholder's expert (coupled with credible testimony at trial) provided sufficient evidence of possible wrongdoing at a corporation, regarding the backdating or spring-loading of stock options that were issued to executive managers to warrant further limited inquiry into the matter through the examination of the corporation's books and records. *La. Mun. Police Emples. Retiremeemt Sys. v. Countrywide Fin. Corp., 2007 Del. Ch. LEXIS 138 (Del. Ch. Oct. 2, 2007).*

Construction with Rule 34. — There is a significant difference in scope between a section 220 action and discovery under Rule 34. The two are, in fact, entirely different procedures. Section 220 is not intended to supplant or circumvent discovery proceedings, nor should it be used to obtain that discovery in advance of the appraisal action itself. If plaintiff wishes to receive the documents it seeks in this action, it must elect to seek appraisal and request them through the discovery process. To now permit plaintiff's additional information beyond the comprehensive disclosure already in the public domain simply because it could receive such information in a later appraisal action through discovery would be putting the cart before the horse. *Polygon Global Opportunities Master Fund v. W. Corp., 2006 Del. Ch. LEXIS 179 (Oct. 12, 2006).*

Effect of deregistration decision. — Delaware law recognizes a corporate board's ability, in a proper exercise of their business judgment, to cause the corporation to take steps to deregister even if, as an incidental matter, deregistration might adversely impact the market for the corporation's securities. The chancery court judge knows of no books and records case where a plaintiff succeeded on its demand solely because the board decided to deregister the company's shares. Without more specific facts that provide a credible basis to suspect wrongdoing, such a demand could not be granted in the instant case.

Stockholder's right to inspect and copy a stocklist is not absolute. Rather, it is a qualified right depending on the facts presented. If a court orders inspection of books and records or stocklists, the court has wide discretion in determining the proper scope of inspection in relation to the stockholder's purpose. The scope of inspection should be circumscribed with precision and limited to those documents that are essential and sufficient to the stockholder's purpose. *Wynnefield Partners Small Cap Value L.P. v. Niagara Corp., 2006 Del. Ch. LEXIS 119 (Del. Ch. June 19, 2006).*

Confidentiality. — Confidential documents are entitled to confidentiality. There must, however, be a reason for insisting upon confidential treatment. It need not be limited to harm to the corporation itself, however, because a corporation's books and records frequently contain, for example, sensitive personal information relating to the various participants in the corporation's activities. Moreover, imposing harm in fact as the standard for maintaining confidentiality would establish too great a burden for the corporation, especially in light of the time constraints on Section 220 compliance. The risk of harm, of whatever nature, must be evaluated on the basis of magnitude and likelihood, an effort that is inherently speculative. *Amalgamated Bank v. UICI, 2005 Del. Ch. LEXIS 82, No. 884-N (June 2, 2005).*

An affirmative defense that might successfully meet a claim investigated through a Section 220 **inspection does not necessarily preclude** access to the pertinent books and records. *Amalgamated Bank v. UICI, 2005 Del. Ch. LEXIS 82, No. 884-N (June 2, 2005).*

Superfluous motions. — A motion to expedite proceedings under subsection (k) of Section 145 is superfluous. The text of the subsection dictates that a proceeding under that provision is "summary." In order to receive summary adjudication of a claim for advancement it is not necessary to file a motion to expedite. If a plaintiff files a motion to expedite it is, in effect, a request to expedite a summary proceeding. Only when unique circumstances are present, e.g., insolvency of the putative indemnitee or inability to retain counsel without advancement, will the chancery court entertain a request to "expedite" a proceeding that is already summary in nature. In the opinion of the chancery court, this reasoning extends to other summary proceedings, such as those brought under this section and Section 225 of the General Corporation Law. *Brown v. Rite Aid Corp., 2004 Del. Ch. LEXIS 29, No. 094-N (May 29, 2004).*

Power of attorney is required under 8 Del. C. § 220(b) only when an attorney or agent makes the demand; implicit in § 220(b) is a requirement that when inspection is to be made by a person other than the stockholder, the corporation be given evidence of that person's authority to act. *Deephaven Risk Arb Trading Ltd. v. UnitedGlobalCom, Inc., 2004 Del. Ch. LEXIS 130 (Aug. 30, 2004).*

A Section 220 action is not the proper forum for litigating a breach of fiduciary duty case. All that the Section 220 plaintiff must show is a credible basis for claiming that "there are legitimate issues of wrongdoing. *Khanna v.*

Covad Communs. Group, 2004 Del. Ch. LEXIS 11. No. 20481-NC (January 23, 2004) .

Adequacy of inspection demand. — The basis for a plaintiff's suspicions under this section can best be addressed after the factual record is developed at trial. The same rationale applies in the context of an evaluation of the adequacy of a plaintiff's inspection demand under this section. *Romero v. Career Educ. Corp., 2005 Del. Ch. LEXIS 112, No. 793-N (July 19, 2005)*.

Preemption. — Both Delaware and federal courts have determined that the Private Securities Litigation Reform Act and Securities Litigation Uniform Standards Act do not necessarily preempt this section. *Romero v. Career Educ. Corp., 2005 Del. Ch. LEXIS 112, No. 793-N (July 19, 2005)*.

Section 220 was not implicitly preempted under U.S. Const. art. VI, cl. 2 by the automatic stay provisions under 15 U.S.C. §§ 77z-1(b)(1), (4), 78u-4(b)(3)(D) of the Private Securities Litigation Reform Act of 1995 and the Securities Litigation Uniform Standards Act since the § 220 action did not seek records that pertained directly to a federal securities law claim asserted in a pending federal action; the shareholder's state action was unrelated to the federal action filed against the corporation in which a stay was imposed under the acts. *Cohen v. El Paso Corp., 2004 Del. Ch. LEXIS 149 (Oct. 18, 2004)*.

There is a dichotomy in section 220 cases between publicly traded companies and closely held companies. With regard to the former, public SEC filings typically provide significant amounts of information about a company, and decisions granting section 220 demands are narrowly tailored to address specific needs, often in response to allegations of wrongdoing. In contrast, stockholders in non-publicly traded companies do not have the wealth of information provided in SEC filings and are often accorded broader relief in section 220 actions. *Polygon Global Opportunities Master Fund v. W. Corp., 2006 Del. Ch. LEXIS 179 (Oct. 12, 2006)*.

Rule 13e-3 disclosures. — In the case of a going private transaction governed by SEC Rule 13e-3, the amount of information made publicly available is even more comprehensive than that required in standard SEC periodic filings. Through its preliminary and final proxy materials, and its Schedule 13E-3, and amendments, defendants would appear to have disclosed all material information necessary for plaintiffs to determine whether or not to seek appraisal. This is not to say that there is a per se rule that the disclosure requirements under Rule 13e-3 are coextensive with the "necessary, essential and sufficient" information standard under section 220 demands for valuing stock in the case of a minority squeeze-out merger. Nevertheless, in the present case, the detail and scope of defendant's disclosures makes this so. *Polygon Global Opportunities Master Fund v. W. Corp., 2006 Del. Ch. LEXIS 179 (Oct. 12, 2006)*.

Limitations. — Although a shareholder was entitled to inspect a corporation's books and records to determine if the board of director's had committed misconduct during a merger with another corporation, the right of inspection was limited to records created on or after the date the

shareholder purchased his shares and to the corporations in which he owned shares, and did not include the right to inspect records created by third parties who advised the corporations during the merger to determine if a separate cause of action existed against those parties. *Saito v. McKesson HBOC, Inc., 2001 Del. Ch. LEXIS 96 (July 10, 2001)*.

Voluntary motion to dismiss complaint filed by named shareholders in derivative suit was granted, where the dismissal was with prejudice as to the named shareholders only, and not to the putative class of shareholders; defendant directors had sought dismissal of the complaint following receipt of the named shareholders' demand to review the corporate books under this section. *Taubenfeld v. Marriott Int'l, Inc., 2003 Del. Ch. LEXIS 108 (Del. Ch. Oct. 28, 2003)*.

Inspection stay granted. — When corporation appealed an order allowing its stockholder to inspect the books and records of corporation's subsidiary, it was appropriate to stay the order pending the appeal because, unless a stay was entered, it was likely that the full production required could be accomplished before an appeal was heard, thus mooting the appeal, and the law authorizing this inspection was new and raised fair ground for litigation over its scope and meaning. *Orloff v. Weinstein Enters., 2004 Del. Ch. LEXIS 85 (June 22, 2004)*.

Obstruction complaint dismissed. — Complaint (that alleged an officer obstructed directors from obtaining corporate information they were entitled to) was dismissed for failing to state a claim, as it did not allege any denial of the directors' rights of inspection under subsection (d) of this section, or that they were hindered in the performance of their directorial duties. *Haseotes v. Bentas, 2002 Del. Ch. LEXIS 106 (Sept. 3, 2002)*.

Limited access granted. — Subject to confidentiality agreements, the court concluded that two unrelated stockholders should have access to lists of other stockholders to further investigate their suspicions of mismanagement; but, between the two of them, the court granted access to books and records as to only one specific transaction, since the primary purposes for their other requests had not been well substantiated. *Marathon Partners, L.P. v. M&F Worldwide Corp., 2004 Del. Ch. LEXIS 101 (July 30, 2004)*.

Shareholder's inspection of corporate books and records was limited to the proper purposes for its investigation: (1) the investigation of potential wrongdoing, mismanagement, or breaches of fiduciary duties by members of the corporation's board of directors in connection with the granting of stock options to corporate executives; and (2) the assessment of the ability of the corporate board to impartially consider a demand for action, related to the items described in the demand letter. *La. Mun. Police Emples. Retirememt Sys. v. Countrywide Fin. Corp., 2007 Del. Ch. LEXIS 138 (Del. Ch. Oct. 2, 2007)*.

Shareholder established "some credible basis" to support an inference of corporate waste or mismanagement, in support of a demand to inspect corporate records, given a formal Securities and Exchange

Commission investigation of the corporation's accounting practices, the corporation's revisions of financial statements, and the commencement of litigation by other shareholders after the precipitous decline of the value of the corporation's stock. *Freund v. Lucent Techs, 2003 Del. Ch. LEXIS 3 (Jan. 9, 2003).*

Shareholder's 8 Del. C. § 220 action had a credible basis, as it was filed after the corporation announced a one billion dollar write-down as a result of improper accounting and after the Securities and Exchange Commission launched a formal investigation into the corporation's accounting practices; nothing supported the corporation's assertion that the shareholder was attempting to aid the plaintiffs in a federal class action against the corporation in which discovery had been stayed, as there were no ties between the shareholder and plaintiffs in that action. *Cohen v. El Paso Corp., 2004 Del. Ch. LEXIS 149 (Oct. 18, 2004).*

Inspection demand fully satisfied. — In a case brought under this section which involved cross motions for summary judgment, the court granted defendants' motion for summary judgment concluding, based on the record before it, that defendants had fully satisfied plaintiffs' demand for inspection of the corporation's books and records. *Messina v. Klugiewicz, 2004 Del. Ch. LEXIS 47 (Apr. 30, 2004).*

Examining records in anticipation of class action. — Transferable rights beneficial holder alleged sufficient facts under oath to survive a corporation's Ch. Ct. R. 12(b)(6) motion to dismiss its 8 Del. C. § 220 summary action to inspect corporate records after the number of available oversubscription rights to acquire the corporation's common stock (at a price less than the then current market value) substantially decreased; utilization of 8 Del. C. § 220 was encouraged for the purpose of meeting Ch. Ct. R. 23.1 specificity requirements, before filing a derivative suit to contest acts (mismanagement, dilution, preferential treatment, or selling to insiders) that might have caused the corporation to have breached its rights offering obligations. *Deephaven Risk Arb Trading Ltd. v. UnitedGlobalCom, Inc., 2004 Del. Ch. LEXIS 130 (Aug. 30, 2004).*

Individual stockholder incidentally part of class action. — Filing of a derivative action did not preclude a shareholder from bringing an action seeking disclosure of corporate records as well, since: disclosure had originally been demanded long before filing of the derivative action; and, it would not have been necessary if the corporation had properly responded to the demand in a timely manner. *Khanna v. Covad Communs. Group, Inc., 2004 Del. Ch. LEXIS 11 (Jan. 23, 2004).*

Stock warrants insufficient for right to inspection. — Though a stockholder successfully maintained an action against defendants to enforce his rights of inspection of a corporation's books and records pursuant to 8 Del. C. § 220, such stockholder lacked standing to serve as co-lead plaintiff in a derivative action in as much as the stockholder had incurred a lapse of stock ownership for a five month period, which caused the continuous ownership requirement of 8 Del. C. § 327 and Del. Ch. Ct. R. 23.1 not

to have been met; ownership of stock warrants was insufficient to satisfy the continuous ownership requirement, as such warrants were contractual, convertible entitlements that did not establish him as a stockholder. *In re New Valley Corp. Derivative Litig., 2004 Del. Ch. LEXIS 107 (June 28, 2004).*

Shareholder satisfied the requirement of presenting credible evidence of possible corporate wrongdoing entitling the shareholder to enforcement of the right to inspect corporate documents, but the court placed various limits on disclosure; it would determine document by document which were protected as work product or under attorney-client privilege and precluded the shareholder from obtaining access to those documents that related primarily to claims arising out of the shareholder's employment-based claims (as opposed to claims arising out of stock ownership). *Khanna v. Covad Communs. Group, Inc., 2004 Del. Ch. LEXIS 11 (Jan. 23, 2004).*

Statement under oath. — Verification under oath that the statements therein are true and accurate, signed by a corporate representative with a notation signed by a notary that it has been "sworn to and subscribed before" him clearly fulfilled the "under oath" requirement of 8 Del. C. § 220; 8 Del. C. § 220's use of "includes" was read to authorize use of an affirmation under penalty of perjury as an alternative to swearing an oath before a notary public in the more traditional sense. *Deephaven Risk Arb Trading Ltd. v. UnitedGlobalCom, Inc., 2004 Del. Ch. LEXIS 130 (Aug. 30, 2004).*

Stockholder who sought an order allowing inspection of the books and records of a corporation did not have to prove that there was mismanagement before being entitled to such an order; evidence that the stockholder presented, although hearsay, was sufficient to raise questions about whether the corporation made improper loans to one of its officers and decisions that affected the value of the stockholder's shares, and those questions could only be resolved by allowing the stockholder to inspect the corporation's stock list, books, and records. *Marmon v. Arbinett-Thexchange, Inc., 2004 Del. Ch. LEXIS 44 (Apr. 28, 2004).*

Former director's inspection rights. — Company was granted summary judgment on an employee's demand to inspect the company's books and records pursuant to subsection (d) of this section where the employee was removed as a director of the company after leaving its employ, therefore losing standing to pursue the claim for inspection under that subsection. *Jacobson v. Dryson Acceptance Corp., 2002 Del. Ch. LEXIS 4 (Jan. 9, 2002).*

Potential individual claims. — Mere existence of potential individual (as contrasted with shareholder) claims against the corporation or its officers and directors does not necessarily defeat inspection rights under this section. On the other hand, the existence of such potential personal claims provides a basis for further inquiry into the shareholder's purpose. *Khanna v. Covad Communs. Group, 2004 Del. Ch. LEXIS 11. No. 20481-NC (January 23, 2004).*

Attorney's fees. — Chairman and a vice president of a business corporation were liable for the director's and the

Corporations

shareholder corporation's reasonable attorneys' fees to a director and a shareholder corporation that owned stock in the business corporation, as the chairman and the vice president denied the director the right of access to the corporate records; however, the chairman and the vice president were not liable for the fees the director and the shareholder corporation incurred in prosecuting an action for recovery of those fees, because the chairman's and the vice president's opposition to the director's and the shareholder corporation's request for attorneys' fees was not egregious or in bad faith. *Carlson v. Hallinan, 2006 Del. Ch. LEXIS 58 (Del. Ch. Mar. 21, 2006)*.

Stockholder was not entitled to an award of attorney's fees, because: (1) the stockholder did not show a clear right to all requested documents based on an alleged valuation purpose or that the corporation acted in bad faith in opposing the stockholder's requests; (2) the stockholder did not show a clear right to the requested documents for the purpose of determining whether the corporation engaged in corporate waste or mismanagement until late in the litigation, if at all; (3) the corporation produced documents on multiple occasions before trial and the court was not aware of any instance in which the corporation intentionally misrepresented material facts to the court; and (4) the corporation did not engage to any material extent in an improper merits defense to any of the shareholder's claimed purposes for inspecting the corporation's books and records. *Norman v. US Mobil-Comm, Inc., 2006 Del. Ch. LEXIS 81 (Del. Ch. Apr. 28, 2006)*.

Illustrative cases. — Trial court granted the corporation's cross-motion for summary judgment as to the purported shareholder's demand for inspection of the corporation's books and records; the purported shareholder had not included the statutorily-required statement in the demand that the purported stockholder's documentary evidence of stock beneficial ownership was a "true and correct copy of what it purports to be." *Seinfeld v. Verizon Communications Inc., 2005 Del. Ch. LEXIS 9 (Jan. 21, 2005)*.

Where stockholders asserted they wanted to examine the corporation's books and records, their reasons of wanting to evaluate their stock values (as well as waste and mismanagement) were proper purposes. *Dobler v. Montgomery Cellular Holding Co., 2001 Del. Ch. LEXIS 126 (Del. Ch. Oct. 19, 2001)*.

Shareholder's demand to view records was granted as the shareholder established the requisite essential and sufficient relationship between his stated purpose and the records and books that he sought to inspect, where he asserted that mismanagement had occurred. *Magid v. Acceptance Ins. Cos., 2001 Del. Ch. LEXIS 141 (Nov. 15, 2001)*.

Access to documents prior to death of original owner. — Given the purposes of 8 Del. C. § 220 and the rationales stated by the plaintiff shareholder in action to investigate allegations of self-dealing by a controlling corporate board member and the member's brother, access to documents relating to the enjoyment of salary and benefits by both members for the period commencing one full fiscal year before the death of the original corporate owner was granted. *Sutherland v. Dardanelle Timber Co., 2005 Del. Ch. LEXIS 181 (Del. Ch. Nov. 18, 2005)*.

Demand based on suspicion or curiosity. — After viewing the evidence in the light most favorable to a stockholder, the court held that stockholder failed to carry the burden of showing that there was a credible basis from which the court could infer that the corporate board of directors committed waste or mismanagement in compensating 3 executives during the relevant period of time, but instead clearly established that the stockholder's 8 Del. C. § 220 demand was made merely on the basis of suspicion or curiosity. *Seinfeld v. Verizon Communs., Inc., 2005 Del. Ch. LEXIS 185 (Del. Ch. Nov. 23, 2005)*.

Filing of a derivative action did not preclude a shareholder from pursuing an action to compel disclosure of corporate records where it was the failure to timely disclose materials properly sought that led to the overlap in actions, and the shareholder had shown a proper purpose all along and had appropriately narrowed the demand; therefore, the court adhered to its original decision denying a motion to dismiss the action under 8 Del. C. § 220, and refused to reconsider it. *Romero v. Career Educ. Corp., 2005 Del. Ch. LEXIS 172 (Del. Ch. Nov. 4, 2005)*.

8 Del. C. § 220 actions were not conclusively precluded by the filing of related derivative litigation; a motion to stay a stockholder's books and records action until a special litigation committee had completed its investigation into the matters alleged in a separate derivative litigation was denied. *Kaufman v. Computer Assocs. Int'l, 2005 Del. Ch. LEXIS 192 (Del. Ch. Dec. 13, 2005)*.

Demonstrated entitlement to inspection. — Founder and shareholders of a health maintenance organization (HMO) were improperly denied their right to an inspection of the books and records of a holding company that acquired the HMO and affiliated companies that provided services to the HMO; the responses that were made to the inspection demands by the founder, who was forced out of a management position at the HMO, were inadequate. *Horbal v. Three Rivers Holdings, Inc., 2006 Del. Ch. LEXIS 53 (Del. Ch. Mar. 10, 2006)*.

Demonstrated entitlement to inspection. — Shareholder's demand letter complied with the technical requirements of *8 Del. C. § 220(b)* because the demand was in writing, under oath, directed to the corporation's principal place of business, and purported to state a proper purpose for the inspection of the corporation's books and records; in addition, the shareholder filed the action after the expiration of the 5-day response period provided to the corporation by *8 Del. C. § 220(c)*. *La. Mun. Police Emples. Retiremt Sys. v. Countrywide Fin. Corp., 2007 Del. Ch. LEXIS 138 (Del. Ch. Oct. 2, 2007)*.

Relitigation of prior determination. — When, in dismissing on demand excusal grounds, another court has denied discovery and leave to amend, it would undermine that decision for this court to permit the same plaintiff to pursue a section 220 action solely targeted at gaining information to relitigate that prior determination. *West*

Coast Mgmt. & Capital, LLC v. Carrier Access Corp., 2006 Del. Ch. LEXIS 195 (Nov. 14, 2006).

Stay denied. — Plaintiff previously demonstrated a credible basis for suspecting possible wrongdoing and proved its entitlement to inspect books and records. If the court grants the stay, plaintiff likely will lose that right forever. Conversely, if the court denies the stay, defendant's right to appellate review may be mooted. In the unique circumstances of this case, i.e., where the grant of a stay will likely permanently deprive plaintiff of its Section 220 inspection right, the court concludes that the substantial harm plaintiff will suffer as a result of a stay outweighs the harm defendant will suffer in the absence of a stay. *Wynnefield Ptnrs. Small Cap Value L.P. v. Niagara Corp., 2006 Del. Ch. LEXIS 144 (Aug. 9, 2006).*

Pretextual purposes. — Chancery Court denied relief to an equity fund that sought an inspection of the books and records of a corporation; while the fund stated 2 proper purposes for seeking the inspection, those purposes were pretextual, and the fund's real purpose in seeking the inspection was to further its position regarding a proxy contest for control of the corporation's board of directors. *Highland Select Equity Fund, L.P. v. Motient Corp., 2007 Del. Ch. LEXIS 37 (Del. Ch. Feb. 26, 2007).*

Plaintiff established a proper purpose for inquiring into the offering where his allegations turned on a decision to raise capital in a way that triggers a controlling shareholder's contractual right in spite of either (i) a lack of necessity for the decision or (ii) a viable or preferable alternative to the financing that has a less negative impact on minority shareholders or the corporation. *Robotti & Co., LLC v. Gulfport Energy Corp., 2007 Del. Ch. LEXIS 94 (July 3, 2007).*

Corporation's motion to compel discovery under Ch. Ct. R. 37 was granted pursuant to Ch. Ct. R. 26(b)(1), because: (1) the corporation's request for a solicitation letter sent to the stockholders by their counsel was reasonably calculated to lead to evidence potentially relevant to the stockholders' claim; (2) the stockholders' purpose in seeking an inspection of books and records under 8 Del. C. § 220 was at issue; and (3) the attorney-client privilege was implicitly waived by the stockholders. *Meltzer v. CNET Networks, 2007 Del. Ch. LEXIS 132 (Del. Ch. Sept. 6, 2007).*

CASE NOTES — OTHER STATES

Alabama

Statement of purpose not required. — Under the law of the State of Delaware, a stockholder who seeks to enforce his right to inspect the books and records of a corporation in which he holds an interest need only demand of the directors of that corporation that such an inspection be permitted; he need not set out his purpose in seeking such an inspection, before or at the time of the filing of a petition. *Birwood Paper Co. v. Damsky, 285 Ala. 685, 235 So. 2d 825 (1970).*

California

Construction with California law. — Although Delaware law might not require a corporation to allow stockholders to inspect the list, it does not prohibit it; compliance with a California statute requiring access for inspection leads to no violation of *Delaware law. Valtz v. Penta Investment Corp., 139 Cal. App. 3d 803, 188 Cal. Rptr. 922 (1983).*

Illinois

By its express terms the section purports only to regulate the conduct of business in its own state, and clearly was not intended to follow the corporation into other states wherein Delaware corporations might be licensed to do business. *McCormick v. Statler Hotels Delaware, 30 Ill. 2d 86, 195 N.E.2d 172 (1963).*

Massachusetts

No amendment rule. — This Massachusetts trial court is unable to predict, and probably should not attempt to do so, whether the Delaware Supreme Court's comments in *Panic* will be limited to efforts to amend a complaint only after an unsuccessful appeal or, rather, will also apply at the trial stage. It would not be surprising for Delaware to decide that the no-amendment rule should also apply in its Chancery or Superior courts after an unsuccessful result on a motion to dismiss. *In re Sonus* *Networks, Inc., 2007 Mass. Super. LEXIS 547 (December 7, 2007).*

This kind of let's-see-what-the-judge-does-on-the-motion-attacking-present-complaint-first,-and-then-move-to-amend-later approach is not favored in a busy session of the superior court. Further, with this particular court, the plaintiff's counsel—at least his local counsel—must be deemed to have been fully aware of this court's approach to these kinds of cases, particularly the reliance on the Delaware Supreme Court's decision in *White v. Panic* to decline leave to amend. *In re Am. Tower Corp. Derivative Litig., 23 Mass. L. Rep. 337, 2007 Mass. Super. LEXIS 517 (November 27, 2007).*

New York

Valuation proper basis. — The valuation of a significant minority shareholder's stock in anticipation of a sale is a proper basis for inspection of books and records under Delaware law; once established, any ulterior purpose is irrelevant. Generally, absent an agreement providing otherwise, shareholders have the right to sell their shares to whomever they wish. The preservation of family ownership is permissible if in furtherance of the independent good of the corporation itself. However, the interests of the controlling shareholder are not necessarily the interests of the corporation. *Leviton Manufacturing Co., Inc. v. Blumberg, 242 A.D.2d 205, 660 N.Y.S.2d 726 (1997).*

Demand made in petition does not meet any of the requirements of Delaware Corporation Law § 220. Even to the extent that such a request could have been served directly upon defendant as a corporate officer at the time of the institution of this action, none of the other aforementioned statutory criteria were met as they would have pertained to him. Moreover, there is every reason to believe that defendant essentially complied with the substance of the request when he made all surviving corporate records available to plaintiff, plaintiff's wife and his attorney, for inspection over at least a two day period in 2003. Accordingly the first cause of action seeking inspection of the corporate books and records, to the extent that they have not already been provided to plaintiff, is dismissed. *Potter v. Arrington, 2006 NY Slip Op 26062, 2006 N.Y. Misc. LEXIS 300 (Feb. 6, 2006).*

Texas

Burden of establishing bad faith demand. — Bad faith Delaware law requires proof that the demand for inspection is made in bad faith. The corporation bears the burden of proving that the demand is for an improper purpose. Any doubt must be resolved in favor of the statutory right of the stockholder to have an inspection. Contacting other stockholders to determine if they wish to join in a suit is a proper purpose under Delaware law. *In re Halter, 1999 Tex. App. LEXIS 6478 (1999).*

Virginia

The Delaware Court of Chancery has exclusive jurisdiction to order inspection under Del. Code tit. 8, § 220. *Foti v. Western Sizzlin Corporation, 64 Va. Cir. 64 (2004).*

CASE NOTES — FEDERAL

Second Circuit

Right of inspection construed strictly. — Persons who supply equity capital to a corporation and directly elect its directors, but who are not stockholders of record, have no right to inspect corporate records, for Delaware has created a statutory right of inspection in favor of a stockholder. Del. Code. Ann. tit. 8 § 220(b), has defined "stockholder" to mean a stockholder of record. Del. Code Ann. tit. 8 § 220(a) has provided that the stock ledger shall be the only evidence as to who are the stockholders entitled to examine the stock ledger, the list required by this section or the books of the corporation under Del. Code Ann. tit. 8 § 219(c). The statutory right of inspection has been construed strictly, and the Delaware Supreme Court has held that establishing oneself as a stockholder of record is a mandatory condition precedent to the right to make a demand for inspection under Del. Code Ann. tit. 8 § 220. *Shaw v. Agri-Mark, Inc., 50 F.3d 117 (2d Cir. 1995).*

New York court lacked subject matter jurisdiction. — This statute vests the Delaware Court of Chancery with exclusive jurisdiction to determine whether or not the person seeking inspection is entitled to the inspection sought. Thus, defendants argue, New York court lacks subject matter jurisdiction to adjudicate this claim. The court agrees. *Reserve Solutions, Inc. v. Vernaglia, 2006 U.S. Dist. LEXIS 41430 (D.N.Y. June 20, 2006).*

Equitable relief not available. — Plaintiff unsuccessfully argues that the court may, and should, require defendants to allow plaintiff access to its books and records not pursuant to the Delaware statute, but pursuant to the court's power to fashion equitable remedies. However, plaintiff has not made a showing that equitable relief is warranted here. That plaintiff will likely have access to corporate books and records in discovery requires him to make an even more heightened showing regarding why he needs those records at this time. This he has failed to do. *Reserve Solutions, Inc. v. Vernaglia, 2006 U.S. Dist. LEXIS 41430 (D.N.Y. June 20, 2006).*

Fifth Circuit

A qualified shareholder enjoys a near absolute right to inspect a corporation's "stock ledger" or "list of stockholders." Inspection of these documents will be bridled only upon a showing by the corporation that the shareholder's purpose is improper. *In re LTV Litigation, 89 F.R.D. 595 (N.D.Tex 1981).*

The inspection statute may not be used to compel disclosure to a stockholder of matters which would otherwise be protected by the attorney-client privilege of the directors. *In re LTV Litigation, 89 F.R.D. 595 (N.D.Tex 1981).*

Seventh Circuit

Use by those contemplating derivative action. — Delaware law prohibits a plaintiff in a shareholder derivative action from using discovery under civil procedure rules until the case survives a motion to dismiss under the heightened pleading standard of Del. Ch. Ct. R. 23.1. In fact, because civil discovery is not readily available in derivative actions, the Delaware courts have repeatedly instructed shareholders contemplating a derivative action to use "the tools at hand," including Del. Code Ann. tit. 8, § 220, to obtain information needed to investigate and prepare a demand and later derivative action. *City of Austin Police Retirement System v. ITT Educational Services, Inc., 2005 U.S. Dist. LEXIS 1646 (S.D.Ind. 2005).*

Del. Code Ann. tit. 8, § 220 actions differ from standard civil discovery in at least two important respects. First, § 220 is limited to the right to inspect existing records and documents. It does not provide the tools of depositions, interrogatories, requests for admission, or inspections of places or things. Second, § 220 involves direct court supervision of the disclosure of information, which differs from the standard civil discovery practice of having opposing parties handle their own exchange of information, with court intervention only as needed. *City of Austin Police Retirement System v. ITT Educational Services, Inc., 2005 U.S. Dist. LEXIS 1646 (S.D.Ind. 2005).*

In substance, a Del. Code Ann. tit. 8, § 220 action is a judicially controlled procedure for forcing a corporation to provide a form of discovery to stockholders. *City of Austin Police Retirement System v. ITT Educational Services, Inc., 2005 U.S. Dist. LEXIS 1646 (S.D.Ind. 2005).*

Under Del. Code Ann. tit. 8, § 220, a plaintiff shareholder must make a credible showing that there are legitimate issues of wrongdoing and must have a proper purpose. *City of Austin Police Retirement System v. ITT Educational Services, Inc., 2005 U.S. Dist. LEXIS 1646 (S.D.Ind. 2005).*

Discovery request. — Generally speaking, the prevailing view seems to be that, in a derivative action, discovery should not be allowed during the pendency of a motion to dismiss. *Sylvia Piven As Tr. for the Leonard Piven Trust Uad 05/21/81 v. Ryan, 2006 U.S. Dist. LEXIS 8274 (N.D. Ill. Mar. 1, 2006).*

The court is being asked to decide whether, under the particular circumstances presented here - where there are parallel state court derivative actions proceeding, where there is a fully-briefed motion to dismiss or stay the action pending before the district court, where there is no allegation that evidence or documents may be compromised or destroyed, and where the facts of the case suggest that dismissal for lack of standing is a distinct possibility — the court should exercise its discretion to delay the disclosure and production of documents. On balance, the court is persuaded that it should. Accordingly, the court denies the motion to compel discovery. *Sylvia Piven As Tr. for the Leonard Piven Trust Uad 05/21/81 v. Ryan, 2006 U.S. Dist. LEXIS 8274 (N.D. Ill. Mar. 1, 2006).*

Ninth Circuit

Proxy solicitation is a proper purpose for the inspection of stock ledgers. *Cenergy Corp. v. Bryson Oil & Gas P.L.C., 662 F. Supp. 1144 (D.Nev. 1987).*

In order for proxy solicitation to be a proper purpose for the inspection of stock ledgers, the shareholder seeking the ledgers must have formed a bona fide intention to solicit proxies. *Cenergy Corp. v. Bryson Oil & Gas P.L.C., 662 F. Supp. 1144 (D.Nev. 1987).*

The court may look beyond the shareholder's statement of purpose to determine whether a shareholder had a proper purpose in seeking a stock ledger. The surrounding circumstances are relevant. *Cenergy Corp. v. Bryson Oil & Gas P.L.C., 662 F. Supp. 1144 (D.Nev. 1987).*

District of Columbia Circuit

Statutory and common-law right. — Delaware recognizes both a statutory right to inspect a corporation's books and records and a common-law right permitting the same. The statutory right supplements and does not supplant the common-law right to inspect books and records. *Fleisher Development Corp. v. Home Owners Warranty Corp., 670 F. Supp. 27 (D.D.C. 1987).*

Classification of common-law action. — Delaware common law treats petitions to examine a corporation's books and records as applications for a writ of mandamus. Such a writ will issue only when a court, in its sound discretion, determines that the facts presented justify inspection. In exercising this discretion, Delaware courts recognize that a stockholder or member's right to inspect a corporation's books and records is a qualified one. Inspection will be ordered only if a member establishes a proper purpose for the inspection. *Fleisher Development Corp. v. Home Owners Warranty Corp., 670 F. Supp. 27 (D.D.C. 1987).*

Presumption against permitting inspection. — Under the United State Supreme Court's formula, there is a presumption that inspection will go forward unless it is for speculative purposes or to gratify idle curiosity or to aid a blackmailer. To the contrary, Delaware has created a presumption against permitting inspection of a corporation's books and records unless there is a specific dispute between the shareholder or member and the corporation in aid of which examination is necessary. Delaware requires a plaintiff to plead this proper purpose with particularity. A plaintiff's failure to be sufficiently specific will result in the dismissal of his or her request to inspect for failure to make out a prima facie case of proper purpose. Delaware appears to have added this requirement to ensure that an inspection will advance the interests of the corporation and is not a mere "fishing expedition." *Fleisher Development Corp. v. Home Owners Warranty Corp., 670 F. Supp. 27 (D.D.C. 1987).*

The inspection rights set out in § 220 do not apply to members of nonstock corporations. *Fleisher Dev. Corp. v. Home Owners Warranty Corp., 647 F. Supp. 661 (D.D.C. 1986).*

§ 221. Voting, inspection and other rights of bondholders and debenture holders

DELAWARE CASE NOTES — REPORTED

Reasonable restrictions valid. — Reasonable restrictions on the right of an individual holder of 1 or more of a series of corporate bonds, either in respect to the obligation or of the security, are generally valid and enforceable. *Japha v. Delaware Valley Util. Co., 40 Del. 599, 15 A.2d 432 (1940).*

But strictly construed. — Restrictions upon corporate bondholders' rights of action, being in derogation of the common-law rights of creditors, are to be strictly construed and are effective only insofar as they are clear and reasonably free from doubt. *Japha v. Delaware Valley Util. Co., 40 Del. 599, 15 A.2d 432 (1940).*

And entire instrument considered. — In construing provisions of a trust indenture securing corporation's bonds, effect must be given to all parts of the instrument, and a construction which gives a reasonable meaning to all its provisions will be preferred to one which must totally reject a portion as repugnant or inexplicable. *Japha v. Delaware Valley Util. Co., 40 Del. 599, 15 A.2d 432 (1940).*

DELAWARE CASE NOTES — UNREPORTED

Noteholders standing to challenge seating of directors. — Corporate noteholders of a corporation that merged with another corporation did not have standing to challenge the manner in which directors were seated in the post-merger board of the surviving corporation. *Law Debenture Trust Co. v. Petrohawk Energy Corp., 2007 Del. Ch. LEXIS 113 (Del. Ch. Aug. 1, 2007).*

CASE NOTES — OTHER STATES

California

Defining the corporations' obligation. — The relationship between a corporation and the holders of its debt securities, even convertible debt securities, is contractual in nature. Arrangements among a corporation, the underwriters of its debt, trustees under its indentures and sometimes ultimate investors are typically thoroughly negotiated and massively documented. The rights and obligations of the various parties are or should be spelled out in that documentation. The terms of the contractual relationship agreed to and not broad concepts such as fairness define the corporation's obligation to its bond-holders. *Pittelman v. Pearce, 6 Cal. App. 4th 1436, 8 Cal. Rptr. 2d 359 (1992).*

Bondholder not entitled to any special protection. — A bondholder, even of a convertible debenture, is simply a creditor of the corporation. He or she is not entitled to any special protections which he or she has failed to negotiate for him- or herself at the time of the purchase of the bond. It is not enough to argue that the marketplace has become more dangerous. Absent fraud, or other similar misconduct, the courts have no brief to interfere in an established business relationship. *Pittelman v. Pearce, 6 Cal. App. 4th 1436, 8 Cal. Rptr. 2d 359 (1992).*

CASE NOTES — FEDERAL

Second Circuit

May be owed fiduciary duties. — have Under Delaware law, convertible debenture holders do not possess all the rights of shareholders with respect to actions taken by corporate directors or majority share-holders. In certain circumstances, a holder of a convertible debenture is entitled to different treatment from a mere creditor of a corporation, and a cause of action for breach of fiduciary duty may lie under Delaware law apart from the express terms of an indenture agreement. *Green v. Hamilton International Corp., 1981 U.S. Dist. LEXIS 13439 (S.D.N.Y. 1981).*

§ 222. Notice of meetings and adjourned meetings

DELAWARE CASE NOTES — REPORTED

Applicability. — This section refers to an adjournment after a meeting has convened and is not relevant to the issue of a postponement of a meeting after it has been designated, but before it is convened. *Aprahamian v. HBO & Co., 531 A.2d 1204 (Del. Ch. 1987).*

Board of director's fiduciary duty of disclosure. — Delaware law imposes upon a board of directors the fiduciary duty to disclose fully and fairly all material facts within its control that would have a significant effect upon a stockholder vote; however, the board is not required to disclose all available information. *Stroud v. Grace, 606 A.2d 75 (Del. 1992).*

Where a board issues a notice of annual meeting with the intention of amending its certificate of incorporation, the general corporation law requires two separate disclosures, under subsection (a) and *8 Del. C. § 242(b)(1)*; significantly, the law does not require any further disclosures in the absence of a proxy solicitation. *Stroud v. Grace, 606 A.2d 75 (Del. 1992).*

Notice required for regularly scheduled annual meetings. — Subsection (a) does not require the board to disclose the purpose of, or matters to be discussed at, regularly scheduled annual meetings. *Stroud v. Grace, 606 A.2d 75 (Del. 1992).*

Notice prerequisite to validity of meeting. — In the absence of waiver, consent or estoppel, reasonable notice to stockholders entitled to vote is a prerequisite to the validity of a special meeting of stockholders. *Bryan v. Western Pac. R.R. Corp., 28 Del. Ch. 13, 35 A.2d 909 (1944).*

Where the means of notification were patently insufficient to fulfill the requirement of notice of a stockholders' meeting, any action should not be accorded the significance and consequence which are attendant upon action of stockholders at a meeting validly called and held. *Bryan v. Western Pac. R.R. Corp., 28 Del. Ch. 13, 35 A.2d 909 (1944).*

But supplying brokers with copies of notice of a stockholders' meeting was not adequate or appropriate means of notifying the particular group of shareholders to whom the corporation wrongfully failed to give notice. *Bryan v. Western Pac. R.R. Corp., 28 Del. Ch. 13, 35 A.2d 909 (1944).*

And preliminary injunction proper relief. — A preliminary injunction to prevent a corporation from recognizing as valid, action taken at any assemblage in which the corporation had wrongfully given notice so as to exclude certain stockholders is a proper and suitable form of relief. *Bryan v. Western Pac. R.R. Corp., 28 Del. Ch. 13, 35 A.2d 909 (1944).*

Advancement of bylaw date of stockholders' meeting. — The advancement by directors of the bylaw date of a stockholders' meeting, for purposes of perpetuating "managing directors" in office and obstructing the legitimate efforts of dissident stockholders in the exercise of their rights to undertake a proxy contest against management, may not be permitted to stand. *Schnell v. Chris-Craft Indus., Inc., 285 A.2d 437 (Del. 1971).*

Conversion of nonprofit association to for-profit. — A nonprofit, nonstock mutual benefit association could be reconverted into a for-profit stock corporation without dissolution (and attendant distribution of assets), merger, consolidation or compensation to affected members; nor need notice be given, either before action is taken or afterwards, to nonvoting members, or, in the case of corporations with stock outstanding, to stockholders without entitlement to vote. *Farahpour v. DCX, Inc., 635 A.2d 894 (Del. 1994)*.

§ 223. Vacancies and newly created directorships

DELAWARE CASE NOTES — REPORTED

"Vacancy" implies a previous incumbency. *McWhirter v. Washington Royalties Co., 17 Del. Ch. 243, 152 A. 220 (1930); Grossman v. Liberty Leasing Co., 295 A.2d 749 (Del. Ch. 1972)*.

Majority of remaining directors may elect. — Majority of the remaining directors, referred to in this section, means that a majority of the remaining directors may elect regardless of whether a quorum of the board is left in office or not. *In re Chelsea Exch. Corp., 18 Del. Ch. 287, 159 A. 432 (1932)*.

Unless otherwise provided in certificate or by-laws. — Majority of remaining directors in office, whether or not they constitute a quorum, can fill the vacancies unless otherwise provided in the certificate or bylaws. *Tomlinson v. Loew's, Inc., 36 Del. Ch. 516, 134 A.2d 518, aff'd, 135 A.2d 136 (Del. 1957)*.

This section does not prevent stockholders from filling new directorships. *Campbell v. Loew's, Inc., 36 Del. Ch. 563, 134 A.2d 852 (1957)*.

De jure and de facto directors not distinguished. — This section does not distinguish between vacancies caused by retirement of de jure directors or de facto directors. *McWhirter v. Washington Royalties Co., 17 Del. Ch. 243, 152 A. 220 (1930)*.

Attempt to fill vacancy by less than majority held invalid. — The election, by 3 of the 7 directors then in office, of a director to fill a purported vacancy on the board was invalid, where the certificate of incorporation was completely silent concerning interim elections to fill vacancies and newly created directorships and the bylaws did not specify the voting strength necessary to elect a director to fill a vacancy or newly created directorship. *Dillon v. Berg, 326 F. Supp. 1214 (D. Del.), aff'd, 453 F.2d 876 (3d Cir. 1971); Dillon v. Scotten, Dillon Co., 335 F. Supp. 566 (D. Del. 1971)*.

Ratification of illegal election. — There was no implied ratification of an illegal election where at subsequent meetings the illegally elected director was accepted as a class A director at a time when there were present sufficient class A directors to have so elected him, because ratification requires knowledge of what is being done and where there was a complete absence of such knowledge on the part of the class A directors, the defense of implied ratification as a basis for considering an individual a validly elected director is without merit. *Young v. Janas, 34 Del. Ch. 287, 103 A.2d 299 (1954)*.

Actions subject to attack by stockholder. — Where certificate of incorporation provides that class A vacancies on board of directors shall be filled by affirmative vote of majority of remaining class A directors, an individual elected class A director to fill vacancy on motion and second by class B directors in a meeting at which only 1 class A director was present was illegally elected and his status was subject to a later attack by a class A stockholder. *Young v. Janas, 34 Del. Ch. 287, 103 A.2d 299 (1954)*.

And contested under § 225. — Director action under this section, whether filling vacancies or staffing newly created directorships, may be contested under § 225 of this title. *Grossman v. Liberty Leasing Co., 295 A.2d 749 (Del. Ch. 1972)*.

DELAWARE CASE NOTES — UNREPORTED

Continuing director provision in indenture agreement. — Continuing director provision in an indenture agreement was not violated by the seating of a board of directors for the surviving corporation in a corporate merger, because the provision simply required that a majority of the incumbent board of the corporation which issued the notes was to approve the nomination or election of new directors if those new directors were to qualify as continuing directors. *Law Debenture Trust Co. v. Petrohawk Energy Corp., 2007 Del. Ch. LEXIS 113 (Del. Ch. Aug. 1, 2007)*.

CASE NOTES — FEDERAL

District of Columbia Circuit

Other alternatives for creation remain. — Section 223(a) provides for two alternative methods for creating a board of directors when none exists but in both instances uses the word "may" rather than "shall," thus impliedly leaving the door open for yet other alternatives, such as simply not filling the vacancies when there is no real need to do so. *In re United Press International, Inc., 60 B.R. 265 (Bankr. D.D.C. 1986)*.

§ 225. Contested election of directors; proceedings to determine validity

DELAWARE CASE NOTES — REPORTED

Purpose. — The purpose of this section is to provide a quick method for review of the corporate election process to prevent a Delaware corporation from being immobilized by controversies about whether a given officer or director is properly holding office. *Box v. Box, 697 A.2d 395 (Del. 1997).*

Section does not operate so as to violate due process; corporate position, not the property of individual officers, is in jeopardy. *Grossman v. Liberty Leasing Co., 295 A.2d 749 (Del. Ch. 1972).*

And section is not exclusive, and Court of Chancery may entertain action to prevent fraud in solicitation of proxies, and may enjoin such solicitation and voting of proxies procured thereby. *Empire S. Gas Co. v. Gray, 29 Del. Ch. 95, 46 A.2d 741 (1946).*

But section is broad in language and purpose; it is in no way limited to a contest arising out of an election by stockholders. *Grossman v. Liberty Leasing Co., 295 A.2d 749 (Del. Ch. 1972).*

Section based upon common law. — The power of the Chancery Court to review a determination of "who is validly elected" in proxy contests has always been an aspect of the Court's common law and statutory authority. *Allison v. Preston, 651 A.2d 772 (Del. Ch. 1994).*

And section's manifest purpose is to right wrongs done to a corporation, not to its individual stockholders, through the unlawful usurpation of its management and offices by persons not entitled thereto. *Fleer v. Frank H. Fleer Corp., 14 Del. Ch. 277, 125 A. 411 (1924).*

Where grievance common to entire corporate body. — Where proceeding under this section is invoked not to assert an individual's claim to office, but to ascertain whether corporation's entire affairs have been unlawfully usurped by individuals through wrongful conduct and trickery at a stockholders' meeting, the grievance is common to entire corporate body. *Fleer v. Frank H. Fleer Corp., 14 Del. Ch. 277, 125 A. 411 (1924).*

Where proceeding under this section involved entire control of corporation's activities, grievance alleged was not grievance accruing to an individual, but one common to entire corporate body. *Standard Scale & Supply Corp. v. Chappel, 16 Del. Ch. 331, 141 A. 191 (1928).*

This section provides for review of grievances which are common to entire corporate body and so provides every stockholder with an interest thereunder. *Young v. Janas, 37 Del. Ch. 14, 136 A.2d 189 (1954).*

Under former wording of section, jurisdiction of court of chancery could be invoked only on application of stockholder. *In re Chelsea Exch. Corp., 18 Del. Ch. 287, 159 A. 432 (1932).*

Equitable holder of stock is entitled to maintain action under this section. *Rosenfield v. Standard Elec. Equip. Corp., 32 Del. Ch. 238, 83 A.2d 843 (1951).*

Determination of stock ownership. — In review proceedings under this section the court may enter upon a question of disputed ownership and determine who is the owner for voting purposes, the record ownership notwith-

standing. *Italo Petro. Corp. of Am. v. Producers Oil Corp. of Am., 20 Del. Ch. 283, 174 A. 276 (1934).*

Where alleged stock ownership was proved by the corporate records, no other primary proof is necessary to sustain their right to maintain action to determine the validity of election of corporate directors. *McLain v. Lanova Corp., 28 Del. Ch. 176, 39 A.2d 209 (1944).*

Where conflicting stock claims arise in connection with the review of an election under this section, the Court of Chancery has the power to decide who had the right to vote the stock in dispute; this does not constitute a binding determination of ownership as between the conflicting claimants unless they are parties who have been served with effective process. *Rosenfield v. Standard Elec. Equip. Corp., 32 Del. Ch. 238, 83 A.2d 843 (1951).*

Quantum of proof. — Before a court declares invalid a corporate election that was held 37 years ago, and thereby upsets long-settled expectations and reliance upon assumed events, it is entitled to demand clear and convincing evidence that the election was, in fact, invalid. *Oberly v. Kirby, 592 A.2d 445 (Del. 1991).*

Proceeding under this section is summary proceeding. *Cavender v. Curtiss-Wright Corp., 30 Del. Ch. 314, 60 A.2d 102 (1948).*

To preserve an expedited remedy, a proceeding brought pursuant to this section is a summary proceeding, limited to narrow issues; thus, an action brought under this section is not to be used for trying purely collateral issues, issues of director misconduct or other breaches of duty. *Box v. Box, 697 A.2d 395 (Del. 1997).*

Standing limited for bidder for target corporation. — Competing bidder for a target corporation, alleging that a violation of the transfer limitations of the target corporation's stock with enhanced voting rights, had standing to pursue a challenge, as it was of immediate and continuing interest to all of the target stockholders; since the competing bidder had purchased stock after a proposed merger had been announced, it lacked standing to pursue claims of breach of fiduciary duties, but it did not lack standing to pursue a claim that it clearly could have pursued after the merger had been completed, under subsection (b) of this section. *Omnicare, Inc. v. NCS Healthcare, Inc., 809 A.2d 1163 (Del. Ch. 2002), appeal dismissed, 822 A.2d 397 (Del. 2002).*

Standing of former directors to contest removal. — Material issues of fact precluded judgment on the pleadings for defendants in action by former directors challenging their removal by shareholders because the plaintiffs may have standing to assert the corporation's contractual rights in support of their claim to office and because the shareholders' agreement did not unambiguously entitle the defendants to such judgment. *Agranoff v. Miller, 734 A.2d 1066 (Del. Ch. 1999).*

Voting trust certificate holder. — The fact that the complainant is the holder of a voting trust certificate does not disqualify him or her as a party who is entitled to call for a review of an election. *Chandler v. Bellanca Aircraft Corp., 19 Del. Ch. 57, 162 A. 63 (1932)*.

Right of stockholder to vote is not such right as requires him or her to be present before court can assume to decide that his or her vote should not have been counted. *In re Diamond State Brewery, Inc., 22 Del. Ch. 364, 2 A.2d 254 (1938)*.

"Withhold authority" proxy cards were required to be counted. — Where the corporation's nominees were not re-elected because the "withhold authority" proxy cards were required to be counted, the nominees continued to be in office as holdovers and had a right to remain in office only until their successors were elected and qualified. *North Fork Bancorporation, Inc. v. Toal, 825 A.2d 860 (Del. Ch. 2000), aff'd, 781 A.2d 693 (Del. 2001)*.

Legality of issuance of stock cannot be passed upon in a proceeding to review a corporate election to which proceeding that person was not a party. *Standard Scale & Supply Corp. v. Chappel, 16 Del. Ch. 331, 141 A. 191 (1928)*.

Legality of issuance of stock cannot be adjudicated adversely to an absent holder. *In re Diamond State Brewery, Inc., 22 Del. Ch. 364, 2 A.2d 254 (1938)*.

Issue of stock ownership is not properly before the Court in a proceeding under this section when a claimant to such stock is not a party. *North Am. Uranium & Oil Corp. v. South Tex. Oil & Gas Co., 36 Del. Ch. 298, 129 A.2d 407 (1957)*.

Court not bound by showing made on books. — Court of Chancery in the exercise of its reviewing jurisdiction over elections of directors is not bound by showing made on books. *In re Canal Constr. Co., 21 Del. Ch. 155, 182 A. 545 (1936); In re Diamond State Brewery, Inc., 22 Del. Ch. 364, 2 A.2d 254 (1938)*.

The Chancellor, in determining the right and power of persons claiming to own stock to vote is not confined in his inquiry to a mere inspection of the stock ledger and the Chancellor is empowered to examine all pertinent evidence with the view of reaching a determination of where justice lies. *In re Canal Constr. Co., 21 Del. Ch. 155, 182 A. 545 (1936)*.

Registered shareholder's vote may be rejected where his voting is found to be in violation of another's rights. *Ringling Bros. — Barnum & Bailey Combined Shows, Inc. v. Ringling, 29 Del. Ch. 610, 53 A.2d 441 (1947); Tracy v. Brentwood Village Corp., 30 Del. Ch. 296, 59 A.2d 708 (1948)*.

Trustees of an Employee Retirement Income Security Act of 1974 (see *29 U.S.C. § 1103*) plan violated their fiduciary duty by casting ballots for directors contrary to the wishes of plan participants, as expressed by duly mailed proxies; plan participants' wishes had to be honored. *Allison v. Preston, 651 A.2d 772 (Del. Ch. 1994)*.

Conversion of nonvoting into voting shares by trustee of voting trust. — Where the corporate charter had been amended to permit conversion of nonvoting stock into voting stock only after "beneficial ownership" had been transferred to a person who was not an initial holder, it was held that, upon execution of a voting trust agreement designed to accomplish divestiture of a certain stockholder's interest in the corporation, such stockholder

no longer retained beneficial ownership of its nonvoting shares, that the trustee's conversion of the shares into voting stock was valid, and that the trustee was entitled to vote the converted shares. *Sundlun v. Executive Jet Aviation, Inc., 273 A.2d 282 (Del. Ch. 1970)*.

Presence of quorum at stockholders' meeting is a proper subject by Court of Chancery in a proceeding under this section in order to inquire into the actual facts. *Atterbury v. Consolidated Coppermines Corp., 26 Del. Ch. 1, 20 A.2d 743 (1941)*.

Notices given by de facto officers calling stockholders' meeting are valid as if they would have had that right as de jure officers. *Drob v. National Mem. Park, 28 Del. Ch. 254, 41 A.2d 589 (1945)*.

Estoppel cannot be relied on in determining how many directors shall be elected at a stockholders' meeting. *In re Ivey & Ellington, Inc., 28 Del. Ch. 298, 42 A.2d 508 (1945)*.

Forgery in execution of proxy. — Court of Chancery will hear and determine an issue of forgery raised in connection with the execution of a proxy. *Investment Assocs. v. Standard Power & Light Corp., 29 Del. Ch. 225, 48 A.2d 501 (1946), aff'd, 29 Del. Ch. 593, 51 A.2d 572 (1947)*.

A strict rule of proof should be required in the Court of Chancery of those who would have a proxy invalidated on the ground of forgery in the execution thereof; nothing less than the testimony of the person whose signature was allegedly forged should be recognized, unless such testimony is unavailable for reasons having substantial merit. *Investment Assocs. v. Standard Power & Light Corp., 29 Del. Ch. 225, 48 A.2d 501 (1946), aff'd, 29 Del. Ch. 593, 51 A.2d 572 (1947)*.

Trickery in securing absence of opposing directors. — Since a quorum obtained by trickery is invalid, and the reasoning which forbids trickery in securing a quorum applies equally well to securing the absence of opposing directors from a meeting by representing that such a meeting will not be held, actions taken at such a meeting are void and the officers and directors remain unchanged. *Schroder v. Scotten, Dillon Co., 299 A.2d 431 (Del. Ch. 1972)*.

Rationale of notice requirement. — When there is a notice requirement for a directors' meeting, the rationale of that requirement is not only to convenience directors, but also to assure that the corporate body, including its stockholders, is given the "benefit of the judgment, counsel and influence of all" of its directors, in a meeting to elect officers. *Schroder v. Scotten, Dillon Co., 299 A.2d 431 (Del. Ch. 1972)*.

Meeting without notice unlawful. — Special meeting held without due notice to all directors as required by the bylaws is not lawful and all acts done at such a meeting are void. *Schroder v. Scotten, Dillon Co., 299 A.2d 431 (Del. Ch. 1972)*.

When meeting was held in accordance with federal district court order, the board of directors of the corporation at the close of the meeting will be found to consist of those validly in office at the time of the meeting (whose terms carried through it) plus those who were elected to office at the meeting. *Schroder v. Scotten, Dillon Co., 299 A.2d 431 (Del. Ch. 1972).*

This section determines validity of removal of individual defendants as directors and election of others to replace them. Essential *Enter. Corp. v. Automatic Steel Prods., Inc., 39 Del. Ch. 93, 159 A.2d 288 (1960).*

It would not be logical to read this section as providing for judicial review of what stockholders do, but not of director action on the same subject, i.e., election of directors. *Grossman v. Liberty Leasing Co., 295 A.2d 749 (Del. Ch. 1972).*

Material misrepresentation during proxy solicitation. — The court may exercise discretion in determining whether even material misrepresentations made during a proxy solicitation campaign warrant the ordering of a new election. *In re Seminole Oil & Gas Corp., 38 Del. Ch. 246, 150 A.2d 20 (1959), appeal dismissed, 159 A.2d 276 (Del. 1960).*

Court of chancery will not take cognizance of alleged violation of securities exchange act when the action constituting the violation would be unobjectionable under the controlling law. *Investment Assocs. v. Standard Power & Light Corp., 29 Del. Ch. 225, 48 A.2d 501 (1946), aff'd, 29 Del. Ch. 593, 51 A.2d 572 (1947).*

Election fairly held should not be set aside for irregularities not affecting substantive rights of stockholders. *Magill v. North Am. Refractories Co., 36 Del. Ch. 305, 129 A.2d 411 (1957).*

Bill to cancel illegal stock and secure another election may be properly filed, but it does not follow that because both purposes may be pursued in 1 bill, neither can be pursued alone. *In re Diamond State Brewery, Inc., 22 Del. Ch. 364, 2 A.2d 254 (1938).*

But seeking to cancel not prerequisite to challenging election. — If a complaining stockholder does not choose to seek the cancellation of another stockholder's stock, he or she should not be compelled to do so as a condition precedent to his or her right to challenge the result of an election of directors. *In re Diamond State Brewery, Inc., 22 Del. Ch. 364, 2 A.2d 254 (1938).*

Action moot where contested board terms have expired. — An action seeking to invoke the Court of Chancery's general equity jurisdiction and its statutory authority to determine the outcome of a contested election under this section was moot, since the terms of the elected board members had expired. *Loudon v. Archer-Daniels-Midland Co., 700 A.2d 135 (Del. 1997).*

Admissibility of parol evidence. — Although minutes of directors' meeting are best evidence of what took place, parol evidence is admissible to supplement or contradict events as reported in the minutes. *Schroder v. Scotten, Dillon Co., 299 A.2d 431 (Del. Ch. 1972).*

Chancery court rule 23(e) is applicable to dismissal and compromise of actions brought under this section. *Borer v. Associated Gen. Util. Co., 35 Del. Ch. 123, 111 A.2d 707 (1955).*

Exercise of discretion under this section must be based on facts of the case and upon a finding of whether irregularity operated prejudicially to the rights of the party complaining. *Magill v. North Am. Refractories Co., 36 Del. Ch. 305, 129 A.2d 411 (1957).*

Subjective intent may be relevant. — Where fraud or a breach of duty is alleged, the court may wish to inquire into the subjective intent of the record owner or beneficial owner, even though this is not a proper inquiry under usual circumstances. *Allison v. Preston, 651 A.2d 772 (Del. Ch. 1994).*

Defendants not deemed interpleaders. — When individual defendants, management, and corporation actively opposed a stockholder's contest of an election under this section, the Court cannot put an interpleader label on any of those defendants. *Liese v. Jupiter Corp., 241 A.2d 492 (Del. Ch. 1968).*

Injunctive relief not factor. — Since reviews of election take place after those directors whose title is contested have taken office, injunctive relief is normally not a factor. *Levin v. Metro-Goldwyn-Mayer, Inc., 43 Del. Ch. 168, 221 A.2d 499 (1966).*

Second-filed action in another jurisdiction. — In the normal course of events, a proceeding under this section should be heard and decided before a second-filed action in another jurisdiction. *Box v. Box, 697 A.2d 395 (Del. 1997).*

Bad faith resistance to action under this section. — Given officers' and directors' clear incentives to contest an action under this section for ulterior reasons unrelated to the merits, the record amply supported a finding that the defendants opposed the action in bad faith, thus warranting an award of legal fees to the majority shareholder who brought the action. *Arbitrium (Cayman Islands) Handels AG v. Johnston, 705 A.2d 225 (Del. Ch. 1997).*

Attorney's fees. — In a stockholder's action under this section, wherein a stockholder seeks attorney's fees, the fact that summary judgment is granted in favor of the corporation does not mean that the cause is without merit where the claims are preserved by taking an appeal. *Baron v. Allied Artists Pictures Corp., 395 A.2d 375 (Del. Ch. 1978), aff'd, 413 A.2d 876 (Del. 1980).*

Although a stockholder's challenge to the election of directors was dismissed on appeal as moot due to a corporate merger, where the stockholder had a meritorious action at the time the case was filed and where the defendants failed to carry their burden on the causal connection between the merger and the lawsuit, the stockholder would be entitled to attorney fees. *Baron v. Allied Artists Pictures Corp., 395 A.2d 375 (Del. Ch. 1978), aff'd, 413 A.2d 876 (Del. 1980).*

Where a stockholder challenges the election of directors, but action by the defendants renders the matter moot, under circumstances which would justify an award of counsel fees and costs, and where the various monetary benefits allegedly flowing to the stockholders of the corporate entity surviving the merger, while perhaps incidental to and resulting from the action taken by the defendants in mooting the matter, were not benefits sought by the stockholder according to the complaints that he or she filed, there is no basis to consider them in awarding a fee to such stockholder's counsel. *Baron v.*

Allied Artists Pictures Corp., 395 A.2d 375 (Del. Ch. 1978), aff'd, 413 A.2d 876 (Del. 1980).

Noncompliance with deadline. — Defendant clearly had not one but two reasonable opportunities to submit its nominations and missed those opportunities out of neglect or indecision, or perhaps to gain a tactical advantage by remaining a 13G filer even while it was preparing to wage a proxy contest. Whatever the reason, the facts are clear that defendant did not comply with any deadline under any reasonable reading of the bylaws. *Openwave Sys. v. Harbinger Capital Partners Master Fund I, Ltd, 924 A.2d 228; 2007 Del. Ch. LEXIS 67 (May 18, 2007).*

Noninterference with stockholder franchise. — Considering the evidence and the testimony of the directors, the court concludes that the reduction in the number of board seats was not a defensive measure designed to interfere with the stockholder franchise. The reduction in the number of board seats occurred nearly two months before defendant launched its proxy contest and was promptly disclosed. At the time the board seat was eliminated, defendant had just filed a Schedule 13G, indicating that its ownership of plaintiff's stock was for investment purposes only. At the time of the board reduction, plaintiff knew only that defendant had acquired a significant stake in plaintiff's common stock and that defendant was an activist hedge fund that in some circumstances attempted to influence the control of the companies it invested in, but in others was a passive investor. When this information is combined with defendant's Schedule 13G filing for investment purposes only, it is a reasonable conclusion that defendant was not a credible threat to the existing board's control of plaintiff's at the time of the board reduction. Openwave Sys. v. Harbinger Capital Partners Master Fund I, Ltd, 924 A.2d 228; 2007 Del. Ch. LEXIS 67 (May 18, 2007).

DELAWARE CASE NOTES — UNREPORTED

Disclosure of vote buying arrangements. — Even those academic commentators who have endeavored to justify tolerance of forms of vote buying as having benefits to diversified investors have emphasized the need for fair disclosure of such arrangements. *Portnoy v. Cryo-Cell Int'l, Inc., 2008 Del. Ch. LEXIS 6 (January 15, 2008). [For the full text of this case opinion, please see the Appendix at the end of this Volume.]*

A mere offer of a position on a management slate should not be considered a vote-buying arrangement subject to a test of entire fairness. *Portnoy v. Cryo-Cell Int'l, Inc., 2008 Del. Ch. LEXIS 6 (January 15, 2008). [For the full text of this case opinion, please see the Appendix at the end of this Volume.]*

Accumulation of voting power. — In keeping with the traditional vigilance this court has displayed in ensuring the fairness of the corporate election process, and in particular the process by which directors are elected, purposely inequitable conduct in the accumulation of voting power will not be tolerated. *Portnoy v. Cryo-Cell Int'l, Inc., 2008 Del. Ch. LEXIS 6 (January 15, 2008). [For the full text of this case opinion, please see the Appendix at the end of this Volume.]*

Plaintiffs can utilize an expedited summary proceeding under this section to challenge director elections. *President & Fellows of Harvard Coll. v. Glancy, 2003 Del. Ch. LEXIS 25 (Mar. 21, 2003).*

Superfluous motions. — A motion to expedite proceedings under subsection (k) of Section 145 is superfluous. The text of the subsection dictates that a proceeding under that provision is "summary." In order to receive summary adjudication of a claim for advancement it is not necessary to file a motion to expedite. If a plaintiff files a motion to expedite it is, in effect, a request to expedite a summary proceeding. Only when unique circumstances are present, e.g., insolvency of the putative indemnitee or inability to retain counsel without advancement, will the chancery court entertain a request to "expedite" a proceeding that is already summary in nature. In the opinion of the chancery court, this reasoning extends to other summary proceedings, such as those brought under Section 220 and this section of the General Corporation Law. *Brown v. Rite Aid Corp., 2004 Del. Ch. LEXIS 29, No. 094-N (May 29, 2004).*

Apartment cooperative. — Despite normal deference to actions of duly elected directors, a chancery court exercised its equitable powers to recognize that less deference was due to directors of an apartment cooperative, who were simply fellow unitholders, and to protect the right that the court had granted to the cooperative members as a whole, in earlier litigation, to determine whether the cooperative should accept another corporation's offer to purchase an underground parking garage and other properties owned by the cooperative; therefore, summary judgment was entered in favor of the anti-sale group, as their position comported with the results of the membership election. *Baring v. Condrell, 2004 Del. Ch. LEXIS 148 (Oct. 18, 2004).*

Refusal of removed director to leave office. — Officer and director of a Delaware corporation acted in bad faith and wasted the time and resources of a parent corporation through refusal to vacate office after the parent corporation voted for the director's removal; the court awarded attorneys' fees and costs to a director of the parent corporation who sued the director of the Delaware corporation for removal. *Stavrou v. Contogouris, 2002 Del. Ch. LEXIS 121 (Oct. 11, 2002).*

Director defendants decided in good faith to investigate the travel expenses and the involvement of senior management. They selected investigator with reasonable care and they acted with the reasonable belief that he was capable of carrying out the investigation. They appropriately monitored and supervised his work. When done, they, in good faith and reasonably, relied upon his findings and his advice. *Perlegos v. Atmel Corp., 2007 Del. Ch. LEXIS 25 (February 8, 2007).*

Court will not disturb the special committee's decision to terminate the plaintiffs where it was not the product of pretext but of a fair and reasonable process. Supporting the special committee's decision is a careful

Corporations

and competent, although somewhat distant from ideal, investigation, a second opinion as to the good faith basis that existed for independent directors to rely on the initial findings, and the professional advice received from two others. That is all that the court can require. Aspects of initial investigation may have been worthy of improvement, but the evidence offered by the plaintiffs does not support a conclusion that the special committee's dismissal for cause was a pretext for ridding the company of the plaintiffs. *Perlegos v. Atmel Corp., 2007 Del. Ch. LEXIS 25 (February 8, 2007).*

Invalid proceeding to remove CEO. — CEO's' motion for partial summary judgment was granted in an action pursuant to this section and it was determined that CEO retained the position; directors' attempt to remove the CEO failed where the board of directors did not unanimously consent to the action in writing as required by 8 Del. C. § 141(f). *Solstice Capital II, Ltd. P'ship v. Ritz, 2004 Del. Ch. LEXIS 39 (Apr. 6, 2004).*

Super majority provision amended by implication. — Shareholders who were attempting to acquire control of a holding company stated a cognizable claim that a supermajority provision in the company's by-laws was amended by implication because the board of directors acted as though it did not exist, and that the board of directors was estopped from relying on the supermajority provision to block a shareholders' vote in favor of changing the board. *Dousman v. Kobus, 2002 Del. Ch. LEXIS 67 (June 6, 2002).*

Super majority erroneously required. — Although a vote was invalid under 8 Del. C. § 225(b), because a corporation's members were erroneously led to believe that 8 Del.C. § 271(a) required a 75 percent majority, the members were entitled to another opportunity to express their will regarding the sale. *Baring v. Watergate E., Inc., 2004 Del. Ch. LEXIS 17 (Feb. 25, 2004).*

Immaterial vote miscounting. — Allegation that an immaterial number of votes were miscounted was not sufficient to state a claim under this section. *A.R. DeMarco Enters. v. Ocean Spray Cranberries, Inc., 2002 Del. Ch. LEXIS 135 (Nov. 26, 2002).*

Entitlement to advance notice. — Board member and chief executive officer of company (CEO) with voting control was entitled to advance notice of a proposal to bring in cash and a replacement CEO, as he possessed the contractual power to prevent the passage of the proposal, and given that the actions depriving the CEO of the opportunity to do so were unfair and would not be countenanced by the court; actions removing and replacing CEO on the board could be undone, in an action brought under this section. *Adlerstein v. Wertheimer, 2002 Del. Ch. LEXIS 13 (Jan. 25, 2002).*

Failure of subsection (b) action. — In an action under subsection (b) of this section, shareholders opposing a merger of publicly traded global providers of computers and computer-related products and services failed to prove the corporation in which they held shares: (1) misrepresented material facts regarding the integration of the corporations' businesses; or (2) used coercion to obtain proxies from a bank that voted its shares and managed shares based upon the promise of future business to the bank. *Hewlett v. Hewlett-Packard Co., 2002 Del. Ch. LEXIS 35 (Apr. 30, 2002).*

Personal jurisdiction for voting power determinations. — Although it is critical that the Chancery Court have jurisdiction over persons if it is to issue an order invalidating the preferred stock they receive, the Court can, as part of a contest under this section, determine whether that stock is part of a corporation's voting power without having personal jurisdiction over those persons. *Chandler v. Ciccoricco, 2003 Del. Ch. LEXIS 47 (May 5, 2003).*

Equity jurisdiction. — Since equity jurisdiction was proper as to one sibling's claim seeking a declaration (that another sibling was no longer a director) with a further request for specific performance and injunctive relief, the chancery court could also hear a related claim for damages. *Jacobson v. Ronsdorf, 2005 Del. Ch. LEXIS 2 (Jan. 6, 2005).*

Inequitable election behavior. — When a corporate manager's only reason for casting doubt on a strategic partner's ongoing relationship with the corporation has nothing to do with the best interests of the corporation, except insofar as the manager believes her own re-election is critical, using the threat of future non-cooperation is the simple use of a corporate, not personal, asset as leverage to extract a vote. That is inequitable behavior. *Portnoy v. Cryo-Cell Int'l, Inc., 2008 Del. Ch. LEXIS 6 (January 15, 2008). [For the full text of this case opinion, please see the Appendix at the end of this Volume.]*

If an electoral contestant assumes the role of presiding over the meeting, she has an obligation to do so fairly. The CEO in the instant case did not do so. She stalled so that her side could win the game, knowing that if the game ended when it was scheduled to end, her side would lose. Then she was dishonest about the reasons for delay. This was a serious breach of duty which helped taint the election. *Portnoy v. Cryo-Cell Int'l, Inc., 2008 Del. Ch. LEXIS 6 (January 15, 2008). [For the full text of this case opinion, please see the Appendix at the end of this Volume.]*

An action under this section is not to be used for trying purely collateral issues and a claim is collateral to a § 225 proceeding if it would not help the court determine the proper composition of the corporation's board or management. All plaintiff had was damages claim for improper termination, and nothing more. The claim created no uncertainty about who the current officers of the corporation were and there were no remaining issues concerning the appropriate composition of the corporation's board or management. *Stengel v. Rotman, 2001 Del. Ch. LEXIS 22 (Feb. 26, 2001).*

Unclean hands is a doctrine designed to protect the integrity of a court of equity, not a weapon to be wielded by parties seeking to excuse their own inequitable behavior by pointing out a trifling instance of impropriety by their counterpart, especially when the defendants cannot show that plaintiff's conduct caused any harm to defendant as a corporation or to its disinterested stockholders. Plaintiff's conduct, while being far from pristine, falls well short of disqualifying him from seeking relief. *Portnoy v. Cryo-Cell Int'l, Inc., 2008 Del. Ch. LEXIS 6 (January 15, 2008). [For the full text of this case opinion, please see the Appendix at the end of this Volume.]*

Dismissal without prejudice. — Where plaintiffs sought declarations relating to the corporation's board elections, plaintiffs' motion for dismissal without prejudice under Del. Ch. Ct. R. 41(a)(2) was granted because the court found that the interests of justice were best served if the dismissal was without prejudice. *Messina v. Klugiewicz, 2004 Del. Ch. LEXIS 47 (Apr. 30, 2004).*

Reimbursement of attorneys' fees. — Taken together, these actions and the questionable conduct of defendants during the earlier proceedings regarding registration, lead the chancery court to infer that defendant behavior in the Section 225 portion of this litigation was either the result of subjective bad faith or a negligent, frivolous and oppressive disregard of the rights of its Series B stockholder. Therefore, plaintiffs are entitled to reimbursement of at least some of their attorneys' fees in connection with the prosecution of that portion of the case. *FGC Holdings Ltd. v. Teltronics, Inc., 2007 Del. Ch. LEXIS 14 (Jan. 22, 2007).*

Interests of minor children. — Trial court erred in ruling in favor of a corporate officer in an action pursuant to *8 Del. C. § 225* challenging the officer's election, because the officer improperly voted stock shares owned by the officer's minor children in the election; *Conn. Gen. Stat. § 45a-631(a)* only allowed a court-appointed guardian to vote the stock under the circumstances, as the voting of the stock represented a use of a valuable asset. *B.F. Rich & Co., A Del. Corp. v. Gray, 2007 Del. LEXIS 404 (Del. Sept. 11, 2007).*

Noteholder standing to challenge seating of directors. — Corporate noteholders of a corporation that merged with a second corporation did not have standing to challenge the manner in which directors were seated in the post-merger board of the surviving corporation. *Law Debenture Trust Co. v. Petrohawk Energy Corp., — A.2d —, 2007 Del. Ch. LEXIS 113 (Del. Ch. Aug. 1, 2007).*

CASE NOTES — OTHER STATES

Pennsylvania

Enjoinable director conduct. — Tinkering with corporate elections to interfere with shareholders' electoral rights violates a director's fiduciary duty to shareholders and is enjoinable. *Jewelcor Management, Inc. v. Thistle Group Holdings, Co., 2002 Phila. Ct. Com. Pl. LEXIS 79 (2004).*

Irreparable harm. — Under Delaware law, the deprivation of a shareholder's right to vote is irreparable harm. *Alan Wurtzel Commerce Program v. Park Towne Place Apartments Limited Partnership, 2001 Phila. Ct. Com. Pl. LEXIS 79 (2001).*

CASE NOTES — FEDERAL

Second Circuit

De facto status. — Under Delaware law, a director who assumes office pursuant to an irregular election achieves only de facto status which may be successfully attacked by the stockholders. Where stockholders challenge officer conduct not primarily involving third parties, courts may void those actions. *In re Trump Hotels Shareholder Derivative Litig., 2000 U.S. Dist. LEXIS 13550 (S.D.N.Y. 2000).*

§ 226. Appointment of custodian or receiver of corporation on deadlock or for other cause

DELAWARE CASE NOTES — REPORTED

Legislative intent. — In enacting paragraph (1) of subsection (a) of this section the General Assembly intended to create a more liberal and readily available remedy in stockholder-deadlock situations. *Giuricich v. Emtrol Corp., 449 A.2d 232 (Del. 1982).*

Appointment not automatic. — If the appointment of a custodian or receiver were intended to be automatic and not within the court's discretion, there was no reason to use the permissive word "may" rather than the mandatory "shall." *Paulman v. Kritzer Radiant Coils, Inc., 37 Del. Ch. 348, 143 A.2d 272 (1958).*

Court of Chancery may, but is not required to, appoint a receiver in case of actual stockholder deadlock. *Hall v. John S. Isaacs & Sons Farms, 37 Del. Ch. 530, 146 A.2d 602 (1958),* aff'd, *39 Del. Ch. 244, 163 A.2d 288 (1960).*

And failure to elect deemed insufficient grounds. — A bare showing of failure to elect directors for two successive annual meetings because of stockholder deadlock is not sufficient to require the court to appoint a receiver. *Paulman v. Kritzer Radiant Coils, Inc., 37 Del. Ch. 348, 143 A.2d 272 (1958).*

Showing of "irreparable injury" not prerequisite to relief in stockholder-deadlock situation. — The provision of subsection (a)(2) of this section requiring a showing of "irreparable injury" as a prerequisite to relief in a director-deadlock situation is inapplicable to a petition under paragraph (1) of subsection (a) of this section in a stockholder-deadlock situation. *Giuricich v. Emtrol Corp., 449 A.2d 232 (Del. 1982).*

Powers of custodian under paragraph (1) of subsection (a) are not as unlimited as powers of receiver appointed under the general equitable powers of the Court. *Giuricich v. Emtrol Corp., 449 A.2d 232 (Del. 1982).*

Involvement of court and custodian in corporation's business. — The involvement of the Court of Chancery and its custodian in a corporation's business and affairs should be kept to a minimum and should be exercised only insofar as the goals of fairness and justice require. *Giuricich v. Emtrol Corp., 449 A.2d 232 (Del. 1982).*

Liquidating receivers for solvent corporations. — Under some circumstances courts of equity will appoint liquidating receivers for solvent corporations, but the power to do so is always exercised with great restraint and only upon a showing of gross mismanagement, positive misconduct by the corporate officers, breach of trust, or extreme circumstances showing imminent danger of great loss to the corporation which, otherwise, cannot be prevented. *Hall v. John S. Isaacs & Sons Farms, 39 Del. Ch. 244, 163 A.2d 288 (1960).*

DELAWARE CASE NOTES — UNREPORTED

Auction. — After 4 years of director deadlock, an auction of a closely-held corporation was ordered, by the court, which found that an auction was one of several alternatives that a board could consider among various transactional possibilities; under subsection (b) of this section, the trial court had the power to order an asset division, among other things, but the court chose the alternative of an auction. *Bentas v. Haseotes, 2003 Del. Ch. LEXIS 24 (Mar. 27, 2003).*

Custodial relief unavailable. — Since stockholder agreement, which was a voting trust, was unenforceable under 8 Del. C. § 218 because it was not executed, the court dismissed a minority shareholders' claims related to: (1) the controller's alleged breach of that agreement; (2) shareholder's alleged detrimental reliance on the voting trust when the shares were bought; and (3) since the trust was not enforceable and since there was not the voting deadlock that there could have been had the trust been enforceable, the claim for 8 Del. C. § 226 custodial relief. *Dweck v. Albert Nassar & Kids Int'l Corp., 2005 Del. Ch. LEXIS 183 (Del. Ch. Nov. 23, 2005).*

CASE NOTES — FEDERAL

Ninth Circuit

Receivership claims not derivative. — The language of subsection (a) of this section and section 291 are nearly identical and both provide that an application for an appointment of a receiver may be brought by any stockholder. Neither statute limits the claims to derivative claims. Because these statutes are clear on their face and because defendant has adduced no authority the contrary, the court concludes that the current claims may be brought by an individual stockholder such as plaintiff. *Glenbrook Capital L.P. v. Mali Kuo, 525 F. Supp. 2d 1130, 2007 U.S. Dist. LEXIS 68353 (ND CA, September 6, 2007).*

§ 227. Powers of Court in elections of directors

CASE NOTES — OTHER STATES

Pennsylvania

Enjoinable director conduct. — Tinkering with corporate elections to interfere with shareholders' electoral rights violates a director's fiduciary duty to shareholders and is enjoinable. *Jewelcor Management, Inc. v. Thistle Group Holdings, Co., 2002 Phila. Ct. Com. Pl. LEXIS 79 (2004).*

§ 228. Consent of stockholders or members in lieu of meeting

DELAWARE CASE NOTES — REPORTED

Applicability. — Provisions of this section are applicable to any Delaware company unless the certificate of incorporation restricts its use. *Allen v. Prime Computer, Inc., 540 A.2d 417 (Del. 1988).*

Scope of section. — This section is not limited to situations in which a single shareholder or a small group of shareholders controls the corporate machinery but includes all Delaware corporations and does not limit in any way those shareholders or groups of shareholders who may exercise their right to effectuate corporate action by written consents. *Pabst Brewing Co. v. Jacobs, 549 F. Supp. 1068 (D. Del. 1982).*

Construction of section with § 242 of this title. — Subsection (c) of this section does not modify § 242(b) of this title to provide that persons who execute a written consent proposing a charter amendment need not be directors of the corporation at that time, so long as the consent is delivered to the corporation before the document that evidences the shareholders' consent to the amendment. *AGR Halifax Fund, Inc. v. Fiscina, 743 A.2d 1188 (Del. Ch. 1999).*

Consruction of section with § 262 of this title. — Because of the general applicability of this section, the absence of specific language regarding written consent in § 262(b)(1) of this title does not compel the conclusion that the market exception applies only to mergers approved at a meeting of shareholders; this section allows approval by written consent for any action which is required to be taken at a meeting of shareholders and thus § 262(b)(1) need not separately mention written consent for this section to apply. *Klotz v. Warner Communications, Inc., 674 A.2d 878 (Del. 1995).*

Construction with § 211. — The mandatory requirement of § 211 of this title that an annual meeting of

Corporations

shareholders be held is not satisfied by shareholder action by written consents pursuant to this section. *Hoschett v. TSI Int'l Software, LTD., 683 A.2d 43 (Del. Ch. 1996).*

Directors elected by written consents hold office only until the next meeting of the shareholders; elections by this method do not affect the obligation under § 211 of this title to hold an annual meeting. *Hoschett v. TSI Int'l Software, LTD., 683 A.2d 43 (Del. Ch. 1996).*

Right to act immediately by majority written consent may be modified or eliminated only by certificate of incorporation. — Because this section clearly and unambiguously permits a majority of the stockholders of a corporation to act immediately and without prior notice to the minority, the statute must be given its plain meaning. The exercise of the right to act immediately by majority written consent may be modified or eliminated only by the certificate of incorporation; thus, bylaws which effectively abrogate the exercise of this right are invalid. *Allen v. Prime Computer, Inc., 540 A.2d 417 (Del. 1988).*

Policies underlying proxy contests equally applicable to contest by consents. — The policies underlying a proxy contest, where the shareholders must decide what persons are to serve as directors, are equally applicable to a contest by consents, where the shareholders must make the same decision. *Pabst Brewing Co. v. Jacobs, 549 F. Supp. 1068 (D. Del. 1982).*

Consent forms must permit choice from among nominees. — In an election contest, consent forms, like proxy cards, must permit the shareholders to make a selective choice from among the nominees for directors. *Pabst Brewing Co. v. Jacobs, 549 F. Supp. 1068 (D. Del. 1982).*

Consents are only valid for 60-day period set forth in subsection (a) of § 213 of this title. *Pabst Brewing Co. v. Jacobs, 549 F. Supp. 1068 (D. Del. 1982).*

The 60-day time period for submission of written consents pursuant to this section should not be confused with the 3-year period of validity for proxies pursuant to § 212 of this title. *Viele v. Devaney, 679 A.2d 993 (Del. Ch. 1996).*

Statement in solicitation that consents are valid for longer period is materially misleading. — A statement in a solicitation for consents that the consents will remain in full force and effect for a period longer than the 60-day period set forth in subsection (a) of § 213 of this title is materially misleading. *Pabst Brewing Co. v. Jacobs, 549 F. Supp. 1068 (D. Del. 1982).*

Setting of record date by board of directors. — Where setting of record date by corporation's board of directors was not in violation of § 213 of this title, the board's action was likewise not in violation of this section; the board of directors of a corporation is not mandated to set a record date which would give any stockholder an advantage with respect to taking action by written consent. *Empire of Carolina, Inc. v. Deltona Corp., 501 A.2d 1252 (Del. Ch. 1985), aff'd, 505 A.2d 452 (Del. 1985).*

Setting date of record by consent. — In order to establish certainty as to when a record date has been set and what corporate action shareholders are pursuing under this section, the soliciting shareholder must communicate to the corporation the date that the first written consent has been executed and the substance of the proposed corporate action to be taken. *Empire of Carolina, Inc. v. Deltona Corp., 514 A.2d 1091 (Del. 1985).*

Individual dating of consent required. — When individual stockholder consents to a board proposal were not individually dated, in violation of this section's subsection (c), they were invalid because there was no way to determine adherence to the time requirement. *H-M Wexford LLC v. Encorp, Inc., 832 A.2d 129 (Del. Ch. 2003).*

Revocation of consents is governed by same general principles applicable to revocation of proxies. *Pabst Brewing Co. v. Jacobs, 549 F. Supp. 1068 (D. Del. 1982).*

In a post record-date sale of corporate stock, the purchaser had a right to revoke the owner/seller's consent to remove corporate directors. *Commonwealth Assocs. v. Providence Health Care, Inc., 641 A.2d 155 (Del. Ch. 1993).*

Timely delivery to the corporation's secretary of revocation of consent to remove corporate directors satisfies the delivery requirements of subsection (a). *Commonwealth Assocs. v. Providence Health Care, Inc., 641 A.2d 155 (Del. Ch. 1993).*

Votes should be disenfranchised. — Votes ostensibly procured in the form of consents in writing for the election of applicants' slate of proposed directors, having been procured through the use of options to purchase such shares in return for which a consideration was paid, should be disenfranchised. *Chew v. Inverness Mgt. Corp., 352 A.2d 426 (Del. Ch. 1976).*

Bylaw concerning review of action taken by shareholder consent. — This section does not bar a board of directors from adopting a bylaw which would impose minimal essential provisions for ministerial review of the validity of the action taken by shareholder consent. *Datapoint Corp. v. Plaza Sec. Co., 496 A.2d 1031 (Del. 1985).*

Requirement for ministerial review of actions taken by shareholder consent. — A bylaw which imposed minimal essential provisions for ministerial review of the validity of the action taken by shareholder consent would serve the purposes of this section. *Allen v. Prime Computer, Inc., 540 A.2d 417 (Del. 1988).*

Bylaw held invalid for intruding on fundamental shareholder rights. — A bylaw imposing an arbitrary delay upon shareholder action in lieu of meeting by postponing accomplishment of such action until 60 days after the corporation's receipt of a shareholder's notice of intent to solicit consents, which intrudes upon fundamental stockholder rights guaranteed by this section, is invalid. *Datapoint Corp. v. Plaza Sec. Co., 496 A.2d 1031 (Del. 1985).*

Bylaw amendments held not inequitable. — Bylaw amendments, which required attendance of all directors for a quorum and unanimous approval of the board of directors before board action could be taken, were not inequitable where the restrictions placed on the board were intended to limit the board's anti-takeover maneu-

Corporations

vering after the acquiring corporation had gained control of the corporation; the bylaw amendments were a permissible part of the acquiring corporation's attempt to avoid its disenfranchisement as a majority shareholder. *Frantz Mfg. Co. v. EAC Indus., 501 A.2d 401 (Del. 1985).*

DELAWARE CASE NOTES — UNREPORTED

Disclosure duty. — Unlike the federal securities laws, the Delaware General Corporation Law (DGCL) imposes no affirmative duty to provide financial information or other substantive information about the corporation in public filings. Even where the DGCL mandates stockholder action, the provisions dealing with notice to stockholders of the proposed action do not require the corporation to supply substantive information to the stockholders relating to the exercise of their franchise. Instead, this statutory void is filled with the equitable principles embodied in the fiduciary duties of the board of directors. *Unanue v. Unanue, 2004 Del. Ch. LEXIS 153, No. 204-N (November 3, 2004).*

Unlike a proxy solicitation, persons organizing other stockholders to act by written consent under section 228 generally are not bound by an affirmative duty to disclose under the federal securities laws. Moreover, because action by written consent requires individual acts of volition by the stockholders, the potential for abuse that gives rise to the federal proxy rules is not present. *Unanue v. Unanue, 2004 Del. Ch. LEXIS 153, No. 204-N (November 3, 2004).*

Charter provision was valid and its plain terms established the record date for consent solicitation. Both subdivision (b)(1) of Section 102 and subsection (a) of Section 141 of the Delaware Corporation Law ("DGCL") provide authority for charter provisions to restrict the authority that directors have to manage firms, unless those restrictions are "contrary to the laws of this State." These statutory provisions are important expressions of the wide room for private ordering authorized by the DGCL, when such private ordering is reflected in the corporate charter. The charter provision is a valid exercise of authority under those sections and is not contrary to law, in the sense that our courts have interpreted that phrase. A consideration of subsection (b) of Section 213 terms and legislative history, as well as of the related statutory section governing consent solicitations, this section, reveals that no public policy set forth in the DGCL (or in Delaware's common law of corporations) is contravened by the charter provision at issue. Given the absence of any conflict with a mandatory aspect of Delaware corporate law, the charter provision's restriction on the board's authority to set a record date was valid. *Jones Apparel Group v. Maxwell Shoe Co., 2004 Del. Ch. LEXIS 74, No. 365-N (May 27, 2004).*

Delivery of action to affected partner required. — Delivery was required under this section in order for actions of shareholders removing the general partner to take effect; the absence of a comparable delivery requirement in the Delaware Revised Uniform Limited Partnership Act, specifically 6 Del. C. § 17-302, was intended since in all other material respects the 2 provisions are parallel. *Alpine Inv. Partners v. LJM2 Capital Mgmt., L.P., 2002 Del. Ch. LEXIS 30 (Mar. 14, 2002).*

CASE NOTES — OTHER STATES

Louisiana

This statute does not require advance notice; it only requires that prompt notice of the taking of the corporate action without a meeting by less than unanimous written consent must be given to those stockholders or members who have not consented in writing. *Crutcher v. Tufts, 898 So. 2d 529 (La. App. 4 Cir. 1995).*

"Any action" is defined to include shareholder action to remove directors from office. *Crutcher v. Tufts, 898 So. 2d 529 (La. App. 4 Cir. 1995).*

Minnesota

In general. — The statute expressly requires a meeting of the shareholders to amend certificates of incorporation, courts interpreting the Delaware General Corporation Code allow for corporate action by written consent. Written consent in lieu of a meeting is specifically available. *Ahlberg v. Timm Medical Technologies, Inc., 2003 Minn. App. LEXIS 1370 (2003).*

While many jurisdictions allow written action by unanimous consent, Delaware is one of a handful of states that allows written action by less than unanimous consent. Any corporate action taken under Del. Code Ann. tit. 8, § 228 is effective only upon delivery of the proper number of valid and unrevoked consents to the corporation. Courts have approved bylaws imposing some minimal essential provisions for ministerial review of the validity of the action taken by shareholder consent, but have disallowed bylaws abrogating this important shareholder right. *Ahlberg v. Timm Medical Technologies, Inc., 2003 Minn. App. LEXIS 1370 (2003).*

The statute clearly and unambiguously permits a majority of the stockholders of a corporation to act immediately and without notice to the minority. *Ahlberg v. Timm Medical Technologies, Inc., 2003 Minn. App. LEXIS 1370 (2003).*

New York

Prompt notice not specified under subsection (e). — Unlike the 8 Del. C. § 228(c) requirement, with which compliance or lack thereof is clear on the face of the consents, the "prompt notice" requirement of 8 Del. C. § 228(e) does not specify when notice need be given. Consequently, where plaintiffs have conceded that notice was provided within one month and have cited to no cases indicating that provision of notice within this time frame violates the statute, there is no reason not to dismiss the claim. *Oppman v. IRMC Holdings, Inc., 2007 NY Slip Op 50093U, 2007 N.Y. Misc. LEXIS 117 (Jan. 23, 2007).*

CASE NOTES — FEDERAL

Second Circuit

This section does not permit a corporation to adopt bylaws delaying the effectiveness of a shareholder vote. They contain no implication that a court, notwithstanding a significant showing of likely fraud, would nonetheless be powerless to stay the effectiveness of shareholder votes pending a hearing on whether the votes were procured through fraud. We see nothing in Delaware law that would prevent the consents collected by defendant from being filed within the permissible 60 day period, so as to preserve their potential effectiveness, subject to a court order staying their effectiveness and perhaps even staying

the counting and public disclosure of the consents, until challenges to their validity have been tried. In this fashion, plaintiff can be protected from any harm resulting from the filing of the consents, even assuming they were procured by fraud. We therefore conclude that plaintiff has failed to demonstrate that the mere act of filing the consents would cause it to suffer irreparable harm. Under the standards of Fed. R. Civ. P. 65, plaintiff is therefore not entitled to preliminary injunctive relief barring defendant from filing the consents. *Delcath Sys. v. Ladd, 466 F.3d 257, 2006 U.S. App. LEXIS 24234 (Sept. 25, 2006).*

§ 229. Waiver of notice

DELAWARE CASE NOTES — REPORTED

Waiver not permitted to be given by party who no longer is in position which would have entitled the party to notice. *In re Seminole Oil & Gas Corp., 38 Del. Ch. 549, 155 A.2d 887 (1959).*

Waiver not permitted when party attends Special meetings for election purposes. — This section permits

waiver of notice of any meeting, including those called under a provision for special meeting called for election purposes. *Grossman v. Liberty Leasing Co., 295 A.2d 749 (Del. Ch. 1972).*

DELAWARE CASE NOTES — UNREPORTED

Waiver not permitted when party attends meeting. — Where plaintiffs sought a summary declaration relating to the corporation's bylaws, the case was dismissed without prejudice for failure to state a claim because 8 Del. C. § 111 did not provide a cause of action for plaintiffs; in addition, under this section, the director

had no grounds to sue for the corporation's failure to provide the director with 60 days' notice of proposed bylaws changes because the director attended the relevant meetings, but did not attend for the sole purpose of objecting to lack of notice. *Messina v. Klugiewicz, 2004 Del. Ch. LEXIS 47 (Apr. 30, 2004).*

§ 231. Voting procedures and inspectors of elections

DELAWARE CASE NOTES — REPORTED

Proxies as part of determination of presence of a quorum. — Nothing in the language of this section requires that proxies be presented as part of the determination of the presence of a quorum. Consequently, failure

to present property settlement agreement setting out voting rights did not defeat the quorum of the annual meeting. *Lobato v. Health Concepts IV, Inc., 606 A.2d 1343 (Del. Ch. 1991).*

CASE NOTES — OTHER STATES

Pennsylvania

Enjoinable director conduct. — Tinkering with corporate elections to interfere with shareholders' electoral rights violates a director's fiduciary duty to shareholders and is enjoinable. *Jewelcor Management, Inc. v. Thistle Group Holdings, Co., 2002 Phila. Ct. Com. Pl. LEXIS 79 (2004).*

Irreparable harm. — Under Delaware law, the deprivation of a shareholder's right to vote is irreparable harm. *Alan Wurtzel Commerce Program v. Park Towne Place Apartments Limited Partnership, 2001 Phila. Ct. Com. Pl. LEXIS 79 (2001).*

Subchapter VIII.
Amendment of Certificate of Incorporation; Changes in Capital and Capital Stock

§ 241. Amendment of certificate of incorporation before receipt of payment for stock

DELAWARE CASE NOTES — REPORTED

Shareholder approval not required. — Normally, a proposed amendment to the certificate of incorporation

must be submitted to a vote of the corporation's stockholders entitled to vote thereon; there are two exceptions which are pertinent: first, if a corporation has not yet received payment for its shares, the board of directors may amend the certificate by board action alone; second, if a corporation has no capital stock, the governing body may approve a certificate amendment, on its own. *Farahpour v. DCX, Inc., 635 A.2d 894 (Del. 1994).*

CASE NOTES — FEDERAL

Second Circuit

Proof of informal method. — Under Delaware law, the amendment of fundamental corporate documents by implication, acquiescence, any informal method must be established by clear proof of a definite and uniform custom or usage, not in accord with the bylaws regularly adopted, and by acquiescence therein. *Management Techs. v. Morris, 961 F. Supp. 640 (S.D.N.Y. 1997).*

§ 242. Amendment of certificate of incorporation after receipt of payment for stock; nonstock corporations

DELAWARE CASE NOTES — REPORTED

This section was designed primarily for convenience of corporation. *State ex rel. RCA v. Benson, 32 Del. 576, 128 A. 107 (1924).*

Legislative intent of subsections (b)(2) and (b)(3). — The contrasting provisions of subsections (b)(2) and (b)(3) regarding class approval of decisions which might adversely affect the class reflect a legislative intent to provide fewer voting rights, of pure statutory origin, to members of nonstock corporations in the adoption of amendments to the certificate of incorporation; in sum, such members have neither a right to vote on an amendment generally nor a right to vote on an amendment as a class member unless the certificate of incorporation provides otherwise. *Farahpour v. DCX, Inc., 635 A.2d 894 (Del. 1994).*

Construction of section with § 228 of this title. — Section 228(c) of this title does not modify subsection (b) of this section to provide that persons who execute a written consent proposing a charter amendment need not be directors of the corporation at that time, so long as the consent is delivered to the corporation before the document that evidences the shareholders' consent to the amendment. *AGR Halifax Fund, Inc. v. Fiscina, 743 A.2d 1188 (Del. Ch. 1999).*

There is general right to amend corporate charter, by changing the nature of its capital stock. *Aldridge v. Franco Wyo. Oil Co., 24 Del. Ch. 126, 7 A.2d 753 (1939),* aff'd, *24 Del. Ch. 349, 14 A.2d 380 (1940).*

. A corporate charter may be amended, increasing an authorized capital stock issue, by the appropriate vote of the stockholders. *Hartford Accident & Indem. Co. v. W.S. Dickey Clay Mfg. Co., 26 Del. Ch. 16, 21 A.2d 178 (1941),* aff'd, *26 Del. Ch. 411, 24 A.2d 315 (1942).*

This section confers broad powers of amendment upon an affirmative vote of a majority of shares having general voting power. Such affirmative vote is always necessary to the adoption of an amendment. *Hartford Accident & Indem. Co. v. W.S. Dickey Clay Mfg. Co., 26 Del. Ch. 411, 24 A.2d 315 (1942).*

Under Delaware law, a corporation, incorporated in the State may make fundamental changes in its structure and purposes, through amendment of its articles of incorporation. *Farahpour v. DCX, Inc., 635 A.2d 894 (Del. 1994).*

Contract rights of shareholders do not rest upon unchangeable base. — The contract rights of the shareholders, in the sense of interrelations inter sese, do not rest upon an unchangeable base, but are subject to alteration under the amendatory provisions of the general law. *Hartford Accident & Indem. Co. v. W.S. Dickey Clay Mfg. Co., 26 Del. Ch. 411, 24 A.2d 315 (1942).*

If the right to change or alter the stockholder's contract be reserved in a proper way, then no shareholder can complain against a proposed change therein, for the very plain reason that one of the terms by which the stockholder holds his or her contract is that the same may be altered. *Peters v. United States Mtg. Co., 13 Del. Ch. 11, 114 A. 598 (1921).*

A corporation, in the sale and issuance of its stock, assumes a contractual relation to the shareholder and for the terms of the contract, the rights of the stockholder and the obligations of the corporation, reference is to be made to the appropriate provisions of the certificate of incorporation and the law of the sovereign conferring the corporate franchise and unless there be some provision in either the law or the corporate certificate reserving the power to do so, there can be no alteration in the terms of the contract under which the shareholder, as such, possesses his or her rights, without his or her consent. *Peters v. United States Mtg. Co., 13 Del. Ch. 11, 114 A. 598 (1921).*

The terms of the agreement between the shareholders, both as to the internal management of the corporation and as to their beneficial interests therein, are but conditions on which the corporate franchise may be exercised, and that the reserved power of the State, gives the State the unqualified right to alter or amend the privilege, or to confer upon the shareholders the right so to do, irrespective of the nature and character of the right invaded. *Keller v. Wilson & Co., 21 Del. Ch. 391, 190 A. 115 (1936).*

Since the power to amend a corporate charter and the method of exercising the power are parts of the contract between the corporation and its shareholders, U.S. Const., art. I, § 10, forbidding laws impairing the obligation of contracts, does not apply. *Hartford Accident & Indem. Co. v. W.S. Dickey Clay Mfg. Co., 26 Del. Ch. 411, 24 A.2d 315 (1942).*

There can be no constitutional objections to amendment when the State has the right to reserve to itself, or a majority or more of the stockholders, the power to change the contract between the corporation and its stockholders or between its different classes of stockholders by an amendment to the charter after such contracts are made, even if a particular class of stockholders must suffer slightly. *Goldman v. Postal Tel., Inc., 52 F. Supp. 763 (D. Del. 1943).*

Board of director's fiduciary duty of disclosure. — Delaware law imposes upon a board of directors the fiduciary duty to disclose fully and fairly all material facts within its control that would have a significant effect upon a stockholder vote; however, the board is not required to disclose all available information. *Stroud v. Grace, 606 A.2d 75 (Del. 1992).*

Burden of proof. — Stockholder approval of an organic, statutory change must comply with the statutory procedure and must be based on full and fair disclosure; the burden rests on the party relying on stockholder approval to establish that the approval resulted from a full informed electorate and that all material facts relevant to the transaction were fully disclosed. *Williams v. Geier, 671 A.2d 1368 (Del. 1996).*

Only by demonstrating that the board of directors breached its fiduciary duties may the presumption of the business judgment rule be rebutted, thereby shifting the burden to the board to demonstrate that the transaction complained of was entirely fair to the stockholders. *Williams v. Geier, 671 A.2d 1368 (Del. 1996).*

Amendments to certificates of incorporation are accomplished by submitting them to stockholders "entitled to vote" at a meeting of stockholders called and held upon notice. *Salt Dome Oil Corp. v. Schenck, 28 Del. Ch. 433, 41 A.2d 583 (1945).*

Exceptions to stockholder approval requirement. — Normally, a proposed amendment to the certificate of incorporation must be submitted to a vote of the corporation's stockholders entitled to vote thereon; there are two exceptions which are pertinent to the present inquiry: first, if a corporation has not yet received payment for its shares, the board of directors may amend the certificate by board action alone; second, if a corporation has no capital stock, the governing body may approve a certificate amendment, on its own. *Farahpour v. DCX, Inc., 635 A.2d 894 (Del. 1994).*

No distinction exists between amendments by statutory method and amendments by charter-created methods. *Sellers v. Joseph Bancroft & Sons Co., 23 Del. Ch. 13, 2 A.2d 108 (1938).*

Proposed amendment must in any case conform to procedure and requirements of this section. *Sellers v. Joseph Bancroft & Sons Co., 23 Del. Ch. 13, 2 A.2d 108 (1938).*

Amendment is not part of charter until it is filed with secretary of state. *Rice & Hutchins, Inc. v. Triplex Shoe Co., 16 Del. Ch. 298, 147 A. 317 (1929),* aff'd, *17 Del. Ch. 356, 152 A. 342 (1930).*

Right of secretary of state to refuse to file amendment. — The Secretary of State has the right, and it is his or her duty, to refuse to file an amendment to a certificate of incorporation that is sought to be made under a section of the law that does not authorize the proposed amendment, but if the thing sought to be done might be legally done under the amendment offered, the Secretary has no right to refuse to file it because he or she thinks the corporation may do something thereunder which could only be legally done under a different section of the law. *State ex rel. RCA v. Benson, 32 Del. 576, 128 A. 107 (1924).*

Amendment of certificate of incorporation limiting duration of corporation is a legally permissible action for corporate activity and must be judged as an independent and distinct transaction unrelated to other sections of the general corporation law. *Willard v. Harrworth Corp., 267 A.2d 577 (Del. 1970).*

Right to amend must be exercised fairly and impartially. — The right of the controlling stockholders to amend, though pursuant to charter authority, must be exercised with fair and impartial regard for the rights and interest of all of the corporate stockholders of every class; and not for the sole benefit of particular classes, to the clear prejudice of other outstanding issues. *Hartford Accident & Indem. Co. v. W.S. Dickey Clay Mfg. Co., 26 Del. Ch. 16, 21 A.2d 178 (1941),* aff'd, *26 Del. Ch. 411, 24 A.2d 315 (1942).*

Presumption of fairness. — Where a majority of the stockholders and directors of a Delaware corporation, acting in good faith, speak for the corporation by taking action under appropriate statutory and charter provisions, a presumption of fairness arises in favor of such action. *Bailey v. Tubize Rayon Corp., 56 F. Supp. 418 (D. Del. 1944).*

Under the Delaware decisional and statutory law an amendment will not be condemned unless it is so unfair as to amount to constructive fraud. Unless the act of the majority of the directors and stockholders is so palpably unfair as to afford no basis for a difference of opinion among reasonable persons, the court should not substitute its judgment for that of the stockholders and directors. *Bailey v. Tubize Rayon Corp., 56 F. Supp. 418 (D. Del. 1944).*

Exercise of power to amend is subject to review by court of equity. — The exercise of grant of power to amend, under Delaware statute, the certificate of incorporation, altering or changing preferences if the majority of stockholders affected by the amendment vote in favor of it, is subject to historical processes of court of equity to gauge whether there has been an oppressive exercise of power granted. *Goldman v. Postal Tel., Inc., 52 F. Supp. 763 (D. Del. 1943).*

Assuming the grant of power by this section, action taken by the majority is not clothed thereby with a superior sanctity vesting such power with the attributes of tyranny; but the exercise of such grant is always subject to the historical processes of a court of equity to gauge whether there has been an oppressive exercise of the power granted. *Barrett v. Denver Tramway Corp., 53 F. Supp. 198 (D. Del. 1943),* aff'd, *146 F.2d 701 (3d Cir. 1944).*

Written consents void. — Written consents to a charter amendment were void ab initio where the persons purporting to take action binding the corporation were not its duly elected directors. *AGR Halifax Fund, Inc. v. Fiscina, 743 A.2d 1188 (Del. Ch. 1999).*

Corporations

Members of nonstock corporation not denied equal protection. — This section did not violate equal protection on the grounds that an amendment of the certificate of incorporation of a stock corporation requires consent of stockholders while amendment of certificate of nonstock corporation does not require consent of members. *Gulcz v. Delaware Polish Beneficial Ass'n, 20 Del. Ch. 52, 169 A. 595 (1933).*

Delaware law authorizes change from a nonprofit, nonstock mutual benefit corporation into a for-profit stock corporation without the vote of its members. *Farahpour v. DCX, Inc., 635 A.2d 894 (Del. 1994).*

Voting rights may be changed by amendment. *Gottlieb v. Heyden Chem. Corp., 32 Del. Ch. 231, 83 A.2d 595 (1951),* rev'd on other grounds, *92 A.2d 594 (Del. 1952).*

The right to vote is not such a change in property rights as to be exempt from the tampering effect of amendment where general power to amend is reserved. It is but an alteration which concerns the internal management of the corporation, and being such is not beyond the reach of an authorized general power to amend. *Morris v. American Pub. Util. Co., 14 Del. Ch. 136, 122 A. 696 (1923).*

Special rights, such as cumulative voting, may be resigned by the appropriate vote of the majority of those enjoying them. *Maddock v. Vorclone Corp., 17 Del. Ch. 39, 147 A. 255 (1929).*

The right of stock to vote cumulatively at an election for directors is a special right of a share within the meaning of this section and it is therefore a right susceptible of change. *Maddock v. Vorclone Corp., 17 Del. Ch. 39, 147 A. 255 (1929).*

An amendment which changes the voting power of the stock of a corporation, and which has no purpose further than that, is not conceived in fraud. *Topkis v. Delaware Hdwe. Co., 23 Del. Ch. 125, 2 A.2d 114 (1938).*

The right to vote is not such a change in property rights as to be exempt from the tampering effect of amendment where general power to amend is reserved. It is but an alteration which concerns the internal management of the corporation, and being such is not beyond the reach of an authorized general power to amend. *Aldridge v. Franco Wyo. Oil Co., 24 Del. Ch. 126, 7 A.2d 753 (1939),* aff'd, *24 Del. Ch. 349, 14 A.2d 380 (1940).*

The word "special," as applied to a right attached to stock, was used in this section in the sense of shares having some unusual or superior quality not possessed by another class of shares. In this sense a relative right is a special right. But the relative position of 1 class of shares in the scheme of capitalization is not to be confused with rights incident to that class as compared with other classes of shares. Where the corporate amendment does no more than to increase the number of the shares of a preferred or superior class, the relative position of subordinated shares is changed in the sense that they are subjected to a greater burden. The peculiar, or special, quality with which they are endowed, and which serves to distinguish them from shares of another class, remains the same. *Hartford Accident & Indem. Co. v. W.S. Dickey Clay Mfg. Co., 26 Del. Ch. 411, 24 A.2d 315 (1942).*

"Vested" rights of stockholders may not be taken away by amendment over objection. *Gottlieb v. Heyden Chem. Corp., 32 Del. Ch. 231, 83 A.2d 595 (1951),* rev'd on other grounds, *92 A.2d 594 (Del. 1952).*

If the subject corporation is a stock corporation with some paid-for shares outstanding, it cannot amend its certificate by board action alone under subsection (b)(1). *Farahpour v. DCX, Inc., 635 A.2d 894 (Del. 1994).*

Subsection (b)(2) expressly provides that a class of stockholders is entitled to a class vote on a proposed amendment whether or not the class is entitled to vote thereon by the certificate of incorporation if the amendment adversely affects the rights of the class. *Farahpour v. DCX, Inc., 635 A.2d 894 (Del. 1994).*

Rights to profits of dissolution are not vested. — As there is no vested right to share in the assets of a corporation prior to dissolution or the declaration of a nonstock dividend, loss of rights to receive assets in dissolution would be a natural consequence of loss of membership status; it would appear that there is no legal or statutory bar to the elimination of membership with the consequent inability of such members to share in the assets upon dissolution. *Farahpour v. DCX, Inc., 635 A.2d 894 (Del. 1994).*

Stockholder may be estopped from objecting to amendment by his or her express or implied acquiescence therein. Any acts indicating an acceptance by a stockholder of the amendment bind the stockholder and bar his or her suit. Acquiescence may sometimes grow out of a stockholder's silence or delay under circumstances that called on the stockholder to dissent if he or she so intended. *Trounstine v. Remington Rand, Inc., 22 Del. Ch. 122, 194 A. 95 (1937).*

A stockholder cannot attack a wrongful or ultra vires act, where the stockholder has accepted pecuniary benefits thereunder, with knowledge of the facts. Acceptance of dividends resulting from the act or thing complained of has in several instances been held to work an estoppel. *Trounstine v. Remington Rand, Inc., 22 Del. Ch. 122, 194 A. 95 (1937).*

A stockholder is barred from complaining against a certificate amendment by the estoppel of his or her acquiescence or by circumstances showing laches in the assertion of his or her objection. *Romer v. Porcelain Prods., Inc., 23 Del. Ch. 52, 2 A.2d 75 (1938).*

A dissenting stockholder to an amendment to a corporate charter which illegally attempts to deprive a nonconsenting stockholder, having notice of such amendment of vested rights in certain accrued and unpaid dividends on his or her stock, cannot delay action or stand by in silence in order to determine if such amendment will be to his or her advantage. *Bay Newfoundland Co. v. Wilson & Co., 24 Del. Ch. 30, 4 A.2d 668 (1939).*

When the facts justify it, even a stockholder who originally objected to a charter amendment, and whose stock was voted against such amendment, may be barred from asserting his or her rights against the corporation by the estoppel of his or her acquiescence or by circumstances showing laches in the assertion of his or her objections.

Frank v. Wilson & Co., 24 Del. Ch. 237, 9 A.2d 82 (1939), aff'd, *27 Del. Ch. 292, 32 A.2d 277 (1943).*

In most cases when the bill is filed within the time prescribed by the statute governing somewhat similar actions at law, the equitable rule, with respect to laches, is not ordinarily based on the mere delay of a complainant in asserting his or her rights, but on delay that works a disadvantage to another, after notice of the invasion of such rights. *Frank v. Wilson & Co., 24 Del. Ch. 237, 9 A.2d 82 (1939),* aff'd, *27 Del. Ch. 292, 32 A.2d 277 (1943).*

The acceptance of dividends on stock, issued pursuant to a charter amendment, alleged to be ultra vires so far as the complainant is concerned, will sometimes operate as an estoppel. *Frank v. Wilson & Co., 24 Del. Ch. 237, 9 A.2d 82 (1939),* aff'd, *27 Del. Ch. 292, 32 A.2d 277 (1943).*

The promptness of action demanded of a stockholder objecting to the accomplishment of a proposed corporate act which, although unauthorized, is capable of ratification, is dependent in a large degree upon the effect of his or her delay on others; and where many persons will be affected by an act that involves a change of capital structure and a material alteration of rights attached to stock ownership, the stockholder, having knowledge of the contemplated action, owes a duty both to the corporation and to the stockholders to act with the promptness demanded by the particular circumstances. *Federal United Corp. v. Havender, 24 Del. Ch. 318, 11 A.2d 331 (1940).*

Where stockholder knew of plan for reclassification of stock and reduction of capital, and subsequently of amendment to charter and filing of certificate of reduction, but waited until more than 87 percent of holders of old stock had changed their position and new securities had been traded on stock exchange before filing bill of complaint, his conduct constituted laches. *Shanik v. White Sewing Mach. Corp., 25 Del. Ch. 371, 19 A.2d 831 (1941).*

Acts indicating an acceptance by a stockholder of an amendment to a corporate charter bind such stockholder and bar his or her suit. *Frank v. Wilson & Co., 27 Del. Ch. 292, 32 A.2d 277 (1943).*

An objecting stockholder need not, in every case, move to enjoin a proposed corporate action such as a certificate of incorporation amendment in order to escape the imputation of laches; but it is incumbent on such stockholder to give notice in plain and unambiguous terms that the intended trespass upon his or her rights would be contested. *Frank v. Wilson & Co., 27 Del. Ch. 292, 32 A.2d 277 (1943).*

Where the conduct of a stockholder, subsequent to the transaction objected to, e.g., amendment to the certificate of incorporation, is such as reasonably to warrant the conclusion that the stockholder has accepted or adopted it, the stockholder's ratification is implied through his or her acquiescence. *Frank v. Wilson & Co., 27 Del. Ch. 292, 32 A.2d 277 (1943).*

It is within the doctrine of acquiescence to hold that assent to a proposed corporate act will be inferred in a case where a stockholder, with full knowledge of an intended invasion of his or her rights and an opportunity to dissent, stands by during the progress of a proceeding which, although unauthorized, is ratifiable, and allows,

without objection, his or her stock to be dealt with in a manner inconsistent with his rights of ownership. *Bay Newfoundland Co. v. Wilson & Co., 27 Del. Ch. 344, 37 A.2d 59 (1944).*

Even where the dissenting shareholder is in a position to assert that it is not within the power of the majority to bind him or her by an amendment, his or her right to relief may be lost through his or her acquiescence, by ratification, or by laches. *Bay Newfoundland Co. v. Wilson & Co., 27 Del. Ch. 344, 37 A.2d 59 (1944).*

This section authorizes alteration of preferences. — This section, which is to be read into the original certificate of incorporation of a corporation in providing that no change or alteration in the preferences of any class of stock shall be made unless a majority of the shares of the class concerned in the change votes in favor thereof, clearly indicates that a change or alteration of any preference may be made. *Morris v. American Pub. Util. Co., 14 Del. Ch. 136, 122 A. 696 (1923).*

One of the conditions upon which the stockholders as preferred stockholders enjoy a preference is that it might at any time be changed and altered upon the approval of a majority of its holders. *Morris v. American Pub. Util. Co., 14 Del. Ch. 136, 122 A. 696 (1923).*

The rate of dividend which preferred stock is to receive can be altered by amendment to the certificate of incorporation. *Morris v. American Pub. Util. Co., 14 Del. Ch. 136, 122 A. 696 (1923).*

The right to the preference in future dividends may be lawfully altered. *Keller v. Wilson & Co., 21 Del. Ch. 13, 180 A. 584 (1935),* rev'd on other grounds, *21 Del. Ch. 391, 190 A. 115 (1936).*

Where defendant corporation possessed the power of self-amendment by virtue of this section, a preferred stockholder's right to receive unpaid dividends in preference to payment of dividend on common stock was not a "vested right of property" and preferred stockholder was not protected by the contract clause of the federal Constitution. *Hottenstein v. York Ice Mach. Corp., 136 F.2d 944 (3d Cir. 1943),* cert. denied, *325 U.S. 886, 65 S. Ct. 1573, 89 L. Ed. 2000 (1945).*

Preferred stockholders of a Delaware corporation buy into a particular enterprise subject to the provision that preferences may be changed by a requisite majority vote and accordingly consent in advance that whatever their preferences may be at the time they are subject to change by the vote of the proper majority. *Goldman v. Postal Tel., Inc., 52 F. Supp. 763 (D. Del. 1943).*

Where stockholders of Delaware corporation have been called to change preferential rights of preferred stockholders by amendment to charter of incorporation under Delaware statute and to approve sale of assets 1 meeting is sufficient, even though separate meetings could have been arranged. *Goldman v. Postal Tel., Inc., 52 F. Supp. 763 (D. Del. 1943).*

An amendment to a certificate of incorporation to change or alter preferences is subject under Delaware statute to protection afforded against arbitrary action in the requirement that a majority of those affected by the

Corporations

amendment must vote in favor of it. *Goldman v. Postal Tel., Inc., 52 F. Supp. 763 (D. Del. 1943).*

Execution of a contract for the sale of assets, not binding on the corporation until approved by vote of stockholders, did not accelerate the preferential right of preferred stockholders into a "vested right" which could not thereafter be altered by amendment of the certificate of incorporation changing preferences by requisite majority vote. *Goldman v. Postal Tel., Inc., 52 F. Supp. 763 (D. Del. 1943).*

The rule is that the preferential right of the class A stockholders to receive $100 in liquidation gives them no present interest in any portion of the corporation's assets. That right would arise only upon the liquidation of the corporation and, since the corporation is engaged in a profitable going business, it is impossible to foresee ultimate liquidation values of the company. *Bailey v. Tubize Rayon Corp., 56 F. Supp. 418 (D. Del. 1944).*

Action of board of directors in recommending amendment and recapitalization to the stockholders constituted neither a breach of fiduciary duty nor an impermissible effort at entrenchment, both of which were claimed to rebut the business judgment presumption and implicate entire fairness review, where record showed: (1) no non-pro rata or disproportionate benefit accrued to the majority interest on the face of the recapitalization, although the dynamics of how the plan would work in practice had the effect of strengthening the majority's interest control; (2) no evidence adduced to show that a majority of the board was interested or acted for purposes of entrenching themselves in office; (3) no evidence was offered to show that the board was dominated or controlled by the majority interest; and (4) there was no evidence of violation of fiduciary duty by the board. *Williams v. Geier, 671 A.2d 1368 (Del. 1996).*

This section authorizes decrease in the number of shares of no par stock issued, as well as authorized and unissued. *State ex rel. RCA v. Benson, 32 Del. 576, 128 A. 107 (1924).*

Language of subsection (a) authorizing consolidation of changes into 1 certificate of amendment permissive. — The language of subsection (a) of this section, providing that "any or all such changes or alterations may be effected by 1 certificate of amendment" is permissive, not mandatory. *Chrysler Corp. v. State, 457 A.2d 345 (Del. 1983).*

Filing of 2 separate amendments for 2 changes consolidated in 1 resolution is permissible under subsection (a) of this section. *Chrysler Corp. v. State, 457 A.2d 345 (Del. 1983).*

And corporation not required to file a single amendment. — Where a Delaware corporation consolidated 2 separate changes allowable under subsection (a) of this section into 1 resolution to amend its certificate of incorporation, the corporation was not required by the statute to file a single amendment. *Chrysler Corp. v. State, 457 A.2d 345 (Del. 1983).*

Consolidation of 2 changes into 1 resolution before shareholders does not render them substantially 1 transaction. — Where a Delaware corporation, by means of a single resolution, amended its certificate of

incorporation so as to increase its authorized capital stock and to reclassify its stock from par value to no par, the consolidation of the 2 changes, listed as separate allowable changes under subsection (a) of this section, into 1 resolution before the shareholders did not render them substantially 1 transaction. *Chrysler Corp. v. State, 457 A.2d 345 (Del. 1983).*

Plaintiff failed to establish his right to order restraining implementation of amendment authorizing the increase in number of authorized shares to an amount sufficient to enable a 2-for-1 stock split, where the amendment was adopted by an overwhelming majority according to this section and plaintiff failed to establish a threat of immediate and irreparable injury, loss or damage. *Levin v. Metro-Goldwyn-Mayer, Inc., 43 Del. Ch. 168, 221 A.2d 499 (1966).*

Relinquishment of stockholder's rights not shown. — Plaintiff stockholder, in not voting in favor of plan of recapitalization, in having her attorney advise defendant 10 days after the plan was approved by other stockholders that she would litigate, in instituting her suit in court, in returning all dividend checks sent to her by defendant, and in retaining the certificates representing old stock, did not indicate a relinquishment of rights as a stockowner. *Dunn v. Wilson & Co., 51 F. Supp. 655 (D. Del. 1943).*

Motive for change not relevant consideration. — If directors or stockholders of a corporation, by appropriate action, have the power to effect a particular change, their motive for doing so is not a relevant consideration in determining the question of objective fairness. *Bailey v. Tubize Rayon Corp., 56 F. Supp. 418 (D. Del. 1944).*

The reasons for an amendment changing the stock structure or the business necessity behind it are not matters for judicial determination. *Bailey v. Tubize Rayon Corp., 56 F. Supp. 418 (D. Del. 1944).*

Amendment cannot relate back to validate void issue of stock. — While an amendment passed at a stockholders' meeting might cure certain irregularities, imperfections and defects in a stock issue that is authorized by the charter and laws of the State, it cannot relate back and validate a stock that was issued without any corporate authority for if the stock issue was void, there was nothing to validate, nothing upon which the amendment could operate. *Triplex Shoe Co. v. Rice & Hutchins, Inc., 17 Del. Ch. 356, 152 A. 342 (1930).*

Stock reclassification plan, to be held unfair, must amount to at least constructive fraud. *Barrett v. Denver Tramway Corp., 146 F.2d 701 (3d Cir. 1944).*

Shareholder vote held effective. — Shareholder vote, following recommendation by board of directors, approving an amendment and recapitalization, was effective where there was no basis for a finding that the amendment and recapitalization involved waste, fraud, or manipulative or other inequitable conduct. *Williams v. Geier, 671 A.2d 1368 (Del. 1996).*

Shareholder vote on recommendation by board of directors of amendment and recapitalization plan was effective; although it might benefit a majority interest, there is no requirement under the Delaware General

Corporation Law that the transaction be structured or conditioned so as to require an affirmative vote of a majority of the minority group of outstanding shares, and the failure to obtain a majority of the minority does not give rise to any adverse inference of invalidity. *Williams v. Geier, 671 A.2d 1368 (Del. 1996).*

This section recognizes rights of stock as a class in matters of change and amendment of its preferences, special rights and powers, and segregates such classes into separate voting groups. *Sellers v. Joseph Bancroft & Sons Co., 23 Del. Ch. 13, 2 A.2d 108 (1938).*

Where a corporate charter required the vote of 75 percent of holders of certain class of stock in order to change the designations, preferences, and voting powers of that class, required percentage was not reached when 1 of the coexecutors of estate of deceased shareholder objected to the proposed changes, since coexecutors must agree on vote to make it legal. *Sellers v. Joseph Bancroft & Sons Co., 25 Del. Ch. 268, 17 A.2d 831 (1941).*

Protection afforded by class vote against effects of amendment is, however, restricted to 3 situations. Where the proposed amendment would alter or change preferences, or special rights or powers, given to a class of shares so as to affect adversely the class, the holders of the shares of that class are entitled to vote on the amendment separately as a class, and a majority of the shares of the class must vote in approval of the amendment. Where the proposed amendment would increase or decrease the amount of the authorized stock of a class, a class vote is required, and a majority of the shares of the class must consent. Where the proposed amendment would increase or decrease the par value of a class of shares, an affirmative vote of a majority in interest of the class is necessary to the adoption of the amendment. *Hartford Accident & Indem. Co. v. W.S. Dickey Clay Mfg. Co., 26 Del. Ch. 411, 24 A.2d 315 (1942).*

Effect given provision requiring greater than majority vote. — When the class of stock is segregated into a voting group, this section prescribes the rule of majority voting for the ascertainment of the group judgment. But § 102 of this title provides that the certificate of incorporation may require for any corporate action the vote of a larger proportion of the stock or any class thereof than is required by any other provisions of the act. Therefore, in the case of a corporation which has designated a vote of a large portion for corporate action the majority rule of this section is supplanted by the designated voting rule contained in the certificate when the stock class to be affected by a proposed amendment is called upon to vote with respect to matters adversely affecting the specified rights to which the voting rule is applicable. *Sellers v. Joseph Bancroft & Sons Co., 23 Del. Ch. 13, 2 A.2d 108 (1938).*

Measure of protection afforded to nonassenting stockholders in any prospective plan of reorganization is applicable only to those stockholders whose rights are, in some way, affected by the plan, and it does not include those persons who voluntarily and with knowledge become stockholders long after the plan has become effective. *Shanik v. White Sewing Mach. Corp., 25 Del. Ch. 371, 19 A.2d 831 (1941).*

Preference given secured creditor valid. — The exercise of a secured creditor's right to elect a majority of the board of directors of its debtor was a valid corporate act, where the creditor's election right was created as part of a complex scheme to protect its substantial investment in the debtor, wherein the common shareholder knowingly bargained away its right to control the board and such an agreement did not effectuate an amendment of the certificate of incorporation. *In re Bicoastal Corp., 600 A.2d 343 (Del. 1991).*

DELAWARE CASE NOTES — REPORTED

Pleading recapitalization. —Because transactions were many and complex, the public shareholders, when repleading direct claims, were required to walk the court through the recapitalization's essential parts, fact-by-fact; the shareholders were to explain by what mechanism an inflated liquidation value permitted the preferred shareholders to receive more in the recapitalization then they otherwise would have. *Gatz v. Ponsoldt, 2005 Del. Ch. LEXIS 158 (Del. Ch. Oct. 13, 2005).*

CASE NOTES — OTHER STATES

Minnesota

Two-step process. — The statute authorizes certain amendments to certificates of incorporation, including those that increase or decrease the authorized capital stock. It also sets out the process for making and approving the amendments. The Delaware courts have construed the section to provide a two-step process that must be followed in precise sequence to amend a certificate of incorporation. First, the board of directors must adopt a resolution proposing the amendment, declaring its advisability and calling for a shareholder vote at a special or annual shareholder meeting. Second, the proposed amendment must be considered and voted upon at a special meeting of the stockholders. *Ahlberg v. Timm Medical Technologies, Inc., 2003 Minn. App. LEXIS 1370 (2003).*

The statute expressly requires a meeting of the shareholders to amend certificates of incorporation, courts interpreting the Delaware General Corporation Code allow for corporate action by written consent. Written consent in lieu of a meeting is specifically available. *Ahlberg v. Timm Medical Technologies, Inc., 2003 Minn. App. LEXIS 1370 (2003).*

Pennsylvania

Supermajority votes. — The Delaware Corporation Code requires a supermajority vote to amend a supermajority provision in a corporate charter. *Alan Wurtzel Commerce Program v. Park Towne Place Apartments Limited Partnership, 2001 Phila. Ct. Com. Pl. LEXIS 79 (2002).*

Unless otherwise provided for, the amendment of corporate charters, like other shareholder action, is generally by majority vote. Supermajority voting provisions have the negative effect of giving minority shareholders the power to veto the will of the majority, effectively disenfranchising the majority. Courts will enforce supermajority voting requirements in corporate charters and bylaws only where the provisions are "clear and unambiguous." *Alan Wurtzel Commerce Program v. Park Towne Place Apartments Limited Partnership, 2001 Phila. Ct. Com. Pl. LEXIS 79 (2001).*

CASE NOTES — FEDERAL

Second Circuit

Proof of informal method. — Under Delaware law, the amendment of fundamental corporate documents by implication, acquiescence, any informal method must be established by clear proof of a definite and uniform custom or usage, not in accord with the bylaws regularly adopted, and by acquiescence therein. *Management Techs. v. Morris, 961 F. Supp. 640 (S.D.N.Y. 1997).*

§ 243. Retirement of stock

CASE NOTES — FEDERAL

Seventh Circuit

Construction with other law. — Del. Code Ann. tit. 8, § 160 provides that a corporation may not redeem its own shares when the capital of the corporation is impaired or when such purchase or redemption would cause any impairment of the capital of the corporation, except that a corporation may purchase or redeem out of capital any of its own shares which are entitled upon any distribution of its assets, whether by dividend or in liquidation, to a preference over another class or series of its stock if such shares will be retired upon their acquisition and the capital of the corporation reduced in accordance with Del. Code Ann. tit. 8, §§ 243, 244. A corporation redeeming its own shares would impair its capital within the meaning of § 160 unless it redeems shares out of surplus. *Wright v. Heizer Corp., 503 F. Supp. 802 (N.D. Ill. 1980).*

§ 244. Reduction of capital

DELAWARE CASE NOTES — REPORTED

This section was designed primarily for the protection of the creditors and stockholders of the corporation. *State ex rel. RCA v. Benson, 32 Del. 576, 128 A. 107 (1924).*

Requirement in this section that no reduction shall be made in the capital stock of a corporation until all its debts are paid means that the capital of the corporation, which is the creditors' security, shall not be impaired. *State ex rel. RCA v. Benson, 32 Del. 576, 128 A. 107 (1924).*

The method of reducing capital by purchasing shares at private sale for retirement may be invoked to eliminate a substantial number of shares held by a stockholder at odds with management policy, provided of course that the transaction is clear of any fraud or unfairness. *Martin v. American Potash & Chem. Corp., 33 Del. Ch. 234, 92 A.2d 295 (1952).*

This section confers upon a corporation power to reduce capital by purchasing shares for retirement at private sale, without a pro rata offering to all holders of stock of the class affected. *Martin v. American Potash & Chem. Corp., 33 Del. Ch. 234, 92 A.2d 295 (1952).*

CASE NOTES — FEDERAL

Seventh Circuit

Construction with other law. — Del. Code Ann. tit. 8, § 160 provides that a corporation may not redeem its own shares when the capital of the corporation is impaired or when such purchase or redemption would cause any impairment of the capital of the corporation, except that a corporation may purchase or redeem out of capital any of its own shares which are entitled upon any distribution of its assets, whether by dividend or in liquidation, to a preference over another class or series of its stock if such shares will be retired upon their acquisition and the capital of the corporation reduced in accordance with Del. Code Ann. tit. 8, §§ 243, 244. A corporation redeeming its own shares would impair its capital within the meaning of § 160 unless it redeems shares out of surplus. *Wright v. Heizer Corp., 503 F. Supp. 802 (N.D. Ill. 1980).*

Subchapter IX.
Merger, Consolidation or Conversion

§ 251. Merger or consolidation of domestic corporations and limited liability company

DELAWARE CASE NOTES — REPORTED

Supremacy of federal bankruptcy law. — General corporation law of the State of Delaware addressed the required procedures for merger or consolidation corporations under this section and *8 Del. C. §§ 252, 253*, but the "notwithstanding any otherwise applicable nonbankruptcy law" language of *11 U.S.C. § 1123*(a) overrode the requirements of the state provisions; if there was any doubt about the Bankruptcy Code trumping the state law provisions, *8 Del. C. § 303* dispelled it by specifically providing for mergers under a *Chapter 11 plan. In re Stone & Webster, Inc., 286 Bankr. 532 (Bankr. D. Del. 2002)*.

Section must be read into charter. — The provisions of this section have been a part of the general corporation law since its first adoption, and must be read into a Delaware corporation's charter to the same extent as though they had actually been inserted in it. *Havender v. Federal United Corp., 24 Del. Ch. 96, 6 A.2d 618 (1939)*, rev'd on other grounds, *24 Del. Ch. 318, 11 A.2d 331 (1940)*.

Statute retroactively applied. — The language of the merger statute, with its right of stock appraisement and payment in cash and withdrawal from the enterprise, permits of no reasonable doubt that a retrospective operation was intended. *Federal United Corp. v. Havender, 24 Del. Ch. 318, 11 A.2d 331 (1940)*.

Acceptance of shares constitutes notice. — Because the power to merge is conferred by statute, every stockholder in a Delaware corporation accepts his or her shares with notice thereof. *Singer v. Magnavox Co., 380 A.2d 969 (Del. 1977)*, overruled on other grounds by *Weinberger v. UOP, Inc., 457 A.2d 701 (Del. 1983)*.

Language of merger statutes negatives narrow or technical construction if the purpose for which they were enacted is to be accomplished. *Federal United Corp. v. Havender, 24 Del. Ch. 318, 11 A.2d 331 (1940)*.

Vice latent in corporate merger carried out in disregard of statutory rules is that the rights of creditors or stockholders may be thereby impaired. *Heilbrunn v. Sun Chem. Corp., 37 Del. Ch. 552, 146 A.2d 757 (1958)*, aff'd, *38 Del. Ch. 321, 150 A.2d 755 (1959)*.

Merger ordinarily contemplates continuance of enterprise and of the stockholder's investment therein, though in altered form. *Sterling v. Mayflower Hotel Corp., 33 Del. Ch. 293, 93 A.2d 107 (1952)*.

Corporate mergers are encouraged and favored. *MacFarlane v. North Am. Cement Corp., 16 Del. Ch. 172, 157 A. 396 (1928)*.

In the absence of any evidence of fraud, bad faith or intentional wrongdoing, there must be a presumption that those favoring the merger are acting honestly, according to their best judgment and for the advantage of the companies they seek to consolidate. *MacFarlane v. North Am. Cement Corp., 16 Del. Ch. 172, 157 A. 396 (1928)*.

Mergers are encouraged to the extent that they tend to conserve and promote corporate interests. *Federal United Corp. v. Havender, 24 Del. Ch. 318, 11 A.2d 331 (1940)*.

Merger should not promote interests of 1 class of stockholders to detriment of another. — A merger should not be permitted if its real and only purpose is to promote the interests of 1 class of stockholders to the detriment, or at the expense of another class, even though the latter may be in the decided minority. *MacFarlane v. North Am. Cement Corp., 16 Del. Ch. 172, 157 A. 396 (1928)*.

Merger may be said to "involve" sale of assets, in the sense that the title to the assets is by operation of law transferred from the constituent corporation to the surviving corporation; but it is not the same thing. *Sterling v. Mayflower Hotel Corp., 33 Del. Ch. 293, 93 A.2d 107 (1952)*.

A merger can be accomplished through an exchange of cash for stock. *Texaco Ref. & Mktg., Inc. v. Delaware River Basin Comm'n, 824 F. Supp. 500 (D. Del. 1993)*, aff'd, *30 F.3d 1488 (3d Cir. 1994)*.

Doctrine of de facto mergers means that there has been a sale of all its assets by 1 corporation to another, the stockholders of the former becoming stockholders in the latter, notwithstanding there was no technical merger or any statutory authority for one, and the transferee corporation will be held to a liability for its transferor's debts. *Gott v. Live Poultry Transit Co., 17 Del. Ch. 288, 153 A. 801 (1931)*.

Assuming that there may be a merger de facto of 2 corporations, the rule as to colorable compliance which is applicable to the existence of a corporation de facto ought likewise to prevail as to de facto mergers; where there was no colorable compliance with the statutory provision, no merger took place when the so-called attempt was made. *Blackstone v. Chandler, 15 Del. Ch. 1, 130 A. 34 (1925)*.

There can be no consolidated corporation de facto where there can be no de jure one. *Gott v. Live Poultry Transit Co., 17 Del. Ch. 288, 153 A. 801 (1931)*.

The doctrine of de facto merger has been invoked in cases of sales of assets for the protection of creditors or stockholders who have suffered an injury by reason of failure to comply with the statute governing such sales. *Heilbrunn v. Sun Chem. Corp., 38 Del. Ch. 321, 150 A.2d 755 (1959)*.

No injury has been inflicted upon the purchaser's stockholders, where their corporation has simply acquired property and paid for it in shares of stock. The business of the purchaser will go on as before, with additional assets, the purchaser's stockholders are not forced to accept stock in another corporation, and the reorganization has not changed the essential nature of the enterprise of the purchasing corporation. Hence, the purchaser's stockholders have no right to raise the question of de facto merger. *Heilbrunn v. Sun Chem. Corp., 38 Del. Ch. 321, 150 A.2d 755 (1959).*

Where a sale of assets is effected under § 271 of this title in consideration of shares of stock of the purchasing corporation and the agreement of sale embodies also a plan to dissolve the selling corporation and distribute the shares so received to the stockholders of the seller, so as to accomplish the same result as would be accomplished by a merger of the seller into the purchaser, such a sale was held to be proper. *Hariton v. Arco Elecs., Inc., 41 Del. Ch. 74, 188 A.2d 123 (1963).*

Valid merger does not require that merging corporations be going concerns, nor does such a requirement appear reasonable or desirable. *Hottenstein v. York Ice Mach. Corp., 45 F. Supp. 436 (D. Del. 1942), aff'd, 136 F.2d 944 (3d Cir. 1943), cert. denied, 325 U.S. 886, 65 S. Ct. 1573, 89 L. Ed. 2000 (1945).*

A statutory merger results in a combination of two corporations with the surviving corporation attaining the property, rights, and privileges of the absorbed corporation, as well as retaining its own property, rights, and privileges. *Texaco Ref. & Mktg., Inc. v. Delaware River Basin Comm'n, 824 F. Supp. 500 (D. Del. 1993), aff'd, 30 F.3d 1488 (3d Cir. 1994).*

Reasons for merger or business necessity behind it are not matters for judicial determination. *MacCrone v. American Capital Corp., 51 F. Supp. 462 (D. Del. 1943); Bruce v. E.L. Bruce Co., 40 Del. Ch. 80, 174 A.2d 29 (1961); Singer v. Magnavox Co., 367 A.2d 1349 (Del. Ch. 1976), aff'd in part and rev'd in part, 380 A.2d 969 (Del. 1977).*

Delaware courts will not inquire into the reasons motivating a merger or the business justification for it as a part of determining its validity. *Singer v. Magnavox Co., 367 A.2d 1349 (Del. Ch. 1976), aff'd in part and rev'd in part, 380 A.2d 969 (Del. 1977).*

Under this section, 2 (or more) Delaware corporations may merge into a single corporation and, generally speaking, whether such a transaction is good or bad, enlightened or ill-advised, selfish or generous is beside the point. *Tanzer v. International Gen. Indus., Inc., 402 A.2d 382 (Del. Ch. 1979).*

Comparison with tender offer. — A tender offer is distinct from a merger, and does not implicate the requirements and protections of this section. *Texaco Ref. & Mktg., Inc. v. Delaware River Basin Comm'n, 824 F. Supp. 500 (D. Del. 1993), aff'd, 30 F.3d 1488 (3d Cir. 1994).*

Tender offers are fairly common in back-end mergers, but a successful tender offer merely results in the purchase of the stock, not the assets, of a corporation. *Texaco Ref. & Mktg., Inc. v. Delaware River Basin Comm'n, 824 F. Supp. 500 (D. Del. 1993), aff'd, 30 F.3d 1488 (3d Cir. 1994).*

Notice of stockholders' meeting. — The Delaware General Assembly intended that the 20-day period of giving notice before stockholders' meeting should in all cases be sufficient, but that a board of directors in the exercise of its informed judgment might fix a period of more than 20 days when the circumstances required it. *MacCrone v. American Capital Corp., 51 F. Supp. 462 (D. Del. 1943).*

The 20 days' notice required in this section shall be given by mail for a period not less than 20 full days before the date of the stockholders' meeting. *MacCrone v. American Capital Corp., 51 F. Supp. 462 (D. Del. 1943).*

A bylaw provision permitting less than 20 days' notice for stockholders' meetings so far as it was applicable to this section, was invalid and of no effect, and the action taken by the directors in fixing the record date of meeting thereunder must be disregarded. *MacCrone v. American Capital Corp., 51 F. Supp. 462 (D. Del. 1943).*

Approval functions responsibility of board. — Where the question of the independence of the members of a special committee that recommended a merger turned upon the reality of the interests and incentives affecting the independent directors, the full board of directors had to act to approve a merger agreement and recommend the merger to the stockholders for approval; a committee could not be empowered to perform that necessary board function, under subsection (b) of this section and *8 Del. C. § 141(c). Krasner v. Moffett, 826 A.2d 277 (Del. 2003).*

Duty of disclosure. — This section and § 252 of this title do not explicitly require a company to inform stockholders of all material facts; the duty of disclosure is a judicially imposed fiduciary duty which applies as a corollary to the statutory requirements. *Arnold v. Society for Savs. Bancorp., 678 A.2d 533 (Del. 1996).*

Public policy does not permit dissenting shareholder to veto fair merger. — There may be shareholders who will be dissatisfied with the effect of the terms of the merger proposal upon the rights attached to their shares. While their right to dissent is admitted, the public policy of the State declared by this section, somewhat analogous to the right of eminent domain, does not permit a dissenting shareholder, as against an affirmative vote, to veto a merger agreement if its terms are fair and equitable in the circumstances of the case. Within the time and in the manner provided by § 262 of this title, the dissatisfied stockholder, if he or she so desires, may demand and receive the money value of his or her shares as that value has been agreed upon or has been determined by an impartial appraisement. *Federal United Corp. v. Havender, 24 Del. Ch. 318, 11 A.2d 331 (1940).*

Burden of establishing fairness of merger plan. — A corporate majority stockholder and the directors of the subsidiary as nominees of the majority stockholder occupy, in relation to the minority, a fiduciary position in dealing with the subsidiary's property and bear the burden of establishing the fairness of a merger plan, and it must pass the test of careful scrutiny by the courts. *Sterling v. Mayflower Hotel Corp., 33 Del. Ch. 293, 93 A.2d 107 (1952); Singer v. Magnavox Co., 380 A.2d 969 (Del. 1977), overruled on other grounds by Weinberger v. UOP, Inc., 457 A.2d 701 (Del. 1983); Young v. Valhi, Inc., 382 A.2d 1372 (Del. Ch. 1978).*

In a minority shareholders' suit alleging breach of fiduciary duty, when defendants stand on both sides of the transaction through control of the corporate machinery, the burden of proof of fairness shifts to defendants, who must also establish there to be a business purpose for the merger other than a freeze-out of the minority. *Harman v. Masoneilan Int'l, 442 A.2d 487 (Del. 1982).*

Fiduciary duty is owed by majority stockholders to minority stockholders of the corporation when dealing with the latter's property. *Roland Int'l Corp. v. Najjar, 407 A.2d 1032 (Del. 1979), overruled on other grounds, 457 A.2d 701 (Del. 1983).*

And duty may not be circumvented by full compliance with procedures required by corporation statutes, nor is it discharged by remitting minority shareholders to a statutory appraisal remedy (often based upon the status of the market and the elements of an appraisal), the timing of which is entirely within the control of the majority. *Roland Int'l Corp. v. Najjar, 407 A.2d 1032 (Del. 1979), overruled on other grounds, 457 A.2d 701 (Del. 1983).*

Lock-ups (options to purchase assets of corporation) and related agreements are permitted under Delaware law where their adoption is untainted by director interest or other breaches of fiduciary duty. *Revlon, Inc. v. MacAndrews & Forbes Holdings, Inc., 506 A.2d 173 (Del. 1985).*

Failure to include fiduciary out clause. — Target's board was required to contract for an effective "fiduciary out" clause to exercise its continuing fiduciary responsibilities to the minority stockholders; although the issues in the appeal did not involve the general validity of either stockholder voting agreements or the authority of directors to insert a subsection (c) provision under this section in a merger agreement, in the instant case, the target's board combined those two otherwise valid actions and caused them to operate in concert as an absolute merger lock up, in the absence of an effective "fiduciary out" clause in the merger agreement. *Omnicare, Inc. v. NCS Healthcare, Inc., 818 A.2d 914 (Del. 2003).*

Conversion of stock is not sale, exchange or transfer. — The statutory conversion of stock in a constituent corporation into stock in the surviving corporation that is effected by a stock for stock merger ought not be construed to constitute a sale, transfer or exchange of that stock for purposes of an agreement among shareholders restricting their power to transfer their stock; merger is a corporate act, which effects by operation of law a transmutation of the stock interest in a constituent corporation. *Shields v. Shields, 498 A.2d 161 (Del. Ch. 1985).*

Fiduciary duties continue. — Any board has authority to give the proponent of a recommended merger agreement reasonable structural and economic defenses, incentives, and fair compensation if the transaction is not completed; to the extent that defensive measures are economic and reasonable, they may become an increased cost to the proponent of any subsequent transaction; just as defensive measures cannot be draconian, however, they cannot limit or circumscribe the directors' fiduciary duties;

notwithstanding a corporation's insolvent condition, the corporation's board has no authority to execute a merger agreement that subsequently prevents it from effectively discharging its ongoing fiduciary responsibilities. *Omnicare, Inc. v. NCS Healthcare, Inc., 818 A.2d 914 (Del. 2003).*

Fiduciary duty applies in context of merger. — Mergers which present a classic "going private" transaction, with the majority having complete control over the timing of the "squeeze play" on the public stockholders — a timing conceivably selected to favor the majority only, based upon the status of the market and the elements of an appraisal — call for the strictest observance of the law of fiduciary duty. *Roland Int'l Corp. v. Najjar, 407 A.2d 1032 (Del. 1979), overruled on other grounds, 457 A.2d 701 (Del. 1983).*

The fiduciary obligation owed by the majority stockholders to the minority stockholders in the context of a merger, be it long or short, is singular, and falls alike on those who control at least 90 percent of the outstanding shares, and those who control a majority but less than 90 percent. *Roland Int'l Corp. v. Najjar, 407 A.2d 1032 (Del. 1979), overruled on other grounds, 457 A.2d 701 (Del. 1983).*

A director may not abdicate his or her fiduciary duty to act in an informed and deliberate manner in determining whether to approve an agreement of merger before submitting the proposal to the stockholders by leaving to the stockholders alone the decision to approve or disapprove the agreement. *Smith v. Van Gorkom, 488 A.2d 858 (Del. 1985); Sealy Mattress Co. v. Sealy, Inc., 532 A.2d 1324 (Del. Ch. 1987).*

Where a cohesive group of stockholders with majority voting power is irrevocably committed to the merger transaction, effective representation of the financial interests of the minority shareholders imposes upon the board an affirmative responsibility to protect those minority shareholders' interests; the board cannot abdicate its fiduciary duties to the minority by leaving it to the stockholders alone to approve or disapprove the merger agreement where stockholders already combine to establish a majority of the voting power that makes the outcome of the stockholder vote a foregone conclusion. *Omnicare, Inc. v. NCS Healthcare, Inc., 818 A.2d 914 (Del. 2003).*

A director may not abdicate the duty imposed by subsection (b) regarding the agreement of merger. *Paramount Communications, Inc. v. Time Inc., 571 A.2d 1140 (Del. 1989).*

Business judgment rule applies to subsection (b). — A board's response to an offer to merge is traditionally tested by the business judgment rule since a statutory merger transaction prerequisite in subsection (b) is approval by the board of directors. *Unitrin, Inc. v. American Gen. Corp., 651 A.2d 1361 (Del. 1995).*

Application of business judgment standard to fiduciaries of zone of insolvency merger target corporation. — Chancery court denied minority shareholders of zone-of-insolvency target corporation a preliminary injunction to stop merger of target into acquirer (in favor of a subsequent merger offer potentially more favorable to shareholders); fiduciaries satisfied business judgment standard considering interests of shareholders and creditors of target. *In re NCS Healthcare, Inc., 825 A.2d 240 (Del. Ch. 2002).*

Exercise of statutory right of merger is always subject to nullification for fraud. *Cole v. National Cash Credit Ass'n, 18 Del. Ch. 47, 156 A. 183 (1931).*

Mere fact that those who initiate merger will receive some benefit does not make it fraudulent. *MacCrone v. American Capital Corp., 51 F. Supp. 462 (D. Del. 1943); Singer v. Magnavox Co., 367 A.2d 1349 (Del. Ch. 1976), aff'd in part and rev'd in part, 380 A.2d 969 (Del. 1977).*

Mere inadequacy of price will not reveal fraud inducing a consolidation. The inadequacy must be so gross as to lead the court to conclude that it was due not to an honest error of judgment but rather to bad faith, or to a reckless indifference to the right of others interested. *Cole v. National Cash Credit Ass'n, 18 Del. Ch. 47, 156 A. 183 (1931); Muschel v. Western Union Corp., 310 A.2d 904 (Del. Ch. 1973).*

Gross undervaluation of shares of minority stockholders may be constructively fraudulent. — In a merger under this section and § 252 of this title, gross undervaluation of the shares of minority stockholders may be shocking to the court's conscience and, therefore, constructively fraudulent. *Stauffer v. Standard Brands, Inc., 40 Del. Ch. 202, 178 A.2d 311, aff'd, 187 A.2d 78 (Del. 1962), overruled on other grounds by Roland Int'l Corp. v. Najjar, 407 A.2d 1032 (Del. 1979).*

Premium alone not adequate basis for assessing fairness in merger. — A substantial premium alone does not provide an adequate basis upon which to assess the fairness of an offering price for a merger. *Smith v. Van Gorkom, 488 A.2d 858 (Del. 1985).*

Fraud not indicated by honest error of judgment. — Where fraud in a merger is charged, the unfairness must be of such character and must be so clearly demonstrated as to impel the conclusion that it emanates from acts of bad faith, or a reckless indifference to the rights of others interested, rather than from an honest error of judgment. *MacCrone v. American Capital Corp., 51 F. Supp. 462 (D. Del. 1943).*

Fraudulent valuation must show conscious abuse of discretion. — In order to enjoin a proposed merger on the theory of constructive fraud based on a claimed discriminatory undervaluation or overvaluation of corporate assets, it must be plainly demonstrated that the overvaluation or undervaluation, as the case may be, is such as to show a conscious abuse of discretion before fraud at law can be made out. *Muschel v. Western Union Corp., 310 A.2d 904 (Del. Ch. 1973).*

Wide discretion in matter of valuation is confided to directors, and as long as they appear to act in good faith, with honest motives, and for honest ends, the exercise of their discretion will not be interfered with. *Muschel v. Western Union Corp., 310 A.2d 904 (Del. Ch. 1973).*

Board of directors enjoys presumption of sound business judgment, and its decisions will not be disturbed if they can be attributed to any rational business purpose. *Muschel v. Western Union Corp., 310 A.2d 904 (Del. Ch. 1973).*

Where evidence did not establish that the board of directors of the acquiring corporation failed to make an informed judgment when the merger plan was presented, they were entitled to the presumption of having made an informed judgment in good faith which could be attributed to a rational business purpose. *Muschel v. Western Union Corp., 310 A.2d 904 (Del. Ch. 1973).*

Good faith analysis. — Pursuant to the judicial scrutiny required under Unocal's two-stage analysis (*Unocal Corp. v. Mesa Petro. Co., Del. Supr., 493 A.2d 946 (1985)*), directors must: first demonstrate that they have reasonable grounds for believing that a danger to corporate policy and effectiveness exists; the second stage of the Unocal test requires the directors to demonstrate that their defensive response was reasonable in relation to the threat posed. *Omnicare, Inc. v. NCS Healthcare, Inc., 818 A.2d 914 (Del. 2003).*

Enhanced judicial review under revlon. — Board's decision to enter into a merger transaction that does not involve a change in control is entitled to judicial deference pursuant to the procedural and substantive operation of the business judgment rule; when a board decides to enter into a merger transaction that will result in a change of control, however, enhanced judicial scrutiny under *Revlon, Inc. v. MacAndrews & Forbes Holdings, Inc., Del. Supr., 506 A.2d 173 (1985)* is the standard of review. *Omnicare, Inc. v. NCS Healthcare, Inc., 818 A.2d 914 (Del. 2003).*

Defensive devices. — When the focus of judicial scrutiny shifts to the range of reasonableness, *Unocal Corp. v. Mesa Petro. Co., Del. Supr., 493 A.2d 946 (1985)* requires that any defensive devices must be proportionate to the perceived threat to the corporation and its stockholders if the merger transaction is not consummated. *Omnicare, Inc. v. NCS Healthcare, Inc., 818 A.2d 914 (Del. 2003).*

Latitude a board will have in either maintaining or using the defensive devices it has adopted to protect the merger it has approved will vary according to the degree of benefit or detriment to the stockholders' interests that is presented by the value or terms of the subsequent competing transaction. *Omnicare, Inc. v. NCS Healthcare, Inc., 818 A.2d 914 (Del. 2003).*

Disclosure of reasons for recommending merger not required. — While a board may formulate a statement of reasons for recommending a merger under subsection (b), it does not have an obligation to do so, nor must it disclose the grounds of the board members' judgments for or against a proposed shareholder action. The law requires only a full and candid disclosure of the material facts. *Newman v. Warren, 684 A.2d 1239 (Del. Ch. 1996).*

Burden of proof upon objecting stockholders. — In considering the alleged unfairness of the terms of a merger, the burden of proof is upon the objecting stockholders. *Hottenstein v. York Ice Mach. Corp., 45 F.*

Supp. 436 (D. Del. 1942), aff'd, *136 F.2d 944 (3d Cir. 1943),* cert. denied, *325 U.S. 886, 65 S. Ct. 1573, 89 L. Ed. 2000 (1945).*

Where the required statutory majorities have the right to merge 2 or more corporations, there is a presumption of bona fides of purpose with a resultant burden on dissidents to demonstrate that the terms of the merger are so unfair as to amount to constructive fraud. *MacCrone v. American Capital Corp., 51 F. Supp. 462 (D. Del. 1943).*

Court will not substitute its own notions of what is or is not sound business judgment. *Muschel v. Western Union Corp., 310 A.2d 904 (Del. Ch. 1973).*

Rights of minority shareholders compared. — The rights of minority shareholders under a merger governed by this section are no greater than those under a merger governed by § 253 of this title. *Singer v. Magnavox Co., 367 A.2d 1349 (Del. Ch. 1976),* aff'd in part and rev'd in part, *380 A.2d 969 (Del. 1977).*

Although there are procedural differences between this section and a merger under § 253 of this title, the fiduciary duties owed by a majority shareholder to the minority are the same. *Najjar v. Roland Int'l Corp., 387 A.2d 709 (Del. Ch. 1978),* aff'd, *407 A.2d 1032 (Del. 1979).*

Elimination of minority shareholders. — A merger, under this section, made for the sole purpose of freezing out minority stockholders, is an abuse of the corporate process; and a complaint, which so alleges, states a cause of action for violation of a fiduciary duty for which the court may grant such relief as it deems appropriate under the circumstances. *Singer v. Magnavox Co., 380 A.2d 969 (Del. 1977),* overruled on other grounds by *Weinberger v. UOP, Inc., 457 A.2d 701 (Del. 1983).*

The use of technically correct but devious corporate action on the part of a parent corporation, for the purpose of accomplishing a merger designed to eliminate minority stockholders of the subsidiary, is a manipulation of corporate machinery contrary to the strict standards of fiduciary behavior required of majority stockholders by the *Supreme Court of Delaware. Young v. Valhi, Inc., 382 A.2d 1372 (Del. Ch. 1978).*

Fiduciary duty violated when minority shareholders are "cashed out." — The fiduciary duty is violated when those who control a corporation's voting machinery use that power to "cash out" minority shareholders, that is, to exclude them from continued participation in the corporate life, for no reason other than to eliminate them. *Roland Int'l Corp. v. Najjar, 407 A.2d 1032 (Del. 1979),* overruled on other grounds, *457 A.2d 701 (Del. 1983).*

Chancery jurisdiction. — "Fairness" suits for alleged fraud and breach of fiduciary duty brought by minority shareholders fall within the Court of Chancery's exclusive, and not its concurrent, jurisdiction. *Harman v. Masoneilan Int'l, 442 A.2d 487 (Del. 1982).*

Merger not enjoined unless clearly injurious or unfair. — The court should not, by its injunctive process, prevent a merger unless it is clear that it would be so injurious and unfair to some minority complaining stockholders as to be shocking, and the court is convinced that it is so grossly unfair to such stockholders as to be

fraudulent. *MacFarlane v. North Am. Cement Corp., 16 Del. Ch. 172, 157 A. 396 (1928).*

Any dealings with the rights of stockholders of any class in merger proceedings will be enjoined upon the application of any properly interested party, if the same is ultra vires fraudulent, or otherwise inequitable. *Havender v. Federal United Corp., 24 Del. Ch. 96, 6 A.2d 618 (1939),* rev'd on other grounds, *24 Del. Ch. 318, 11 A.2d 331 (1940).*

If the plan adopted in a corporate merger is not fair and equitable to the interested stockholders, it will always be enjoined by a court of equity. *Havender v. Federal United Corp., 24 Del. Ch. 96, 6 A.2d 618 (1939),* rev'd on other grounds, *24 Del. Ch. 318, 11 A.2d 331 (1940).*

A court of equity will not permit the merger to affect injuriously the rights of objecting stockholders. *Havender v. Federal United Corp., 24 Del. Ch. 96, 6 A.2d 618 (1939),* rev'd on other grounds, *24 Del. Ch. 318, 11 A.2d 331 (1940).*

In actions to enjoin the operation of a plan of merger, under the law of Delaware, the court may afford relief only if it finds that the plan is so unfair as to shock the conscience of the court and to amount to fraud. *Hottenstein v. York Ice Mach. Corp., 45 F. Supp. 436 (D. Del. 1942),* aff'd, *136 F.2d 944 (3d Cir. 1943),* cert. denied, *325 U.S. 886, 65 S. Ct. 1573, 89 L. Ed. 2000 (1945).*

Absent fraud or a showing that the terms of a proposed merger are so unfair as to shock the conscience of the court, the courts of Delaware permit contracting corporations to take advantage of statutory devices for corporate consolidation furnished by legislative act. *Bruce v. E.L. Bruce Co., 40 Del. Ch. 80, 174 A.2d 29 (1961); Singer v. Magnavox Co., 367 A.2d 1349 (Del. Ch. 1976),* aff'd in part and rev'd in part, *380 A.2d 969 (Del. 1977).*

While a court of equity should stand ready to prevent corporate fraud and any overreaching by fiduciaries of the rights of stockholders, the court should not impede the consummation of an orderly merger under the Delaware statutes, an efficient and fair method having been furnished which permits a judicially protected withdrawal from a merger by a disgruntled stockholder. *David J. Greene & Co. v. Schenley Indus., Inc., 281 A.2d 30 (Del. Ch. 1971).*

Remedy to vindicate mandate of subsection (b) and policy of full disclosure. — Preliminary injunction against proposed parent-subsidiary is a proper remedy to vindicate mandate of subsection (b) and the policies underlying the fiduciary obligation of full disclosure by the board of directors where such board has made no informed decision regarding a proposed merger, the board is uniquely situated to make determinations regarding a company's values, and the board has not disclosed material facts to the minority stockholders. *Sealy Mattress Co. v. Sealy, Inc., 532 A.2d 1324 (Del. Ch. 1987).*

Delay may lead to denial of injunctive relief. — In cases involving the sale of corporate assets or their merger with those of another corporation, slight delay may lead to the denying of a motion for injunctive relief where such an order would involve a complex undoing of an accomplished

Corporations

corporate act. *Elster v. American Airlines, 36 Del. Ch. 213, 128 A.2d 801 (1957).*

Shareholders' application for preliminary injunction denied. — Where shareholders had not established probability of ultimate success, their application for a preliminary injunction to prevent the filing of the documents necessary to consummate merger was denied. *Muschel v. Western Union Corp., 310 A.2d 904 (Del. Ch. 1973).*

Injunction of merger through preferred shareholder class action denied. — See *Jedwab v. MGM Grand Hotels, Inc., 509 A.2d 584 (Del. Ch. 1986).*

Laches. — An objecting stockholder need not, in every case, move to enjoin a proposed corporate action in order to escape the imputation of laches; but it is to be said that prompt action means unambiguous and decisive action; and it is, at the least, incumbent on such stockholder to give notice in plain and unequivocal terms that the intended invasion of rights will be contested. *Federal United Corp. v. Havender, 24 Del. Ch. 318, 11 A.2d 331 (1940).*

Sitting by inactive and in what amounts to silence, when every consideration for the rights of others demanded prompt and vigorous action, and until affairs had become so complicated that a restoration of former status was difficult, if not impossible, is conduct amounting to laches. *Federal United Corp. v. Havender, 24 Del. Ch. 318, 11 A.2d 331 (1940).*

Estoppel. — When an informed minority shareholder either votes in favor of the merger, or accepts the benefits of the transaction, he or she cannot thereafter attack its fairness. *Bershad v. Curtiss-Wright Corp., 535 A.2d 840 (Del. 1987).*

Coercion standard. — Standard for determining stockholder coercion is that a stockholder vote may be nullified by wrongful coercion where the board or some other party takes actions which have the effect of causing the stockholders to vote in favor of the proposed transaction for some reason other than the merits of that transaction. *Omnicare, Inc. v. NCS Healthcare, Inc., 818 A.2d 914 (Del. 2003).*

Coercion not found. — Delaware law does not impose a duty of entire fairness on controlling stockholders making a non-coercive tender or exchange offer to acquire shares directly from the minority holders and in place of an entire fairness standard, a court examines both the structure of the transaction to insure that it is voluntary in nature and information disclosed to insure its adequacy and completeness; and where the court finds an offer to be both structurally non-coercive and fully disclosed, the court has left the decision whether to tender or not up to the stockholders. *Next Level Communs., Inc. v. Motorola, Inc., 834 A.2d 828 (Del. Ch. 2003), review denied, 817 A.2d 804 (Del. 2003).*

Applicability of higher bid injunction analysis. — When another higher bid has been made, an injunction against the target board's chosen deal has the effect of ensuring a fair auction in which the highest bidder will prevail, at comparatively little risk to target stockholders. Indeed, in most circumstances, this means that the chances for a later damages proceeding are greatly minimized given the competition between rival bidders. *In re Netsmart Techs., Inc. S'holders Litig, 924 A.2d 171; 2007 Del. Ch. LEXIS 35 (March 14, 2007).*

When the chancery court is asked to enjoin a transaction and another higher-priced alternative is not immediately available, it has been appropriately modest about playing games with other people's money. But even in that context, the court has not hesitated to use its injunctive powers to address disclosure deficiencies. When stockholders are about to make a decision based on materially misleading or incomplete information, a decision not to issue an injunction maximizes the potential that the crudest of judicial tools (an appraisal or damages award) will be employed down the line, because the stockholders' chance to engage in self-help on the front end would have been vitiated and lost forever. In re Netsmart Techs., Inc. S'holders Litig, 924 A.2d 171; 2007 Del. Ch. LEXIS 35 (March 14, 2007).

Waiver not required. — There is nothing under Delaware law that requires the offeror in a tender offer to waive enforceable rights that it has as a holder of preferred stock of the target corporation or as a lender to the target corporation (or to provide some blanket assurance that it will do so); nor does the fact that the offeror has chosen to commence a tender offer without the consent of the target's board of directors give rise to such an obligation. *Next Level Communs., Inc. v. Motorola, Inc., 834 A.2d 828 (Del. Ch. 2003), review denied, 817 A.2d 804 (Del. 2003).*

Remedy for objection as to share value is appraisal. — When an inadequate cash price per share is the basis for objection to a corporate merger, the remedy of the dissatisfied shareholders is to seek an appraisal of the value of their shares pursuant to the procedures set forth under the appraisal statute, § 262 of this title. *Singer v. Magnavox Co., 367 A.2d 1349 (Del. Ch. 1976), aff'd in part and rev'd in part, 380 A.2d 969 (Del. 1977).*

Consideration must be given to all relevant factors entering into the determination of value. However, this does not mean that any one factor is in every case important or that it must be given a definite weight in the evaluation; the relative importance of several tests of value depends on the circumstances. *Sterling v. Mayflower Hotel Corp., 33 Del. Ch. 293, 93 A.2d 107 (1952).*

Liquidating value of stock is not sole test. — In ascertaining the value of stock in appraisal proceedings under the merger statute, the liquidating value of the stock is not the sole test of value; all relevant factors must be considered. *Sterling v. Mayflower Hotel Corp., 33 Del. Ch. 293, 93 A.2d 107 (1952).*

Market price is most significant element in judging fairness of merger. — Market price, when it can be established by free trading in an open forum, is the most significant element to be taken into consideration in reaching a judgment on the overall fairness of a corporate merger. *David J. Greene & Co. v. Schenley Indus., Inc., 281 A.2d 30 (Del. Ch. 1971).*

Net asset value is 1 factor to be considered in determining the fairness of a plan of merger. *Sterling v. Mayflower Hotel Corp., 33 Del. Ch. 293, 93 A.2d 107 (1952).*

Fair value for fractional shares. — Corporation was statutorily allowed to issue fractional shares to some stockholders but not to others in the same transaction (based upon the size of each stockholder's holdings) as stockholders did not always have to be treated equally, just fairly; the law dealing with the appraisal remedy allows that a price based on New York Stock Exchange closing prices over a 10-day period may amount to "fair value." *Applebaum v. Avaya, Inc., 805 A.2d 209 (Del. Ch. 2002).*

This section recognized possibility of conversion of shares into "shares or other securities." The reference is therefore clearly broader than to stock only. Under this section shares could have been converted into redeemable bonds. *Coyne v. Park & Tilford Distillers Corp., 37 Del. Ch. 558, 146 A.2d 785 (1958),* aff'd, *38 Del. Ch. 514, 154 A.2d 893 (1959).*

Accumulations of dividends on the preference stock of a corporation were lawfully compounded, where the preferred shareholders were put to their election, either to demand payment in money of the value of their preferred shares as agreed upon, or as ascertained by an appraisement, or to accept the exchange of securities offered by the merger plan. *Federal United Corp. v. Havender, 24 Del. Ch. 318, 11 A.2d 331 (1940).*

In Delaware a parent corporation may merge with a wholly owned subsidiary and thereby cancel old preferred stock and the rights of the holders thereof to the unpaid, accumulated dividends, by substituting in lieu thereof stocks of the surviving corporation. *Langfelder v. Universal Lab., Inc., 68 F. Supp. 209 (D. Del. 1946),* aff'd, *163 F.2d 804 (3d Cir. 1947).*

Determination of recoverable losses. — The court committed error in apparently capping recoverable loss under an entire fairness standard of review at the fair value of a share of stock on the date of approval of the merger; under the entire fairness standard of review, a party may have a legally cognizable injury regardless of whether the tender offer and cash-out price is greater than the stock's fair value as determined for statutory appraisal purposes. *Cede & Co. v. Technicolor, Inc., 634 A.2d 345 (Del. 1993).*

Stockholders face a threat of irreparable injury if an injunction does not issue until such time as the board discloses additional information, to wit, the full November 18, 2006 revenue and earnings projections including the years 2010 and 2011. Absent such disclosure, the company's shareholders will vote without important information regarding their management's and best estimates regarding the future cash flow of the company. In a cash-out transaction, this information is highly material, as the stockholders are being asked to give up the possibility of future gains from the on-going operation of the company in exchange for an immediate cash payment. That is especially so when management is staying in the game, leaving the public stockholders behind with their exit payment as compensation for forsaking any share of future gains. *In re Netsmart Techs., Inc. S'holders Litig, 924 A.2d 171; 2007 Del. Ch. LEXIS 35 (March 14, 2007).*

Specific performance denied. — Because it has failed to meet its burden of demonstrating that the common understanding of the parties permitted specific performance of the merger agreement, plaintiff's petition for specific performance is denied. *United Rentals, Inc. v. Ram Holdings, Inc., 937 A.2d 810, 2007 Del. Ch. LEXIS 181 (December 21, 2007). **[For the full text of this case opinion, please see the Appendix at the end of this Volume.]***

DELAWARE CASE NOTES — UNREPORTED

Special committees. — The composition of the special committee is of central importance. Members of a special committee negotiating a parent-subsidiary merger must, of course, be independent and willing to perform their job. This independence is the *sina qua non* of the entire negotiation process. The court necessarily places more trust in a multiple-member committee than in a committee where a single member works free of the oversight provided by at least one colleague. But, in those rare circumstances when a special committee is comprised of only one director, Delaware courts have required the sole member, like Caesar's wife, to be above reproach. *Gesoff v. IIC Indus., 2006 Del. Ch. LEXIS 91 (Del. May 18, 2006).*

In addition to being independent and, preferably, having more than one member, a well constituted special committee should be given a clear mandate setting out its powers and responsibilities in negotiating the interested transaction. Evidently, this mandate should include the power to fully evaluate the transaction at issue, and, ideally, include what the chancery court has called the "critical power" to say "no" to the transaction. The

controller's commitment to leave the essential fate of the transaction in the hands of the special committee is a significant one, because it ensures that the merger offer is not negotiated in the shadow of punitive action by the controller if the minority resists the merger. Delaware courts have also noted that, when questioned, members of a special committee should be able to articulate the extent of their authority. The source of that requirement, simply enough, is the common sense principle that no mandate, however clear, is sufficient if the special committee does not understand its considerable powers. *Gesoff v. IIC Indus., 2006 Del. Ch. LEXIS 91 (Del. May 18, 2006).*

The discussions between the parent and the special committee should be conducted in a way that is consistent with arm's-length negotiations. These negotiations need not, of course, be a "death struggle." But they should be vigorous and spirited, and provide evidence that the special committee and the parent are not colluding to injure the minority stockholders. At a minimum, the special committee should have control over its own sources of information and should have the loyalty of its advisors

Corporations

throughout the process. *Gesoff v. IIC Indus., 2006 Del. Ch. LEXIS 91 (Del. May 18, 2006).*

The goal of the process established by the board of the subsidiary must be to come as close as possible to simulating arm's-length bargaining with the parent. For obvious reasons, a transaction that is by its terms dependent on the special committee process will struggle to evidence fair dealing if that process withers under scrutiny. *Gesoff v. IIC Indus., 2006 Del. Ch. LEXIS 91 (Del. May 18, 2006).*

Equitable challenge. — Stockholders who do not vote for a transaction and who simply accept the transactional consideration rather than seek appraisal are not barred from making or participating in an equitable challenge to the transaction. Notably, that conclusion did not rest simply on an examination of this court's case law, but more importantly a consideration of the issue in the light of our Supreme Court's jurisprudence, which among other things had made it clear that appraisal was simply one means by which to challenge a long-form merger, with the bringing of an equitable action being another, even more common means. In re PNB Holding Co. S'holders Litig., 2006 Del. Ch. LEXIS 158 (Aug. 18, 2006).

Standstill agreement. — What competing bidder is asking for is release from the prior restraint on it, a prior restraint that prevents defendants' stockholders from choosing another higher-priced deal. Given that the board has decided to sell the company, and is not using the standstill agreement for any apparent legitimate purpose, its refusal to release competing bidder justifies an injunction. Otherwise, the defendant's stockholders may be foreclosed from ever considering competing offer, a result that, under precedent, threatens irreparable injury. *Upper Deck. Co. v. Topps Co. (In re Topps Co. S'holders Litig.), 2007 Del. Ch. LEXIS 82 (June 14, 2007).*

CEO's material economic motivations. — Because the CEO might rationally have expected a going private transaction to provide him with a unique means to achieve his personal objectives, and because the merger in fact secured for the CEO the joint benefits of immediate liquidity and continued employment that he sought just before negotiating that merger, the stockholders are entitled to know that the CEO harbored material economic motivations that differed from their own that could have influenced his negotiating posture. Given that the special committee delegated to the CEO the sole authority to conduct the merger negotiations, this concern is magnified. As such, an injunction will issue preventing the vote on the merger vote until such time as the shareholders are apprised of the CEO's overtures to the board concerning his retirement benefits. In re Lear Corp. S'holder Litig., 2007 Del. Ch. LEXIS 88 (June 15, 2007).

Equitable challenge. — Stockholders who do not vote for a transaction and who simply accept the transactional consideration rather than seek appraisal are not barred from making or participating in an equitable challenge to the transaction. Notably, that conclusion did not rest simply on an examination of this court's case law, but more importantly a consideration of the issue in the light of our Supreme Court's jurisprudence, which among other

things had made it clear that appraisal was simply one means by which to challenge a long-form merger, with the bringing of an equitable action being another, even more common means. *In re PNB Holding Co. S'holders Litig., 2006 Del. Ch. LEXIS 158 (Aug. 18, 2006).*

Contents of the merger agreement. — Plaintiff had no right to argue that the merger was invalid under subsection (b) on the grounds that the merger agreement itself did not specify how the series A preferred stock was to be treated, because plaintiff knew about the term sheet and demanded that it be kept confidential; therefore, plaintiff could not have been injured in any manner by the failure of the merger agreement itself to describe the term sheet. *RGC Int'l Investors, LDC v. Greka Energy Corp., 2000 Del. Ch. LEXIS 157 (Nov. 6, 2000).*

Certificates of merger. — Continuing director provision in an indenture agreement, adopting resolutions approving the nomination and election of the post-merger directors as set forth in the certificate of merger, was not violated by the boards of 2 corporations, (including the corporation which issued the notes); nor did the filing of a certificate of merger that simply identified the post-merger directors as the surviving corporation's board, after the stockholders of both corporations approved the merger agreement, violate that provision. *Law Debenture Trust Co. v. Petrohawk Energy Corp., 2007 Del. Ch. LEXIS 113 (Del. Ch. Aug. 1, 2007).*

Merging parties were permitted to use a certificate of merger to seat a board of directors, so long as that board was consistent with the expectations of the voting stockholders; even if this method of seating the post-merger directors was different than the proxy statement suggested would be used, the method was agreed upon by the boards of both corporations. *Law Debenture Trust Co. v. Petrohawk Energy Corp.,2 007 Del. Ch. LEXIS 113 (Del. Ch. Aug. 1, 2007).*

Failure to hold shareholder meeting. — Because only a unanimous board could act by written consent under 8 Del. C. § 141(f), and because the company the shareholder owned shares in never met to consider the merger, the merger was never validly approved by the company in accordance with Del. Code Ann. subsection (b) of this section. *Tansey v. Trade Show News Networks, Inc., 2001 Del. Ch. LEXIS 142 (Nov. 27, 2001).*

Sale of shares during pendency of suit opposing merger share price. — Where the court approved a settlement increasing target corporation's cash price per public share from $ 5.45 to $ 6.60 in merger with acquiring corporation, the court held (citing this section and § 253 of this title) that objecting shareholders who sold their shares during the pendency of the litigation could not share in the increased price. *In re Prodigy Communications Corp., 2002 Del. Ch. LEXIS 95 (July 26, 2002).*

Revlon trigger. — In the context of defensive devices implemented to protect a merger agreement, the adoption of structural safety devices alone does not trigger *Revlon, Inc. v. MacAndrews & Forbes Holdings, Inc., Del. Supr., 506 A.2d 173 (1985);* rather, such devices are properly subject to a *Unocal Corp. v. Mesa Petro. Co., Del. Supr.,*

493 A.2d 946 (1985) analysis. *Omnicare, Inc. v. Health-care, Inc., 2003 Del. LEXIS 196 (Apr. 4, 2003).*

Muddled, dishonest, process. — The process established by the defendants unilaterally imposed on the minority a price of the parent's own choosing, established a deceptive negotiation between the parties, and left the minority's putative special committee almost entirely powerless against its parent. This muddled, dishonest, process is emphatically not what the Supreme Court meant by fair dealing in *Weinberger*, and will not be tolerated here. *Gesoff v. IIC Indus., 2006 Del. Ch. LEXIS 91 (Del. May 18, 2006).*

Preliminary injunction against the procession of the merger vote should issue until such time as: (1) the defendant board discloses several material facts not contained in the corporation's "proxy statement," including facts regarding assurances from current purchaser that he would retain existing management after the merger; and (2) competing purchaser is released from the standstill for purposes of: (a) publicly commenting on its negotiations with defendant; and (b) making a non-coercive tender offer on conditions as favorable or more favorable than those it has offered to the defendant's board. *Upper Deck. Co. v. Topps Co. (In re Topps Co. S'holders Litig.), 2007 Del. Ch. LEXIS 82 (June 14, 2007).*

Corporations

CASE NOTES — OTHER STATES

Georgia

Delaware appraisal action only appropriate remedy. — When plaintiffs did not appeal the trial court's denial of injunctive relief before the merger and then failed to assert on this appeal that such denial was error, they waived any argument they may have had concerning that decision. Moreover, to the extent that the plaintiffs viewed defendant corporation's value in the rosy light of a recovery for the same wrongs alleged in their complaint, and were therefore aggrieved by the price they were offered for their shares, they were required to pursue their remedy in the form of a Delaware appraisal action. When the plaintiffs chose not to pursue this remedy, the trial court was within its rights to deny them relief by granting defendant's motion to dismiss. *Paul & Suzie Schutt Irrevocable Family Trust v. NAC Holding, 283 Ga. App. 834; 642 S.E.2d 872; 2007 Ga. App. LEXIS 209 (March 1, 2007).*

Illinois

Termination fees not coercive. — The fact that shareholders knew that voting to disapprove the merger would result in activating a portion of the termination fees does not constitute coercion in this case. The termination fees were clearly disclosed to shareholders and the reciprocal termination fees, drafted to protect both companies in the event that the merger was not consummated, appear to have been an integral part of the transaction. Further, nothing in the present record suggests that the termination fee provisions had the effect of causing shareholders to vote in favor of the proposed merger based on anything other than the merits. Accordingly, the court finds that the termination fee provisions were not impermissibly coercive and that the argument that Omnicare applies was misplaced. *Shaper v. Bryan, 371 Ill. App. 3d 1079; 864 N.E.2d 876; 2007 Ill. App. LEXIS 195; 309 Ill. Dec. 635 (March 8, 2007).*

Indiana

Effective date. — Under Delaware law, a corporate merger with a foreign corporation becomes effective when adopted, approved, certified, executed, and acknowledged by each of the constituent corporations in accordance with the laws under which it is formed, and is evidenced by an agreement of merger or a certificate of merger filed with the secretary of state. The statute provides the method for a merger. Corporate instruments are effective upon the filing date. *Keybank National Association v. Mochael, 737 N.E.2d 834 (Ind. 2000).*

Massachusetts

Eighty percent approval requirement permissible. — It would be permissible for the certificate of incorporation to require an 80% vote for approval of a merger under the authority of §102(b)(4) as opposed to the simple majority vote required by §251(c). This would simply be calling for "the vote of a larger portion of the stock" than is required by other parts of the chapter. *Seibert v. Milton Bradley Company, 380 Mass. 656, 405 N.E.2d 131 (1980).*

Michigan

Fraud. — The exercise of the statutory right of merger is always subject to nullification for fraud, and that the allocation of equities in the surviving corporation between the old preferred and common stockholders may be so unfair as to amount to constructive fraud. *Dratz v. Occidental Hotel Company, 325 Mich. 699, 39 N.W.2d 341 (1949).*

New York

Effective date. — It is indisputable that notwithstanding all of the acts and procedures contemplated and those actually performed subsequent to the signing of the instrument, the agreement to merge could not and did not become effective or enforceable until it was approved by a majority of shareholders. *Federal Deposit Insurance Corporation v. Commissioner of Taxation & Finance, 189 A.D.2d 39, 594 N.Y.S.2d 447 (1993).*

Texas

Construction with other law. — In a long-form merger, Delaware law provides that the board of directors of a corporation will compile certain information and then submit that information to the shareholders of the corporation. After the report of the board has been furnished to the shareholders, the shareholders are entitled to vote on the merger. The same is not true when a short-form merger occurs under Section 253. *Warren v.*

Warren Equip. Co., 2006 Tex. App. LEXIS 1247, 2006 Tex. App. LEXIS 1247 (Feb. 16, 2006).

Washington

Fixation of stock value. — The authority for the consolidation and merger of its domestic corporations is given in Delaware by statute. It has also given to a nonconsenting stockholder in either of the consolidating corporations the right to have paid to him or her the value of his or her stock, and has provided a procedure whereby he or she may have that value fixed and a method by which such value may be recovered from the resulting corporation. A part of the statutory right is to have the value of the stock fixed by appraisers selected by the interested parties. If this cannot be accomplished, the chancellor of Delaware is authorized by statute to designate appraisers. When the appraisers fix the value of the stock, their decision is binding on the corporation, and, if it does not pay such value to the stockholder, he or she is given a right of action to recover a judgment therefor. *Grant v. Pacific Gamble Robinson Company, 22 Wash.2d 65, 154 P.2d 301 (1944).*

Wisconsin

There is no duty under Delaware law to get an independent appraisal of a subsidiary before a merger. *Stauffacher v. Checota, 149 Wis. 2d 762, 441 N.W.2d 755 (Wis. App. 1979).*

CASE NOTES — FEDERAL

First Circuit

Retention of key employees. — Just as a board of directors may legitimately attempt to retain key executives during a hostile tender offer in order to secure their advice, the board may legitimately do the same regarding a disputed election for control of the company. A golden parachute agreement adopted in the face of a tender offer is a legitimate means to retain key employees. *Nault v. XTRA Corp., 1992 U.S. Dist. LEXIS 10512 (D.Mass. 1992).*

Second Circuit

Fiduciary duty to maximize value. — When a corporate board of directors authorizes management to engage in merger negotiations, the board has a fiduciary duty to maximize the value of the corporation for the stockholders' benefit. *Caruso v. Metex Corp., 1992 U.S. Dist. LEXIS 14556 (E.D.N.Y. 1992).*

Fiduciary duty to actively oversee. — A board of directors of a corporation, to fulfill their fiduciary responsibilities, must actively and directly oversee matters relating to the sale or merger of the corporation. *Caruso v. Metex Corp., 1992 U.S. Dist. LEXIS 14556 (E.D.N.Y. 1992).*

"Entire fairness" review. — Under Delaware law, majority shareholders have a fiduciary duty to minority shareholders in a corporate merger, and the court must scrutinize the circumstances of the merger for compliance with the rule of "entire fairness." *Richardson v. White, Weld & Co., 1979 U.S. Dist. LEXIS 12417 (S.D.N.Y. 1979).*

Measure of fair value. — Because mergers are permitted under Delaware law, and the accomplishment of a merger necessarily involves adjusting the rights of shareholders, a shareholder's preferential rights are subject to defeasance. Stockholders are charged with knowledge of this possibility at the time they acquire their shares. Moreover, Delaware provides specific protection to shareholders who believe that they have received insufficient value for their stock as the result of a merger: they may obtain an appraisal under § 262. Furthermore, the decision to merge with another company does not relieve the corporation or its directors of the duty to accord to the minority fair and equitable terms of conversion. The measure of fair value, however, is the amount equal to the corporation, not the stated redemption or liquidation value of the shares. *Rauch v. RCA Corp., 1987 U.S. Dist. LEXIS 3323 (S.D.N.Y. 1987).*

Under Delaware law, the desire to go private is sufficient reason for undertaking the merger. In the absence of fraudulent or deceptive conduct, merely concentrating a company's control in the hands of a few is, by itself, an insufficient ground for complaint. *Loengard v. Santa Fe Industries, Inc., 639 F. Supp. 673 (S.D.N.Y. 1986).*

Consideration due warrant holders. — Under Delaware law, warrant holders under the warrant agreement at issue in that case were entitled to receive the same consideration that any other corporate shareholder had received in a merger. *R.A. Mackie & Co., L.P. v. Petrocorp Inc., 244 F. Supp. 2d 279 (S.D.N.Y. 2003).*

"Liquidation". — Under Delaware law, neither a tender offer nor a merger is a liquidation. The term "liquidation" when applied to a corporation, means the winding up of the affairs of the corporation by getting in its assets, settling with the creditors and debtors, and apportioning the amount of profit and loss. *Sedighim v. Donaldson, Lufkin & Jenrette, Inc., 167 F. Supp. 2d 639 (S.D.N.Y. 2001).*

A merger is distinct from a sale of assets under Delaware law, and the distinction is not merely one of form but of substance. When an actual transfer of assets is structured as a merger, Delaware courts may consider the substance of the transaction in determining whether the transaction is a "sale of assets." *Sedighim v. Donaldson, Lufkin & Jenrette, Inc., 167 F. Supp. 2d 639 (S.D.N.Y. 2001).*

Under Delaware law, minority stock interests may be eliminated by merger. Also, where a merger of corporations is permitted by law, a shareholder's preferential rights are subject to defeasance. Stockholders are charged with knowledge of this possibility at the time they acquire their shares. *Satterfield v. Monsanto Co., 88 F. Supp. 2d 288 (S.D.N.Y. 2000).*

Standing to maintain derivative claim. — Under Delaware law, a plaintiff must have been a shareholder at the time of the challenged transaction to have standing to maintain a shareholder derivative suit. In addition, Delaware courts require that plaintiff remain a shareholder at the time of the filing of the suit and throughout the litigation. A plaintiff who ceases to be a shareholder, whether by reason of a merger or for any other reason, loses standing to continue a derivative suit. Delaware courts, however, recognize two exceptions to the general rule that a plaintiff loses standing where the shareholder loses stock as a result of a merger. These exceptions apply (1) where the merger itself is the subject of a claim of fraud; or (2) where the merger is in reality a reorganization not affecting plaintiff's ownership in the business enterprise. *Solow v. Stone, 994 F. Supp. 173 (S.D.N.Y. 1998).*

Under Delaware law, a merger agreement is binding only if a majority of all issued and outstanding company shares approve it. *Mony Group, Inc. v. Highfields Capital Management, L.P., 368 F.3d 138 (2d Cir. 2004).*

Proxy votes. — Under Delaware law, any merger or consolidation of domestic corporations must meet a number of statutory requirements, including that, at a special meeting for the purpose of acting on the merger agreement, a majority of the outstanding stock of the corporation entitled to vote thereon shall be voted for the adoption of the agreement. Thus, in the context of a proxy vote to approve a merger agreement under Delaware law, a majority of all outstanding shares must vote "yes" in order to approve the merger; an abstention (or any vote other than "yes") is tantamount to a "no" vote. Moreover, when two proxies are offered bearing the same name, then the proxy that appears to have been last executed will be accepted and counted under the theory that the latter — that is, more recent — proxy constitutes a revocation of the former. *Mony Group, Inc. v. Highfields Capital Management, L.P., 368 F.3d 138 (2d Cir. 2004).*

Third Circuit

Survival of claims. — Any claim of a merged corporation becomes the property of the surviving corporation. *Kanbar v. U.S. Healthcare, Inc., 1989 U.S. Dist. LEXIS 13474 (E.D.Pa. 1989).*

Standing to maintain derivative claim. — Delaware law requires that a derivative action plaintiff must be a shareholder both at the time of the alleged wrong and at the time of suit. The only exceptions to this rule are: (a) where the merger itself is the subject of a claim of fraud, i.e., where the merger was perpetrated to derive the merged corporation of its claim; or (b) where the merger is in reality a reorganization which does not affect plaintiff's ownership of the business enterprise. The second exception is limited to a merger which is merely a share for share merger with a newly formed holding company, which retained the old company a wholly owned subsidiary of the new holding company with the shareholders of the old company owning all the shares of the new holding company. The structure of the old and new companies is virtually identical. *Kanbar v. U.S. Healthcare, Inc., 1989 U.S. Dist. LEXIS 13474 (E.D.Pa. 1989).*

Under Delaware law, in the context of a corporate merger, a derivative shareholder must not only be a stockholder at the time of the alleged wrong and at time of commencement of suit but that he or she must also maintain shareholder status throughout the litigation.

Amalgamated Bank v. Yost, 2005 U.S. Dist. LEXIS 1280 (E.D.Pa. 2005).

Presumed knowledge of shareholder. — It is elementary that the substantial elements of the merger and consolidation provisions of the General Corporation Law are written into every corporate charter. The shareholder has notice that the corporation whose shares he or she has acquired may be merged with another corporation if the required majority of the shareholders agree. He or she is informed that the merger agreement may prescribe the terms and conditions of the merger, the mode of carrying it into effect, and the manner of converting the shares of the constituent corporations into the shares of the resulting corporation. A well-understood meaning of the word "convert" is to alter in form, substance, or quality. Substantial rights of shareholders, as is well known, may include rights in respect of voting, options, preferences, and dividends. The average intelligent mind must be held to know that dividends may accumulate on preferred stock, and that in the event of a merger of the corporation issuing the stock with another corporation, the various rights of shareholders, including the right to dividends on preference stock accrued but unpaid, may, and perhaps must, be the subject of reconcilement and adjustment. *Langfelder v. Universal Laboratories, Inc., 163 F.2d 804 (3d Cir. 1947).*

Fifth Circuit

"Business combination". — Delaware law defines "merger" and "consolidation" as a transaction involving two or more entities, where the legal existence of one or more entities ceases to exist. A "business combination" can be a merger or consolidation, or various other transactions involving the corporation or its subsidiary and an interested shareholder. *Newsouth Communications Corp. v. Universal Telephone Co., LLC, 2002 U.S. Dist. LEXIS 18969 (E.D.La. 2002).*

Sixth Circuit

Standing to maintain derivative claim. — In the seminal *Anderson* case, the Delaware Supreme Court, interpreting relevant statutory provisions of the Delaware Corporation Law, held that in order to maintain standing, a derivative shareholder must not only be a stockholder at the time of the alleged wrong and at time of commencement of suit but that he must also maintain shareholder status throughout the litigation. That court further clarified that a plaintiff who ceases to be a shareholder, whether by reason of a merger or for any other reason, loses standing to continue a derivative suit. That court recognized but two narrow exceptions to the continuing ownership requirement for standing: (1) where the merger itself is the subject of a claim of fraud, and (2) where the merger is in reality a reorganization which does not affect plaintiff's ownership of the business enterprise. *Prince v. Palmer, 2005 U.S. App. LEXIS 14239 (6th Cir. 2005).*

The *Anderson* reorganization exception does not apply to two distinct corporations, each with its own board of directors, officers, assets and stockholders, whose merger was far more than a corporate reshuffling, and which resulted in plaintiffs' possessing property interests distinctly different from that which they held as share-holders of the old corporation. *Prince v. Palmer, 2005 U.S. App. LEXIS 14239 (6th Cir. 2005).*

Seventh Circuit

Director duties generally. — Under Delaware law, directors owe a fiduciary duty of fairness to a class of minority shareholders. Fairness requires fair dealing and fair price. Fair dealing involves the duty of candor and the duty to conduct the merger in a way that protects the interests of minority shareholders. The state of incorpora-tion determines the fiduciary obligations owed by directors to their shareholders. The duty of candor or disclosure is defined in terms almost identical to those used under federal securities laws: the limited function of a court is to determine whether defendants disclosed all information in their "possession" germane to the transaction in issue. Germane means information such as a reasonable shareholder would consider important in deciding whether to sell or retain stock. *Eliasen v. Hamilton, 1987 U.S. Dist. LEXIS 1826 (N.D.Ill. 1987).*

Standing to maintain derivative claim. — In Delaware, direct attacks on corporate restructurings may be maintained even after the transaction has been completed. Accordingly, a former shareholder may directly challenge a merger which terminated the shareholder's status, if the merger itself is the subject of a claim of fraud. *Lynch v. Marklin of America, Inc., 724 F. Supp. 595 (N.D.Ill. 1989).*

Presumption of fairness applied. — Where both an employees' stock purchase plan and the plan and agreement of merger have received the favorable vote of more than two-thirds of the stockholders, such employees' stock purchase plan and such plan and agreement of merger are presumed to be fair and cannot be successfully attacked by dissident stockholders except upon a showing of actual or constructive fraud. *Krantman v. Liberty Loan Corp., 152 F. Supp. 705 (N.D. Ill. 1956).*

De facto mergers. — Delaware courts, recognize the "de facto merger" doctrine only in very limited contexts. In only a few instances involving sales of assets have Delaware courts applied the doctrine of de facto merger and only then for the protection of creditors or stockhold-ers who have suffered by reason of failure to comply with the statute governing such sales. *Binder v. Bristol-Myers Squibb, Co., 184 F. Supp. 2d 762 (N.D.Ill. 2001).*

A de facto merger may be found where an asset sale took place that amounted to a merger. *Binder v. Bris-tol-Myers Squibb, Co., 184 F. Supp. 2d 762 (N.D.Ill. 2001).*

Ninth Circuit

Prerequisites to application of business judgment rule in takeover context. — The business judgment rule may protect directors of a corporation when they are responding to a takeover threat. However, in such circumstances there is an omnipresent specter that a board may be acting primarily in its own interests. Before the business judgment rule will be applied in such a context, it must be established that: (1) there were reasonable grounds for believing that corporate policy and effectiveness were endangered; after which, (2) the defensive measure chosen must be reasonable in relation to the threat posed. The directors may satisfy this burden by showing good faith and reasonable investigation. This is called the *Unocal* analysis. If a defensive mechanism is intended to act primarily as an anti-takeover device, the *Unocal* analysis will apply in determining the propriety of the mechanism. If it has some other purpose, and only incidentally acts as an anti-takeover device, then the business judgment rule applies. *NL Industries, Inc. v. Lockheed Corp., 1992 U.S. Dist. LEXIS 22652 (C.D.Cal. 1992).*

Absent a "special injury" affecting only certain shareholders, a claim for breach of the fiduciary duty of care must be brought derivatively on behalf of the corporation. *In re McKesson HBOC, Inc. Securities Litigation, 126 F. Supp. 2d 1248 (N.D.Cal. 2000).*

Tenth Circuit

Effect of consolidation. — A consolidation effects the dissolution of the original corporations and brings into existence a new corporation. Also, upon consolidation being effected under statutory provisions, absent language indicating a contrary intent, the constituent corporations will be deemed to be dissolved and their powers, privi-leges, and property vested in the consolidated corporation as a new corporation created by the act of consolidation. *Jones v. Noble Drilling Co., 135 F.2d 721 (10th Cir. 1943).*

Eleventh Circuit

The preferred stockholder is entitled to vote on any proposal for merger or consolidation. *Penfield v. Davis, 105 F. Supp. 292 (N.D. Ala. 1952).*

No absolute right to interest in corporation. — It is clear that the Delaware legislature has determined that a stockholder has no absolute right to his or her interest in the corporation and may be forced to surrender his or her shares for a fair cash price. *Grimes v. Donaldson, Lufkin & Jenrette, Inc., 392 F. Supp. 1393 (N.D. Fla. 1974).*

Standing to maintain derivative claim. — As a general rule of Delaware law, a derivative shareholder must not only be a stockholder at the time of the alleged wrong and at time of commencement of suit but must also maintain shareholder status throughout the litigation. To the extent their claims are derivative, plaintiffs may have standing under an exception to the general rule where the merger itself is the subject of a claim of fraud. This exception applies when the merger was perpetrated to deprive the corporation on whose behalf the suit is brought of its claim against the individual defendants. *Sturm v. Marriott Marquis Corp., 85 F. Supp. 2d 1356 (N.D.Ga. 2000).*

District of Columbia Circuit

The separate corporate existence of a constituent corporation ceases upon merger into another corpora-tion. *Kanuth v. Prescott, Ball & Turben, Inc., 1992 U.S. Dist. LEXIS 3943 (D.D.C. 1992).*

§ 252. Merger or consolidation of domestic and foreign corporations; service of process upon surviving or resulting corporation

DELAWARE CASE NOTES — REPORTED

Supremacy of federal bankruptcy laws. — General corporation law of the State of Delaware addressed the required procedures for merger or consolidation corporations under this section and *8 Del. C. §§ 251, 253*, but the "notwithstanding any otherwise applicable nonbankruptcy law" language of *11 U.S.C. § 1123*(a) overrode the requirements of the state provisions; if there was any doubt about the Bankruptcy Code trumping the state law provisions, *8 Del. C. § 303* dispelled it by specifically providing for mergers under a *Chapter 11 plan. In re Stone & Webster, Inc., 286 Bankr. 532 (Bankr. D. Del. 2002).*

Estoppel. — When an informed minority shareholder either votes in favor of the merger, or accepts the benefits of the transaction, he or she cannot thereafter attack its fairness. *Bershad v. Curtiss-Wright Corp., 535 A.2d 840 (Del. 1987).*

Delaware attachment laws cannot be construed to authorize the attachment of shares of a foreign corporation. Thus, where a Delaware corporation, some of whose shares had been validly attached, merged, under Delaware law, with a New Jersey corporation and the shares were converted into the shares of the latter corporation, the effect of the merger was to terminate any jurisdiction the Court of Chancery had over the seized property. *Union Chem. & Materials Corp. v. Cannon, 38 Del. Ch. 203, 148 A.2d 348 (1959).*

Duty of disclosure. — This section and § 251 of this title do not explicitly require a company to inform stockholders of all material facts; the duty of disclosure is a judicially imposed fiduciary duty which applies as a corollary to the statutory requirements. *Arnold v. Society for Savs. Bancorp., 678 A.2d 533 (Del. 1996).*

CASE NOTES — OTHER STATES

Indiana

Effective date. — Under Delaware law, a corporate merger with a foreign corporation becomes effective when adopted, approved, certified, executed, and acknowledged by each of the constituent corporations in accordance with the laws under which it is formed, and is evidenced by an agreement of merger or a certificate of merger filed with the secretary of state. The statute provides the method for a merger. Corporate instruments are effective upon the filing date. *Keybank National Association v. Mochael, 737 N.E.2d 834 (Ind. 2000).*

Michigan

Fraud. — The exercise of the statutory right of merger is always subject to nullification for fraud, and that the allocation of equities in the surviving corporation between the old preferred and common stockholders may be so unfair as to amount to constructive fraud. *Dratz v. Occidental Hotel Company, 325 Mich. 699, 39 N.W.2d 341 (1949).*

§ 253. Merger of parent corporation and subsidiary or subsidiaries

DELAWARE CASE NOTES — REPORTED

Purpose. — Read in connection with the general and unrestricted authority conferred by § 251 of this title, this section is declaratory of the right of all Delaware corporations to consolidate or merge, its immediate purpose being not a grant of power, but a simplification of procedure with respect to mergers of parent corporations with their subsidiaries. *Federal United Corp. v. Havender, 24 Del. Ch. 318, 11 A.2d 331 (1940).*

The purpose of this section is to provide the parent corporation with a means of eliminating the minority shareholder's interest in the enterprise. *Stauffer v. Standard Brands, Inc., 41 Del. Ch. 7, 187 A.2d 78 (1962), overruled on other grounds by Roland Int'l Corp. v. Najjar, 407 A.2d 1032 (Del. 1979).*

This section is designed to give the parent corporation "a means of eliminating the minority stockholders' interest in the enterprise"; the parent corporation at its election may adopt either method. *In re Delaware Racing Ass'n, 42 Del. Ch. 406, 213 A.2d 203 (1965).*

This section is modeled upon that of New York. *Stauffer v. Standard Brands, Inc., 41 Del. Ch. 7, 187 A.2d 78 (1962), overruled on other grounds by Roland Int'l Corp. v. Najjar, 407 A.2d 1032 (Del. 1979).*

Supremacy of federal bankruptcy. — General corporation law of the State of Delaware addressed the required procedures for merger or consolidation corporations under this section and *8 Del. C. §§ 251, 252*, but the "notwithstanding any otherwise applicable nonbankruptcy law" language of *11 U.S.C. § 1123*(a) overrode the requirements of the state provisions; if there was any doubt about the Bankruptcy Code trumping the state law provisions, *8 Del. C. § 303* dispelled it by specifically providing for mergers under a *Chapter 11 plan. In re Stone & Webster, Inc., 286 Bankr. 532 (Bankr. D. Del. 2002).*

Construction of section with § 262 of this title. — Despite similarities between the short-form merger procedure and merger approval by written consent, the lack of a paragraph granting appraisal in the latter circumstance is a crucial difference. *Klotz v. Warner Communications, Inc., 674 A.2d 878 (Del. 1995).*

Creditors of a corporation who accepted, but failed to exercise, warrants that entitled them to purchase stock were bound by the plain language of the warrants to the rights set forth therein; therefore, they failed to state a claim against the controlling shareholder, after a short-form merger pursuant to *8 Del. C. § 253*, either for breach of an implied duty of good faith and fair dealing (since their remedies were limited by contract) or for denial of appraisal rights pursuant to *8 Del. C. § 262. Aspen Advisors LLC v. United Artists Theatre Co., 843 A.2d 697 (Del. Ch. 2004)*, aff'd, *861 A.2d 1251 (Del. 2004)*.

Warrantholders whose right to exercise their warrants disappeared when the corporation in which they held the warrants was merged into another, and who could not show that any duty to them was violated by the short-form merger, were properly compensated according to the terms of their warrants by the same value received by other common stockholders, less the cost of exercising their warrants; the right to a statutory appraisal remedy applied only to stockholders, a status that the warrantholders could have held, but, because they had declined to exercise their options, did not hold. *Aspen Advisors LLC v. United Artists Theatre Co., 861 A.2d 1251 (Del. 2004)*.

Majority shareholders must establish proper purpose for the short-form merger. *Roland Int'l Corp. v. Najjar, 407 A.2d 1032 (Del. 1979)*, overruled on other grounds, *457 A.2d 701 (Del. 1983)*.

This section does not require that minority stockholders be forced out of resulting corporation in all short-form mergers. *In re Delaware Racing Ass'n, 42 Del. Ch. 406, 213 A.2d 203 (1965)*.

Rule that majority stockholders have fiduciary duty to minority stockholders applies to a short-form merger under the Delaware general corporation law. *Roland Int'l Corp. v. Najjar, 407 A.2d 1032 (Del. 1979)*, overruled on other grounds, *457 A.2d 701 (Del. 1983)*.

In every merger under Delaware law, whether it be long-form or short-form, the essential consideration must be the fiduciary duty of fairness and good faith owed by the majority to the minority stockholders. *Coleman v. Taub, 638 F.2d 628 (3d Cir. 1981)*.

Fairness required. — The exclusive standard of judicial review in examining the propriety of an interested cash-out merger transaction by a controlling or dominating shareholder is entire fairness. *Kahn v. Lynch Communication Sys., 638 A.2d 1110 (Del. 1994)*.

In parent-subsidiary merger transactions the issues are those of fairness — fair price and fair dealing. *Bershad v. Curtiss-Wright Corp., 535 A.2d 840 (Del. 1987)*.

Delaware law does not impose a duty of entire fairness on controlling stockholders making a non-coercive tender or exchange offer to acquire shares directly from the minority holders and in place of an entire fairness standard, a court examines both the structure of the transaction to insure that it is voluntary in nature and information disclosed to insure its adequacy and completeness; and where the court finds an offer to be both structurally non-coercive and fully disclosed, the court has left the decision whether to tender or not up to the stockholders. *Next Level Communs., Inc. v. Motorola, Inc., 834 A.2d 828 (Del. Ch. 2003)*, review denied, *817 A.2d 804 (Del. 2003)*.

Parent-subsidiary merger was the product of fair dealing where the parent did not dictate the terms of the transaction, other than to prescribe that it would be a stock-for-stock merger, the transaction was negotiated on the subsidiary's behalf by a committee of directors totally independent of the parent, it was made subject to the approval of a majority of the subsidiary's minority stockholders, and the parent caused its subsidiary director nominees to absent themselves from the negotiations and decisionmaking process. *Citron v. E.I. Du Pont de Nemours & Co., 584 A.2d 490 (Del. Ch. 1990)*.

Conditions under which a tender offer is non-coercive. — Delaware law should consider an acquisition tender offer by a controlling stockholder non-coercive only when: (1) it is subject to a non-waivable majority of the minority tender condition; (2) the controlling stockholder promises to consummate a prompt merger at the same price if it obtains more than 90% of the shares; and (3) the controlling stockholder has made no retributive threats, as these protections minimize the distorting influence of the tendering process on voluntary choice, and also recognize the adverse conditions that confront stockholders who find themselves owning what have become very thinly traded shares. *In re Pure Res., Inc., 808 A.2d 421 (Del. Ch. 2002)*, appeal denied, *808 A.2d 421 (Del. Ch. 2002)*.

Vice latent in corporate merger carried out in disregard of statutory rules is that the rights of creditors or stockholders may be thereby impaired. *Heilbrunn v. Sun Chem. Corp., 37 Del. Ch. 552, 146 A.2d 757 (1958)*, aff'd, *38 Del. Ch. 321, 150 A.2d 755 (1959)*.

Merger between domestic and alien corporations is precluded. — The merger statute, by necessary implication, precludes mergers between domestic corporations and alien corporations, that is, those created under the laws of a foreign country. *Braasch v. Goldschmidt, 41 Del. Ch. 519, 199 A.2d 760 (1964)*.

But domestic corporation may merge with domestic subsidiary of alien corporation. — A merger between Delaware corporations is not prohibited where 1 of the corporations is a wholly owned subsidiary of an alien corporation. *Braasch v. Goldschmidt, 41 Del. Ch. 519, 199 A.2d 760 (1964)*.

By virtue of merger, derivative rights to sue pass to surviving corporation. *Braasch v. Goldschmidt, 41 Del. Ch. 519, 199 A.2d 760 (1964)*.

Upon a merger the old company could not thereafter have instituted an action against its directors and others for an accounting, and since the old corporation was itself barred because the right of action was transferred to the surviving company, the stockholders of the old company were without derivative status. *Braasch v. Goldschmidt, 41 Del. Ch. 519, 199 A.2d 760 (1964)*.

Determination of earnings and asset value at time of merger. — See *Francis I. DuPont & Co. v. Universal City Studios, Inc., 312 A.2d 344 (Del. Ch. 1973)*, aff'd, *334 A.2d 216 (Del. 1975)*.

Book value, which is the original cost of an enterprise's assets, is regarded as of minor importance in assessing the fairness of a stock-for-stock merger exchange. *Citron v.*

E.I. Du Pont de Nemours & Co., 584 A.2d 490 (Del. Ch. 1990).

Measure of value is same as that for long-form merger. — There is no difference in the measure of value in appraisal proceeding growing out of a short-form merger under this section from the measure of value in appraisal proceeding growing out of a long-form merger under § 251 of this title. *In re Delaware Racing Ass'n, 42 Del. Ch. 406, 213 A.2d 203 (1965).*

Rights of minority shareholders compared. — The rights of minority shareholders under a merger governed by § 251 of this title are no greater than those under a merger governed by this section. *Singer v. Magnavox Co., 367 A.2d 1349 (Del. Ch. 1976), aff'd in part and rev'd in part, 380 A.2d 969 (Del. 1977).*

A determination as to whether or not the strict standards of fiduciary duty imposed on a majority stockholder in a merger based on this section has been properly carried out requires no less scrutiny by the trial court than that called for in a case in which the rights of minority stockholders have been allegedly diminished by a merger based on § 251 of this title. *Kemp v. Angel, 381 A.2d 241 (Del. Ch. 1977).*

Although there are procedural differences between § 251 of this title and a merger under this section, the fiduciary duties owed by a majority shareholder to the minority are the same. *Najjar v. Roland Int'l Corp., 387 A.2d 709 (Del. Ch. 1978), aff'd, 407 A.2d 1032 (Del. 1979).*

Fiduciary duty may not be circumvented by full compliance with the procedures of the corporation statutes, nor is it discharged by remitting minority shareholders to a statutory appraisal remedy (often based upon the status of the market and the elements of an appraisal), the timing of which is entirely within the control of the majority. *Roland Int'l Corp. v. Najjar, 407 A.2d 1032 (Del. 1979), overruled on other grounds, 457 A.2d 701 (Del. 1983).*

The fiduciary duty is violated when those who control a corporation's voting machinery use that power to "cash out" minority shareholders, that is, to exclude them from continued participation in the corporate life, for no reason other than to eliminate them. *Roland Int'l Corp. v. Najjar, 407 A.2d 1032 (Del. 1979), overruled on other grounds, 457 A.2d 701 (Del. 1983).*

This section authorizes adoption of plan by which shares are exchanged for cash alone. *Coyne v. Park & Tilford Distillers Corp., 37 Del. Ch. 558, 146 A.2d 785 (1958), aff'd, 38 Del. Ch. 514, 154 A.2d 893 (1959).*

The possibility of a merger plan providing cash for shares and the existence of a right to an appraisal in such a case are perfectly compatible. *Coyne v. Park & Tilford Distillers Corp., 37 Del. Ch. 558, 146 A.2d 785 (1958), aff'd, 38 Del. Ch. 514, 154 A.2d 893 (1959).*

Under this section, the terms of a merger may provide that the stockholders of the merged corporation be given no option but to accept cash for their stock. *Carl Marks & Co. v. Universal City Studios, Inc., 43 Del. Ch. 391, 233 A.2d 63 (1967).*

Use of independent special committee. — Where an independent special committee is used to simulate an arm's length transaction in an interested cash-out merger, the majority shareholder must not dictate the terms of the merger; the special committee must also have real bargaining power that it can exercise with the majority shareholder on an arm's length basis. *Kahn v. Lynch Communication Sys., 638 A.2d 1110 (Del. 1994).*

Burden of establishing fairness of merger plan. — In a minority shareholders' suit alleging breach of fiduciary duty, when defendants stand on both sides of the transaction through control of the corporate machinery, the burden of proof of fairness shifts to defendants, who must also establish there to be a business purpose for the merger other than a freeze-out of the minority. *Harman v. Masoneilan Int'l, 442 A.2d 487 (Del. 1982).*

In a parent-subsidiary merger context, shareholder ratification operates only to shift the burden of persuasion, not to change the substantive standard of review which should be entire fairness; nor does the fact that the merger was negotiated by a committee of independent, disinterested directors alter the review standard. *Citron v. E.I. Du Pont de Nemours & Co., 584 A.2d 490 (Del. Ch. 1990).*

Where there is only dispute as to value, there is no remedy except appraisal. *Stauffer v. Standard Brands, Inc., 41 Del. Ch. 7, 187 A.2d 78 (1962), overruled on other grounds by Roland Int'l Corp. v. Najjar, 407 A.2d 1032 (Del. 1979).*

Notice to stockholders is required to be sent only after consummation of the merger. *Carl Marks & Co. v. Universal City Studios, Inc., 43 Del. Ch. 391, 233 A.2d 63 (1967).*

Purpose of merger notice requirement. — A Notice of Merger filed pursuant to this section and § 262 of this title is primarily intended to notify the stockholders of action being taken by the parent corporation and to apprise the stockholders of their appraisal remedy. *Zirn v. VLI Corp., 681 A.2d 1050 (Del. 1996).*

Disclosure required for shareholder ratification. — Stockholder vote approving merger was fully informed and valid where the proxy statement disclosed all facts material to the subsidiary's minority stockholders' decision to approve or disapprove the proposed merger. *Citron v. E.I. Du Pont de Nemours & Co., 584 A.2d 490 (Del. Ch. 1990).*

Short form merger notice requirements. — Notice of a short-form merger issued immediately after the conclusion of a hotly contested tender offer did not satisfy the parent company's fiduciary duty of disclosure when that notice contained merely the statutorily mandated information about the mechanics of perfecting a demand for appraisal and no other information relating to the value of the merged entity or its securities; even when adequate, current information is found in the total mix of publicly available information, the fiduciary duty of disclosure requires that a notice of short-form merger either be accompanied by detailed disclosures, or disclose summary financial information that adequately advises stockholders where and how to obtain more detailed information. *Gilliland v. Motorola, Inc., 859 A.2d 80 (Del. Ch. 2004).*

Corporations

Stockholder's objection to merger could not, in itself, be read as making a demand for payment. *Carl Marks & Co. v. Universal City Studios, Inc., 43 Del. Ch. 391, 233 A.2d 63 (1967).*

Letters in which certain minority stockholders objected to a merger did not constitute a written demand for payment within the meaning of this section. *Abraham & Co. v. Olivetti Underwood Corp., 42 Del. Ch. 95, 204 A.2d 740 (1964), aff'd, 42 Del. Ch. 588, 217 A.2d 683 (1966).*

Spin off of subsidiary. — Prior to the date of distribution the interests held by a spin off subsidiary's prospective stockholders were insufficient to impose fiduciary obligations on the parent and the subsidiary's directors, thus, corporate parent and directors of a wholly-owned subsidiary did not owe fiduciary duties to the prospective stockholders of the subsidiary after the parent declares its intention to spin off the subsidiary. *Anadarko Petro. Corp. v. Panhandle E. Corp., 545 A.2d 1171 (Del. 1988).*

Chancery jurisdiction. — "Fairness" suits for alleged fraud and breach of fiduciary duty brought by minority shareholders fall within the Court of Chancery's exclusive, and not its concurrent, jurisdiction. *Harman v. Masoneilan Int'l, 442 A.2d 487 (Del. 1982).*

Freeze-out that both complies with statutory procedures, and fails to breach a fiduciary duty, does not run afoul of *Delaware law. Coleman v. Taub, 638 F.2d 628 (3d Cir. 1981).*

When complaint attacking merger "alleges" that sole purpose of merger is to eliminate minority interests, such a complaint is virtually immune from a motion to dismiss for failure to state a cause of action. *Najjar v. Roland Int'l Corp., 387 A.2d 709 (Del. Ch. 1978), aff'd, 407 A.2d 1032 (Del. 1979).*

On a motion for summary judgment, plaintiff-shareholder carries burden of establishing that there exists no valid purpose for merger attempted under this section. *Temple v. Combined Properties Corp., 410 A.2d 1375 (Del. Ch. 1979).*

The case of *Roland Int'l Corp. v. Najjar, Del. Supr., 407 A.2d 1032 (1979)*, does not stand for the proposition that a

defendant charged with a breach of fiduciary duty, in order successfully to oppose a motion for summary judgment, must affirmatively establish that there was a valid business purpose for the merger in question. *Temple v. Combined Properties Corp., 410 A.2d 1375 (Del. Ch. 1979).*

Estoppel. — When an informed minority shareholder either votes in favor of the merger, or accepts the benefits of the transaction, he or she cannot thereafter attack its fairness. *Bershad v. Curtiss-Wright Corp., 535 A.2d 840 (Del. 1987).*

Waiver not required. — There is nothing under Delaware law that requires the offeror in a tender offer to waive enforceable rights that it has as a holder of preferred stock of the target corporation or as a lender to the target corporation (or to provide some blanket assurance that it will do so); nor does the fact that the offeror has chosen to commence a tender offer without the consent of the target's board of directors give rise to such an obligation. *Next Level Communs., Inc. v. Motorola, Inc., 834 A.2d 828 (Del. Ch. 2003), review denied, 817 A.2d 804 (Del. 2003).*

Coercion not found. — In the context of a tender offer, generally, reports of factual matters that are neutrally stated and not threatening do not amount to wrongful coercion; moreover, the reality of the situation is required to be disclosed clearly and not couched in vague or euphemistic language. *Next Level Communs., Inc. v. Motorola, Inc., 834 A.2d 828 (Del. Ch. 2003), review denied, 817 A.2d 804 (Del. 2003).*

Where there is no suggestion of bad faith on the record that the offeror's decision in a tender offer to cease funding the corporation (target) is the subject of the tender offer, it cannot amount to inequitable coercion for the offeror to disclose that decision in its tender offer where, indeed, it is undoubtedly also true that the offeror has an affirmative duty, under both federal and state law, to include a disclosure about this decision in its tender offer materials. *Next Level Communs., Inc. v. Motorola, Inc., 834 A.2d 828 (Del. Ch. 2003), review denied, 817 A.2d 804 (Del. 2003).*

DELAWARE CASE NOTES — UNREPORTED

This section implicates only the right to vote on a merger, as opposed to a right to consent or approve. This section states that a parent corporation must own at least 90% of each class of stock entitled to "vote on such merger." Inherent in the language of this section is the recognition that there can be and are classes of stock which are not entitled to vote on a merger. *Matulich v. Aegis Communs. Essar Invs., Ltd., 2008 Del. LEXIS 20 (January 15, 2008).*

Contractual, statutory rights distinguished. — Series B shareholders' contractual right to consent and approve does not constitute a statutory right to vote on the merger. Therefore, the court of chancery properly concluded that the contractual rights of the Series B Preferred Shareholders were irrelevant in calculating whether company Focus had the statutory voting power necessary to execute a short-form merger. Consequently, as a matter of law, plaintiff's challenge to the merger is

without merit. *Matulich v. Aegis Communs. Essar Invs., Ltd., 2008 Del. LEXIS 20 (January 15, 2008).*

Construction with other law. — An analysis of § 253 in the context of the entire General Corporation Law provides no reason to assume that the General Assembly wished to prevent a corporation from providing a class of shareholders with a right of collective dissent without, at the same time, preventing a majority shareholder from exercising a right to employ a short form merger. As already noted, § 212(b) contemplates the ability of a shareholder both to vote and to consent. Section 253 implicates only the right to *vote* on a merger, as opposed to a general right to assent. The difference in language allows investors to agree, *ex ante,* to order their affairs the way they wish. On the one hand, investors may agree to provide preferred shareholders with a right of refusal and, at the same time, provide minority shareholders with protection against a short-form merger. If so, the preferred stock may be granted voting rights. If, on the other hand, preferred shareholders desire a collective right to block any merger, but see no advantage in granting protection to minority shareholders, those shares may bear a right to consent, but not a right to vote on the merger itself. Although the reasons for an investor to choose one set of protections over the other is not entirely clear, the law contemplates the ability to select either structure. *Matulich v. Aegis Communs. Group, Inc., 2007 Del. Ch. LEXIS 80 (May 31, 2007).*

Collective right to refuse to assent without vote. — Nothing in the General Corporation Law suggests that a corporation may not authorize a series of shares such that those shareholders have a collective right to refuse their assent to a merger without exercising that right through a vote. So long as a corporation organizes itself within the boundaries of Delaware statutory law, it is given great flexibility in its internal governance structures, as well as great freedom to modify the rights and limitations of shareholder rights, particularly those of preferred shareholders, through private agreement. This flexibility provides particularly rich and flexible threads with which corporate actors can weave their agreements, ensuring a diversity of forms of share ownership appropriate to varying situations. Matulich v. Aegis Communs. Group, Inc., 2007 Del. Ch. LEXIS 80 (May 31, 2007).

Quasi appraisal scheme. — After court determined that the majority shareholder did not give adequate notice to the minority shareholders so as to allow them to make an informed decision about whether or not to ask for an appraisal under 8 Del. C. § 253, the court devised a "quasi appraisal" scheme so that minority shareholders could affirmatively opt in if they desired, and would be entitled to the appraised amount that the court determined was equitable; opt-in shareholders were required to pay a price per share into an escrow account before the stock was appraised. *Gilliland v. Motorola, Inc., 2005 Del. Ch. LEXIS 33 (Mar. 4, 2005).*

Applicability of fairness standard. — Because short-form mergers, under this section were designed to be a summary process, Delaware courts did not entertain entire fairness claims or allegations of unfair dealing in relation to short-form mergers; even though the entire fairness standard did not apply, the valuation analysis presented to the stockholders in the instant case was found to be so bereft of actual information that the corporation had a duty to provide at least some further indication of the company's value to the corporation's stockholders. *Erickson v. Centennial Beauregard Cellular LLC, 2003 Del. Ch. LEXIS 38 (Apr. 11, 2003).*

CASE NOTES — OTHER STATES

Maryland

The person attacking the merger has the burden of demonstrating some basis for invoking the fairness obligation, and when the corporate action has been approved by an informed vote of a majority of the minority shareholders, he or she has the burden of showing that the transaction was unfair to the minority. *Walter J. Schloss Associates v. Chesapeake and Ohio Railway Company, 73 Md. App. 727, 536 A.2d 147 (1988).*

Michigan

Fraud. — The exercise of the statutory right of merger is always subject to nullification for fraud, and that the allocation of equities in the surviving corporation between the old preferred and common stockholders may be so unfair as to amount to constructive fraud. *Dratz v. Occidental Hotel Company, 325 Mich. 699, 39 N.W.2d 341 (1949).*

New York

Short-form merger. — Under Delaware law, a parent corporation, which owns 90% or more of the stock of a subsidiary, can merge with that subsidiary without advance notice or consent of the minority stockholders upon approval by the parent's board of directors. No corporate purpose is statutorily required for a short-form merger; rather, the very purpose of such mergers is to provide the parent corporation with a means of eliminating the minority shareholder's interest in the enterprise. Upon approval of the merger, the parent corporation must make payment in cash to the minority for their stock. If a minority stockholder is dissatisfied with the offer made by the parent corporation for his or her shares, he or she has the right to have a court-appointed appraiser determine the fair value and the right to receive a decree from the Delaware Court of Chancery ordering the surviving corporation to pay for his or her shares at the resulting appraised value. *Green v. Santa Fe Industries, Inc., 70 N.Y.2d 244, 514 N.E.2d 105, 519 N.Y.S.2d 793 (1997).*

Non-survival of derivative action. — A stockholder, who has instituted a derivative action on behalf of the corporation, does not continue to have the right to prosecute the action after there has been a merger under § 253 of the as a result of which the plaintiff's stock was converted into the right only to receive a fixed sum in cash from the surviving corporation. *Rubinstein v. Catacosinos, 91 A.D.2d 445, 459 N.Y.S.2d 286 (1983).*

Rhode Island

Inactive subsidiary. — Under Delaware law a parent corporation may merge with a wholly owned inactive subsidiary pursuant to a plan cancelling preferred stock and the rights of holders thereof to unpaid accumulated dividends and substituting in lieu thereof stock of the surviving corporation. *Bove v. The Community Hotel Corp. of Newport, Rhode Island, 105 R.I. 36; 249 A.2d 89 (1969).*

Texas

In general. — Short-form merger under this section is a unilateral act by the parent company. The merger is complete upon resolution of the board of directors of the

Corporations

parent company and the filing of a certificate of ownership and merger. A short-form merger under this section does not implicate stockholders, stockholders of record, or voting rights; ownership is the only question. By statute, the directors are the ones who vote on the short-form merger; shareholders are not entitled to vote. When a stockholder deposits stock in a voting trust, the stockholder parts with his voting rights but retains beneficial ownership of the stock. *Warren v. Warren Equip. Co., 2006 Tex. App. LEXIS 1247, 2006 Tex. App. LEXIS 1247 (Feb. 16, 2006).*

Construction with other law. — In a long-form merger, Delaware law provides that the board of directors of a corporation will compile certain information and then submit that information to the shareholders of the corporation. After the report of the board has been furnished to the shareholders, the shareholders are entitled to vote on the merger. The same is not true when a short-form merger occurs under this section. *Warren v. Warren Equip. Co., 2006 Tex. App. LEXIS 1247, 2006 Tex. App. LEXIS 1247 (Feb. 16, 2006).*

Wisconsin

There is no duty under Delaware law to get an independent appraisal of a subsidiary before a merger. *Stauffacher v. Checota, 149 Wis. 2d 762, 441 N.W.2d 755 (Wis. App. 1979).*

CASE NOTES — FEDERAL

Second Circuit

Section 253 of the Delaware Corporation Law permits a parent corporation owning at least 90% of the stock of a subsidiary to merge with the subsidiary upon approval by the parent's board of directors. The vote of the stockholders of the subsidiary is not required. *Elfenbein v. American Financial Corp., 487 F. Supp. 619 (S.D.N.Y. 1980).*

Third Circuit

A short-form merger effected solely to "squeeze out" minority shareholders amounts to a violation of the majority shareholder's fiduciary duty. *Flynn v. Bass Bros. Enters., 456 F. Supp. 484 (E.D. Pa. 1978).*

Seventh Circuit

Upon merger, the derivative rights on behalf of the merged corporation pass to the surviving corporation. In this respect, shareholders of the merged corporation then lose their standing to maintain a derivative suit on behalf of the merged corporation against the surviving corporation. This principle also has been applied to the situation where the merger occurs also during the course of the litigation. *Kreindler v. Marx, 85 F.R.D. 612 N.D.Ill. 1979).*

Eleventh Circuit

It is clear that the Delaware legislature has determined that a stockholder has no absolute right to his or her interest in the corporation and may be forced to surrender his or her shares for a fair cash price. *Grimes v. Donaldson, Lufkin & Jenrette, Inc., 392 F. Supp. 1393 (N.D. Fla. 1974).*

§ 254. Merger or consolidation of domestic corporation and joint-stock or other association

CASE NOTES — OTHER STATES

Michigan

Fraud. — The exercise of the statutory right of merger is always subject to nullification for fraud, and that the allocation of equities in the surviving corporation between the old preferred and common stockholders may be so unfair as to amount to constructive fraud. *Dratz v. Occidental Hotel Company, 325 Mich. 699, 39 N.W.2d 341 (1949).*

§ 255. Merger or consolidation of domestic nonstock corporations

CASE NOTES — OTHER STATES

Michigan

Fraud. — The exercise of the statutory right of merger is always subject to nullification for fraud, and that the allocation of equities in the surviving corporation between the old preferred and common stockholders may be so unfair as to amount to constructive fraud. *Dratz v. Occidental Hotel Company, 325 Mich. 699, 39 N.W.2d 341 (1949).*

§ 256. Merger or consolidation of domestic and foreign nonstock corporations; service of process upon surviving or resulting corporation

CASE NOTES — OTHER STATES

Michigan

Fraud. — The exercise of the statutory right of merger is always subject to nullification for fraud, and that the allocation of equities in the surviving corporation between the old preferred and common stockholders may be so unfair as to amount to constructive fraud. *Dratz v. Occidental Hotel Company, 325 Mich. 699, 39 N.W.2d 341 (1949).*

§ 257. Merger or consolidation of domestic stock and nonstock corporations

DELAWARE CASE NOTES — REPORTED

Changing to a for-profit corporation. — Delaware law authorizes change from a nonprofit, nonstock mutual benefit corporation into a for-profit stock corporation without the vote of its members. *Farahpour v. DCX, Inc., 635 A.2d 894 (Del. 1994).*

CASE NOTES — OTHER STATES

Michigan

Fraud. — The exercise of the statutory right of merger is always subject to nullification for fraud, and that the allocation of equities in the surviving corporation between the old preferred and common stockholders may be so unfair as to amount to constructive fraud. *Dratz v. Occidental Hotel Company, 325 Mich. 699, 39 N.W.2d 341 (1949).*

§ 258. Merger or consolidation of domestic and foreign stock and nonstock corporations

CASE NOTES — OTHER STATES

Michigan

Fraud. — The exercise of the statutory right of merger is always subject to nullification for fraud, and that the allocation of equities in the surviving corporation between the old preferred and common stockholders may be so unfair as to amount to constructive fraud. *Dratz v. Occidental Hotel Company, 325 Mich. 699, 39 N.W.2d 341 (1949).*

§ 259. Status, rights, liabilities, of constituent and surviving or resulting corporations following merger or consolidation

DELAWARE CASE NOTES — REPORTED

This section is in accord with the general law even without a statute or an agreement. Western *Air Lines v. Allegheny Airlines, 313 A.2d 145 (Del. Ch. 1973).*

It supplies the rationale for the general rule that creditors will not be allowed to prevent a merger. *Western Air Lines v. Allegheny Airlines, 313 A.2d 145 (Del. Ch. 1973).*

Identity of merged corporation is absorbed. — When a consolidation or merger has taken place under statute, the old corporations have their identity absorbed into that of the new corporation or the one into which they were merged. *Argenbright v. Phoenix Fin. Co., 21 Del. Ch. 288, 187 A. 124 (1936).*

Public policy, clearly expressed in this section, holds that the obligations of the extinguished corporation in a merger survive as obligations of the surviving corporation. *Western Air Lines v. Allegheny Airlines, 313 A.2d 145 (Del. Ch. 1973).*

If the merger agreement does not specifically state that it is not applicable to successors and assigns, the policy of the law is so clear that survival should be taken as the normal course of events. Contracts must be written and construed in light of generally accepted legal principles. *Western Air Lines v. Allegheny Airlines, 313 A.2d 145 (Del. Ch. 1973).*

Creation and enlargement of rights. — One's voluntary act cannot create or enlarge one's rights by imposing liability on, or enlarging the liability of, another, apart from statute or other special circumstance, as is the case in this section. *Pioneer Nat'l Title Ins. Co. v. Child, Inc., 401 A.2d 68 (Del. 1979).*

Corporate existence is terminated on date of merger. *Beals v. Washington Int'l, Inc., 386 A.2d 1156 (Del. Ch. 1978).*

And corporation ceases to exist on merger for all purposes, unless general assembly provides

otherwise. *Beals v. Washington Int'l, Inc., 386 A.2d 1156 (Del. Ch. 1978).*

A statutory merger results in a combination of two corporations with the surviving corporation attaining the property, rights, and privileges of the absorbed corporation, as well as retaining its own property, rights, and privileges. *Texaco Ref. & Mktg., Inc. v. Delaware River Basin Comm'n, 824 F. Supp. 500 (D. Del. 1993),* aff'd, *30 F.3d 1488 (3d Cir. 1994).*

Claims or causes of action pass to surviving corporation. — When a merger becomes effective all assets of the merged corporation, including any causes of action which might exist on its behalf, pass by operation of law to the surviving company. *Heit v. Tenneco, Inc., 319 F. Supp. 884 (D. Del. 1970).*

When first corporation merges into other corporations when plaintiff's derivative action is pending, neither plaintiff nor other former stockholders of first corporation had standing to maintain suit and first corporation could not institute or maintain suit. *Heit v. Tenneco, Inc., 319 F. Supp. 884 (D. Del. 1970).*

By virtue of a merger, stockholders' derivative rights pass to the surviving corporation. *Braasch v. Goldschmidt, 41 Del. Ch. 519, 199 A.2d 760 (1964).*

Derivative actions based upon corporation's claim for damages against another corporation, if these actions have merit, are assets of the corporation on whose behalf they were commenced, and pass upon merger as provided in this section. *Bokat v. Getty Oil Co., 262 A.2d 246 (Del. 1970).*

Following merger or consolidation, claims sued upon in a derivative action on behalf of 1 party to the merger, and against the other corporate party, become moot. *Bokat v. Getty Oil Co., 262 A.2d 246 (Del. 1970).*

Corporation into which another corporation was merged, is liable for all the debts, liabilities and duties of the merged corporation. *Beals v. Washington Int'l, Inc., 386 A.2d 1156 (Del. Ch. 1978).*

Section 261 of this title relates solely to the impact of merger on abatement of pending causes of action of constituent parties to the merger and does not impinge or amend this section as to the transfer of ownership of choses in action from merged party to surviving party. *Lewis v. Anderson, 477 A.2d 1040 (Del. 1984).*

Through merger, the derivative standing of former shareholders of a merged corporation to pursue pre-merger claims existing against their former officers and directors is lost and whether the merger takes place before or after the suit is brought is immaterial; a merger which eliminates ownership of stock eliminates standing to pursue a derivative suit. *Lewis v. Anderson, 477 A.2d 1040 (Del. 1984).*

This section and §§ 261 and 327 of this title, read individually and collectively, permit one result which is not only consistent but sound: A plaintiff who ceases to be a shareholder, whether by reason of a merger or for any other reason, loses standing to continue a derivative suit; § 327 of this title alone addresses standing to commence and to pursue a derivative suit. *Lewis v. Anderson, 477 A.2d 1040 (Del. 1984).*

Claimants may sue on contract or in tort against transferee corporation. — Where 1 corporation transfers all of its assets to another corporation, and payment is made in stock, issued by the transferee directly to the shareholders of the transferring corporation, in exchange for their stock in that corporation, the transferee agreeing to assume all the debts and liabilities of the transferor, persons having claims against the transferor may, in most cases, at least, proceed at law in the first instance, against the transferee and procure a personal judgment against that corporation; and this is true whether the claim and the action based thereon be in contract or in tort. *Drug, Inc. v. Hunt, 35 Del. 339, 168 A. 87 (1933).*

Agreement of parties to terminate contractual obligations. — Notwithstanding this section, contractual obligations do not pass if the parties by their objective contractual language contemplated that such obligations would not pass. *Mesa Partners v. Phillips Petro. Co., 488 A.2d 107 (Del. Ch. 1984).*

This section deals with rights and liens of creditors against property of corporation, not with attachment liens against property of the stockholders. *Union Chem. & Materials Corp. v. Cannon, 38 Del. Ch. 203, 148 A.2d 348 (1959).*

Section does not guarantee creditors jurisdictions in which to assert remedies. — When this section preserves remedies generally to creditors in consolidation and merger cases, it does not undertake to guarantee to them jurisdictions in which to assert the remedies. *Cole v. National Cash Credit Ass'n, 18 Del. Ch. 47, 156 A. 183 (1931).*

There is nothing in this section that purports to deal with rights of shareholders. *Federal United Corp. v. Havender, 24 Del. Ch. 318, 11 A.2d 331 (1940).*

Change in majority control of stock. — There is a clear distinction between a change in the majority control of the stock of a corporation and the sale of one of the corporation's assets. *Texaco Ref. & Mktg., Inc. v. Delaware River Basin Comm'n, 824 F. Supp. 500 (D. Del. 1993),* aff'd, *30 F.3d 1488 (3d Cir. 1994).*

Delaware corporation may not avoid its contractual obligations by merger; those duties "attach" to the surviving corporation and may be "enforced against it." *Fitzsimmons v. Western Airlines, 290 A.2d 682 (Del. Ch. 1972).*

Although they arise under federal law or collective bargaining agreement. — Contractual duties which survive a merger are enforceable under Delaware law and they are not made less so because those duties arise under federal law or because they arise from a collective bargaining agreement. *Fitzsimmons v. Western Airlines, 290 A.2d 682 (Del. Ch. 1972).*

This section is broad and certainly does not exclude from its purview a duty arising from a contract with a union. *Fitzsimmons v. Western Airlines, 290 A.2d 682 (Del. Ch. 1972).*

Hence, merger does not terminate employees' rights under collective bargaining contract. — Under Delaware corporation law, the rights of employees who are covered by collective bargaining contracts between their employer and union will not be automatically terminated by merger of the employer with another corporation. *Fitzsimmons v. Western Airlines, 290 A.2d 682 (Del. Ch. 1972).*

Successor employer may be required to arbitrate with union. — The disappearance by merger of a corporate employer which has entered into a collective bargaining agreement with the union does not automatically terminate all rights of the employees covered by the agreement, and, in appropriate circumstances, the successor employer may be required to arbitrate with the union under the agreement. *Fitzsimmons v. Western Airlines, 290 A.2d 682 (Del. Ch. 1972).*

Principle applies although merger may never eventuate. — Although merger of the 2 companies may never be a reality, the threatened breach of contract aspect of the dispute, whether the bargain agreements of the constituent corporation will survive the merger with the right of plaintiff to injunctive relief if successful, brings the case within the principle of this section. *Fitzsimmons v. Western Airlines, 290 A.2d 682 (Del. Ch. 1972).*

Rights based on warranties pass to successor. — Upon the formation of the successor corporation, the rights of the constituent corporations based on warranties denying any claim against one of the predecessor corporations pass to their successor pursuant to the agreement of merger and to this section. *Levitt v. Bouvier, 287 A.2d 671 (Del. 1972).*

Surviving corporation is liable for misrepresentation in nonsurviving corporation's proxy statement. — The surviving corporation after a merger is liable for any material misrepresentation contained in a proxy statement issued by the nonsurviving corporation in connection with the merger. *Gould v. American Hawaiian S.S. Co., 331 F. Supp. 981 (D. Del. 1971).*

Derivative suit constitutes chose in action vesting in new corporation upon merger. — Shareholder's derivative claim against officers and directors of corporation was a property right of the corporation and upon merger, the corporation's assets and liabilities passed and became vested in the new corporation so that under subsection (a) of this section, the shareholder's derivative claim constituted a chose in action which became "vested"

in the new corporation. *Lewis v. Anderson, 477 A.2d 1040 (Del. 1984).*

Standing in post-merger derivative action. — To have post-merger standing to carry on a derivative suit, derivative shareholder must not only be a stockholder at the time of the alleged wrong and at the time of commencement of the suit but must also maintain shareholder status throughout the litigation. *Lewis v. Anderson, 477 A.2d 1040 (Del. 1984).*

In the context of a corporate merger, the former shareholders of the merged corporation lose standing to maintain a derivative suit once their ownership of stock is eliminated. *Alabama By-Products Corp. v. Cede & Co. ex rel. Shearson Lehman Bros., 657 A.2d 254 (Del. 1995).*

Former shareholder in a merged company, who had become a shareholder in the successor company, lacked standing to pursue a pre-existing derivative claim under the rule of *Lewis v. Anderson, 477 A.2d 1040 (Del. 1984)*, to which the high court adhered; the shareholder argued that the merger was arranged in a fraudulent attempt to avoid the derivative action, but failed to plead fraud with any particularity. *Lewis v. Ward, 852 A.2d 896 (Del. 2004).*

Service of process upon merged corporation. — Corporation which has been merged into another corporation can be served with process after the merger, even if the action seeks a rescission of the merger. *Beals v. Washington Int'l, Inc., 386 A.2d 1156 (Del. Ch. 1978).*

Function of state court where 2 airlines merge. — In a merger between 2 airlines both federal and Delaware law require the surviving corporation to assume the duties of a constituent corporation in the merger, but the duties which are imposed cannot be decided simply under general principles of either contract or corporate law, since the operation of the airline and its employee relations are governed by federal law and regulation; and there are federal agencies which make determinations as to these. The function of the state court is to step aside until that is completed and then consider any application under this section to enforce the duties and/or to determine any aspect of the contract dispute which remains unsettled. *Fitzsimmons v. Western Airlines, 290 A.2d 682 (Del. Ch. 1972).*

DELAWARE CASE NOTES — UNREPORTED

Loss of standing. — A derivative plaintiff must maintain ownership throughout the course of litigation. This section, section 261, and section 327, read individually and collectively, permit one result which is not only consistent but sound: A plaintiff who ceases to be a shareholder, whether by reason of a merger or for any other reason, loses standing to continue a derivative suit. *Strategic Asset Mgmt. v. Nicholson, 2004 Del. Ch. LEXIS 178, No. 20360-NC (November 30, 2004).*

Continuing director provision in indenture agreement. — Not only did the surviving corporation succeed to the obligations of an acquired corporation that issued notes of indebtedness as the "Company" under the indenture agreement for the notes, but also to the acquired corporation's rights under the indenture

agreement, which included allowing the surviving corporation to be treated as the "Company" under the continuing director provision of the indenture agreement; thus, the continuing director provision of the indenture agreement was not violated by the merger. *Law Debenture Trust Co. v. Petrohawk Energy Corp., 2007 Del. Ch. LEXIS 113 (Del. Ch. Aug. 1, 2007).*

Realty tax consequences. — Merging retail complex entities were subject to the realty transfer tax, despite not filing a deed for the merger, where the business purpose of the merger was a transfer of assets to a surviving entity (considered to be a sale of the real estate). *Acadia Brandywine Town Ctr., LLC v. New Castle County, — A.2d —, 2004 Del. Super. LEXIS 286 (Del. Super. Ct. Sept. 10, 2004).*

CASE NOTES — OTHER STATES

Illinois

Non-surviving corporation in a merger under Delaware law ceases to exist for the purposes of the laws of Delaware only. *NDC, LLC v. Topinka, 2007 Ill. App. LEXIS 665 (June 15, 2007).*

Iowa

Non-survival of derivative action. — By virtue of a merger derivative rights pass to the surviving corporation and neither the corporation which disappeared in the merger nor its former stockholder may maintain an action thereon. *Berger v. General United Group, Inc., 268 N.W.2d 630 (Iowa 1978).*

Massachusetts

Absorption of old identity. — When a consolidation or merger has taken place, the old corporations have their identity absorbed into that of the new corporation or the one into which they were merged. *Aspinook Corporation v. Commissioner, 326 Mass. 327, 94 N.E.2d 366 (1950).*

Pennsylvania

Amenability to personal jurisdiction. — The action and conduct of a constituent corporation can be attributed to its successor following a merger for the purpose of determining the successor's amenability to personal jurisdiction for the liability of its predecessor. *Simmers v. American Cyanamid Corp., 394 Pa. Super. 464, 576 A.2d 376 (1989).*

Liability. — The surviving corporation in a merger remains liable to the merged corporations' voluntary and involuntary creditors and for their warranties. *Ready Food Products, Inc. v. APV Crepaco, Inc., 28 Phila. 194 (1994).*

Texas

Under Delaware law, a successor may incur liability for its predecessor's torts by expressly or impliedly assuming liability. *Lockheed Martin Corp. v. Gordon, 16 S.W.3d 127 (Tex. App. 2000).*

CASE NOTES — FEDERAL

Second Circuit

Under Delaware law it is settled that the separate corporate existence of a constituent corporation ceases upon merger and the emerging corporation is the only corporation with capacity to be sued and process cannot be served on the constituent corporation. *Sevits v. Mckiernan-Terry Corp., 264 F. Supp. 810 (S.D.N.Y. 1966).*

Under Delaware law, a merged corporation and its stockholders lose the right to sue derivatively. *Voege v. Ackerman, 364 F. Supp. 72 (S.D.N.Y. 1973).*

Under the law of Delaware, once a corporation has been merged out of existence, its rights, privileges and very identity are merged into the remaining corporation. By virtue of a merger, the merged corporation loses its capacity to sue the corporation into which it has been merged, and the stockholders of the merged corporation lose the right to sue derivatively. *Basch v. Talley industries, Inc., 53 F.R.D. 9 (S.D.N.Y. 1971).*

An action cannot be maintained against a corporation that has been merged out of existence. *Damon Alarm Corp. v. American Dist. Tel. Co., 304 F. Supp. 83 (S.D.N.Y. 1969).*

Third Circuit

Any claim of a merged corporation becomes the property of the surviving corporation. *Kanbar v. U.S. Healthcare, Inc., 1989 U.S. Dist. LEXIS 13474 (E.D.Pa. 1989).*

Delaware law requires that a derivative action plaintiff must be a shareholder both at the time of the alleged wrong and at the time of suit. The only exceptions to this rule are: (a) where the merger itself is the subject of a claim of fraud, i.e., where the merger was perpetrated to derive the merged corporation of its claim; or (b) where the merger is in reality a reorganization which does not affect plaintiff's ownership of the business enterprise. The second exception is limited to a merger which is merely a share for share merger with a newly formed holding company, which retained the old company a wholly owned subsidiary of the new holding company with the shareholders of the old company owning all the shares of the new holding company. The structure of the old and new companies is virtually identical. *Kanbar v. U.S. Healthcare, Inc., 1989 U.S. Dist. LEXIS 13474 (E.D.Pa. 1989).*

Under Delaware law, the effect of a merger is that the companies become one corporation and the rights and obligations of each of the constituent corporations continues to exist under the one surviving corporation. *Caciolo v. American Aluminum & Insulation Co., 2004 U.S. Dist. LEXIS 11804 (E.D.Pa. 2004).*

Under Delaware law, the separate corporate existence of a constituent corporation ceases upon merger, and the emerging corporation is the only corporation with capacity to be sued and process cannot be served on the constituent corporation. *Allegany Envtl. Action v. Westinghouse Elec. Corp., 1998 U.S. Dist. LEXIS 1883 (W.D.Pa. 1998).*

Fourth Circuit

Long-arm jurisdiction. — where a predecessor corporation would have been amenable to long-arm jurisdiction in an action on its contract in another state, the surviving merged corporation remains liable to be haled into court in that state in connection with its liability on that contract. *Maryland Nat'l Bank v. Shaffer Stores Co., 240 F. Supp. 777 (D. Md. 1965).*

In general. — Delaware law provides that when there is a merger, any causes of action which might have existed pass by operation of law to the surviving company. *Bunker Ramo-Eltra corp. v. Fairchild Industries, Inc., 639 F. Supp. 409 (D.Md. 1986).*

Sixth Circuit

Maintenance of standing. — in the seminal *Anderson* case, the Delaware supreme court, interpreting relevant statutory provisions of the Delaware corporation law, held that in order to maintain standing, a derivative shareholder must not only be a stockholder at the time of the alleged wrong and at time of commencement of suit but that he must also maintain shareholder status throughout the litigation. That court further clarified that a plaintiff who ceases to be a shareholder, whether by reason of a merger or for any other reason, loses standing to continue a derivative suit. That court recognized but two narrow exceptions to the continuing ownership requirement for standing: (1) where the merger itself is the subject of a claim of fraud, and (2) where the merger is in reality a reorganization which does not affect plaintiff's ownership of the business enterprise. *Prince v. Palmer, 2005 U.S. App. LEXIS 14239 (6th Cir. 2005).*

The *anderson* reorganization exception does not apply to two distinct corporations, each with its own board of directors, officers, assets and stockholders, whose merger was far more than a corporate reshuffling, and which resulted in plaintiffs' possessing property interests distinctly different from that which they held as shareholders of the old corporation. *Prince v. Palmer, 2005 U.S. App. LEXIS 14239 (6th Cir. 2005).*

Seventh Circuit

In Delaware, direct attacks on corporate restructurings may be maintained even after the transaction has been completed. Accordingly, a former shareholder may directly challenge a merger which terminated the shareholder's status, if the merger itself is the subject of a claim of fraud. *Lynch v. Marklin of America, Inc., 724 F. Supp. 595 (N.D.Ill. 1989).*

Delaware courts recognize the "de facto merger" doctrine only in very limited contexts. In only a few instances involving sales of assets have Delaware courts applied the doctrine of de facto merger and only then for the protection of creditors or stockholders who have suffered by reason of failure to comply with the statute governing such sales. *Binder v. Bristol-Myers Squibb, Co., 184 F. Supp. 2d 762 (N.D.Ill. 2001).*

A de facto merger may be found where an asset sale took place that amounted to a merger. *Binder v. Bristol-Myers Squibb, Co., 184 F. Supp. 2d 762 (N.D.Ill. 2001).*

Eighth Circuit

Under Delaware law, it is settled that the separate corporate existence of a constituent corporation ceases upon merger and the emerging corporation is the only corporation with capacity to be sued and process cannot be served on the constituent corporation. *Beam v. Monsanto co., 414 F. Supp. 570 (W.D. Ark. 1976).*

Capacity to sue. — under the law of Delaware, once a corporation has been merged out of existence, its rights, privileges and very identity are merged into the remaining

corporation. By virtue of the merger, the merged corporation loses its capacity to sue the corporation into which it has been merged. *Beam v. Monsanto Co., 414 F. Supp. 570 (W.D. Ark. 1976).*

Premise behind successor liability. — under basic principles of corporation law, when one corporate entity merges into another, the surviving corporation inherits all the rights, powers, and liabilities of the merged corporation. Thus, the entire premise behind successor liability is that the surviving corporation is liable for the acts of the predecessor corporation regardless of any showing of wrongdoing on its part. *Propane Industrial, Inc. v. United States Department of Energy, 1991 U.S. Dist. LEXIS 9014 (W.D.Mo. 1991).*

Tenth Circuit

Effect of consolidation. — A consolidation effects the dissolution of the original corporations and brings into existence a new corporation. Also, upon consolidation being effected under statutory provisions, absent language indicating a contrary intent, the constituent corporations will be deemed to be dissolved and their powers, privileges, and property vested in the consolidated corporation as a new corporation created by the act of consolidation. *Jones v. Noble Drilling Co., 135 f.2d 721 (10th Cir. 1943).*

Eleventh circuit

Sec. 259 does not provide for the cessation of the merged corporation's existence. It is clear that only the separate existence of the constituent corporation ceases to exist, and that all of the property, rights, privileges, powers, and franchises theretofore enjoyed by the nonsurvivor become the property of the survivor. *Vulcan Materials Co. v. United States, 308 F. Supp. 53 (N.D.Ala. 1969).*

The corporation that survives following a merger has primary liability for the predecessor entities' liabilities and obligations. *Driver Logistics Serv. v. United States, 197 F. Supp. 2d 1346 (M.D.Fla. 2002).*

Maintenance of standing. — As a general rule of Delaware law, a derivative shareholder must not only be a stockholder at the time of the alleged wrong and at time of commencement of suit but must also maintain shareholder status throughout the litigation. To the extent their claims are derivative, plaintiffs may have standing under an exception to the general rule where the merger itself is the subject of a claim of fraud. This exception applies when the merger was perpetrated to deprive the corporation on whose behalf the suit is brought of its claim against the individual defendants. *Sturm v. Marriott Marquis Corp., 85 F. Supp. 2d 1356 (n.d.ga. 2000).*

District of Columbia Circuit

A surviving corporation assumes all rights and liabilities of the merged corporation. *Kanuth v. Prescott, Ball & Turben, Inc., 1992 U.S. Dist. LEXIS 3943 (D.D.D.C. 1992).*

Tax Court

A power of attorney is not one of the "rights, privileges, powers and franchises" which survive a merger on the name of the resulting corporation. *Malone & Hyde, Inc., T.C. memo 1992-661 (Tax Ct. 1992).*

§ 260. Powers of corporation surviving or resulting from merger or consolidation; issuance of stock, bonds or other indebtedness

CASE NOTES — OTHER STATES

Kansas

It is not necessary for a corporation to show a "valid corporate purpose" for eliminating minority stockholders. *In re Hesstom Corporation, 254 Kan. 941, 870 P.2d 17 (1994).*

CASE NOTES — FEDERAL

Tenth Circuit

Effect of consolidation. — A consolidation effects the dissolution of the original corporations and brings into existence a new corporation. Also, upon consolidation being effected under statutory provisions, absent language indicating a contrary intent, the constituent corporations will be deemed to be dissolved and their powers, privileges, and property vested in the consolidated corporation as a new corporation created by the act of consolidation. *Jones v. Noble Drilling Co., 135 F.2d 721 (10th Cir. 1943).*

§ 261. Effect of merger upon pending actions

DELAWARE CASE NOTES — REPORTED

Standing of shareholder to maintain derivative suit on behalf of constituent corporation not preserved. — This section does not preserve the standing of a shareholder to maintain a shareholder's derivative suit where, as a result of merger, the plaintiff no longer owns shares in the corporation on whose behalf the suit was brought. *Lewis v. Anderson, 453 A.2d 474 (Del. Ch. 1982), aff'd, 477 A.2d 1040 (Del. 1984).*

DELAWARE CASE NOTES — UNREPORTED

Loss of standing. — A derivative plaintiff must maintain ownership throughout the course of litigation. This section, section 259, and section 327, read individually and collectively, permit one result which is not only consistent but sound: A plaintiff who ceases to be a shareholder, whether by reason of a merger or for any other reason, loses standing to continue a derivative suit. *Strategic Asset Mgmt. v. Nicholson, 2004 Del. Ch. LEXIS 178, No. 20360-NC (November 30, 2004).*

CASE NOTES — OTHER STATES

New York

Accounting for gain not available. — When the relief sought is to set aside a merger and an accounting for a gain, the latter is not available, as its equivalent has been provided for by the right of refusal and having the stock appraised. *Albert v. Salzman, 41 A.D.2d 501, 344 N.Y.S.2d 457 (1973).*

CASE NOTES — FEDERAL

Third Circuit

Maintenance of standing. — Delaware law requires that a derivative action plaintiff must be a shareholder both at the time of the alleged wrong and at the time of suit. The only exceptions to this rule are: (a) where the merger itself is the subject of a claim of fraud, i.e., where the merger was perpetrated to derive the merged corporation of its claim; or (b) where the merger is in reality a reorganization which does not affect plaintiff's ownership of the business enterprise. The second exception is limited to a merger which is merely a share for share merger with a newly formed holding company, which retained the old company a wholly owned subsidiary of the new holding company with the shareholders of the old company owning all the shares of the new holding company. The structure of the old and new companies is virtually identical. *Kanbar v. U.S. Healthcare, Inc., 1989 U.S. Dist. LEXIS 13474 (E.D.Pa. 1989).*

Seventh Circuit

A saving clause for derivative suits provides that any action or proceeding, whether civil, criminal or administrative, pending by or against any corporation which is a party to a merger or consolidation shall be prosecuted as if such merger or consolidation had not taken place, or the corporation surviving or resulting from such merger of consolidation may be substituted in such action or proceeding. The plain purpose of § 261 is to save pending lawsuits. The complaint must be filed by a person who is a shareholder of the corporation on whose behalf the suit is brought, regardless of whether the suit is brought against a corporation or third parties. *Kreindler v. Marx, 85 F.R.D. 612 N.D.Ill. 1979).*

District of Columbia Circuit

An indictment against a corporation is not abated by the merger of the defendant into another corporation. *United States v. Maryland & Virginia Milk Producers, Inc., 145 F. Supp. 374 (D.D.C. 1956).*

Tax Court

A power of attorney is not an "action of proceeding" which continues in force after the merger of the principal into another corporation. *Malone & Hyde, Inc., T.C. Memo 1992-661 (Tax Ct. 1992).*

§ 262. Appraisal rights

DELAWARE CASE NOTES — REPORTED

Purpose. — The primary purpose of this section is to protect the contractual rights of stockholders objecting to a corporate merger. *Root v. York Corp., 28 Del. Ch. 203, 39 A.2d 780 (1944).*

The purpose of the appraisal statute is to replace the stockholder's veto power with a means of withdrawing from the company at a judicially determined price. *Salomon Bros. v. Interstate Bakeries Corp., 576 A.2d 650 (Del. Ch. 1989)Cede & Co. v. Technicolor, Inc., 684 A.2d 289 (Del. 1996).*

The purpose of an appraisal action is not to punish the respondent corporation. The court must only award interest to fairly compensate dissenting shareholders for their losses incurred during the pendency of an appraisal; there is no punitive aspect of an appraisal proceeding. *Rapid-American Corp. v. Harris, 603 A.2d 796 (Del. 1992).*

Legislative intent. — Clearly, there is a legislative intent to fully compensate shareholders for whatever their loss may be, subject only to the narrow limitation that one cannot take speculative effects of the merger into account. *Weinberger v. UOP, Inc., 457 A.2d 701 (Del. 1983).*

An appraisal proceeding is a limited legislative remedy intended to provide shareholders dissenting from a merger on grounds of inadequacy of the offering price with a judicial determination of the intrinsic worth (fair value) of their shareholdings. *Cede & Co. v. Technicolor, Inc., 542 A.2d 1182 (Del. 1988).*

The appraisal remedy is entirely a creature of statute; it is a limited legislative remedy developed initially as a means to compensate shareholders of Delaware corporations for the loss of their common law right to prevent a merger or consolidation by refusal to consent to such transactions. *Alabama By-Products Corp. v. Cede & Co. ex rel. Shearson Lehman Bros., 657 A.2d 254 (Del. 1995).*

Appraisal remedy is intended to provide those shareholders who dissent from a merger on the basis of inadequacy of offering price with an independent judicial determination of the fair value of their shares. *Alabama By-Products Corp. v. Cede & Co. ex rel. Shearson Lehman Bros., 657 A.2d 254 (Del. 1995).*

Liberal construction of the appraisal statute requires the avoidance of complexities in proceedings under it, particularly where the corporation will not be subjected to risks of liability. *In re Northeastern Water Co., 28 Del. Ch. 139, 38 A.2d 918 (1944).*

This section is clearly for the protection of objecting shareholders, and it should be liberally construed to that end. *Schenck v. Salt Dome Oil Corp., 27 Del. Ch. 234, 34 A.2d 249 (1943), rev'd on other grounds, 28 Del. Ch. 433, 41 A.2d 583 (1945), overruled on other grounds, Raynor v.*

LTV Aerospace Corp., 331 A.2d 393 (Del. Ch. 1975); In re Universal Pictures Co., 28 Del. Ch. 72, 37 A.2d 615 (1944).

While this section should be liberally construed for the protection of objecting shareholders, a liberal construction does not call for an abandonment of orderly procedure prescribed by the statute. *In re Northeastern Water Co., 28 Del. Ch. 139, 38 A.2d 918 (1944).*

The design of this section requires the avoidance of complexities in proceedings under it. *Lichtman v. Recognition Equip., Inc., 295 A.2d 771 (Del. Ch. 1972); Kaye v. Pantone, Inc., 395 A.2d 369 (Del. Ch. 1978).*

The requirements of this section are to be liberally construed for the protection of objecting stockholders, within the boundaries of orderly corporate procedures and the purpose of the requirement. *Raab v. Villager Indus., Inc., 355 A.2d 888 (Del.), cert. denied, 429 U.S. 853, 97 S. Ct. 147, 50 L. Ed. 2d 129 (1976).*

Construction of section with § 228 of this title. — Because of the general applicability of § 228 of this title, the absence of specific language regarding written consent in paragraph (b)(1) of this section does not compel the conclusion that the market exception applies only to mergers approved at a meeting of shareholders; § 228 allows approval by written consent for any action which is required to be taken at a meeting of shareholders and thus paragraph (b)(1) of this section need not separately mention written consent for § 228 to apply. *Klotz v. Warner Communications, Inc., 674 A.2d 878 (Del. 1995).*

Construction of section with § 253 of this title. — Despite similarities between the short-form merger procedure and merger approval by written consent, the lack of a paragraph granting appraisal in the latter circumstance is a crucial difference. *Klotz v. Warner Communications, Inc., 674 A.2d 878 (Del. 1995).*

Creditors of a corporation who accepted, but failed to exercise, warrants that entitled them to purchase stock were bound by the plain language of the warrants to the rights set forth therein; therefore, they failed to state a claim against the controlling shareholder, after a short-form merger pursuant to *8 Del. C. § 253*, either for breach of an implied duty of good faith and fair dealing (since their remedies were limited by contract) or for denial of appraisal rights pursuant to *8 Del. C. § 262. Aspen Advisors LLC v. United Artists Theatre Co., 843 A.2d 697 (Del. Ch. 2004), aff'd, 861 A.2d 1251 (Del. 2004).*

Warrantholders whose right to exercise their warrants disappeared when the corporation in which they held the warrants was merged into another, and who could not show that any duty to them was violated by the short-form merger, were properly compensated according to the terms of their warrants by the same value received by other common stockholders, less the cost of exercising their warrants; the right to a statutory appraisal remedy applied only to stockholders, a status that the warrantholders could have held, but, because they had declined to exercise their options, did not hold. *Aspen Advisors LLC v. United Artists Theatre Co., 861 A.2d 1251 (Del. 2004).*

Strict compliance required. — Strict compliance with this section is necessary for a shareholder to withdraw or be dismissed from an appraisal action. *Alabama By-Products Corp. v. Cede & Co. ex rel. Shearson Lehman Bros., 657 A.2d 254 (Del. 1995).*

Scope of section. — This section does not extend appraisal rights if a merger was approved by written consents when the market exception would otherwise apply. *Klotz v. Warner Communications, Inc., 674 A.2d 878 (Del. 1995).*

Applicability of equitable principles. — There is no basis for expanding the limited remedy which is provided for in this section by the invocation of equitable principles. *In re Enstar Corp., 604 A.2d 404 (Del. 1992).*

Purpose of notice requirement. — A Notice of Merger filed pursuant to this section and § 262 of this title is primarily intended to notify the stockholders of action being taken by the parent corporation and to apprise the stockholders of their appraisal remedy. *Zirn v. VLI Corp., 681 A.2d 1050 (Del. 1996).*

Requirements for notice of merger. — The corporation did not comply with the requirements of *8 Del. C. § 262*, because it delayed in mailing notice of the merger to petitioners 17 days beyond the time statutorily permitted, and the notice violated subsection (d)(2) by not including a copy of the appraisal statute. *Borruso v. Communications Telesystems Int'l, 753 A.2d 451 (Del. Ch. 1999).*

Notice of a short-form merger issued immediately after the conclusion of a hotly contested tender offer did not satisfy the parent company's fiduciary duty of disclosure when that notice contained merely the statutorily mandated information about the mechanics of perfecting a demand for appraisal and no other information relating to the value of the merged entity or its securities; even when adequate, current information is found in the total mix of publicly available information, the fiduciary duty of disclosure requires that a notice of short-form merger either be accompanied by detailed disclosures, or disclose summary financial information that adequately advises stockholders where and how to obtain more detailed information. *Gilliland v. Motorola, Inc., 859 A.2d 80 (Del. Ch. 2004).*

Authority to reform settlement agreement premised upon unilateral mistake. — The provision in this section which gives the Court of Chancery authority to impose "just terms" as a condition of its approval of a statutory appraisal proceeding, does not give it authority to reform a settlement agreement that was premised upon a unilateral mistake. *In re Enstar Corp., 604 A.2d 404 (Del. 1992).*

Cases decided under this section must be considered in determining stockholders' rights. *In re*

Delaware Racing Ass'n, 42 Del. Ch. 175, 206 A.2d 664, aff'd, *42 Del. Ch. 406, 213 A.2d 203 (1965).*

Comparative acquisition approach held proper. — The Court of Chancery acted in accordance with the parameters of this section by making a per share value determination of a company on the basis of a comparative approach applied by an expert, using the premia that he attributed to the company's controlling interests in two subsidiaries. *M.G. Bancorporation, Inc. v. Le Beau, 737 A.2d 513 (Del. 1999).*

This section furnishes orderly method for withdrawal from corporation by shareholders who dissent from a merger or consolidation. *Loeb v. Schenley Indus., Inc., 285 A.2d 829 (Del. Ch. 1971).*

Availability of appraisal rights should be taken into account as factor in assessing whether transaction is entirely fair, even though its existence alone is insufficient to establish that the transaction is fair. *Tanzer v. International Gen. Indus., Inc., 402 A.2d 382 (Del. Ch. 1979).*

Right to appraisal is given by this section. By this section, a stockholder is required to comply with certain prescribed conditions precedent before his or her right to an appraisal and payment can arise. These conditions must be satisfied before the right to payment arises: If there is no right to payment, there can be no right to an appraisal. *Stephenson v. Commonwealth & S. Corp., 18 Del. Ch. 91, 156 A. 215 (1931),* aff'd, *19 Del. Ch. 447, 168 A. 211 (1933).*

The appraisal right is given to the stockholder in compensation for the stockholder's former right at common law to prevent a merger. *Heilbrunn v. Sun Chem. Corp., 38 Del. Ch. 321, 150 A.2d 755 (1959).*

A dissenting stockholder has an absolute right to an appraisal. *Felder v. Anderson, Clayton & Co., 39 Del. Ch. 76, 159 A.2d 278 (1960); Kaye v. Pantone, Inc., 395 A.2d 369 (Del. Ch. 1978).*

The right to an appraisal in a merger proceeding is entirely a creature of statute. *Loeb v. Schenley Indus., Inc., 285 A.2d 829 (Del. Ch. 1971); Kaye v. Pantone, Inc., 395 A.2d 369 (Del. Ch. 1978).*

The right to appraisal is purely statutory. It is limited to stockholders of the merged corporation. *Lichtman v. Recognition Equip., Inc., 295 A.2d 771 (Del. Ch. 1972).*

The right of a dissentient to appraisal is perfected by compliance with the statutory requirements of written objection to the merger and demand for payment of the value of the dissentient's shares. *Lichtman v. Recognition Equip., Inc., 295 A.2d 771 (Del. Ch. 1972).*

The statutory right of appraisal is given the shareholder as compensation for the abrogation of the common-law rule that a single shareholder could block a merger. *Francis I. duPont & Co. v. Universal City Studios, Inc., 343 A.2d 629 (Del. Ch. 1975); Kaye v. Pantone, Inc., 395 A.2d 369 (Del. Ch. 1978).*

Stockholders objecting to merger are entitled to preserve their statutory rights to an appraisal of the intrinsic value of their shares. *Weinberger v. United Fin. Corp., 405 A.2d 134 (Del. Ch. 1979).*

The right to an appraisal is limited to stockholders of the merged corporations. *Kaye v. Pantone, Inc., 395 A.2d 369 (Del. Ch. 1978).*

An appraisal decision will be overturned only if the trial court abused its discretion. *Rapid-American Corp. v. Harris, 603 A.2d 796 (Del. 1992).*

A court abuses its discretion in an appraisal proceeding when its factual findings do not have record support, and its valuation is not the result of an orderly and logical deductive process. *Rapid-American Corp. v. Harris, 603 A.2d 796 (Del. 1992).*

When inadequate cash price per share is the basis for objection to a corporate merger, the remedy of the dissatisfied shareholders is to seek an appraisal of the value of their shares pursuant to the procedures set forth under this section. *Singer v. Magnavox Co., 367 A.2d 1349 (Del. Ch. 1976),* aff'd in part and rev'd in part, *380 A.2d 969 (Del. 1977).*

Analogy to eminent domain. — The power of a stockholder majority to override minority dissenters and remit to them the cash appraisal remedy is analogous to the right of eminent domain. *Francis I. duPont & Co. v. Universal City Studios, Inc., 343 A.2d 629 (Del. Ch. 1975).*

An appraisal is a method of paying a shareholder for taking the shareholder's property. *Francis I. duPont & Co. v. Universal City Studios, Inc., 343 A.2d 629 (Del. Ch. 1975).*

An appraisal under this section is a method for compensating a stockholder for the involuntary taking of the shareholder's property. *Kaye v. Pantone, Inc., 395 A.2d 369 (Del. Ch. 1978).*

Stockholder's status is expressly defined in an appraisal proceeding. The stockholder has lost for the time being all the substantial rights of a stockholder — the right to vote, the right to receive dividends, and the right to receive any distribution upon the shares. The shareholder's status is primarily that of a monetary claimant against the consolidated or surviving corporation, and is more nearly analogous to that of a creditor than to that of a stockholder. *Southern Prod. Co. v. Sabath, 32 Del. Ch. 497, 87 A.2d 128 (1952).*

The effect of an appraisal action is to convert the status of the plaintiffs therein from that of stockholders of the corporation to that of creditors thereof. *Braasch v. Goldschmidt, 41 Del. Ch. 519, 199 A.2d 760 (1964); Kaye v. Pantone, Inc., 395 A.2d 369 (Del. Ch. 1978).*

Unregistered stockholder may not dissent from merger and demand appraisal of his or her stock. *Salt Dome Oil Corp. v. Schenck, 28 Del. Ch. 433, 41 A.2d 583 (1945); American Hdwe. Corp. v. Savage Arms Corp., 37 Del. Ch. 59, 136 A.2d 690 (1957); Coyne v. Schenley Indus., Inc., 38 Del. Ch. 535, 155 A.2d 238 (1959); Olivetti Underwood Corp. v. Jacques Coe & Co., 42 Del. Ch. 588, 217 A.2d 683 (1966); Carl M. Loeb, Rhoades & Co. v. Hilton Hotels Corp., 43 Del. Ch. 206, 222 A.2d 789 (1966).*

Registered holder must be presumed to be "stockholder." — Where there are no facts indicating that a person was not within the statutory classification of this section, unless such facts appear, such person, as a registered holder, must be presumed to be a "stockholder."

In re Universal Pictures Co., 28 Del. Ch. 72, 37 A.2d 615 (1944), overruled on other grounds in *Raynor v. LTV Aerospace Corp., 331 A.2d 393 (Del. Ch. 1975).*

Purchase of stock with notice of contested transaction. — The term "stockholder" as used in this section should not be construed to exclude one who purchases with notice of the contested transaction. *Salomon Bros. v. Interstate Bakeries Corp., 576 A.2d 650 (Del. Ch. 1989).*

The right to appraisal is not lost for the reason that the stockholder purchased those shares after the terms of a merger had been announced. *Salomon Bros. v. Interstate Bakeries Corp., 576 A.2d 650 (Del. Ch. 1989).*

Persons whose shares are held in "street" or nominee names are not "stockholders of record." *Enstar Corp. v. Senouf, 535 A.2d 1351 (Del. 1987).*

Where shares of publicly traded corporations are held in the name of brokers or fiduciaries (commonly called "street name") for the account of the beneficial owners, the brokers or fiduciaries are the stockholders of record. *Berlin v. Emerald Partners, 552 A.2d 482 (Del. 1988).*

Obligation of corporation under section. — A corporation of this State, engaged in proceedings under this section, shall have an obligation to issue specific instructions to its stockholders as to the correct manner of executing and filing a valid demand under this section. As a general rule in the future, failure by the corporation to furnish such instructions will result in the resolution in favor of the stockholder of all doubt as to the sufficiency, for corporate purposes, of the demand. *Raab v. Villager Indus., Inc., 355 A.2d 888 (Del.),* cert. denied, *429 U.S. 853, 97 S. Ct. 147, 50 L. Ed. 2d 129 (1976); Tabbi v. Pollution Control Indus., Inc., 508 A.2d 867 (Del. Ch. 1986),* overruled on other grounds, *535 A.2d 1351 (Del. 1987).*

General assembly has expressly granted appraisal right only under the merger statutes and not under the sale of assets statutes. This difference in treatment of the rights of dissenting stockholders may well have been deliberate in order to allow even greater freedom of action to corporate majorities in arranging combinations than is possible under the merger statutes. *Hariton v. Arco Elecs., Inc., 40 Del. Ch. 326, 182 A.2d 22 (1962),* aff'd, *41 Del. Ch. 74, 188 A.2d 123 (1963).*

Appraisal unnecessary in purchase of fractional shares. — Supreme court agreed that *8* Del. *C.* § 155 permitted the corporation, as part of a reverse-forward stock split, to treat its stockholders unequally by cashing out the stockholders who owned only fractional interests while opting not to dispose of fractional interests of stockholders who held more than one share of stock after the reverse split; the use of a 10-day average stock market trading price fulfilled the fair price requirement of § 155 (as a fair compromise to guard against price fluctuation risk), making an appraisal similar to that required under this section unnecessary since the corporation's stock was widely held and actively traded. *Applebaum v. Avaya, Inc., 812 A.2d 880 (Del. 2002).*

Court of chancery is given general control over appraisal in a proceeding in the nature of a class suit, to which the corporation and all dissenting stockholders are made parties and in which they are subjected to the jurisdiction of the Court. *Southern Prod. Co. v. Sabath, 32 Del. Ch. 497, 87 A.2d 128 (1952); Raynor v. LTV Aerospace Corp., 317 A.2d 43 (Del. Ch. 1974).*

Powers given by this section are not within inherent jurisdiction of court of chancery. — The rights and powers given by this section are in no sense declaratory of the ancient equity jurisdiction of the English Court of Chancery, and are not within the original inherent jurisdiction of this Court of Chancery; they are additional powers given by the General Assembly, pursuant to Art. IV, § 20, *Del. Const. Schenck v. Salt Dome Oil Corp., 27 Del. Ch. 234, 34 A.2d 249 (1943),* rev'd on other grounds, *28 Del. Ch. 433, 41 A.2d 583 (1945).*

Under certain circumstances chancellor's power to fashion appropriate relief is broad. — Under certain circumstances, particularly where fraud, misrepresentation, self-dealing, deliberate waste of corporate assets or gross and palpable overreaching are involved, the chancellor's powers are complete to fashion any form of equitable and monetary relief as may be appropriate, including rescissory damages. *Weinberger v. UOP, Inc., 457 A.2d 701 (Del. 1983).*

Chancellor's discretion is not limited to single remedial formula for monetary damages in cash-out merger. *Weinberger v. UOP, Inc., 457 A.2d 701 (Del. 1983).*

Issues, parties, etc., to action. — In an appraisal action, the only litigable issue is the determination of the value of the appraisal petitioners' shares on the date of the merger, the only party defendant is the surviving corporation and the only relief available is a judgment against the surviving corporation for the fair value of the dissenters' shares. *Cede & Co. v. Technicolor, Inc., 542 A.2d 1182 (Del. 1988).*

Claims of wrongdoing. — The court correctly denied the motion to amend and enlarge the appraisal action to include a claim for rescissory relief for conspiracy, illegality, fraud, and breach of fiduciary duty, as a determination of fair value does not involve an inquiry into claims of wrongdoing in the merger. *Cede & Co. v. Technicolor, Inc., 542 A.2d 1182 (Del. 1988).*

A fraud action asserting fair dealing and fair price claims affords an expansive remedy and is brought against the alleged wrongdoers to provide whatever relief the facts of a particular case may require and the approach to determining relief may be the same as that employed in determining fair value; however, an appraisal action may not provide a complete remedy for unfair dealing or fraud because a damage award in a fraud action may include "rescissory damages if the [trier of fact] considers them susceptible of proof and a remedy appropriate to all issues of fairness before him." *Cede & Co. v. Technicolor, Inc., 542 A.2d 1182 (Del. 1988).*

Where the wrongdoing alleged by minority stockholder in his stock appraisal action under this section directly related to the fair value of his stock, and not to the validity of the merger itself; the claim was more personal than derivative, and the corporate opportunity claim was properly asserted in the § 262 proceeding. *Cavalier Oil Corp. v. Harnett, 564 A.2d 1137 (Del. 1989).*

A company was entitled to summary judgment in an action by minority shareholders seeking appraisal rights, because the issue of whether shares beneficially owned by one of the minority shareholders through the company's employee stock option plan (ESOP) should have been eligible for appraisal was beyond the proper scope of relief where the shareholder conceded that no appraisal demand was made for ESOP shares; whether the employer breached its fiduciary duty as trustee was essentially between the employee as beneficial holder and the employer as record holder of the stock. *Union Ill. 1995 Inv. L.P. v. Union Fin. Group, Ltd., 847 A.2d 340 (Del. Ch. 2003).*

This section does not preclude stockholders from exercising tactical options, such as the partial withdrawal of shares by a beneficial holder who did not vote any shares in favor of a merger; therefore, a shareholder who did what it could to stop a merger by voting all of its shares against it, but hedged its bets on an appraisal award by withdrawing some of the its shares from the subsequent appraisal, was entitled to summary judgment on the issue of the validity of its attempt to withdraw only a portion of its shares. *Union Ill. 1995 Inv. L.P. v. Union Fin. Group, Ltd., 847 A.2d 340 (Del. Ch. 2003).*

Formality and legal technicality required of demand. — A demand under this section requires the formality and legal technicality befitting a last step in the final transaction between the corporation and its dissenting stockholder. *Raab v. Villager Indus., Inc., 355 A.2d 888 (Del.),* cert. denied, *429 U.S. 853, 97 S. Ct. 147, 50 L. Ed. 2d 129 (1976).*

Corporation, like stockholder, is given right to initiate proceeding and bring the stockholder into court for the purpose of appraising his or her stock. *Southern Prod. Co. v. Sabath, 32 Del. Ch. 497, 87 A.2d 128 (1952).*

A determination of the value of corporate stock may be commenced by the surviving corporation or any stockholder who timely demands an appraisal. *Kaye v. Pantone, Inc., 395 A.2d 369 (Del. Ch. 1978).*

This section provides for payment of cash as well as securities to an objecting stockholder. *In re Delaware Racing Ass'n, 42 Del. Ch. 175, 206 A.2d 664,* aff'd, *42 Del. Ch. 406, 213 A.2d 203 (1965).*

This section purports to furnish exclusive remedy to a dissenting shareholder and is to be distinguished from a stockholder's common-law right to seek to have a merger enjoined. *Loeb v. Schenley Indus., Inc., 285 A.2d 829 (Del. Ch. 1971).* But see *Andra v. Blount, 772 A.2d 183 (Del. Ch. 2000).*

Not exclusive remedy. — Nothing in this section expressly states that appraisal is an exclusive remedy. *Andra v. Blount, 772 A.2d 183 (Del. Ch. 2000).* But see *Loeb v. Schenley Indus., Inc., 285 A.2d 829 (Del. Ch. 1971).*

Proof establishing right to appraisal. — Since stockholders are given an absolute right to proceed under this section, proof that they have complied with its requirements is enough to establish their right to an appraisal. *Kaye v. Pantone, Inc., 395 A.2d 369 (Del. Ch. 1978).*

Parties entitled to participate. — Once an appraisal action is commenced, all stockholders who have demanded an appraisal are entitled to participate in the proceedings and awards. *Kaye v. Pantone, Inc., 395 A.2d 369 (Del. Ch. 1978).*

Dissenting shareholders are not entitled to preliminary determination by court. — Dissenting stockholders who elect to have their shares appraised are required to await the outcome of the statutory scheme before receiving payment for their shares with interest and are not entitled to have the court make a preliminary determination (without benefit of an appraiser's report) fixing a minimum value for their shares and ordering the payment of such value pending formal appraisal. *Loeb v. Schenley Indus., Inc., 285 A.2d 829 (Del. Ch. 1971).*

Persons no longer record stockholders at merger date. — Persons who were record stockholders as of the record date for the vote on the merger, and who filed a timely demand for appraisal, but who were no longer stockholders of record as of the merger date were not entitled to appraisal. *Tabbi v. Pollution Control Indus., Inc., 508 A.2d 867 (Del. Ch. 1986),* overruled on other grounds, *535 A.2d 1351 (Del. 1987).*

A valid demand must be executed by or on behalf of the holder of record, whether that holder is the beneficial owner, a trustee, agent or nominee. *Enstar Corp. v. Senouf, 535 A.2d 1351 (Del. 1987).*

Signatures required for demand. — A demand under this section must be properly and formally signed by or for all stockholders of record. *Raab v. Villager Indus., Inc., 355 A.2d 888 (Del.),* cert. denied, *429 U.S. 853, 97 S. Ct. 147, 50 L. Ed. 2d 129 (1976).*

As a general proposition dissenting stockholders are put to election by this section. *Cole v. National Cash Credit Ass'n, 18 Del. Ch. 47, 156 A. 183 (1931).*

A stockholder objecting to a merger or consolidation may withdraw from the enterprise and obtain payment in money for the value of his or her stock by following the procedure prescribed by the statute. As a general proposition dissenting stockholders are thus put to an election by the statute. *Porges v. Vadsco Sales Corp., 27 Del. Ch. 127, 32 A.2d 148 (1943).*

The objectant to a merger has an election of remedies. He or she may dissent and then receive in the manner fixed by the statute the value of his or her stock, or, if no dissent, then he or she is bound by the merger. *Langfelder v. Universal Lab., Inc., 68 F. Supp. 209 (D. Del. 1946),* aff'd, *163 F.2d 804 (3d Cir. 1947).*

Upon the completion of the steps required to perfect the right to appraisal, the stockholder has made an election to withdraw from the corporate enterprise and take the value of his or her stock. *Southern Prod. Co. v. Sabath, 32 Del. Ch. 497, 87 A.2d 128 (1952); Lichtman v. Recognition Equip., Inc., 295 A.2d 771 (Del. Ch. 1972).*

Estoppel. — When an informed minority shareholder either votes in favor of the merger, or accepts the benefits of the transaction, he or she cannot thereafter attack its fairness. *Bershad v. Curtiss-Wright Corp., 535 A.2d 840 (Del. 1987).*

Choice of remedies. — Stockholders should not have been required to elect between the statutory right to an appraisal and the opportunity to litigate the allegation of fraud in the merger although they may not recover duplicative judgments. *Cede & Co. v. Technicolor, Inc., 542 A.2d 1182 (Del. 1988).*

Exercise of statutory right of merger is always subject to nullification for fraud. *Cole v. National Cash Credit Ass'n, 18 Del. Ch. 47, 156 A. 183 (1931).*

There are exceptional circumstances under which a stockholder is not obliged to make an election to accept the merger or to demand the value of his or her stock in money, but may enlist the aid of a court of equity to restrain the consummation of the merger. The exercise of the statutory right of merger is always subject to nullification for fraud. *Porges v. Vadsco Sales Corp., 27 Del. Ch. 127, 32 A.2d 148 (1943).*

Business purpose requirement rule abrogated. — In view of the fairness test which has long been applicable to parent-subsidiary mergers, the expanded appraisal remedy now available to shareholders, and the broad discretion of the chancellor to fashion such relief as the facts of a given case may dictate, no additional meaningful protection is afforded minority shareholders by the business purpose requirement of the trilogy of *Singer v. Magnavox Co., Del. Supr., 380 A.2d 969 (1977); Tanzer v. International Gen. Indus., Inc., Del. Supr., 379 A.2d 1121 (1977); Roland Int'l Corp. v. Najjar, Del. Supr., 407 A.2d 1032 (1979),* and their progeny, accordingly, such requirement shall no longer be of any force or effect. *Weinberger v. UOP, Inc., 457 A.2d 701 (Del. 1983).*

This section does not require corporation to state its position or defenses in petition or stockholder's list. *In re Universal Pictures Co., 28 Del. Ch. 72, 37 A.2d 615 (1944),* overruled on other grounds in *Raynor v. LTV Aerospace Corp., 331 A.2d 393 (Del. Ch. 1975).*

Disclosure of persons claiming appraisal rights. — For the protection of dissenting stockholders, a corporation should be expected to make full disclosure of all persons who claim appraisal rights and of all documents received which might possibly be deemed to constitute objections and demands, but to ask for that kind of disclosure, and at the same time to lean toward a construction of the disclosures as admissions of legal sufficiency of the acts of the claimants would seem most inconsistent. *In re Universal Pictures Co., 28 Del. Ch. 72, 37 A.2d 615 (1944),* overruled on other grounds in *Raynor v. LTV Aerospace Corp., 331 A.2d 393 (Del. Ch. 1975).*

Request of appraisal relinquishes ownership rights. — A shareholder who elects to seek an appraisal rather than accept the terms of the merger loses the traditional benefits of stock ownership: the right to vote stock and to receive payment of dividends or other distribution upon the shares. *Alabama By-Products Corp. v. Cede & Co. ex rel. Shearson Lehman Bros., 657 A.2d 254 (Del. 1995).*

Stockholder need not vote against the proposed merger in order to qualify for an appraisal. *Lewis v.*

Corroon & Reynolds Corp., 30 Del. Ch. 200, 57 A.2d 632 (1948).

But he or she must not vote in favor of merger if he or she intends to qualify for an appraisal of his or her shares. *Lewis v. Corroon & Reynolds Corp., 30 Del. Ch. 200, 57 A.2d 632 (1948).*

Appraisal is ordinary remedy. — Although a plaintiff's remedy in response to a successful challenge to a merger transaction should ordinarily be confined to an appraisal, in cases where fraud, misrepresentation, self-dealing, deliberate waste of corporate assets, or gross and palpable overreaching exists, appraisal might well be inadequate. *Joseph v. Shell Oil Co., 498 A.2d 1117 (Del. Ch. 1985).*

Stockholder may split vote and apply for appraisal as to some of his or her shares. — With respect to the majority stockholders, no disadvantage is occasioned to them if a stockholder is permitted to split his or her vote and apply for appraisal as to some of his or her shares. *Colonial Realty Corp. v. Reynolds Metals Co., 40 Del. Ch. 515, 185 A.2d 754 (1962), aff'd, 190 A.2d 752 (Del. 1963).*

It certainly cannot be said that the statute expressly, or by unavoidable intendment, disqualifies a stockholder who has voted some of his or her shares in favor of a merger from seeking an appraisal of other shares as to which he or she has fully complied with the statutory requirements. *Colonial Realty Corp. v. Reynolds Metals Co., 40 Del. Ch. 515, 185 A.2d 754 (1962), aff'd, 190 A.2d 752 (Del. 1963).*

Claimant cannot subsequently split holdings to seek appraisal of portion. — A claimant who has demanded of the surviving corporation payment of the value of his or her shares may not subsequently split his or her holdings to seek appraisal of a portion only. *Lichtman v. Recognition Equip., Inc., 295 A.2d 771 (Del. Ch. 1972).*

Late filing of claim. — If a "late" filing of a claim for appraisal of stock will not unduly interfere with the orderly procedure of appraisal, the court should permit the claim to be filed, unless there is evidence of bad faith. *Jacques Coe & Co. v. Minneapolis-Moline Co., 32 Del. Ch. 1, 84 A.2d 815 (1949).*

Burden of proof of compliance with statutory requirements is on stockholder claiming right to appraisal. *In re Hilton Hotels Corp., 42 Del. Ch. 283, 210 A.2d 185, aff'd, 43 Del. Ch. 206, 222 A.2d 789 (1965).*

Primary purpose of requiring written communication by stockholder prior to meeting called to vote upon the proposed merger is to inform the corporation and other stockholders of the number of possible dissenters and, as such, potential demandants of cash for their shares. *In re Zeeb, 32 Del. Ch. 486, 87 A.2d 123 (1952); Colonial Realty Corp. v. Reynolds Metals Co., 40 Del. Ch. 515, 185 A.2d 754 (1962), aff'd, 190 A.2d 752 (Del. 1963).*

No presumption as to the time of delivery will be raised. *In re Hilton Hotels Corp., 42 Del. Ch. 283, 210 A.2d 185, aff'd, 43 Del. Ch. 206, 222 A.2d 789 (1965).*

Action by stockholder's agent. — *See In re Zeeb, 32 Del. Ch. 486, 87 A.2d 123 (1952).*

Stockholder's written communication must have been made before vote on the consolidation agreement had been taken. *Stephenson v. Commonwealth & S. Corp., 19 Del. Ch. 447, 168 A. 211 (1933).*

And it need not be artfully worded. *In re Atlas Powder Co., 32 Del. Ch. 14, 78 A.2d 1 (1951), rev'd on other grounds, 32 Del. Ch. 486, 87 A.2d 123 (1952).*

But it must be reasonably absolute. *In re Atlas Powder Co., 32 Del. Ch. 14, 78 A.2d 1 (1951), rev'd on other grounds, 32 Del. Ch. 486, 87 A.2d 123 (1952).*

Where stock is held by husband and wife as tenants by the entirety, rights must be exercised jointly by the husband and wife, and the actions prescribed by this section are defective where the wife did not join in them. *In re Northeastern Water Co., 28 Del. Ch. 139, 38 A.2d 918 (1944).*

A demand signed by 1 spouse alone, who does not purport to act for the other spouse therein, is inadequate to cover the stock held by them as joint owners and is therefore invalid. *Raab v. Villager Indus., Inc., 355 A.2d 888 (Del.), cert. denied, 429 U.S. 853, 97 S. Ct. 147, 50 L. Ed. 2d 129 (1976).*

Demand letter which was not delivered until morning of stockholders' meeting was untimely, and did not entitle the shareholders who sent it to an appraisal. *Tabbi v. Pollution Control Indus., Inc., 508 A.2d 867 (Del. Ch. 1986), overruled on other grounds, 535 A.2d 1351 (Del. 1987).*

Burden of proving timely delivery of demand. — When controverted, the claimants have the burden of proving timely delivery of their demand. *Raab v. Villager Indus., Inc., 355 A.2d 888 (Del.), cert. denied, 429 U.S. 853, 97 S. Ct. 147, 50 L. Ed. 2d 129 (1976).*

Minority stockholder's rejection of offer held to be demand for appraisal. — Where a minority stockholder explicitly rejected a $ 150 per share offer from majority stockholders perfecting a merger under § 253 of this title, this was a demand for the only available alternative under this section. *Bell v. Kirby Lumber Corp., 413 A.2d 137 (Del. 1980).*

Statutory formalities for dissent have been strictly enforced. *Lutz v. A.L. Garber Co., 340 A.2d 186 (Del. Ch. 1974), aff'd, 340 A.2d 188 (Del. 1975).*

Right of appraisal granted to dissenting shareholders preempted by Subchapter III of Chapter 113 of Interstate Commerce Act (49 U.S.C. § 11341 et seq.). — See *Bruno v. Western Pac. R.R., 498 A.2d 171 (Del. Ch. 1985), aff'd, 508 A.2d 72 (Del. 1986), cert. denied, 482 U.S. 927, 107 S. Ct. 3209, 96 L. Ed. 2d 696 (1987).*

Section contemplates determination of stockholders entitled to appraisal remedy. — Only after hearing shall the Court of Chancery determine the stockholders who have complied with the provisions of this section and become entitled to the valuation of and payment for their shares. *Raynor v. LTV Aerospace Corp., 317 A.2d 43 (Del. Ch. 1974).*

This section does not require the Court of Chancery to determine which stockholders have perfected their right to the appraisal remedy until after a hearing. *Raynor v. LTV Aerospace Corp., 317 A.2d 43 (Del. Ch. 1974).*

Only 1 petition is necessary to require the court of chancery to hold a hearing. *Raynor v. LTV Aerospace Corp., 317 A.2d 43 (Del. Ch. 1974).*

This section has been recognized as providing a single procedure in which all the dissenting stockholders who have perfected their right to appraisal will participate. *Raynor v. LTV Aerospace Corp., 317 A.2d 43 (Del. Ch. 1974).*

To require each dissenting stockholder to file his or her own separate petition would be unwieldy and unreasonable. *Raynor v. LTV Aerospace Corp., 317 A.2d 43 (Del. Ch. 1974).*

Once a petition is filed, other dissenting stockholders had a right to rely on the language of this section and believe that their stock would be valued in the appraisal proceeding. *Raynor v. LTV Aerospace Corp., 317 A.2d 43 (Del. Ch. 1974).*

Those dissenting stockholders who are not petitioners will not be deprived of their rights under this section simply because they have apparently decided to "go along for the ride." *Raynor v. LTV Aerospace Corp., 317 A.2d 43 (Del. Ch. 1974).*

Filing date not extended merely because resulting corporation not shown prejudiced. — It is neither the policy of this State nor the intention of the General Assembly to extend the filing date merely because there is no showing of prejudice to the resulting corporation. To so hold would defeat the orderly procedure which this section sets forth. *Schneyer v. Shenandoah Oil Corp., 316 A.2d 570 (Del. Ch. 1974).*

The resulting or surviving corporation need not, as an element to its defense of the statutory filing period, produce evidence that it has suffered prejudice. *Schneyer v. Shenandoah Oil Corp., 316 A.2d 570 (Del. Ch. 1974).*

Key date for fixing both liability and damages is date of merger. *Francis I. duPont & Co. v. Universal City Studios, Inc., 343 A.2d 629 (Del. Ch. 1975).*

While a certain amount of retrospective analysis and backdating are required, the whole statutory scheme is keyed to the date of the merger because that is the date on which the shareholder's property is taken. *Francis I. duPont & Co. v. Universal City Studios, Inc., 343 A.2d 629 (Del. Ch. 1975).*

Shareholders have burden of establishing their right to appraisal. *Schneyer v. Shenandoah Oil Corp., 316 A.2d 570 (Del. Ch. 1974).*

Perfected claim for appraisal not lost. — Once a shareholder perfects the right to appraisal, the shareholder's status is transformed from that of an equity owner of the corporation to that of a quasi-creditor with a monetary claim against the surviving corporation; this change of status can be reversed only if the shareholder satisfies one of the express statutory conditions. *Alabama By-Products Corp. v. Cede & Co. ex rel. Shearson Lehman Bros., 657 A.2d 254 (Del. 1995).*

Orderliness and certainty of appraisal proceeding are to be maintained even though this section is construed liberally in favor of the shareholder. *Schneyer v. Shenandoah Oil Corp., 316 A.2d 570 (Del. Ch. 1974).*

There is nothing which would authorize the Court to depart from the general rules developed to govern appraisal proceedings simply because of the nature of the corporate enterprise. *Bell v. Kirby Lumber Corp., 395 A.2d 730 (Del. Ch. 1978), modified, 413 A.2d 137 (Del. 1980).*

Where period for demanding appraisal expires on Sunday. — Where the period in which a shareholder may petition the Court of Chancery for a determination of the value of the stock of all such shareholders expires on a Sunday, the statutory period for filing a petition does not toll until the following day. *Schneyer v. Shenandoah Oil Corp., 316 A.2d 570 (Del. Ch. 1974).*

Value of stock. — It is the value of the stock that is considered the damage principal for the purpose of the award. *Francis I. duPont & Co. v. Universal City Studios, Inc., 343 A.2d 629 (Del. Ch. 1975).*

It is stock that is the property subject to the taking and it is the value of the stock which constitutes the measure of the statutory recovery by the judgment. *Francis I. duPont & Co. v. Universal City Studios, Inc., 343 A.2d 629 (Del. Ch. 1975).*

The sole issue raised by an action seeking an appraisal should be the value of the dissenting stockholder's stock. *Kaye v. Pantone, Inc., 395 A.2d 369 (Del. Ch. 1978).*

Fair value measures that which has been taken from the shareholder; a proportionate interest in a going concern. In the appraisal process the corporation is valued as an entity, not merely as a collection of assets, or by the sum of the market price of each share of its stock. The corporation must be viewed as an on-going enterprise, occupying a particular market position in the light of future prospects. *In re Shell Oil Co., 607 A.2d 1213 (Del. 1992).*

Evidence supported Court of Chancery's valuation conclusions. *In re Shell Oil Co., 607 A.2d 1213 (Del. 1992).*

In an appraisal action to determine the fair value of dissenting shareholders' stock in a company, the chancery court determined that the fair value of the stock was almost half of that sought by the dissenting shareholders because it was based on the value of the merger, which was the best evidence of fair value where there was no evidence that the board of the company sought to achieve anything other than the highest possible value, minus synergies, to account for the company being valued as a going concern. *Union Ill. 1995 Inv. L.P. v. Union Fin. Group, Ltd., 847 A.2d 340 (Del. Ch. 2003).*

More liberal approach to stock valuation must include proof of value by any techniques or methods which are generally considered acceptable in the financial community and otherwise admissible in court, subject only to the court's interpretation of subsection (h) of this section. *Weinberger v. UOP, Inc., 457 A.2d 701 (Del. 1983).*

The scope of the Chancellor's inquiry into fair value is limited only by the express exclusion of any element of value arising from the accomplishment or expectation of the merger, and the *Rules of Evidence. In re Shell Oil Co., 607 A.2d 1213 (Del. 1992).*

Approach used to value shares in determining fairness of merger is no different than that employed in an appraisal proceeding under this section. *Weinberger*

Corporations

v. UOP, Inc., 426 A.2d 1333 (Del. Ch. 1981), rev'd on other grounds, *457 A.2d 701 (Del. 1983)*, aff'd, *497 A.2d 792 (Del. 1985)*.

Cost of equity. — Providing an estimate of the cost of equity for an acquiring company is a practice that is not acceptable when valuing a company as a stand-alone entity under this section. *Gilbert v. MPM Enters., Inc., 709 A.2d 663 (Del. Ch. 1997)*.

Evidence of post-merger offers for stock valuation. — Evidence of post-merger offers were not admissible as valid indications of merger-date fair value because they were not known or susceptible of proof as of the date of the merger, but instead arose from the accomplishment or expectation of the merger. *Kahn v. Household Acquisition Corp., 591 A.2d 166 (Del. 1991)*.

Terms of certificate of designation. — Properly expressed terms of a certificate of designation of preferred stock may establish the consideration to which holders of the stock will be entitled in the event of a merger and, when the documents creating the security do so, that the amount so fixed or determined constitutes the "fair value" of the stock for the purposes of dissenters' rights under this section. *In re Ford Holdings, Inc. Preferred Stock, 698 A.2d 973 (Del. Ch. 1997)*.

A prior version of this section gave appraiser great latitude in seeking evidence from which he or she could ascertain the value of the shares to be appraised. *In re General Realty & Utils. Corp., 29 Del. Ch. 480, 52 A.2d 6 (1947)*.

In a proceeding under this section the appraiser was free to ascertain evidence of value apart from that supplied him by the parties. *In re General Realty & Utils. Corp., 29 Del. Ch. 480, 52 A.2d 6 (1947)*.

In an appraisal proceeding, because of its purpose of placing a true, intrinsic value on the shares of corporate stock, the appraiser should not be deprived by any party of the opportunity to consider materials which the appraiser feels to be relevant. *Bell v. Kirby Lumber Corp., 395 A.2d 730 (Del. Ch. 1978)*, modified, *413 A.2d 137 (Del. 1980)*.

And he is not bound to accept appraisal report. — The appraiser, in carrying out his or her duty to make a valuation of the stock, is not bound to accept the conclusions of an appraisal report prepared at the request of the corporation, regardless of what the parties might be bound by estoppel to accept. *Bell v. Kirby Lumber Corp., 395 A.2d 730 (Del. Ch. 1978)*, modified, *413 A.2d 137 (Del. 1980)*.

But corporation has duty to disclose report. — Under the duty of complete candor imposed on a majority stockholder, a corporation has a duty to disclose the existence of an appraisal report prepared in preparation for a merger. *Bell v. Kirby Lumber Corp., 395 A.2d 730 (Del. Ch. 1978)*, modified, *413 A.2d 137 (Del. 1980)*.

Credibility of expert valuations. — The weight to be ascribed to expert valuations necessarily depends on the validity of the assumptions underlying them and where those assumptions are values supplied by others, the conduct of such other persons is probative of their credibility and of the information being supplied to the expert. *Alabama By-Products Corp. v. Neal, 588 A.2d 255 (Del. 1991)*.

Expert witnesses appointed by the court of chancery. — If the Court is limited to the biased presentation of the parties, it is often forced to pick and choose from a limited record without the benefit of objective analysis and opinion. To compensate for this handicap, the Court of Chancery should consider, in a proper case, appointing its own expert witnesses. *In re Shell Oil Co., 607 A.2d 1213 (Del. 1992)*.

Appraiser must arrive at dollar and cents appraisal; consequently, the appraiser should state the value of the elements given independent weight and the weight given to each in arriving at the appraisal value. This procedure will render the valuation process a little less arbitrary and will permit a review at least on a degree basis. *Jacques Coe & Co. v. Minneapolis-Moline Co., 31 Del. Ch. 368, 75 A.2d 244 (1950)*.

Weight to be given to conflicting appraisals attributable to the same party, as well as the motivations going into such appraisals, should be subjected to close scrutiny by the appraiser. *Bell v. Kirby Lumber Corp., 395 A.2d 730 (Del. Ch. 1978)*, modified, *413 A.2d 137 (Del. 1980)*.

Adoption of valuation views of expert. — Although the Court of Chancery is entitled to deference on the mixed fact/law issue of fair value under this section, the question of whether the Court of Chancery may adopt an expert's valuation views is a question of law. *Gonsalves v. Straight Arrow Publishers, 701 A.2d 357 (Del. 1997)*.

The valuation process was fatally flawed, demanding reversal, where the Court of Chancery's valuation determination in adopting the valuation of one expert as definitive reflected an "either-or" approach, which was at variance with the Court's statutory obligation to engage in an independent valuation exercise. *Gonsalves v. Straight Arrow Publishers, 701 A.2d 357 (Del. 1997)*.

Factors in ascertaining stock value. — A corporation's earnings, along with the market value of its stock, asset value, dividend record, earning prospects and other factors reflecting on a corporation's financial stability and prospects for growth, are all relevant matters for inquiry in ascertaining the value of stock held by dissenting stockholders. *Universal City Studios, Inc. v. Francis I. duPont & Co., 334 A.2d 216 (Del. 1975)*.

Value of stock of insolvent corporation. — Where the company is not able to refinance its debt, is insolvent and on the verge of bankruptcy, the appraisal value of its stock, insofar as affected by its debts, is determined by reference to the amount of its legal liability to pay its debt. *In re Vision Hdwe. Group, Inc., 669 A.2d 671 (Del. Ch. 1995)*.

Compilation of factors mandatory. — A compilation of as many factors as are pertinent to a given case has been held mandatory in arriving at the intrinsic value of stock held by shareholders who wish to disassociate themselves from an impending merger. *Universal City Studios, Inc. v. Francis I. duPont & Co., 334 A.2d 216 (Del. 1975)*.

Distinction between test of fair value and test of just compensation in condemnation cases. — The distinction between the constitutional test of just compensation in condemnation cases and the statutory test of fair value in appraisal proceedings is substantial. The condemnation cases do not involve contract rights, while complainant's contract when he purchased the stock contained as a term thereof the appraisal section. *Meade v. Pacific Gamble Robinson Co., 29 Del. Ch. 406, 51 A.2d 313 (1947), aff'd, 30 Del. Ch. 509, 58 A.2d 415 (1948).*

Concept of fairness has 2 basic aspects: Fair dealing and fair price. *Weinberger v. UOP, Inc., 457 A.2d 701 (Del. 1983).*

In parent-subsidiary merger transactions the issues are those of fairness — fair price and fair dealing. *Bershad v. Curtiss-Wright Corp., 535 A.2d 840 (Del. 1987).*

Concept of fair dealing embraces questions of when the transaction was timed, how it was initiated, structured, negotiated, disclosed to the directors, and how the approvals of the directors and the stockholders were obtained. *Weinberger v. UOP, Inc., 457 A.2d 701 (Del. 1983).*

Concept of fair price relates to the economic and financial considerations of the proposed merger, including all relevant factors: Assets, market value, earnings, future prospects, and any other elements that affect the intrinsic or inherent value of a company's stock. *Weinberger v. UOP, Inc., 457 A.2d 701 (Del. 1983).*

Joinder of appraisal and unfair dealing actions unauthorized. — Court of Chancery properly dismissed the claim for unfair dealing, noting that to authorize the joinder of appraisal and unfair dealing actions would result in a hybrid appraisal action, effectively broadening the legislative remedy afforded under this section. *Alabama By-Products Corp. v. Neal, 588 A.2d 255 (Del. 1991).*

Three elements of value are generally given major consideration, namely market value, asset value and earnings value. *Levin v. Midland-Ross Corp., 41 Del. Ch. 276, 194 A.2d 50 (1963).*

Appraiser should state weight given each substantial element in determining value. — An appraiser appointed under this section should state the monetary value which he or she has ascribed to the more substantial elements of value considered and the weight he or she has given each such element in arriving at the appraised value. *Jacques Coe & Co. v. Minneapolis-Moline Co., 31 Del. Ch. 368, 75 A.2d 244 (1950).*

Assets must be judged on "going concern" basis. *Sporborg v. City Specialty Stores, Inc., 35 Del. Ch. 560, 123 A.2d 121 (1956).*

The basic concept of value under the appraisal statute is that the stockholder is entitled to be paid for that which has been taken from him or her, his or her proportionate interest in a going concern. *In re Tri-Continental Corp., 31 Del. Ch. 523, 74 A.2d 71 (1950).*

The shares of stockholders dissenting to a merger must be valued on a going concern basis. *Heller v. Munsingwear, Inc., 33 Del. Ch. 593, 98 A.2d 774 (1953).*

A dissenting stockholder is entitled to receive the intrinsic value of his or her share in a going concern. This can mean only that he or she is entitled to receive that sum which represents the amount he or she would have received as a stockholder in one way or another as long as the company continued in business. *In re Delaware Racing Ass'n, 42 Del. Ch. 175, 206 A.2d 664, aff'd, 42 Del. Ch. 406, 213 A.2d 203 (1965).*

Earnings history, stability and future prospects. — The Court must examine historical earnings and peruse the corporation's stability and future prospects as of the date of merger. *Universal City Studios, Inc. v. Francis I. duPont & Co., 334 A.2d 216 (Del. 1975).*

Determination of earnings must be based upon historical earnings rather than on the basis of prospective earnings. *Francis I. DuPont & Co. v. Universal City Studios, Inc., 312 A.2d 344 (Del. Ch. 1973), aff'd, 334 A.2d 216 (Del. 1975).*

Earnings determined by averaging over reasonable period of time. — For appraisal purposes earnings are to be determined by averaging the corporation's earnings over a reasonable period of time. *Francis I. DuPont & Co. v. Universal City Studios, Inc., 312 A.2d 344 (Del. Ch. 1973), aff'd, 334 A.2d 216 (Del. 1975).*

Five-year period immediately preceding merger is ordinarily considered to be most representative and reasonable period of time over which to compute average earnings. *Francis I. DuPont & Co. v. Universal City Studios, Inc., 312 A.2d 344 (Del. Ch. 1973), aff'd, 334 A.2d 216 (Del. 1975).*

Important purpose behind practice of averaging over 5-year period is to balance extraordinary profits and/or losses which might distort the earnings data if a period of only 1 or 2 years was used. *Francis I. DuPont & Co. v. Universal City Studios, Inc., 312 A.2d 344 (Del. Ch. 1973), aff'd, 334 A.2d 216 (Del. 1975).*

Prospective financial condition of corporation and risk factor inherent in the corporation and the industry within which it operates are vital factors to be considered in arriving at a realistic present earnings value. *Universal City Studios, Inc. v. Francis I. duPont & Co., 334 A.2d 216 (Del. 1975).*

Appraiser's determination of multiplier for arriving at an earnings valuation when determining the value of stock will not be disturbed as long as it is within the range of reason. *Bell v. Kirby Lumber Corp., 395 A.2d 730 (Del. Ch. 1978), modified, 413 A.2d 137 (Del. 1980).*

Where the multiplier used by appraiser in arriving at an earnings valuation when determining value of stock is within the range of reason, the Court of Chancery will not alter it. *Bell v. Kirby Lumber Corp., 395 A.2d 730 (Del. Ch. 1978), modified, 413 A.2d 137 (Del. 1980).*

Judgment in application of multiplier. — The application of a multiplier to average earnings in order to capitalize them lies within the realm of judgment for which there is no hard and fast rule. *Universal City Studios, Inc. v. Francis I. duPont & Co., 334 A.2d 216 (Del. 1975).*

Multiplier of 16.1 in determining earnings value at time of merger approved. — See *Francis I. DuPont & Co. v. Universal City Studios, Inc., 312 A.2d 344 (Del. Ch. 1973), aff'd, 334 A.2d 216 (Del. 1975).*

Dividends largely reflect same value as earnings and so should not be separately considered in valuing

Corporations

shares. *Francis I. DuPont & Co. v. Universal City Studios, Inc.*, *312 A.2d 344 (Del. Ch. 1973), aff'd, 334 A.2d 216 (Del. 1975).*

In absence of reliable market for stock, a reconstructed market value must be given consideration, if one can be made. *Francis I. DuPont & Co. v. Universal City Studios, Inc.*, *312 A.2d 344 (Del. Ch. 1973), aff'd, 334 A.2d 216 (Del. 1975).*

Use of price-earnings ratios of comparable businesses on the date of merger as a factor in evaluating another company, and as a vital first step in arriving at a multiplier, is reasonable. *Universal City Studios, Inc. v. Francis I. duPont & Co., 334 A.2d 216 (Del. 1975).*

Ratios of comparable companies on day of merger. — The determination of value as of the day of merger being the Court's endeavor, it is appropriate that the price-earnings ratios of comparable companies, serving as barometers of risk within the industry, be referred to solely on the day of merger in the absence of extraordinary deviation from the past price-earnings record. *Universal City Studios, Inc. v. Francis I. duPont & Co., 334 A.2d 216 (Del. 1975).*

Multiplier will be low if the financial outlook for corporation is poor, or high if prospects are encouraging. *Universal City Studios, Inc. v. Francis I. duPont & Co., 334 A.2d 216 (Del. 1975).*

Liquidation value of the stock may not be accepted as the sole measure of value, since value is to be fixed on a going concern basis. *In re Tri-Continental Corp., 31 Del. Ch. 523, 74 A.2d 71 (1950); Bell v. Kirby Lumber Corp., 395 A.2d 730 (Del. Ch. 1978), modified, 413 A.2d 137 (Del. 1980).*

Liquidation or sales value should not be used in arriving at asset value since this would be contrary to the main purpose of finding the going concern value of assets to the company whose shares are being appraised. *Levin v. Midland-Ross Corp., 41 Del. Ch. 276, 194 A.2d 50 (1963).*

Stockholders are entitled to be paid the intrinsic value of their shares determined on a going concern basis, which excludes a valuation based solely upon the liquidating value, or an aliquot share in the value of the assets of the merged corporation. *In re Delaware Racing Ass'n, 42 Del. Ch. 406, 213 A.2d 203 (1965).*

Asset value as the sole controlling factor in determining the value of stock, where merger proceedings are objected to, is not the law of *Delaware. Root v. York Corp., 29 Del. Ch. 351, 50 A.2d 52 (1946).*

The value per share of the preferred stock cannot be determined by dividing the number of preferred shares into the asset value of the corporation. Neither the net asset value nor any other single factor can be the controlling element in an appraisal under this section. *Root v. York Corp., 29 Del. Ch. 351, 50 A.2d 52 (1946).*

Asset value, while a factor, must not be overemphasized in arriving at a determination of appraised value of stock, because other factors such as the value based on prospective earnings are vitally important. *In re General Realty & Utils. Corp., 29 Del. Ch. 480, 52 A.2d 6 (1947).*

Net asset value is entitled to weight, but it must be remembered that an appraisal is not a liquidation, and that the stock must be appraised on a going concern basis with the possibility in different cases that the value of the stock may be substantially above or below net asset or break-up value. *In re General Realty & Utils. Corp., 29 Del. Ch. 480, 52 A.2d 6 (1947).*

Net asset value is a theoretical liquidating value to which the share would be entitled upon the company going out of business. Its very nature indicates that it is not the value of stock in a going concern. *In re Tri-Continental Corp., 31 Del. Ch. 523, 74 A.2d 71 (1950).*

Discount may be applied to net asset value to determine on any day a theoretical or constructed market value of the common stock of a closed-end investment company with leverage. *In re Tri-Continental Corp., 31 Del. Ch. 523, 74 A.2d 71 (1950).*

The asset value is to be determined by finding the going concern value of the assets to the company whose shares are being appraised. *Felder v. Anderson, Clayton & Co., 39 Del. Ch. 76, 159 A.2d 278 (1960).*

No rule of thumb is applicable to weighting of asset value in an appraisal pursuant to this section; rather, the rule becomes one of entire fairness and sound reasoning in the application of traditional standard and settled Delaware law to the particular facts of each case. *Bell v. Kirby Lumber Corp., 413 A.2d 137 (Del. 1980).*

Earnings and dividends of a corporation are ordinarily of prime importance in valuing common stock in appraisal proceedings. *In re Tri-Continental Corp., 31 Del. Ch. 523, 74 A.2d 71 (1950).*

The existence of evidence showing actual earnings immediately subsequent to the merger date to be in excess of the estimate future earnings calculated on the basis of long-range considerations does not render erroneous the use of the estimated earnings as a factor in ascertaining the value of the shares. *In re General Realty & Utils. Corp., 29 Del. Ch. 480, 52 A.2d 6 (1947).*

Normally much greater weight is accorded the earnings value element, but the asset value element must be given somewhat greater weight where for some time the corporation was using more than an average amount of its assets to expand and improve its business activities and much of this was not yet reflected in earnings. *Sporborg v. City Specialty Stores, Inc., 35 Del. Ch. 560, 123 A.2d 121 (1956).*

Rather than immediate prospective income, the average income to be expected over a reasonable period of time is the rule to be followed in making an appraisal. *Sporborg v. City Specialty Stores, Inc., 35 Del. Ch. 560, 123 A.2d 121 (1956).*

Capitalized earnings value is not entitled to exclusive consideration under this section in the absence of the most unusual circumstances. *Felder v. Anderson, Clayton & Co., 39 Del. Ch. 76, 159 A.2d 278 (1960).*

Capitalized earnings are given independent and significant weight in arriving at the appraised value of the shares. Asset value is not necessarily zero because capitalized earnings amount to zero. *Felder v. Anderson, Clayton & Co., 39 Del. Ch. 76, 159 A.2d 278 (1960).*

The fair value of assets at a given date is not necessarily fully reflected in capitalized earnings as of that date. *Felder v. Anderson, Clayton & Co., 39 Del. Ch. 76, 159 A.2d 278 (1960).*

Annual earnings that have been influenced by an unusual factor should be disregarded. In re Delaware Racing Ass'n, 42 Del. Ch. 175, 206 A.2d 664, aff'd, 42 Del. Ch. 406, 213 A.2d 203 (1965).

The appraiser was basically right in accepting the corporation's own earnings figures where the corporation accounts in question were kept in accordance with accepted practices and that the methods of depreciation used by management were acceptable. *In re Delaware Racing Ass'n, 42 Del. Ch. 175, 206 A.2d 664, aff'd, 42 Del. Ch. 406, 213 A.2d 203 (1965).*

Where a race track cannot be actually classified as a public utility in the light of its competitive position vis-a-vis both thoroughbred and trotting racing in the area from which patrons must be attracted, high multiplier of earnings used by the appraiser was clearly unwarranted. *In re Delaware Racing Ass'n, 42 Del. Ch. 175, 206 A.2d 664, aff'd, 42 Del. Ch. 406, 213 A.2d 203 (1965).*

A long and undisturbed history of no payment of dividends by a race track must be given recognition and not merely ignored, even though there is little doubt but that had there not been governmental obstacles to such course of action some dividends could well have been paid out during the life of the track. *In re Delaware Racing Ass'n, 42 Del. Ch. 175, 206 A.2d 664, aff'd, 42 Del. Ch. 406, 213 A.2d 203 (1965).*

The general rule that in determining the actual value of stock, consideration should be given to the various relevant factors of value including earnings, dividends, market price, assets and any other pertinent factors on a "going concern" basis, is the rule in fraud cases and is also the approach to valuation in stock appraisal proceedings under this section. *Poole v. N.V. Deli Maatschappij, 43 Del. Ch. 283, 224 A.2d 260 (1966).*

Special dividends. — When merger consideration includes partial cash and stock payments, shareholders are entitled to appraisal rights. So long as payment of the special dividend remains conditioned upon shareholder approval of the merger, shareholders should not be denied their appraisal rights simply because their directors are willing to collude with a favored bidder to "launder" a cash payment. As defendant corporation failed to inform shareholders of their appraisal rights, the meeting must be enjoined for at least the statutorily required notice period of twenty days. *La. Mun. Police Emples. Ret. Sys. v. Crawford, 918 A.2d 1172; 2007 Del. Ch. LEXIS 27 (February 23, 2007).*

Market value is not the sole or exclusive criterion of value in appraisal proceedings, and due weight under the circumstances must be accorded to other relevant elements of value. *In re Tri-Continental Corp., 31 Del. Ch. 101, 66 A.2d 910 (1949), rev'd on other grounds, 31 Del. Ch. 523, 74 A.2d 71 (1950).*

"Value" as used in subsection (c) of this section is not synonymous with market value. *Chicago Corp. v. Munds, 20 Del. Ch. 142, 172 A. 452 (1934).*

In determining value under subsection (c) of this section, the appraisers are in a better position to gauge the fair value of the stock than the outside public, and therefore the market prices need not control but are only 1 factor in determining value. *Chicago Corp. v. Munds, 20 Del. Ch. 142, 172 A. 452 (1934).*

If there is an actual market value uninfluenced by the merger in existence, it would be error to disregard it in an appraisal of stock, but the absence of such an element does not require the construction of a hypothetical market value to be given effect in the final determination of value. *In re Tri-Continental Corp., 31 Del. Ch. 523, 74 A.2d 71 (1950).*

Market value should not be given any independent weight where the evidence shows that there was no dependable market value at or about the effective date of the merger. *Sporborg v. City Specialty Stores, Inc., 35 Del. Ch. 560, 123 A.2d 121 (1956).*

Market value is 1 of the elements to be considered in an appraisal proceeding. *Sporborg v. City Specialty Stores, Inc., 35 Del. Ch. 560, 123 A.2d 121 (1956).*

Delaware law compels the inclusion of a "control premium" where a parent company's 100% ownership interest in its subsidiaries is clearly a relevant valuation factor and the rejection of the "control premium" implicitly places a disproportionate emphasis on pure market value. *Rapid-American Corp. v. Harris, 603 A.2d 796 (Del. 1992).*

The trial court's decision to exclude the control premium at the corporate level of a parent company with a 100% ownership interest in three valuable subsidiaries practically discounted the parent's entire inherent value. The exclusion of a "control premium" artificially and unrealistically treated the parent as a minority shareholder. *Rapid-American Corp. v. Harris, 603 A.2d 796 (Del. 1992).*

Fair value may also include damages stockholders sustain as class. — When the trial court deems it appropriate, fair value also includes any damages, resulting from the taking, which the stockholders sustain as a class. *Weinberger v. UOP, Inc., 457 A.2d 701 (Del. 1983).*

Original value may be a convenient figure for certain purposes, but it hardly reflects present asset value and that is what the stockholder is entitled to have considered in arriving at the going concern value of his or her stock. *Heller v. Munsingwear, Inc., 33 Del. Ch. 593, 98 A.2d 774 (1953).*

Use of depreciated original cost to determine asset value would be almost meaningless because of the lapse of time. *Heller v. Munsingwear, Inc., 33 Del. Ch. 593, 98 A.2d 774 (1953).*

Depreciated reproduction cost should be used, if at all, only as evidence of asset value. *Felder v. Anderson, Clayton & Co., 39 Del. Ch. 76, 159 A.2d 278 (1960).*

If there is no better evidence of asset value, depreciated reproduction cost (adjusted downward by weighting) is useful, particularly where the depreciation is based upon the actual condition of the plant structures. *Felder v. Anderson, Clayton & Co., 39 Del. Ch. 76, 159 A.2d 278 (1960).*

Depreciated reproduction cost is not the end-all in arriving at asset value. The Delaware cases do not require that "net asset value" be determined on the basis of depreciated reproduction cost. *Felder v. Anderson, Clayton & Co., 39 Del. Ch. 76, 159 A.2d 278 (1960).*

Obsolescence factor arising out of the unfavorable outlook for the industry can be more appropriately considered when a determination is made as to the proper multiplier to be applied in computing earnings value. *Levin v. Midland-Ross Corp., 41 Del. Ch. 276, 194 A.2d 50 (1963).*

"Sales value" or "investment value," based on the hypothesis that all earnings of a mercantile venture must come from its sales, and that management "can" convert an ascertainable portion of the sales into earnings, need not be used as an independent element of value. It is in effect but another and even more theoretical method of determining earnings value. It thus duplicates that element without purpose. *Sporborg v. City Specialty Stores, Inc., 35 Del. Ch. 560, 123 A.2d 121 (1956).*

Capitalization of net rental value of stores seems to be a well-recognized approach and is a proper method of finding an asset value for such real property. *Sporborg v. City Specialty Stores, Inc., 35 Del. Ch. 560, 123 A.2d 121 (1956).*

Highest and best use of land. — Where on the basis of nonspeculative expert testimony the appraiser found that the land of the subsidiary and resulting corporations had a particular value on the date of merger and from this figure he or she subtracted the cost of razing the existing plant, in order that the highest and best use of the land might be realized, which, according to the evidence, would be residential development, these findings were not disturbed despite objectants' contention that as a speculation, use of the land for industry would no doubt mean a greatly higher per acre valuation. *In re Delaware Racing Ass'n, 42 Del. Ch. 175, 206 A.2d 664, aff'd, 42 Del. Ch. 406, 213 A.2d 203 (1965).*

Insurance appraisal, while not conclusive, is admissible as reflecting the current value of the fixed assets actually being used by defendant in its going concern. *Heller v. Munsingwear, Inc., 33 Del. Ch. 593, 98 A.2d 774 (1953).*

Average of prices on last trading day preceding announcement of merger reflected a fair market price and constituted compliance with the statute. *Levin v. Midland-Ross Corp., 41 Del. Ch. 276, 194 A.2d 50 (1963).*

Leverage, in the valuation of the common stock of closed-end investment companies, must be considered and given effect if it is an operating element at the time value is to be determined. *In re Tri-Continental Corp., 31 Del. Ch. 523, 74 A.2d 71 (1950).*

It is not appropriate to include claim for the value of stock options lost by the claimant as a result of the merger. *Lichtman v. Recognition Equip., Inc., 295 A.2d 771 (Del. Ch. 1972).*

Right of appraisal was not available to corporate executive's, who were option holders; their argument that under principles of equity, their options should be treated as having already been exercised before the merger and converted into "stock," and that the resulting hypothetical "stock" should be included in the appraisal action was rejected. *Andaloro v. PFPC Worldwide, Inc., 830 A.2d 1232 (Del. Ch. 2003).*

Full value of corporate assets to regulated closed-end corporation is not the same as the value of those assets to the common stockholder because of the factor of discount. To fail to recognize this conclusion in the valuing of common stock of a regulated closed-end company with leverage is to fail to face the economic facts and to commit error. Discount is an element of value which must be given independent effect in the valuing of common stock of regulated closed-end investment companies with leverage, and is not confined solely to the construction of a hypothetical market value. *In re Tri-Continental Corp., 31 Del. Ch. 523, 74 A.2d 71 (1950).*

Where corporate property has been completely amortized, yet has a value, that value should be included in arriving at net asset value. In the absence of evidence that the fully amortized items are of value it cannot be assumed that such is the case. *Jacques Coe & Co. v. Minneapolis-Moline Co., 31 Del. Ch. 368, 75 A.2d 244 (1950).*

Determination of value of assets of motion picture corporation. — See *Francis I. DuPont & Co. v. Universal City Studios, Inc., 312 A.2d 344 (Del. Ch. 1973), aff'd, 334 A.2d 216 (Del. 1975).*

Excessive compensation. — In the absence of a derivative claim attacking excessive compensation, the underlying issue of whether such costs may be adjusted may not be considered in an appraisal proceeding. *Gonsalves v. Straight Arrow Publishers, 701 A.2d 357 (Del. 1997).*

No special value given for company's long-pending but unproductive antitrust claim. — Where minority shareholders sought an appraisal under this section, no special value was given to the shares by reason of the prior pendency of a lawsuit in the form of a long-pending but so far unproductive antitrust claim made by the company. *Lebman v. National Union Elec. Corp., 414 A.2d 824 (Del. Ch. 1980).*

Effect of proposed alternative to cash-out merger. — If a corporation proposes an alternative to a cash-out merger, the effect would be to deprive the minority of any right to an appraisal under this section, since appraisal rights are not available on a sale of assets, nor are they available for shares of stock which are listed on a national securities exchange and which are exchanged upon a merger for shares of stock listed on a national securities exchange. *Tanzer v. International Gen. Indus., Inc., 402 A.2d 382 (Del. Ch. 1979).*

Consideration of "synergistic effect." — If, in a minority shareholder suit to enjoin a merger, it is argued that a summary judgment must be granted because the benefit by way of saving from the merger (called "the synergistic effect") must be shared on some basis between all the entities and cannot be allocated solely to 1 party, such an argument must be rejected for 2 reasons: (1) This section presently precludes such a consideration; and (2) even if a possible synergistic effect should be recognized and given value, there must be evidence that the premium offered by the surviving corporation for the stock owned by the minority stockholders does not adequately compensate the minority for such possible synergistic effect. *Tanzer v. International Gen. Indus., Inc., 402 A.2d 382 (Del. Ch. 1979).*

Value not attributable to possibility of alternative post-merger cost pattern. — Where the corporation's going forward business plan is to retain the same management, a dissenting shareholder seeking appraisal may not seek to attribute value to an alternative cost pattern that may occur post-merger. *Gonsalves v. Straight Arrow Publishers, 701 A.2d 357 (Del. 1997).*

Valuation in "2-step" mergers. — In a 2-step merger, where value is added to the the going concern by the majority acquiror during the transient period of the 2-step merger, such value accrues to the benefit of all shareholders and must be included in the appraisal process on the date of the merger. *Cede & Co. v. Technicolor, Inc., 684 A.2d 289 (Del. 1996).*

The accomplishment or expectation of the merger exception is very narrow and does not encompass known elements of value, including those which exist on the date of the merger because of a majority acquiror's interim action in a 2-step merger. *Cede & Co. v. Technicolor, Inc., 684 A.2d 289 (Del. 1996).*

Permissive counterclaim in appraisal actions should be looked upon with disfavor. *Kaye v. Pantone, Inc., 395 A.2d 369 (Del. Ch. 1978).*

Assertion of a permissive counterclaim by the surviving corporation in a stockholder appraisal action would have a "chilling effect" upon the exercise of statutory appraisal rights by dissenting stockholders and might cause others who might seek an appraisal arising out of the merger not to participate in the action. *Kaye v. Pantone, Inc., 395 A.2d 369 (Del. Ch. 1978).*

Reopening case. — When failure to present evidence of present worth factors was not the result of "mistake, inadvertence, surprise or excusable neglect," and the evidence is not "newly discovered," there is no justification for reopening a stock appraisal case. *Poole v. N.V. Deli Maatschappij, 257 A.2d 241 (Del. Ch. 1969).*

Costs. — This section confides the apportionment of costs to the discretion of the Court of Chancery. To justify a modification of the order for costs, the Supreme Court would have to find an abuse of judicial discretion. *Meade v. Pacific Gamble Robinson Co., 30 Del. Ch. 509, 58 A.2d 415 (1948).*

It is reasonable to construe this section as permitting the Court of Chancery to tax all appraisal costs against the surviving corporation where there appears no basis for concluding that the shareholder acted in bad faith, or occasioned unnecessary expense, or made use of the procedure for the purpose of being "bought off" by the corporation rather than for the purpose of obtaining a fair value for his or her shares. *Meade v. Pacific Gamble Robinson Co., 30 Del. Ch. 509, 58 A.2d 415 (1948).*

In the absence of a showing of bad faith on the part of the dissenting stockholders, or a showing that the statutory procedure was made use of for the purpose of being "bought off," it is reasonable to tax all costs against the surviving corporation. *In re Tri-Continental Corp., 31 Del. Ch. 523, 74 A.2d 71 (1950).*

Costs are generally assessed against the resulting corporation in an appraisal proceeding, but this rule is altered if bad faith or other such factors appear. *Sporborg v. City Specialty Stores, Inc., 35 Del. Ch. 560, 123 A.2d 121 (1956).*

Stockholders entitled to an appraisal in a valuation proceeding following a merger but who have not either personally or by counsel taken any active part in the actual proceedings may not be required to contribute proportionately to the defraying of counsel and expert witness fees incurred by those stockholders who through their attorneys and others have pulled the laboring oar not only before the appraiser but before the court. *Levin v. Midland-Ross Corp., 41 Del. Ch. 352, 194 A.2d 853 (1963).*

This section leaves the appointment of costs to the discretion of the Court. *Kaye v. Pantone, Inc., 395 A.2d 369 (Del. Ch. 1978).*

The General Assembly had determined that even should bad faith ultimately be found on the part of a stockholder, the only remedy for the corporation is the apportionment of the costs of the proceeding. *Kaye v. Pantone, Inc., 395 A.2d 369 (Del. Ch. 1978).*

An apportionment of the costs of an appraisal proceeding is not done until after the actual appraisal process has been concluded and the fair value of the petitioner's shares has been determined. It is impossible for the Court to determine if the proceedings have been brought in bad faith until the price offered by the corporation can be compared with the value arrived at in the appraisal proceedings. *Kaye v. Pantone, Inc., 395 A.2d 369 (Del. Ch. 1978).*

In the absence of an equitable exception, the plaintiff in an appraisal proceeding should bear the burden of paying its own expert witnesses and attorneys. *Cede & Co. v. Technicolor, Inc., 684 A.2d 289 (Del. 1996).*

Interest. — The matter of allowing interest is left to the court's discretion. *Felder v. Anderson, Clayton & Co., 39 Del. Ch. 76, 159 A.2d 278 (1960); Bell v. Kirby Lumber Corp., 413 A.2d 137 (Del. 1980); Lebman v. National Union Elec. Corp., 414 A.2d 824 (Del. Ch. 1980).*

Interest is not designed to increase the statutory recovery of the principal award. *Francis I. duPont & Co. v. Universal City Studios, Inc., 343 A.2d 629 (Del. Ch. 1975).*

Interest represents damages for the delay in payment and compensation for the use of plaintiffs' money. *Francis I. duPont & Co. v. Universal City Studios, Inc., 343 A.2d 629 (Del. Ch. 1975).*

Interest should not itself carry additional interest solely due to the entry of an order. *Francis I. duPont & Co. v. Universal City Studios, Inc., 343 A.2d 629 (Del. Ch. 1975).*

It is unlikely that the legislature intended that the statutory discretionary award of interest, with the court balancing the equities, itself would be subject to post-judgment interest as a normal judgment right under a general appraisal case order fixing the value of stock. *Francis I. duPont & Co. v. Universal City Studios, Inc., 343 A.2d 629 (Del. Ch. 1975).*

Corporations

There was not an abuse of discretion in a vice-chancellor's award of 7 percent simple interest from the date of merger to date of payment. *Bell v. Kirby Lumber Corp., 413 A.2d 137 (Del. 1980).*

The trial court did not abuse its discretion in awarding only simple interest where it did not state a rationale for its ruling. *Rapid-American Corp. v. Harris, 603 A.2d 796 (Del. 1992).*

Under subsection (i) of this section, the trial court is vested with the clear discretion to award either simple or compound interest. It must take into account all relevant factors in reaching its decision. While not exhaustive, some of these factors can include the considerations enumerated in subsection (h) of this section. *Rapid-American Corp. v. Harris, 603 A.2d 796 (Del. 1992).*

Evidence supported award of simple interest. *In re Shell Oil Co., 607 A.2d 1213 (Del. 1992).*

The decision to award either pre-judgment or post-judgment interest is entirely within the discretion of the Court of *Chancery. Alabama By-Products Corp. v. Cede & Co. ex rel. Shearson Lehman Bros., 657 A.2d 254 (Del. 1995).*

The Court of Chancery has broad discretion in both the fixing of the rate of interest and the period of its application in an appraisal proceeding; its determination will not be disturbed unless arbitrary or capricious. *Gonsalves v. Straight Arrow Publishers, 701 A.2d 357 (Del. 1997).*

An award of interest pursuant to subsection (h) of this section may be said to support 2 goals: first, the award compensates petitioner for the loss of the use of the fair value of his or her shares during the pendency of the proceeding; and second, the award forces the corporation to disgorge any benefits it obtained from the use of the fair value of petitioner's shares during the pendency of the proceeding. *Gilbert v. MPM Enters., Inc., 709 A.2d 663 (Del. Ch. 1997).*

This section provides discretion to choose a rate of interest on a case-by-case basis, but, because explanation is required for the choice, remand of a case was necessary for elaboration by the Court of Chancery upon its decision to award compound interest. *M.G. Bancorporation, Inc. v. Le Beau, 737 A.2d 513 (Del. 1999).*

Type and computation of interest. — Compound interest was required fairly to compensate petitioners for having to wait to be paid fair value for their shares, and this interest was to be compounded quarterly from the date of the merger until the date of final judgment. *Borruso v. Communications Telesystems Int'l, 753 A.2d 451 (Del. Ch. 1999).*

Court of chancery has established rate of return available to ordinary prudent investor by averaging the return from a mixed portfolio of short-, medium-, and long-term United States Treasury bills, savings deposits held in commercial banks, savings deposits held in mutual savings banks, Moody's triple A corporate bond average, and the values found in the Dow Jones industrial common stock average. *Lebman v. National Union Elec. Corp., 414 A.2d 824 (Del. Ch. 1980).*

Court of chancery may properly focus on what would have been the rate of interest at which a prudent investor could have invested money rather than on how much it would have cost the corporation to borrow the money in determining an award of interest pursuant to this section. *Lebman v. National Union Elec. Corp., 414 A.2d 824 (Del. Ch. 1980).*

Court of chancery entitled to deference. — The Court of Chancery's determination under subsection (h) of this section has traditionally been granted a high level of deference by the Delaware Supreme Court; this deference reflects a recognition that appraisal cases tend to be factually intensive and often involve competing valuation methodologies. *Gonsalves v. Straight Arrow Publishers, 701 A.2d 357 (Del. 1997).*

Consideration of terms of merger and prior offers. — Court of Chancery did not err in admitting the terms of the merger and evidence of prior offers and did not abuse its discretion in refusing to give any weight to these values in its appraisal of the dissenter's shares. *M.P.M. Enters. v. Gilbert, 731 A.2d 790 (Del. 1999).*

Liberal test for reviewing appraisal proceedings. — The innate impreciseness of a chosen multiplier has necessitated the adoption of a liberal test for reviewing decisions in appraisal proceedings. *Universal City Studios, Inc. v. Francis I. duPont & Co., 334 A.2d 216 (Del. 1975).*

Lower tribunal's choice of multiplier will be upheld if it is within range of reason. *Universal City Studios, Inc. v. Francis I. duPont & Co., 334 A.2d 216 (Del. 1975).*

And if there is no clear abuse of discretion. — The "imponderables of the valuation process" and the concomitant broad discretion traditionally granted to evaluators of corporate shares of stock, compel an acceptance of the method of determining a multiplier unless there is a clear abuse of discretion amounting to an error at law, i.e., such as the use of only one value factor at the expense of other factors. *Universal City Studios, Inc. v. Francis I. duPont & Co., 334 A.2d 216 (Del. 1975).*

Federal security law. — For discussion of appraisal rights under federal security law, see *Valente v. PepsiCo., Inc., 454 F. Supp. 1228 (D. Del. 1978).*

DELAWARE CASE NOTES — UNREPORTED

Only the record holder possesses and may perfect appraisal rights. The statute simply does not allow consideration of the beneficial owner in this context. *In re Appraisal of Transkaryotic Therapies, Inc., 2007 Del. Ch. LEXIS 57 (May 2, 2007).*

A beneficial owner, who acquires shares after the record date, does not have to prove that each of its specific shares for which it seeks appraisal was not voted in favor of the merger. *In re Appraisal of Transkaryotic Therapies, Inc., 2007 Del. Ch. LEXIS 57 (May 2, 2007).*

Delaware Court of Chancery lacks the power in a 8 Del. C. § 262 appraisal proceeding to disregard a pre-merger issuance of stock, even if that transaction is claimed to be improperly dilutive; a wrongful dilution claim was not cognizable, as it fell outside the scope of issues the Court of Chancery was empowered to decide in the § 262 appraisal proceeding, making it necessary that the Chancery Court base its examinations of the appraisers' appraisals on the number of shares outstanding on the date of the appraisal (which was the date of the back-end merger in which the minority shares were acquired). *Prescott Group Small Cap, L.P. v. Coleman Co., 2004 Del. Ch. LEXIS 131 (Sept. 8, 2004).*

The only "sale value" that this section and the case law proscribe are valuation techniques that improperly include synergistic elements of value and minority and illiquidity discounts. *Prescott Group Small Cap, L.P. v. Coleman Co., 2004 Del. Ch. LEXIS 131, No. 17802 (September 8, 2004).*

Excluded values. — Synergistic and minority value are excluded under this section. Control value — the value derived from a sale of the company as a whole without any discounts for minority status or premia for synergies — is not a proscribed measure of going concern value under this section. *Prescott Group Small Cap, L.P. v. Coleman Co., 2004 Del. Ch. LEXIS 131, No. 17802 (September 8, 2004).*

Share dilution inquiry barred. — Faithfulness to this section and cases interpreting it precludes the Court from inquiring into allegations that shareholders had dilution claims arising months before the merger. *Gentile v. Singlepoint Fin., 2003 Del. Ch. LEXIS 21, No. 18677-NC (March 5, 2003).*

Determination of proper address. — Notice of a merger effectuated under 8 Del. C. § 262(d)(2) must be given to the stockholders entitled to appraisal rights. This subsection, however, does not specify the means by which the sender of the notice is to ascertain the proper addresses of the stockholders. Other provisions of the Delaware General Corporation Law, *see, e.g.,* 8 Del. C. §§ 222(b), 251(c), 253(c), make clear that statutory notice, in general, is sufficient if appropriately directed to the address shown on the records of the corporation. Any other perspective, moreover, would beg the question: if not that address, then what address? *Konfirst v. Willow CSN, Inc., 2006 Del. Ch. LEXIS 211 (Dec. 14, 2006).*

The discrepancy between independent appraiser's DCF and the Delaware fair value standard does not support a disclosure claim. To rule otherwise would turn proxy statements into law review surveys, with directors having to describe the twists and turns of § 262 jurisprudence — such as how to make a comparable company analysis comport with the fair value standard and relate that to the banker's work. Our law does not require that. So long as the valuation work is accurately described and appropriately qualified, that is sufficient. Here, the disclosure met that mark. Moreover, the valuation methodology was fairly disclosed. Stockholders were cautioned that the value reached was a "subjective" estimate and that an appraisal in this court could result in a different value. Finally, in terms of materiality, it is worth noting that the proxy statement disclosed that the appraisal gave only a 20% weight to its dividend-based DCF analysis, with 80% of the final weight resting on its

other analyses. *In re PNB Holding Co. S'holders Litig., 2006 Del. Ch. LEXIS 158 (Aug. 18, 2006).*

Interest in appraisal actions. — As to form, the case law regarding this statute has logically evolved in favor of awarding compound interest in appraisal actions because it better comports with fundamental economic reality. It is simply not credible in today's financial markets that a person sophisticated enough to perfect his or her appraisal rights would be unsophisticated enough to make an investment at simple interest. Neither are today's companies, nor the companies that lend them money, generally unsophisticated enough to invest or lend at a simple rate of interest. Thus, with respect to both intended purposes of the interest award, reimbursing lost opportunity cost or disgorgement of assets and their benefits, compound interest is generally more appropriate to accomplishing those purposes. *Finkelstein v. Liberty Digital, Inc., 2005 Del. Ch. LEXIS 53, No. 19598 (April 25, 2005).*

Reading 8 Del. C. § 262(h) and (i) together demonstrates that an interest award necessarily has 2 components — a rate of interest and a form of interest; the Delaware Court of Chancery must determine both parts in fashioning an interest award that is fair to the dissenting stockholder as well as to the surviving corporation. *Dobler v. Montgomery Cellular Holding Co., 2004 Del. Ch. LEXIS 139 (Sept. 30, 2004).*

There is no precise formula the court must use in determining the appropriate rate of interest under this section, and each party bears the burden of proving the appropriate rate under the circumstances; thus, where petitioners fail to develop a credible record on the issue, the court looks to the legal rate of interest, as defined by 6 Del. C. § 2301. *Doft & Co. v. Travelocity.com Inc., 2004 Del. Ch. LEXIS 75 (May 20, 2004).*

Subsections (h) and (i) of this section, when read together, demonstrate that an interest award necessarily has 2 components (a rate of interest and a form of interest), and a court must determine both parts in fashioning an interest award that is fair to the dissenting stockholder as well as to the surviving corporation; an award of compound interest is generally the form of interest most likely to fulfill the purposes of Delaware's appraisal statute. *Taylor v. Am. Specialty Retailing Group, Inc., 2003 Del. Ch. LEXIS 75 (July 25, 2003).*

Burden of proof for establishing value. — Fair value, as used in an appraisal setting, is defined as the value of the company to the stockholder as a going concern, rather than its value to a third party as an acquisition; thus, in a statutory appraisal proceeding, both sides have the burden of proving their respective valuation positions by a preponderance of the evidence, and the court may exercise independent judgment to assess the fair value of the shares if neither party meets its burden. *Doft & Co. v. Travelocity.com Inc., 2004 Del. Ch. LEXIS 75 (May 20, 2004).*

Despite the fact that neither a group of minority shareholders nor a controlled company and its two holding companies met their burden in an appraisal action filed by the shareholders pursuant to 8 Del. C. § 262 of proving valuation of common stock held by the controlled company, the opinion provided by the shareholders' expert was accepted by the court; the shareholders' expert looked to third-party insight and performed a comparable transactions analysis. *Dobler v. Montgomery Cellular Holding Co.*, 2004 Del. Ch. LEXIS 139 (Del. Ch. Sept. 30, 2004).

The Supreme Court of Delaware will accept the Court of Chancery's factual determinations if they turned on a question of credibility and the acceptance or rejection of particular pieces of testimony; a factual finding made by the Court of Chancery based on a weighing of expert opinion would be overturned only if arbitrary or lacking evidential support. *Cede & Co. v. Technicolor, Inc.*, 2005 Del. LEXIS 177 (May 4, 2005).

Equitable tolling. — This section's statutory formalities, particularly with regards to demand for appraisal, deserve strict enforcement. At the same time, the certainty and fairness offered by deadlines can be outweighed in appropriate circumstances, where the interests of justice require vindication of the plaintiff's rights. *Encompass Servs. Holding Corp. v. Prosero Inc.*, 2005 Del. Ch. LEXIS 17, No 578-N (February 3, 2005).

Because plaintiff abided by all the technical requirements of this section and appears likely to have timely filed its action in a court of competent jurisdiction, equity supports tolling of the deadline under this section. Plaintiff did not sleep on its rights. Furthermore, defendant had actual and timely notice of the action at all times and was not prejudiced by the delay. *Encompass Servs. Holding Corp. v. Prosero Inc.*, 2005 Del. Ch. LEXIS 17, No 578-N (February 3, 2005).

Quasi appraisal. — After court determined that the majority shareholder did not give adequate notice to the minority shareholders so as to allow them to make an informed decision about whether or not to ask for an appraisal under 8 Del. C. § 253, the court devised a "quasi appraisal" scheme so that minority shareholders could affirmatively opt in if they desired, and would be entitled to the appraised amount that the court determined was equitable; opt-in shareholders were required to pay a price per share into an escrow account before the stock was appraised. *Gilliland v. Motorola, Inc.*, 2005 Del. Ch. LEXIS 33 (Mar. 4, 2005).

Quasi-appraisal award granted. — For that failure as a fiduciary, bank holding company, which benefited as an appraisal respondent, owes a duty to the estate's beneficiaries to pay the beneficiaries the amount necessary to make them whole — specifically, a quasi-appraisal award. A quasi-appraisal remedy is appropriate for plaintiffs who may have been wrongfully deprived, even indirectly, of the statutory remedy of appraisal. Here, the beneficiaries have made a showing that they suffered an equitable injury at the hands of the respondent. Simply stated, company withdrew as executor and did not find a replacement when it knew the beneficiaries of the estate were dissenting themselves and would likely request them to dissent on behalf of the estate's shares. *In re PNB Holding Co. S'holders Litig.*, 2006 Del. Ch. LEXIS 158 (Aug. 18, 2006).

Merger violated this section where the notice and information required to be sent to the shareholder by the merging companies was never sent and the absence of the statutorily-required information was accompanied by a failure to make any attempt to disclose to the shareholder the facts material to his decision whether to accept the consideration offered in the merger or to seek appraisal. *Tansey v. Trade Show News Networks, Inc.*, 2001 Del. Ch. LEXIS 142 (Nov. 27, 2001).

Comparable transaction approach. — In appraisal proceeding by dissenting shareholders following a merger, the shareholders' comparable transaction approach to determine value was adopted by the court, as the analytical methodology properly and reasonably reflected all relevant facts; fair value, as used in subsection (h) under this section was defined as the value of the company to the stockholder as a going concern, rather than the company's value to a third party as an acquisition. *Gentile v. SinglePoint Fin., Inc.*, 2003 Del. Ch. LEXIS 21 (Mar. 5, 2003).

Excusable delay. — Where a bankruptcy court arguably had exclusive jurisdiction and held that it had "related to" jurisdiction of a debtor-in-possession's enforcement of its dissent and appraisal rights (which were property of the estate), the debtor-in-possession's delay in making its demand under 8 Del. C. § 262 past the 120-day deadline was excusable under the circumstances, particularly since the debtor-in-possession acted promptly as soon as the bankruptcy court abstained from exercising its jurisdiction. *Encompass Servs. Holding Corp. v. Prosero Inc.*, 2005 Del. Ch. LEXIS 17 (Feb. 3, 2005).

Shareholders in an appraisal suit against a company were held entitled to the fair value of the company's common stock as of the merger date at $1.64 per share as well as compounded monthly interest at the rate of 6.21 percent where the court determined, considering all relevant factors, that such amount was the proper fair value of the common shares of the company in light of the timing of the merger just as the company's new business model was beginning to take hold, as well as the adoption of a very speculative and exaggerated 2002 budget on the part of the company. *Gholl v. eMachines, Inc.*, 2004 Del. Ch. LEXIS 171 (Nov. 24, 2004).

Shared synergies, sum-of-the-parts analysis. — In an *8 Del. C. § 262* proceeding seeking judicial appraisal of equity holdings as a result of a merger, weighting a modified shared synergies analysis at 75 percent and a modified sum-of-the-parts analysis at 25 percent, the fair value on the date of the merger was found to be $24.97 per share. *Highfields Capital v. Axa Fin.*, 2007 Del. Ch. LEXIS 126 (Del. Ch. Aug. 17, 2007).

Independent valuation. — Because the shareholders of the acquired companies and the acquiring corporation failed to meet their burden of proof regarding the fair value of the acquired companies in an appraisal action by the shareholders, the court made an independent valuation of the companies to determine their fair value as of the merger date, and weighted the results of the discounted cash flows and comparative transactions analyses in determining the fair value of the companies.

In re U.S. Cellular Operating Company, 2005 Del. Ch. LEXIS 1 (Jan. 6, 2005).

Court did not rely upon the cellular corporation's valuation expert for several reasons, including, that the expert: (1) did not rely on an industry expert to arrive at assumptions used in the discounted cash flow (DCF) analysis; (2) relied on gross national product for an assumed growth rate without comparing to industry growth rates; (3) valued the corporation as a stand alone company without using its existing synergies; and (4) relied on the government's "C-Block auction" unrealstic values (outdated data, different technology, an emerging market, and inexperienced bidders). *Dobler v. Montgomery Cellular Holding Co., 2004 Del. Ch. LEXIS 139 (Sept. 30, 2004).*

Enterprise value. — Court found tentative value of a shareholder's publishing holding company's shares acquired in a merger was determined according to a formula it outlined based in part upon enterprise value (capitalization rate derived from comparable companies, multiplied times weighted five-year earnings before interest and taxes (EBIT)) otherwise adjusted. *Gonsalves v. Straight Arrow Publishers, Inc., 2002 Del. Ch. LEXIS 105 (Sept. 10, 2002).*

Comparable company analysis, rather than a discounted cash flow analysis (DCF), was used to determine the fair value of a merging corporation's stock in a statutory appraisal action because the most fundamental input used by the experts in the DCF, the projections of future revenues, expenses, and cash flows, were not shown to be reasonably reliable. *Doft & Co. v. Travelocity.com Inc., 2004 Del. Ch. LEXIS 75 (May 20, 2004).*

Delaware law recognizes that there is an inherent minority trading discount in a comparable company analysis because the valuation method depends on comparisons to market multiples derived from trading information for minority blocks of the comparable companies and the equity valuation produced in a comparable company analysis does not accurately reflect the intrinsic worth of a corporation on a going concern basis; therefore, the court, in appraising the fair value of the equity, must correct this minority trading discount by adding back a premium designed to correct it. *Doft & Co. v. Travelocity.com Inc., 2004 Del. Ch. LEXIS 75 (May 20, 2004).*

Indicia of fair value: discounted cash flow as a factor. — Discounted cash flow is a final valuation that does not need any additional correction, such as a control premium. *Dobler v. Montgomery Cellular Holding Co., 2004 Del. Ch. LEXIS 139 (Sept. 30, 2004).*

Value of membership in larger marketing network. — As a going concern, a corporation already had contractual relationships with other cellular providers making it more valuable than if its subscribers were confined to its licensed area; the minority shareholders were entitled to this value, as the benefits of being part of a wider regional network. *Dobler v. Montgomery Cellular Holding Co., 2004 Del. Ch. LEXIS 139 (Sept. 30, 2004).*

Fee shifting. — Behavior of the corporation did not rise to the level necessary for the court to invoke its equitable powers and award fees and costs; fee shifting is a narrow exception, seldom invoked by the Delaware Court of Chancery. *Dobler v. Montgomery Cellular Holding Co., 2004 Del. Ch. LEXIS 139 (Sept. 30, 2004).*

Interest awards. — After determining the fair value of a dissenting shareholder's shares, the trial court determined that simple post-judgment interest was a fair rate to both the corporation and the shareholder, considering "all relevant factors" pursuant to subsection (h) of this section, which included the procedural posture and relative change in position of the parties and the post-judgment goal of putting the parties back in the position they would have been had the judgment been paid; the court awarded the statutory legal rate of interest on the principal amount only. *Cede & Co. v. Technicolor, Inc., 2003 Del. Ch. LEXIS 146 (Dec. 31, 2003).*

Because the parties in an appraisal action brought by stockholders failed to meet their burden of proof regarding an appropriate interest rate, the court, after determining the fair value of 2 companies, awarded interest to the stockholders at a floating rate, compounded on a quarterly basis, equal to the legal rate, under 6 Del. C. § 2301(a), because the award appeared to best serve the dual purposes of disgorging any benefit received by the acquiring corporation from its use of the stockholders' funds and compensating the stockholders for the loss of use of their money during the pendency of the action. *In re U.S. Cellular Operating Company, 2005 Del. Ch. LEXIS 1 (Jan. 6, 2005).*

Appraisal proceeding claimant was entitled to interest on its award, once the fair value of the shares was ascertained, at the rate of 6.27 percent, compounded monthly, from the date of the corporate merger to the date of the judgment, pursuant to subdivisions (h) and (i) of this section; the court reached its determination by weighting the cost of borrowing of seven percent and the prudent investor rate of return of 5.54 percent equally. *In re Emerging Communs., Inc. S'holders Litig., 2004 Del. Ch. LEXIS 70 (May 3, 2004).*

In a 8 Del. C. § 262 appraisal proceeding, since the corporation's actual costs of borrowing, and the minority shareholders' opportunity cost were not adequately developed on the record, Delaware case law (and the court, in the instant case) held that the legal interest rate could (and was to) serve as a default rate for pre-judgment interest. *Prescott Group Small Cap, L.P. v. Coleman Co., A.2d 2004 Del. Ch. LEXIS 131 (Sept. 8, 2004).*

In determining the fair rate of interest in an action pursuant to 8 Del. C. § 262, a group of minority shareholders (by relying completely on the rates as of the merger date) failed in meeting their burden of establishing the appropriate rate of interest for the entire time period; in those circumstances, the court looked to the legal rate of interest, which was 5 percent over the Federal Reserve discount rate, and held that the appropriate rate was 8.25 percent, compounded quarterly. *Dobler v. Montgomery Cellular Holding Co, 2004 Del. Ch. LEXIS 139 (Sept. 30, 2004).*

Law of the case doctrine governed the minority shareholder's entitlement to pre-judgment interest following the retrial of their statutory appraisal action; accordingly, the minority shareholders were entitled to prejudgment interest up to the remanded final judgment entry date consistent with the initial determination of the chancery court, and were thereafter entitled to post-judgment interest at the legal rate. *Cede & Co. v. Technicolor, Inc., 2005 Del. LEXIS 177 (May 4, 2005).*

In an action by a corporate shareholder for a determination of the fair value of the corporation's common stock as of the date of a merger, interest compounded monthly was found to be appropriate pursuant to 8 Del. C. § 262(i), as the record showed that the shareholder was a sophisticated businessman who probably would not have invested in anything which returned only simple interest; the corporation's only argument that simple interest should be awarded, its view that the shareholder should not prosper through delay in pursuing the action, had already been rejected. *Lane v. Cancer Treatment Ctrs. of Am., Inc., 2004 Del. Ch. LEXIS 108 (July 30, 2004).*

Finding the corporation's expert generally more credible than the shareholder's expert (particularly on the point of the long-term growth prospects of a cigar company), but noting that the varying valuations could not be reconciled with each other, the court reached its own conclusions using predominantly a discounted cash flow analysis, and awarded appropriate interest, compounded monthly. *Cede & Co. v. JRC Acquisition Corp., 2004 Del. Ch. LEXIS 12 (Feb. 10, 2004).*

Where a shareholder dissented from a cash-out merger and sought appraisal, the court determined credibility issues with respect to each party's expert's valuations, which were based on the discounted cash flow method; the court analyzed a particular merger plan, evaluated the free cash flow projections and terminal value of each corporate business, examined the discount rate, and then applied the pre-judgment and post-judgment interest rates as applicable to arrive at the price per share. *Cede & Co. v. Technicolor, Inc., 2003 Del. Ch. LEXIS 146 (Dec. 31, 2003).*

Discounted cash flow analysis. —A discounted cash flow (DCF) analysis involves: (1) projecting operating cash flows out to a valuation horizon, (2) determining a terminal value which represents the business' value at the horizon, and (3) discounting all cash flows to their present value; a DCF analysis is an exercise in appraising the present value at a set date of the expected future cash flows earned by the company. *Henke v. Trilithic Inc., 2005 Del. Ch. LEXIS 170 (Del. Ch. Oct. 28, 2005).*

Where the court developed its own valuation as of the date of the merger, which was 10 years before, using the discounted cash flow methodology, the court considered all relevant factors that were known or which could be ascertained as of the date of the merger involving the corporation's value, including: (1) the rate of revenue growth, (2) the appropriate tax rate, (3) the discount rate, (4) the rate of change in working capital, (5) the rate of growth during the terminal period, (6) the value of the corporation's debt, and (7) the value of nonoperating assets sold shortly after the merger. *Henke v. Trilithic Inc., 2005 Del. Ch. LEXIS 170 (Del. Ch. Oct. 28, 2005).*

Build-up method. — In determining the corporation's value, the discount rate was determined under the build-up method; the "build-up" method begins with a risk-free rate of return as a base, then additional rates that represent the corporation's security's unique risks are added to that risk-free base to determine a discount rate. *Henke v. Trilithic Inc., 2005 Del. Ch. LEXIS 170 (Del. Ch. Oct. 28, 2005).*

Independent valuation. —Where neither appraiser satisfied burden to prove corporate valuation, the court conducted its own independent valuation. *Henke v. Trilithic Inc., 2005 Del. Ch. LEXIS 170 (Del. Ch. Oct. 28, 2005).*

Debt. —Court determined the value of the corporation's debt to be the debt that the corporation was required to pay back versus the debt that the corporation was required to pay back if it timely paid back that debt; therefore, debt that was not timely paid and that had been called as of the date of the valuation, and with respect to which the corporation could not take advantage of certain incentives which would have reduced the debt payable, was valued at the higher amount that the corporation was required to pay. *Henke v. Trilithic Inc., 2005 Del. Ch. LEXIS 170 (Del. Ch. Oct. 28, 2005).*

Tax rate. — Because of the transitory nature of tax deductions and credits and the requirement that firms eventually paid their deferred taxes, the court considered it more reasonable to use a marginal tax rate of 40 percent where the corporation's financial statements indicated that the corporation had a 34 percent federal tax rate and a 6 percent state tax rate for income tax purposes. *Henke v. Trilithic Inc., 2005 Del. Ch. LEXIS 170 (Del. Ch. Oct. 28, 2005).*

Evidence regarding one of the corporation's employee estimates of the number of hours of free time donated by employees to produce a product was admissible, even though those estimates were not reflected in a contemporaneous document. *Henke v. Trilithic Inc., 2005 Del. Ch. LEXIS 170 (Del. Ch. Oct. 28, 2005).*

Appraiser's use of the subject corporation's single transaction that occurred 4 years before the valuation date was unreasonable to value the corporation because, inter alia, other lines of business had been introduced and some lines of business were no longer as predominant. *Henke v. Trilithic Inc., 2005 Del. Ch. LEXIS 170 (Del. Ch. Oct. 28, 2005).*

Corporation's projections presented to a state government agency to obtain a loan and to demonstrate that the loan could be paid was presumably not false or misleading and was adopted in part by the court to value the corporation. *Henke v. Trilithic Inc., 2005 Del. Ch. LEXIS 170 (Del. Ch. Oct. 28, 2005).*

Strict compliance with statutory standards. — Several stockholders whose appraisal demands are rejected in this letter opinion submitted separate written arguments in support of their right to appraisal. Many of them set forth understandable reasons for their failure to comply strictly with the statutory requirements. The statutory requirements, however, are just that: they are strict and can only be avoided, if ever, in extraordinary circumstances. The circumstances here are not extraordinary. Appraisal rights are created by statute and, in order to partake in those rights, strict compliance with the precise statutory standards is essential. *Konfirst v. Willow CSN, Inc., 2006 Del. Ch. LEXIS 211 (Dec. 14, 2006).*

Illustrative cases. — Where credibility of valuation experts who testified for dissenting shareholder and acquiring corporation was suspect, the court adopted the nearly contemporaneous valuation prepared by an independent appraiser in connection with another proposed merger involving the same acquired company. *Gray v. Cytokine Pharmasciences, Inc., 2002 Del. Ch. LEXIS 48 (Del. Fam. Ct. Apr. 25, 2002).*

Trial court determined that, in minority shareholder's appraisal rights proceeding, where minority shareholder refused to consent to the conversion of corporation from subchapter C to subchapter S, necessitating a cash-out merger and minority shareholder's removal as a shareholder, the appropriate tax rate for projected future tax expenses was as a subchapter C corporation, that the staff and officer compensation, as well as the annual rental expenses, were properly included as deductions from gross revenues, and that the "net asset value" employed as a method of valuation was not inappropriate because it was not the exclusive method of valuation. *Ng v. Heng Sang Realty Corp., 2004 Del. Ch. LEXIS 69 (Apr. 22, 2004).*

Appraisal rights claimant in a two-step "privatization" of a corporation was entitled to $38.05 per share as the fair value, rather than the $10.25 that was arrived at during the privatization, together with interest, based on use of later projections for an appropriate and reliable discounted cash flow valuation; calculations included arrival at the appropriate discount rate, a determination of the cost of equity which included various premiums such as a hurricane damage risk and small firm/small stock, and which declined to use others such as the supersmall firm premium, did not rely on adoption of the "enterprise value," and gave little or no weight to the stock market price and the corporate opportunity claim. *In re Emerging Communs., Inc. S'holders Litig., 2004 Del. Ch. LEXIS 70 (May 3, 2004).*

Where dissenting shareholders' and a corporation's valuation of stock (had a proposed merger not taken place) were widely divergent, the chancery court, guided by principles of reasonableness, reached its own valuation; the court was guided primarily by a constant growth model, given that the pharmaceutical company that did not seem likely to attain any comparatively large, new market share in the near future. *Cede & Co. v. Medpointe HealthCare, Inc., 2004 Del. Ch. LEXIS 124 (Aug. 16, 2004).*

While the chancery court's valuation model in a statutory appraisal action, following a cash-out merger of minority shareholders, was supported by record evidence and was the product of an orderly and logical deductive process, a different discount rate from that used by the chancery court was required by the law of the case doctrine, resulting in a different per share value for the stock found by the chancery court. *Cede & Co. v. Technicolor, Inc., 2005 Del. LEXIS 177 (May 4, 2005).*

CASE NOTES — OTHER STATES

California

Minority shareholders have an "additional interest" in their shares beyond their bare monetary value; that interest is the right to remain shareholders until their elimination serves a bona fide corporate purpose. *Stephenson v. Drever, 16 Cal. 4th 1167, 69 Cal. Rptr. 2d 764, 947 P.2d 1301 (1997).*

Entire fairness test. — Analysis of a breach of fiduciary duty claim involves application of the "entire fairness test." "Entire fairness" requires consideration of fair dealing and fair price. The former embraces questions of when the transaction was timed, how it was initiated, structured, negotiated, disclosed to the directors, and how the approvals of the directors and the stockholders were obtained. The latter aspect of fairness relates to the economic and financial considerations of the proposed merger, including all relevant factors: assets, market value, earnings, future prospects, and any other elements that affect the intrinsic or inherent value of a company's stock. However, the test for fairness is not a bifurcated one as between fair dealing and price. All aspects of the issue must be examined as a whole since the question is one of entire fairness. *Interactive Multimedia Artists v. Superior Court, 62 Cal. App. 4th 1546, 73 Cal. Rptr. 2d 462 (1998).*

The purpose of this statute is to protect the shareholder by providing the shareholder with a judicial determination of the fair value of its shareholdings. *Sagi v. Capital, 2005 Cal. App. Unpub. LEXIS 1409 (2005).*

Colorado

Equitable relief. — Where fraud, misrepresentation, self-dealing, deliberate waste of corporate assets, or gross and palpable overreaching are involved, a dissenting shareholder may bring an equitable action. In Delaware, a dissenting shareholder may receive rescissory damages in an equitable action. In this situation, the court awards rescissory damages when a traditional form of equitable relief, like rescission, is not feasible. *Szaloczi v. John R. Behrmann Revocable Trust, 90 P.3d 835 (Colo. 2002).*

Georgia

Delaware appraisal action only appropriate remedy. — When plaintiffs did not appeal the trial court's denial of injunctive relief before the merger and then failed to assert on this appeal that such denial was error, they waived any argument they may have had concerning that decision. Moreover, to the extent that the plaintiffs viewed defendant corporation's value in the rosy light of a recovery for the same wrongs alleged in their complaint, and were therefore aggrieved by the price they were offered for their shares, they were required to pursue their remedy in the form of a Delaware appraisal action. When the plaintiffs chose not to pursue this remedy, the trial court was within its rights to deny them relief by granting defendant's motion to dismiss. *Paul & Suzie Schutt*

Irrevocable Family Trust v. NAC Holding, 283 Ga. App. 834; 642 S.E.2d 872; 2007 Ga. App. LEXIS 209 (March 1, 2007).

Illinois

Director disclosure duties. — Delaware courts address the duty of disclosure by corporate directors only with respect to the following five scenarios: mergers, proxy solicitations, tender offers, self-tender offers, and stockholder votes. *Sims v. Tezak, 296 Ill. App. 3d 503, 694 N.E.2d 1015, 230 Ill. Dec. 737.Dec. 737 (1998).*

Duty of candor. — Corporate directors of a closely held corporation do not owe minority shareholders a fiduciary duty of candor with respect to a repurchase of the minority shareholders' shares. *Sims v. Tezak, 296 Ill. App. 3d 503, 694 N.E.2d 1015, 230 Ill. Dec. 737 (1998).*

Kansas

It is not necessary for a corporation to show a "valid corporate purpose" for eliminating minority stockholders. *In re Hesstom Corporation, 254 Kan. 941, 870 P.2d 17 (1994).*

A corporation is required to disclose all material facts relevant to a merger. *In re Hesstom Corporation, 254 Kan. 941, 870 P.2d 17 (1994).*

Massachusetts

Block approach. — The Delaware courts have adopted a general approach to the appraisal of stock which a Massachusetts judge might appropriately follow. The Delaware procedure, known as the "Delaware block approach," calls for a determination of the market value, the earnings value, and the net asset value of the stock, followed by the assignment of a percentage weight to each of the elements of value. *Piemonte v. New Boston Garden Corporation, 377 Mass. 719. 387 N.E.2d 1145 (1979).*

Corporate earnings approach. — Delaware case law has established a method of computing value of stock based on corporate earnings. The appraiser generally starts by computing the average earnings of the corporation for the past five years. Extraordinary gains and losses are excluded from the average earnings calculation. The appraiser then selects a multiplier — to be applied to the average earnings — which reflects the prospective financial condition of the corporation and the risk factor inherent in the corporation and the industry. In selecting a multiplier, the appraiser generally looks to other comparable corporations. The appraiser's choice of a multiplier is largely discretionary and will be upheld if it is "within the range of reason." *Piemonte v. New Boston Garden Corporation, 377 Mass. 719, 387 N.E.2d 1145 (1979).*

Maine

"Fair value". — The question for the court becomes direct and simple: What is the best price a single buyer could reasonably be expected to pay for the firm as an entirety? This formulation is not to be confused with the market value of the corporation because, taken by itself, a business's market value may not accurately reflect its fair, intrinsic value. Nonetheless, although the legal notion of fair value is distinct from fair market value, "fair value" is still obtained by considering the behavior of market forces. *In re: Valuation of Common Stock of Penobscot Shoe Company, 2003 Me. Super. LEXIS 140 (2003).*

Block method. — While recognizing that the precise process was a function of the particular circumstances of the subject corporation, the "Delaware block method" of business appraisal requires consideration of a corporation's "stock market price, investment value, and net asset value." The appraiser must then determine the relative degrees of weight to be assigned to the results of those three separate analyses. This comparative approach does not foreclose the appraiser from concluding that one or more of those results is not worthy of weight; nonetheless, each of the three conclusions must at least be considered. *In re: Valuation of Common Stock of Penobscot Shoe Company, 2003 Me. Super. LEXIS 140 (2003).*

Opening of appraisal process. — The Supreme Court of Delaware rejected a valuation method that is limited to the three Delaware block method and opened the appraisal process to any relevant and admissible valuation technique. *In re: Valuation of Common Stock of Penobscot Shoe Company, 2003 Me. Super. LEXIS 140 (2003).*

The appraisal of the dissenters' shares must be determined on the basis of information and data which are known or susceptible of proof as of the date of the merger. *In re: Valuation of Common Stock of Penobscot Shoe Company, 2003 Me. Super. LEXIS 140 (2003).*

New Jersey

"Stockholder", "stock", "share". — The word stockholder means a holder of record of stock in a stock corporation and also a member of record of a nonstock corporation; the words "stock" and "share" mean and include what is ordinarily meant by those words and also membership or membership interest of a member of a nonstock corporation. *Berger v. Berger, 249 N.J. Super. 305, 592 A.2d 321 (1991).*

Beneficial owners of stock held in a street name could assert statutory rights. *Berger v. Berger, 249 N.J. Super. 305, 592 A.2d 321 (1991).*

To deprive the beneficial owners of the appraisal statute would violate the spirit of the law and work a forfeiture merely on a hyper-technical basis. To do justice to the beneficial owners where no injury, prejudice, or damage will result to the detriment of the defendant, the right of the beneficial owners to bring an action must be sustained, and the court so upholds that right. It is in keeping with the policy that the state's appraisal statute be construed liberally in favor of dissenting stockholders that the court recognizes the plaintiffs' right to bring this action. *Berger v. Berger, 249 N.J. Super. 305, 592 A.2d 321 (1991).*

New Mexico

Construction with other law. — Though the Delaware appraisal statute does not have an express exclusivity provision, Delaware case law provides a comprehensive analysis of the scope of the appraisal remedy. That analysis is not incompatible with the New Mexico statute, which contains both an apparent ambiguity when applied to freeze out mergers, and an express exception for fraudulent or unlawful conduct. *McMinn v. MBF Operating Acquisition Corp. 2007 NMSC 40; 164 P.3d 41; 2007 N.M. LEXIS 330 (June 27, 2007).*

Exclusivity. — Even if a claim challenges director decision-making related to valuation of shares, that claim will not be precluded by appraisal if such decision-making was accompanied, as it was here, by a conflict of interest. *McMinn v. MBF Operating Acquisition Corp., 2007 NMSC 40; 164 P.3d 41; 2007 N.M. LEXIS 330 (June 27, 2007).*

New York

Merger. — Under Delaware law, a parent corporation, which owns 90% or more of the stock of a subsidiary, can merge with that subsidiary without advance notice or consent of the minority stockholders upon approval by the parent's board of directors. No corporate purpose is statutorily required for a short-form merger; rather, the very purpose of such mergers is to provide the parent corporation with a means of eliminating the minority shareholder's interest in the enterprise. Upon approval of the merger, the parent corporation must make payment in cash to the minority for their stock. If a minority stockholder is dissatisfied with the offer made by the parent corporation for his or her shares, he or she has the right to have a court-appointed appraiser determine the fair value and the right to receive a decree from the Delaware Court of Chancery ordering the surviving corporation to pay for his or her shares at the resulting appraised value. *Green v. Santa Fe Industries, Inc., 70 N.Y.2d 244, 514 N.E.2d 105, 519 N.Y.S.2d 793 (1997).*

Under the laws of Delaware, a merger is authorized and given effect except under exceptional circumstances but, in any event, a non-assenting stockholder may refuse to accept the merger and obtain money for the value of his stock by proceeding according to the terms of the statute. *Langfelder v. Universal Laboratories, Inc., 293 N.Y. 200, 56 N.E.2d 550 (1944).*

When the relief sought is to set aside a merger and an accounting for a gain, the latter is not available, as its equivalent has been provided for by the right of refusal and having the stock appraised. *Albert v. Salzman, 41 A.D.2d 501, 344 N.Y.S.2d 457 (1973).*

Valuation factors. — The value of a shareholder's interest is to be determined by consideration of various factors, including asset value, earning prospects, and facts known or ascertainable at the time of a merger that shed light on the future prospects of the corporation. Non-party corporations may be subject to disclosure concerning value if reasonable and necessary. *In re Wolf Popper Ross Wolf & Jones, 179 A.D.2d 389, 578 N.Y.S.2d 159 (1992).*

Ohio

Protection of business judgement rule. — The law of Delaware is well established that in the absence of evidence of fraud or unfairness, a corporation's repurchase of its capital stock, at a premium over market from a dissident shareholder is entitled to the protection of the business judgment rule. *Drage v. Ameritrust Corp., 1988 Ohio App. LEXIS 3972 (1988).*

Washington

Right incorporated into corporate contract. — It appeared on the face of the Delaware statute that appellants in that case had a statutory right incorporated into their corporate contract to have respondent's shares appraised by an appraiser appointed by a Delaware court. *State ex rel. Starkey v. Alaska Airlines, Inc., 68 Wash.2d 318, 413 P.2d 352 (1966).*

Merger. — The authority for the consolidation and merger of its domestic corporations is given in Delaware by statute. It has also given to a nonconsenting stockholder in either of the consolidating corporations the right to have paid to him or her the value of his or her stock, and has provided a procedure whereby he or she may have that value fixed and a method by which such value may be recovered from the resulting corporation. A part of the statutory right is to have the value of the stock fixed by appraisers selected by the interested parties. If this cannot be accomplished, the chancellor of Delaware is authorized by statute to designate appraisers. When the appraisers fix the value of the stock, their decision is binding on the corporation, and, if it does not pay such value to the stockholder, he or she is given a right of action to recover a judgment therefor. *Grant v. Pacific Gamble Robinson Company, 22 Wash.2d 65, 154 P.2d 301 (1944).*

Designation of appraisers. — Proceedings relative to the designation of appraisers by the chancellor of Delaware must be had and taken in that state, as provided by the Delaware statute. *Grant v. Pacific Gamble Robinson Company, 22 Wash.2d 65; 154 P.2d 301 (1944).*

Wisconsin

Comparison with fraud action. — In an appraisal action the only litigable issue is the determination of the value of the appraisal petitioners' shares on the date of the merger, the only party defendant is the surviving corporation and the only relief available is a judgment against the surviving corporation for the fair value of the dissenters' shares. In contrast, a fraud action asserting fair-dealing and fair-price claims affords an expansive remedy and is brought against the alleged wrongdoers to provide whatever relief the facts of a particular case may require. In evaluating claims involving violations of entire fairness, the trial court may include in its relief any damages sustained by the shareholders. In a fraud claim, the approach to determine relief may be the same as that employed in determining fair value under § 262. However, an appraisal action may not provide a complete remedy for unfair dealing or fraud because a damage award in a fraud action may include rescissory damages if the trier of fact considers them susceptible of proof and a remedy appropriate to all issues of fairness before him or her. *Stauffacher v. Checota, 149 Wis. 2d 762, 441 N.W.2d 755 (Wis. App. 1979).*

Going-concern approach. — In all instances, shares are to be valued on a going-concern basis, rather than on a liquidated basis, by which of course is meant as if the merger had never been conceived. These approaches to measuring value govern all appraisal proceedings.

Stauffacher v. Checota, 149 Wis. 2d 762, 441 N.W.2d 755 (Wis. App. 1979).

The liberalized approach to valuation includes proof of value by any techniques or methods which are generally considered acceptable in the financial community and otherwise admissible in court. The court may consider elements of future value, including the nature of the enterprise, which are known or susceptible of proof as of the date of the merger. When the trial court deems it appropriate, fair value also includes any damages, resulting from the taking, which the stockholders sustain as a class. However, the court may not consider the speculative elements of value arising from the accom-

plishment or expectation of the merger. The Delaware Block method has not been abolished if properly supported in the record. The Delaware Block method simply is no longer the exclusive method of valuation. *Stauffacher v. Checota, 149 Wis. 2d 762, 441 N.W.2d 755 (Wis. App. 1979).*

Good faith, honest motives irrelevant. — While the issues of good faith and honest motives are relevant in an action to enjoin or rescind a merger because of fraud, such concerns are irrelevant in a statutory appraisal proceeding, which involves a judicial determination of the fair value of the shareholder's stock. *Stauffacher v. Checota, 149 Wis. 2d 762, 441 N.W.2d 755 (Wis. App. 1979).*

CASE NOTES — FEDERAL

Second Circuit

In general. — Under Delaware law, a dissenting stockholder has a right of appraisal, which is available in cases of merger or consolidation but not in cases of sales of assets even when immediately followed by dissolution. *Barnett v. Anaconda Co., 238 F. Supp. 766 (S.D.N.Y. 1956).*

Protection of shareholders. — Because mergers are permitted under Delaware law, and the accomplishment of a merger necessarily involves adjusting the rights of shareholders, a shareholder's preferential rights are subject to defeasance. Stockholders are charged with knowledge of this possibility at the time they acquire their shares. Moreover, Delaware provides specific protection to shareholders who believe that they have received insufficient value for their stock as the result of a merger: they may obtain an appraisal under § 262. Furthermore, the decision to merge with another company does not relieve the corporation or its directors of the duty to accord to the minority fair and equitable terms of conversion. The measure of fair value, however, is the amount equal to the corporation, not the stated redemption or liquidation value of the shares. *Rauch v. RCA Corp., 1987 U.S. Dist. LEXIS 3323 (S.D.N.Y. 1987).*

Exclusive remedy. — Under Delaware law, the exclusive remedy for minority shareholders who dispute the fair value of their shares is to seek a judicial appraisal. *Loengard v. Santa Fe Industries, Inc., 639 F. Supp. 673 (S.D.N.Y. 1986).*

Under Delaware law, absent an allegation that appraisal is an inadequate remedy in a corporate merger, appraisal is the exclusive remedy available to minority shareholders who object to a merger and who seek the fair value of their shares. *Weinstein v. Appelbaum, 193 F. Supp. 2d 774 (S.D.N.Y. 2002).*

Under Delaware law, the general rule is that a minority shareholder's exclusive remedy of appraisal yields only to an exception where the stockholder properly alleges bad faith which goes beyond the issues of mere inadequacy of price. *Weinstein v. Appelbaum, 193 F. Supp. 2d 774 (S.D.N.Y. 2002).*

Under Delaware law, appraisal is not an inadequate remedy simply because an investor in a corporation does not fare as well as he hoped to when he

or she invested. *Weinstein v. Appelbaum, 193 F. Supp. 2d 774 (S.D.N.Y. 2002).*

Fourth Circuit

Delaware law provides that courts in appraisal cases shall determine a stock's fair value exclusive of any element of value arising from the accomplishment or expectation of a disputed transaction. *Williams v. 5300 Columbia Pike Corp., 891 F. Supp. 1169 (E.D.Va. 1995).*

Delaware is one of the small minority of states where appraisal is generally not available after a sale of all or substantially all of a corporation's assets. Delaware courts have declined to find that a properly executed sale of assets may be treated as a "de facto merger" to which appraisal rights extend. Where minority shareholders challenge a sale of assets, as opposed to a merger, valuation may take into account an increase in the assets' value that is attributable to the sale itself. *Williams v. 5300 Columbia Pike Corp., 891 F. Supp. 1169 (E.D.Va. 1995).*

Sixth Circuit

Equitable relief. — Under Delaware law, cashed-out minority shareholders should generally be required to use the liberalized appraisal process adopted in that case to obtain the fair value of their shares. However, the appraisal remedy may be inadequate where fraud, misrepresentation, self-dealing, deliberate waste of corporate assets, or gross and palpable overreaching are involved, thus allowing a court to grant equitable relief, including monetary damages. *Krieger v. Gast, 179 F. Supp. 2d 762 (W.D.Mich. 2001).*

Delaware courts permit cashed-out minority shareholders to challenge the "entire fairness" of a merger outside of an appraisal proceeding under the rubric of fair dealing and fair price, even in the face of allegations that the alleged harm could be remedied in an appraisal. *Krieger v. Gast, 179 F. Supp. 2d 762 (W.D.Mich. 2001).*

Seventh Circuit

In general. — Del. Code Ann. tit. 8, § 262, governs the rights of dissenting shareholders in cash-out mergers. Under this statute, a dissenting shareholder, who makes a statutory demand, is entitled to an appraisal by the court of Chancery of the fair value of the stockholder's shares of stock. *Connector Service Corp. v. Briggs, 1998 U.S. Dist. LEXIS 18864 (N.D.Ill. 1998).*

A minority shareholder has a statutory right to object to any proposed merger of his or her corporation with any other corporation, and to have his or her stock appraised and the appraised value paid to him or her by the surviving corporation. *Krantman v. Liberty Loan Corp., 152 F. Supp. 705 (N.D. Ill. 1956).*

The issue raised by an action seeking an appraisal should be the value of the dissenting stockholders' stock. A dissenting stockholder's shares will be valued on a going-concern basis. The concept of fair price when valuing shares of stock in an appraisal relates to the economic and financial considerations of the proposed merger, including all relevant factors: assets, market value, earnings, future prospects, and any other elements that affect the intrinsic or inherent value of a company's stock. However, one cannot take speculative effects of the merger into account. *Wanninger v. SPNV Holdings, 1989 U.S. Dist. LEXIS 9502 (N.D.Ill. 1989).*

Ninth Circuit

Appraisal upon objection to consolidation. — Section 61 of the Delaware law provides that any stockholder who has objected in writing to the consolidation shall have the right, within 20 days after the effective date of the consolidation, to demand payment of the value of his or her stock from the corporation resulting from the consolidation. There is a provision for appraisal in the event of inability to agree on values. *National Supply Co.*

v. Leland Stanford Junior University, 134 F.2d 689 (9th Cir. 1943).

The statutory imperatives of timely objection and demand are of the very substance of the consolidation. Stockholders are entitled to rely on the status of things as they appear on the date of the meeting and to govern themselves accordingly. They have the right to be advised of the number of shares objecting to the merger, since these objections foreshadow money demands to be made upon the new company. The extent of such foreseen demands is necessarily of influence with stockholders in appraising the wisdom of consolidation and in persuading them whether or not they should themselves object and claim the value of their holdings. The governing boards of the constituent corporations must similarly rely on the presence or absence of substantial dissent in determining whether the tentative agreement should be adhered to or abandoned. More important still, perhaps, is the statutory purpose of creating a fixed condition in order that the public, in acquiring securities of the corporation growing out of the merger, may not be prejudiced by objections belatedly asserted. *National Supply Co. v. Leland Stanford Junior University, 134 F.2d 689 (9th Cir. 1943).*

Eleventh Circuit

It is clear that the Delaware legislature has determined that a stockholder has no absolute right to his or her interest in the corporation and may be forced to surrender his or her shares for a fair cash price. *Grimes v. Donaldson, Lufkin & Jenrette, Inc., 392 F. Supp. 1393 (N.D. Fla. 1974).*

§ 263. Merger or consolidation of domestic corporation

CASE NOTES — OTHER STATES

Michigan

Fraud. — The exercise of the statutory right of merger is always subject to nullification for fraud, and that the allocation of equities in the surviving corporation between the old preferred and common stockholders may be so unfair as to amount to constructive fraud. *Dratz v. Occidental Hotel Company, 325 Mich. 699, 39 N.W.2d 341 (1949).*

Washington

Statutory right to appraisal. — The authority for the consolidation and merger of its domestic corporations is given in Delaware by statute. It has also given to a nonconsenting stockholder in either of the consolidating

corporations the right to have paid to him or her the value of his or her stock, and has provided a procedure whereby he or she may have that value fixed and a method by which such value may be recovered from the resulting corporation. A part of the statutory right is to have the value of the stock fixed by appraisers selected by the interested parties. If this cannot be accomplished, the chancellor of Delaware is authorized by statute to designate appraisers. When the appraisers fix the value of the stock, their decision is binding on the corporation, and, if it does not pay such value to the stockholder, he or she is given a right of action to recover a judgment therefor. *Grant v. Pacific Gamble Robinson Company, 22 Wash.2d 65, 154 P.2d 301 (1944).*

§ 264. Merger or consolidation of domestic corporation and limited liability company

CASE NOTES — OTHER STATES

Michigan

The exercise of the statutory right of merger is always subject to nullification for fraud, and that the allocation of equities in the surviving corporation between the old

preferred and common stockholders may be so unfair as to amount to constructive fraud. *Dratz v. Occidental Hotel Company, 325 Mich. 699, 39 N.W.2d 341 (1949).*

§ 266. Conversion of a domestic corporation to other entities.

CASE NOTES — FEDERAL

Tenth Circuit

Determination of conversion status upon motion to dismiss. — The Delaware statutes provide that the conversion constitutes a continuation of the other entity and is not a dissolution of the other entity unless otherwise agreed, or unless otherwise provided in a resolution of conversion. Thus, determining whether corporation in fact was dissolved or continued may require resort to internal corporate documents. Also, the record before the court does not establish that the corporation necessarily took the appropriate steps internally to convert the corporation to a limited liability company. The certificate issued by the Delaware Secretary of State constitutes only prima facie evidence of the conversion, not conclusive proof. As such, this matter is not appropriate for resolution on a motion to dismiss. While the court recognizes that this issue ultimately may prove to be a mere technicality, it nonetheless presents an issue of fact that this court will not resolve on a motion to dismiss. *JP Morgan Trust Co. v. Mid-America Pipeline Co., 2006 U.S. Dist. LEXIS 4820 (D. Kan. Feb. 7, 2006).*

Judicial notice of certificates. — In the instant case, the court will exercise its discretion and, without converting the motion to one for summary judgment, will take judicial notice of the fact that the certificate of formation and the certificate of conversion were both filed with the Delaware Secretary of State on July 30, 2002, and that the Delaware Secretary of State issued a certificate stating that the appropriate conversion documents were filed. These documents are public records which are properly authenticated. Thus, the fact that they were filed with and issued by the Delaware Secretary of State, as well as their contents, are not subject to reasonable dispute. Indeed, public documents filed with the secretary of state such as those at issue here generally satisfy the judicial notice standard and district courts routinely take judicial notice of such documents in resolving motions to dismiss. *JP Morgan Trust Co. v. Mid-America Pipeline Co., 2006 U.S. Dist. LEXIS 4820 (D. Kan. Feb. 7, 2006).*

Subchapter X.
Sale of Assets, Dissolution and Winding Up

§ 271. Sale, lease or exchange of assets; consideration; procedure

DELAWARE CASE NOTES — REPORTED

Corporation has right to sell or dispose of its assets. — A corporation has a right to sell and dispose of substantially all its assets. *Butler v. New Keystone Copper Co., 10 Del. Ch. 371, 93 A. 380 (1915).*

The right of the specified majority to sell all the assets is absolute insofar as the fact of sale, and whether one should be made, is concerned. *Allied Chem. & Dye Corp. v. Steel & Tube Co. of Am., 14 Del. Ch. 1, 120 A. 486 (1923).*

It is the right of the majority in a corporation to practically desert the corporate venture by selling out its assets and, thereby, in the case of a highly profitable concern, deprive their associates of the opportunity to reap gains in the future by continuing in the business, provided the terms and conditions of the sale are fair to the corporation. *Allaun v. Consolidated Oil Co., 16 Del. Ch. 318, 147 A. 257 (1929).*

The right of the majority of stockholders to authorize a sale of assets is absolute even though dissenting stockholders are thereby deprived of the opportunity for future profits, provided that the price to be paid, the manner of payment and such like questions meet the test of the corporation's best interest. *Baron v. Pressed Metals of Am., Inc., 35 Del. Ch. 325, 117 A.2d 357 (1955), aff'd, 35 Del. Ch. 581, 123 A.2d 848 (1956).*

The right of a corporation to sell all of its assets for stock in another corporation is expressly accorded by this section. The stockholder is, in contemplation of law, aware of this right when he or she acquires his or her stock. The stockholder is also aware of the fact that the situation might develop whereby he or she would be ultimately forced to accept a new investment. *Hariton v. Arco Elec., Inc., 40 Del. Ch. 326, 182 A.2d 22 (1962), aff'd, 41 Del. Ch. 74, 188 A.2d 123 (1963).*

There is no statutory limitation on the right of a Delaware corporation to sell its assets on such terms and conditions and for such consideration as its board of directors deems expedient and for the best interests of the corporation. *Alcott v. Hyman, 40 Del. Ch. 449, 184 A.2d 90 (1962), aff'd, 42 Del. Ch. 233, 208 A.2d 501 (1965).*

Two things with respect to sale are contemplated: (a) An authorization of sale by the stockholders, and (b) a fixing of the terms and conditions by the directors. *Allied Chem. & Dye Corp. v. Steel & Tube Co. of Am., 14 Del. Ch. 1, 120 A. 486 (1923).*

Stockholders must consent to sale. — The essential requirement for a sale of all the assets of a corporation is that the stockholders shall consent thereto. *Robinson v. Pittsburgh Oil Ref. Corp., 14 Del. Ch. 193, 126 A. 46 (1924).*

Terms and conditions of sale must conform to best interests of corporation. — The right of the directors to define terms and conditions of sale is circumscribed by a discretion which must consult not only expediency, but as well the best interests of the corporation. *Allied Chem. & Dye Corp. v. Steel & Tube Co. of Am., 14 Del. Ch. 1, 120 A. 486 (1923).*

When this section is to be construed, the test that the terms and conditions must be expedient and in the best interests of the corporation is to be applied in the light of the fact that the corporation in making the sale must find a purchaser; in other words, the best interests of the corporation are those of a corporation desiring to sell. *Allied Chem. & Dye Corp. v. Steel & Tube Co. of Am., 14 Del. Ch. 64, 122 A. 142 (1923).*

This section does not require shareholder approval prior to board action. *Clarke Mem. College v. Monaghan Land Co., 257 A.2d 234 (Del. Ch. 1969).*

This section does not require notice of terms of proposed sale. *Clarke Mem. College v. Monaghan Land Co., 257 A.2d 234 (Del. Ch. 1969).*

Sale of less than all or substantially all assets is not covered by negative implication from this section. *Gimbel v. Signal Cos., 316 A.2d 599 (Del. Ch.), aff'd, 316 A.2d 619 (Del. 1974).*

Sale of vital assets. — Issue of whether or not the sale of certain limited partnership assets constituted a sale of substantially all of the assets, requiring approval of the limited partners, was not decided on summary judgment; this section required the court to focus not on the interpretation of the words "substantially all," but upon whether a transaction involved the sale of assets quantitatively vital to the operation of the corporation. *In re Nantucket Island Assocs., 810 A.2d 351 (Del. Ch. 2002).*

This section was designed as a protection for rational owners of capital; its proper interpretation requires the court to focus on the economic importance of the businesses involved, and not their aesthetic worth. *Hollinger Inc. v. Hollinger Int'l, Inc., 858 A.2d 342 (Del. Ch. 2004).*

Under 8 Del. C. § 271, "all or substantially all" did not mean "more than 50 percent." *Hollinger Inc. v. Hollinger Int'l, Inc., 858 A.2d 342 (Del. Ch. 2004).*

Exchange of assets not affecting corporate purpose. — Where foundation was in the business of holding investment securities and donating its profits to charity, the exchange of one portfolio of securities for another portfolio of similar value did not substantially affect the corporate purpose, and member approval was not required under the charter. *Oberly v. Kirby, 592 A.2d 445 (Del. 1991).*

Test as to when shareholder approval required can be somewhat qualitatively defined. — This section requires shareholder approval upon the sale of "all or substantially all" of the corporation's assets. While this test does not lend itself to a strict mathematical standard to be applied in every case, the qualitative factor can be defined to some degree notwithstanding the limited Delaware authority. *Gimbel v. Signal Cos., 316 A.2d 599 (Del. Ch.), aff'd, 316 A.2d 619 (Del. 1974).*

Critical factor in determining character of sale of assets is generally considered not the amount of property sold but whether the sale is in fact an unusual transaction or one made in the regular course of business of the seller. *Gimbel v. Signal Cos., 316 A.2d 599 (Del. Ch.), aff'd, 316*

A.2d 619 (Del. 1974); Katz v. Bregman, 431 A.2d 1274 (Del. Ch. 1981).

Trustees of voting trust have right to vote shares which they hold on a stockholder's resolution authorizing the sale of substantially all corporate assets. *Clarke Mem. College v. Monaghan Land Co., 257 A.2d 234 (Del. Ch. 1969).*

Stockholder who paid lower price should not be denied voice. — A stockholder who has paid less for his or her stock than another should not for that reason be denied a voice upon a question of sale simply because in the event of liquidation, he or she will, while receiving the same identical amount on distribution as his or her higher cost fellow stockholder, nevertheless make more on his or her investment. *Allied Chem. & Dye Corp. v. Steel & Tube Co. of Am., 14 Del. Ch. 1, 120 A. 486 (1923).*

Rights of controlling shareholders. — Controlling shareholders have no inalienable right to usurp the authority of boards of directors that they elect, since a central premise of the *8 Del. C. § 141* vests most managerial power over the corporation in the board (and not in the stockholders); that the majority of a company's voting power is concentrated in one stockholder does not mean that that stockholder must be given a veto over board decisions when such a veto would not also be afforded to dispersed stockholders who collectively own a majority of the votes. *Hollinger Inc. v. Hollinger Int'l, Inc., 858 A.2d 342 (Del. Ch. 2004).*

Stockholder-creditors not inhibited from voting for sale. — Stockholders who happen also to be overdue creditors may not be inhibited from using their voting power in favor of a fair sale of the corporation's assets where the only claim of tainting fraud is that their debts as well as others will result in being paid. If the ensuing of that sort of result can properly be called a personal advantage, it is not such a personal advantage as could in reason be regarded as indicating a fraud. *Allaun v. Consolidated Oil Co., 16 Del. Ch. 318, 147 A. 257 (1929).*

Improper delegation of directors' authority to corporate officers. — Delegation by the board of directors to its president and secretary to determine whether a sale of assets of the corporation would be made, and if so, upon what terms, is a violation of this section and of the stockholder's resolution empowering the board to sell, because former subsection (c) of § 141 of this title authorized delegation of directors' powers to 2 or more directors, not to officers. *Clarke Mem. College v. Monaghan Land Co., 257 A.2d 234 (Del. Ch. 1969).*

Sale presupposes willing buyer and willing seller. — Fundamentally the fair price of corporate assets is the resultant of the 2 opposing views of a willing seller and a willing purchaser, the former of whom is not compelled to sell and the latter of whom is not required to buy. *Allied Chem. & Dye Corp. v. Steel & Tube Co. of Am., 14 Del. Ch. 64, 122 A. 142 (1923).*

The value in a sale of corporate assets is not one of cost or replacement value but of value in connection with a sale; that such a sale presupposes a willing buyer and a willing seller; that a buyer can be expected to anticipate a profit, and that majority stockholders of a selling

Corporations

corporation are not guilty of improper motives in wanting to make a speculative profit. *Baron v. Pressed Metals of Am., Inc.*, 35 Del. Ch. 325, 117 A.2d 357 (1955), aff'd, 35 Del. Ch. 581, 123 A.2d 848 (1956).

Test of fairness of price, the sale being regarded as made by those who stand in a fiduciary relation towards the complainants, is whether it is to their injury and damage, regardless of whether it is also to the profit of the alleged fiduciaries. *Allied Chem. & Dye Corp. v. Steel & Tube Co. of Am.*, 14 Del. Ch. 64, 122 A. 142 (1923).

Fairness judged in light of conditions existing at time of sale. — The fairness of a price for selling assets must be judged in the light of conditions as they exist at the time of sale disregarding subsequent events. *Marks v. Wolfson*, 41 Del. Ch. 115, 188 A.2d 680 (1963).

Fairness determined in part by opportunity for profit. — Where a seller desires to sell the corporate assets, the fairness of a selling price must be in part determined by the proposed purchaser's opportunity for profit. *Allaun v. Consolidated Oil Co.*, 16 Del. Ch. 318, 147 A. 257 (1929).

Small number of possible purchasers should be taken into account. — In considering the fairness of the price for which it is proposed to sell the assets of a corporation, it is proper to take into account the fact that the possible purchasers are exceedingly few in number. *Allied Chem. & Dye Corp. v. Steel & Tube Co. of Am.*, 14 Del. Ch. 64, 122 A. 142 (1923).

If sale of assets of corporation is only "freezing out" by which the majority use their power to sell to themselves in another guise and thereby carry on in the business without their former associates of the minority, equity would doubtless restrain it regardless of the fairness of price. *Allaun v. Consolidated Oil Co.*, 16 Del. Ch. 318, 147 A. 257 (1929).

Valuation should be based on actual figures. — As between the valuation based on a forecast of the future and one based on actual figures, the latter method seems preferable. *Marks v. Wolfson*, 41 Del. Ch. 115, 188 A.2d 680 (1963).

Assets properly valued as of date offer approved by vote. — Corporate directors, in receiving offer to purchase corporate assets, acted reasonably when they valued the assets as of the date when the offer was approved by the stockholders' vote rather than the date when the directors accepted the offer. *Schiff v. RKO Pictures Corp.*, 34 Del. Ch. 329, 104 A.2d 267 (1954).

Selling value of corporate assets may be more or less than actual value. *Allaun v. Consolidated Oil Co.*, 16 Del. Ch. 318, 147 A. 257 (1929).

When the price to be paid in a sale of corporate assets case is under attack, the question to be decided is what is the value of such assets for sale purposes, selling value having the quality according to the circumstances of the particular transaction of being more or less than actual value. *Abelow v. Symonds*, 40 Del. Ch. 36, 173 A.2d 167 (1961).

Market price on stock exchange is not reliable criterion of the true value of corporate property when dealing with a proposed sale of corporate assets, but the earning record made by the selling corporation and future prospects based on the use of such assets by the selling corporation and by prospective purchasers are pertinent and important factors. *Schiff v. RKO Pictures Corp.*, 34 Del. Ch. 329, 104 A.2d 267 (1954).

Book value is of far less importance than earning power. *Cottrell v. Pawcatuck Co.*, 36 Del. Ch. 169, 128 A.2d 225 (1956), cert. denied, 355 U.S. 12, 78 S. Ct. 54, 2 L. Ed. 2d 20 (1957).

Earning power will control replacement cost in considering value in a sale. *Allied Chem. & Dye Corp. v. Steel & Tube Co. of Am.*, 14 Del. Ch. 64, 122 A. 142 (1923).

Sound, or replacement, values are no fair indication of market or commercial value, and the fact that such values are quoted to the investing public when securities of the owning company are to be sold does not alter the situation. *Allied Chem. & Dye Corp. v. Steel & Tube Co. of Am.*, 14 Del. Ch. 64, 122 A. 142 (1923).

Reproduction cost less depreciation and valuations for insurance purposes are of little help in determining market value of plant and equipment. *Cottrell v. Pawcatuck Co.*, 36 Del. Ch. 169, 128 A.2d 225 (1956), cert. denied, 355 U.S. 12, 78 S. Ct. 54, 2 L. Ed. 2d 20 (1957).

Good will is fleeting, intangible asset which depends largely upon the individual or the personality and ability of the officers and employees of the corporation. *Lawson v. HFC*, 17 Del. Ch. 343, 152 A. 723 (1930).

If proposed sale is fraud on minority, it cannot stand. *Allied Chem. & Dye Corp. v. Steel & Tube Co. of Am.*, 14 Del. Ch. 1, 120 A. 486 (1923).

Fraud cannot fairly be predicated upon failure to purchase goodwill when a corporation sells its assets, unless a showing of special facts justifies it. *Argenbright v. Phoenix Fin. Co.*, 21 Del. Ch. 288, 187 A. 124 (1936).

Any "ordinary and regular course of the business" test obviously is not intended to limit the directors to customary daily business activities. *Gimbel v. Signal Cos.*, 316 A.2d 599 (Del. Ch.), aff'd, 316 A.2d 619 (Del. 1974).

Every transaction out of normal routine does not necessarily require shareholder approval. *Gimbel v. Signal Cos.*, 316 A.2d 599 (Del. Ch.), aff'd, 316 A.2d 619 (Del. 1974).

While it is true that a transaction in the ordinary course of business does not require shareholder approval, the converse is not true. *Gimbel v. Signal Cos.*, 316 A.2d 599 (Del. Ch.), aff'd, 316 A.2d 619 (Del. 1974).

Shareholders (both the controlling shareholder and the other shareholders) did not have the right to vote on the corporation's sale of a group of newspapers and publications located in England, because, the "all or substantially all" test was not met; based upon a primarily a quantitative, versus a qualitative analysis, the unsold components of the corporation (which were primarily a group of newspapers and publications located in the Chicago, Illinois area), left the corporation viable, substantial, and ongoing from both an asset valuation and earnings (primarily viewed through the earnings approach used in the publications arena — "EBITDA" — earnings before income taxes, depreciation, and amortization) standpoint. *Hollinger Inc. v. Hollinger Int'l, Inc., 858 A.2d 342 (Del. Ch. 2004).*

Unusual nature of transaction must strike at the heart of the corporate existence and purpose. *Gimbel v. Signal Cos., 316 A.2d 599* (Del. Ch.), aff'd, *316 A.2d 619 (Del. 1974).*

If the sale is of assets quantitatively vital to the operation of the corporation and is out of the ordinary and substantially affects the existence and purpose of the corporation, then it is beyond the power of the board of directors. *Gimbel v. Signal Cos., 316 A.2d 599* (Del. Ch.), aff'd, *316 A.2d 619 (Del. 1974).*

"Interest" of director should be fact considered when and if a charge is made that an agreement was negotiated at the expense of the corporation. Where the votes of such interested directors are necessary to make a quorum, the burden of showing fairness would be shifted to these directors. *Smith v. Good Music Station, Inc., 36 Del. Ch. 262, 129 A.2d 242 (1957).*

Sale not condemned because seller's officers were retained by purchaser. — A sale of corporate assets is not to be condemned as fraudulent on the bare showing that 2 or 3 officers of the seller were, after the sale, engaged to render services for the purchaser similar to the services theretofore rendered by them to the seller at the same compensation which they had formerly received. *Mitchell v. Highland-Western Glass Co., 19 Del. Ch. 326, 167 A. 831 (1933).*

Duty of loyalty. — The shareholder vote provided by this section does not supersede the duty of loyalty owed by control persons; rather, this statutorily conferred power must be exercised within the constraints of the duty of loyalty. *Thorpe v. CERBCO, Inc., 676 A.2d 436 (Del. 1996).*

Presumption that directors acted in good faith. — The directors of a corporation who are not acting in self-interest are clothed with that presumption which the law accords to them of being actuated in their conduct by a bona fide regard for the interests of the corporation whose affairs the stockholders have committed to their charge. This being so, a sale of corporate assets must be examined with the presumption in its favor that the directors who negotiated it honestly believed that they were securing terms and conditions which were expedient and for the corporation's best interests. *Robinson v. Pittsburgh Oil Ref. Corp., 14 Del. Ch. 193, 126 A. 46 (1924).*

The judgment of the directors in fixing the terms and conditions of the sale of corporate assets is entitled to the presumption in its favor that it was exercised honestly and in good faith. *Allaun v. Consolidated Oil Co., 16 Del. Ch. 318, 147 A. 257 (1929).*

A presumption exists that corporate action, whether by stockholders or directors, in the sale of assets is in the best interests of the corporation. *Mercantile Trading Co. v. Rosenbaum Grain Corp., 17 Del. Ch. 325, 154 A. 457 (1931).*

A sale of corporate assets must be examined with the presumption in its favor that the directors who negotiated it honestly believed that they were securing terms and conditions which were expedient and for the corporation's

best interests. *Mitchell v. Highland-Western Glass Co., 19 Del. Ch. 326, 167 A. 831 (1933).*

In the absence of evidence to the contrary, the judgment of directors in fixing the terms and conditions of a sale of the corporate assets as in any other corporate act is entitled to the presumption that it was exercised honestly and in good faith. Such presumption falls, however, when the votes of interested directors are necessary for approval of the corporate action. *Gropper v. North Cent. Tex. Oil Co., 35 Del. Ch. 198, 114 A.2d 231 (1955).*

There is a presumption that directors act honestly and in the best interests of the stockholders in negotiating a contract for the sale of corporate assets. *Baron v. Pressed Metals of Am., Inc., 35 Del. Ch. 325, 117 A.2d 357 (1955),* aff'd, *35 Del. Ch. 581, 123 A.2d 848 (1956).*

Not every disparity between price and value will be allowed to upset proposed sale of corporate assets. The disparity must be sufficiently great to indicate that it arises not so much from an honest mistake in judgment concerning the value of the assets, as from either improper motives underlying the judgment of those in whom the right to judge is vested or a reckless indifference to or a deliberate disregard of the interests of the whole body of stockholders including, of course, the minority. *Allaun v. Consolidated Oil Co., 16 Del. Ch. 318, 147 A. 257 (1929).*

Inadequacy of price when the corporate assets are sold will not suffice to condemn the transaction as fraudulent, unless the inadequacy is so gross as to display itself as a badge of fraud and so long as the inadequacy of price may reasonably be referred to an honest exercise of sound judgment, it cannot be denominated as fraudulent. *Allied Chem. & Dye Corp. v. Steel & Tube Co. of Am., 14 Del. Ch. 1, 120 A. 486 (1923).*

The directors and majority of stockholders who resolve on a sale owe the duty of obtaining a fair and adequate price for the assets; but a mere inadequacy of price will not suffice to condemn the transaction as fraudulent, unless the inadequacy is so gross as to display itself as a badge of fraud. *Mitchell v. Highland-Western Glass Co., 19 Del. Ch. 326, 167 A. 831 (1933).*

Plaintiff ordinarily has burden of proving fraud or inadequacy of price. — When disparity is alleged between the value of the assets sold and the consideration received, the party attacking the sale of corporation assets has the burden of showing such a gross disparity as will raise an inference of improper motives or reckless indifference to or intentional disregard of stockholders' interests. *Baron v. Pressed Metals of Am., Inc., 35 Del. Ch. 581, 123 A.2d 848 (1956).*

Even where corporate action has been allegedly taken to benefit majority stockholders, the burden of proving bad faith and the like rests on the plaintiff. *Marks v. Wolfson, 41 Del. Ch. 115, 188 A.2d 680 (1963).*

It was incumbent on plaintiffs to prove that the defendants against whom relief is sought were either guilty of actual fraud or that the price fixed for the sale of assets was so clearly inadequate as constructively to carry the badge of fraud. *Marks v. Wolfson, 41 Del. Ch. 115, 188 A.2d 680 (1963).*

Tender offer and sale of corporate assets held protected by business judgment rule. — See *Thompson v. Enstar Corp., 509 A.2d 578 (Del. Ch. 1984)*.

Stockholder approval shifted burden to plaintiffs opposing purchase by single stockholder. — In a stockholders' class action to enjoin the corporation from accepting the offer of a single stockholder to purchase all the corporate assets, even assuming that, otherwise, the board of directors would have the burden of showing the fairness of the transaction on the theory that the dominant stockholder controlled the board of directors, nevertheless, the independent majority stockholder approval had the effect of shifting that burden back to the plaintiffs. *Schiff v. RKO Pictures Corp., 34 Del. Ch. 329, 104 A.2d 267 (1954)*.

Burden of proof rests on those espousing transaction when seller is dominated by purchaser, and independent stockholder ratification cannot be given. *Abelow v. Symonds, 40 Del. Ch. 462, 184 A.2d 173 (1962)*, aff'd, *189 A.2d 675 (Del. 1963)*.

Discovery. — Where there is a legal attack on a sale of assets made under the statute, those attacking the sale are not entitled to discovery to search for possible causes of action in the absence of a fairly substantial showing that they may possibly exist. *Garbarino v. Albercan Oil Corp., 109 A.2d 824 (Del. Ch. 1954)*.

Aggrieved party may invoke protection of court of equity. — When the power to sell corporate assets is sought to be used, it is competent for anyone who conceives himself or herself aggrieved thereby to invoke the processes of a court of equity for protection against its oppressive exercise. *Allied Chem. & Dye Corp. v. Steel & Tube Co. of Am., 14 Del. Ch. 1, 120 A. 486 (1923)*.

Restraining order against approval of sale. — A restraining order will issue against the receipt by a corporation of the votes of a majority of its shareholders for approval of a proposed sale of substantially all of its assets to 1 of 2 possible buyers when the offers of both would-be buyers are essentially the same, each buyer having waived all conditions precedent, except that the latter offers more money, so that stockholder approval of the proposed sale to the former would not be in the best interest of the corporation. *Thomas v. Kempner, 398 A.2d 320 (Del. Ch. 1979)*.

When a corporation desires to sell substantially all of its assets, and enters into negotiations for such a sale to 1 party, who offers a certain price, along with certain nonpecuniary terms and conditions, and another party subsequently proposes to buy these same assets at a higher price, a restraining order will issue that will provide for the further adjournment of a presently noticed meeting of the corporation's stockholders, so as to permit the corporation's board of directors to invite and receive bids for the sale of the corporate assets in issue, such bids to be based on the nonpecuniary terms and conditions of the first party's proposal, and to thereafter submit the bid so conditioned containing the highest cash offer to the corporation's stockholders for their vote. *Thomas v. Kempner, 398 A.2d 320 (Del. Ch. 1979)*.

Where a proposed sale would, if consummated, constitute a sale of substantially all of the assets of a corporation, as presently constituted, an injunction should issue preventing the consummation of such sale at least until it has been approved by a majority of the outstanding stockholders of the corporation entitled to vote at a meeting duly called on at least 20 days' notice. *Katz v. Bregman, 431 A.2d 1274 (Del. Ch. 1981)*.

Requisite vote authorizing sale normally prevents review by court of chancery. — In the absence of a showing that directors and majority stockholders are in some manner to share in profits arising from a sale of assets, the requisite vote of stockholders authorizing the sale normally prevents the Court of Chancery from review of a sale of assets. *Baron v. Pressed Metals of Am., Inc., 35 Del. Ch. 325, 117 A.2d 357 (1955)*, aff'd, *35 Del. Ch. 581, 123 A.2d 848 (1956)*.

Delay may lead to denial of injunctive relief. — In cases involving the sale of corporate assets or their merger with those of another corporation, slight delay may lead to the denying of a motion for injunctive relief where such an order would involve a complex undoing of an accomplished corporate act. *Elster v. American Airlines, 36 Del. Ch. 213, 128 A.2d 801 (1957)*.

The doctrine of de facto mergers means that there has been a sale of all its assets by 1 corporation to another, the stockholders of the former becoming stockholders in the latter, notwithstanding there was no technical merger or any statutory authority for one, and the transferee corporation will be held to a liability for its transferor's debts. *Gott v. Live Poultry Transit Co., 17 Del. Ch. 288, 153 A. 801 (1931)*.

Assuming that there may be a merger de facto of 2 corporations, the rule as to colorable compliance which is applicable to the existence of a corporation de facto ought likewise to prevail as to de facto mergers; where there was no colorable compliance with the statutory provision, no merger took place when the so-called attempt was made. *Blackstone v. Chandler, 15 Del. Ch. 1, 130 A. 34 (1925)*.

There can be no consolidated corporation de facto where there can be no de jure one. *Gott v. Live Poultry Transit Co., 17 Del. Ch. 288, 153 A. 801 (1931)*.

The doctrine of de facto merger has been invoked in cases of sales of assets for the protection of creditors or stockholders who have suffered an injury by reason of failure to comply with the statute governing such sales. *Heilbrunn v. Sun Chem. Corp., 38 Del. Ch. 321, 150 A.2d 755 (1959)*.

No injury has been inflicted upon the purchaser's stockholders where their corporation has simply acquired property and paid for it in shares of stock. The business of the purchaser will go on as before, with additional assets; the purchaser's stockholders are not forced to accept stock in another corporation; and the reorganization has not changed the essential nature of the enterprise of the purchasing corporation. Hence, the purchaser's stockholders have no right to raise the question of de facto merger. *Heilbrunn v. Sun Chem. Corp., 38 Del. Ch. 321, 150 A.2d 755 (1959)*.

Where a sale of assets is effected under this section in consideration of shares of stock of the purchasing corporation and the agreement of sale embodies also a plan to dissolve the selling corporation and distribute the shares so received to the stockholders of the seller so as to accomplish the same result as would be accomplished by a merger of the seller into the purchaser, such a sale was held to be proper. *Hariton v. Arco Elec., Inc., 41 Del. Ch. 74, 188 A.2d 123 (1963).*

No board or stockholder approval required where transactions involved no attempt to sell stock. — Where a group of investors set out to acquire the complete ownership of a corporation, first by acquiring 92.6 percent stock interest through competitive biddings, then attempted to obtain the remaining shares through a properly registered tender offer and finally through use of a short-form merger, although the effect could be viewed as a sale of assets, there was no attempt to sell the stock pursuant to this section and, consequently, the transactions did not require approval by the board and by the stockholders of the corporation. *Field v. Allyn, 457 A.2d 1089* (Del. Ch.), aff'd, *467 A.2d 1274 (Del. 1983).*

Special classes of stock. — A Delaware corporation may structure the rights and obligations by and among itself and its shareholders through the issuance of special classes of stock, and where not otherwise prohibited by statute or public policy, the corporation may limit or expand such rights as it sees fit. *Winston v. Mandor, 710 A.2d 835 (Del. Ch. 1997)*, appeal dismissed, *713 A.2d 932 (Del. Ch. 1998).*

Liability of transferee. — A corporation which has either directly or indirectly come into possession of all the assets of predecessor corporations against which taxes were assessed is liable as the transferee of those assets to any income and excess profits taxes that were assessed against the predecessor companies, provided the assessments were duly made. *Gott v. Live Poultry Transit Co., 17 Del. Ch. 288, 153 A. 801 (1931).*

In an ordinary sale whereby the selling corporation receives and holds the consideration paid, the transferee corporation is under no liability to the transferor's debtors. *McKee v. Standard Minerals Corp., 18 Del. Ch. 97, 156 A. 193 (1931).*

The liability of an acquiring company, when it acquires the assets of another corporation but fails to provide for the payment of debts of the other corporation, is not greater than the value of the assets received to which the creditor was formerly entitled to look for satisfaction when the same were in the hands of his or her debtor. *McKee v. Standard Minerals Corp., 18 Del. Ch. 97, 156 A. 193 (1931).*

If stockholders of 1 corporation turn over its assets to another corporation, receiving unto themselves the stock of the transferee in payment, the transaction is void as against the creditors of the former, and they may look to the latter for satisfaction to the extent of the value of the assets received when the selling corporation fails to provide for the payment of its debts. When a transaction of that sort takes place, it is a fraud on creditors and is void as to them. *McKee v. Standard Minerals Corp., 18 Del. Ch. 97, 156 A. 193 (1931).*

If a transaction between 2 corporations constituted a bona fide sale for value of all of the assets and property of 1 corporation to another, under this section the purchaser would not be liable for the debts or for damages caused by a tortious act committed by the selling corporation before the sale was consummated. *Drug, Inc. v. Hunt, 35 Del. 339, 168 A. 87 (1933).*

Legal, yet inequitable reallocation of control. — The actions of directors in structuring the proposed transaction through the bankruptcy process they did resulted in a theoretically legal, yet undeniably inequitable, reallocation of control over the corporate enterprise. That reallocation does not withstand close judicial scrutiny. *Esopus Creek Value L.P. v. Hauf, 913 A.2d 593; 2006 Del. Ch. LEXIS 200 (Nov. 29, 2006).*

CASE NOTES — OTHER STATES

California

Disclosure. — Directors and majority shareholders must disclose all facts which would have been viewed by a reasonable investor as having significantly altered the "total mix" of information made available. *Neubauer v. Goldfard, 108 Cal. App. 4th 47, 133 Cal. Rptr. 2d 218 (2003).*

Whether a reasonable shareholder would consider a particular piece of information "important" or "significantly altering the total mix" of information made available is generally a question for the trier of fact. *Neubauer v. Goldfarb, 108 Cal. App. 4th 47, 133 Cal. Rptr. 2d 218 (2003).*

Illinois

Scope of fiduciary duty. — A majority shareholder, or a group of shareholders who combine to form a majority, has a fiduciary duty to the corporation and to its minority shareholders if the majority shareholder dominates the board of directors and controls the corporation. The circumstances of the challenged action or inaction dictate the scope of the fiduciary duty. If a shareholder plaintiff can prove that the majority shareholder has used his or her control over the corporation's board of directors to engage in self-dealing, Delaware law requires judgment of the self-dealing action of the dominated board by the entire fairness test. Self-dealing occurs when the majority shareholders cause the dominated corporation to act in such a way that the majority shareholders receive something from the corporation to the exclusion and detriment of the minority shareholders. The entire fairness test remains applicable even when an independent committee is utilized because the underlying factors that raise the specter of impropriety can never be eradicated completely and still require careful judicial scrutiny. This rule reflects the reality that in a transaction such as the sale of interest in a corporation, the controlling shareholder will continue to dominate the company regardless of the outcome of the transaction. *Feldheim v. Sims, 344 Ill. App. 3d 135, 800 N.E.2d 410, 279 Ill. Dec. 342 (2003).*

Maryland

Self-flagellation not required. — Under Delaware law, corporate fiduciaries are not required to engage in self-flagellation, as their duty of disclosure does not oblige them to characterize their conduct in such a way as to admit wrongdoing. *Paskowitz v. Wohlstadter, 151 Md. App. 1, 822 A.2d 1272 (2003).*

Necessary damages. — Under corporate case law in Delaware, director disclosure violations that negatively impact voting or economic rights support a direct shareholder claim, and require proof of actual damages; disclosure violations that do not negatively impact voting or economic rights may be dismissed for failure to state a claim. *Paskowitz v. Wohlstadter, 151 Md. App. 1, 822 A.2d 1272 (2003).*

Massachusetts

Inapplicable in bankruptcy trustee action. — A Delaware statute requiring an affirmative vote of a majority of stock issued and outstanding, or the written consent of the holders of a majority of the voting stock, to authorize the sale, lease, or exchange of all the assets of a corporation, did not enable the trustee in bankruptcy representing the corporation and its creditors to question the validity of a mortgage of all its assets authorized only by a vote of its directors. One reason assigned for this holding, and stated to be persuasive, is that such statutes as the one relied on are intended for the protection of stockholders and have nothing to do with the interests and rights of creditors, and that creditors have no standing to plead statutory requirements not intended for their protection. *Atlas Finance Corporation v. Trocchi, 302 Mass. 477, 19 N.E.2d 722 (1939).*

Entire fairness test. — Delaware law protects minority shareholders by reviewing those transactions where a controlling shareholder benefits from a transaction in a way that goes beyond the benefits accorded to other stockholders. This analysis, referred to as the "entire fairness test," requires the controlling shareholder(s) to prove the "entire fairness" of such a transaction. The "entire fairness" doctrine is designed to deal with those situations where a controlling shareholder has his or her own interest in the outcome of a transaction that might cloud his or her otherwise objective business judgment. *Olsen v. Seifert, 9 Mass. L. Rep. 268 (Super. 1998).*

Minnesota

New corporation may receive assets. — A corporation has the power to transfer its assets to, and accept the stock of, a new corporation. *Dworsky v. The Buzza Company, 215 Minn. 282, 9 N.W.2d 767 (1943).*

Sale through other channel not precluded. — A statute of Delaware authorizes the sale of all the property and assets of a corporation by its board of directors when and as authorized by the stockholders. The statute fixes the sole manner in which the directors can sell such assets and good will; but that does not mean that the stockholders who own the corporation may not decide to sell through some other channel. *Bacich v. Northland Transportation Company, 185 Minn. 544, 242 N.W. 379 (1932).*

New York

In general. — Under Delaware law, a corporation may sell all of its property and assets when authorized by the vote of a majority of the outstanding stock, unless it is shown that the disparity between the money received and the value of the assets sold is so great that the court will infer that those passing judgment are guilty of improper motives or are recklessly indifferent to or intentionally disregarding the interest of the whole body of stockholders. *Alcott v. Hyman, 16 Misc. 2d 192, 183 N.Y.S.2d 359 (1958).*

Demand on stockholders is not necessary under Delaware law in any case where the wrongs complained of are beyond the power of ratification by a majority of the stockholders. *Newman Plaintiffs, v. Baldwin, 13 Misc. 2d 897, 179 N.Y.S.2d 19 (1958).*

Addendum provision. — Del. Corp. Law § 64-a provides for the sale of the assets and franchises of a corporation when and as authorized by the affirmative vote of the holders of a majority of the stock issued and outstanding, or when authorized by the written consent of the majority thereof. The addendum provision allows the company to require in its certificate for said action the vote or written consent of a larger proportion of the stockholders. *Wattley v. National Drug Stores Corp., 122 Misc. 533, 204 N.Y.S. 254 (Sup. 1924).*

Ohio

Sale of assets subjects directors to enhanced scrutiny. — Generally, the management of the business and affairs of a Delaware corporation is entrusted to its directors, who are the duly elected and authorized representatives of the stockholders. Under normal circumstances, the business judgment rule mandates deference to directors' decisions, presuming that in making a business decision the directors of a corporation acted on an informed basis, in good faith, and in the honest belief that the action taken was in the best interests of the company. However, a sale of all assets is considered an extraordinary transaction, and subjects the directors' conduct to enhanced scrutiny to ensure that it is reasonable. *Huang v. Landixe Thermocomposites, Inc., 144 Ohio App. 3d 289, 760 N.E.2d 14 (2001).*

Duty to obtain best value. — When deciding to sell the assets or control of a company, the governing board of directors has a fiduciary duty to obtain the best value reasonably available to the shareholders. *Huang v. Landixe Thermocomposites, Inc., 144 Ohio App. 3d 289, 760 N.E.2d 14 (2001).*

Texas

Assumption of liability. — Under Delaware law, a successor may incur liability for its predecessor's torts by expressly or impliedly assuming liability. *Lockheed Martin Corp. v. Gordon, 16 S.W.3d 127 (Tex. App. 2000).*

CASE NOTES — FEDERAL

Second Circuit

Active oversight of board during merger. — A board of directors of a corporation, to fulfill their fiduciary responsibilities, must actively and directly oversee matters relating to the sale or merger of the corporation. *Caruso v. Metex Corp., 1992 U.S. Dist. LEXIS 14556 (E.D.N.Y. 1992).*

A merger is distinct from a sale of assets under Delaware law, and the distinction is not merely one of form but of substance. When an actual transfer of assets is structured as a merger, Delaware courts may consider the substance of the transaction in determining whether the transaction is a "sale of assets." *Sedighim v. Donaldson, Lufkin & Jenrette, Inc., 167 F. Supp. 2d 639 (S.D.N.Y. 2001).*

Shareholder approval. — Under Delaware corporation law, approval by stockholders holding a majority of shares is sufficient to authorize the sale of all of the assets of a corporation, and dissolution may be authorized by stockholders holding two-thirds of the shares. *Barnett v. Anaconda Co., 238 F. Supp. 766 (S.D.N.Y. 1956).*

Third Circuit

Assumption of obligations not automatic. — Under Delaware successor liability law, a company that purchases the assets of another does not by so doing automatically assume the obligations of the purchased corporation. *Diamond International Corp. v. Sulzer Bros., Inc., 1989 U.S. Dist. LEXIS 9820 (E.D.Pa. 1989).*

Standards of equity. — In the absence of statutory provisions to that effect, equity imposes a standard which the terms, conditions and expedience of a sale must meet. Majority stockholders and directors cannot appropriate to themselves the assets of a corporation, and this may not be done indirectly by their personally sharing in the profits of the sale of the corporate assets. Moreover they owe a duty to the minority stockholders to see that the assets are sold for a fair and adequate price. *Gomberg v. Midvale Co., 157 F. Supp. 132 (E.D. Pa. 1955).*

Fourth Circuit

Fiduciary duty to obtain fair price. — A corporation may sell all or substantially all of its assets, but the directors have a fiduciary duty to obtain a fair price. A fair price is one to which a reasonable and willing seller and a reasonable and willing buyer, under all circumstances, would agree. Ordinarily, determination of assets' fair value is within the directors' business judgment and discretion, and the burden of proof is on a dissenting shareholder to demonstrate unfairness. But where directors and shareholders who approved a sale have an interest in the transaction, the burden shifts to the proponents of a sale to show the directors' utmost good faith and the transaction's scrupulous fairness. *Williams v. 5300 Columbia Pike Corp., 891 F. Supp. 1169 (E.D.Va. 1995).*

Appraisal generally not available post-sale. — Delaware is one of the small minority of states where appraisal is generally not available after a sale of all or substantially all of a corporation's assets. Delaware courts have declined to find that a properly executed sale of assets may be treated as a "de facto merger" to which appraisal rights extend. Where minority shareholders challenge a sale of assets, as opposed to a merger, valuation may take into account an increase in the assets' value that is attributable to the sale itself. *Williams v. 5300 Columbia Pike Corp., 891 F. Supp. 1169 (E.D.Va. 1995).*

Seventh Circuit

Delaware courts recognize the "de facto merger" doctrine only in very limited contexts. In only a few instances involving sales of assets have Delaware courts applied the doctrine of de facto merger and only then for the protection of creditors or stockholders who have suffered by reason of failure to comply with the statute governing such sales. *Binder v. Bristol-Myers Squibb, Co., 184 F. Supp. 2d 762 (N.D.Ill. 2001).*

A de facto merger may be found where an asset sale took place that amounted to a merger. *Binder v. Bristol-Myers Squibb, Co., 184 F. Supp. 2d 762 (N.D.Ill. 2001).*

Tenth Circuit

Violation of Del. Code Ann. tit. 8, § 271 would be gross negligence if the board completely failed to even attempt to comply with its statutory obligation. *Geer v. Cox, 242 F. Supp. 2d 1009 (D.Kan 2003).*

Determination of sale. — Delaware courts have long held that determination of whether there is a sale of substantially all assets so as to trigger Del. Code Ann. tit. 8, § 271 depends upon the particular qualitative and quantitative characteristic of the transaction at issue. Thus, a transaction must be viewed in terms of its overall effect on the corporation, and there is no necessary qualifying percentage. Such an inquiry is factual in nature. Delaware courts have favored a contextual approach, focusing on whether a transaction involves the sale of assets quantitatively vital to the operation of the corporation and is out of the ordinary and substantially affects the existence and purpose of the corporation. *Geer v. Cox, 242 F. Supp. 2d 1009 (D.Kan 2003).*

§ 273. Dissolution of joint venture corporation having 2 stockholders

DELAWARE CASE NOTES — REPORTED

Purpose of section. — This section was enacted in order to provide a speedy method of bringing about the dissolution of a joint venture corporation as well as supervision of the distribution of its assets. *In re Arthur Treacher's Fish & Chips, Inc., 386 A.2d 1162 (Del. Ch. 1978).*

Substantive equity right. — This section creates a substantive equity right and that right is a stockholder's right to protect his or her investment in a corporation, the operations of which have become paralyzed by corporate deadlock. Such a substantive equity right is enforceable and protectible by a federal court's equity powers. *In re English Seafood (USA), Inc., 743 F. Supp. 281 (D. Del. 1990)*.

State interest. — The State of Delaware has a strong interest in the formation and termination of corporations under its laws and in the uniform development and application of the statutory scheme that the state legislature and courts have created to regulate those corporations. This state interest is sufficiently strong that federal court's should abstain from exercising its subject matter jurisdiction and equity powers in proceeding under this section. *In re English Seafood (USA), Inc., 743 F. Supp. 281 (D. Del. 1990)*.

Joint venturers owe each other fiduciary duty of utmost good faith, fairness and honesty with respect to their relationship to each other and to the enterprise. *In re Arthur Treacher's Fish & Chips, Inc., 386 A.2d 1162 (Del. Ch. 1978)*.

Granting of dissolution is discretionary. — The General Assembly's use of the word "may" in subsection (b) of this section clearly indicates that dissolution was not intended to be granted automatically upon the filing of a petition for dissolution but rather that the granting of such form of relief is discretionary. *In re Arthur Treacher's Fish & Chips, Inc., 386 A.2d 1162 (Del. Ch. 1978)*.

Court may take positive action. — In matters brought under this section, the Court is not powerless to take positive action. *In re Arthur Treacher's Fish & Chips, Inc., 386 A.2d 1162 (Del. Ch. 1978)*.

Diversity jurisdiction. — Proceedings under this section are adversary proceedings sufficient to fulfill the controversy requirement for federal diversity jurisdiction. *In re English Seafood (USA), Inc., 743 F. Supp. 281 (D. Del. 1990)*.

DELAWARE CASE NOTES — UNREPORTED

Stay granted. — This section is an important provision of Delaware corporate law. It enables deadlocked joint venturers "to bring closure to what has become an inefficient and unworkable relationship." Its saliency as a dispute resolution mechanism, though, is somewhat lessened when the party invoking it has, on numerous occasions, initiated (and lost) litigation in another jurisdiction where the main goal was to substantially the same relief as a Delaware court could provide if a dissolution action had been brought here in the first place. Certainly, a court should be wary when this section is invoked as a statutory panacea by a purported joint venturer who, having failed before in its effort to break up the company and having eschewed the power of this court for so long, suddenly maintains that a rapid and summary dissolution is the appropriate method through which the corporation's best interests will be served. In the circumstances present here, the equitable powers this court enjoys to manage its own docket and to provide for the efficient and orderly administration of justice outweigh, at least in the foreseeable future, this particular petitioner's statutory right to an immediate dissolution under this section. *Xpress Mgmt. v. Hot Wings Int'l, Inc., 2007 Del. Ch. LEXIS 74 (May 30, 2007)*.

§ 275. Dissolution generally; procedure

DELAWARE CASE NOTES — REPORTED

This section provides method of voluntary dissolution by the directors, by authority of the stockholders. *Harned v. Beacon Hill Real Estate Co., 9 Del. Ch. 232, 80 A. 805 (1911)*, aff'd, *9 Del. Ch. 411, 84 A. 229 (1912)*.

Directors cannot of themselves dissolve corporation. The first step in a dissolution, however, is the adoption of a resolution to that end by the directors. A resolution by the directors carries great weight with the stockholders, and, therefore, the personnel of the directorate is of considerable consequence in a matter of a corporation's dissolution. As the judgment of the directors carries most weight with the stockholders, every assurance that is reasonably possible should be provided, so that the directors are led to their conclusions solely by a regard for the interests of the corporation and its stockholders. *Lippard v. Parish, 22 Del. Ch. 25, 191 A. 829 (1937)*.

Distribution of all assets would clearly be winding up, which could legally be done only in the method provided by law. *Butler v. New Keystone Copper Co., 10 Del. Ch. 371, 93 A. 380 (1915)*.

Fairness of plan. — A plan of distribution in dissolving a corporation could be so designed as to force small investors to sell their interests. Such a plan would obviously be suspect if accompanied by an unreasonably small offer by the dominating stockholder. It becomes of importance, therefore, to determine whether or not the dominating shareholder's offering price was reasonable under the circumstances. *Shrage v. Bridgeport Oil Co., 31 Del. Ch. 203, 68 A.2d 317 (1949)*.

If, through stock ownership, an individual was in a position to require a corporation to dissolve pursuant to this section, the individual was under an obligation to adopt a plan of dissolution which would be fair to all the stockholders of the corporation. *Shrage v. Bridgeport Oil Co., 31 Del. Ch. 203, 68 A.2d 317 (1949)*.

While the majority stockholders have a right to dissolve the corporation, in doing so, they must consider its overall fairness. An unfair plan may not be forced on the small shareholder merely because of its happy tax consequences for the large shareholders. *Shrage v. Bridgeport Oil Co., 31 Del. Ch. 305, 71 A.2d 882 (1950)*.

Where a plan for dissolution calling for distribution of assets in kind is unfair to the small shareholders, effectuation of the plan should be enjoined pending a determination of the appropriate fair value per share of the corporation's stock, and it should be ordered that the per-share value when obtained will be offered by the corporation to the stockholders for a reasonable fixed time as an alternative to distribution under the unfair plan.

Shrage v. Bridgeport Oil Co., 31 Del. Ch. 305, 71 A.2d 882 (1950).

Mere fact that corporation has quit doing business does not necessarily constitute de facto dissolution if it is still solvent. *Shanghai Power Co. v. Delaware Trust Co., 316 A.2d 589 (Del. Ch. 1974),* aff'd in part and rev'd in part, *378 A.2d 624 (Del. 1977).*

DELAWARE CASE NOTES — UNREPORTED

This section on its face does not contain a reasonableness requirement, or any other requirement as to the timing of the filing of the certificate of dissolution.

Belanger v. Fab Indus., 2005 Del. Ch. LEXIS 30, No. 054-N (February 17, 2005).

CASE NOTES — OTHER STATES

New York

After certificate issued. — When the certificate of dissolution was issued, the corporation had ceased to function. The statute, however, permitted its continuance for three years after the date of dissolution, for purposes of suit by or against the corporation, to dispose of its property, and to divide its capital stock. Under Delaware law the directors continue as directors and not as trustees to close up the business of the corporation, but only for the three-year period. After that time the stockholders might have asked for the appointment of a receiver. The law seems well settled that a corporation which has become defunct by dissolution in the state of its creation is defunct in every

CASE NOTES — FEDERAL

Second Circuit

Delaware corporate law treats members the same as stockholders for the purposes of dissolution. *Securities and Exchange Commission v. American Board of Trade, 719 F. Supp. 186 (S.D.N.Y. 1989).*

"Liquidation". — Under Delaware law, neither a tender offer nor a merger is a liquidation. The term "liquidation" when applied to a corporation, means the winding up of the affairs of the corporation by getting in its assets, settling with the creditors and debtors, and apportioning the amount of profit and loss. *Sedighim v. Donaldson, Lufkin & Jenrette, Inc., 167 F. Supp. 2d 639 (S.D.N.Y. 2001).*

Stockholder authorization. — Under Delaware corporation law, approval by stockholders holding a majority of shares is sufficient to authorize the sale of all of the assets of a corporation, and dissolution may be authorized by stockholders holding two-thirds of the shares. *Barnett v. Anaconda Co., 238 F. Supp. 766 (S.D.N.Y. 1956).*

Dissolution under Delaware law is authorized by an appropriate vote of the stockholders and becomes effective upon the proper filing of a certificate of dissolution. *New York v. Panex Industries, Inc., 1996 U.S. Dist. LEXIS 9418 (W.D.N.Y. 1996).*

There is no common law dissolution under Delaware law, the remedy being exclusively statutory. *Marcus v. Lincolnshire Mgmt., Inc., 409 F. Supp. 2d 474, 2006 U.S. Dist. LEXIS 1281 (S.D.N.Y. 2006).*

Choice of law. — As this is a diversity case, the choice of law is controlled by New York choice of law principles. And New York adheres to the internal affairs doctrine pursuant to which the internal affairs of a corporation are governed by the law of the state of its incorporation. No "affair" is more "internal" than a claim that could result in the termination of the existence of the corporation. No state has a greater interest in that question than the state of incorporation. In this instance, Delaware. Accordingly, the complaint fails to state a claim upon which dissolution may be granted. *Marcus v. Lincolnshire Mgmt., Inc., 409 F. Supp. 2d 474, 2006 U.S. Dist. LEXIS 1281 (S.D.N.Y. 2006).*

Eighth Circuit

Two methods of corporate dissolution are provided: (1) the adoption of a plan by action of the board of directors followed by a meeting of shareholders upon three weeks' published notice and a vote in favor of such plan by a two-thirds majority of stockholders there present; or (2) in lieu of such notice the written consent of 100% of the shareholders. *Winton v. Kelm, 122 F. Supp. 649 (D. Minn. 1954).*

§ 276. Dissolution of nonstock corporation; procedure

CASE NOTES — FEDERAL

Second Circuit

Delaware corporate law treats members the same as stockholders for the purposes of dissolution.

Securities and Exchange Commission v. American Board of Trade, 719 F. Supp. 186 (S.D.N.Y. 1989).

§ 277. Payment of franchise taxes before dissolution or merger

CASE NOTES — OTHER STATES

Virginia

Not threshold requirement for use of winding-up period. — Under Del. Gen. Corp. Law tit. 8, § 277, a corporation may not dissolve until all franchise taxes due or assessable have been paid by the corporation. Compliance with Del. Gen. Corp. Law tit. 8, § 277 is not a threshold requirement for a corporation to take advantage of the three-year winding-up period, but rather is a bar to complete dissolution protection until a Delaware corporation pays its state taxes. *Hoopes Construction, Inc. v. Wilcher, 1998 Va. Cir. LEXIS 440 (1998).*

§ 278. Continuation of corporation after dissolution for purposes of suit and winding up affairs

DELAWARE CASE NOTES — REPORTED

Intent of this section is merely to permit the Court of Chancery, in its discretion, and prior to the expiration of 3 years from the date of dissolution, to continue corporate existence for such an additional period of time beyond 3 years as might be required in order to permit a corporation to complete the winding up of its affairs. *In re Citadel Indus., Inc., 423 A.2d 500 (Del. Ch. 1980).*

This section creates new right of substance, for at common law a dissolved corporation could neither sue nor be sued. *International Pulp Equip. Co. v. St. Regis Kraft Co., 54 F. Supp. 745 (D. Del. 1944).*

Section liberally construed. — When considered together, this section, authorizing suit within 3 years after dissolution, and § 321 of this title, concerning service of legal process on corporation, both remedial in nature, must be liberally construed. *International Pulp Equip. Co. v. St. Regis Kraft Co., 54 F. Supp. 745 (D. Del. 1944).*

Section expands equitable doctrine precluding escheat. — This section is in effect a statutory expansion of the equitable doctrine that upon dissolution of a corporation its property, notwithstanding the technical rules of the early common law, does not escheat to the sovereign or revert to the original grantor, and will be administered in chancery for the purpose of winding up the corporate affairs and distributing the assets to those equitably entitled to them. *Addy v. Short, 47 Del. 157, 89 A.2d 136 (1952).*

Section compared to § 279. — The statutory scheme seems to contemplate 2 situations, one where the dissolved corporation has continuing legal existence and is capable of winding up its affairs through its own officers and directors, and the other where the dissolved corporation can no longer wind up its unfinished business because it has no legal existence, or where it is unable or unwilling to do so through its own officers and directors. This section applies to the first situation; § 279 of this title to the second. *In re Citadel Indus., Inc., 423 A.2d 500 (Del. Ch. 1980).*

This section is not the exclusive method for the enforcement of claims for or against a dissolved corporation, since § 279 of this title permits the appointment of a trustee or receiver to take charge of the corporation's property, and to do all other acts necessary for the final settlement of the unfinished business of the corporation; although the two sections are interrelated, a petition under § 279 is directed to the restoration of corporate existence once terminated under this section or otherwise by the action of its officers and directors. *City Investing Co. Liquidating Trust v. Continental Cas. Co., 624 A.2d 1191 (Del. 1993).*

In tandem, this section and § 279 of this title ensure that whether a corporation is dissolved voluntarily by its shareholders or for nonpayment of taxes, it remains a viable entity authorized to possess property as well as to sue and be sued incident to the winding up of its affairs. *City Investing Co. Liquidating Trust v. Continental Cas. Co., 624 A.2d 1191 (Del. 1993).*

This section is not, in itself, a statute of limitations. *Smith-Johnson S.S. Corp. v. United States, 231 F. Supp. 184 (D. Del. 1964).*

This section does not operate as an act of limitations on an application made under § 279, and though the corporate existence for a winding up by the officers of the company is limited to 3 years from dissolution, the power of the Court of Chancery to administer the winding up proceedings is not limited thereby. *Harned v. Beacon Hill Real Estate Co., 9 Del. Ch. 232, 80 A. 805 (1911),* aff'd, *9 Del. Ch. 411, 84 A. 229 (1912).*

But decisions interpreting such statutes may be applied. — This section is a clear expression of a legislative policy normally prohibiting the commencement of actions by or against dissolved corporations more than 3 years after their dissolution and, as such, by way of analogy justifies the application of decisions interpreting statutes of limitations. *Smith-Johnson S.S. Corp. v. United States, 231 F. Supp. 184 (D. Del. 1964).*

Dissolved corporation has power to close its affairs. *Gamble v. Penn Valley Crude Oil Corp., 34 Del. Ch. 359, 104 A.2d 257 (1954).*

But it cannot carry on business for which it was established. *Gamble v. Penn Valley Crude Oil Corp., 34 Del. Ch. 359, 104 A.2d 257 (1954).*

After 3 years, corporate officers have no power to continue further their winding up duties. *Harned v. Beacon Hill Real Estate Co., 9 Del. Ch. 232, 80 A. 805 (1911),* aff'd, *9 Del. Ch. 411, 84 A. 229 (1912).*

Trustee may wind up corporate affairs. — This section does not require the directors or officers of a dissolved corporation to execute personally every aspect of winding up, nor does it prohibit them from vesting such power in a trustee. *Lone Star Indus., Inc. v. Redwine, 757 F.2d 1544 (5th Cir. 1985).*

The establishment of a liquidation trust is entirely consistent with the orderly winding up process contemplated by this section, provided it does not serve as a basis for the avoidance of corporate liabilities. *City Investing Co. Liquidating Trust v. Continental Cas. Co., 624 A.2d 1191 (Del. 1993).*

Claim beyond three-year period held viable. — A dissolved corporation, which established a liquidating trust to administer its assets during a post-dissolution period, was subject, under the terms of the agreement which established the trust, to a claim asserted beyond the three-year period established under this section. *City Investing Co. Liquidating Trust v. Continental Cas. Co., 624 A.2d 1191 (Del. 1993).*

Corporation can still serve as repository of title and as obligor of debt even though the corporation has been dissolved for 3 years or more. *Sanders v. Vari, 37 Del. Ch. 353, 143 A.2d 275 (1958).*

During the 3-year period of winding up, the corporation functions exactly as it had functioned before dissolution, with the important qualification that its powers are limited to closing its affairs and do not extend to carrying on the business for which it was established, but as concerns the property it had at the time of dissolution, its title and possession are unimpaired. *Addy v. Short, 47 Del. 157, 89 A.2d 136 (1952).*

Taking of property under will not related to closing of corporate business. — Where a corporation had power to acquire and hold property, and to dispose of the same, and all these powers were terminated upon the expiration of the corporate charter except those which were extended for the 3-year period of grace, and these were only such powers as were necessary to wind up the affairs of the corporation, the taking of property under the residuary clause of a will would not in anywise be connected with or related to the setting and closing of the corporate business, it would be rather the exercise of power granted by the original charter to acquire property, and, instead of contemplating a winding up, it would look forward rather to a continuance of the business first authorized. *McBride v. Murphy, 14 Del. Ch. 242, 124 A. 798 (1924), aff'd, 130 A. 283 (Del. 1925).*

Dissolution did not work extinguishment of possibility of reverter. — Neither the dissolution of the company nor the expiration of the 3-year period worked an extinguishment of the possibility of reverter retained by deed, and upon the abandonment of the land the possibility was enlarged to a fee simple title and as statutory successors to the rights and powers of the corporation, trustees in dissolution are now entitled to maintain their action. *Addy v. Short, 47 Del. 157, 89 A.2d 136 (1952).*

Transferable character of stocks is destroyed by dissolution with some equitable limitations. *Gamble v. Penn Valley Crude Oil Corp., 34 Del. Ch. 359, 104 A.2d 257 (1954).*

Restricted power of dissolved corporation does not include right to issue additional capital stock as, generally speaking, the acquisition of additional capital would seem to be the very antithesis of winding up. *Gamble v. Penn Valley Crude Oil Corp., 34 Del. Ch. 359, 104 A.2d 257 (1954).*

Abatement. — Any suit against a dissolved corporation which was filed before dissolution or during the 3-year statutory wind-up period does not abate, even on the expiration of the wind-up period. *In re RegO Co., 623 A.2d 92 (Del. Ch. 1992).*

This section keeps dissolved corporation alive for 3 years for purpose of suit. *Frederic G. Krapf & Son v. Gorson, 243 A.2d 713 (Del. 1968).*

Automatic extension of corporate existence. — This section provides an automatic extension of corporate existence for three years. In addition, the Court of Chancery may extend the three-year period for any purpose relating to litigation or where additional time is needed for the winding up process. *City Investing Co. Liquidating Trust v. Continental Cas. Co., 624 A.2d 1191 (Del. 1993).*

Corporation does not continue to exist for purposes of affirmative cross-libel or counterclaim. — Voluntarily dissolved corporation does not continue to exist for the purposes of an affirmative cross-libel or counterclaim interposed in a pending suit after the 3-year period specified in this section has expired. *Smith-Johnson S.S. Corp. v. United States, 231 F. Supp. 184 (D. Del. 1964).*

Service of notice of income tax deficiency and penalty constituted commencement of "proceeding" against defendant within the meaning of this section. *Ross v. Venezuelan-American Indep. Oil Producers Ass'n, 230 F. Supp. 701 (D. Del. 1964).*

Appointment of receiver does not continue corporate existence beyond statutory period. — Dissolution of a corporation by the Governor pursuant to *8 Del. C. § 511,* extension of corporate life under this section, and failure of Court of Chancery to extend beyond the statutory period caused corporation to cease to exist as a corporation, even though a receiver was appointed under *8 Del. C. § 279,* and such corporation owes no federal income tax for years when it was not in existence. *United States v. McDonald & Eide, Inc., 670 F. Supp. 1226 (D. Del. 1987), aff'd, 865 F.2d 73 (3d Cir. 1989).*

Attorneys were entitled to recover a judgment for legal services for corporate defendant despite fact that action was not brought within 3 years from time corporate defendant was dissolved. *Ross v. Venezuelan-American Indep. Oil Producers Ass'n, 230 F. Supp. 701 (D. Del. 1964).*

Where there is breach by corporation of its assumed valid option contract in a situation where holder of stock option cannot get his or her stock solely because of the dissolution, ordinarily his or her remedy would be an action for damages for breach of contract, but such a remedy is inadequate because an attempt by a jury to fix money damages would be fair neither to the option holder nor to the corporation and the other stockholders because the option holder's claim is for the value of the shares in dissolution and the ascertainment of such value is dependent upon the prior deduction of such value factors as dissolution charges, undetermined tax liability and other obligations of the corporation which will not be known exactly at the time a jury would be called upon to determine the amount of plaintiff's damages. *Gamble v. Penn Valley Crude Oil Corp., 34 Del. Ch. 359, 104 A.2d 257 (1954).*

Stockholder consent is not necessary to assign corporate trademarks representing the corporation's entire assets, where the corporation's charter has been repealed and the corporation dissolved under Delaware law, since the corporation can continue for limited purposes including that of disposing and conveying any and all property it possesses. *Storm Waterproofing Corp. v. L. Sonneborn Sons, 31 F.2d 992 (D. Del. 1929).*

DELAWARE CASE NOTES — UNREPORTED

Enforcement of judgment against dissolved corporation. — Under Delaware law, because a corporation continued in existence for at least 3 years after its dissolution, a foreign judgment, rendered the year after the corporation was dissolved, was not rendered against a nonexistent entity; thus, the corporation's corporate dissolution did not deprive the foreign courts of subject matter jurisdiction or otherwise render the foreign judgment void. *Akande v. Transamerica Airlines, Inc. (In re Transamerica Airlines, Inc.), 2007 Del. Ch. LEXIS 68 (Del. Ch. May 25, 2007).*

CASE NOTES — OTHER STATES

California

Rights preserved in full vigor. — During the three-year period of winding up, the corporation functions exactly as it had functioned before dissolution, with the important qualification that its powers are limited to closing its affairs and do not extend to carrying on the business for which it was established. But as concerns the property it had at the time of dissolution, its title and possession are unimpaired. Whatever rights it had, of whatever nature, are preserved in full vigor during the three-year period. Any other conclusion would contravene the plain language of the statute. The suggestion that the act of dissolution in itself in some fashion works a forfeiture or extinguishment of a legal right, by analogy to the death of an individual, is therefore on the face of the statute unsound. *Elk River Mill & Lumber Co. v. Georgia-Pacific Corp., 164 Cal. App. 2d 459, 330 P.2d 404 (1958).*

Connecticut

Receiver may be appointed post wind-up. — Notwithstanding the expiration of the three-year period, a dissolved corporation may be made a defendant to a suit in the Delaware Court of Chancery for the appointment of a receiver, and such receiver may be appointed at any time when cause therefor appears. *Millbrook Owner's Association, Inc. v. Hamilton Standard, 1996 Conn. Super. LEXIS 1504 (1996).*

Continuation as body corporate post wind-up. — All corporations, whether they expire by their own limitation or are otherwise dissolved, shall nevertheless be continued, for the term of three years from such expiration or dissolution or for such longer period as the court of chancery shall in its discretion direct, bodies corporate for the purpose of prosecuting and defending suits, whether civil, criminal or administrative, by or against them, and of enabling them gradually to settle and close their business, to dispose of and convey their property, to discharge their liabilities and to distribute to their stockholders any remaining assets, but not for the purpose of continuing the business for which the corporation is organized. With respect to any action, suit or proceeding begun by or against the corporation either prior to or within three years after the date of its expiration or dissolution the action shall not abate by reason of the dissolution of the corporation; the corporation shall, solely for the purpose of such action, suit or proceeding, be continued as a body corporate beyond the three-year period and until any judgments, orders or decrees therein shall be fully executed, without the necessity for any special direction to that effect by the court of chancery. *Sankaran v. Jarvis, 1993 Conn. Super. LEXIS 3077 (1993).*

Kansas

Not a statute of limitations. — While § 278 represents a legislative policy declaring that all suits by or against dissolved corporations must be commenced within three years after dissolution, it is not, in itself, a statute of limitations. This clearly appears from the ensuing § 279 authorizing the Court of Chancery at any time, either before or after the corporation's affairs have been wound up, to appoint a receiver to prosecute or defend suits by or on behalf of the corporation. *Patterson v. Missouri Valley Steel, Inc., 229 Kan. 481, 625 P.2d 483 (1981).*

Actions during wind-up binding. — The law of Delaware provides that corporations shall be continued bodies corporate for a term of three years after dissolution for the purpose of enabling them gradually to settle and close their business, to dispose of and convey their property and to divide their capital stock. In such case they remain intact as corporations. Their acts are those of a corporation and binding upon the stockholders. *Republic Natural Gas Company v. Axe, 197 Kan. 91, 415 P.2d 406 (1966).*

Minnesota

Legally dead. — A corporation expiring by its own limitation or "otherwise dissolved" shall be continued for a period of three years for the purpose of winding up and liquidating its business, but not for the purpose for which the corporation was organized. A corporation whose charter has become void and whose powers have become inoperative by reason of nonpayment of taxes has been otherwise dissolved within the meaning of the statute. Where a corporation has expired by its own limitation or its charter has become void and its powers inoperative by reason of nonpayment of taxes, the powers of the corporation are terminated. It is legally dead and without power to perform any of its corporate functions. *Kratky v. Andrews, 224 Minn. 386, 28 N.W.2d 624 (1947).*

Limited purpose of wind-up period. — Expired corporations are granted a continued existence for three years. But the additional three years of life is granted for only the limited purpose of prosecuting and defending suits and of enabling the corporation gradually to settle and close its business, to dispose of and convey its property and to divide its capital stock. In order that there might be no implication of powers beyond those specifically named, the section proceeds to deny to any corporation to which it applies any right to continue as a corporation for the purpose of conducting the business for which it was established. *Kratky v. Andrews, 224 Minn. 386, 28 N.W.2d 624 (1947).*

Under Delaware law, a corporation's existence continues unmodified for three years while its officers and directors wind up its affairs unless application is made for the appointment of a trustee or receiver. *Benchmark Computer Systems, Inc. v. London, 417 N.W.2d 714 (Minn. App. 1988).*

The authority of Delaware corporate officers continues after dissolution unless a trustee or receiver is appointed, and service on such officers is therefore sufficient to establish jurisdiction over the corporation. *Benchmark Computer Systems, Inc. v. London, 417 N.W.2d 714 (Minn. App. 1988).*

New York

After certificate issued. — When the certificate of dissolution was issued, the corporation had ceased to function. The statute, however, permitted its continuance for three years after the date of dissolution, for purposes of suit by or against the corporation, to dispose of its property, and to divide its capital stock. Under Delaware law, the directors continue as directors and not as trustees to close up the business of the corporation, but only for the three-year period. After that time the stockholders might have asked for the appointment of a receiver. The law seems well settled that a corporation which has become defunct by dissolution in the state of its creation is defunct in every other state. *Lehrich v. Sixth Avenue Bancorporation, Inc., 251 A.D. 391, 296 N.Y.S. 358 (1937).*

North Carolina

Can still be party defendant. — A corporation whose charter had been revoked for nonpayment of taxes could be sued in its own name as a party defendant. *Amicare Nursing Inns, Inc. v. CHC Corp., 34 N.C. App. 310, 237 S.E.2d 873 (1977).*

Ohio

Three-year-period. — Delaware corporate law provides that a dissolved corporation has three years after its date of dissolution in which it continues to exist for

purposes of prosecuting and defending suits. *O'Dell v. Dana Corporation, 1994 Ohio App. LEXIS 3510 (1994).*

Pennsylvania

Three-year-period. — Under the Delaware Code, corporations exist for purposes of suit for three years after dissolution. *Lichtman v. Taufer, 2004 Phila. Ct. Com. Pl. LEXIS 68 (2004).*

Virginia

Non-payment of taxes. — A corporation whose charter is "void and powers inoperative" due to nonpayment of taxes is considered dissolved. A corporation's nonpayment of taxes makes the charter void, and all powers upon the corporation inoperative, and thus dissolved. Del. Gen. Corp. Law tit. 8, § 278 is interpreted as allowing a dissolving corporation to nevertheless exist for a period of three years for the purposes of winding up its corporate and business affairs. This includes bringing suit as well as defending suits brought by others. *Hoopes Construction, Inc. v. Wilcher, 1998 Va. Cir. LEXIS 440 (1998).*

Construction with other law. — Under Del. Gen. Corp. Law tit. 8, § 277, a corporation may not dissolve until all franchise taxes due or assessable have been paid by the corporation. Compliance with Del. Gen. Corp. Law tit. 8, § 277 is not a threshold requirement for a corporation to take advantage of the three-year winding-up period, but rather is a bar to complete dissolution protection until a Delaware corporation pays its state taxes. *Hoopes Construction, Inc. v. Wilcher, 1998 Va. Cir. LEXIS 440 (1998).*

Washington

Suit process. — Under Delaware law, suit may be instituted against a Delaware corporation within three years after a certificate of dissolution has been filed, by service of process upon the secretary of state. *Williams v. Steamship Mutual Underwriting Association, Limited, 45 Wash.2d 209, 273 P.2d 803 (1954).*

Virgin Islands

Continuation of trust. — Under Delaware law, corporate existence does not cease upon dissolution, but may be continued, generally through a liquidating trust, for the limited purpose of winding up corporate affairs. A trust whose existence continues beyond the time contemplated by the terms of the trust for the purpose of winding up corporate affairs continues the corporation as a viable entity authorized to possess property as well as sue and be sued incident to the winding up of its affairs. *Harthman v. Texaco, 30 V.I. 308; 157 F.R.D. 367 (1994).*

Under the common law and Del. Gen. Corp. Law tit. 8 § 279, a trustee may prosecute and defend an action in the name of the corporation. *Harthman v. Texaco, 30 V.I. 308; 157 F.R.D. 367 (1994).*

While a dissolved corporation is not continued for the purpose of doing the business for which it is created, it is continued in order that, for the period of three years, the corporation itself may settle and close its business, and, if it fails to do, that thereafter its creditors and stockholders may, by application to a court, secure the appointment of trustees or receivers who shall make a final settlement of the unfinished business of the corporation. Any property which may not have been disposed of by the company before dissolution, or during the succeeding three years, is not lost, but remains the property of the corporation, so that it may be sold and disposed of for the benefit of its creditors and stockholders. *Town View, Inc. v. Young, 15 V.I. 266 (1978).*

CASE NOTES — FEDERAL

First Circuit

Delaware, like most states, has a statute that prolongs the life of a corporation in order to allow the corporation to dispose of its affairs in an orderly fashion. *College-Town v. U.S. Tradewinds, Inc., 1986 U.S. Dist. LEXIS 26005 (D.Mass. 1986).*

Second Circuit

Section 278 of the Delaware General Corporation Law provides that a dissolved corporation continues in existence as a body corporate until any judgments in actions pending at the time of dissolution are fully executed. *American Renaissance Lines, Inc. v. Saxis Steamship Co., 71 F.R.D. 703 (E.D.N.Y. 1976).*

Three-year extension. — During a corporation's extended period post-dissolution to wind up its affairs, it may sue or be sued on claims connected with the dissolution. Delaware corporation law specifically grants a dissolved corporation an extended period of three years during which it may prosecute or defend suits for the purpose of completing any unfinished business. A corporation in the aftermath of dissolution may close out its business by disposing of property, discharging liabilities, and distributing to stockholders any remaining assets. *Deerfield Specialty Papers, Inc. v. Black Clawson Co., 751 F. Supp. 1578 (S.D.N.Y. 1990).*

Delaware law extends the period in which a dissolved corporation may be sued to three years. *Sherman v. Chicago Communications Service, Inc., 1980 U.S. Dist. LEXIS 10028 (S.D.N.Y. 1980).*

Under Delaware law, all corporations, whether they expire by their own limitation or are otherwise dissolved, shall nevertheless be continued, for the term of three years from such expiration or dissolution for the purpose of prosecuting and defending suits. Specifically with respect to litigation begun by or against the corporation either prior to or within three years after the date of its expiration or dissolution, the action shall not abate by reason of the dissolution of the corporation; the corporation shall, solely for the purpose of such action, suit or proceeding, be continued as a body corporate beyond the three-year period and until any judgments, orders or decrees therein shall be fully executed. *Shared Communication Services. v. Goldenberg Rosenthal, LLP, 2004 U.S. Dist. LEXIS 23270 (S.D.N.Y. 2004).*

Del. Code Ann. tit. 8, § 278 keeps a dissolved Delaware corporation alive for three years for purposes of litigation. *Old Republic Insurance Co. v. Hansa World Cargo Service, Inc., 170 F.R.D. 361 (S.D.N.Y. 1997).*

The provision extending the life of a dissolved corporation cannot be used to support the maintenance of an action against a corporation which has ceased to exist as a result of a merger. *Damon Alarm Corp. v. American Dist. Tel. Co., 304 F. Supp. 83 (S.D.N.Y. 1969).*

Modern statutory remedies have effectively replaced the trust fund doctrine. There are sound reasons for abiding by the wind-up period established by this section. Therefore, the court of appeals concludes that the district court correctly held that the State's claims against the shareholder-distributees are barred by this section. *Marsh v. Rosenbloom, 499 F.3d 165, 2007 U.S. App. LEXIS 20555 (2nd Cir., NY, August 28, 2007).*

Pre-emption. — State has not shown such a conflict between Delaware law and the congressional policy manifested in CERCLA as to lead us to conclude that Congress intended to preempt Delaware's corporate wind-up period, which protects dissolved corporations' and their former shareholders' interests in finality. CERCLA does not suggest that the entire corpus of state corporation law is to be replaced simply because a plaintiff's cause of action is based upon a federal statute, or because it would net the government more money, which is essentially all the State has shown here. That is not sufficient to justify preemption. *Marsh v. Rosenbloom, 499 F.3d 165, 2007 U.S. App. LEXIS 20555 (2nd Cir., NY, August 28, 2007).*

Effect of 1941 amendment. — The Delaware law provided for continuance of corporate existence until execution of the decree in suits brought by the corporation, but not in those brought against it, if the suit was started during the three year period following dissolution. By the 1941 amendment suits in which the corporation was defendant were put on the same base as those in which it was plaintiff. *Trounstine v. Bauer, Pogue & Co., 144 F.2d 379 (2d Cir. 1944).*

Where a corporation asks for affirmative relief the corporation becomes an actor in the litigation, and the action may be considered as one brought by it, within the meaning of Del. Rev. Code § 2074. *Trounstine v. Bauer, Pogue & Co., 144 F.2d 379 (2d Cir. 1944).*

Third Circuit

Under the Delaware statute. the corporate entity was preserved for the purposes of a proceeding before the National Labor Relations Board and that an enforcement proceeding is but a continuation of that one within the contemplation of the statute. *National Labor Relations Board v. Weirton Steel Co., 135 F.2d 494 (3d Cir. 1943).*

Fourth Circuit

The continued existence of the corporation is strictly limited under Delaware law to a few specific situations: First, under Del. Code Ann. tit. 8, § 278, a corporation's existence is continued for three years after dissolution. During that time, the corporation may not conduct the business for which it was originally incorporated. It may conduct only such business as is "incidental and necessary to wind up. Second, the three-year winding up period may be extended by the Court of Chancery. Third, automatic prolongation of the life of the corporation beyond the three-year period is provided for for the limited purpose of allowing actions previously commenced by and against the corporation to continue to their expiration. Fourth, the statute provides that the Court of Chancery may at any time appoint receivers or trustees to conduct the business of the corporation. *Johnson v. Helicopter & Airplane Services Corp., 404 F. Supp. 726 (D. Md 1975).*

The dissolution of a corporation does not extinguish its liability in pending criminal proceedings against it. *Melrose Distillers, Inc. v. United States, 258 F.2d 726 (4th Cir. 1958).*

Liberal construction. — Section 2074, of the Revised Code of Delaware of 1935, Delaware Corporation Law § 42, is broadly remedial and should be liberally construed in order to permit a dissolved corporation to resist any claim made against it within three years after the date of dissolution. The Delaware statute explicitly provides for continued corporate existence for as long as may be necessary to reach a final determination of any "proceeding" as well as any "action or suit" begun by or against a corporation within three years of its dissolution. The word "proceeding" is obviously broader than action or suit and should be given full effect in order to achieve the fundamental purpose of the statute. *Bahen & Wright, Inc. v. Commissioner, 176 F.2d 538 (4th Cir. 1949).*

Sixth Circuit

Three-year extension. — Section 42 of the Delaware Corporation Law, Rev. Code 1935, § 2074, after providing that a dissolved corporation continues in existence for three years for the purpose of winding up, then provides that with respect to any suit commenced against it prior to such expiration, the corporation shall for the purpose of such suit be continued as a body corporate beyond the three-year period and until any judgment therein shall be fully executed. *Louisville Trust Co. v. Glenn, 66 F. Supp. 872 (W.D.Ky. 1946).*

Seventh Circuit

The term "otherwise dissolved" in § 278 of the Delaware Corporation Law applies to a dissolution for nonpayment of franchise taxes. Thus, a Delaware corporation dissolved for nonpayment of state franchise taxes falls within the purview of § 278 and continues to exist as a body corporate for the purposes stated therein. *Illinois C. G. R. Co. v. Arbox Three Corp., 700 F. Supp. 389 (N.D.Ill. 1988).*

It is clear from Delaware law that Del. Code Ann. tit. 8, § 278, represents a legislative policy declaring that all suits by dissolved corporations must be commenced within three years after dissolution and prohibits the commencement of actions by or against dissolved corporations more than three years after their dissolution. *Centagon, Inc. v. Board of Directors, 2001 U.S. Dist. LEXIS 19148 (N.D.Ill. 2001).*

Eighth Circuit

State of coma. — A Delaware corporation which has forfeited its charter but has not dissolved is in a state of coma during which it is still subject to suit. *Missouri v. Bliss, 1985 U.S. Dist. LEXIS 12751 (E.D.Mo. 1985).*

Limitation on transfer of assets. — Under Delaware law, an inactive corporation can still have assets. These assets cannot be transferred, however, unless the corporation is revived. *Field Hybrids, LLC v. Toyota Motor Corp., 2004 U.S. Dist. LEXIS 23201 (D.Minn. 2004).*

Ninth Circuit

"Suit". — In Delaware, a corporation is continued after dissolution for the purpose of prosecuting and defending suits by or against them. The word "suit" is seldom used when referring to a criminal prosecution. *United States v. Safeway Stores, Inc., 140 F.2d 834 (9th Cir. 1944).*

Delaware law provides an automatic three year extension of corporate existence for the purpose of prosecuting or defending any lawsuit begun prior to or within three years after corporate dissolution. *Yukon Recovery, L.L.C. v. Certain Abandoned Property, 205 F.3d 1189 (9th Cir. 2000).*

Tenth Circuit

A criminal prosecution brought against a dissolved Delaware corporation does not survive. *United States v. United States Vanadium Corp., 230 F.2d 646 (10th Cir. 1956).*

Eleventh Circuit

Three-year extension. — Del. Code Ann. tit. 8, § 278, provides that all corporations, whether they expire by their own limitation or are otherwise dissolved, shall nevertheless be continued, for the term of three years from such expiration or dissolution, bodies corporate for the purpose of prosecuting and defending suits, whether civil, criminal or administrative, by or against them, and of enabling them gradually to settle and close their business to dispose of and convey their property, to discharge their liabilities and to distribute to their stockholders any remaining assets, but not for the purpose of continuing the business for which the corporation was organized. *Dunkle v. Denko, 1997 U.S. Dist. LEXIS 16412 (N.D.Fla. 1997).*

United States Court of Federal Claims

Three-year extension. — Delaware, in its general corporation law, continues the existence of dissolved corporations for a term of three years, or for such longer period as the court of chancery may direct, for the purposes of prosecuting or defending suits and of enabling them gradually to settle and close their business, but not for the purpose of continuing the business for which the corporation was organized. Unless an action or proceeding by or against the corporation is commenced either prior to or within three years after the date of its dissolution, a dissolved corporation has no capacity to sue or be sued. *BLH, Inc. v. United States, 2 Cl. Ct. 463 (Cl. Ct. 1983).*

The statute allows dissolved corporations to continue to carry on significant activities and transactions, including: to hold substantial assets, to retain a board of directors, to hold regular meetings, to issue shareholder reports, to file state and federal tax returns, to invest corporate assets beyond the three-year period and to contract for insurance. Such activities do not extend the three-year limitation on the corporation's existence or continue its capacity to sue or be sued in actions that have not been commenced prior to dissolution or within three years thereafter. *BLH, Inc. v. United States, 2 Cl. Ct. 463 (Cl. Ct. 1983).*

Under Delaware law, a corporation whose charter has expired is given three years in which to wind up its affairs. The Delaware chancellor may appoint a receiver at any time, even after the expiration of the three-year period, to wind up the affairs of a dissolved corporation. *In re Government of Norway, 145 Ct. Cl. 470 (Ct. Cl. 1959).*

United States Supreme Court

Continuation of proceeding. — Any "proceeding" begun by or against a corporation before or within three years after dissolution shall continue until any judgments, orders, or decrees therein shall be fully executed. The term "proceeding" is elsewhere used in the Delaware Code as including criminal prosecutions. *Melrose Distillers, Inc. v. United States, 359 U.S. 271, 79 S. Ct. 763, 3 L. Ed. 2d 800 (U.S. 1959).*

§ 279. Trustees or receivers for dissolved corporations; appointment; powers; duties

DELAWARE CASE NOTES — REPORTED

This section provides remedy for creditors and stockholders of the dissolved corporation which may be invoked for their protection at any time if the company refuses, fails or neglects to settle and close its business. *Harned v. Beacon Hill Real Estate Co., 9 Del. Ch. 411, 84 A. 229 (1912).*

This section provides a remedy for stockholders and creditors of a dissolved corporation which may be invoked for their protection at any time in order to settle and wind up the corporate affairs. *Addy v. Short, 46 Del. 178, 81 A.2d 300 (1951), rev'd on other grounds, 47 Del. 157, 89 A.2d 136 (1952).*

This section functions primarily for the benefit of shareholders and creditors, where assets remain undisposed of after dissolution. *In re Citadel Indus., Inc., 423 A.2d 500 (Del. Ch. 1980).*

Action is in rem. — A dissolution proceeding is an in rem action; those who have claims against the corporation can have those claimed corporate obligations affected in the domestic rehabilitation or dissolution, upon notice and opportunity to be heard, whether or not they are subject to in personam jurisdiction in the state where the dissolution or rehabilitation is taking place. *In re Nat'l Heritage Life Ins. Co., 656 A.2d 252 (Del. Ch. 1994).*

Appointment of receiver for dissolved corporation may be within inherent power of court of equity. *Levin v. Fisk Rubber Corp., 27 Del. Ch. 200, 33 A.2d 546 (1943).*

It is elementary that on a proper showing a court of competent jurisdiction may appoint a receiver to judicially dissolve a domestic corporation. *In re Nat'l Heritage Life Ins. Co., 656 A.2d 252 (Del. Ch. 1994).*

Section compared to § 278. — This statutory scheme seems to contemplate 2 situations, one where the dissolved corporation has continuing legal existence and is capable of winding up its affairs through its own officers and directors, and the other where the dissolved corporation can no longer wind up its unfinished business because it has no legal existence, or where it is unable or unwilling to do so through its own officers and directors. Section 278 of this title applies to the first situation; this section to the second. *In re Citadel Indus., Inc., 423 A.2d 500 (Del. Ch. 1980).*

Section 278 of this title is not the exclusive method for the enforcement of claims for or against a dissolved corporation, since this section permits the appointment of a trustee or receiver to take charge of the corporation's property, and to do all other acts necessary for the final settlement of the unfinished business of the corporation; although the two sections are interrelated, a petition under this section is directed to the restoration of corporate existence once terminated under § 278 or otherwise by the action of its officers and directors. *City Investing Co. Liquidating Trust v. Continental Cas. Co., 624 A.2d 1191 (Del. 1993).*

In tandem, § 278 of this title and this section ensure that whether a corporation is dissolved voluntarily by its shareholders or for nonpayment of taxes, it remains a viable entity authorized to possess property as well as to sue and be sued incident to the winding up of its affairs. *City Investing Co. Liquidating Trust v. Continental Cas. Co., 624 A.2d 1191 (Del. 1993).*

Section 278 does not operate as act of limitations on application made under this section, and though the corporate existence for a winding up by the officers of the company is limited to 3 years from dissolution, the power of the Court of Chancery to administer the winding up proceedings is not limited thereby. *Harned v. Beacon Hill Real Estate Co., 9 Del. Ch. 232, 80 A. 805 (1911), aff'd, 9 Del. Ch. 411, 84 A. 229 (1912).*

Section 282 does not limit recovery of fraudulently transferred funds. — Section 282 of this title is not intended to limit the ability of a court to recover, for the benefit of creditors or for a receiver appointed under this section, funds fraudulently conveyed to a corporation's stockholders prior to dissolution, the transfer of which left the corporation insolvent. *In re RegO Co., 623 A.2d 92 (Del. Ch. 1992).*

Appointment of receiver is within sound discretion of court. *Levin v. Fisk Rubber Corp., 30 Del. Ch. 31, 52 A.2d 741 (1947).*

Caution exercised in appointing receiver for solvent corporation. — Conceding the inherent power of a court of equity to appoint a receiver for a solvent corporation, the right must be exercised with great caution, and only when there is real imminent danger of material loss that cannot be otherwise prevented. *Lichens Co. v. Standard Com. Tobacco Co., 28 Del. Ch. 220, 40 A.2d 447 (1944).*

This section permits the court to appoint receiver after 3 years from dissolution, and at any time when there is property or assets of the dissolved company to be administered by a receiver. *Slaughter v. Moore, 9 Del. Ch. 350, 82 A. 963 (1912).*

Even after the expiration of 3 years from the dissolution of the company by proclamation, jurisdiction is given to the Court of Chancery to take charge of the unfinished business of the company and its undisposed assets for proper administration thereof for the stockholders and creditors of the company, all of which is involved in the words "at any time," used in this section; the jurisdiction is not lost if the application be made by a bill in which the corporation is named as the defendant. *Harned v. Beacon Hill Real Estate Co., 9 Del. Ch. 232, 80 A. 805 (1911),* aff'd, *9 Del. Ch. 411, 84 A. 229 (1912).*

This section is sufficiently broad to include the appointment of a trustee even after the 3-year period of grace under § 278 of this title. *Addy v. Short, 46 Del. 178, 81 A.2d 300 (1951),* rev'd on other grounds, *47 Del. 157, 89 A.2d 136 (1952).*

Court may require showing of reason for displacing corporate officers. — If a corporation at the time of its dissolution is an active one, and even to a small extent pursues the objects for which it was created, then the court might require some reason to be shown why the officers should be displaced by a receiver to wind up its affairs. *Harned v. Beacon Hill Real Estate Co., 9 Del. Ch. 232, 80 A. 805 (1911),* aff'd, *9 Del. Ch. 411, 84 A. 229 (1912).*

Power of trustees in dissolution stems solely from statute defining the rights and liabilities of a dissolved corporation. *Gamble v. Penn Valley Crude Oil Corp., 34 Del. Ch. 359, 104 A.2d 257 (1954).*

Fiduciary nature of appointment. — Where a corporation had in effect, though not in form, become dissolved, and the 3 directors constituted trustees to wind up its affairs, it followed, necessarily, that they were subject to all the limitations put on trustees in dealing with the trust property for their own benefit. *Eberhardt v. Christiana Window Glass Co., 9 Del. Ch. 284, 81 A. 774 (1911).*

Directors, in addition to the duties towards the stockholders which they had in common with all directors of other corporations, assumed a special and peculiar relation to those who had been legally stockholders, and still were stockholders equitably, upon becoming trustees for the dissolution and winding up of the corporation affairs; they held the relationship of trustee and cestui que trust. They could not sell and convey the trust property to themselves, or to one of them, without the knowledge of the cestui que trust. If they did so, the cestui que trust could either repudiate the conveyance, or ratify it and obtain an accounting for the value received by the trustees. *Eberhardt v. Christiana Window Glass Co., 9 Del. Ch. 284, 81 A. 774 (1911).*

Duties of trustee. — A trustee is obliged to see that the trust estate is productive but a trustee's overriding duty is to see that corpus is preserved and protected. *Lockwood v. OFB Corp., 305 A.2d 636 (Del. Ch. 1973).*

A trustee is prohibited from making an investment which endangers security of corpus. *Lockwood v. OFB Corp., 305 A.2d 636 (Del. Ch. 1973).*

Equality among receivers of same GRADE. — If trustees or receivers are appointed, equality among all of the same grade, and preference for none, is the rule upon which the liquidation proceeds. *Amussen v. Quaker City Corp., 18 Del. Ch. 28, 156 A. 180 (1931).*

Receiver will not be appointed because of mere errors of judgment in business management. *Lichens Co. v. Standard Com. Tobacco Co., 28 Del. Ch. 220, 40 A.2d 447 (1944).*

Appointment of receiver does not continue corporate existence beyond statutory period. — Dissolution of a corporation by the Governor pursuant to *8 Del. C. § 511,* extension of corporate life under *8 Del. C. § 278,* and failure of Court of Chancery to extend beyond the statutory period caused corporation to cease to exist as a corporation, even though a receiver was appointed under this section, and such corporation owes no federal income tax for years when it was not in existence. *United States v. McDonald & Eide, Inc., 670 F. Supp. 1226 (D. Del. 1987),* aff'd, *865 F.2d 73 (3d Cir. 1989).*

Terms upon which trustee may conduct sale must be judged upon the facts of each individual case: A trustee is bound to use the care and prudence of a reasonably skillful and diligent person. *Lockwood v. OFB Corp., 305 A.2d 636 (Del. Ch. 1973).*

Burden on objectors to show loss to trust from trustees' negligence. — Where objectors do not charge the trustees with self-dealing or other conflict of interest, but they say simply that the trustees were negligent, the burden of showing loss to the trust rests upon the objectors. *Lockwood v. OFB Corp., 305 A.2d 636 (Del. Ch. 1973).*

Leave to bring suit is often matter within discretion of court, even when a receiver has been appointed. *Levin v. Fisk Rubber Corp., 30 Del. Ch. 31, 52 A.2d 741 (1947).*

Where receiver's authority to sue in federal court is challenged. — Inasmuch as the authority of a receiver of a dissolved corporation to sue in federal court is challenged by the defendant, the burden rests upon the receiver to establish that authority and unless, within a period of 15 days, the receiver presents to the Court of Chancery an application for authority to continue the prosecution of the instant suit and to retain an attorney for the purpose, the suit will be dismissed and the purported sequestration of defendant's property will be vacated. *D'Angelo v. Petroleos Mexicanos, 373 F. Supp. 1076 (D. Del. 1974).*

Receiver would be proper party to seek vacation of allegedly void judgment against the corporation. *Rhoads v. Mitchell, 43 Del. 343, 47 A.2d 174 (1946).*

Receiver and the complainant's counsel should be impartial between and independent of stockholders and creditors, and neither the complainant, nor the complainant's solicitor, should be appointed receiver of such corporation, or act as counsel for a receiver. *Cahall v. Lofland, 12 Del. Ch. 125, 107 A. 769 (1919).*

The legal adviser of the receiver should be impartial between all interests, and it is unwise and unfair, and, therefore, wrong for the court to appoint or the receiver to

Corporations

select, as his or her adviser his or her personal counsel or the legal adviser of a stockholder or creditor who are interested parties in a receivership. *Cahall v. Lofland, 12 Del. Ch. 125, 107 A. 769 (1919).*

Stockholder's solicitor properly retained as solicitor for receiver. — Where a dissolved corporation without creditors is being wound up by the directors as statutory trustees, and 1 of the stockholders obtains the appointment of a liquidating receiver to supplant the directors, it being alleged that the directors before dissolution had fraudulently dealt with assets of the corporation, and subsequently the receiver filed a bill against the directors and others to enforce restitution, it was not improper for the solicitor for the stockholder to act as solicitor for the receiver in bringing and prosecuting the suit. *Cahall v. Lofland, 12 Del. Ch. 125, 107 A. 769 (1919).*

Possibility of reverter constitutes "unfinished business" of corporation. *Addy v. Short, 47 Del. 157, 89 A.2d 136 (1952).*

Service of process upon corporate officers. — The General Assembly did not intend that a receiver should be appointed, even for a dissolved corporation, in an ex parte proceeding, if there were any of its officers in existence who could be served with process, and, therefore, it must have intended that the corporation should be made party defendant. *Harned v. Beacon Hill Real Estate Co., 9 Del. Ch. 411, 84 A. 229 (1912).*

Administration of assets by court of chancery after winding-up period. — Any asset of the corporation, vested or contingent, not disposed of during the winding-up period may in a proper case be administered by the Court of Chancery under this section and the rights of creditors and stockholders protected. *Addy v. Short, 47 Del. 157, 89 A.2d 136 (1952).*

CASE NOTES — OTHER STATES

Kansas

Construction with other law. — While § 278 represents a legislative policy declaring that all suits by or against dissolved corporations must be commenced within three years after dissolution, it is not, in itself, a statute of limitations. This clearly appears from the ensuing § 279 authorizing the Court of Chancery at any time, either before or after the corporation's affairs have been wound up, to appoint a receiver to prosecute or defend suits by or on behalf of the corporation. *Patterson v. Missouri Valley Steel, Inc., 229 Kan. 481, 625 P.2d 483 (1981).*

Minnesota

Under Delaware law, a corporation's existence continues unmodified for three years while its officers and directors wind up its affairs unless application is made for the appointment of a trustee or receiver. *Benchmark Computer Systems, Inc. v. London, 417 N.W.2d 714 (Minn. App. 1988).*

The authority of Delaware corporate officers continues after dissolution unless a trustee or receiver

is appointed, and service on such officers is therefore sufficient to establish jurisdiction over the corporation. *Benchmark Computer Systems, Inc. v. London, 417 N.W.2d 714 (Minn. App. 1988).*

Virgin Islands

In general. — Under Delaware law, corporate existence does not cease upon dissolution, but may be continued, generally through a liquidating trust, for the limited purpose of winding up corporate affairs. A trust whose existence continues beyond the time contemplated by the terms of the trust for the purpose of winding up corporate affairs continues the corporation as a viable entity authorized to possess property as well as sue and be sued incident to the winding up of its affairs. *Harthman v. Texaco, 30 V.I. 308; 157 F.R.D. 367 (1994).*

Under the common law and Del. Gen. Corp. Law tit. 8 § 279, a trustee may prosecute and defend an action in the name of the corporation. *Harthman v. Texaco, 30 V.I. 308; 157 F.R.D. 367 (1994).*

CASE NOTES — FEDERAL

First Circuit

Appointment. — Under Delaware law a receiver or a trustee (if a former director of the dissolved corporation) is appointed only on motion of a creditor or stockholder to a Delaware chancery court. *College-Town v. U.S. Tradewinds, Inc., 1986 U.S. Dist. LEXIS 22709 (D.Mass. 1986).*

Third Circuit

Vested title. — Under § 4408 of the Revised Code of Delaware a receiver appointed by the Court of Chancery for the dissolution of a corporation is vested with title to the corporate assets. *Wachsman v. Tobacco Products Corp., 129 F.2d 815 (3d Cir. 1942).*

Standing in other state. — The standing of a dissolution receiver of Delaware to maintain a suit in behalf of

the corporation in another state would be recognized by a court of that state. *Wachsman v. Tobacco Products Corp., 129 F.2d 815 (3d Cir. 1942).*

It was necessary for the plaintiffs to be able to aver that they made an unavailing effort to obtain through the Delaware receiver the action which they desired in respect of the defendant corporation's tax claim or to set forth legally sufficient reasons for their failure so to act. If the receiver is a general receiver, in whom title to the corporate assets is vested, a demand of him or her for action must be made by stockholders before they may maintain a derivative suit. *Wachsman v. Tobacco Products Corp., 129 F.2d 815 (3d Cir. 1942).*

Seventh Circuit

Construction with other law. — Once the period established pursuant to Section 278 has expired, the corporation may not be revived. Rather, a hopeful plaintiff must apply to the Court of Chancery for the appointment of a receiver who would then defend suits on behalf of the corporation. *Weyerhaeuser Co. v. Edward Hines Lumber Co., 1991 U.S. Dist. LEXIS 11980 (N.D.Ill. 1991).*

Tax Court

Power to act. — Where the resolution of dissolution appointed the president of the corporation as trustee for

winding up the affairs of the corporation, another director and stockholder had no power to act in the name of the corporation by purporting to commence an action for tax relief. *Falls City Pontiac Co. v. Commissioner, 15 T.C. 977 (Tax Ct. 1950).*

§ 280. Notice to claimants; filing of claims

DELAWARE CASE NOTES — REPORTED

Legislative intent. — The 1987 and 1990 legislation that enacted §§ 280-282 of this title was designed, at least in part, to provide a mechanism with which uncertainty could be dissipated and fairness to future as well as present corporate claimants could be presently established through adjudication. *In re RegO Co., 623 A.2d 92 (Del. Ch. 1992).*

Purpose. — Sections 280-282 of this title provide a judicial mechanism designed to afford fair treatment to foreseeable future, yet unknown, claimants of a dissolved corporation, while providing corporate directors with a mechanism that will both permit distributions on corporate dissolution, and avoid risk that a future corporate claimant will, at some future time, be able to establish that such distribution was in violation of any duty owed to the corporation's creditors on dissolution. *In re RegO Co., 623 A.2d 92 (Del. Ch. 1992).*

Default provision. — Section 281(b), despite its location, is the base-line provision of the procedure; it is a default provision that governs every corporation in dissolution that does not elect to pursue the elective procedure set forth in this section and in § 281(a). *In re RegO Co., 623 A.2d 92 (Del. Ch. 1992).*

Security arrangement. — The Court of Chancery is not prevented from approving a security arrangement under subsection (c) of this section if that arrangement is funded by all of the dissolving corporation's assets and is fair to all classes of present and future claimants. *In re RegO Co., 623 A.2d 92 (Del. Ch. 1992).*

Inadequacy of assets in offering full security. — In the situation in which a dissolved corporation is dedicating all of its assets to the security arrangement offered under subsection (c) of this section, the inadequacy of those assets to offer full security ought not to deprive the directors of the corporation from proceeding under this section and § 281(a); sufficiency of the security agreement may be achieved in spite of the inability to assure or secure future compensation in full to all foreseeable future claimants. *In re RegO Co., 623 A.2d 92 (Del. Ch. 1992).*

Effects of court approval of plan of security. — The effects of court approval of a plan of security for corporate claimants include: (1) the preclusion of liability on the part of the directors of the dissolved corporation to claimants of the dissolved corporation for matters arising out of the making of liquidation distributions; (2) the limitation of potential liability of stockholders to the lesser of a pro rata share of each claim against the corporation, or the amount distributed in dissolution; and (3) the establishment of a limitations period for actions against stockholders on claims against the corporation. *In re RegO Co., 623 A.2d 92 (Del. Ch. 1992).*

Determination of liability cut-off date. — In adopting the limitation provision contained in subsection (c) of this section, the General Assembly left the determination of an appropriate liability cut-off date to the substantive law of the state in which the claim arises. *In re RegO Co., 623 A.2d 92 (Del. Ch. 1992).*

DELAWARE CASE NOTES — REPORTED

The purpose of sections 280 to 282 is to provide a judicial mechanism to afford fair treatment to foreseeable future, yet unknown, claimants of a dissolved corporation, while providing corporate directors with a mechanism that will both permit distributions on corporate dissolution and avoid risk that a future corporate claimant will, at a later time, be able to establish that such distribution was in violation of a duty owed to the corporation's creditors on dissolution. *Akande*

v. Transamerica Airlines, Inc. (In re Transamerica Airlines, Inc.), 2006 Del. Ch. LEXIS 47 (Del. Ch. Feb. 28, 2006).

Delaware case law recognizes that a director breaches her fiduciary duty to creditors if she fails to comply with the dissolution procedures set forth in 8 *Del. C.* §§ 280-282. *Akande v. Transamerica Airlines, Inc. (In re Transamerica Airlines, Inc.), 2006 Del. Ch. LEXIS 47 (Del. Ch. Feb. 28, 2006).*

§ 281. Payment and distribution to claimants and stockholders

DELAWARE CASE NOTES — REPORTED

Legislative intent. — The 1987 and 1990 legislation that enacted §§ 280-282 of this title was designed, at least

in part, to provide a mechanism with which uncertainty could be dissipated and fairness to future as well as present corporate claimants could be presently established through adjudication. *In re RegO Co., 623 A.2d 92 (Del. Ch. 1992).*

Purpose. — Sections 280-282 of this title provide a judicial mechanism designed to afford fair treatment to foreseeable future, yet unknown, claimants of a dissolved corporation, while providing corporate directors with a mechanism that will both permit distributions on corporate dissolution, and avoid risk that a future corporate claimant will, at some future time, be able to establish that such distribution was in violation of any duty owed to the corporation's creditors on dissolution. *In re RegO Co., 623 A.2d 92 (Del. Ch. 1992).*

Default provision. — Subsection (b) of this section, despite its location, is the base-line provision of the procedure; it is a default provision that governs every corporation in dissolution that does not elect to pursue the elective procedure set forth in § 280 and subsection (a) of this section. *In re RegO Co., 623 A.2d 92 (Del. Ch. 1992).*

Inadequacy of assets in offering full security. — In the situation in which a dissolved corporation is dedicating all of its assets to the security arrangement offered under § 280(c), the inadequacy of those assets to offer full security ought not to deprive the directors of the corporation from proceeding under § 280 and subsection (a) of this section; sufficiency of the security agreement may be achieved in spite of the inability to assure or secure future compensation in full to all foreseeable future claimants. *In re RegO Co., 623 A.2d 92 (Del. Ch. 1992).*

All outstanding stock is entitled to ratable participation in distribution. — All outstanding stock, whatever its source, is entitled, in the absence of statute or of a contract provision to the contrary, to a ratable participation in the distribution of the capital to which all have contributed. *Gaskill v. Gladys Belle Oil Co., 16 Del. Ch. 289, 146 A. 337 (1929).*

Inability to pay both present and future creditors. — Subsection (b) must mean that a corporation in dissolution which cannot pay both its present creditors and make adequate provision for contingent and future claims, and which follows subsection (b) procedure, is not to pay its current creditors in full but to pay them ratably. *In re RegO Co., 623 A.2d 92 (Del. Ch. 1992).*

Interests of preferred stockholders. — Section 281(b)(i) is designed to protect the valid interests of creditors of a dissolved company, and says nothing about the rights and interests of preferred stockholders. The cases that have been brought under this section involve claimants challenging the adequacy of some reserve and requesting the court's independent review to protect their potential claims against the company. This court has never applied this section to protect the company's decision to reserve the full dollar-for-dollar amount of a contingent liability which has the effect of favoring a single class of preferred stockholders. Stated differently, the fact that Section 281(b)(i) permits the board to create a dollar-for- dollar

reserve does not speak to the allocation issues among preferred stockholders when the creation of such a generous reserve advantages one class over another. Blue Chip Capital Fund II L.P. v. Tubergen, 906 A.2d 827; 2006 Del. Ch. LEXIS 152 (Aug. 22, 2006).

Priorities of preferred shares are satisfied first. — Common stockholders are entitled only to what might be left after satisfaction of the priorities of the preferred stock. *Cox v. Sellers, 27 Del. Ch. 50, 29 A.2d 914 (1943),* rev'd on other grounds, *33 A.2d 548 (Del. 1943).*

Upon dissolution and distribution of assets, preferred stock may have sufficient preference rights to take it all to the exclusion of the common stock. *Robinson v. Pittsburgh Oil Ref. Corp., 14 Del. Ch. 193, 126 A. 46 (1924).*

There is no requirement that dividends be paid from profits. *Penington v. Commonwealth Hotel Constr. Corp., 17 Del. Ch. 394, 155 A. 514 (1931).*

Nor is there any inhibition against payment of dividends from any existing assets, including capital. *Penington v. Commonwealth Hotel Constr. Corp., 17 Del. Ch. 394, 155 A. 514 (1931).*

Dividends to be paid must be those accrued while company was going concern. — The dividends to be paid on the dissolution proceedings must be those dividends which had accrued while the company was a going concern and which would have been paid from surplus or profits had such funds existed. *Penington v. Commonwealth Hotel Constr. Corp., 17 Del. Ch. 394, 155 A. 514 (1931).*

Partly paid shares brought into equality with fully paid shares prior to distribution. — Upon corporate dissolution, before any distribution is made to either preferred or common stock, there must be an equalization in each class of all shares, whereby the partly paid shares are brought to the same footing as the fully paid ones. *Penington v. Commonwealth Hotel Constr. Corp., 17 Del. Ch. 188, 151 A. 228 (1930),* rev'd in part on other grounds, *17 Del. Ch. 394, 155 A. 514 (1931).*

Right of corporate officer to be repaid money "advanced" to company should not be less highly respected in dissolution proceedings in a court of equity than in a court of law having regard to principles of justice and right. *Grone v. Economic Life Ins. Co., 38 Del. Ch. 158, 80 A. 809 (1911).*

Former version of § 280 (see now § 283) of this title conferred upon court of chancery exclusive jurisdiction over matters pertaining to trustees under this section. *John Julian Constr. Co. v. Monarch Bldrs., Inc., 324 A.2d 208 (Del. 1974).*

Judgment creditor cannot be heard to assert that garnishees are "trustees" within the meaning of this section while denying that Chancery has jurisdiction of the issue by virtue of § 280 (see now § 283) of this title. *John Julian Constr. Co. v. Monarch Bldrs., Inc., 324 A.2d 208 (Del. 1974).*

DELAWARE CASE NOTES — UNREPORTED

Triggering event. — Holding that indemnification rights of former officers and directors fall within subpara-

graph (i), as opposed to subparagraph (iii) of subsection (b) of this section, does not mean that the corporation should not take into account the likelihood of a triggering event in determining what is a reasonable provision. Indeed, one could foresee many cases where the likelihood of a triggering event at the time of distribution approaches zero, leading to the logical conclusion that no provision for future indemnification claims is reasonable. *In re Delta Holdings, Inc., 2004 Del. Ch. LEXIS 104, No. 18604 (July 26, 2004).*

Amendment of pleadings. — When a judgment creditor alleged a judgment debtor's breach of fiduciary duty, the evidence showed that the debtor had notice of the creditor's suit against it and the resulting judgment, so that, when the debtor dissolved (if that dissolution were pursuant to the elective procedures in 8 Del. C. §§ 280(a)(1) and subsection (a) of this section, the debtor would be obligated to provide the creditor with notice of the dissolution (which it admittedly did not provide) and

make provision for the creditor; in that regard, amending the creditor's breach of fiduciary duty claim was not futile, for purposes of a motion to amend. *Akande v. Transamerica Airlines, Inc. (In re Transamerica Airlines, Inc.), 2006 Del. Ch. LEXIS 47 (Del. Ch. Feb. 28, 2006).*

When a judgment creditor alleged a judgment debtor's breach of fiduciary duty, the evidence showed that the debtor had notice of the creditor's suit against it and the resulting judgment, so (when the debtor dissolved) if that dissolution was pursuant to the default procedure in subsection (b) of this section, the debtor was obligated to make provision for the creditor; given that fact, amending the creditor's breach of fiduciary duty claim was not futile, for purposes of a motion to amend. *Akande v. Transamerica Airlines, Inc. (In re Transamerica Airlines, Inc.), 2006 Del. Ch. LEXIS 47 (Del. Ch. Feb. 28, 2006).*

CASE NOTES — FEDERAL

Third Circuit

Common law creditor recovery. — Under Delaware common law, where a corporation distributes assets to its shareholders while leaving creditors unsatisfied, those creditors are entitled to recovery directly from the shareholders, without result to fraudulent conveyance law and without have to first obtain a prior judgment against the corporate debtor. *Protocomm Corp. v. Novell Advanced Services, Inc., 171 F. Supp. 2d 459 (E.D.Pa. 2001).*

United States Court of Federal Claims

Unsatisfied creditor remedies. — Under Delaware law if all of a corporation's assets are disposed of without consideration or distributed among its shareholders, a creditor of the corporation is entitled to pursue those assets. Where a corporation distributes assets to a shareholder leaving unsatisfied creditors, the creditors may recover directly from the distributees. *Sharples v. United States, 209 Ct. Cl. 509, 533 F.2d 550 (Ct. Cl. 1976).*

§ 282. Liability of stockholders of dissolved corporations

DELAWARE CASE NOTES — REPORTED

Legislative intent. — The 1987 and 1990 legislation that enacted §§ 280-282 of this title was designed, at least in part, to provide a mechanism with which uncertainty could be dissipated and fairness to future as well as present corporate claimants could be presently established through adjudication. *In re RegO Co., 623 A.2d 92 (Del. Ch. 1992).*

Purpose. — Sections 280-282 of this title provide a judicial mechanism designed to afford fair treatment to foreseeable future, yet unknown, claimants of a dissolved corporation, while providing corporate directors with a mechanism that will both permit distributions on corporate dissolution, and avoid risk that a future corporate claimant will, at some future time, be able to establish that such distribution was in violation of any duty owed to the corporation's creditors on dissolution. *In re RegO Co., 623 A.2d 92 (Del. Ch. 1992).*

No intent to limit recovery of fraudulently transferred funds. — This section is not intended to limit the ability of a court to recover, for the benefit of creditors or for a receiver appointed under § 279, funds fraudulently conveyed to a corporation's stockholders prior to dissolution, the transfer of which left the corporation insolvent. *In re RegO Co., 623 A.2d 92 (Del. Ch. 1992).*

Upon dissolution, all pending actions against corporation abate unless saved by statute. *In re International Reinsurance Corp., 29 Del. Ch. 34, 48 A.2d 529 (1946).*

If appointment of receivers does not result in dissolution, pending actions against corporation do not abate. *In re International Reinsurance Corp., 29 Del. Ch. 34, 48 A.2d 529 (1946).*

A claim of fraudulent conveyance is not a claim against the corporation within the meaning of this section. *In re RegO Co., 623 A.2d 92 (Del. Ch. 1992).*

§ 283. Jurisdiction

DELAWARE CASE NOTES — REPORTED

Section 1901 of Title 10 is available to judgment creditor for transfer of its claims to Court of Chancery. *John Julian Constr. Co. v. Monarch Bldrs., Inc., 324 A.2d 208 (Del. 1974).*

Former law conferred upon Court of Chancery exclusive jurisdiction over matters pertaining to § 281 trustees. *John Julian Constr. Co. v. Monarch Bldrs., Inc., 324 A.2d 208 (Del. 1974).*

Judgment creditor cannot be heard to assert that garnishees are "trustees" within the meaning of (former version of) § 281 of this title while denying that Chancery Court has jurisdiction of the issue by virtue of this section. *John Julian Constr. Co. v. Monarch Bldrs., Inc., 324 A.2d 208 (Del. 1974).*

Where receiver of dissolved corporation is officer of Court of Chancery, his or her action in administering the estate is subject to the Court's supervision. *D'Angelo v. Petroleos Mexicanos, 373 F. Supp. 1076 (D. Del. 1974).*

§ 284. Revocation or forfeiture of charter; proceedings

DELAWARE CASE NOTES — REPORTED

Actions under this section are not prosecutions, and the civil complaint filed by the Attorney General is not a "process." *Young v. National Ass'n for Advancement of White People, 35 Del. Ch. 10, 109 A.2d 29 (1954).*

Right to exact forfeiture of charter for nonuser of franchises existed at common law, and this common law right is neither annulled nor abridged, expressly or by implication, by this section. *Morford ex rel. Gray v. Trustees of Middletown Academy, 25 Del. Ch. 58, 13 A.2d 168 (1940).*

Court of Chancery will forfeit corporate charter where abuse of its privileges and franchises is clear. *Young v. National Ass'n for Advancement of White People, 35 Del. Ch. 10, 109 A.2d 29 (1954).*

Courts are reluctant to pronounce a sentence of death upon a corporation for abuse of franchise. Where, however, there is a clear case of abuse of corporate privileges and franchises, courts will not hesitate to pass the sentence. *Southerland ex rel. Snider v. Decimo Club, Inc., 16 Del. Ch. 183, 142 A. 786 (1928).*

Sustained course of fraud, immorality or violations must be shown. — Generally, Courts of Chancery in forfeiture proceedings, perhaps reluctant to take a subjective position on what ultra vires activities injure the general welfare or contravene public policy, look for and find a sustained course of fraud, immorality or violations of statutory law before deciding that there has been an abuse of charter privileges. *Young v. National Ass'n for Advancement of White People, 35 Del. Ch. 10, 109 A.2d 29 (1954).*

Continued criminal violations may constitute misuse of charter. — The Court of Chancery does not enforce the criminal laws. However, the Court has been given statutory jurisdiction to revoke a charter for abuse. Continued serious criminal violations by corporate agents in the course of the discharge of their duties could very well constitute the misuse of a charter. *Craven v. Fifth Ward Republican Club, Inc., 37 Del. Ch. 524, 146 A.2d 400 (1958).*

Indefinite absence of stockholder action may result in corporate dissolution under this section upon the initiative of any stockholder. *Wife W. v. Husband W., 307 A.2d 812 (Del. Super. Ct. 1973), aff'd, 327 A.2d 754 (Del. 1974).*

Misuse of charter by nonprofit corporation which sought profits. — Where the evidence shows the defendant, organized as a nonprofit corporation, is engaged in misusing and abusing its corporate powers, privileges and franchises by seeking as 1 of the principal objects of its existence to make profits for the use of itself and members, a decree of revocation and forfeiture as authorized by this section must be entered. *Southerland ex rel. Snider v. Decimo Club, Inc., 16 Del. Ch. 183, 142 A. 786 (1928).*

Injunction to prevent abuse of charter. — Since the court has the power by virtue of statute to revoke the charter for abuses, it also has the ancillary discretionary power to act by way of injunction to prevent such abuses at an interlocutory stage. *Craven v. Fifth Ward Republican Club, Inc., 37 Del. Ch. 524, 146 A.2d 400 (1958).*

CASE NOTES — FEDERAL

Eighth Circuit

State of coma. — A Delaware corporation which has forfeited its charter but has not dissolved is in a state of coma during which it is still subject to suit. *Missouri v. Bliss, 1985 U.S. Dist. LEXIS 12751 (E.D.Mo. 1985).*

§ 285. Dissolution or forfeiture of charter by decree of court; filing

CASE NOTES — FEDERAL

Eighth Circuit

State of coma. — A Delaware corporation which has forfeited its charter but has not dissolved is in a state of coma during which it is still subject to suit. *Missouri v. Bliss, 1985 U.S. Dist. LEXIS 12751 (E.D.Mo. 1985).*

Subchapter XI.
Insolvency; Receivers and Trustees

§ 291. Receivers for insolvent corporations; appointment and powers

DELAWARE CASE NOTES — REPORTED

Purpose. — The purpose of this section is to protect the rights of stockholders and creditors in cases of insolvency. *Jones v. Maxwell Motor Co., 13 Del. Ch. 76, 115 A. 312 (1921).*

This section is remedial statute, giving to the Court of Chancery power it did not theretofore possess. *Thoroughgood v. Georgetown Water Co., 9 Del. Ch. 84, 77 A. 720 (1910).*

This section does not confer upon creditors the right to have a receiver appointed, although the insolvency of the corporation may be palpable, hopeless and attended by indisputable fraud or mismanagement, but it makes possible a new remedy because it confers upon the chancellor a new power, but because that which the statute confers is merely a remedy, the statute cannot affect proceedings in the federal courts sitting in equity. *Pusey & Jones Co. v. Hanssen, 261 U.S. 491, 43 S. Ct. 454, 67 L. Ed. 763 (1923).*

Act is calculated to secure proper adjustment of affairs of corporation and a just and equitable distribution of its assets among its creditors. The purpose of the bill is to secure a full administration of the property of the defendant as an insolvent corporation. *Jones v. Mutual Fid. Co., 123 F. 506 (C.C.D. Del. 1903).*

Appointment of receiver is remedy of auxiliary and incidental nature and cannot be the sole object of the bill; and in most cases, some other primary relief against alleged fraudulent or inequitable conduct by a defendant in breach of fiduciary obligations is also specifically prayed for. *Drob v. National Mem. Park, 28 Del. Ch. 254, 41 A.2d 589 (1945).*

A right to assert an interest now exists where it did not exist before. The assets, where insolvency arises, may now be taken from the hands of those who theretofore exercised sole dominion over the property and be drawn into equity where a receiver named by the court shall hold and manage them for the benefit of creditors and stockholders. The appointment of the receiver is not the final relief. Such appointment is only ancillary to the primary relief, which is to protect and preserve and ultimately dispose of the corporate assets in harmony with the conception that this section has conferred upon the classes named a right to have the assets impressed with a beneficial interest common to all. *Mackenzie Oil Co. v. Omar Oil & Gas Co., 14 Del. Ch. 36, 120 A. 852 (1923).*

Apart from statute, the appointment of a receiver is merely a remedy incidental and ancillary to the primary object of litigation, and cannot itself constitute such primary object. *Myers v. Occidental Oil Corp., 288 F. 997 (D. Del. 1923).*

The appointment of a receiver for the protection of property is 1 of the oldest remedies in equity. But it is a remedy of an auxiliary and incidental nature, and cannot be the only real relief sought by the bill. *Lichens Co. v. Standard Com. Tobacco Co., 28 Del. Ch. 220, 40 A.2d 447 (1944).*

Complainants must be stockholders or creditors. — Unless the complainants occupy the status of stockholders or creditors of the corporation, a petition for a receiver of an insolvent corporation will be denied, for it is only to persons occupying such status that this section accords the right to seek a receiver on the ground of insolvency. *Frantz v. Templeman Oil Corp., 15 Del. Ch. 203, 134 A. 100 (1926).*

Words "any creditor" appearing in this section embrace simple contract creditors. *Mackenzie Oil Co. v. Omar Oil & Gas Co., 14 Del. Ch. 36, 120 A. 852 (1923).*

The statute creates and confers on simple contract creditors as well as judgment creditors a substantial right of a purely equitable nature and a purely equitable procedure to enforce it. No action at law by a nonjudgment creditor nor any legal process on behalf of a judgment creditor, can enforce such a right. An exhaustion of the legal remedy for the collection of the pecuniary demands of complainants, proceeding under the statute, would not only fail to secure to them the relief prayed for, but necessarily deprive them of it. *Jones v. Mutual Fid. Co., 123 F. 506 (C.C.D. Del. 1903).*

It is not necessary that the complainant be a judgment creditor in order for a receiver to be appointed for an insolvent corporation. *Sill v. Kentucky Coal & Timber Dev. Co., 11 Del. Ch. 93, 97 A. 617 (1916).*

A creditor under the statute need not be a judgment creditor. *Pusey & Jones Co. v. Hanssen, 279 F. 488 (3d Cir. 1922),* rev'd on other grounds, *261 U.S. 491, 43 S. Ct. 454, 67 L. Ed. 763 (1923).*

The word "creditor" is a term of very broad meaning and it is defined as to embrace, not alone judgment or lien creditors, but also general or simple contract creditors, or creditors at large and when used in this section its ordinary meaning must be given to it, unless something inheres in the nature and purpose of this section which necessarily compels a restriction of its definition to a limited class. *Mackenzie Oil Co. v. Omar Oil & Gas Co., 14 Del. Ch. 36, 120 A. 852 (1923).*

"Any creditor," as used in this section, includes an unsecured simple contract creditor. *Pusey & Jones Co. v. Hanssen, 261 U.S. 491, 43 S. Ct. 454, 67 L. Ed. 763 (1923).*

The term "creditor" as used in the section is not confined to one having a judgment or lien. It embraces a simple contract creditor. *Velcut Co. v. United States Wrench Mfg. Co., 16 Del. Ch. 40, 140 A. 801 (1928).*

A creditor possessing a claim for damages for breach of contract is a creditor within the meaning of this section.

Velcut Co. v. United States Wrench Mfg. Co., 16 Del. Ch. 40, 140 A. 801 (1928).

Holder of instrument is creditor within statute. Pusey & Jones Co. v. Hanssen, 279 F. 488 (3d Cir. 1922), rev'd on other grounds, 261 U.S. 491, 43 S. Ct. 454, 67 L. Ed. 763 (1923).

Bondholders held creditors within meaning of section. — The right under this section to appeal to the chancellor to appoint a receiver for an insolvent corporation is given by the terms of the section to "any creditor or stockholder." Those that hold the bonded obligations of the corporation which are not yet due and on which matured interest coupons are in default are creditors. Noble v. European Mtg. & Inv. Corp., 19 Del. Ch. 216, 165 A. 157 (1933).

Creditor of stockbroker in receivership was regarded only as general creditor to the extent of any dividends paid to the stockbroker on certain shares in which the stockbroker had no equitable interest, in the absence of a showing tracing the dividends into a specific account or fund. NYSE v. Pickard & Co., 274 A.2d 148 (Del. Ch. 1971).

Corporation is not dissolved by appointment of receiver. The books of the corporation contain evidence of its organization and continued corporate existence; but to deprive it of these books and papers would not in effect work a dissolution of the company. Hirschfield v. Reading Fin. & Sec. Co., 9 Del. Ch. 344, 82 A. 690 (1912).

The appointment of the receiver did not dissolve the corporation, or cut short its legal existence. DuPont v. Standard Arms Co., 9 Del. Ch. 315, 81 A. 1089 (1912).

Principles enunciated in cases in which corporations have been dissolved are irrelevant to a receivership proceeding under this section, for the reason that under this section corporate life is not terminated by the appointment of receivers. In re International Reinsurance Corp., 29 Del. Ch. 34, 48 A.2d 529 (1946).

Although the decree of the court appointing a receiver has the effect of transforming the assets of the corporation into a fund to be held in the nature of a trust for the creditors and stockholders, the appointment of a receiver in such case does not work a dissolution of the company. Haas v. Sinaloa Exploration & Dev. Co., 17 Del. Ch. 253, 152 A. 216 (1930).

Where a receiver is appointed under this section the continuity of the corporation's life is in nowise interrupted. State v. Surety Corp. of Am., 19 Del. Ch. 17, 162 A. 852 (1932).

The appointment of a receiver for a corporation does not result in its dissolution. Carpenter v. Griffith Mtg. Corp., 20 Del. Ch. 132, 172 A. 447 (1934).

The appointment of a receiver for a corporation does not dissolve its corporate entity. Hannigan v. Italo Petroleum Corp., 37 Del. 227, 181 A. 660 (1935).

Technically, the appointment of a receiver does not dissolve a corporation. Lichens Co. v. Standard Com. Tobacco Co., 28 Del. Ch. 220, 40 A.2d 447 (1944).

Appointment of receiver does not disturb or interfere with existing liens. McGlinn v. Wilson Line, 20 Del. Ch. 315, 174 A. 365 (1934).

Appointment of receiver lies in discretion of chancellor. Stone v. Jewett, Bigelow & Brooks Coal Co., 14 Del. Ch. 256, 125 A. 340 (1924).

The fact that there is discretion in the chancellor to refuse to appoint a receiver does not destroy the right given by this section, any more than it could be said that the discretion which equity always exercises in administering the remedy of specific performance strips the right which underlies that remedy of its equitable character. Mackenzie Oil Co. v. Omar Oil & Gas Co., 14 Del. Ch. 36, 120 A. 852 (1923).

When the fact of insolvency is so shown, it does not follow that the appointment of a receiver will be made as a matter of course because it will yet be necessary to find such facts in the case as will make a favorable appeal to the discretion of the chancellor. Manning v. Middle States Oil Corp., 15 Del. Ch. 321, 137 A. 79 (1927).

The appointment of a receiver for an insolvent corporation is discretionary under this section. Velcut Co. v. United States Wrench Mfg. Co., 16 Del. Ch. 40, 140 A. 801 (1928).

Even when insolvency is shown, the appointment of a receiver is always a question that rests in the sound discretion of the chancellor. Kenny v. Allerton Corp., 17 Del. Ch. 219, 151 A. 257 (1930); Banks v. Cristina Copper Mines, Inc., 34 Del. Ch. 44, 99 A.2d 504 (1953).

Chancellor may, upon his or her own motion, appoint receiver, provided the facts and circumstances are such as to justify him or her in so doing. Gray ex rel. Cooch v. Council of Newark, 9 Del. Ch. 171, 79 A. 735 (1911).

Appointment should not be made in case of serious doubt. — If the court should entertain any serious doubt, a complaint asking for the appointment of a receiver should be denied. Banks v. Cristina Copper Mines, Inc., 34 Del. Ch. 44, 99 A.2d 504 (1953).

Receiver will never be appointed except under special circumstances of great exigency and when some real beneficial purpose will be served thereby. Drob v. National Mem. Park, 28 Del. Ch. 254, 41 A.2d 589 (1945).

Management's inability to hold an election. — Pursuant to 8 Del. C. § 322, the Court of Chancery enjoys the ability to appoint a receiver when and if a corporation "refuse[s], fail[s], or neglect[s] to obey any order or decree of any [Delaware court]. . . ." Though 8 Del. C. § 322 does not expound upon the powers and duties of a receiver so appointed, 8 Del. C. § 291 does discuss those powers and duties, albeit in the context of an insolvent company. That statute provides that a receiver may "take charge of [the corporation's] assets, estate, effects, business and affairs . . . and do all other acts which might be done by the corporation and which may be necessary and proper." Pursuant to the doctrine of in pari materia, the court observes that, if one became necessary to effectuate the terms of the order, a duly appointed receiver would accede to similar powers and duties. The court now has no occasion to consider whether or not circumstances justifying the appointment of a receiver could arise in this case, either under section 322 or more general principles of equity. Nevertheless, it is important to note that a state law process is available to deal with management's inability to properly fulfill its duty to hold an election-a process well capable of protecting the interests of all constituent groups. *Esopus Creek Value L.P. v. Hauf, 913 A.2d 593; 2006 Del. Ch. LEXIS 200 (Nov. 29, 2006).*

Receiver necessary to protect the company's creditors. — Motion to dismiss a company's creditor's claim seeking a receiver under *8 Del. C. § 291* was denied, as the company's actions of permitting the de facto controlling stockholder to repeatedly expand that stockholder's own position as a fully secured creditor to the detriment of other creditors in the event of liquidation and allowing the controlling stockholder's family members to continue to receive lucrative payments as consultants of the company supported the rational inference that a receiver was necessary to protect the company's creditors. *Prod. Res. Group, L.L.C. v. NCT Group, Inc., 863 A.2d 772 (Del. Ch. 2004).*

Appointment of receiver must serve some beneficial purpose to stockholders. — The rule has been stated that the court should not interfere by appointing a receiver, even for purposes of preservation, unless there is a present danger to the interests of the stockholders consisting of a serious suspension of or interference with the conduct of the business, and a threatened depreciation of the value of the assets consequent thereupon, which may be met and remedied by a receiver. It must appear that the appointment of a receiver will serve some beneficial purpose to the stockholders. *Salnita Corp. v. Walter Holding Corp., 19 Del. Ch. 426, 168 A. 74 (1933).*

Appointment of receiver is for benefit of all interested parties, including those who may ultimately establish rights in the case. *Hannigan v. Italo Petro. Corp. of Am., 37 Del. 180, 181 A. 4 (1935).*

Receiver is not appointed in interest of corporation. *Jones v. Maxwell Motor Co., 13 Del. Ch. 76, 115 A. 312 (1921).*

Involvement of court and custodian in corporation's business. — The involvement of the Court of Chancery and its custodian in a corporation's business and affairs should be kept to a minimum and should be exercised only insofar as the goals of fairness and justice require. *Giuricich v. Emtrol Corp., 449 A.2d 232 (Del. 1982).*

Creditor or stockholder may have benefit of this section in federal court, but the allegation of insolvency of the defendant corporation must be proved. *Myers v. Occidental Oil Corp., 288 F. 997 (D. Del. 1923).*

Presence of assets of corporation in state is not prerequisite to the appointment of a receiver under this section. *Adler v. Campeche Laguna Corp., 257 F. 789 (D. Del. 1919).*

When corporation has no assets, no useful purpose can be subserved by naming a receiver (an officer of the court whose function under this section is to take, hold, manage and administer assets); and in such case, the receiver ought not to be appointed. *Jones v. Maxwell Motor Co., 13 Del. Ch. 76, 115 A. 312 (1921); Freeman v. Hare & Chase, Inc., 16 Del. Ch. 207, 142 A. 793 (1928).*

In addition to primary assets of corporation there are other assets recoverable by receiver. One kind is conditional in character, the liability of a stockholder for the unpaid par value of his or her shares to pay creditors of the company when the assets of the company are insufficient for the purpose. There must be a preliminary determination by the court that there is such a deficiency and the amount thereof before particular authority to make an assessment and the amount thereof is given by the court to the receiver as well as orders or instructions as to the recovery thereof by suit. *Cahall v. Lofland, 12 Del. Ch. 162, 108 A. 752 (1920).*

Contention regarding management's ability to develop leased properties had no bearing on insolvency. — Where it is contended in the complaint that a corporation will never be successful under its present management in its effort to develop the properties which it holds under leases and that it has been able to maintain its existence only by the selling of additional stock and by advances made by certain of its officers and directors, this fact has no bearing upon disclosing insolvency necessary for receivership. *Banks v. Cristina Copper Mines, Inc., 34 Del. Ch. 44, 99 A.2d 504 (1953).*

Complainant must show condition of insolvency existing when his or her bill was filed. *Manning v. Middle States Oil Corp., 15 Del. Ch. 321, 137 A. 79 (1927); Rogers v. Bancokentucky Co., 18 Del. Ch. 23, 156 A. 217 (1931).*

Receiver should not be appointed if condition of insolvency is subsequently removed. — While insolvency must be shown at the time the bill is filed, if since the bill was filed the condition of insolvency has been removed, a receiver should not be appointed. *Freeman v. Hare & Chase, Inc., 16 Del. Ch. 207, 142 A. 793 (1928); Kenny v. Allerton Corp., 17 Del. Ch. 219, 151 A. 257 (1930); Banks v. Cristina Copper Mines, Inc., 34 Del. Ch. 44, 99 A.2d 504 (1953).*

Receiver not appointed where readjustment plan was being successfully carried out. — Where insolvent corporation had formulated and was successfully carrying out a readjustment plan for the purpose of liquidating its affairs with least loss to certificate holders, and those administering the plan were entirely separate from directors in charge when insolvency developed, court would not appoint receiver. *Wright v. Mortgage Guar. Co., 20 Del. Ch. 340, 174 A. 271 (1934).*

Insolvency under this section may be of 2 kinds, a deficiency of assets below liabilities with no reasonable prospect that the business can be successfully continued in the face thereof, or an inability to meet maturing obligations as they fall due in the usual course of business. *Freeman v. Hare & Chase, Inc., 16 Del. Ch. 207, 142 A. 793 (1928).*

There are 2 definitions of insolvency, one based on an inability to pay debts as they become due in the usual course of business and the other on a deficiency of assets over liabilities, but neither one is to be adopted to the entire exclusion of the other, for the needs of corporations and their stockholders and creditors, based on financial and commercial circumstances, conditions of the corporations, and the character of their business, vary so widely that no rule is universally applicable. *Sill v. Kentucky Coal & Timber Dev. Co., 11 Del. Ch. 93, 97 A. 617 (1916).*

Insolvency may consist of a deficiency of assets over liabilities, or inability to meet financial obligations as they mature in the usual course of business. *Whitmer v. William Whitmer & Sons, 11 Del. Ch. 222, 99 A. 428 (1916); Bruch v. National Guar. Credit Corp., 13 Del. Ch. 180, 116 A. 738 (1922).*

Insolvency under the statute exists where the liabilities exceed the assets, or where there is an inability to meet current maturing obligations in the ordinary course of business. *Kenny v. Allerton Corp., 17 Del. Ch. 219, 151 A. 257 (1930).*

Bare showing of insolvency alone will not result in appointment of receiver as a matter of course. Inasmuch as the appointment is discretionary with the chancellor, the appointment will not be made, even though the jurisdictional fact of insolvency exists, if the chancellor in the proper exercise of his or her discretion deems it unwise under the circumstances to make the appointment. *Noble v. European Mtg. & Inv. Corp., 19 Del. Ch. 216, 165 A. 157 (1933).*

Insolvency is jurisdictional fact. *Manning v. Middle States Oil Corp., 15 Del. Ch. 321, 137 A. 79 (1927); Kenny v. Allerton Corp., 17 Del. Ch. 219, 151 A. 257 (1930); Shaten v. Volco Cement Corp., 23 Del. Ch. 101, 2 A.2d 152 (1938); Banks v. Cristina Copper Mines, Inc., 34 Del. Ch. 44, 99 A.2d 504 (1953).*

And proof in support of it should be clear and convincing. *Manning v. Middle States Oil Corp., 15 Del. Ch. 321, 137 A. 79 (1927); Kenny v. Allerton Corp., 17 Del. Ch. 219, 151 A. 257 (1930); Shaten v. Volco Cement Corp., 23 Del. Ch. 101, 2 A.2d 152 (1938); Banks v. Cristina Copper Mines, Inc., 34 Del. Ch. 44, 99 A.2d 504 (1953).*

Technical liability to subsidiary does not constitute insolvency. — When a corporation organizes its activities into different subsidiary corporate units, a technical liability of it to one of its subsidiaries being but in substance a liability to itself is not such an insolvency as is contemplated by this section authorizing receiverships. *Manning v. Middle States Oil Corp., 15 Del. Ch. 321, 137 A. 79 (1927).*

Corporation should not be pronounced insolvent so long as there is reasonable prospect of success and the corporation is able to respond to the lawful demands of creditors. *Sill v. Kentucky Coal & Timber Dev. Co., 11 Del. Ch. 93, 97 A. 617 (1916).*

Corporation should have chance to adjust what appear to be temporary troubles. — To precipitate a corporation into a receivership before it has had a fair chance to adjust what appears to be only temporary troubles would be an unwise use of the chancellor's discretionary power, even if it be assumed that it is technically insolvent. *Kenny v. Allerton Corp., 17 Del. Ch. 219, 151 A. 257 (1930).*

Failure to pay claim because of dispute as to amount cannot constitute insolvency. — Failure to pay a claim, so long as such failure is due not to inability to pay but to a dispute as to its amount or validity, cannot

constitute insolvency. *Velcut Co. v. United States Wrench Mfg. Co., 16 Del. Ch. 40, 140 A. 801 (1928).*

Insolvency not established where debts can be met by using credit resources. — Insolvency within the meaning of this section is not made out where the corporation's situation is such that whatever debts are properly chargeable against it can be taken care of by the corporation's use of its credit resources. *McKee v. Standard Minerals Corp., 18 Del. Ch. 97, 156 A. 193 (1931).*

If a corporation which is charged to be insolvent only in the sense that it cannot pay its current bills has sufficient credit to raise funds with which to meet them, the Court of Chancery ought not generally to appoint a receiver for it. *Shaten v. Volco Cement Corp., 23 Del. Ch. 101, 2 A.2d 152 (1938).*

If a corporation which is charged to be insolvent only in the sense that it cannot pay its current bills has sufficient credit upon which to raise funds to pay those bills, a court ought not generally appoint a receiver. *Banks v. Cristina Copper Mines, Inc., 34 Del. Ch. 44, 99 A.2d 504 (1953).*

Use of borrowed money to pay debts does not constitute inability to pay obligations. — The fact that the money which was used to pay debts was borrowed money does not constitute an inability to pay obligations as they mature, so as to constitute the ground of insolvency. *Freeman v. Hare & Chase, Inc., 16 Del. Ch. 207, 142 A. 793 (1928); Banks v. Cristina Copper Mines, Inc., 34 Del. Ch. 44, 99 A.2d 504 (1953).*

Fact that holding company has subsidiary which is bad investment, so bad that, if it were liquidated, the parent company would lose its investment therein, does not necessarily mean that a receiver should be appointed for the parent where the ground relied on is insolvency due to inability to meet current obligations. *Shaten v. Volco Cement Corp., 23 Del. Ch. 101, 2 A.2d 152 (1938).*

Exclusion of shareholder from management does not warrant appointment of receiver. — The bare fact that the owner of one half of the outstanding stock was excluded from any participation in the management has been held not enough to warrant the appointment of a receiver. *Salnita Corp. v. Walter Holding Corp., 19 Del. Ch. 426, 168 A. 74 (1933).*

Receiver is not indispensably necessary to recovery of alleged secret profits made by the officers and directors of an insolvent corporation. *Boggs v. Bellevue, Inc., 18 Del. Ch. 108, 156 A. 202 (1931).*

Corporate president has no implied or inherent power to consent to appointment of a receiver for the purpose of winding up its affairs. *Bruch v. National Guar. Credit Corp., 13 Del. Ch. 180, 116 A. 738 (1922).*

Receiver will not be appointed where court can find another and less stringent means of protecting the rights of the parties. *Moore v. Associated Producing & Ref. Corp., 14 Del. Ch. 97, 121 A. 655 (1923).*

Failure of officers to furnish information did not justify appointment of receiver. — Complainant was entitled to reasonable information relating to the activities and financial condition of the corporation, but the failure of its officers to furnish it did not justify the appointment of a receiver. *Lichens Co. v. Standard Com. Tobacco Co., 28 Del. Ch. 220, 40 A.2d 447 (1944).*

Mere differences of opinion among stockholders or directors as to business policy or methods pursued or to be pursued by the corporation cannot of themselves constitute a legitimate ground on which to vest in a receiver control and management of the corporate property and franchises. *Carson v. Allegany Window Glass Co., 189 F. 791 (D. Del. 1911).*

A receiver will not be appointed to wind up the affairs of a corporation merely because of dissensions among stockholders where it appears that the corporation is solvent and its business prosperous. *Salnita Corp. v. Walter Holding Corp., 19 Del. Ch. 426, 168 A. 74 (1933).*

Mere dissensions among corporate stockholders, whether over internal matters or otherwise, will seldom justify the appointment of a receiver. *Drob v. National Mem. Park, 28 Del. Ch. 254, 41 A.2d 589 (1945).*

No mere differences of opinion among stockholders or directors as to business policy or methods pursued by the corporation can of themselves constitute a legitimate ground for the appointment of a receiver. *Banks v. Cristina Copper Mines, Inc., 34 Del. Ch. 44, 99 A.2d 504 (1953).*

Receiver is officer of court appointing him or her. A receiver is appointed for the benefit of all parties who may establish rights in the cause. *Stockbridge v. Beckwith, 6 Del. Ch. 72, 33 A. 620 (1887).*

The receiver is but the creature of the court. He or she has no powers except such as are conferred upon him or her by the order of his or her appointment. *Stockbridge v. Beckwith, 6 Del. Ch. 72, 33 A. 620 (1887).*

When appointment takes effect. — If a receiver has been appointed on a designated day and the record shows nothing as to the precise hour of his or her appointment, it is to be regarded in law as having taken effect at the beginning of that day. *Ferris v. Chic-Mint Gum Co., 14 Del. Ch. 270, 125 A. 343 (1924).*

Equality among receivers of same grade. — If trustees or receivers are appointed, equality among all of the same grade and preference for none is the rule upon which the liquidation proceeds. *Amussen v. Quaker City Corp., 18 Del. Ch. 28, 156 A. 180 (1931).*

Receiver and his or her counsel should be impartial between and independent of stockholders and creditors, and neither the complainant nor his or her solicitor should be appointed receiver of such corporation, or act as counsel for a receiver. *Cahall v. Lofland, 12 Del. Ch. 125, 107 A. 769 (1919).*

The legal adviser of the receiver should be impartial between all interests, and it is unwise and unfair, and, therefore, wrong for the court to appoint, or the receiver to select, as his or her adviser his or her personal counsel, or the legal adviser of a stockholder or creditor who are interested parties in a receivership. *Cahall v. Lofland, 12 Del. Ch. 125, 107 A. 769 (1919).*

Stockholder's solicitor properly retained as solicitor for receiver. — Where a dissolved corporation without creditors is being wound up by the directors as statutory trustees, and 1 of the stockholders obtains the appointment of a liquidating receiver to supplant the directors, it being alleged that the directors before dissolution had fraudulently dealt with assets of the corporation, and subsequently the receiver filed a bill against the directors and others to enforce restitution, it was not improper for the solicitor for the stockholder to act as solicitor for the receiver in bringing and prosecuting the suit. *Cahall v. Lofland, 12 Del. Ch. 125, 107 A. 769 (1919).*

Receiver has no extraterritorial power of official action; none which the court appointing him or her can confer with authority to enable him or her to go into a foreign jurisdiction to take possession of the debtor's property; none which can give him or her, upon the principle of comity, a privilege to sue in a foreign court or another jurisdiction, as the judgment creditor himself or herself might have done, where his or her debtor may be amenable to the tribunal which the creditor may seek. *Stockbridge v. Beckwith, 6 Del. Ch. 72, 33 A. 620 (1887).*

Receiver's right to possession of debtor's property is limited to the jurisdiction of his or her appointment; and he or she has no lien upon the property of the debtor except for that which he or she may get the possession of without suit, or for that which, after having been permitted to sue for, he or she may reduce into possession in that way. *Stockbridge v. Beckwith, 6 Del. Ch. 72, 33 A. 620 (1887).*

Continuation of business by receiver. — A proper showing made to the chancellor, he or she under the powers vested in him or her, may make such modification of his or her decree as may be necessary to authorize receivers appointed by him or her to continue the business of a corporation for the express purpose of conserving its assets and restoring it to a condition of solvency. *Baden-hausen Co. v. Kidwell, 12 Del. Ch. 370, 107 A. 297 (1919).*

Although receivers appointed under this section proceed to liquidate a corporation and ultimately terminate its existence, the section does not necessarily contemplate that in every instance corporate assets shall be turned into cash and distributed and its business and affairs wound up. Cases may exist where the court will deem it best to continue to operate the company's business through a receiver and at a later time turn the corporation back to the stockholders and officers as a going concern. *In re International Reinsurance Corp., 29 Del. Ch. 34, 48 A.2d 529 (1946).*

Custody of corporate seal. — An order to the officers of the company to deliver to the receiver of the company all the property, effects, etc., of the company, including the corporate seal and all books relating to the past transactions of the company does not necessarily mean that the receiver has a right to sell the corporate seal, but probably would be an authority that the custody of the seal should be given to the receiver to be used for whatever proper purpose it may be found useful in winding up or administering the affairs and assets of the company. *Hirschfield v. Reading Fin. & Sec. Co., 9 Del. Ch. 344, 82 A. 690 (1912).*

Maintenance and defense of suits. — The right to sue its officers for mismanagement of its affairs is a right of the corporation; if money is recovered it belongs to the corporation; and if the corporation becomes insolvent and a receiver of all its estate and effects is appointed, the receiver is the proper person to bring the suit; for by the appointment of the receiver the court, through its receiver, assumes jurisdiction of all the estate and affairs of the corporation, for the benefit of all those whom the court shall ultimately adjudge to be entitled to such estate. *Du Pont v. Standard Arms Co., 9 Del. Ch. 315, 81 A. 1089 (1912).*

A receiver appointed under the authority of this section represents not alone the corporation of which he or she is receiver, but as well the interests of all creditors, and may sue to set aside corporate transfers and conveyances made in fraud of creditors. *Keedy v. Sterling Elec. Appliance Co., 115 A.2d 359 (Del. Ch. 1921).*

A cause of action belonging to a corporation may and should be asserted by a general receiver appointed for it. *McKee v. Rogers, 18 Del. Ch. 81, 156 A. 191 (1931).*

While a general receiver with title vested in him or her may as a matter of comity be recognized for purposes of suit in jurisdictions foreign to his or her appointment, an equity receiver, appointed as temporary custodian of local assets, is not extended the right to sue in assertion of causes of action in courts outside the jurisdiction of his or her appointment. *McKee v. Rogers, 18 Del. Ch. 81, 156 A. 191 (1931).*

Receiver takes assets as trustee of insolvent. — A receiver appointed under this section is not a purchaser for value without notice but takes the assets of the company as a trustee and as a representative of the insolvent, and such receiver acquires no greater interest in the estate than the corporation had, and its assets are subject to setoffs, liens and encumbrances as they exist at the time of the appointment. *Greif v. James H. Wright Co., 10 Del. Ch. 308, 91 A. 205 (1914).*

In the distribution of the assets of a bankrupt corporation, a receiver occupies a position toward both creditors and stockholders somewhat analogous to that of a trustee. In enforcing alleged rights of action in the collection of corporate assets, a receiver usually acts as the representative of the corporation, and has no greater rights or powers. Where, however, the insolvent corporation has perpetrated a fraud on its creditors, by an illegal and improper disposition of its assets, a somewhat different situation arises. Under such circumstances, it seems that the receiver may enforce the rights of creditors, and in so doing has even greater rights than the corporation could have had. *Bovay v. H.M. Byllesby & Co., 26 Del. Ch. 69, 22 A.2d 138 (1941).*

Receiver has power to collect unpaid stock subscriptions because the relation between the stockholder and the company is contractual and the unpaid subscription an asset of the corporation. *John W. Cooney Co. v. Arlington Hotel Co., 11 Del. Ch. 430, 106 A. 39 (1918).*

The acceptance of shares of stock under a law similar to § 162 of this title, without subscription, raises an implied promise to pay for them. Some courts call such a liability an equitable asset, but, whatever it may be called, it is a liability that may be enforced to pay the debts of the corporation, and by no one more properly than a receiver appointed under the insolvency statute. *John W. Cooney Co. v. Arlington Hotel Co., 11 Del. Ch. 430, 106 A. 39 (1918).*

The amount due to the company for stock issued and not paid for is an asset of the company for the benefit of its creditors when it is insolvent. *Cooper v. Eastern Horse & Mule Co., 12 Del. Ch. 210, 110 A. 666 (1920).*

An order may be entered adjudging the amount of the unpaid indebtedness of a corporation and assessing upon the subscribers to and holders of stock who have not paid in full therefor such portion of the amount due thereon as is necessary to pay the adjudicated indebtedness and the costs and expenses of administration. *Carpenter v. Griffith Mtg. Corp., 20 Del. Ch. 132, 172 A. 447 (1934).*

Debt due receiver cannot be set off against debt due company. — A debt due to the receiver, as distinguished from a debt due to the company, cannot be set off as against a debt due from the company. *Greif v. James H. Wright Co., 10 Del. Ch. 308, 91 A. 205 (1914).*

Seller of property on trial basis could assert rights against receiver. — Where property is sold on trial basis and buyer has not accepted and seller has not disaffirmed sale at time buyer becomes insolvent and receivers are appointed, no title to the property has passed, and seller can assert against the receivers same rights as he or she could assert against buyer. *James Bradford Co. v. United Leather Co., 11 Del. Ch. 76, 97 A. 620 (1915).*

Receiver has the right to terminate all unfulfilled contracts made by the company before his or her appointment is clear. He or she may choose to continue one and terminate another. A receiver is not bound by the executory contracts of the corporation over whose property he or she is appointed, and, subject to the control of the court, a receiver may abandon and repudiate them, if in his or her opinion it would not be profitable or desirable to adopt and perform them, and he or she is entitled to a reasonable time within which to make his or her election. *DuPont v. Standard Arms Co., 9 Del. Ch. 315, 81 A. 1089 (1912); Conover v. Sterling Stores Co., 14 Del. Ch. 26, 120 A. 740 (1923).*

If the contract is one of personal service, it is settled that as between individuals, the death of the employer discharges or terminates a contract for personal service. The receiver is the arm of the court, the powers of the officers of the company to deal with its affairs are suspended, and the receiver may rightly suspend the executory contracts made by the company. When a receiver so elects, the situation is the same as when by death the individual employee is stripped of his or her power to further continue the contract. This possibility of a termination of contracts made with corporations is contemplated by the parties to the contract and is made an unexpressed but implied condition of it. It is the suspension, temporary or permanent, of corporate activities by the act of the court in taking possession of the property and affairs of the company, which operates to at least suspend the right to continue the service or recover compensation for a termination of the service from the assets which the court has taken into its charge through

Corporations

its receiver. *DuPont v. Standard Arms Co., 9 Del. Ch. 315, 81 A. 1089 (1912).*

A contract of lease having a period yet to run falls within the general rule that the receiver or trustee in bankruptcy may, if it is deemed burdensome to the estate, elect to repudiate it. *Conover v. Sterling Stores Co., 14 Del. Ch. 26, 120 A. 740 (1923).*

Court of equity has power to appoint receiver pendente lite, but that power should not be exercised except in a clear case when it is necessary for the prevention of manifest wrong and injury, and where the plaintiff would otherwise be in danger of suffering irreparable loss. *Gray ex rel. Cooch v. Council of Newark, 9 Del. Ch. 171, 79 A. 735 (1911).*

While there is no statutory power to appoint a receiver pendente lite, the inherent, or implied, and certainly well established powers of the Court of Chancery administered by the chancellor are such as to vest in him or her the jurisdiction to take possession of the assets and affairs of a corporation, by a receiver pendente lite, in order to prevent loss to those interested. *Whitmer v. William Whitmer & Sons, 11 Del. Ch. 222, 99 A. 428 (1916).*

When insolvency is denied and the evidence on the point is conflicting, a motion for a receiver pendente lite should not be granted. *Whitmer v. William Whitmer & Sons, 11 Del. Ch. 222, 99 A. 428 (1916).*

To sustain a motion for the appointment of a receiver pendente lite, it is not necessary to decide in favor of complainant upon the merits, nor is it necessary that such a case be presented as will entitle the complainant, beyond all doubt, to a decree upon the final hearing. *Hanssen v. Pusey & Jones Co., 276 F. 296 (D. Del. 1921), aff'd, 279 F. 488 (3d Cir. 1922), rev'd on other grounds, 261 U.S. 491, 43 S. Ct. 454, 67 L. Ed. 763 (1923).*

While it is settled that a court of equity has the power to appoint a receiver pendente lite, it is equally well settled that such power should not be exercised except in a clear case, when it is necessary for the prevention of manifest wrong and injury, and where the plaintiff would otherwise be in danger of suffering irreparable loss. *Moore v. Associated Producing & Ref. Corp., 14 Del. Ch. 97, 121 A. 655 (1923).*

A receiver pendente lite should not be appointed solely on the ground that on final hearing a permanent receiver might, or even probably would be appointed unless there are facts indicating that unless the receiver is appointed, threatened or impending injury or loss is in danger of being visited upon the complainant. *Moore v. Associated Producing & Ref. Corp., 14 Del. Ch. 97, 121 A. 655 (1923).*

Where a claim for an income tax refund could not be expected to be pressed with confidence in its merits by the present officers and directors of a corporation who, if the facts upon which the merits of the claim for refund rest were true, were guilty of so manipulating the corporation's financial showing as to make a false appearance of profits out of which dividends were declared by them; and where the corporation is entitled to have the merits of the claim for refund intelligently and sincerely urged before the commissioner to the end that resort to suit for collection of the overpaid taxes with its necessary expense and delay

might possibly be avoided; and where it would not be reasonable to permit the fate of the claim for refund to be left under the possibility of a withdrawal by the officers and directors of the corporation whose personal interests were in opposition to it, accordingly an order appointing a receiver pendente lite is justified. *Satterthwaite ex rel. Irving Trust Co. v. Eastern Bankers' Corp., 17 Del. Ch. 310, 154 A. 475 (1931).*

A receiver pendente lite for a corporation actively functioning is never justified except under circumstances that show an urgent need for immediate protection against injury which is either in the course of actual infliction or reasonably to be apprehended. *Salnita Corp. v. Walter Holding Corp., 19 Del. Ch. 426, 168 A. 74 (1933).*

Power of court to appoint receiver for solvent corporation. — Where corporate insolvency does not exist, the right to appoint a receiver can only be found in the general equity powers of the court sitting as a Court of Chancery. *Carson v. Allegany Window Glass Co., 187 F. 791 (D. Del. 1911).*

Originally, jurisdiction to appoint a receiver in order to wind up a solvent corporation was largely denied on the theory that it was equivalent to a decree for dissolution, which was generally within the sole province of the legislative body. *Lichens Co. v. Standard Com. Tobacco Co., 28 Del. Ch. 220, 40 A.2d 447 (1944).*

Courts of equity have often recognized their inherent right to wind up the affairs of a solvent going corporation and to appoint a receiver for that purpose for the protection of minority stockholders when fraud and gross mismanagement by corporate officers, causing real imminent danger of great loss, clearly appears and cannot be otherwise prevented. *Drob v. National Mem. Park, 28 Del. Ch. 254, 41 A.2d 589 (1945).*

The court will exercise its power to appoint a receiver for a solvent corporation with great restraint. *Vale v. Atlantic Coast & Inland Corp., 34 Del. Ch. 50, 99 A.2d 396 (1953).*

In order to state a claim for the appointment of a receiver for a solvent corporation, plaintiff must show fraud, gross mismanagement or extreme circumstances causing imminent danger of great loss which cannot be otherwise prevented. *Vale v. Atlantic Coast & Inland Corp., 34 Del. Ch. 50, 99 A.2d 396 (1953).*

Mismanagement of corporate affairs is not necessary element of bill for appointment of receiver. *Sill v. Kentucky Coal & Timber Dev. Co., 11 Del. Ch. 93, 97 A. 617 (1916).*

Allegations as to mismanagement did not make bill multifarious. — Where the appointment of a receiver on the basis of insolvency was the main and only real relief properly sought by a bill, allegations as to mismanagement, being immaterial, could not make the bill multifarious. *Hopper v. Fesler Sales Co., 11 Del. Ch. 209, 99 A. 82 (1916).*

Chancery court lacks jurisdiction of receiver's counterclaim based on securities exchange act. — Exclusive jurisdiction of any claim under the federal Securities Exchange Act is vested in the federal courts. Thus, the Chancery Court lacks jurisdiction over the counterclaim of a brokerage house's receiver, where the gravamen of such claim is an allegation that plaintiff, a stock exchange, had failed to enforce compliance by the brokerage house with the *Securities Exchange Act. NYSE v. Pickard & Co., 282 A.2d 651 (Del. Ch. 1971).*

Joinder of claims. — Where several creditors respectively holding separate and distinct claims join in pursuing such a remedy against a common fund as that given by the statute against the assets of an insolvent corporation, where the relief to be accorded of necessity reaches and affects the claims of all creditors entitled to the benefits of the act, and where it is immaterial to the defendant how the fund in the possession of the court is to be distributed among creditors, such joinder is of those who claim under a common right inherent in the nature of the statutory remedy. However separate and distinct their respective claims, when considered apart from the remedy resorted to and the relief sought, the complainants have a common, if not a joint interest in such remedy and relief; and consequently their claims may be joined for jurisdictional purposes. *Jones v. Mutual Fid. Co., 123 F. 506 (C.C.D. Del. 1903).*

Constitutional provision for jury trial not pertinent. — Having jurisdiction to appoint receivers for insolvent corporation, the chancellor may proceed to pass on all matters necessary to a determination, notwithstanding that among such matters there may be questions which also in other connections may be heard at law before juries and in such cases the constitutional provision that trial by jury shall be as heretofore has no pertinency. *Mackenzie Oil Co. v. Omar Oil & Gas Co., 14 Del. Ch. 36, 120 A. 852 (1923).*

Cross-examination. — In a receivership proceeding, when a right to cross-examine the claimant is reserved, it is not the duty of a master to prod the reserver in order to find out if he or she desires to follow it, but it is incumbent on the one for whom the reservation is made, when he or she discovers that the court or master is proceeding on the assumption that the right has been abandoned, to promptly call attention to the fact that the assumption is an erroneous one. *Haas v. Sinaloa Exploration & Dev. Co., 17 Del. Ch. 334, 155 A. 4 (1931).*

Effect of appointment of receiver in foreign state. — Where every asset of every description had been transferred to a receiver of courts in other jurisdictions and duly sold under authority of those courts, and the funds realized therefrom had not as yet been distributed and the receiver discharged, there was no necessity for the appointment of a receiver whose only activity, if he or she was appointed, could be to seek to induce the courts in those jurisdictions to resign their control in its very last stage to an officer of this court. *Jones v. Maxwell Motor Co., 13 Del. Ch. 76, 115 A. 312 (1921).*

The appointment by a court of another state of a receiver of the assets of a Delaware corporation located in such other state cannot serve to deprive a chancery court in Delaware of its jurisdiction to appoint a general receiver for the same corporation. *Frankland v. Remington Phonograph Corp., 13 Del. Ch. 312, 119 A. 127 (1922).*

The appointment of a receiver of a Delaware corporation ought to be made in all cases where a foreign court has appointed a receiver, provided the necessary jurisdictional facts exist. *Stone v. Jewett, Bigelow & Brooks Coal Co., 14 Del. Ch. 256, 125 A. 340 (1924); Manning v. Middle States Oil Corp., 15 Del. Ch. 321, 137 A. 79 (1927).*

The fact that a foreign court has taken charge of the assets of a Delaware corporation located within its jurisdiction and has appointed a receiver therefor with powers not alone over the assets but as well with powers of a general nature over the corporation, does not oust the Court of Chancery of Delaware from its jurisdiction under this section to appoint a general receiver. *Stone v. Jewett, Bigelow & Brooks Coal Co., 14 Del. Ch. 256, 125 A. 340 (1924).*

Where, because of the extent to which a foreign court has gone in administering the corporate assets, it is manifest that the appointment of a receiver in Delaware would be an utterly vain and useless thing, there is a good reason for refusing to act. *Stone v. Jewett, Bigelow & Brooks Coal Co., 14 Del. Ch. 256, 125 A. 340 (1924).*

While the existence elsewhere of a general receiver for a Delaware corporation is a circumstance of very great, if not decisive, weight on the question of discretion, where the essential element of insolvency is shown, such circumstance has no relevancy whatever to the question of whether insolvency exists. Unless the fact of insolvency is either admitted in the foreign proceedings or judicially found upon evidence in a suit of which the finding court has jurisdiction, the Court of Chancery should, in determining whether insolvency is shown, view the case entirely aside from what the foreign court has seen fit to do and decline to allow the existence of the foreign receivership to have any prejudicial influence in the judicial act of forming a judgment upon the evidence. *Manning v. Middle States Oil Corp., 15 Del. Ch. 321, 137 A. 79 (1927).*

This section confers the jurisdiction to appoint a receiver only when insolvency exists. It does not make the existence of a receivership elsewhere a ground for appointment here. *Rogers v. Bancokentucky Co., 18 Del. Ch. 23, 156 A. 217 (1931).*

In passing upon the fact of insolvency under this section, the fact of the appointment of a receiver in another state is of no relevancy where the receivership there was not based on insolvency. *Rogers v. Bancokentucky Co., 18 Del. Ch. 23, 156 A. 217 (1931).*

A receiver elsewhere would as a general rule prompt an exercise of the discretion in Delaware in favor of the appointment, with the qualification that the necessary jurisdictional facts, including of course insolvency, must be shown to exist. *Rogers v. Bancokentucky Co., 18 Del. Ch. 23, 156 A. 217 (1931).*

Limitation of actions. — In administering a receivership estate, the court will not allow the period of the receivership to be reckoned in calculating the time for the running of the statute of limitations. *Haas v. Sinaloa Exploration & Dev. Co., 17 Del. Ch. 253, 152 A. 216 (1930).*

Even if the receiver has the technical right to plead the statute of limitations because of the lapse of time since the receivership, he or she ought not to do so. *Haas v. Sinaloa Exploration & Dev. Co., 17 Del. Ch. 253, 152 A. 216 (1930).*

DELAWARE CASE NOTES — UNREPORTED

Individual creditors of a Delaware corporation that is either insolvent or in the zone of insolvency have no right to assert direct claims for breach of fiduciary duty against corporate directors. Creditors may nonetheless protect their interest by bringing derivative claims on behalf of the insolvent corporation or any other direct nonfiduciary claim that may be available for individual creditors. *N. Am. Catholic Educ. Programming Found., Inc. v. Gheewalla, 2007 Del. LEXIS 227 (May 18,. 2007).*

CASE NOTES — OTHER STATES

Pennsylvania

Neither Pennsylvania or Delaware recognizes a cause of action for deepening insolvency. *Miller v.* *Santilli, 2007 Phila. Ct. Com. Pl. LEXIS 252 (September 20, 2007).*

CASE NOTES — FEDERAL

Third Circuit

Limitation on "deepening insolvency" actions in Third Circuit. — In Trenwick, the Vice Chancellor put to rest the notion that there is such a thing as a cause of action for so-called "deepening insolvency" in Delaware law This effectively prevents extending our holding in Official Comm. of Unsecured Creditors v. R.F. Lafferty & Co., 267 F.3d 340, 347 (3d Cir. 2001), in which we decided that the cause of action exists in Pennsylvania, to Delaware cases (and supersedes those few Delaware District and Bankruptcy Court cases that have done so). *Teleglobe Communs. Corp. v. BCE, Inc. (In re Teleglobe Communs. Corp.), 2007 U.S. App. LEXIS 16942 (3d Cir. July 17, 2007).*

Seventh Circuit

Mere insolvency is not enough to allow piercing of the corporate veil. If creditors could enter judgments against shareholders every time that a corporation becomes unable to pay its debts as they become due, the limited liability characteristic of the corporate form would be meaningless. *Judson Atkinson Candies, Inc. v. Latini-Hohberger Dhimantec, 476 F. Supp. 2d 913, 2007 U.S. Dist. LEXIS 15834 (N.D. Ill. March 6, 2007).*

Ninth Circuit

Receivership claims not derivative. — The language of subsection (a) of section 226 and this section are nearly identical and both provide that an application for an appointment of a receiver may be brought by any stockholder. Neither statute limits the claims to derivative claims. Because these statutes are clear on their face and because defendant has adduced no authority the contrary, the court concludes that the current claims may be brought by an individual stockholder such as plaintiff. *Glenbrook Capital L.P. v. Mali Kuo, 525 F. Supp. 2d 1130, 2007 U.S. Dist. LEXIS 68353 (ND CA, September 6, 2007).*

§ 292. Title to property; filing order of appointment; exception

DELAWARE CASE NOTES — REPORTED

It is duty of receiver to search for, collect and administer assets of the corporation committed to his or her charge. *Brill v. Southerland, 30 Del. Ch. 467, 14 A.2d 408 (1940).*

Receiver takes property with notice of outstanding rights and equities. — A receiver appointed by a court of chancery to wind up the affairs of an insolvent company is like a receiver in bankruptcy, in that it takes the property of the company as a purchaser from the company with notice of all outstanding rights and equities. *James Bradford Co. v. United Leather Co., 11 Del. Ch. 110, 97 A. 622 (1916).*

Lien cannot attach after receiver has been appointed because on the appointment date title to the company's assets are vested in the receiver by operation of this section. *In re Fader Motor Co., 245 A.2d 156 (Del. Ch. 1968).*

Where records do not show exact time of appointment of receiver, it is assumed that such appointment took effect on the beginning of that day and a judgment filed at 4:30 p.m. of that day could not become a lien. *Ferris v. Chic-Mint Gum Co., 14 Del. Ch. 270, 125 A. 343 (1924).*

§ 295. Creditors' proofs of claims; when barred; notice

DELAWARE CASE NOTES — REPORTED

Court has discretion to fix deadline for filing of claims. — A court of equity, in the exercise of a proper judicial discretion, can always fix a deadline for filing of claims, even though this results in eliminating as participants in the assets some person who might have been able to qualify to participate in the corporate assets if a more extended period of time for the filing of claims had been fixed by the court. *In re International Reinsurance Corp., 29 Del. Ch. 34, 48 A.2d 529 (1946).*

A court of equity, in fixing the time within which claims shall be filed for the purpose of participating in the estate of a corporation, will regard, on the one hand, the substantial right of all creditors to share in the debtor's property, and, on the other hand, the necessity for expeditious administration. Giving due consideration to both, the court must make rules which are practical, as well as equitable. *In re International Reinsurance Corp., 29 Del. Ch. 34, 48 A.2d 529 (1946).*

§ 296. Adjudication of claims; appeal

DELAWARE CASE NOTES — REPORTED

Section does not set standard for allowance of claims. — This section does not purport to set up the standard by which the court shall allow or disallow a particular claim. *In re International Reinsurance Corp., 29 Del. Ch. 34, 48 A.2d 529 (1946).*

This section does not require the court to investigate the merits of a claim which has been reduced to judgment. *In re* International *Reinsurance Corp., 29 Del. Ch. 34, 48 A.2d 529 (1946).*

Mere filing of claim does not constitute pleading. — The mere filing of a claim by an alleged creditor of a corporation with its receiver, while it gives notice of the claim, is not in itself a pleading or an intervention in the receivership action. *Hannigan v. Italo Petroleum Corp., 37 Del. 227, 181 A. 660 (1935).*

Claim of director. — The relationship of a director to a corporation is not, in and of itself, such a relationship as would justify denial or postponement of the director's claim in an insolvency proceeding, although the courts subject the claims of directors to careful scrutiny and insist that their bona fides be conclusively established. *NYSE v. Pickard & Co., 296 A.2d 143 (Del. Ch. 1972).*

Collateral security. — Independent of statute, a creditor with collateral shall have the right to prove and receive payment on his or her full claim against an insolvent corporation administered in a court of equity, without deducting from such claim the amount collected by him or her from his or her collateral, provided, of course, that in no event shall such secured creditor receive more than his or her full debt from either or both sources. *Mark v. American Brick Mfg. Co., 10 Del. Ch. 58, 84 A. 887 (1912).*

Subordination agreements are contracts and the court has the power to distribute the insolvent corporation's assets in accord with the rights of the parties as fixed by their own contract. *NYSE v. Pickard & Co., 296 A.2d 143 (Del. Ch. 1972).*

Priority must be founded upon statute or rule of law. — Any priority among insolvency claimants of the same class must be founded upon a statute or upon the operation of some general rule of law; a claimant seeking priority based upon general equitable principles must demonstrate something in the intrinsic nature of his or her claim which confers upon him or her an equity superior to those of competing claimants of the same class. *NYSE v. Pickard & Co., 296 A.2d 143 (Del. Ch. 1972).*

Claims based upon notes, bonds and book accounts are on equal footing. — When the claims filed against an insolvent corporation are based upon promissory notes, bonds and book accounts, all these claims are on an equal footing, no one of them bearing priority of payment over the other. *Blair v. Clayton Enter. Co., 9 Del. Ch. 95, 77 A. 740 (1910).*

Preference is given to payment of rent in administering the estate of an insolvent corporation. Rent is a profit issuing out of land. It cannot reasonably include the cost of repairs which the tenant should have made. *Bailey v. Lightwell Steel Sash Co., 12 Del. Ch. 60, 105 A. 376 (1918).*

Necessity for tracing commingled funds. — Where on insolvency of consignee, the proceeds of the sale of the consigned goods could not be traced into a specific fund in the hands of the receiver, the claim for such proceeds could not be allowed as a preferred claim, but was payable as a general claim. *Jones v. United Tire & Rubber Corp., 14 Del. Ch. 51, 120 A. 744 (1923).*

When the facts are represented to be that the moneys received by the insolvent for goods consigned to it for sale were deposited in a bank and mingled with its general funds and that the bank account in which the proceeds of sale were deposited never fell below the amount thereof, and was in excess thereof at the time of the appointment of the receivers, the money belonging to the consignors is sufficiently traced and identified and its payment to the consignors entitled to it should be ordered. *Curran v. Smith-Zollinger Co., 17 Del. Ch. 187, 151 A. 217 (1930).*

Interest on claims against an insolvent corporation should be calculated on claims down to the date of the order of the appointment of a receiver. *Blair v. Clayton Enter. Co., 9 Del. Ch. 95, 77 A. 740 (1910).*

There should be no difference between claims which bear interest according to the terms of the instrument upon which they are based and those which do not, for the duty to pay debts when due applies to all kinds of claims, whether interest is demanded by virtue of contract, or awarded by usage as it is an incident to the duty of payment and the probable obligation of the debtor, whether he or she has agreed to pay interest or not. *Blair v. Clayton Enter. Co., 9 Del. Ch. 95, 77 A. 740 (1910).*

In distributing assets of an insolvent corporation, if a creditor does not, in the sworn statement of his or her claim, demand interest, it is to be assumed that he or she has either waived it, or that he or she is not entitled to it by agreement or some other circumstance. *Blair v. Clayton Enter. Co., 9 Del. Ch. 95, 77 A. 740 (1910).*

Holders of mortgages are entitled to interest on their mortgages until the order for payment of the mortgages by the receiver of the corporation, as against other creditors, if the proceeds of sale of the mortgaged premises applicable to the payment thereof is sufficient. *Walter v. Peninsula Cut Stone Co., 9 Del. Ch. 374, 82 A. 961 (1912).*

As against the assets of an insolvent company when its affairs are being administered by a chancery receiver, interest is not allowed beyond the date of the appointment of the receiver, except on liens which bear interest. *John W. Cooney Co. v. Arlington Hotel Co., 11 Del. Ch. 286, 101 A. 879 (1917),* modified, *11 Del. Ch. 430, 106 A. 39 (1918).*

Attorney's fees. — The only ground upon which an exception to a claim for attorney's fees is based is that the services rendered were not of the value claimed, and where the services were rendered before the receivership and the amount claimed as compensation was submitted to and approved by the board of directors of the corpora-tion and there is no pretense that fraud induced the directors' approval, the exception will be cleared. *Haas v. Sinaloa Exploration & Dev. Co., 17 Del. Ch. 334, 155 A. 4 (1931).*

Effect of court order approving allowance of claim. — If a receiver allows a claim filed, the order of the court approving his or her action is a determination of its existence and amount, and that the claimant has the right to share in the assets of the corporation impounded by the court, and to be distributed by it. *Hannigan v. Italo Petroleum Corp., 37 Del. 227, 181 A. 660 (1935).*

§ 298. Compensation, costs and expenses of receiver or trustee

DELAWARE CASE NOTES — REPORTED

Receivers and their counsel are entitled to be compensated for their services. *R.H. McWilliams, Jr., Co. v. Missouri-Kansas Pipe Line Co., 21 Del. Ch. 308, 190 A. 569 (1936),* aff'd sub nom. *In re Missouri-Kansas Pipe Line Co., 25 Del. Ch. 400, 22 A.2d 388 (1941).*

Ordinarily, a receiver is entitled to compensation for authorized services performed by him or her, measured by the reasonable value thereof. An allowance made to a receiver is an expense of the receivership. Likewise, the claim of the receiver's counsel for such compensation as is properly due him or her ranks as a part of the expense of the receivership. *Brill v. Southerland, 30 Del. Ch. 467, 14 A.2d 408 (1940).*

As a general rule a receiver's compensation and expenses are payable from the funds in his or her hands, and no part is taxable against the party at whose instance the receiver was appointed. Where there is no fund out of which expenses can be paid, or the fund is insufficient, the usual rule is that the party at whose instance the receiver was appointed should be required to provide the means of payment. *Brill v. Southerland, 30 Del. Ch. 467, 14 A.2d 408 (1940).*

Both the receiver of a corporation and the receiver's attorney are agents of the Court of Chancery and are entitled to reasonable compensation for their services and to reimbursement for incidental necessary expenses. *Veeder v. Public Serv. Holding Corp., 29 Del. Ch. 396, 51 A.2d 321 (1947),* aff'd, *70 A.2d 22 (Del. 1949).*

But they cannot expect more than "moderate compensation." *R.H. McWilliams, Jr., Co. v. Missouri-Kansas Pipe Line Co., 21 Del. Ch. 308, 190 A. 569 (1936),* aff'd sub nom. *In re Missouri-Kansas Pipe Line Co., 25 Del. Ch. 400, 22 A.2d 388 (1941).*

Amount of compensation is discretionary and based upon particular facts in each case. *Deputy v. Delmar Lumber Mfg. Co., 10 Del. Ch. 101, 85 A. 669 (1913).*

But courts in fixing compensation, should consider responsibility assumed by receiver, the labor and acts involved, and due regard should be had to the price usually paid for similar services in connection with the particular kind of business managed by the receiver. *Deputy v. Delmar Lumber Mfg. Co., 10 Del. Ch. 101, 85 A. 669 (1913).*

Counsel should be compensated only for work requiring special legal skill. — Compensation to counsel for a receiver should be limited to such work done for the receiver as requires special legal skill, and not for such things as the receiver himself or herself is capable of performing. *Deputy v. Delmar Lumber Mfg. Co., 10 Del. Ch. 101, 85 A. 669 (1913).*

Allowance should be denied if receiver was negligent. — The receiver's petition for allowances should be denied if he or she was negligent in the performance of his or her duties. *Frazer v. Consolidated Novelty Co., 17 Del. Ch. 37, 157 A. 431 (1929).*

If the receiver fails to adhere strictly to terms of the court's order of sale, and loss in excess of that which he or she asks in the way of allowances was caused thereby, the allowances should be denied. *Frazer v. Consolidated Novelty Co., 17 Del. Ch. 37, 157 A. 431 (1929).*

Receivers not compensated for efforts in connection with reorganization plan. — Where a claim was made on behalf of the receivers that their time and effort were used in endeavoring to work out a plan by which the assets of the company should be turned over to creditors through a new corporation, and so avoid the expense of a receivership, it was held that this should not be taken into account in fixing the compensation of the receivers as it was not their duty to create a new enterprise and they had no authority of the court to do so and it is not the duty of the receiver to formulate or promote 1 or other proposed plan of reorganization. *Deputy v. Delmar Lumber Mfg. Co., 10 Del. Ch. 101, 85 A. 669 (1913).*

Receiver's expenses as lien upon property of corporation. — Courts of equity have to a limited extent, and sparingly, exercised the power to make the expenses of a receiver of a public corporation a lien upon the property of the company, superior to prior liens. *Central Trust & Sav. Co. v. Chester County Elec. Co., 9 Del. Ch. 247, 80 A. 801 (1911).*

Where the general receiver has assets other than the mortgaged property sufficient to properly compensate him or her and his or her counsel, there should be an apportionment of such between the general creditors and encumbrancers, each class paying for the services of which it derived the benefit. *Central Trust & Sav. Co. v. Chester County Elec. Co., 9 Del. Ch. 247, 80 A. 801 (1911).*

Corporations

Where it appears that a receiver has been appointed for an insolvent corporation, and the receiver has rendered services in caring for the property of the company, keeping it in operation and improving its condition, and the whole of the plant of the company is afterwards sold in a foreclosure suit brought by the trustee under a mortgage to secure bonds of the company, the general receiver and his or her counsel will be entitled to some compensation from the fund arising from the sale of the mortgaged property, if the other general assets are not sufficient for a proper compensation, even though the proceeds of sale be insufficient to pay the bonds. *Central Trust & Sav. Co. v. Chester County Elec. Co., 9 Del. Ch. 247, 80 A. 801 (1911).*

Voluntary services, amounting to a mere duplication of the efforts of the duly authorized agents of the Court of Chancery are seldom compensable from corporate funds. A different rule would result in a waste of assets. A receivership is comparable to a creditors' bill, and if the common fund is augmented or preserved by the independent or even supplemental efforts of representatives of stockholders, reasonable compensation may be allowed. *Veeder v. Public Serv. Holding Corp., 29 Del. Ch. 396, 51 A.2d 321 (1947), aff'd, 70 A.2d 22 (Del. 1949).*

Voluntary committees who are mere agents of creditors or stockholders are entitled to be compensated and only in the same degree as their principals would be, that is to say, only to the extent that they have incurred expenses in the business of creating or preserving the common fund. Any expenses they have incurred in other connections as for instance in watching the progress of the administration, conferring with the receivers, gratuitously advising them and assuming generally to act as overseers of the receivers, cannot be compensated for out of the estate. *R.H. McWilliams, Jr., Co. v. Missouri-Kansas Pipe Line Co., 21 Del. Ch. 308, 190 A. 569 (1936), aff'd sub nom.*

In re Missouri-Kansas Pipe Line Co., 25 Del. Ch. 400, 22 A.2d 388 (1941).

A committee of stockholders, being but an agent for stockholders, must expect its claim for allowance to be tested by the same principles which would be applied if the stockholders had themselves done the committee's work in negotiating for its insolvent corporation. Any obligation that the committee incurred to save, protect or create the common fund, should be borne by the fund. Compensation for personal services or reimbursement of personal expenses that are not directly related to any of these ends, cannot be allowed. The committee must look to its principals for personal compensation. *R.H. McWilliams, Jr., Co. v. Missouri-Kansas Pipe Line Co., 21 Del. Ch. 308, 190 A. 569 (1936), aff'd sub nom. In re Missouri-Kansas Pipe Line Co., 25 Del. Ch. 400, 22 A.2d 388 (1941).*

Lawyers for stockholder's protection committee were entitled to compensation for the value of that portion of the services which directly contributed to the administration of the receivership estate, and, in a very substantial sense, proved a valuable contribution to the labor of its settlement and liquidation, that portion which benefitted the receivership primarily and was availed of by it. *Penington v. Commonwealth Hotel Constr. Corp., 18 Del. Ch. 238, 158 A. 140 (1931).*

Compensation for services rendered by creditor's attorney. — Where a creditor of an insolvent company brings an action for the appointment of a receiver, and to wind up its affairs, compensation will be allowed to his or her attorney for services rendered in bringing such suit for the appointment of a receiver, the same is to be paid from the fund in the hands of the receiver, provided such services prove beneficial to the other creditors. *Ross v. South Del. Gas Co., 10 Del. Ch. 236, 89 A. 593 (1914).*

§ 300. Employee's lien for wages when corporation insolvent

DELAWARE CASE NOTES — REPORTED

There is no repugnancy between this section and § 4931 of Title 10. *Di Angelo v. McCormick Bros., 19 Del. Ch. 307, 168 A. 79 (1933).*

This section applies only to insolvent corporations. *Di Angelo v. McCormick Bros., 19 Del. Ch. 307, 168 A. 79 (1933).*

But § 4931 of title 10 is applicable in case of any corporation, whether insolvent or solvent, as well as to any person or persons or associations. *Di Angelo v. McCormick Bros., 19 Del. Ch. 307, 168 A. 79 (1933).*

Wage preference given by this section is subordinate to existing liens. *Di Angelo v. McCormick Bros., 19 Del. Ch. 307, 168 A. 79 (1933).*

It was not intended that a lien fairly and in good faith obtained by a vigilant and active creditor, before the adjudication of insolvency, should thereafter become second to the claims of laborers. *Clough v. Superior Equip. Corp., 18 Del. Ch. 65, 156 A. 249 (1931).*

The word "assets" in this section is to be construed as meaning the property interest of the corporation that is

left after prior encumbrances are satisfied. *Clough v. Superior Equip. Corp., 18 Del. Ch. 65, 156 A. 249 (1931).*

But preference given by § 4931 of Title 10 is senior in rank to existing liens. *Di Angelo v. McCormick Bros., 19 Del. Ch. 307, 168 A. 79 (1933).*

Section denies priority to officers of corporation. — The evident purpose and meaning of the last phrase of this section is to deny priority to every person who served the company as an officer, whatever may have been the character of the labor or service which he or she rendered to the company. *Walter v. Peninsula Cut Stone Co., 9 Del. Ch. 348, 82 A. 689 (1912).*

And director is officer within meaning of section. *Walter v. Peninsula Cut Stone Co., 9 Del. Ch. 348, 82 A. 689 (1912).*

Contractor for special service employing others to assist the contractor in carrying out a contract with an insolvent corporation claim for priority does not fall within the purview of this section. *Garretson v. Delaware State Fair, Inc., 14 Del. Ch. 367, 128 A. 919 (1925).*

§ 303. Proceeding under the Federal Bankruptcy Code of the United States; effectuation

DELAWARE CASE NOTES — REPORTED

Supremacy of federal bankruptcy laws over state merger laws. — While the General Corporation Law of the State of Delaware addressed the required procedures for merger or consolidation corporations under *8 Del. C. §§ 251 to 253*, the "notwithstanding any otherwise applicable nonbankruptcy law" language of *11 U.S.C.* § 1123(a) overrode the requirements of the state provisions; if there was any doubt about the Bankruptcy Code trumping the state law provisions, this section dispelled it by specifically providing for mergers under a *Chapter 11 plan. In re Stone & Webster, Inc., 286 Bankr. 532 (Bankr. D. Del. 2002).*

CASE NOTES — FEDERAL

Second Circuit

Delaware law permits the cancellation of common stock pursuant to a Chapter 11 plan without further action by the board of directors or stockholders. *Abel v. Shugrue, 184 B.R. 648 (S.D.N.Y. 1995).*

Sixth Circuit

The plain language of the Delaware statute clearly contemplates the restructuring of shareholder voting rights. This provision of the governing state law is not inconsistent with the general thrust of the Bankruptcy Code which exists to provide the opportunity to restructure obligations allowing the debtor to continue as a viable and productive entity. *In re Federated Dep't Stores, Inc., 133 B.R. 886 (S.D.Ohio 1991).*

District of Columbia Circuit

The plain intent of § 303 is to recognize and accord plenary authority for the reorganization court to issue decrees and orders relative to the reorganization. Hence, § 303 should be construed broadly to effectuate that intent rather than narrowly and restrictively, in derogation of that intent. *In re United Press International, Inc., 60 B.R. 265 (Bankr. D.D.C. 1986).*

Section 303 supplies sufficient Delaware statutory authorization for a debtor to operate, during the pendency of its reorganization proceedings, without a board of directors. *In re United Press International, Inc., 60 B.R. 265 (Bankr. D.D.C. 1986).*

Subchapter XII.
Renewal, Revival, Extension and Restoration of Certificate of Incorporation or Charter

§ 311. Revocation of voluntary dissolution

DELAWARE CASE NOTES — REPORTED

This section provides for revocation of voluntary corporate dissolution and applies to corporations which have been dissolved under § 275 of this title. *Willard v.* *Harrworth Corp., 258 A.2d 914 (Del. Ch. 1969), aff'd, 267 A.2d 577 (Del. 1970).*

§ 312. Renewal, revival, extension and restoration of certificate of incorporation

DELAWARE CASE NOTES — REPORTED

This section is expressly applicable to any corporation whose limited time for existence has not expired. *Willard v. Harrworth Corp., 258 A.2d 914 (Del. Ch. 1969),* aff'd, *267 A.2d 577 (Del. 1970).*

This section applies to corporations "whose certificate of incorporation has expired by reason of failure to renew it," and arguably has no application to a certificate which expired by reason of a date limitation written into it by way of amendment. *Willard v. Harrworth Corp., 267 A.2d 577 (Del. 1970).*

Name of revived corporation. — If the name used in the revival proceeding is sufficient to clearly and unmistakably identify the original corporation which it is sought to revive, it is, within the meaning of the law, the same name, and the requirement of the statute is met. *Pippin v. McMahon Bros., 33 Del. 42, 130 A. 37 (1925).*

Where it is clear that the corporation named is the corporation intended, or where because of similarity of name or description it cannot be regarded as another and different corporation, technical difference in name will not be permitted to defeat the purpose of the statute. *Pippin v. McMahon Bros., 33 Del. 42, 130 A. 37 (1925).*

Where the only difference between the original name and the revival name consists in well recognized abbreviations, and the discrepancy or difference in the words is not at all likely to cause anyone to believe that a new corporation, or one different from the original is intended, the corporation named in the revival proceeding is the same as the one named in the original certificate. *Pippin v. McMahon Bros., 33 Del. 42, 130 A. 37 (1925).*

When its charter is renewed, corporation is restored to its old franchises. It changes from a corporation with limited powers to be used only in course of winding up, to a corporation reinvigorated by the State with all of its former franchises. *McKee v. Standard Minerals Corp., 18 Del. Ch. 97, 156 A. 193 (1931).*

Attack upon renewed existence should be brought by state. — If the records in the office of the Secretary of State disclose the life of the corporation was properly renewed, but the record embodies a falsehood, it is a matter about which the State should complain. A complainant seeking the appointment of a receiver cannot attack the renewed existence of the corporation. That the State could avoid the renewal, there could be no doubt. *McKee v. Standard Minerals Corp., 18 Del. Ch. 97, 156 A. 193 (1931).*

Once a charter has been renewed and revived only the State can institute proceedings to void it on the ground that the parties applying for such renewal and revival were not authorized to do so. Once the charter has been revived, a receiver cannot be appointed under the statutory authority to appoint receivers for corporations

whose charters have been forfeited. *Engstrum v. Paul Engstrum Assocs., 36 Del. Ch. 19, 124 A.2d 722 (1956).*

Section 510 of this title must be read in light of subsection (e) of this section. — Section 510 of this title provides that, upon forfeiture of a charter for failure to pay franchise taxes, all of the corporation's powers become inoperative, but this provision must be read in the light of subsection (e) of this section, which provides that upon reinstatement of a charter all contracts and other matters done and performed by the corporate officers during the time the charter was inoperative shall be validated, and be the exclusive liability of the corporation. *Frederic G. Krapf & Son v. Gorson, 243 A.2d 713 (Del. 1968).*

The president of a corporation, the charter of which has been proclaimed for failure to pay franchise taxes, may not be held personally liable upon a contract entered into by him in behalf of the corporation after the proclamation of the charter and before its revival. *Frederic G. Krapf & Son v. Gorson, 243 A.2d 713 (Del. 1968).*

CASE NOTES — OTHER STATES

Nevada

Retroactive affirmation. — Under Delaware law, reinstatement of the corporate charter retroactively confirms a corporation's standing to sue with respect to a

lawsuit commenced in the forfeiture period. *Atlantic Commercial Development Corp. v. Boyles, 103 Nev. 35, 732 P.2d 1360 (1987).*

CASE NOTES — FEDERAL

Second Circuit

Resuscitation from coma. — Under Delaware law, a corporation which has been proclaimed forfeited for nonpayment of taxes is not completely dead. It is in a state of coma from which it can be easily resuscitated, but until this is done its powers as a corporation are inoperative and the exercise of these powers is a criminal offense. It still can serve as repository of title and as obligor of debt. *Board of Managers v. City of New York, 2005 U.S. Dist. LEXIS 9139 (S.D.N.Y. 2005).*

Seventh Circuit

Validation of prior acts. — Under Delaware law, reinstatement of a corporate charter validates the acts

taken by the corporation during the periods when the charter was voided, and makes liabilities incurred during these periods the exclusive liabilities of the corporation. Officers are therefore absolved from personal liability. *Hosiery Mfg. Corp. v. Williams, 1989 U.S. Dist. LEXIS 15445 (N.D.Ill. 1989).*

Eighth Circuit

State of coma. — A Delaware corporation which has forfeited its charter but has not dissolved is in a state of coma during which it is still subject to suit. *Missouri v. Bliss, 1985 U.S. Dist. LEXIS 12751 (E.D.Mo. 1985).*

§ 314. Status of corporation

CASE NOTES — FEDERAL

Seventh Circuit

Validation of prior acts. — Under Delaware law, reinstatement of a corporate charter validates the acts taken by the corporation during the periods when the charter was voided, and makes liabilities incurred during these periods the exclusive liabilities of the corporation. Officers are therefore absolved from personal liability.

Hosiery Mfg. Corp. v. Williams, 1989 U.S. Dist. LEXIS 15445 (N.D.Ill. 1989).

Eighth Circuit

State of coma. — A Delaware corporation which has forfeited its charter but has not dissolved is in a state of coma during which it is still subject to suit. *Missouri v. Bliss, 1985 U.S. Dist. LEXIS 12751 (E.D.Mo. 1985).*

Corporations

Subchapter XIII.
Suits Against Corporations, Directors, Officers or Stockholders

§ 321. Service of process on corporations

DELAWARE CASE NOTES — REPORTED

General intent of section is to give that notice which will in the nature of things bring the attention of the corporation to the commencement of proceedings against it. *Keith v. Melvin L. Joseph Constr. Co., 451 A.2d 842 (Del. Super. Ct. 1982).*

Section does not present exclusive method of procedure. *Wax v. Riverview Cem. Co., 41 Del. 424, 24 A.2d 431 (1942).*

Section liberally construed. — When considered together, § 278 of this title, authorizing suit within 3 years after dissolution and this section, concerning service of legal process on corporation, both remedial in nature, must be liberally construed. *International Pulp Equip. Co. v. St. Regis Kraft Co., 54 F. Supp. 745 (D. Del. 1944).*

Service of process, where corporate registered agent is corporation sought to be notified, may be made by any method authorized by this section for service on a corporate registered agent or upon a corporation. *Keith v. Melvin L. Joseph Constr. Co., 451 A.2d 842 (Del. Super. Ct. 1982).*

This section and § 324(b) of this title read together, as necessity requires, clearly indicate that an attachment of shares of stock may be made by leaving with the corporate resident agent a certified copy of the original writ in the same manner as corporate resident agents are served with process under this section; that is, that service may be made by serving a certified copy of the original writ on the officers as indicated in this section. *Brainard v. Canaday, 49 Del. 182, 112 A.2d 862 (1955).*

Service of writ of summons upon resident agent is as complete and valid as if the service had been made upon the president or other head officer. *Penn Cent. Light & Power Co. v. Central E. Power Co., 36 Del. 74, 171 A. 332 (1934).*

Subpoena duces tecum may be directed to corporation. *Kolyba Corp. v. Banque Nationale De Paris, 316 A.2d 585 (Del. Ch. 1973).*

And may be served on resident agent. — Service of a subpoena duces tecum upon the resident agent of a Delaware corporation is valid and effective. *Kolyba Corp. v. Banque Nationale De Paris, 316 A.2d 585 (Del. Ch. 1973).*

Effective legal process can be had on a corporation in this State by serving its resident agent. *Kolyba Corp. v. Banque Nationale De Paris, 316 A.2d 585 (Del. Ch. 1973).*

Service upon secretary of state. — The Secretary of State's capacity to accept service on behalf of a dissolved corporation is 1 of the conditions upon which a corporation pursues its right to do business under a Delaware charter. *International Pulp Equip. Co. v. St. Regis Kraft Co., 54 F. Supp. 745 (D. Del. 1944).*

Where dissolution of corporation had been proclaimed more than 4 years prior to commencement of action, service upon corporation through service on Secretary of State was valid. *Ross v. Venezuelan-American Indep. Oil Producers Ass'n, 230 F. Supp. 701 (D. Del. 1964).*

Corporation has right to determine who shall appear for it. — Subpoena is directed to the corporation and it has the right to determine, initially, at least, who shall appear for it. *Kolyba Corp. v. Banque Nationale De Paris, 316 A.2d 585 (Del. Ch. 1973).*

But party causing subpoena to be issued does not. — In making service the party causing the subpoena to be issued cannot thereby "choose" the person who is to appear on behalf of the corporation. *Kolyba Corp. v. Banque Nationale De Paris, 316 A.2d 585 (Del. Ch. 1973).*

Return showing proper service prerequisite to granting of default judgment against defendant. *Keith v. Melvin L. Joseph Constr. Co., 451 A.2d 842 (Del. Super. Ct. 1982).*

Landlord's leasing agent's acceptance of service of an injured tenant's negligence complaint was binding on the corporate landlord, meaning that the agent's unexplained failure to turn over the complaint to someone in authority as not excusable neglect entitling the landlord to either consideration of any meritorious defenses or relief from a default judgment subsequently obtained; minimal informal communications between the parties did not amount to an appearance by the landlord entitling it to notice of the motion for default. *Apt. Cmtys. Corp. v. Martinelli, 859 A.2d 67 (Del. 2004).*

Return complete and regular on its face is prima facie evidence of facts stated thereon and strong and convincing proof is required to rebut the presumption of its verity. *Keith v. Melvin L. Joseph Constr. Co., 451 A.2d 842 (Del. Super. Ct. 1982).*

Use of abbreviated form of defendant's name does not constitute irregularity on face of return where the summons clearly indicates the full name of the defendant at several locations. *Keith v. Melvin L. Joseph Constr. Co., 451 A.2d 842 (Del. Super. Ct. 1982).*

Failure to state precise time of day service was effected is not an irregularity on the face of the return. *Keith v. Melvin L. Joseph Constr. Co., 451 A.2d 842 (Del. Super. Ct. 1982).*

Service held insufficient. — Where a subpoena was directed to and served personally on 3 persons in a suit against the defendant company, and the 3 persons were part of the board of 9 directors of the company, the complainant being another, this was an insufficient service. *Thoroughgood v. Georgetown Water Co., 9 Del. Ch. 84, 77 A. 720 (1910).*

In a former employee's racial discrimination action against a former employer, the employee's method of service by mailing the handwritten summons to 2 of the employer's retail stores did not meet the requirements of *Fed. Civ. P. R. 4, 8 Del. C. § 321* and *10 Del. C. § 3111*; because the employee provided no good cause for failing to properly serve the employer when the employee had an additional 120 days to re-serve the employer, the employee's action was subject to dismissal. *Thompson v. Target Stores, 501 F. Supp. 2d 601 (D. Del. 2007)*.

Typographical error in naming defendant corporation in the original complaint which delayed service beyond three years after dissolution of the corporation did not mandate dismissal of the action. *Resource Ventures, Inc. v. Resources Mgt. Int'l, Inc., 42 F. Supp. 2d 423 (D. Del. 1999)*.

Return. — The sheriff is not required to spell out in his or her return, affirmatively and expressly, that each and all of the prerequisites for legal services of process were complied with, but if the sheriff states anything in the return which shows that a requirement was not observed, the return may be fatally defective. *Abbott Supply Co. v. Shockley, 50 Del. 261, 128 A.2d 794 (1956)*, aff'd, *135 A.2d 607 (Del. 1957)*, overruled on other grounds by *Brown v. Federal Nat'l Mtg. Ass'n, 359 A.2d 661 (Del. 1976)*.

CASE NOTES — UNREPORTED

Customer properly served the grocery store, as the sheriff's return indicated that the sheriff had effected service in accordance with C.P. Ct. Civ. R. 4(f)(III) and 8 Del. C. § 321(a); the store's conclusory argument that service was improper was insufficient to rebut the presumption in favor of proper service. *Bailey v. ACME/ASCO/Albertson's Inc., 2006 Del. Super. LEXIS 58 (Del. Super. Ct. Feb. 21, 2006)*.

CASE NOTES — FEDERAL

Second Circuit

Service upon the secretary of state is permitted only when the process server cannot "by due diligence" serve an officer or the registered agent. *A. M. Simon Co. v. William McWilliams Indus., 286 F. Supp. 564 (S.D.N.Y. 1968)*.

Fifth Circuit

Proper service upon Secretary of State. — Where a Delaware corporation has become inoperative and void for nonpayment of taxes, service of process upon the Secretary of State's Office in the State of Delaware is proper. *Schoemann v. Natural Energy Corp., 2000 U.S. Dist. LEXIS 3361 (E.D.La. 2000)*.

§ 322. Failure of corporation to obey order of court; appointment of receiver

DELAWARE CASE NOTES — REPORTED

Management's inability to hold an election. — Pursuant to 8 Del. C. § 322, the Court of Chancery enjoys the ability to appoint a receiver when and if a corporation "refuse[s], fail[s], or neglect[s] to obey any order or decree of any [Delaware court]. . . ." Though 8 Del. C. § 322 does not expound upon the powers and duties of a receiver so appointed, 8 Del. C. § 291 does discuss those powers and duties, albeit in the context of an insolvent company. That statute provides that a receiver may "take charge of [the corporation's] assets, estate, effects, business and affairs . . . and do all other acts which might be done by the corporation and which may be necessary and proper." Pursuant to the doctrine of in pari materia, the court observes that, if one became necessary to effectuate the terms of the order, a duly appointed receiver would accede to similar powers and duties. The court now has no occasion to consider whether or not circumstances justifying the appointment of a receiver could arise in this case, either under section 322 or more general principles of equity. Nevertheless, it is important to note that a state law process is available to deal with management's inability to properly fulfill its duty to hold an election-a process well capable of protecting the interests of all constituent groups. *Esopus Creek Value L.P. v. Hauf, 913 A.2d 593; 2006 Del. Ch. LEXIS 200 (Nov. 29, 2006)*.

§ 324. Attachment of shares of stock or any option, right or interest therein; procedure; sale; title upon sale; proceeds

DELAWARE CASE NOTES — REPORTED

Stock is personal property and is subject to attachment. — Shares of stock are personal property in the state of the residence of the corporation and can be taken in execution or reached by attachment. *Haskell v. Middle States Petro. Corp., 35 Del. 380, 165 A. 562 (1933)*.

The words "or any person's option to acquire such shares, or his right or interest in such shares" are clearly indicative of the legislative intention to subject to attachment all rights and interests, legal and equitable, in shares of stock of Delaware corporations. *Spoturno v. Woods, 38 Del. 378, 192 A. 689 (1937)*.

Effect of former 6 DEL. C. § 8-317. — The amendment of former 6 Del. C. § 8-317 in 1983 was not intended to modify the effect of the situs statute (*8 Del. C. § 169*) or attachment mechanisms employed to bring stock into court. *Castro v. ITT Corp., 598 A.2d 674 (Del. Ch. 1991)*.

Power to sequester stock springs from equity. — The power of the court to sequester stock does not have its origin in this section but springs from the historic and inherent power of equity. *Baker v. Gotz, 387 F. Supp. 1381 (D. Del.), aff'd, 523 F.2d 1050 (3d Cir. 1975)*.

Attachment of shares of stock is made under this section exclusively. *Central Nat'l Bank v. Rubenstein, 35 Del. 154, 160 A. 871 (1932)*.

But such attachment is not attachment or garnishment of corporation; and the corporation, upon giving a certificate for the number of shares owned by the defendant, has complied with the requirements of this section. *Central Nat'l Bank v. Rubenstein, 35 Del. 154, 160 A. 871 (1932)*.

Under this section the corporation is not attached or summoned as garnishee, but an officer of the company gives to the sheriff a certificate of the number of shares held by the debtor in such company, and is not inconsistent with, or limited in its operation, by *10 Del. C. § 3502*. *Morgan v. Ownbey, 29 Del. 379, 100 A. 411 (1916), aff'd, 30 Del. 297, 105 A. 838 (1919), aff'd, 256 U.S. 94, 41 S. Ct. 433, 65 L. Ed. 837 (1921)*.

Negotiable instrument other than stock is not subject to sequestration without seizure of the instrument. This was also the intended effect of former 6 Del. C. § 8-317 in the form enacted by the *General Assembly*. *Baker v. Gotz, 387 F. Supp. 1381 (D. Del.), aff'd, 523 F.2d 1050 (3d Cir. 1975)*.

Attachment is in nature of ex parte proceeding. — Attachment looking toward the sale of shares of stock is in the nature of an ex parte proceeding, not a garnishment, and the company in whose hands the attachment is laid makes no answer and does nothing but give a certificate of the number of shares standing in the name of the debtor on the books of the company and is not a party to the suit. *State ex rel. Cooke v. New York-Mexican Oil Co., 32 Del. 244, 122 A. 55 (1923)*.

Subsection (b) of this section and § 321 of this title read together, as necessity requires, clearly indicate that an attachment of shares of stock may be made by leaving with the corporate resident agent a certified copy of the original writ in the same manner as corporate resident agents are served with process under § 321 of this title; that is, that service may be made by serving a certified copy of the original writ on the officers as indicated in § 321 of this title. *Brainard v. Canaday, 49 Del. 182, 112 A.2d 862 (1955)*.

Suit in equity barred where adequate remedy at law available under this section. — Where a corporation transferred all of its assets to a second corporation in consideration for stock in the second corporation, simple contract creditors of the first corporation could not sue in equity to enforce payment of debt against the second corporation because they had an adequate legal remedy through seizure and sale of the stock received in satisfac-

tion of judgment under this section. *Ozan Lumber Co. v. Davis Sewing Mach. Co., 284 F. 161 (D. Del. 1922), aff'd, 292 F. 135 (3d Cir. 1923)*.

Attachment of shares of stock rests wholly on judicial process, and its legality depends on the due pursuit of the steps prescribed by the law for its prosecution. It can borrow no aid from the volunteered acts or waiver of technicalities by the corporation with a certain officer of which the copy of the process should be left. Such acts are regarded as void, so far as they interfere with the rights of the defendant or with other third parties. *Brainard v. Canaday, 49 Del. 182, 112 A.2d 862 (1955)*.

This section requires cancellation of old shares and registration of new shares on the corporation books in the name of the purchaser at the statutory sale. It must also require the issuance of new certificates to the purchaser. In this situation no question of an overissue could arise. *Bartlett v. GMC, 36 Del. Ch. 131, 127 A.2d 470 (1956)*.

If this section is to accomplish its intended purpose, it must be construed to require the corporation to give the purchaser new certificates and to cancel the old registrations. Otherwise, a sale under this section would give the purchaser practically nothing. *Bartlett v. GMC, 36 Del. Ch. 131, 127 A.2d 470 (1956)*.

Building and loan association stock is subject to attachment. — Stock of a building and loan association has many features that distinguish it from ordinary corporation stock. The shares are not owned by the members in the sense that corporation stock is ordinarily owned; it is not issued and paid for in the way that corporation stock is usually issued and paid for. But the shares have a money value, dependent mainly on the amount the member has paid into the association in the way of dues. Such value can be readily ascertained by the company at any time, and is what may be called "surrender value." The shares of stock sought to be attached in this case are shares of the defendants in an incorporated company of Delaware; they have some ascertainable money value to the defendants, and are subject to attachment for debt under the clear and general language of this section. *Central Nat'l Bank v. Rubenstein, 35 Del. 154, 160 A. 871 (1932)*.

Court may determine ownership without physical seizure of certificate. — The Court of Chancery has the right to determine the ownership of stock of Delaware corporations without physical seizure of the certificate. *Haas v. Haas, 35 Del. Ch. 392, 119 A.2d 358 (1955)*.

Certificate not essential to validity of attachment. — Certificate required to be delivered by the corporation to the sheriff attaching shareholder's interest is not essential to the validity of the attachment. *Gibson v. Gillespie, 33 Del. 381, 138 A. 600 (1927)*.

Duplicate original of writ of attachment. — If the original is a valid writ, then a duplicate original should be said to be the equivalent of a certified copy. Thus, shares of stock would be validly attached by the sheriff leaving with the corporate resident agent a duplicate original of the writ of attachment. *Brainard v. Canaday, 49 Del. 182, 112 A.2d 862 (1955)*.

Corporations

Writ invalid where not signed by prothonotary. — An original writ of attachment is invalid where it was not signed by the Prothonotary in accordance with Superior Court Civil Rule 4(c). *Brainard v. Canaday, 49 Del. 182, 112 A.2d 862 (1955).*

Judgment in divorce proceeding may be enforced by attachment and sale of stock. — A judgment in a divorce proceeding entered by the Superior Court under *13 Del. C. § 1513* may be enforced by a writ of attachment and order for sale under this section as to shares of stock. *Bartlett v. GMC, 36 Del. Ch. 131, 127 A.2d 470 (1956).*

Foreign attachment is purely statutory proceeding. *Omnium De Participations Indus. De Luxe v. Spoturno, 39 Del. 100, 196 A. 194 (1937).*

Stock registered in name of third person was not subject to foreign attachment in a proceeding against the real owner; the court was thereby without jurisdiction to enter an order for the sale of the stock to satisfy any judgment in personam which might be entered against the owner. *Womack v. De Witt, 40 Del. 304, 10 A.2d 504 (1939).*

Defendant's right to attack foreign attachment was not waived by the filing by the resident agent for a corporation of a certificate designating the shares registered in the name of the defendant. *Brainard v. Canaday, 49 Del. 182, 112 A.2d 862 (1955).*

Seizure of stock for purpose of compelling appearance of nonresidents. — In seizing shares of stock for the purpose of compelling nonresident corporate defendants to appear, the Court of Chancery was not

governed by the provisions of attachment at law under this section. *Greene v. Johnston, 34 Del. Ch. 115, 99 A.2d 627, 42 A.L.R.2d 906 (1953).*

Due process of law, as applied to notice of proceedings under a statute resulting in judgment, means notice directed by the statute itself, and not a voluntary or gratuitous notice resting in favor or discretion; and the statutory provisions must not leave open clear opportunities for a commission of fraud or injustice, and must be such as to indicate that, if complied with, there is a reasonable probability, the defendant will receive actual notice. *Spoturno v. Woods, 38 Del. 378, 192 A. 689 (1937).*

Where the plaintiff sought to attach stock of a nonresident, the attachment was void where the stock was listed on the corporate books as belonging to the defendant's broker and therefore could not be construed as implied notice to the defendant and was insufficient notice under the due process clause, regardless of the fact that the defendant made a general appearance during his lifetime; but because of the general appearance, the action could be prosecuted against the deceased defendant's administrators. *Omnium De Participations Indus. De Luxe v. Spoturno, 39 Del. 100, 196 A. 194 (1937).*

Where buyer of stock at judicial sale knows that previous owner parted with title before attachment, buyer cannot compel transfer in corporate books, by mandamus, unless buyer surrenders stock certificate or furnishes bond against outstanding interest. *State ex rel. Cooke v. New York-Mexican Oil Co., 32 Del. 244, 122 A. 55 (1923).*

DELAWARE CASE NOTES — UNREPORTED

This section does not prohibit attachment of unissued shares or uncertificated securities. In fact, subsection (a) merely refers to "shares," not "issued shares" of stock. That provision also states that with regard to all stocks except uncertificated securities, attachment is not laid and no order of sale shall issue unless § 8-112 of Title 6 has been satisfied. *Livingston v. Ramunno, 1999 Del. Super. LEXIS 292 (1999).*

The responding corporation to a stock attachment is different than the typical garnishee in a debt attachment or wage attachment. An attachment of shares of stock of a corporation is not an attachment or garnishment of the corporation. When the attaching process is duly returned, neither the corporation nor its officer is required, like garnishees, to make answer upon the garnishment and the officer's certificate indicating the number of shares

attached is all that is required. *Harrington v. Hollingsworth, 1996 Del. Super. LEXIS 556 (1996).*

This section and section 169 do not apply to shares of stock which are the subject of an appraisal proceeding under Section 262. *Ums Ptnrs v. Jackson, 1995 Del. Super. LEXIS 250 (1995).*

Limitations.—This section does not authorize the attachment of "rights" belonging to shares of stock which themselves are not subject to attachment. In other words, this section permits attachment of rights "belonging" to shares only where the "shares" themselves are subject to attachment. *Ums Ptnrs v. Jackson, 1995 Del. Super. LEXIS 250 (1995).*

Manner of sale. — The sale of stock, especially closely held stock, is unique, but it is to be conducted in the same manner as other personalty. *Atlantic Properties Group v. Deibler, 1994 Del. Super. LEXIS 32 (1994) .*

§ 325. Actions against officers, directors or stockholders to enforce liability of corporation; unsatisfied judgment against corporation

DELAWARE CASE NOTES — REPORTED

The purpose of this section is to prescribe the manner in which actions are pursued and not to restrict causes of action that have traditionally been available to creditors independently of the corporation law. *Lone Star Indus., Inc. v. Redwine, 757 F.2d 1544 (5th Cir. 1985).*

Judgment and unsatisfied execution against corporation as condition precedent. — Obtaining a judgment and unsatisfied execution against the corporation is a condition precedent to the employment of the remedies mentioned in this section by the creditor directly against the stockholders. The law does not permit a creditor to collect a claim from stockholders if the creditor can recover it from the corporation, and the only way the creditor's inability to do this can be shown to the court is by a judgment and unsatisfied execution. But if the creditor proceeds independently of that statute, by a bill asking for the appointment of receivers on the ground of insolvency, a judgment and execution are not required because the court is compelled to determine the very fact that the judgment and execution are designed to establish. *John W. Cooney Co. v. Arlington Hotel Co., 11 Del. Ch. 430, 106 A. 39 (1918).*

This section is plainly irrelevant in copyright infringement action, since it is not a suit against an officer, director or stockholder for the debts of a corporation. *Hideout Records & Distribs. v. El Jay Dee, Inc., 601 F. Supp. 1048 (D. Del. 1984).*

Joint liability. — A director who joins with his or her associate directors in the wrongful authorization of the management is jointly liable with them for the injury which it did to the corporation. *Eshleman v. Keenan, 21 Del. Ch. 259, 187 A. 25 (1936).*

Unpaid subscriptions. — The debts of the company not having been ascertained and there being no showing that the assessment or collection on an unpaid subscrip-

tion was necessary either for the payment of debts of the corporation or for the purpose of equalization among the stockholders, suit could not be maintained on a stock subscription note against a stockholder by a receiver for the unpaid subscription. *Philips v. Slocomb, 35 Del. 462, 167 A. 698 (1933).*

Mere act of voting did not justify charge of participation in conspiracy. — The mere act of a large corporate shareholder in a transferee corporation in voting in favor of a purchase of assets at an allegedly grossly exaggerated price could not of itself justify a charge against the shareholder of wrongful participation in an alleged conspiracy. *Heil v. Standard Gas & Elec. Co., 17 Del. Ch. 214, 151 A. 303 (1930).*

Sole ownership of stock and common directors and officers between parent and subsidiary are only some of the factors to be considered by courts in determining whether or not the corporate fiction should be disregarded and the shareholders held liable. *Scott-Douglas Corp. v. Greyhound Corp., 304 A.2d 309 (Del. Super. Ct. 1973).*

It requires a strong case to induce a court to consider 2 corporations as 1 on account of 1 owning all the capital stock of the other. *Scott-Douglas Corp. v. Greyhound Corp., 304 A.2d 309 (Del. Super. Ct. 1973).*

CASE NOTES — OTHER STATES

Connecticut

Special circumstances rule. — In Delaware, although the officers and directors of a corporation generally owe no duties to the creditors of their corporation apart from those arising under the creditors' contracts with the corporation, they owe certain "extra duties" to corporate creditors when there are special circumstances which affect their rights as creditors of the corporation, e.g. fraud, insolvency, or a violation of a statute. *Bennett Restructuring Fund, L.P. v. Hamburg, 2003 Conn. Super. LEXIS 61 (2003).*

With respect to a claim that a corporate officer or director of a Delaware corporation owes a fiduciary duty to

any creditor of the corporation whom he or she defrauds, the courts of Delaware have long rejected that claim. With respect to whether under the "special circumstances rule" the extra duties imposed upon corporate officers and directors who defraud corporate creditors are fiduciary duties, for breach of which defrauded creditors can sue offending officers and directors both for fraud and for breach of fiduciary duty, Delaware courts conclude that such "extra duties" are not fiduciary in nature, and have dismissed a plaintiff's breach-of-fiduciary-duty claim while permitting its parallel fraud claim to proceed. *Bennett Restructuring Fund, L.P. v. Hamburg, 2003 Conn. Super. LEXIS 61 (2003).*

CASE NOTES — FEDERAL

Second Circuit

Necessity of prior judgment. — Section 278 applies to claims against shareholders that arise before dissolution, so therefore section 325(b) also applies and the State must obtain judgment against corporation before pursuing its claim against the shareholder-distributees. *Marsh v. Rosenbloom, 499 F.3d 165, 2007 U.S. App. LEXIS 20555 (2nd Cir., NY, August 28, 2007).*

Pre-emption. — State has not shown such a conflict between Delaware law and the congressional policy manifested in CERCLA as to lead us to conclude that Congress intended to preempt Delaware's corporate wind-up period, which protects dissolved corporations' and their former shareholders' interests in finality. CERCLA does not suggest that the entire corpus of state corporation law is to be replaced simply because a plaintiff's cause of action is based upon a federal statute, or because it would

net the government more money, which is essentially all the State has shown here. That is not sufficient to justify preemption. *Marsh v. Rosenbloom, 499 F.3d 165, 2007 U.S. App. LEXIS 20555 (2nd Cir., NY, August 28, 2007).*

Third Circuit

Del. Code Ann. tit. 8, § 325 does not work to restrict causes of action traditionally available to creditors independent of corporate law. *Protocomm Corp. v. Novell Advanced Services, Inc., 171 F. Supp. 2d 459 (E.D.Pa. 2001).*

Construction of prior court opinion. — A prior decision did not determine that Del. Code Ann. tit. 8, § 325 could be used to provide standing for a claim brought under Del Code Ann. tit. 8, § 174. Rather, the court essentially provided that the cause of action be brought under the common-law fraudulent conveyance claim.

Protocomm Corp. v. Novell Advanced Services, Inc., 171 F. Supp. 2d 459 (E.D.Pa. 2001).

This statute is not authority for the proposition that individual directors and officers may sue an accounting firm for breach of contract with the corporations. *Neuberger v. Shapiro, 110 F. Supp. 2d 373 (E.D.Pa. 2000).*

Continued liability to judgment creditor. — One who was a stockholder at the time of a wrongful distribution may be liable to a judgment creditor of the corporation under § 325 even though the distributee is no longer a stockholder at the time of the action by the creditor. *ProtoComm Corp. v. Novell, Inc., 55 F. Supp. 2d 319 (E.D.Pa 1999).*

Seventh Circuit

Common law actions not restricted. — If the officers, directors, or shareholders of a corporation are otherwise liable for the corporation's debts under statutory law, a corporate creditor may sue any or all of them, after first obtaining judgment and an unsatisfied execution against the corporation. Statutory corporate law provides no means for holding shareholders of the corporation liable for its debts. However, the statute does not restrict causes of action traditionally available to corporate creditors at common law. *Pinellas County v. Great American Industrial Group, Inc., 1991 U.S. Dist. LEXIS 17517 (N.D.Ill. 1991).*

Direct recovery from shareholders. — Where a corporation distributes its assets to its shareholders, leaving creditors unsatisfied, those creditors are entitled to recover directly from the shareholders, without resort to fraudulent conveyance law, and without obtaining a prior judgment against the corporate debtor. *Pinellas County v. Great American Industrial Group, Inc., 1991 U.S. Dist. LEXIS 17517 (N.D.Ill. 1991).*

Ninth Circuit

Insolvency triggers director fiduciary duties to creditors. — Typically, directors do not owe fiduciary duties to creditors because the relationship between debtor and creditor is contractual in nature. At the moment a corporation becomes insolvent, however, the insolvency triggers fiduciary duties for directors for the benefit of creditors. Such duties exist when a company becomes "insolvent in fact," that is, when it is within the "zone" or "vicinity" of insolvency, a poorly defined state that may exist when the corporation cannot generate and/or obtain enough cash to pay for its projected obligations and fund its business requirements for working capital and capital expenditures with a reasonable cushion to cover the variability of its business needs over time. Creditors have a right to expect that directors will not divert, dissipate, or unduly risk assets necessary to satisfy their claims. Notably, in insolvency the duty runs not directly to the creditors but to the "community of interest." Thus, while this duty does not necessarily place creditor interests ahead of the interests of stockholders, it requires the board to maximize the corporation's long-term wealth-creating capacity. *Official Committee of Bond Holders v. Official Committee of Trade Creditors, 2004 U.S. Dist. LEXIS 19497 (N.D.Cal. 2004).*

§ 327. Stockholder's derivative action; allegation of stock ownership

DELAWARE CASE NOTES — REPORTED

Purpose. — The policy embodied in this section is the prevention of the evil of purchasing stock in order to maintain a derivative action designed to attack a transaction which occurred prior to the purchase of the stock. *Newkirk v. W.J. Rainey, Inc., 31 Del. Ch. 433, 76 A.2d 121 (1950).*

The sole purpose of this section is to prevent what has been considered an evil, namely, the purchasing of shares in order to maintain a derivative action designed to attack a transaction which occurred prior to the purchase of the stock. *Blasband v. Rales, 971 F.2d 1034 (3d Cir. 1992).*

This section prevents a stockholder from attacking transactions completed before he or she becomes a stockholder. It was designed principally to prevent the purchasing of stock to be used for the purpose of filing a derivative action attacking transactions occurring prior to such purchase. There is nothing in the policy behind this section which would call for a construction favoring its application in situations where inexcusable inaction on the part of corporate personnel might make it less likely that wrongdoing would be discovered. *Maclary v. Pleasant Hills, Inc., 35 Del. Ch. 39, 109 A.2d 830 (1954).*

This section should be construed so as to reasonably effectuate its primary purpose to discourage a type of strike suit — it should not be construed so as to unduly encourage the camouflaging of transactions and prevent reasonable opportunities to rectify corporate aberrations. *Maclary v. Pleasant Hills, Inc., 35 Del. Ch. 39, 109 A.2d 830 (1954).*

This section is aimed primarily at purchases made for the purpose of maintaining suits attacking transactions taking place prior to such purchases. Where a customer has at all times been the owner of stock and the broker in fact held shares for that account, it is difficult to see how anything more should be required to satisfy the policy reflected in the statute. *Saks v. Gamble, 35 Del. Ch. 378, 118 A.2d 793 (1955), aff'd, 35 Del. Ch. 503, 122 A.2d 120 (1958).*

This section was enacted to prevent what has been considered an evil; namely, the purchasing of shares in order to maintain a derivative action designed to attack a transaction which occurred prior to the purchase of the stock. *Helfand v. Gambee, 37 Del. Ch. 51, 136 A.2d 558 (1957).*

This section was enacted to eliminate strike suits and other abuses which developed along with the derivative suit. *Harff v. Kerkorian, 324 A.2d 215 (Del. Ch. 1974), modified, 347 A.2d 133 (Del. 1975); Jones v. Taylor, 348 A.2d 188 (Del. Ch. 1975).*

Corporations

The purpose of the rule requiring the plaintiff to be a shareholder at the time of the transaction of which he or she complains is to prevent what is considered to be a wrong, namely, the purchasing of shares in order to maintain a derivative action so as to attack a transaction which occurred prior to the purchase of stock. *Jones v. Taylor, 348 A.2d 188 (Del. Ch. 1975).*

The policy behind this section is to prevent so-called strike suits, whereby individuals purchase shares in a corporation with litigious motives. *Schreiber v. Bryan, 396 A.2d 512 (Del. Ch. 1978).*

A primary purpose of the contemporaneous ownership requirement is to curtail strike suits by prohibiting potential plaintiffs from buying into a lawsuit through the purchase of shares of stock in a corporation after an alleged wrong has occurred. *Brambles USA, Inc. v. Blocker, 731 F. Supp. 643 (D. Del. 1990).*

As a matter of policy, one who buys shares with knowledge of a purported wrongdoing should not be permitted to bring suit to challenge that wrongdoing. *Brambles USA, Inc. v. Blocker, 731 F. Supp. 643 (D. Del. 1990).*

No state of mind exception. — Although this court has often recognized that a primary purpose of this section is to prevent plaintiffs from buying stock in order to maintain a derivative suit, there is no indication in the unambiguous text of the statute that that is its only purpose or that a plaintiff has standing when he otherwise would not simply because he was ignorant of the wrongdoing before he acquired the stock. This court cannot supplant the plain language of a Delaware statute with conjecture about that statute's underlying public policy. Indeed, plaintiff does not cite to any legislative history underlying the enactment of this section in support of his public policy argument, but rather to decisions of this court that merely attempt to explain the statute. Those decisions could not and did not alter the plain language of the statute. This section is clear that stock ownership at the time of challenged conduct is a prerequisite to maintaining a derivative action and the General Assembly has not legislated a state of mind exception to that requirement. *Desimone v. Barrows, 924 A.2d 908; 2007 Del. Ch. LEXIS 75 (June 7, 2007).*

This section was not passed to prevent correction of corporate wrongdoing. *Maclary v. Pleasant Hills, Inc., 35 Del. Ch. 39, 109 A.2d 830 (1954); Helfand v. Gambee, 37 Del. Ch. 51, 136 A.2d 558 (1957).*

Construction of section. — This section should be liberally construed in situations where its primary purpose will not be frustrated thereby. *Jones v. Taylor, 348 A.2d 188 (Del. Ch. 1975); Brambles USA, Inc. v. Blocker, 731 F. Supp. 643 (D. Del. 1990).*

The provisions of this section are not inflexible standards, and a court of equity must examine carefully the particular circumstances of each case. *Schreiber v. Carney, 447 A.2d 17 (Del. Ch. 1982).*

This section does not create the right to sue derivatively but rather restricts that right. *Harff v. Kerkorian, 324 A.2d 215 (Del. Ch. 1974), modified, 347 A.2d 133 (Del. 1975).*

What is derivative action. — A derivative action is in reality one brought by a stockholder on behalf of the corporation, not to redress a wrong done to the stockholder individually, but to obtain recovery or relief in favor of the corporation and all similar stockholders so as to compensate the corporation for some wrong done to it as a whole. *Reeves v. Transport Data Communications, Inc., 318 A.2d 147 (Del. Ch. 1974).*

Nature of derivative suit is twofold: First, it is the equivalent of a suit by the stockholders to compel the corporation to sue; and second, it is a suit by the corporation, asserted by the stockholders in its behalf, against those liable to it. *Harff v. Kerkorian, 324 A.2d 215 (Del. Ch. 1974), modified, 347 A.2d 133 (Del. 1975).*

What is a double derivative action. — In a double derivative suit, a stockholder of a parent corporation seeks recovery for a cause of action belonging to a subsidiary corporation. *Rales v. Blasband, 634 A.2d 927 (Del. 1993).*

Plaintiff must be shareholder at time of challenged transaction. — Under Delaware law, a plaintiff must have been a shareholder at the time of the challenged transaction to have standing to maintain a shareholder derivative suit. *Blasband v. Rales, 971 F.2d 1034 (3d Cir. 1992).*

In an action contesting the terms of a private placement, the plaintiff was required to prove that it was a stockholder as of the time the terms of the private placement were decided, not as of the time the shares were transferred; the timing of the allegedly wrongful transaction must be determined by identifying the acts which are susceptible of being remedied in a legal tribunal. *7547 Partners v. Beck, 682 A.2d 160 (Del. 1996).*

Stockholder's derivative suit is distinct and peculiarly equitable action, and nothing about it compels the Chancery Court to follow traditional accounting procedure in what amounts to an action for damages flowing from breach of contract. *Levien v. Sinclair Oil Corp., 300 A.2d 28 (Del. Ch. 1972).*

A stockholder's suit, a derivative action, must in this State be brought in equity. Consequently, it does involve an equitable remedy. *Rosenthal v. Burry Biscuit Corp., 30 Del. Ch. 299, 60 A.2d 106 (1948).*

The derivative action was developed by equity to enable stockholders to sue in the corporation's name where those in control of the corporation refused to assert a claim belonging to the corporation. *Harff v. Kerkorian, 324 A.2d 215 (Del. Ch. 1974), modified, 347 A.2d 133 (Del. 1975).*

Corporation is proper and necessary party in an adverse action against it by stockholders to enjoin the corporation from carrying out a stock option plan. *Elster v. American Airlines, 34 Del. Ch. 500, 106 A.2d 202 (1954).*

Corporation is adverse party in a stockholder's derivative action. *Elster v. American Airlines, 34 Del. Ch. 500, 106 A.2d 202 (1954).*

Benefit of action results to all shareholders equally. — The benefit of an action brought by a corporation, or a derivative action on its behalf, necessarily results to all of the shareholders equally, even when some of them have been wrongdoers, or have by acquiescence, or ratification, forfeited their equitable claims to redress; but the best method to work out the rights of the parties in a case of this kind is to preserve the fiction of corporate entity. *Keenan v. Eshleman, 23 Del. Ch. 234, 2 A.2d 904, 120 A.L.R. 227 (1938).*

The relief to be obtained in a derivative action is relief to the corporation in which all stockholders, whether guilty or innocent of the wrongs complained of, shall share indirectly. *Taormina v. Taormina Corp., 32 Del. Ch. 18, 78 A.2d 473 (1951); Abelow v. Symonds, 38 Del. Ch. 572, 156 A.2d 416 (1959).*

And result would not be different even if suing stockholder owned all stock of the wronged corporation. *Abelow v. Symonds, 38 Del. Ch. 572, 156 A.2d 416 (1959).*

Stockholders in derivative action are not entitled to recover in their own right. *Bokat v. Getty Oil Co., 262 A.2d 246 (Del. 1970).*

Relief inures to benefit of corporation. — Stockholders who proceed in maintaining a derivative action do so on behalf of the corporation whose cause of action they assert. Their right is strictly a derivative one, and the relief obtained belongs to the corporation and not to themselves. *Harden v. Eastern States Pub. Serv. Co., 14 Del. Ch. 156, 122 A. 705 (1923).*

When a stockholder sues in his or her derivative right as a stockholder, the wrong against which the stockholder complains is one that was done to the corporation. Any relief which may be afforded is in its behalf and inures to its benefit. The complainant as a stockholder is interested in the alleged wrong and in the relief only in an indirect and derivative sense. *Ainscow v. Sanitary Co. of Am., 21 Del. Ch. 35, 180 A. 614 (1935).*

Any relief which may be afforded in a stockholder derivative action is in the corporation's behalf and inures to its benefit. The complainant as a stockholder is interested in the alleged wrong and in the relief only in an indirect and derivative sense. *Eshleman v. Keenan, 22 Del. Ch. 82, 194 A. 40 (1937), aff'd, 23 Del. Ch. 234, 2 A.2d 904 (1938).*

Limited standing for bidder for target corporation. — Competing bidder for a target corporation, alleging that a violation of the transfer limitations of the target corporation's stock with enhanced voting rights, had standing to pursue a challenge, as it was of immediate and continuing interest to all of the target stockholders; since the competing bidder had purchased stock after a proposed merger had been announced, it lacked standing to pursue claims of breach of fiduciary duties, but did not lack standing to pursue a claim that it clearly could have pursued after the merger had been completed, under *8 Del. C. § 225(b). Omnicare, Inc. v. NCS Healthcare, Inc., 809 A.2d 1163 (Del. Ch. 2002), appeal dismissed, 822 A.2d 397 (Del. 2002).*

Read literally, this section does not provide that only stockholders have standing to sue derivatively. *Harff v. Kerkorian, 324 A.2d 215 (Del. Ch. 1974), modified, 347 A.2d 133 (Del. 1975).*

But only one who was stockholder at time of transaction or one whose shares devolved upon him or her by operation of law may maintain a derivative action.

Harff v. Kerkorian, 324 A.2d 215 (Del. Ch. 1974), modified, 347 A.2d 133 (Del. 1975); Schreiber v. Bryan, 396 A.2d 512 (Del. Ch. 1978).

Stockholder status at the time of the transaction being attacked and throughout the litigation is essential. *Harff v. Kerkorian, 324 A.2d 215 (Del. Ch. 1974), modified, 347 A.2d 133 (Del. 1975).*

Plaintiff in derivative action must be qualified to serve in fiduciary capacity as a representative of a class, whose interest is dependent upon the representative's adequate and fair prosecution. *Youngman v. Tahmoush, 457 A.2d 376 (Del. Ch. 1983).*

Equitable owner of stock can maintain action. — Under the common law of Delaware as applicable to proceedings in equity, an equitable owner of stock can maintain a stockholder's derivative action, and the term "stockholder" as employed in this section, therefore, includes an equitable owner. *Rosenthal v. Burry Biscuit Corp., 30 Del. Ch. 299, 60 A.2d 106 (1948).*

For many purposes, such as voting, dividend payments and appraisal proceedings, the corporation must have a rather inflexible basis of stockholder identity. That rigidity is not needed where the equitable owner of stock is seeking to protect the corporate interests. It places no undue burden on a corporation to permit an equitable owner to sue in a derivative action because the owner must prove ownership in order to maintain the action, and the need for the same certainty which prompted the courts to recognize only registered stockholders in other situations is therefore not apparent. *Rosenthal v. Burry Biscuit Corp., 30 Del. Ch. 299, 60 A.2d 106 (1948).*

An equitable stockholder can maintain a stockholder's derivative suit. A stockholder whose stock is held on margin under the usual contract with the broker permitting the broker to repledge the shares is an equitable stockholder. *Gamble-Skogmo, Inc. v. Saks, 35 Del. Ch. 503, 122 A.2d 120 (1956).*

In addition to this section's requirements, the Delaware courts require that the plaintiff remain a shareholder at the time of the filing of the suit and throughout the litigation. This requirement ensures that the plaintiff has sufficient incentive to represent adequately the corporation's interests during litigation. *Blasband v. Rales, 971 F.2d 1034 (3d Cir. 1992).*

Stock held in a margin account under the terms of which a broker has the right to sell or repledge stock held for the stockholder entitles its equitable owner to maintain a derivative action; the rule that an equitable owner of stock may sue derivatively has also been recognized in trust cases. *Brown v. Dolese, 38 Del. Ch. 471, 154 A.2d 233 (1959), aff'd, 39 Del. Ch. 1, 157 A.2d 784 (1960).*

An equitable stockholder, that is, one who owns in street name, may maintain a stockholder's derivative suit or a representative suit. *Braasch v. Goldschmidt, 41 Del. Ch. 519, 199 A.2d 760 (1964).*

Rule 23.1, Ch. Ct. R., was designed to militate against the wrong of buying into a derivative law suit and should not be allowed to bar an action by a stockholder with a long standing equitable interest in a corporation.

Theodora Holding Corp. v. Henderson, 257 A.2d 398 (Del. Ch. 1969).

For purposes of a derivative action, an equitable owner is considered a stockholder. *Harff v. Kerkorian, 324 A.2d 215 (Del. Ch. 1974), modified, 347 A.2d 133 (Del. 1975).*

For purposes of a derivative action, the term "stockholder" as employed in this section includes an equitable owner. *Jones v. Taylor, 348 A.2d 188 (Del. Ch. 1975).*

Holder of option to purchase stock is not equitable stockholder of corporation. *Harff v. Kerkorian, 324 A.2d 215 (Del. Ch. 1974), modified, 347 A.2d 133 (Del. 1975).*

Nor are debenture holders stockholders. *Harff v. Kerkorian, 324 A.2d 215 (Del. Ch. 1974), modified, 347 A.2d 133 (Del. 1975).*

Debenture holders lack standing to sue derivatively because they are not "stockholders" under this section. *Harff v. Kerkorian, 347 A.2d 133 (Del. 1975).*

Nor is holder of convertible bond a stockholder, by contract, in equity any more than at law. *Harff v. Kerkorian, 324 A.2d 215 (Del. Ch. 1974), modified, 347 A.2d 133 (Del. 1975).*

Holders of convertible debentures are creditors of the corporation and simply do not have standing to maintain a stockholder's derivative action under *Delaware law. Harff v. Kerkorian, 324 A.2d 215 (Del. Ch. 1974), modified, 347 A.2d 133 (Del. 1975).*

Plaintiff must be continuous owner of stock. — It is implicit in this section and in Rule 23.1, Ch. Ct. R., that a stockholder-plaintiff must at the time he or she files a complaint have been the continuous owner of some of the stock held at the time of the alleged wrongful transaction. But neither this section nor Rule 23.1 literally requires that the plaintiff must allege that he or she owns the same stock which he or she owned at the time of the transaction of which he or she complains. *Dann v. Chrysler Corp., 40 Del. Ch. 103, 174 A.2d 696 (1961).*

If the organization of a specific subsidiary under a specific agreement for the purpose of engaging in oil operations in a specific country is the transaction under attack and capable of correction by a derivative suit, plaintiff stockholder must have held his or her stock at the time of the transaction in order to have standing to bring the suit. *Levien v. Sinclair Oil Corp., 261 A.2d 911 (Del. Ch. 1969), rev'd in part on other grounds, 280 A.2d 717 (Del. 1971).*

A plaintiff bringing a derivative suit on behalf of a corporation must be a stockholder of the corporation at the time he or she commences the suit and must maintain that status throughout the course of the litigation. *Heit v. Tenneco, Inc., 319 F. Supp. 884 (D. Del. 1970).*

In order to maintain a derivative suit, stockholder status at the time of the transaction being attacked and during the litigation is essential. *Jones v. Taylor, 348 A.2d 188 (Del. Ch. 1975).*

Requirement that a plaintiff who brings a derivative suit on behalf of a corporation must be a stockholder of the corporation at the time he or she commences the suit is not without exception. *Schreiber v. Carney, 447 A.2d 17 (Del. Ch. 1982).*

Intervention. — The weight of persuasive authority favors intervention as a method of curing a standing deficiency in a stockholder's derivative action. *NL Indus., Inc. v. Maxxam, Inc., 698 A.2d 949 (Del. Ch. 1996).*

Standing in post-merger derivative actions. — To have post-merger standing to carry on a derivative suit, derivative shareholder must not only be a stockholder at the time of the alleged wrong and at the time of commencement of the suit but he or she must also maintain shareholder status throughout the litigation. *Lewis v. Anderson, 477 A.2d 1040 (Del. 1984).*

Plaintiff was without standing to pursue his stockholder derivative claims as a result of the consummated cash-out merger and plaintiff's failure to challenge the fairness of the underlying merger itself. *Kramer v. Western Pac. Indus., 546 A.2d 348 (Del. 1988).*

Shareholder who bought stock subsequent to merger did not have standing to pursue a derivative action based upon agreements entered into prior to the merger where the underlying transaction complained of was complete at the time of the merge and was not a continuing wrong. *Brambles USA, Inc. v. Blocker, 731 F. Supp. 643 (D. Del. 1990).*

Former shareholder in a merged company, who had become a shareholder in the successor company, lacked standing to pursue a pre-existing derivative claim under the rule of *Lewis v. Anderson, 477 A.2d 1040 (Del. 1984),* to which the high court adhered; the shareholder argued that the merger was arranged in a fraudulent attempt to avoid the derivative action, but failed to plead fraud with any particularity. *Lewis v. Ward, 852 A.2d 896 (Del. 2004).*

Continuing transactions. — If, in a derivative action, the wrong complained of is a continuing one and has not been consummated, a transferee of stock may sue although the wrong commenced before the transfer. *Newkirk v. W.J. Rainey, Inc., 31 Del. Ch. 433, 76 A.2d 121 (1950).*

Once it is decided that certain stock purchases are the "transactions" of which plaintiffs complain in a stockholder's derivative action, and such transactions were consummated prior to the date plaintiffs acquired their stock, then under this section the suit cannot be maintained; such purchases are not continuing wrongs against the corporation and allegations concerning conspiracy refer back to the alleged original wrongs. *Newkirk v. W.J. Rainey, Inc., 31 Del. Ch. 433, 76 A.2d 121 (1950).*

Where stockholder brings action against corporation attempting to enjoin its issuance of stock under an option plan, the fact that the allegedly wrongful acts were committed prior to the earliest sale on which the stockholder had acquired stock in the corporation precludes the court from holding that the wrong was a continuing one, and stockholder is not entitled to proceed. *Elster v. American Airlines, 34 Del. Ch. 94, 100 A.2d 219 (1953).*

Where the issuance of stock is authorized and where certificates are presumably to be issued therefor at once, and that is the very action under attack, the transaction is not complete for purposes of applying this section until the

Corporations

certificates are issued. *Maclary v. Pleasant Hills, Inc., 35 Del. Ch. 39, 109 A.2d 830 (1954).*

Where the transaction of which plaintiff complained was legally completed when the stockholders voted their approval and this approval was admittedly given after plaintiff became a stockholder, the transaction of which plaintiff complained was not completed before plaintiff became a stockholder. The plaintiff's claim was therefore not barred by this section or by *Rule 23.1, Ch. Ct. R. Lavine v. Gulf Coast Leaseholds, Inc., 35 Del. Ch. 539, 122 A.2d 550 (1956).*

In a case of alleged continuing wrongs against a corporation, the test for determining the time at which stock must have been purchased in order to provide the stockholder with standing to maintain a derivative action concerns whether the wrong complained of is in actuality a continuing one or is one which has been consummated. *Schreiber v. Bryan, 396 A.2d 512 (Del. Ch. 1978).*

Mere allegations that later grants of the same nature were made do not suffice to invoke the narrow continuing wrong exception to the clear statutory mandate that a derivative plaintiff must have owned stock at the time the transaction he attacks occurred in order to have standing to challenge that transaction on the corporation's behalf. Therefore, consistent with long-standing precedent, plaintiff is barred by this section from attacking the options grants made before he became a stockholder. *Desimone v. Barrows, 924 A.2d 908; 2007 Del. Ch. LEXIS 75 (June 7, 2007).*

Request or demand upon corporation. — A request or demand is not necessary in all cases of derivative actions. When it is manifest from the circumstances that a demand would be a useless form, the same is not required as a condition precedent to the right of the stockholders to proceed. Where the demand if made would be directed to the particular individuals who themselves are the alleged wrongdoers and who therefore would be invited to sue themselves, the rule is settled that a demand and refusal is not requisite. *Fleer v. Frank H. Fleer Corp., 14 Del. Ch. 277, 125 A. 411 (1924).*

The right of a stockholder to prosecute a derivative suit is limited to situations where the stockholder has demanded that the directors pursue the corporate claim and they have wrongfully refused to do so or where demand is excused because the directors are incapable of making an impartial decision regarding such litigation. *Rales v. Blasband, 634 A.2d 927 (Del. 1993).*

A stockholder may under certain circumstances sue in equity in right of the corporation. Where a stockholder does so, however, he or she asserts the right of the corporation. This the stockholder is not permitted to do, unless the circumstances be such that the corporation will not sue. Its unwillingness to act must be evidenced by a refusal after proper demand, or by facts which show that by reason of hostile interest or guilty participation in the wrongs complained of, the responsible managers of the corporation cannot be expected to sue, or would be improper persons to conduct the litigation. In the latter case, a demand upon them and a refusal are not required as a condition precedent to the stockholder's right to proceed. *Baker v. Bankers Mtg. Co., 14 Del. Ch. 427, 129 A. 775 (1925).*

A stockholder may sue to enforce a corporate right without any demand on the corporation if the circumstances are such that the directors, whether by reason of hostile interest or guilty participation in the wrongs complained of, cannot be expected to institute a corporate suit, or where even if they did institute such a suit, it is apparent that they would not be the proper persons to conduct the litigation incident thereto. *Sohland v. Baker, 15 Del. Ch. 431, 141 A. 277 (1927).*

Before the shareholder is permitted in his or her own name to institute and conduct a litigation which usually belongs to the corporation, the shareholder should show, to the satisfaction of the court, that he or she has exhausted all the means within his or her reach to obtain, within the corporation itself, the redress of his or her grievances, or action in conformity to his or her wishes. The shareholder must make an earnest, not a simulated effort, with the managing body of the corporation to induce remedial action on their part, and this must be made apparent to the court. *Sohland v. Baker, 15 Del. Ch. 431, 141 A. 277 (1927).*

If by reason of hostile interest or guilty participation in the wrongs complained of, the directors cannot be expected to institute suit, or if a suit is instituted it is apparent that the directors would not be the proper persons to conduct it, no demand upon them to institute suit is requisite to enable a stockholder to sue in behalf of the corporation. *Miller v. Loft, Inc., 17 Del. Ch. 301, 153 A. 861 (1931).*

A stockholder cannot be permitted as a general rule to invade the discretionary field committed to the judgment of the directors and sue in the corporation's behalf when the managing body refuses. A stockholder may sue in equity in his or her derivative right to assert a cause of action on behalf of the corporation, without prior demand upon the directors to sue, when it is apparent that a demand would be futile, that the officers are under an influence that sterilizes discretion and could not be proper persons to conduct the litigation. *McKee v. Rogers, 18 Del. Ch. 81, 156 A. 191 (1931).*

A stockholder has no right to file a bill in the corporation's behalf in a derivative action unless he or she has first made demand on the corporation that it bring the suit and the demand has been answered by a refusal, or unless the circumstances are such that because of the relation of the responsible officers of the corporation to the alleged wrongs, a demand would be obviously futile or, if complied with, it is apparent that the officers are not the proper persons to conduct the litigation. *Ainscow v. Sanitary Co. of Am., 21 Del. Ch. 35, 180 A. 614 (1935).*

Demand on the board was excused because the amended complaint alleged particularized facts creating a reasonable doubt that a majority of the board would be disinterested or independent in making a decision on a demand. *Rales v. Blasband, 634 A.2d 927 (Del. 1993).*

Necessity for action should be alleged. — The necessity of the stockholder's showing that the corporation cannot secure relief except through the gratuitous assumption by the stockholder of its championship, is what imposes upon the stockholder the requirement that appropriate allegations shall be made in his or her bill of complaint of facts upon which the court can see the basis on which the necessity rests for the stockholder's derivative action. They are very material allegations. Being material to allege, they are material to prove, unless admitted; and if they are neither proved nor admitted, the bill should be dismissed even after answer has been filed and the cause has gone to final hearing. *Ainscow v. Sanitary Co. of Am., 21 Del. Ch. 35, 180 A. 614 (1935).*

Demand futility test. — A court must determine whether the particularized factual allegations of a derivative stockholder complaint create a reasonable doubt that, as of the time the complaint is filed, the board of directors could have properly exercised its independent and disinterested business judgment in responding to a demand; if the derivative plaintiff satisfies this burden, then demand will be excused as futile. *Rales v. Blasband, 634 A.2d 927 (Del. 1993).*

A court should not apply the *Aronson v. Lewis, Del. Supr., 473 A.2d 805, 814 (1984)* test for demand futility where the board that would be considering the demand did not make a business decision which is being challenged in the derivative suit; this situation would arise in three principal scenarios: (1) Where a business decision was made by the board of a company, but a majority of the directors making the decision have been replaced; (2) where the subject of the derivative suit is not a business decision of the board; and (3) where the decision being challenged was made by the board of a different corporation. *Rales v. Blasband, 634 A.2d 927 (Del. 1993).*

A plaintiff in a double derivative suit is still required to satisfy the *Aronson v. Lewis, Del. Supr., 473 A.2d 805, 814 (1984)* test in order to establish that demand on the subsidiary's board is futile. *Rales v. Blasband, 634 A.2d 927 (Del. 1993).*

Stockholder electing appraisal remedy thereafter barred from suing derivatively. — A stockholder of a Delaware corporation who elects to pursue his or her appraisal remedy under the Delaware general corporation law cannot thereafter sue derivatively on behalf of the corporation. *Dofflemyer v. W.F. Hall Printing Co., 558 F. Supp. 372 (D. Del. 1983).*

Proper remedy against exploitation of corporation by its dominant stockholder is by suit in behalf of the corporation to redress the wrongs when done, not by a proceeding to prevent the acquisition of control which makes the exploitation possible. Certainly it is not against the policy of the law for 1 stockholder to own a majority of a corporation's stock. *Francis v. Medill, 16 Del. Ch. 129, 141 A. 697 (1928).*

Dissolved or nonresident corporations. — Where all the known assets of a dissolved corporation have been distributed, and it is truly civiliter mortuus, thus placing a cause of action directly in the hands of its stockholders, or where the corporate entity of a nonresident corporation can be shown to be a fiction or sham, there would seem to be no compelling reason for holding that the presence of such corporation in court is required for jurisdictional purposes. But where there is no doubt but that the nonresident corporation can be served with process, it would be contrary to settled principles of law to permit service of process on it to be dispensed with in Delaware solely because of a claimed inability to serve those charged with wrongdoing at the corporate domicile. *Striker v. Chesler, 39 Del. Ch. 193, 161 A.2d 576 (1960).*

Any defense available against corporation is available against plaintiff in stockholder's derivative action. *Schleiff v. B & O R.R., 36 Del. Ch. 342, 130 A.2d 321 (1955).*

Motive which inspired stockholder to file suit in his derivative right to require officers of the corporation to account for wrongs they committed against it is immaterial as a defense to the suit. *Millstein v. Arcade Cafeteria, Inc., 23 Del. Ch. 99, 2 A.2d 158 (1938).*

If the complainant in a stockholder's derivative action can show a good case, he or she is not disqualified from doing so because of any supposed ugly motive which may inspire him or her to assert it. *Millstein v. Arcade Cafeteria, Inc., 23 Del. Ch. 99, 2 A.2d 158 (1938).*

Ratification and acquiescence. — While a stockholder who has ratified or acquiesced in a corporate wrong may be estopped from filing a suit in behalf of the corporation, the fact that he or she may reap indirect benefit from a derivative suit filed by another stockholder who is under no estoppel will have no adverse effect upon the suit by the latter. *Eshleman v. Keenan, 22 Del. Ch. 82, 194 A. 40 (1937), aff'd, 23 Del. Ch. 234, 2 A.2d 904 (1938).*

Where the action is a derivative one, brought on behalf of the corporation, the complaint and the defenses are to be considered as though the corporation itself were suing the defendants, and releases, ratifications or waivers are ineffective. *Keenan v. Eshleman, 23 Del. Ch. 234, 2 A.2d 904 (1938).*

Where the action is a derivative one, brought for the benefit of a going corporation, equitable principles demand that the theory of the action be recognized and that the whole recoverable amount be decreed to be paid to the corporation, notwithstanding releases, ratifications or waivers after the event. *Keenan v. Eshleman, 23 Del. Ch. 234, 2 A.2d 904 (1938).*

To permit recovery to be diminished by an amount in proportion to the stock holdings of the stockholders who have ratified the wrongful acts would tend to encourage fraud; the effect would be to transform, by molding the decree, a derivative action into one for the benefit of the individual, and would not accord with the theory of the complaint, the prayer for relief, or the inherent nature of the wrong sought to be redressed. It would tend to weaken, if not to destroy, the efficacy of a stockholder's action to correct a corporate wrong; and would compel the complaining stockholder to accept that for which he or she had not sued. *Keenan v. Eshleman, 23 Del. Ch. 234, 2 A.2d 904 (1938).*

Ratification of fraudulent acts by a majority of the stockholders does not inure to the benefit of the defendants to the extent that the decree against them should be in such amount as to redress the wrong suffered by the dissenting stockholders by causing to be paid to them a

Corporations

dividend of the recoverable amount measured by their stock holdings. *Keenan v. Eshleman, 23 Del. Ch. 234, 2 A.2d 904 (1938)*.

A stockholder cannot complain of corporate action in which, with full knowledge of all the facts, he or she has concurred. *Elster v. American Airlines, 34 Del. Ch. 94, 100 A.2d 219 (1953)*.

A limitation on stockholder derivative actions, somewhat analogous to the ownership proscription, is called, for want of a better title, estoppel; stockholder cannot complain of corporate action in which he or she has concurred. *Schreiber v. Bryan, 396 A.2d 512 (Del. Ch. 1978)*.

Motion to strike for sham, under Rule 11, Ch. Ct. R., does not test the legal sufficiency of the claim stated, but whether the attorney who signed the pleading met the standards fixed by the rule. *Halpern v. Barran, 272 A.2d 118 (Del. Ch. 1970)*.

To achieve its purpose a motion to strike for sham, under Rule 11, Ch. Ct. R., will be granted not only when counsel knew the allegations of the pleadings were false and when they had their genesis in material unknown to him or her; it will also be granted when there is a substantial overbreadth of pleading compared with the knowledge on which it is based. *Halpern v. Barran, 272 A.2d 118 (Del. Ch. 1970)*.

Every inference should favor the pleader. But when there is no reasonable relationship between the charges made and the information on which they are based, then the pleading lacks good ground to support it, it is sham and will be dismissed under *Rule 11, Ch. Ct. R. Halpern v. Barran, 272 A.2d 118 (Del. Ch. 1970)*.

In the case of a stockholder's derivative suit, where plaintiff sues to enforce rights of his or her corporation, his or her inability to meet the test of a motion to strike for sham, under Rule 11, Ch. Ct. R., should not foreclose other stockholders or the corporation itself from asserting like charges when able to support them, so that the charges in the complaint subject to the Rule 11 motion should be dismissed with prejudice as to plaintiff only. *Singer v. Creole Petro. Corp., 301 A.2d 327 (Del. Ch.), modified, 311 A.2d 859 (Del. 1973)*.

Denial of motion for summary judgment. — Where the affidavits filed in a case do not disclose the circumstances under which the corporate officers are alleged to have appropriated a corporate opportunity and, beyond the naked allegations, no information is furnished relative to the circumstances under which the alleged appropriation of a corporate opportunity occurred, until such evidence is presented the court can form no conclusion with reference thereto and a motion for summary judgment will be denied. *Gottlieb v. McKee, 34 Del. Ch. 537, 107 A.2d 240 (1954)*.

Motion for summary judgment survived motion to dismiss. — Minority shareholders alleged sufficient individual injury — unconditionally resulting from the controlling shareholder's manipulation of a subsidiary holding in a manner designed to dilute both the cash value and voting rights of the minority stockholder — for their claims to survive a motion to dismiss under Chancery

Court Rule 12(b)(6). *In re Tri-Star Pictures, Inc., 634 A.2d 319 (Del. 1993)*.

Burden of proof in action alleging usurping of corporate opportunity. — In a derivative action alleging that the controlling stockholder committed waste and usurped a corporate opportunity from 1 subsidiary by creating another, the defendant has the burden of proving that the first subsidiary was not stripped of a corporate opportunity. *Schreiber v. Bryan, 396 A.2d 512 (Del. Ch. 1978)*.

Determination of adequate compensation in intercorporate transaction. — In a derivative action presenting the question of whether a subsidiary corporation was adequately compensated in an intercorporate transaction, if the court finds that ordinary business persons might differ as to whether or not the subsidiary corporation was adequately compensated, the court must validate the transaction. *Schreiber v. Bryan, 396 A.2d 512 (Del. Ch. 1978)*.

Complaint seeking remedy for alleged personal injury to class of stockholders. — Plaintiffs should not be summarily denied the right to couch their complaint in terms which seek a remedy for alleged personal injury to a class of stockholders as opposed to the theoretical injury to a corporate entity. *Abelow v. Symonds, 38 Del. Ch. 572, 156 A.2d 416 (1959)*.

Derivative claims of corporation merged into second corporation against second corporation moot. — Since a corporation cannot sue itself for its own benefit, the derivative claims asserted on behalf of a corporation merged into a second corporation against the second corporation must be dismissed as moot. *Dofflemyer v. W.F. Hall Printing Co., 558 F. Supp. 372 (D. Del. 1983)*.

Claim for special injury to stockholder not derivative action. — Where there is injury to the corporation and also special injury to the individual stockholder, a stockholder, if he or she should so desire, may proceed on his or her claim for the protection of his or her individual rights rather than in the right of the corporation and such action would then not constitute a derivative action. *Elster v. American Airlines, 34 Del. Ch. 94, 100 A.2d 219 (1953)*.

If the injury complained of is to the stockholder individually, and not to the corporation, then the cause of action is individual, not derivative. *Reeves v. Transport Data Communications, Inc., 318 A.2d 147 (Del. Ch. 1974)*.

Acquiring stock from shareholder who participated or acquiesced in corporate wrong. — One who acquires stock from a shareholder who participated in or acquiesced in a corporate wrong lacks the capacity to complain of it. *Courtland Manor, Inc. v. Leeds, 347 A.2d 144 (Del. Ch. 1975)*.

A shareholder may not complain of acts of corporate mismanagement if he or she acquired his or her shares from those who participated or acquiesced in the wrongful transaction. *Courtland Manor, Inc. v. Leeds, 347 A.2d 144 (Del. Ch. 1975)*.

The basis for the rule that a shareholder may not complain of acts of corporate mismanagement if he or she acquired his or her shares from those who participated or acquiesced in the wrongful transaction is that where shareholders have purchased all or substantially all of the shares of a corporation at a fair price, they have personally sustained no injury from wrongs which occurred prior to their purchase, and consequently, any recovery on their part for such prior wrongs would constitute a windfall and would enable such shareholders to obtain funds to which they had no just title or claim. *Courtland Manor, Inc. v. Leeds, 347 A.2d 144 (Del. Ch. 1975).*

Plaintiff may not improperly characterize action as nonderivative. — A plaintiff may not characterize an action as nonderivative when in fact it seeks relief for a wrong to his corporation. *Abelow v. Symonds, 38 Del. Ch. 572, 156 A.2d 416 (1959).*

Mere assertion that plaintiff is suing derivatively does not make action derivative. *Reeves v. Transport Data Communications, Inc., 318 A.2d 147 (Del. Ch. 1974).*

Examples of suits maintained individually by stockholders. — Actions which are based on a wrongful refusal to issue a stock certificate or a refusal to recognize a proper transfer of stock are examples of suits which are maintained individually by stockholders. *Reeves v. Transport Data Communications, Inc., 318 A.2d 147 (Del. Ch. 1974).*

Mismanagement. — Mismanagement which depresses value of stock is wrong to corporation, and therefore to the stockholders collectively, and thus is one which must be remedied through a derivative action. *Reeves v. Transport Data Communications, Inc., 318 A.2d 147 (Del. Ch. 1974).*

Suits by stockholders alleging mismanage- ment on the part of the directors are included within the umbrella of a derivative action. *Harff v. Kerkorian, 324 A.2d 215 (Del. Ch. 1974), modified, 347 A.2d 133 (Del. 1975).*

A claim of mismanagement resulting in corporate waste, if proven, represents a direct wrong to the corporation that is indirectly experienced by all shareholders. Any devaluation of stock is shared collectively by all the shareholders, rather than independently by the plaintiff or any other individual shareholder. Thus, the wrong alleged is entirely derivative in nature. *Kramer v. Western Pac. Indus., 546 A.2d 348 (Del. 1988).*

Allegations required in action for breach of fiduciary duty. — In a derivative action for breach of fiduciary duty, a stockholder must allege (1) the existence of a fiduciary relationship, (2) a breach of the fiduciary's duty, and (3) knowing participation in that breach by the defendants. *Penn Mart Realty Co. v. Becker, 298 A.2d 349 (Del. Ch. 1972).*

Burden of proof for breach of fiduciary duty of disclosure. — Although it is clear that claims for common law fraud, misrepresentation, or equitable fraud do require plaintiffs to show quantifiable damage, damages need not always be proven in a case involving breach of fiduciary duty of disclosure. *In re Tri-Star Pictures, Inc., 634 A.2d 319 (Del. 1993).*

Multifarious complaint. — A complaint is multifarious if the complainant seeks the relief of cancellation of a stock subscription alleged to have been obtained on the ground of fraud and at the same time seeks relief against the corporation which only a stockholder is entitled to

receive. *Miller v. Loft, Inc., 17 Del. Ch. 301, 153 A. 861 (1931).*

Executor deemed to have had notice of pendency of action. — When a derivative suit was pending at the time of the defendant's death, the executor must be deemed to have had actual notice of the pendency of this action when he came into court and suggested the death on the record. *Wimpfheimer v. Goldsmith, 298 A.2d 778 (Del. Ch. 1972).*

Chancery rules fixing procedure for taking exception to account do not apply to derivative suits. — Chancery Rules 123-129 fix the procedure to be followed when an exception is taken to an account in a procedure similar to that followed under the old federal equity practice; they have no application to a derivative suit, which is to be considered as if the injured corporation itself were suing defendants. *Levien v. Sinclair Oil Corp., 300 A.2d 28 (Del. Ch. 1972).*

Forum non conveniens. — Factors to be considered in ruling on a motion to dismiss a derivative suit on the ground of forum non conveniens are: (1) Whether Delaware law is applicable; (2) the relative ease of access to proof; (3) the availability of compulsory process for witnesses; (4) the possibility of the view of premises; (5) all other practical considerations which would make the trial easy, expeditious and inexpensive; and (6) the pendency or nonpendency of a similar action or actions in another jurisdiction. *Parvin v. Kaufmann, 43 Del. Ch. 461, 236 A.2d 425 (1967).*

An action to assert a derivative claim on behalf of a corporation will ordinarily not be dismissed on the ground of forum non conveniens except in the rare case in which the combination of the factors to be considered tips the scales overwhelmingly in favor of the defendants. *Parvin v. Kaufmann, 43 Del. Ch. 461, 236 A.2d 425 (1967).*

Discovery and inspection. — In a stockholder's derivative action to enjoin corporation's activity on stock option, where the questions propounded under an interrogatory relate to the identity of persons who may have knowledge of relevant facts and to matters relevant to the issue, the interrogatory is proper and should be answered. *Elster v. American Airlines, 34 Del. Ch. 500, 106 A.2d 202 (1954).*

In a stockholder's derivative action, interrogatories could ask corporation to describe the nature, terms and subject matter of each of certain documents called for by the interrogatory, and although objection is made to the interrogatory on the ground that it will require corporation to summarize and to state the effect of the documents referred to, where stockholder asserts that he or she is only asking for such information as will enable him or her to identify a paper for the purpose of ordering its production, the objection fails. *Elster v. American Airlines, 34 Del. Ch. 500, 106 A.2d 202 (1954).*

In a stockholder's derivative action to enjoin corporation's activity, stockholder in interrogatories could ask for the total number of shares held of record and not of record by each optionee which have been acquired otherwise than by the exercise of the options. *Elster v. American Airlines, 34 Del. Ch. 500, 106 A.2d 202 (1954).*

In stockholder's derivative action against directors of the corporation, where stockholder failed to produce at the request of corporation certain income tax returns, and there was nothing to explain the failure of stockholder to produce such returns, nor when they would be produced, and it was also not clear as to whether or not the failure of stockholder to produce them was due to refusal or negligence or because of inability on his part to obtain copies of the same from the office of the Bureau of Internal Revenue, the court would not issue an order dismissing the action for failure of the stockholder to comply with the order of the court, but the burden was upon the stockholder to explain satisfactorily the failure to comply. *Gottlieb v. McKee, 34 Del. Ch. 537, 107 A.2d 240 (1954).*

When a corporation for whose benefit a derivative action is brought objects to requests for discovery, the Court of Chancery must apply the same rules of discovery as govern other parties. *Garbarino v. Albercan Oil Corp., 109 A.2d 824 (Del. Ch. 1954).*

A corporation is entitled to prevent even its stockholders from engaging in unrestricted discovery in search of "something" even in a derivative suit for the benefit of the corporation. *Garbarino v. Albercan Oil Corp., 109 A.2d 824 (Del. Ch. 1954).*

Inspection of records allowed: (1) before the date the shareholder acquired his shares, as Del. C. 8, § 327 did not limit the dates of a permissible Del. C. 8, § 220 inspection); (2) irrespective of the source of the records; and (3) on records given to the corporation by the target before or after the merger. *Saito v. McKesson HBOC, Inc., 806 A.2d 113 (Del. 2002).*

Traditional requirements respecting pleadings held less significant. — The speed with which the defendant corporation withdrew from the transaction which was under attack after the filing of stockholder's derivative action renders the traditional requirements with respect to pleadings less significant because plaintiff was not afforded opportunities to amend the pleadings which are customarily available. *Iroquois Indus., Inc. v. Lewis, 318 A.2d 134 (Del. 1974).*

Settlement. — In reviewing the approval of a settlement of a derivative action, the function of the Delaware Supreme Court is merely to determine whether or not the court below has committed an act of judicial indiscretion in approving the settlement in the exercise of business judgment; it does not exercise its own judgment to determine anew the question of the intrinsic fairness of the settlement. *Rutman v. Kaminsky, 43 Del. Ch. 303, 226 A.2d 122 (1967).*

The recovery of monetary damages from director defendants is not a sine qua non to settlement of a derivative action. *Prince v. Bensinger, 244 A.2d 89 (Del. Ch. 1968).*

A proposed settlement may be approved if, although the corporation will not receive immediate tangible benefits upon approval of the proposed settlement, probable long-term benefits to the stockholders may properly be anticipated. *Prince v. Bensinger, 244 A.2d 89 (Del. Ch. 1968).*

Under this section and Rule 23.1, Ch. Ct. R., the Chancery Court's responsibility is to determine whether or not the proposed settlement terms are fair, reasonable and adequate, a settlement hearing not being in any sense a rehearsal of a trial. *Prince v. Bensinger, 244 A.2d 89 (Del. Ch. 1968).*

When notice of settlement hearings for a derivative action contain a statement that the file in question would be open for examination in Wilmington, as well as summarize the pleadings, the evidence, plaintiffs' position, the terms of settlement, and set forth a new bonus plan in its entirety, it complies with Delaware requirements. *Prince v. Bensinger, 244 A.2d 89 (Del. Ch. 1968).*

If the settlement of a derivative action is ultimately consummated, an evaluation of plaintiffs' contribution and appropriate attorneys' fees thereto will be made by the court after a duly scheduled hearing. *Prince v. Bensinger, 244 A.2d 89 (Del. Ch. 1968).*

The courts of Delaware do not adhere to the stringent federal rules governing the use of prospectuses for marketing corporate securities, when testing the sufficiency of notices of settlement hearings, under this section and *Rule 23.1, Ch. Ct. R. Prince v. Bensinger, 244 A.2d 89 (Del. Ch. 1968).*

A motion to set aside a settlement will be granted when a plaintiff-stockholder died more than 18 months before the stipulation of settlement was signed, since while the action is derivative, counsel derives their agency and authority from the plaintiff-stockholder. *Paolozzi v. Barber, 260 A.2d 176 (Del. Ch. 1969).*

When the corporation, for whose benefit suits were brought, puts a value on the claims against one defendant, many times what the court approved in settling claims against other defendants who have a joint and several liability, the court cannot let the order stand. *Paolozzi v. Barber, 260 A.2d 176 (Del. Ch. 1969).*

Costs and attorney's fees. — An exception to the rule that the losing litigant must pay its own counsel exists in derivative actions where the defendant corporation, even though prevailing, has been specifically and substantially benefited by the action. *Gottlieb v. Heyden Chem. Corp., 34 Del. Ch. 436, 105 A.2d 461 (1954).*

In stockholders derivative actions, attorneys engaged in the litigation are entitled to be paid from the fund resulting therefrom, to the extent that their services were helpful in the creation of such fund, or in the preservation of an existing fund. *Brady v. Pennroad Corp., 30 Del. Ch. 517, 64 A.2d 412 (1948).*

A corporation may defend a stockholder's derivative action (although theoretically any recovery rebounds to the benefit of the corporation) if the corporate interests are threatened by the suit, and in connection with the defense the corporation may properly pay counsel fees. *Blish v. Thompson Automatic Arms Corp., 30 Del. Ch. 538, 64 A.2d 581 (1948).*

In a successful stockholder's derivative action, counsel is entitled to be compensated for services and expenses which can be demonstrated to have either created or preserved the fund resulting from the litigation. *Aaron v. Parsons, 37 Del. Ch. 407, 144 A.2d 155 (1958).*

In determining the amount of an allowance consideration should be given to: (1) The amount recovered by the action; (2) the standing and ability of the counsel involved; (3) the difficulty of the litigation; and (4) the amount of time and effort of counsel in connection with the case. *Aaron v. Parsons, 37 Del. Ch. 407, 144 A.2d 155 (1958).*

The filing of a derivative action against a corporation will justify the award of fees to plaintiff's counsel only where the action confers some benefit upon the corporation, and the action, when filed, was meritorious and had a causal connection to the conferred benefit. *Chrysler Corp. v. Dann, 43 Del. Ch. 252, 223 A.2d 384 (1966).*

Although the general rule in Delaware is that a litigant must defray the costs of his or her own counsel, an exception is recognized where a suit by 1 member of a class results in the creation of a fund that inures to the benefit of all members of the class, as is the case in stockholder's derivative suits and creditor's bills. *Tri State Mall Assocs. v. A.A.R. Realty Corp., 298 A.2d 368 (Del. Ch. 1972).*

Ordinarily, in shareholder derivative actions, a losing plaintiff must pay his or her own counsel and bear the burden of his or her costs. However, when such litigation results in a benefit to the corporation or to the members of a class, a successful plaintiff is entitled to an allowance of counsel fees based upon the fund or property or benefit which his or her efforts have created, and in this regard it is not necessary that the benefit be measured in precise monetary standards. *Baron v. Allied Artists Pictures Corp., 395 A.2d 375 (Del. Ch. 1978), aff'd, 413 A.2d 876 (Del. 1980).*

To be entitled to an award of counsel fees and expenses in a stockholder derivative action, it is not necessary that the shareholder-plaintiff be successful in the sense that he or she obtain a favorable judgment in the litigation. *Baron v. Allied Artists Pictures Corp., 395 A.2d 375 (Del. Ch. 1978), aff'd, 413 A.2d 876 (Del. 1980).*

A plaintiff in a derivative suit rendered moot by subsequent corporate action is not required in the first instance to affirmatively demonstrate that the corporate action was induced by the prosecution of his suit in order to recover counsel fees and expenses. *Baron v. Allied Artists Pictures Corp., 395 A.2d 375 (Del. Ch. 1978), aff'd, 413 A.2d 876 (Del. 1980).*

The amount of an allowance for counsel fees, particularly in a corporate derivative action, is a matter left to the discretion of the court. *Baron v. Allied Artists Pictures Corp., 395 A.2d 375 (Del. Ch. 1978), aff'd, 413 A.2d 876 (Del. 1980).*

The number of hours spent in a derivative suit is not the controlling element on which an allowance of attorney's fees is to be based. Rather, the court must look to the nature of the action, the work accomplished and the result achieved, as well as to the time expended, in arriving at what would appear to be a reasonable fee for the effort. *Baron v. Allied Artists Pictures Corp., 395 A.2d 375 (Del. Ch. 1978), aff'd, 413 A.2d 876 (Del. 1980).*

Res judicata. — In a stockholder's derivative suit a judgment entered either after trial on the merits or upon an approved settlement is res judicata and bars subsequent suit on the same claim in behalf of the corporation. *Ezzes v. Ackerman, 43 Del. Ch. 420, 234 A.2d 444 (1967).*

DELAWARE CASE NOTES — UNREPORTED

Plaintiff must be shareholder at time of challenged transaction. — Stockholder who brought a derivative action lacked standing to seek relief with respect to challenged stock option grants that were made prior to the stockholder's purchase of shares in the corporation; the actual disposition of those claims depended on further proceedings undertaken to determine whether or not there was another stockholder who had standing to intervene to protect the right of the stockholders and the corporation to seek redress for the very early option grants alleged in the complaint. *Conrad v. Blank, 2007 Del. Ch. LEXIS 130 (Del. Ch. Sept. 7, 2007).*

Plaintiff must be continuous owner of stock. — Cofounder could not pursue breach of fiduciary duty claims, because no equitable exception to the continuous stock ownership requirement under *8 Del. C. § 327* and Ch. Ct. R. 23.1 operated, which would have allowed the cofounder to continue asserting derivative claims after the merger of a corporation with 2 partnerships. *Feldman v. Cutaia, 2007 Del. Ch. LEXIS 111 (Del. Ch. Aug. 1, 2007).*

Loss of standing. — A derivative plaintiff must maintain ownership throughout the course of litigation. This section, section 261, and section 327, read individually and collectively, permit one result which is not only consistent but sound: A plaintiff who ceases to be a shareholder, whether by reason of a merger or for any other reason, loses standing to continue a derivative suit.

Strategic Asset Mgmt. v. Nicholson, 2004 Del. Ch. LEXIS 178, No. 20360-NC (November 30, 2004).

Warrants are not a sufficient basis in the instant case for satisfaction of the continuous ownership requirement. *In re New Valley Corp. Derivative Litig., 2004 Del. Ch. LEXIS 107, No. 17649-NC (June 28, 2004).*

Dilution claim was derivative action. — Where minority shareholders claimed that the voting interest of their shares was diluted as a result of the majority shareholder's conversion of the corporation's promissory notes at a price that was about one-tenth of the employee stock option conversion price and about one-fifteenth of the price under the merger that was concluded 6 months later, that claim was a derivative claim rather than a direct claim, since the shareholders' voting power after its decrease from 39 percent to 7 percent was not a material change in voting power. *Gentile v. Rossette, 2005 Del. Ch. LEXIS 160 (Del. Ch. Oct. 20, 2005).*

Majority shareholder/director's conversion of debt to equity was considered to be either a benefit or a detriment to the corporation for purposes of determining that the minority shareholder dilution claim was a derivative claim rather than a direct claim; that conclusion was reached, in part, because the remedy for any detriment that the corporation suffered would be pursued on behalf of the corporation. *Gentile v. Rossette, , 2005 Del. Ch. LEXIS 160 (Del. Ch. Oct. 20, 2005).*

Corporations

No longer had standing to pursue claim. — Where minority shareholders claimed that the value of their shares was diluted as a result of the majority shareholder's conversion of the corporation's promissory notes at a fraction of both the employee stock option conversion price and the price under the merger that was concluded 6 months later, that claim was a derivative claim that expired upon the merger; the shareholders were not shareholders in the corporation after the merger and so no longer had standing to pursue that derivative claim against the successor entity. *Gentile v. Rossette, 2005 Del. Ch. LEXIS 160 (Del. Ch. Oct. 20, 2005).*

Direct/derivative classification not possible at summary judgment stage. — Where defendant controlling shareholder/director undertook a self-interested transaction in which defendant received benefits not shared with those to whom fiduciary duties were owed, whether plaintiff minority shareholders' claim was direct or derivative could not be resolved on summary judgment. *Gentile v. Rossette, 2005 Del. Ch. LEXIS 160 (Del. Ch. Oct. 20, 2005).*

Minority shareholders' claim that majority shareholder's self-dealt receipt of put options for shares received in the corporation's merger reduced the value of their shares and was a condition of the merger; the claim was potentially a direct claim since the put option benefit was alleged to be entirely related to the merger; summary judgment was not granted against minority shareholders in order that the court could consider the material facts in dispute, which included the valuation of the put options on the date of the merger, the effect upon the value of the corporation, and the minority shareholders' interests in that corporate value. *Gentile v. Rossette, 2005 Del. Ch. LEXIS 160 (Del. Ch. Oct. 20, 2005).*

Shareholder did not have standing to challenge option grants by a corporation prior to the date when it first acquired stock in the corporation. *La. Mun. Police Emples. Retirememt Sys. v. Countrywide Fin. Corp., 2007 Del. Ch. LEXIS 138 (Del. Ch. Oct. 2, 2007).*

Shareholders' derivative suit may have been barred because *8 Del. C. § 327* required ownership of stock contemporaneously with the wrongs challenged in a derivative suit; the wrong actually complained of occurred before the shareholders obtained their stock. *In re Coca-cola Enters., 2007 Del. Ch. LEXIS 147 (Del. Ch. Oct. 17, 2007).*

CASE NOTES — OTHER STATES

California

The purpose of Delaware's requirement for contemporaneous ownership is to prevent so-called strike suits, whereby stock in a corporation is purchased with purely litigious motives, that is, for the sole purpose of prosecuting a derivative action to attack transactions that occurred before the stock purchase. The Delaware courts have construed Del. Code Ann. tit. 8, § 327 and Del. Ch. Ct. R. 23.1 as further requiring that the derivative plaintiff retain stock ownership for the duration of the litigation. *Grosset v. Wenaas, 2008 Cal. LEXIS 1414 (February 14, 2008).*

The issue with respect to whether an action is a direct or derivative action must turn solely on the following questions: (1) who suffered the alleged harm (the corporation or the suing stockholders, individually); and (2) who would receive the benefit of any recovery or other relief obtained. *Schuster v. Gardner, 127 Cal. App. 4th 305, 25 Cal. Rptr. 3d 468 (2005).*

An action brought by a shareholder against corporate officers was a derivative suit, where the corporation suffered the alleged harm, and where it would receive the benefit of any recovery, rather than individual stockholders. The shareholder lacked standing to pursue the action under both *California and Delaware law. Schuster v. Gardner, 127 Cal. App. 4th 305, 25 Cal. Rptr. 3d 468 (2005).*

Quantifiable damage is not a necessary element of a cause of action for breach of fiduciary duty. *Sagi v. Capital, 2005 Cal. App. Unpub. LEXIS 1409 (2005).*

The duty of the court in deciding whether an action is a direct or derivative action is to look at the nature of the wrong alleged, not merely at the form of the words used in the complaint. A claim is not "direct" simply because it is pleaded that way. Instead, the court must look to all the facts of the complaint and determine for itself whether a direct claim exists. *Schuster v. Gardner, 127 Cal. App. 4th 305, 25 Cal. Rptr. 3d 468 (2005).*

Inference of demand futility not found. — A board's failure to appoint a special litigation committee to investigate the claims made in a derivative suit cannot raise an inference of demand futility because there is no necessity to appoint a special litigation committee if the board itself is disinterested. *Oakland Raiders v. National Football League. 93 Cal. App. 4th 572, 113 Cal. Rptr. 2d 255 (2001).*

Bondholder protections. — A bondholder, even of a convertible debenture, is simply a creditor of the corporation. He or she is not entitled to any special protections which he or she has failed to negotiate for him- or herself at the time of the purchase of the bond. It is not enough to argue that the marketplace has become more dangerous. Absent fraud, or other similar misconduct, the courts have no brief to interfere in an established business relationship. *Pittelman v. Pearce, 6 Cal. App. 4th 1436, 8 Cal. Rptr. 2d 359 (1992).*

Entire fairness test. — Analysis of a breach of fiduciary duty claim involves application of the "entire fairness test." "Entire fairness" requires consideration of fair dealing and fair price. The former embraces questions of when the transaction was timed, how it was initiated, structured, negotiated, disclosed to the directors, and how the approvals of the directors and the stockholders were obtained. The latter aspect of fairness relates to the economic and financial considerations of the proposed merger, including all relevant factors: assets, market value, earnings, future prospects, and any other elements that affect the intrinsic or inherent value of a company's stock. However, the test for fairness is not a bifurcated one as between fair dealing and price. All aspects of the issue must be examined as a whole since the question is one of entire fairness. *Interactive Multimedia Artists v. Superior Court, 62 Cal. App. 4th 1546, 73 Cal. Rptr. 2d 462 (1998).*

When a controlling-shareholder defendant is charged with self-dealing in a transaction, the defendant has the burden of establishing the entire fairness of the transaction. The concept of fairness has two basic aspects: fair dealing and fair price. The former embraces questions of when the transaction was timed, how it was initiated, structured, negotiated, disclosed to the directors, and how the approvals of the directors and the stockholders were obtained. The latter aspect of fairness relates to the economic and financial considerations of the proposed merger, including all relevant factors: assets, market value, earnings, future prospects, and any other elements that affect the intrinsic or inherent value of a company's stock. *Sagi v. Capital, 2005 Cal. App. Unpub. LEXIS 1409 (2005).*

Review of settlement. — A court reviews the settlement of a derivative suit as a means of protecting the interests of those who are not directly represented in the settlement negotiations. The court must therefore scrutinize the proposed settlement agreement to the extent necessary to reach a reasoned judgment that the agreement is not the product of fraud or overreaching by, or collusion between, the negotiating parties, and that the settlement, taken as a whole, is fair, reasonable and adequate to all concerned. *Robbins v. Alibrandi, 2005 Cal. App. Unpub. LEXIS 1019 (2005).*

The derivative action provides a means for shareholders to assert a claim of misuse of managerial power on behalf of the corporation. *Shaev. Claflin, 2004 Cal. App. Unpub. LEXIS 5840 (2004).*

Exhaustion of intracorporate remedies. — Before undertaking the prosecution of a derivative claim, a shareholder must first make a demand on the corporation's board of directors to consider pursuing the proposed action. This rule is designed to insure that the stockholder exhaust intracorporate remedies and also to provide an early screening mechanism to prevent abuse of the derivative action. *Shaev v. Claflin, 2004 Cal. App. Unpub. LEXIS 5840 (2004).*

Demand bypass. — Where the shareholder complains about acts of the board itself, the question arises whether the board would be able to pursue the claim with impartiality, since doing so would require that the board sue itself on behalf of the corporation. In such a case, a derivative plaintiff may bypass the demand on the board. However, under Delaware law the plaintiff must allege with particularity why such a demand was excused or would have been futile. *Shaev v. Claflin, 2004 Cal. App. Unpub. LEXIS 5840 (2004).*

In order to demonstrate demand futility, the plaintiff must allege facts sufficient to raise a reasonable doubt that: (1) the directors are disinterested and independent or that (2) the challenged transaction was otherwise the product of a valid exercise of business judgment. *Shaev v. Claflin, 2004 Cal. App. Unpub. LEXIS 5840 (2004).*

Although the demand-futility test is often analyzed separately, the question whether the business judgment rule applies to the challenged actions determines both the sufficiency of the complaint on the merits and the threshold demand-futility issue. *Shaev v. Claflin, 2004 Cal. App. Unpub. LEXIS 5840 (2004).*

A plaintiff seeking to avoid the protection of the business judgment rule must allege facts showing that the directors engaged in self-dealing or wasted corporate assets. *Shaev v. Claflin, 2004 Cal. App. Unpub. LEXIS 5840 (2004).*

Colorado

The standard for reviewing a special litigation committee's decision varies depending on whether the decision arises in the context of determining whether to sue (in cases where demand is made) or in the context of deciding whether to pursue litigation already ongoing (in cases where demand was futile). *Hirsch v. Jones Intercable, Inc., 984 P.2d 629 (Colo. 1999).*

Connecticut

Delaware law excuses the failure to make a demand when, inter alia, particularized allegations in the complaint raise a reasonable doubt as to whether the directors exercised proper business judgment. *Noble v. Baum, 1991 Conn. Super. LEXIS 1231*

Classic derivative claim. — The underlying duty to maximize corporate assets, upon whose breach the claim is based, is owed directly to corporation itself, and only indirectly to individual creditors as members of the broader community of interests that comprise the corporation. Therefore, such a claim is a classic derivative claim that can only be asserted either by or on behalf of the corporation, if it is not in bankruptcy, or by the bankruptcy trustee if bankruptcy proceedings have begun. *Bennett Restructuring Fund, L.P. v. Hamburg, 2003 Conn. Super. LEXIS 61 (2003).*

Rejection of bootstrap futility claims. — Simply naming the directors as defendants does not excuse demand. To construe it as sufficient would mean that plaintiffs could readily circumvent the demand requirement merely by naming as defendants all members of the derivative corporation's board. Merely naming disinterested directors as defendants does not allow the prosecutor of a derivative suit to avoid his duty to make a demand on them. Allegations that demand is futile because the directors would be suing themselves are also insufficient to excuse demand. The law of the State of Delaware is clear that an allegation of demand futility must go further than naming all the directors as defendants. Accordingly, there appears to be consensus among the courts to reject bootstrap allegations of futility, based on claims of directional participation coupled with a reluctance by directors to sue themselves. *Noble v. Baum, 1991 Conn. Super. LEXIS 1231 (1991).*

Decision to refrain from action. — The business judgment rule operates only in the context of director action. Technically speaking, it has no role where directors have either abdicated their functions, or absent a conscious decision, have failed to act. But it also follows that under applicable principles, a conscious decision to refrain from acting may nonetheless be a valid exercise of business judgment and enjoy the protection of the rule. *Noble v. Baum, 1991 Conn. Super. LEXIS 1231 (1991).*

A demand is futile only when a reasonable doubt is created that: (1) the directors are disinterested and independent and (2) the challenged transaction was otherwise the product of a valid exercise of business judgment. Thus, there is a two-tiered test whereby two inquiries are made, one into the independence and disinterestedness of the directors and the other into the substantive nature of the challenged transaction and the board's approval thereof. As to the latter inquiry, the court does not assume that the transaction is a wrong to the corporation requiring corrective steps by the board. Rather, the alleged wrong is substantively viewed against the factual background alleged in the complaint. As to the former inquiry, directorial independence and disinterestedness, the court reviews the factual allegations to decide, whether they raise a reasonable doubt, as a threshold matter, that the protections of the business judgment rule are available to the board. *Noble v. Baum, 1991 Conn. Super. LEXIS 1231 (1991).*

A demand could be futile when the directors' judgment is so unwise or unreasonable as to fall outside the permissible grounds of the directors' sound discretion. *Noble v. Baum, 1991 Conn. Super. LEXIS 1231 (1991).*

Good faith protections. — The business judgment rule provides that directors or officers will not be held liable for breach of fiduciary duty to a corporation or its stockholders for mistakes of fact or law that cause harm to the corporation or its stockholders, if the directors acted in good faith. Under the business judgment doctrine, acts of directors, within the powers of a corporation, in furtherance of its business, made in good faith and in the exercise of honest judgment, are valid and conclude the corporation and its stockholders; questions of management policy, contract expediency, and adequate consideration are left to the directors honest and unselfish decision, judgment and discretion and may not be interfered with or restrained. *Noble v. Baum, 1991 Conn. Super. LEXIS 1231 (1991).*

Board decisions carry a strong presumption of good faith and validity. This good-faith presumption can only be overcome by facts pleaded with particularity. *Noble v. Baum, 1991 Conn. Super. LEXIS 1231 (1991).*

Waiver of business judgment protections. — In rare cases a transaction may be so egregious on its face that board approval cannot meet the test of business judgment, and a substantial likelihood of director liability therefore exists. Absent particularized facts, however, the protections of the business judgment rule are waived only in the case of improperly motivated corporate decisions, not in the case of poor ones. *Noble v. Baum, 1991 Conn. Super. LEXIS 1231 (1991).*

The business judgment rule does not apply when the corporate decision lacks a business purpose, is tainted by a conflict of interest, is so egregious as to amount to a no-win decision, or results from an obvious or prolonged failure to exercise oversight or supervision. *Noble v. Baum, 1991 Conn. Super. LEXIS 1231 (1991).*

Reasonable doubt as to applicability of business judgment rule. — The conscious decision to sign off on forms required to be filed with a federal investigative body was intended as a vouching for the accuracy and integrity of the information there provided and, if it is established at trial that that information was materially false and misleading, a bevy of remedies — both criminal and civil — are available to address that wrong. The potential imposition of such sanctions on skilled professionals whose portfolios rest as much upon their personal integrity as it does on their financial acumen cannot be underestimated since, for these directors (and their families), this is a far more significant outcome than is the potential need to resign from other boards on which they presently serve or not being asked to serve on the next board. Therefore, there is reasonable doubt these directors (all — as opposed to a mere majority) are disinterested and independent and there is, thus, reasonable doubt that the protections of the business judgment rule are available to them. *Fina v. Calarco, 2005 Conn. Super. LEXIS 2984 (Sept. 16, 2005).*

District of Columbia

Bar on later assertion of futility. — Under the law of Delaware and the states that follow its lead, a shareholder who makes demand may not later assert that demand was in fact excused as futile. *Flocco v. State Farm Mut. Auto. Ins. Co., 752 A.2d 147 (D.C. App. 2000).*

Illinois

Standing of equitable owner. — According to Delaware law, in any derivative suit instituted by a stockholder of a corporation, it shall be averred in the complaint that the plaintiff was a stockholder of the corporation at the time of the transaction of which such stockholder complains or that such stockholder's stock thereafter devolved upon such stockholder by operation of law. Pursuant to Delaware law, for purposes of instituting a derivative action, an "equitable" owner is considered a stockholder with standing to sue. *Housman v. Albright, 368 Ill. App. 3d 214, 857 N.E.2d 724, 2006 Ill. App. LEXIS 698; 306 Ill. Dec. 325 (Aug. 9, 2006).*

Bar on later assertion of futility. — Under the law of Delaware and the states that follow its lead, a shareholder who makes demand may not later assert that demand was in fact excused as futile. It would be a waste of time and resources to allow a shareholder to make a demand and have the claim investigated by the company, only to allow the shareholder to declare the investigation meaningless when unhappy with the results. *Miller v. Thomas, 275 Ill. App. 3d 779, 656 N.E.2d 89 211 Ill. Dec. 897 (1995).*

Attorney fees. — Delaware follows the American Rule under which absent statutory authority or a contractual agreement to the contrary, the prevailing party in a suit is ordinarily responsible for the payment of his or her own legal fees. However, there is an exception to this rule as to actions that result in a benefit to a corporation or its stockholders. In the context of corporate litigation, a court, in its discretion, may order the payment of counsel fees and related expenses to a plaintiff whose efforts result in a creation of a common fund or a corporate benefit inuring to the benefit of the corporation or its shareholders. A party may obtain an award of attorney's fees under this exception only if: (1) the action was meritorious when filed; (2) a benefit is produced in factor of the corporation or the shareholders; and (3) there is a causal connection between the litigation and the claimed benefit. *Foley v. Santa Fe Pacific Corporation, 267 Ill. App. 3d 555, 641 N.E.2d 992, 204 Ill. Dec. 562 (1994).*

Successful derivative or class action suits which result in the recovery of money or property wrongfully diverted from the corporation, or which result in the imposition of changes in internal operating procedures that are designed to produce such monetary savings in the future, are typically viewed as fund-creating actions. However, the definition of a corporate benefit is much more elastic as the benefit need not be measurable in economic terms. Changes in corporate policy or a heightened level of corporate disclosure, if attributable to the filing of a meritorious suit, may justify an award of counsel fees. Once it is determined that an action benefiting the corporation chronologically followed the filing of a meritorious suit, the burden is upon the corporation to demonstrate that the lawsuit did not in any way cause their action. *Foley v. Santa Fe Pacific Corporation, 267 Ill. App. 3d 555, 641 N.E.2d 992, 204 Ill. Dec. 562 (1994).*

Demand futility test. — The test employed in determining whether a demand upon a corporate board of directors would be futile consists of an examination of whether, taking the well-pleaded facts as true, the allegations in the complaint raise a reasonable doubt that (i) the directors are disinterested and independent, and (ii) the directors exercised proper business judgment in approving the challenged transaction. The first prong of this test is applied as of the time the litigation was commenced. Thus, the court must review the factual allegations of the complaint to determine whether they create a reasonable doubt as to the disinterest and independence of the directors at the time the complaint was filed. *Seinfeld v. Bays, 230 Ill. App. 3d 412; 595 N.E.2d 69; 172 Ill. Dec. 6 (1992).*

Directorial interest exists whenever divided loyalties are present, or a director either has received, or is entitled to receive, a personal financial benefit from the challenged transaction which is not equally shared by the stockholders. Independence of directors is determined by examination of the influences upon the directors' performance of their duties generally, and more specifically, in respect to the challenged transaction. Demand typically is deemed to be futile when a majority of the directors have participated in or approved the alleged wrongdoing or are otherwise financially interested in the challenged transactions. *Seinfeld v. Bays, 230 Ill. App. 3d 412, 595 N.E.2d 69, 172 Ill. Dec. 6 (1992).*

Individual action standing. — Shareholders may bring direct actions, both as individuals and as a class, for injuries done to them in their individual capacities by corporate fiduciaries. Yet, in order to properly assert an individual claim, a plaintiff is required to assert more than an injury resulting from a wrong to the corporation. A plaintiff must allege either an injury which is separate and distinct from that suffered by other shareholders, or a wrong involving a contractual right of a shareholder which exists independently of any right of the corporation. For a plaintiff to have standing to bring an individual action, he or she must be injured directly or independently of the corporation. *Seinfeld v. Bays, 230 Ill. App. 3d 412, 595 N.E.2d 69, 172 Ill. Dec. 6 (1992).*

Determination of nature of action. — Whether a cause of action is individual or derivative must be determined from the nature of the wrong alleged and the relief, if any, which could result if plaintiff were to prevail. In determining the nature of the wrong alleged, a court must look to the body of the complaint rather than to the plaintiff's designation or stated intention. *Seinfeld v. Bays, 230 Ill. App. 3d 412, 595 N.E.2d 69, 172 Ill. Dec. 6 (1992).*

Claims of devaluation of stock and of corporate waste are claims which accrue to the corporation rather than to individual shareholders. Such suits must be brought derivatively on behalf of the corporation and its shareholders. *Seinfeld v. Bays, 230 Ill. App. 3d 412, 595 N.E.2d 69, 172 Ill. Dec. 6 (1992).*

Corporate opportunity. — Where a business opportunity is presented to an officer in his or her individual capacity, rather than in his or her official capacity as an officer or director, and the opportunity is one not essential to the corporation nor in which the corporation has any interest or expectancy, the opportunity is that of the officer and not of the corporation. The test of whether a particular opportunity is an individual or corporate one seems to be whether there is a specific duty, on the part of the officer sought to be held liable, to act or contract in regard to the particular matter as the representative of the corporation, all of which is largely a question of fact. Whether a corporate officer seizes a corporate opportunity for his or her own depends not on any single factor nor is it determined by any fixed standard. Numerous factors are to be weighed, including the manner in which the offer is communicated to the officer, the good faith of the officer, the use of corporate assets to acquire the opportunity, the financial ability of the corporation to acquire the opportunity, the degree of disclosure made to the corporation, the action taken by the corporation with reference thereto, and the need or interest of the corporation in the opportunity. The presence or absence of any single factor is not determinative of the issue of corporate opportunity. *Paulman v. Kritzer, 74 Ill. App. 2d 284, 219 N.E.2d 541 (1966).*

Participants in employee stock ownership plan equitable owners. — In the instant case, the employee stock ownership plan (ESOP) specifically stated that a participating employee's interest in the ESOP was invested in shares of company stock, which were held for the employee's benefit by the trustee. Both plaintiffs owned several shares of stock that were fully vested and credited to their ESOP accounts. Although the "Committee" had the right to vote and exercise other rights of a company stockholder, in the event of a corporate matter involving a merger or consolidation, recapitalization, reclassification, liquidation, dissolution, or sale or transfer of substantially all the assets of the company, the participating employee was entitled to direct the trustee how to vote the company stock allocated to his or her account. Moreover, all of the stock is owned through the ESOP plan. If the ESOP participants are not permitted to participate in a shareholders' derivative suit, no one can sue other than the trustee, who refused to sue. The Delaware legislature could not have intended such an absurd result. ESOP stockholders must be left with some type of recourse if the trustee is unable or unwilling to sue the officers of the corporation for a breach of their fiduciary duties. Hence, the ESOP participants in the present case are equitable stockholders and have standing to maintain a shareholders' derivative suit pursuant to Delaware law. *Housman v. Albright, 368 Ill. App. 3d 214, 857 N.E.2d 724, 2006 Ill. App. LEXIS 698, 306 Ill. Dec. 325 (Aug. 9, 2006).*

Iowa

Corporate concession rule. — Under Delaware corporations law, a shareholder who elects to make a demand upon the board of directors concedes or waives the right to challenge the independence of a majority of the board to respond to the demand. This rule is sometimes referred to as the "corporate concession." *Whalen v. Connelly, 593 N.W.2d 147 Iowa 1999).*

Maryland

Demand futility test. — With respect to shareholder's derivative actions, the balance struck by the Delaware Supreme Court, in determining whether a pre-suit demand would have been futile, is for the trial court to decide, under the particularized facts alleged, whether a reasonable doubt is created that: (1) the directors are disinterested and independent and (2) the challenged transaction is otherwise the product of a valid exercise of business judgment. Only if the particularized facts support a reasonable doubt that the challenged transaction is the product of a valid exercise of business judgment is a demand excused. As applied by the Delaware courts, that formulation is an exacting requirement. *Werbowsky v. Collomb, 362 Md. 581, 766 A.2d 123 (2001).*

In determining whether a pre-suit demand in a shareholder's derivative action would have been shown futile, the Delaware Supreme Court made clear that the shorthand shibboleth of dominated and controlled directors is insufficient, and that it is not enough to charge that a director was nominated by or elected at the behest of those controlling the outcome of a corporate decision, for that is the usual way a person becomes a corporate director. Nor is mere directorial approval of a transaction, absent particularized facts supporting a breach of fiduciary duty claim, or otherwise establishing the lack of independence or disinterestedness of a majority of the directors sufficient to excuse demand. *Werbowsky v. Collomb, 362 Md. 581, 766 A.2d 123 (2001).*

Interest or dependence may not be found merely from the fact that directors are paid for their services or on speculative, non-specific allegations that they act in order to secure their retention as directors. With respect to allegations of corporate waste, the test, both as to ultimate liability and with respect to demand futility, is whether what the corporation has received is so inadequate in value that no person of ordinary, sound business judgment would deem it worth that which the corporation has paid. *Werbowsky v. Collomb, 362 Md. 581, 766 A.2d 123 (2001).*

Under Delaware law, there are two requirements that a plaintiff must meet to proceed with a derivative claim. First, the plaintiff must satisfy the continuous ownership rule. Under that rule, the plaintiff must have been a shareholder at the time of the corporate action that is the subject of his complaint. Second, the plaintiff must meet the demand futility rule. That rule requires the plaintiff to have made demand on the corporation's board of directors to take action, which the board then refused; or to be excused from making demand because it would have been futile. This rule is described as a matter of substantive law embodied in the procedural requirements of Rule 23.1. *Paskowitz v. Wohlstadter, 151 Md. App. 1, 822 A.2d 1272 (2003).*

Derivative versus direct claims. — A derivative action is a claim asserted by a shareholder plaintiff on behalf of the corporation to redress a wrong against the corporation. The defendant in a derivative action may be a corporate fiduciary, such as a director, who committed a wrong against the corporation. The action is derivative because it is brought for the benefit of the corporation, not for the shareholder plaintiff. For that reason, ordinarily, damages recovered in a derivative suit are paid to the corporation. By contrast, a direct action is a claim asserted by a shareholder, individually, against a corporate fiduciary, such as a director, to redress an injury personal to the shareholder. Because damages recovered in a direct action are to remedy the shareholder plaintiff individually, they are payable to him, not to the corporation. Direct claims often are filed as class actions. *Paskowitz v. Wohlstadter, 151 Md. App. 1, 822 A.2d 1272 (2003).*

Disclosure obligations. — Under Delaware corporate law, the members of the board of directors of a Delaware corporation are corporate fiduciaries who owe a triad of duties to the corporation's shareholders: the duties of care, loyalty, and good faith. These fiduciary duties give rise to certain disclosure obligations. Often, the obligation to disclose will arise in the context of a communication being made by the directors to the shareholders about stockholder action that is being considered or solicited. *Paskowitz v. Wohlstadter, 151 Md. App. 1, 822 A.2d 1272 (2003).*

The Delaware law of the fiduciary duties of directors, as developed in judicial decisions, establishes a general duty of directors to disclose to stockholders all material information reasonably available when seeking stockholder action. Whether or not a failure to fulfill that duty will result in personal liability for damages against directors depends upon the nature of the stockholder action that was the object of the solicitation of stockholder votes and the misstated or omitted disclosures in connection with that solicitation. The mere fact that a director breaches his or her duty to disclose material information when seeking stockholder action, i.e., votes, does not necessarily result in personal liability on the director's part. Whether the stockholder has suffered an injury depends on the nature of the stockholder action that was the object of the solicitation of votes. *Paskowitz v. Wohlstadter, 151 Md. App. 1, 822 A.2d 1272 (2003).*

Self-flagellation not required. — Under Delaware law, corporate fiduciaries are not required to engage in self-flagellation, as their duty of disclosure does not oblige them to characterize their conduct in such a way as to admit wrongdoing. *Paskowitz v. Wohlstadter, 151 Md. App. 1, 822 A.2d 1272 (2003).*

Massachusetts

Standing. — A plaintiff must be a shareholder at the time of the filing of the derivative suit and must remain a shareholder throughout the litigation. *Kessler v. Sinclair, 37 Mass. App. Ct. 573, 641 N.E.2d 135 (1994).*

A double derivative action is a derivative action maintained by the shareholders of a parent corporation or holding company on behalf of a subsidiary company. The wrongs addressed include wrongs directly incurred by the parent corporation as well as those indirectly incurred, because of wrongs suffered by the subsidiary company. *Kessler v. Sinclair, 37 Mass. App. Ct. 573, 641 N.E.2d 135 (1994).*

Excusing demand. — Two alternative tests for excusing demand are: (1) whether threshold presumptions of director disinterest or independence are rebutted by well-pleaded facts; and, if not, (2) whether the complaint pleads particularized facts sufficient to create a reasonable doubt that the challenged transaction was the product of a valid exercise of business judgment. *Kessler v. Sinclair, 37 Mass. App. Ct. 573, 641 N.E.2d 135 (1994).*

If a derivative plaintiff fails to carry the burden of demonstrating that demand should be excused, the complaint must be dismissed. *In re Sonus Networks, Inc., 18 Mass. L. Rep. 295 (Super.2004).*

A derivative plaintiff is required to plead with particularity that "reasonable doubt" exists either that: (1) a majority of the board of directors is disinterested and independent; or (2) that the challenged transaction was a valid exercise of business judgment. Thus, in determining demand futility, the court must make two inquiries, one into the independence and disinterestedness of the directors and the other into the substantive nature of the challenged transaction and the board's approval thereof. *In re Sonus Networks, Inc., 18 Mass. L. Rep. 295 (Super. 2004).*

To satisfy the requirement of alleging with particularity the reasons for a derivative plaintiff's failure to demand action from a board of directors, the stockholder plaintiff must overcome the powerful presumptions of the business judgment rule by alleging sufficient particularized facts to support an inference that demand is excused because the board is incapable of exercising its power and authority to pursue the derivative claims directly. *In re Sonus Networks, Inc., 18 Mass. L. Rep. 295 (Super. 2004).*

The question of directors' independence flows from an analysis of the factual allegations pertaining to the influences upon the directors' performance of their duties generally, and more specifically in respect to the challenged transaction. *In re Sonus Networks, Inc., 18 Mass. L. Rep. 295 (Super. 2004),*

Presumption of director propriety. — In determining the disinterestedness and independence of members of a board of directors, a presumption of propriety must be the starting point in the absence of clear allegations to the contrary. *In re Sonus Networks, Inc., 18 Mass. L. Rep. 295 (Super. 2004).*

Directors are not interested or lacking in independence merely because they share outside professional associations or relationships. *In re Sonus Networks, Inc., 18 Mass. L. Rep. 295 (Super. 2004).*

In general. — A cardinal precept of the General Corporation Law of the State of Delaware is that directors, rather than shareholders, manage the business and affairs of the corporation. The existence and exercise of this power carries with it certain fundamental fiduciary obligations to the corporation and its shareholders. Moreover, a stockholder is not powerless to challenge director action which results in harm to the corporation. The machinery of corporate democracy and the derivative suit are potent tools to redress the conduct of a torpid or unfaithful management. The derivative action developed in equity to enable shareholders to sue in the corporation's name where those in control of the company refused to assert a claim belonging to it. The nature of the action is two-fold. First, it is the equivalent of a suit by the shareholders to compel the corporation to sue. Second, it is a suit by the corporation, asserted by the shareholders on its behalf, against those liable to it. *South Shore Gastroninterology UA v. Richard F. Selden, 17 Mass. L. Rep. 673 (Super. 2004).*

Demand threshold. — By its very nature the derivative action impinges on the managerial freedom of directors. Hence, the demand requirement of Del. Ch. Ct. R. 23.1 exists at the threshold, first to insure that a stockholder exhausts his or her intracorporate remedies, and then to provide a safeguard against strike suits. Thus, by promoting this form of alternate dispute resolution, rather than immediate recourse to litigation, the demand requirement is a recognition of the fundamental precept that directors manage the business and affairs of corporations. In determining demand futility the court must make two inquiries, one into the independence and disinterestedness of the directors and the other into the substantive nature of the challenged transaction and the board's approval thereof. *South Shore Gastroninterology UA v. Richard F. Selden, 17 Mass. L. Rep. 673 (Super. 2004).*

Director independence. — To satisfy the requirement of alleging with particularity the reasons for a shareholder's failure to demand action from a board of directors, the stockholder plaintiff must overcome the powerful presumptions of the business judgment rule by alleging sufficient particularized facts to support an inference that demand is excused because the board is incapable of exercising its power and authority to pursue the derivative claims directly. A demand on the board is excused only if the complaint contains particularized factual allegations raising a reasonable doubt that either: (1) the directors are disinterested and independent, or (2) the challenged transaction was otherwise the product of a

Corporations

valid exercise of business judgment. However, the mere threat of personal liability for approving a questioned transaction, standing alone, is insufficient to challenge either the independence or disinterestedness of directors, although in rare cases a transaction may be so egregious on its face that board approval cannot meet the test of business judgment, and a substantial likelihood of director liability therefore exists. The question of independence flows from an analysis of the factual allegations pertaining to the influences upon the directors' performance of their duties generally, and more specifically in respect to the challenged transaction. *South Shore Gastroninterology UA v. Richard F. Selden, 17 Mass. L. Rep. 673 (Super. 2004).*

Allegation of particularized facts. — In the demand-futile context a derivative-action plaintiff charging domination and control of one or more directors must allege particularized facts manifesting a direction of corporate conduct in such a way as to comport with the wishes or interests of the corporation (or persons) doing the controlling. The court looks next at the question of whether a reasonable doubt is created that the challenged transactions were otherwise than the product of valid exercises of business judgment. *South Shore Gastroninterology UA v. Richard F. Selden, 17 Mass. L. Rep. 673 (Super. 2004).*

There is a very large — though not insurmountable — burden on stockholders who believe they should pursue the remedy of a derivative suit instead of selling their stock or seeking to reform or oust these directors from office. Delaware has pleading rules and an extensive judicial gloss on those rules that must be met in order for a stockholder to pursue a derivative remedy. Sound policy supports these rules. *South Shore Gastroninterology UA v. Richard F. Selden, 17 Mass. L. Rep. 673 (Super. 2004).*

Demand futility test. — Under Delaware law, where, as here, there is no specific challenge to a particular decision by a board of directors to act or refrain from acting, the applicable test for determining demand futility is whether or not the particularized factual allegations of a derivative stockholder complaint create a reasonable doubt that, as of the time the complaint is filed, the board of directors could have properly exercised its independent and disinterested business judgment in responding to a demand. If the derivative plaintiff satisfies this burden, then demand will be excused as futile. *In re PolyMedica Corp. Shareholder Derivative Litigation, 15 Mass. L. Rep. 115, 2002 Mass. Super. LEXIS 271 (2002).*

The purpose of the distinction between interested and disinterested directors is to ensure that the directors voting on a plaintiff's demand can exercise their business judgment in the best interests of the corporation, free from significant contrary personal interests and apart from the domination and control of those who are alleged to have participated in wrongdoing. *In re PolyMedica Corp. Shareholder Derivative Litigation, 15 Mass. L. Rep. 115, 2002 Mass. Super. LEXIS 271 (2002).*

Entire fairness test. — Delaware law protects minority shareholders by reviewing those transactions where a controlling shareholder benefits from a transaction in a way that goes beyond the benefits accorded to other stockholders. This analysis, referred to as the "entire fairness test," requires the controlling shareholder(s) to prove the "entire fairness" of such a transaction. The "entire fairness" doctrine is designed to deal with those situations where a controlling shareholder has his or her own interest in the outcome of a transaction that might cloud his or her otherwise objective business judgment. *Olsen v. Seifert, 9 Mass. L. Rep. 268 (Super. 1998).*

Standing. — Under Delaware law a plaintiff must retain his or her status as a shareholder throughout the litigation in order to continue to prosecute a derivative action. A plaintiff who ceases to be a shareholder, whether by reason of a merger, or for any other reason, loses standing to continue a derivative suit. *Kessler v. Sinclair, 4 Mass. L. Rep. 38 (Super 1995).*

Length of the board's investigation, five months, is not sufficient evidence to find that the investigation was unreasonable without some particularized facts demonstrating that the investigation was actually delayed or obstructed by the board. *Lichtenfeld v. Bucknum, 2006 Mass. Super. LEXIS 48 (Jan. 31, 2006).*

All of the evidence suggests that the board acted appropriately in response to plaintiff's demand. Such actions included: (1) setting up the committee; (2) the committee's retention of separate counsel; (3) interviewing approximately thirty individuals; (4) examining telephone and email records; (5) conferrrng with the SEC; and (5) excluding the individual defendants from the investigative process and vote. No admissible evidence contradicts the legal presumption that the Board acted reasonably and in good faith. Plaintiff, therefore, lacks the requisite standing to bring his derivative claims. *Lichtenfeld v. Bucknum, 2006 Mass. Super. LEXIS 48 (Jan. 31, 2006).*

Minnesota

Derivative versus direct claims. — Derivative claims are those brought by shareholders to enforce the right of a corporation when the corporate entity itself has failed to enforce a right that may properly be asserted against it. In a derivative claim, the injury is direct to the corporation but indirect to the stockholders bringing the suit. By contrast, "individual" or "direct" claims are those premised upon: (1) an injury that a plaintiff suffers that is separate and distinct from that suffered by other shareholders; or (2) a wrong involving a contractual right of a shareholder which exists independently from any right of the corporation. For a plaintiff to have standing to bring an individual action, he must be injured directly or independently of the corporation. The line of distinction between derivative and direct/individual claims is often a narrow one. The determination of whether a claim is direct or derivative is a substantive issue. *Erickson v. Horing, 2002 Minn. App. LEXIS 1137 (2002).*

Whether a cause of action is individual or derivative must be determined from the nature of the wrong alleged and the relief, if any, which could result if plaintiff were to prevail. In determining the nature of the wrong alleged, a court must look to the body of the complaint, not to the designation assigned to a claim by the plaintiff. *Erickson v. Horing, 2002 Minn. App. LEXIS 1137 (2002).*

Demand futility test. — In normal double-derivative pleadings where the decision being challenged was made by the board of a different corporation, the test for demand futility is whether the complaint raises a reasonable doubt regarding the ability of a majority of the board of directors to exercise properly its business judgment in a decision on a demand at the time of the complaint. *Professional Management. Associates. v. Coss, 2001 Minn. App. LEXIS 800 (2001).*

In general. — The demand requirement protects the corporate structure by recognizing that the directors of a corporation, and not the shareholders, have the power to manage the business and affairs of the corporation. Thus, a shareholder may not bring a cause of action to enforce the rights of the corporation unless the shareholder demands that the directors pursue the claim and the directors wrongfully refuse to do so or the shareholder shows that demand is excused because the directors cannot make an impartial decision. *Professional Management. Associates. v. Coss, 2001 Minn. App. LEXIS 800 (2001).*

In a double-derivative suit, the plaintiff shareholder must make a demand on both the parent corporation and the subsidiary or demonstrate that demand is excused for both. *Professional Management. Associates. v. Coss, 2001 Minn. App. LEXIS 800 (2001).*

Standard of review. — If the plaintiff shareholder makes a demand and the board of directors refuses to pursue the action, the court does not end its inquiry but reviews the board's decision under the traditional business-judgment rule by examining the good faith and reasonableness of the board's investigation and decision. Absent an abuse of discretion by the board, the court will respect the board's decision not to pursue the action and will grant the board's motion to dismiss it. *Professional Management. Associates. v. Coss, 2001 Minn. App. LEXIS 800 (2001).*

In Delaware, the innocent-shareholder equitable principle might allow a case to go forward under the proper circumstances. *Professional Management. Associates. v. Coss, 2001 Minn. App. LEXIS 800 (2001).*

Failure to take action. — A board of directors' failure to take action, even if it is aware of wrongdoing, does not demonstrate futility. *Professional Management. Associates. v. Coss, 2001 Minn. App. LEXIS 800 (2001).*

In general. — Under Delaware law, before filing a derivative action, shareholders must either make a pre-suit demand on the board of directors or demonstrate that such demand is excused because it would be futile. *Professional Management Associates v. Coss, 598 N.W.2d 406 (Minn. App. 1999).*

Standing. — Under Delaware law, a plaintiff who ceases to be a shareholder, whether by reason of a merger or for any other reason, loses standing to continue a derivative suit. The only exceptions to this rule are where: (a) the merger itself is the subject of a claim of fraud; and (b) the merger is in reality a reorganization which does not affect the plaintiff's ownership of the business enterprise. *Professional Management Associates v. Coss, 598 N.W.2d 406 (Minn. App. 1999).*

In general, under Delaware law, to bring a double derivative suit, a plaintiff shareholder must make a demand twice, once of the subsidiary company and once of the holding company. *Professional Management Associates v. Coss, 598 N.W.2d 406 (Minn. App. 1999).*

Excuse of demand. — Demand Under Delaware law, a pre-suit demand is excused if the particularized factual allegations in the complaint (including, where appropriate, the contents of documents referenced therein) create a reasonable doubt that (1) the directors were disinterested and independent; or that (2) the challenged transaction was otherwise the result of a valid exercise of business judgment. *Professional Management Associates v. Coss, 574 N.W.2d 107 (Minn. App. 1999).*

Lack of independence. — Where the facts alleged, if proven, would demonstrate that a majority of the directors who would have received the demand letter are "interested" in the challenged transaction or "lack independence" because of domination by an interested party, pre-suit demand will be excused. To establish lack of independence, allegations of control must be coupled with such facts as would demonstrate that through personal or other relationships, the directors are beholden to the controlling person. *Professional Management Associates v. Coss, 574 N.W.2d 107 (Minn. App. 1999).*

The directors' ability to affect the continued employment and remuneration of other directors as corporate officers raises a reasonable doubt that those directors could act independently. *Professional Management Associates v. Coss, 574 N.W.2d 107 (Minn. App. 1999).*

Burden of proof. — The business judgment rule posits a powerful presumption that a court will not interfere with decisions made by a loyal and informed board. It is the claimant's burden to rebut the presumption with evidence that directors, in reaching their challenged decision, breached any one of the triads of their fiduciary duty— good faith, loyalty, or due care. If the plaintiffs meet their burden, then the business judgment rule will not apply, and the directors will have to show the "entire fairness" of the challenged transaction to the shareholder-creditor plaintiffs. If the rule does apply, if the decision is found to have been made by a loyal and informed board, then the decision will not be overturned by the courts unless it cannot be attributed to any rational business purpose. *Potter v. Pohlad, 560 N.W.2d 389 (Minn. App. 1997).*

As part of their fiduciary duties, corporate officers have a duty to inform themselves, prior to making a business decision, of all material information reasonably available to them. Having become so informed, they must then act with requisite care in the discharge of their duties. The duty of care is judged under a gross negligence standard. The court's role in evaluating the duty is to provide an objective review of the process by which the officers reached the decision under review. *Potter v. Pohlad, 560 N.W.2d 389 (Minn. App. 1997).*

Gross negligence for breach of a fiduciary duty is defined as reckless indifference to or a deliberate disregard of the whole body of stockholders or actions that are without the bounds of reason. *Potter v. Pohlad, 560 N.W.2d 389 (Minn. App. 1997).*

An informed decision to delegate a task is as much an exercise of business judgment as any other. The amount of information that it is prudent to have before a decision is made is itself a business judgment. *Potter v. Pohlad, 560 N.W.2d 389 (Minn. App. 1997).*

Bad faith. — A showing that the directors of a corporation acted in bad faith will rebut the presumption of the business judgment rule. Courts analyzing claims of bad faith generally inquire into the motives of the board members. *Potter v. Pohlad, 560 N.W.2d 389 (Minn. App. 1997).*

Duty of candor. — To the extent that a duty of candor exists separate from the duties of care and good faith, it entails the obligation to disclose all material information to shareholders when seeking shareholder approval. *Potter v. Pohlad, 560 N.W.2d 389 (Minn. App. 1997).*

New Jersey

Appointment of special litigation committee. — Delaware law also permits a corporation's board to seek dismissal of a derivative suit in a demand-excused context. In such demand-excused cases, the board may appoint a special litigation committee to investigate whether the suit is in the best interest of the corporation. *In re PSE&G Shareholder Litigation, 173 N.J. 258, 801 A.2d 295 (2002).*

A board's decision to reject the demand will not be overturned unless it is wrongful. A board's refusal is only wrongful if it is not a valid exercise of its business judgment. There is a presumption under the business judgment rule that disinterested directors act on an informed basis, in good faith, and in the honest belief that their actions are in the corporation's best interest. If the refusal to proceed with the litigation is protected by the business judgment rule, the shareholder may not continue the derivative proceeding. *In re PSE & G Shareholder Litigation, 315 N.J. Super. 323, 801 A.2d 295 (2002).*

In order to be protected by the business judgment rule, the directors making a business decision must have become fully informed and acted in good faith and in the honest belief that their actions are in the corporation's best interest. The court must determine whether the directors made a fully informed judgment when they rejected the shareholder's demand and that the rejection was in the best interests of the corporation. *In re PSE & G Shareholder Litigation, 315 N.J. Super. 323, 801 A.2d 295 (2002).*

Appointment of special litigation committee. — When a majority of directors decide that they should not consider the demand either because too many of them are named as defendants or they may be interested parties, they may appoint a special litigation committee to investigate the demand. *In re PSE & G Shareholder Litigation, 315 N.J. Super. 323, 801 A.2d 295 (2002).*

Burden of proof. — A corporation bears the burden of establishing the decisionmakers' independence, lack of bias, good faith, and thoroughness of its investigation is fair and just. Even if the corporation shows that the committee's process was fair, the court still must determine whether the committee reached a reasonable and principle decision. The adoption of a modified business judgment rule, the key feature being that the corporation, not the shareholder, would have to meet an initial burden of proof is more consistent with the realities of shareholder-corporate existence. *In re PSE & G Shareholder Litigation, 315 N.J. Super. 323, 801 A.2d 295 (2002).*

Directoral independence. — Directoral interest exists when divided loyalties are present, or where the director stands to receive a personal financial gain from the transaction not equally shared by the shareholders. Directoral independence means that a director's decision is based on the corporate merits of the subject before the board rather than extraneous considerations or influences. *In re Prudential Insurance Company Derivative Litigation, 282 N.J. Super. 256, 659 A.2d 961 (1995).*

The business judgment rule operates only in the context of director action. Technically speaking, it has no role where directors have either abdicated their functions or, absent a conscious decision, failed to act. *In re Prudential Insurance Company Derivative Litigation, 282 N.J. Super. 256, 659 A.2d 961 (1995).*

Demand not excused. — Where directors are sued derivatively because they have failed to do something, such as a failure to oversee subordinates, demand should not be excused automatically in the absence of allegations demonstrating why the board is incapable of considering a demand. Indeed, requiring demand in such circumstances is consistent with the board's managerial prerogatives because it permits the board to have the opportunity to take action where it has not previously considered doing so. *In re Prudential Insurance Company Derivative Litigation, 282 N.J. Super. 256, 659 A.2d 961 (1995).*

Beneficial owners of stock held in a street name could assert statutory rights. *Berger v. Berger, 249 N.J. Super. 305, 592 A.2d 321 (1991).*

New York

In general. — Delaware law requires, generally, that as a condition precedent to a plaintiff bringing a shareholder derivative lawsuit, said plaintiff must make a presuit demand upon the board of directors to prosecute the contemplated action. A plaintiff need not meet this requirement if he or she sets forth in the complaint particularized factual allegations sufficient to create a reasonable doubt either as to whether the directors are disinterested and independent or whether the transaction at issue resulted from a valid exercise of business judgment. Where a derivative claim complains of the board's nonfeasance, as opposed to a business decision, a court need only determine whether or not the particularized factual allegations create a reasonable doubt that the board of directors could have properly exercised its independent and disinterested business judgment in responding to a demand. *Simon v. Becherer, 7 A.D.3d 66, 775 N.Y.S.2d 313 (2004).*

A stockholder may not pursue a derivative suit to assert a claim of the corporation unless: (1) the stockholder has first demanded that all directors pursue the corporate claim, and they have wrongfully refused to do so; or (2) such demand is excused, because the directors are deemed incapable of making an impartial decision regarding the pursuit of the litigation. *Adams v. Banc of America Securities LLC, 2005 NY Slip Op 50714U, 7 Misc. 3d 1023A (2005).*

Fiduciary duties. — Under Delaware law, corporate officers, directors, and controlling shareholders owe their corporation and its minority shareholders a fiduciary obligation of honesty, loyalty, good faith, and fairness. Delaware law imposes a duty upon corporations to disclose all available material information when obtaining shareholder approval. Only damages caused by the breach of fiduciary duty are compensable. *Lama Holding Company v. Smith Barney Inc., 88 N.Y.2d 413, 668 N.E.2d 1370, 646 N.Y.S.2d 76 (1996).*

Misappropriation of corporate opportunity. — Governing Delaware law does not necessarily require proof that a director has personally obtained a tangible benefit for purposes of a derivative claim for misappropriation of corporate opportunity, but only that he or she acquiesced in approving a wrongful transaction or failed to protect the interests of the corporation and the minority shareholders. *Brinckerhoff v. JAC Holding Corp., 10 A.D.3d 520, 782 N.Y.S.2d 58 (2004).*

Directorial interest. — A director is considered interested where he or she will receive a personal financial benefit from a transaction that is not equally shared by the stockholders. Directorial interest also exists where a corporate decision will have a materially detrimental impact on a director, but not on the corporation and the stockholders. In such circumstances, a director cannot be expected to exercise his or her independent business judgment without being influenced by the adverse personal consequences resulting from the decision. Directors who are sued for failure to oversee subordinates have a disabling interest when the potential for liability is not a mere threat but instead may rise to a substantial likelihood. *Simon v. Becherer, 7 A.D.3d 66, 775 N.Y.S.2d 313 (2004).*

Where the wrong alleged is the inaction of the board of directors rather than a conscious decision approving some action taken by the corporation, the business judgment rule is inapplicable. The standard by which futility is assessed involves deciding what board members would have done had they been presented with a demand to investigate the alleged wrongdoing at the time the complaint was filed. In response to the demand, it is expected that the directors will determine the best method of informing themselves about the alleged misconduct and weigh available alternatives, including "internal corrective action and commencing legal proceedings." A director is considered disqualified from being able to make an independent decision in response to the demand if "interested" in its subject matter. Director interest is defined as the receipt of a "personal financial benefit from a transaction that is not equally shared by the stockholders." Alternatively, "interest also exists where a corporate decision will have a materially detrimental impact on a director, but not on the corporation and the stockholders."

Miller v. Schreyer, 257 A.D.2d 358, 683 N.Y.S.2d 51 (1999).

Excuse of demand. — Under Delaware law, a demand on the directors of a corporation will be excused only when a plaintiff alleges with particularity facts which create a reasonable doubt that the directors' action is protected by the business judgment rule. In determining the futility of such a demand, the trial court must decide whether a reasonable doubt is created that the directors are disinterested and independent or that the challenged transaction is otherwise the product of a valid exercise of business judgment. *O'Donnell v. Patrick Ferro, 303 A.D.2d 567, 756 N.Y.S.2d 485 (2003).*

Share of control premium. — Under Delaware law, majority shareholders have no nonderivative fiduciary duty to share proportionately with minority shareholders the "control premium" received from the sale of a majority share in the corporation. *Herzog, Heine, Geduld, Inc. v. NCC Industries, Inc., 251 A.D.2d 173, 673 N.Y.S.2d 910 (1998).*

Demand requirement. — Under Delaware law, as elsewhere, the requirement of a demand upon directors of a corporation to pursue a derivative complaint is a recognition of the inherent powers of the board to manage the affairs of the corporation, which includes making decisions about whether or not to pursue such litigation. *Wilson v. Tully, 243 A.D.2d 229, 676 N.Y.S.2d 531 (1998).*

Stockholders must overcome powerful presumptions. — The Delaware Supreme Court has observed that stockholders often do not make a demand upon directors of a corporation to pursue a derivative complaint, but instead bring suit, claiming that demand is excused. However, because such derivative suits challenge the propriety of decisions made by directors pursuant to their managerial authority, the Delaware Supreme Court has repeatedly held that stockholder plaintiffs must overcome the powerful presumptions of the business judgment rule before they will be permitted to pursue the derivative claim. *Wilson v. Tully, 243 A.D.2d 229, 676 N.Y.S.2d 531 (1998).*

Although no demand upon directors of a corporation to pursue a derivative complaint will be required where it would be futile, the Delaware Supreme Court has held that the entire question of demand futility is inextricably bound to issues of business judgment and the standards of that doctrine's applicability. The business judgment rule is an acknowledgement of the managerial prerogatives of Delaware directors and is a presumption that in making a business decision the directors of a corporation acted on an informed basis, in good faith, and in the honest belief that the action taken was in the best interests of the company. Proper business judgment includes both substantive due care (the terms of the transaction) and procedural due care (an informed decision). *Wilson v. Tully, 243 A.D.2d 229, 676 N.Y.S.2d 531 (1998).*

Approval of a transaction by a majority of independent, disinterested directors almost always bolsters a presumption that the business judgment rule attaches to transactions approved by a board of directors that are later attacked on grounds of lack of due care. In such cases, a heavy burden falls on a plaintiff to avoid presuit demand upon directors of a corporation to pursue a derivative complaint. *Wilson v. Tully, 243 A.D.2d 229, 676 N.Y.S.2d 531 (1998).*

The business judgment rule is a presumption that in making a business decision, not involving self-interest, the directors of a corporation acted on an informed basis, in good faith and in the honest belief that the action taken was in the best interests of the company. If a board's decision can be attributed to any rational business purpose, a court will not substitute its judgment for that of a board. When the challenged transaction is approved by a board, the majority of whom are outside, nonmanagement directors, a heavy burden falls on plaintiffs to avoid presuit demand. *Frankel v. American Film Technologies, Inc., 177 Misc. 2d 279, 675 N.Y.S.2d 837 (1998).*

Directorial independence. — Where there is no claim that a majority of defendant directors are not disinterested and independent, the mere threat of personal liability for approving a questioned transaction, standing alone, is insufficient to challenge either the independence or disinterestedness of directors, although in rare cases a transaction may be so egregious on its face that board approval cannot meet the test of business judgment, and a substantial likelihood of director liability therefore exists. *Wilson v. Tully, 243 A.D.2d 229, 676 N.Y.S.2d 531 (1998).*

Exemption from liability. — Where the certificate of incorporation exempts directors from liability, the risk of liability does not disable them from considering a demand to pursue a derivative complaint fairly unless particularized pleading permits the court to conclude that there is a substantial likelihood that their conduct, such as bad faith, intentional misconduct, knowing violation of law, or any other conduct for which the directors may be liable, falls outside the exemption. *Wilson v. Tully, 243 A.D.2d 229, 676 N.Y.S.2d 531 (1998).*

Demand futility review. — The entire review is factual in nature and, in determining demand futility, a court in the proper exercise of its discretion must decide whether, under the particularized facts alleged, a reasonable doubt is created that: (1) the directors are disinterested and independent and (2) the challenged transaction was otherwise the product of a valid exercise of business judgment. Similarly, a court should not apply the test for demand futility where the board that would be considering the demand did not make the business decision that is being challenged. *Wilson v. Tully, 243 A.D.2d 229, 676 N.Y.S.2d 531 (1998).*

Where inaction, rather than action, by a board is charged and directors are sued derivatively because they have failed to do something (such as a failure to oversee subordinates), demand should not be excused automatically in the absence of allegations demonstrating why the board is incapable of considering a demand. Indeed, requiring demand in such circumstances is consistent with the board's managerial prerogatives because it permits the board to have the opportunity to take action where it has not previously considered doing so. In such a case, it is appropriate to examine whether the board that would be

addressing the demand can impartially consider its merits without being influenced by improper considerations. A court must determine whether or not the particularized factual allegations of a derivative stockholder complaint create a reasonable doubt that, as of the time the complaint is filed, the board of directors could have properly exercised its independent and disinterested business judgment in responding to a demand. *Wilson v. Tully, 243 A.D.2d 229, 676 N.Y.S.2d 531 (1998).*

Insufficient evidence to excuse demand. — It is well-settled that mere allegations of participation in the approval of a challenged transaction are insufficient to excuse a pre-suit demand upon directors of a corporation to pursue a derivative complaint and conclusory allegations of recklessness or gross negligence are insufficient to overcome the strong presumption of propriety afforded by the business judgment rule. *Wilson v. Tully, 243 A.D.2d 229, 676 N.Y.S.2d 531 (1998).*

A demand upon directors of a corporation to pursue a derivative complaint would not be excused absent specific allegations of self-dealing or bias on the part of a majority of the board. Derivative suits are almost invariably directed at major, allegedly illegal, corporate transactions. By virtue of their offices, directors ordinarily participate in the decision making involved in such transactions. Excusing demand on the mere basis of prior board acquiescence, therefore, would obviate the need for demand in practically every case. *Wilson v. Tully, 243 A.D.2d 229, 676 N.Y.S.2d 531 (1998).*

Gross negligence, which, in the corporate context, means reckless indifference to or a deliberate disregard of the whole body of stockholders' or actions which are without the bounds of reason. *Wilson v. Tully, 243 A.D.2d 229, 676 N.Y.S.2d 531 (1998).*

A director is independent if that director is capable of making decisions for the corporation based on the merits of the subject rather than extraneous considerations or influences. *Wilson v. Tully, 243 A.D.2d 229, 676 N.Y.S.2d 531 (1998).*

No particular "reasonable doubt" standard. — The Delaware Supreme Court has refused to establish a particular "reasonable doubt" standard and each court must employ an objective analysis to determine whether a plaintiff's complaint contains the facts necessary to support a finding of reasonable doubt of director disinterest or independence, or proper business judgment. *Wilson v. Tully, 243 A.D.2d 229, 676 N.Y.S.2d 531 (1998).*

Excuse standard very high. — In seeking to excuse demand futility (a demand upon directors of a corporation to pursue a derivative complaint), whether improper action or inaction is alleged, that standard is very high in Delaware. *Wilson v. Tully, 243 A.D.2d 229, 676 N.Y.S.2d 531 (1998).*

If it can be established that a board is incapable of fairly assessing a demand for a suit, a shareholder may arrogate to himself the board's authority to decide whether to commence litigation on the corporation's behalf. The shareholder's pleading burden in this case is a heavy one. The pre-argument demand is waived only when the complaint contains well-pleaded, factually specific allegations which rebut the presumption of director independence. *Miller v. Schreyer, 200 A.D.2d 492, 606 N.Y.S.2d 642 (1994).*

Discovery is not permitted in shareholder derivative suits unless plaintiff has presented factual allegations of evidentiary value to establish charges of improper conduct. *Teachers' Retirement System of Louisiana v. Welch, 244 A.D.2d 231, 664 N.Y.S.2d 38 (1997).*

The Delaware rule is that the pre-litigation demand can only be excused where facts are alleged with particularity which create a reasonable doubt that the directors' action was entitled to the protections of the business judgment rule. *Teachers' Retirement System of Louisiana v. Welch, 244 A.D.2d 231, 664 N.Y.S.2d 38 (1997).*

Under Delaware law, every shareholder derivative complaint shall: allege with particularity the efforts, if any, made by the plaintiff to obtain the action he or she desires from the directors or comparable authority and the reasons for his or her failure to obtain the action or for not making the effort. *Katz v. Emmett, 226 A.D.2d 588, 641 N.Y.S.2d 131 (1996).*

Demand futility test. — A demand on the directors can be excused only when the plaintiff alleges "with particularity" facts that create a reasonable doubt that the directors' action was entitled to the protections of the business judgment rule. In determining the futility of a demand the trial court, in the proper exercise of its discretion, must decide whether, under the particularized facts alleged, a reasonable doubt is created that: (1) the directors were independent and disinterested and (2) the challenged transaction was otherwise the product of a valid exercise of business judgment. *Katz v. Emmett, 226 A.D.2d 588, 641 N.Y.S.2d 131 (1996).*

No pre-litigation demand is necessary if the complaint alleges acts for which a majority of the directors may be liable and plaintiff reasonably concluded that the board would not be responsive to a demand. *Miller v. Schreyer, 200 A.D.2d 492, 606 N.Y.S.2d 642 (1994).*

Limitation on stock purchases. — Delaware law authorizes an officer or director to purchase the stock of the corporation with which he or she is associated except where the company involved has a policy of reacquiring its own stock, the director or officer takes advantage of superior or insider information or wrongly applies corporate resources to facilitate the purchase. *Ault v. Soutter, 167 A.D.2d 38, 570 N.Y.S.2d 280 (1991).*

Limitation on director opportunity. — When there is presented to a corporate officer a business opportunity which the corporation is financially able to undertake, and which, by its nature, falls into the line of the corporation's business and is of practical advantage to it, or is an opportunity in which the corporation has an actual or expectant interest, the officer is prohibited from permitting his or her self-interest to be brought into conflict with the corporation's interest and may not take the opportunity for him- or herself. *Ault v. Soutter, 167 A.D.2d 38, 570 N.Y.S.2d 280 (1991).*

Standing. — The only standing requirement for maintaining a derivative suit is that a plaintiff be a stockholder of the corporation at the time of the transaction(s) in question and that he or she is qualified to serve in a fiduciary capacity as a representative of a class. *Ault v. Soutter, 167 A.D.2d 38, 570 N.Y.S.2d 280 (1991).*

Under Delaware law, an equitable owner of shares in a corporation is considered to have shareholder status. *Petrou v. Karl Ehmer International Foods, Inc., 167 A.D.2d 338, 561 N.Y.S.2d 48 (1990).*

Under Delaware law, a plaintiff in a shareholder derivative action, to have standing, must show both shareholder status at the time of the complained of transaction and qualification to serve in a fiduciary capacity as a representative of the shareholder class. *CPF Acquisition Co., Inc. v. CPF Acquisition Co., Inc., 255 A.D.2d 200, 682 N.Y.S.2d 3 (1998).*

A stockholder, who has instituted a derivative action on behalf of the corporation, does not continue to have the right to prosecute the action after there has been a merger as a result of which the plaintiff's stock was converted into the right only to receive a fixed sum in cash from the surviving corporation. *Rubinstein v. Catacosinos, 91 A.D.2d 445, 459 N.Y.S.2d 286 (1983).*

Under Delaware law, a merger that eliminates a derivative plaintiff's ownership of shares of the corporation for whose benefit the former shareholder sued, terminates the standing to pursue the derivative claims. *Adams v. Banc of America Securities LLC, 2005 NY Slip Op 50714U, 7 Misc. 3d 1023A (2005).*

Diminution in value. — Courts have repeatedly held that an allegation of diminution in the value of stock based on a breach of fiduciary duty gives rise to a derivative action only. *Hart v. General Motors Corporation, 129 A.D.2d 179, 517 N.Y.S.2d 490 (1987).*

Standard of review. — In a derivative action brought by a shareholder, the court in the proper exercise of its discretion must decide whether, under the particularized facts alleged, a reasonable doubt is created that: (1) the directors are disinterested and independent and (2) the challenged transaction was otherwise the product of a valid exercise of business judgment. *Frankel v. American Film Technologies, Inc., 177 Misc. 2d 279, 675 N.Y.S.2d 837 (1998).*

Waiver upon demand. — If the stockholders make a demand on the board, then they waive any claim that they might otherwise have had that the board act independently on the demand, but they do not waive the right to claim that the board has wrongfully refused the demand. Thus, if the board rejects the demand, the board is entitled to the presumption of the business judgment rule, unless the stockholder can allege facts with particularity creating a reasonable doubt that the board is entitled to the presumption. *Adams v. Banc of America Securities LLC, 2005 NY Slip Op 50714U, 7 Misc. 3d 1023A (2005).*

Individual harm analysis. — Under Delaware law, in order to determine whether the plaintiffs' claims are derivative or individual, the court should look to the nature of the wrong and to whom the relief should go. The stockholder's claimed direct injury must be independent of any alleged injury to the corporation. The stockholder must demonstrate that the duty breached was owed to the stockholder and that he or she can prevail without showing an injury to the corporation. The analysis must be based solely on who suffered the alleged harm the corporation or the suing stockholder individually and who would receive the benefit of the recovery or other remedy. Thus, under both New York and Delaware law, the plaintiffs' individual claims must allege harm independent from the alleged injury suffered by the corporation. *Alpert v. National Association of Securities Dealers, LLC, 2004 NY Slip Op 51872U, 7 Misc. 3d 1010A (2005).*

Particularity of futility pleading. — Under Delaware law, shareholders seeking to bring a derivative action on behalf of the corporation must make a demand on the board of directors, unless such demand would be futile. Del. Ch. Ct. R. 23.1 provides that every shareholder derivative complaint must allege with particularity the efforts, if any, made by the plaintiff to obtain the action he or she desires from the directors or comparable authority and the reasons for his or her failure to obtain the action or for not making the effort. A plaintiff bears the burden of pleading futility. *Spear v. Conway, 2003 NY Slip Op 51749U, 6 Misc. 3d 1023A (2003).*

The *Aronson* test, under Delaware law, for determining whether a derivative complaint adequately pleads demand futility is whether the particular facts alleged create a reasonable doubt that: (1) the directors were independent and disinterested; and (2) the challenged transaction was otherwise the product of a valid exercise of business judgment. Where inaction rather than action by a board is charged, the inquiry is limited to the first prong of the *Aronson* test. *Spear v. Conway, 2003 NY Slip Op 51749U, 6 Misc. 3d 1023A (2003).*

In the demand-futile context, a plaintiff charging domination and control of one or more directors must allege particularized facts manifesting a direction of corporate conduct in such a way as to comport with the wishes or interests of the corporation (or persons) doing the controlling. *Frankel v. American Film Technologies, Inc., 177 Misc. 2d 279, 675 N.Y.S.2d 837 (1998).*

Under Delaware law, before a derivative suit can be brought, the futility of making a demand on the corporate board must be pleaded with particularity. *Wilmoth v. Sandor, 259 A.D.2d 252, 686 N.Y.S.2d 388 (1999).*

Examination when inaction of board charged. — Where inaction, rather than action, by a board is charged and directors are sued derivatively because they have failed to do something, it is appropriate to examine whether the board that would be addressing the demand can impartially consider its merits without being influenced by improper considerations. Thus, a trial court must determine whether or not the particularized factual allegations of a derivative stockholder complaint create a reasonable doubt that, as of the time the complaint is filed, the board of directors could have properly exercised its independent and disinterested business judgment in responding to a demand. *Spear v. Conway, 2003 NY Slip Op 51749U, 6 Misc. 3d 1023A (2003).*

Lack of reasonable oversight claim. — The Delaware Chancery Court has stated that generally where a claim of directorial liability for corporate loss is predicated upon ignorance of liability creating activities within the corporation, only a sustained or systematic failure of the board to exercise oversight-such as an utter failure to attempt to assure a reasonable information and reporting system exists-will establish the lack of good faith that is a necessary condition to liability. Such a test of liability—lack of good faith as evidenced by sustained or systematic failure of a director to exercise reasonable oversight—is quite high. *Spear v. Conway, 2003 NY Slip Op 51749U, 6 Misc. 3d 1023A (2003).*

Special litigation committee. — The burden is upon the movant to prove the independence of the special litigation committee, and that it conducted a reasonable investigation of the matters alleged in the complaint in good faith. *Weiser v.Grace, 179 Misc. 2d 116, 683 N.Y.S.2d 781 (1998).*

The court, in the exercise of its discretion, may permit the parties to engage in limited discovery to assist the court in its inquiry regarding the good faith and independence of the special litigation committee as well as the bases supporting the special litigation committee's conclusions. *Weiser v.Grace, 179 Misc. 2d 116, 683 N.Y.S.2d 781 (1998).*

When assessing the good faith and reasonableness of the special litigation committee's investigation, the court must also determine whether the committee's reliance on counsel was in good faith. To successfully challenge the committee's good-faith reliance on counsel, plaintiffs must show overreaching by counsel or neglect by the special litigation committee. *Weiser v.Grace, 179 Misc. 2d 116, 683 N.Y.S.2d 781 (1998).*

Contents of complaint. — Particularity in pleaIn a derivative action brought by one or more shareholders or members to enforce a right of a corporation or of an unincorporated association, the corporation or association having failed to enforce a right which may properly be asserted by it, the complaint shall allege that the plaintiff was a shareholder or member at the time of the transaction of which the plaintiff complains or that the plaintiff's share or membership thereafter devolved on the plaintiff by operation of law. The complaint shall also allege with particularity the efforts, if any, made by the plaintiff to obtain the action the plaintiff desires from the directors or comparable authority and the reasons for the plaintiff's failure to obtain the action or for not making the effort. *Frankel v. American Film Technologies, Inc., 177 Misc. 2d 279, 675 N.Y.S.2d 837 (1998).*

When demand not necessary. — A demand on stockholders as a whole prior to filing a derivative suit is not necessary under Delaware law in any case where the wrongs complained of are beyond the power of ratification by a majority of the stockholders. *Newman v. Baldwin, 13 Misc. 2d 902, 1958 N.Y. Misc. LEXIS 3250*

Claim of individual harm shown. — Under Delaware law, a shareholder may bring a direct claim where he or she has suffered harm not suffered by the corporation generally, and will be individually entitled to the benefit of the remedy obtained. A claim that a transaction was handled in a discriminatory fashion so that plaintiffs and similarly situated minority shareholders received a lesser benefit than other shareholders, sets forth a form of harm suffered individually rather than by the corporation. *Brinckerhoff v. JAC Holding Corp., 10 A.D.3d 520, 782 N.Y.S.2d 58 (2004).*

Applicability of Delaware law. — Cause of action brought as a derivative action under BCL § 626, while allowed under BCL § 1319 for jurisdictional purposes, must still be adjudicated herein by application of Delaware law. *Potter v. Arrington, 2006 NY Slip Op 26062, 2006 N.Y. Misc. LEXIS 300 (Feb. 6, 2006).*

Merger. — Even if plaintiff's causes of action were direct claims that survived the merger, they would not state a cognizable cause of action because defendants did not hold a majority of the preferred shares and, accordingly, were powerless to compel the merger. Further, the record shows that the merger was approved by the board of directors, and plaintiff failed to allege sufficient facts to overcome the business judgment rule. *Nemazee v. Premier Purch. Partners, L.P., 2005 NY Slip Op 9429, 806 N.Y.S.2d 22, 2005 N.Y. App. Div. LEXIS 13894 (Dec. 8, 2005).*

Insufficient wrongdoing demand. — Fifth cause of action should be dismissed because petitioners did not make a procedurally sufficient demand in that there are no specific assertions of wrongdoing upon which the corporation could seek correction or redress. The claim essentially is that the shareholders wish to know why the company went out of business. That factor does not support the necessary claim of breach of fiduciary duties which would give rise to the derivative suit sought here. *Potter v. Arrington, 2006 NY Slip Op 26062, 2006 N.Y. Misc. LEXIS 300 (Feb. 6, 2006).*

North Carolina

A director qualifies as interested when he or she will obtain a personal financial benefit from the transaction at issue. Such a benefit disqualifies a director as independent when stockholders do not equally share that benefit. A director is also not independent if the transaction will adversely affect him, but not the corporation or other shareholders. *Marcoux v. Prim, 2004 NCBC 5 (N.C. Super. Ct. 2004).*

To establish lack of independence, a plaintiff meets his or her burden by showing that the directors are either beholden to the controlling shareholder or so under its influence that their decision is sterilized. *Marcoux v. Prim, 2004 NCBC 5 (N.C. Super. Ct. 2004).*

Insider trading. — Under Delaware law, to make out a prima facie claim for insider trading, a plaintiff must allege that each sale by each individual defendant was entered into and completed on the basis of and because of, adverse material non-public information. Such burden was not met in the instant case. Plaintiff's insider trading claim does little more than suggest a mere threat of liability for defendant director. It does not state what insider information defendant possessed at the time he sold stock — only that because of his position in the company, he was in a position to know insider information. Plaintiff does not tie either of defendant's two alleged trades to any specific knowledge on his part or even state that the transactions were based on or motivated in any way by such knowledge. Plaintiff merely alleges that defendant generally possessed material non-public information at the time of each sale. Moreover, plaintiff fails to give any indication of the size of the two sales relative to his total ownership of the stock. *Egelhof v. Szulik, 2006 NCBC 4, 2006 NCBC LEXIS 5 (Mar. 13, 2006).*

Restating earnings. — Were the court to recognize demand futility on the grounds asserted by plaintiff, the demand requirement would be rendered void in all cases where a company opts to restate earnings. Such a ruling would be inconsistent with the public policy that corporations act diligently to correct reported earnings when mistakes or inconsistencies are discovered or where current accounting practices dictate a change in reporting practices. Plaintiff's conclusory demand futility arguments with respect to the five members of the audit committee are insufficient for the court to find that his failure to make demand is excused. *Egelhof v. Szulik, 2006 NCBC 4, 2006 NCBC LEXIS 5 (Mar. 13, 2006).*

The mere adoption and approval of annual fees and moderate increases or stock option grants for directors is not enough to cast a reasonable doubt on a defendant directors' disinterest. *Egelhof v. Szulik, 2006 NCBC 4, 2006 NCBC LEXIS 5 (Mar. 13, 2006).*

Ohio

Decisions of disinterested directors. — The business judgment rule is a tool of judicial review, not a standard of conduct. When the director's personal liability in damages is at issue, liability is predicated upon concepts of gross negligence. However, when the justification of a particular transaction is at issue, the court adopts a standard of judicial review whereby it must weigh the objective reasonableness of the business decision. Where the elements of the rule are satisfied in a transactional justification case, that decisions of disinterested directors will not be disturbed if they can be attributed to any rational business purpose. *Gries Sports Enterprises, Inc. v. Cleveland Browns Football Co., Inc., 26 Ohio St. 3d 15, 496 N.E.2d 959 (1986).*

Under Delaware law, a director is interested if he or she appears on both sides of a transaction or he or she has or expects to derive personal financial benefit not equally received by the stockholders. A director is independent if his or her decision is based on the corporate merits of the subject before the board rather than extraneous considerations or influences. A director is not independent when he or she is dominated by or beholden to another person through personal or other relationships. A director is informed if he or she makes a reasonable effort to become familiar with the relevant and reasonably available facts prior to making a business judgment. *Gries Sports Enterprises, Inc. v. Cleveland Browns Football Co., Inc., 26 Ohio St. 3d 15, 496 N.E.2d 959 (1986).*

Corporations

A transaction not given protection by the business judgment rule is subject to strict scrutiny, and the directors have the burden of showing the transaction was fair. *Gries Sports Enterprises, Inc. v. Cleveland Browns Football Co., Inc., 26 Ohio St. 3d 15, 496 N.E.2d 959 (1986).*

Necessary allegations. — Under Delaware law, directors cannot be accused of a breach of fiduciary duty in the absence of allegations that the business judgment rule does not protect a board's decisionmaking. Such allegations must rise above the assertion that a corporate board acted against the interests of the corporation or engaged in bad decisionmaking and include, for example, allegations that the board was self-interested or that the board failed to exert any deliberative effort in making its decision. *NCS Healthcare, Inc., Plaintiff-Appellant v. Candlewood Partners, LLC, 160 Ohio App. 3d 421, 2005 Ohio 1669, 827 N.E.2d 797 (2005).*

The heightened judicial scrutiny called for by the test of intrinsic or entire fairness is not called forth simply by a demonstration that a controlling shareholder fixes the terms of a transaction and, by exercise of voting power or by domination of the board, compels its effectuation. It is in each instance essential to show as well that the fiduciary has an interest with respect to the transaction that conflicts with the interests of minority shareholders. *Huang v. Landixe Thermocomposites, Inc., 144 Ohio App. 3d 289, 760 N.E.2d 14 (2001).*

Sale of all assets. — Generally, the management of the business and affairs of a Delaware corporation is entrusted to its directors, who are the duly elected and authorized representatives of the stockholders. Under normal circumstances, the business judgment rule mandates deference to directors' decisions, presuming that in making a business decision the directors of a corporation acted on an informed basis, in good faith, and in the honest belief that the action taken was in the best interests of the company. However, a sale of all assets is considered an extraordinary transaction, and subjects the directors' conduct to enhanced scrutiny to ensure that it is reasonable. *Huang v. Landixe Thermocomposites, Inc., 144 Ohio App. 3d 289, 760 N.E.2d 14 (2001).*

Actions of interested directors are evaluated according to a higher standard than are those of disinterested directors. As defined by Delaware law, an interested director is one who either appears on both sides of a transaction or, through the transaction, acquires a personal financial benefit not equally received by the corporation or its stockholders. *Huang v. Landixe Thermocomposites, Inc., 144 Ohio App. 3d 289, 760 N.E.2d 14 (2001).*

Duty to obtain best value. — When deciding to sell the assets or control of a company, the governing board of directors has a fiduciary duty to obtain the best value reasonably available to the shareholders. *Huang v. Landixe Thermocomposites, Inc., 144 Ohio App. 3d 289, 760 N.E.2d 14 (2001).*

Acceptance of futility argument concern. — Courts have expressed concern that the acceptance of the argument that it is futile for a shareholder to request a board of directors to sue itself would abrogate Rule 23.1 and weaken the managerial powers of directors. *Drage v. Procter & Gamble, 119 Ohio App. 3d 19, 694 N.E.2d 479 (1997).*

Under Delaware law, demand upon the directors of a corporation is excused when the plaintiff's claims raise a "reasonable doubt" as to "whether the directors exercised proper business judgment in approving the challenged transactions." *Drage v. Procter & Gamble, 119 Ohio App. 3d 19, 694 N.E.2d 479 (1997).*

The business judgment rule is a presumption that in making a business decision the directors of a corporation acted on an informed basis, in good faith, and in the honest belief that the action taken was in the best interests of the company. *Drage v. Ameritrust Corp., 1988 Ohio App. LEXIS 3972 (1988).*

Use of business judgment rule. — In order to utilize the business judgment rule as a defense, the directors of a corporation must initially make several showings at trial. The directors must show that they had reasonable grounds for believing that a danger to corporate policy and effectiveness existed. They satisfy the burden by showing good faith, and reasonable investigation. In addition, the directors must show that the defensive mechanism was reasonable in relation to the threat posed. Moreover, that proof is materially enhanced where a majority of the board favoring the proposal consisted of outside independent directors who have acted in accordance with the foregoing standards. *Drage v. Ameritrust Corp., 1988 Ohio App. LEXIS 3972 (1988).*

Repurchase of capital stock. — The law of Delaware is well established that in the absence of evidence of fraud or unfairness, a corporation's repurchase of its capital stock, at a premium over market from a dissident shareholder is entitled to the protection of the business judgment rule. *Drage v. Ameritrust Corp., 1988 Ohio App. LEXIS 3972 (1988).*

Application of modified business judgment rule. — When decisions are made by directors in actual or threatened take-over situations, the modified business judgment rule applies. *Drage v. Ameritrust Corp., 1988 Ohio App. LEXIS 3972 (1988).*

Fiduciary duty of shareholder. — Delaware law declares that a shareholder does not have a fiduciary duty to other shareholders as a result of stock ownership unless it has a majority interest or has exercised actual domination or control of the corporation. *Drage v. Ameritrust Corp., 1988 Ohio App. LEXIS 3972 (1988).*

A stockholder can maintain an individual action against the corporation if he has sustained a special injury, which the courts impliedly define as a wrong inflicted upon him or her alone or a wrong affecting any particular right which he or she is asserting, such as his or her preemptive rights as a stockholder, rights involving the control of the corporation, or a wrong affect the stockholders and not the corporation. *Drage v. Ameritrust Corp., 1988 Ohio App. LEXIS 3972 (1988).*

To set out an individual action, plaintiff must allege either an injury which is separate and distinct from that suffered by other shareholders, or a wrong involving a contractual right of a shareholder, such as the right to vote, or to assert majority control, which exists independently of any right of the corporation. *Drage v. Ameritrust Corp., 1988 Ohio App. LEXIS 3972 (1988).*

Pennsylvania

Courts' use of own business judgment. — Delaware law permits a court in some cases ("demand excused" cases) to apply its own business judgment in the review process when deciding to honor the directors' decision to terminate derivative litigation. *Cuker v. Mikalauskas, 547 Pa. 600, 692 A.2d 1042 (1997).*

Rhode Island

Applicability of business judgment rule. — The business judgment rule is a presumption that in making a business decision the directors of a corporation acted on an informed basis, in good faith and in the honest belief that the action taken was in the best interests of the company. This presumption, which protects a board-approved transaction, can only be claimed by disinterested directors, meaning that directors can neither appear on both sides of a transaction nor expect to derive any personal financial benefit from it in the sense of self-dealing, as opposed to a benefit which devolves upon the corporation or all stockholders generally. If the transaction at issue is an "interested" director transaction, the business judgment rule will be rendered inapplicable. When, however, the business judgment rule does apply, directors will be protected from liability, and the party challenging the transaction has the burden of rebutting the presumption. *Lynch v. John W. Kennedy Co., 2005 R.I. Super. LEXIS 103.*

In essence, the business judgment rule creates a rebuttable presumption that directors have acted properly. *Heritage Healthcare Services, Inc. v. The Beacon Mutual Insurance Company, 2004 R.I. Super. LEXIS 29 (2004).*

South Carolina

Under Delaware law, demand may be excused even if the threshold presumptions of director disinterest or independence are not rebutted by well-pleaded facts, if the complaint pleads particularized facts sufficient to create a reasonable doubt that the challenged transaction was the product of a valid exercise of business judgment. *Carolina First Corporation v. Whittle, 343 S.C. 176, 539 S.E.2d 402 (S.C. App. 2000).*

Tennessee

Derivative versus direct suits. — Delaware courts distinguish between derivative and direct suits on the basis of injury rather than duty. A shareholder can maintain a direct action only when he or she sustains a "special injury." That is, an injury distinct from that suffered by other shareholders or a wrong involving a contractual right of a shareholder. Wrongs involving contractual rights of a shareholder are such rights as the right to vote or the right of the majority shareholder to exert control over rights which exists independent of corporation rights. Mismanagement which depresses the value of stock is a wrong to the corporation, i.e., the

stockholders collectively, to be enforced by a derivative action. *Bayberry Associates v. Jones, 783 S.W.2d 553 (Tenn. 1990).*

Texas

When applicable. — Under some circumstances, an individual shareholder may not recover for the injury to his stock alone, but must seek recovery derivatively on behalf of the corporation. Under Delaware law, the test used to distinguish between a shareholder derivative claim and an individual claim is whether the plaintiff has suffered a "special injury." If a plaintiff has not suffered a special injury, the suit must be brought derivatively. *Estate of Peterson v. Glenmede Corporation, 1996 Tex. App. LEXIS 4897 (1996).*

Derivative versus direct suits. — The Delaware court has articulated the standard for analyzing whether a stockholders' suit is direct or derivative as follows: The analysis must be based solely on the following questions: Who suffered the alleged harm — the corporation or the suing stockholders, individually — and who would receive the benefit of any recovery or other remedy? To decide if the harm was to the corporation or to the stockholder individually, the most relevant question is whether the stockholder can prevail without showing an injury to the corporation. A court should look to the nature of the wrong and to whom the relief should go. The stockholder's claimed direct injury must be independent of any alleged injury to the corporation. The stockholder must demonstrate that the duty breached was owed to the stockholder and that he or she can prevail without showing a corresponding injury to the corporation. *Shirvanian v. Defrates, 161 S.W.3d 102 (Tex. App. 2005).*

When an injury to corporate stock falls equally upon all shareholders, an individual shareholder may not recover for the injury to his or her stock alone, but must seek recovery derivatively on behalf of the corporation. To determine whether a complaint states a derivative or individual cause of action, the court must examine the nature of the wrongs alleged in the complaint, not the label employed by the plaintiff. *Estate of Peterson v. Glenmede Corporation, 1996 Tex. App. LEXIS 4897 (1996).*

Standing. — A plaintiff bringing a derivative suit on behalf of a corporation must be a shareholder of the corporation at the time he commences the suit and must maintain that status throughout the course of the litigation. *Estate of Peterson v. Glenmede Corporation, 1996 Tex. App. LEXIS 4897 (1996).*

Virginia

A derivative action is an equitable proceeding in which a shareholder asserts, on behalf of the corporation, a claim that belongs to the corporation rather than the shareholder. *Simmons v. Miller, 261 Va. 561, 544 S.E.2d 666 (2001).*

Applicable to trust relationships. — Even the State of Delaware permits equitable owners of stock to sue derivatively in instances where a trust relationship is involved. *Milstead v. Bradshaw, 43 Va. Cir. 428 (1997).*

Necessary pleadings. — Delaware Code tit. 8, § 327 provides that in any derivative suit instituted by a stockholder of a corporation, it shall be averred in the complaint that the plaintiff was a stockholder of the corporation at the time of the transaction of which he complains or that his stock thereafter devolved on him by operation of law. *Milstead v. Bradshaw, 43 Va. Cir. 428 (1997)*.

Washington

Special litigation committee. — Before bringing a shareholders' derivative action, shareholders must present their claims to the corporation and give the corporation an opportunity to pursue the case. Under Delaware law, the corporation has a variety of options, one of which is to form a special litigation committee (SLC) to evaluate the shareholders' claims. If the SLC concludes that the suit is in the corporation's best interest, the corporation may assume the shareholders' place and pursue the suit on its own. However, if the SLC concludes the action is not in the corporation's best interest, the corporation may bring a motion to terminate the suit. If the court does not grant the motion, the court may permit the shareholders to prosecute the suit on the corporation's behalf. *Dreiling v. Jain, 151 Wash.2d 900, 93 P.3d 861 (2004)*.

Under Delaware law, a corporation seeking to dismiss a derivative action is required to prepare and submit an special litigation committee (SLC) report to the court. *Dreiling v. Jain, 151 Wash.2d 900, 93 P.3d 861 (2004)*.

West Virginia

Standing. — Under the common law of Delaware as applicable to proceedings in equity an equitable owner of stock can maintain a stockholder's derivative action. The rigidity of stockholder lists is not necessary where the equitable owner seeks to protect corporate interests. The statute does not limit to "holders of record" those who can file a shareholder derivative suit. In any derivative suit instituted by a stockholder of a corporation, it shall be averred in the complaint that the plaintiff was a stockholder of the corporation at the time of the transaction of which he or she complains or that his or her stock thereafter devolved upon him or her by operation of law. The Delaware Code does limit those who can maintain a derivative suit to parties who were shareholders at the time of the transaction. *State ex rel. Elish v. Wilson, 189 W. Va. 739, 434 S.E.2d 411 (1993)*.

Wisconsin

Short merger disclosures. — In a merger, the duty of complete candor requires that majority shareholders must reveal to minority shareholders all facts which a reasonable shareholder would consider material or germane to a decision whether to vote for a merger. Even in a situation where there is no voting, as in a short-form merger, the parent corporation has a duty to disclose to minority shareholders what appraisal information it has. Nevertheless this breach of duty should be evaluated in light of the observation that it would be difficult to imagine a case under the short merger statute in which there could be such actual fraud as would entitle a minority to set aside the merger. *Stauffacher v. Checota, 149 Wis. 2d 762, 441 N.W.2d 755 (Wis. App. 1979)*.

There is no duty under Delaware law to get an independent appraisal of a subsidiary before a merger. *Stauffacher v. Checota, 149 Wis. 2d 762, 441 N.W.2d 755 (Wis. App. 1979)*.

CASE NOTES — FEDERAL

First Circuit

Preliminary obligation. — When offering a lawsuit on behalf of a corporation, plaintiffs have an obligation to show clearly, as a preliminary matter, that the corporation lacks the capacity to protect its own interests. When they fail to do this, dismissal is proper. *Sachs v. Sprague, 401 F. Supp. 2d 159, 2005 U.S. Dist. LEXIS 29181 (D. Mass. 2005)*.

Standing. — A plaintiff may not maintain a derivative action if he did not own stock in the corporation when he filed the lawsuit. *Malone v. Network Switching Systems, Inc., 1987 U.S. Dist. LEXIS 3287 (D.Mass. 1987)*.

A director is interested if he or she will be materially affected, either to his or her benefit or detriment, by a decision of the board, in a manner not shared by the corporation and the stockholders. In such circumstances, a director cannot be expected to exercise his or her independent business judgment without being influenced by the adverse personal consequences resulting from the decision. The "mere threat" of personal liability is insufficient to challenge the disinterestedness of a director. A plaintiff must articulate particularized facts showing that a director faces "a substantial likelihood" of liability. *Caviness v. Evans, 2005 U.S. Dist. LEXIS 17350 (D.Mass. 2005)*.

Demand futility. — Under Delaware law, *Aronson v. Lewis*, remains the seminal precedent on the circumstances for demand futility when a shareholder challenges a decision by the board of the corporation as a whole. *Aronson* and its progeny provide that demand futility is established if, accepting the well-pleaded facts of the complaint as true, the alleged particularized facts raise a reasonable doubt that either (1) the directors are disinterested or independent with respect to the challenged transaction or (2) the challenged transaction was the product of a valid exercise of the directors' business judgment. *Landy v. D'Alessandro, 316 F. Supp. 2d 49 (D.Mass. 2004)*.

Aronson applies only to challenged transactions that were made by the board as a whole. For transactions made by individual directors or subsets of the board, Delaware law turns to the *Rales* test. *Landy v. D'Alessandro, 316 F. Supp. 2d 49 (D.Mass. 2004)*.

Under *Rales*, a court must determine whether or not the particularized factual allegations of a derivative stockholder complaint create a reasonable doubt that, as of the time the complaint is filed, the board of directors could have properly exercised its independent and disinterested business judgment in responding to a demand. If the derivative plaintiff satisfies this burden, then demand will be excused as futile. *Landy v. D'Alessandro, 316 F. Supp. 2d 49 (D.Mass. 2004).*

Both *Aronson* and *Rales* rely on a "reasonable doubt" standard. It is important to note that the Delaware Supreme Court has concluded that it would be neither practicable nor wise to attempt to formulate a criterion of general application for determining reasonable doubt. Reasonable doubt must be decided by the trial court on a case-by-case basis employing an objective analysis. Aronson, which introduced the term reasonable doubt into corporate derivative jurisprudence, made expressly clear that the entire review is factual in nature. *Landy v. D'Alessandro, 316 F. Supp. 2d 49 (D.Mass. 2004).*

The court in *Aronson* has concluded that in the demand-futile context a plaintiff charging domination and control of one or more directors must allege particularized facts manifesting a direction of corporate conduct in such a way as to comport with the wishes or interests of the corporation (or persons) doing the controlling. *Landy v. D'Alessandro, 316 F. Supp. 2d 49 (D.Mass. 2004).*

The court in *Aronson* has explained the second prong of the test for demand futility in the following way: in determining demand futility, the court in the proper exercise of its discretion must decide whether, under the particularized facts alleged, a reasonable doubt is created that the challenged transaction was otherwise the product of a valid exercise of business judgment. The court makes an inquiry into the substantive nature of the challenged transaction and the board's approval thereof. Under Delaware law this is a heavy burden. *Landy v. D'Alessandro, 316 F. Supp. 2d 49 (D.Mass. 2004).*

A court employs a standard other than *Aronson* when determining whether plaintiff should have made demand on the board before bringing a derivative suit with respect to these types of decisions or transactions. Under *Rales*, a court must determine whether or not the particularized factual allegations of a derivative stockholder complaint create a reasonable doubt that, as of the time the complaint is filed, the board of directors could have properly exercised its independent and disinterested business judgment in responding to a demand. If the derivative plaintiff satisfies this burden, then demand will be excused as futile. *Landy v. D'Alessandro, 316 F. Supp. 2d 49 (D.Mass. 2004).*

If an action is derivative in nature, the shareholders must first make a demand on the corporate officers or directors to bring the suit on behalf of the corporation. This demand requirement can only be excused where facts are alleged with particularity which create a reasonable doubt that the directors' action was entitled to the protections of the business judgment rule. The business judgment rule is a presumption that in making a business decision the directors of a corporation acted on an informed basis, in good faith, and in the honest belief that the action taken was in the best interests of the company. Absent an abuse of discretion, that judgment will be respected by the courts. The burden is on the party challenging the decision to establish facts rebutting the presumption. *Niehoff v. Maynard, 2000 U.S. Dist. LEXIS 22009 (D.R.I. 2000).*

The business judgment rule can insulate unlawful conduct. As the Delaware Supreme Court has explained in *Aronson*, the business judgment rule is a presumption that in making a business decision the directors of a corporation acted on an informed basis, in good faith, and in the honest belief that the action taken was in the best interests of the company. One can reasonably conceive of numerous situations in which directors might act on an informed basis, in good faith, and in the honest belief that an action taken is in the best interests of the company and yet approve a transaction that, in the end, proves to be unlawful. *Landy v. D'Alessandro, 316 F. Supp. 2d 49 (D.Mass. 2004).*

The *Aronson* standard of reasonable doubt is not meant to alter or affect the definition of business judgment. The question in *Aronson* is whether the facts create an objective, reasonable doubt that the board exercised business judgment. *Landy v. D'Alessandro, 316 F. Supp. 2d 49 (D.Mass. 2004).*

The court in *Aronson* has articulated the basic principle of board interest: from the standpoint of interest, this means that directors can neither appear on both sides of a transaction nor expect to derive any personal financial benefit from it in the sense of self-dealing, as opposed to a benefit which devolves upon the corporation or all stockholders generally. *Landy v. D'Alessandro, 316 F. Supp. 2d 49 (D.Mass. 2004).*

Limited partnership actions. — Under Delaware law, the determination of whether a fiduciary duty lawsuit involving a limited partnership is derivative or direct in nature is similar to that involving a corporation. *Niehoff v. Maynard, 2000 U.S. Dist. LEXIS 22009 (D.R.I. 2000).*

To assess whether a plaintiff has brought a derivative or direct action in the context of a limited partnership, a court must look to the nature of the wrongs alleged in the body of plaintiff's complaint, not plaintiff's characterization or stated intention. In addition, a court must also look to the relief that the plaintiff would be entitled if he were to prevail. In short, the gravamen of the complaint must portray injury to the partnership and not to the partner individually to raise a derivative claim. *Niehoff v. Maynard, 2000 U.S. Dist. LEXIS 22009 (D.R.I. 2000).*

A shareholder may bring a direct suit against the corporation if he or she has alleged a "special injury;" that is, if he or she alleges an injury which is separate and distinct from that suffered by other shareholders, or a wrong involving a contractual right of a shareholder, such as the right to vote, or to assert majority control, which exists independently of any right of the corporation. If a plaintiff cannot show either factor, his or her claims are derivative. Stated differently, for a plaintiff to bring an individual action, he or she must be injured directly or independently of the corporation. The test is whether the plaintiff has suffered an injury distinct from that suffered by other shareholders. *Niehoff v. Maynard, 2000 U.S. Dist. LEXIS 22009 (D.R.I. 2000).*

The following activities give rise to derivative actions: actions against directors or officers for breach of fiduciary duty to the corporation (e.g., waste of corporate assets, self-dealing, mismanagement of corporate business, misappropriation of corporate assets or business opportunities) and actions to recover damages for a consummated ultra vires act. *Niehoff v. Maynard, 2000 U.S. Dist. LEXIS 22009 (D.R.I. 2000).*

The following activities give rise to direct actions: fraudulent statements which directly affect the value of securities held by the shareholder; a suit brought to inspect corporate books and records; a suit against directors for fraud in the sale or purchase of the individual shareholder's stock; actions to compel payment of dividends; actions to preserve shareholders' rights to vote; a claim that a transaction improperly dilutes a shareholder's ownership interest or infringes the shareholder's preemptive rights; a claim that a proposed merger, recapitalization, or similar transaction unfairly affects minority shareholders; and a claim that a proposed corporate action should be enjoined as ultra vires, fraudulent, or designed to harm a specific shareholder illegitimately. *Niehoff v. Maynard, 2000 U.S. Dist. LEXIS 22009 (D.R.I. 2000).*

Tendency to discuss defendants in "collective terminology" evinces a failure to heed the numerous admonitions by judiciary for derivative plaintiffs to obtain books and records before filing a complaint. *Sachs v. Sprague, 401 F. Supp. 2d 159, 2005 U.S. Dist. LEXIS 29181 (D. Mass. 2005).*

Second Circuit

In general. — The stockholders as a body have no power to bring suit on behalf of the corporation; that power, as an incident to the general powers of management, is confided to the board of directors. A stockholder may institute and conduct the litigation in behalf of the corporation only on a showing that he or she has exhausted all the means within his or her reach to obtain, within the corporation itself, the redress of his or her grievances, or action in conformity with his or her wishes. The corporation, having refused to institute proceedings, the only way that its rights could be brought before the court was by a bill filed by a stockholder. *Steinberg v. Hardy, 90 F. Supp. 167 (D. Conn. 1950).*

Derivative actions, which are an extremely useful check on directors' faithful performance of their duties, are justified in the face of directors' inaction, whether a failure to act diligently or an unjustified refusal to act. Action by the directors may be prompted by a demand, thereby vitiating the need for a lawsuit. Refusal to act can then be overcome, in protection of the corporation and its shareholders, by the derivative lawsuit. Nonetheless, the board should have the initial opportunity to make the decision. Excusing a demand will not provide the directors an opportunity to seek to impose responsibility on the actual wrongdoers. Faced with a demand, no action may be taken, but the directors should not be denied the opportunity. *Citron v. Daniell, 796 F. Supp. 649 (D.Conn. 1992).*

Standing. — A shareholder need not be a shareholder of record in order to institute and maintain a stockholder's derivative action. As an equitable owner of stock in a corporation, i.e., a non-record or equitable stockholder, he

or she may maintain a derivative action. *Marco v. Dulles, 177 F. Supp. 533 (S.D.N.Y. 1959).*

An equitable owner, under Delaware law, may bring a derivative action. *Steinberg v. Hardy, 90 F. Supp. 167 (D. Conn. 1950).*

An equitable shareholder cannot maintain a derivative suit in Delaware especially where there is no showing of complicity between a legal owner of the shares and directors of a corporation or no other circumstances tending to bar the equitable holder from all relief if permission to sue is not granted. *Bankers National Corp. v. Barr, 7 F.R.D. 305 (S.D.N.Y. 1945).*

The attitude of Delaware courts is to construe "stockholder" as meaning "registered holder." *Bankers National Corp. v. Barr, 7 F.R.D. 305 (S.D.N.Y. 1945).*

Only shareholders have the right to sue derivatively on behalf of a corporation. The right to sue derivatively is an attribute of ownership, justified on the theory that the plaintiff in such a suit seeks to recover what belongs to the corporation, because as a co-owner, it also belongs to him or her. A creditor's interest, on the other hand, is limited to ensuring the corporation's continuing ability to pay him or her what it owes. *Brooks v. Weiser, 57 F.R.D. 491 (S.D.N.Y. 1972).*

Special injury test. — To satisfy the special injury test, a plaintiff must allege an injury that is either: (1) separate and distinct from that suffered by other shareholders; or (2) based on a contractual right, such as a shareholder's right to vote or to assert majority control, that exists independently of any right of the corporation. *Solow v. Stone, 994 F. Supp. 173 (S.D.N.Y. 1998).*

Although the first branch of the special injury test assumes the existence of multiple shareholders, one of whom suffered an injury separate and distinct from the others, the inquiry does not turn on that assumption. The ultimate issue is whether the injury about which a plaintiff complains resulted from a direct harm to the plaintiff or a general harm to the corporation. If the harm is to the corporation, and therefore affects the entire corporate structure, an individual plaintiff has not suffered a particularized injury, regardless of whether he or she is the corporation's sole creditor. *Solow v. Stone, 994 F. Supp. 173 (S.D.N.Y. 1998).*

The second branch of the special injury test recognizes that, in limited situations, a shareholder may bring an individual action to vindicate a right that belongs to him or her by virtue of his or her status as a shareholder. The paradigmatic example of such a right is the right to vote or the right to assert majority control in a corporation. *Solow v. Stone, 994 F. Supp. 173 (S.D.N.Y. 1998).*

Demand futility. — Under Delaware law, demand is excused by demonstrating futility under the following standard: the particularized allegations of the complaint must raise a reasonable doubt as to (i) director disinterest or independence or (ii) whether the directors exercised proper business judgment in approving the challenged transaction. The entire review is factual in nature and is within the sound discretion of the court. *Oye v. Schwartz, 762 F. Supp. 510 (E.D.N.Y. 1991).*

Acts of self-dealing which involve a majority of the directors will generally support the excusing of demand. *Oye v. Schwartz, 762 F. Supp. 510 (E.D.N.Y. 1991).*

Stockholders' derivative suits are equitable and the rules of equity that demand first be made on a trustee to sue, and demand refused, or reason shown why such demand would be useless, and that the trustee be made a party to the suit so as to avoid harassing a defendant are applicable. *Bankers National Corp. v. Barr, 7 F.R.D. 305 (S.D.N.Y. 1945).*

The requirements of the Delaware Court of Chancery have been interpreted as dispensing with the necessity of a demand on other shareholders where facts are alleged showing that fraud or illegality on the part of the offending directors was involved. *Marco v. Dulles, 177 F. Supp. 533 (S.D.N.Y. 1959).*

Under Delaware law, failure to make a demand upon the board will be excused only if such a demand would be futile. To plead demand futility adequately, a plaintiff must allege with particularity facts creating a reasonable doubt that: (1) the directors are disinterested and independent or (2) the challenged transaction was otherwise the product of a valid exercise of business judgment. *Ryan v. Aetna Life Ins. Co., 765 F. Supp. 133 (S.D.N.Y. 1991).*

As to the first *Aronson* inquiry, the Court reviews the factual allegations of the complaint to determine whether they create a reasonable doubt as to the disinterestedness and independence of the directors at the time the complaint was filed. In order to raise a reasonable doubt in this respect, plaintiff must allege that the directors expected a personal benefit from the challenged transaction or appeared on both sides of the transaction, showing divided loyalties. *Ryan v. Aetna Life Ins. Co., 765 F. Supp. 133 (S.D.N.Y. 1991).*

Delaware law holds that demand must be made upon the board if the disputed transaction has been approved by a majority consisting of the disinterested directors. *Ryan v. Aetna Life Ins. Co., 765 F. Supp. 133 (S.D.N.Y. 1991).*

Under the second prong of the *Aronson* test, the Court must look to the allegations of impropriety in the exercise of both substantive due care (purchase terms), and procedural due care (an informed decision). On the issue of substantive due care, Delaware courts focus on whether the transaction represents a fair exchange. *Ryan v. Aetna Life Ins. Co., 765 F. Supp. 133 (S.D.N.Y. 1991).*

Approval of a transaction by a majority of independent, disinterested directors almost always bolsters a presumption that the business judgment rule attaches to transactions approved by a board of directors that are later attacked on grounds of procedural due care. In such cases, a heavy burden falls on a plaintiff to avoid presuit demand. *Ryan v. Aetna Life Ins. Co., 765 F. Supp. 133 (S.D.N.Y. 1991).*

The Delaware Supreme Court has not defined what degree of factual specificity is required to establish reasonable doubt sufficient to excuse a demand; however, particularized facts are required, thus the pleading requirements are more stringent than they would be on a motion to dismiss for failure to state a claim under Fed. R.

Civ. P. 12(b)(6). *In re Trump Hotels Shareholder Derivative Litig., 2000 U.S. Dist. LEXIS 13550 (S.D.N.Y. 2000).*

To establish lack of independence, a plaintiff meets his or her burden by showing that the directors are either beholden to the controlling shareholder or so under its influence that their discretion is sterilized. *In re Trump Hotels Shareholder Derivative Litig., 2000 U.S. Dist. LEXIS 13550 (S.D.N.Y. 2000)*

In 1936, the laws of Delaware did not require a demand on other shareholders as a condition precedent to a stockholder's derivative action. *Marco v. Dulles, 177 F. Supp. 533 (S.D.N.Y. 1959).*

Convertible debenture holders. — Under Delaware law, convertible debenture holders do not possess all the rights of shareholders with respect to actions taken by corporate directors or majority shareholders. In certain circumstances, a holder of a convertible debenture is entitled to different treatment from a mere creditor of a corporation, and a cause of action for breach of fiduciary duty may lie under Delaware law apart from the express terms of an indenture agreement. *Green v. Hamilton International Corp., 1981 U.S. Dist. LEXIS 13439 (S.D.N.Y. 1981).*

A convertible debenture has the qualities of a debt and an equity security. If the wrongs alleged in a derivative action against a corporation impact upon the securities so as to undermine the debtor-creditor relationship, a contract analysis is appropriate, and plaintiffs, as creditors of the corporation, are owed no special duty outside the bounds of the contract. If the wrongs alleged impinge upon the equity aspects, then the analysis more properly treats plaintiffs like shareholders to whom the majority shareholders and directors of a corporation owe a duty of honesty, loyalty, good faith, and fairness. *Green v. Hamilton International Corp., 1981 U.S. Dist. LEXIS 13439 (S.D.N.Y. 1981).*

Power to make litigation decisions. — The power of the board to manage the corporation without improper judicial or shareholder interference includes within its scope the power to conduct the corporation's litigation for example, whether to institute litigation in the first instance, abandon the litigation, or settle the action. *Abramowitz v. Posner, 513 F. Supp. 120 (S.D.N.Y. 1981).*

Because Delaware law empowers a board of directors to delegate all of its authority to a committee, a properly authorized independent committee has the authority, to the extent provided in the board's resolution, to seek the termination of litigation charging fellow directors with wrongdoing. Moreover, even if a majority of directors are interested in the transactions at issue, a board can still delegate its authority to a committee of disinterested directors. *Stein v. Bailey, 531 F. Supp. 684 (S.D.N.Y. 1982).*

A stockholder cannot sue on a corporation's behalf when the managing body of the corporation refuses. Moreover, a decision such as whether to proceed with a derivative action may be approved in the exercise of independent business judgment by the independent directors. Whether or not a corporation shall seek to enforce in the courts a cause of action for damage is, like other business questions, ordinarily a matter of internal management, and is left to the discretion of the directors, in the absence of instruction by vote of the stockholders. *Seigal v. Merrick, 1979 U.S. Dist. LEXIS 7851 (S.D.N.Y. 1979).*

Delaware law authorizes a corporation's outside directors to terminate a stockholder's derivative action. The procedure followed by the corporation's board of directors in delegating its decision-making authority to a special committee is an appropriate method of insulating the corporation from shareholder interference by meeting the requirements of the business judgment rule. A corporation is specifically authorized to establish an independent committee of outside directors. Thus, under the business judgment rule, as followed by the courts of Delaware, a special review committee of outside directors is authorized to terminate a stockholder's derivative action. *Seigal v. Merrick, 1979 U.S. Dist. LEXIS 7851 (S.D.N.Y. 1979).*

Under Delaware law, a corporation may appoint a special review committee of disinterested, independent directors with authority to refuse a stockholder's demand or to terminate a stockholders' derivative suit. *Seigal v. Merrick, 1979 U.S. Dist. LEXIS 7851 (S.D.N.Y. 1979).*

Under Delaware law, a decision such as whether to proceed with a derivative action may be approved in the exercise of independent business judgment by the independent directors. The corporation may choose to establish an independent committee to determine whether to prosecute a derivative action. *Siegal v. Merrick, 84 F.R.D. 106 (S.D.N.Y. 1979).*

Both New York and Delaware law contemplate that a special litigation committee be represented by independent counsel. *In re Par Pharmaceutical, Inc. Derivative Litigation, 750 F. Supp. 641 (S.D.N.Y. 1990).*

Merger. — Under Delaware law, a merged corporation and its stockholders lose the right to sue derivatively. *Voege v. Ackerman, 364 F. Supp. 72 (S.D.N.Y. 1973).*

Under the law of Delaware, once a corporation has been merged out of existence, its rights, privileges and very identity are merged into the remaining corporation. By virtue of a merger, the merged corporation loses its capacity to sue the corporation into which it has been merged, and the stockholders of the merged corporation lose the right to sue derivatively. *Basch v. Talley Industries, Inc., 53 F.R.D. 9 (S.D.N.Y. 1971).*

Proxy claims. — Under Delaware law, a plaintiff asserting proxy claims need not comply with the federal demand requirement. False proxy claims are not subject to the demand requirement of Del. Ch. Ct. R. 23.1. *Katz v. Pels, 774 F. Supp. 121 (S.D.N.Y. 1991).*

Mutual fund fees and expenses. — A pro rata bearing of expenses by individual shareholders seems to fall within the very essence of an injury which is not independent from that suffered by the corporation. Indeed, if the only injury to an investor is the indirect harm which consists of the diminution in the value of his or her shares, the suit must be derivative. *In re Goldman Sachs Mut. Funds Fee Litig., 2006 U.S. Dist. LEXIS 1542 (S.D.N.Y. Jan. 13, 2006).*

Excessive distribution and management fees. — Plaintiffs argue that the alleged excessive distribution and management fees at issue here were borne directly by shareholders, and that therefore the shareholders suffered an injury independent of the corporation. This court is unpersuaded that the alleged financial harm of overcharges harms the individual investor independently of the harm to the funds. Rather, a pro rata bearing of expenses by individual shareholders seems to fall within the very essence of an injury which is not independent from that suffered by the corporation. The alleged injury suffered by plaintiffs occurred only secondarily and as a function of and in proportion to their pro rata investment in the funds. *In re Evergreen Mut. Funds Fee Litig., 423 F. Supp. 2d 249, 259 (D.N.Y. Mar. 24, 2006).*

Demand futility found. — This is not a case where the directors had no grounds for suspicion or were blamelessly unaware of the conduct leading to the corporate liability. Rather, plaintiffs allege that the director-committee members conscientiously permitted a known violation of law by the corporation to occur. This is precisely the type of case the Delaware Chancery Court was contemplating when it recently held that a claim that an audit committee or board had notice of serious misconduct and simply failed to investigate, for example, would survive a motion to dismiss, even if the committee or board was well constituted and otherwise functioning. If true, plaintiffs allegations that the committee failed to exercise appropriate attention to potentially illegal corporate activities would constitute a breach of loyalty, subjecting directors to a substantial likelihood of liability. Thus, plaintiffs' allegations raise a reasonable doubt that these director-committee members were disinterested and capable objectively deciding whether or not to prosecute this litigation on the corporation's behalf. Accordingly, demand would have been futile. *Veeco Instruments, Inc. v. Braun (In re Veeco Instruments, Inc. Sec. Litig.), 434 F. Supp. 2d 267 (D.N.Y. June 14, 2006).*

Third Circuit

Demand generally. — A shareholder lacks standing to bring a shareholder derivative action unless he or she pleads with particularity that demand was made (termed "demand refusal" cases) or that demand would have been futile (termed "demand excused" cases). Where demand is made on the board, its refusal to investigate the allegations is deemed an exercise of reasonable business judgment, unless the plaintiff pleads facts with particularity to create a reasonable doubt that the refusal is protected by the business judgment rule, i.e., sufficient facts to support an inference of wrongful refusal. The business judgment rule is a presumption that in making a decision not involving self-interest, the directors of a corporation acted on an informed basis in good faith and in the honest belief that the action taken was in the best interests of the company. The burden is on the plaintiff to establish facts rebutting this presumption. The business judgment rule may not be invoked where there is an absence of good faith or evidence of self-dealing. *Abrams v. Koether, 1992 U.S. Dist. LEXIS 16295 (D.N.J. 1992).*

By electing to make a demand, a shareholder plaintiff tacitly concedes the independence of a

majority of the board to respond. Therefore, when a board refuses a demand, the only issues to be examined are the good faith and reasonableness of its investigation. Absent an abuse of discretion, if the requirements of the traditional business judgment rule are met, the board of directors' decision not to pursue the derivative claim will be respected by the courts. In such cases, a board of directors' motion to dismiss an action filed by a shareholder, whose demand has been rejected, must be granted. Thus, for demand-refused cases the sole question for the court is whether the complaint contains sufficient facts to create a doubt as to the good faith of the directors or the reasonableness of their investigation. By conceding independence when demand is made, the plaintiff cannot raise issues of non-independence in demand-refused cases. *Abrams v. Koether, 1992 U.S. Dist. LEXIS 16295 (D.N.J. 1992).*

Under Delaware law, a shareholder who makes a demand on the board tacitly acknowledges the absence of facts to support a finding of futility, and the question of whether demand is excused is moot. *Abrams v. Koether, 1992 U.S. Dist. LEXIS 16295 (D.N.J. 1992).*

In a demand-excused case, the plaintiff-shareholder must plead with particularity facts to create a reasonable doubt as to the directors' disinterestedness or independence, or whether the directors exercised proper business judgment. A reasonable doubt as to the directors' independence may be created by alleging facts demonstrating that the directors are dominated or otherwise controlled by one interested in the transaction, or that the board is "so under his influence that its discretion is sterilized." The directors must be disinterested to gain protection of the business judgment rule, i.e., they cannot appear on both sides of a transaction or expect to derive any personal financial benefit from it. *Abrams v. Koether, 1992 U.S. Dist. LEXIS 16295 (D.N.J. 1992).*

Demand is also excused where the plaintiff pleads with particularity that the directors failed to exercise proper business judgment. Proper business judgment is the exercise of substantive due care (fairness in the terms of the transaction) and procedural due care (making an informed decision). Due care is absent where the directors make an uninformed or undeliberated decision, or where the directors reach a decision in which the terms are so inadequate that no person of ordinary business judgment would assent to them (such as corporate waste). *Abrams v. Koether, 1992 U.S. Dist. LEXIS 16295 (D.N.J. 1992).*

Demand futility. — Delaware law excuses demand as futile where facts are pleaded with sufficient particularity to create a reasonable doubt that the directors are disinterested and independent, or that the challenged transaction was otherwise the product of a valid exercise of business judgment. Where the allegations of a complaint raise a reasonable doubt as to the disinterestedness of the directors, demand is excused and the court does not proceed to the second part of the test. *Abrams v. Koether, 1992 U.S. Dist. LEXIS 16295 (D.N.J. 1992).*

Under Delaware law, the decision to bring a lawsuit or to refrain from litigating a claim on behalf of the corpora-

tion is a decision concerning the management of the corporation and consequently is the responsibility of the directors. Because the derivative action impinges on the managerial freedom of directors, the demand requirement exists at the threshold, first to insure that a stockholder exhausts his or her intracorporate remedies, and then to provide a safeguard against strike suits. Demand may be excused if futile. *In re Cendant Corp. Derivative Action Litigation, 96 F. Supp. 2d 394 (D.N.J. 2000).*

Futility is determined by looking to the composition of the board at the time the derivative action claim is asserted. *In re Cendant Corp. Derivative Action Litigation, 96 F. Supp. 2d 394 (D.N.J. 2000).*

In determining the sufficiency of a complaint to withstand demand futility, the trial court is confronted with two questions: whether threshold presumptions of director disinterest or independence are rebutted by well-pleaded facts; and, if not, whether the complaint pleads particularized facts sufficient to create a reasonable doubt that the challenged transaction was the product of a valid exercise of business judgment. The entire review is factual in nature, and in order for demand to be excused, the trial court must be satisfied that a plaintiff has alleged facts with particularity which, taken as true, support a reasonable doubt as to a director's interest or independence or that the challenged transaction was the product of a valid exercise of business judgment. In its determination, the trial court must not rely on any one factor but must examine the totality of the circumstances and consider all of the relevant factors. *In re Cendant Corp. Derivative Action Litigation, 189 F.R.D. 117 (D.N.J. 1999).*

With regard to demand futility in a shareholder's derivative action, the court reviews the factual allegations of the complaint to determine whether they create a reasonable doubt as to the disinterestedness and independence of the directors at the time the complaint was filed. If the transaction at issue is an "interested" director transaction, such that the business judgment rule is inapplicable to the board majority approving the transaction, then the inquiry ceases. Directorial interest exists whenever divided loyalties are present, or where the director stands to receive a personal benefit from the transaction not equally shared by the shareholders. A director is also interested when a corporate decision will have a materially detrimental impact on a director. Directorial independence requires a director's decision to be based on the corporate merits of the subject before the board rather than extraneous considerations or influences. *In re Cendant Corp. Derivative Action Litigation, 189 F.R.D. 117 (D.N.J. 1999).*

Pertaining to a shareholder derivative suit, when no demand is made on the board, the stockholder must plead particularized facts as to why demand would have been futile. Futility in this context does not mean that there is no likelihood that a board will agree to the demand. Rather, demand is futile where a reasonable doubt exists that the board has the ability to exercise its managerial power, in relation to the decision to prosecute, within the strictures of its fiduciary obligations. If the board's disability as to a particular transaction is attributable to self-interest or lack of independence, then presuit demand is not required. *Coyer v. Hemmer, 901 F. Supp. 872 (D.N.J. 1995).*

Pertaining to Delaware's demand futility test, control will not be presumed merely because one is a majority shareholder. It is not enough to charge that a director was nominated by or elected at the behest of those controlling the outcome of a corporate election. It is the care, attention, and sense of individual responsibility to the performance of one's duties, not the method of election, that generally touches upon independence. *Coyer v. Hemmer, 901 F. Supp. 872 (D.N.J. 1995).*

Under Delaware law, the rule that a shareholder must make a demand upon a corporation's directors before initiating a derivative suit, unless such demand would be futile, is more than mere pleading; it is a substantive right. Notice pleading is not enough. Generalities, artistically ambiguous, all-encompassing conclusory allegations are not enough. What is required are pleadings that are specific and, if conclusory, supported by sufficient factual allegations that corroborate the conclusion and support the proposition that demand is futile. *Coyer v. Hemmer, 901 F. Supp. 872 (D.N.J. 1995).*

Under Delaware law, derivative plaintiffs must satisfy one of two tests to establish that demand is excused. When a plaintiff's claims arise from an affirmative business decision made by a corporation's board of directors, courts apply the two-prong *Aronson* test laid. Under the *Aronson* test, courts will excuse pre-suit demand if the complaint alleges, with particularity, sufficient facts to create a reasonable doubt that (1) the majority of the directors are disinterested and independent, or (2) the challenged transaction is otherwise the product of the directors' valid exercise of business judgment. If either prong is satisfied, demand is excused. *Amalgamated Bank v. Yost, 2005 U.S. Dist. LEXIS 1280 (E.D.Pa. 2005).*

When a derivative plaintiff does not challenge an affirmative business decision, Delaware courts employ the modified *Rales* test. Under the *Rales* test, courts will excuse pre-suit demand if the complaint makes particularized factual allegations that create a reasonable doubt that the board of directors could have properly exercised its independent and disinterested business judgment in response to a demand. *Amalgamated Bank v. Yost, 2005 U.S. Dist. LEXIS 1280 (E.D.Pa. 2005).*

Delaware courts perform demand futility analysis for each separate claim in a derivative suit. *Amalgamated Bank v. Yost, 2005 U.S. Dist. LEXIS 1280 (E.D.Pa. 2005).*

Under the first prong of Delaware's *Aronson*'s test, a derivative plaintiff seeking to excuse demand must use particularized facts to create a reasonable doubt that the directors are disinterested and independent. To satisfy its burden, a plaintiff must show that at least half of the board was either interested or not independent. Directors are interested when they appear on both sides of a challenged transaction or expect to derive a personal financial benefit from a transaction that is not shared by stockholders generally. *Amalgamated Bank v. Yost, 2005 U.S. Dist. LEXIS 1280 (E.D.Pa. 2005).*

Director independence. — In Delaware, neither mere personal friendships alone, nor mere outside business relationships alone, are sufficient to raise a reasonable doubt regarding a director's independence for purposes of excusing pre-suit demand in a derivative action. *Amalgamated Bank v. Yost, 2005 U.S. Dist. LEXIS 1280 (E.D.Pa. 2005).*

In Delaware, allegations that directors are paid for their services, without more, do not establish any financial interest for purposes of excusing pre-suit demand in a derivative action. *Amalgamated Bank v. Yost, 2005 U.S. Dist. LEXIS 1280 (E.D.Pa. 2005).*

In Delaware, a plaintiff charging domination must allege particularized facts; the shorthand shibboleth of dominated and controlled directors is insufficient for purposes of excusing pre-suit demand in a derivative action. *Amalgamated Bank v. Yost, 2005 U.S. Dist. LEXIS 1280 (E.D.Pa. 2005).*

A controlling director's involvement in selecting each of the directors is insufficient to create a reasonable doubt about their independence for purposes of excusing pre-suit demand in a derivative action. *Amalgamated Bank v. Yost, 2005 U.S. Dist. LEXIS 1280 (E.D.Pa. 2005).*

Even if a plaintiff fails to create a reasonable doubt about the board's independence, a court will excuse the demand requirement if a plaintiff raises a reasonable doubt that the directors exercised proper business judgment in the transaction. Even if directors appear disinterested and independent, if they acted illegally in approving a transaction, their interest in avoiding personal liability automatically and absolutely disqualifies them from passing on a shareholder's demand. *Amalgamated Bank v. Yost, 2005 U.S. Dist. LEXIS 1280 (E.D.Pa. 2005).*

The majority of the board must be "interested", i.e., on both sides of a transaction or receiving personal financial benefit from the transaction which did not devolve on the shareholders generally. In addition, the board is not disinterested where it has divided loyalties. Conclusory allegations are insufficient to create the requisite reasonable doubt. Nor can a plaintiff employ a "bootstrap" argument that demand is excused by alleging that the directors would otherwise have to sue themselves to create the requisite reasonable doubt. Moreover, mere approval of the allegedly injurious transaction does not incapacitate a board for purposes of considering a demand under demand futility analysis. *Abrams v. Koether, 1992 U.S. Dist. LEXIS 16295 (D.N.J. 1992).*

Under the *Cinerama* formulation for determining if the interest of one or more directors was material to the independence of the entire board, a complaint fails to rebut the business judgment rule unless it alleges facts from which one could infer that the director defendants, through their dominance over the other board members, so infected or affected the deliberative process of the board as to disarm the board of its presumption of regularity and respect. *In re Cendant Corp. Derivative Action Litigation, 189 F.R.D. 117 (D.N.J. 1999).*

Removal of business judgment presumption. — Delaware law does not authorize the automatic removal of the business judgment presumption from every considered decision of a company owned by a controlling shareholder. The presumption is removed only when the corporation affirmatively deals with the controlling shareholder or one of its controlled entities. *In re Cendant Corp. Derivative Action Litigation, 189 F.R.D. 117 (D.N.J. 1999).*

Under Delaware law, the independence of the majority of the board must be challenged to strip the individual directors of the business judgment presumption. *In re Cendant Corp. Derivative Action Litigation, 189 F.R.D. 117 (D.N.J. 1999).*

To rebut the business judgment rule's presumption, a plaintiff has the burden of coming forward with evidence sufficient to show that the board breached its duty of care, breached its duty of loyalty, or abused its discretion. That burden of production is difficult to carry; a court will not substitute its judgment for that of a board if the latter's decision can be attributed to any rational business purpose. *Gregory v. Correction Connection, Inc., 1991 U.S. Dist. LEXIS 3659 (E.D.Pa. 1991).*

If a board satisfies its burden of proof under both prongs of a threshold judicial analysis, the presumption of the business judgment rule takes effect, and the burden of proof shifts to the plaintiff to rebut the presumption by showing by a preponderance of the evidence that the directors' decisions were: (1) motivated by a lack of good faith, (2) made without adequate information, (3) primarily based on perpetuating themselves in office, or (4) either fraudulent or characterized by overreaching. Absent such a showing, a court will not substitute its judgment for that of the board. *Gregory v. Correction Connection, Inc., 1991 U.S. Dist. LEXIS 3659 (E.D.Pa. 1991).*

Standing. — Delaware law requires that a derivative action plaintiff must be a shareholder both at the time of the alleged wrong and at the time of suit. The only exceptions to this rule are: (a) where the merger itself is the subject of a claim of fraud, i.e., where the merger was perpetrated to derive the merged corporation of its claim; or (b) where the merger is in reality a reorganization which does not affect plaintiff's ownership of the business enterprise. The second exception is limited to a merger which is merely a share for share merger with a newly formed holding company, which retained the old company a wholly owned subsidiary of the new holding company with the shareholders of the old company owning all the shares of the new holding company. The structure of the old and new companies is virtually identical. *Kanbar v. U.S. Healthcare, Inc., 1989 U.S. Dist. LEXIS 13474 (E.D.Pa. 1989).*

Under Delaware law, in the context of a corporate merger, a derivative shareholder must not only be a stockholder at the time of the alleged wrong and at time of commencement of suit but that he or she must also maintain shareholder status throughout the litigation. *Amalgamated Bank v. Yost, 2005 U.S. Dist. LEXIS 1280 (E.D.Pa. 2005).*

Under Delaware law an equitable or beneficial owner is permitted to maintain a derivative action. *Murdock v. Follansbee Steel Corp., 213 F.2d 570 (3d Cir. 1954).*

Derivative versus individual claim. — To determine whether a complaint states a derivative or an individual cause of action, the court must look to the nature of the wrongs alleged in the body of the complaint, not to the plaintiff's designation or stated intention. Delaware courts have long recognized that actions charging mismanagement which depress the value of the stock allege a wrong to the corporation, i.e., the shareholders collectively, to be enforced by a derivative action. A claim of mismanagement resulting in corporate waste, if proven, represents a direct wrong to the corporation that is indirectly experienced by all shareholders. Any devaluation of stock is shared collectively by all the shareholders, rather than independently by the plaintiff or any other individual shareholder. A plaintiff alleges a special injury and may maintain an individual action only if he complains of an injury distinct from that suffered by other shareholders or a wrong involving one of his or her contractual rights as a shareholder. *Furst v. Feinberg, 2002 U.S. App. LEXIS 26174 (3d Cir. 2002).*

Waste. — In Delaware, a shareholder's allegations that a board of directors committed waste by authorizing the issuance of stock for inadequate consideration are derivative in nature. Waste of corporate assets injures the corporation itself. On the other hand, when it is alleged that a board issued stock with the primary and wrongful intent of entrenching itself, and when the consideration paid for such stock is not the basis for allegations of waste, an individual action lies to the extent that the alleged entrenching activity directly impairs some right the plaintiff possesses as a shareholder. *Gregory v. Correction Connection, Inc., 1991 U.S. Dist. LEXIS 3659 (E.D.Pa. 1991).*

Merger. — In order to state a direct claim with respect to a merger, a stockholder must challenge the validity of the merger itself, usually by charging the directors with breaches of fiduciary duty resulting in unfair dealing and/or unfair price. *Furst v. Feinberg, 2002 U.S. App. LEXIS 26174 (3d Cir. 2002).*

Rales **analysis.** — Although the analysis under *Rales* requires only a singular inquiry, it nonetheless embodies the concerns relevant to both the first and second prongs of *Aronson*. For example, where a complaint alleges self dealing by three members of a seven member board, the *Rales* inquiry, like the first prong of *Aronson*, will focus on whether the remaining four directors would be able to act independently of the three interested directors. However, when a complaint alleges wrongful conduct by a majority of the board the court must address the same concerns considered by the second prong of *Aronson*. Accordingly, if the directors will face a substantial likelihood of personal liability, their ability to impartially consider a demand under *Rales* would be compromised. It is against this procedural and substantive framework that the Court will address the parties' arguments. *In re Merck & Co., Inc. Derivative & ERISA Litig., 2006 U.S. Dist. LEXIS 27861 (D.N.J. May 5, 2006).*

Self-dealing. — Receipt of a bonus, the size of which is tied to the overall profitability of the corporation does not substantiate a claim of self-dealing absent a specific allegation that the voting of the bonuses themselves or the calculation thereof, involved some form of self-dealing. *In re Merck & Co., Inc. Derivative & ERISA Litig., 2006 U.S. Dist. LEXIS 27861 (D.N.J. May 5, 2006).*

Insider trading. — Although the proceeds defendants received from stock sales seem substantial, the allegations in the complaint are insufficient to create an inference of insider trading. Plaintiffs do not provide particularized facts as to what percentage of each defendants overall stock ownership the sales represent. Likewise, the complaint fails to specify the directors' previous trading practices or whether defendant imposed restrictions on the timing of director trading. Plaintiffs have failed to allege any particularized facts tying even a single stock sale to specific adverse non-public information in the possession of these directors. *In re Merck & Co., Inc. Derivative & ERISA Litig., 2006 U.S. Dist. LEXIS 27861 (D.N.J. May 5, 2006).*

Ignoring safety risks. — Plaintiffs contend that the directors' alleged disregard of known risks associated with the use of Vioxx constitutes egregious conduct and actions in bad faith. Ignoring safety risks can be more easily characterized as "egregious" where the information lies in the hand of those officers involved in actually running the corporation on a day to day basis, as opposed to a group of predominantly outside directors with little involvement in the operations of the corporation. Second, there is a significant difference between the safety warnings given to the officers in *Tower Air,* and those allegedly before defendant's board. The safety information provided to the officers in *Tower Air* revealed documented problems with aircraft maintenance and repair work. These reports were unquestionably negative and illustrated serious risks to public safety. Here, plaintiffs' own allegations assert that defendants approved and monitored Merck's marketing and sales plans despite receiving a body of scientific evidence which questioned the cardiovascular risk safety of Vioxx. Plaintiffs have, therefore, failed to allege particularized facts that would suggest that the directors' conduct was "egregious," or in bad faith. *In re Merck & Co., Inc. Derivative & ERISA Litig., 2006 U.S. Dist. LEXIS 27861 (D.N.J. May 5, 2006).*

Fund injuries. — The first two forms of alleged injury — payment of excessive distribution and advisory fees out of fund assets — are derivative in nature. That is, the injury they allegedly caused fund shareholders (depletion of fund assets) is indistinguishable from injury they caused the funds themselves: the mere fact that fund assets ultimately belong to the fund shareholders does not render depletion of those assets injury suffered by shareholders that is distinct from injury suffered by the funds. The same may be said with regard to the third form of injury — diminished marginal returns on shareholder investment — allegedly caused by broker compensation practices: this injury is indistinguishable from injury to the funds themselves, as each investor's diminished marginal return on investment is merely a reflection of the funds' overall diminished performance. *In re Lord Abbett Mut. Funds Fee Litig., 2005 U.S. Dist. LEXIS 37492 (D.N.J. Dec. 28, 2005).*

Potential liability from other, unrelated litigation would not make directors interested in the decision to consider a demand for this specific derivative suit. For example, if directors were faced with damages from an ERISA suit, and if plaintiffs made demand on the board for an unrelated claim, it is unlikely that the specter of the ERISA damages would so worry the directors as to cause them to reject plaintiffs' demand. Were that to be the standard for directors' interest, any possible future litigation could serve to create demand futility. Judgment counsels against such an open-ended course and its unintended consequences; thus district court's opinion as to plaintiff's not establishing demand futility was upheld. *Fagin v. Gilmartin, 432 F.3d 276 (3rd Cir. December 15, 2005).*

Fourth Circuit

Demand generally. — It is a cardinal precept of the Delaware General Corporation Law that directors, rather than shareholders, manage the business and affairs of the corporation. Because by its very nature the derivative action impinges upon the managerial freedom of directors, strict demand requirements are imposed. In situations where derivative plaintiffs are attacking an affirmative business decision made by the board, a court of chancery in the proper exercise of its discretion must decide whether, under the particularized facts alleged, a reasonable doubt is created that: (1) the directors are disinterested and independent and (2) the challenged transaction was otherwise the product of a valid exercise of business judgment. Further, a derivative plaintiff must establish that a majority of the board is interested or lacks independence in order to excuse demand on that ground. *In re Mut. Funds Investent Litigation, 2005 U.S. Dist. LEXIS 18082 (D.Md. 2005).*

The test for determining whether demand is excused in a derivative action is disjunctive, because demand is excused if a plaintiff has pleaded facts raising a reasonable doubt either that a majority of the members of the board are not disinterested or independent, or that the challenged decision was not otherwise a product of a valid exercise of business judgment. *In re Mut. Funds Investent Litigation, 2005 U.S. Dist. LEXIS 18082 (D.Md. 2005).*

In cases where derivative plaintiffs are not challenging an affirmative decision made by the present board, a modified test for whether demand is excused applies to cases in which the board is charged with a failure of oversight. Under the modified test, a court is to determine (in addition to making an appropriate inquiry under the first prong of the test) whether or not the particularized factual allegations of a derivative stockholder complaint create a reasonable doubt that, as of the time the complaint is filed, the board of directors could have properly exercised its independent and disinterested business judgment in responding to a demand. *In re Mut. Funds Investent Litigation, 2005 U.S. Dist. LEXIS 18082 (D.Md. 2005).*

Effect of indemnification provision. — While Delaware courts have allowed dismissal of a complaint for failure to make a pre-suit demand when the pleadings alleged solely a violation of the fiduciary duty of care on the grounds that the claim was barred by the corporation's exculpatory provision in its charter, indemnification provisions in corporate governing documents issued pursuant to Del. Code Ann. tit. 8, § 102(b)(7) cannot be invoked to bar duty of loyalty and good-faith claims. Thus, where the complaint alleges well-pleaded facts that implicate the duty of loyalty and good faith, as well as the duty of care, the indemnification provision will not subject the complaint to dismissal. *Miller v. U.S. Foodservice, Inc., 361 F. Supp. 2d 470 (D.Md. 2005).*

Fifth Circuit

Under Delaware law, a derivative action is an action brought by one or more shareholders or members to enforce a right of a corporation or of an unincorporated association. If a stockholder complains of an indirect injury sustained as a result of a wrong done to the corporation, such action will be treated as a derivative action. Any devaluation of stock is shared collectively by all the shareholders, rather than independently by an individual shareholder; therefore, the wrong is entirely derivative in nature. *H.I.G. P-Xi Holding, Inc., 2001 U.S. Dist. LEXIS 5074 (E.D.La. 2001).*

In a derivative action, Delaware courts often apply the business judgment rule, a rebuttable presumption that directors do not breach their duty of care. Only a disinterested corporate director can assert the business judgment rule as a defense to a derivative action. A disinterested director is a director who has not appeared on both sides of a business transaction and who has not received a personal financial benefit from the transaction. *H.I.G. P-Xi Holding, Inc., 2001 U.S. Dist. LEXIS 5074 (E.D.La. 2001).*

Standing. — To bring a derivative action, stockholder status at the time of the transaction being attacked and during the entire litigation is essential. For purposes of a derivative action, an equitable owner is considered a stockholder. On the other hand, debenture holders are not considered stockholders by Delaware courts. Holders of convertible debentures are creditors of a corporation and do not have standing to maintain a stockholder's derivative action under Delaware law. Similarly, a holder of an option to purchase stock is not considered an equitable owner. *H.I.G. P-Xi Holding, Inc., 2001 U.S. Dist. LEXIS 5074 (E.D.La. 2001).*

Delaware courts have allowed for standing by one director of a charitable corporation against the corporation in situations where warring factions of the board dispute the actions of a corporate board. Directors of charitable corporations have standing to maintain an action on behalf of the corporation for breach of fiduciary duty. As a fiduciary, the trustee of a charitable trust or director of a charitable corporation has a sufficiently concrete interest in the outcome of litigation involving a breach of fiduciary duty to the charitable entity that he or she has standing. *Hand of Help USA v. Hand of Help Romania, 2002 U.S. Dist. LEXIS 3828 (N.D.Tex 2002).*

Under Delaware law, the corporation is an adverse party in a stockholders' derivative action.

Although a derivative suit is asserted by a stockholder on behalf of the corporation, it is also a suit by a stockholder to compel the corporation to sue, and the corporation is a nominal defendant. *H.I.G. P-Xi Holding, Inc., 2001 U.S. Dist. LEXIS 5074 (E.D.La. 2001).*

Unfair actions or breaches of corporate duties are usually challenged by shareholders in derivative actions because the directors who abused their positions are unlikely to sue themselves. Under Delaware law, a corporation can, however, sue its directors for breaches of corporate duties. *H.I.G. P-Xi Holding, Inc., 2001 U.S. Dist. LEXIS 5074 (E.D.La. 2001).*

Under the business judgment rule, plaintiffs in a derivative action have the burden of showing that the defendants acted without the requisite due care or in bad faith or disloyally, failing to exercise reasonable business judgment. It is a very difficult standard. *Cohn v. Nelson, 375 F. Supp. 2d 844 (E.D.Miss. 2005).*

To prove a violation of the "duty to monitor" in a derivative action, a plaintiff must plead and prove facts that demonstrate a sustained or systematic failure of the board to exercise oversight — such an utter failure to attempt to assure a reasonable information and reporting system exists. Liability is premised on a showing that the directors were conscious of the fact that they were not doing their jobs. This is a difficult standard to allege, let alone prove on summary judgment or at trial. *Cohn v. Nelson, 375 F. Supp. 2d 844 (E.D.Miss. 2005).*

Under Delaware law, the distinction between derivative and direct actions depends upon whether the individual shareholder or the corporation as a whole is directly injured by the alleged wrongdoing. When the corporation as a whole is injured, a derivative action permits an individual stockholder to bring suit on behalf of the corporation provided the shareholder has first made a demand on the board of directors to take remedial action. However, if a stockholder can demonstrate injury distinct from that suffered by the corporation, no pre-suit demand is required, and he may pursue relief in a direct action. The Delaware Supreme Court has recently clarified that standard and has stated that in order to assert a direct action, the stockholder must demonstrate that his injury is independent of any alleged injury to the corporation. That is, the stockholder must show that the duty breached was owed to the stockholder and that he or she can prevail without showing an injury to the corporation. *Hogan v. Baker, 2005 U.S. Dist. LEXIS 16888 (N.D.Tex. 2005).*

Under Delaware law, a shareholder may sue on his or her own behalf or derivatively, on behalf of the corporation. The distinction between derivative and individual actions rests upon the party being directly injured by the alleged wrongdoing. Shareholders may bring direct actions for injuries done to them in their individual capacities by corporate fiduciaries. Recovery in these individual actions goes to the suing shareholders. Thus, to have standing to sue individually, rather than derivatively on behalf of the corporation, the plaintiff must allege an injury that is separate and distinct from that suffered by other shareholders. In other words, for a plaintiff to have standing to bring an individual action, he or she must be injured directly or independently of the corporation. *Kunzweiler v. Zero.net, Inc., 2002 U.S. Dist. LEXIS 12080 (N.D.Tex. 2002).*

Whether a cause of action is individual or derivative must be determined from the nature of the wrong alleged and the relief, if any, that could result if the plaintiff were to prevail. In determining the nature of the wrong alleged, a court must look to the body of the complaint, not to the plaintiff's designation or stated intention. *Kunzweiler v. Zero.net, Inc., 2002 U.S. Dist. LEXIS 12080 (N.D.Tex. 2002).*

Where a shareholder's complaint articulates a cause of action that is both individual and derivative, the shareholder may proceed with the individual action. *Southdown, Inc. v. Moore McCormack Resources, Inc., 686 F. Supp. 595 (S.D.Tex. 1988).*

A shareholder may not personally recover damages for a wrong done solely to the corporation, even though the shareholder may be injured by that wrong. To recover individually, a stockholder must prove a personal cause of action and personal injury. Injuries suffered by the corporation which merely result in the depreciation of the value of shareholders' stock do not give shareholders a separate and independent right of action. *King v. Douglass, 973 F. Supp. 707 (S.D.Tex. 1996).*

Under Delaware law, one looks to the nature of the wrongs alleged in the body of the complaint, and not to a plaintiff's designation or stated intention, to determine whether a cause of action is a personal one asserted by a shareholder or by a number of plaintiffs a class action, or a derivative one. An individual or class action may be maintained only when the shareholder plaintiffs have been injured directly, rather than indirectly through harm to the corporation. The test to distinguish between derivative and individual harm is whether the plaintiffs have suffered a "special injury," i.e., an injury distinct from that suffered by all shareholders generally or one involving the shareholder's contractual rights, such as the right to vote. *King v. Douglass, 973 F. Supp. 707 (S.D.Tex. 1996).*

The distinction between derivative and individual actions rests upon the party being directly injured by the alleged wrongdoing. To have standing to sue individually, rather than derivatively on behalf of the corporation, the plaintiff must allege more than an injury resulting from a wrong to the corporation. For a plaintiff to have standing to bring an individual action, he or she must be injured directly or independently of the corporation. An alleged wrong involving a corporation is individual in nature when it injures the shareholders directly or independently of the corporation. A wrong is derivative in nature when it injures the shareholders indirectly and dependently through direct injury to the corporation. *King v. Douglass, 973 F. Supp. 707 (S.D.Tex. 1996).*

Delaware courts characterize suits alleging mismanagement that depresses the value of stock as a wrong to the corporation or stockholders collectively that should be enforced by a derivative action. Any devaluation of the stock is shared collectively by the shareholders, rather than independently by the plaintiff or other individual shareholder. Thus the wrong alleged is entirely derivative in nature. *King v. Douglass, 973 F. Supp. 707 (S.D.Tex. 1996).*

The Delaware Supreme Court discarded the "special injury" test and in its place articulated the following test for determining whether a claim is derivative or direct: The analysis must be based solely on the following questions: Who suffered the alleged harm — the corporation or the suing stockholder individually — and who would receive the benefit of the recovery or other remedy? According to the Delaware Supreme Court, this approach is to be applied henceforth in determining whether a stockholder's claim is derivative or direct. Smith v.Waste Management Inc., 407 F.3d 381 (5th Cir. 2005).

In determining whether a stockholder's claim is derivative or direct in Delaware, the proper analysis has been and should remain that a court should look to the nature of the wrong and to whom the relief should go. The stockholder's claimed direct injury must be independent of any alleged injury to the corporation. The stockholder must demonstrate that the duty breached was owed to the stockholder and that he or she can prevail without showing an injury to the corporation. *Smith v. Waste Management Inc., 407 F.3d 381 (5th Cir. 2005).*

Under Delaware law, fundholders may bring a derivative suit to obtain relief for breaches of fiduciary duty directors and officers owe the corporation. An individual cause of action exists only if damages to the shareholders were not incidental to damages to the corporation. Further, a claim of mismanagement, resulting in a devaluation of stock, represents a direct wrong to the corporation that is indirectly experienced by all shareholders. *Hogan v. Baker, 2005 U.S. Dist. LEXIS 16888 (N.D.Tex. 2005).*

Demand requirement. — Where the corporation is a Delaware corporation, the substantive corporation law of Delaware determines whether or not the demand requirements of Fed. R. Civ. P. 23.1 have been satisfied. Delaware law requires a stockholder to make a demand on the board of directors to pursue the corporate claim, or to show why demand is excused because the directors are incapable of making an impartial decision regarding such litigation. *Spector v. Sidhu, 2004 U.S. Dist. LEXIS 876 (N.D.Tex. 2004).*

Delaware law requires a stockholder to make a demand on the board of directors **to** pursue the corporate claim because directors are empowered to manage, or direct the management of, the business and affairs of the corporation. *Kaltman v. Sidhu, 2004 U.S. Dist. LEXIS 2818 (N.D. Tex. 2004).*

In the context of Fed. R. Civ. P. 23.1, under Delaware law, the *Rales* test is employed where directors are sued because they have failed to do something; demand should not be excused automatically in the absence of allegations demonstrating why the board is incapable of considering a demand. The court must consider whether the particularized factual allegations of a derivative stockholder complaint create a reasonable doubt that, as of the time the complaint is filed, the board of directors could have properly exercised its independent and disinterested business judgment in responding to a demand. To create a doubt that the board of directors could exercise its independent and disinterested business judgment, the plaintiff would need to allege with particularity facts that create a reasonable doubt that the board is capable of acting free from personal financial interest and improper extraneous influences. *Spector v. Sidhu, 2004 U.S. Dist. LEXIS 876 (N.D.Tex. 2004).*

A director is considered interested where he or she will receive a personal financial benefit from a transaction that is not equally shared by the stockholders, or where a corporate decision will have a materially detrimental impact on a director, but not on the corporation and the stockholders. To establish lack of independence, plaintiff must show that the directors are beholden to the interested director or so under his influence that their discretion would be sterilized. *Kaltman v. Sidhu, 2004 U.S. Dist. LEXIS 2818 (N.D. Tex. 2004).*

The mere threat of personal liability for approving a questioned transaction, standing alone, is insufficient to challenge either the independence or disinterestedness of directors. Only when the potential for liability rises from a mere threat of personal liability to a substantial likelihood of personal liability will directors be considered interested. *Kaltman v. Sidhu, 2004 U.S. Dist. LEXIS 2818 (N.D. Tex. 2004).*

The mere fact that the board has elected not to sue before the derivative action was filed should not of itself indicate interestedness. It is the board's inaction in most every case which is the raison d'etre for Fed. R. Civ. P. 23.1. *Kaltman v. Sidhu, 2004 U.S. Dist. LEXIS 2818 (N.D. Tex. 2004).*

Under Delaware law, the mere threat of personal liability for approving a questioned transaction, standing alone, is insufficient to challenge either the independence or disinterestedness of directors. Only when the potential for liability rises from a mere threat of personal liability to a substantial likelihood of personal liability will directors be considered interested. *Spector v. Sidhu, 2004 U.S. Dist. LEXIS 876 (N.D.Tex. 2004).*

Under Delaware law, to establish a lack of independence, plaintiffs must show that the outside directors are "beholden" to the interested directors or so under their influence that their discretion would be sterilized. Plaintiffs must allege particularized facts manifesting a direction of corporate conduct in such a way as to comport with the wishes or interests of the corporation (or persons) doing the controlling. *Spector v. Sidhu, 2004 U.S. Dist. LEXIS 876 (N.D.Tex. 2004).*

Under Delaware law, the mere fact that the board has elected not to sue before the derivative action was filed should not of itself indicate "interestedness." It is the board's inaction in most every case which is the raison d'etre from Fed. R. Civ. P. 23.1. *Spector v. Sidhu, 2004 U.S. Dist. LEXIS 876 (N.D.Tex. 2004).*

The mere existence of an "insured vs. insured" exclusion clause in the directors' and officers' liability insurance coverage, without more, is insufficient to excuse demand.

Spector v. Sidhu, 2004 U.S. Dist. LEXIS 876 (N.D.Tex. 2004).

The business judgment rule is a purely defensive rule, and not a basis for granting a motion to dismiss a stockholders' derivative suit against a corporation and its directors alleging a breach of fiduciary duty when the corporate directors, or a committee thereof, in their collective business judgment, determined that the suit was not in the best interests of the corporation. *Maher v. Zapata Corp., 490 F. Supp. 348 (S.D. Tex. 1980).*

Under Delaware law, when the presumption of the business judgment rule has been rebutted, the burden shifts to the defendants to demonstrate the unfairness of the board's action. The concept of fairness has two basic aspects: fair dealing and fair price. The former embraces questions of when the transaction was timed, how it was initiated, structured, negotiated, disclosed to the directors, and how the approvals of the directors and the stockholders were obtained. The latter aspect of fairness relates to the economic and financial considerations of the proposed transaction, including all relevant factors. The test for fairness is not a bifurcated one as between fair dealing and price. All aspects of the issue must be examined as a whole since the question is one of entire fairness. *King v. Douglass, 973 F. Supp. 707 (S.D.Tex. 1996).*

A plaintiff-shareholder must overcome the presumptions of the business judgment rule, when it is asserted by a defendant, before they will be permitted to pursue derivative claims. The business judgment rule requires the trial court to presume that directors have acted in good faith and in the honest belief that their actions served the corporation's best interest. *King v. Douglass, 973 F. Supp. 707 (S.D.Tex. 1996).*

Ordinarily, the business judgment rule provides a presumption that in making a business decision the directors of a corporation acted only after they were appropriately informed and after they had honestly determined that the action taken was in the best interests of the company. Because contests for control have an omnipresent specter that a board may be acting primarily in its own interests, the directors have an enhanced duty to prove that they had reasonable grounds for believing that a danger to corporate policy and effectiveness existed because of another person's stock ownership. *Southdown, Inc. v. Moore McCormack Resources, Inc., 686 F. Supp. 595 (S.D.Tex. 1988).*

Direct claims found. — Allegations that (1) the majority owners of the company failed to provide the minority members the same information on which to make the investment decision, and that, lacking any expectation of significant future work, the plaintiffs did not invest in the financing round and their shares were thereby diluted and that (2) this misrepresentation was an attempt to wipe out this group of shareholders and seize control of the company for the larger institutional shareholders who were privy to information about this contract appear on their face to be a direct claims under Delaware law, as they all involve controlling shareholders increasing their interests in the company at the expense of a group of minority shareholders. Accordingly, resolving in the insured's favor any doubts as to whether the facts alleged in the underlying petition fall within coverage, the court concludes that these three claims are not derivative claims, and thus the claims are not excluded from coverage as a "derivative action" under the terms of the policy. *Federal Ins. Co. v. Infoglide Corp., 2006 U.S. Dist. LEXIS 53734 (D. Texas July 18, 2006).*

Sixth Circuit

Demand requirement. — Where a conscious decision by corporate directors to act or refrain from acting is made, the demand requirement for a shareholder to bring a derivative action is excused when under the particularized facts alleged, a reasonable doubt is created that: (1) a majority of the directors are disinterested and independent; or (2) the challenged transaction was otherwise the product of a valid exercise of business judgment. Under the first prong, independence requires that a director's decision be based on the corporate merits of the subject before the board rather than extraneous considerations or influences. This standard is satisfied if a majority of the board that was in office at the time of filing was free from personal interest or domination and control, and thus capable of objectively evaluating a demand and, if necessary, remedying the alleged injury. It is no answer to say that demand is necessarily futile because: (a) the directors would have to sue themselves, thereby placing the conduct of the litigation in hostile hands; or (b) that they approved the underlying transaction. *Salsitz v. Nasser, 208 F.R.D. 589 (E.D. Mich. 2002).*

Where a conscious decision by corporate directors to act or refrain from acting is made, the demand requirement for a shareholder to bring a derivative action is excused when under the particularized facts alleged, a reasonable doubt is created that: (1) a majority of the directors are disinterested and independent; or (2) the challenged transaction was otherwise the product of a valid exercise of business judgment. Under the second prong, the business judgment rule provides that whether a judge or jury considering a business decision after the fact, believes a decision substantively wrong, or degrees of wrong extending through stupid to egregious or irrational, provides no ground for director liability, so long as the court determines that the process employed was either rational or employed in a good faith effort to advance corporate interests. Thus, a court may not consider the content of the board decision that leads to corporate loss, apart from consideration of the good faith or rationality of the process employed. *Salsitz v. Nasser, 208 F.R.D. 589 (E.D. Mich. 2002).*

Under Delaware law, a basic premise of corporate governance is that the board of directors manages the affairs of the corporation, not the shareholders. Frequently, derivative suits have challenged the propriety of decisions made by directors pursuant to their managerial authority. In such situations, a shareholder seeking to demonstrate demand futility must either: (1) create a reasonable doubt as to the disinterest and independence of the directors or (2) create a reasonable doubt as to whether the challenged decision was the product of a valid

exercise of the business judgment rule. *In re Concord EFS, Inc. Derivative Litigations., 2004 U.S. Dist. LEXIS 25569 (W.D.Tenn. 2004).*

Under Delaware law, futility of making demand upon a board of directors to file suit on behalf of a corporation must be determined before the action commences, not afterwards. *In re Concord EFS, Inc. Derivative Litigations., 2004 U.S. Dist. LEXIS 25569 (W.D.Tenn. 2004).*

Under the *Rales* test, the court must determine whether or not the particularized factual allegations create a reasonable doubt that, as of the time the complaint was filed, a majority of the board of directors could have properly exercised its independent and disinterested business judgment in responding to a demand. To establish a reasonable doubt, plaintiffs are not required to plead facts that would be sufficient to support a judicial finding of demand futility. Nor must plaintiffs demonstrate a reasonable probability of success on the merits. Whether plaintiffs have alleged facts sufficient to create a reasonable doubt concerning the disinterestedness and independence of a majority of the board must be determined from the accumulation of all the facts taken together. *McCall v. Scott, 239 F.3d 808 (6th Cir. 2001).*

The relevant time period for the inquiry of whether demand is excused upon the allegations of the complaint is the time at which the board rejected the stockholders' demand that the corporation sue certain of its current and/or former directors or officers. Only if a demand is excused as futile do Delaware courts go beyond the pleadings and treat a subsequent defense motion to terminate akin to proceedings on summary judgment or a hybrid summary judgment motion for dismissal. The relevant time period for this inquiry is the time at which the special litigation or other committee of the board decided to seek to terminate the stockholders' derivative suit. *Consumers Power Co. Derivative Litigation, 132 F.R.D. 455 (E.D.Mich. 1990).*

Evidentiary rules. — Facts in existence before derivative claims are filed but not discovered until later, may be considered in determining demand futility. *McCall v. Scott, 239 F.3d 808 (6th Cir. 2001).*

Inaction by the board will not excuse the failure to make a demand because it would deprive the board of the opportunity to be "prodded" into action, which is a fundamental goal of the demand requirement. *McCall v. Scott, 239 F.3d 808 (6th Cir. 2001).*

Powerful presumptions of business judgment rule. — Because derivative suits challenge the propriety of decisions made by directors under their authority, stockholder plaintiffs must overcome the powerful presumptions of the business judgment rule before they will be permitted to pursue the derivative claim. *McCall v. Scott, 239 F.3d 808 (6th Cir. 2001).*

Analysis when business judgment rule inapplicable. — Infrequently, a derivative suit will be filed where there is no conscious decision by the directors to act or refrain from acting. Such lack of decision by the board makes it impossible to apply the business judgment rule. In these situations, it is appropriate to examine whether the board that would be addressing the demand can impartially consider its merits without being influenced by improper considerations. *In re Concord EFS, Inc. Derivative Litigations., 2004 U.S. Dist. LEXIS 25569 (W.D.Tenn. 2004).*

Need for particularized facts. — Under Delaware law, shareholder plaintiffs cannot merely posit, without any particularized facts, that individual corporate management defendants knew of, or directly participated in, the allegedly material misstatements. *In re Concord EFS, Inc. Derivative Litigations., 2004 U.S. Dist. LEXIS 25569 (W.D.Tenn. 2004).*

To excuse demand on grounds of corporate waste, shareholder plaintiffs must allege particularized facts that the consideration received by the corporation was so inadequate that no person of ordinary sound business judgment would deem it worth that which the corporation has paid. *In re Concord EFS, Inc. Derivative Litigations., 2004 U.S. Dist. LEXIS 25569 (W.D.Tenn. 2004).*

Failure of oversight. — Where plaintiff shareholders allege ignorance of liability-creating activities by individual corporate management defendants, only a sustained or systematic failure of the board to exercise oversight, such as an utter failure to attempt to assure a reasonable information and reporting system exists, will establish the lack of good faith that is a necessary condition to liability. Only through gross negligence may a director be found to have breached the duty of care. *In re Concord EFS, Inc. Derivative Litigations., 2004 U.S. Dist. LEXIS 25569 (W.D.Tenn. 2004).*

Standing. — Whether a plaintiff maintains standing to pursue a shareholder derivative action under the Delaware corporation statutes is an issue of statutory standing. *Prince v. Palmer, 2005 U.S. App. LEXIS 14239 (6th Cir. 2005).*

In the seminal *Anderson* case, the Delaware Supreme Court, interpreting relevant statutory provisions of the Delaware Corporation Law, held that in order to maintain standing, a derivative shareholder must not only be a stockholder at the time of the alleged wrong and at time of commencement of suit but that he must also maintain shareholder status throughout the litigation. That court further clarified that a plaintiff who ceases to be a shareholder, whether by reason of a merger or for any other reason, loses standing to continue a derivative suit. That court recognized but two narrow exceptions to the continuing ownership requirement for standing: (1) where the merger itself is the subject of a claim of fraud, and (2) where the merger is in reality a reorganization which does not affect plaintiff's ownership of the business enterprise. *Prince v. Palmer, 2005 U.S. App. LEXIS 14239 (6th Cir. 2005).*

The *Anderson* reorganization exception does not apply to two distinct corporations, each with its own board of directors, officers, assets and stockholders, whose merger was far more than a corporate reshuffling, and which resulted in plaintiffs' possessing property interests distinctly different from that which they held as shareholders of the old corporation. *Prince v. Palmer, 2005 U.S. App. LEXIS 14239 (6th Cir. 2005).*

A director is considered interested when, for example, he or she will receive a personal financial benefit from a transaction that is not equally shared by the stockholders, or when a corporate decision will have a materially detrimental impact on a director but not the corporation or its stockholders. While the mere threat of personal liability is not sufficient, reasonable doubt as to the disinterestedness of a director is created when the particularized allegations in the complaint present "a substantial likelihood" of liability on the part of a director. *McCall v. Scott, 239 F.3d 808 (6th Cir. 2001).*

Seventh Circuit

Illinois case law follows Delaware case law in determining the proper tests for demand futility. *McSparran v. Larson, 2006 U.S. Dist. LEXIS 53773 (D. Ill. May 3, 2006).*

A wrong to the corporation. — Stockholder actions charging mismanagement which depresses the value of stock allege a wrong to the corporation, i.e., the stockholders collectively, to be enforced by a derivative action. *Lynch v. Marklin of America, Inc., 724 F. Supp. 595 (N.D.Ill. 1989).*

Plaintiff shareholders typically bring claims of corporate mismanagement as derivative actions because no shareholder suffers a harm independent of that visited upon the corporation and other shareholders. *Miller v. Loucks, 1992 U.S. Dist. LEXIS 16966 (N.D.Ill. 1992).*

Under Delaware law, the "time of the challenged transaction" for purposes of Del. Code Ann. tit. 8, § 327 depends on precisely what about the transaction is being challenged. Where the plaintiff in a shareholder's derivative suit complains of the terms, rather than the actual consummation, of a transaction, the "time of the challenged transaction" is when the terms of the transaction are established. *Montgomery v. Aetna Plywood, Inc., 231 F.3d 399 (7th Cir. 2000).*

Standing. — Under Delaware law, an individual has standing to challenge corporate mismanagement only if he or she can allege some "special injury" distinct from that suffered by the corporation and other shareholders. *Miller v. Loucks, 1992 U.S. Dist. LEXIS 16966 (N.D.Ill. 1992).*

In Delaware, in order for an individual to pursue derivative claims, not only must he have been a shareholder of the nominal defendant corporation at the time of the challenged transaction, but he or she must also remain a shareholder at the time of the filing of the suit and throughout the litigation. *In re Gen. Instrument Corp. Securities Litigation, 2000 U.S. Dist. LEXIS 17082 (N.D.Ill. 2000).*

A plaintiff who ceases to be a shareholder, whether by reason of merger or for any other reason, loses standing to continue a derivative suit. *In re Gen. Instrument Corp. Securities Litigation, 2000 U.S. Dist. LEXIS 17082 (N.D.Ill. 2000).*

Termination of shareholder's power. — Under Delaware law, a shareholder's power to bring a derivative action on behalf of the corporation is terminated once a presuit demand has been made and rejected. Thus, just as a corporate board's decisions regarding the routine business transactions of the corporation are accorded great deference under the business judgment rule, its decision not to pursue legal recourse pursuant to a shareholder's complaint is given the same treatment. Following a refused demand, a shareholder can only maintain a derivative action if he or she can demonstrate that the board's decision not to sue was improperly motivated or tainted with self-interest such that the directors were not acting in the best interests of the corporation. *Lewis v. Hilton, 648 F. Supp. 725 (N.D.Ill. 1986).*

Demand and business judgment inextricably bound. — According to Delaware law, the demand requirements are predicated upon and inextricably bound to issues of business judgment. *Miller v. Loucks, 1992 U.S. Dist. LEXIS 16966 (N.D.Ill. 1992).*

The Delaware Supreme Court establishes the standards for excusing the demand requirement in derivative suits against Delaware corporations. The court notes that the derivative nature of shareholder suits extends from the primary right of a corporation to pursue its own legal interests. Hence, under ordinary circumstances, a corporation through its board of directors, should be able to make the decision whether to pursue legal remedies for injuries to the corporate entity. As with other corporate decisionmaking processes, the decision of whether to sue is accorded great deference by the courts under the business judgment rule. *Cottle v. Hilton Hotels Corp., 635 F. Supp. 1094 (N.D.Ill. 1986).*

To excuse demand, plaintiffs must offer a particularized, legally recognized reason for the board of directors' inability to consider objectively a demand to pursue the derivative claims directly. *Miller v. Loucks, 1992 U.S. Dist. LEXIS 16966 (N.D.Ill. 1992).*

Under Delaware law, the sufficiency of a complaint pleading demand futility is tested by making two determinations: (1) whether the well-pleaded facts rebut the threshold presumptions of director disinterest or independence; and, if not, (2) whether the well-pleaded facts create a reasonable doubt that the challenged transaction was the product of a valid exercise of business judgment. *Miller v. Loucks, 1992 U.S. Dist. LEXIS 16966 (N.D.Ill. 1992).*

Under Delaware law, the mere threat of personal liability for approving a questioned transaction, standing alone, is insufficient to challenge either the independence or disinterestedness of directors, although in rare cases a transaction may be so egregious on its face that board approval cannot meet the test of business judgment, and a substantial likelihood of director liability therefore exists. *Miller v. Loucks, 1992 U.S. Dist. LEXIS 16966 (N.D.Ill. 1992).*

Under Delaware law, the rule that a shareholder must make a demand upon a corporation's directors before initiating a derivative suit, unless such demand would be futile, is more than a mere pleading requirement; it is a substantive right. The standard for determining whether a complaint adequately alleges demand futility is: whether taking the well-pleaded facts as true, the allegations raise

a reasonable doubt as to (i) director disinterest or independence or (ii) whether the directors exercised proper business judgment in approving the challenged transaction. Moreover, conclusory allegations of fact or law contained in the complaint need not be considered true in determining demand futility unless they are supported by specific facts. *Shields v. Erikson, 1989 U.S. Dist. LEXIS 10079 (N.D.Ill. 1989).*

Delaware law, like federal law, recognizes the demand requirement in Fed. R. Civ. P. 23.1 as based on the fundamental precept that directors manage the corporation, not shareholders. Demand is excused if the complaint demonstrates that the directors are not disinterested. However, the mere fact that the lawsuit will subject the directors to liability is insufficient to show interest. Nor is there interest merely because the board receives payment for its services. Vague allegations of control or domination of the board of directors will not suffice to excuse demand. Allegations that the entire board participates in the wrongs or approves of them is also insufficient. *Shields on behalf of Sundstrand Corp. v. Erickson, 710 F. Supp. 68 (N.D.Ill. 1989).*

The demand requirement has been described as a substantive right of the corporation and not simply a procedural prerequisite to the derivative action. Thus, the substantive right to a demand on the corporation must be kept conceptually apart from the procedural requirement of Fed. R. Civ. P. 23.1 that the plaintiff shareholder plead with particularity his or her efforts to obtain relief from the corporation or the reasons for not making such an effort. *Cottle v. Hilton Hotels Corp., 635 F. Supp. 1094 (N.D.Ill. 1986).*

In paring considerations down to a test for determining the futility of the shareholder demand requirement, the Delaware Supreme Court requires that a trial court must decide whether, under the particularized facts alleged, a reasonable doubt is created that: (1) the directors are disinterested and independent and (2) the challenged transaction was otherwise the product of a valid exercise of business judgment. Hence, the court must make two inquiries, one into the independence and disinterestedness of the directors and the other into the substantive nature of the challenged transaction and the board's approval thereof. If a reasonable doubt has been raised with respect to either the directors' disinterestedness and independence or whether the decision was otherwise a valid business judgment, the demand requirement will be excused and the shareholder permitted to pursue the derivative action. *Cottle v. Hilton Hotels Corp., 635 F. Supp. 1094 (N.D.Ill. 1986).*

The mere fact that directors participated in and authorized the disputed transactions underlying the derivative suit is not enough by itself to excuse demand. If this were the only prerequisite to excusing demand, the demand requirement would be effectively repealed since, by definition, the directors have a hand in all corporate transactions of any consequence. *Cottle v. Hilton Hotels Corp., 635 F. Supp. 1094 (N.D.Ill. 1986).*

As the first part of the *Aronson* test suggests, the allegations must create a reasonable doubt that the underlying corporate transactions were made by disinterested and independent directors. *Cottle v. Hilton Hotels Corp., 635 F. Supp. 1094 (N.D.Ill. 1986).*

A plaintiff-shareholder can also be excused from demand under *Aronson* if he or she can allege particularized facts which create a reasonable doubt that the challenged transaction was the product of a valid business judgment notwithstanding the directors' disinterestedness and independence. This aspect of the test has not been examined as thoroughly by the courts, though the *Aronson* court alluded to the narrowness of this exception when it noted that in rare cases a transaction may be so egregious on its face that board approval cannot meet the test of business judgment, and a substantial likelihood of director liability therefore exists. *Cottle v. Hilton Hotels Corp., 635 F. Supp. 1094 (N.D.Ill. 1986).*

The *Rales* court found that the "essential predicate" for applying the *Aronson* test was that a decision of the board of directors is being challenged in the derivative suit. The court in *Rales* stated that where the board that would be considering the demand did not make a business decision which is being challenged in the derivative suit, there are three scenarios in which the *Aronson* test would not apply: (1) where a business decision was made by the board of a company, but a majority of the directors making the decision have been replaced, (2) where the subject of the derivative suit is not a business decision of the board, and (3) where the decision being challenged was made by the board of a different corporation. *In re Abbott Labs. Derivative Shareholders Litigation, 325 F.3d 795 (7th Cir. 2003).*

The animating principle of the demand futility doctrine is that the directors can not faithfully decide whether proceeding with the corporation's litigation is in the corporation's best interest when the complaint seeks redress for the conduct that gives rise to the personal financial benefit for which the directors alone have received. The case law makes it clear that the personal benefit must arise from the challenged transaction. *In re General Instrument Corp., 23 F. Supp. 2d 867 (N.D.Ill. 1998).*

A saving clause for derivative suits provides that any action or proceeding, whether civil, criminal or administrative, pending by or against any corporation which is a party to a merger or consolidation shall be prosecuted as if such merger or consolidation had not taken place, or the corporation surviving or resulting from such merger of consolidation may be substituted in such action or proceeding. The plain purpose of § 261 is to save pending lawsuits. The complaint must be filed by a person who is a shareholder of the corporation on whose behalf the suit is brought, regardless of whether the suit is brought against a corporation or third parties. *Kreindler v. Marx, 85 F.R.D. 612 N.D.Ill. 1979).*

In reviewing a report by an independent committee, the court should first look at the independence of the committee, whether its recommendations were made in good faith, and whether the committee made a reasonable investigation. The court can then, in its own discretion, move to a second step and apply its own business judgment to determine whether the suit should be pursued. *Grafman v. Century Broadcasting Corp., 762 F. Supp. 215 (N.D.Ill. 1991).*

Independent director. — A disinterested director can neither appear on both sides of a transaction nor expect to derive any personal financial benefit from the challenged transaction in the sense of self-dealing, as opposed to a benefit which devolves upon the corporation or all stockholders generally. *In re Abbott Labs. Derivative Shareholders Litigation, 325 F.3d 795 (7th Cir. 2003).*

Independence exists when a director's decision is based on the corporate merits of the subject before the board rather than extraneous considerations or influences. *In re Abbott Labs. Derivative Shareholders Litigation, 325 F.3d 795 (7th Cir. 2003).*

A director is independent when he or she is able to reach his or her decision solely on the merits without being governed by outside influences or considerations. To show a lack of independence, the plaintiff must demonstrate that outside considerations influenced the decisions of the committee. *Grafman v. Century Broadcasting Corp., 762 F. Supp. 215 (N.D.Ill. 1991).*

Under Delaware law, a corporation itself has the initial, preemptive opportunity to investigate derivative claims, and to determine whether the corporation should pursue them. The directors of a Delaware corporation may make this determination by appointing a committee. The directors may delegate to this committee the power both to investigate and to terminate derivative litigation. A dissatisfied shareholder may attack the committee's conclusion only after the corporation adopts it.. *Grafman v. Century Broadcasting Corp., 743 F. Supp. 544 (N.D.Ill. 1990).*

Derivative versus individual action. — Whether a shareholder's complaint in a diversity case stated a derivative (as opposed to individual) claim is dependent upon the characterization of the claim under state law. Under Delaware law, where the claimed injury will be sustained by all of the shareholders solely by virtue of their status as shareholders, the action is a derivative action. In order to make out an individual cause of action under Delaware law, a plaintiff must allege either an injury which is separate and distinct from that suffered by other shareholders, or a wrong involving a contractual right of a shareholder, such as the right to vote, or to assert majority control, which exists independent of any right of the corporation. *Rosenfield v. Becor Western, Inc., 1987 U.S. Dist. LEXIS 14276 (E.D.Wis. 1987).*

A shareholder may bring an individual action where there is an injury, which is separate, and distinct from that suffered by other shareholders. If the cause of action is based on unlawful acts affecting only the stock owned by the plaintiff, an individual action is appropriate. *Newell Co. v. Vermont American Corp., 725 F. Supp. 351 (N.D.Ill. 1989).*

Disqualification of plaintiff. — A plaintiff in a derivative action must adequately and fairly represent the interests of the shareholders. The plaintiff is not automatically disqualified from bringing a derivative suit simply because that shareholder is also the potential acquirer. To be disqualified, defendant must show that the plaintiff-representative's interests are intrinsically at variance with those of the other shareholders. The court may look to extrinsic factors to determine the adequacy of representation; the most important consideration being antagonistic economic interests. *Air Line Pilots Association, International v. UAL Corp., 717 F. Supp. 575 (N.D.Ill. 1989)*.

Evidentiary rules. — Delaware law prohibits a plaintiff in a shareholder derivative action from using discovery under civil procedure rules until the case survives a motion to dismiss under the heightened pleading standard of Del. Ch. Ct. R. 23.1. In fact, because civil discovery is not readily available in derivative actions, the Delaware courts have repeatedly instructed shareholders contemplating a derivative action to use "the tools at hand," including Del. Code Ann. tit. 8, § 220, to obtain information needed to investigate and prepare a demand and later derivative action. *City of Austin Police Retirement System v. ITT Educational Services, Inc., 2005 U.S. Dist. LEXIS 1646 (S.D.Ind. 2005)*.

Waste and misappropriation of corporate assets are harms against the corporation and must be brought derivatively. Delaware law, however, also recognizes the special injury exception to this rule, permitting a shareholder to litigate individually if the wrong to the corporation inflicts a distinct and disproportionate injury on the investor. *Minor v. Albright, 2001 U.S. Dist. LEXIS 19436 (N.D.Ill. 2001)*.

Under Delaware law, a shareholder seeking declaratory judgment as to the ownership of the shares of a Delaware corporation need not proceed derivatively. *Weinstein v. Schwartz, 2005 U.S. App. LEXIS 18976 (7th Cir. 2005)*.

Standard of pleadings review. — The totality of the allegations in a complaint based on demand futility for directors' conscious inaction need only support a reasonable doubt of business judgment protection, not a judicial finding that the directors' actions are not protected by the business judgment rule. *In re Abbott Labs. Derivative Shareholders Litigation, 325 F.3d 795 (7th Cir. 2003)*.

Corporate boards have an obligation to undertake a good faith obligation to ensure that reporting systems are in place that alert board members to significant risks faced by the company. As such, plaintiffs are excused from making a demand upon the board of directors based on the doctrine of demand futility. It is not only the public pronouncements by newspapers, analysts, and litigants that arguably created a duty for the board to act. Instead, if the allegations in the complaint are true, the public pronouncements were merely a symptom of the ills brought upon corporation by massive oversight failures or intentional manipulation of financial and enrollment figures. *McSparran v. Larson, 2006 U.S. Dist. LEXIS 3787 (N.D. Ill. Jan. 27, 2006)*.

Discovery request. — Generally speaking, the prevailing view seems to be that, in a derivative action, discovery should not be allowed during the pendency of a motion to dismiss. *Sylvia Piven As Tr. for the Leonard Piven Trust Uad 05/21/81 v. Ryan, 2006 U.S. Dist. LEXIS 8274 (N.D. Ill. Mar. 1, 2006)*.

The court is being asked to decide whether, under the particular circumstances presented here — where there are parallel state court derivative actions proceeding, where there is a fully-briefed motion to dismiss or stay the action pending before the district court, where there is no allegation that evidence or documents may be compromised or destroyed, and where the facts of the case suggest that dismissal for lack of standing is a distinct possibility — the court should exercise its discretion to delay the disclosure and production of documents. On balance, the court is persuaded that it should. Accordingly, the court denies the motion to compel discovery. *Sylvia Piven As Tr. for the Leonard Piven Trust Uad 05/21/81 v. Ryan, 2006 U.S. Dist. LEXIS 8274 (N.D. Ill. Mar. 1, 2006)*.

There is no substantial reason to question the independence of a majority of board of directors. Plaintiff has not put forth any allegations that outside directors have their salary set by any board member, or are otherwise financially dependent upon other directors. If mere social acquaintances and prior business relationships with other board members coupled with the receipt of directorial fees destroyed a board member's independence, few boards would have any independent members. While certain directors are officers of the corporation and therefore have their salaries set by other directors, thereby eliminating their independence, the majority of the directors remain independent. *McSparran v. Larson, 2006 U.S. Dist. LEXIS 53773 (D. Ill. May 3, 2006)*.

Two claims of misconduct by former employees at a large corporation do not establish a systematic lack of board oversight. Even if such claims give rise to class action securities fraud cases or government investigations, that does not alter the fact that the only allegations of misconduct come from two of thousands of current and former employees. To allow such claims to give rise to demand futility would significantly diminish the protections of the demand requirement for all large corporations, which are likely to have several lawsuits and employee claims pending at any given time. Not every lawsuit means a board was negligent in its oversight and not every government investigation means a company's board must relinquish control over litigation on behalf of the corporation. *McSparran v. Larson, 2006 U.S. Dist. LEXIS 53773 (D. Ill. May 3, 2006)*.

Eighth Circuit

Demand futility. — Under Delaware law, a shareholder must satisfy a stringent pleading standard and allege particularized facts justifying any failure to make a demand. In a derivative action brought by one or more shareholders the complaint shall also allege with particularity the efforts, if any, made by the plaintiff to obtain the action desired from the directors or the reasons for the plaintiff's failure to make such efforts. A demand is considered futile and may be excused only if the particularized facts alleged in the complaint create a reasonable doubt that: (1) the directors are disinterested and independent; or (2) the challenged transaction was otherwise the product of a valid exercise of business judgment. *Wesenberg v. Zimmerman, 2002 U.S. Dist. LEXIS 11868 (D.Minn. 2002).*

Under Delaware law, it is clear that a plaintiff may only establish futility and therefore excuse a demand by creating a reasonable doubt that either: (1) the directors are independent or disinterested for the purposes of responding to the demand; or (2) the underlying transaction is protected by the business judgment rule. These prongs are in the disjunctive. *Wesenberg v. Zimmerman, 2002 U.S. Dist. LEXIS 11868 (D.Minn. 2002).*

The mere threat of personal liability for approving a questioned transaction, standing alone, is insufficient to challenge either the independence or disinterestedness of directors. To succeed with such an argument, the shareholder would need to show that there is a "substantial likelihood" that the directors will have to pay damages to the company. *Wesenberg v. Zimmerman, 2002 U.S. Dist. LEXIS 11868 (D.Minn. 2002).*

Review of committee's decision to dismiss lawsuit. — In exercising its own business judgment, the court should carefully consider and weigh the strength of the corporate interest in dismissal when faced with a nonfrivolous lawsuit and, when appropriate, give special consideration to matters of law and public policy in addition to the corporation's best interests. Ethical, commercial, promotional, public and employee relations, and fiscal, as well as legal factors should be considered in analyzing the committee's decision to terminate a particular lawsuit, and in exercising the court's own business judgment. *Watts v. Des Moines Register & Tribune, 525 F. Supp. 1311 (S.D. Iowa 1981).*

The four-pronged analysis to be applied in evaluating a dismissal motion premised upon an independent litigation committee's exercise of business judgment requires a judicial assessment of: (1) the procedural propriety of a complaining shareholder's initiation of suit; (2) whether the board committee is endowed with the requisite corporate power to seek dismissal of a derivative suit; (3) whether the movants have adequately demonstrated the disinterest, independence and good faith of committee members, the bases for the conclusions of such members and the appropriateness and sufficiency of their investigative techniques; and (4) whether, in the court's exercise of its own independent business judgment, dismissal of derivative counts is warranted. *Watts v. Des Moines Register & Tribune, 525 F. Supp. 1311 (S.D. Iowa 1981).*

Demand excuse tests compared. — The court discerns no real difference between the *Levine* and *Rales* standards. The true effect of *Rales* is to remove the second prong from *Levine*, and creates a standard for different board cases that is very similar to the first prong from *Levine. In re Am. Italian Pasta Co. Secs. Litig., 2006 U.S. Dist. LEXIS 40548 (D. Mo. June 19, 2006).*

Timing of demand. — Demand is to be made on the board at the time the derivative complaint is filed, and subsequent changes to the board do not "cancel" a finding of futility once it is made. In attempting to demonstrate futility, Plaintiffs appear to be focusing on the board as it existed when the first derivative complaint was filed prior

to the consolidation of cases against defendant corporation. This appears to be inappropriate: no futility was found at that time, and the strong interests favoring normal corporate governance counsel against analyzing futility based on the board's composition prior to the filing of the complaint spawning the futility analysis. Therefore, the proper analysis would focus on the board's composition at the time the amended complaint was filed. *In re Am. Italian Pasta Co. Secs. Litig., 2006 U.S. Dist. LEXIS 40548 (D. Mo. June 19, 2006).*

Ninth Circuit

The determination of whether a claim is direct or derivative under Delaware law **depends on** the following factors: Who suffered the alleged harm — the corporation or the suing stockholder individually — and who would receive the benefit of the recovery or other remedy? The stockholder's claimed direct injury must be independent of any alleged injury to the corporation. The existence of a fiduciary relationship between the majority and minority shareholders does not excuse the need for independent and direct harm to the minority shareholders. *In re At Home Corp., 154 Fed. Appx. 666; 2005 U.S. App. LEXIS 25407 (9th Cir. Nov. 23, 2005).*

Special litigation committee. — Delaware law endows a corporation in a derivative suit with the power to form a special litigation committee (SLC) of the board of directors, and to either terminate or assume prosecution of the suit based upon the SLC's review and recommendation. *Johnson v. Hui, 811 F. Supp. 479 (N.D.Cal. 1991).*

A special litigation committee has the power to terminate a derivative action to the extent allowed by the law of the state of incorporation. Under Delaware law, a special litigation committee has the power to terminate a derivative action under certain circumstances. *Johnson v. Hui, 811 F. Supp. 479 (N.D.Cal. 1991).*

A special litigation committee may terminate a derivative action with leave of the court following an appropriate motion to terminate by the affected corporation. *Johnson v. Hui, 811 F. Supp. 479 (N.D.Cal. 1991).*

The Supreme Court of Delaware has laid out a two-step standard of review applicable to motions to terminate derivative actions based on the recommendation of a special litigation committee: first, the court should inquire into the independence and good faith of the committee and the bases supporting its conclusions. Limited discovery may be ordered to facilitate such inquiries. The corporation should have the burden of proving independence, good faith and reasonable investigation. If the court determines either that the committee is not independent or has not shown reasonable bases for its conclusions the court shall deny the corporations motion. If, however, the court is satisfied under Fed. R. Civ. P. 56 standards that the committee was independent and showed reasonable bases for good-faith findings and recommendations, the court may proceed, in its discretion, to the next step. Second, the court should determine applying its own independent business judgment, whether the motion should be granted. *Johnson v. Hui, 811 F. Supp. 479 (N.D.Cal. 1991).*

Corporations

Under Delaware law, the right of a stockholder to prosecute a derivative suit is limited to situations where the stockholder has demanded that the directors pursue the corporate claim and they have wrongfully refused to do so or where demand is excused because the directors are incapable of making an impartial decision regarding such litigation. In general, demand is excused where, under the particularized facts alleged, a reasonable doubt is created that a majority of the directors are disinterested and independent or that the challenged transaction was otherwise the product of a valid exercise of business judgment. *In re Sagent Technology, Inc, 278 F. Supp. 2d 1079 (N.D.Cal 2003).*

Demand futility. — To show futility under Delaware law, a plaintiff must allege particularized facts creating a reasonable doubt that (1) the directors are disinterested and independent, or (2) the challenged transaction was otherwise the product of a valid exercise of business judgment. *Janas v. McCracken, 183 F.3d 970 (9th Cir. 1999).*

Under Delaware law, demand may be excused where, under the particularized facts alleged, a reasonable doubt is created that: (1) the directors are disinterested and independent and (2) the challenged transaction was otherwise the product of a valid exercise of business judgment. *In re Silicon Graphics, Inc., 1996 U.S. Dist. LEXIS 16989 (N.D.Cal. 1996).*

Demand futility cannot be pleaded merely on the basis of allegations that directors acted or would act to preserve their positions. *In re Sagent Technology, Inc, 278 F. Supp. 2d 1079 (N.D.Cal 2003).*

Waste. — The essence of a claim of waste of corporate assets is the diversion of corporate assets for improper or unnecessary purposes. Corporate waste entails an exchange of corporate assets for consideration so disproportionately small as to lie beyond the range at which any reasonable person might be willing to trade. Most often the claim is based on a transfer of corporate assets that serves no purpose for the corporation or for which no consideration is received. A cause of action for corporate waste must be asserted in a derivative action, because a cause of action for impairment or destruction of the corporation's business vests in the corporation rather than in the individual shareholders. *In re Sagent Technology, Inc, 278 F. Supp. 2d 1079 (N.D.Cal 2003).*

Under Delaware law, directors are interested if they are on both sides of a transaction, or if they benefit financially from a transaction. One director's interest in a challenged transaction is insufficient, without more, to deprive the board of protection under the business judgment rule. *In re Silicon Graphics, Inc., 1996 U.S. Dist. LEXIS 16989 (N.D.Cal. 1996).*

To recover for individual harm, rather than derivative harm, a shareholder must show that he or she has suffered special injury. A special injury is established where there is a wrong suffered by the individual stockholder that was not suffered by all stockholders generally or where the wrong involves a contractual right of the stockholders, such as the right to

vote. *Frankston v. Aura Systems, 1998 U.S. App. LEXIS 20531 (9th Cir. 1998).*

Tenth Circuit

Standing. — A plaintiff suing derivatively must have shareholder status not only at the time of the transaction of which he complains but at the time suit is brought as well; however, Delaware has also recognized two exceptions to this rule, one being where the transaction or merger by which the putative plaintiff lost his or her shareholder status is the subject of a claim of fraud. *Eastwood v. National Bank of Commerce, 673 F. Supp. 1068 (W.D.Okla 1987).*

Demand futility. — Demand on the board of directors is excused as futile where, taking the well-pleaded facts as true, the allegations raise a reasonable doubt as to the directors' disinterest or whether the directors exercised proper business judgment in approving the challenged transaction. *In re Storage Technology Corp. Securities Litigation, 804 F. Supp. 1368 (D.Colo. 1992).*

To excuse demand on a corporation's board under Delaware law, plaintiff must allege facts which create a reasonable doubt that (1) the directors are disinterested and independent or (2) the challenged transaction was otherwise the product of a valid exercise of business judgment. To satisfy the first prong under the federal pleading standard, plaintiff must plead particularized facts demonstrating either a financial interest or entrenchment on the part of the directors. To satisfy the second prong, plaintiff must plead particularized facts which raise a reasonable doubt that the directors exercised proper business judgment in the transaction. *Grogan v. O'Neil, 307 F. Supp. 2d 1181 (D.Kan. 2004).*

In a derivative action against a corporation, to excuse demand under Delaware law, a plaintiff must allege facts which create a reasonable doubt that: (1) the directors are disinterested and independent, or (2) the challenged transaction was otherwise the product of a valid exercise of business judgment. *Grogan v. O'Neil, 292 F. Supp. 2d 1282 (D.Kan. 2003).*

In a derivative action against a corporation, to satisfy the first prong of *Aronson* under the federal pleading standard, a plaintiff must plead particularized facts demonstrating either a financial interest or entrenchment on the part of the directors. To satisfy the second prong of *Aronson*, the plaintiff must plead particularized facts which raise a reasonable doubt that the directors exercised proper business judgment in the transaction. *Grogan v. O'Neil, 292 F. Supp. 2d 1282 (D.Kan. 2003).*

Under Delaware law, demand on a corporation's board of directors will be excused only if under the particularized facts alleged, a reasonable doubt is created that: (1) the directors are disinterested and independent or (2) the challenged transaction was otherwise the product of a valid exercise of business judgment. The test is disjunctive. In order to satisfy the first prong of the *Aronson* test, a plaintiff must plead particularized facts demonstrating either a financial interest or entrenchment on the part of the directors. In order to satisfy the second prong of the *Aronson* test, the plaintiff must plead particularized facts, which raise a reasonable doubt that the directors exercised proper business judgment in the transaction. Proper business judgment means both substantive due care (terms of the transaction) and procedural due care (an informed decision). *Geer v. Cox, 242 F. Supp. 2d 1009 (D.Kan 2003).*

Direct versus derivative action. — The distinction between a derivative action and an individual or direct action depends upon the nature of the wrong alleged and the relief, if any, which could result if plaintiff were to prevail. To pursue a direct action, a stockholder must allege more than an injury resulting from a wrong to the corporation. Instead, a shareholder must state a claim for an injury which is separate and distinct from that suffered by other shareholders, or a wrong involving a contractual right of a shareholder which exists independently of any right of the corporation. *Grogan v. O'Neil, 307 F. Supp. 2d 1181 (D.Kan. 2004).*

A plaintiff who asserts only indirect injury to shareholders based on their pro rata shares of the corporation cannot maintain a direct claim. *Grogan v. O'Neil, 307 F. Supp. 2d 1181 (D.Kan. 2004).*

The distinction between a derivative action and an individual or direct action depends upon the nature of the wrong alleged and the relief, if any, which could result if plaintiff were to prevail. To pursue a direct action, a stockholder must allege more than an injury resulting from a wrong to the corporation. Instead, a shareholder must state a claim for an injury which is separate and distinct from that suffered by other shareholders, or a wrong involving a contractual right of a shareholder which exists independently of any right of the corporation. *Grogan v. O'Neil, 292 F. Supp. 2d 1282 (D.Kan. 2003).*

State law determines whether a shareholder may maintain a direct, nonderivative action. Delaware law distinguishes between direct individual and derivative actions based on the nature of the wrong alleged and the relief, if any, which could result if plaintiff were to prevail. Thus, if the relief sought flows primarily to the corporation, the action must be brought as a derivative action on behalf of the corporation. In analyzing whether the complaint states a derivative or direct claim, the court must look to the nature of the alleged wrong rather than the designation used by plaintiff. A plaintiff may maintain a direct action if the shareholder complains of an injury distinct from that suffered by other shareholders, or a wrong involving one of the shareholder's contractual rights as a shareholder. *Geer v. Cox, 242 F. Supp. 2d 1009 (D.Kan 2003).*

A corporate waste claim ordinarily involves board approval of an exchange of corporate assets for consideration so disproportionately small as to lie beyond the range at which any reasonable person might be willing to trade. *Grogan v. O'Neil, 292 F. Supp. 2d 1282 (D.Kan. 2003).*

As a practical matter on a corporate waste claim, a stockholder plaintiff must generally show that the board irrationally squandered corporate assets, for example, where the challenged transaction served no corporate purpose or where the corporation received no considera-

tion at all. *Grogan v. O'Neil, 292 F. Supp. 2d 1282 (D.Kan. 2003).*

A corporate waste claim must fail if there is any substantial consideration received by the corporation, and there is a good-faith judgment that in the circumstances the transaction is worthwhile. Courts are ill-fitted to weigh the adequacy of consideration or after the fact, to judge appropriate degrees of business risk. Absent some reasonable doubt that the board proceeded based on a good-faith assessment of the corporation's best interests, the board's decisions are entitled to deference under the business judgment rule. *Grogan v. O'Neil, 292 F. Supp. 2d 1282 (D.Kan. 2003).*

Domination or control. — Plaintiff must assert particularized, non-conclusory facts showing domination or control. Plaintiff does not provide any citation to the amended complaint, nor does plaintiff explain demonstrated facts to support his assertion that defendant maintained control over the board in his consultant position. Plaintiff essentially invites this court to presume facts, not pled in the complaint, which suggest a consultation agreement necessarily creates a reasonable doubt that defendant exercised dominion or control over a majority of the board. The district court declines plaintiff's invitation. Delaware law does not allow the court to excuse demand by innuendos raised in Plaintiff's complaint. Moreover, the facts, as pled by plaintiff, demonstrate that prior to the initiation of the law suit, Defendant corporation voluntarily conducted an internal investigation, took corrective action, and self-reported a matter to the SEC. It is difficult to conceive that a majority of the board was so beholden to individual defendant, yet they were able to initiate an internal investigation and force his retirement. Accordingly, plaintiff's argument as to dominion or control is unavailing. *Andropolis v. Snyder, 2006 U.S. Dist. LEXIS 54073 (D. Colo. Aug. 3, 2006).*

Red flags. — Plaintiff does not assert particularized facts to suggest that: (1) the director defendants knew of the alleged "culture;" and (2) this "culture" allowed individual defendant to charge more than one million dollars in personal expenses to corporation defendant. Claimed red flags are only useful when they are either waived in one's face or displayed so that they are visible to the careful observer. Thus, plaintiff's allegation that the director defendants' ignored a red flag that gave rise to individual defendant malfeasance and thereby gives rise to a substantial likelihood of liability for breaching their fiduciary duties to defendant corporation is unavailing. *Andropolis v. Snyder, 2006 U.S. Dist. LEXIS 54073 (D. Colo. Aug. 3, 2006).*

Insider trading. — Plaintiff has not pled particularized facts showing that individual defendants possessed material non-public information on the dates of the aforementioned sales. Simply because defendants sat on the board at the time they sold stock does not necessarily support the conclusion that those directors face a substantial threat of liability for insider selling such that demand requirement was futile. *Andropolis v. Snyder, 2006 U.S. Dist. LEXIS 54073 (D. Colo. Aug. 3, 2006).*

Corporations

Eleventh Circuit

Standing. — As a general rule of Delaware law, a derivative shareholder must not only be a stockholder at the time of the alleged wrong and at time of commencement of suit but must also maintain shareholder status throughout the litigation. To the extent their claims are derivative, plaintiffs may have standing under an exception to the general rule where the merger itself is the subject of a claim of fraud. This exception applies when the merger was perpetrated to deprive the corporation on whose behalf the suit is brought of its claim against the individual defendants. *Sturm v. Marriott Marquis Corp., 85 F. Supp. 2d 1356 (N.D.Ga. 2000).*

Direct versus derivative action. — Delaware law allows an individual shareholder to prevail against officers or directors of a corporation only when alleging direct and not derivative injury. A shareholder seeking direct relief must allege "special injury." The Delaware courts have developed a two-prong test for distinguishing direct and derivative claims. A plaintiff seeking individual relief must allege either "an injury which is separate and distinct from that suffered by other shareholders" or a wrong involving a contractual right of a shareholder, such as the right to vote, or to assert majority control, which exists independently of any right of the corporation." *Chalk Line Mfg. v. Frontenac Venture V, Ltd., 1994 Bankr. LEXIS 1087 (Bankr N.D.Ala. 1994)*

Although a plaintiff may not change the nature of a claim from derivative to direct simply by so designating it, a court should not summarily deny plaintiffs the right to assert claims for direct injury. If the plaintiff can prove that the defendants' actions caused an injury to the plaintiffs directly, and not that the defendants' actions injured the corporation primarily and the plaintiffs only secondarily, then the plaintiffs' are entitled to recovery. The court will not deny plaintiffs the opportunity to proceed unless their complaint alleges no claims for direct or "special injury." *Chalk Line Mfg. v. Frontenac Venture V, Ltd., 1994 Bankr. LEXIS 1087 (Bankr N.D.Ala. 1994).*

Minority shareholders may bring a direct action under Delaware law against majority shareholders who interfere with their voting rights. Interference with the minority stockholders' right to participation does no injury to the corporation. Where relief to the corporation would not cure the wrong, a direct action lies. *Chalk Line Mfg. v. Frontenac Venture V, Ltd., 1994 Bankr. LEXIS 1087 (Bankr N.D.Ala. 1994).*

In deciding whether a complaint states an individual or a derivative shareholder claim, the court is not bound by the designation chosen by the plaintiff. Instead, the nature of the action is judged by the body of the complaint. To set out an individual action, the plaintiff must allege either an injury which is separate and distinct from that suffered by other shareholders, or a wrong involving a contractual right of a shareholder, such as the right to vote, or to assert majority control, which exists independently of any right of the corporation. Where a shareholder's complaint sets out a cause of action that is both individual and derivative, the shareholder may proceed with the individual action. *Sturm v. Marriott Marquis Corp., 85 F. Supp. 2d 1356 (N.D.Ga. 2000).*

Special litigation committee. — Under Delaware law, a court must review the totality of the circumstance to determine whether the members of a special litigation committee are in a position to base a decision that the maintenance of the derivative suit is not in the best interests of the corporation on the merits of the issue rather than being governed by extraneous, considerations and influences. Delaware courts generally look to a number of factors when applying the totality of the circumstances test: (1) a committee member's status as a defendant, and potential liability; (2) a committee member's participation in or approval of the alleged wrongdoing; (3) a committee member's past or present business dealings with the corporation; (4) a committee member's past or present business or social dealings with individual defendants; (5) the number of directors on the committee; and (6) the structural bias of the committee. *Klein v. FPL Group, Inc., 2004 U.S. Dist. LEXIS 919 (S.D.Fla. 2004).*

Where a special litigation or litigation evaluation committee's role is only advisory, it is entitled to less deference than where it possesses unconditional authority to act on behalf of the board in investigating the allegations of a suit and in establishing the corporation's position with respect to the suit. *Klein v. FPL Group, Inc., 2004 U.S. Dist. LEXIS 919 (S.D.Fla. 2004).*

In determining when it is appropriate to dismiss derivative actions where the board has an inherent conflict of interest and has therefore appointed an "independent investigation committee" to make a decision, the question has been treated by some courts as one of the "business judgment" of the board committee. If a committee, composed of independent and disinterested directors, conducted a proper review of the matters before it, considered a variety of factors and reached in good faith, a business judgment that the action was not in the best interest of the corporation, the action must be dismissed. The issues become solely independence, good faith, and reasonable investigation. The ultimate conclusion of the committee, under that view, is not subject to judicial review. However, that acceptance of the "business judgment" rational at the discovery stage of derivative litigation is a proper balancing point. The court must be mindful that directors are passing judgment on fellow directors in the same corporation and fellow directors who designated them to serve both as directors and committee members. The court thus steers a middle course between those cases which yield to the independent business judgment of a board committee and a case which would yield to unbridled plaintiff stockholder control. *Klein v. FPL Group, Inc., 2003 U.S. Dist. LEXIS 19979 (S.D.Fla. 2003).*

The bulk of the plaintiff's "demand futility" allegations are mere conclusions of law masquerading as allegations of fact. Even within the forgiving confines of notice pleading, the court must eschew reliance on bald assertions and unsupported conclusions. In sum, the plaintiff fails to allege any particularized facts raising a reasonable doubt that board member was capable of making corporate decisions on the merits rather than on extraneous considerations or influences. By failing to allege facts sufficient to raise a reasonable doubt as to his independence or disinterestedness as a board member, the plaintiff fails to allege that a majority of board of directors are incapable of impartially considering the demand. *Story v. Kang, 2006 U.S. Dist. LEXIS 4354 (M.D. Fla. Jan. 20, 2006).*

District of Columbia Circuit

Derivative actions disfavored. — When the corporation is injured by a third party, the corporation's directors are left to exercise their business judgment in deciding whether bringing suit is in the best interests of the corporation, and that the individual stockholders must rely on their directors to manage the firm. Only in "exceptional situations," where a corporate concern may not be resolved through the processes of business judgment is a shareholder derivative suit on behalf of the corporation permitted. A derivative action is disfavored because it is an encroachment upon the prerogative of the board of directors to manage the corporation. *Labovitz v. Washington Times Corp., 900 F. Supp. 500 (D.D.C. 1995).*

Individual versus derivative claims. — Under Delaware law, shareholders can bring an individual claim if they suffer injuries directly or independently of the corporation. Claims based on injury to the corporation, however, are derivative in nature and any damages suffered are owed to the corporation. To determine whether claims are individual or derivative, courts must look to the nature of the wrongs alleged in the body of the complaint, not to a plaintiff's designation or stated intention. A plaintiff must allege a "special injury" to himself, apart from that suffered by the corporation. This injury can arise in two situations: first, where the allegedly wrongful conduct violates a duty to the complaining shareholder independent of the fiduciary duties owed that party along with all other shareholders, or second, where the conduct causes an injury to the shareholders distinct from any injury to the corporation itself. *Labovitz v. Washington Times Corp., 172 F.3d 897 (D.C. Cir. 1999).*

A shareholder who suffers an injury peculiar to himself should be able to maintain an individual action, even though the corporation also suffers an injury from the same wrong. *Labovitz v. Washington Times Corp., 172 F.3d 897 (D.C. Cir. 1999).*

A shareholder may not sue as an individual if the alleged wrong is primarily against the corporation. The one exception to this general rule is that a stockholder may maintain an individual action against the corporation if that stockholder has sustained a "special injury," as when there is a wrong suffered by an individual stockholder that was not suffered by all stockholders generally or where the wrong involves a contractual right of the stockholders, such as the right to vote. A "special injury" occurs where there has been stock dilution and a corresponding reduction in stockholder's voting power, and where a stock exchange agreement has violated shareholder voting rights because management gained veto power over all shareholder actions, but not where corporate mismanagement has depressed stock value, where the manipulation of corporate machinery has not directly prohibited a proxy contest, or where directors have approved "golden parachutes," and paid other unnecessary fees and expenses. *Labovitz v. Washington Times Corp., 900 F. Supp. 500 (D.D.C. 1995).*

If the gravamen of the complaint is injury to the corporation or if the shareholder's damages are the indirect result of an injury to the corporation, the shareholder may not sue individually. *Labovitz v. Washington Times Corp., 900 F. Supp. 500 (D.D.C. 1995).*

The court is not bound by the designation employed by the pleader in determining whether a cause of action is individual or derivative; the nature of the action is instead controlled by the substance of the claim. Under Delaware law, a shareholder must have suffered a special injury, distinct from that suffered by the corporation or the other stockholders, before he or she can bring an action individually. In order to constitute a special injury, the wrong complained of must violate a duty to the complaining shareholder independent of the fiduciary duties owed that party along with all other shareholders, or it must cause an injury to the shareholders distinct from any injury to the corporation itself. *Washington Bancorporation v. Washington, 1989 U.S. Dist. LEXIS 11437 (D.D.C. 1989).*

The court's search for a special injury is a broad one, not restricted to whether a contractual right or other such right has been interfered with. The court must look ultimately to whether the plaintiff has alleged special injury, in whatever form. *Washington Bancorporation v. Washington, 1989 U.S. Dist. LEXIS 11437 (D.D.C. 1989).*

Demand requirements. — Under Delaware law, a shareholder must first make a demand of the corporation's board of directors before bringing a derivative action on behalf of the corporation. The demand requirement is a recognition of the fundamental precept that directors manage the business and affairs of corporations and its principal goal is to give the board of directors an opportunity to address the grievance themselves, to alert it to problems of which it may be unaware, and to give it the opportunity to use the corporation's own resources in championing causes of action the board deems meritorious. *Washington Bancorporation v. Washington, 1989 U.S. Dist. LEXIS 11437 (D.D.C. 1989).*

The requirement of a demand, however, may be excused as futile when the presumption that the directors would exercise good business judgment in evaluating the demand is overcome. Because it is presumed that in making a business decision the directors of a corporation act on an informed basis, in good faith, and in the honest belief that the action is in the best interests of the corporation, the party challenging the decision has the burden of rebutting that presumption. *Washington Bancorporation v. Washington, 1989 U.S. Dist. LEXIS 11437 (D.D.C. 1989).*

United States Supreme Court

Applicability of New Jersey statute. — That a corporation which was the subject of a stockholder's derivative action in New Jersey was organized under the laws of Delaware does not make inapplicable a New Jersey statute providing that the plaintiff may be required

to give security for reasonable expenses of the corporation. *Cohen v. Beneficial Industrial Loan Corp., 337 U.S. 541, 69 S. Ct. 1221, 93 L. Ed. 1528 (U.S. 1949).*

§ 328. Effect of liability of corporation on impairment of certain transactions

DELAWARE CASE NOTES — REPORTED

Creditors cannot ordinarily prevent merger or consolidation. — As a general proposition, it is not permitted to a creditor of a corporation to prevent its merger or consolidation with another if the statutory law of its creation authorizes it. *Cole v. National Cash Credit Ass'n, 18 Del. Ch. 47, 156 A. 183 (1931).*

The express conference upon creditors by statute of a right of action generally by which not only the assets of their debtor but as well the entire assets of the consolidated company, whether derived from the debtor constituent or not, may be seized in satisfaction, renders less defensible the right of creditors to prevent a consolidation. *Cole v. National Cash Credit Ass'n, 18 Del. Ch. 47, 156 A. 183 (1931).*

The fact that the quick asset condition of the consolidated company will, in relation to its liabilities, render it

less desirable as a debtor from the viewpoint of current financial soundness than the constituent debtor, if true as alleged, cannot serve to justify an enjoining of the consolidation on the creditor's complaint. *Cole v. National Cash Credit Ass'n, 18 Del. Ch. 47, 156 A. 183 (1931).*

Void transaction. — If stockholders of one corporation turn over its assets to another corporation, receiving unto themselves the stock of the transferee in payment, the transaction is void as against the creditors of the former, and they may look to the latter for satisfaction to the extent of the value of the assets received when the selling corporation fails to provide for the payment of its debts. When a transaction of that sort takes place, it is a fraud on creditors and is void as to them. *McKee v. Standard Minerals Corp., 18 Del. Ch. 97, 156 A. 193 (1931).*

§ 329. Defective organization of corporation as defense

DELAWARE CASE NOTES — REPORTED

Corporate existence of corporation de facto cannot be inquired into collaterally. It is only by quo warranto proceedings in the name of the State that its right to exist can be determined. *Wilmington City Ry. v. Wilmington & Brandywine Springs Ry., 8 Del. Ch. 468, 46 A. 12 (1900).*

When a corporation has an existence de facto, the rightfulness of its existence can only be questioned by the State, and cannot be questioned collaterally in a litigation between it and a private party. *Wilmington City Ry. v. Wilmington & Brandywine Springs Ry., 8 Del. Ch. 468, 46 A. 12 (1900).*

Disregarding corporate entity. — The fiction of a legal corporate entity should be ignored when it has been used as a shield for fraudulent or other illegal acts. *Martin v. D.B. Martin Co., 10 Del. Ch. 211, 88 A. 612 (1913).*

In dealing with corporations with interlocking directors, and other devices, legal and illegal, useful and harmless, or fraudulent and harmful, for the control of other corporations, the court may rightly ignore corporate

existence, when such existence serves as a barrier to the righting of wrong done to the stockholders of the dominant corporation. *Martin v. D.B. Martin Co., 10 Del. Ch. 211, 88 A. 612 (1913).*

Where 1 corporation owns all the shares of another corporation, cooperating in the same business, the former financing the latter, and the same persons are officers of both corporations, the latter is for certain purposes to be considered as an agency, adjunct or instrumentality of the former and for the protection of the rights of stockholders of the dominant, or parent company, and for righting of wrongs done them by means of the control of the dominant, or parent, company of the allied companies, the latter are to be treated as agents of the former, or even as identical with each other. *Martin v. D.B. Martin Co., 10 Del. Ch. 211, 88 A. 612 (1913).*

Judgment creditor who sues a corporation as such thereby admits the legality of its incorporation, and is estopped from denying it in that suit. *Bellis v. Morgan Trucking, Inc., 375 F. Supp. 862 (D. Del. 1974).*

CASE NOTES — UNREPORTED

Corporate status was res judicata. — Although the corporate status of a swimming pool construction business was never completed because it was not authorized by the Delaware Secretary of State, the owners of the business

could not be held liable in buyers' breach of contract action because another court's ruling that the business was a de facto corporation was res judicata. *Bishop v. Murphy, 2006 Del. Super. LEXIS 131 (Del. Super. Ct. Apr. 10, 2006).*

Subchapter XIV.
Close Corporations; Special Provisions

§ 341. Law applicable to close corporation

DELAWARE CASE NOTES — REPORTED

Applicability of § 350 of this title. — Section 350 of this title only applies under this section to a close corporation, within the statutory definition, which elects to be treated as such under § 344 of this title. *Chapin v. Benwood Found., Inc., 402 A.2d 1205 (Del. Ch. 1979)*, aff'd, *415 A.2d 1068 (Del. 1980)*.

Minority investors. — It would run counter to the spirit of the doctrine of independent legal significance, and

would be inappropriate judicial legislation, for the Supreme Court to fashion a special judicially-created rule for minority investors when the subject entity does not fall within statutes concerning close corporations, or when there are no negotiated special provisions in the certificate of incorporation, by-laws, or stockholder agreements. *Nixon v. Blackwell, 626 A.2d 1366 (Del. 1993)*.

CASE NOTES — UNREPORTED

Reformation is unavailable in this case as a matter of law under the Waggoner test for the simple reason that defendant corporation cannot establish the intent of "all parties interested," including all of defendant corporation's present and past stockholders. According to publicly available information, defendant corporation has 13.15 million shares outstanding and an average daily volume over the past three months of over 70,000 shares. At this rate, defendant corporation had literally thousands

of record and beneficial holders as of the record date for the 2005 annual meeting and it has literally thousands of record and beneficial stockholders today. It is simply impossible for defendant corporation to show that all present and past shareholders intended the provisions to read as defendant corporation now claims. *Lions Gate Entm't Corp. v. Image Entm't, Inc., 2006 Del. Ch. LEXIS 108 (Del. June 5, 2006)*.

CASE NOTES — FEDERAL

Second Circuit

In general. — Under Delaware law, a close corporation may restrict or interfere with the discretion or powers of the board of directors through a provision in the shareholder's agreement. Section 350 only applies under Del.

Code Ann. tit. 8, § 341 to a close corporation, within the statutory definition, which elects to be treated as such. *USA Soccer Properties, Inc. v. Aegis Group PLC, 1992 U.S. Dist. LEXIS 11513 (S.D.N.Y. 1992)*.

§ 342. Close corporation defined; contents of certificate of incorporation

DELAWARE CASE NOTES — REPORTED

Minority investors. — It would run counter to the spirit of the doctrine of independent legal significance, and would be inappropriate judicial legislation, for the Supreme Court to fashion a special judicially-created rule for minority investors when the subject entity does not fall

within statutes concerning close corporations, or when there are no negotiated special provisions in the certificate of incorporation, by-laws, or stockholder agreements. *Nixon v. Blackwell, 626 A.2d 1366 (Del. 1993)*.

CASE NOTES — OTHER STATES

Illinois
Limitation on special relief. — Minority shareholders in a closely held, but not a "close corporation" as defined by the statute, are barred from receiving any special relief not afforded to minority shareholders in a publicly traded corporation. *Sims v. Tezak, 296 Ill. App. 3d 503, 694 N.E.2d 1015, 230 Ill. Dec. 737 (1998)*.

Massachusetts
The special protections provided under Delaware law apply only to a corporation designated as a "close corporation" in its certificate of incorporation, and which fulfills other requirements, including a limitation to 30 on the number of stockholders, that all classes of stock have to have at least one restriction on transfer, and that there

be no public offering. *Harrison v. Netcentric Corparation, 433 Mass. 465, 744 N.E.2d 622 (2001)*.

Protection of minority shareholders. — In Delaware, no special judicially created rules will be recognized to protect minority shareholders in closely held corporations. Instead, such parties can establish greater protection only by contract or by incorporation as a statutory "close corporation" under Del. Code Ann. tit. 8, § 342. *Clemmer v. Cullinane, 62 Mass. App. Ct. 904, 815 N.E.2d 651 (2004)*.

If the corporation has not been designated a close corporation under Del. Code tit. 8, § 342, which offers greater protections for the minority shareholder by permitting shareholder agreements and alternate governance arrangements, then the remedies available to a minority shareholder are few. *Clemmer v. Cullinane, 2002 Mass. Super. LEXIS 248 (2002).*

Fairness test proper approach. — In Delaware, in cases where the controlling shareholders stood personally to benefit by the actions alleged to constitute the freezeout, the entire fairness test, correctly applied and articulated, is the proper judicial approach. Indeed, majority stockholders may well owe fiduciary duties where a plaintiff's termination might amount to a wrongful freezeout of his or her stock interest. *Clemmer v. Cullinane, 62 Mass. App. Ct. 904, 815 N.E.2d 651 (2004).*

There is not a heightened fiduciary duty on shareholders in a close corporation governed by Delaware law. *Davidson v. General Morots Corop., 57 Mass. App. Ct. 637, 786 N.E.2d 845 (2003).*

Delaware does not impose a heightened fiduciary duty on shareholders in a close corporation. *Lorenc v. Be Free, Inc., 16 Mass. L. Rep. 638 (Super. 2003).*

Delaware law does not impose broad fiduciary duties on stockholders of a closely held corporation. *Olsen v. Seifert, 9 Mass. L. Rep. 268 (Super. 1998).*

CASE NOTES — FEDERAL

Second Circuit

In general. — The formation of a Delaware close corporation is controlled by Del. Code Ann. tit. 8, §§ 343 and 344. In order to be considered a close corporation, a company's certificate of incorporation must contain a heading stating the name of the corporation and that it is a close corporation. In addition, the certificate of incorporation must require that, among other prerequisites, no more than 30 persons hold issued stock of all classes and that no public offering of the corporation's stock will be

made. *USA Soccer Properties, Inc. v. Aegis Group PLC, 1992 U.S. Dist. LEXIS 11513 (S.D.N.Y. 1992).*

Third Circuit

In general. — Close corporations are defined as those having a relatively small number of shareholders who (1) tend to have a substantial portion of their wealth invested in the corporation, (2) tend to be intimately involved in its management, and (3) tend to restrict management in the corporation. *Gregory v. Correction Connection, Inc., 1991 U.S. Dist. LEXIS 3659 (E.D.Pa. 1991).*

§ 343. Formation of a close corporation

CASE NOTES — FEDERAL

Second Circuit

The formation of a Delaware close corporation is controlled by Del. Code Ann. tit. 8, §§ 343 and 344. In order to be considered a close corporation, a company's certificate of incorporation must contain a heading stating the name of the corporation and that it is a close corpora-

tion. In addition, the certificate of incorporation must require that, among other prerequisites, no more than 30 persons hold issued stock of all classes and that no public offering of the corporation's stock will be made. *USA Soccer Properties, Inc. v. Aegis Group PLC, 1992 U.S. Dist. LEXIS 11513 (S.D.N.Y. 1992).*

§ 344. Election of existing corporation to become a close corporation

DELAWARE CASE NOTES — REPORTED

Applicability of § 350 of this title. — Section 350 of this title only applies under § 341 of this title to a close corporation, within the statutory definition, which elects

to be treated as such under this section. *Chapin v. Benwood Found., Inc., 402 A.2d 1205 (Del. Ch. 1979), aff'd, 415 A.2d 1068 (Del. 1980).*

CASE NOTES — OTHER STATES

New York

In general. — Any Delaware corporation can elect to become a close corporation by filing an appropriate certificate of amendment and by such amendment approved by the holders of all of its outstanding stock may

include in its certificate provisions restricting directors' authority. *Zion v. Kurtz, 50 N.Y.2d 92, 405 N.E.2d 681, 428 N.Y.S.2d 199 (1980).*

CASE NOTES — FEDERAL

Second Circuit

Construction with other law. — Under Delaware law, a close corporation may restrict or interfere with the discretion or powers of the board of directors through a provision in the shareholder's agreement. Section 350 only applies under Del. Code Ann. tit. 8, § 341 to a close corporation, within the statutory definition, which elects

to be treated as such. *USA Soccer Properties, Inc. v. Aegis Group PLC, 1992 U.S. Dist. LEXIS 11513 (S.D.N.Y. 1992).*

The formation of a Delaware close corporation is controlled by Del. Code Ann. tit. 8, §§ 343 and 344. In order to be considered a close corporation, a company's certificate of incorporation must contain a heading stating the name of the corporation and that it is a close corporation. In addition, the certificate of incorporation must require that, among other prerequisites, no more than 30 persons hold issued stock of all classes and that no public offering of the corporation's stock will be made. *USA Soccer Properties, Inc. v. Aegis Group PLC, 1992 U.S. Dist. LEXIS 11513 (S.D.N.Y. 1992).*

Delaware law does provide a means for an extant corporation to alter its status to become a close corporation; however, the fact that this provision requires a filing stating the intent to become a close corporation re-enforces the notion that a corporation can not be considered closely held simply because its shares are held by a small number of investors. *USA Soccer Properties, Inc. v. Aegis Group PLC, 1992 U.S. Dist. LEXIS 11513 (S.D.N.Y. 1992).*

§ 347. Issuance or transfer of stock of a close corporation in breach of qualifying conditions

CASE NOTES — OTHER STATES

Massachusetts
Protection of minority shareholders. — Delaware has not adopted a duty of utmost good faith and loyalty for shareholders in a close corporation. Instead under Delaware law, minority shareholders can protect themselves by contract, for example by negotiating for protection in stock agreements or employment contracts, before investing in the corporation. Additionally, founding shareholders can elect to incorporate the company as a statutory close corporation under Delaware law, which provides special relief to shareholders of such corporations. *Harrison v. Netcentric Corporation, 433 Mass. 465, 744 N.E.2d 622 (2001).*

§ 350. Agreements restricting discretion of directors

DELAWARE CASE NOTES — REPORTED

Applicability of section. — This section only applies under § 341 of this title to a close corporation, within the statutory definition, which elects to be treated as such under § 344 of this title. *Chapin v. Benwood Found., Inc., 402 A.2d 1205 (Del. Ch. 1979),* aff'd, *415 A.2d 1068 (Del. 1980).*

When members of charitable corporation are members only because they are trustees of the corporation, their membership status is coincidental with their fiduciary obligation to manage the affairs of the corporation in keeping with its charitable purpose to benefit deserving members of the public. As such, they are not stockholders, have no personal ownership rights which they can contract away and are not governed by this section and § 218 of this title, which recognize and enforce agreements among stockholders. *Chapin v. Benwood Found., Inc., 402 A.2d 1205 (Del. Ch. 1979),* aff'd, *415 A.2d 1068 (Del. 1980).*

CASE NOTES — OTHER STATES

Massachusetts
In general. — Under Delaware law the stockholders of a closely held corporation can expressly provide for duties not otherwise implied for a Delaware corporation. *Davidson v. General Motors Corp., 57 Mass. App. Ct. 637, 786 N.E.2d 845 (2003).*

New York
A written agreement between the holders of a majority of a corporation's stock is not invalid, as between the parties to the agreement, on the ground that it so relates to the conduct of the business and affairs of the corporation as to restrict or interfere with the discretion or powers of the board of directors or on the ground that it is an attempt by the parties to the agreement or by the stockholders of the corporation to treat the corporation as if it were a partnership. *Zion v. Kurtz, 50 N.Y.2d 92, 405 N.E.2d 681, 428 N.Y.S.2d 199 (1980).*

Liberal construction of internal agreements. — The public policy of Delaware does not proscribe a provision contained in a shareholders' agreement even though it takes all management functions away from the directors. Although some decisions outside Delaware have sustained reasonable restrictions upon director discretion contained in stockholder agreements, the theory of Del. Corp. Laws § 350 is to declare unequivocally, as a matter of public policy, that stockholder agreements of this character are not invalid, that § 351 recognizes a special subclass of close corporations which operate by direct stockholder management, and with respect to § 354 that it should be liberally construed to authorize all sorts of internal agreements and arrangements which are not affirmatively improper or, more particularly, injurious to third parties. *Zion v. Kurtz, 50 N.Y.2d 92, 405 N.E.2d 681, 428 N.Y.S.2d 199 (1980).*

Any Delaware corporation can elect to become a close corporation by filing an appropriate certificate of amendment and by such amendment approved by the holders of all of its outstanding stock may include in its certificate provisions restricting directors' authority. *Zion v. Kurtz, 50 N.Y.2d 92, 405 N.E.2d 681, 428 N.Y.S.2d 199 (1980).*

CASE NOTES — FEDERAL

Second Circuit

Applicability. — Under Delaware law, a close corporation may restrict or interfere with the discretion or powers of the board of directors through a provision in the shareholder's agreement. Section 350 only applies under Del. Code Ann. tit. 8, § 341 to a close corporation, within the statutory definition, which elects to be treated as such. *USA Soccer Properties, Inc. v. Aegis Group PLC, 1992 U.S. Dist. LEXIS 11513 (S.D.N.Y. 1992).*

Corporations which are not closely held are not governed by Del. Code Ann. tit. 8, § 350. Delaware law otherwise forbids any substantial limitation on a director's discretion in acting on behalf of a corporation. So long as the corporate form is used as it is presently provided by Delaware's statutes, a court cannot give legal sanction to agreements which have the effect of removing from directors in a very substantial way their duty to use their own best judgment on management matters. *USA Soccer Properties, Inc. v. Aegis Group PLC, 1992 U.S. Dist. LEXIS 11513 (S.D.N.Y. 1992).*

§ 351. Management by stockholders

CASE NOTES — OTHER STATES

Massachusetts

In general. — Under Delaware law, the stockholders of a closely held corporation can expressly provide for duties not otherwise implied for a Delaware corporation. *Davidson v. General Motors Corp., 57 Mass. App. Ct. 637, 786 N.E.2d 845 (2003).*

New York

The certificate of incorporation of a close corporation may provide that the business of the corporation shall be managed by the stockholders of the corporation rather than the board of directors and that such a provision may be inserted in the certificate by amendment if all holders of record of all of the outstanding stock so authorize. *Zion v. Kurtz, 50 N.Y.2d 92, 405 N.E.2d 681, 428 N.Y.S.2d 199 (1980).*

Liberal construction of internal agreements. — The public policy of Delaware does not proscribe a

provision contained in a shareholders' agreement even though it takes all management functions away from the directors. Although some decisions outside Delaware have sustained reasonable restrictions upon director discretion contained in stockholder agreements, the theory of Del. Corp. Laws § 350 is to declare unequivocally, as a matter of public policy, that stockholder agreements of this character are not invalid, that § 351 recognizes a special subclass of close corporations which operate by direct stockholder management, and with respect to § 354 that it should be liberally construed to authorize all sorts of internal agreements and arrangements which are not affirmatively improper or, more particularly, injurious to third parties. *Zion v. Kurtz, 50 N.Y.2d 92, 405 N.E.2d 681, 428 N.Y.S.2d 199 (1980).*

Subchapter XV.
Foreign Corporations

§ 371. Definition; qualification to do business in State; procedure

DELAWARE CASE NOTES — REPORTED

Primary object of this section is to secure to the State and its people a way to serve process on a corporation which is organized elsewhere and which comes here to act through officers or agents. *Farmers Bank v. Sinwellan Corp., 367 A.2d 180 (Del. 1976).*

This section permits foreign corporation to qualify to do business in Delaware. *In re Trust Estate of Saulsbury, 43 Del. Ch. 400, 233 A.2d 739 (1967).*

Although a corporation is a person, not a citizen entitled to the equal protection of the laws, and may be excluded by a foreign state from doing business within its borders, statutes such as this section and § 380, the first of which permits a foreign corporation to do business in Delaware and the second of which allows a qualified foreign corporation to serve as a trustee in Delaware, are modifications of the rule. *In re Trust Estate of Saulsbury, 43 Del. Ch. 400, 233 A.2d 739 (1967).*

Foreign corporation must comply with statutory regulations. — When a foreign corporation comes into this State by branch office, or agents, or representatives, located here to do a particular kind of business, it must comply with the statutory regulations prescribed for those who transact that kind of business. *E.A. Strout Co. v. Howell, 27 Del. 31, 85 A. 666 (1913).*

Effect of noncompliance with section. — Noncompliance with this section bars a foreign corporation from maintaining "any action" in the courts of this *State. Farmers Bank v. Sinwellan Corp., 367 A.2d 180 (Del. 1976).*

Regulations not violative of commerce clause. — 8 *Del. C. § 371* et seq., do not cause a foreign corporation to be subjected to regulations inconsistent with those for domestic corporations, and thus do not create a burden violative of the commerce clause of the *United States*

Constitution. Sternberg v. O'Neil, 550 A.2d 1105 (Del. 1988).

Test for applicability of this section is whether the foreign corporation does "any business in this State," not whether it is "doing business" here. *Farmers Bank v. Sinwellan Corp., 367 A.2d 180 (Del. 1976).*

"Tests" compared. — The "any" business test under this section is more comprehensive in meaning than the "doing business" test under § 382 of this title. *Farmers Bank v. Sinwellan Corp., 367 A.2d 180 (Del. 1976).*

Activities in state clearly beyond minimum requirements of "any" business criterion. — Where it was undisputed that plaintiff maintained a Delaware bank account in its corporate name, advertised in 2 Delaware newspapers of general circulation, stored its financial records in this State, executed contracts in Delaware with Delaware residents, sold or attempted to sell securities in this State, engaged in credit transactions with Delaware residents, and provided taxi service in Delaware to transport persons to and from places in this State, in the aggregate, at least, plaintiff's activities in Delaware clearly go beyond the minimum requirements of the "any" business criterion in this section. *Farmers Bank v. Sinwellan Corp., 367 A.2d 180 (Del. 1976).*

Jurisdiction over foreign corporations. — A foreign corporation's ownership of a Delaware corporate subsidiary constitutes a due process minimum contact which permits Delaware courts to assert specific jurisdiction over the foreign parent corporation in a double derivative action. *Sternberg v. O'Neil, 550 A.2d 1105 (Del. 1988).*

When a corporation qualified as a foreign corporation pursuant to this section, and appointed a registered agent for the service of process pursuant to *8 Del. C. § 376*, the corporation consented to the exercise of general jurisdiction by the courts of *Delaware. Sternberg v. O'Neil, 550 A.2d 1105 (Del. 1988).*

Curing delinquency. — While this section was intended to prevent a nonqualified foreign corporation from invoking the processes of the Delaware court system to the disadvantage of a Delaware resident or qualified entity as a penalty for refusal to pay the applicable franchise fee, the statute also provides an incentive for curing that delinquency. *Hudson Farms, Inc. v. McGrellis, 620 A.2d 215 (Del. 1993).*

A nonqualified foreign corporation may achieve registration during the pendency of a lawsuit, notwithstanding the lack of such status when the litigation was commenced; the statutory scheme does not require dismissal of an action if compliance is effected during maintenance of the suit. *Hudson Farms, Inc. v. McGrellis, 620 A.2d 215 (Del. 1993).*

DELAWARE CASE NOTES — UNREPORTED

The primary object of this section is to secure to the State and its people a way to serve process on a corporation that is organized elsewhere and that comes to Delaware to act through officers or agents. The General Assembly has codified penalties when foreign corporations fail to meet their obligations to appoint an appropriate registered agent. *Del. Code Ann. tit. 8, § 383(a) (2001). Verizon Del. v. Baldwin Line Constr. Co., 2004 Del. LEXIS 124 (2004).*

The process by which a foreign corporation shall appoint a registered agent is clearly prescribed in the Delaware General Corporation Law. Del. Code Ann. tit. 8, § 371(b)(2) (2001). Likewise, in the event a foreign corporation wishes to change its registered agent, the process for effecting that change also is prescribed by the Delaware General Corporation Law. Del. Code Ann. tit. 8, § 377. *Verizon Del. v. Baldwin Line Constr. Co., 2004 Del. Super. LEXIS 124 (2004).*

§ 376. Service of process upon qualified foreign corporations

DELAWARE CASE NOTES — REPORTED

Foreign corporation qualified in Delaware is subject to service of process in Delaware on any transitory cause of action. *D'Angelo v. Petroleos Mexicanos, 378 F. Supp. 1034 (D. Del. 1974).*

This section does not in terms limit amenability to service of a qualified foreign corporation to one which does business in Delaware or with respect to a cause of action arising in *Delaware. D'Angelo v. Petroleos Mexicanos, 378 F. Supp. 1034 (D. Del. 1974).*

Jurisdiction over foreign corporations. — When a corporation qualified as a foreign corporation pursuant to *8 Del. C. § 371*, and appointed a registered agent for the service of process pursuant to this section, the corporation consented to the exercise of general jurisdiction by the courts of *Delaware. Sternberg v. O'Neil, 550 A.2d 1105 (Del. 1988).*

A foreign corporation's ownership of a Delaware corporate subsidiary constitutes a due process minimum contact which permits Delaware courts to assert specific jurisdiction over the foreign parent corporation in a double derivative action. *Sternberg v. O'Neil, 550 A.2d 1105 (Del. 1988).*

§ 377. Change of registered agent

DELAWARE CASE NOTES — UNREPORTED

Appointment and change of agent. — The process by which a foreign corporation shall appoint a registered agent is clearly prescribed in the Delaware General Corporation Law. Del. Code Ann. tit. 8, § 371(b)(2) (2001). Likewise, in the event a foreign corporation wishes to change its registered agent, the process for effecting that change also is prescribed by this section. *Verizon Del. v. Baldwin Line Constr. Co., 2004 Del. Super. LEXIS 124 (2004).*

Excusable neglect not found. — Where a contractor did not appoint a new registered agent for almost two years after it became aware of the death of its registered agent, its failure to answer a properly served complaint could not be characterized as "excusable neglect" permitting default judgment to be vacated. *Verizon Del. v. Baldwin Line Constr. Co., 2004 Del. Super. LEXIS 124 (2004).*

§ 382. Service of process on nonqualifying foreign corporations

DELAWARE CASE NOTES — REPORTED

This section refers only to corporations, and does not apply to individuals. *Wier v. Fairfield Galleries, Inc., 377 A.2d 28 (Del. Ch. 1977).*

Section does not confer jurisdiction to extent permissible under due process clause. *Cropper v. Rego Distribution Center, Inc., 461 F. Supp. 529 (D. Del. 1978).*

But section reflects "minimum contacts" test of *International Shoe Co. v. Washington, 326 U.S. 310, 66 S. Ct. 154, 90 L. Ed. 95 (1945). Cropper v. Rego Distribution Ctr., Inc., 461 F. Supp. 529 (D. Del. 1978).*

Service of process on corporation is procedural incident of assertion of court's jurisdiction over it. *Eastman Kodak Co. v. Studiengesellschaft Kohle, 392 F. Supp. 1152 (D. Del. 1975).*

This section provides mechanism for service of process upon foreign corporations not qualified to do business in Delaware under certain circumstances. *Scott Paper Co. v. Scott's Liquid Gold, Inc., 374 F. Supp. 184 (D. Del. 1974).*

Regulations not violative of commerce clause. — 8 *Del. C. § 371* et seq., do not cause a foreign corporation to be subjected to regulations inconsistent with those for domestic corporations, and thus do not create a burden that violates the commerce clause of the *United States Constitution. Sternberg v. O'Neil, 550 A.2d 1105 (Del. 1988).*

Section compared with § 371 of this title. — The "any" business test under § 371 of this title is more comprehensive in meaning than the "doing business" test under this section. *Farmers Bank v. Sinwellan Corp., 367 A.2d 180 (Del. 1976).*

Section compared with § 383 of this title. — Although the definition of "doing business" has been broadened for purposes of this section, it is viewed narrowly for purposes of § 383 of this title. *Coyle v. Peoples, 349 A.2d 870 (Del. Super. Ct. 1975), aff'd, 372 A.2d 539 (Del. 1977).*

The "doing business" test is applicable for purposes of the long-arm statute but not for maintenance of an action within the meaning of § 383 of this title. *Farmers Bank v. Sinwellan Corp., 367 A.2d 180 (Del. 1976).*

Section compared with § 3104(c)(4) of Title 10. — The jurisdiction requirements of this section for foreign corporation are stricter than those of paragraph (4) of subsection (c) of § 3104 of Title 10, for any nonresident. This section not only requires that the defendant transact business generally in Delaware, it also requires that the civil action in question arise or grow out of the business conducted in this State. Paragraph (4) of subsection (c) of § 3104 of Title 10 does not have this section requirement and is therefore an expansion beyond this section. *Hill v. Equitable Trust Co., 562 F. Supp. 1324 (D. Del. 1983).*

While a pattern of activity must be proven to establish jurisdiction under this section, a single act may suffice under *10 Del. C. § 3104. Mid-Atlantic Mach. & Fabric, Inc. v. Chesapeake Shipbuilding, Inc., 492 A.2d 250 (Del. Super. Ct. 1985).*

Section liberally defined. — This section indicates an intent to adopt a liberal definition of "transacting business" within the *State. County Plumbing & Heating Co. v. Strine, 272 A.2d 340 (Del. Super. Ct. 1970).*

This section indicates an intent to adopt a liberal definition of "doing business within the State." *Gentry v. Wilmington Trust Co., 321 F. Supp. 1379 (D. Del. 1970).*

In view of the evolution of the Delaware long-arm statute, it has been held that a "liberal definition" should govern the application of this section. *Nacci v. Volkswagen of Am., Inc., 297 A.2d 638 (Del. Super. Ct. 1972).*

Delaware courts have held that a "liberal definition should govern the application of the current Delaware long-arm statute." *Scott Paper Co. v. Scott's Liquid Gold, Inc., 374 F. Supp. 184 (D. Del. 1974).*

The language of this section should be liberally construed in favor of finding jurisdiction. *Perry v. AMC, 353 A.2d 589 (Del. Super. Ct. 1976).*

A broad definition of "doing business" in this section has been adopted as a protective measure to ensure that wrongdoing corporations cannot escape liability. *Fehl v. S.W.C. Corp., 433 F. Supp. 939 (D. Del. 1977).*

The "transacting business generally" requirement of this section is construed liberally. *Cropper v. Rego Distribution Center, Inc., 461 F. Supp. 529 (D. Del. 1978).*

Precedent uniformity dictates a liberal construction of this section, favoring the exercise of jurisdiction. *Waters v. Deutz Corp., 460 A.2d 1332 (Del. Super. Ct. 1983).*

When section authorizes service. — This section permits substituted service in a suit brought against a foreign corporation which transacts business, including the solicitation of orders, in Delaware in a cause of action which arises or grows out of the business transacted in *Delaware. La Chemise Lacoste v. General Mills, Inc., 53 F.R.D. 596 (D. Del. 1971), aff'd, 487 F.2d 312 (3d Cir. 1973).*

In order for this section to authorize service on a nonqualified foreign corporation both: (1) The corporation must be transacting business generally in Delaware and (2) the suit must arise or grow out of a particular business transaction which occurred in the *State. Simpson v. Thiele, Inc., 344 F. Supp. 7 (D. Del. 1972); Delaware Lead*

Constr. Co. v. Young Indus., Inc., 360 F. Supp. 1244 (D. Del. 1973); General Foods Corp. v. Haines & Co., 458 F. Supp. 1167 (D. Del. 1978).

This section requires that two conditions be met before it can properly be invoked: First, the corporate defendant must be transacting business generally in Delaware and, second, the suit must arise from business transacted in the *State. Scott Paper Co. v. Scott's Liquid Gold, Inc., 374 F. Supp. 184 (D. Del. 1974).*

The two-pronged test of amenability to process under this section is: (1) The corporation must be transacting business generally in this State; and (2) the suit must arise or grow out of a particular business transaction which occurred in this *State. Perry v. AMC, 353 A.2d 589 (Del. Super. Ct. 1976); Cropper v. Rego Distribution Center, Inc., 461 F. Supp. 529 (D. Del. 1978).*

Court must first determine jurisdiction. — When the personal jurisdiction of the court is challenged or denied, it is the duty of the court, on application of a party or on its own motion, to determine the question of jurisdiction before proceeding with other aspects of the case. *General Foods Corp. v. Haines & Co., 458 F. Supp. 1167 (D. Del. 1978).*

Intent to waive due process right required. — In order for an out-of-state corporation to have waived its constitutional rights of due process in respect to service of process, it must have intended to waive such rights. *A.A.R. Realty Corp. v. United States Fire Ins. Co., 335 A.2d 271 (Del. Super. Ct. 1975).*

Determination of reach of section does not resolve venue question. — A determination of the reach of this section does not necessarily answer the question whether it was doing business in this district for venue purposes. *Scott Paper Co. v. Scott's Liquid Gold, Inc., 374 F. Supp. 184 (D. Del. 1974).*

Plaintiff has burden of sustaining jurisdiction. — Jurisdiction having been challenged, the burden rests on plaintiff to sustain it. *Simpson v. Thiele, Inc., 344 F. Supp. 7 (D. Del. 1972); Cropper v. Rego Distribution Center, Inc., 461 F. Supp. 529 (D. Del. 1978).*

Facts which may be relevant to the determination whether a defendant corporations' business activities subject them to this "long arm" statute may include: Identity of ownership and control of the chain of corporations between manufacture and sale of the product to the public, the actual relationship of those corporations; the contracts establishing the rights and responsibilities of the several corporations with respect to the franchise, and the distribution of the product; control by each corporation over the business actions of another; the power to cancel the relationship and the duration of the contractual relationship; the exclusiveness of the right to handle the product; the practice or requirement of exclusiveness as between this manufacturer's products and products of other manufacturers; the advertising practices and the control over advertising by the respective corporations; control over the manner of sale, prices and services to be provided; control over services permitted or required to be performed or actually performed by each corporation with respect to the movement, promotion or servicing of the product; the relationship of the corporations with respect to the warranty of the product and their relationship with respect to the performance, or reimbursement for performance of warranty obligations, including contractual obligations of the corporations with respect to defective materials and work. *Nacci v. Volkswagen of Am., Inc., 297 A.2d 638 (Del. Super. Ct. 1972).*

Licensor "transacting business." — Since in the event of a dispute between licensor and a Delaware licensee over the terms of a license, personal jurisdiction over licensor would properly lie in this forum, licensor is "transacting business" in Delaware under the meaning of this section. *Eastman Kodak Co. v. Studiengesellschaft Kohle, 392 F. Supp. 1152 (D. Del. 1975).*

To meet standard of transacting business, something more is required than a finding that the transaction which gave rise to the lawsuit occurred in *Delaware. General Foods Corp. v. Haines & Co., 458 F. Supp. 1167 (D. Del. 1978).*

Section requires that defendant perform some act in Delaware with respect to the claim by which it has purposefully availed itself of the privileges and protections of this *State. Cropper v. Rego Distribution Center, Inc., 461 F. Supp. 529 (D. Del. 1978).*

Claim relating only generally to nonresident's business in Delaware may not satisfy "arising out of" requirement. *Eastman Kodak Co. v. Studiengesellschaft Kohle, 392 F. Supp. 1152 (D. Del. 1975).*

Slight irregularities in mechanics of service do not require dismissal. — When the notice letter is mistakenly addressed to a nonexistent corporation, but is received in good order by the properly named defendant, and when a second complaint which lacks an accompanying notice letter is served on the same defendant, these errors in the mechanics of service are only slight irregularities and do not require dismissal under subsection (c) of this section. *Cropper v. Rego Distribution Center, Inc., 461 F. Supp. 529 (D. Del. 1978).*

Corporate entities must be respected. *Fehl v. S.W.C. Corp., 433 F. Supp. 939 (D. Del. 1977).*

But separate corporate entity may be disregarded where it would otherwise shield a parent or alter ego corporation from liability for acts attributable to it. *Fehl v. S.W.C. Corp., 433 F. Supp. 939 (D. Del. 1977).*

Effect of merger or reorganization. — If one company absorbs another through merger or reorganization, it would not offend notions of fairness to require the first to submit to the jurisdiction of the Delaware courts although there is no independent basis for jurisdiction. *Fehl v. S.W.C. Corp., 433 F. Supp. 939 (D. Del. 1977).*

Personal jurisdiction under section may be assumed over successor corporation, on the basis of acts of its predecessor, in cases where a merger or continuation has preserved the same corporate entity intact. *Fehl v. S.W.C. Corp., 433 F. Supp. 939 (D. Del. 1977).*

Hearing conducted when evidence in conflict. — See *Harry David Zutz Ins., Inc. v. H.M.S. Assocs., 360 A.2d 160 (Del. Super. Ct. 1976).*

Activities held sufficient for jurisdiction. — Where the record showed that a corporation solicited business in

Corporations

Delaware, received a contract to do a substantial job in Delaware, came to Delaware to perform under its contract, got a license to permit it to do so, and the litigation which ensued dealt with the work it is alleged to have contracted to do in Delaware, the corporation did in fact engage in a course or practice of carrying on business in Delaware such that service on the Secretary of State as agent for the corporation was proper. *Crowell Corp. v. Topkis Constr. Co., 267 A.2d 613 (Del. Super. Ct. 1970).*

The activities of a manufacturer in soliciting orders, selling products and visiting customers amounts to "a course or practice of carrying on business activities" by "solicitation of business orders in this State" as those terms are used in this section. *County Plumbing & Heating Co. v. Strine, 272 A.2d 340 (Del. Super. Ct. 1970).*

The activities of a manufacturer's representative in systematically soliciting orders from Delaware customers, forwarding the orders to a foreign corporation, and occasionally conducting displays of the corporation's products in Delaware were sufficient to subject the corporation to the jurisdiction of Delaware courts. *Gentry v. Wilmington Trust Co., 321 F. Supp. 1379 (D. Del. 1970).*

Where corporation has conscientiously pursued objective of doing business by utilizing commission brokers over a substantial period of time to solicit orders in Delaware and clearly it would be carrying on business activities in Delaware if this same function had been performed by its employees, the fact that it has elected to pay for these services through commissions rather than salaries does not alter the business reality of the matter that corporation was transacting business in the *State. Scott Paper Co. v. Scott's Liquid Gold, Inc., 374 F. Supp. 184 (D. Del. 1974).*

Where national advertising is intended to and apparently does generate a consumer demand in Delaware for defendant's products and the demand, in turn, generates corresponding demand among Delaware retailers, the benefit from that demand is reaped, in part, through the solicitation of orders in Delaware by defendant's commission brokers and the end result of that solicitation and defendant's systematic cultivation of the Delaware market is a continuous flow of its products into the *State. Scott Paper Co. v. Scott's Liquid Gold, Inc., 374 F. Supp. 184 (D. Del. 1974).*

An automobile manufacturer whose automobiles are sold in this State through a wholly owned subsidiary, who advertises extensively in this State and who provides a heavily advertised and allegedly extensive warranty to buyers of its automobiles was found to transact business in this State within the meaning of this section. *Perry v. AMC, 353 A.2d 589 (Del. Super. Ct. 1976).*

Activities not sufficient for jurisdiction. — Where defendant received an order from the purchaser, the defendant manufactured the packer at its plant in Pennsylvania, defendant did not solicit the order in Delaware and it was in Pennsylvania that defendant installed the packer on a chassis which was delivered to it in Pennsylvania and after installing the packer on the chassis a representative of the purchaser picked both the chassis and packer up in Pennsylvania and brought them back to Delaware, it was held that no incidents of the transaction occurred in *Delaware. Simpson v. Thiele, Inc., 344 F. Supp. 7 (D. Del. 1972).*

Since all of defendant's transactions took place in New York, the fact that 1 of the locations provided for under an insurance package prepared by defendant was situated in Delaware is not such a significant transaction involving contact by defendant in Delaware as would make the corporation subject to service in this *State. A.A.R. Realty Corp. v. United States Fire Ins. Co., 335 A.2d 271 (Del. Super. Ct. 1975).*

Although several employees of predecessor company, which sold a certain product line to New York corporate purchaser of the assets of the predecessor company, were later employed by the purchaser, the corporate purchaser was not a continuation of the predecessor company, so that business transactions in Delaware by predecessor company would be attributed to corporate purchaser for purpose of establishing diversity jurisdiction in employee's action against corporate purchaser for injuries incurred while using product line. *Fehl v. S.W.C. Corp., 449 F. Supp. 48 (D. Del. 1978).*

When a corporation's only contact with the State is to send a representative to negotiate a guarantee agreement, this is insufficient to amount to a course or practice of doing business. *General Foods Corp. v. Haines & Co., 458 F. Supp. 1167 (D. Del. 1978).*

In a suit by a former employee alleging age discrimination in his discharge by a foreign corporation, where the decision to discharge was made by the corporation in New Jersey, and arose out of the former employee's relationship to his employer, not out of his or his employer's sales activity in Delaware, the cause of action did not grow out of any business transacted in Delaware, and the foreign corporation is not amenable to service of process under this section. *Magid v. Marcal Paper Mills, Inc., 517 F. Supp. 1125 (D. Del. 1981).*

§ 383. Actions by and against unqualified foreign corporations

DELAWARE CASE NOTES — REPORTED

Section compared with § 382 of this title. — Although the definition of "doing business" has been broadened for purposes of § 382 of this title, it is viewed narrowly for purposes of this section. *Coyle v. Peoples, 349 A.2d 870 (Del. Super. Ct. 1975),* aff'd, *372 A.2d 539 (Del. 1977).*

The "doing business" test is applicable for purposes of the long-arm statute but not for maintenance of an action within the meaning of this section. *Farmers Bank v. Sinwellan Corp., 367 A.2d 180 (Del. 1976).*

Effect of noncompliance with § 371 of title. — Noncompliance with § 371 of this title bars a foreign corporation from maintaining "any action" in the courts of this

State. Farmers Bank v. Sinwellan Corp., 367 A.2d 180 (Del. 1976).

When section inapplicable. — This section is not applicable if the corporation is not "doing business" in this State for purposes of this section and is thus not required to register under § 371 of this title. *Coyle v. Peoples, 349 A.2d 870 (Del. Super. Ct. 1975),* aff'd, *372 A.2d 539 (Del. 1977).*

Litigation barred by section. — This section only bars litigation by foreign corporations which have done business in Delaware without qualifying therefor. *Financeamerica Private Brands, Inc. v. Harvey Hall, Inc., 366 A.2d 836 (Del. Super. Ct. 1976).*

And must be raised at outset of suit. — See *G.R. Sponaugle & Sons v. McKnight Constr. Co., 304 A.2d 339 (Del. Super. Ct. 1973).*

The failure of a foreign corporation to qualify is a matter of defense to be raised in the pleadings. *G.R. Sponaugle & Sons v. McKnight Constr. Co., 304 A.2d 339 (Del. Super. Ct. 1973).*

The capacity of a corporation to enforce a contract can be raised only by a plea in abatement. *G.R. Sponaugle & Sons v. McKnight Constr. Co., 304 A.2d 339 (Del. Super. Ct. 1973).*

Raising issue of foreign corporation's capacity. — The issue of the capacity of a foreign corporation as limited by this section is a matter to be raised as provided in Super. Ct. Civ. R. 9(a). *Financeamerica Private Brands, Inc. v. Harvey Hall, Inc., 366 A.2d 836 (Del. Super. Ct. 1976).*

Capacity of corporation to file mechanic's lien action. — See *G.R. Sponaugle & Sons v. McKnight Constr. Co., 304 A.2d 339 (Del. Super. Ct. 1973).*

Compliance during pendency of action. — A nonqualified foreign corporation may achieve registration during the pendency of a lawsuit, notwithstanding the lack of such status when the litigation was commenced; the statutory scheme does not require dismissal of an action if compliance is effected during maintenance of the suit. *Hudson Farms, Inc. v. McGrellis, 620 A.2d 215 (Del. 1993).*

Activities insufficient for jurisdiction. — An unlicensed broker's foreign corporation is not required to be a qualified corporation in order to enforce a contract for a sales commission, where the unlicensed broker conducted only a single transaction in this State in conjunction with a broker of this State, since the transaction does not constitute "doing business" under this section. *Coyle v. Peoples, 349 A.2d 870 (Del. Super. Ct. 1975),* aff'd, *372 A.2d 539 (Del. 1977).*

DELAWARE CASE NOTES — UNREPORTED

Construction with Section 371. — The primary object of Del. Code Ann. tit. 8, § 371 is to secure to the State and its people a way to serve process on a corporation that is organized elsewhere and that comes to Delaware to act through officers or agents. The General Assembly has codified penalties when foreign corporations fail to meet their obligations to appoint an appropriate registered agent under subsection (a) of this section. *Verizon Del. v. Baldwin Line Constr. Co., 2004 Del. Super. LEXIS 124 (2004).*

Subchapter XVII.
Miscellaneous Provisions

§ 391. Taxes and fees payable to Secretary of State upon filing certificate or other paper

DELAWARE CASE NOTES — REPORTED

The 1982 amendment to subsection (b) of this section will not be applied retrospectively since there is no express provision for retrospective application in the amendment. *Chrysler Corp. v. State, 457 A.2d 345 (Del. 1983).*

Subsections (a)(2) and (b) of this section must be read together. *Chrysler Corp. v. State, 457 A.2d 345 (Del. 1983).*

Paragraph (3) of subsection (a) controls assessment of tax where authorized capital stock not increased. — Since a certificate of amendment which changed shares of common stock from shares having par value to shares without par value did not increase the authorized capital stock, paragraph (3) of subsection (a) of this section, not paragraph (2) of subsection (a) of this section, controlled the assessment of tax on the certificate of amendment. *Chrysler Corp. v. State, 457 A.2d 345 (Del. 1983).*

Consolidation of 2 changes into 1 resolution before shareholders does not render them substantially 1 transaction. — Where a Delaware corporation, by means of a single resolution, amended its certificate of incorporation so as to increase its authorized capital stock and to reclassify its stock from par value to no par, the consolidation of the 2 changes, listed as separate allowable changes under subsection (a) of § 242 of this title, into 1 resolution before the shareholders did not render them substantially 1 transaction. *Chrysler Corp. v. State, 457 A.2d 345 (Del. 1983).*

Schedule of taxes and fees is subject to change. — The schedule of taxes and fees to be paid to the State by corporations is subject to change, and has been changed from time to time, and to what extent corporations shall be assessed is a matter for legislative determination. *State v. Bethlehem Steel Corp., 37 Del. 441, 184 A. 873 (1936).*

§ 394. Reserved power of State to amend or repeal chapter; chapter part of corporation's charter or certificate of incorporation

DELAWARE CASE NOTES — REPORTED

State's reserved power becomes part of charter. — The reservation of power to alter or revoke a grant necessarily becomes a part of the charter of every corporation formed under the general statute providing for the formation of corporations. *Wilmington City Ry. v. Wilmington & Brandywine Springs Ry., 8 Del. Ch. 468, 46 A. 12 (1900).*

There is impliedly written into every corporate charter in this State, as a constituent part thereof, every pertinent provision of the Delaware Constitution and statutes. *Peters v. United States Mtg. Co., 13 Del. Ch. 11, 114 A. 598 (1921); Morris v. American Pub. Util. Co., 14 Del. Ch. 136, 122 A. 696 (1923); Hartford Accident & Indem. Co. v. W.S. Dickey Clay Mfg. Co., 26 Del. Ch. 411, 24 A.2d 315 (1942).*

All future amendments to the General Corporation Law are written by this section into a corporation's charter as effectively as was the original act. *Davis v. Louisville Gas & Elec. Co., 16 Del. Ch. 157, 142 A. 654 (1928).*

The provisions of § 251 of this title have been a part of the General Corporation Law since its first adoption, and must be read into a Delaware corporation's charter to the same extent as though they had actually been inserted in it. *Havender v. Federal United Corp., 24 Del. Ch. 96, 6 A.2d 618 (1939), rev'd on other grounds, 24 Del. Ch. 318, 11 A.2d 331 (1940).*

Where a corporation was created under the General Corporation Law, every pertinent provision of the Constitution and of that law is impliedly written into and composes a part of its charter. *Aldridge v. Franco Wyo. Oil Co., 24 Del. Ch. 126, 7 A.2d 753 (1939), aff'd, 24 Del. Ch. 349, 14 A.2d 380 (1940).*

The provisions of the Delaware Corporation Law are a part of the charter of every corporation. *Voege v. American Sumatra Tobacco Corp., 241 F. Supp. 369 (D. Del. 1965).*

Buyers of stock have knowledge that law may be changed. — Buyers of stock of Delaware corporations become stockholders with actual or imputed knowledge that the Corporation Law may be changed, and the corporate charter thereby amended subject to the limitation that rights must be protected. *Weinberg v. Baltimore Brick Co., 34 Del. Ch. 586, 108 A.2d 81 (1954), aff'd, 35 Del. Ch. 225, 114 A.2d 812 (1955).*

Power of alteration and amendment is not without limit. The alterations must be reasonable; they must be made in good faith, and be consistent with the scope and object of the act of incorporation. *Wilmington City Ry. v. Wilmington & Brandywine Springs Ry., 8 Del. Ch. 468, 46 A. 12 (1900).*

Reserved power may be exercised to alter existing contracts. — The power reserved by the State to amend its General Corporation Law may be exercised, not only to alter the contract as it exists between the State and the corporate entity, but as well to alter the contract existing between the corporation and its stockholders, and the stockholders inter sese. *Davis v. Louisville Gas & Elec. Co., 16 Del. Ch. 157, 142 A. 654 (1928).*

The terms of the agreement between the shareholders, both as to the internal management of the corporation and as to their beneficial interests therein, are but conditions on which the corporate franchise may be exercised, and the reserved power of the State gives the State the unqualified right to alter or amend the privilege, or to confer upon the shareholders the right so to do, irrespective of the nature and character of the right invaded. *Keller v. Wilson & Co., 21 Del. Ch. 391, 190 A. 115 (1936).*

Provisions such as those contained in this section have been construed to authorize the enactment of statutes changing the rights of stockholders in regard to shares acquired prior to such enactment. *Coyne v. Park & Tilford Distillers Corp., 38 Del. Ch. 514, 154 A.2d 893 (1959).*

Vested rights. — A power reserved to the General Assembly to alter, amend or repeal a charter, authorizes it to make any alteration or amendment of a charter granted subject to it which will not defeat, or substantially impair, the object of the grant, or any rights vested under it, and which the General Assembly may deem necessary to secure either that object or any public right. *Wilmington City Ry. v. Wilmington & Brandywine Springs Ry., 8 Del. Ch. 468, 46 A. 12 (1900).*

The corporate charter may be repealed or amended, and, within limits, the interrelations of State, corporation and stockholders may be changed; but neither vested property rights nor the obligation of contracts of third persons may be destroyed or impaired. *Keller v. Wilson & Co., 21 Del. Ch. 391, 190 A. 115 (1936).*

No vested right in pre-amendment version of charter. — Shareholders did not have a vested right to a charter provision subsequently amended; such a claim did not fall within the ambit of this section, which provides perhaps the only vested right, the prohibition of a statutory charter amendment that takes away or impairs any remedy against a corporation or its officers for any liability previously incurred. *Kidsco Inc. v. Dinsmore, 674 A.2d 483 (Del. Ch. 1995).*

DELAWARE CASE NOTES — UNREPORTED

Limitations. — The substantive effect of this section is to engraft the statutory rules provided in the Delaware General Corporation Laws onto every charter, to relieve drafters of charters of the burden of explicitly specifying

every single one of those rules that they wish to adopt. Thus, had charter not included any provision at all governing the setting of record dates for consent solicitations, this section would incorporate the terms of subsection (b) of Section 213 into the charter. But, the charter provision does provide a method for setting the record date. This section does not create ambiguity where there is none, and does not incorporate statutory terms back into a charter provision when the drafters have chosen to deviate from those terms. *Jones Apparel Group v. Maxwell Shoe Co., 2004 Del. Ch. LEXIS 74, No. 365-N (May 27, 2004).*

CHAPTER 5.
CORPORATION FRANCHISE TAX

§ 501. Corporations subject to and exempt from franchise tax

DELAWARE CASE NOTES — REPORTED

Franchise tax is debt due state. *State v. Surety Corp. of Am., 19 Del. Ch. 17, 162 A. 852 (1932).*

Although this section designates an imposition of this kind as a license fee or franchise tax, it plainly is not a tax upon corporate franchises. In fact, it is not, strictly speaking, a tax at all, nor has it the elements of one. It is in reality an arbitrary imposition laid upon the corporation, without regard to the value of its property or of its franchises, and without regard to whether it exercises the latter or not, solely as a condition of its continued existence. *State v. Surety Corp. of Am., 19 Del. Ch. 17, 162 A. 852 (1932).*

Tax exempt hospital should render emergency aid. — A hospital which was a private, nonprofit, no stock, charitable hospital corporation but receiving tax exemptions on the basis that it was open to the public, should be required at all times to render reasonable needed aid in those instances where an emergency involving death or serious bodily impairment might reasonably be said to exist. *Manlove v. Wilmington Gen. Hosp., 53 Del. 338, 169 A.2d 18, aff'd, 174 A.2d 135 (Del. 1961).*

Mere retention by corporation of its charter creates obligation to pay tax, irrespective of whether or not the corporation is in the active conduct of the business which it was created to carry on. *State v. Surety Corp. of Am., 19 Del. Ch. 17, 162 A. 852 (1932).*

Tax payable out of assets in hands of receiver. — If the receivership of a corporation is a liquidating one from the beginning, the franchise tax is payable out of the corporation's assets in the hands of the receiver. *State v. Surety Corp. of Am., 19 Del. Ch. 17, 162 A. 852 (1932).*

In a purely liquidating receivership, franchise taxes assessed by the State upon a corporation for its privilege to exist are payable out of the estate in the hands of the receiver, notwithstanding such taxes have accrued since the date of his appointment, and notwithstanding the corporate franchise was of no value to the receiver and that he had never in fact made any use of it. *State v. Surety Corp. of Am., 19 Del. Ch. 17, 162 A. 852 (1932).*

§ 502. Annual franchise tax report; contents; failure to file and pay tax; duties of Secretary of State

DELAWARE CASE NOTES — REPORTED

Purpose of law in requiring corporations to make annual reports to the Secretary of State is to enable that officer to determine the basis of their annual license fees, especially when such determination rests wholly or in part upon the information that can be acquired only from the corporations themselves, as for instance the character of the business pursued and the amount thereof transacted within and without the *State of Delaware. State v. Coppermines Co., 25 Del. 400, 80 A. 145 (1911).*

Corporation must make full and accurate annual report. — As the law contemplates an annual taxation on the basis of an annual authorized capitalization, the law requires a corporation in making its annual report to give accurately, truthfully and fully the status of its capitaliza-

tion for the whole year, with reference to which its report is required to be made. *State v. Coppermines Co., 25 Del. 400, 80 A. 145 (1911).*

Report not binding on secretary of state or on corporation. — Annual report filed on amount of authorized stock is not binding on either the Secretary of State or the corporation. *State v. R.H. Perry & Co., 33 Del. 530, 140 A. 474 (1928).*

Errors in annual report of the corporation to the Secretary of State can be shown like any other defense to the amount claimed to be due in an action to collect franchise tax. *State v. R.H. Perry & Co., 33 Del. 530, 140 A. 474 (1928).*

§ 507. Collection of tax; preferred debt

DELAWARE CASE NOTES — REPORTED

Priority of debts owed united states. — The provisions of Article 6 of the Constitution of the United States, which declare that the laws of the United States made in pursuance of the Constitution shall be the supreme law of the land, require that the priority conferred by *31 U.S.C.*

§ 191, relating to debts owed the United States, should outrank the preference which is given to the State by this section. *West Coast Power Co. v. Southern Kan. Gas Co., 20 Del. Ch. 130, 172 A. 414 (1934).*

§ 510. Failure to pay tax or file a complete annual report for 1 year; charter void; extension of time

DELAWARE CASE NOTES — REPORTED

Corporate franchise tax act is purely revenue measure. *Wax v. Riverview Cem. Co., 41 Del. 424, 24 A.2d 431 (1942).*

Failure to pay franchise taxes is an issue solely between the corporation and the State since the franchise tax statutes are for revenue-raising purposes alone. *Frederic G. Krapf & Son v. Gorson, 243 A.2d 713 (Del. 1968).*

Effect of this section is not limited by §§ 511 and 512 of this title dealing with the proclamation; hence, the doing of things directed by §§ 511 and 512 of this title is not a prerequisite to the voidance of a charter for nonpayment of taxes. *Wuerfel v. F.H. Smith Co., 25 Del. Ch. 82, 13 A.2d 601 (1940).*

Corporate franchise tax itself does not accrue during period charter is inoperative. *Wax v. Riverview Cem. Co., 41 Del. 424, 24 A.2d 431 (1942).*

Tax not collectible for more than 2 years. — Since under this section the charter becomes void when the franchise tax is unpaid for 2 consecutive years, the claim of the State will be allowed for franchise taxes falling due only while the corporation was alive and the tax is not collectible for more than 2 years. *State v. Surety Corp. of Am., 19 Del. Ch. 17, 162 A. 852 (1932).*

Corporation which has forfeited its charter for nonpayment of taxes is not completely dead; it is in a state of coma from which it can be easily resuscitated, but until this is done its powers as a corporation are inoperative, and the exercise of these powers is a criminal offense. *Wax v. Riverview Cem. Co., 41 Del. 424, 24 A.2d 431 (1942).*

So long as there is a statutory right to be reinstated, the proclamation of forfeiture for nonpayment of taxes does no more than forfeit the corporate right to do business, but does not extinguish the corporation as a legal entity. *Wax v. Riverview Cem. Co., 41 Del. 424, 24 A.2d 431 (1942).*

The word "void" as used in this section with regard to the status of the corporate charter was never intended in the sense of absolutely invalid, for there has always been provision for reinstatement which could not occur if the charter had become absolutely void. *Wax v. Riverview Cem. Co., 41 Del. 424, 24 A.2d 431 (1942).*

Contracts validated upon reinstatement of charter. — This section provides that, upon forfeiture of a charter for failure to pay franchise taxes, all of the corporation's powers become inoperative, but this provision must be read in the light of subsection (e) of § 312 of this title, which provides that upon reinstatement of a charter all contracts and other matters done and performed by the corporate officers during the time the charter was inoperative shall be validated, and be the exclusive liability of the corporation. *Frederic G. Krapf & Son v. Gorson, 243 A.2d 713 (Del. 1968).*

The president of a corporation, the charter of which has been proclaimed for failure to pay franchise taxes, may not be held personally liable upon a contract entered into by him or her in behalf of the corporation after the proclamation of the charter and before its revival. *Frederic G. Krapf & Son v. Gorson, 243 A.2d 713 (Del. 1968).*

CASE NOTES — OTHER STATES

Virginia

Prosecution of civil suit. — Del. Gen. Corp. Law tit. 8 § 510 grants limited capabilities to dissolving corporations. The prosecution of a civil suit by a delinquent corporation, however, sharply contrasts passive functions, such as serving as a repository of title and an obligor of debt, allowed by the Delaware courts. *Hoopes Construction, Inc. v. Wilcher, 1998 Va. Cir. LEXIS 440 (1998).*

The language of Del. Gen. Corp. Law tit. 8, § 510 states that all powers conferred upon the corporation are declared inactive. The ability to sue, under the plain meaning of the § 510, no longer exists because it is a "power conferred upon a corporation." *Hoopes Construction, Inc. v. Wilcher, 1998 Va. Cir. LEXIS 440 (1998).*

Construction with other law. — A corporation whose charter is "void and powers inoperative" due to nonpayment of taxes is considered dissolved. A corporation's nonpayment of taxes makes the charter void, and all powers upon the corporation inoperative, and thus dissolved. Del. Gen. Corp. Law tit. 8, § 278 is interpreted as allowing a dissolving corporation to nevertheless exist for a period of three years for the purposes of winding up its corporate and business affairs. This includes bringing suit as well as defending suits brought by others. *Hoopes Construction, Inc. v. Wilcher, 1998 Va. Cir. LEXIS 440 (1998).*

Under Del. Gen. Corp. Law tit. 8, § 277, a corporation may not dissolve until all franchise taxes due or assessable have been paid by the corporation. Compliance with Del. Gen. Corp. Law tit. 8, § 277 is not a threshold requirement for a corporation to take advantage of the three-year winding-up period, but rather is a bar to complete dissolution protection until a Delaware corporation pays its state taxes. *Hoopes Construction, Inc. v. Wilcher, 1998 Va. Cir. LEXIS 440 (1998).*

CASE NOTES — FEDERAL

Sixth Circuit

Patent assignment enforceable. — If a contract entered into by a corporate officer after the forfeiture of the charter is considered binding on the corporation under Delaware law, there is no principled reason why a patent assignment executed by a corporate officer after an inadvertent forfeiture should not be similarly upheld and enforced. *Parker v. Cardiac Sci., Inc., 2006 U.S. Dist. LEXIS 90014 (D. Mich. Nov. 27, 2006).*

§ 511. Repeal of charters of delinquent corporations; report to Governor and proclamation

CASE NOTES — FEDERAL

Second Circuit

State of coma. — Under Delaware law, a corporation which has been proclaimed forfeited for nonpayment of taxes is not completely dead. It is in a state of coma from which it can be easily resuscitated, but until this is done its powers as a corporation are inoperative and the exercise of these powers is a criminal offense. It still can serve as repository of title and as obligor of debt. *Board of Managers v. City of New York, 2005 U.S. Dist. LEXIS 9139 (S.D.N.Y. 2005).*

§ 513. Acting under proclaimed charter; penalty

DELAWARE CASE NOTES — REPORTED

This section provides remedy for state against corporation, the officers of which persist in exercising its corporate powers after the charter forfeiture. *Frederic G. Krapf & Son v. Gorson, 243 A.2d 713 (Del. 1968).*

And section has no bearing in contest between private parties. *Frederic G. Krapf & Son v. Gorson, 243 A.2d 713 (Del. 1968).*

Alternative Entities

TITLE 6
COMMERCE AND TRADE

SUBTITLE II.
OTHER LAWS RELATING TO COMMERCE AND TRADE

CHAPTER 15.
DELAWARE REVISED UNIFORM PARTNERSHIP ACT

Subchapter I. General Provisions

§ 15-110.   Indemnification

CASE NOTES — FEDERAL COURTS

Second Circuit

Expectation of payment of legal expenses. — The statute that governed partnership gives it the authority to indemnify and hold harmless any partner or other person from and against any and all claims and demands whatsoever. This includes the authority to advance defense costs prior to final judgment. Company had an unbroken track record of paying the legal expenses of its partners and employees incurred as a result of their jobs, without regard to cost. All of the defendants therefore had, at a minimum, every reason to expect that company would pay their legal expenses in connection with the government's investigation and, if they were indicted, defending against any charges that arose out of their employment by the company. *United States v. Stein, 2006 U.S. Dist. LEXIS 42915 (D. N.Y. June 26, 2006).*

Government interference. — The fact that advancement of legal fees occasionally might be part of an obstruction scheme or indicate a lack of full cooperation by a prospective defendant is insufficient to justify the government's interference with the right of individual criminal defendants to obtain resources lawfully available to them in order to defend themselves, regardless of the legal standard of scrutiny applied. *United States v. Stein, 2006 U.S. Dist. LEXIS 42915 (D. N.Y. June 26, 2006).*

Violation of 5th and 6th Amendment found. — So much of the memorandum and the activities of the prosecution as threatened to take into account, in deciding whether to indict partnership, whether partners would advance attorneys' fees to present or former employees in the event they were indicted for activities undertaken in the course of their employment interfered with the rights of such employees to a fair trial and to the effective assistance of counsel and therefore violated the Fifth and Sixth Amendments to the Constitution. *United States v. Stein, 2006 U.S. Dist. LEXIS 42915 (D. N.Y. June 26, 2006).*

Subchapter II.
Nature of Partnership

§ 15-202.   Formation of partnership; powers

DELAWARE CASE NOTES — UNREPORTED

Partnership not created by colloquial reference to another as a "partner". — No static and ascertainable relationship existed between 2 businesspersons, such that it could be considered a Delaware general partnership under 6 Del. C. § 15-202, where they were simply trying to negotiate a mutually binding, formal relationship as members of a limited liability company that was to conduct a business endeavor; the mere fact that 1 of the 2 colloquially used the word "partners" publicly at certain meetings/documents did not overcome their inability to establish a binding, business relationship by contract. *Ramone v. Lang, 2006 Del. Ch. LEXIS 71 (Del. Ch. Apr. 3, 2006).*

Subchapter III.
Relations of Partners to Persons Dealing with Partnership

§ 15-205.   Admission without contribution or partnership interest

CASE NOTES — FEDERAL COURTS

Seventh Circuit

Inference of "partner" status. — Since neither the partnership agreement nor the Partnership Act excludes "contract partners" from the partnership, there is no basis to find as a matter of law that the firm did not owe plaintiff a fiduciary relationship. The requirement that she execute the partnership agreement and her alleged treatment as a "partner" for purposes of state and federal income taxes is sufficient to create an inference that she was a "partner" for purposes of partnership law and therefore owed a fiduciary duty by the firm. *Beesen-Dwars v. Duane Morris LLP, 2007 U.S. Dist. LEXIS 54947 (D. Ill. July 24, 2007).*

§ 15-306.   Partner's liability

DELAWARE CASE NOTES — REPORTED

Nature of partners. — Because partners have equal rights in the management of general partnerships, and because they are not protected by limited liability, partners in general partnerships are unlikely to be passive investors who profit solely on the efforts of others. *Great Lakes Chem. Corp. v. Monsanto Co., 96 F. Supp. 2d 376 (D. Del. 2000).*

CASE NOTES — FEDERAL COURTS

Fifth Circuit

In general. — Under Delaware law general partners are liable for all obligations of the partnership. *Peter v. GC Services L.P., 310 F.3d 344 (5th Cir. 2002).*

Seventh Circuit

In general. — Delaware partnership law provides that all partners are liable jointly and severally for everything chargeable to the partnership. It is well-established that under the law of partnerships, knowledge and actions of one partner are imputed to all others. The partnership is liable for acts performed in its name and within the scope of its business, and the partners are liable for all debts and obligations of the partnership. The same liabilities apply to a general partner in a limited partnership. *Randle v. GC Services, L.P., 25 F. Supp. 2d 849 (N.D.Ill. 1998).*

§ 15-307.   Actions by and against partnership and partners

CASE NOTES — FEDERAL COURTS

Third Circuit

In Delaware, general partners have the power to sue directly on behalf of the partnership on the partnership's claims. *HB Gen. Corp. v. Manchester Partners, 95 F.3d 1185 (3d Cir. 1996).*

Subchapter IV.
Relations of Partners to Each Other and to Partnership

§ 15-401.   Partner's rights and duties

CASE NOTES — FEDERAL COURTS

Seventh Circuit

Under Delaware law one partner owes the other partners fiduciary duties. *Niki Development Corp. v. HOB Hotel Chicago Partners, L.P., 2001 U.S. Dist. LEXIS 1544 (N.D.Ill. 2001).*

A general partner owes his partners utmost good faith, fairness, and loyalty in his or her partnership dealings. This duty exists concurrently with the obligations set forth in the partnership agreement whether or not expressed therein. *Niki Development Corp. v. HOB Hotel Chicago Partners, L.P., 2001 U.S. Dist. LEXIS 1544 (N.D.Ill. 2001).*

§ 15-404. General standards of partner's conduct

Seventh Circuit

Under Delaware law one partner owes the other partners fiduciary duties. *Niki Development Corp. v. HOB Hotel Chicago Partners, L.P., 2001 U.S. Dist. LEXIS 1544 (N.D.Ill. 2001).*

A general partner owes his partners utmost good faith, fairness, and loyalty in his or her partnership dealings. This duty exists concurrently with the obligations set forth in the partnership agreement whether or not expressed therein. *Niki Development Corp. v. HOB Hotel Chicago Partners, L.P., 2001 U.S. Dist. LEXIS 1544 (N.D.Ill. 2001).*

§ 15-405. Actions by partnership and partners; derivative actions

No automatic revival of right of action upon dissolution. — It is clear under the Revised Uniform Partnership Act (*6 Del. C. § 15-101* et seq.) that a right of action arising during the life of a partnership is not revived merely because a dissolution occurs, and a separate right to an accounting on dissolution arises. *Fike v. Ruger, 754 A.2d 254 (Del. Ch. 1999).*

First Circuit

Accounting exception adopted. — While one might question the public policy of requiring an accounting in situations such as the one presently before the court, as the law presently stands an accounting remains a condition precedent to an action at law between limited partners under Delaware law. On this point, the court finds it particularly noteworthy that in 2001 a Revised Uniform Limited Partnership Act ("RULPA") was approved and recommended for adoption and enactment in all the states. The RULPA contains a provision that allows direct action by a limited partner against the limited partnership or another partner, with or without an accounting, if the partner can plead and prove an actual or threatened injury that is not solely the result of an injury suffered or threatened to be suffered by the limited partnership. This section was derived from the Revised Uniform Partnership Act ("RUPA"), § 405(b). While Delaware has incorporated into the Delaware Revised Uniform Partnership Act the provision in RUPA that allows direct action by one partner against another in a general partnership, Del. Code. Ann. tit. 6 § 15-405(b), it has not adopted the provision in RULPA creating the same limited exception to the accounting rule in the case of actions between limited partners. In the absence of such statutory authority, or the applicability of a recognized exception, plaintiffs' direct claims against their co-limited partners are necessarily barred as premature for failure to first pursue an equitable action for an accounting. *Drenis v. Haligiannis, 452 F. Supp. 2d 418, 2006 U.S. Dist. LEXIS 68488 (D.N.Y. Sept. 25, 2006).*

Subchapter VIII.
Winding Up Partnership Business or Affairs

§ 15-801. Events causing dissolution and winding up of partnership business or affairs

Effect of withdrawal on partnership. — The limited partners' withdrawal dissolved the limited partnership because Delaware law dissolves a limited partnership as a matter of law after all limited partners have withdrawn. *Continental Ins. Co. v. Rutledge & Co., 750 A.2d 1219 (Del. Ch. 2000).*

Virginia

Construction with other law. — The provision of a narrower dissolution statute for limited partnerships evinced a legislative intent that the broader provisions of the General Partnership statute not apply to limited partnerships. *First Union National Bank v. Allen Lorey Family Limited Partnership, 34 Va. Cir. 474 (1994).*

RUPA

§ 15-802. Partnership continues after dissolution

CASE NOTES — OTHER STATES

Virginia

Construction with other law. — The provision of a narrower dissolution statute for limited partnerships evinced a legislative intent that the broader provisions of the General Partnership statute not apply to limited partnerships. *First Union National Bank v. Allen Lorey Family Limited Partnership, 34 Va. Cir. 474 (1994).*

CHAPTER 17.
LIMITED PARTNERSHIPS

Subchapter I.
General Provisions

§ 17-101.   Definitions

DELAWARE CASE NOTES — REPORTED

Ambiguities interpreted contrary to drafting partner. — In interpreting a partnership agreement, ambiguities were resolved against the drafting general partner and in favor of the limited partners' reasonable expectations, with consent being required to amend the partnership agreement to affect the limited partners' substantive rights; if parties to a partnership agreement desire to establish separate 'classes' or 'groups' of limited partners, such classes or groups should be expressly specified, with the relative rights, powers, and duties of the limited partners in such classes or groups expressly set forth in the partnership agreement. *In re Nantucket Island Assocs., 810 A.2d 351 (Del. Ch. 2002).*

"Limited partnerships". — Limited partnerships in Delaware are formed pursuant to this section and are comprised of general partners and limited partners. *Great Lakes Chem. Corp. v. Monsanto Co., 96 F. Supp. 2d 376 (D. Del. 2000).*

Waiver. — While agreement contained a choice of law clause providing that Delaware law is to govern, both parties have cited only Missouri law in their arguments on the enforceability of the nonsolicitation clause. Parties to a contract may waive the provisions of their contract by their conduct. Therefore, by not citing any Delaware law on customer nonsolicitation clauses, the parties have

waived the Delaware choice of law clause in the operating agreement. *JTL Consulting, L.L.C. v. Shanahan, 2006 Mo. App. LEXIS 92 (Jan. 24, 2006).*

Limited partnerships' contract theory-based structure provides incentives for parties to opt for the limited partnership over other forms of business organizations. As such, parties, otherwise unwilling to shoulder fiduciary burdens, maintain the opportunity to form limited partnerships precisely because the parties can contract around some or all of the fiduciary duties the general partner typically owes the limited partners. *Continental Ins. Co. v. Rutledge & Co., 750 A.2d 1219, 2000 Del. Ch. LEXIS 18 (Del. Ch. 2000).*

Liability of limited partners. — The general policy of DRULPA is that the liability of limited partners of a Delaware limited partnership is limited. *In re LJM2 Co-Investment, L.P., 866 A.2d 762, 2004 Del. Ch. LEXIS 195 (Del. Ch. 2004).*

Interpretation of agreements. — Because DRULPA embodies the policy of freedom of contract and maximum flexibility, the process of engrafting default statutory provisions onto an agreement of limited partnership should be undertaken with caution. *In re LJM2 Co-Investment, L.P., 866 A.2d 762, 2004 Del. Ch. LEXIS 195 (Del. Ch. 2004).*

DELAWARE CASE NOTES — UNREPORTED

Delaware law permits partners of a limited partnership to operate their business as they choose, insofar as their actions do not conflict with specific commands of public policy. *Active Asset Recovery, Inc. v. Real Estate Asset Recovery Servs., 1999 Del. Ch. LEXIS 179 (Del. Ch. Sept. 10, 1999).*

Contractual relationship. — The relationship between limited partners and the general partner in a limited partnership is more like that of a corporation to its preferred shareholders — primarily contractual in nature. *In re Cencom Cable Income Partners, L.P. Litig., 1996 Del. Ch. LEXIS 17 (Del. Ch. Feb. 15, 1996).*

§ 17-105.   Service of process on domestic limited partnerships

DELAWARE CASE NOTES — REPORTED

Service held proper. — Service of process was proper when made upon person whose interest in limited partnership had been sold but where this change had not

been publicly recorded by amendment of the certificate of limited partnership. *Harry David Zutz Ins., Inc. v. H.M.S. Assocs., 360 A.2d 160 (Del. Super. Ct. 1976).*

DELAWARE CASE NOTES — UNREPORTED

The service of process statutory scheme contemplates adequate notice and presumes proper service when made on a general partner of a registered foreign limited partnership when the general partner is located in Delaware. Only when the general partner cannot be found in this state and when the limited partnership has not

registered to do business in Delaware, does the statutory scheme presume designation of the Secretary of State as agent to accept service of process. The legislature then requires the Secretary of State to accept service of process for the unregistered foreign limited partnership. In essence, the statutes create a continuum for service of process based upon the nature of the limited partnership's contact with Delaware. The statutes do not address the scenario where an unregistered foreign limited partnership has a Delaware corporation as its general partner. *Macklowe v. Planet Hollywood, 1994 Del. Ch. LEXIS 179 (Del. Ch. Oct. 13, 1994).*

Illustrative cases. — Selection by an unregistered foreign limited partnership of a Delaware resident corporation as its general partner constitutes a reasonable basis for concluding it expected its general partner to be served and accept service of process in the event it was doing business in Delaware. *Macklowe v. Planet Hollywood, 1994 Del. Ch. LEXIS 179 (Del. Ch. Oct. 13, 1994).*

While failure to amend a certificate of limited partnership to reflect the current address of the partnership may in some circumstances estop the defendant from claiming ineffective service of process, in this case the plaintiff failed to take reasonable steps to notify the defendant by either delivering a copy of the complaint personally to the general partner, or by leaving it as his home or other place of business. At the same time, plaintiff's counsel knew that the defendant still owned the property at a certain address and in fact sent correspondence there after a default judgment was obtained. Moreover, the plaintiff had general partner's phone number and could have contacted him to get his address. Under the circumstances, the plaintiff could have effectuated service in the manner provided for by §17-105(a) and was not justified in resorting to service on the Secretary of State pursuant to §17-105(b). *Webster v. Ferm, 1986 Del. Super. LEXIS 1180 (Del. Super. Ct. Apr. 24, 1986).*

Certified mail is not an appropriate method of serving the summons and complaint on a domestic limited partnership. certified mail is not an appropriate method of serving the summons and complaint on a domestic limited partnership. *Shomide v. ILC Dover LP, 2006 U.S. Dist. LEXIS 50246 (D. Del. July 20, 2006).*

§ 17-108.   Indemnification

DELAWARE CASE NOTES — UNREPORTED

Section 18-108 of the Limited Liability Company Act is verbatim § 17-108 of the Delaware Revised Uniform Limited Partnership Act ('DRULPA'). Both DRULPA and LLCA allow the contracting parties to determine the extent of indemnification in their agreements. In granting the advances on claims of indemnification in a limited partnership setting, it has been held that courts should interpret language so as to achieve where possible the beneficial purposes that indemnification can afford. *Morgan v. Grace, 2003 Del. Ch. LEXIS 113, No. 20430 (2003).*

In general. — The best reading of this section is that it permits a limited partnership to indemnify a partner or other person even in the absence of a provision in the partnership agreement contemplating that result. *Active Asset Recovery, Inc. v. Real Estate Asset Recovery Servs., 1999 Del. Ch. LEXIS 179 (Del. Ch. Sept. 10, 1999).*

The public policy of Delaware is to allow advancement, if the partnership agreement so provides, even in cases in which the plaintiff is a limited partner and the claims are for breach of fiduciary duty. This has regularly been done under corporate indemnification provisions which are somewhat more restrictive than DRULPA. *Delphi Easter Partners Ltd. Partnership v. Spectacular Partners, Inc., 1993 Del. Ch. LEXIS 159 (Del. Ch. Aug. 6, 1993).*

In the absence of an agreement, this section leaves a limited partnership with the power but not the duty to indemnify. Given that the power to indemnify would seem broader than — and, indeed, inclusive of — the power to advance litigation expenses, it seems reasonable to infer that a limited partnership also has the power of advancement. *Active Asset Recovery, Inc. v. Real Estate Asset Recovery Servs., 1999 Del. Ch. LEXIS 179 (Del. Ch. Sept. 10, 1999).*

This section, enacted in 1985, is broadly enabling. It might be compared to the partnership indemnification provision, which provides for mandatory indemnification in a narrower set of cases, and is also broader than the statutory indemnification provision applicable to corporations. In fact, this section defers completely to the contracting parties to create and delimit rights and obligations with respect to indemnification and advancement of expenses. The statute itself creates no rights to indemnification. *Delphi Easter Partners Ltd. Partnership v. Spectacular Partners, Inc., 1993 Del. Ch. LEXIS 159 (Del. Ch. Aug. 6, 1993).*

Interpretation of agreements. — In construing contractual language under DRULPA conferring rights of indemnification, courts should interpret language so as to achieve where possible the beneficial purposes that indemnification can afford. Those benefits include the allocation of certain risks at the outset of a contractual relation in order to make the contractual structure feasible or more attractive to participants. *Delphi Easter Partners Ltd. Partnership v. Spectacular Partners, Inc., 1993 Del. Ch. LEXIS 159 (Del. Ch. Aug. 6, 1993).*

§ 17-109.   Service of process on partners and liquidating trustees

DELAWARE CASE NOTES — REPORTED

No retroactive application. — Because the General Assembly did not provide for the retroactive application of this section, the court lacked personal jurisdiction where the partnership's certificate was filed before its effective date. *CRI Liquidating Reit, Inc. v. A.F. Evans Co., 730 A.2d 1244 (Del. Ch. 1997).*

DELAWARE CASE NOTES — UNREPORTED

Limited partners.–This chapter contains no provision that would subject a limited partner to personal jurisdiction solely on the basis of his status as a limited partner. Until 1988, there was no provision subjecting general partners to jurisdiction within this State. This was corrected by the 1988 enactment of this section. Further amendments to § 17-109, effective August, 1990, include provisions that would allow a partner to consent to the jurisdiction of the Delaware courts. If mere status as a limited partner constituted implied consent to jurisdiction, the General Assembly would not have found it necessary to provide for jurisdiction by express consent in subsection (d). *Regency Housing & Drilling Ltd. Partnership I v. Cohen, 1991 Del. Super. LEXIS 341 (1991).*

Consent to jurisdiction. — As a matter of law, by accepting the position of general partner, a corporation consents to be subjected to a Delaware court's jurisdiction if the limited partnership has chosen to incorporate under Delaware law. *RJ Assocs. v. Health Payors' Org. Ltd. P'ship., 1999. Del. Ch. LEXIS 161 (Del. Ch. July 16, 1999).*

Illustrative case. — The wrongs alleged in the instant case go essentially to the management of a Delaware limited partnership. Defendants voluntarily undertook to mange the funds and received millions of dollars in compensation for doing so. Now, limited partners in the Delaware entity seek to hold them accountable for alleged wrongs they committed. It is both necessary and proper for the courts of this state to ensure that the managers of a Delaware entity are held responsible for their actions in managing the Delaware entity. When a person manages a Delaware entity, and receives substantial benefit from doing so, he should reasonably expect to be held responsible for his wrongful acts relating to the Delaware entity in Delaware. *Albert v. Alex. Brown Mgmt. Servs., 2005 Del. Ch. LEXIS 133 (Del. Ch. Aug. 26, 2005).*

§ 17-110.   Contested matters relating to general partners; contested votes

RULPA

DELAWARE CASE NOTES — UNREPORTED

This section is the partnership analogue to Title 8, Section 225. Adirondack GP v. American Power Corp., 1996 Del. Ch. LEXIS 143 (Del. Ch. Nov. 13, 1996).

Construction with other law. — What is in dispute in the instant case is not the title to the office, but general partner's performance of its obligations under the funding and partnership agreements. The dispute, therefore, fits squarely within the provisions of section 17-111, as it is an action to interpret, apply or enforce the provisions of an agreement. *Adirondack GP v. American Power Corp., 1996 Del. Ch. LEXIS 143 (Del. Ch. Nov. 13, 1996).*

§ 17-111.   Interpretation and enforcement of partnership agreement

DELAWARE CASE NOTES — REPORTED

Equity jurisdiction. — A request for enforcement of any statutory rights pursuant to the Delaware Revised Uniform Limited Partnership Act (*6 Del. C. § 17-101* et seq.) by a general partner in a limited partnership against that partnership or its co-partners is properly brought in the Court of *Chancery. Schwartzberg v. Critef Assocs., 685 A.2d 365 (Del. Ch. 1996).*

DELAWARE CASE NOTES — UNREPORTED

Sole jurisdiction. — Delaware courts have consistently interpreted this section as maintaining the former rule that Chancery has sole jurisdiction over internal partnership affairs, except after some event has occurred, such as an accounting or drafting a separate instrument, that obviates equity's superior ability to resolve all outstanding matters between the parties. This makes sense in light of the fact that disputes between partners will almost always involve equitable issues. It also enhances Delaware's attractiveness as a home for partnerships by providing managers of those entities with a secure, highly expert forum to resolve disputes involving how they do their jobs. *Albert v. Alex. Brown Mgmt. Servs., 2004 Del. Super. LEXIS 303 (2004).*

Construction with other law. — What is in dispute in the instant case is not the title to the office, but general partner's performance of its obligations under the funding and partnership agreements. The dispute, therefore, fits squarely within the provisions of this section, as it is an action to interpret, apply or enforce the provisions of an agreement. *Adirondack GP v. American Power Corp., 1996 Del. Ch. LEXIS 143 (Del. Ch. Nov. 13, 1996).*

Subchapter II.
Formation; Certificate of Limited Partnership

§ 17-201.   Certificate of limited partnership

CASE NOTES — OTHER STATES

Massachusetts

Termination. — The filing of a certificate of cancellation of a limited partnership terminates the limited partnership's existence. *Smyth v. Field, 40 Mass. App. Ct. 625, 666 N.E.2d 1008 (1996).*

Pennsylvania

Default consent. — Where a limited partnership does not address the approval of a merger, a merger requires the consent of all general partners and the consent of the limited partners with a simple majority of the interest in profits. *Alan Wurtzel Commerce Program v. Park Towne Place Apartments Limited Partnership, 2001 Phila. Ct. Com. Pl. LEXIS 79 (2002).*

CASE NOTES — FEDERAL COURTS

Seventh Circuit

Permissive "common name" statute. — Under Delaware partnership law, plaintiffs are entitled to sue both the limited partnership and its general partners. Delaware has a "common name" statute which allows a limited partnership to be sued as an entity. An unincorporated association of persons, including a partnership, using a common name may sue and be sued in such common name. Such statutes are permissive, not mandatory; suit may still be brought against the general partners liable for the partnership obligation. Under Delaware law, individuals comprising groups or associations may continue to be sued as individuals, just as individual partners may be sued without resort to the partnership name. *Randle v. GC Services, L.P., 25 F. Supp. 2d 849 (N.D.Ill. 1998).*

Subchapter III.
Limited Partners

§ 17-301.   Admission of limited partners

CASE NOTES — OTHER STATES

Pennsylvania

Tender offer disclosure standard. — Under Delaware law the standard for disclosure in a tender offer is that a corporate director or majority shareholder owes a fiduciary duty to their stockholders to disclose all facts material to the transaction in an atmosphere of entire candor. Similar standards have been applied in the context of limited partnerships. In extending an offer to the limited partners to buy their limited partnership units, the general partner owes a duty of full disclosure of material information respecting the business and value of the partnership which is in its possession. *Wurtzel. v. Park Towne Place Associates Limited Partnership, 2002 Phila. Ct. Com. Pl. LEXIS 29.*

In extending an offer to the limited partners to buy their limited partnership units, the general partner owes a duty of full disclosure of material information respecting the business and value of partnership which is in its possession. *Wurtzel. v. Park Towne Place Associates Limited Partnership, 2002 Phila. Ct. Com. Pl. LEXIS 29 (2002).*

Corporate directors owe a fiduciary duty to their shareholders to disclose fully all facts material to the transaction in an atmosphere of entire fairness. A fact is material if the plaintiff shows a substantial likelihood that under all circumstances, the omitted fact would have assumed actual significance in the deliberations of the reasonable shareholder. A corporate general partner owes a fiduciary duty to limited partners of the limited partnership of which it is a general partner. Because the relationship between general partners and limited partners is similar to the relationship between directors and shareholders, general fiduciary principles for directors apply to general partners. Thus, a general partner has a like duty of full and fair disclosure. *Alan Wurtzel Commerce Program v. Park Towne Place Apartments Limited Partnership, 2001 Phila. Ct. Com. Pl. LEXIS 79 (2001).*

§ 17-302.   Classes and voting

DELAWARE CASE NOTES — REPORTED

Manner of amending partnership agreement. — In interpreting a partnership agreement, ambiguities were resolved against the drafting general partner and in favor of the limited partners' reasonable expectations, with consent being required to amend the partnership agreement to affect the limited partners' substantive rights;

subsection (f) of this section reinforced the need for a specific articulation of the manner in which partnership agreement amendments could be effected and clarified. *In re Nantucket Island Assocs., 810 A.2d 351 (Del. Ch. 2002).*

The absence of a delivery requirement in DRULPA is particularly noteworthy, because the counterpart provision of the Delaware General Corporation Law ("DGCL") mandates the delivery of written consents. Subsection (a) of the latter provision expressly requires that written consents evincing shareholder action taken without a meeting "shall be delivered to the corporation by delivery to its registered office." Except for the requirement that written consents be delivered to the corporation, the provisions of Section 17-302(e) of the DRULPA and of Section 228(a) of the DGCL are parallel in all material respects. *Alpine Inv. Partners v. LJM2 Capital Mgmt., L.P., 794 A.2d 1276, 2002 Del. Ch. LEXIS 23 (Del. Ch. 2002).*

Construction of statute. — It is a well-established principle of statutory construction that the General Assembly is presumed to have inserted every provision into a legislative enactment for some useful purpose and construction, and when different terms are used in various parts of a statute, it is reasonable to assume that a distinction between the was intended. In the case of limited partnerships, the intent of the General Assembly was that the requirement of delivery of written consents would be the subject of contract, rather than of legislative mandate. *Alpine Inv. Partners v. LJM2 Capital Mgmt., L.P., 794 A.2d 1276, 2002 Del. Ch. LEXIS 23 (Del. Ch. 2002).*

Implied prohibition. — The provision in Section 17-302(e) that actions by written consent require only that consents representing the requisite number of limited partner votes be "signed," carries with it an implied prohibition against creating any additional requirements, including a requirement that the consents be "delivered." *Alpine Inv. Partners v. LJM2 Capital Mgmt., L.P., 794 A.2d 1276, 2002 Del. Ch. LEXIS 23 (Del. Ch. 2002).*

DELAWARE CASE NOTES — UNREPORTED

This section does not create a presumption or rule of construction against assignees having voting rights. Arvida/JMB Partners, L.P. v. Vanderbilt Income & Growth Assocs., 1997 Del. Ch. LEXIS 79 (Del. Ch. May 23, 1997)

§ 17-303.   Liability to third parties

DELAWARE CASE NOTES — REPORTED

"Control." –The Delaware Revised Uniform Limited Partnership Act (*6 Del. C. § 17-101* et seq.) defines 'control' solely for the purpose of limiting liability of limited partners to third parties, which does not necessarily equate to the threshold for finding a passive investor under federal securities laws. *Steinhardt Group Inc. v. Citicorp, 126 F.3d 144 (3d Cir. 1997).*

Partner as independent contractor. — Provisions of agreement between a general partner and the partnership itself which provided that the partner would manage the company as an independent contractor was not an effective limitation on the partner's authority to bind the partnership in other contracts because such provisions would allow general partners to create, by contract, a nonstatutory limited partnership without complying with the provisions of this subchapter. *Harper v. Delaware Valley Broadcasters, Inc., 743 F. Supp. 1076 (D. Del. 1990); 932 F.2d 959 (3rd Cir. 1991).*

DELAWARE CASE NOTES — UNREPORTED

Fiduciary duties. — Although the Delaware Revised Uniform Limited Partnership Act does not specifically state that a limited partner owes a fiduciary duty to a general partner it, by reference to the Delaware Uniform Partnership Act, so provides. Therefore, to the extent that a partnership agreement empowers a limited partner discretion to take actions affecting the governance of the limited partnership, the limited partner may be subject to the obligations of a fiduciary, including the obligation to act in good faith as to the other partners. *KE Property Management, Inc. v. 275 Madison Management Corp., 1993 Del. Ch. LEXIS 147 (Del. Ch. July 21, 1993).*

§ 17-305.   Access to and confidentiality of information; records

DELAWARE CASE NOTES — REPORTED

Access for substituted limited partners. — Plaintiff who became a 'substitute limited partner' of the partnerships, rather than merely an assignee of economic rights of its transferor, was entitled to a copy of the current list of names, addresses, and ownership interests of the limited partners. *In re American Tax Credit Properties Ltd. Partnerships, 714 A.2d 87 (Del. Ch. 1997),* aff'd sub. nom. *American Tax Credit Properties v. Everest, Properties, Inc., 707 A.2d 765 (Del. 1998).*

Hearing. — As a general rule, the court will not entertain outside claims or collateral issues within a hearing under this section, but will hear only those matters that pertain to the limited partner's demand to inspect the books. *Gotham Partners v. Hallwood Realty Partners, 714 A.2d 96 (Del. Ch. 1998).*

Partnership agreement requires disclosure of list of investors. — Under the partnership agreement contract defendant limited partnership was required to provide the plaintiff, a non-limited partner investor in the

RULPA

defendant through its ownership of Beneficial Unit Certificates (BUC) issued by the defendant, with a list of the names and addresses of the defendant's partners, as well as other BUC owners, to conduct a mini-tender offer for 4.9% of the defendant's outstanding partnership interests. *Bond Purchase, L.L.C. v. Patriot Tax Credit Props., L.P., 746 A.2d 842 (Del. Ch. 1999).*

Production of records for valuing limited partnership interests. — Court, in part, denied and granted the relief sought by requiring requiring real estate limited partnerships and their general partners to disclose to limited partners for their legitimate purpose of valuing their interests: (1) property appraisals (to include those for properties held less than 5 years); (2) limited partnership agreements (to determine other obligations, such as to managers or general partners); (3) non-public subsidiary financial statements; but (4) not loan and security documents (as the request unreasonably assumed liquidations might occur). *Madison Ave. Inv. Partners, LLC v. Am. First Real Estate Inv. Partners, L.P., 806 A.2d 165 (Del. Ch. 2002).*

Application of the 'improper purpose defense.' — While the 'improper purpose defense' has only been applied to a partner's contractual right to a list of partners, it follows from its contract law origins and the similarities between the Beneficial Unit Certificate (BUC) holders in this case and the general or limited partners in the cases in which the Court has applied it, that the 'improper purpose defense' also applies to plaintiff's contractual right to a list of BUC holders. *Bond Purchase, L.L.C. v. Patriot Tax Credit Props., L.P., 746 A.2d 842 (Del. Ch. 1999).*

'Improper purpose defense' must prove disclosure would be adverse to interests of partnership as a whole. — Because the partnership failed to prove by a preponderance of the evidence that disclosure of the investor list to plaintiff pursuant to plaintiff's contractual right in the partnership agreement would be adverse to the interests of the partnership as a whole, plaintiff could not be denied access to the investor list on the basis of the 'improper purpose defense'. *Bond Purchase, L.L.C. v. Patriot Tax Credit Props., L.P., 746 A.2d 842 (Del. Ch. 1999).*

Defenses to disclosure under subsection (b). — Where the defendant's general partner in good faith believed that disclosing the list of the names and addresses of the defendant's partners and other Beneficial Unit Certificate (BUC) owners to the plaintiff was not in the best interest of the defendant partnership, the defendant was entitled to deny the plaintiff access to the list. *Bond Purchase, L.L.C. v. Patriot Tax Credit Props., L.P., 746 A.2d 842 (Del. Ch. 1999).*

"Personal and adverse effects". — The concept of a proper purpose, whether found in statute or contract, is different than the concept of a defense based upon a showing that the purpose is personal to the partner and adverse to the partnership. A showing that a purpose is personal and has adverse effects does not make that purpose "improper" and a request for access to a partnership list may be justifiably denied upon showing that the purpose is personal and has adverse effects regardless of whether that purpose is "proper." Thus, the basis of the defense is more appropriately characterized as founded on "personal and adverse effects" rather than on an "improper purpose." *In re Paine Webber Qualified Plan Prop. Fund Three, 698 A.2d 389, 1997 Del. Ch. LEXIS 22 (Del. Ch. 1997).*

Denial of access warranted. — In the absence of an explicit contractual provision or statutory language to the contrary, and in circumstances in which, as here, a partner denying another partner access to partnership business records can show that the partner seeking access is doing so for a purpose personal to that partner and adverse to the interests of the partnership considered jointly, the court is warranted in denying the request for access. *Schwartzberg v. Critef Assocs. Ltd. Pshp., 685 A.2d 365, 1996 Del. Ch. LEXIS 59 (Del. Ch. 1996).*

DELAWARE CASE NOTES — UNREPORTED

Proper purpose found. — Plaintiffs' stated purposes, to investigate mismanagement and to value their investments in the fund, were proper where they have shown that the fund's value has plummeted over the last few years while the general partner and special limited partner made substantial fees and there was testimony that bank made highly profitable investments that the fund did not participate in. While these facts fall well short of actually proving wrongdoing, they do provide a credible basis for inferring mismanagement of the fund. In addition, the fund is comprised of several non-typical investments which make valuing the plaintiffs' interest in the fund difficult. Coupled with the facts that the fund has written down many of its investments and that the overall value of the fund has plunged by 75%, the plaintiffs have good reason to want to properly value their interests in the fund. *Forsythe v. CIBC Emple. Private Equity Fund I, L.P., 2005 Del. Ch. LEXIS 104 , No. 657-N (July 7, 2005).*

A partnership agreement can create a contractual inspection right that is in addition to and separate from the statutory inspection right. *Arbor Place, L.P. v. Encore Opportunity Fund, 2002 Del. Ch. LEXIS 102 (Del. Ch. Jan. 29, 2002).*

Clarity in agreement. — If the broader power to restrict access contemplated by this section is to be the argued litmus test for access, it should be made manifestly clear in the agreement and not left in doubt, especially when the partnership agreement also has a provision that on its face creates a less restrictive right to access the partnership's information. *Bond Purchase, L.L.C. v. Patriot Tax Credit Props., L.P., 1999 Del. Ch. LEXIS 170 (Del. Ch. Aug. 16, 1999).*

Presumption of exclusion. — Where language exists in a partnership agreement that creates on its face fair and reasonable access to partnership information, with every opportunity for the drafters to limit access if the partnership and investors so choose, the chancery court

RULPA

cannot in good conscience assume the negative and conclude that there is a presumption of exclusion. *Bond Purchase, L.L.C. v. Patriot Tax Credit Props., L.P., 1999 Del. Ch. LEXIS 170 (Del. Ch. Aug. 16, 1999).*

There is nothing in partnership law requiring a general partner to meet with limited partners at their every request. The rights of a limited partner to see information about the limited partnership are limited by either the partnership agreement or, in the absence of anything in that agreement, by the fiduciary duty owed by the general partner to the limited partner. *Dean v. Dick, 1999 Del. Ch. LEXIS 121 (Del. Ch. June 10, 1999).*

Improper purpose found. — Here, plaintiffs have no plans to use the limited partnership lists to increase the value of their current investments in the defendant limited partnerships. Rather, plaintiffs are using their plaintiffs' nominal investment in the defendant limited partnerships purely as a legal vehicle to obtain the lists in anticipation of a possible tender offer, to be conducted by a separate entity and in which the plaintiffs' participation would at best be token. Thus, the use of the lists to aid in that tender offer is a purpose that relates solely to the investment fund's interest as a potential buyer, not to the plaintiffs' interest as limited partners. That purpose is therefore not proper under this section. *In re Paine Webber Ltd. Pshp., 1996 Del. Ch. LEXIS 117 (Del. Ch. Sept. 17, 1996).*

Timeliness of motion to compel production. — Motion to compel unredacted versions of documents (in a proceeding to inspect the books and records of a Delaware limited partnership under 6 Del. C. § 17-305) was not time-barred, even though the time for filing an appeal had passed; inherent in the court's power under Ch. Ct. R. 59(f) is the concept that an order requiring a redaction log contemplates that there could be further proceedings as to the sufficiency of the explanations given for the redactions, allowing the trial court to retain jurisdiction. *Forsythe v. Cibc Emple., 2006 Del. Super. LEXIS 71 (Del. Ch. Mar. 22, 2006).*

§ 17-306. Remedies for breach of partnership agreement by limited partner

CASE NOTES — FEDERAL COURTS

First Circuit

Accounting exception not adopted. — While one might question the public policy of requiring an accounting in situations such as the one presently before the court, as the law presently stands an accounting remains a condition precedent to an action at law between limited partners under Delaware law. On this point, the court finds it particularly noteworthy that in 2001 a Revised Uniform Limited Partnership Act ("RULPA") was approved and recommended for adoption and enactment in all the states. The RULPA contains a provision that allows direct action by a limited partner against the limited partnership or another partner, with or without an accounting, if the partner can plead and prove an actual or threatened injury that is not solely the result of an injury suffered or threatened to be suffered by the limited partnership. This section was derived from the Revised Uniform Partnership Act ("RUPA"), § 405(b). While Delaware has incorporated into the Delaware Revised Uniform Partnership Act the provision in RUPA that allows direct action by one partner against another in a general partnership, Del. Code. Ann. tit. 6 § 15-405(b), it has not adopted the provision in RULPA creating the same limited exception to the accounting rule in the case of actions between limited partners. In the absence of such statutory authority, or the applicability of a recognized exception, plaintiffs' direct claims against their co-limited partners are necessarily barred as premature for failure to first pursue an equitable action for an accounting. *Drenis v. Haligiannis, 452 F. Supp. 2d 418, 2006 U.S. Dist. LEXIS 68488 (D.N.Y. Sept. 25, 2006).*

Subchapter IV.
General Partners

§ 17-403. General powers and liabilities

DELAWARE CASE NOTES — REPORTED

Equity jurisdiction. — A request for enforcement of any statutory rights pursuant to the Delaware Revised Uniform Limited Partnership Act (*6 Del. C. § 17-101* et seq.) by a general partner in a limited partnership against that partnership or its co-partners is properly brought in the Court of *Chancery. Schwartzberg v. Critef Assocs., 685 A.2d 365 (Del. Ch. 1996).*

DELAWARE CASE NOTES — UNREPORTED

Winding up. — The DRULPA give a general partner the right to recoup reasonable litigation expenses necessary to the winding up of a limited partnership. *Active Asset Recovery, Inc. v. Real Estate Asset Recovery Servs., 1999 Del. Ch. LEXIS 179 (Del. Ch. Sept. 10, 1999).*

Binding partnership. — The stated purpose of the limited partnership is significant because if the proposed transaction is itself within the purpose of the partnership than, of course, the general partner may lawfully authorize and effectuate the transaction. However, as the general partner's powers are the same as those of a partners of a general partnership, the general partner may not bind the partnership to a transaction which is not apparently for the carrying on of the business of the partnership in the usual way. *Kansas RSA 15 Ltd. Partnership v. SBMS RSA, 1995 Del. Ch. LEXIS 14 (Del. Ch. Mar. 8, 1995).*

Duty of limited partner to general partner. — Although the Delaware Revised Uniform Limited Partnership Act does not specifically state that a limited partner owes a fiduciary duty to a general partner it, by reference to the Delaware Uniform Partnership Act, so provides. Therefore, to the extent that a partnership agreement empowers a limited partner discretion to take actions affecting the governance of the limited partnership, the limited partner may be subject to the obligations of a fiduciary, including the obligation to act in good faith as to the other partners. *KE Property Management, Inc. v. 275 Madison Management Corp., 1993 Del. Ch. LEXIS 147 (Del. Ch. July 21, 1993).*

Delegation of authority. — Delaware law does not contain an express provision allowing general partners to delegate their authority to a committee. Rather, the specific rights and responsibilities of parties in a general or limited partnership are determined by the parties' particular partnership agreement. *Katell v. Morgan Stanley Group, Inc., 1993 Del. Ch. LEXIS 92 (Del. Ch. June 8, 1993).*

CASE NOTES — FEDERAL COURTS

First Circuit

Standing. — Under Delaware's Revised Limited Partnership Act, the general partner of a limited partnership is authorized to enforce the rights and obligations of the limited partnership. Therefore, in Delaware, general partners have the power to sue directly on behalf of the partnership on the partnership's claims. *Rivera Siaca v. DCC Operating, Inc. (In re Olympic Mills Corp.), 333 B.R. 540, 2005 Bankr. LEXIS 2306, 45 Bankr. Ct. Dec. (LRP) 190 (B.A.P. 1st Cir. 2005).*

Although Delaware has a common name statute which allows partnerships to sue and be sued in the partnership name, its use, although often convenient, is not mandatory. Accordingly, as a matter of law, general partner, was authorized to bring the district court action in its own name without naming the limited partnership, and it did not waive that right. *Rivera Siaca v. DCC Operating, Inc. (In re Olympic Mills Corp.), 333 B.R. 540, 2005 Bankr. LEXIS 2306, 45 Bankr. Ct. Dec. (LRP) 190 (B.A.P. 1st Cir. 2005).*

Third Circuit

In Delaware, general partners have the power to sue directly on behalf of the partnership on the partnership's claims. *HB Gen. Corp. v. Manchester Partners, 95 F.3d 1185 (3d Cir. 1996).*

Seventh Circuit

In general. — Delaware partnership law provides that all partners are liable jointly and severally for everything chargeable to the partnership. It is well established that, under the law of partnerships, knowledge and actions of one partner are imputed to all others. The partnership is liable for acts performed in its name and within the scope of its business, and the partners are liable for all debts and obligations of the partnership. The same liabilities apply to a general partner in a limited partnership. *Randle v. GC Services, L.P., 25 F. Supp. 2d 849 (N.D.Ill. 1998).*

Under Delaware law one partner owes the other partners fiduciary duties. *Niki Development Corp. v. HOB Hotel Chicago Partners, L.P., 2001 U.S. Dist. LEXIS 1544 (N.D.Ill. 2001).*

A general partner owes his partners utmost good faith, fairness, and loyalty in his or her partnership dealings. This duty exists concurrently with the obligations set forth in the partnership agreement whether or not expressed therein. *Niki Development Corp. v. HOB Hotel Chicago Partners, L.P., 2001 U.S. Dist. LEXIS 1544 (N.D.Ill. 2001).*

Personal participation in wrongs; enrichment. — To hold a parent corporation liable for breaches of the general partner's fiduciary duties, a plaintiff limited partner must raise sufficient issue of material fact to support the conclusion that the general partner personally participated in the wrongs complained of and utilized partnership assets under their control to enrich themselves at the expense of the limited partners. *Niki Development Corp. v. HOB Hotel Chicago Partners, L.P., 2003 U.S. Dist. LEXIS 4949 (N.D.Ill. 2003).*

Directors and corporate parents of general partners can only be subject to fiduciary liability for implementing unfair, self-dealing transactions, or, in other words, for participating in alleged fiduciary breaches in which they themselves benefit. *Niki Development Corp. v. HOB Hotel Chicago Partners, L.P., 2003 U.S. Dist. LEXIS 4949 (N.D.Ill. 2003).*

Tenth Circuit

Derivative versus direct actions. — Delaware law allows a limited partner to bring a derivative action after demand upon the general partner or without demand if it would be futile. Generally, whether an action is direct or derivative depends upon whether the injury alleged is independent of the injury suffered by the limited partnership. Where the claim belongs to the partnership, limited partners ordinarily cannot enforce their proportional interest in a partnership claim as their individual claim. At the same time, limited partners can bring a direct action when the injury can be differentiated from that suffered by the other partners. Courts have allowed claims for (1) an accounting, (2) fiduciary breach, and (3) breach of the partnership agreement to proceed as individual claims in varying circumstances. *United States Cellular Investment Co. v. Southwestern Bell Mobile Systems, Inc., 1997 U.S. App. LEXIS 31865 (10th Cir. 1997).*

Eleventh Circuit

Liability under the FDCPA. — Under Delaware law, general partners are vicariously liable for the acts of the limited partnership, including violations of the Fair Debt

Collections Practices Act. *Belin v. Litton Loan Servicing, 2006 U.S. Dist. LEXIS 47953 (D. Fla. July 14, 2006).*

Court of Federal Claims

Unlimited liability. — General partners of limited partnerships have the liabilities of a partner in a partner- ship without limited partners to persons other than the partnership and the other partners. In other words, general partners assume unlimited liability for partnership debts. *Transpac Drilling Venture v. United States, 26 Cl. Ct. 1245 (Cl. Ct. 1992).*

§ 17-406. Remedies for breach of partnership agreement by general partner

DELAWARE CASE NOTES — UNREPORTED

Construction with other business entities law. — Certainly partnerships are amenable to greater freedom contractually to shape the set of legal relationships that constitute the partnership than are corporations, and this freedom may include clear contracting with respect to fiduciary duties. But there may be less to this difference between corporations and limited partnerships (or other entities) in this respect than meets the eye. First, there is modernly great flexibility in the corporate form. The corporate charter may, for example, particularize director and officers' duties. Thus, there is no reason why corporate charters cannot contain provisions dealing with corporate opportunities or dealing with the ability of officers or directors to compete with the corporation. Second, and equally importantly, investors in limited partnership or other more explicitly contractual entities (to the extent they are informed) have a limited incentive to invest in entities that broadly and explicitly repudiate a duty of loyalty. Thus, under Delaware law, all forms of business organization that entail passive investors and active managers permit parties at the time of contracting to specify a great deal bearing on the exercise of managerial power, and passive investors in all forms of enterprise have a powerful incentive, insofar as self-interested transactions by the managers are involved, to retain the possibility of later judicial review under a fairness standard. In fact, the underlying principles of fiduciary analysis in both the corporate and the partnership context reflect a similar principle: given no defect in process (e.g., fraud, nondisclosure, or manipulation) explicitly negotiated and validly adopted provisions of a constitutional document will be enforced. *U.S. WEST, Inc. v. Time Warner Inc., 1996 Del. Ch. LEXIS 55 (Del. Ch. June 6, 1996).*

Sufficient grounds for removal. — General partner's self-interested $ 1.3 million loan to an affiliate constituted a material breach of fiduciary duty, and was therefore a sufficient ground under the partnership agreement for removal as the general partner without prior notice and an opportunity to cure. *Knetzger v. Centre City Corp., 1999 Del. Ch. LEXIS 145 (Del. Ch. June 30, 1999).*

It is clear that general partner should be removed immediately as general partner. The partnership agreement contemplates removal for fraud which is material and detrimental to the Partnership or for gross negligence. Although this provision is phrased awkwardly, it is clear that general partner's conduct was in bad faith, worse than grossly negligent, and purposely misleading. Therefore, "removal provision is easily satisfied." *McGovern v. General Holding, Inc., 2006 Del. Ch. LEXIS 93 (Del. Ch. June 2, 2006).*

Dissolution and liquidation order. — Consistent with court's reluctance to place a 90% owner under substitute management, it is rational and necessary to order the dissolution and liquidation of limited partnership as it is impractical for the business to continue given the fractious relations and the recent death of one of the two limited partners. A receiver will be appointed, from recommendations made by surviving limited partner that are shared with general partner for comment, to lead the dissolution process and oversee the operation of limited partnership until its affairs are completely wound up. The receiver shall select an investment bank to auction the limited partnership, in whole or in discrete parts, in order to obtain the highest possible value. *McGovern v. General Holding, Inc., 2006 Del. Ch. LEXIS 93 (Del. Ch. June 2, 2006).*

CASE NOTES — FEDERAL COURTS

Seventh Circuit

Under Delaware law one partner owes the other partners fiduciary duties. *Niki Development Corp. v. HOB Hotel Chicago Partners, L.P., 2001 U.S. Dist. LEXIS 1544 (N.D.Ill. 2001).*

A general partner owes his partners utmost good faith, fairness, and loyalty in his or her partnership dealings. This duty exists concurrently with the obligations set forth in the partnership agreement whether or not expressed therein. *Niki Development Corp. v. HOB Hotel Chicago Partners, L.P., 2001 U.S. Dist. LEXIS 1544 (N.D.Ill. 2001).*

RULPA

Subchapter V.
Finance

§ 17-502.   Liability for contribution

DELAWARE CASE NOTES — REPORTED

Limited liability. — The general policy of DRULPA is that the liability of limited partners of a Delaware limited partnership is limited. *In re LJM2 Co-Investment, L.P., 866 A.2d 762, 2004 Del. Ch. LEXIS 195 (Del. Ch. 2004).*

Contribution obligation. — To the extent a partnership agreement requires a partner to make a contribution, the partner is obligated, except to the extent such obligation is modified by the terms of the partnership agreement, to make such contribution to a limited partnership. *In re LJM2 Co-Investment, L.P., 866 A.2d 762, 2004 Del. Ch. LEXIS 195 (Del. Ch. 2004).*

Default rule of unanimity. — Unanimous consent requirement of subdivision (b)(1) of this section was "required hereunder" within the meaning of the third proviso to section 13.1 of the partnership agreement. The "contract" at issue — the partnership agreement — contained no provision relating to the compromise of contribution obligations. By choosing to include no such express provision, the parties to that agreement understood that the default rule of unanimity would govern their relations and the conduct of the partnership. Thus, it is appropriate to construe the third proviso to section 13.1 as including the uncontradicted statutory default of unanimity necessary for the compromise of capital calls. For these reasons, the court concludes that the amendment to section 3.1(f) required unanimous approval. *In re LJM2 Co-Investment, L.P., 866 A.2d 762, 2004 Del. Ch. LEXIS 195 (Del. Ch. 2004).*

The power to rescind is not the same as the power to compromise, which impliedly includes a power to discriminate among limited partners and, thus, the power of rescission is not necessarily subject to the unanimous consent requirement of subdivision (b)(1) of this section. *In re LJM2 Co-Investment, L.P., 866 A.2d 762, 2004 Del. Ch. LEXIS 195 (Del. Ch. 2004)*

Subchapter VI.
Distributions and Withdrawal

§ 17-604.   Distribution upon withdrawal

DELAWARE CASE NOTES — REPORTED

The General Assembly intended to include within the coverage of § 17-604 only partners withdrawing under § 602 or 603 and to exclude from the coverage of § 17-604 partners who "otherwise cease[d] for any reason" to be a partner. *Hillman v. Hillman, 910 A.2d 262; 2006 Del. Ch. LEXIS 217 (Aug. 23, 2006).*

Capital contribution not forfeited. — A partner who is expelled pursuant to a partnership agreement is entitled to receive fair value for his partnership interest. Therefore, though not literally addressed in the DRULPA, turning to Delaware's general partnership acts leads to the same result as if § 17-604 governed the "event of withdrawal" caused by a partner's removal. Thus, contrary to former general partner's assertions, his inability to elect to become a limited partner does not result in a forfeiture of his capital contribution. At the very least, his economic investment would be protected from forfeiture if he filed an equitable action to recover that amount. *Hillman v. Hillman, 910 A.2d 262, 2006 Del. Ch. LEXIS 217 (Aug. 23, 2006).*

§ 17-607.   Limitations on distribution

DELAWARE CASE NOTES — UNREPORTED

Sitting on rights. — Nothing in this section suggests an intention to permit a plaintiff, who claims that a limited partner's demand for withdrawal was a per se breach of the limited partnership agreement and that the contract compromising that demand for payment was invalid, to sit on its rights until payments under that supposedly invalid contract are actually made. *Pomeranz v. Museum Partners, L.P., 2005 Del. Ch. LEXIS 10, No. 20211 (Jan. 24, 2005).*

Subchapter VII.
Assignment of Partnership Interests

§ 17-701.   Nature of partnership interest

CASE NOTES — OTHER STATES

Pennsylvania

Tender offer disclosure standard. — Under Delaware law the standard for disclosure in a tender offer is that a corporate director or majority shareholder owes a fiduciary duty to their stockholders to disclose all facts material to the transaction in an atmosphere of entire candor. Similar standards have been applied in the context of limited partnerships. In extending an offer to the limited partners to buy their limited partnership units, the general partner owes a duty of full disclosure of material information respecting the business and value of the partnership which is in its possession. *Wurtzel. v. Park Towne Place Associates Limited Partnership, 2002 Phila. Ct. Com. Pl. LEXIS 29.*

In extending an offer to the limited partners to buy their limited partnership units, the general partner owes a duty of full disclosure of material information respecting the business and value of partnership which is in its possession. *Wurtzel. v. Park Towne Place Associates*

Limited Partnership, 2002 Phila. Ct. Com. Pl. LEXIS 29 (2002).

Corporate directors owe a fiduciary duty to their shareholders to disclose fully all facts material to the transaction in an atmosphere of entire fairness. A fact is material if the plaintiff shows a substantial likelihood that under all circumstances, the omitted fact would have assumed actual significance in the deliberations of the reasonable shareholder. A corporate general partner owes a fiduciary duty to limited partners of the limited partnership of which it is a general partner. Because the relationship between general partners and limited partners is similar to the relationship between directors and shareholders, general fiduciary principles for directors apply to general partners. Thus, a general partner has a like duty of full and fair disclosure. *Alan Wurtzel Commerce Program v. Park Towne Place Apartments Limited Partnership, 2001 Phila. Ct. Com. Pl. LEXIS 79 (2001).*

§ 17-703.   Partner's partnership interest subject to charging order.

DELAWARE CASE NOTES — UNREPORTED

To successfully invoke the provisions of this section, plaintiff must reduce her foreign judgment to a domestic judgment bearing an "amount". To hold otherwise would be to go far beyond the requisites of full faith and credit and would erode, if not eviscerate the protections accorded by the rule that execution may not be issued directly on a foreign judgment. *MacDonald v. MacDonald, 1986 Del. Ch. LEXIS 400 (Del. Ch. May 9, 1986).*

The Superior Court seems clearly the appropriate court to reduce the foreign judgment to a Delaware judgment stating an "amount". Once Superior Court reduces the California judgment to a Delaware judgment bearing a stated amount, it may then charge the defendant's interest in partnership as contemplated by this section. *MacDonald v. MacDonald, 1986 Del. Ch. LEXIS 400 (Del. Ch. May 9, 1986)*

Subchapter VIII.
Dissolution

§ 17-801.   Nonjudicial dissolution

CASE NOTES — OTHER STATES

Virginia

Construction with other law. — The provision of a narrower dissolution statute for limited partnerships evinced a legislative intent that the broader provisions of

the General Partnership statute not apply to limited partnerships. *First Union National Bank v. Allen Lorey Family Limited Partnership, 34 Va. Cir. 474 (1994).*

§ 17-802.   Judicial dissolution

DELAWARE CASE NOTES — UNREPORTED

The test of Section 17-802 is whether it is reasonably practicable to carry on the business of a limited partnership, and not whether it is impossible. *In re Silver Leaf, L.L.C., 2005 Del. Ch. LEXIS 119 (Del. Ch. Aug. 18, 2005).*

In evaluating whether to dissolve a partnership pursuant to § 17-802, courts must determine the business of the partnership and the general partner's ability to achieve that purpose in conformity with the partnership agree-

RULPA

ment. *In re Silver Leaf, L.L.C., 2005 Del. Ch. LEXIS 119 (Del. Ch. Aug. 18, 2005)*.

Dissolution date. — Reading into this statute the authority to declare a partnership dissolved on the date on which the events necessary to the court's determination of reasonable impracticability had occurred would work a significant extension of this section. As a general matter, this court's power to dissolve a partnership where events have made it "reasonably impractical" for the partnership to continue in accordance with the partnership agreement is a "limited" one and should be exercised with corresponding care. *Active Asset Recovery, Inc. v. Real Estate Asset Recovery Servs., 1999 Del. Ch. LEXIS 179 (Del. Ch. Sept. 10, 1999)*.

Disappointing past returns inappropriate basis. — In effect, limited partner urges the court to compare the partnership's ideal degree of financial success with the actual figures and use this as a basis for dissolving the partnership. Such a comparison, while perhaps demonstrating disappointing past returns, is an inappropriate basis on which to order dissolution. Although limited partner may be disappointed in its investment, it has not demonstrated that the cellular business can no longer be sustained. *Cincinnati Bell Cellular Sys. Co. v. Ameritech Mobile Phone Serv., 1996 Del. Ch. LEXIS 116 (Del. Ch. Sept. 3, 1996)*.

Frightened of future competition inappropriate basis. — Absent some limitation on competition against the partnership in the partnership agreement (or some indication that had the parties considered it ex ante, they would have included such a provision in the partnership agreement), the fact that plaintiff limited partner is frightened of future competition is not a basis for unilaterally dissolving a viable business at the request of one limited partner. *Cincinnati Bell Cellular Sys. Co. v. Ameritech Mobile Phone Serv., 1996 Del. Ch. LEXIS 116 (Del. Ch. Sept. 3, 1996)*.

Illustrative cases. — About all of this, when seen in the context of the legal test for judicial dissolution, it must be said that even if plaintiffs were right about all of it, it would constitute much ado about very little indeed. In fact the record discloses that no substantial violation of the rights of the limited partners had occurred. Surely the modest charitable and promotional use of partnership resources does not constitute a breach of duty so long as a reasonable business person might conclude that any potential advantage was worth the marginal cost. As to the non-charitable or non-promotional items they are de minimis in all events and the partnership will be provided the compensation to which it is entitled. These uses of show elements however, do not provide any basis for concluding that the partnership should be dissolved. *Red Sail Easter Ltd. Partners, L.P. v. Radio City Music Hall Prods., Inc., 1993 Del. Ch. LEXIS 154 (Del. Ch. July 28, 1993)*.

Based on the uncontradicted evidence presented during the trial, the court has no choice but to find that it is no longer "reasonably practicable" to carry on the business of this partnership, within the meaning of this section. The partnership's business involves the heavily leveraged purchase of a property, for which debt service was to be made largely from rent payments received from a single lessee. That lessee is now insolvent and no further payments are forthcoming. Petitioner's witness offered unchallenged testimony that, given the current depressed real estate market in Dallas, procuring new tenants is practically impossible without large financial incentives or extensive renovations, which the partnership is currently unable to undertake. The property is operating at a projected annual $ 6 million loss. And the outstanding debt on the property, which is without recourse, is far in excess of its value. In short, the petitioner has shown by overwhelming evidence that "it is not reasonably practicable to carry on the business" for the purpose stated in the partnership agreement, namely, to use the property "for profit and as an investment." *PC Tower Center, Inc. v. Tower Center Dev. Associates Ltd. Partnership, 1989 Del. Ch. LEXIS 72 (Del. Ch. June 8, 1989)*.

Dissolution and liquidation order. — Consistent with court's reluctance to place a 90% owner under substitute management, it is rational and necessary to order the dissolution and liquidation of limited partnership as it is impractical for the business to continue given the fractious relations and the recent death of one of the two limited partners. "A receiver" will be appointed, from recommendations made by surviving limited partner that are shared with general partner for comment, to lead the dissolution process and oversee the operation of limited partnership until its affairs are completely wound up. The receiver shall select an investment bank to auction the limited partnership, in whole or in discrete parts, in order to obtain the highest possible value. *McGovern v. General Holding, Inc., 2006 Del. Ch. LEXIS 93 (Del. Ch. June 2, 2006)*.

CASE NOTES — OTHER STATES

Virginia

Construction with other law. — The provision of a narrower dissolution statute for limited partnerships evinced a legislative intent that the broader provisions of the General Partnership statute not apply to limited partnerships. *First Union National Bank v. Allen Lorey Family Limited Partnership, 34 Va. Cir. 474 (1994)*.

RULPA

§ 17-804.   Distribution of assets

CASE NOTES — OTHER STATES

North Carolina

One who seeks to serve as a liquidator may not pick and choose among the assets of the partnership that he will supervise, but instead must be willing to accept responsi-bility for the full and complete winding up of the partnership's affairs within this state. *Piedmont Venture Partners., L.P. v. Deloitte & Touche, L.P.P., 2007 NCBC 6; 2007 NCBC LEXIS 6 (March 5, 2007).*

§ 17-804.   Distribution of assets

DELAWARE CASE NOTES — UNREPORTED

Not an appraisal statute. — Under the DRULPA, the court must determine the value of the limited partnership's assets and distribute them to the partners, not provide the limited partners with the value of their proportionate ownership interests in the limited partnership as a going concern. The General Assembly knows how to draft an appraisal statute, see Title 8, Section 262. This section is not one. *Active Asset Recovery, Inc. v. Real Estate Asset Recovery Servs., 1999 Del. Ch. LEXIS 179 (Del. Ch. Sept. 10, 1999).*

Applicable to derivative claimants. — This section establishes a process by which the rights of parties to which the partnership has an obligation (or may have an obligation) are protected. Absent an indication that subsection (b) of this section was intended to be limited to creditors, the court must conclude that its provisions are intended to protect the rights of derivative claimants as well as the rights of creditors and partners. *In re CC&F Fox Hill Assocs., 1997 Del. Ch. LEXIS 111 (Del. Ch. July 7, 1997).*

Request for an accounting in instant case provided notice of a claim which falls within the category of "contingent, conditional or unmatured claims and obligations, known to the limited partnership" under this section. Defendants have failed to explain how they made, or attempted to make, reasonable provisions to cover plaintiffs' notice. *In re CC&F Fox Hill Assocs. Ltd. Pshp., 1997 Del. Ch. LEXIS 89 (Del. Ch. June 12, 1997).*

CASE NOTES — OTHER STATES

New York

Priority of creditors. — Upon winding up of a limited partnership, the assets must be distributed to creditors, including partners who are creditors, to the extent otherwise permitted by law, in satisfaction of liabilities of the limited partnership. By the terms of the statute, the priority of those who follow creditors can be modified by the partnership agreement, while no such provision exists for the creditors. Therefore, the priority of creditors, unlike the priorities of those who follow them, is not a modifiable default provision. *Mizrahi v. Chanel, Inc., 193 Misc. 2d 1, 746 N.Y.S.2d 878 (2001).*

Subchapter IX.
Conversion; Merger; Domestication; and Transfer

§ 17-910.   Service of process on registered foreign limited partnerships

DELAWARE CASE NOTES — UNREPORTED

The service of process statutory scheme contemplates adequate notice and presumes proper service when made on a general partner of a registered foreign limited partnership when the general partner is located in Delaware. Only when the general partner cannot be found in this state and when the limited partnership has not registered to do business in Delaware, does the statutory scheme presume designation of the Secretary of State as agent to accept service of process. The legislature then requires the Secretary of State to accept service of process for the unregistered foreign limited partnership. In essence, the statutes create a continuum for service of process based upon the nature of the limited partnership's contact with Delaware. The statutes do not address the scenario where an unregistered foreign limited partnership has a Delaware corporation as its general partner. *Macklowe v. Planet Hollywood, 1994 Del. Ch. LEXIS 179 (Del. Ch. Oct. 13, 1994).*

Selection by an unregistered foreign limited partnership of a Delaware resident corporation as its general partner constitutes a reasonable basis for concluding it expected its general partner to be served and accept service of process in the event it was doing business in Delaware. *Macklowe v. Planet Hollywood, 1994 Del. Ch. LEXIS 179 (Del. Ch. Oct. 13, 1994).*

RULPA

§ 17-911.   Service of process on unregistered foreign limited partnerships

DELAWARE CASE NOTES — UNREPORTED

The service of process statutory scheme contemplates adequate notice and presumes proper service when made on a general partner of a registered foreign limited partnership when the general partner is located in Delaware. Only when the general partner cannot be found in this state and when the limited partnership has not registered to do business in Delaware, does the statutory scheme presume designation of the Secretary of State as agent to accept service of process. The legislature then requires the Secretary of State to accept service of process for the unregistered foreign limited partnership. In essence, the statutes create a continuum for service of process based upon the nature of the limited partnership's contact with Delaware. The statutes do not address the scenario where an unregistered foreign limited partnership has a Delaware corporation as its general partner. *Macklowe v. Planet Hollywood, 1994 Del. Ch. LEXIS 179 (Del. Ch. Oct. 13, 1994).*

Illustrative cases. — Selection by an unregistered foreign limited partnership of a Delaware resident corporation as its general partner constitutes a reasonable basis for concluding it expected its general partner to be served and accept service of process in the event it was doing business in Delaware. *Macklowe v. Planet Hollywood, 1994 Del. Ch. LEXIS 179 (Del. Ch. Oct. 13, 1994).*

A foreign limited partnership who consents to jurisdiction through a forum selection clause "does business" for purposes of this section and can be served through the Secretary of State. *Alstom Power v. Duke, 2005 Del. Super. LEXIS 54 (Del. Super. Ct. Jan. 31, 2005).*

Subchapter X.
Derivative Actions

§ 17-1001.   Right to bring action

DELAWARE CASE NOTES — REPORTED

Actions involving limited partnerships. — Corporate standards apply to limited partnerships in the 'demand excused' analysis; accordingly, the statutory test for derivative actions in the partnership context is nearly identical to corporation case law. *Seaford Funding Ltd. Partnership v. M & M Assocs. II, 672 A.2d 66 (Del. Ch. 1995).*

Business judgment rule. — Reviewing a general partner's refusal of demand under the business judgment rule creates 3 issues: (1) whether the general partner acted independently and not interestedly; (2) whether the general partner reasonably investigated the basis for the proposed litigation; and (3) whether the general partner refused to act in good faith. *Seaford Funding Ltd. Partnership v. M & M Assocs. II, 672 A.2d 66 (Del. Ch. 1995).*

General partners may not claim the protection of the business judgment rule when appearing on both sides of the transaction or when deriving a personal benefit in the sense of self-dealing; furthermore, general partners may not use the business judgment rule as a shield if they are not informed of material information reasonably available to them before making a business decision. *Seaford Funding Ltd. Partnership v. M & M Assocs. II, 672 A.2d 66 (Del. Ch. 1995).*

Demand generally required in derivative action. — Where a claim is derivative in nature, Delaware law requires plaintiffs either to make a demand on the general partners or allege in the complaint why such a demand was not made; and assertions in a complaint that the general partners mismanaged the partnership were insufficient to show that demand should be excused due to the inapplicability of the business judgment rule to the general partners' conduct. Therefore, because plaintiffs failed to meet the requirements of this chapter, they lacked standing to prosecute. *Litman v. Prudential-Bache Properties, Inc., 611 A.2d 12 (Del. Ch. 1992).*

Effect of refusal after demand. — When limited partners make demand and the general partner refuses to pursue the action after informed consideration and in good faith, the business judgment rule comes into play; the plaintiffs' power to maintain the derivative action is terminated by the refusal. *Seaford Funding Ltd. Partnership v. M & M Assocs. II, 672 A.2d 66 (Del. Ch. 1995).*

DELAWARE CASE NOTES — UNREPORTED

The General Assembly has expressed its intent to retroactively apply its 1998 amendment giving standing to assignees in this section. *Gotham Partners, L.P. v. Hallwood Realty Partners, L.P., 2000 Del. Ch. LEXIS 152 (Del. Ch. Oct. 20, 2000)*

Applicability of corporate cases. — The determination of whether a claim is derivative or direct in nature is substantially the same for corporate cases as it is for limited partnership cases. *Albert v. Alex. Brown Mgmt. Servs., 2005 Del. Ch. LEXIS 133 (Del. Ch. Aug. 26, 2005).*

Binding effect. — Considerations of fairness and judicial economy require that an action to redress a wrong to a limited partnership be litigated derivatively, so that it may be resolved once and for all in a single lawsuit. The result is binding on the partnership and precludes any other limited partner from bringing the same claim. *Katell v. Morgan Stanley Group, 1993 Del. Ch. LEXIS 5, Fed. Sec. L. Rep. (CCH) P97437 (Del. Ch. Jan. 14, 1993).*

RULPA

Iowa

Delaware law requires that a complaint in a derivative action must allege with particularity the effort, if any, made to secure the action desired from the general partner and the reasons the effort failed or why they chose not to make the effort. *Whalen v. Connelly, (Iowa 1999).*

Role of general partner. — Once a demand is received, the general partner has the responsibility to decide whether to bring the law suit on behalf of the partnership and must exercise business judgment whether to pursue the course of action demanded by the plaintiff. A plaintiff's power to maintain a derivative action is terminated by the general partner's proper refusal to take the demanded action. Delaware statutory law, however, does not articulate when a general partner must take action and does not address the consequences of making a demand for action to a general partner with a clear conflict of interest amounting to self-dealing. *Whalen v. Connelly, 593 N.W.2d 147 (Iowa 1999).*

Wrongful refusal of demand. — When a general partner refuses a limited partner's demand, in order for the plaintiff-limited partner's derivative action to go forward, the plaintiff must allege with particularity facts that create a reasonable doubt that the board of directors wrongfully refused the demand. In determining whether a demand was wrongfully refused, a court reviews the decision according to the traditional business judgment rule. The business judgment rule is a presumption that in making a business decision, not involving self-interest, the directors of a corporation acted on an informed basis, in good faith and in the honest belief that the action taken was in the best interests of the company. The burden is on the party challenging the decision to establish facts rebutting the presumption. *Whalen v. Connelly, 593 N.W.2d 147 (Iowa 1999).*

Judicial review of a board's refusal of a demand under the business judgment rule creates three issues for the court: (1) whether the general partner acted independently and not self interestedly; (2) whether the general partner reasonably investigated the basis for the proposed litigation; and (3) whether the general partner refused to act in good faith. *Whalen v. Connelly, 593 N.W.2d 147 (Iowa 1999).*

A pre-suit demand by a limited partner to the general partner in a derivative suit waives any contention that the general partner was incapable of acting on the demand. Conversely, making a demand assumes that the general partner is capable of acting on the demand. Whalen v. Connelly, 593 N.W.2d 147 (Iowa 1999).

Demand. — When a claim against a partnership is derivative, Delaware law requires the plaintiff to either make a demand on the general partners to instigate litigation or plead an explanation of why such a demand was not made. *Whalen v. Connelly, 593 N.W.2d 147 (Iowa 1999).*

North Carolina

The purpose behind the statutory demand requirement is the same in both North Carolina and Delaware. North Carolina law requires plaintiffs to pursue and exhaust intra-corporate remedies through demand on directors to assure corporate management the opportunity to pursue alternative remedies, thus avoiding unnecessary litigation. Delaware's statutory demand requirement is based on the same principles: The demand requirement is premised on the idea that the decision of whether to bring a lawsuit is a business one that is properly in the hands of the corporation's directors, whose role it is to manage the business and affairs of the corporation. Its purpose is to ensure that the derivative action remains an exception to the general rule that the appropriate party to bring suit is the corporation acting through its directors. *Ray v. Deloitte & Touche, L.L.P., 2006 NCBC 5, 2006 NCBC LEXIS 7 (April 21, 2006).*

Under Delaware law, a plaintiff may not bring a derivative claim in the right of a limited partnership unless the general partner has refused to do so, or any demand that the general partner do so would be futile. *Cabaniss v. Deutsche Bank Securities, Inc., 611 S.E.2d 878 (N.C. App. 2005).*

In derivative actions, the complaint must state with particularity what effort the plaintiffs made to get a general partner to initiate an action by a general partner or explain why it has not done so. This rule is one of substantive right, not simply a technical rule of pleading. The purpose of this rule is to allow the general partner, on behalf of the limited partnership, the opportunity to rectify the alleged wrong without suit or to control any litigation brought for its benefit. *Cabaniss v. Deutsche Bank Securities, Inc., 611 S.E.2d 878 (N.C. App. 2005).*

Limitation on complaint. — When a plaintiff accepts the terms of a partnership agreement which discloses conflicts of interest or self-dealing, he or she is precluded from bringing a derivative claim based on facts disclosed in that agreement. A stockholder cannot complain of corporate action in which he or she has concurred. *Cabaniss v. Deutsche Bank Securities, INC., 611 S.E.2d 878 (N.C. App. 2005).*

Futility may not be assumed merely because there was no one upon whom demand could be made. As applied to this case, Plaintiffs must instead show why it was, in fact, impractical to comply with the procedures set out in the partnership agreements for appointing a successor general partner or liquidator. *Ray v. Deloitte & Touche, L.L.P., 2006 NCBC 5, 2006 NCBC LEXIS 7 (April 21, 2006).*

Proper remedy here (under both Delaware and North Carolina law) is dismissal without prejudice. First, the present action is not a typical futility of demand case where the complaint is dismissed for the plaintiff's failure to plead facts with sufficient particularity due to an inadequate investigation before filing suit. Rather, decision to dismiss the complaint is based on the plaintiffs' failure to identify and then make a pre-suit demand on the proper representatives of the funds. Second, the present action involves an unusual set of facts. Specifically, this case concerns two nonfunctioning entities with no leadership due to the bankruptcy of the managing bodies. And

finally, contrary to the defendants' contention, plaintiffs may in fact be able to cure the statutory defects in their pleading. *Ray v. Deloitte & Touche, L.L.P., 2006 NCBC 5, 2006 NCBC LEXIS 7 (April 21, 2006).*

CASE NOTES — FEDERAL COURTS

Third Circuit

Personal participation in wrongs; enrichment. — To hold a parent corporation liable for breaches of the general partner's fiduciary duties, a plaintiff limited partner must raise sufficient issue of material fact to support the conclusion that the general partner personally participated in the wrongs complained of and utilized partnership assets under their control to enrich themselves at the expense of the limited partners. *Niki Development Corp. v. HOB Hotel Chicago Partners, L.P., 2003 U.S. Dist. LEXIS 4949 (N.D.Ill. 2003).*

Directors and corporate parents of general partners can only be subject to fiduciary liability for implementing unfair, self-dealing transactions, or, in other words, for participating in alleged fiduciary breaches in which they themselves benefit. *Niki Development Corp. v. HOB Hotel Chicago Partners, L.P., 2003 U.S. Dist. LEXIS 4949 (N.D.Ill. 2003).*

Not exclusive remedy. — The Revised Uniform Limited Partnership Act (RULPA) adopted in both New Jersey and Delaware, recognizes the availability of a derivative action but does not mandate that a suit such as this be brought exclusively as a derivative action. Derivative claims are not the exclusive vehicle available to limited partners. *Blystra v. Fiber Tech Group, Inc., 2005 U.S. Dist. LEXIS 38117 (D.N.J. Dec. 29, 2005).*

Choice of law. — Delaware law applies to determine whether the limited partners have standing. Where limited partnership is organized under the laws of Delaware, Delaware law controls the determination of whether a limited partner's suit is individual or derivative. *Blystra*

v. Fiber Tech Group, Inc., 2005 U.S. Dist. LEXIS 38117 (D.N.J. Dec. 29, 2005).

Sixth Circuit

Under Delaware law, limited partners cannot control the business' assets or activities, and may sue on its behalf only under limited circumstances. *Winn v. Seidman Financial Services, 726 F. Supp. 170 (W.D.Mich. 1989).*

Tenth Circuit

Derivative versus direct actions. — Delaware law allows a limited partner to bring a derivative action after demand upon the general partner or without demand if it would be futile. Generally, whether an action is direct or derivative depends upon whether the injury alleged is independent of the injury suffered by the limited partnership. Where the claim belongs to the partnership, limited partners ordinarily cannot enforce their proportional interest in a partnership claim as their individual claim. At the same time, limited partners can bring a direct action when the injury can be differentiated from that suffered by the other partners. Courts have allowed claims for (1) an accounting, (2) fiduciary breach, and (3) breach of the partnership agreement to proceed as individual claims in varying circumstances. *United States Cellular Investment Co. v. Southwestern Bell Mobile Systems, Inc., 1997 U.S. App. LEXIS 31865 (10th Cir. 1997).*

§ 17-1002. Proper plaintiff

DELAWARE CASE NOTES — REPORTED

Limited partners claims were direct, not derivative — Where limited partners of an investment fund claimed that the general partner withdrew the funds in violation of the partnership agreement, that the withdrawal exceeded the balance in the account, and that timely disclosure of the withdrawal was not given, the court found that while a diminution of the value of a business was classically derivative in nature, the operation and function of the instant fund diverged so radically

from the traditional corporate model that the claims were properly brought as direct claims, by the limited partners, all of which had withdrawn from the fund by the time the action was filed; that portion of defendants' motions to dismiss contending that the limited partners lacked standing to bring the action because they were not partners, was rejected, as this section did not apply. *Anglo Am. Sec. Fund, L.P. v. S.R. Global Int'l Fund, L.P., 829 A.2d 143 (Del. Ch. 2003).*

DELAWARE CASE NOTES — UNREPORTED

Standing by contract. — This section provides only one way for parties to a limited partnership to confer standing by contract to bring a derivative suit upon a partner who obtains its interest after the disputed transaction. That one circumstance occurs when the interest is transferred pursuant to terms of the partnership agreement from a person who was a partner at the time of the

transaction. *Flynn v. Bachow, 1998 Del. Ch. LEXIS 181 (Del. Ch. Sept. 18, 1998).*

There is no language in DRULPA § 17-1002 that grants parties to a limited partnership the right to create conditions establishing standing to bring a derivative action by contract. *Flynn v. Bachow, 1998 Del. Ch. LEXIS 181 (Del. Ch. Sept. 18, 1998).*

Judgment of general partner. — On the obvious level, the general partners do have control over derivative suits. The statutory test for determining derivative actions in the partnership context is almost identical to case law language in the corporations context. Neither § 17-1001 nor § 17-1003 of the partnership law provides enough guidance as to determine exactly which derivative suits general partners must pursue. As a result, general partners must exercise their judgment in pursuing litigation against their partnership due to demand made on them. In light of this exercise of judgment, a plaintiff may experience a situation where demand on the general partners would be futile. Therefore, the issues in determining demand futility for partnership law appear identical to those in corporation law. *Litman v. Prudential-Bache Properties, 1993 Del. Ch. LEXIS 13, Fed. Sec. L. Rep. (CCH) P97313 (Del. Ch. Jan. 4, 1993).*

CASE NOTES — OTHER STATES

Iowa

Role of general partner. — Once a demand is received, the general partner has the responsibility to decide whether to bring the law suit on behalf of the partnership and must exercise business judgment whether to pursue the course of action demanded by the plaintiff. A plaintiff's power to maintain a derivative action is terminated by the general partner's proper refusal to take the demanded action. Delaware statutory law, however, does not articulate when a general partner must take action and does not address the consequences of making a demand for action to a general partner with a clear conflict of interest amounting to self-dealing. *Whalen v. Connelly, 593 N.W.2d 147 (Iowa 1999).*

§ 17-1003. Complaint

DELAWARE CASE NOTES — REPORTED

Demand generally required in derivative action. — Where a claim is derivative in nature, Delaware law requires plaintiffs either to make a demand on the general partners or allege in the complaint why such a demand was not made; and assertions in a complaint that the general partners mismanaged the partnership were insufficient to show that demand should be excused due to the inapplicability of the business judgment rule to the general partners' conduct. Therefore, because plaintiffs failed to meet the requirements of this chapter, they lacked standing to prosecute. *Litman v. Prudential-Bache Properties, Inc., 611 A.2d 12 (Del. Ch. 1992).*

DELAWARE CASE NOTES — UNREPORTED

Judgment of general partner. — On the obvious level, the general partners do have control over derivative suits. The statutory test for determining derivative actions in the partnership context is almost identical to case law language in the corporations context. Neither § 17-1001 nor § 17-1003 of the partnership law provides enough guidance as to determine exactly which derivative suits general partners must pursue. As a result, general partners must exercise their judgment in pursuing litigation against their partnership due to demand made on them. In light of this exercise of judgment, a plaintiff may experience a situation where demand on the general partners would be futile. Therefore, the issues in determining demand futility for partnership law appear identical to those in corporation law. *Litman v. Prudential-Bache Properties, 1993 Del. Ch. LEXIS 13, Fed. Sec. L. Rep. (CCH) P97313 (Del. Ch. Jan. 4, 1993).*

Demand excused. — Demand by limited partners was excused, where the facts alleged in the partners' complaint were: (1) sufficient to support an inference that the general partner exercised no oversight; and (2) created a substantial likelihood of the general partner's liability for gross negligence in discharging its oversight duty, or a material breach of a partnership agreement. *Forsythe v. ESC Fund Mgmt. Co. (U.S.), 2007 Del. Ch. LEXIS 140 (Del. Ch. Oct. 9, 2007).* **[For the full text of this case opinion, please see the Appendix at the end of this Volume.]**

Illustrative case. — It is very persuasive that where the general partner is 100% owned by one person, and the general partner would be required to bring suit against that person, there is at least some doubt as to the disinterest of that person. In the instant case, where the only party against whom relief is sought is the 100% owner of the party that would be requested to prosecute the lawsuit—what could be closer to beholdenness? General partner is beholden to plaintiff because general partnership is 100% owned by plaintiff. And so, demand is excused. *Dean v. Dick, 1999 Del. Ch. LEXIS 121 (Del. Ch. June 10, 1999).*

CASE NOTES — OTHER STATES

Iowa

Wrongful refusal of demand. — When a general partner refuses a limited partner's demand, in order for the plaintiff-limited partner's derivative action to go forward, the plaintiff must allege with particularity facts that create a reasonable doubt that the board of directors wrongfully refused the demand. In determining whether a demand was wrongfully refused, a court reviews the decision according to the traditional business judgment rule. The business judgment rule is a presumption that in making a business decision, not involving self-interest, the directors of a corporation acted on an informed basis, in good faith and in the honest belief that the action taken was in the best interests of the company. The burden is on

RULPA

the party challenging the decision to establish facts rebutting the presumption. *Whalen v. Connelly, 593 N.W.2d 147 (Iowa 1999).*

Judicial review of a board's refusal of a demand under the business judgment rule creates three issues for the court: (1) whether the general partner acted independently and not self interestedly; (2) whether the general partner reasonably investigated the basis for the proposed litigation; and (3) whether the general partner refused to act in good faith. *Whalen v. Connelly, 593 N.W.2d 147 (Iowa 1999).*

Corporate concession. — Under Delaware corporations law, a shareholder who elects to make a demand upon the board of directors concedes or waives the right to challenge the independence of a majority of the board to respond to the demand. This rule is sometimes referred to as the "corporate concession." *Whalen v. Connelly, 593 N.W.2d 147 (Iowa 1999).*

A pre-suit demand by a limited partner to the general partner in a derivative suit waives any contention that the general partner was incapable of acting on the demand. Conversely, making a demand assumes that the general partner is capable of acting on

the demand. *Whalen v. Connelly, 593 N.W.2d 147 (Iowa 1999).*

Demand. — When a claim against a partnership is derivative, Delaware law requires the plaintiff to either make a demand on the general partners to instigate litigation or plead an explanation of why such a demand was not made. *Whalen v. Connelly, 593 N.W.2d 147 (Iowa 1999).*

North Carolina

Purpose of particularity requirement. — In derivative actions, the complaint must state with particularity what effort plaintiffs made to get a general partner to initiate an action by a general partner or explain why it has not done so. This rule is one of substantive right, not simply a technical rule of pleading. The purpose of this rule is to allow the general partner, on behalf of the limited partnership, the opportunity to rectify the alleged wrong without suit or to control any litigation brought for its benefit. *Cabaniss v. Deutsche Bank Securities, Inc., 611 S.E.2d 878 (N.C. App. 2005).*

CASE NOTES — FEDERAL COURTS

Seventh Circuit

Personal participation in wrongs; enrichment. — To hold a parent corporation liable for breaches of the general partner's fiduciary duties, a plaintiff limited partner must raise sufficient issue of material fact to support the conclusion that the general partner personally

participated in the wrongs complained of and utilized partnership assets under their control to enrich themselves at the expense of the limited partners. *Niki Development Corp. v. HOB Hotel Chicago Partners, L.P., 2003 U.S. Dist. LEXIS 4949 (N.D.Ill. 2003).*

Subchapter XI.
Miscellaneous

§ 17-1101. Construction and application of chapter and partnership agreement

DELAWARE CASE NOTES — REPORTED

Recourse against general partner. — When the actions of the general partner violate the express terms of the partnership agreement, recourse may be sought in contract law, and not simply under partnership regulations. *Gotham Partners, L.P. v. Hallwood Realty Partners, L.P., 795 A.2d 1 (Del. Ch. 2001).*

In a case involving a series of transactions in which a general partner controlling group's control was entrenched by an increase in percentage interest from 5.1 percent to 29.7 percent (66.67 percent was required to remove a general partner), interpreting former paragraph (d)(2) of this section, the Delaware Supreme Court held that a limited partnership agreement could provide for contractually created fiduciary duties substantially mirroring traditional fiduciary duties that apply in the corporation law (for example, the entire fairness standard), but a limited partnership agreement could not eliminate the fiduciary duties or liabilities of a general partner; the court affirmed the joint and several liability of the controlling groups but remanded for a rationally articulated recission-substitute remedy, which could include recission,

sterilization, and damages, to put the plaintiff limited partner in the position it would have been in if the controlling group had complied with the partnership agreement. *Gotham Partners, L.P. v. Hallwood Realty Partners, L.P., 805 A.2d 882 (Del. 2002).*

Application of (d)(1). — Former subsection (d)(1) of this section only applies where the court finds the clause upon which the defendants rely is ambiguous. If the limited partnership agreement remains unambiguous, then former (d)(1) does not apply because a general partner cannot wrongly rely in good faith on a misinterpretation of a contract clause if it is subject to only one plausible interpretation. *Continental Ins. Co. v. Rutledge & Co., 750 A.2d 1219 (Del. Ch. 2000).*

Good faith reliance. — Breach of fiduciary duty claim dismissed where plaintiff partner failed to plead that defendant partner acted in bad faith; a general partner acting in good faith reliance on the provisions of the partnership agreement is shielded from liability for breach of fiduciary duty by subsection (d) of this section. *United*

States Cellular Inv. Co. v. Bell Atl. Mobile Sys., 677 A.2d 497 (Del. 1996).

Compromise of responsibility. — A partner who accepted the role of a general partner, and had an obligation pursuant to the limited partnership agreement to manage the partnership in a manner consistent with the common law duties of a fiduciary, could not compromise this responsibility barring a provision modifying or contracting away that responsibility. *Davenport Group v. Strategic Inv. Partners, Inc., 685 A.2d 715 (Del. Ch. 1996).*

In general. — Limited partnerships' contract theory-based structure provides incentives for parties to opt for the limited partnership over other forms of business organizations. As such, parties, otherwise unwilling to shoulder fiduciary burdens, maintain the opportunity to form limited partnerships precisely because the parties can contract around some or all of the fiduciary duties the general partner typically owes the limited partners. *Continental Ins. Co. v. Rutledge & Co., 750 A.2d 1219, 2000 Del. Ch. LEXIS 18 (Del. Ch. 2000).*

Application of default fiduciary duties. — Determinations of whether the provisions of a limited partnership agreement are inconsistent with the application of default fiduciary duties are necessarily imprecise and often require close judgment calls. While demanding that the parties to a limited partnership agreement make their intentions to displace fiduciary duties plain, the cases have erred on the side of flexibility regarding the type of evidence sufficient to support a judicial finding that such an intention existed. Resisting the temptation to resolve hairsplitting questions by reference to maxims of interpre-tation, our courts have thus far adhered as a general matter to a close examination of whether the application of default fiduciary duties can be reconciled with the practical and efficient operation of the terms of the limited partnership agreement. Where such a reconciliation is possible, the court will apply default fiduciary duties in the absence of clear contractual language disclaiming their applicability. But where the use of default fiduciary duties would intrude upon the contractual rights or expectations of the general partner or be insensible in view of the contractual mechanisms governing the transaction under consideration, the court will eschew fiduciary concepts and focus on a purely contractual analysis of the dispute. *R.S.M. Inc. v. Alliance Capital Mgmt. Holdings L.P., 790 A.2d 478, 2001 Del. Ch. LEXIS 45 (Del. Ch. 2001).*

Intent to preempt fiduciary principles. — The irreconcilability of fiduciary duty principles with the operation of the partnership agreement can itself be evidence of the clear intention of the parties to preempt fiduciary principles. *R.S.M. Inc. v. Alliance Capital Mgmt. Holdings L.P., 790 A.2d 478, 2001 Del. Ch. LEXIS 45 (Del. Ch. 2001).*

Subsection (c) of this section statutorily authorized the parties to the partnership agreement to restrict the fiduciary duties owed to the defendants. Principles of contract preempt fiduciary principles where the parties to a limited partnership have made their intentions to do so plain. *Brickell Partners v. Wise, 794 A.2d 1, 2001 Del. Ch. LEXIS 106 (Del. Ch. 2001).*

RULPA

DELAWARE CASE NOTES — UNREPORTED

In general. — As a matter of statutory law, the traditional fiduciary duties among and between partners are defaults that may be modified by partnership agreements. This flexibility is precisely the reason why many choose the limited partnership form in Delaware. Decisional law also has recognized and given illumination to this principle. The cases have gone so far as to suggest that partnership agreements act as safe harbors for actions that might otherwise quality as breaches of fiduciary duties under the traditional default rules. *Kahn v. Icahn, 1998 Del. Ch. LEXIS 223 (Del. Ch. Nov. 12, 1998).*

Construction with other business entities law. — Certainly partnerships are amenable to greater freedom contractually to shape the set of legal relationships that constitute the partnership than are corporations, and this freedom may include clear contracting with respect to fiduciary duties. But there may be less to this difference between corporations and limited partnerships (or other entities) in this respect than meets the eye. First, there is modernly great flexibility in the corporate form. The corporate charter may, for example, particularize director and officers' duties. Thus, there is no reason why corporate charters cannot contain provisions dealing with corporate opportunities or dealing with the ability of officers or directors to compete with the corporation. Second, and equally importantly, investors in limited partnership or other more explicitly contractual entities (to the extent they are informed) have a limited incentive to invest in entities that broadly and explicitly repudiate a duty of loyalty. Thus, under Delaware law, all forms of business organization that entail passive investors and active managers permit parties at the time of contracting to specify a great deal bearing on the exercise of managerial power, and passive investors in all forms of enterprise have a powerful incentive, insofar as self-interested transactions by the managers are involved, to retain the possibility of later judicial review under a fairness standard. In fact, the underlying principles of fiduciary analysis in both the corporate and the partnership context reflect a similar principle: given no defect in process (e.g., fraud, nondisclosure, or manipulation) explicitly negotiated and validly adopted provisions of a constitutional document will be enforced. *U.S. WEST, Inc. v. Time Warner Inc., 1996 Del. Ch. LEXIS 55 (Del. Ch. June 6, 1996).*

Duties of limited partner. — Although the Delaware Revised Uniform Limited Partnership Act does not specifically state that a limited partner owes a fiduciary duty to a general partner it, by reference to the Delaware Uniform Partnership Act, so provides. Therefore, to the extent that a partnership agreement empowers a limited partner discretion to take actions affecting the governance of the limited partnership, the limited partner may be subject to the obligations of a fiduciary, including the obligation to act in good faith as to the other partners. *KE Property Management, Inc. v. 275 Madison Management Corp., 1993 Del. Ch. LEXIS 147 (Del. Ch. July 21, 1993).*

Nothing in DRULPA or our case law expressly prohibits a limited partnership agreement from providing that limited partners are subject to duties that the common law or equity does not independently impose upon them. *Cantor Fitzgerald, L.P. v. Cantor, 2000 Del. Ch. LEXIS 43 (Del. Ch. Mar. 13, 2000).*

Safe harbor for general partner. — The Delaware Revised Limited Partnership Act recognizes partners may modify fiduciary duties through contract. In other words, whether a general partner acts in good faith, with due care or with requisite loyalty may be determined by the consistency to which the general partner adheres to its contractual obligations. Put another way, the limited partnership agreement may authorize actions creating a "safe harbor" for the general partner under circumstances which might otherwise be questionable or impose a stricter standard of scrutiny than the norm. *In re Cencom Cable Income Partners, L.P. Litig., 1996 Del. Ch. LEXIS 17 (Del. Ch. Feb. 15, 1996).*

Delegation of authority. — Delaware law does not contain an express provision allowing general partners to delegate their authority to a committee. Rather, the specific rights and responsibilities of parties in a general or limited partnership are determined by the parties' particular partnership agreement. *Katell v. Morgan Stanley Group, Inc., 1993 Del. Ch. LEXIS 92 (Del. Ch. June 8, 1993).*

Illustrative case. — Holding that the parties to the 1996 partnership agreement could bargain to impose a fiduciary duty of loyalty on the limited partners is not remotely offensive to any concerns of public policy. To the contrary, upholding the right of these partners to agree by a mutual exchange of dependent promises that they will not act in ways that threaten to destroy the common mission and purpose 'of the partnership upholds DRUPLA's policy of affording partners the broadest possible discretion in drafting their partnership agreements. The duty of loyalty proclaimed in the 1996 partnership agreement requires no dependency upon a default concept to a narrow definition derived from corporate common law. The scope of the duties owed by the parties must be determined by reference to the nature of this particular business enterprise. *Cantor Fitzgerald, L.P. v. Cantor, 2000 Del. Ch. LEXIS 43 (Del. Ch. Mar. 13, 2000).*

Obligation to act fairly and prove fairness. — What general partner could not cause limited partnership to do was to pursue a business strategy that could only benefit himself personally, to the exclusion of the limited partnership and its other investors. Under Delaware law, a general partner and its representative must manage the partnership in the best interests of the partnership and deal fairly with the limited partners. Unless an agreement between the partners makes clear that the partners intended to preempt fundamental fiduciary duties, a general partner is obligated to act fairly and prove fairness when making self-interested decisions. If general partner was correct in his view that limited partnership could not benefit from the new technologies and only his wholly-owned company would benefit, it was clearly wrongful and disloyal for him to cause limited partnership to develop them. *McGovern v. General Holding, Inc., 2006 Del. Ch. LEXIS 93 (Del. Ch. June 2, 2006).*

CASE NOTES — OTHER STATES

Connecticut

Good-faith reliance. — A general partner acting in good-faith reliance on the provisions of a partnership agreement is shielded from liability for breach of fiduciary duty. *Greenwich Global, LLC. v. Clairvoyant Capital, LLC., 2002 Conn. Super. LEXIS 2834 (2002).*

Restriction of fiduciary obligations. — Arbitration panel made a rational and logical decision that the covenant not to sue, if not the release, unequivocally applied to the plaintiffs' claims in question. The arbitrators found that there was no violation of public policy because of Delaware law as embodied in the Delaware Revised Uniform Limited Partnership Act (DRULPA) which permits parties to agree to restrict fiduciary obligations. *Merrick v. Cummin, 2005 Conn. Super. LEXIS 2706 (Oct. 11, 2005)*

Maryland

Limitations on fiduciary duties. — Under Delaware law, while partners are free to limit their fiduciary duties by contract, the parties to a limited partnership must make plain their intention to do so. Where there is no clear contractual language that preempts default fiduciary duty rules, the courts of Delaware will continue to apply them. *Westbard Apts., LLC v. Westwood Joint Venture, LLC, 2007 Md. App. LEXIS 80 (May 25, 2007).*

New York

Diversion of opportunity claim dismissed. — Partnership agreement permitted its partners to engage in other real estate business, and such other business clauses allow partners to pursue business opportunities that might otherwise have gone to the partnership. Thus, to the extent that claims allege that defendants diverted an opportunity from first limited partnership to second limited partnership, they were properly dismissed based on documentary evidence. *Barrett v. Toroyan, 2006 NY Slip Op 2829, 2006 NY Slip Op 2829; 28 A.D.3d 331; 813 N.Y.S.2d 415; 2006 N.Y. App. Div. LEXIS 4461 (Apr. 18, 2006).*

Misappropriation/waste claim allowed to proceed. — To the extent claims allege that defendants misappropriated original limited partnership's goodwill and asset management fees and committed waste by spending its money for the benefit of the second limited partnership, they should not have been dismissed, since the documentary evidence does not utterly refute plaintiff's factual allegations, conclusively establishing a defense as a matter of law Under Delaware law, a limited partnership agreement can limit, but not eliminate, the general partner's fiduciary duties and previous court opinion in the state was careful to say that an other business clause does not permit self-dealing or self-interested transactions. *Barrett v. Toroyan, 2006 NY Slip Op 2829, 2006 NY Slip Op 2829; 28 A.D.3d 331; 813 N.Y.S.2d 415; 2006 N.Y. App. Div. LEXIS 4461 (Apr. 18, 2006).*

Pennsylvania

Fiduciary duty. — Unless expanded or limited by the partnership agreement, a general partner has the fiduciary duty to manage the partnership in its interest and in the interests of the limited partners. *Alan Wurtzel Commerce Program v. Park Towne Place Apartments Limited Partnership, 2001 Phila. Ct. Com. Pl. LEXIS 79 (2001).*

§ 17-1105. Cases not provided for in this chapter

CASE NOTES — OTHER STATES

New York

As to the fiduciary duties which are owed by and to the limited partners, every partner must account to the partnership for any benefit, and hold as trustee for it any profits, derived by him or her without the consent of the other partners from any transaction connected with the conduct of the partnership or from any use by him or her of its property. *Mizrahi v. Chanel, Inc., 193 Misc. 2d 1, 746 N.Y.S.2d 878 (2001).*

RULPA

Subchapter I.
General Provisions

§ 18-101. Definitions

DELAWARE CASE NOTES — REPORTED

"Limited liability companies". — Limited liability companies are hybrid entities that combine desirable characteristics of corporations, limited partnerships, and general partnerships. *Great Lakes Chem. Corp. v. Monsanto Co., 96 F. Supp. 2d 376 (D. Del. 2000).*

Limited liability companies are entitled to partnership status for federal income tax purposes under certain circumstances, which permits limited liability companies members to avoid double taxation. *Great Lakes Chem. Corp. v. Monsanto Co., 96 F. Supp. 2d 376 (D. Del. 2000).*

CASE NOTES — OTHER STATES

Missouri

Promise not to compete. — A limited liability company formed under section 18-101 et seq. of the Delaware code shares many similarities with partnerships and close corporations. An operating agreement between a limited liability company and its members would fall within the class of contracts or relationships that would give a limited liability company a legitimate interest sufficient to sustain a promise not to compete by a member. *JTL Consulting, L.L.C. v. Shanahan, 2006 Mo. App. LEXIS 92 (Jan. 24, 2006).*

New York

Sections 18-101 and 18-301 are concerned primarily with fixing the time at which a person should be deemed to have been admitted to an LLC, not with denning the substantive requirements for membership. Insofar as the statute permits an LLC operating agreement to be oral, a person could be a member without that fact being reflected in the LLC's records. *Kim v. Ferdinand Capital LLC, 2007 N.Y. Misc. LEXIS 5431; 238 N.Y.L.J. 23 (July 9, 2007).*

§ 18-102. Name set forth in certificate

CASE NOTES — FEDERAL COURTS

Second Circuit

Under Delaware law, "LLC" indicates that the entity of that name is a limited liability company organized under the Limited Liability Company Act. *Independence*

Realty, LLC v. Travelers Indemnity Co., 2002 U.S. Dist. LEXIS 6585 (S.D.N.Y. 2002).

§ 18-106. Nature of business permitted; powers

DELAWARE CASE NOTES — UNREPORTED

Representation in court. — Because of the limited liability inherent in the limited liability company and the contractual nature of this entity, the court found that the Delaware Legislature did not intend a member or manager of an limited liability company could appear in Court to represent the entity without representation by Delaware legal counsel. Ultimately, regulation of the practice

of law rests in the Delaware Supreme Court, not the legislature. The underlying purpose of the rule prohibiting the appearance of a corporation by anyone other than a member of the Delaware Bar also applies to the representation of limited liability companies. *Poore v. Fox Hollow Enters., 1994 Del. Super. LEXIS 193 (1994).*

§ 18-108. Indemnification

DELAWARE CASE NOTES — REPORTED

Right to advancement of legal fees. — Limited Liability Company Act (*6 Del. C. § 18-101* et seq.) grants limited liability companies broad authority to provide for indemnification by contract in their operating agreements; hence, former managers of a limited liability company were entitled to advancement of legal fees in current manager's action for breach of contract and breach of fiduciary duties

according to the provision in the company's operating agreement. *Senior Tour Players 207 Mgmt. Co. LLC v. Golftown 207 Holding Co. LLC, 853 A.2d 124 (Del. Ch. 2004).*

"Hold harmless". — Advancement cases that rely on § 108 of the Limited Liability Company Act and the Limited Partnership Act never look to the phrase "hold

LLC

harmless" as providing the authority to grant mandatory advancement rights. Indeed, the legal authority for an LLC agreement to grant mandatory advancement rights has never been questioned in this court. The point of § 108 is that the parties to these agreements have complete freedom of contract—they are free to contract for advancement because neither the statute nor any principle of law or equity prohibits it. To hold that the phrase "hold harmless" automatically includes a right to advancement would, in fact, risk infringing upon that freedom by creating a potential trap for a careless draftsperson accidentally to include contractual advancement rights that were not intended. *Majkowski v. Am. Imaging Mgmt. Servs., LLC, 913 A.2d 572, 2006 Del. Ch. LEXIS 204 (Dec. 6, 2006).*

"Indemnify and hold harmless" is a legal term of art that does not include the unique concept of advancement as it functions within the rubric of Delaware's law of limited liability companies. The public policy in favor of advancement rights, much like the public policy in favor of arbitration, does not trump basic principles of contract interpretation, and does not alter the fact that a limited liability company will only be obligated to advance litigation expenses to an officer when its LLC agreement expressly states the company's intention to mandate advancement. *Majkowski v. Am. Imaging Mgmt. Servs., LLC, 913 A.2d 572, 2006 Del. Ch. LEXIS 204 (Dec. 6, 2006).*

DELAWARE CASE NOTES — UNREPORTED

Section 18-108 of the Limited Liability Company Act is verbatim § 17-108 of the Delaware Revised Uniform Limited Partnership Act ('DRULPA'). Both DRULPA and LLCA allow the contracting parties to determine the extent of indemnification in their agreements. In granting the advances on claims of indemnification in a limited partnership setting, it has been held that courts should interpret language so as to achieve where possible the beneficial purposes that indemnification can afford. *Morgan v. Grace, 2003 Del. Ch. LEXIS 113, No. 20430 (2003).*

"Expense". — The chancery court is unwilling to conclude that the mere use of the word 'expense' can be read to support a requirement of advancement. Delaware law is well settled that the right to indemnification and the right to advancement are distinct. And, as previously addressed, in a limited liability company setting, the language of the agreement will be honored as reflecting the intent of the parties. The LLCA clearly provides broad authority for the contracting parties to include both indemnification and advancement in their agreement. For whatever reason, the parties at hand chose to expressly allow advancement in the agreement of one LLC and not in the other. The court will not rewrite those agreements to provide for a right the parties clearly did not intend. *Morgan v. Grace, 2003 Del. Ch. LEXIS 113, No. 20430 (2003).*

Effect of conversion. — Corporation's bylaws providing a mandatory right of advancement to its officers and directors should not be read to apply equally to the former managers of the limited liability company (LLC), even where the LLC's operating agreement provided for indemnification but not for mandatory advancement. The right to indemnification or advancement for claims that arose during the life of the LLC continues to be governed by the terms of the old operating agreement. *Bernstein v. Tractmanager, Inc., 2007 Del. Ch. LEXIS 172 (November 20, 2007). [For the full text of this case opinion, please see the Appendix at the end of this Volume.]*

Limited liability companies and corporations differ in important ways, most pertinently in regard to indemnification: mandating it in the case of corporate directors and officers who successfully defend themselves, but leaving the indemnification of managers or officers of limited liability companies to private contract. While the business of the LLC continued on in the corporate form following the 2003 conversion, there is no reason to infer that the directors who approved the new certificate of incorporation and bylaws intended to change, adjust, or expand any of the existing rights or duties governing the LLC. *Bernstein v. Tractmanager, Inc., 2007 Del. Ch. LEXIS 172 (November 20, 2007). [For the full text of this case opinion, please see the Appendix at the end of this Volume.]*

Construction with other law. — Although (unlike the Delaware General Corporation Law in 8 Del. C. § 145(e)) the Limited Liability Company Act (LLCA) is entirely mute on the subject of advancement, 6 Del. C. § 18-108 of the LLCA gives broad authority to members of LLCs to set the terms for indemnification in their operating agreements; given that the broad freedom of members of LLCs to define their obligations inter sese by contract is germane to the formation and interpretation of LLC agreements, persons forming LLCs clearly have the authority to require a written undertaking as a condition to advancement. *Senior Tour Players 207 Mgmt. Co. LLC v. Golftown 207 Holding Co. LLC, 2004 Del. Ch. LEXIS 22 (Mar. 10, 2004).*

Governing statutory scheme for limited liability companies, including 8 Del. C. § 145 and 6 Del. C. § 18-108, does not support the implication that any party receiving an advancement would be obligated to execute a written undertaking to repay; therefore, because the operating agreement of a limited liability company was silent on the issue of a written undertaking, the court would not read such a requirement into the contract. *Senior Tour Players 207 Mgmt. Co. LLC v. Golftown 207 Holding Co. LLC, 2004 Del. Ch. LEXIS 22 (Del. Ch. Mar. 10, 2004).*

CASE NOTES — FEDERAL COURTS

Fourth Circuit

The word "issuer" in subsection (e) of this section does not include transfer agents. *Mellon Investor Servs., LLC v. Longwood Country Garden Centers, Inc., 2008 U.S. App. LEXIS 2631 (4th Cir., N.C., February 6, 2008).*

Fifth Circuit

Unenforceable provision. — Indemnification provision at issue does not specifically focus attention on the fact that by agreement LLC was assuming liability for the other entities' own negligence. Thus, under Delaware law, the LLC agreement language is not sufficiently clear and unequivocal such that the Court can affirmatively conclude that LLC expressly agreed to indemnify the other entities for their own negligence, albeit active or passive. Accordingly, the court finds the provision unenforceable under Delaware law. *Motiva Enters., LLC v. Liberty Mut. Ins. Co., 2006 U.S. Dist. LEXIS 81373 (D.Tex. Nov. 6, 2006).*

§ 18-109.   Service of process on managers and liquidating trustees

DELAWARE CASE NOTES — REPORTED

This section, like § 3114 of title 10, is a consent statute, providing that when a nonresident accepts a position as a manager of a Delaware limited liability company the nonresident consents that service upon the nonresident's own statutory agent will amount to in personam jurisdiction over the nonresident for any claims covered by the statute. *Assist Stock Mgt. L.L.C. v. Rosheim, 753 A.2d 974 (Del. Ch. 2000).*

DELAWARE CASE NOTES — UNREPORTED

Nonresidents. — When nonresidents agree to serve as directors or managers of Delaware entities, it is only reasonable that they anticipate that under certain circumstances they will be subject to personal jurisdiction in Delaware courts. The same principle that governs jurisdiction over corporate directors under 10 Del. C. § 3114 applies to this section: it is the rights, duties, and obligations which have to do with service as a director of a Delaware corporation which make a director subject to personal service in Delaware. *Palmer v. Moffat, 2001 Del. Super. LEXIS 386 (2001).*

Subsection (a) satisfied. — The confusion about ownership arises out of disputed managerial acts. Did the companies promise to issue units to in 1997 and to certain other employees and managers in 2000? That is, the question of who owns what units depends in a material way on actions they took as managers of the Companies. Likewise, these issues also bear a relationship to the validity of the votes removing manager because they relate to the question of whether the plaintiffs had sufficient voting power to cast him out. That is, all of these issues relate to the business of the companies and therefore satisfy the literal terms of subsection (a) of this section. *Cornerstone Techs. L.L.C. v. Unger, 2003 Del. Ch. LEXIS 34, No. 19712-NC (Mar. 31, 2003).*

§ 18-110.   Contested matters relating to managers; contested votes

DELAWARE CASE NOTES — UNREPORTED

Disclaimer of manager status does not divest jurisdiction. — By the plain terms of this section, the Court of Chancery may hear and determine the validity of any admission, election, appointment, removal or resignation of a manager of a limited liability company. And, the plaintiffs may constructively serve manager under subsection (a) because he is a 'person . . . whose right to serve as a manager is contested.' If, upon reflection, he adheres to his view that he was never a manager of either company, he is free to enter into a stipulated judgment to that effect. But his disclaimer of that status does not operate to divest this court of personal jurisdiction over him under subsection (a). *Cornerstone Techs. L.L.C. v. Unger, 2003 Del. Ch. LEXIS 34, No. 19712-NC (Mar.h 31, 2003).*

§ 18-111.   Interpretation and enforcement of limited liability company agreement

DELAWARE CASE NOTES — UNREPORTED

Waiver. — While agreement contained a choice of law clause providing that Delaware law is to govern, both parties have cited only Missouri law in their arguments on the enforceability of the nonsolicitation clause. Parties to a contract may waive the provisions of their contract by their conduct. Therefore, by not citing any Delaware law on customer nonsolicitation clauses, the parties have waived the Delaware choice of law clause in the operating agreement. *JTL Consulting, L.L.C. v. Shanahan, 2006 Mo. App. LEXIS 92 (Jan. 24, 2006).*

Arbitration provisions. —Plaintiffs' suit against defendants which involved interpretation of defendant limited liability company's (LLC) limited liability agreement and which sought dissolution of the LLC, was dismissed because the agreement unequivocally called for arbitration of all disputes arising out of or relating to it, and the agreement did not carve out dissolution or other claims from arbitration. *Terex Corp. v. STV USA, Inc., 2005 Del. Ch. LEXIS 159 (Del. Ch. Oct. 20, 2005).*

LLC

Subchapter II.
Formation; Certificate of Formation

§ 18-201. Certificate of formation

CASE NOTES — UNREPORTED

Amendment of certificate of formation, as to members. — Managing partner and managing copartner of a limited liability company (LLC) were the members of the LLC, in spite of the fact that the LLC's certificate of formation filed with the Delaware Secretary of State stated that the copartner's son was the member of the LLC, because the LLC agreement which the partner and the copartner signed after the filing of the certificate of formation (superseding the certificate of formation) and the documentary evidence made it clear that the partner and the copartner were the members of the LLC; the certificate of formation was not required to be amended when the partner and the copartner became the members. *In re Grupo Dos Chiles, LLC, 2006 Del. Ch. LEXIS 54 (Del. Ch. Mar. 10, 2006).*

CASE NOTES — FEDERAL COURTS

First Circuit

In general. — A limited liability company (LLC) is a form of statutory business organization that combines some of the advantages of a partnership with some of the advantages of a corporation. Under Delaware law, an LLC is a separate legal entity distinct from its members. As in a corporation, investors have limited liability, Del. Code Ann. tit. 6, § 18-303, own undivided interests in the company's property, Del. Code Ann. tit. 6, § 18-701, are bound by the terms of their agreement, and share in the overall profits and losses ratably according to their investment or as otherwise provided by the organizing agreement, Del. Code Ann. tit. 6, § 18-503. *Fraser v. Major League Soccer, L.L.C., 97 F. Supp. 2d 130 (D.Mass 2000).*

Second Circuit

Piercing the corporate veil. — Under Delaware law, a limited liability is a "separate legal entity" distinct from the members who own an interest in the limited liability company. Delaware law, however, permits a court to pierce the corporate veil of an entity where there is fraud or where the entity is in fact a mere instrumentality or alter ego of its owner. *SR International Business Insurance Co. v. World Trade Center Props., LLC, 375 F. Supp. 2d 238 (S.D.N.Y. 2005).*

CASE NOTES — OTHER STATES

Connecticut

Invalid conversion. — Without the authorization of the general partner, the attempted conversion of a limited partnership to a limited liability company was invalid under Delaware law. *Greenwich Global, LLC. v. Clairvoyant Capital, LLC., 2002 Conn. Super. LEXIS 2834 (2002).*

§ 18-202. Amendment to certificate of formation

CASE NOTES — UNREPORTED

Amendment as to members. — Managing partner and managing copartner of a limited liability company (LLC) were the members of the LLC, in spite of the fact that the LLC's certificate of formation filed with the Delaware Secretary of State stated that the copartner's son was the member of the LLC, because the LLC agreement which the partner and the copartner signed after the filing of the certificate of formation (superseding the certificate of formation) and the documentary evidence made it clear that the partner and the copartner were the members of the LLC; the certificate of formation was not required to be amended when the partner and the copartner became the members. *In re Grupo Dos Chiles, LLC, 2006 Del. Ch. LEXIS 54 (Del. Ch. Mar. 10, 2006).*

§ 18-209. Merger and consolidation

CASE NOTES — OTHER STATES

Illinois

Tax liability. — Plaintiff, as the surviving domestic limited liability company, is responsible for the additional franchise tax due as a result of the increase in the predecessor corporation's paid-in capital prior to the merger. *NDC, LLC v. Topinka, 2007 Ill. App. LEXIS 665 (June 15, 2007).*

§ 18-211.   Certificate of correction

CASE NOTES — UNREPORTED

Amendment of certificate of formation, as to members. — Managing partner and managing copartner of a limited liability company (LLC) were the members of the LLC, in spite of the fact that the LLC's certificate of formation filed with the Delaware Secretary of State stated that the copartner's son was the member of the LLC, because the LLC agreement which the partner and the copartner signed after the filing of the certificate of formation (superseding the certificate of formation) and the documentary evidence made it clear that the partner and the copartner were the members of the LLC; the certificate of formation was not required to be amended when the partner and the copartner became the members. *In re Grupo Dos Chiles, LLC, 2006 Del. Ch. LEXIS 54 (Del. Ch. Mar. 10, 2006).*

§ 18-214.   Conversion of certain entities to a limited liability company.

CASE NOTES — FEDERAL COURTS

Tenth Circuit

Determination of conversion status upon motion to dismiss. — The Delaware statutes provide that the conversion constitutes a continuation of the other entity and is not a dissolution of the other entity unless otherwise agreed, or unless otherwise provided in a resolution of conversion. Thus, determining whether corporation in fact was dissolved or continued may require resort to internal corporate documents. Also, the record before the court does not establish that the corporation necessarily took the appropriate steps internally to convert the corporation to a limited liability company. The certificate issued by the Delaware Secretary of State constitutes only prima facie evidence of the conversion, not conclusive proof. As such, this matter is not appropriate for resolution on a motion to dismiss. While the court recognizes that this issue ultimately may prove to be a mere technicality, it nonetheless presents an issue of fact that this court will not resolve on a motion to dismiss. *JP Morgan Trust Co. v. Mid-America Pipeline Co., 2006 U.S. Dist. LEXIS 4820 (D. Kan. Feb. 7, 2006).*

Judicial notice of certificates. — In the instant case, the court will exercise its discretion and, without converting the motion to one for summary judgment, will take judicial notice of the fact that the certificate of formation and the certificate of conversion were both filed with the Delaware Secretary of State on July 30, 2002, and that the Delaware Secretary of State issued a certificate stating that the appropriate conversion documents were filed. These documents are public records which are properly authenticated. Thus, the fact that they were filed with and issued by the Delaware Secretary of State, as well as their contents, are not subject to reasonable dispute. Indeed, public documents filed with the secretary of state such as those at issue here generally satisfy the judicial notice standard and district courts routinely take judicial notice of such documents in resolving motions to dismiss. *JP Morgan Trust Co. v. Mid-America Pipeline Co., 2006 U.S. Dist. LEXIS 4820 (D. Kan. Feb. 7, 2006).*

Subchapter III.
Members

§ 18-301.   Admission of members

CASE NOTES — OTHER STATES

New York

Sections 18-101 and 18-301 are concerned primarily with fixing the time at which a person should be deemed to have been admitted to an LLC, not with denning the substantive requirements for membership. Insofar as the statute permits an LLC operating agreement to be oral, a person could be a member without that fact being reflected in the LLC's records. *Kim v. Ferdinand Capital LLC, 2007 N.Y. Misc. LEXIS 5431; 238 N.Y.L.J. 23 (July 9, 2007).*

§ 18-302.   Classes and voting

DELAWARE CASE NOTES — REPORTED

Alternative voting arrangements. — In a lender's suit seeking to call the borrower's members' reserve capital obligations to the lender regarding a defaulted loan, the members could consent to an amendment of the limited liability company (LLC) agreement in a manner other than affirmative vote at a meeting or by written consent, because the LLC agreement provided for alternative methods of consent. *Chase Manhattan Bank v. Iridium Afr. Corp., __ F. Supp. 2d __, 2004 U.S. Dist. LEXIS 2332 (D. Del. Feb. 13, 2004).*

LLC

§ 18-303.   Liability to 3rd parties

DELAWARE CASE NOTES — REPORTED

No protection under federal securities laws. — In comparison with limited partnerships, the Limited Liability Company Act (*6 Del. C. § 18-101* et seq.) permits a member in a limited liability company to be an active participant in management and still to retain limited liability; thus, there is no statutory basis, as with limited partnerships, to presume that limited liability company members are passive investors entitled to protection under the federal securities laws. *Great Lakes Chem. Corp. v. Monsanto Co., 96 F. Supp. 2d 376 (D. Del. 2000).*

DELAWARE CASE NOTES — UNREPORTED

Purposes of chapter. — A limited liability company, a relatively new entity, was created to allow tax benefits similar to a partnership, while still providing limited liability protection, much like a corporation. As with a corporation, a member of a limited liability company may not be held liable for the debts, obligations and liabilities of the company. It follows that this Court has no jurisdiction to pierce the corporate veil of a limited liability company, just as it would not with a corporation. *Thomas v. Hobbs, 2005 Del. Super. LEXIS 164 (2005).*

Member liability for preformation conduct. — If a person makes material misrepresentations to induce a purchaser to purchase a parcel of land at a price far above fair market value, and thereafter forms an LLC to purchase and hold the land, that person can not later claim that his status as an LLC member protects him from liability to the purchaser under this section. *Pepsi-Cola Bottling Co. v. Handy, 2000 Del. Ch. LEXIS 52 (Del. Ch. 2000).*

CASE NOTES — OTHER STATES

California

Alter ego doctrine. — While membership alone may not cause personal liability, nothing in the statute refers to or precludes the application of the alter ego doctrine. Indeed, a member is not insulated from personal liability; he or she may agree to be obligated personally for the debts, obligations and liabilities of the limited liability company. *Allison v. Danilovic, 2004 Cal. App. Unpub. LEXIS 10988 (2004).*

Connecticut

This section plainly provides that a limited liability company member cannot be held liable for the malfeasance of a limited liability company by virtue of his membership in the limited liability company alone; in other words, he must do more than merely be a member in order to be liable personally for an obligation of the limited liability company. *Weber v. U. S. Sterling Secs., Inc., 282 Conn. 722; 924 A.2d 816; 2007 Conn. LEXIS 235 (June 19, 2007).*

This section does not preclude individual liability for members of a limited liability company if that liability is not based simply on the member's affiliation with the company. *Weber v. U. S. Sterling Secs., Inc., 282 Conn. 722; 924 A.2d 816; 2007 Conn. LEXIS 235 (June 19, 2007).*

North Carolina

Construction with other law. — Under this section and the comparable North Carolina statute, absent an agreement to the contrary, member-managers are specifically shielded from liability when acting as LLC managers. Thus, when a member-manager acts in its managerial capacity, it acts *for* the LLC, and obligations incurred while acting in that capacity are those *of* the LLC. Accordingly, when a member-manager is managing the LLC's business, its liability is inseparable from that of the LLC. *Hamby v. Profile Prods., L.L.C., 361 N.C. 630; 652 S.E.2d 231; 2007 N.C. LEXIS 1105 (November 9, 2007).*

CASE NOTES — FEDERAL COURTS

First Circuit

In general. — A limited liability company (LLC) is a form of statutory business organization that combines some of the advantages of a partnership with some of the advantages of a corporation. Under Delaware law, an LLC is a separate legal entity distinct from its members. As in a corporation, investors have limited liability, Del. Code Ann. tit. 6, § 18-303, own undivided interests in the company's property, Del. Code Ann. tit. 6, § 18-701, are bound by the terms of their agreement, and share in the overall profits and losses ratably according to their investment or as otherwise provided by the organizing agreement, Del. Code Ann. tit. 6, § 18-503. *Fraser v. Major League Soccer, L.L.C., 97 F. Supp. 2d 130 (D.Mass 2000).*

Eighth Circuit

The members of a limited liability company can agree to be personally liable for any or all debts, obligations, and liabilities of the limited liability company if they wish. *Frontier Traylor Shea, LLC v. Metropolitan Airports Commission, 132 F. Supp. 2d 1193 (D.Minn. 2000).*

LLC

§ 18-304.   Events of bankruptcy

DELAWARE CASE NOTES — REPORTED

Assignee of economic rights. — After a power company's minority shareholder filed a petition for bankruptcy, an ipso facto clause in the limited liability company (LLC) agreement was preempted to the extent it would deprive the minority owner of the economic rights available to an assignee of an LLC membership interest under *6 Del. C. § 18-702(b)(2)* of the Delaware LLC Act, but the minority owner had been divested of its right to participate in the power company's management and only retained the economic rights of a transferee pursuant to the *LLC Act. Milford Power Co., LLC v. PDC Milford Power, LLC, 866 A.2d 738 (Del. Ch. 2004).*

§ 18-305.   Access to and confidentiality of information; records

CASE NOTES — OTHER STATES
New York

Effect of Delaware exclusive jurisdiction clause. — As a threshold issue, although limited liability company was incorporated in Delaware, that does not divest New York of its interest in adjudicating this matter. The defendants-respondents' allegation that New York lacks jurisdiction to decide this case is based solely on the fact that Delaware Commerce and Trade Law, 6 Del. C. § 18-305(f), vests exclusive jurisdiction over this dispute in the Delaware Court of Chancery. That, however, does not mandate that this case be tried in Delaware. This Court has repeatedly held that a statute or rule of another state granting the courts of that state exclusive jurisdiction over certain controversies does not divest the New York courts of jurisdiction over such controversies. *Sachs v. Adeli, 2005 NY Slip Op 9049, 804 N.Y.S.2d 731, 2005 N.Y. App. Div. LEXIS 13419 (Nov. 29, 2005).*

Inspection of tax records. — Even if instant case were controlled by Delaware law, the outcome would remain the same. Delaware Commerce and Trade Law § 18-305(a) states in pertinent part that each member of a limited liability company has the right to obtain from the limited liability company from time to time upon reasonable demand for any purpose reasonably related to the member's interest true and full information regarding the status of the business and financial condition a copy of the limited liability company's federal, state and local income tax returns for each year. Because the plaintiff is a one-third owner in the limited liability company, and the tax records of the company's subsidiary are both necessary and otherwise unavailable for his fraud litigation, the plaintiff is entitled to inspect the tax records of the subsidiary. *Sachs v. Adeli, 2005 NY Slip Op 9049, 804 N.Y.S.2d 731, 2005 N.Y. App. Div. LEXIS 13419 (Nov. 29, 2005).*

§ 18-306.   Remedies for breach of limited liability company agreement by member

CASE NOTES — OTHER STATES
Connecticut

A member of a limited liability company may bring a derivative action on behalf of the company against another member which has breached a fiduciary duty to the company or which has failed to perform a promise to the company. *Taurus Advisory Group, Inc. v. Sector Management, Inc., 1996 Conn. Super. LEXIS 2272 (2002).*

Subchapter IV.
Managers

§ 18-402.   Management of limited liability company

DELAWARE CASE NOTES — UNREPORTED

Enhanced scrutiny test for corporate interests in Orban v. Field, — A.2d — (Del. Ch. Apr. 1, 1997), was met where board of directors of limited liability company (LLC) approved the sale of substantially all of the assets where the LLC was bordering on the brink of default and bankruptcy, business prospects were declining, and no better transaction was available. *Blackmore v. Link Energy LLC, 2005 Del. Ch. LEXIS 155 (Del. Ch. Oct. 14, 2005).*

Sale of substantially all assets. — The fact that unit holders were left with nothing after a sale of substantially all of the assets of the limited liability company, given a context in which the chief alternative substantiated by evidence was an equally barren bankruptcy proceeding, did not suffice to rebut the presumption that the directors were acting in the good faith exercise of their fiduciary duties, or to establish a claim of waste. *Blackmore v. Link Energy LLC, 2005 Del. Ch. LEXIS 155 (Del. Ch. Oct. 14, 2005).*

An "understanding" is not a substitute for an agreement, especially where, as here, there is no evidence that this "understanding" was shared by or with the other

LLC

contracting parties. In sum, the defendants have failed to prove the existence of a limited liability company agreement, including the possibility that the shareholder's agreement served as a stand-in; the governance of the child care entity, accordingly, was under the default provisions of 6 Del.C. § 18-402. *Facchina v. Malley, 2006 Del. Ch. LEXIS 142 (Aug. 1, 2006)*.

Applicable state law. — Under Delaware law, the use of written consents, without a meeting of the members, was sufficient as a procedural matter. In short, the defendants argue that California law controls the internal governance of a Delaware limited liability company with its principal (and, in this instance, only) place of business in California. Delaware law, however, governs the internal affairs of a Delaware limited liability company, regardless of its place of operations. Thus, the designation of plaintiff as managing member was, as a matter of Delaware law, effective. *Facchina v. Malley, 2006 Del. Ch. LEXIS 142 (Aug. 1, 2006)*.

CASE NOTES — OTHER STATES

North Carolina

Restructuring transaction within protection of business judgment rule. — The decisions of the management committee surrounding the transactions at issue here are entitled to the protection of the business judgment rule under Delaware law, and the court will not upset those decisions. The management committee chose to pursue a buyout, and when the buyout fell through, they had the right to restructure the transaction as a merger. *Wachovia Capital Partners, LLC v. Frank Harvey Inv. Family L.P., 2007 NCBC 7; 2007 NCBC LEXIS 7 (March 5, 2007)*.

Rhode Island

Construction with general corporation law. — As a general rule, under Delaware law, managers of a LLC are held to the same fiduciary bar as a director of a corporation. *Marsh v. Billington Farms, LLC, 2006 R.I. Super. LEXIS 119 (Aug. 31, 2006)*.

Subchapter V.
Finance

§ 18-502.   Liability for contribution

CASE NOTES — OTHER STATES

Connecticut

A member of a limited liability company may bring a derivative action on behalf of the company against another member which has breached a fiduciary duty to the company or which has failed to perform a promise to the company. *Taurus Advisory Group, Inc. v. Sector Management, Inc., 1996 Conn. Super. LEXIS 2272 (2002)*.

§ 18-503.   Allocation of profits and losses

CASE NOTES — FEDERAL COURTS

First Circuit

In general. — A limited liability company (LLC) is a form of statutory business organization that combines some of the advantages of a partnership with some of the advantages of a corporation. Under Delaware law, an LLC is a separate legal entity distinct from its members. As in a corporation, investors have limited liability, Del. Code Ann. tit. 6, § 18-303, own undivided interests in the company's property, Del. Code Ann. tit. 6, § 18-701, are bound by the terms of their agreement, and share in the overall profits and losses ratably according to their investment or as otherwise provided by the organizing agreement, Del. Code Ann. tit. 6, § 18-503. *Fraser v. Major League Soccer, L.L.C., 97 F. Supp. 2d 130 (D.Mass 2000)*.

Subchapter VI.
Distributions and Resignation

§ 18-607.   Limitations on distribution

CASE NOTES — UNREPORTED

Other claims not barred. — This section prohibits the stripping of corporate assets so as to render an LLC insolvent, and creates a corporate cause of action against LLC members who improperly receive a distribution of those assets. However, this section does not shield LLC members against any other claims against them, i.e., against all claims except those that arise under this section. Nothing in this section so provides. *Pepsi-Cola Bottling Co. v. Handy, 2000 Del. Ch. LEXIS 52 (Del. Ch. 2000)*.

LLC

Subchapter VII.
Assignment of Limited Liability Company Interests

§ 18-701. Nature of limited liability company interest

CASE NOTES — FEDERAL COURTS

First Circuit

In general. — A limited liability company (LLC) is a form of statutory business organization that combines some of the advantages of a partnership with some of the advantages of a corporation. Under Delaware law, an LLC is a separate legal entity distinct from its members. As in a corporation, investors have limited liability, Del. Code Ann. tit. 6, § 18-303, own undivided interests in the company's property, Del. Code Ann. tit. 6, § 18-701, are bound by the terms of their agreement, and share in the overall profits and losses ratably according to their investment or as otherwise provided by the organizing agreement, Del. Code Ann. tit. 6, § 18-503. *Fraser v. Major League Soccer, L.L.C., 97 F. Supp. 2d 130 (D.Mass 2000).*

Second Circuit

Piercing the corporate veil. — Under Delaware law, a limited liability is a "separate legal entity" distinct from the members who own an interest in the limited liability company. Delaware law, however, permits a court to pierce the corporate veil of an entity where there is fraud or where the entity is in fact a mere instrumentality or alter ego of its owner. *SR International Business Insurance Co. v. World Trade Center Props., LLC, 375 F. Supp. 2d 238 (S.D.N.Y. 2005).*

§ 18-702. Assignment of limited liability company interest

DELAWARE CASE NOTES — UNREPORTED

The policy that underlies subdivision (b)(3) of this section is that it is far more tolerable to have to suffer a new passive co-investor one did not choose than to endure a new co-manager without consent. That is particularly the case where, as here, an LLC is closely held. When an LLC is closely held, members often work closely with co-owners and, therefore, prefer to select their associates. Transfers of membership interests, then, introduce potential new conflicts of interest and change and perhaps complicate decision-making. *Eureka VIII LLC v. Niagara Falls Holdings LLC, 899 A.2d 95, 117 (Del. Ch. June 6, 2006).*

Appropriate remedial conclusions. — These statutory expressions of policy clearly evince the General Assembly's understanding that it is legitimate for a member of an LLC to craft provisions mandating that its fellow member either retain certain characteristics or lose its membership status. Thus, the statutes reinforce the remedial conclusions clearly suggested by the provisions of the LLC agreement in the instant case that were breached: plaintiff should not be bound to manage and operate an LLC with a co-member with which it never intended or agreed to go into business. To redress the situation plaintiff finds itself in, it is appropriate that defendant be remitted to holding merely the economic interest of an assignee of a members' interest in the redevelopment company. *Eureka VIII LLC v. Niagara Falls Holdings LLC, 899 A.2d 95, 117 (Del. Ch. June 6, 2006).*

DELAWARE CASE NOTES — REPORTED

Economic performance to assignee in bankruptcy. — Because subdivision (b)(2) of this section, did not excuse the companies from rendering economic performance to an assignee, the court concluded that *11 U.S.C. § 365(e)(2)(A)* did not apply; the default provision was unenforceable as an ipso facto provision. *Northrop Grumman Tech. Servs. v. Shaw Goup Inc. (In re IT Group, Inc.), 302 B.R. 483 (D. Del. 2003).*

After a power company's minority shareholder filed a petition for bankruptcy, an ipso facto clause in the limited liability company (LLC) agreement was preempted to the extent it would deprive the minority owner of the economic rights available to an assignee of an LLC membership interest under *6 Del. C. § 18-702(b)(2)* of the Delaware LLC Act, but the minority owner had been divested of its right to participate in the power company's management and only retained the economic rights of a transferee pursuant to the *LLC Act. Milford Power Co., LLC v. PDC Milford Power, LLC, 866 A.2d 738 (Del. Ch. 2004).*

Subchapter VIII.
Dissolution

§ 18-802. Judicial dissolution

DELAWARE CASE NOTES — UNREPORTED

Intervention. — Creditor could not intervene under Ch. Ct. R. 24(a) in statutory dissolution action under *6 Del. C. § 18-802* as: (1) there was no statute that conferred on it an unconditional right to intervene, and the creditor had no interest in the property or transaction that was the subject of the petition; (2) the petition concerned whether

LLC

it was reasonably practicable to carry on the business of a limited liability company in conformity with the limited liability company agreement; (3) the creditor had no interest relating to that subject, and was not possibly threatened with any adverse effect from whatever judgment was ultimately reached on that subject; and (4) if a judicial dissolution was ordered, the winding up and distribution of assets would be governed by *6 Del. C. §§ 18-803* and *18-804*, which fully protected the creditor's interests. *Follieri Group v. Follieri/Yucaipa Invs.*, 2007 Del. Ch. LEXIS 125 (Del. Ch. Aug. 23, 2007).

Creditor could not intervene under Ch. Ct. R. 24(b) in statutory dissolution action under *6 Del. C. § 18-802* as: (1) there was no statute that conferred on it an unconditional right to intervene, and the creditor had no interest in the property or transaction that was the subject of the petition; (2) the creditor's entire argument was that its claim for payment and the dissolution action had a question of law or fact in common; and (3) the dissolution action had nothing to do with the creditor's claimed indebtedness. *Follieri Group v. Follieri/Yucaipa Invs.*, 2007 Del. Ch. LEXIS 125 (Del. Ch. Aug. 23, 2007).

Dissolution granted. — Given its ownership structure and operating agreement, limited liability company was no longer able to carry on its business in a reasonably practicable manner. The vote of the members was deadlocked and the operating agreement provided no means around the deadlock. Moreover, limited liability company had no business to operate. Therefore, upon application of

a member, the court dissolved the company. *In re Silver Leaf, L.L.C.*, 2005 Del. Ch. LEXIS 119, No. 20611 (Aug. 18, 2005).

Duty to scriven with precision. — With the contractual freedom granted by the LLC Act comes the duty to scriven with precision. Regrettably for defendants, the drafters of the LLC Agreement in the instant case crafted an unwieldy dispute resolution scheme that gives parties alleging claims for compulsory relief the right to litigate, rather than arbitrate, their claims. The claims raised by plaintiff primarily involve a request for mandatory injunctive relief and specific performance. In the alternative, plaintiff seeks dissolution. By the LLC Agreement's own terms, plaintiff is permitted to seek relief in court, rather than in arbitration, for each of these claims. As such, defendant's motion to dismiss in favor of arbitration is denied. *Willie Gary LLC v. James & Jackson LLC*, 2006 Del. Ch. LEXIS 3 (Del. Ch. Jan. 10, 2006).

Illustrative case. — When the LLC Agreement at issue explicitly defines a dissolution event as involving a "judicial determination" that certain events require that the business be dissolved, it is difficult to conclude that the parties had agreed that any party seeking such a determination was duty-bound to proceed before an arbitrator, rather than a member of the judiciary who could make a "judicial determination." *Willie Gary LLC v. James & Jackson LLC*, 2006 Del. Ch. LEXIS 3 (Del. Ch. Jan. 10, 2006).

§ 18-803.   Winding up

DELAWARE CASE NOTES — UNREPORTED

Intervention. — Creditor could not intervene under Ch. Ct. R. 24(a) in statutory dissolution action under *6 Del. C. § 18-802* as: (1) there was no statute that conferred on it an unconditional right to intervene, and the creditor had no interest in the property or transaction that was the subject of the petition; (2) the petition concerned whether it was reasonably practicable to carry on the business of a limited liability company in conformity with the limited liability company agreement; (3) the creditor had no

interest relating to that subject, and was not possibly threatened with any adverse effect from whatever judgment was ultimately reached on that subject; and (4) if a judicial dissolution was ordered, the winding up and distribution of assets would be governed by *6 Del. C. §§ 18-803* and *18-804*, which fully protected the creditor's interests. *Follieri Group v. Follieri/Yucaipa Invs.*, 2007 Del. Ch. LEXIS 125 (Del. Ch. Aug. 23, 2007).

CASE NOTES — FEDERAL

Second Circuit

Capacity defense. — A lay litigant, even an unusually sophisticated one such as the plaintiff in the instant case, can certainly be forgiven for not immediately understanding the consequences of this section and section 18-804, for seeking clarification in discovery (which was apparently never provided) of the exact status of limited liability

company, or for not asserting a capacity defense until further information was obtained. Plaintiff has thus provided a reasonable explanation for the delay in advancing the defense. *Byong Kwon v. Yun*, 2008 U.S. Dist. LEXIS 4232 (SD NY, January 22, 2008).

§ 18-804.   Distribution of assets

DELAWARE CASE NOTES — REPORTED

Inadequate provision made for claim likely to arise. — Where former member of limited liability corporation (LLC) argued that, based on facts known to the LLC through its employees, the member's claim for breach of the LLC agreement was likely to arise or to

become known to the LLC within 10 years after the date of dissolution, and yet the LLC failed to make such provision as would be reasonably likely to be sufficient to provide compensation for that claim, in violation of subdivision (b)(3) of this section, the complaint plead facts that supported the inference that the LLC was wound up in contravention of the Limited Liability Company Act (*6 Del. C. § 18-101* et seq.). *Metro Commun. Corp. BVI v.*

Advanced Mobilecomm Techs. Inc., 854 A.2d 121 (Del. Ch. 2004).

DELAWARE CASE NOTES — UNREPORTED

Intervention. — Creditor could not intervene under Ch. Ct. R. 24(a) in statutory dissolution action under *6 Del. C. § 18-802* as: (1) there was no statute that conferred on it an unconditional right to intervene, and the creditor had no interest in the property or transaction that was the subject of the petition; (2) the petition concerned whether it was reasonably practicable to carry on the business of a limited liability company in conformity with the limited liability company agreement; (3) the creditor had no

interest relating to that subject, and was not possibly threatened with any adverse effect from whatever judgment was ultimately reached on that subject; and (4) if a judicial dissolution was ordered, the winding up and distribution of assets would be governed by *6 Del. C. §§ 18-803* and *18-804*, which fully protected the creditor's interests. *Follieri Group v. Follieri/Yucaipa Invs., 2007 Del. Ch. LEXIS 125 (Del. Ch. Aug. 23, 2007).*

CASE NOTES — FEDERAL

Second Circuit

Capacity defense. — A lay litigant, even an unusually sophisticated one such as the plaintiff in the instant case, can certainly be forgiven for not immediately understanding the consequences of this section and section 18-804, for seeking clarification in discovery (which was apparently

never provided) of the exact status of limited liability company, or for not asserting a capacity defense until further information was obtained. Plaintiff has thus provided a reasonable explanation for the delay in advancing the defense. *Byong Kwon v. Yun, 2008 U.S. Dist. LEXIS 4232 (SD NY, January 22, 2008).*

Subchapter X.
Derivative Actions

§ 18-1001. Right to bring action

CASE NOTES — OTHER STATES

Connecticut

A member of a limited liability company may bring a derivative action on behalf of the company against another member which has breached a fiduciary duty to the company or which has failed to perform a promise to the company. *Taurus Advisory Group, Inc. v. Sector Management, Inc., 1996 Conn. Super. LEXIS 2272 (2002).*

New York

A member of a limited liability company may bring an action in the right of such company if members with authority to do so have refused to bring the action or if an effort to cause those members to bring the action is not likely to succeed. *Vertical Computer Systems, Inc. v. Ross Systems, Inc., 11 A.D.3d 375, 784 N.Y.S.2d 499 (2004).*

§ 18-1002. Proper plaintiff

CASE NOTES — OTHER STATES

New York

Plaintiff does, in fact, have standing to assert a derivative claim under Delaware law on behalf of the limited liability company for material misrepresentation. In this court's view, plaintiff can be an adequate and fair representative of the LLC members in pursuing a claim for

material misrepresentation. As stated earlier, plaintiff is not precluded from representing LLC members necessarily because it is embroiled in litigations with the LLC. *Delta Fin. Corp. v. Morrison, 2006 NY Slip Op 52097U, 13 Misc. 3d 1232A, 2006 N.Y. Misc. LEXIS 3186 (Nov. 2, 2006).*

Subchapter XI.
Miscellaneous

§ 18-1101. Construction and application of chapter and limited liability company agreement

DELAWARE CASE NOTES — REPORTED

Limiting liability of directors. — Despite a limited liability company agreement containing an exculpatory

clause protecting the company's directors from a breach of the duty of care, a motion to dismiss filed by the company and the directors was denied, in a former equity unit holders' suit asserting breach of fiduciary duty, because the former equity unit holders alleged sufficient facts in the complaint to support a claim for disloyal conduct, which was enough to survive the motion to dismiss. The complaint alleged that the approval of a transaction that resulted in the distribution to the company's creditors of 100 percent of available funds — an amount that exceeded the total amount of their claims and which rendered the equity units of the company worthless — was violative because the directors failed to consider alternative transactions that would have provided a better result for the company's equity holders, particularly in light of the alleged fact that the company was in no way insolvent at the time of the transaction. *Blackmore Partners, L.P. v. Link Energy LLC, 864 A.2d 80 (Del. Ch. 2004).*

Compliance with arbitration provision ordered. — A managing member of a limited liability company and its affiliates were entitled to an order compelling the minority members to arbitrate their breach of fiduciary duty claims in accordance with an arbitration provision of the limited liability company agreement pursuant to Del. Code Ann. tit. 6, § 18-1101(c)(2). *Douzinas v. Am. Bureau of Shipping, Inc., 888 A.2d 1146, 2006 Del. Ch. LEXIS 6 (Del. Ch. 2006).*

DELAWARE CASE NOTES — UNREPORTED

Enforceability of arbitration agreement. — The Court of Chancery does not have jurisdiction over claims that are properly committed to arbitration because the availability of arbitration provides an adequate legal remedy. Delaware public policy favors resolution of disputes through arbitration and requires that any doubt regarding the arbitrability of a dispute be resolved in favor of arbitration. If a potentially applicable arbitration provision exists, the court will only conclude a dispute is not covered when the court finds either an express provision excluding the dispute from the coverage of the arbitration clause or the most forceful evidence of purpose to exclude. *CAPROC Manager, Inc. v. Policemen's & Firemen's Ret. Sys., 2005 Del. Ch. LEXIS 50, No. 1059-N (Apr. 18, 2005).*

Limited liability company agreement did not exhibit forceful evidence of a purpose to exclude from arbitration disputes the purported removal of a managing shareholder. Thus, in the circumstances of the instant case, plaintiff failed to rebut the strong presumption in favor of arbitration. *CAPROC Manager, Inc. v. Policemen's & Firemen's Ret. Sys., 2005 Del. Ch. LEXIS 50, No. 1059-N (Apr. 18, 2005).*

CASE NOTES — OTHER STATES

New York

A party may breach the implied covenant of good faith and fair dealing without violating an express term of the contract. The implied covenant is designed to protect the spirit of an agreement when, without violating an express term of the agreement, one side uses oppressive or underhanded tactics to deny the other side the fruits of the parties' bargain. *Lerner v. Westreich, 2006 NY Slip Op 51058U, 12 Misc. 3d 1164A; 2006 N.Y. Misc. LEXIS 1377 1 (N.Y. Misc. June 5, 2006).*

Dilution of distribution rights. — If the facts alleged in the complaint were proven, if manager left an obligation unfulfilled at the time of his resignation as manager, with the intention of taking actions after his resignation that would dilute limited liability company's distribution rights, a finder of fact could conclude that manager had violated the implied covenant of good faith and fair dealing. *Lerner v. Westreich, 2006 NY Slip Op 51058U, 12 Misc. 3d 1164A; 2006 N.Y. Misc. LEXIS 1377 1 (N.Y. Misc. June 5, 2006).*

CASE NOTES — FEDERAL

Sixth Circuit

The good faith duties of a member of an LLC include a duty of candor to the LLC's other members. *Dickey v. Bull Mt. Dev. Co., 2006 U.S. Dist. LEXIS 74172 (D. Tenn. Oct. 11, 2006).*

§ 18-1107. Taxation of limited liability companies

CASE NOTES — UNREPORTED

Restoration of good standing. — Good standing of a limited liability company (LLC) with the State of Delaware was not properly restored by a copartner who paid the LLC's overdue taxes; the copartner could not unilaterally restore the LLC's good standing, pursuant to 6 Del. C. § 18-1107(i), when the copartner and the partner were involved in litigation that the partner brought to dissolve the LLC. *In re Grupo Dos Chiles, LLC, 2006 Del. Ch. LEXIS 54 (Del. Ch. Mar. 10, 2006).*

TITLE 12.
DECEDENTS' ESTATES AND FIDUCIARY RELATIONS

Part V.
Fiduciary Relations

CHAPTER 38.
TREATMENT OF DELAWARE STATUTORY TRUSTS

Subchapter I.
Domestic Statutory Trusts

§ 3801.　Definitions

DELAWARE CASE NOTES — REPORTED

Advancement of expenses authorized. — The Business Trust Act does not prohibit a business trust from advancing litigation expenses to trustees. *Nakahara v. NS 1991 Am. Trust*, 739 A.2d 770 (Del. Ch. 1998).

§ 3806.　Management of statutory trust

CASE NOTES — FEDERAL COURTS

Second Circuit

Imposition of reciprocal duties. — Without more explicit authority under Delaware law, a court will not presume to find through silent implication an affirmation in Del. Code Ann. tit.12 § 3806(a) of anything as substantial as the imposition of reciprocal fiduciary duties on arms' length commercial parties simply because they make use of the convenient device of a Delaware business trust to apportion use of trademarks. *Calvin Klein Trademark Trust v. Wachner, 123 F. Supp. 2d 731 (S.D.N.Y. 2000)*.

§ 3817.　Indemnification

DELAWARE CASE NOTES — REPORTED

Advancement of expenses authorized. — The Business Trust Act does not prohibit a business trust from advancing litigation expenses to trustees. *Nakahara v. NS 1991 Am. Trust*, 739 A.2d 770 (Del. Ch. 1998).

DELAWARE COURT OF CHANCERY

TITLE 10
COURTS AND JUDICIAL PROCEDURE

PART I.
ORGANIZATION, POWERS, JURISDICTION AND OPERATION OF COURTS

CHAPTER 3.
COURT OF CHANCERY

Subchapter III.
General Jurisdiction and Powers

§ 341.   Matters and causes in equity

In Delaware there remains an historic and constitutional separation of law and equity; under Del. Const., art. IV, § 7, the Superior Court's jurisdiction relates to all civil causes at "common law" while Del. Const., art. IV, § 10 and this section make clear the Court of Chancery's jurisdiction to hear and determine all matters and causes in equity. *Monroe Park v. Metropolitan Life Ins. Co., 457 A.2d 734 (Del. 1983).*

Equity jurisdiction. — The term "equity jurisdiction," means the aggregate of the controversies in which the Court of Chancery may properly exercise its power to grant equitable relief. *Clark v. Teeven Holding Co., 625 A.2d 869 (Del. Ch. 1992).*

Court has all the equitable jurisdiction of this state. — The Court of Chancery has all the equitable jurisdiction of the State; all of the jurisdiction that was possessed by the high court of chancery in England at the time of the separation of the colonies. *First Nat'l Bank v. Andrews, 26 Del. Ch. 344, 28 A.2d 676 (1942).*

The Court of Chancery, as a court of limited jurisdiction, exercises jurisdiction only over all matters and causes in equity, and has the same jurisdiction as the English High Court of Chancery had in 1776. *Clark v. Teeven Holding Co., 625 A.2d 869 (Del. Ch. 1992).*

The Court of Chancery may exercise jurisdiction in matters that were unknown in 1776 but where there is today no adequate remedy in any other court. *Clark v. Teeven Holding Co., 625 A.2d 869 (Del. Ch. 1992).*

Section guarantees people equitable remedies. — This section is a guarantee to the people of the State that equitable remedies will at all times be available for their protection and this guarantee the General Assembly may not ignore. *duPont v. duPont, 32 Del. Ch. 413, 85 A.2d 724 (1951).*

And equity gives relief as justice and conscience require. — The function of a Court of Chancery is to give such relief as justice and good conscience may require, and under the changing conditions of society and the increasing number of corporate enterprises, its powers are not necessarily limited by a lack of early precedents. *Lichens Co. v. Standard Com. Tobacco Co., 28 Del. Ch. 220, 40 A.2d 447 (1944).*

But real interested person must be a party. — No bill in equity can be maintained without the real interested person being a party to the action. *Hunter v. McCarthy, 28 Del. Ch. 27, 36 A.2d 261 (1944).*

Denial of alleged constitutional rights. — The Court of Chancery is always open to restrain or vindicate the denial of alleged constitutional rights. *Parson v. Keve, 413 F. Supp. 111 (D. Del. 1976).*

Suit is brought in equity by a bill filed. — In the absence of some rule of court or statutory provision, the usual method of bringing suit in equity is by bill filed. *Root v. York Corp., 28 Del. Ch. 203, 39 A.2d 780 (1944).*

Allegations in complaint and what the plaintiff is really seeking determine jurisdiction. — Whether or not equitable jurisdiction exists is to be determined by an examination of the allegations of the complaint viewed in light of what the plaintiff really seeks to gain by bringing his or her cause of action. *Hughes Tool Co. v. Fawcett Publications, Inc., 297 A.2d 428 (Del. Ch. 1972),* rev'd on other grounds, *315 A.2d 577 (Del. 1974).*

Since the existence of jurisdiction is to be ascertained as of the time of the filing of the complaint, the subject-matter jurisdiction of the Chancery Court depends solely upon the allegations of the complaint and a determination of what the plaintiff really seeks by the complaint. *Diebold*

Chancery Court

Computer Leasing, Inc. v. Commercial Credit Corp., 267 A.2d 586 (Del. 1970).

Where Court of Chancery observed that corporate plaintiffs seeking monetary damages from another corporation did not advance any claim under a statute that vested jurisdiction in the Court of Chancery, but only asserted common law claims sounding in tort and contract (i.e., specific performance of defendant's contractual obligation to obtain liability insurance covering damage caused to plaintiffs' property), the Court of Chancery determined that under *10 Del. C. § 341*, it did not have equitable subject matter jurisdiction, because plaintiffs failed to allege that they had no adequate remedy at law; more importantly, even if plaintiffs had alleged that they had an inadequate remedy at law, a realistic assessment of whether money damages were sufficient to remedy the alleged breach of contract demonstrated that such an allegation would be a facade. *Candlewood Timber Group, LLC v. Pan Am. Energy, LLC, 859 A.2d 989 (Del. 2004).*

Discretionary jurisdiction. — The decision to exercise discretionary jurisdiction over claims for which there is an adequate remedy at law is at the discretion of the Court of Chancery which may in its discretion continue to hear the legal claims or to transfer those claims to the appropriate law court. *Clark v. Teeven Holding Co., 625 A.2d 869 (Del. Ch. 1992).*

Of great importance for the Court of Chancery in deciding whether to continue to hear legal claims or transfer those claims to the appropriate law court is whether the facts involved in the legal and in the equitable claims are so intertwined that it would be undesirable or impossible to sever them. *Clark v. Teeven Holding Co., 625 A.2d 869 (Del. Ch. 1992).*

The Court of Chancery, when deciding if a case would be an appropriate case for the court to exercise its discretion to hear the legal claims, should consider whether the claims are primarily the type that are usually tried before a jury, since depriving the law courts of jurisdiction would also deprive a party of a jury trial. *Clark v. Teeven Holding Co., 625 A.2d 869 (Del. Ch. 1992).*

Amendments to complaint liberally permitted to attain jurisdiction. — When on the face of the complaint a showing of a traditional equitable jurisdiction is not strong, but is adequately strengthened by an amendment to the complaint tendered by the plaintiff, leave to file the amendment should be granted under the liberal amendment policy of Chancery Rule 15. *Diebold Computer Leasing, Inc. v. Commercial Credit Corp., 267 A.2d 586 (Del. 1970).*

Equity will apply statutes of limitations to legal rights. — As a general proposition, while statutes of limitations are in terms applicable to actions at law, a court of equity will apply the terms of the statute in bar of a purely legal right which happens to be drawn into its cognizance where, had the action been at law, it would have been barred there. *Haas v. Sinaloa Exploration & Dev. Co., 17 Del. Ch. 253, 152 A. 216 (1930).*

A court of equity will not have its hand stayed by any technical omission or matter of form in the act complained of, which might be resorted to for the purpose of avoiding a statute, or which would be useless under the facts and circumstances of the particular case. *Brown v. Wilmington & Brandywine Leather Co., 9 Del. Ch. 39, 74 A. 1105 (1910).*

Where the complainant should have appeared for examination in an equity suit but was ignorant of the requirements of judicial procedure, and the equity court was satisfied that the complainant's motives were not really improper nor does the equity court find the defendant suffered injury, the court will not bar complainant's relief when he or she appears at a later date and is fully examined. *Jones v. Bodley, 28 Del. Ch. 191, 39 A.2d 413 (1944); 59 A.2d 463 (Del. 1947).*

"Subject matter jurisdiction" speaks to power of court to adjudicate a particular kind of controversy. In the case of the court of chancery, that power is limited to matters and causes in equity where there is no sufficient remedy by common law or statute, and to all other matters where jurisdiction is specifically conferred by statute. *Heathergreen Commons Condominium Ass'n v. Paul, 503 A.2d 636 (Del. Ch. 1985).*

The Court of Chancery does not hold a monopoly on deciding cases based on equitable principles. *Clark v. Teeven Holding Co., 625 A.2d 869 (Del. Ch. 1992).*

Exercising subject matter jurisdiction. — A decision by the Court of Chancery that it will assume "equity jurisdiction" over a particular controversy because there is not adequate remedy at law is not void if wrong and is subject only to direct attack. *Clark v. Teeven Holding Co., 625 A.2d 869 (Del. Ch. 1992).*

If a controversy contains any equitable feature that would provide the Court of Chancery with subject-matter jurisdiction over any part of a controversy, the court may, in its discretion, take jurisdiction over the entire controversy. *Clark v. Teeven Holding Co., 625 A.2d 869 (Del. Ch. 1992).*

Once equity obtains jurisdiction, it will determine the whole matter. — When a court of equity has obtained jurisdiction over some portion of a controversy, it will determine the whole matter if relief is sought by proper pleadings. *Root v. York Corp., 28 Del. Ch. 203, 39 A.2d 780 (1944).*

Once in equity you must pursue your remedy there. — Where defendant elected to first invoke relief in the Court of Chancery it was necessary to pursue that remedy until a decision was reached there before Superior Court would entertain application to set aside judgment. *First Nat'l Bank v. Lieberman, 15 Del. 367, 41 A. 90 (1895).*

Complete remedy may be granted. — The Court of Chancery has the discretion to take jurisdiction over and to decide law claims in the course of resolving any equitable features of a controversy. *Clark v. Teeven Holding Co., 625 A.2d 869 (Del. Ch. 1992).*

Any relief granted a complainant in equity must correspond with the case alleged in the bill. *Jones v. Bodley, 28 Del. Ch. 191, 39 A.2d 413 (1944); 59 A.2d 463 (Del. 1947).*

When a resulting trust is alleged in a bill, there can be no decree for an express trust. *Jones v. Bodley,*

28 Del. Ch. 191, 39 A.2d 413 (1944); 59 A.2d 463 (Del. 1947).

Court of chancery has jurisdiction to dismiss a bill of complaint in such a manner as to terminate the controversy involved. *Perrine v. Pennroad Corp., 28 Del. Ch. 342, 43 A.2d 721 (1945); 29 Del. Ch. 531, 47 A.2d 479 (1946).*

Or for lack of jurisdiction. — The Court of Chancery has the power to dismiss an action for lack of equity jurisdiction sua sponte. *Clark v. Teeven Holding Co., 625 A.2d 869 (Del. Ch. 1992).*

Costs of equity proceeding. — Costs of the proceeding at equity may be imposed even upon the successful party if such an imposition of costs seems equitable to the Chancellor. *Simon v. Pyrites Co., 32 Del. 581, 128 A. 370 (1925).*

The court of chancery may award a money judgment. *Clark v. Teeven Holding Co., 625 A.2d 869 (Del. Ch. 1992).*

An equitable right may be remedied by the award of a money judgment in appropriate instances, and the fact that such relief is the only relief sought does not deprive the Court of Chancery of jurisdiction. *Bird v. Lida, Inc., 681 A.2d 399 (Del. Ch. 1996).*

An action at law will not abate by reason of the pendency of a proceeding in equity. *Simon v. Pyrites Co., 32 Del. 581, 128 A. 370 (1925).*

Supreme court's determination binding on equity. — Supreme Court's determination of an issue on appeal is conclusive when that issue is again raised, after reversal, on remand to Court of *Chancery. Lee Bldrs., Inc. v. Wells, 34 Del. Ch. 307, 103 A.2d 918 (1954).*

Also equity is bound by its own prior decisions. — The Court of Chancery is bound by its prior decisions which are affirmed by the Supreme Court although a point in question may not have been raised in the Supreme Court for if the ruling is to be changed it should come before the *Supreme Court or the General Assembly. Young v. Janas, 34 Del. Ch. 287, 103 A.2d 299 (1954).*

Valid trusts will be enforced and protected in equity. — Where a trust is valid, it is a fundamental maxim and principle of equity, that the trust shall be protected and enforced by a court of equity. *State v. Griffith, 2 Del. Ch. 392 (1847); 2 Del. Ch. 421 (1848).*

So court will not allow a trust to fail for want of a trustee. — A Court of Chancery never allows a trust to fail for want of a trustee. *State v. Griffith, 2 Del. Ch. 392 (1847); 2 Del. Ch. 421 (1848).*

Court will not appoint trustee to do what can be done directly. — Personal property constituting a part of the trust estate would necessarily come into the hands of the executor or administrator of the deceased trustee, whose duty it would be to pay it over to the beneficiary, and the court finds no need to appoint a new trustee to act merely as a conduit for the purpose of such transfer, which might be made directly. *In re Estate of Kittinger, 9 Del. Ch. 71, 77 A. 24 (1910).*

Trustees take legal title for the benefit of someone else. — Testamentary trustees take the legal title to the trust property, though in equity they hold it for the benefit of some other person. *Roberts v. Downs, 28 Del. Ch. 293, 42 A.2d 315 (1945).*

Court may remove trustee. — The power of this Court to remove a trustee, appointed by a deed or will, is merely ancillary to its duty to see that the trust is administered properly, and in most cases will be exercised sparingly. *In re Trust Estate of Catell, 28 Del. Ch. 115, 38 A.2d 466 (1944).*

Testator's intentions usually control the trust. — The testator's intention is generally the controlling factor in the creation of a trust and a clear direction to a trustee to accumulate a fund cannot be disregarded unless some rule of law or well-defined rule of public policy is violated thereby. *Lewes Trust Co. v. Smith, 28 Del. Ch. 64, 37 A.2d 385 (1944).*

The fundamental rationale for applying cy pres or deviation is that accomplishment of the primary purpose of the testator is the matter of primary importance, and its achievement must be the object of any judicial permission to change or deviate from the trust terms. *Bank of Del. v. Buckson, 255 A.2d 710 (Del. Ch. 1969).*

But court's finding of intention is reviewable. — The determination of the Chancery Court as to the intent of the parties to a trust agreement is reviewable to the extent of ascertaining whether that Court was clearly wrong in its finding, with due regard for its opportunity to adjudge the credibility of witnesses. *Cleveland Trust Co. v. Wilmington Trust Co., 258 A.2d 58 (Del. 1969).*

Court may direct trustee to deviate from trust terms. — An equity court has the power to direct the trustee of a charitable trust to deviate or change from a trust term if because of circumstances not known to or anticipated by the trustor, compliance would substantially impair the accomplishment of his or her purpose. *Bank of Del. v. Buckson, 255 A.2d 710 (Del. Ch. 1969).*

Racially restricted trust, if private, is constitutional. — Although the Chancery Court may not instruct a trustee to honor racial restrictions in a trust instrument, a trust with racial restrictions which is entirely private and which does not involve, in any way, action by the State or its agents is constitutional. *Milford Trust Co. v. Stabler, 301 A.2d 534 (Del. Ch. 1973).*

The law looks not only to the formal documents creating or structuring the trust or other entity but also to the way in which its affairs are actually conducted, because state action is just as significant in the latter as in the former and any discrimination therein based on race is equally unlawful. *Milford Trust Co. v. Stabler, 301 A.2d 534 (Del. Ch. 1973).*

But court may not advise trustee to illegally discriminate. — The Court may not advise the trustee under a will creating a scholarship fund to reject applications from nonwhites because such advice would amount to state (judicial) enforced discrimination in violation of the *Fourteenth Amendment. Bank of Del. v. Buckson, 255 A.2d 710 (Del. Ch. 1969).*

And may remove such restriction. — When a racial or religious restriction would make impractical the accomplishment of a testator's primary intention, the restriction will be removed. *Bank of Del. v. Buckson, 255 A.2d 710 (Del. Ch. 1969).*

Court will not ordinarily terminate a term trust. — If by the terms of the trust it is provided that the trust shall not terminate until a certain time, or until the happening of a certain event, the Court will not ordinarily decree the termination of the trust until the specified time has arrived or the specified event has occurred, although the sole beneficiary of the trust is under no incapacity, and wishes to terminate the trust. *Lewes Trust Co. v. Smith, 28 Del. Ch. 64, 37 A.2d 385 (1944).*

Court may reform trust for mistake. — It is clear that the Court is empowered to reform a trust instrument for mistake when warranted by the evidence. *Roos v. Roos, 42 Del. Ch. 40, 203 A.2d 140 (1964).*

Court may grant specific performance if all evidence is for the plaintiff. — In a case where the entire evidence is in favor of the complainant, none whatever being adduced by the defendant to overcome its effect, so that the duty of the court, if the case were before a jury, would be to give binding instructions in favor of the plaintiff, a court of equity will decree specific performance in favor of the complainant. *Giammatteo v. Penna, 17 Del. Ch. 25, 147 A. 250 (1929).*

But specific performance is discretionary. — A specific performance of a contract of sale is not a matter of course, but rests entirely in the discretion of the court upon a view of all the circumstances. *Godwin v. Collins, 3 Del. Ch. 189 (1868); 9 Del. Ch. 28 (1869).*

The relief of specific performance lies in the discretion of the court so far, and only so far, that it must necessarily judge whether, under the circumstances of the case, the contract is or is not an inequitable one; that being determined, judicial discretion ceases. *Godwin v. Collins, 3 Del. Ch. 189 (1868); 9 Del. Ch. 28 (1869).*

Thus no specific performance when unable to exact justice between parties. — When under the circumstances of the case, the Court of Chancery is unable to do exact justice between the parties, a specific performance will not be decreed, but the complainant will be left to the complainant's remedy at law. *Godwin v. Collins, 3 Del. Ch. 189 (1868); 9 Del. Ch. 28 (1869).*

But if contract is burdensome to the defendant no specific performance. — Equity will never decree specific performance of a contract where its terms are so unequal that to require the defendant to carry it out would be to load the defendant with hard and oppressive burdens. *Gray Co. v. Alemite Corp., 20 Del. Ch. 244, 174 A. 136 (1934).*

Innocent representations by plaintiff are sufficient to deny specific performance. — Even innocent representations as to material circumstances are sufficient to refuse specific performance if the plaintiffs were induced to sign the contract by reason thereof. *Glenn v. Tide Water Associated Oil Co., 34 Del. Ch. 198, 101 A.2d 339 (1953).*

Bargain forced by plaintiff will not be enforced by the court. — Where a party seeks to enforce a bargain that he or she forced from a badgered board of directors, equity will not lend its aid to the specific performance of

such a contract. *Cook v. Fusselman, 300 A.2d 246 (Del. Ch. 1972).*

But inadequate consideration will not bar specific performance. — Mere inadequacy of consideration, in the absence of any unfairness or overreaching, does not justify a denial of the right of specific performance where in other respects the contract conforms with the rules and principles of equity. *Glenn v. Tide Water Associated Oil Co., 34 Del. Ch. 198, 101 A.2d 339 (1953).*

A contract for the sale of land can be specifically enforced. — A bill for specific performance of a contract for the sale of lands presents a purely equitable controversy for the decision of which the exclusive jurisdiction of the Chancery Court is unquestioned. *Old Time Petroleum Co. v. Turcol, 17 Del. Ch. 276, 153 A. 562 (1931).*

A court of equity will enforce specific performance of contracts concerning land, for all land is assumed to have a peculiar value to those who contract as to it, so that damages for breach of the contract is not an adequate remedy. *F.B. Norman Co. v. E.I. duPont de Nemours & Co., 12 Del. Ch. 155, 108 A. 743 (1920).*

Because damages cannot be exactly measured. — An injury caused by breach of a contract for the conveyance of land is usually not capable of such reasonably exact measurement as to prevent enforcement of an agreement that is not unconscionable. *Lee Bldrs., Inc. v. Wells, 34 Del. Ch. 307, 103 A.2d 918 (1954).*

Plaintiff must have performed own part of contract. — A party seeking a decree for specific performance of a contract for the sale of realty must have performed within the time specified his or her own obligations under the contract. *Wells v. Lee Bldrs., Inc., 34 Del. Ch. 107, 99 A.2d 620 (1953).*

Unless defendant prevented own performance. — The failure of a plaintiff to perform an obligation will be excused if the failure was caused by the other party. *Wells v. Lee Bldrs., Inc., 34 Del. Ch. 107, 99 A.2d 620 (1953).*

Burden is on plaintiff to show defendant prevented plaintiff's performance. — In the absence of proof showing the actual prevention by the vendor of performance by the vendee or a direct refusal to permit the vendee to perform, the vendee has not sustained the burden which is cast upon it of showing circumstances excusing its failure to perform the condition precedent called for by the contract, before it was entitled to a conveyance. *Wells v. Lee Bldrs., Inc., 34 Del. Ch. 107, 99 A.2d 620 (1953).*

A separation agreement is a contract which may be specifically enforced in chancery. *Astle v. Wenke, 297 A.2d 45 (Del. 1972).*

Specific enforcement of settlement agreements. — Specific performance of settlement agreement was ordered in a stockholder's suit against a corporation; the court found money damages were not adequate to compensate the stockholder for requirements such as award of stock options, mutual non-disparagement, and a general release (including settlement of the stockholder's *8 Del. C. § 220* suit). *Loppert v. Windsortech, Inc., 865 A.2d 1282 (Del. Ch. 2004).*

Agreement to renew a lease. — A Court of Chancery has jurisdiction to decree specific performance of an agreement to renew a lease. *Clough v. Cook, 10 Del. Ch. 175, 87 A. 1017 (1913).*

Building contracts. — A court of equity should not order specific performance of any building contract in a situation in which it would be impractical to carry out such an order. *Northern Del. Indus. Dev. Corp. v. E.W. Bliss Co., 245 A.2d 431 (Del. Ch. 1968).*

A court of equity is not without jurisdiction in a proper case to order the completion of an expressly designed and largely completed construction project. *Northern Del. Indus. Dev. Corp. v. E.W. Bliss Co., 245 A.2d 431 (Del. Ch. 1968).*

A court of equity will not order specific performance of a building contract in a situation in which it would be impractical to carry out such an order unless there are special circumstances or the public interest is directly involved. *Ryan v. Ocean Twelve, Inc., 316 A.2d 573 (Del. Ch. 1973).*

Equity may grant damages with a decree of specific performance. — Equity may, when its jurisdiction is invoked to obtain specific performance of a contract, award damages or pecuniary compensation along with specific performance when the decree as awarded does not give complete and full relief. *Tri State Mall Assocs. v. A.A.R. Realty Corp., 298 A.2d 368 (Del. Ch. 1972).*

Implied condition precedent to order of specific performance. — Even where specific performance is ordered, there is an implied condition precedent that the terms of the obligation be fixed and certain and that there is a construction plan "so precisely definite as to make compliance therewith subject to effective judicial supervision." *Ryan v. Ocean Twelve, Inc., 316 A.2d 573 (Del. Ch. 1973).*

Agreement to form a partnership. — While a court of equity will not decree specific performance of an agreement to form a partnership, which being at will is terminable by either party immediately, it will secure to a partner the interest in property to which by the partnership agreement such partner is entitled. *Elliott v. Jones, 11 Del. Ch. 283, 101 A. 872 (1917).*

Court has jurisdiction to grant injunctions. — The Court of Chancery has jurisdiction to hear such traditional, equitable matters as trusts and fiduciary relations, and has jurisdiction to hear claims where the law courts cannot afford an adequate remedy. Thus, it exercises jurisdiction over matters where an injunction is sought. *Clark v. Teeven Holding Co., 625 A.2d 869 (Del. Ch. 1992).*

Equity generally has jurisdiction in a suit for injunction to restrain a threatened injury. *Elster v. American Airlines, 34 Del. Ch. 94, 100 A.2d 219 (1953).*

The injunctive process will never issue to allay mere apprehensions. *Gray Co. v. Alemite Corp., 20 Del. Ch. 244, 174 A. 136 (1934).*

There must be some special reason cognizable in equity other than the mere fact of possible prospective litigation to justify interference by injunction with a party's right to sue. *Gray Co. v. Alemite Corp., 20 Del. Ch. 244, 174 A. 136 (1934).*

Authority of the court of chancery to issue a temporary restraining order and to enforce it through its contempt powers cannot be questioned. *City of Wilmington v. AFSCME, Local 320, 307 A.2d 820 (Del. Ch. 1973).*

Enjoining land encroachment. — A mandatory injunction may be awarded by a Court of Chancery to enjoin the continuance of an encroachment on another's land and compel a removal thereof. *Haitsch v. Duffy, 10 Del. Ch. 280, 92 A. 249 (1914).*

If a land company, organized to develop a seaside summer resort, dedicates a strip of land along the ocean front for public use to be kept open for the ocean view, and is succeeded by a municipality created by the General Assembly, an owner of a lot fronting on the ocean may maintain a bill in equity against the municipality, and a lessee from it, to prevent the lessee from building on the beach front a structure which would obstruct the complainant's view of the ocean. *Poole v. Commissioners of Rehoboth, 9 Del. Ch. 192, 80 A. 683 (1911).*

Right to injunction based on nature of land rights. — The right to a mandatory injunction to require the removal of an encroachment on land is based on the peculiar nature of the right invaded and the subject matter affected--land. *Haitsch v. Duffy, 10 Del. Ch. 280, 92 A. 249 (1914).*

A mandatory preliminary injunction is beyond the power of the chancellor. *Tebo v. Hazel, 38 Del. Ch. 116, 74 A. 841 (1909).*

Equity may enjoin public functionaries. — The general authority of the Court of Chancery to restrain by injunction unauthorized acts of public functionaries, to the detriment of the public, is sustained. *State v. Maury, 2 Del. Ch. 141 (1851).*

A court will review an administrative decision, if the action by the agency was arbitrary or an abuse of discretion, because in the administration of a statutory remedy, a discretion abused or exercised arbitrarily is no remedy at all, and equity will grant relief in such situations if there is no adequate alternative remedy available at law. *Choma v. O'Rourke, 300 A.2d 39 (Del. Ch. 1972).*

A court of equity may restrain a public board from taking action in a field in which it has no powers, where the party seeking injunctive relief can demonstrate that such official action, if improperly carried out, will cause irreparable injury which cannot be adequately redressed at law; thus the Chancery Court has jurisdiction of plaintiff's application for injunctive relief against defendants' reliance on a statute which may not be applicable to plaintiff's bridge operation. *Delaware River & Bay Auth. v. Carello, 43 Del. Ch. 213, 222 A.2d 794 (1966).*

Legal subrogation is the equitable substitution of another person in the place of the creditor to whose rights he or she succeeds in relation to the debt paid. *Eastern States Petro. Co. v. Universal Oil Prod. Co., 28 Del. Ch. 365, 44 A.2d 11 (1945).*

The remedy of subrogation is based on the theory that somewhat the same equity operates which seeks to prevent the unjust enrichment of one person at the expense of another by permitting actions for reimbursement, contribution and exoneration, and in appropriate cases creates a

Chancery Court

relation somewhat analogous to a constructive trust. *Eastern States Petro. Co. v. Universal Oil Prod. Co., 28 Del. Ch. 365, 44 A.2d 11 (1945).*

It is based on equity and justice, not contract rights. — Subrogation is an equitable remedy originally borrowed from the civil law, and its application ordinarily depends upon the principles of equity and justice rather than upon any semblance of contract rights. *Eastern States Petro. Co. v. Universal Oil Prod. Co., 28 Del. Ch. 365, 44 A.2d 11 (1945).*

One who pays the debt of another at the other's direct or indirect request is usually entitled to subrogation, and under such circumstances, a mere contract action at law on an implied promise would not, necessarily, give adequate relief. *Eastern States Petro. Co. v. Universal Oil Prod. Co., 28 Del. Ch. 365, 44 A.2d 11 (1945).*

Debt paid by person not bound thereby. — When the remedy of subrogation is applicable, a debt, extinguished at law by payment made by a person not bound thereby, is treated in equity as still subsisting for his or her benefit. *Eastern States Petro. Co. v. Universal Oil Prod. Co., 28 Del. Ch. 365, 44 A.2d 11 (1945).*

Subrogation does not apply when a complainant merely pays his or her own debt, and not the debt of another, though incidental benefits may thereby accrue to the other. *Eastern States Petro. Co. v. Universal Oil Prod. Co., 28 Del. Ch. 365, 44 A.2d 11 (1945).*

Nor do volunteers have a right to subrogation. — One who pays the debt of another upon his or her own initiative, and without invitation, compulsion or the necessity for self-protection, is usually regarded as a mere volunteer without any standing in equity and cannot rely on subrogation. *Eastern States Petro. Co. v. Universal Oil Prod. Co., 28 Del. Ch. 365, 44 A.2d 11 (1945).*

One induced by fraud to pay a debt is not a volunteer. — One who is induced by fraud to pay the debt of another is, ordinarily, not a mere volunteer, and may rely on subrogation. *Eastern States Petro. Co. v. Universal Oil Prod. Co., 28 Del. Ch. 365, 44 A.2d 11 (1945).*

A surety has rights of subrogation. — A surety may proceed in a court of equity, after a debt becomes due, to compel the creditor to collect the debt out of the principal debtor. *Aetna Cas. & Sur. Co. v. Mayor & Council, 17 Del. Ch. 280, 160 A. 747 (1930).*

But its scope is larger than principal-surety relationship. — Originally, the remedy of subrogation might have been largely confined to cases involving the relation of principal and surety, but it has a much broader application; and when right and justice demand it the tendency is to extend, rather than to restrict, its application. *Eastern States Petro. Co. v. Universal Oil Prod. Co., 28 Del. Ch. 365, 44 A.2d 11 (1945).*

Right of spouse to separate maintenance is enforceable in equity. — The right of a spouse to maintenance is a right secured to spouse by the common law and since it is a purely legal right, it may be enforced in equity as may any other legal right which lacks redress at law. *duPont v. duPont, 32 Del. Ch. 413, 85 A.2d 724 (1951).*

Spouse must show destitute and necessitous circumstances. — In an action for separate maintenance by one spouse against the other, proof of destitute and necessitous circumstances is jurisdictionally necessary before spouse is entitled to an order for his or her own support. *Wife v. Husband, 270 A.2d 180 (Del. Ch. 1970).*

When accounts are complicated so as to confuse a jury. — A case in order that the parties should be decreed to account in the Court of Chancery is where the transactions are so complicated, so long and intricate, that it is impossible for a jury to examine them with accuracy and they will require time, assiduous attention and minute investigation, and are involved in so much confusion and difficulty that no other tribunal, by reason of the forms of proceeding of the courts of law, can afford the plaintiff a remedy. *President, Dirs. & Co. v. Polk, 1 Del. Ch. 167 (1821).*

But not when court cannot clearly ascertain each party's rights. — The Court of Chancery will never undertake to adjust the rights of parties without satisfactory means of ascertaining what their rights are, and if an accounting cannot be safely stated, and the true balance between these parties ascertained, the Court of Chancery cannot proceed. *Davidson v. Wilson, 3 Del. Ch. 307 (1869).*

"Fairness" suits for alleged fraud and breach of fiduciary duty brought by minority shareholders fall within the Court of Chancery's exclusive, and not its concurrent, jurisdiction. *Harman v. Masoneilan Int'l, 442 A.2d 487 (Del. 1982).*

Equity may grant other relief in a bill for accounting. — Where plaintiffs have asked for an accounting and the nature of the accounting is such that equity would have jurisdiction, in the determination of a suit, Court of Chancery has the power to grant such other and incidental relief as may be necessary to afford a complete relief. *Consolidated Solubles Co. v. Consolidated Fisheries Co., 34 Del. Ch. 551, 107 A.2d 639 (1954); 35 Del. Ch. 125, 112 A.2d 30 (1955); 113 A.2d 576 (Del. 1955).*

Equity has the power to appoint a receiver. — The inherent right of a court of equity to appoint a receiver pendente lite in appropriate cases, in order to preserve the property involved in the litigation, has been recognized since an early date. *Lichens Co. v. Standard Com. Tobacco Co., 28 Del. Ch. 220, 40 A.2d 447 (1944).*

But it is an auxiliary remedy. — The appointment of a receiver for the protection of property is one of the oldest remedies in equity. But it is a remedy of an auxiliary and incidental nature, and cannot be the only real relief sought by the bill. *Lichens Co. v. Standard Com. Tobacco Co., 28 Del. Ch. 220, 40 A.2d 447 (1944).*

Court may place a solvent corporation into receivership if imminent danger exists. — Conceding the inherent power of a court of equity to appoint a receiver for a solvent corporation, the right must be exercised with great caution, and only when there is real imminent danger of material loss that cannot be otherwise prevented. *Lichens Co. v. Standard Com. Tobacco Co., 28 Del. Ch. 220, 40 A.2d 447 (1944).*

To protect minority shareholders from fraud and gross mismanagement. — Courts of equity have often recognized their inherent right to wind up the affairs of a solvent going corporation and to appoint a receiver for that purpose for the protection of minority stockholders when fraud and gross mismanagement by corporate officers, causing real imminent danger of great loss, clearly appears, and cannot be otherwise prevented. *Drob v. National Mem. Park, 28 Del. Ch. 254, 41 A.2d 589 (1945).*

But not for mere errors in business management. — A court of equity will not appoint a receiver to wind up a corporation because of mere errors of judgment in business management. *Lichens Co. v. Standard Com. Tobacco Co., 28 Del. Ch. 220, 40 A.2d 447 (1944).*

Corporation should have a fair chance to adjust its own troubles. — To precipitate a corporation into a receivership before it has had a fair chance to adjust what appears to be only temporary troubles, would be an unwise use of the Chancellor's discretionary power, even if it be assumed that it is technically insolvent. *Kenny v. Allerton Corp., 17 Del. Ch. 219, 151 A. 257 (1930).*

Foreign court can appoint a receiver for a Delaware corporation. — That foreign courts can administer the assets of a foreign corporation found in their jurisdiction is beyond doubt, but that they can appoint a general receiver is not tenable. *Frankland v. Remington Phonograph Corp., 13 Del. Ch. 312, 119 A. 127 (1922).*

But court of chancery can appoint a general receiver for the same corporation. — The appointment by a court of another state of a receiver of the assets of a Delaware corporation located in such other state cannot serve to deprive a Chancery in Delaware of its jurisdiction to appoint a general receiver for the same corporation. *Frankland v. Remington Phonograph Corp., 13 Del. Ch. 312, 119 A. 127 (1922).*

In appointing a receiver, equity may also decide legal issues. — Having jurisdiction to appoint receivers for insolvent corporation the Chancellor may proceed to pass on all matters necessary to a determination, notwithstanding that among such matters there may be questions which also in other connections may be heard at law before juries and in such cases, the constitutional provision that trial by jury shall be as heretofore has no pertinency. *Mackenzie Oil Co. v. Omar Oil & Gas Co., 14 Del. Ch. 36, 120 A. 852 (1923).*

A court of equity will not ordinarily set aside a voluntary conveyance absent fraud. — A court of equity will not interfere to set aside a voluntary conveyance, because the conveyance disappoints hopes or expectations, however just and reasonable; not even because it violates obligations, if they are only natural or moral ones. Courts of equity, as well as of law, protect only legal rights and enforce legal obligations; a conveyance will be set aside on the ground of fraud, only when it is in fraud of some legal right and one existing at the time it is made. *Chandler v. Hollingsworth, 3 Del. Ch. 99 (1867).*

It will not insist on equivalence of contracts. — A court of equity does not attempt to weigh the actual value nor to insist upon the equivalent in contracts when each party has equal competence. *Glenn v. Tide Water Associated Oil Co., 34 Del. Ch. 198, 101 A.2d 339 (1953).*

But it will protect the weak and aged. — Equity intervenes justly and properly to protect the weak and the aged against imposition by designing people, and even against manifest improvidence though there is no actual fraud in the other party. *Atkins v. Foreaker, 12 Del. Ch. 335, 114 A. 173 (1921).*

A court of equity cannot compel grantees to furnish to the grantor support stated as a consideration in a deed, and damages at law would not make good their failure to do so; but a court of equity will protect the grantor, an aged and helpless person, dependent on the grantees, by setting aside the conveyance if they had made default to perform the duty stated in the deed. *Atkins v. Foreaker, 12 Del. Ch. 335, 114 A. 173 (1921).*

If contract is fair and equitable, equity will not set aside the conveyance. — Though a grantor be aged, infirm, physically dependent on grantees in such a way as to create a fiduciary relation between them, nevertheless, if it is shown that the grantor is not imposed upon by undue influence, or otherwise, that the agreement for his or her support for life stated as the consideration in the deed is fair and equitable, that he or she is mentally capable of making and understanding the transaction, and did comprehend it, and that the consideration is performed, there is no sufficient reason to set aside the deed. *Atkins v. Foreaker, 12 Del. Ch. 335, 114 A. 173 (1921).*

Equity will protect the illiterate. — If one party's inability to read is known to the other party or is otherwise brought home to the other party, as when the first party makes his or her mark, the first party has no right to make an assumption as to the ability of the other to read, and in such case, the first party is not bound unless he or she in fact knew and agreed to the terms. *Sharpless-Hendler Ice Cream Co. v. Davis, 17 Del. Ch. 321, 155 A. 247 (1931).*

But not where other party is unaware of illiteracy. — Where an illiterate person, unknown to the other party to be illiterate, chose to affix his or her name to an agreement without demanding that it be read to him or her and without being misled in any way by the other party to it, the fact of illiteracy is of no materiality, and the contract is binding. *Sharpless-Hendler Ice Cream Co. v. Davis, 17 Del. Ch. 321, 155 A. 247 (1931).*

Spouse obtaining benefit from other spouse. — Equity raises a presumption against the validity of a transaction by which one spouse obtains a possible benefit at the expense of the other, and casts upon the first spouse the burden of showing affirmatively his or her compliance with all equitable requisites. *Darlak v. Darlak, 34 Del. Ch. 91, 99 A.2d 763 (1953).*

To establish a constructive trust burden of showing fraud is on plaintiff. — When seeking to establish a constructive trust based on an alleged fraudulent procurement by the defendant of the complainant's signature to and acknowledgment of deeds, the burden is on the complainant to support the charge of fraud; where it is sought to turn a deed absolute on its face to one that was in fact in trust, the party that would thus contradict the appearance of so formal and solemn an instrument must support this burden by proof that is clear, full and satis-

Chancery Court

factory, leaving no doubt of the existence of the trust alleged. *Bradford v. Vinton, 17 Del. Ch. 261, 153 A. 678 (1930).*

Fiduciary relationship is of some significance in establishing a constructive trust. — Where a fiduciary relationship is shown whereby one party is in an attitude of dependence upon, or responsive to the control and advice of, another, and the validity of a transaction between the parties is in question, the extent of the significance which the Court attaches to the status of the fiduciary relationship in determining whether or not to impose a constructive trust is that the transaction should be subjected to careful scrutiny with the view of determining whether the person in whom the confidence was reposed or in whom a controlling influence rested, used his or her position to advantage himself or herself. *Bradford v. Vinton, 17 Del. Ch. 261, 153 A. 678 (1930).*

Superior court has concurrent jurisdiction where damages for fraud are sought. — The Superior Court now has at least concurrent jurisdiction with Chancery in cases where fraud is alleged and money damages for the fraud of a party are sought. *Kuhn Constr. Co. v. State, 248 A.2d 612 (Del. Super. Ct. 1968).*

It is not every fraud case that is entitled to be redressed in equity, and if all that is sought in equity as a relief against fraud is nothing more than a judgment for the amount of damages suffered, then equity will not stir itself. *Cochran v. F.H. Smith Co., 20 Del. Ch. 159, 174 A. 119 (1934).*

Equity may reform contracts on grounds of mistake. — One of the Court of Chancery's most important powers is to reform contracts, where the parties, by mistake, have failed to stipulate in terms according to their real intentions. *Cannon v. Collins, 3 Del. Ch. 132 (1867).*

No reformation if no fraud or mutual mistake. — Where a party with full knowledge of what he or she is doing, without the inducement of fraud or the misapprehension caused by mutual mistake, enters into a contract, whatever may be his or her other rights of relief, he or she is not entitled to the relief of reformation. *Arcturus Radio Tube Co. v. Radio Corp. of Am., 20 Del. Ch. 376, 177 A. 899 (1935).*

Deed may be reformed if it affords real relief. — A court of equity will not reform a deed unless some real relief can be had under the corrected instrument. *Rauhut v. O'Donnell, 28 Del. Ch. 58, 37 A.2d 66 (1944).*

Specific performance may be granted with reformation. — Where both reformation of a deed on the ground of a material and mutual mistake and specific performance are sought, the latter remedy is essential to complete relief and in an appropriate case can be had in the same proceeding. *Rauhut v. O'Donnell, 28 Del. Ch. 58, 37 A.2d 66 (1944).*

Equitable estoppel may be applied. — The party in a contract to be charged is estopped to deny his or her assent because of conduct which reasonably justified the other party in believing that assent had been expressed. *Sharpless-Hendler Ice Cream Co. v. Davis, 17 Del. Ch. 321, 155 A. 247 (1931).*

An equitable estoppel arises whenever a party, by voluntary conduct, has either deliberately or unconsciously led another party in reliance upon that conduct to change such other party's position for the worse. *Wolf v. Globe Liquor Co., 34 Del. Ch. 312, 103 A.2d 774 (1954).*

Whenever one party, relying upon conduct of another, changes his or her position to his or her detriment, or puts himself or herself in a position which cannot be undone without substantial expense, the person whose conduct has brought the situation about will be estopped from asserting his or her legal rights against the party so misled, particularly as between parties who have long acquiesced in settlements of accounts or other mutual dealings. *Wolf v. Globe` Liquor Co., 34 Del. Ch. 312, 103 A.2d 774 (1954).*

One who participates in or acquiesces in an action has no standing in a court of equity to complain against it and equity will not hear a complainant stultify himself or herself by complaining against acts in which he or she participated or of which had demonstrated approval by sharing in their benefits. *Gottlieb v. McKee, 34 Del. Ch. 537, 107 A.2d 240 (1954).*

While a bare promise to a charity is at first revocable under the application of the doctrine of promissory estoppel, it does not remain so after the charity, in reliance upon that promise, has put itself into a legal position from which it cannot be expected to extricate itself without substantial injury. *Danby v. Osteopathic Hosp. Ass'n, 34 Del. Ch. 427, 104 A.2d 903 (1954).*

Person sought to be estopped must have had knowledge of facts. — It is essential to the doctrine of estoppel that the party sought to be estopped should have had the means of knowing the facts or have been in such a position that he ought to have known them. *Gottlieb v. McKee, 34 Del. Ch. 537, 107 A.2d 240 (1954).*

Where stockholder had no knowledge of the fact that the resolution in question was to be presented at the annual meeting and was informed that the management of the corporation intended to present no other items of business at the meeting, the stockholder was not estopped from asserting any right relative thereto prior to the execution of the stockholder's proxy. *Gottlieb v. McKee, 34 Del. Ch. 537, 107 A.2d 240 (1954).*

Estoppel in partition proceedings. — The powers of chancery to invoke the equitable principle of estoppel or other equitable principles in partition proceedings is not questioned. *Holladay v. Flinn, 17 Del. Ch. 415, 149 A. 307 (1929).*

An undertaking to do something which is already obligatory will not furnish the basis of an estoppel. *Danby v. Osteopathic Hosp. Ass'n, 34 Del. Ch. 427, 104 A.2d 903 (1954).*

Equity will not generally decide title to real estate. — Court of Chancery, generally speaking, will not decide title to real estate, but where equitable relief is also sought, only a question of the exercise of discretion is involved. *Wolfman v. Jablonski, 34 Del. Ch. 67, 99 A.2d 494 (1953).*

But the jurisdiction of a court of equity to remove clouds on titles is well established. *Newlin v. Phillips, 9 Del. Ch. 165, 80 A. 640 (1911).*

To quiet title plaintiff must rely on the strength of own title. — In an action for declaratory judgment to quiet title, plaintiffs must recover upon the strength of their own title and cannot rely upon the weakness of defendant's title. *Marvel v. Barley Mill Road Homes, Inc., 34 Del. Ch. 417, 104 A.2d 908 (1954).*

Tenancy by the entirety with resulting trust. — Marital property was owned in tenancy by the entirety even though the acquisition money arguably had come from the husband's separate assets which were to remain his under their prenuptial agreement. After the wife sued for divorce and husband's died before the divorce was final, so as not to frustrate their prenuptial agreement and to do equity the tenancy by the entirety property was to be owned 100% by wife for life subject to a resulting trust in 50% for his estate, rather than 100 percent by the wife. *Fischer v. Fischer, 864 A.2d 98 (Del. Ch. 2005).*

A restrictive covenant should be enforced only to the extent that it is reasonable so to do. *Knowles-Zeswitz Music, Inc. v. Cara, 260 A.2d 171 (Del. Ch. 1969).*

Equity has jurisdiction over settlements of stockholders' suits. — In stockholders' suit to cancel a voting trust, where the directors of the corporation produced evidence that they had acted in good faith and free from disqualifying interest in settling the complaint, the suit will be defeated, and with that finding on the corporation's behalf, equity court will not inquire into the merits of the settlement. *Perrine v. Pennroad Corp., 28 Del. Ch. 342, 43 A.2d 721 (1945); 29 Del. Ch. 531, 47 A.2d 479 (1946).*

Where the directors of a corporation seek equity approval of a settlement on a stockholder's complaint for cancellation of a voting trust where the chief reason for the board's approval of the agreement is the uncertainty of the outcome of the litigation and the fact that a final determination would require an indefinite length of time, such that the board was influenced by the very substantial amount of the settlement, and a consideration of the possible profits which the corporation might make by the use of this money, the Court is not called upon to make an appraisal in the nature of an advisory opinion. *Perrine v. Pennroad Corp., 28 Del. Ch. 342, 43 A.2d 721 (1945); 29 Del. Ch. 531, 47 A.2d 479 (1946).*

Where there is controversy in settlement of a stockholder's derivative action, equity court before ordering a dismissal of the suit, will set the application down for hearing, and give notice to stockholders of the corporation concerned, and thus to afford them, as well as the proponents of the settlement, an opportunity to be heard. *Perrine v. Pennroad Corp., 28 Del. Ch. 342, 43 A.2d 721 (1945); 29 Del. Ch. 531, 47 A.2d 479 (1946).*

And which stock has the right to vote. — The Chancellor has the right, in an appropriate proceeding, to cancel shares of no-par stock, because issued without corporate authority, because the consideration had not been fixed as required by law, or for any other reason proper and sufficient in law or in equity. *Triplex Shoe Co. v. Rice & Hutchins, Inc., 17 Del. Ch. 356, 152 A. 342 (1930).*

The Chancellor has the right to determine that any stock, the right of which was disputed, had not the right to vote. *Triplex Shoe Co. v. Rice & Hutchins, Inc., 17 Del. Ch. 356, 152 A. 342 (1930).*

When faced with an illegal strike by public employees, an equity court is generally acknowledged to have the power to apply injunctive coercion wherever it will do the most good. *City of Wilmington v. AFSCME, Local 320, 307 A.2d 820 (Del. Ch. 1973).*

Equity has jurisdiction over threatened breach of contract. — The jurisdiction of the Chancery Court to enjoin a threatened breach of contract, for which breach damages would not be adequate, is unquestioned. *Diebold Computer Leasing, Inc. v. Commercial Credit Corp., 267 A.2d 586 (Del. 1970).*

This is not divested by the declaratory judgment act. — Where subject-matter jurisdiction in chancery appears in a cause in the form of the traditional jurisdiction of equity over threatened breach of contract, that jurisdiction is not divested by the Declaratory Judgment Act, *10 Del. C. § 6501. Diebold Computer Leasing, Inc. v. Commercial Credit Corp., 267 A.2d 586 (Del. 1970).*

Equity can have jurisdiction in a declaratory judgment action. — The Chancery Court has jurisdiction in a declaratory judgment action if there is any underlying basis for equity jurisdiction measured by traditional standards. *Diebold Computer Leasing, Inc. v. Commercial Credit Corp., 267 A.2d 586 (Del. 1970).*

Taxpayer's claim must fall under some traditional equity jurisdiction. — In order for the Chancery Court properly to assume jurisdiction over a taxpayer's claim, it must be found to fall under some traditional head of conventional equity jurisdiction. *Delaware Bankers Ass'n v. Division of Revenue of Dep't of Fin., 298 A.2d 352 (Del. Ch. 1972).*

Federal enforcement of tax lien may be characterized as an "equitable" proceeding, and sequestration procedures of the Court of Chancery may be available in federal court action. *United States v. Stone, 59 F.R.D. 260 (D. Del. 1973).*

A bill to enforce an equitable assignment is a recognized head of equity jurisdiction. *Greene v. Johnston, 34 Del. Ch. 115, 99 A.2d 627, 42 A.L.R.2d 906 (1953).*

Commission de lunatico inquirendo. — It is clearly settled that a Court of Chancery has, independent of statute, jurisdiction to issue a commission de lunatico inquirendo respecting a person who has real estate within the jurisdiction of the Court, though the person is a nonresident. *In re Wilson, 9 Del. Ch. 332, 82 A. 695 (1912).*

Distribution of personal estate. — There can be no question of the Chancery Court's jurisdiction to entertain an action for the distribution of a personal estate or an action to partition realty. *In re Estate of McCracken, 43 Del. Ch. 132, 219 A.2d 908 (1966).*

The court of equity has jurisdiction to superintend the administration of estates, and to decree a distribution of the residue after payment of all debts and charges among the parties entitled either as legatees or distributees.

Chancery Court

Glanding v. Industrial Trust Co., 28 Del. Ch. 499, 45 A.2d 553 (1945).

Equity will not interpret a will granting only legal estates. — A court of equity will never exercise a power to interpret a will which only deals with and disposes of purely legal estates and interests, and which makes no attempt to create any trust relations with respect to the property donated. *Security Trust Co. v. Spruance, 20 Del. Ch. 195, 174 A. 285 (1934).*

Equity abhors a forfeiture, and it will disregard a forfeiture occasioned by failure to comply with the very letter of an agreement when it has been substantially performed. *Jefferson Chem. Co. v. Mobay Chem. Co., 267 A.2d 635 (Del. Ch. 1970).*

Equity has some labor jurisdiction despite general federal preemption. — Although substantially all jurisdiction in labor disputes affecting interstate commerce has been preempted by the federal government, state power may prevent conduct marked by violence and imminent threats to public order, by establishing subject-matter jurisdiction. *Avisun Corp. v. Oil, Chem. & Atomic Workers Local 8-732, 259 A.2d 389 (Del. Ch. 1969).*

Plaintiff must have clean hands. — A court of equity is a court of conscience, and will not aid a complainant who has been guilty of any reprehensible conduct relating to the matter in controversy, which violates the fundamental conceptions of equity jurisprudence. *Jones v. Bodley, 28 Del. Ch. 191, 39 A.2d 413 (1944); 59 A.2d 463 (Del. 1947).*

Hands must have been rendered unclean in the matter in controversy. — In order to invoke the clean hands doctrine as a defense to a bill to enjoin the breach of the negative portion of a convenant, the hands of the complainant must be rendered unclean by reason of some conduct connected with the matter in controversy, for it would be highly unjust to deny to a litigant all right to equitable relief because of generally bad conduct. *Sharpless-Hendler Ice Cream Co. v. Davis, 17 Del. Ch. 161, 151 A. 261 (1930).*

Unclean hands need not be pleaded as a defense. — The maxim that one who comes into equity must do so with clean hands is not one of defense and need not be pleaded; rather, it lays restrictions upon complainants, and tells them that an appeal for relief to a court of conscience by those who have themselves been guilty of unconscionable conduct will not be honored. *Sharpless-Hendler Ice Cream Co. v. Davis, 17 Del. Ch. 161, 151 A. 261 (1930).*

§ 342. Adequate remedy in other courts

DELAWARE CASE NOTES — REPORTED

This section neither grants nor divests equity of any jurisdiction. *Boxer v. Husky Oil Co., 429 A.2d 995 (Del. Ch. 1981).*

The court of chancery must be kept within the limits of its jurisdiction. *Beeson v. Elliott, 1 Del. Ch. 368 (1831).*

Under Delaware law, there was no right to contribution among joint tort-feasors until the enactment of the Uniform Contribution Among Tort-Feasors Act on May 7, 1949, therefore, that right was never a part of equity's traditional jurisdiction in Delaware, and the Court of Claims does not exercise jurisdiction over such claims. *Clark v. Teeven Holding Co., 625 A.2d 869 (Del. Ch. 1992).*

No fixed or limited categories of jurisdiction. — The nature of chancery's particular mission forecloses the development of fixed and limited categories of relationships over which equity will take jurisdiction in an appropriate case, but in all instances it is necessary that the legal remedy either not exist or be found to be inadequate. *McMahon v. New Castle Assocs., 532 A.2d 601 (Del. Ch. 1987).*

Equity must always decide its own jurisdiction. — The Court of Chancery must always consider, whenever and however raised, and even on its own initiative, its right to adjudicate a cause. *Clark v. Sipple, 10 Del. Ch. 51, 84 A. 1 (1912).*

"Subject matter jurisdiction" speaks to power of court to adjudicate a particular kind of controversy. In the case of the court of chancery, that power is limited to matters and causes in equity where there is no sufficient remedy by common law or statute, and to all other matters where jurisdiction is specifically conferred by statute. *Heathergreen Commons Condominium Ass'n v. Paul, 503 A.2d 636 (Del. Ch. 1985).*

Chancery is without jurisdiction if there is sufficient remedy at law. *Broughton v. Warren, 281 A.2d 625 (Del. Ch. 1971); A.M.M. v. J.L.W., 285 A.2d 824 (Del. Ch. 1971); In re Real Property of Wife, K, 297 A.2d 424 (Del. Ch. 1972); Walton v. State, 407 A.2d 535 (Del. 1979).*

In the absence of any express statutory limitation, a court of equity has no jurisdiction where there is an appropriate and adequate remedy in the courts of law, or by some other special mode provided by statute. *Virden v. Board of Pilot Comm'rs, 8 Del. Ch. 1, 67 A. 975 (1895).*

Equitable jurisdiction embodied that complete system of equity jurisprudence as administered by the High Court of Chancery of Great Britain and as brought to this country by the colonists and later enacted into state statute, subject only to the proper application of the ancient rule that equity will not assume to exercise jurisdiction where there exists a complete and adequate remedy at law. *Glanding v. Industrial Trust Co., 28 Del. Ch. 499, 45 A.2d 553 (1945).*

If a plaintiff has sufficient remedy at law the Chancery Court does not have jurisdiction of the matter. *McElroy v. McElroy, 256 A.2d 763 (Del. Ch. 1969).*

Chancery jurisdiction was founded on the absence of adequate remedy at law, and the basic duty enforced was that fixed by law. *Wife v. Husband, 270 A.2d 180 (Del. Ch. 1970).*

The Court of Chancery has no jurisdiction of a cause of action as to which the party seeking relief has an adequate remedy at law. *Reeves v. Transport Data Communications, Inc., 318 A.2d 147 (Del. Ch. 1974).*

In order for the Court of Chancery to assume jurisdiction over a proceeding, there must be an absence of an adequate remedy at law. *Chateau Apts. Co. v. City of Wilmington, 391 A.2d 205 (Del. 1978).*

This is a fundamental limitation on equity. — This section expresses a fundamental principle governing the conduct of litigation in the Chancery Court, that it has no jurisdiction of a cause of action as to which the party seeking relief has an adequate remedy at law. *Hughes Tool Co. v. Fawcett Publications, Inc., 297 A.2d 428 (Del. Ch. 1972),* rev'd on other grounds, *315 A.2d 577 (Del. 1974).*

And this limitation on equity's jurisdiction is historical. — This section is merely declaratory of the ancient rule of equity that the basic jurisdictional fact upon which equity operates is the absence of an adequate remedy in the law courts. *Tull v. Turek, 38 Del. Ch. 182, 147 A.2d 658 (1958).*

This section denying to the Chancellor power to determine any matter wherein sufficient remedy may be had at law is declaratory of a limitation established from ancient times irrespective of statutes. *Kahn v. Orenstein, 12 Del. Ch. 344, 114 A. 165 (1921); 119 A. 444 (Del. 1922).*

The proviso that the Chancellor "shall not have power to determine any matter, wherein sufficient remedy may be had by common law, or statute, before any other court or jurisdiction, of this State; ...," is merely declaratory of the old *English rule. First Nat'l Bank v. Andrews, 26 Del. Ch. 344, 28 A.2d 676 (1942).*

Equitable jurisdiction embodied that complete system of equity jurisprudence as administered by the High Court of Chancery of Great Britain and as brought to this country by the colonists and later enacted into state statute, subject only to the proper application of the ancient rule that equity will not assume to exercise jurisdiction where there exists a complete and adequate remedy at law. *Glanding v. Industrial Trust Co., 28 Del. Ch. 499, 45 A.2d 553 (1945).*

What constitutes an adequate remedy at law. — As meant by this section, an adequate remedy at law is one which (1) is as complete, practical and as efficient to the ends of justice and its prompt administration as the remedy in equity, and (2) is obtainable as of right. *In re Real Property of Wife, K, 297 A.2d 424 (Del. Ch. 1972).*

The mere fact that a litigant may have a remedy at law does not divest chancery of its jurisdiction; it must afford the plaintiffs full, fair and complete relief. *Hughes Tool Co. v. Fawcett Publications, Inc., 315 A.2d 577 (Del. 1974); 350 A.2d 341 (Del. 1975).*

To be adequate the legal remedy must be available as a matter of right. *Family Court v. Department of Labor & Indus. Relations, 320 A.2d 777 (Del. Ch. 1974).*

The legal remedy must be full, fair and complete. *Family Court v. Department of Labor & Indus. Relations, 320 A.2d 777 (Del. Ch. 1974).*

In determining the adequacy of a legal remedy for purposes of jurisdiction, the issue for the equity court is not whether another remedy would be preferable to the plaintiffs, but whether the available remedy at law will provide a full, adequate and complete remedy to the plaintiffs. *Chateau Apts. Co. v. City of Wilmington, 391 A.2d 205 (Del. 1978).*

A remedy at law must be as practical to the ends of justice and to its prompt administration as the remedy in equity. *Elster v. American Airlines, 34 Del. Ch. 94, 100 A.2d 219 (1953); Family Court v. Department of Labor & Indus. Relations, 320 A.2d 777 (Del. Ch. 1974).*

That the law affords a remedy to the complainant is not enough to oust the jurisdiction of equity from the exercise of its remedies; the remedy at law must be adequate and complete. *Hitchens v. Millman, 18 Del. Ch. 404, 162 A. 39 (1932).*

If a complainant has a full, adequate and complete remedy in a court of law, he or she has no right to relief in a court of equity. *O'Neil v. E.I. duPont de Nemours & Co., 12 Del. Ch. 76, 106 A. 50 (1919).*

No adequate remedy at law. — When the answers to the federal issues presented may demonstrate irreparable injury, it is impossible to compute the continuing damages alleged to be accruing from day to day, and a multiplicity of suits may result, this spells out "inadequate remedy at law," so that it is error to dismiss the action on the ground of lack of equity jurisdiction. *Eastern Shore Natural Gas Co. v. Stauffer Chem. Co., 298 A.2d 322 (Del. 1972).*

A legal remedy may not be adequate, although an action for damages could be brought, where the harm suffered will be irreparable or where the injury will occasion a multiplicity of suits. *Chateau Apts. Co. v. City of Wilmington, 391 A.2d 205 (Del. 1978).*

Prevention of future wrongs. — Where plaintiffs wanted money damages for past wrongs committed by defendant, and also wanted to prevent such wrongs in the future, this latter desire does not confer equitable jurisdiction. Absent allegations that a real threat exists that a multiplicity of lawsuits will be required to prevent such wrongs, or that such acts in the future will work irreparable harm, the plaintiffs have a sufficient remedy at law. *IBM Corp. v. Comdisco, Inc., 602 A.2d 74 (Del. Ch. 1991).*

Statute can place jurisdiction in another tribunal. — This section is to the effect that the Chancellor shall not hear and determine any cause where a sufficient remedy exists at law; it is both a restriction upon the Chancellor in the exercise of the general equity powers of the Court of Chancery and, at the same time, an implied grant of authority to the General Assembly to restrict the Chancellor in the exercise of those powers by the creation of a sufficient remedy in some other tribunal and by making such remedy exclusive to the other tribunal. *duPont v. duPont, 32 Del. Ch. 413, 85 A.2d 724 (1951).*

But remedy in other tribunal must be exclusive of and equivalent to chancery. — Chancery jurisdiction remains, notwithstanding the statutory creation of jurisdiction of the subject matter in another court and a remedy elsewhere that may be adequate, unless the new remedy is equivalent and is expressly made exclusive in the other tribunal. *Diebold Computer Leasing, Inc. v. Commercial Credit Corp., 267 A.2d 586 (Del. 1970).*

Chancery Court

If the General Assembly under its implied constitutional authority expressly or by necessary implication confers exclusively upon some other tribunal jurisdiction of causes theretofore heard and determined in the Court of Chancery, that will not prevent the Chancellor from acting unless a remedy is provided in the new tribunal which is the equivalent of the remedy available in the Court of Chancery. *duPont v. duPont, 32 Del. Ch. 413, 85 A.2d 724 (1951).*

Del. Const., art. IV, § 10, Del. Const., art. IV, § 17 and this section give the General Assembly authority to remove equitable matters from Chancery Court's jurisdiction if exclusive jurisdiction is conferred upon some other tribunal and the new tribunal is granted power to provide remedies equivalent to those available in Chancery, and so long as these two requirements are met, constitutional principles are not offended by the delegation of equity powers to some court other than *Chancery. Continental Coach Crafters Co. v. Fitzwater, 415 A.2d 785 (Del. Super. Ct. 1980).*

Where jurisdiction in equity has become established, a statute creating a remedy at law or removing the obstacles at law on the existence of which equity jurisdiction was originally founded does not oust equity of that jurisdiction, unless the statute affirmatively discloses the legislative intent to make the legal remedy exclusive. *Boxer v. Husky Oil Co., 429 A.2d 995 (Del. Ch. 1981).*

If there is an adequate remedy at law, equity must dismiss. — If the requirements for the removal of subject jurisdiction from the Court of Chancery are met, there is a sufficient remedy available before another court, and a suit in equity must be dismissed for lack of jurisdiction. *Wife, S. v. Husband, S., 295 A.2d 768 (Del. Ch. 1972).*

So if there is no special equity a bill will be dismissed if law affords an adequate remedy. — Where there is nothing in the way of a special equity to invoke the jurisdiction of the equity court, a bill should be dismissed because of the adequacy of a remedy at law. *Testardo v. Bresser, 17 Del. Ch. 312, 153 A. 800 (1931).*

Statute proscribes remedy requested. — An order restraining bank from disbursing funds on deposit could not be granted as it was the substantial equivalent of garnishment which is prohibited by *10 Del. C. § 3502. Delaware Trust Co. v. Partial, 517 A.2d 259 (Del. Ch. 1986).*

Granting of equitable jurisdiction is appealable. — An order, even though interlocutory, upholding the jurisdiction of the Court over the objection of the losing party, ordinarily is appealable since a substantial legal issue, viz, jurisdiction, has been determined. *Phillips v. Liberty Mut. Ins. Co., 43 Del. Ch. 388, 232 A.2d 101 (1967).*

Adequate remedy at law test applies to plaintiffs and defendants. — When adequacy of a legal remedy is spoken of as a ground for refusing the interposition of equity, the phrase is not, of course, confined in its application to those who would be plaintiffs at law. It is equally applicable to those who would be defendants; so that if a defendant in a law suit has a defense cognizable before the law court, he or she has an adequate remedy at law and will be turned out of equity because in that forum the defendant asserts a case which is available to him or her as a defense in the law court. *Pefkaros v. Harman, 20 Del. Ch. 238, 174 A. 124 (1934).*

If a defense is cognizable at law, then there is an adequate remedy at law. — Where there is a defense cognizable at law the possessor of it has an adequate remedy at law and equity will not enjoin the adversary from suing. *Gray Co. v. Alemite Corp., 20 Del. Ch. 244, 174 A. 136 (1934).*

Where a defense is one which is clearly cognizable at law, it is not a ground for equitable relief. *Holschumaker v. Etchells, 9 Del. Ch. 33, 74 A. 644 (1909).*

Equity will not interpose its injunctive relief against proceedings at law when the complainant, the defendant in the law action, relies solely upon matters that constitute an adequate defense at law, for the manifest reason that in such a case the law affords an adequate remedy. *Old Time Petroleum Co. v. Turcol, 17 Del. Ch. 276, 153 A. 562 (1931).*

Grounds of defense not used in trial at law. — A party will not be aided in equity after a trial at law unless the party can impeach the justice of the verdict or reports by facts or on grounds of which the party could not have availed himself or herself, or was prevented from doing so by fraud, accident, or act of the opposite party unmixed with negligence or fault on his or her part. *Kersey v. Rash, 3 Del. Ch. 321 (1869).*

To warrant the interference of a court of equity with the operation of a judgment at law upon grounds of defense or evidence which were cognizable at law, but not used at the trial, it must appear that the defendant at law was prevented from availing himself or herself of such grounds of defense or evidence either by fraud or surprise, or by what is termed, in the sense of courts of equity, accident, and without any neglect or default on the part of himself or herself or his or her agents. *Kersey v. Rash, 3 Del. Ch. 321 (1869); Holschumaker v. Etchells, 9 Del. Ch. 33, 74 A. 644 (1909).*

When in a court of law all the issues are legal, and the defense is legal and not an equitable one unavailable at law, still a court of equity has jurisdiction to set aside a judgment obtained in the suit in case there be some equitable ground arising out of, or connected with, the trial itself. *Hudson v. Layton, 12 Del. Ch. 106, 107 A. 785 (1919).*

The powers of the Court of Chancery to relieve a defendant in an action at law against whom there has been entered a judgment at law are (1) where a defendant has an equitable defense not cognizable at law, and (2) where a defendant has a defense available at law. In the former case equity will always give relief against the judgment, but in the latter case will not grant relief unless it appears that the grounds of defense or evidence cognizable at law were not used at the trial because the defendant was prevented from availing himself or herself of such grounds of defense or evidence either by fraud or surprise, or what in the sense of courts of equity is termed accident, and without any neglect or default on his or her own part. *Hudson v. Layton, 12 Del. Ch. 106, 107 A. 785 (1919).*

Where in an action at law a judgment was obtained and the attorney for the defendant failed to make a defense which there was to the action because the attorney had been misled by conduct of the attorney for the plaintiff in the action, and it was shown also that there was a complete defense to the action, the question was raised as to the jurisdiction of the court to vacate the judgment; the cause for vacating the judgment was not that there was a legal or equitable defense to the action, but that it was a matter extrinsic the merits of that cause, the misleading conduct of the attorney for the plaintiff, whereby the action was not so defended. *Kuratle v. Pyle, 12 Del. Ch. 112, 107 A. 788 (1919); 12 Del. Ch. 372, 110 A. 659 (1920).*

The statutory power given to the Superior Court to open a judgment obtained by default and let the defendant into a trial when it appears that the defendant had no notice of the action does not oust the Court of Chancery of jurisdiction where in the conduct of the cause one party misleads his or her adversary to the injury of the latter. The two matters are quite distinct, the Superior Court being authorized to give the statutory relief and a court of equity the equitable relief based on what has been called legal fraud, as distinct from moral fraud. *Kuratle v. Pyle, 12 Del. Ch. 112, 107 A. 788 (1919); 12 Del. Ch. 372, 110 A. 659 (1920).*

A Court of Chancery has the power to prevent the collection of a default judgment by vacating the same so that the defendant may have an opportunity to defend in the law court when defendant's attorney had been misled by the representations of complainant's attorney which caused defendant's failure to assert a valid defense. *Pyle v. Kuratle, 12 Del. Ch. 372, 110 A. 659 (1920).*

Fraud or surprise must be in the procuring of the judgment. — The fraud for which a judgment can be impeached in equity is in some matter other than the issue in controversy in the action and the fraud must relate to the procuring of the judgment or decree, and not the transaction which was the basis of the decree. *Hudson v. Layton, 12 Del. Ch. 106, 107 A. 785 (1919).*

Party who claims fraud must have been reasonably diligent. — If a litigant fails to avail himself or herself of a remedy provided by law and is subsequently barred from pursuing that remedy because of his or her own lack of diligence, the litigant cannot then rely on the absence of a remedy at law as a basis for equitable jurisdiction. *In re Real Property of Wife, K, 297 A.2d 424 (Del. Ch. 1972).*

Where there has been a fair trial at law, neither party having been subjected to an unconscientious disadvantage through fraud, surprise or uncontrollable accident, but the result of the trial has disclosed to a party the lack of some advantage he or she might have used or has put the party on the track of some additional evidence not before known which by reasonable diligence he or she might have discovered, equity will not relieve. *Kersey v. Rash, 3 Del. Ch. 321 (1869).*

Party to judgment at law with equitable defense. — If a party has an equitable defense, one not cognizable at law and which, therefore, the party could not use at law, and consequently has suffered judgment, equity will always relieve against the judgment, not however by compelling a new trial at law, but by dealing with the subject as one of its own original jurisdiction. This involves no conflict of the two jurisdictions, for each court, though acting upon the same subject matter, and to contrary results, deals with distinct rights or relations of the parties, the one with those which are legal, the other with those which are equitable. *Kersey v. Rash, 3 Del. Ch. 321 (1869).*

Multiplicity of suits. — A court of equity will intervene and entertain bills to prevent a multiplicity of actions at law, where the facts under consideration warrant it. *Wise v. Delaware Steeplechase & Race Ass'n, 28 Del. Ch. 532, 45 A.2d 547, 165 A.L.R. 830 (1945).*

While it is true that equity will take jurisdiction of an action over which it would not otherwise have jurisdiction in order to prevent a multiplicity of suits, the threat of such a multiplicity must be shown to be imminent. *Delaware Bankers Ass'n v. Division of Revenue of Dep't of Fin., 298 A.2d 352 (Del. Ch. 1972).*

For equity to assume jurisdiction where a multiplicity of suits is the alleged irreparable harm, the plaintiff must show more than a mere possibility of such litigation; the danger to which the plaintiff is exposed must be a real one. *Chateau Apts. Co. v. City of Wilmington, 391 A.2d 205 (Del. 1978).*

Necessity for chancery jurisdiction to avoid multiplicity of suits at law is not established solely on basis of numerosity of parties or where object of seeking chancery jurisdiction is to obtain a consolidation of actions or to save the expenses of separate actions. *McMahon v. New Castle Assocs., 532 A.2d 601 (Del. Ch. 1987).*

Statutes can create concurrent jurisdiction at law and in equity. — There exist many statutes at law providing a complete and adequate remedy over matters that prior to the enactments fell within the jurisdiction of equity, and the courts of this State throughout the many decisions have directly or by implication at all times recognized a coextensive jurisdiction existing between law and equity commonly referred to as a concurrent jurisdiction. *Glanding v. Industrial Trust Co., 28 Del. Ch. 499, 45 A.2d 553 (1945).*

Unless statute shows intent to remove equity jurisdiction. — The effect of a statute creating a legal remedy depends upon the legislative intent, and unless the statute shows a clear and certain intent that the equitable jurisdiction is no longer to be exercised under the matters within the scope of the statute, then the equitable jurisdiction has not been abrogated. *Glanding v. Industrial Trust Co., 28 Del. Ch. 499, 45 A.2d 553 (1945).*

Once equity has jurisdiction it will retain it. — Once equity has acquired jurisdiction of a cause, it will retain that jurisdiction to give final relief to end the controversy. This remains the rule even though circumstances have arisen after the filing of the complaint which make the equitable relief prayed for impracticable. *Tull v. Turek, 38 Del. Ch. 182, 147 A.2d 658 (1958).*

Where two courts have concurrent jurisdiction, the one which first possesses the cause has the exclusive right of

Chancery Court

exercising jurisdiction. *Beeson v. Elliott, 1 Del. Ch. 368 (1831)*.

In matters of concurrent jurisdiction, if action at law was filed before bill was filed in equity, Chancery Court would not ordinarily assume jurisdiction. *Flaherty v. Industrial Trust Co., 20 Del. Ch. 403, 178 A. 586 (1935)*.

In matters lying in the field of the concurrent jurisdiction of law and equity, when a party has elected to proceed in chancery the Superior Court will not entertain an application for relief in the same connection until the matter is finally determined in chancery. *Flaherty v. Industrial Trust Co., 20 Del. Ch. 403, 178 A. 586 (1935)*.

The fact that Court of Chancery having once taken jurisdiction, will dispose of all matters involved, must of necessity have limitations. *Knowles v. Williams, 34 Del. Ch. 243, 102 A.2d 442 (1954)*.

Where both the Superior Court and the Court of Chancery have concurrent jurisdiction, the court first assuming jurisdiction will usually retain it. *Sterling v. Sekcienski, 34 Del. Ch. 525, 106 A.2d 767 (1954)*.

Once equity obtains jurisdiction, it may go on to decide the whole controversy in appropriate cases. *Getty Ref. & Mktg. Co. v. Park Oil, Inc., 385 A.2d 147 (Del. Ch. 1978)*.

Under settled principles of equity jurisprudence, once equity jurisdiction has attached, the Chancery Court can properly proceed to deal with the whole matter. *Park Oil, Inc. v. Getty Ref. & Mktg. Co., 407 A.2d 533 (Del. 1979)*.

Discretion of court. — Whether a Chancery Court will continue to exercise concurrent jurisdiction over an entire controversy where part of it is cognizable at law and part of it is equitable is discretionary with the Court. *Getty Ref. & Mktg. Co. v. Park Oil, Inc., 385 A.2d 147 (Del. Ch. 1978)*.

If a controversy is vested with "equitable features" which would support Chancery jurisdiction of at least a part of the controversy, then the Chancellor has discretion to resolve the remaining portions of the controversy as well. *Getty Ref. & Mktg. Co. v. Park Oil, Inc., 385 A.2d 147 (Del. Ch. 1978)*.

Court of Chancery can refuse to hear and determine that portion of a controversy which standing alone would not fall within Chancery's jurisdiction for in such a case the Court has discretion to continue to hear the essentially legal portion of the action or to transfer it to the appropriate law court. *Getty Ref. & Mktg. Co. v. Park Oil, Inc., 385 A.2d 147 (Del. Ch. 1978)*.

Absence of precedent is no bar to award of relief by the Court of Chancery. *Severns v. Wilmington Medical Ctr., Inc., 421 A.2d 1334 (Del. 1980)*.

Allegations of complaint viewed in light of what plaintiff seeks to gain. — The question as to whether or not equitable jurisdiction exists is to be determined by an examination of the allegations of the complaint viewed in light of what the plaintiff really seeks to gain by bringing a cause of action. *Reeves v. Transport Data Communications, Inc., 318 A.2d 147 (Del. Ch. 1974)*.

Where only allegations in complaint are claims for debt or money, Court of Chancery would not have subject matter jurisdiction to hear the complaint. *Getty*

Ref. & Mktg. Co. v. Park Oil, Inc., 385 A.2d 147 (Del. Ch. 1978).

Writ of prohibition. — If the petitioner has an adequate remedy at law in the form of a writ of prohibition the Court of Chancery lacks the jurisdiction to determine the merits of this case. *Family Court v. Department of Labor & Indus. Relations, 320 A.2d 777 (Del. Ch. 1974)*.

Fraud lies in the field of the concurrent jurisdiction of law and equity. *Flaherty v. Industrial Trust Co., 20 Del. Ch. 403, 178 A. 586 (1935)*.

There are cases where courts of equity and courts of law have concurrent jurisdiction, though the primary rights violated are of a legal nature, and cases involving fraud are ordinarily in that class. *Bovay v. H.M. Byllesby & Co., 25 Del. Ch. 1, 12 A.2d 178 (1940)*.

Equity retains jurisdiction over instruments despite legal remedies. — Equity will entertain a bill to cancel an instrument on the ground of fraud or forgery, notwithstanding law would afford a defensive remedy based on those grounds; because the remedy at law is not as full as in equity and is therefore not sufficient. *Flaherty v. Industrial Trust Co., 20 Del. Ch. 403, 178 A. 586 (1935)*.

Jurisdiction in equity suits to recover on lost negotiable instruments is well settled. *Townsend Trust Co. v. Reynolds, 20 Del. Ch. 21, 169 A. 295 (1933)*.

The extension of the legal remedies into the field of lost instruments does not destroy the jurisdiction of equity as it theretofore existed over the same subject. *Townsend Trust Co. v. Reynolds, 20 Del. Ch. 21, 169 A. 295 (1933)*.

Chancery has jurisdiction over its own appeal bonds despite legal remedy. — Although there is a remedy at law by an action on an appeal bond given in a chancery case, it does not necessarily follow that the Chancery Court is without jurisdiction. *Ellis D. Taylor, Inc. v. Craft Bldrs., Inc., 260 A.2d 180 (Del. Ch. 1969)*.

Equity retains jurisdiction of forcible entry and detainer cases. — The fact that the General Assembly designed the legal remedy under the (former) forcible entry and detainer statute to be a summary one, is no indication of a legislative intent to exempt that remedy from chancery's interference in cases where, according to settled principles, equity is in the exercise of its appropriate jurisdiction. *Pefkaros v. Harman, 20 Del. Ch. 238, 174 A. 124 (1934)*.

Unless no equities are involved. — Where, in a forcible entry and detainer case, there was no question relating to equitable title which the party could not set up before the justice of the peace, and there were no elements of an equitable estoppel which the legal forum would be disqualified to consider, but the question was one of fact only, equity had no jurisdiction. *Pefkaros v. Harman, 20 Del. Ch. 238, 174 A. 124 (1934)*.

Fraudulent confession of judgment. — If the law in a case where judgment has been entered by confession on a bond and warrant afforded no remedy, there might possibly be some ground for the interposition of equity. *Testardo v. Bresser, 17 Del. Ch. 312, 153 A. 800 (1931)*.

Where warrant of attorney for confession of judgment was forged, legal remedy of setting aside a judgment based on the forged document was not sufficient as compared to equity's power to order cancellation or destruction of the document. *Hollis v. Kinney, 13 Del. Ch. 366, 120 A. 356 (1923).*

Constructive trusts. — When the right asserted is not distinctly equitable in origin, the request for constructive trust will ordinarily succeed in conferring jurisdiction in equity only when a claim to specific property is asserted. *McMahon v. New Castle Assocs., 532 A.2d 601 (Del. Ch. 1987).*

Concurrent jurisdiction of suits by assignees of unassignable choses in action. — The jurisdiction of suits by assignees of unassignable choses in action, formerly exclusive in equity, is not now recognized as even concurrent with law courts, unless it be shown that adequate relief is not afforded at law. *Illinois Fin. Co. v. Interstate Rural Credit Ass'n, 11 Del. Ch. 349, 101 A. 870 (1917).*

And to enforce rights under a mortgage. — While the Court of Chancery has jurisdiction to enforce rights under a mortgage concurrently with the Superior Court, yet the statutory proceeding in the court of law by scire facias sur mortgage is more expeditious and in other respects preferable to a suit in chancery. *Malsberger v. Parsons, 11 Del. Ch. 249, 100 A. 786 (1917).*

Implied condition precedent to ordering specific performance. — Even where specific performance is ordered, there is an implied condition precedent that the terms of the obligation be fixed and certain and that there is a construction plan "so precisely definite as to make compliance therewith subject to effective judicial supervision." *Ryan v. Ocean Twelve, Inc., 316 A.2d 573 (Del. Ch. 1973).*

Accounting by fiduciaries. — The Court of Chancery has historically entertained suits seeking an accounting by fiduciaries and the General Assembly has not enacted any statute transferring that jurisdiction to another court. *Boxer v. Husky Oil Co., 429 A.2d 995 (Del. Ch. 1981).*

An accounting by a nonfiduciary will be required by a court of equity only when the accounts are so complex that the legal remedy is likely to prove inadequate and given the development of broad and liberal discovery rules in the law courts, it seems likely that equity shall rarely, if ever, have to be resorted to in order to determine the state of accounts in a purely commercial relationship. *McMahon v. New Castle Assocs., 532 A.2d 601 (Del. Ch. 1987).*

Building contract. — A court of equity will not order specific performance of a building contract in a situation in which it would be impractical to carry out such an order unless there are special circumstances or the public interest is directly involved. *Ryan v. Ocean Twelve, Inc., 316 A.2d 573 (Del. Ch. 1973).*

Where it would undoubtedly have required a considerable period of time and involved a series of corrective acts on the part of the developer and builder of a condominium to effect satisfaction, where compensatory damages to cover the costs of correcting the wrongs could bring about the same ultimate relief, and where there were no special circumstances existing which would render money damages inadequate, equity would not assume jurisdiction. *Ryan v. Ocean Twelve, Inc., 316 A.2d 573 (Del. Ch. 1973).*

A common law copyright, like its statutory successor, is distinct from that which is copyrighted; it is not a material substance, but is an incorporeal right in the nature of a franchise or privilege of publication and is such a unique interest, devoid as it is of physical substance, that it cannot be recovered in an action at law, and jurisdiction rests in equity. *Hughes Tool Co. v. Fawcett Publications, Inc., 315 A.2d 577 (Del. 1974); 350 A.2d 341 (Del. 1975).*

Separation contracts. — The nonsupport provisions *13 Del. C. §§ 502, 506, and 507* are not such legal remedy as will preclude equity jurisdiction in a case involving a separation contract between spouses, since these provisions supply no remedy for the enforcement of the contract by way of damages and the action is under the control of the State, not of the party to the contract. *Peters v. Peters, 20 Del. Ch. 28, 169 A. 298 (1933).*

The right of a spouse to maintenance, since it is a purely legal right, may be enforced in equity as may any other legal right which lacks redress at law. *duPont v. duPont, 32 Del. Ch. 413, 85 A.2d 724 (1951).*

The award of separate maintenance to a deserted and destitute spouse by a court of equity constitutes nothing more than a fulfillment of equity's historic function, the giving of a remedy for a legal right which otherwise was remediless. *duPont v. duPont, 32 Del. Ch. 413, 85 A.2d 724 (1951).*

Court of chancery has been divested of jurisdiction of child support. — Chapter 114, 58 Del. Laws, codified as § 901 et seq. of this title, creates in the Family Court an adequate remedy at law sufficient to divest the Court of Chancery of jurisdiction in child support cases. *P. v. P., 287 A.2d 409 (Del. Ch. 1972).*

Compelling contributions to support and education of adult child. — In view of the enactment of *1 Del. C. § 701,* the existence of *13 Del. C. § 501,* and the clear intention expressed by the General Assembly by § 902 of this title to place all original civil jurisdiction "over family and child matters" in the Family Court, the Court of Chancery no longer has jurisdiction to entertain an action to compel a parent to contribute to the support and education of an adult child over the age of 18 years. *Scribner v. Chonofsky, 310 A.2d 924 (Del. Ch. 1973).*

Mandamus as adequate remedy at law. — The existence of an adequate remedy in the law court in the form of a mandamus action precludes the concurrent jurisdiction of the Court of *Chancery. Sabo v. Williams, 303 A.2d 696 (Del. Ch. 1973).*

Quo warranto is an adequate remedy to oust public officials. — If a person is disqualified to hold a public office, the law supplies an adequate remedy by way of quo warranto to oust such person, and equity has no jurisdiction by way of injunction against payment to such person of his or her salary, to pass upon the question of his right to hold the office. *Ake v. Bookhammer, 13 Del. Ch. 320, 119 A. 238 (1922).*

Administrative remedy plus a right to appeal is an adequate remedy. — As provided by *30 Del. C. §§ 329 and 331,* an administrative remedy is available for testing the validity of occupational fee charges as well as a right of appeal to the Superior Court from the ruling of the

Chancery Court

Tax Appeal Board, so that equity will not enjoin the collection of a tax alleged to be illegal where there is an adequate remedy at law and there is no real threat of a multiplicity of suits and unreasonable litigation. *Delaware Bankers Ass'n v. Division of Revenue of Dep't of Fin., 298 A.2d 352 (Del. Ch. 1972).*

Specific performance will not be granted where plaintiff has an adequate remedy at law. *Lee Bldrs., Inc. v. Wells, 33 Del. Ch. 439, 95 A.2d 692 (1953).*

The remedy of specific performance of a contract is available only where there is no adequate remedy at law for its breach. *Francis v. Medill, 16 Del. Ch. 129, 141 A. 697 (1928).*

Review of routine agency decisions. — The common law writ of certiorari generally contemplates only a review of the paper record created below to determine whether the lower court or agency has made an evident error of law, thus, where an agency action was not made pursuant to a quasi-judicial hearing and order procedure but was a routine decision by an operating officer of the department, there is no record of the action for the common law writ to act upon. In such circumstances, there may be substantial doubt that the writ of certiorari is meaningfully available. *Couch v. Delmarva Power & Light Co., 593 A.2d 554 (Del. Ch. 1991).*

Contract for the sale of personal property is not enforceable in equity. — Because the law supplies an adequate remedy by way of damages for the breach of the ordinary contract for the delivery of personal property, the remedy of specific performance is generally denied in such cases. *Francis v. Medill, 16 Del. Ch. 129, 141 A. 697 (1928).*

Unless the property is peculiar and individual in character. — Ownership of shares of stock may in certain circumstances possess such peculiar and unique features as warrant the specific enforcement of a contract for their sale and delivery. *Francis v. Medill, 16 Del. Ch. 129, 141 A. 697 (1928).*

A contract concerning the sale of shares of stock may be specifically enforced if the complainant has no adequate remedy at law. *G.W. Baker Mach. Co. v. U.S. Fire Apparatus Co., 11 Del. Ch. 386, 97 A. 613 (1916).*

The power of a Court of Chancery to decree specific performance of contracts respecting personal property is limited to personal property peculiar and individual in character, where for some other cause its value is not measurable by a money value reasonably ascertainable as damages in an action at law. *Elliott v. Jones, 11 Del. Ch. 283, 101 A. 872 (1917).*

A particular horse with unique or peculiar traits and qualities different from horses in general, and which has promises of development by training so as to become valuable for speed in racing contests, has a prospective but now unascertainable value, and, therefore, a contract respecting it is properly a subject for a decree for specific performance, because of the inadequacy of legal remedies. *Elliott v. Jones, 11 Del. Ch. 283, 101 A. 872 (1917).*

Contract of stock sale which gives majority control is specifically enforceable. — One who contracts for the purchase of shares of stock in a corporation in such amount as to give a majority control is entitled to a specific performance of the contract because of the inadequacy of the remedy at law for damages. *Francis v. Medill, 16 Del. Ch. 129, 141 A. 697 (1928).*

As is claim for delivery of new stock certificates. — The Chancery Court has subject-matter jurisdiction of a claim for delivery of new stock certificates based upon improper indorsement of the original certificates even when a bona fide purchaser has submitted the original securities for transfer, and the plaintiff in such case is not limited to an action at law for money damages. *Scott v. Ametek, Inc., 277 A.2d 714 (Del. Ch. 1971).*

Federal enforcement of tax lien may be characterized as an "equitable" proceeding, and sequestration procedures of the Court of Chancery may be available in a federal court action. *United States v. Stone, 59 F.R.D. 260 (D. Del. 1973).*

Violation of uniform fraudulent conveyances act. — Court of Chancery has at least concurrent jurisdiction to hear controversies involving alleged violations of the Uniform Fraudulent Conveyances Act, 6 Del. C. § 1301 et seq., whether the claim has matured or not. *Getty Ref. & Mktg. Co. v. Park Oil, Inc., 385 A.2d 147 (Del. Ch. 1978).*

"Fairness" suits for alleged fraud and breach of fiduciary duty brought by minority shareholders fall within the Court of Chancery's exclusive, and not its concurrent, jurisdiction. *Harman v. Masoneilan Int'l, 442 A.2d 487 (Del. 1982).*

Stockholder liability for debts of delaware corporation. — Court of Chancery has jurisdiction to hear actions where facts are alleged which, if true, would permit the Court to pierce the corporate veil and hold individual stockholders personally liable for debts of a Delaware corporation. *Getty Ref. & Mktg. Co. v. Park Oil, Inc., 385 A.2d 147 (Del. Ch. 1978).*

Right to specific performance does not depend on mutuality of remedy. — Cases of specific performance whether of the pure type or of the related kind are to find their justification in other appropriate principles of general equitable cognizance and are not to be affected by questions concerning mutuality of remedy. *Sharpless-Hendler Ice Cream Co. v. Davis, 16 Del. Ch. 315, 147 A. 305 (1929).*

The right to the equitable relief of specific performance in this State depends not upon mutuality of remedy, but the inadequacy of an action at law. *G.W. Baker Mach. Co. v. U.S. Fire Apparatus Co., 11 Del. Ch. 386, 97 A. 613 (1916).*

Damages are an adequate remedy at law. — Ordinarily a party aggrieved by a claimed breach of contract or injured as a result of a tort has a complete and adequate remedy at law in the form of an action for damages. *Hughes Tool Co. v. Fawcett Publications, Inc., 297 A.2d 428 (Del. Ch. 1972), rev'd on other grounds, 315 A.2d 577 (Del. 1974).*

But equity may award damages as incidental to the equitable relief. — A court of equity has no jurisdiction to entertain a suit brought purely for compensatory damages, those being awarded at law; it may nevertheless award compensatory damages as a part of the final relief in a cause over which it admittedly had jurisdiction. *Tull v. Turek, 38 Del. Ch. 182, 147 A.2d 658 (1958).*

If equity has jurisdiction of the subject matter, it has always been true that it will proceed to determine all facts necessary to a decree, barring such exceptional facts as legal titles, and when a fact to be ascertained is whether money is due, and if so how much, equity otherwise having jurisdiction, will not, simply because it has no jury, decline to ascertain the fact that something is due and, if necessary, how much. *Mackenzie Oil Co. v. Omar Oil & Gas Co., 14 Del. Ch. 36, 120 A. 852 (1923).*

Court of Chancery, when it has once obtained jurisdiction of a cause of purely equitable cognizance, as by injunction, has right to decree, as incidental to the main relief, such damages as may be necessary to do complete justice. *Simon v. Pyrites Co., 32 Del. 581, 128 A. 370 (1925).*

Dealing in matters measurable in dollars. — While it is axiomatic that courts of equity will not deal in matters readily measurable in dollars, one of the recognized exceptions to that rule is where it appears that a money judgment would not produce the dollars, and thus courts of equity often intervene in cases of insolvency and nonresidence. *Bayard v. Martin, 34 Del. Ch. 184, 101 A.2d 329 (1953); 347 U.S. 944, 74 S. Ct. 639, 98 L. Ed. 1092 (1953).*

Equity leaves question of title to real estate to law. — Where an action involves the determination of title to real estate, the Court of Chancery usually requires the issue to be determined in an action at law, even where equitable relief is also sought. *Marvel v. Barley Mill Road Homes, Inc., 34 Del. Ch. 417, 104 A.2d 908 (1954).*

But will enjoin action that will cloud title. — Court of Chancery has jurisdiction, in a proper case, under its inherent powers, to restrain by injunction such action as would cast a cloud upon the title to real property, and it is not necessary for the legal owner to wait until such cloud has been cast before calling upon a Court of Chancery for relief. *Johnson v. Messick, 11 Del. Ch. 454, 106 A. 58 (1919).*

Ejectment of plaintiff has legal title. — The Court of Chancery lacks jurisdiction to entertain ejectment actions; plaintiffs acquire legal title and have an adequate remedy at law. *Burris v. Wilmington Trust Co., 301 A.2d 277 (Del. 1972).*

Protection of defendant in ejectment action whose title is equitable. — Chancery Court has the right to protect a defendant in an ejectment action at law whose title is equitable against the plaintiff in that action, whose claim is a legal one, if the equitable title is a meritorious defense not available as such in the action at law. *Boole v. Johnson, 11 Del. Ch. 364, 102 A. 782 (1917).*

Equity can impose trust on deed. — To charge the grantee, under an ordinary deed, with a trust, upon extrinsic evidence, especially upon parol evidence, is a jurisdiction to be exercised with caution, and only under cogent proof, such as the conscience of the Court of Chancery cannot resist; still the jurisdiction is unquestionable. *Hall v. Livingston, 3 Del. Ch. 348 (1869).*

Cancellation of deed. — As the complainant, seeking cancellation of a deed in an ejectment at law, could not obtain a cancellation of the deed, he or she is entitled to proceed with the suit in the Court of Chancery which will afford the complainant the benefits of the full and complete remedy of cancellation. *Hitchens v. Millman, 18 Del. Ch. 404, 162 A. 39 (1932).*

Lessee's option to purchase is protected by equity. — The Chancery Court has jurisdiction to issue a preliminary injunction restraining a landlord from prosecuting an action at law to dispossess the complainant of certain real estate held by it under a lease containing a clause conferring on the lessee a right to purchase the property at any time during the life of the lease. *Old Time Petroleum Co. v. Turcol, 17 Del. Ch. 276, 153 A. 562 (1931).*

Trespass. — Equity will not relieve against mere trespasses to real property but the trespass must be of such an aggravated nature as to create a case where the injury is irreparable and the remedy at law inadequate for its compensation before equity will interfere. *Nebeker v. Berg, 13 Del. Ch. 6, 115 A. 310 (1921).*

Enjoining commission of crime. — As a general proposition a court of equity cannot enjoin the commission of crime, for its powers relate to civil rights, but where the rights of the public are interfered with, the court has jurisdiction to enjoin the wrongful acts. *Wolcott ex rel. Maloney v. Doremus, 11 Del. Ch. 277, 101 A. 868 (1917).*

Nuisances. — The fact that the keeping of a nuisance is a crime does not deprive the Court of Chancery of power to enjoin the nuisance. *Wolcott ex rel. Maloney v. Doremus, 11 Del. Ch. 277, 101 A. 868 (1917).*

Residual jurisdiction over the administration of estates. — Equity has and will exercise jurisdiction in cases concerning the administration of estates, which have been omitted from the constitutional or statutory grant of probate jurisdiction to other courts, or for which the methods or relief available before such courts are imperfect or inadequate. *In re Estate of Ortiz, 26 Del. Ch. 240, 27 A.2d 368 (1942).*

Statute of limitations will bar equitable action in the absence of fraud. — Where the statute of limitations bars the legal remedy, it shall bar the equitable remedy in an analogous case, in the absence of unusual circumstances, such as in a suit to undo a fraud, where persons in a fiduciary relation have enriched themselves by fraudulent breaches of duty. *Wise v. Delaware Steeplechase & Race Ass'n, 28 Del. Ch. 161, 39 A.2d 212 (1944); 28 Del. Ch. 532, 45 A.2d 547 (1945).*

Dispute as to trustees' commissions is within chancery jurisdiction. — A claim involving a dispute between trustees as to the right to commissions earned by virtue of an appointment made by the Court of Chancery was within the general jurisdiction of the Court of Chancery. *Kimmel v. Wilmington Trust Co., 287 A.2d 760 (Del. Ch. 1972).*

Court must be satisfied prima facie it has jurisdiction of document to be incorporated. — When offered a document for incorporation in an order, the Court of Chancery must be satisfied prima facie that it has subject-matter jurisdiction as to a significant part of what is contained therein, but that determination does not necessarily extend to every part thereof. *A.M.M. v. J.L.W., 285 A.2d 824 (Del. Ch. 1971).*

Parties cannot by order on an agreement confer a jurisdiction which the Court of Chancery may not have, nor can they compel the Court to exercise a discretion to accept jurisdiction. *A.M.M. v. J.L.W., 285 A.2d 824 (Del. Ch. 1971).*

The inclusion of an indemnification provision in a contract, which provides plaintiff with an adequate remedy at law for breach of covenant but does not purport to make monetary relief an exclusive remedy or provide that the penalty for nonperformance be restricted to a certain amount, does not deny plaintiff, on proper showing, appropriate injunctive relief in the event the covenant in issue is found to be enforceable. *Knowles-Zeswitz Music, Inc. v. Cara, 260 A.2d 171 (Del. Ch. 1969).*

Discontinuation of comatose patient's life-support systems. — The Court of Chancery cannot grant nor the Supreme Court order any relief as to discontinuation of a comatose patient's life-support systems without an evidentiary hearing. *Severns v. Wilmington Medical Ctr., Inc., 421 A.2d 1334 (Del. 1980).*

The Court of Chancery has the power to grant relief to a guardian of the person through authorization of the discontinuation of a comatose patient's life-support systems in accordance with the proof which is made and the requirements of justice. There need not be legislation authorizing and providing guidelines for the relief sought. *Severns v. Wilmington Medical Ctr., Inc., 421 A.2d 1334 (Del. 1980).*

Estoppels should be resorted to solely as a means of preventing injustice, and should not be permitted to defeat the law. *Ainscow v. Alexander, 28 Del. Ch. 545, 39 A.2d 54 (1944).*

DELAWARE CASE NOTES — UNREPORTED

Reformation is unavailable in this case as a matter of law under the *Waggoner* test for the simple reason that defendant corporation cannot establish the intent of "all parties interested," including all of defendant corporation's present and past stockholders. According to publicly available information, defendant corporation has 13.15 million shares outstanding and an average daily volume over the past three months of over 70,000 shares. At this rate, defendant corporation had literally thousands of

record and beneficial holders as of the record date for the 2005 annual meeting and it has literally thousands of record and beneficial stockholders today. It is simply impossible for defendant corporation to show that all present and past shareholders intended the provisions to read as defendant corporation now claims. *Lions Gate Entm't Corp. v. Image Entm't, Inc., 2006 Del. Ch. LEXIS 108 (Del. June 5, 2006).*

§ 343.   Injunctions staying actions at law, or to prevent waste

DELAWARE CASE NOTES — REPORTED

Courts must avoid conflicts with each other, as any other policy would destroy all respect for the courts. *Bayard v. Martin, 34 Del. Ch. 184, 101 A.2d 329 (1953); 347 U.S. 944, 74 S. Ct. 639, 98 L. Ed. 1092 (1953).*

Chancery is without jurisdiction if there is sufficient remedy at law. — There are two grounds upon which the Court of Chancery interferes with suits at law: (1) When the defense is an equitable one; (2) when the defense is legal, but equity can aid in making it effectual. *Matthews v. Dodd, 3 Del. Ch. 159 (1867).*

The ground upon which a writ of injunction issues to enjoin an action of law in a Court of Chancery is that the party is making use of the jurisdiction of a court of law contrary to equity and good conscience; and it is commonly suggested in the bill that complainant, for some reasons therein stated, is not able to make his or her defense in such Court, though complainant has a good discharge in equity, or that the Court refuses some rightful advantage, or does injustice to complainant in the proceeding, or has not power to do complainant right. *Conner v. Pennington, 1 Del. Ch. 177 (1821).*

A court of equity does not interfere with judgments at law unless complainant has an equitable defense of which complainant could not avail himself or herself at law, or had a good defense at law which complainant was pre-

vented from availing himself or herself of by fraud or accident, unmixed with negligence of complainant or complainant's agents. *Emerson v. Gray, 38 Del. Ch. 87, 63 A. 768 (1906).*

Where the relief requested is intervention in proceedings pending in a law court, the basis for equitable jurisdiction is a showing that some serious injury is threatened which the law court will not be able to repair, but which a court of equity can either prevent from occurring in the first place or can afterwards repair. *Bayard v. Martin, 34 Del. Ch. 184, 101 A.2d 329 (1953); 347 U.S. 944, 74 S. Ct. 639, 68 L. Ed. 1092 (1953).*

Court must act cautiously. — The Court of Chancery in relieving against judgments at law upon grounds impeaching their justice, has always acted cautiously, and held itself within strict limits. *Kersey v. Rash, 3 Del. Ch. 321 (1869).*

Proper exercise of discretion requires balancing. — It is imperative to a proper exercise of discretion that the Court balance the conveniences of the parties and the possible injuries to them that may be affected by either the granting or withholding of injunctive relief. *Petty v. Penntech Papers, Inc., 347 A.2d 140 (Del. Ch. 1975).*

Power to enjoin challenged conduct prior to a full evidentiary hearing constitutes the strong arm of equity jurisdiction, and should never be utilized unless a clear case of imminent, irreparable injury is presented and the applicant satisfies the court that there is at least a reasonable probability of ultimate success on final hearing. *Petty v. Penntech Papers, Inc., 347 A.2d 140 (Del. Ch. 1975).*

When preliminary injunction granted. — Preliminary injunction may not be granted unless some otherwise inevitable and irreparable injury looms eminent to the party seeking it. *Capital Educators Ass'n v. Camper, 320 A.2d 782 (Del. Ch. 1974).*

A threat of future injury, standing alone, will not justify interlocutory injunctive relief. *Capital Educators Ass'n v. Camper, 320 A.2d 782 (Del. Ch. 1974).*

Holding over or forcible entry and detainer. — There is jurisdiction in the Court of Chancery to restrain proceedings for holding over or forcible entry and detainer. *Butler v. Topkis, 38 Del. Ch. 75, 63 A. 646 (1906).*

Equity can enjoin an action in ejectment. — The Court of Chancery can enjoin an action in ejectment when the defendant in that suit has an equitable title to the land in question. *Boole v. Johnson, 11 Del. Ch. 364, 102 A. 782 (1917).*

Collection of debt on ground of future debt owing. — Chancery will not arrest proceedings at law for the recovery of a debt due and recoverable there on the ground that the plaintiff owes the defendant a sum not yet due, the payment of which he or she may evade, if permitted to recover in his or her suit at law. *Hayes v. Hayes, 2 Del. Ch. 191, 73 Am. Dec. 709 (1859).*

Party to equity suit to stay law judgment. — No injunction can be decreed as against persons to restrain the collection of a judgment by them, their attorneys or agents, unless they were made parties; they must be heard on the question, whether this judgment has been satisfied, before their legal rights can be interfered with. *Davidson v. Wilson, 3 Del. Ch. 307 (1869).*

Advantage gained by fraud at law. — If the plaintiff in an action at law has procured or is responsible for a false return of execution, equity will interfere to restrain the use of an advantage gained in a court of ordinary jurisdiction, which must merely make that court an instrument of injustice, in all cases where such advantage has been gained by the fraud, accident, or mistake of the opposite party. *Emerson v. Gray, 38 Del. Ch. 87, 63 A. 768 (1906).*

Burden of proof. — In an action to enjoin a seller from proceeding with the execution of judgment notes, the burden is squarely upon plaintiffs to make an affirmative showing of whatever is essential to their case. *Bayard v. Martin, 34 Del. Ch. 184, 101 A.2d 329 (1953); 347 U.S. 944, 74 S. Ct. 639, 98 L. Ed. 1092 (1953).*

Proof of probability of succeeding in equity. — In an action to enjoin a seller from proceeding with execution of judgment notes, pending determination of seller's suit in Superior Court, in considering propriety of issuance of temporary injunction, only probability of prevailing which was proper for the Court of Chancery to consider was the probability of prevailing on the issues which Court of Chancery itself was to try and treatment of the fraud issue was not in the jurisdiction of the Court. *Bayard v. Martin, 34 Del. Ch. 184, 101 A.2d 329 (1953); 347 U.S. 944, 74 S. Ct. 639, 98 L. Ed. 1092 (1953).*

Possibility of future judgment against other party being unavailable. — In an action to enjoin a seller from proceeding with the execution of judgment notes, where evidence was not sufficient to establish that subsequent judgment against the seller would be unavailing, motion for temporary injunction would be denied. *Bayard v. Martin, 34 Del. Ch. 184, 101 A.2d 329 (1953); 347 U.S. 944, 74 S. Ct. 639, 98 L. Ed. 1092 (1953).*

Considerations of fairness not grounds for interference. — In an action to enjoin a seller from proceeding with the execution of judgment notes, motion for temporary injunction was denied on theory that considerations of fairness required equity to intervene and regulate proceedings in *Superior Court. Bayard v. Martin, 34 Del. Ch. 184, 101 A.2d 329 (1953); 347 U.S. 944, 74 S. Ct. 639, 98 L. Ed. 1092 (1953).*

To restrain waste a party must have title to land. — A party applying for a writ of injunction to stay waste should have, or establish, a title to the place in which the waste is committed, before an injunction can be issued; and in the party's affidavit the particular title should be set out and it is not sufficient to allege merely that the party is entitled to a fee simple estate. *Thompson v. Lynam, 1 Del. Ch. 64 (1819).*

Purchaser at sheriff's sale can restrain waste before actual conveyance. — Plaintiff, although having no conveyance of the land from the sheriff and the sheriff has not made return of the sale, has at least an equitable title to the land, and perhaps something more, and can prevent waste by a writ of injunction. *Thompson v. Lynam, 1 Del. Ch. 64 (1819).*

Waste of a cotenant. — Although courts of equity will not interfere by injunction to prevent waste in cases of tenants in common, or coparceners or joint tenants, because they have a right to enjoy the estate as they please, yet they will interfere in special cases; as where the party committing the waste is insolvent, or where the waste is destructive of the estate, and not within the usual legitimate exercise of the right of enjoyment of the estate. *Burris v. Jackson, 8 Del. Ch. 345, 68 A. 381 (1899).*

An injunction may go to restrain a tenant from doing damages, and from removing crops and manure except according to custom of the country. *Wilds v. Layton, 1 Del. Ch. 226 (1822).*

Cutting of timber may be restrained. — Cutting of timber from land is an injury irreparable in its nature, and by whomsoever committed is remediable in equity and the remedy by injunction in such cases has been greatly extended, and is applied even to restrain trespasses which are irreparable. *Fleming v. Collins, 2 Del. Ch. 230 (1859).*

The cutting of timber, whether by a tenant (and so constituting technical waste), or by a trespasser, is such an injury as will be prevented by an injunction by decree of the Court of *Chancery. Dill v. Dill, 10 Del. Ch. 257, 91 A. 450 (1914).*

Account and satisfaction for waste. — The Court having jurisdiction to restrain waste will do complete jus-

Chancery Court

tice by decreeing an account and satisfaction for the waste committed. *Fleming v. Collins, 2 Del. Ch. 230 (1859).*

When the Court takes jurisdiction to restrain waste, it will do complete justice by decreeing an accounting and satisfaction for the waste committed. *Ennis v. Smith, 38 Del. Ch. 154, 80 A. 636 (1911).*

§ 348. Mediation proceedings for business disputes

DELAWARE CASE NOTES — UNREPORTED

Injunctive relief. — Homeowners' association was granted a preliminary injunction to enjoin property owners from demolishing a house on an adjacent property which the owners purchased in a community and converting the property to a grassy playfield for the owners' children because the association made a sufficient showing of probable success on the merits, irreparable harm, and the balance of equities to justify the imposition of a preliminary injunction. *Serv. Corp. v. Guzzetta, 2007 Del. Ch. LEXIS 84 (Del. Ch. June 13, 2007).*

SUBCHAPTER IV.
PROCEDURE

§ 361.   Rules of Court

DELAWARE CASE NOTES — REPORTED

Rules are binding on parties and on the court. — The general rules of the Court when made and promulgated have, so long as they remain unrescinded or unmodified, the force and effect of law, and are equally binding on parties and the Court. *In re du Pont, 8 Del. Ch. 442, 68 A. 399 (1899).*

In any case not covered by a rule of court, the Chancellor is remitted to the inherent power of the Court to regulate its practice according to the well defined and authoritative precedents, and the power inheres in the very constitution of the Court to make such general orders covering classes of cases, or such special orders in any particular case as may from time to time be found necessary. *Wilds v. Wilds, 8 Del. Ch. 368, 68 A. 447 (1899).*

Chancery should proceed with caution in reversing its own rules. — The promulgation of a rule of court is a decision by the preceding Chancellor that the power existed; and the present court should proceed cautiously in reversing its own decisions, requiring that it should appear very clearly that the rule which it was sought to ignore was neither authorized by statute law then in force, nor by the inherent powers of the Court of *Chancery. In re du Pont, 8 Del. Ch. 442, 68 A. 399 (1899).*

§ 365.   Compelling appearance of defendant in absence of personal service

DELAWARE CASE NOTES — REPORTED

Equity is given jurisdiction over subject matter in its jurisdiction. — This section gives the Court of Chancery jurisdiction to decide disputes concerning subject matter under its jurisdiction; it embraces in rem actions and provides for service on parties having a possible interest therein including nonresidents. *Abercrombie v. Davies, 35 Del. Ch. 354, 118 A.2d 358 (1955).*

This section's purpose is to give the Court of Chancery jurisdiction to decide disputes concerning subject matter under its jurisdiction. *Arden-Mayfair, Inc. v. Louart Corp., 385 A.2d 3 (Del. Ch. 1978).*

This section must be strictly followed, but this rule does not forbid interpretation. *Perrine v. Pennroad Corp., 19 Del. Ch. 368, 168 A. 196 (1933).*

The legislative expression "out of the state" can be taken to embrace residence in another state. *Perrine v. Pennroad Corp., 19 Del. Ch. 368, 168 A. 196 (1933).*

Where the affidavit undertakes to meet this section by stating that the defendants "reside outside of the State," the averment is equivalent to saying they are "out of the State." *Perrine v. Pennroad Corp., 19 Del. Ch. 368, 168 A. 196 (1933).*

Field of property subject to seizure not enlarged. — This section and *10 Del. C. § 366,* respectively, authorize seizure of property in equity (sequestration) in proceedings strictly in rem and quasi in rem. They do not undertake to enlarge the field of property subject to seizure. *Baker v. Gotz, 387 F. Supp. 1381 (D. Del. 1975); 523 F.2d 1050 (3d Cir. 1975).*

This section is applicable to both residents and nonresidents. *Winitz v. Kline, 288 A.2d 456 (Del. Ch. 1971).*

NONRESIDENTS. — A court has the power to bring nonresidents before it by constructive service unattended by seizure, if the suit is one wherein the relief sought relates to the status, title, or ownership of property actually located within its jurisdiction. *Perrine v. Pennroad Corp., 19 Del. Ch. 368, 168 A. 196 (1933); Krizanek v. Smith, 32 Del. Ch. 513, 87 A.2d 871 (1952); Jacobs v. Tenney, 316 F. Supp. 151 (D. Del. 1970).*

This section is applicable in suits against nonresidents where a decree is sought, not for money payment, but settling the title to personal property. *Perrine v. Pennroad Corp., 19 Del. Ch. 368, 168 A. 196 (1933).*

The fictional situs of stock under § 169 of Title 8 alone does not pass constitutional muster as a predicate for jurisdiction under this section in an action admittedly seeking to obtain personal liability of a nonresident in connection with transactions unrelated to the forum. *U.S. Indus., Inc. v. Gregg, 540 F.2d 142 (3d Cir. 1976); 433 U.S. 908, 97 S. Ct. 2972, 53 L. Ed. 2d 1091 (1977); Barber-Greene Co. v. Walco Nat'l Corp., 428 F. Supp. 567 (D. Del. 1977).*

This section is a statutory grant of power to bring non-residents before the Court of Chancery by constructive service of process, unattended by seizure, if the suit is one wherein the relief sought relates to the status, title or ownership of property actually located within its jurisdiction. *Arden-Mayfair, Inc. v. Louart Corp., 385 A.2d 3 (Del. Ch. 1978).*

Where a suit does not seek to impose monetary liability on the defendant corporation, its president and vice-president, but rather seeks only to clarify and reinforce the voting rights of shareholders with regard to the election of directors, it is one which seeks a decree as to the status and ownership rights of corporate stock having its situs in Delaware and thus, service on nonresident stockholders by publication under this section would have been sufficient. *Arden-Mayfair, Inc. v. Louart Corp., 385 A.2d 3 (Del. Ch. 1978).*

The word "property" has a broad and comprehensive meaning, including legal and equitable interests in both real and personal property. *Blumenthal v. Blumenthal, 28 Del. Ch. 1, 35 A.2d 831 (1944); 59 A.2d 216 (Del. 1945).*

Property need not be seized. — Where the complaint seeks a decree that certain shares of stock in a Delaware corporation are not subject to a voting trust and that the legal title be decreed to the present holders of the voting trust certificates, since the property in question has its situs in this State, and since so far as the trustees are concerned, the suit simply seeks to determine the legal ownership and control of that property, seizure of it is unnecessary as a prerequisite to jurisdiction over the trustees; service upon them by publication is sufficient. *Perrine v. Pennroad Corp., 19 Del. Ch. 368, 168 A. 196 (1933).*

If the property in question has its situs in Delaware, the jurisdiction of the Court of Chancery is clear and its power broad in compelling obedience to its judgment, whether or not seizure of the res has been made prior to substituted service by notice and publication. *Hodson v. Hodson Corp., 32 Del. Ch. 76, 80 A.2d 180 (1951).*

Service by publication upon nonresident trustees of a Delaware voting trust is valid without seizure of the corporate stock constituting the trust res, providing the relief prayed against the individual defendants is in their official capacity as trustees only. *Smith v. Biggs Boiler Works Co., 32 Del. Ch. 287, 85 A.2d 365 (1951).*

A court is not powerless to bring nonresidents before it by constructive service unattended by seizure in a suit to pass upon the validity of a purported voting trust agreement brought against nonresident trustees although the stock was not registered in their names, since the situs of corporate stock is the domicile of the corporation. *Krizanek v. Smith, 32 Del. Ch. 513, 87 A.2d 871 (1952).*

The Court of Chancery has the right to determine the ownership of stock of Delaware corporations without physical seizure of the certificate. *Haas v. Haas, 35 Del. Ch. 392, 119 A.2d 358 (1955).*

The Delaware court of chancery exercises jurisdiction with respect to the stock of delaware corporations on the theory that for certain purposes such property has its situs in *Delaware. Haas v. Haas, 35 Del. Ch. 392, 119 A.2d 358 (1955).*

Response to in rem process does not create personal liability. — When a nonresident appears solely in response to effective in rem process it would be a constructive fraud upon such nonresident to hold that he might thereby be subjected to personal liability; this is true as a matter of law. *Abercrombie v. Davies, 35 Del. Ch. 354, 118 A.2d 358 (1955).*

The nonresident is reasonably entitled to assume that he or she is appearing only to litigate the subject matter which is the basis of the Court's jurisdiction; to assert an entirely new cause of action after the nonresident has appeared would thus be basically unfair. *Townsend Corp. v. Davidson, 40 Del. Ch. 295, 181 A.2d 219 (1962).*

Thus pleadings cannot be amended to assert new cause of action. — Under the in rem procedure of this section it would be a constructive fraud on appearing nonresident defendants to permit an amendment asserting a completely new cause of action. *Townsend Corp. v. Davidson, 40 Del. Ch. 295, 181 A.2d 219 (1962).*

Trustees have no personal liability in an in rem proceeding concerning trust. — If nonresident trustees of a voting trust should appear simply "as trustees, etc.," their act in so appearing should not result in their being treated as present before the Court in their individual capacities and no accounting relief should be afforded against them as individuals. *Perrine v. Pennroad Corp., 19 Del. Ch. 368, 168 A. 196 (1933).*

Absent party must be given sufficient notice of proceedings. — The presence of the res within the State confers jurisdiction over it, and the absence of a party interested in its disposal cannot serve to stay the jurisdiction's full and complete exercise, provided of course the absent person is given notice in some form recognized by the law as sufficient. *Perrine v. Pennroad Corp., 19 Del. Ch. 368, 168 A. 196 (1933).*

When published notice sufficient. — Where the parties suing were named and the three nonresident trustees were disclosed as the parties being sued, the court in which the bill was filed was stated, and the day on or before which the defendants were required to answer was specifically designated, it was held that the published notice was sufficient. *Perrine v. Pennroad Corp., 19 Del. Ch. 368, 168 A. 196 (1933).*

Chancery Court

Chancery can order seizure and deliverance if defendant defaults. — The Court of Chancery is not without power to effectuate its decree declaring that the cloud of a voting trust should be removed from the title to stock in a Delaware corporation without ever calling upon the trustees to do any personal act in aid of the decree's full effectuation. It could in virtue of the express provisions of this section seize the stock and cause its possession to be delivered. *Perrine v. Pennroad Corp., 19 Del. Ch. 368, 168 A. 196 (1933).*

Voluntary participation in conspiracy may be sufficient contact for the constitutional exercise of jurisdiction under the standard of *International Shoe Co. v. Washington, 326 U.S. 310, 66 S. Ct. 154, 90 L. Ed. 95 (1945),* where the participation is with knowledge of an act to be taken in furtherance of the conspiracy in *Delaware.*

Istituto Bancario Italiano SpA v. Hunter Eng'g Co., 449 A.2d 210 (Del. 1982).

Release of corporate shares held for another. — Once it is called to the court's attention that the interest in corporate shares which have been seized is the property of another, or is held for the benefit of another, then justice requires that the property be released. *Life Assurance Co. v. Associated Investors Int'l Corp., 312 A.2d 337 (Del. Ch. 1973).*

A securities broker-dealer which holds shares in its name that are, in actuality, owned by other parties may have such nominee stock, upon seizure pursuant to a sequestration order, released. *Life Assurance Co. v. Associated Investors Int'l Corp., 312 A.2d 337 (Del. Ch. 1973).*

§ 366. Compelling appearance of nonresident defendant

DELAWARE CASE NOTES — REPORTED

Constitutionality. — The Delaware sequestration procedure reflects a "valid governmental interest" sufficient to justify postponement of a hearing on the deprivation of a significant property interest until after the taking. *Gordon v. Michel, 297 A.2d 420 (Del. Ch. 1972).*

An attachment necessary to secure jurisdiction in a state court is clearly a compelling government interest, such that this section is constitutional. *Gordon v. Michel, 297 A.2d 420 (Del. Ch. 1972).*

Sequestration of property of nonresidents having no substantial contact with State does not violate due process. *U.S. Indus., Inc. v. Gregg, 348 F. Supp. 1004 (D. Del. 1972), rev'd, 540 F.2d 142 (3d Cir. 1976), cert. denied, 433 U.S. 908, 97 S. Ct. 2972, 53 L. Ed. 2d 1091 (1977).*

The acquisition of quasi-in-rem jurisdiction by sequestration is constitutional. *U.S. Indus., Inc. v. Gregg, 58 F.R.D. 469 (D. Del. 1973).*

The general appearance requirement of this section does not violate due process. *U.S. Indus., Inc. v. Gregg, 58 F.R.D. 469 (D. Del. 1973).*

The general appearance rule may give a plaintiff an unfair advantage by allowing him to bring suit on a large claim in a jurisdiction where the original basis for jurisdiction is the presence of property having a comparatively small value, but any such unfairness does not rise to constitutional proportions. *U.S. Indus., Inc. v. Gregg, 58 F.R.D. 469 (D. Del. 1973).*

This section is constitutional. *Wiley v. Copeland, 349 A.2d 211 (Del. 1975).*

This section is not unconstitutional per se and may still be utilized in appropriate circumstances to compel the appearance of a nonresident defendant if the defendant had sufficient minimum contacts with Delaware to support personal jurisdiction. *Bank of Am. Nat'l Trust & Sav. Ass'n v. GAC Properties Credit, Inc., 389 A.2d 1304 (Del. Ch. 1978).*

Shaffer v. Heitner, 433 U.S. 186, 98 S. Ct. 2569, 53 L. Ed. 2d 683 (1977) did not strike down the Delaware sequestration statute. *Grynberg v. Burke, 388 A.2d 443 (Del. Ch. 1978).*

There is nothing in *Shaffer v. Heitner, 433 U.S. 186, 98 S. Ct. 2569, 53 L. Ed. 2d 683 (1977),* which indicates that the United States Supreme Court found this section be be unconstitutional per se. *Bank of Am. Nat'l Trust & Sav. Ass'n v. GAC Properties Credit, Inc., 389 A.2d 1304 (Del. Ch. 1978).*

It is not the procedures provided in this section which were held to be constitutionally impermissible by the United States Supreme Court but rather the fact that these procedures had been used to compel appearance in Delaware of nonresidents who had little or no contact with Delaware prior to a suit being filed. *Bank of Am. Nat'l Trust & Sav. Ass'n v. GAC Properties Credit, Inc., 389 A.2d 1304 (Del. Ch. 1978).*

Application of this section carries a Delaware court onto thin constitutional ice, since there remain few situations in which seizure of property may form a proper basis for the exercise of personal jurisdiction. *Cable Adv. Networks, Inc. v. DeWoody, 632 A.2d 1383 (Del. Ch. 1993).*

"Nonresident" defined. — The term "nonresident" in this section refers to a defendant's physical absence from *Delaware. Wife v. Husband, 271 A.2d 51 (Del. Ch. 1970).*

Where there can be a reasonable inference from allegations that defendant did indeed leave his or her usual place of residence and is no longer resident in the State in the sense of "presence" or otherwise, defendant is a nonresident of Delaware within the meaning of this section. *Wife v. Husband, 271 A.2d 51 (Del. Ch. 1970).*

A defendant who leaves the State for a substantial period of time, with no indication of his or her destination, who leaves no evidence of intent to return here, and who has maintained no residence of any kind within the State, is a nonresident in the sense contemplated by this section. *Wife v. Husband, 271 A.2d 51 (Del. Ch. 1970).*

The word "property" has a broad and comprehensive meaning, including legal and equitable interests in both real and personal property. *Blumenthal v. Blumen-*

thal, 28 Del. Ch. 1, 35 A.2d 831 (1944); 59 A.2d 216 (Del. 1945); Weinress v. Bland, 31 Del. Ch. 269, 71 A.2d 59 (1950); U.S. Indus., Inc. v. Gregg, 348 F. Supp. 1004 (D. Del. 1972), rev'd, 540 F.2d 142 (3d Cir. 1976), cert. denied, 433 U.S. 908, 97 S. Ct. 2972, 53 L. Ed. 2d 1091 (1977).

Defendant cannot have waived defenses until after section declared unconstitutional. — A nonresident defendant cannot be held to have waived the defenses of lack of jurisdiction and invalid service of process until after the former contrary line of precedents were struck down by *Shaffer v. Heitner, 433 U.S. 186, 98 S. Ct. 2569, 53 L. Ed. 2d 683 (1977),* which held this section unconstitutional. *Tuckman v. Aerosonic Corp., 394 A.2d 226 (Del. Ch. 1978).*

But, once unconstitutionality known, can waive by delay. — A nonresident defendant's failure to assert the defenses of lack of jurisdiction and insufficiency of process promptly results in a waiver where a lapse of 82 days takes place between the time the defendant files a motion to dismiss and the time the defendant first knows that this section was declared unconstitutional by the *United States Supreme Court. Tuckman v. Aerosonic Corp., 394 A.2d 226 (Del. Ch. 1978).*

Minimum contacts required. — In order to subject a defendant to a judgment, if the defendant is not present within the territory of the forum, the defendant must have certain minimum contacts with it such that the maintenance of the suit does not offend traditional notions of fair play and substantial justice. *Shaffer v. Heitner, 433 U.S. 186, 97 S. Ct. 2569, 53 L. Ed. 2d 683 (1977).*

Relationship among defendant, forum and litigation is central concern of the inquiry into personal jurisdiction. *Shaffer v. Heitner, 433 U.S. 186, 97 S. Ct. 2569, 53 L. Ed. 2d 683 (1977).*

And nonresident defendant must have sufficient contacts, ties or relations with forum state for that state to give its courts jurisdiction over that defendant. *Shaffer v. Heitner, 433 U.S. 186, 97 S. Ct. 2569, 53 L. Ed. 2d 683 (1977).*

Nonresident defendants must have purposefully availed themselves of privilege of conducting activities within Delaware in a way that would justify bringing them before a Delaware tribunal. *Shaffer v. Heitner, 433 U.S. 186, 97 S. Ct. 2569, 53 L. Ed. 2d 683 (1977).*

Where abundance of contacts are present, service of process under this section would not violate constitutional due process, and consequently it would be proper to attach property interests located in Delaware as a means to coerce a nonresident defendant to appear and defend the action on its merits. *Grynberg v. Burke, 388 A.2d 443 (Del. Ch. 1978).*

Number of minimum contacts distinguished by nature of action. — The number of minimum contacts required to support substituted service of process on nonresident defendants is much less in the case of actions alleging the commission of a tort than in actions alleging breach of contract or arising out of doing business. *Bank of Am. Nat'l Trust & Sav. Ass'n v. GAC Properties Credit, Inc., 389 A.2d 1304 (Del. Ch. 1978).*

Conflict of laws. — Although the law of Michigan determines the nature and extent of a residuary legatee's interest in stock constituting part of a residuary estate, the law of Delaware controls the question of whether such interest may be sequestered under this section. *Cheff v. Athlone Indus., Inc., 43 Del. Ch. 394, 233 A.2d 170 (1967).*

Delaware law would clearly apply in determining rights to property having a situs here and seized pursuant to Delaware's sequestration statute. *Wimpfheimer v. Goldsmith, 298 A.2d 778 (Del. Ch. 1972).*

Where a loan transaction was negotiated and closed in Florida, the laws of Florida determine the nature and extent of defendant's interest, if any, in the stock, but the law of Delaware controls the question of whether any such interest may be sequestered under this section. *U.S. Indus., Inc. v. Gregg, 348 F. Supp. 1004 (D. Del. 1972), rev'd, 540 F.2d 142 (3d Cir. 1976), cert. denied, 433 U.S. 908, 97 S. Ct. 2972, 53 L. Ed. 2d 1091 (1977).*

Where an alleged interest in a security arises in a foreign jurisdiction the law of that jurisdiction governs the existence of the interest and presumably its nature, and the law of Delaware determines whether the interest is one which may be sequestered. *Baker v. Gotz, 387 F. Supp. 1381 (D. Del. 1975); 523 F.2d 1050 (3d Cir. 1975).*

This section does not broaden or eliminate federal venue requirements. *United States v. Stone, 59 F.R.D. 260 (D. Del. 1973).*

Before employing state procedures, a party must satisfy federal venue and jurisdiction standards. *United States v. Stone, 59 F.R.D. 260 (D. Del. 1973).*

Sequestration procedures available in federal court action. — Federal enforcement of tax lien may be characterized as an "equitable" proceeding, and sequestration procedures of the Court of Chancery may be available in a federal court action. *United States v. Stone, 59 F.R.D. 260 (D. Del. 1973).*

The sole primary purpose of this section is to compel the appearance of a nonresident in an action in the Court of *Chancery. Weinress v. Bland, 31 Del. Ch. 269, 71 A.2d 59 (1950); E.M. Fleischmann Lumber Corp. v. Resources Corp. Int'l, 33 Del. Ch. 587, 98 A.2d 506 (1953); Lefcourt Realty Corp. v. Sands, 35 Del. Ch. 164, 113 A.2d 428 (1955); Trans World Airlines v. Hughes Tool Co., 41 Del. Ch. 11, 187 A.2d 350 (1962); Wife v. Husband, 271 A.2d 51 (Del. Ch. 1970); Winitz v. Kline, 288 A.2d 456 (Del. Ch. 1971); Hughes Tool Co. v. Fawcett Publications, Inc., 290 A.2d 693 (Del. Ch. 1972).*

The purpose of this section is to compel the personal appearance of a nonresident owning property where a sale of the seized property is necessary to render effectual relief. *United States v. Stone, 59 F.R.D. 260 (D. Del. 1973).*

The purpose of the General Assembly in this section was to confer on the Chancellor wide authority for the compulsion of appearance and the satisfaction of decrees, leaving the Chancellor to devise, in the particular case, the method best suited to accomplish the purpose. *United States v. Loft, Inc., 25 Del. Ch. 363, 19 A.2d 721 (1941); Weinress v. Bland, 31 Del. Ch. 269, 71 A.2d 59 (1950).*

A plaintiff in the Court of Chancery may use this section to seize a nonresident's property not only to force the

Chancery Court

nonresident's appearance, but in case he or she fails to appear, to sell the property to satisfy the plaintiff's claim to the extent of the sequestered property. *Jacobs v. Tenney, 316 F. Supp. 151 (D. Del. 1970).*

The express purpose of the Delaware sequestration procedure is to compel a nonresident to enter a personal appearance. *Shaffer v. Heitner, 433 U.S. 186, 97 S. Ct. 2569, 53 L. Ed. 2d 683 (1977).*

And it authorizes sequestration of nonresident's Delaware property. — The sequestration of property in Delaware owned by a nonresident defendant for the purpose of compelling the appearance of such a defendant in an action for a money judgment is authorized by this section. *Baker v. Gotz, 336 F. Supp. 197 (D. Del. 1971),* aff'd, *492 F.2d 1238 (3d Cir. 1974),* cert. denied, *417 U.S. 955, 94 S. Ct. 3084, 41 L. Ed. 2d 674 (1974).*

Where nonresidence is alleged and a monetary claim in any amount is asserted, a defendant's property may be seized. *Widder v. Leeds, 317 A.2d 32 (Del. Ch. 1974).*

This section, on its face, authorizes the seizure of nonresident defendants' property within the State of Delaware, for purposes of compelling a nonresident to appear in the Court of *Chancery. Cable Adv. Networks, Inc. v. DeWoody, 632 A.2d 1383 (Del. Ch. 1993).*

Sequestration is analogous to foreign attachment. — This section undertakes to provide for equity a procedure analogous to that of foreign attachment at law. *Cantor v. Sachs, 18 Del. Ch. 359, 162 A. 73 (1932); Sands v. Lefcourt Realty Corp., 35 Del. Ch. 340, 117 A.2d 365 (1955); Schwartz v. Miner, 36 Del. Ch. 481, 133 A.2d 599 (1957); Trans World Airlines v. Hughes, 40 Del. Ch. 523, 185 A.2d 762 (1962); Wife v. Husband, 271 A.2d 51 (Del. Ch. 1970); J.B.G. v. P.J.G., 286 A.2d 256 (Del. Ch. 1971); Gordon v. Michel, 297 A.2d 420 (Del. Ch. 1972).*

Sequestration by chancery is analogous to foreign attachment at law in the procedure to be followed in both instances and in the ultimate relief sought by such process; that is, the compulsion upon a nonresident defendant to make a general appearance in the particular court. *Garretson v. Garretson, 306 A.2d 737 (Del. 1973).*

Sequestration in equity is simply analogous to foreign attachment at law. *D'Angelo v. Petroleos Mexicanos, 378 F. Supp. 1034 (D. Del. 1974).*

In enacting the first sequestration statute, sequestration was viewed as analogous to foreign attachment and interpretations of the sequestration statute were often made by referring to the policy that prevailed in foreign attachment. *Papendick v. Bosch, 389 A.2d 1315 (Del. Super. Ct. 1978); 410 A.2d 148 (Del. 1979); 446 U.S. 909, 100 S. Ct. 1837, 64 L. Ed. 2d 262 (1980).*

But sequestration is broader than legal attachment. — Sequestration under this section has been recognized as foreign attachment in equity but there is an important difference between the foreign attachment and sequestration statutes since this section requires only a showing that the defendant "is a nonresident of the State of Delaware" in order to obtain an order of sequestration but § 3506 of this title requires a showing both that the defendant is "not an inhabitant" of the State and also that

the defendant "cannot be found." *Jacobs v. Tenney, 316 F. Supp. 151 (D. Del. 1970).*

Section 3506 of this title relating to foreign attachment at law provides that a writ of foreign attachment may issue upon "proof satisfactory to the Court, ... that plaintiff has a good cause of action against the defendant in a sum exceeding $50," but this section contains neither requirement and if nonresidence is alleged, and a monetary claim in any amount is asserted, the defendant's property may be seized. *Hughes v. TWA, 40 Del. Ch. 552, 185 A.2d 886 (1962).*

Due to wider inherent powers of chancery. — The wider scope of equitable seizure flows primarily from the wider inherent powers of the Court of Chancery over property not attachable at law. *Sands v. Lefcourt Realty Corp., 35 Del. Ch. 340, 117 A.2d 365 (1955).*

Chancery not governed by rules of attachment at law. — In seizing shares of stock for the purpose of compelling nonresident corporate defendants to appear the Court of Chancery is not governed by the provisions of attachment at law. *Greene v. Johnston, 34 Del. Ch. 115, 99 A.2d 627, 42 A.L.R. 2d 906 (1953).*

Sequestration order will be issued as a matter of course. — Upon application for an order of sequestration plaintiff is required by court rule to establish that the nonresident not only owned property in Delaware but that the other requirements of the applicable statute and rule had been met and this having been done, an order of sequestration issued as a matter of course. *Trans World Airlines v. Hughes, 40 Del. Ch. 523, 185 A.2d 762 (1962).*

When this section says that the Court "may" compel appearance by seizure of property, use of the verb "may" is without significance since the litigant is entitled to the process as a matter of right. *Breech v. Hughes Tool Co., 41 Del. Ch. 128, 189 A.2d 428 (1963).*

Ex parte motion for sequestration. — The Court of Chancery has the power to deny an ex parte motion for sequestration. *Cable Adv. Networks, Inc. v. DeWoody, 632 A.2d 1383 (Del. Ch. 1993).*

The issuance of an ex parte order seizing a defendant's property in this state is not a matter of right, in the sense that only ministerial acts are necessary in order to effectuate it; rather, when seizure is employed to effectuate jurisdiction, in order to satisfy the requirements of due process, it is necessary, at a minimum, for a judicial officer to evaluate the exigency that is said to justify the deviation from the procedures normally mandated before a court may constitutionally interfere with the exercise of property rights. *Cable Adv. Networks, Inc. v. DeWoody, 632 A.2d 1383 (Del. Ch. 1993).*

Plaintiff's complaint is within scope of this section. — If a complainant seeks to make use of the benefits of this section providing in substance for attachment in limine of the defendant's property to be held to abide and satisfy the final decree, the complainant must bring his or her case within the plain purview of its terms. *Cantor v. Sachs, 18 Del. Ch. 359, 162 A. 73 (1932).*

Unless the precise requirements of this section are complied with, there may be no order of sequestration. *Gluck v. Chashin, 42 Del. Ch. 325, 210 A.2d 855 (1965).*

Or seizure of property will be vacated. — If the case of the complainants does not fall clearly within the scope of this section the seizure which has been made must be vacated. *Cantor v. Sachs, 18 Del. Ch. 359, 162 A. 73 (1932).*

And party need not be original plaintiff. — The use of the procedure under this section should not be denied to a party merely because it is not an original plaintiff and if a claim for affirmative relief is being asserted by such party against a nonresident. *Trans World Airlines v. Hughes, 40 Del. Ch. 523, 185 A.2d 762 (1962).*

This section was drafted with the idea that limited appearances would not be available. *U.S. Indus., Inc. v. Gregg, 58 F.R.D. 469 (D. Del. 1973).*

There is a legitimate public interest behind the general appearance rule. If a state or federal court is required by a defendant's response to a complaint to try and determine all of the issues upon which an in personam claim turns, there is a public interest in having that expenditure of judicial resources settle the rights of the parties with respect to that claim and in not leaving open the possibility of subsequent, duplicative litigation in the same court or another. *U.S. Indus., Inc. v. Gregg, 58 F.R.D. 469 (D. Del. 1973).*

Nonresidency of the defendant must be apparent from the complaint. — This section does not lay down any requirement as to how the address of the defendant shall be ascertained to which the notice by mail may be sent; all that it provides is that the bill of complaint must show that the defendant is not a Delaware resident. *Cantor v. Sachs, 18 Del. Ch. 359, 162 A. 73 (1932).*

The statutory language of this section is plain on its face and requires the fact of nonresidency to be alleged in the complaint and the language admits of no other meaning, and, consequently, the failure to make the required allegation defeats the right to an order of sequestration. *Gluck v. Chashin, 42 Del. Ch. 325, 210 A.2d 855 (1965).*

This section merely requires that the nonresidence of a defendant be apparent upon reading the complaint. *United States v. Sinclair, 347 F. Supp. 1129 (D. Del. 1972), appeal dismissed, 498 F.2d 847 (3d Cir. 1974).*

A failure to set forth the defendant's nonresidence in the complaint is fatal to an application for an order of sequestration pursuant to that complaint. *United States v. Sinclair, 347 F. Supp. 1129 (D. Del. 1972), appeal dismissed, 498 F.2d 847 (3d Cir. 1974).*

But the language is not so strict as to require the use of the word "nonresident;" it is sufficient if the complaint discloses nonresidency. *United States v. Sinclair, 347 F. Supp. 1129 (D. Del. 1972), appeal dismissed, 498 F.2d 847 (3d Cir. 1974).*

When a complaint alleges that an estate is being administered outside the jurisdiction of the court, this allegation appears to meet the literal requirement of this section that the complaint allege nonresidency. While the word nonresident is not used, the lack of personal jurisdiction over the estate is apparent upon reading the complaint. *United States v. Sinclair, 347 F. Supp. 1129 (D. Del. 1972), appeal dismissed, 498 F.2d 847 (3d Cir. 1974).*

Burden on nonresident defendants who entered general appearances. — Nonresident defendants who entered general appearances which released their Delaware property from sequestration order had the burden of demonstrating at an evidentiary hearing that the reason for entering the general appearances was to obtain release from the sequestration order. *Grynberg v. Burke, 388 A.2d 443 (Del. Ch. 1978).*

The burden is placed upon the nonresident defendant to show that a general appearance was entered by compulsion in response to the sequestration and seizure of his or her property. *Bank of Am. Nat'l Trust & Sav. Ass'n v. GAC Properties Credit, Inc., 389 A.2d 1304 (Del. Ch. 1978).*

Entering general appearance did not waive right to challenge constitutionality of sequestration. — Nonresident defendants, by entering general appearances which released their Delaware property from a sequestration order, did not thereby waive their right to challenge the constitutionality of the sequestration as to them when, as of the time of their decision to enter the general appearances, their constitutional right to resist such process based upon insufficient contacts with Delaware had not been judicially declared to exist. *Grynberg v. Burke, 388 A.2d 443 (Del. Ch. 1978).*

Plaintiff under federal securities act of 1933 has benefit of general appearance rule. — Delaware practice provides for in personam jurisdiction over the defendant if the defendant appears to defend on the merits. Presumably, Congress contemplated that a Delaware plaintiff asserting a claim under the federal Securities Act of 1933 would have the benefit of this rule. *U.S. Indus., Inc. v. Gregg, 58 F.R.D. 469 (D. Del. 1973).*

Nothing in the federal Securities Act of 1933 would provide a basis for a claim that Delaware would be required to apply federal law on limited appearances, and in the absence of some such basis in the federal law, the state courts are free to follow their own rules in a concurrent jurisdiction case. *U.S. Indus., Inc. v. Gregg, 58 F.R.D. 469 (D. Del. 1973).*

There is no need to show that the defendant cannot be found; a showing of nonresidence of a defendant is all that is required to obtain a seizure order under this section. *Jacobs v. Tenney, 316 F. Supp. 151 (D. Del. 1970).*

Notice must be given to the defendant. — This section does direct notice to the defendant in unmistakable terms. *Cantor v. Sachs, 18 Del. Ch. 359, 162 A. 73 (1932).*

Notice of the nature and kind of relief sought is particularly important to a nonresident defendant whose property is seized under this section because he can only defend by entering a general appearance. *Steinberg v. Shields, 38 Del. Ch. 349, 152 A.2d 113 (1959).*

And method of publication must be reasonable. — If the Court should resort to such a method of publication and for such a length of time as would be unreasonable as a vehicle of notice, due process of law would invalidate its proceedings, not because this section is vulnerable but because the Court's method of carrying out its mandatory provisions could not be said reasonably to effect a service upon the defendant. *Cantor v. Sachs, 18 Del. Ch. 359, 162 A. 73 (1932).*

Chancery Court

Publication for once a week for three consecutive weeks, if conducted under circumstances of reasonable notoriety, would alone be sufficient to satisfy the requirements of due process, unless possibly the defendants were known to be so far distant that by no reasonable probability could the notice get to them in time to be of practical value. *Cantor v. Sachs, 18 Del. Ch. 359, 162 A. 73 (1932).*

But sequence of seizure and notice not important. — As between seizure of the res on the one hand and notice to the owner on the other, which shall precede the other seems to be merely a question of regulation or method, so long as notice to the owner and an opportunity to be heard are secured; it is a mere matter of procedural sequence. *Cantor v. Sachs, 18 Del. Ch. 359, 162 A. 73 (1932).*

And the due process clause does not require notice before a sequestration order issues. *Gordon v. Michel, 297 A.2d 420 (Del. Ch. 1972).*

This section must be construed to contemplate an effective seizure. *Greene v. Allen, 33 Del. Ch. 508, 96 A.2d 349 (1953).*

And seizure may be ex parte. — This section empowers the Court of Chancery to seize property having a situs in this State of a nonresident to compel the nonresident's appearance in a pending action; the order is often issued ex parte, without prior notice to the nonresident or opportunity to be heard and notice of the sequestration is thereafter given by mail and publication. *Gordon v. Michel, 297 A.2d 420 (Del. Ch. 1972).*

But seizure must be soon enough to give defendant opportunity to appear. — The object of the seizure is "to compel" the appearance of the defendant. Since the seizure is to bring the defendant before the Court by compulsory appearance, it must follow that any seizure which occurred too late to afford the defendant an opportunity to appear, which it is the object of the seizure to compel, would not be in accordance with the true meaning of this section. *Cantor v. Sachs, 18 Del. Ch. 359, 162 A. 73 (1932).*

Defendant in possession of seized property deemed to have notice. — If there is a seizure under this section the owner-defendant who is deemed to be in possession of the seized property either by personally or through an agent, must be taken to be informed of the seizure as a matter of course. *Cantor v. Sachs, 18 Del. Ch. 359, 162 A. 73 (1932).*

Property must be reasonably identified. — This section contemplates an effective seizure and there can be an effective seizure of equitable interests only where those interests appear of record or are identified with reasonable certainty in a court order. *Cannon v. Union Chem. & Materials Corp., 37 Del. Ch. 399, 144 A.2d 145 (1958).*

A specification of the property to be seized is ordinarily required, and for this purpose a direction to seize all shares of stock of the nonresident defendant in a named corporation is a sufficient identification in respect of shares and interests held of record and appearing on the corporate books, but in respect of unrecorded equitable interests the plaintiff's affidavit and the court's order should not only specify the name of the corporation issuing the shares but should also contain an identification of the shares sufficient to enable the corporation to make adequate notations of the seizure upon its books. *Greene v. Johnston, 34 Del. Ch. 115, 99 A.2d 627, 42 A.L.R. 2d 906 (1953).*

Where no court order directing seizure of stock for the purpose of compelling nonresident corporate defendant to appear has been entered, effective seizure of the stock has not been made. *Greene v. Johnston, 34 Del. Ch. 115, 99 A.2d 627, 42 A.L.R.2d 906 (1953).*

The reason the description of a sequestration order must be made with some particularity is to protect the corporation when it enters a stop transfer order against the sequestered stock and to protect the interest of innocent third parties. *Yancey v. National Trust Co., 251 A.2d 561 (Del. 1969).*

And it is plaintiff's duty to reasonably identify property to be seized. — The responsibility to provide information sufficient to permit the sequestrator to make an effective seizure is upon the party seeking to invoke this statutory jurisdiction. *Greene v. Allen, 33 Del. Ch. 508, 96 A.2d 349 (1953).*

Sequestration vacated where plaintiff does not establish authority to sue. — Inasmuch as plaintiff's authority as a receiver of a dissolved corporation to sue in federal court was challenged by the defendant, the burden rested upon the plaintiff to establish that authority and unless, within a period of 15 days, the plaintiff presented to the Court of Chancery an application for authority to continue the prosecution of the instant suit and to retain an attorney for the purpose, the suit would be dismissed and the purported sequestration of defendant's property would be vacated. *D'Angelo v. Petroleos Mexicanos, 373 F. Supp. 1076 (D. Del. 1974).*

Affidavit held critically incomplete. — Where an affidavit did not state what property garnishee had prior to service of the sequestration order and did not state what property it held which was legally owned by the defendant, and since the order of sequestration was directed to the legal as well as the beneficial title held at or prior to service, the affidavit was incomplete in critical respects. *Kolyba Corp. v. Banque Nationale De Paris, 316 A.2d 585 (Del. Ch. 1973).*

A party who secures a sequestration order cannot have discovery, as a matter of course, against a garnishee. *Kolyba Corp. v. Banque Nationale De Paris, 316 A.2d 585 (Del. Ch. 1973).*

To get discovery, a party securing a sequestration order must do more than simply assert disagreement with the report by the garnishee or a general desire to test it, as the party must make some showing to persuade the Court that discovery is reasonable and necessary. *Kolyba Corp. v. Banque Nationale De Paris, 316 A.2d 585 (Del. Ch. 1973).*

Complainant must aid court in locating defendant. — In view of the duty laid upon the Court to notify the defendant by mail, it would be the duty of the Court to exact some showing from the complainant of where the defendant could be found or some excuse as to why such information is unavailing. *Cantor v. Sachs, 18 Del. Ch. 359, 162 A. 73 (1932).*

Order seizing property not belonging to defendant will be quashed. — When property not owned by a defendant has been seized by order of the Court entered pursuant to this section, the order should be quashed and the property released from sequestration. *Jacobs v. Tenney, 316 F. Supp. 151 (D. Del. 1970).*

Once it is brought to the attention of the Court that the interest seized pursuant to a sequestration order is actually held for the benefit of another, justice requires that it be released. *Widder v. Leeds, 317 A.2d 32 (Del. Ch. 1974).*

Seizure of property does not vest title in sequestrator. — The seizure of property under this section does not vest title in the Court's appointee called, for convenience, a "sequestrator," since in the event the plaintiff procures a judgment, this section calls for a sale of the seized property to satisfy such judgment in the event the property is not released and consequently, the considerations which militate against attaching unmatured and contingent obligations do not apply under the procedure set up by this section. *Weinress v. Bland, 31 Del. Ch. 269, 71 A.2d 59 (1950).*

And sequestrator is not fiduciary within the meaning of federal tax laws. — When property is seized under this section, it is in custodia legis, and the person who was appointed to make the seizure is not a "fiduciary" within the meaning of the federal statutes relating to income tax payments by fiduciaries. *United States v. Loft, Inc., 25 Del. Ch. 363, 19 A.2d 721 (1941).*

But sequestrator does have possession. — A Delaware sequestrator who has seized stock having a statutory situs in Delaware and which can be sold under order of the Chancery Court, is "in possession" thereof within the meaning of the Florida Nonclaim Act, even though sequestrator does not have actual physical possession of the stock certificates. *Wimpfheimer v. Goldsmith, 298 A.2d 778 (Del. Ch. 1972).*

Field of property subject to seizure not enlarged. — Section 365 of this title and this section, respectively, authorize seizure of property in equity (sequestration) in proceedings strictly in rem and quasi in rem. They do not undertake to enlarge the field of property subject to seizure. *Baker v. Gotz, 387 F. Supp. 1381 (D. Del. 1975); 523 F.2d 1050 (3d Cir. 1975).*

Value of property seized must be reasonably related to claim. — There is no limitation contained in this section as to the seizure of a nonresident's property in Delaware, although the property so caused to be seized should always bear some reasonable relationship to the amount of the claim asserted. *Trans World Airlines v. Hughes, 40 Del. Ch. 523, 185 A.2d 762 (1962).*

Property seized under this section is generally released upon the appearance of its owner. *Trans World Airlines v. Hughes, 40 Del. Ch. 523, 185 A.2d 762 (1962).*

The authority of the sequestrator is derived solely from the order of the Court, and it must describe specifically the property to be seized when there is an equitable interest involved. *Winitz v. Kline, 288 A.2d 456 (Del. Ch. 1971).*

Seized property may not be turned over to the plaintiff. — The court can do with the seized property only that which this section permits, and it does not authorize a turnover of such property to a successful plaintiff. *Wife v. Husband, 271 A.2d 51 (Del. Ch. 1970).*

Control of investment of seized property. — A person whose corporate securities are seized in Delaware is normally given the right to control the investment of such seized property pending his or her appearance. *Trans World Airlines v. Hughes Tool Co., 41 Del. Ch. 11, 187 A.2d 350 (1962).*

The burden on the plaintiff under this section to have the court not release defendant's property, in a case concerned with claims against a nonresident based on the nonresident's alleged violation of a covenant not to disclose information he or she acquired as a result of long-term employment by plaintiff, will be to show that if successful in this litigation, the plaintiff will be the beneficiary of a judgment in excess of the unitemized inventory of his or her net assets. *Hughes Tool Co. v. Fawcett Publications, Inc., 290 A.2d 693 (Del. Ch. 1972).*

Upon the entry of a general appearance by a nonresident defendant whose property has been seized, the Court is required to release the property unless the plaintiff can show reasonable possibility of failing to obtain satisfaction of any judgment. The philosophy embodied in this section is clear. Since the entry of a general appearance is the condition of the release of the seized property, the object of seizure is to compel that kind of appearance. *Sands v. Lefcourt Realty Corp., 35 Del. Ch. 340, 117 A.2d 365 (1955).*

Under this section, upon making a general appearance, defendant is entitled to have his or her property released unless plaintiff satisfies the Court that because of other circumstances there is a reasonable possibility that such release may render it substantially less likely that he or she will obtain satisfaction for any judgment secured. *Gordon v. Michel, 297 A.2d 420 (Del. Ch. 1972).*

Negotiable instruments cannot be validly sequestered without physical seizure of the security certificates. *Baker v. Gotz, 387 F. Supp. 1381 (D. Del. 1975); 523 F.2d 1050 (3d Cir. 1975).*

A negotiable instrument, other than stock, was not and is not subject to sequestration without seizure of the instrument. This was also the intended effect of 6 Del. C. § 8-317 in the form enacted by the *General Assembly. Baker v. Gotz, 387 F. Supp. 1381 (D. Del. 1975); 523 F.2d 1050 (3d Cir. 1975).*

This section covers those cases only where a money decree is sought. *Wightman v. San Francisco Bay Toll-Bridge Co., 16 Del. Ch. 200, 142 A. 783 (1928).*

The proceeding by way of seizure of property of nonresidents must be confined to cases where the eventual outcome to which the case looks is a possible sale. *Wightman v. San Francisco Bay Toll-Bridge Co., 16 Del. Ch. 200, 142 A. 783 (1928).*

Chancery Court

This section applies to suits against nonresidents only in cases where a money decree is sought. *Perrine v. Pennroad Corp., 19 Del. Ch. 368, 168 A. 196 (1933).*

This section applies only to cases where a sale is necessary to render effectual the nature of relief which the complainant's bill seeks. *E.M. Fleischmann Lumber Corp. v. Resources Corp. Int'l, 33 Del. Ch. 587, 98 A.2d 506 (1953).*

Proceedings under this section must be confined to cases where the eventual outcome to which the action looks, should the defendant shun the jurisdiction of Delaware, is where a sale of sequestered property is necessary to render effectual the nature of the relief sought in the complaint. *Buechner v. Farbenfabriken Bayer Aktiengesellschaft, 38 Del. Ch. 329, 151 A.2d 125 (1959); 154 A.2d 684 (Del. 1959).*

The argument that by "complaint" this section means "a pleading which states a claim for relief against the nonresident" is invalid; it is sufficient that the complaint, regardless of its merits, is on its face a bona fide one stating a claim for monetary damage. *Hughes v. TWA, 40 Del. Ch. 552, 185 A.2d 886 (1962).*

The sequestration of property in Delaware owned by a nonresident defendant for the purpose of compelling the appearance of such a defendant in an action for a money judgment is authorized by this section. *Baker v. Gotz, 336 F. Supp. 197 (D. Del. 1971),* aff'd, *492 F.2d 1238 (3d Cir. 1974),* cert. denied, *417 U.S. 955, 94 S. Ct. 3084, 41 L. Ed. 2d 674 (1974).*

Or a suit for rescission. — Where the prayer is for rescission and not for a money payment, this section is applicable, because an order for rescission could be entered by this Court and, if not obeyed, then alternative relief in the form of a money judgment and sale could be granted under the general prayer for relief. *E.M. Fleischmann Lumber Corp. v. Resources Corp. Int'l, 33 Del. Ch. 587, 98 A.2d 506 (1953).*

And complaint for general relief will not justify a sequestration order. — Where only prayer for relief which is applicable to the defendants is the prayer for general relief, it doesn't justify the issuance of the sequestration process under this section against the moving defendants, particularly where, the propriety of the process is seasonably attacked; the allegations do not constitute adequate notice to these defendants as to the nature of the remedy, if any, sought against them. *Steinberg v. Shields, 38 Del. Ch. 349, 152 A.2d 113 (1959).*

Nor will suit involving property rights. — If the relief sought in a suit for equitable execution of corporate stock directly involved rights in property, this section will not be applicable to the service of process on a nonresident transferee. *Blumenthal v. Blumenthal, 28 Del. Ch. 1, 35 A.2d 831 (1944); 59 A.2d 216 (Del. 1945).*

This section affords to a nonresident defendant an election as to whether or not to appear or to default. *Townsend Corp. v. Davidson, 40 Del. Ch. 295, 181 A.2d 219 (1962).*

Defendant is made to suffer consequences for not appearing. — If a foreign defendant owning property in Delaware does not voluntarily appear in a suit, it may nevertheless be made to suffer the consequences of any proper decree which may ultimately be rendered against it, provided, it is constructively brought before the Court in the manner provided by the provisions of this section. *Bouree v. Trust Francais, 14 Del. Ch. 332, 127 A. 56 (1924).*

But the special appearance device has been abolished by the rules of court, and this applies to sequestration cases. *Schwartz v. Miner, 36 Del. Ch. 481, 133 A.2d 599 (1957).*

And motion to dismiss for lack of jurisdiction is used. — The purpose formerly served by granting leave to appear specially to attack jurisdiction is now fulfilled by the filing of a motion to dismiss for lack of jurisdiction, etc., as provided by Chancery Court Rule 12(b). If the motion is denied, the defendant may then elect whether or not to subject himself to the Court's jurisdiction generally by continuing to defend the action. *Schwartz v. Miner, 36 Del. Ch. 481, 133 A.2d 599 (1957).*

Test of validity of foreign attachment of indebtedness due from garnishee to nonresident defendant. — It has long been the general rule in Delaware that the test of the validity of a foreign attachment of an indebtedness due from a garnishee to a nonresident defendant is whether the defendant has the right to sue the garnishee in Delaware to recover the debt. If the defendant does, the attachment is valid; if the defendant does not, the indebtedness is beyond the reach of the attachment writ. *D'Angelo v. Petroleos Mexicanos, 378 F. Supp. 1034 (D. Del. 1974).*

Fact that debt sequestered may have been payable outside of Delaware is not important. *D'Angelo v. Petroleos Mexicanos, 378 F. Supp. 1034 (D. Del. 1974).*

Limits of liability when merits not contested. — The judgment finally entered in a proceeding under this section though in form a personal one, is nevertheless effective, in the absence of the appearance of the defendant, only to the extent that the seized property is capable of satisfying it. The jurisdiction of the Court in such case is based solely on the presence of the property within the reach of its process. *Cantor v. Sachs, 18 Del. Ch. 359, 162 A. 73 (1932).*

And when defendant contests merits. — This section does not offer a middle way, permitting a defendant whose property is attached to contest the merits of plaintiff's claim, and if unsuccessful, to have liability limited to the value of the seized property. *Lefcourt Realty Corp. v. Sands, 35 Del. Ch. 164, 113 A.2d 428 (1955).*

There is no limited appearance under this section. — The clear meaning and intent of this section precludes the adoption in Delaware of the limited-appearance rule. *Sands v. Lefcourt Realty Corp., 35 Del. Ch. 340, 117 A.2d 365 (1955).*

But defendant's liability is limited to the causes in the original complaint. — The provision of this section authorizing the entry of an order directing the nonresident defendant to appear is a grant of power based upon a complaint as then filed and the use of the words "in the cause," advises a defendant that he or she is called upon to appear to respond to the charges as then asserted.

Townsend Corp. v. Davidson, 40 Del. Ch. 295, 181 A.2d 219 (1962).

A nonresident whose property has been seized by sequestration is entitled to assume that appearance is to litigate only those causes of action in the original complaint. *Tenney v. Jacobs, 43 Del. Ch. 526, 240 A.2d 138 (1968).*

Nature of property is not material. — The primary purpose of the seizure is to compel appearance in a lawsuit, and to this purpose neither the nature of the property seized nor its incidental connection with the lawsuit seems material. *Breech v. Hughes Tool Co., 41 Del. Ch. 128, 189 A.2d 428 (1963).*

Sequestered property not necessarily coinciding with all property which plaintiff attempted to sequester. — The validity of sequestration does not depend upon the property in fact sequestered coinciding with all of the property which plaintiff has attempted to sequester, as long as some of it does. *D'Angelo v. Petroleos Mexicanos, 378 F. Supp. 1034 (D. Del. 1974).*

Because sequestrator was unable to find all of property sought to be seized does not constitutionally invalidate the seizure of indebtedness which is described in the affidavit. *D'Angelo v. Petroleos Mexicanos, 378 F. Supp. 1034 (D. Del. 1974).*

Interests must be identifiable and saleable. — Even if the defendants had beneficial interests in stock of a corporation at the date the notice of seizure was served, if those interests were not of record, the Court of Chancery would not have obtained jurisdiction unless those interests were sufficiently identified in the papers served upon the corporation to enable the corporation to make appropriate notations of the seizure on its books. *Cannon v. Union Chem. & Materials Corp., 37 Del. Ch. 399, 144 A.2d 145 (1958).*

Where no direct interest subject to sale is held in property there exists no interest subject to sequestration. *Cheff v. Athlone Indus., Inc., 43 Del. Ch. 394, 233 A.2d 170 (1967).*

To be seizable under an order of sequestration based on this section, an equitable interest must be owned beneficially by the nonresident, it must be capable of being sold, it must be capable of effective seizure, and it must be readily identifiable. *Winitz v. Kline, 288 A.2d 456 (Del. Ch. 1971).*

Delaware courts confronted with questions of whether interests in stock were sequesterable, have asked whether the specified interest was cognizable at law or equity, whether it was susceptible of sufficient identification to permit seizure, and whether it was saleable. *U.S. Indus., Inc. v. Gregg, 348 F. Supp. 1004 (D. Del. 1972), rev'd, 540 F.2d 142 (3d Cir. 1976), cert. denied, 433 U.S. 908, 97 S. Ct. 2972, 53 L. Ed. 2d 1091 (1977).*

This section allows the seizure of property in which the defendant has an equitable interest. *Cheff v. Athlone Indus., Inc., 43 Del. Ch. 394, 233 A.2d 170 (1967).*

But it does not allow seizure of property of an entity in which the defendant has an equitable interest. *Cheff v. Athlone Indus., Inc., 43 Del. Ch. 394, 233 A.2d 170 (1967).*

In the absence of a showing of a fraudulent conveyance or the like, stock actually owned by a subsidiary cannot be attached in an equitable action against the parent corporation on the theory that such stock is equitably or beneficially the property of the parent corporation for despite the broad language of this section, property attached thereunder must in some form be the property of the defendant. *Buechner v. Farbenfabriken Bayer Aktiengesellschaft, 38 Del. Ch. 329, 151 A.2d 125 (1959); 154 A.2d 684 (Del. 1959).*

Intangibles may be seized. — The inherent powers of a court of equity extend to the seizure and sale of intangible property. *Greene v. Johnston, 34 Del. Ch. 115, 99 A.2d 627, 42 A.L.R.2d 906 (1953).*

There is no good reason why the General Assembly should see fit to give a remedy by way of a seizure of intangibles in a law action and preclude their seizure in an equity action. *Weinress v. Bland, 31 Del. Ch. 269, 71 A.2d 59 (1950).*

The words "real and personal property" as used in this section should be construed as including intangibles. *Weinress v. Bland, 31 Del. Ch. 269, 71 A.2d 59 (1950).*

Corporate shares held for another will be released. — Once it is called to the Court's attention that the interest in corporate shares which have been seized is the property of another, or is held for the benefit of another, then justice requires that the property be released. *Life Assurance Co. v. Associated Investors Int'l Corp., 312 A.2d 337 (Del. Ch. 1973).*

A securities broker-dealer which holds shares in its name that are, in actuality, owned by other parties may have such nominee stock, upon seizure pursuant to a sequestration order, released. *Life Assurance Co. v. Associated Investors Int'l Corp., 312 A.2d 337 (Del. Ch. 1973).*

Debt owed by resident debtor is sequesterable. — The comprehensive terms employed in this section would seem to indicate an intent to cover every situation which it was constitution-ally possible to cover, including a debt owed by a resident debtor and the fact that a debt is payable in another state is not a reason for excluding such debts from the operation of this section. *Weinress v. Bland, 31 Del. Ch. 269, 71 A.2d 59 (1950).*

Even when the debt is unmatured and contingent. — This section authorizes the seizure of obligations even though they are considered unmatured and contingent in some respects. *Weinress v. Bland, 31 Del. Ch. 269, 71 A.2d 59 (1950).*

Stock of delaware corporation may be sequestered. — It is possible for a complainant who desires to sue a nonresident to force the nonresident's appearance by seizing his or her stock located in *Delaware. Cantor v. Sachs, 18 Del. Ch. 359, 162 A. 73 (1932).*

Shares of stock of Delaware corporations have their situs in Delaware and are therefore subject to seizure. *Cantor v. Sachs, 18 Del. Ch. 359, 162 A. 73 (1932).*

The Court of Chancery exercises jurisdiction with respect to the stock of Delaware corporations on the theory

interest. *Cheff v. Athlone Indus., Inc., 43 Del. Ch. 394, 233 A.2d 170 (1967).*

Chancery Court

that for certain purposes such property has its situs in *Delaware. Haas v. Haas, 35 Del. Ch. 392, 119 A.2d 358 (1955).*

The seized shares have a Delaware situs because the Ford Motor Company is a Delaware corporation and the corporation law to which it owes its existence provides expressly that the situs of ownership of stock of all such corporations, for all purposes of title, action, attachment, garnishment and jurisdiction of all courts in this State shall be regarded as in this *State. Breech v. Hughes Tool Co., 41 Del. Ch. 128, 189 A.2d 428 (1963).*

This section provides that an order of sequestration may be entered for the purpose of compelling appearance of the nonresident defendants and stock of the named defendants seized. *Oil & Gas Ventures, Inc. v. Cheyenne Oil Corp., 43 Del. Ch. 143, 220 A.2d 785 (1966).*

The situs of stock in a Delaware corporation, by reason of *8 Del. C. § 169,* is in Delaware for purposes of sequestration despite the removal of the certificates from the country. *Yancey v. National Trust Co., 251 A.2d 561 (Del. 1969).*

Interests in stock of a Delaware corporation coming within the scope of this section are sequesterable in Delaware for the purpose of compelling the appearance of nonresident defendants. *U.S. Indus., Inc. v. Gregg, 348 F. Supp. 1004 (D. Del. 1972),* rev'd, *540 F.2d 142 (3d Cir. 1976),* cert. denied, *433 U.S. 908, 97 S. Ct. 2972, 53 L. Ed. 2d 1091 (1977).*

The Delaware situs statute, § 169 of Title 8, as construed by the Delaware courts and as applied in a nonresident stock sequestration proceeding, does not comport with the constitutional requirement that jurisdiction be predicated on minimum contacts with the forum. *U.S. Indus., Inc. v. Gregg, 540 F.2d 142 (3d Cir. 1976); 433 U.S. 908, 97 S. Ct. 2972, 53 L. Ed. 2d 1091 (1977).*

The single fact of statutory situs of stock under § 169 of Title 8 does not suffice to give Delaware sufficient contact or affiliation with a sequestration litigation to satisfy constitutional standards. *U.S. Indus., Inc. v. Gregg, 540 F.2d 142 (3d Cir. 1976); 433 U.S. 908, 97 S. Ct. 2972, 53 L. Ed. 2d 1091 (1977).*

Where a company's incorporation is the only genuine contact a litigation has with Delaware, the fictional situs of stock in Delaware under § 169 of Title 8 does not pass constitutional muster as a predicate for jurisdiction in an action admittedly seeking to obtain personal liability of a nonresident in connection with transactions unrelated to the forum. *U.S. Indus., Inc. v. Gregg, 540 F.2d 142 (3d Cir. 1976); 433 U.S. 908, 97 S. Ct. 2972, 53 L. Ed. 2d 1091 (1977).*

It strains reason to suggest that anyone buying securities in a corporation formed in Delaware impliedly consents to subject oneself to Delaware's jurisdiction on any cause of action. *Shaffer v. Heitner, 433 U.S. 186, 97 S. Ct. 2569, 53 L. Ed. 2d 683 (1977).*

Where the sole connection of the defendant California corporation, its president and vice-president with Delaware is that they are the owners of corporate stock which, by statute, has its fictional and legal situs in Delaware, and where action by the plaintiff locally domiciled corporation concedes defendants' ownership of the stock in the local corporation and seeks only to determine the voting rights of such stock at an annual election of directors as such rights may or may not be affected by the California statutes on which the defendants rely, under "traditional notions of fair play and substantial justice" defendants have a constitutionally protected right to be free from appearing in the Delaware courts in such suit. *Arden-Mayfair, Inc. v. Louart Corp., 385 A.2d 3 (Del. Ch. 1978).*

Even though the sequestration procedure in this section, as applied to the sequestration of stock with a situs, under § 169 of Title 8, in Delaware was ultimately invalidated by the United States Supreme Court, a plaintiff will not be held civilly liable for prior reliance upon that procedure. *U.S. Indus., Inc. v. Gregg, 457 F. Supp. 1293 (D. Del. 1978); 605 F.2d 1199 (3d Cir. 1979); 444 U.S. 1076, 100 S. Ct. 1023, 63 L. Ed. 2d 758 (1980).*

But stock of foreign corporation may not be seized. — Attachment laws cannot be construed to authorize the attachment of shares of a foreign corporation. *Union Chem. & Materials Corp. v. Cannon, 38 Del. Ch. 203, 148 A.2d 348 (1959).*

The injunctive powers of chancery over a corporation do not give the Court jurisdiction over a nonresident's property where the property is not within the jurisdiction and the writ of injunction may not be employed to accomplish the same purposes as a foreign attachment for the foundation of the Court's jurisdiction is the situs of the stock and once that situs was transferred elsewhere the power of the Court over the shares, and hence its jurisdiction, was lost. *Union Chem. & Materials Corp. v. Cannon, 38 Del. Ch. 203, 148 A.2d 348 (1959).*

Stock of nonresident owners with bare legal title may be seized. — While seizure of registered shares on the basis of a bare legal title may result in the seizure of property equitably owned by a third party, that is one of the hazards of the separation of the legal and beneficial ownership and the shares so registered are seizable under the law. *Rebstock v. Lutz, 39 Del. Ch. 25, 158 A.2d 487 (1960).*

But generally will be released on application from beneficial owners. — If the shares seized are in fact equitably owned by a third party or parties, such persons have a remedy on application to the Court. *Rebstock v. Lutz, 39 Del. Ch. 25, 158 A.2d 487 (1960); Chasin v. Gluck, 42 Del. Ch. 538, 216 A.2d 142 (1965).*

It is generally true that stock to which a nonresident holds only bare legal title will be released from sequestration on application of the beneficial owners, but it nevertheless may be seized initially. *Yancey v. National Trust Co., 251 A.2d 561 (Del. 1969).*

"Bare legal title" (i.e., registered ownership) is sequesterable, the property being subject to release only upon showing that its retention or sale would defeat or interfere with equitable interests therein. *U.S. Indus., Inc. v. Gregg, 348 F. Supp. 1004 (D. Del. 1972),* rev'd, *540 F.2d 142 (3d Cir. 1976),* cert. denied, *433 U.S. 908, 97 S. Ct. 2972, 53 L. Ed. 2d 1091 (1977).*

Determination of status as beneficial owner. — Before the Court acts upon the defendant's motion to vacate the sequestration as to shares of stock, plaintiff should have an opportunity to attempt to confirm or disaffirm the position asserted that the defendant is not the beneficial owner. *Steinberg v. Shields, 38 Del. Ch. 423, 153 A.2d 599 (1959).*

Sequestration possible in derivative suit. — In a derivative stockholder's suit a corporate debt can be sequestered. *Weinress v. Bland, 31 Del. Ch. 269, 71 A.2d 59 (1950).*

Seized property might be sold to satisfy any decree that might be obtained in a derivative action affording relief to the corporation notwithstanding it stands of record as a technical defendant. *Cantor v. Sachs, 18 Del. Ch. 359, 162 A. 73 (1932).*

Equitable jurisdiction in a stockholder's derivative suit for directors to account for wrongs to the corporation rests upon the derivative nature of the suit, which is cognizable only in equity. *Rebstock v. Lutz, 39 Del. Ch. 25, 158 A.2d 487 (1960).*

The interest of a state in aiding its citizens in prosecuting claims against nonresident defendants with property in the state has long been recognized and such an interest is clearly present in a stockholder's derivative suit. *Gordon v. Michel, 297 A.2d 420 (Del. Ch. 1972).*

But is not designed to provide jurisdiction over nominal defendants. — It is a false assumption that the sequestration law was designed to provide a means of compelling the appearance not only of real defendants named in a derivative action, but also of the corporation for whose benefit the suit is brought. *Levine v. Milton, 42 Del. Ch. 597, 219 A.2d 145 (1966).*

Interest of executors in the personal property of their decedent is properly subject to sequestration, since they hold both legal and equitable title for the purpose of settling the estate. *Yancey v. National Trust Co., 251 A.2d 561 (Del. 1969).*

Self-sequestration. — Self-sequestration under the mechanics of this section is as effective to accomplish the so-called primary purpose of the sequestration statute, to compel an appearance, as is sequestration against a nonparty. *Weinress v. Bland, 31 Del. Ch. 269, 71 A.2d 59 (1950).*

A sequestration results in a sale of the defendant's claim against the debtor, and the so-called incongruity existing where a plaintiff at law is both a judgment creditor and a judgment debtor, if self-attachment is permitted, does not exist in the case of equitable self-sequestration. *Weinress v. Bland, 31 Del. Ch. 269, 71 A.2d 59 (1950).*

Bank's exemption from attachment does not exempt from sequestration. — Section 3502 of this title, which exempts banks from attachment, does not serve to exempt a bank, acting as trustee for a nonresident spouse, in the case of sequestration proceedings brought by the other spouse to compel the nonresident spouse to comply with a support order. *J.B.G. v. P.J.G., 286 A.2d 256 (Del. Ch. 1971).*

Application of "long-arm" jurisdiction. — There is no valid policy reason why this section should not be construed in conjunction with *Rule 4(e), Fed. R. Civ. P.*, to permit the sequestration of a nonresident defendant's property even though he may be amenable to personal service outside the state under the "long-arm" service provisions of *15 U.S.C. § 78aa. Jacobs v. Tenney, 316 F. Supp. 151 (D. Del. 1970).*

Sequestration places lien on stock. — A sequestration made in compliance with this section and the rules of court reaches and liens the interest in the stock to which it is directed, and proceeds upon the premise that such interest is seized for the purpose of compelling appearance by the person who holds that interest. *Nickson v. Filtrol Corp., 265 A.2d 425 (Del. Ch. 1970).*

Where the stock was personal property which was seized by the sequestrator by virtue of both this section and an order entered by the Court, sequestration, in effect, constitutes a lien on the stock. *Wimpfheimer v. Goldsmith, 298 A.2d 778 (Del. Ch. 1972).*

The practical effect of a sequestration order signed under this section is not to deprive the defendant of the possession or control of property, but only to impose a lien upon it, which would not impair a sale, but would pass to the proceeds of such a sale. *U.S. Indus., Inc. v. Gregg, 457 F. Supp. 1293 (D. Del. 1978); 605 F.2d 1199 (3d Cir. 1979); 444 U.S. 1076, 100 S. Ct. 1023, 63 L. Ed. 2d 758 (1980).*

But lien is lost if possession is lost. — If possession of tangible personalty by the court's officer is lost otherwise than by a tortious removal by the owner, the lien is lost and with it the jurisdiction of the court over the property since the test of the continued efficacy of the lien is the continued possession of the officer and if that possession is lost by lawful removal of the property to a foreign jurisdiction, the lien is lost. *Union Chem. & Materials Corp. v. Cannon, 38 Del. Ch. 203, 148 A.2d 348 (1959).*

Or conversion of stock by merger can defeat lien. — Conversion of shares of stock by merger is not a transfer or assignment and the principle of law that the owner of property attached may not by alienating it defeat the attachment does not apply. *Union Chem. & Materials Corp. v. Cannon, 38 Del. Ch. 203, 148 A.2d 348 (1959).*

Husband estopped from denying ownership of partnership interest so as to defeat order of sequestration. — See *Widder v. Leeds, 317 A.2d 32 (Del. Ch. 1974).*

For the purpose of this section, a counterclaim is a "complaint" and a defendant who counterclaims is a "plaintiff." *Breech v. Hughes Tool Co., 41 Del. Ch. 128, 189 A.2d 428 (1963).*

Mere technical errors causing no prejudice to the defendants do not affect the validity of the sequestration order. *United States v. Sinclair, 347 F. Supp. 1129 (D. Del. 1972), appeal dismissed, 498 F.2d 847 (3d Cir. 1974).*

The denial of a motion to quash a sequestration order issued in accordance with this section is not appealable under *28 U.S.C. § 1291* as an appeal of a "final order." *United States v. Estate of Pearce, 498 F.2d 847 (3d Cir. 1974).*

Promulgation of rules by chancellor. — This section does not purport to require the promulgation of rules as a condition of its operation; its language is not mandatory but it is permissive and the rules the Chancellor may make are such as may be necessary. *Cantor v. Sachs, 18 Del. Ch. 359, 162 A. 73 (1932).*

Indemnity against loss to owner of property. — So unreasonable is it that a nonresident's property might be seized on mesne process and held an indefinite length of time, only in the end possibly to be turned back to him, without provision for indemnity against loss or damage occasioned to the owner, that if there be any reasonable construction of this section possible which would yield the indemnity, such construction ought to be unhesitatingly adopted and such construction of this section is to a limited extent at least reasonably permissible. *Cantor v. Sachs, 18 Del. Ch. 359, 162 A. 73 (1932).*

Filing by Delaware corporation of registration statement with delaware securities commissioner does not support substituted service of process pursuant to this section. *Bank of Am. Nat'l Trust & Sav. Ass'n v. GAC Properties Credit, Inc., 389 A.2d 1304 (Del. Ch. 1978).*

Relation of § 3114 to this section. — Section 3114 of this title does not limit or affect any existing method of service of process, including that under this section. *Bank of Am. Nat'l Trust & Sav. Ass'n v. GAC Properties Credit, Inc., 389 A.2d 1304 (Del. Ch. 1978).*

Language of subsection (d) of § 3114 of this title specifically preserves the right to use this section in appropriate circumstances. *Bank of Am. Nat'l Trust & Sav. Ass'n v. GAC Properties Credit, Inc., 389 A.2d 1304 (Del. Ch. 1978).*

Order refusing to vacate a sequestration is an appealable one when it determines substantial questions against a nonresident. *Breech v. Hughes Tool Co., 41 Del. Ch. 128, 189 A.2d 428 (1963).*

§ 369. Issues of fact triable by jury

DELAWARE CASE NOTES — REPORTED

Referral to jury discretionary with court. — If a party is allowed a jury trial on a question of fact by a court of equity, it is not as a matter of right, but of the court's discretion. *Aetna Cas. & Sur. Co. v. Mayor & Council, 18 Del. Ch. 324, 160 A. 749 (1932).*

The granting of an application to direct an issue to be tried by a jury at law is not a matter of right, but falls completely within the sound discretion of the Court of Chancery. *Saunders v. Saunders, 31 Del. Ch. 514, 71 A.2d 258 (1950).*

If a cause is properly in the Court of Chancery, no right exists in either party to the litigation to say that a fact necessary to be determined in the course of the proceeding, although it may be said to be a subject for cognizance in a court of law before a jury, cannot also be determined in equity without the intervention of a jury. *Saunders v. Saunders, 31 Del. Ch. 514, 71 A.2d 258 (1950).*

Jury trial in chancery is advisory only. *Getty Ref. & Mktg. Co. v. Park Oil, Inc., 385 A.2d 147 (Del. Ch. 1978).*

And advisory jury verdict is not entirely equivalent to jury verdict at law. *Getty Ref. & Mktg. Co. v. Park Oil, Inc., 385 A.2d 147 (Del. Ch. 1978).*

Fact that plaintiff joins legal and equitable claims should not automatically deprive defendant of right to trial by jury on purely legal issues. This is so because otherwise a plaintiff could deprive a defendant of a jury trial merely by adding a spurious equitable claim to a demand for money damages and commencing the action in Chancery instead of at law. *Getty Ref. & Mktg. Co. v. Park Oil, Inc., 385 A.2d 147 (Del. Ch. 1978).*

Questions of fact concerning the title to land should not be decided by chancery, but should be sent to a jury in a law court. *Dill v. Dill, 10 Del. Ch. 257, 91 A. 450 (1914).*

Once jurisdiction of the subject matter has been properly ascertained equity will proceed to determine all facts essential to a decree, except the determination of facts necessary to adjudicate the legal title to land. *Saunders v. Saunders, 31 Del. Ch. 514, 71 A.2d 258 (1950).*

Matter must be material to be referred to jury. — This section does not operate if in reference to the matter and cause to be heard and determined in the Court, the subject is not material. *Comly v. Waters, 2 Del. Ch. 72 (1840).*

The chancellor is not bound by a jury's finding of fact, but the Chancellor will not arbitrarily disregard or even lightly consider such findings. *Scotton v. Wright, 14 Del. Ch. 124, 122 A. 541 (1923).*

§ 371. Sale of land to enforce judgment

DELAWARE CASE NOTES — REPORTED

Jurisdiction of court of chancery. — A Court of Chancery's order directing judgment be transferred to the records of the Superior Court did not divest the Court of Chancery of jurisdiction over the cause of action. *Handler Constr., Inc. v. Corestates Bank, 633 A.2d 356 (Del. 1993).*

Concurrent jurisdiction in the Court of Chancery over the foreclosure of mortgages has persisted, without interruption or limitation, under the constitutional and statutory law of this *State. Handler Constr., Inc. v. Corestates Bank, 633 A.2d 356 (Del. 1993).*

Foreclosure of an equitable mortgage is vested exclusively within the jurisdiction of the Court of *Chancery.*

Handler Constr., Inc. v. Corestates Bank, 633 A.2d 356 (Del. 1993).

Mortgage foreclosure. — A mortgagee may elect to have a mortgage, which has been executed with the requisite legal formalities, foreclosed either at law by a writ of scire facias sur mortgea in Superior Court, pursuant to § 5061 of this title, or by a bill in equity filed in the Court of Chancery pursuant to this section. *Handler Constr., Inc. v. Corestates Bank, 633 A.2d 356 (Del. 1993).*

Jury trial. — There is no constitutional right to a trial by jury in a mortgage foreclosure proceeding. *Money Store/Delaware, Inc. v. Kamara, 704 A.2d 282 (Del. Super. Ct. 1997).*

§ 372.   Power to appoint Masters

DELAWARE CASE NOTES — REPORTED

Decisions subject to de novo review. — A Special Discovery Master's decisions are recommendations which, absent the consent of the parties, are subject to de novo review by the *Superior Court. Playtex FP, Inc. v. Columbia Cas. Co., 609 A.2d 1083 (Del. Super. Ct. 1991).*

Scope of appointment. — A judge of a Court of Chancery may appoint a master to hear and evaluate all claims presented in an entire case unless otherwise provided by statute or rule of court. *DiGiacobbe v. Sestak, 743 A.2d 180 (Del. Super. Ct. 1999).*

Limit on master's authority. — Since masters are appointed by the Chancellor, they may not exercise judi-cial authority. *DiGiacobbe v. Sestak, 743 A.2d 180 (Del. Super. Ct. 1999).*

Review of master's report. — The master's rulings, findings of fact, conclusions of law, and recommended disposition have no effect until they are adopted by a judge after a meaningful review. *DiGiacobbe v. Sestak, 743 A.2d 180 (Del. Super. Ct. 1999).*

Timely objections to the master's finding's and conclusions must be reviewed de novo by the judge and, for a review of the evidence to be meaningful, there must be a transcript of the proceedings before the master. *DiGiacobbe v. Sestak, 743 A.2d 180 (Del. Super. Ct. 1999).*

DELAWARE COURT OF CHANCERY

CHANCERY COURT RULES

I. SCOPE OF RULES — ONE FORM OF ACTION

Rule 1.   Scope and purpose of Rules

DELAWARE CASE NOTES — REPORTED

Rules should be construed to aid in disposition of cases. — These Rules should not be construed to operate without regard to their primary purpose, namely, to aid in the disposition of cases in the light of all the material facts which can reasonably and seasonably be made available to the Court. *DuPont v. Equitable Sec. Trust Co., 35 Del. Ch. 261, 115 A.2d 482 (1955), aff'd, 122 A.2d 429 (Del. 1956).*

And absent prejudice to a defendant, addition or deletion of parties should be made freely in order to carry out the spirit and purpose expressed in this rule, "to secure the just, speedy and inexpensive determination of every proceeding." *Diner Foods, Inc. v. City of Dover, 43 Del. Ch. 331, 229 A.2d 495 (1967).*

II. COMMENCEMENT OF ACTION; SERVICE OF PROCESS, PLEADINGS, MOTIONS, AND ORDERS; DEPOSIT AND SECURITY FOR COSTS

Rule 4.   Process

DELAWARE CASE NOTES — REPORTED

This rule is designed to curb "fishing expeditions," which would be permissible under statute in the absence of restriction. *Rebstock v. Lutz, 39 Del. Ch. 25, 158 A.2d 487 (1960).*

The substance of paragraph (db) was adopted to curb so-called "fishing expeditions" which would otherwise be permissible under the broad terms of *10 Del. C. § 366. Chasin v. Gluck, 42 Del. Ch. 538, 216 A.2d 142 (1965).*

The purpose of paragraph (db) of rule is to thwart "fishing expeditions." *Baker v. Gotz, 336 F. Supp. 197 (D. Del. 1971), aff'd, 492 F.2d 1238 (3d Cir. 1974), cert. denied, 417 U.S. 955, 94 S. Ct. 3084, 41 L. Ed. 2d 674 (1974).*

And compliance with the affidavit requirement of paragraph (db) is a condition to the sequestration of property owned by a nonresident defendant. *Baker v. Gotz, 336 F. Supp. 197 (D. Del. 1971), aff'd, 492 F.2d 1238 (3d Cir. 1974), cert. denied, 417 U.S. 955, 94 S. Ct. 3084, 41 L. Ed. 2d 674 (1974).*

It is not a jurisdictional but a procedural requirement. *Rebstock v. Lutz, 39 Del. Ch. 25, 158 A.2d 487 (1960).*

Requirements of the affidavit pertaining to a description of the property to be seized and its estimated amount and value have been held to be procedural and not jurisdictional. *Chashin v. Gluck, 42 Del. Ch. 201, 207 A.2d 30 (1964), rev'd on other grounds, 210 A.2d 855 (Del. 1965).*

Compliance with 10 DEL. C. § 366. — Upon application for an order of sequestration, the plaintiff is required by this rule to establish that the nonresident not only owned property in Delaware, but that the other requirements of *10 Del. C. § 366* and the rule have been met; this having been done, an order of sequestration is issued as a

matter of course. *Trans World Airlines v. Hughes, 40 Del. Ch. 523, 185 A.2d 762, aff'd, 185 A.2d 886 (Del. Ch. 1962).*

No sequestration may be had in Chancery unless the plaintiff by his complaint brings himself within the terms of *10 Del. C. § 366,* so as to confer upon the Court the power to seize property to compel an appearance. *Gluck v. Chashin, 42 Del. Ch. 325, 210 A.2d 855 (1965).*

Unless the precise requirements of *10 Del. C. § 366* are complied with, there may be no order of sequestration. *Gluck v. Chashin, 42 Del. Ch. 325, 210 A.2d 855 (1965).*

Rule contemplates a large measure of discretion by the chancellor in its application, as the order of sequestration must be submitted to him for his consideration and approval, and his approval signifies that he has found substantial compliance with the procedural requirements of the rule. *Rebstock v. Lutz, 39 Del. Ch. 25, 158 A.2d 487 (1960).*

If the affidavit states upon information and belief that the defendant's property consists of shares of stock in certain corporations, the inference is that the deponent is referring to shares standing in the names of defendants in the various corporations so that the affidavit is not required to state that the defendants are believed to have a legal title in the shares to be seized, for this is a valid statement of defendant title and interest in property sought to be seized. *Lutz v. Boas, 38 Del. Ch. 563, 156 A.2d 96 (1959).*

Where the affidavit in support of sequestration not only gives the addresses of the nonresident defendants but avers that the property of the defendants proposed to be seized consists of shares of common stock of a named corporation "standing in the names or held for the benefit of the aforesaid defendants," stating on information and belief not only the number of shares thought to be individually owned by the defendants, but also stating the number of shares which stand in the names of nominees, the plaintiff has clearly not thrown out a dragnet; rather, he has met the basic requirements of *10 Del. C. § 366* and Ch. Ct. R. 4(db). *Chasin v. Gluck, 42 Del. Ch. 538, 216 A.2d 142 (1965).*

Shares properly sequestered. — Where the record before the Court indicates that the requirements of *10 Del. C. § 366* and paragraph (db), have been satisfied, then, until satisfactory evidence is provided to the contrary, the Court can only conclude that the shares have been properly sequestered. *Life Assurance Co. v. Associated Investors Int'l Corp., 312 A.2d 337 (Del. Ch. 1973).*

Sequestration vacated if dissolved corporation's receiver does not establish authority to sue. — When plaintiff's authority as a receiver of dissolved corporation to sue in federal court has been challenged by the defendant, the burden rests upon the plaintiff to establish that authority, and unless within a period of 15 days the plaintiff presents to the Court of Chancery an application for authority to continue the prosecution of the suit and to retain an attorney for the purpose, the suit will be dismissed and the purported sequestration of defendant's property will be vacated. *D'Angelo v. Petroleos Mexicanos, 373 F. Supp. 1076 (D. Del. 1974).*

Seizure is not effective without court order. — Where no Court order directing seizure of stock for the purpose of compelling a nonresident corporate defendant to appear has been entered, effective seizure of the stock has not been made. *Greene v. Johnston, 34 Del. Ch. 115, 99 A.2d 627 (1953).*

However, service by publication upon nonresident trustees of a delaware voting trust is valid without seizure of the corporate stock constituting the trust res, providing the relief prayed against the individual defendants is in their official capacity as trustees only. *Smith v. Biggs Boiler Works Co., 32 Del. Ch. 287, 85 A.2d 365 (1951).*

If shares seized are in fact equitably owned by third parties, such persons have a remedy on application to the Court. *Chasin v. Gluck, 42 Del. Ch. 538, 216 A.2d 142 (1965).*

Entry of an alias order of sequestration signifies a finding of substantial compliance with the procedural requirements of the rule. *Chasin v. Gluck, 42 Del. Ch. 538, 216 A.2d 142 (1965).*

Omission under paragraph (db)(1)(b) need not be sanctioned by the court upon due application because of subparagraph (5) of paragraph (db) and compliance with paragraph (db)(1)(b)(v). *Lutz v. Boas, 38 Del. Ch. 563, 156 A.2d 96 (1959).*

But the plaintiff may state a reason for noncompliance in accordance with paragraph (db)(1)(b)(v) of this rule; and, if on its face the reason is sufficient, the rule is complied with. *Rebstock v. Lutz, 39 Del. Ch. 25, 158 A.2d 487 (1960).*

But such deals only with preceding paragraphs. — Paragraph (db)(1)(b)(v) of this rule deals only

with the requirements of paragraph (db)(1)(b)(i)-(iv), whereas paragraph (db)(5) deals with any part of the entire rule. *Rebstock v. Lutz, 39 Del. Ch. 25, 158 A.2d 487 (1960).*

The required statements under paragraph (db)(1)(b)(v) are only those necessary under paragraphs (db)(1)(b)(i)-(iv) and include, as to the property of each defendant sought to be seized, a reasonable description, the estimated amount and value, the nature of the defendant's title or interest and the source of the affiant's information as to any of the items stated upon information and belief, which are the only statements which may be excused under paragraph (db)(1)(b)(v). *Baker v. Gotz, 336 F. Supp. 197 (D. Del. 1971), aff'd, 492 F.2d 1238 (3d Cir. 1974), cert. denied, 417 U.S. 955, 94 S. Ct. 3084, 41 L. Ed. 2d 674 (1974).*

Paragraph (db)(5) is intended to provide a method by which plaintiffs who are for some reason unable to meet the general requirements of paragraph (db) can be relieved from doing so if judicial approval is obtained after an application therefor has been filed, subject to the exception that the statements necessary under paragraph (db)(1)(b)(i)-(iv) of this rule can be met by an affidavit which satisfies paragraph (db)(1)(b)(v) of this rule. *Baker v. Gotz, 336 F. Supp. 197 (D. Del. 1971), aff'd, 492 F.2d 1238 (3d Cir. 1974), cert. denied, 417 U.S. 955, 94 S. Ct. 3084, 41 L. Ed. 2d 674 (1974).*

If a sequestration order is to be granted upon the basis of an affidavit which fails to specify the property of each defendant sought to be seized, it can be done, if at all, only by following the procedure stated in paragraph (db)(5). *Baker v. Gotz, 336 F. Supp. 197 (D. Del. 1971), aff'd, 492 F.2d 1238 (3d Cir. 1974), cert. denied, 417 U.S. 955, 94 S. Ct. 3084, 41 L. Ed. 2d 674 (1974).*

However, the mere fact that the sequestration order is signed is not compliance with paragraph (db)(5), the object of which is to require the attention of the Court to be specifically directed to an omission not curable under paragraph (db)(1)(b)(v) before a sequestration order is entered. *Baker v. Gotz, 336 F. Supp. 197 (D. Del. 1971), aff'd, 492 F.2d 1238 (3d Cir. 1974), cert. denied, 417 U.S. 955, 94 S. Ct. 3084, 41 L. Ed. 2d 674 (1974).*

Statement of not knowing amount and value of property complies. — If the plaintiffs are justified in saying that they do not know the amount of property owned by a defendant, they cannot give the estimated value, and a statement that plaintiffs do not know the amount and value of property complies with the requirement of paragraph (db)(1)(b)(v) of this rule; it in effect gives the reason for failure to give the estimated value of the property seized. *Lutz v. Boas, 38 Del. Ch. 563, 156 A.2d 96 (1959).*

Amendment supplying allegations of nonresidency does not cure complaint deficiency. — Since the fact of the residency of the individual defendants cannot be said to have arisen out of the original occurrence complained of, an amendment supplying allegations of nonresidency of the defendants after a motion to vacate sequestration does not cure the deficiency in the complaint. *Gluck v. Chashin, 42 Del. Ch. 325, 210 A.2d 855 (1965).*

Service upon personal representative. — This rule does not contain a method for effecting substituted service upon, or giving notice to, a personal representative of a decedent. *Tabas v. Crosby, 444 A.2d 250 (Del. Ch. 1982).*

Rule 5. Service and filing of pleadings and other papers; appearance and withdrawal thereof

DELAWARE CASE NOTES — REPORTED

Discovery materials as part of trial record. — The inclusion of discovery materials in the trial record, once required, is now severely restricted; accordingly, in civil matters, discovery materials are no longer filed with the trial courts. *Delaware Elec. Coop. v. Duphily, 703 A.2d 1202 (Del. 1997).*

Discovery material is not a part of the record in the trial court unless admitted into evidence or entered into the record through motion; a resulting corollary is that, if the discovery material does not find acceptance in the trial record, it forms no part of the record on appeal. *Delaware Elec. Coop. v. Duphily, 703 A.2d 1202 (Del. 1997).*

Appeal of judgments maintaining sealing orders. — Supreme court (1) granted a corporation's motion to dismiss a former inhouse counsel's appeal of a motion to disqualify outside counsel as moot, and (2) denied the corporation's motion to dismiss counsel's appeal from a final judgment that maintained a prior sealing order as timely filed, so as to avoid unsealing under subdivision (g)(7) of this rule. *Hallett v. CARNET Holding Corp., 809 A.2d 1159 (Del. 2002).*

Rule 6. Time

DELAWARE CASE NOTES — REPORTED

First day excluded while last day included. — The general rule for the computation of time under a statute, in the absence of anything showing a contrary intent, is that the first day should be excluded, but the day on which the act is to be done should be included. *Santow v. Ullman, 39 Del. Ch. 427, 166 A.2d 135 (1960).*

Meaning of phrase "at least." — The prefixing of the phrase "at least" before the number of days required simply means, on its face, that the specified time is the minimum time. *Santow v. Ullman, 39 Del. Ch. 427, 166 A.2d 135 (1960).*

In the rule of time computation prevailing in the Courts, the day of the event is not included, but the last day of the period is included. *Bierczynski v. Rogers, 239 A.2d 218 (Del. 1968).*

The phrase "at least" does not evidence a specific legislative intent to require a longer time than that required by the general rule; if the General Assembly intends to depart from the general rule, it may readily find appropriate language to indicate an intention to do so. *Santow v. Ullman, 39 Del. Ch. 427, 166 A.2d 135 (1960).*

Period not tolled on Sunday. — Where 4-month period for demanding a determination of the value of the stock of all shareholders by an appraiser expired on a Sunday, the statutory period for filing a petition did not toll until the following day. *Schneyer v. Shenandoah Oil Corp., 316 A.2d 570 (Del. Ch. 1974).*

Motion to strike granted where excusable neglect not shown. — Where defendants fail to respond to the Court's order and file belated answers without the leave of Court in violation of paragraph (b), making no showing that their neglect was excusable, a motion to strike such answers will be granted. *Oil & Gas Ventures, Inc. v. Cheyenne Oil Corp., 43 Del. Ch. 143, 220 A.2d 785 (1966).*

III. PLEADINGS AND MOTIONS

Rule 8. General rules of pleading

DELAWARE CASE NOTES — REPORTED

Party desiring modification of an existing maintenance order should proceed by petition setting forth the basis for the particular request, whereupon the opposing party may then file an appropriate answer setting forth his defenses, if any. *Du Pont v. Du Pont, 34 Del. Ch. 320, 103 A.2d 783 (1954).*

Plaintiffs need not necessarily draw their complaint with such definiteness that defendants can argue that the statute of limitations is applicable on the basis of allegations of the complaint itself. *Dann v. Chrysler Corp., 40 Del. Ch. 103, 174 A.2d 696 (1961).*

Pleading must be particular for DEL. CH. CT. R. 23.1 demand. — To determine whether Del. Ch. Ct. R. 23.1 demand would be futile, the Chancery Court of Delaware must determine whether the particular facts, as alleged, create a reason to doubt that (1) the directors are disinterested and independent; or (2) the challenged transaction is otherwise the product of a valid exercise of business judgment, and the complaint must plead with sufficient particularity the facts to support demand futility; this is more than the notice pleading requirement under Del. Ch. Ct. R. 8(a), but is not to the level of evidence — the complaint must set forth particularized factual statements that are essential to the claim and mere speculation or opinion is not enough. *In re Walt Disney Co. Derivative Litig., 825 A.2d 275 (Del. Ch. 2003).*

Fraud allegation lacked particularity. — In making fraud allegations, the failure of limited partners in an investment fund to assert with particularity actual and reasonable reliance on the financial statement at issue, and the failure to allege the particular facts connecting the alleged fraud to the claimed injury, resulted in a dismissal of the fraud claim for failure to state a cause of action upon which relief could be granted; although notice pleading, under Del. Ch. Ct. R. 8, was sufficient to survive a motion to dismiss under Del. Ch. Ct. R. 12(b)(6), Del. Ch. Ct. R. 9(b) required that the circumstances constituting any alleged fraud be stated with particularity, which the complaint failed to do. *Anglo Am. Sec. Fund, L.P. v. S.R. Global Int'l Fund, L.P., 829 A.2d 143 (Del. Ch. 2003).*

Essential element for application of doctrine of laches is a finding of unreasonable delay. *Harman v. Masoneilan Int'l, 442 A.2d 487 (Del. 1982).*

The statute of limitations or laches should not, on motion to dismiss a complaint, be applied to bar recovery, as these defenses should be affirmatively pleaded and established at trial on merits. *Brown v. Dolese, 38 Del. Ch. 471, 154 A.2d 233 (1959), aff'd, 157 A.2d 784 (Del. 1960).*

And defense based on pretext is insufficient to support satisfaction. — A defense based upon a pretext to avoid the discharge of an obligation or one which is merely set up for the purpose of avoiding a just claim is not sufficient to support an attempted satisfaction of the claim by a partial payment. *Modern Dust Bag Co. V. Commercial Trust Co., 34 Del. Ch. 354, 104 A.2d 378 (1954).*

Pleadings should state the ultimate facts, not conclusions of law. *Suplee v. Eckert, 35 Del. Ch. 550, 122 A.2d 918 (1956).*

Notice of breach of contract claims. — Allegations in a complaint were sufficient to put defendants on notice of plaintiff's claims against them, where: the complaint averred that a contract between one defendant and plaintiff existed; that the licensed technology was being used in a product of both defendants in contravention of the contract between plaintiff and the first defendant; and that plaintiff was damaged as a result. *VLIW Tech., L.L.C. v. Hewlett-Packard Co., 840 A.2d 606 (Del. 2003).*

"Impertinence" in equity pleading signifies that which is irrelevant and which does not in consequence belong in the pleading; the word does not include the idea of offending propriety. *Suplee v. Eckert, 35 Del. Ch. 550, 122 A.2d 918 (1956).*

Before the allegation in a complaint will be stricken as impertinent, the matter criticized must be so unrelated to the plaintiff's claim as to be unworthy of any consideration; however, it must be remembered that the degree of relevancy is not deemed material. *Suplee v. Eckert, 35 Del. Ch. 550, 122 A.2d 918 (1956).*

Pleadings under chancery rule 23.1 must comply with the mandate of subsection (e) of this rule that they be "simple, concise and direct", therefore, a prolix complaint larded with conclusory language does not comply with these fundamental pleading mandates. *Brehm v. Eisner, 746 A.2d 244 (Del. 2000).*

DELAWARE CASE NOTES — UNREPORTED

Federal fiduciary duty pleading standard. — Given that the Third Circuit has emphasized the view that the Federal Rules of Civil Procedure do not require a plaintiff to plead detailed facts to make out a claim for breach of fiduciary duties under Delaware law, district court is bound to hold that the plaintiff's allegations are sufficient in instance case. *IT Group, Inc. v. D'Aniello, 2005 U.S. Dist. LEXIS 27869 (D. Del. Nov. 15, 2005).*

Rule 9. Pleading special matters

DELAWARE CASE NOTES — REPORTED

Paragraph (a) is limited to pleading special matters relating to capacity or status to maintain an action and not to "legal existence" as a factual or evidentiary issue. *Brunswick Corp. v. Colt Realty, Inc., 253 A.2d 216 (Del. Ch. 1969).*

Applicability of (b) to fraudulent conveyances. — The pleading requirements of subsection (b) of this Rule apply to a claim under *6 Del. C. § 1307,* concerning conveyances made with intent to defraud. *Geyer v. Ingersoll Publications Co., 621 A.2d 784 (Del. Ch. 1992).*

Applicability of (b) to CFA and UDTPA. — Claims made by the state of Delaware under the Consumer Fraud Act and the Uniform Deceptive Trade Practices Act are not subject to subsection (b)'s requirements of particularity, because the remedial goals of these two acts are inconsistent with the application of the particularized pleading requirements of this rule to enforcement actions brought by the Attorney General to protect the consuming public. *State ex rel. Brady v. Publishers Clearing House, 787 A.2d 111 (Del. Ch. 2001).*

Grounds for reformation must be pleaded with particularity. — In order to obtain reformation of a contract, the party seeking such form of relief must plead with particularity the ingredients on which it is based, namely mutual mistake or fraud. *Gracelawn Mem. Park v. Eastern Mem. Consultants, Inc., 280 A.2d 745 (Del. Ch. 1971), aff'd, 291 A.2d 276 (Del. 1972).*

While subsection (b) of this rule provides that knowledge may be averred generally, when pleading a claim of fraud that has at its core the charge that the defendant knew something, there must at least be sufficient well-pleaded facts from which it can reasonably be inferred that this "something" was knowable and that the defendant was in a position to know it. *Metro Commun. Corp. BVI v. Advanced Mobilecomm Techs. Inc., 854 A.2d 121 (Del. Ch. 2004).*

"Fraud" distinct from "bad faith." — The definition of "fraud" is distinct from that of "bad faith." *Desert Equities, Inc. v. Morgan Stanley Leveraged Equity Fund, 624 A.2d 1199 (Del. 1993).*

The word "fraud" not sufficient. — Using the word "fraud" or its equivalent in any form is not a substitute for the statement of sufficient facts to make the basis of the charge reasonably apparent. *Dann v. Chrysler Corp., 40 Del. Ch. 103, 174 A.2d 696 (1961).*

Similarly, use of the word "constructive" rather than "actual" fraud alters the rule requirement that the "circumstances" be stated with particularity. *Dann v. Chrysler Corp., 40 Del. Ch. 103, 174 A.2d 696 (1961).*

And complaint not so complying will be dismissed with leave to amend. — The Supreme Court will affirm dismissal of a complaint for the reformation of a contract, with a right to amend, by reason of paragraph (b) of this rule, which requires that a party seeking reformation of a contract must plead with particularity the facts on which the prayer is based, where the complaint does not satisfy this requirement, and the Court will specifically affirm a reservation made by the Vice-Chancellor to the plaintiff of the right to amend that portion of the complaint seeking reformation of the contract. *Gracelawn Mem. Park v. Eastern Mem. Consultants, Inc., 291 A.2d 276 (Del. 1972).*

Where the plaintiff has been ordered to state his charges of fraud with particularity, as required by paragraph (b), and failed to do so, this failure is ground for dismissal, and Ch. Ct. R. 12(a) (now see R. 12(b)) itself contemplates sanctions, drastic if necessary. *Mayer v. Adams, 40 Del. Ch. 94, 174 A.2d 313 (1961).*

Fraud allegation lacked particularity. — In making fraud allegations, the failure of limited partners in an investment fund to assert with particularity actual and reasonable reliance on the financial statement at issue, and the failure to allege the particular facts connecting the alleged fraud to the claimed injury, resulted in a dismissal of the fraud claim for failure to state a cause of action upon which relief could be granted; although notice pleading, under Del. Ch. Ct. R. 8, was sufficient to survive a motion to dismiss under Del. Ch. Ct. R. 12(b)(6), Del. Ch. Ct. R. 9(b) required that the circumstances constituting any alleged fraud be stated with particularity, which the complaint failed to do. *Anglo Am. Sec. Fund, L.P. v. S.R. Global Int'l Fund, L.P., 829 A.2d 143 (Del. Ch. 2003).*

Former shareholder in a merged company, who had become a shareholder in the successor company, lacked standing to pursue a pre-existing derivative claim under the rule of *Lewis v. Anderson, 477 A.2d 1040 (Del. 1984),* to which the high court adhered; the shareholder had argued that the merger was arranged in a fraudulent attempt to avoid the derivative action, but failed to plead fraud with any particularity. *Lewis v. Ward, 852 A.2d 896 (Del. 2004).*

Investment bank failed to sufficiently plead a claim for fraud against former employees who, in conversations with investors, expressed satisfaction with their employment while they were planning their departure to a competing firm; the remarks were of a general nature, and it was inconceivable that any hard-nosed investor would make an investment decision based on a fund manager's expressions of contentment with employment. *Lazard Debt Recovery GP, LLC v. Weinstock, 864 A.2d 955 (Del. Ch. 2004).*

Fraudulent misrepresentation re-quired to be pleaded with particularity to toll statute of limitations. — Where a plaintiff relies upon fraudulent misrepresentation to suspend the operation of the statute of limitation, he is required under this rule to plead with particularity the circumstances constituting fraud. Those allegations must have "particularity sufficient to advise the charged defendant of the basis of the claim, and mere use of the word "fraud,' or its equivalent, is not a sufficiently particular statement of the circumstances relied upon." *Halpern v. Barran, 313 A.2d 139 (Del. Ch. 1973).*

Where in a complaint of fraudulent concealment there is no reference whatever to fraud and, in particular, there is no recitation of any specific artifice or misrepresentation by which it is claimed that defendants succeeded in concealing from plaintiffs the wrongs of which they complain, these allegations may be fairly characterized as mere generalizations, anchored to no specific acts of concealment by defendants, and the complaint therefore fails to assert with the requisite particularly fraudulent acts sufficient to toll the statute of limitations. *Halpern v. Barran, 313 A.2d 139 (Del. Ch. 1973).*

The rationale for requiring a claim of fraud to be pleaded with particularity does not apply to an allegation of bad faith, which relates to state of mind; while a claim of fraud has five components, a claim of bad faith hinges on a party's tortious state of mind, and under paragraph (b) of this Rule, state of mind may be pled generally. *Desert Equities, Inc. v. Morgan Stanley Leveraged Equity Fund, 624 A.2d 1199 (Del. 1993).*

A claim of conspiracy to defraud must be pled with particularity. A complaint alleging conspiracy must allege facts which, if true, show the formation and operation of a conspiracy, the wrongful act or acts done pursuant thereto, and the damage resulting from such acts. Facts, not legal conclusions, must be pled, including facts showing damages. *Atlantis Plastics Corp. v. Sammons, 558 A.2d 1062 (Del. Ch. 1989).*

Summary judgment for defendant proper where the plaintiff fails to state the circumstances constituting fraud with particularity as required by paragraph (b) of this rule and the allegations are insufficient to raise genuine issues of material fact. *Siple v. Corbett, 447 A.2d 1184 (Del. 1982).*

Failure to disclose recapitalization's dilution factor to minority shareholder. — Breach of fiduciary duty claim where the directors failed to disclose fully the contemplated recapitalization and the extent to which the minority shareholder's equity position in the corporation would be diluted was not dismissed. Acker v. Transurgical, Inc., (Del. Ch. Apr. 8, 2004).

Dismissal lying within chancellor's discretion. — This rule, which provides that in all averments of fraud the circumstances thereof shall be stated with particularity, is a rule of procedure, and the action of the Chancellor in refusing or granting a motion to dismiss the complaint upon this ground is a matter lying within his discretion. *Fish Eng'g Corp. v. Hutchinson, 39 Del. Ch. 215, 162 A.2d 722 (1960).*

Although vagueness alone does not warrant dismissal of the action, it may be attacked by a proper motion under CH. CT. R. 12, especially when the plaintiff asserts fraud. *Mayer v. Adams, 40 Del. Ch. 94, 174 A.2d 313 (1961).*

Condition of mind may be averred generally. *Fetters v. Mayor of Wilmington, 31 Del. Ch. 338, 73 A.2d 644 (1950).*

Particularization of allegations of fraudulent intent not required. — Fraud was stated with sufficient particularity where plaintiff alleged, upon information and belief, the knowledge and intent of defendants, as Del. Ch. Ct. R. 9(b) did not require particularization of allegations

of fraudulent intent; Del. Ch. Ct. R. 9(b) provided that malice, intent, knowledge, and other condition of mind of a person necessary to plead fraud could be averred generally, and in some contexts the particularity requirement had to be applied in light of the facts of the case, with less particularity being required when the facts laid more in the knowledge of the opposing party than of the pleading party. *H-M Wexford LLC v. Encorp, Inc., 832 A.2d 129 (Del. Ch. 2003).*

Motions arising under this rule necessarily involve the drawing of inferences from a combination of facts and circumstances. *Fetters v. Mayor of Wilmington, 31 Del. Ch. 338, 73 A.2d 644 (1950).*

Rule 10.   Form of pleadings

DELAWARE CASE NOTES — REPORTED

It is not sufficient just to make charges against "certain" parties, etc.; such claims must be made more definite in these areas. *Dann v. Chrysler Corp., 40 Del. Ch. 103, 174 A.2d 696 (1961).*

"Particularity" is not an issue. — Complaining that the statement of each claim is not stated with sufficient

particularity as to each defendant is another issue and not a violation of the requirements of paragraph (b) of this *Rule. Dann v. Chrysler Corp., 40 Del. Ch. 103, 174 A.2d 696 (1961).*

Rule 11.   Signing of pleadings, motions, and other papers; representations to Court; sanctions

DELAWARE CASE NOTES — REPORTED

Fundamental purpose of rule to establish standards. — While "good ground" may be tested by objective facts, a fundamental purpose of this rule is to establish standards for the attorney who signs the pleading, and when his pleading is a substantial overstatement of his information or when there is no reasonable relationship between the two, the rule is properly invoked, but the attorney is not obliged to have in hand a complete defense for summary judgment or other motion purposes. *Halpern v. Barran, 313 A.2d 139 (Del. Ch. 1973).*

But not fine line. — This rule has a place in the processing of litigation, but it does not provide a workable standard for fine-line comparison of pleading and knowledge. *Halpern v. Barran, 313 A.2d 139 (Del. Ch. 1973).*

Imposition of sanctions is mandatory. — Because this rule now states that if a party violates the rule, the court "shall impose ... an appropriate sanction," the court no longer has discretion to decline to impose sanctions, and discretion exists only with respect to the nature and extent of the sanctions. *Hurst v. General Dynamics Corp., 583 A.2d 1334 (Del. Ch. 1990).*

It is not basis for early-on kind of CH. CT. R. 12(B) motion. *Halpern v. Barran, 313 A.2d 139 (Del. Ch. 1973).*

A motion to strike does not test the legal sufficiency of the claim stated, but tests whether the attorney who signed the pleading met the standards fixed by this rule. *Halpern v. Barran, 272 A.2d 118 (Del. Ch. 1970).*

The granting of a motion to strike under this rule constitutes a "dismissal" of the action when the plaintiff has shown no good ground for any of the allegations found to be sham and has not merely pleaded overbroadly.

Singer v. Creole Petro. Corp., 301 A.2d 327 (Del. Ch.), modified, 311 A.2d 859 (Del. 1973).

Every inference should favor the pleader, but when there is no reasonable relationship between the charges made and the information on which they are based, the pleading lacks good ground to support it; it is sham and will be dismissed under the rule. *Halpern v. Barran, 272 A.2d 118 (Del. Ch. 1970).*

With prejudice as to plaintiff only. — In the case of a stockholder's derivative suit, where the plaintiff sues to enforce the rights of his corporation, his inability to meet the test of this rule should not foreclose other stockholders or the corporation itself from asserting like charges when able to support them, so that the charges in the complaint subject to this rule should be dismissed with prejudice as to the plaintiff only. *Singer v. Creole Petro. Corp., 301 A.2d 327 (Del. Ch.), modified, 311 A.2d 859 (Del. 1973).*

Test as to whether dismissal should be with prejudice. — The test as to whether the dismissal of the allegations in a complaint as "sham" under this rule should be with prejudice is the same as for a dismissal under Ch. Ct. R. 41(b), that is, if it is upon the merits of the action or involves a situation in which the defendant must incur the inconvenience of preparing to meet the merits because there is no initial bar to the court's reaching them. *Singer v. Creole Petro. Corp., 301 A.2d 327 (Del. Ch.), modified, 311 A.2d 859 (Del. 1973).*

Objective of rule not limited to testing counsel's conduct. — While an attorney certifies or authenticates a pleading by his signature (and all that implies), the objective of this rule is not limited to testing the conduct of counsel. *Halpern v. Barran, 272 A.2d 118 (Del. Ch. 1970).*

Good ground not measured by subjective standard. — While this rule speaks in terms of an attorney's "knowledge, information and belief," it does not follow that good ground is measured by a subjective standard. *Halpern v. Barran, 272 A.2d 118 (Del. Ch. 1970).*

Rather, standard applied is objective one. — Although the motive for filing a suit may be relevant in weighing the credibility of the plaintiff, where an attack is made on a pleading under this rule, the standard applied is an objective one; that is, whether the knowledge and information on which the allegations are based constitute "good ground" for the complaint. *Weinschel Eng'g Co. v. Midwest Microwave, Inc., 297 A.2d 443 (Del. Ch. 1972).*

Thus, the rule permits a party to invoke and argue objective facts in testing for "good ground" support; indeed, affidavits may be permissible for that purpose. *Halpern v. Barran, 272 A.2d 118 (Del. Ch. 1970).*

Allegations of fact. — When reviewing pleadings and other documents for compliance with subdivision (b)(3) of this rule, a court is apt to allow less latitude to those parts making allegations of fact than to those merely arguing inferences or conclusions from the facts alleged. *In re BHC Communications, Inc. Shareholder Litig., 789 A.2d 1 (Del. Ch. 2001).*

When burden shifts to plaintiff. — Where defendants' affidavits in support of their motions make prima facie showing, the burden shifts to the plaintiff to come forward with further evidence to demonstrate that there is a genuine issue of material fact on the question to prevent granting of the defendant's motion for dismissal under this rule. *Singer v. Creole Petro. Corp., 297 A.2d 440 (Del. Ch. 1972), supplemental opinion, 301 A.2d 327 (Del. Ch. 1973), modified, 311 A.2d 859 (Del. 1973).*

Overbreadth of pleading compared to knowledge. — To achieve its purpose, a motion under this rule will be granted not only when counsel knew the allegations of the pleadings were false and when they had their genesis in material unknown to him; it will also be granted when there is a substantial overbreadth of pleading compared with the knowledge on which it is based. *Halpern v. Barran, 272 A.2d 118 (Del. Ch. 1970).*

Where the plaintiff disclaims any knowledge of particular transactions alleged in the charge, the charge will be dismissed as a sham under this rule. *Singer v. Creole Petro. Corp., 297 A.2d 440 (Del. Ch. 1972), supplemental opinion, 301 A.2d 327 (Del. Ch. 1973), modified, 311 A.2d 859 (Del. 1973).*

Order not to file causes of action. — The court properly ordered the plaintiff not to file, and the register not to accept, any causes of action based upon previously addressed claims where (1) the case was on the docket for nearly 30 years, (2) nearly four years after the affirmance of the dismissal of the action, the plaintiff filed a motion to reactivate the suit, without offering any justification for relief, and (3) the arguments advanced in his motion were a mere rehashing of his previously rejected claims. *Yancey v. National Trust Co., 712 A.2d 476 (Del. 1998).*

Dismissal without prejudice granted. — Highest court: (1) redefined a test to determine if the shareholders' claim was a separate or a derivative claim under Del. Ch. Ct. R. 23.1; (2) found they did not state a derivative claim; (3) found they did not state a ripe separate claim upon which relief could be granted, but that that issue was not argued; and, (4) affirmed the dismissal, but reversed the judgment and remanded for the trial court to dismiss the case (without prejudice) with leave to replead under Del. Ch. Ct. R. 11. *Tooley v. Donaldson, Lufkin, & Jenrette, Inc., 845 A.2d 1031 (Del. 2004).*

Plaintiff's counsel was found to have prosecuted a purported class action suit against a software company in bad faith by filing false and misleading complaints and by withholding material information during discovery; the trial court ordered plaintiff and counsel jointly and severally to pay $25,000 to the defendant as well as ordered the law firm and lawyers to pay $2,500 to the trial court for the waste of the court's resources and time. *Beck v. Atl. Coast Plc., 868 A.2d 840 (Del. Ch. 2005).*

Trial courts are obligated to diligently sanction discovery abuse, because the burden rests on the trial courts to promptly and effectively take corrective action to secure the just, speedy, and inexpensive determination of every proceeding before them. *Beck v. Atl. Coast Plc., 868 A.2d 840 (Del. Ch. 2005).*

Rule 12. Defenses and objections — When and how presented — By pleading or motion — Motion for judgment on pleadings

DELAWARE CASE NOTES — REPORTED

I. GENERAL CONSIDERATION.

Plaintiffs alleged adequate specific facts to support their claim that the officers, affiliates and parents utilized partnership assets which they controlled to enrich themselves at the expense of the limited partners. *Wallace v. Wood, 752 A.2d 1175 (Del. Ch. 1999).*

Burden of proof. — On a subdivision (b)(2) motion, the burden is on the plaintiff to make a specific showing that the Chancery Court has jurisdiction under a long-arm statute. *Werner v. Miller Tech. Mgmt., L.P., 831 A.2d 318 (Del. Ch. 2003).*

II. WHEN PRESENTED.

Sanctions contemplated where fraud charges not stated with particularity. — Where the plaintiff has been ruled to state his charges of fraud with particularity, as required by Ch. Ct. R. 9(b) but has failed to do so, this failure is ground for dismissal, and paragraph (b) of this rule itself contemplates sanctions, drastic if necessary. *Mayer v. Adams, 40 Del. Ch. 94, 174 A.2d 313 (1961).*

III. HOW PRESENTED.

A. JURISDICTION OVER SUBJECT MATTER.

Dismissal where no "actual controversy." — Where a plaintiff's sworn answers fail to show the required "actual controversy," a motion to dismiss for lack of jurisdiction over the subject matter must be granted. *Wilmington Manor, Inc. v. Grant, 34 Del. Ch. 487, 105 A.2d 783 (1954).*

But error to dismiss when inadequate remedy at law. — When the answers to issues presented may demonstrate irreparable injury, it is impossible to compute the continuing damages alleged to be accruing from day to day, and a multiplicity of suits may result, this spells out "inadequate remedy at law," so that it is error to dismiss the action on the ground of lack of equity jurisdiction. *Eastern Shore Natural Gas Co. v. Stauffer Chem. Co., 298 A.2d 322 (Del. 1972).*

Court may decline to make final ruling where uncertainty. — Because of uncertainty as to whether parts of a contract are still a matter of contract between the parties, the Chancery Court may decline to make a final ruling on a defendant's motion to dismiss for lack of jurisdiction over the subject matter, giving counsel an opportunity to supplement the record. *City of Wilmington v. Delaware Coach Co., 43 Del. Ch. 343, 230 A.2d 762 (1967).*

No jurisdiction over appeal of nonbinding advisory statement issued by board. — Nonbinding declaratory statement issued by the Public Employment Relations Board pursuant to *19 Del. C. § 1306* and *14 Del. C. § 4006(h)(4)*, regarding an interpretation controversy as to parity provisions in public employee collective bargaining agreements, did not constitute a decision of the PERB under *19 Del. C. § 1308* and, therefore, was not subject to statutory appeal under *19 Del. C. § 1309*; the legislative intent of the statutory scheme embodied in the Public Employment Relations Act, *19 Del. C. §§ 1301-1316*, indicates that binding orders of the PERB, but not nonbinding advisory statements, carry a right of appeal to the *Delaware Chancery Court. AFSCME Locals 1102, Local 320 v. City of Wilmington, 858 A.2d 962 (Del. Ch. 2004).*

Complaint to enjoin arbitration was time barred and dismissed. — Where a contractor participated in arbitration proceedings for almost one year before filing a complaint to enjoin the arbitration, the contractor's request for an injunction was time barred, as the right to seek court intervention, pursuant to *10 Del. C. § 5702(c)*, was not without restriction; a motion to dismiss the contractor's complaint, brought pursuant to Del. Ch. Ct. R. 12(b)(1), based upon a lack of subject matter jurisdiction, was granted. *Fid. & Deposit Co. of Md. v. State Dep't of Admin. Servs., 830 A.2d 1224 (Del. Ch. 2003).*

B. JURISDICTION OVER PERSON.

Primacy of personal jurisdiction challenge. — Before reaching the merits of their motion to dismiss under subdivision (b)(6) of this rule, the Chancery Court must first consider a defendant's motion to dismiss for lack of personal jurisdiction pursuant to subdivision (b)(2); the analyses of motions to dismiss under subdivision (b)(2) and subdivision (b)(6) are separate and distinct, and examination of a document for subdivision 12(b)(2) purposes does not warrant consideration of the document for subdivision (b)(6) purposes. *Werner v. Miller Tech. Mgmt., L.P., 831 A.2d 318 (Del. Ch. 2003).*

Condition precedent. — A court's finding of personal jurisdiction is a condition precedent to a proper exercise of its own judicial authority and is determinative of the course of other litigation between the same parties. *Branson v. Exide Elecs. Corp., 625 A.2d 267 (Del. 1993).*

Prima facie showing. — When personal jurisdiction is challenged by a motion to dismiss pursuant to subsection (b)(2) of this rule, the plaintiff bears the burden of showing a basis for the Chancery Court's exercise of jurisdiction over the nonresident defendant; generally, the Chancery Court will engage in a two-step analysis: (1) determining whether service of process on the nonresident is authorized by statute, and (2) considering whether the exercise of jurisdiction is, in the circumstances presented, consistent with due process. *Werner v. Miller Tech. Mgmt., L.P., 831 A.2d 318 (Del. Ch. 2003).*

"Choice of law" provisions. — While a "Choice of Law" provision should not be ignored in a jurisdictional analysis, such a provision does not by itself confer jurisdiction; here the Court of Cancery dismissed claims against defendants for lack of personal jurisdiction and decided the provision in a partnership agreement was essentially standing alone, it cannot be said to bestow personal jurisdiction on the defendants; the partners can, if they chose, avail themselves of Delaware law through a forum selection clause in the partnership agreement. *Werner v. Miller Tech. Mgmt., L.P., 831 A.2d 318 (Del. Ch. 2003).*

Conspiracy theory. — To validly exercise jurisdiction under a conspiracy theory a court must find that a five-part test has been satisfied; the test requires (1) there is the existence of a conspiracy to defraud; (2) the defendant must be a member of that conspiracy; (3) a substantial act or substantial effect in furtherance of the conspiracy occurs in Delaware; (4) the defendant knows or has reason to know of the act in Delaware or that acts outside Delaware would have an effect in Delaware; and (5) the act in or effect on Delaware is a direct and foreseeable result of the conduct in furtherance of the conspiracy; more importantly, this test is a strict test that should be construed narrowly, and therefore, application of personal jurisdiction under the conspiracy theory requires factual proof of each enumerated element; without some showing that some act or effect occurred in Delaware, a plaintiff cannot satisfy the third element of the conspiracy theory test, and his claim for personal jurisdiction on this ground must fail. *Werner v. Miller Tech. Mgmt., L.P., 831 A.2d 318 (Del. Ch. 2003).*

Special appearance abolished. — Terminology and procedure surrounding the special or limited appearance has been replaced by the *Rules of Court. Abercrombie v. Davies, 35 Del. Ch. 354, 118 A.2d 358 (1955).*

The special appearance has been abolished by the *Rules of Court. Schwartz v. Miner, 36 Del. Ch. 481, 133 A.2d 599 (1957).*

Now, function of a special appearance is amply discharged by the use of remedies provided by this rule. *Abercrombie v. Davies, 35 Del. Ch. 354, 118 A.2d 358 (1955).*

The purpose formerly served by granting leave to appear specially to attack jurisdiction is now fulfilled by the filing of a motion to dismiss for lack of jurisdiction as provided by paragraph (b) of this rule. *Schwartz v. Miner, 36 Del. Ch. 481, 133 A.2d 599 (1957).*

Motion not made without submitting to jurisdiction. — A Ch. Ct. R. 12(b)(6) motion cannot be made without the defendant first submitting himself to the jurisdiction of the Court. *Widder v. Leeds, 317 A.2d 32 (Del. Ch. 1974).*

A nonresident defendant may always attack the jurisdiction of this court, thereby making in effect a special appearance. *Lefcourt Realty Corp. v. Sands, 35 Del. Ch. 164, 113 A.2d 428, aff'd, 117 A.2d 365 (Del. 1955).*

Nonresident advisory board. — Chancery Court determined that the individual nonresident advisory board members who provided only ideas to Delaware partnership was not to be construed as ability to manage the partnership and did not constitute contact with Delaware for the purposes of *19 Del. C. § 3104(c)* and the U.S. Const. amend. XIV and dismissed the claims against them under a subdivision (b)(2) motion to dismiss. *Werner v. Miller Tech. Mgmt., L.P., 831 A.2d 318 (Del. Ch. 2003).*

By motion or answer. — The right to raise the matters formerly incorporated in a special appearance, including an attack upon the Court's jurisdiction over the person or property, are preserved and may now be done either by motion or, in some cases, in the answer. *Abercrombie v. Davies, 35 Del. Ch. 354, 118 A.2d 358 (1955).*

But merits of plaintiff's claim may not be so attacked. — An attack on the jurisdiction of the Court over a nonresident may always be made by a special appearance but such an attack may not include an attack on the merits of plaintiff's claim. *Hughes v. TWA, 40 Del. Ch. 552, 185 A.2d 886 (1962).*

Attack on the merits of the plaintiff's claim may not be made under the guise of a special appearance by a nonresident defendant to contest the jurisdiction of the Court over him. *Widder v. Leeds, 317 A.2d 32 (Del. Ch. 1974).*

Only other type of appearance nonresident may make is general appearance. *Lefcourt Realty Corp. v. Sands, 35 Del. Ch. 164, 113 A.2d 428, aff'd, 117 A.2d 365 (Del. 1955).*

If motion is denied, the defendant may then elect whether or not to subject himself to the Court's jurisdiction generally by continuing to defend the action. *Schwartz v. Miner, 36 Del. Ch. 481, 133 A.2d 599 (1957).*

Court cannot grant a motion under subdivision (b)(2) simply by accepting the well pleaded allegations of the complaint as true, because the pleader has no obligation to plead facts that show the amenability of the defendant to service of process; it is not open to defendant to restrict a subdivision (b)(2) motion to the face of the complaint. *Hart Holding Co. v. Drexel Burnham Lambert Inc., 593 A.2d 535 (Del. Ch. 1991).*

Subdivision (b)(2) motion presents a factual matter. — A motion under subdivision (b)(2) presents a factual matter, not a legal question alone. That factual question will concern the connection that the defendant has had, directly or indirectly, with the forum. The legal questions presented — whether that connection constitutes "doing business," whether it satisfies some aspect of a long-arm statute, or whether the assertion of personal jurisdiction conforms to conventional notions of fair play and substantial justice — cannot be resolved until the court determines these predicate factual matters. *Hart Holding Co. v. Drexel Burnham Lambert Inc., 593 A.2d 535 (Del. Ch. 1991).*

Discovery. — A plaintiff has an evidentiary burden when a subdivision (b)(2) motion is brought, and she may not be precluded from attempting to prove that a defendant is subject to the jurisdiction of the court, and may not ordinarily be precluded from reasonable discovery in aid of mounting such proof. Only where the facts alleged in the complaint make any claim of personal jurisdiction over defendant frivolous, might the trial court, in the exercise of its discretionary control over the discovery process, preclude reasonable discovery in aid of establishing personal jurisdiction. *Hart Holding Co. v. Drexel Burnham Lambert Inc., 593 A.2d 535 (Del. Ch. 1991).*

Argument on nature of dispute pending between parties does not transform an appearance to attack jurisdiction into a general one and does not constitute a waiver of objections to jurisdiction. *Hana Ranch, Inc. v. Lent, 424 A.2d 28 (Del. Ch. 1980).*

C. IMPROPER VENUE.

A derivative claim on behalf of a corporation will ordinarily not be dismissed on the ground of forum non conveniens except in the rare case in which the combination of the factors to be considered tips the scales overwhelmingly in favor of the defendants. *Parvin v. Kaufmann, 43 Del. Ch. 461, 236 A.2d 425 (1967).*

Factors to be considered in ruling on a motion to dismiss a derivative suit on the ground of forum non conveniens are (1) whether Delaware law is applicable, (2) the relative ease of access to proof, (3) the availability of compulsory process for witnesses, (4) the possibility of the view of premises, (5) all other practical considerations which would make the trial easy, expeditious and inexpensive, and (6) the pendency or nonpendency of a similar action or actions in another ju-

Chancery Court

risdiction. *Parvin v. Kaufmann, 43 Del. Ch. 461, 236 A.2d 425 (1967).*

D. FAILURE TO STATE CLAIM.

Relationship to Del. Ch. Ct. R. 23.1. — Since the standard under Del. Ch. Ct. R. 12(b)(6) is less stringent than the standard under Del. Ch. Ct. R. 23.1, a complaint that survives a Rule 23.1 motion to dismiss generally will also survive a Del. Ch. Ct. R. 12(b)(6) motion to dismiss, assuming that it otherwise contains sufficient facts to state a cognizable claim. *In re Walt Disney Co. Derivative Litig., 825 A.2d 275 (Del. Ch. 2003).*

A complaint will be dismissed on motion if it is clearly without merit, and the lack of merit may be either a matter of law or of fact. *Morgan v. Wells, 32 Del. Ch. 108, 80 A.2d 504 (1951); Cohen v. Mayor of Wilmington, 34 Del. Ch. 39, 99 A.2d 393 (1953).*

A subdivision (b)(6) motion will be granted if it appears with reasonable certainty that the plaintiff could not prevail on any set of facts that can be inferred from the pleading. *Kohls v. Kenetech Corp., 791 A.2d 763 (Del. Ch. 2000).*

Or when plaintiff not entitled to relief under any state of facts. — A complaint will not be dismissed for failure to state a claim unless it appears to a certainty that under no state of facts which could be proved to support the claim asserted would the plaintiff be entitled to relief. *Morgan v. Wells, 32 Del. Ch. 108, 80 A.2d 504 (1951); Cohen v. Mayor of Wilmington, 34 Del. Ch. 39, 99 A.2d 393 (1953); Danby v. Osteopathic Hosp. Ass'n, 101 A.2d 308 (Del. Ch. 1953), aff'd, 104 A.2d 903 (Del. 1954); Penn Mart Realty Co. v. Becker, 298 A.2d 349 (Del. Ch. 1972); Delaware State Troopers Lodge No. 6 v. O'Rourke, 403 A.2d 1109 (Del. Ch. 1979); Weinberger v. UOP, Inc., 409 A.2d 1262 (Del. Ch. 1979).*

However, if the complaint states a claim upon which the pleader might recover, the complaint should not be dismissed without a trial or motion for summary judgment. *Cohen v. Mayor of Wilmington, 34 Del. Ch. 39, 99 A.2d 393 (1953).*

Only those matters referred to in pleadings are to be considered. *Haber v. Bell, 465 A.2d 353 (Del. Ch. 1983).*

In the absence of conversion of a motion to dismiss for failure to state a claim into a motion for summary judgment, the chancery court should not have considered technical advice memoranda and other Internal Revenue Service documents, as well as news stories, in determining that a retailer was on inquiry notice that its practice of insuring its employees' lives was going to run into retrospective disallowances of deductions as well as claims by employees' estates. *Wal-Mart Stores, Inc. v. AIG Life Ins. Co., 860 A.2d 312 (Del. 2004).*

Matters outside the pleading may be presented in connection with a motion to dismiss the complaint, not as an aid to that motion, but to convert the motion to one for summary judgment under Rule 56. *Good v. Getty Oil Co., 518 A.2d 973 (Del. Ch. 1986).*

A motion to dismiss a complaint for failure to state a claim upon which relief can be granted pursuant to subdivision (b)(6) is treated as one for summary judgment when the parties filed evidentiary matter outside the pleadings during the course of briefing. *Dave Greytak Enters., Inc. v. Mazda Motors of Am., Inc., 622 A.2d 14 (Del. Ch. 1992), aff'd, 609 A.2d 668 (Del. 1992).*

In the absence of an affirmative indication from the trial judge, a reviewing court will not presuppose that the trial court relied on evidence outside of the complaint when deciding a motion to dismiss under subsection (b). *In re Tri-Star Pictures, Inc., 634 A.2d 319 (Del. 1993).*

Extraneous material may cause treatment as motion for summary judgment. — It is well settled that when a party moves to dismiss for failure to state a claim pursuant to subsection (b), and submits matters outside the pleadings, the motion will be treated as one for summary judgment under Court of Chancery Rule 56. *In re Tri-Star Pictures, Inc., 634 A.2d 319 (Del. 1993).*

If a party presents documents in support of its Rule 12(b)(6) motion and the court considers the documents, it generally must treat the motion as one for summary judgment. *In re Santa Fe Pac. Corp. Shareholder Litig., 669 A.2d 59 (Del. 1995).*

The consideration of a document outside of the scope of the pleadings converts a proceeding from a 12(b)(6) motion to dismiss to a motion for summary judgment. *Vanderbilt Income & Growth Assocs. v. ARVIDA/JMB Managers, Inc., 691 A.2d 609 (Del. 1996).*

Exceptions to pleading requirements. — The exceptions to the subdivision (b)(6) prohibition against considering documents outside of the pleadings are usually limited to two situations: (1) when the document is integral to a plaintiff's claim and incorporated into the complaint; and (2) when the document is not being relied upon to prove the truth of its contents. *Vanderbilt Income & Growth Assocs. v. ARVIDA/JMB Managers, Inc., 691 A.2d 609 (Del. 1996).*

Vagueness or lack of detail is not sufficient grounds alone to dismiss a complaint for failure to state a claim. *Morgan v. Wells, 32 Del. Ch. 108, 80 A.2d 504 (1951); Cohen v. Mayor of Wilmington, 34 Del. Ch. 39, 99 A.2d 393 (1953); Danby v. Osteopathic Hosp. Ass'n, 101 A.2d 308 (Del. Ch. 1953), aff'd, 104 A.2d 903 (Del. 1954).*

Mere vagueness does not justify dismissal. *Mayer v. Adams, 40 Del. Ch. 94, 174 A.2d 313 (1961).*

Although vagueness alone does not warrant dismissal of the action, it may be attacked by a proper motion under the rule, especially when the plaintiff assets fraud. *Mayer v. Adams, 40 Del. Ch. 94, 174 A.2d 313 (1961).*

Fraud allegation lacked particularity. — In making fraud allegations, the failure of limited partners in an investment fund to assert with particularity actual and reasonable reliance on the financial statement at issue, and the failure to allege the particular facts connecting the alleged fraud to the claimed injury, resulted in a dismissal of the fraud claim for failure to state a cause of action upon which relief could be granted; although notice pleading, under Del. Ch. Ct. R. 8, was sufficient to survive a motion to dismiss under Del. Ch. Ct. R. 12(b)(6), Del. Ch. Ct. R. 9(b) required that the circumstances constituting any alleged fraud be stated with particularity, which the complaint failed to do. *Anglo Am. Sec. Fund, L.P. v. S.R. Global Int'l Fund, L.P., 829 A.2d 143 (Del. Ch. 2003).*

Former shareholder in a merged company, who had become a shareholder in the successor company, lacked standing to pursue a pre-existing derivative claim under the rule of *Lewis v. Anderson, 477 A.2d 1040 (Del. 1984),* to which the high court adhered; the shareholder had argued that the merger was arranged in a fraudulent attempt to avoid the derivative action, but failed to plead fraud with any particularity. *Lewis v. Ward, 852 A.2d 896 (Del. 2004).*

Nevertheless, on a motion to dismiss, all well-pleaded allegations must be accepted as true. *Danby v. Osteopathic Hosp. Ass'n, 101 A.2d 308 (Del. Ch. 1953),* aff'd, *104 A.2d 903 (Del. 1954); Delaware State Troopers Lodge No. 6 v. O'Rourke, 403 A.2d 1109 (Del. Ch. 1979); Weinberger v. UOP, Inc., 409 A.2d 1262 (Del. Ch. 1979).*

When a defendant seeks dismissal for failure to state a claim upon which relief can be granted, the court accepts as true all the well-pleaded facts and takes no evidence with respect to them. The motion, thus, presents only a legal question. *Hart Holding Co. v. Drexel Burnham Lambert Inc., 593 A.2d 535 (Del. Ch. 1991).*

With complaint construed in most favorable light. — The Court, on a motion to dismiss for failure to state a claim, construes a complaint in the light most favorable to the plaintiff. *Morgan v. Wells, 32 Del. Ch. 108, 80 A.2d 504 (1951).*

On a Rule 12(b)(6) motion, the complaint must be viewed in the light most favorable to the plaintiff. *Delaware State Troopers Lodge No. 6 v. O'Rourke, 403 A.2d 1109 (Del. Ch. 1979).*

In reviewing dismissal under subdivision (b)(6), the reviewing court must determine whether it appears with reasonable certainty that, under any set of facts which could be proven to support the claim, plaintiffs would not be entitled to relief; that review is also limited to the well-pled facts contained in the complaint which, viewing all inferences in a light most favorable to the plaintiff, must be taken as true. *In re Tri-Star Pictures, Inc., 634 A.2d 319 (Del. 1993).*

Chancery court's grant of a motion to dismiss a breach of contract action was reversed, where plaintiff's complaint alleged the existence of a contract, breach of the contract's confidentiality requirements, resulting damages, and plaintiff provided a reasonable reading of the contract that the confidentiality provisions had not expired but remained. *VLIW Tech., L.L.C. v. Hewlett-Packard Co., 840 A.2d 606 (Del. 2003).*

As well as all inferences. — In considering a defense motion under subdivision (b)(6) to dismiss a complaint for failure to state a claim, all inferences must be construed in favor of the plaintiff. *Penn Mart Realty Co. v. Becker, 298 A.2d 349 (Del. Ch. 1972); Weinberger v. UOP, Inc., 409 A.2d 1262 (Del. Ch. 1979).*

Upon a motion to dismiss a complaint for failure to state a claim, the court must accept the inference which favors the sufficiency of the complaint. *Vale v. Atlantic Coast & Inland Corp., 34 Del. Ch. 50, 99 A.2d 396 (1953).*

On a Rule 12(b)(6) motion, all inferences must be accepted which favor the sufficiency of the complaint. *Delaware State Troopers Lodge No. 6 v. O'Rourke, 403 A.2d 1109 (Del. 1979).*

When considering a motion to dismiss a counterclaim under subdivision (b)(6) of this rule for failure to state a claim upon which relief could be granted, although all facts of the pleadings and reasonable inferences to be drawn therefrom were accepted as true, neither inferences nor conclusions of fact unsupported by allegations of specific facts were accepted as true; a trial court did not need to blindly accept as true all allegations, nor did the trial court have to draw all inferences from them in plaintiff's favor, unless they were reasonable inferences, and the court could consider, for certain limited purposes, the content of documents that were integral to or were incorporated by reference into the counterclaim. *Gloucester Holding Corp. v. U.S. Tape & Sticky Prods., LLC, 832 A.2d 116 (Del. Ch. 2003).*

Except those nonsupported. — A challenge to a complaint necessarily admits all facts of pleadings and the reasonable inferences to be drawn therefrom, but it does not admit either inferences or conclusions of fact not supported by allegations of specific facts upon which the inferences or conclusions rest are conclusions of law. *Cohen v. Mayor of Wilmington, 34 Del. Ch. 39, 99 A.2d 393 (1953).*

A motion to dismiss for failure to state a claim upon which relief can be granted does not concede pleaded conclusions of law or fact where there are no allegations of specific facts which would support such conclusions. *Weinberger v. UOP, Inc., 409 A.2d 1262 (Del. Ch. 1979).*

Ruling upon motion to dismiss for lack of personal jurisdiction. — The Court of Chancery erred by granting the individual defendants' motions to dismiss for failure to state a claim without first ruling expressly upon the individual defendants' Rule 12(b)(2) motions to dismiss for lack of personal jurisdiction. *Branson v. Exide Elecs. Corp., 625 A.2d 267 (Del. 1993).*

Though evidence upon which claim is based need not be pleaded. — To determine a defendant's motion to dismiss a complaint for failure to state a claim upon which relief can be granted, the plaintiff is only required to state a claim; he need not plead the evidence upon which the claim is based. *Cohen v. Mayor of Wilmington, 34 Del. Ch. 39, 99 A.2d 393 (1953).*

Differing reasonable interpretations. — On a motion to dismiss for failure to state a claim, a court cannot choose between two differing reasonable interpretations of ambiguous documents. *Vanderbilt Income & Growth Assocs. v. ARVIDA/JMB Managers, Inc., 691 A.2d 609 (Del. 1996).*

The use of a motion to dismiss to disprove the allegations of the complaint is inappropriate; such motions assume that the well-pleaded allegations of the complaint are true. *Good v. Getty Oil Co., 518 A.2d 973 (Del. Ch. 1986).*

Chancery Court

Court should have complete account as well as relief sought. — In order to test the sufficiency of a complaint, in whole or in part, the Court should have a reasonably complete account not only of the transactions allegedly causing the injury, giving pertinent dates and places, but also a statement of the appropriate relief sought. *Helfand v. Gambee, 37 Del. Ch. 51, 136 A.2d 558 (1957).*

But question of fact cannot be resolved on such motion. — Whether there was or was not to be a binding agreement to give an option until it was reduced to writing is a question of fact which cannot be resolved on a motion to dismiss but which must await the unfolding of the evidence. *Vale v. Atlantic Coast & Inland Corp., 34 Del. Ch. 50, 99 A.2d 396 (1953).*

And where there is a serious dispute as to the title of property, the court will not dismiss the complaint for failure to state a cause of action but will retain jurisdiction pending the determination of the question. *Cohen v. Mayor of Wilmington, 34 Del. Ch. 39, 99 A.2d 393 (1953).*

Likewise, enforcement of reduced royalties. — The unilateral undertaking by a licensor to accept a lesser amount of royalty than that provided in the license agreement does not destroy the licensor's right thereafter to enforce such agreement at the reduced royalty or subject that enforcement action to dismissal for failure to state a claim. *Components, Inc. v. Western Elec. Co., 267 A.2d 579 (Del. 1970).*

But action against lender dismissed. — Where the plaintiff as guarantor seeks to enjoin the endorsement of the notes against the defendant and the lending institution, and the lender is not an original party to the guaranty agreement between the plaintiff and defendant, action against the lender will be dismissed. *Danby v. Osteopathic Hosp. Ass'n, 101 A.2d 308 (Del. Ch. 1953), aff'd, 104 A.2d 903 (Del. 1954).*

Court does not assume sufficient remedy otherwise. — Where defendants entered the plaintiff's premises during the plaintiff's absence, after they had assured the plaintiff that no action would be taken until he had been advised and, without the institution of condemnation proceedings, proceeded to trespass upon the plaintiff's property and to seriously damage the same, the Court would not assume, upon a motion to dismiss, that any damages which the plaintiff might receive upon condemnation proceedings, which had not at that time been instituted, would be a sufficient remedy. *Cohen v. Mayor of Wilmington, 34 Del. Ch. 39, 99 A.2d 393 (1953).*

Subsequent review of dismissal. — Where first vice chancellor denied defendants' motion to dismiss under subdivision (b)(6) of this rule on one ground, another vice chancellor, under Rule 41(b), was not precluded from finding on another ground where he simply resolved the ambiguity that the first vice chancellor had identified under a different procedural standard. *Oberly v. Kirby, 592 A.2d 445 (Del. 1991).*

Shareholder's derivative action against a corporation and the corporate directors was dismissed pursuant to Del. Ch. Ct. R. 12(b)(6), where: the factors necessary to show usurpation of a corporate opportunity were not met; the directors had no duty to monitor the personal activities of the corporate founder; and a split-dollar insurance policy on behalf of the founder was disclosed and was not shown to be unlawful. *Beam v. Stewart, 833 A.2d 961 (Del. Ch. 2003), aff'd, 845 A.2d 1040 (Del. 2004).*

In minority shareholder's action claimimg that corporation and its board of directors breached their fiduciary duty by disclosure violations when they offered a voluntary buy-sell program, which the instant shareholder participated in to sell her shares, at the same time that negotiations were ongoing and which resulted, shortly after the shareholder's sale, of a corporate merger with a larger corporation that caused the market value of the shares to double, the shareholder did not have to rely on the "fraud on the market" theory because reliance was established by the corporation's request for shareholder action, the merger negotiations were material, and dismissal was denied as to the board; although dismissal was granted as to the corporation because it had no fiduciary duty of disclosure to the shareholder. *Alessi v. Beracha, 849 A.2d 939 (Del. Ch. 2004).*

Shareholder relief not granted. — Former shareholders' claim that the value received for their shares in a merger (due to wrongdoing by the corporation's founder and former chair) was clearly a derivative claim, not an individual one against the founder; therefore, since they were no longer shareholders after the merger, they lacked standing to bring such a claim, leading their complaint to be dismissed with prejudice. *In re Syncor Int'l Corp. S'holders Litig., 857 A.2d 994 (Del. Ch. 2004).*

Investor claims dismissed where documents relied upon contradicted allegations. — Claims based upon a private placement memorandum, which an investor claimed was misleading, but which was not expressly referred to in the subsequently executed purchase agreement, were dismissed for failure to state a cause of action, as the investor represented itself as an "accredited investor," as defined by federal securities regulations, and, as such, the investor presumptively understood the ramifications of the integration and disclaimer clauses within the purchase agreement; under Del. Ch. Ct. R. 12(b)(6), a claim could, despite allegations to the contrary, be dismissed where the unambiguous language of the documents upon which the claim was based contradicted the complaint's allegations. *H-M Wexford LLC v. Encorp, Inc., 832 A.2d 129 (Del. Ch. 2003).*

Creditors of a corporation who accepted (but failed to exercise) warrants that entitled them to purchase stock were bound by the plain language of the warrants to the rights set forth therein; therefore, they failed to state a claim against the controlling shareholder, after a short-form merger pursuant to 8 Del. C. § 253, either for breach of an implied duty of good faith and fair dealing (since their remedies were limited by contract) or for denial of appraisal rights pursuant to 8 Del. C. § 262. *Aspen Advisors LLC v. United Artists Theatre Co., 843 A.2d 697 (Del. Ch. 2004), aff'd, 861 A.2d 1251 (Del. 2004).*

Allegations sufficient to state claim that proposed corporate merger is unfair. — A complaint does not have to allege the particulars of why a merger is unfair so long as it alleges a use of its position by a majority shareholder to cash-out the minority on inadequate terms for no sufficient business purpose other than to get rid of them. Such general allegations coupled with factual assertions showing a use of the majority position is sufficient to state a cause of action and to place the burden on the majority shareholder, as part of its fiduciary duty, to prove the fairness of the merger terms as opposed to requiring the plaintiff to prove that they were unfair. *Weinberger v. UOP, Inc., 409 A.2d 1262 (Del. Ch. 1979).*

Fiduciary duties. — Plain and unambiguous language of the partnership agreement displaced traditional fiduciary duty principles; therefore, the limited partner failed to state a claim of action in its derivative suit challenging the partnership's acquisition of a company owned by the general partner. *Brickell Partners v. Wise, 794 A.2d 1 (Del. Ch. 2001).*

Investment bank failed to state claims against former fund managers for breach of contract (except on one small issue), breach of fiduciary responsibility, or fraud after the fund managers quit with no notice and went to work for a competing firm; a chancery court would not protect a sophisticated firm that had been unwilling to pay additional consideration to protect itself by imposing limits on employees that did not relate to the faithful performance of their fund management duties or to any term of their contract. *Lazard Debt Recovery GP, LLC v. Weinstock, 864 A.2d 955 (Del. Ch. 2004).*

Despite a limited liability company agreement containing an exculpatory clause protecting the company's directors from a breach of the duty of care, a motion to dismiss filed by the company and the directors was denied, in a former equity unit holders' suit asserting breach of fiduciary duty, because the former equity unit holders alleged sufficient facts in the complaint to support a claim for disloyal conduct, which was enough to survive the motion to dismiss. The complaint alleged that the approval of a transaction that resulted in the distribution to the company's creditors of 100 percent of available funds–an amount that exceeded the total amount of their claims and which rendered the equity units of the company worthless–was violative because the directors failed to consider alternative transactions that would have provided a better result for the company's equity holders, particularly in light of the alleged fact that the company was in no way insolvent at the time of the transaction. *Blackmore Partners, L.P. v. Link Energy LLC, 864 A.2d 80 (Del. Ch. 2004).*

Limited partners claims were direct, not derivative. — Where limited partners of an investment fund claimed that the general partner withdrew the funds in violation of the partnership agreement, that the withdrawal exceeded the balance in the account, and that timely disclosure of the withdrawal was not given, the court found that while a diminution of the value of a business was classically derivative in nature, the operation and function of the instant fund diverged so radically from the traditional corporate model that the claims were properly brought as direct claims, by the limited partners, all of which had withdrawn from the fund by the time the action was filed; that portion of defendants' motions to dismiss, brought pursuant to Del. Ch. Ct. R. 12(b)(6), contending that the limited partners lacked standing to bring the action because they were not partners, was rejected, as *6 Del. C. § 17-1002* did not apply. *Anglo Am. Sec. Fund, L.P. v. S.R. Global Int'l Fund, L.P., 829 A.2d 143 (Del. Ch. 2003).*

Laches. — The rule that a complaint may not be dismissed for alleged failure to state a claim unless it appears to a reasonable certainty that under no statement of facts which could be proved would plaintiff be entitled to relief applies to a motion to strike the remedy portion of a complaint on the ground that it is barred by laches. *Harman v. Masoneilan Int'l, 442 A.2d 487 (Del. 1982).*

E. FAILURE TO JOIN PARTY.

Failure of the plaintiff to join indispensable parties should be attacked by a motion to dismiss under this rule rather than by motion for judgment on the pleadings. *Goldhar v. Rosenfeld, 38 Del. Ch. 233, 149 A.2d 753 (1959).*

IV. JUDGMENT ON PLEADINGS.

A motion for judgment on pleadings under this rule is a convenient device for determining a matter without trial where the pleadings show no dispute as to the material facts, though it is conceivable that a decision on such a motion would reveal the possible materiality of facts which were not before the Court when it ruled on the motion. *Du Pont v. Equitable Sec. Trust Co., 35 Del. Ch. 261, 115 A.2d 482 (1955), aff'd, 122 A.2d 429 (Del. 1956).*

Nonetheless, motions under this rule are not favored because of their delaying effect. *Helfand v. Gambee, 37 Del. Ch. 51, 136 A.2d 558 (1957).*

A court may grant a motion for judgment on the pleadings where there is no material fact in dispute and where the moving party is entitled to judgment as a matter of law; that is, a court should not grant such a motion unless it appears to a reasonable certainty that the nonmovant would not be entitled to relief for its claims under any set of facts that could be proven in support of its allegations. *Desert Equities, Inc. v. Morgan Stanley Leveraged Equity Fund, 624 A.2d 1199 (Del. 1993).*

Scope of court's review. — In passing on a motion to dismiss a complaint under subdivision (b)(6) of this rule for failure to state a claim upon which relief can be granted, the court is to assume the truthfulness of all well-pleaded allegations of fact in the complaint and may also consider, for certain limited purposes, the content of documents that are integral to or are incorporated by reference into the complaint; however, neither inferences nor conclusions of fact unsupported by allegations of specific facts are accepted as true, and a trial court need not blindly accept as true all allegations, nor must it draw all inferences from them in plaintiffs' favor unless they are reasonable inferences. *In re BHC Communications, Inc. Shareholder Litig., 789 A.2d 1 (Del. Ch. 2001).*

Online at http://cscde.lexisnexis.com

Chancery Court

Pleaded facts and inferences construed in most favorable light. — In determining a motion under subsection (c) of this Rule for judgment on the pleadings, a trial court is required to view the facts pleaded and inferences to be drawn from such facts in a light most favorable to the non-moving party. *Desert Equities, Inc. v. Morgan Stanley Leveraged Equity Fund, 624 A.2d 1199 (Del. 1993).*

Construction through federal decisional law. — Since subsection (c) of this Rule is identical with *Federal Rule of Civil Procedure 12(c),* the court may look to federal decisional law in construing this *Rule. Desert Equities, Inc. v. Morgan Stanley Leveraged Equity Fund, 624 A.2d 1199 (Del. 1993).*

The rule governing motions for judgment on pleadings requires that pleadings be closed before such a motion is filed, for, if the pleadings have not been closed within the meaning of the rule, the motion will be denied because it was prematurely filed. *Vale v. Atlantic Coast & Inland Corp., 34 Del. Ch. 50, 99 A.2d 396 (1953).*

And on a motion for judgment on pleadings the court is confined to pleadings in disposing of such a motion. *Schleiff v. B. & O.R.R., 36 Del. Ch. 342, 130 A.2d 321 (1955).*

Reference to outside documents. — Chancery Court may consider, for certain limited purposes, the content of documents that are integral to or are incorporated by reference into the complaint and under subdivision (b)(6) of this rule, a complaint may, despite allegations to the contrary, be dismissed where the unambiguous language of documents upon which the claims are based contradict the complaint's allegations. *Werner v. Miller Tech. Mgmt., L.P., 831 A.2d 318 (Del. Ch. 2003).*

Proxy statements were considered by the court in determining whether to grant judgment on the pleadings in favor of defendants, a corporation and the majority shareholder corporation with which it merged, as well as the directors, and their investment banker, who provided shareholders of the corporation with information regarding the fairness of the proposed cash-out merger; it was not enough for the shareholder challengers, in claiming insufficient disclosure, to argue that the investment banker should have performed analyses other than the one it performed, or to argue that they disagreed with the investment banker's recommendations as a matter of judgment. *In re JCC Holding Co., 843 A.2d 713 (Del. Ch. 2003).*

Allegations that negate each other. — With respect to a subdivision (b)(6) motion to dismiss under this rule, a Chancery Court is hardly bound to accept as true a demonstrable mischaracterization and the erroneous allegations that flow from it; a claim may be dismissed if allegations in the complaint or in the exhibits incorporated into the complaint effectively negate the claim as a matter of law. *Werner v. Miller Tech. Mgmt., L.P., 831 A.2d 318 (Del. Ch. 2003).*

Dismissal of stockholder action on pleadings improper. — Dismissal of a stockholder action on the pleadings, pursuant to Del. Ch. Ct. R. 12(b)(6), was improper where the question of the independence of the members of a special committee that recommended a merger was a question that turned upon the reality of the interests and incentives affecting the independent directors; the full board of directors had to act to approve a merger agreement and recommend the merger to the stockholders for approval, and a committee could not be empowered to perform that necessary board function, pursuant to 8 Del. C. §§ 141(c) and 251(b). *Krasner v. Moffett, 826 A.2d 277 (Del. 2003).*

V. AMENDMENT.

Sufficient cause. — A stockholder information form is analogous to a defense under this rule and the right to amend for cause is consistent with the language set forth in the form. *In re Enstar Corp., 513 A.2d 206 (Del. Ch. 1986).*

VI. EFFECT OF DISMISSAL.

Preclusion of subsequent action. — The operative effect of a dismissal pursuant to (b) depends upon the basis selected for granting the motion; a dismissal for lack of jurisdiction or improper venue does not preclude a subsequent action in an appropriate forum, whereas a dismissal for failure to state a claim upon which relief can be granted is with prejudice. *Branson v. Exide Elecs. Corp., 625 A.2d 267 (Del. 1993).*

When a California court voluntarily dismissed a stockholder's original complaint with leave to amend, this did not amount to a dismissal with prejudice under Del. Ch. Ct. R. 12(b)(6) because the California dismissal was not final. *Dieterich v. Harrer, 857 A.2d 1017 (Del. Ch. 2004).*

Rule 13.   Counterclaim and cross-claim

DELAWARE CASE NOTES — REPORTED

Power to adopt rule on compulsory counterclaims. — Court of equity has historically entertained cross bills seeking affirmative relief if the claim asserted by cross bill arose out of the same transaction that formed the basis of the complainant's claim. Therefore, the Court of Chancery under its rule-making power could properly adopt paragraph (a) dealing with compulsory counterclaims seeking affirmative relief. *Delaware Chems., Inc. v.*

Reichhold Chems., Inc., 35 Del. Ch. 493, 121 A.2d 913 (1956).

Court's jurisdiction over intervening parties and claims. — The Court has personal jurisdiction over a party not originally joined, but who meets the test of Rule 24, and who asserts a counterclaim arising out of the same facts as those alleged in the complaint. *In re RJR Nabisco, Inc. Shareholders Litig., 576 A.2d 654 (Del. Ch. 1990).*

Court's ancillary jurisdiction extends to compulsory counterclaims asserted by persons with a right under Rule 24(a) to intervene. *In re RJR Nabisco, Inc. Shareholders Litig., 576 A.2d 654 (Del. Ch. 1990).*

When the facts alleged in the intervenor's new "claim" in effect constitute the same factors or transaction as put in issue by the existing pleadings, and when the proposed intervenors, far from being strangers to the existing parties, allegedly acted in the transaction in question at the behest of the defendants, the Court has ancillary jurisdiction over the compulsory and permissive claims of every kind arising from the transaction that could be asserted by the original parties and the intervenors. *In re RJR Nabisco, Inc. Shareholders Litig., 576 A.2d 654 (Del. Ch. 1990).*

This rule is similar to Fed. R. Civ. P. 13. *Kaye v. Pantone, Inc., 395 A.2d 369 (Del. Ch. 1978).*

Proceedings under this rule must be actually directed against potential counter-claimant. *In re Arthur Treacher's Fish & Chips of Ft. Lauderdale, Inc., 386 A.2d 1162 (Del. Ch. 1978).*

Possible benefit from relief sought not enough. — It is not enough, in meeting the requirements of this rule, that a party may benefit from the relief sought. *In re Arthur Treacher's Fish & Chips of Ft. Lauderdale, Inc., 386 A.2d 1162 (Del. Ch. 1978).*

A counterclaim for malicious prosecution may not be interposed in the action which is the basis of the claim. *Alexander v. Petty, 35 Del. Ch. 5, 108 A.2d 575 (1954).*

This rule deals with matured claims, as indicated by the special manner in which the rule handles claims maturing after suit is commenced. *Alexander v. Petty, 35 Del. Ch. 5, 108 A.2d 575 (1954).*

Counterclaim from a related foreign state action can also be asserted inasmuch as the spirit of the rules

generally favors the filing of all related claims. *Bata v. Hill, 37 Del. Ch. 363, 143 A.2d 728 (1958).*

Court has discretion to refuse to entertain a permissive counterclaim. *Kaye v. Pantone, Inc., 395 A.2d 369 (Del. Ch. 1978).*

Permissive counterclaim in appraisal actions should be looked upon with disfavor. *Kaye v. Pantone, Inc., 395 A.2d 369 (Del. Ch. 1978).*

When the defendant does not file his tendered cross-claim prior to the trial of his case, he should not be permitted to supplement the record after failing to seek a timely amendment to his pleadings and introduce affirmative evidence on his alleged contractual rights when he had the opportunity. *Cook v. Fusselman, 300 A.2d 246 (Del. Ch. 1972).*

After trial, at which he has had a full opportunity to participate, a defendant will not be given leave to file a proposed cross-claim for specific performance of an alleged contract and have his right to such form of relief preserved by the issuance of a preliminary injunction. *Cook v. Fusselman, 300 A.2d 246 (Del. Ch. 1972).*

Basic purpose of paragraph (h) is to encourage, and even compel, the joining in one case of all interested parties for the purpose of obtaining a final and comprehensive judicial determination of all aspects of a particular transaction or occurrence. *Trans World Airlines v. Hughes, 40 Del. Ch. 523, 185 A.2d 762, aff'd, 185 A.2d 886 (Del. Ch. 1962).*

Sua sponte joinder of wife with husband. — It is improper for the Court sua sponte to join a wife personally as a party over her husband's objection and then to use that joinder for the benefit of the husband when she is not individually a party and does not even present evidence in defense to the claim because of the husband's refusal to allow her joinder. *Astle v. Wenke, 297 A.2d 45 (Del. 1972).*

Rule 14.   Third-party practice

DELAWARE CASE NOTES — REPORTED

Subject matter jurisdiction of third cause of action. — Where the third party complaint, the affidavit and the prior pleadings, taken together, state an actual controversy prior to the time where a remedy would be

traditionally available, the Chancery Court has subject matter jurisdiction of the third cause of action. *Rollins Int'l, Inc. v. International Hydronics Corp., 295 A.2d 592 (Del. Ch. 1972), aff'd, 303 A.2d 660 (Del. 1973).*

Rule 15.   Amended and supplemental pleadings

DELAWARE CASE NOTES — REPORTED

I. General Consideration.
II. Amendments.
III. Relation Back.

I. GENERAL CONSIDERATION.

Legislative intent. — Subsection (aaa) of this rule, limiting a plaintiff's ability to amend a complaint, embodied a legislative-type finding that, by the time a responsive brief was due to be filed in opposition to a motion to dismiss of the type described in the rule, the party-plaintiff would have enough information from which to decide whether to stand on the complaint as alleged or, instead,

to re-plead. *Stern v. LF Capital Partners, LLC, 820 A.2d 1143 (Del. Ch. 2003).*

Purpose. — Purpose of subsection (aaa) of this rule was to eliminate (or at least sharply curtail) instances in which a trial court was required to adjudicate multiple motions to dismiss the same action, and the rule was designed to accomplish that objective by requiring plaintiffs, when confronted by a motion to dismiss pursuant to any of Ch. Ct. R. 12(b)(6), (c) or 23.1, to elect either to stand on the complaint and answer the motion or, instead, to amend or seek leave to amend the complaint before the response to the motion was due; the rule enforced this requirement by providing that, if a plaintiff chose to file an answering brief in opposition to a motion to dismiss rather than amend the complaint, any subsequent dismissal pursuant to the motion was with prejudice unless the court for good cause shown found that dismissal with prejudice would not be just under all the circumstances. *Stern v. LF Capital Partners, LLC, 820 A.2d 1143 (Del. Ch. 2003).*

Applicability. — There was substantial interplay between subsection (aaa) of this rule, limiting a plaintiff's right to amend its complaint, and Del. Ch. Ct. R. 41(a), regarding voluntary dismissal, and those rules were to be construed, to the extent possible, to give effect to both. *Stern v. LF Capital Partners, LLC, 820 A.2d 1143 (Del. Ch. 2003).*

Although failure to join an indispensable party in a land use action would be grounds for dismissal under this rule and Del. Ch. Ct. R. 19, the court declined to dismiss landowners' complaint challenging a zoning ordinance on those grounds because it found that the holder of a remainder interest in the property at issue whose interested never vested and which had, in any case, been transferred to a party was not an indispensable party. *Lynch v. City of Rehoboth,* (Del. Ch. May 28, 2004).

"Without prejudice". — Dismissals with and without prejudice are equally appealable as final judgments. The phrase "without prejudice" in an order of dismissal by a Delaware judge is not to be construed as an implicit invitation to file an amended complaint. Instead, the phrase "without prejudice" will mean only that the otherwise final judgment does not operate as a res judicata bar to preclude a subsequent lawsuit on the same cause of action. If leave to amend a complaint is contemplated by a Delaware judge following a dismissal without prejudice, there must be an express statement to that effect in the order, in which case the order will be an interlocutory decree. Our holdings are intended to avoid future confusion and provide certainty regarding the ability to file an amendment, the finality of a judgment of dismissal without prejudice, and the time in which to file an appeal. *Braddock v. Zimmerman, 906 A.2d 776, 2006 Del. LEXIS 468 (Sept. 12, 2006).*

Scope. — In order to give subsection (aaa) of this rule, limiting a plaintiff's right to amend a complaint, its intended scope, once the time for amendment had passed under that rule, a party-plaintiff was not permitted to resort to Ch. Ct. R. 41(a), 23 or 23.1 to file a "without prejudice" dismissal of its action. *Stern v. LF Capital Partners, LLC, 820 A.2d 1143 (Del. Ch. 2003).*

Standard of review. — Under subsection (a) of this rule, leave to amend was to be freely given when justice so required, but under subsection (aaa), by contrast, a dismissal was to be "with prejudice," i.e. without leave to amend, unless the court for good cause shown found that dismissal with prejudice would not be just under all the circumstances. *Stern v. LF Capital Partners, LLC, 820 A.2d 1143 (Del. Ch. 2003).*

II. AMENDMENTS.

This rule is written upon the assumption that pleadings are not an end in themselves but are designed to assist, not deter, the disposition of litigation on its merits. *Brunswick Corp. v. Colt Realty, Inc., 253 A.2d 216 (Del. Ch. 1969).*

Nevertheless, motions to amend pleadings are always addressed to the discretion of the trial judge. *Brunswick Corp. v. Colt Realty, Inc., 253 A.2d 216 (Del. Ch. 1969); Bokat v. Getty Oil Co., 262 A.2d 246 (Del. 1970).*

While leave to amend should be granted freely when justice requires it, it is always, however, a discretionary matter with the trial judge, reviewable on appeal solely for abuse of discretion. *Bokat v. Getty Oil Co., 262 A.2d 246 (Del. 1970).*

And serious prejudice is to party reasonable limitation. — Although liberality of amendment to a pleading is a tradition in the courts of Delaware, under this rule serious prejudice to one opposing the motion is a reasonable limitation on that liberality. *Bowl-Mor Co. v. Brunswick Corp., 297 A.2d 61 (Del. Ch.), appeal dismissed, 297 A.2d 67 (Del. 1972).*

Amendment of statutory claim. — To permit a party to amend a statutory claim to include fraud claims would impermissibly broaden the legislative remedy. *Cede & Co. v. Technicolor, Inc., 542 A.2d 1182 (Del. 1988).*

Procedural bar. — In an action that was, at least partly, a derivative action, against an investment fund, after plaintiffs elected to stand on their complaint in response to defendants' motion to dismiss, rather than amend their complaint, their subsequent motion to amend, before the trial court ruled on the motion to dismiss, was precluded under subsection (aaa) of this rule. *Stern v. LF Capital Partners, LLC, 820 A.2d 1143 (Del. Ch. 2003).*

Dropping of party defendant. — When this rule is employed to drop a party defendant, the proper function of the Court is to prevent any undue prejudice to the party affected by a motion to drop and, except where a plaintiff proposes to drop an entire controversy before the filing of an answer or a motion for summary judgment, the Court, while empowered to permit the dropping of a named party defendant, must do so only on terms that are fair and proper and usually in the early stages of the litigation. *Oil & Gas Ventures, Inc. v. Cheyenne Oil Corp., 43 Del. Ch. 143, 220 A.2d 785 (1966).*

A conditional allowance has a place in the exercise of the court's discretion under this rule. *Brunswick Corp. v. Colt Realty, Inc., 253 A.2d 216 (Del. Ch. 1969).*

Consideration of form, time or harassment. — In considering objections to the filing of amendments, the Court, absent an unusual showing, looks only to objections involving questions of form, time or harassment. *E.M. Fleischmann Lumber Corp. v. Resources Corp. Int'l, 34 Del. Ch. 509, 106 A.2d 205 (1954).*

When on the face of the complaint a showing of traditional equitable jurisdiction is not strong, but is adequately strengthened by an amendment to the complaint tendered by the plaintiff, leave to file the amendment should be granted under the liberal amendment policy of this rule. *Diebold Computer Leasing, Inc. v. Commercial Credit Corp., 267 A.2d 586 (Del. 1970).*

Subsection (a) was drafted to facilitate decision on merits, not as an end in itself. *Levinson v. American Accident Reinsurance Group, 503 A.2d 632 (Del. Ch. 1985).*

III. RELATION BACK.

Amend only matter arising out of that set forth. — Paragraph (c) of this rule, providing that an amendment to a complaint relates back to the date of filing of the complaint, refers only to matter which "arose out of the conduct, transaction or occurrence set forth." *Gluck v. Chashin, 42 Del. Ch. 325, 210 A.2d 855 (1965).*

Subsection (aaa) of this rule was itself sufficiently clear to preclude a plaintiff who had chosen to respond to a motion to dismiss (rather than amend) from voluntarily dismissing in order to file a new action alleging amended claims. *Stern v. LF Capital Partners, LLC, 820 A.2d 1143 (Del. Ch. 2003).*

Amendments which do not relate back. — Proposed amendment to complaint which would add sole stockholder of plaintiff corporation as a plaintiff and assert a claim of fraud against certain defendants did not relate back to the original complaint and was barred due to failure to assert the claim within the 3-year statute of limitations period of *10 Del. C. § 8106. Atlantis Plastics Corp. v. Sammons, 558 A.2d 1062 (Del. Ch. 1989).*

DELAWARE CASE NOTES — UNREPORTED

Rule 15(aaa) did not preclude plaintiffs from amending their complaint at least with respect to standing. Plaintiffs' proposed amendments, however, address more than the standing defense. In that regard, plaintiffs have violated the spirit, if not the letter, of Rule 15(aaa) because the new allegations contained in their proposed complaint go well beyond the facts necessary to address defendants' standing defense and include several

matters germane to issues defendants did fairly raise in their motion and opening brief. Nevertheless, based on the court's preference for resolving matters on the merits and the absence of material prejudice to defendants, plaintiffs' motion to amend in its entirety is granted. *Franklin Balance Sheet Inv. Fund v. Crowley, 2006 Del. Ch. LEXIS 188 (Oct. 19, 2006).*

IV. PARTIES

Rule 17. Parties plaintiff and defendant; capacity

DELAWARE CASE NOTES — REPORTED

I. General Consideration.
II. Real Party in Interest.
III. Infants and Incompetents.

I. GENERAL CONSIDERATION.

Cross references. — As to assignee suing in own name, see § 3902 of Title 10. As to action by 1 or more on behalf of a class, see Rule 23 of the Court of Chancery.

II. REAL PARTY IN INTEREST.

Trustees of an express trust have standing to bring suit for reformation of the trust by paragraph (a) of this rule. *Roos v. Roos, 42 Del. Ch. 40, 203 A.2d 140 (1964).*

And reasonable time must be allowed for substitution of such party. — Although the executor or administrator is the proper party to assert claims in behalf of a decedent's estate, since this rule provides that no action shall be dismissed on the ground that it is not prosecuted in the name of the real party in interest until a reasonable time has been allowed for the substitution of such party, the Court

may allow plaintiffs who have brought an action in their own name time within which to comply with this *Rule. Krajewski v. Blair, 297 A.2d 70 (Del. Ch. 1972).*

An order realigning parties is appealable since it might well determine a substantial right of defendants, viz., the right to be sued by the real party in interest as required by this rule. *Phillips v. Liberty Mut. Ins. Co., 43 Del. Ch. 388, 232 A.2d 101 (1967).*

III. INFANTS AND INCOMPETENTS.

Guardian ad litem appointed for voting stock. — When there is a possible conflict between the personal interest of a guardian, who by voting his wards' stock is in a position to gain control of the affairs of a corporation, and his fiduciary duty as a guardian of minors, this rule provides that a guardian ad litem may be appointed for the minor trust beneficiaries who have a right to have their stock voted in their own best interest. *Wilmington Trust Co. v. Lee, 298 A.2d 358 (Del. Ch. 1972).*

Rule 18. Joinder of claims and remedies

DELAWARE CASE NOTES — REPORTED

The old doctrine of multifariousness has little application today. Bennett v. Breuil Petro. Corp., 34 Del. Ch. 6, 99 A.2d 236 (1953).

Thus, a complaint asserting both a personal and a derivative cause of action is not defective because of improper joinder. Bennett v. Breuil Petro. Corp., 34 Del. Ch. 6, 99 A.2d 236 (1953).

Rule 19.   Joinder of persons needed for just adjudication

DELAWARE CASE NOTES — REPORTED

This rule is mandatory in letter as well as in spirit, and joinder will be ordered once the Court finds that its terms are met. *Hughes Tool Co. v. Fawcett Publications, Inc., 350 A.2d 341 (Del. 1975).*

Paragraph (a) depends upon availability to process. — Paragraph (a) of this rule is written in terms of one who is "subject to service of process" and, in that sense, its efficacy depends upon availability to process. *Hughes Tool Co. v. Fawcett Publications, Inc., 350 A.2d 341 (Del. 1975).*

Testing motion under paragraph (a). — Rather than by placing the burden on the moving party to show that the nonparty in question is subject to service, a motion under paragraph (a) of this rule should be tested on its own facts which are before the Court. *Hughes Tool Co. v. Fawcett Publications, Inc., 350 A.2d 341 (Del. 1975).*

Paragraph (b) of this rule contemplates a finding that one who should be joined "cannot be made a party" before the Court begins applying the factors which determine the fate of the action. *Hughes Tool Co. v. Fawcett Publications, Inc., 350 A.2d 341 (Del. 1975).*

Determination where person cannot be made party lies within discretion of court according to the circumstances of each case. *Hunt v. DelCollo, 317 A.2d 545 (Del. Ch. 1974).*

Where the person is foreign corporation, joinder under paragraph (a) is not feasible, absent a showing by the plaintiff to the contrary. *Rollins Int'l, Inc. v. International Hydronics Corp., 295 A.2d 592 (Del. Ch. 1972),* aff'd, *303 A.2d 660 (Del. 1973).*

"Indispensable parties" defined. — Indispensable parties are persons who not only have an interest in the controversy but an interest of such a nature that a final decree cannot be made without either affecting that interest or leaving the controversy in such a condition that its final termination may be wholly inconsistent with equity and good conscience. *Elster v. American Airlines, 34 Del. Ch. 500, 106 A.2d 202 (1954).*

Indispensability rests upon facts of case. — The question of whether or not parties to any action shall be considered as indispensable parties is frequently not easy to determine; and, in most instances, that determination must rest upon the facts of the particular case. *Elster v. American Airlines, 34 Del. Ch. 500, 106 A.2d 202 (1954).*

The governmental interests of Argentina would be a relevant factor if defendant corporation had moved to dismiss plaintiff corporation's suit for monetary damages under Ch. Ct. R. 19, on the basis that the Argentine governmental entities were indispensable parties, such that defendant would be prejudiced if the case proceeded in Delaware without the presence of those Argentine governmental entities; defendant did advance the argument that the Argentine courts had exclusive jurisdiction, but rather than decide that jurisdictional issue directly, the Court of Chancery improperly injected the exclusive jurisdiction issue into its forum non conveniens analytic

framework. *Candlewood Timber Group, LLC v. Pan Am. Energy, LLC, 859 A.2d 989 (Del. 2004).*

However, all parties to a contract sought to be cancelled are indispensable parties to the suit for cancellation, unless it is obvious that one not joined has no interest whatever in the subject matter of the suit. *Elster v. American Airlines, 34 Del. Ch. 500, 106 A.2d 202 (1954).*

Likewise, where claims of a local and its parent union are to the same assets, the local is a necessary and indispensable party to an action brought by the parent union. *United Elec., Radio & Mach. Workers v. Derrickson, 34 Del. Ch. 263, 102 A.2d 921 (1954).*

And a corporation is a proper and necessary party in an adverse action against it by stockholders to enjoin the corporation from carrying out a stock option plan. *Elster v. American Airlines, 34 Del. Ch. 500, 106 A.2d 202 (1954).*

Failure to join indispensable nonresident corporate defendant requires that the complaint be dismissed. *Istituto Bancario Italiano SpA v. Hunter Eng'g Co., 428 A.2d 19 (Del. Ch. 1981),* modified, *449 A.2d 210 (Del. 1982).*

Where the issue concerns the validity of a charitable trust, the attorney general is a necessary party. *Carlisle v. Delaware Trust Co., 34 Del. Ch. 133, 99 A.2d 764 (1953).*

Additionally, persons interested in the object of a suit must be made parties; it is not sufficient that they be given merely an opportunity to appear. *Elster v. American Airlines, 34 Del. Ch. 500, 106 A.2d 202 (1954); Sterling v. Sekcienski, 34 Del. Ch. 525, 106 A.2d 767 (1954).*

If the subject matter of the suit is an agreement, transfer or conveyance between the corporation, acting by its directors or managers and some other person or corporation, it is proper and necessary to make such other person or corporation a party defendant to the suit because that other person or corporation has a substantial interest in the determination of whether or not the agreement in question is really within the powers or without the powers of the corporation. *Elster v. American Airlines, 34 Del. Ch. 500, 106 A.2d 202 (1954).*

Determination of the rights of the optionees in a stockholders' action to enjoin the carrying out of a stock option without making them parties thereto would be contrary to the principles of equity and good conscience. *Elster v. American Airlines, 34 Del. Ch. 500, 106 A.2d 202 (1954).*

Unless unaffected or interested persons are so numerous. — All persons materially interested in the object of a suit in equity and who would be affected by the decree must be made parties thereto, except where the rights of persons not actually made parties are not affected or where the interested persons are so numerous that it would be impracticable to make them all parties. *United Elec., Radio & Mach. Workers v. Derrickson, 34 Del. Ch. 263, 102 A.2d 921 (1954).*

Joinder of parties whose properties adjoined lake was not required in a case involving alleged public right-of-way where access did not include properties that adjoined the lake, and where any final decree could be crafted so as not to affect adversely the interests of the lakefront property owners. *Scureman v. Judge, 626 A.2d 5 (Del. Ch. 1992)*.

Although failure to join an indispensable party in a land use action would be grounds for dismissal under this rule and Del. Ch. Ct. R. 15, the court declined to dismiss landowners' complaint challenging a zoning ordinance on those grounds because it found that the holder of a remainder interest in the property at issue whose interested never vested and which had, in any case, been transferred to a party was not an indispensable party. *Lynch v. City of Rehoboth, (Del. Ch. May 28, 2004)*.

Rule 21.   Misjoinder and nonjoinder of parties

DELAWARE CASE NOTES — REPORTED

The purpose of this rule is to eliminate the serious consequences of nonjoinder or misjoinder of parties which existed at common law. *Diner Foods, Inc. v. City of Dover, 43 Del. Ch. 331, 229 A.2d 495 (1967)*.

The court of chancery should not dismiss a suit for nonjoinder if presently unnamed parties can be joined. *Goldhar v. Rosenfeld, 38 Del. Ch. 233, 149 A.2d 753 (1959)*.

Thus, an indispensable party to a lawsuit, either a plaintiff or a defendant, may be added at any stage of the proceeding, either on motion of a party or by the Court sua sponte, but only if no prejudice results to the other side as a result of the addition of the new party. *Diner Foods, Inc. v. City of Dover, 43 Del. Ch. 331, 229 A.2d 495 (1967)*.

Absent prejudice to a defendant, the addition or deletion of parties should be made freely in order to carry out the spirit and purpose expressed in Ch. Ct. R. 1, "to secure the just, speedy and inexpensive determination of every proceeding." *Diner Foods, Inc. v. City of Dover, 43 Del. Ch. 331, 229 A.2d 495 (1967)*.

When this rule is employed to drop a party defendant, the proper function of the Court is to prevent any undue prejudice to the party affected by a motion to drop; and, except where a plaintiff proposes to drop an entire controversy before the filing of an answer or a motion for summary judgment, the Court, while empowered to permit the dropping of a named party defendant, must do so only on terms that are fair and proper and usually in the early stages of the litigation. *Oil & Gas Ventures, Inc. v. Cheyenne Oil Corp., 43 Del. Ch. 143, 220 A.2d 785 (1966)*.

Rule 23.   Class actions

DELAWARE CASE NOTES — REPORTED

I. General Consideration.
II. Requisites to Class Action.
III. Class Actions Maintainable.
IV. Determination by Order, etc.
V. Dismissal or Compromise.

I. GENERAL CONSIDERATION.

Cross references. — As to derivative actions by shareholders, see Rule 23.1 of the Court of Chancery. As to actions relating to unincorporated associations, see Rule 23.2 of the Court of Chancery. As to voluntary dismissals see Rule 41(a) of the Court of Chancery. As to dismissals for inaction, see Rule 41(e) of the Court of Chancery.

II. REQUISITES TO CLASS ACTION.

The first test for maintaining class action is that the claimed class is so numerous that the joinder of all members of such class is impractical. *Delaware Bankers Ass'n v. Division of Revenue of Dep't of Fin., 298 A.2d 352 (Del. Ch. 1972)*.

Impracticality of joinder. — With respect to the requirement in subsection (a) that a class be "so numerous that joinder of all members is impracticable," the test is not impossibility of joinder, but impracticality. *Leon N. Weiner & Assocs. v. Krapf, 584 A.2d 1220 (Del. 1991)*.

Composition of class. — A class homogeneous and cohesive in grievances, rights and interests is indispensable under subdivision (b)(2) because the remedy contemplated is final injunctive or declaratory relief with respect to the class as a whole. *Nottingham Partners v. Dana, 564 A.2d 1089 (Del. 1989)*.

Common issues of fact and law. — Because of the predominance of common issues of law and fact, class action certification was appropriate for beneficiaries of express trusts based on claims relating to the disclosure of fees charged by defendant bank for investments of trust funds. *Price v. Wilmington Trust Co., 730 A.2d 1236 (Del. Ch. 1997)*.

Past mental or physical infirmities of plaintiff did not prevent her from being an adequate class representative. *Price v. Wilmington Trust Co., 730 A.2d 1236 (Del. Ch. 1997)*.

In the case of defendant class certification, close scrutiny is given the fourth prerequisite, that the named defendant adversary will "fairly and adequately protect the interests of the class," largely because of the risk that plaintiff will seek out weak adversaries to represent the class. *Leon N. Weiner & Assocs. v. Krapf, 584 A.2d 1220 (Del. 1991)*.

Because of questions regarding manageability of the class, class action certification was not appropriate for beneficiaries of express trusts based on claims relating to certain "sweep fees" charged by defendant bank. *Price v. Wilmington Trust Co., 730 A.2d 1236 (Del. Ch. 1997)*.

Mere reluctance of the designated defendant to serve as a class representative is not a basis for rejecting class action certification if the reluctance relates primarily to burden-sharing and not to a lack of commitment to oppose the asserted claims for relief. *Leon N. Weiner & Assocs. v. Krapf, 584 A.2d 1220 (Del. 1991).*

Existence of equitable right must be demonstrated. — Before the Chancery Court can be deemed to have jurisdiction over an action brought on behalf of a class, there would appear to be the need of demonstrating the existence of an equitable right arising out of the fact that no clear legal remedy is available. *Delaware Bankers Ass'n v. Division of Revenue of Dep't of Fin., 298 A.2d 352 (Del. Ch. 1972)Dieter v. Prime Computer, Inc., 681 A.2d 1068 (Del. Ch. 1996).*

Black persons constitute definite class for determining educational admissions. — Those Delaware citizens of black descent who are legally interested in obtaining a college education and legally interested in a determination of their constitutional right with respect to admission to a specific educational institution constitute a definite class within the meaning of this rule. *Parker v. University of Del., 31 Del. Ch. 381, 75 A.2d 225 (1950).*

However, the president of a parent union cannot represent members of the local in a class action, for he is not a member of that class. *United Elec., Radio & Mach. Workers v. Derrickson, 34 Del. Ch. 263, 102 A.2d 921 (1954).*

Rejection predominantly based on financial considerations erroneous. — The trial court committed legal error in premising its rejection of plaintiff's motion for defendant class certification predominantly on financial considerations, in particular the cost of compliance with the notice requirements of this Rule, rather than due process concerns. *Leon N. Weiner & Assocs. v. Krapf, 584 A.2d 1220 (Del. 1991).*

Adequacy of representation. — The certification of an action as a class action involves important judicial determinations, including the adequacy of representation. *Derdiger v. Tallman, 773 A.2d 1005 (Del. Ch. 2000).*

III. CLASS ACTIONS MAINTAINABLE.

Class action is essentially a procedural device designed so that mere numbers may not impede large groups of individuals from either enforcing their rights or jointly defending against alleged wrongs on their part. *Delaware Bankers Ass'n v. Division of Revenue of Dep't of Fin., 298 A.2d 352 (Del. Ch. 1972).*

Which is particularly appropriate for equal protection questions. — A class action is particularly appropriate where the question to be determined involves the application of 1 of the great guarantees of the Constitution of the United States — the equal protection of the laws. *Parker v. University of Del., 31 Del. Ch. 381, 75 A.2d 225 (1950).*

Equitable fraud not a proper subject. — A class action may not be maintained in a purely common law or equitable fraud case since individual questions of law or fact, particularly as to the element of justifiable reliance, will inevitably predominate over common questions of law or fact. *Dieter v. Prime Computer, Inc., 681 A.2d 1068 (Del. Ch. 1996).*

This rule is procedural, not jurisdictional, and is designed to enable the chancellor to determine early in the case whether to treat a suit which has been properly brought in equity as a class action. *Wilmington Trust Co. v. Schneider, 320 A.2d 709 (Del. 1974); Harman v. Masoneilan Int'l, Inc., 418 A.2d 1004 (Del. Ch. 1980), rev'd on other grounds, 442 A.2d 487 (Del. 1982).*

It does not confer jurisdiction upon chancery court of case which ought to be in law court. *Wilmington Trust Co. v. Schneider, 320 A.2d 709 (Del. 1974).*

And assuming jurisdiction solely because of multiplicity would broaden such without approval. — Treating the rule as one authorizing equity to assume jurisdiction solely because of multiplicity would have the effect of broadening the scope of equity jurisdiction without constitutional or even statutory approval; yet Delaware has consistently been diligent in preserving the distinction between law and equity. *Wilmington Trust Co. v. Schneider, 320 A.2d 709 (Del. 1974).*

Also, mere fact that several cases involve same legal question is not a compelling reason for the exercise of equitable jurisdiction. *Wilmington Trust Co. v. Schneider, 320 A.2d 709 (Del. 1974).*

Burden of proof. — The plaintiff has the burden of satisfying the court that it has met the requirements of this rule for maintaining a class action. *Dieter v. Prime Computer, Inc., 681 A.2d 1068 (Del. Ch. 1996).*

Class action suits are not necessarily mutually exclusive; an action may be certified under more than one subdivision of paragraph (b) in appropriate circumstances. *Leon N. Weiner & Assocs. v. Krapf, 584 A.2d 1220 (Del. 1991).*

Court of chancery has jurisdiction to try a class suit for damages, as such suits have been long recognized as being a party of equity jurisprudence. *Abelow v. Symonds, 38 Del. Ch. 572, 156 A.2d 416 (1959).*

Suits seeking monetary compensation. — Although subdivision (b)(2) is primarily a vehicle for injunctive or declaratory relief it may include suits seeking monetary compensation, provided this is not the predominant remedy. *Nottingham Partners v. Dana, 564 A.2d 1089 (Del. 1989).*

"Typicality" requirement of subsection (a)(3). — Stockholders who purchased their shares after the announcement of the challenged merger were not typical of the class of stockholders who contested the terms of the transaction. *Dieter v. Prime Computer, Inc., 681 A.2d 1068 (Del. Ch. 1996).*

Sufficiency of contact with state. — Where the issue is whether a plaintiff class may be bound to an adjudication of the equitable duty of loyalty created by the law of the incorporating state, the purchase (or merely holding) of the shares of a corporation of that state itself creates a sufficient relationship with that jurisdiction to permit that jurisdiction to be one in which rights attaching to stock of the corporation may be conclusively adjudicated. *Hynson v. Drummond Coal Co., 601 A.2d 570 (Del. Ch. 1991).*

Difference between creditor and shareholder status requires consideration. — While there may be no prohibition against the joining of shareholders and debenture holders in 1 class, the difference between creditor status and shareholder status requires careful consideration under this rule. *Fins v. Pearlman, 424 A.2d 305 (Del. 1980).*

Where derivative rather than class action required. — Where the principal harm plaintiffs have alleged is that the prices of a corporation's stock plummeted after a revised restructuring plan was announced, and the causes of action allege a waste of corporate assets or a decrease in the value of stock which falls equally on all stockholders, claims were direct wrongs to the corporation and should have been brought as a derivative action, and not as a class action. *Brug v. Enstar Group, Inc., 755 F. Supp. 1247 (D. Del. 1991).*

Individual vs. class claims. — Judgment on the pleadings in favor of corporate defendants on plaintiff minority shareholders' inadequate disclosure claims did not mandate elimination of so many of the minority shareholder plaintiffs as to cause them to fail the numerosity test; since the challenged merger involved a corporation's merger with its majority shareholder, the entire fairness doctrine applied, and minority shareholders who voted for the merger or who accepted consideration were not necessarily barred from participating in a subsequent class action challenge. *In re JCC Holding Co., 843 A.2d 713 (Del. Ch. 2003).*

IV. DETERMINATION BY ORDER, ETC.

Provision as to determining if class action is necessary is mandatory. — The provision of this rule relating to a determination by order as to whether or not a class action should be maintained is mandatory. The Court may not do this merely by judicial notice, nor is a motion for summary judgment (without more) an appropriate way to have the determination made. *Koffler v. McBride, 283 A.2d 855 (Del. Ch. 1971).*

However, this rule should be liberally construed. *Parker v. University of Del., 31 Del. Ch. 381, 75 A.2d 225 (1950).*

But not to extend or limit jurisdiction. — Chancery Ct. R. 82 provides that this rule, as is the case with all other Rules of the court, "shall not be construed to extend or limit the jurisdiction of the Court of Chancery." *Delaware Bankers Ass'n v. Division of Revenue of Dep't of Fin., 298 A.2d 352 (Del. Ch. 1972).*

Discovery of presence of 1 or 2 Delaware residents as members of plaintiff class, long after substituted service of process was completed, cannot cure the individual nonresident defendant's objection to the use of substituted service of process to compel their appearance. *Bank of Am. Nat'l Trust & Sav. Ass'n v. GAC Properties Credit, Inc., 389 A.2d 1304 (Del. Ch. 1978).*

Application for certification of case as class action premature. — In light of the fact that the requisite vote for approval of a proposed merger may not be obtained at the stockholders' meeting and the case may thus become moot, and because, in any event, consummation of such merger will not become effective for up to 60 days after the stockholders' meeting, in a situation in which the plaintiff has not, as yet, been deposed, his application for certification of the case as a class action is premature.

Weinberger v. United Fin. Corp., 405 A.2d 134 (Del. Ch. 1979).

Showing required for disqualification. — Before a plaintiff can be found to be disqualified to maintain an action under this rule, a defendant must show that a serious conflict of interest exists, by virtue of 1 factor or a combination of factors, and that the plaintiff cannot be expected to act in the interests of others because doing so would harm his other interests. *Youngman v. Tahmoush, 457 A.2d 376 (Del. Ch. 1983).*

Opt out right. — Chancery Court has discretionary power under subdivision (d)(2) to provide an opt out right and to require notice thereof be given, if it finds that an opt out right is necessary to protect the interests of absent class members. *Nottingham Partners v. Dana, 564 A.2d 1089 (Del. 1989).*

An action which consists primarily of equitable claims with an ancillary request for monetary damages will not require a provision for opting-out. *In re MCA, Inc., 598 A.2d 687 (Del. Ch. 1991).*

The device of a properly administered class action may be employed, without affording opt-out rights, to bind all absent shareholder/plaintiffs to a final judgment in an action seeking to vindicate rights attaching to corporate stock, whether those rights are sought to be protected by injunction or compensated by an award of money. *Hynson v. Drummond Coal Co., 601 A.2d 570 (Del. Ch. 1991).*

Standard of review of determination of an action's qualification for class action certification under this Rule is whether the Court erred as a matter of law in its consideration of legal precepts involving subject matter jurisdiction, and in this respect, the scope of review is *de novo*. *Leon N. Weiner & Assocs. v. Krapf, 584 A.2d 1220 (Del. 1991).*

Assuming a correct formulation by the trial court of the legal precepts underlying this Rule, the standard of review of the Court's findings of fact, in application of those precepts to its ultimate determination, is whether they are supported by the record and the product of an orderly and logical deductive process. *Leon N. Weiner & Assocs. v. Krapf, 584 A.2d 1220 (Del. 1991).*

Stay issues when another action is pending. — Delaware courts, in the interests of comity and judicial economy, will normally stay after-filed suits when previously-filed suits stating similar claims are pending in another court; this is particularly so where the primary claims are based on federal laws and a federal action is already pending in a federal court. *Prezant v. De Angelis, 636 A.2d 915 (Del. 1994).*

Allocation of costs. — Plaintiff's motion for defendant class certification should not shift to the named defendants the court costs incidental to the class action certification. *Leon N. Weiner & Assocs. v. Krapf, 584 A.2d 1220 (Del. 1991).*

Federal practice on cost bearing is applicable to this *Rule. Leon N. Weiner & Assocs. v. Krapf, 584 A.2d 1220 (Del. 1991).*

Chancery Court

V. DISMISSAL OR COMPROMISE.

This rule is intended to guard against surreptitious buy-outs of representative plaintiffs, leaving other class members without recourse. *Wied v. Valhi, Inc., 466 A.2d 9 (Del. 1983)*, cert. denied, *465 U.S. 1026, 104 S. Ct. 1284, 79 L. Ed. 2d 687 (1984)*.

Purpose of paragraph (e). — The purpose behind the exception in paragraph (e) of this rule is to dispose of class actions where there is no inclination to press for a judicial determination and where that attitude has not been influenced by the receipt of anything of value. *Hutchison v. Bernhard, 43 Del. Ch. 139, 220 A.2d 782 (1965)*.

One of the purposes of paragraph (e) of this rule is to forestall the buying out of a plaintiff in a class action. *Jaeger v. Muscat, 43 Del. Ch. 178, 221 A.2d 607 (1966)*.

Due process. — The due process clause is satisfied when a subdivision (b)(2) class action is settled without providing objectors means of opting out because objectors are (1) adequately represented by the named plaintiffs; (2) represented by qualified counsel; (3) given notice of proposed settlement; (4) given opportunity to object to settlement and (5) assured settlement will take place only if trial judge finds it fair, adequate and reasonable. *Nottingham Partners v. Dana, 564 A.2d 1089 (Del. 1989)*.

Due process for absent class members. — Notice and the opportunity to opt out of a class action which is eventually settled, without adequate representation, does not satisfy due process requirements; notice and an opt-out opportunity are no substitute for extensive document examination, depositions of adverse witnesses, securing expert advice on complicated issues and aggressive negotiation at arms length. *Prezant v. De Angelis, 636 A.2d 915 (Del. 1994)*.

The requirement that leave of court be obtained to dismiss a class action suit is not a mere technicality; it serves an important function in ensuring that class representatives are faithful in carrying out the fiduciary duties which they owe to class members. *De Angelis v. Salton/Maxim Housewares, Inc., 641 A.2d 834 (Del. Ch. 1993)*, rev'd on other grounds and remanded sub nom. *Prezant v. DeAngelis, 636 A.2d 915 (Del. 1994)*.

Propriety of compromise. — Provisions of compromise determined not to be abuse of Court's discretion. *In re Resorts Int'l Shareholders Litig. Appeals, 570 A.2d 259 (Del. 1990)*.

Court's responsibility to determine if settlement fair. — The court's function in the settlement of a class action suit is to consider the nature of the plaintiff's claim, the possible defenses thereto, the legal and factual circumstances of the case and then to apply its own business judgment in deciding whether the settlement is reasonable in light of these factors. *Prezant v. De Angelis, 636 A.2d 915 (Del. 1994)*.

In class action suits, as in other litigation, courts strongly favor the voluntary settlement of suits; subsection (e) requires that the chancery court review proposed settlements of class action suits in order to guard against surreptitious buyouts of representative plaintiff, leaving other class members without recourse. *De Angelis v. Salton/Maxim Housewares, Inc., 641 A.2d 834 (Del. Ch. 1993)*, rev'd on other grounds and remanded sub nom. *Prezant v. DeAngelis, 636 A.2d 915 (Del. 1994)*.

Not only must the terms of a settlement be carefully examined, but the court must also scrutinize the process by which the settlement is procured; a settlement will be examined with heightened scrutiny, and an enhanced standard of review will be applied, if the settlement process appears likely to be unfair. *De Angelis v. Salton/Maxim Housewares, Inc., 641 A.2d 834 (Del. Ch. 1993)*, rev'd on other grounds and remanded sub nom. *Prezant v. DeAngelis, 636 A.2d 915 (Del. 1994)*.

Settlement of a stockholder class action was approved, over the objection of a class member, where there was no evidence of a conflict or antagonism involving plaintiff and plaintiff was exposed to the same economic terms and other conditions as all of the other stockholders; Delaware courts favored the voluntary settlement of complex corporate litigation and the job of the court, in reviewing a proposed settlement, was to ascertain that the settlement's terms were fair and reasonable. *Blank v. Belzberg, 858 A.2d 336 (Del. Ch. 2003)*.

Judicial standard for settlement approval. — The factors to be considered in determining whether a settlement should be approved include: (1) the probable validity of the claims, (2) the apparent difficulties in enforcing the claims throughout the courts, (3) the collectability of any judgment recovered, (4) the delay, expense and trouble of litigation, (5) the amount of the compromise as compared with the amount and collectability of a judgment, and (6) the views of the parties involved, pro and con. *De Angelis v. Salton/Maxim Housewares, Inc., 641 A.2d 834 (Del. Ch. 1993)*, rev'd on other grounds and remanded sub nom. *Prezant v. DeAngelis, 636 A.2d 915 (Del. 1994)*.

In every class action settlement, the Court of Chancery is required to make an explicit determination on the record of the propriety of the class action according to the requisites of paragraphs (a) and (b) of this rule. This determination, which is equivalent to class certification, may be made at the conclusion of the settlement hearing when a temporary settlement class has been established to facilitate effectuation of a proposed settlement, or it may be made at some earlier time, such as in conjunction with notice to the class. However, class certification is required in every class action settlement. *Prezant v. De Angelis, 636 A.2d 915 (Del. 1994)*.

Paragraph (e) has primary application to dismissals voluntarily entered or consented to by plaintiff. *Hutchison v. Bernhard, 43 Del. Ch. 139, 220 A.2d 782 (1965)*.

Enforcement of settlement agreement by court. — A paragraph (e) dismissal of a class action under this rule normally occurs when a plaintiff who has lost confidence in his case tacitly or actively goes along with a Ch. Ct. R. 41(e) motion to dismiss for inaction. *Jaeger v. Muscat, 43 Del. Ch. 178, 221 A.2d 607 (1966)*.

To have a complaint dismissed with prejudice to a plaintiff, but without prejudice to others of his class, paragraph (e) of this rule requires a motion supported by an affidavit to the effect that no compensation in any form has passed directly or indirectly from any of the defendants to the plaintiff or plaintiff's attorney, and no promise to give any such compensation has been made in connection with the dismissal proposed. *Jaeger v. Muscat, 43 Del. Ch. 178, 221 A.2d 607 (1966).*

Use of temporary settlement classes. — When using the temporary settlement class device, a formal class ruling may be deferred until the settlement hearing, however, such a ruling must be made before a settlement can be approved. *Prezant v. De Angelis, 636 A.2d 915 (Del. 1994).*

Since judicial economy is served by a comprehensive settlement hearing rather than piecemeal litigation, and since temporary settlement classes foster settlement of contested issues (a favored result under Delaware law), the use of temporary settlement classes to accomplish these ends is approved so long as the strictures of this Rule are ultimately satisfied. *Prezant v. De Angelis, 636 A.2d 915 (Del. 1994).*

Representative plaintiff must be adequate. — When claims of absent class members are being compromised, the appropriate course is for the Court of Chancery to make an explicit finding on the record that the action satisfies the criteria of subsections (a) and (b) and is thus properly maintainable as a class action; this would include finding that all class members were adequately represented. *Prezant v. De Angelis, 636 A.2d 915 (Del. 1994).*

Because adequacy of a class representative is a requirement of this Rule and is constitutionally mandated (see U.S. Const., amend. XIV), a determination to that effect is essential to court approval of a class action settlement; accordingly, without reaching the merits of the settlement, the reviewing court will reverse and remand for an appropriate determination if one has not yet been made. *Prezant v. De Angelis, 636 A.2d 915 (Del. 1994).*

The Court of Chancery's use of heightened scrutiny in its evaluation of the merits of the settlement was not a proper substitute for the continued involvement of an adequate class representative. *Prezant v. De Angelis, 636 A.2d 915 (Del. 1994).*

The court may exercise discretion even under the exception in this rule to do justice. *Hutchison v. Bernhard, 43 Del. Ch. 139, 220 A.2d 782 (1965).*

State court settlement bars action in federal court. — When a state court settlement of a class action releases all claims which arise out of the challenged transaction and is determined to be fair and to have met all due process requirements, the class members are bound by the release or the doctrine of issue preclusion. Class members cannot subsequently relitigate the claims barred by the settlement in a federal court. *In re MCA, Inc., 598 A.2d 687 (Del. Ch. 1991).*

Order of court directing that losing plaintiffs pay the cost of giving notice to the class of the pendency of the action is at the discretion of the judge. *Wood v. Coastal States Gas Corp., 401 A.2d 932 (Del. 1979).*

The defendants' motion to dismiss because of the plaintiff's sale of his stock after commencing the action should be considered as one coming within paragraph (e) of this rule, because to allow a dismissal without Court control would make possible one of the very abuses sought to be controlled by the notice requirement of the rule, i.e., the buy-off of an objector without regard to the rights of the stockholders generally, and the court may order the other stockholders to be notified. *Hutchison v. Bernhard, 43 Del. Ch. 139, 220 A.2d 782 (1965).*

The provisions are applicable to the dismissal and compromise of actions brought to review corporate elections under *8 Del. C. § 225,* since this rule purports to apply to all class actions, and there is therefore no compelling reason why an exception should be made. *Borer v. Associated Gen. Util. Co., 35 Del. Ch. 123, 111 A.2d 707 (1955).*

This rule for a hearing on dismissal of a class action throws a heavy burden on the court, particularly when objection is forcibly made. *Duane v. Menzies, 37 Del. Ch. 416, 144 A.2d 229 (1958).*

And approval of a class action settlement requires more than a cursory scrutiny by the Court of the issues presented. The function of the Court is discharged, however, when the nature of the claim, the possible defenses to it and the legal and factual obstacles facing the plaintiff in the event of trial are weighed and considered. *Rome v. Archer, 41 Del. Ch. 404, 197 A.2d 49 (1964).*

Absent plaintiffs in class action suit are bound by judgment despite the fact that they were not personally served and did not appear in the rendering court so long as the due process requirements of proper notice and adequate representation were satisfied. *Geller v. Tabas, 462 A.2d 1078 (Del. 1983).*

Intervening class members. — Permitting an individual class member to intervene at any stage of a class action is somewhat antithetical to the representative nature of such a proceeding. *Giammalvo v. Sunshine Mining Co., 644 A.2d 407 (Del. 1994).*

Motions to intervene on appeal are seldom granted, especially when the movant declined to join in the proceedings at trial. *Giammalvo v. Sunshine Mining Co., 644 A.2d 407 (Del. 1994).*

Dismissal not permitted. — In order to give Ch. Ct. R. 15(aaa), limiting a plaintiff's right to amend a complaint, its intended scope, once the time for amendment had passed under that rule, a party-plaintiff was not permitted to resort to this rule Ch. Ct. R. 41(a), or 23.1 to file a "without prejudice" dismissal of its action. *Stern v. LF Capital Partners, LLC, 820 A.2d 1143 (Del. Ch. 2003).*

Determination of attorney fees. — The adoption of a mandatory method or mathematical model for determining attorney's fees in common fund cases would be the antithesis of the equitable principles from which the concept of such awards originated; the court therefore approved an award of fees based on the percentage of the common fund claimed by the potential class members. *Goodrich v. E.F. Hutton Group, Inc., 681 A.2d 1039 (Del. 1996).*

The common fund doctrine permits an attorney to independently request an award of fees from the settlement fund, at which point the attorney's role changes from that of a fiduciary for the clients to that of a claimant against the fund. This divergence of interests requires a court to continue its third party role in reviewing fee applications and to make a determination of reasonableness on behalf of the common fund's beneficiaries before approving a fee award. *Goodrich v. E.F. Hutton Group, Inc., 681 A.2d 1039 (Del. 1996).*

Notice requirements for settlement hearings. — While subsection (e) of this rule and Rule 23.1 do not specifically address notice requirements with respect to settlement hearings, it is the Delaware Court of Chancery's general practice that settling parties provide notice to class members between 30 and 45 days prior to the settlement hearing. *In re Coleman Co. Shareholders Litig., 750 A.2d 1202 (Del. Ch. 1999).*

Rule 23.1.   Derivative actions by shareholders

DELAWARE CASE NOTES — REPORTED

I. GENERAL CONSIDERATION.

Purpose. — The derivative action was developed by equity to enable stockholders to sue in the corporation's name where those in control of the corporation refused to assert a claim belonging to the corporation. *Harff v. Kerkorian, 324 A.2d 215 (Del. Ch. 1974),* modified, *347 A.2d 133 (Del. 1975).*

This rule is one of substantive right, not simply a technical rule of pleading. *Haber v. Bell, 465 A.2d 353 (Del. Ch. 1983); Lewis v. Aronson, 466 A.2d 375 (Del. Ch. 1983),* rev'd on other grounds, *473 A.2d 805 (Del. 1984).*

Design of rule. — This rule is designed to give a corporation, on whose behalf a derivative suit is brought, the opportunity to rectify the alleged wrong without suit or to control any litigation brought for its benefit. *Haber v. Bell, 465 A.2d 353 (Del. Ch. 1983); Lewis v. Aronson, 466 A.2d 375 (Del. Ch. 1983),* rev'd on other grounds, *473 A.2d 805 (Del. 1984).*

The "demand" contemplated by this rule is really a form of notice designed to afford to the corporation's board an opportunity to consider the facts asserted and to exercise its business judgment whether to press any arguable claim the corporation may possess or to take other action; the board has no obligation to take any specific type of action to comply with a demand under this rule. *Schick Inc. v. Amalgamated Clothing & Textile Workers Union, 533 A.2d 1235 (Del. Ch. 1987).*

The purpose of pre-suit demand is to assure that the stockholder affords the corporation the opportunity to address an alleged wrong without litigation, to decide whether to invest the resources of the corporation in litigation, and to control any litigation which does occur. *Spiegel v. Buntrock, 571 A.2d 767 (Del. 1990).*

The foundation of this rule is the requirement that management retain control over corporate claims except where conditions of director disqualification exist. *Good v. Getty Oil Co., 518 A.2d 973 (Del. Ch. 1986).*

Pleadings under this rule must comply with the mandate of chancery rule 8(e) that they be "simple, concise and direct", therefore, a prolix complaint larded with conclusory language does not comply with these fundamental pleading mandates. *Brehm v. Eisner, 746 A.2d 244 (Del. 2000).*

Relationship to Del. Ch. Ct. R. 12(b)(6). — Since the standard under Del. Ch. Ct. R. 12(b)(6) is less stringent than the standard under Del. Ch. Ct. R. 23.1, a complaint that survives a Rule 23.1 motion to dismiss generally will also survive a Del. Ch. Ct. R. 12(b)(6) motion to dismiss, assuming that it otherwise contains sufficient facts to state a cognizable claim. *In re Walt Disney Co. Derivative Litig., 825 A.2d 275 (Del. Ch. 2003).*

In a stockholder's derivative action, the corporation is an adverse party. *Elster v. American Airlines, 34 Del. Ch. 500, 106 A.2d 202 (1954).*

However, this rule does not alter substantive rights such as the nature or quantum of recovery for the corporation after the establishment of liability, but it does create procedural requirements which did not exist in Delaware equity practice prior to its formulation. *Mayer v. Adams, 36 Del. Ch. 466, 133 A.2d 138 (1957).*

The fundamental basis of a derivative stockholder's action is to enforce corporate right. *Taormina v. Taormina Corp., 32 Del. Ch. 18, 78 A.2d 473 (1951).*

Whether conditions of director disqualification exist is a substantive issue; its consideration does not end when the complaint is found to be sufficient. *Good v. Getty Oil Co., 518 A.2d 973 (Del. Ch. 1986).*

Complaint must allege particularized facts. — To survive a Rule 23.1 motion to dismiss in a due care case where an expert has advised the board in its decision-making process, the complaint must allege particularized facts, not conclusions. *Brehm v. Eisner, 746 A.2d 244 (Del. 2000).*

Complaints lacked essential requirements for stating a claim of waste premised on failure of the directors to exercise due care. *Grobow v. Perot, 539 A.2d 180 (Del. 1988).* But see *Brehm v. Eisner, 746 A.2d 244 (Del. 2000).*

Demand futility. — The complaint did not satisfy the requirements of this rule in that it did not create a reasonable doubt that the directors are disinterested and independent or that the challenged transaction was the product of a valid exercise of business judgment. *Good v. Getty Oil Co., 514 A.2d 1104 (Del. Ch. 1986).*

Trial court correctly dismissed suits under this rule for failure of plaintiffs to make presuit demand upon the board of directors. *Grobow v. Perot, 539 A.2d 180 (Del. 1988).* But see *Brehm v. Eisner, 746 A.2d 244 (Del. 2000).*

Where plaintiff alleged that the board failed to prevent its chairman from misrepresenting the corporation's financial condition and conspired with him to misrepresent the value of the corporation's stock, but did not challenge any specific board action that approved these alleged wrongdoings, plaintiff failed to demonstrate that demand would have been futile. *Seminaris v. Landa, 662 A.2d 1350 (Del. Ch. 1995).*

When claim is meritorious. — A claim is meritorious within the meaning of this rule if it can withstanding a motion to dismiss on the pleadings if, at the same time, the plaintiff possesses knowledge of provable facts which hold out some reasonable likelihood of ultimate success. It is not necessary that factually there be absolute assurance of ultimate success, but only that there be some reasonable hope. *Palley v. McDonnell Co., 295 A.2d 762 (Del. Ch. 1972),* aff'd, *310 A.2d 635 (Del. 1973).*

Challenge to "dead hand" provision in rights plan. — Shareholders' claims challenging the validity of a "dead hand" provision in a poison pill rights plan were not subject to dismissal under this rule because they were individual, not derivative, and even if they were derivative, the complaint satisfied the requirements for demand excusal. *Carmody v. Toll Bros., 723 A.2d 1180 (Del. Ch. 1998).*

Burden of proof. — Where the complaint alleged that the directors "looked the other way" while the chairman made misleading earnings statements and conspired to inflate stock values and thus subjected the company to securities lawsuits, in order to hold the directors liable, plaintiff would have to demonstrate that they were grossly negligent in failing to supervise. *Seminaris v. Landa, 662 A.2d 1350 (Del. Ch. 1995).*

In determining pleading sufficiency under this rule, the court is merely reading the language of a pleading and applying to that pleading statutes, case law and the requirements of this rule. *Brehm v. Eisner, 746 A.2d 244 (Del. 2000).*

Nature of derivative suit is twofold. — First, it is the equivalent of a suit by the stockholders to compel the corporation to sue; and second, it is a suit by the corporation, asserted by the stockholders in its behalf, against those liable to it. *Harff v. Kerkorian, 324 A.2d 215 (Del. Ch. 1974),* modified, *347 A.2d 133 (Del. 1975).*

Stockholder may sue in own name for benefit of corporation. — Generally, a cause of action belonging to a corporation can be asserted only by the corporation. However, whenever a corporation possesses a cause of action which it either refuses to assert or, by reason of circumstances, is unable to assert, equity will permit a stockholder to sue in his own name for the benefit of the corporation solely for the purpose of preventing injustice when it is apparent that the corporation's rights would not be protected otherwise. *Taormina v. Taormina Corp., 32 Del. Ch. 18, 78 A.2d 473 (1951).*

Suits by stockholders mismanagement on part of directors are included within the umbrella of a derivative action. *Harff v. Kerkorian, 324 A.2d 215 (Del. Ch. 1974),* modified, *347 A.2d 133 (Del. 1975).*

Adequate protection of shareholder interests. — Defendants motion to dismiss the derivative plaintiffs as unable to adequately and fairly protect the interests of the corporation and its shareholders was denied because each plaintiff, although not fully familiar with the action, was aware of the basic facts or nature of his or her claims and defendants adduced no evidence that either plaintiff had interests antagonistic to the interests he or she purported to represent, or that class counsel was incompetent or inexperienced to meet the minimum adequacy requirements. *In re Fuqua Indus., Consol., 752 A.2d 126 (Del. Ch. 1999).*

Where the wrong of which a stockholder complains is not a wrong inflicted upon him alone or a wrong affecting any particular right which he is asserting but is an indirect injury as a result of the wrong done to the corporation, such action will be treated as a derivative action. *Elster v. American Airlines, 34 Del. Ch. 94, 100 A.2d 219 (1953).*

A claim of mismanagement resulting in corporate waste, if proven, represents a direct wrong to the corporation that is indirectly experienced by all shareholders. Any devaluation of stock is shared collectively by all the shareholders, rather than independently by the plaintiff or any other individual shareholder. Thus, the wrong alleged is entirely derivative in nature. *Kramer v. Western Pac. Indus., 546 A.2d 348 (Del. 1988).*

Transactional creativity. — As a matter of form, the recapitalization consisted of two transactions that occurred simultaneously, with the result that to an outside observer, the controlling stockholder never held the benefits of the expropriation for any length of time that the naked human eye could discern. In the supreme court's view, that difference in form, which is a product of transactional creativity, should not affect how the law views the substance of what truly occurred, or how the public shareholders' claim for redress should be characterized. In both cases the fiduciary exercises its control over the corporate machinery to cause an expropriation of economic value and voting power from the public shareholders. That the fiduciary does not retain the direct benefit from the expropriation but chooses instead to convert that benefit to cash by selling it to a third party, is not a circumstance that can justify depriving the injured public shareholders of the right they would otherwise have to seek redress in a direct action. Accordingly, the supreme court concludes that although the court of chancery correctly determined that the recapitalization claim could be brought derivatively, it erred in concluding that that claim was exclusively derivative. *Gatz v. Ponsoldt, 925 A.2d 1265; 2007 Del. LEXIS 167 (April 16, 2007).*

Corporate waste. — In determining whether corporate directors committed waste by granting certain stock options, the precise issue becomes whether the particularized factual allegations of the complaint create a reason to doubt that reasonable directors could have expected the corporation to benefit from the grant of the options. *Zupnick v. Goizueta, 698 A.2d 384 (Del. Ch. 1997).*

Dismissal of second suit. — That a second stockholder's derivative suit must as a matter of law be dismissed under the common-law principle of another action pending is not a rule of unbending rigor, but one of justice and expediency. In cases of successive derivative suits by stockholders it should be applied with caution. Although the cause of action may be the same, yet the suing plaintiffs are different, and the suits are both in right of the corporation, but it is always possible that stockholders other than the one first suing may have a legitimate reason to file suit. *Auerbach v. Cities Serv. Co., 37 Del. Ch. 381, 143 A.2d 904 (1958).*

Relief to be obtained in a derivative action is relief to the corporation in which all stockholders, whether guilty or innocent of the wrongs complained of, shall share indirectly. *Taormina v. Taormina Corp., 32 Del. Ch. 18, 78 A.2d 473 (1951).*

Where there is injury to corporation as well as special injury to the individual stockholder, a stockholder, if he should so desire, may proceed on his claim for the protection of his individual rights rather than in the right of the corporation, and such action would then not constitute a derivative action. *Elster v. American Airlines, 34 Del. Ch. 94, 100 A.2d 219 (1953).*

Adequacy of representation. — A stockholder derivative claim may be maintained although it does not have the support of a majority of the corporation's shareholders or even the support of all the minority stockholders. *Emerald Partners v. Berlin, 564 A.2d 670 (Del. Ch. 1989).*

An objecting stockholder is in a different category from that of a plaintiff required to comply with this rule. *Steigman v. Berry, 42 Del. Ch. 53, 203 A.2d 463 (1964).*

To allege that officers and directors should be called upon to justify certain transactions is not to say anything legally in a stockholder's derivative action. *Dann v. Chrysler Corp., 40 Del. Ch. 103, 174 A.2d 696 (1961).*

Complaint must be read in its entirety and should not be construed in a piecemeal manner. *Lewis v. Aronson, 466 A.2d 375 (Del. Ch. 1983),* rev'd on other grounds, *473 A.2d 805 (Del. 1984).*

Particularity requirement not satisfied by unsupported allegation of domination and control. — An allegation of domination and control, unsupported by underlying facts, does not satisfy the requirement of particularity. *Bergstein v. Texas Int'l Co., 453 A.2d 467 (Del. Ch. 1982).*

Discretion of court. — A decision on a motion under this rule, whether based on demand-excused or demand-refused, involves essentially a discretionary ruling on a predominantly factual issue. *Scattered Corp. v. Chicago Stock Exch., 701 A.2d 70 (Del. 1997).*

Amended complaint after new board in place. — When an amended derivative complaint is filed, the existence of a new independent board of directors is relevant to a Rule 23.1 demand inquiry only as to derivative claims in the amended complaint that are not already validly in litigation. Three circumstances must exist to excuse a plaintiff from making demand under Rule 23.1 when a complaint is amended after a new board of directors is in place: first, the original complaint was well pleaded as a derivative action; second, the original complaint satisfied the legal test for demand excusal; and third, the act or transaction complained of in the amendment is essentially the same as the act or transaction challenged in the origi-

nal complaint. A fortiori for Rule 23.1 demand purposes, a complaint that has been dismissed is not validly in litigation. *Braddock v. Zimmerman, 906 A.2d 776, 2006 Del. LEXIS 468 (Sept. 12, 2006).*

Dismissed complaint. — A complaint that is dismissed without prejudice but with express leave to amend is nevertheless a dismissed complaint. It constitutes a judicial determination that the original complaint was either not well pleaded as a derivative action or did not satisfy the legal test for demand excusal. Following such a dismissal, for purposes of a Rule 23.1 demand inquiry, the complaint is not validly in litigation. Consequently, where a complaint is amended with permission following a dismissal without prejudice, even if the act or transaction complained of in the amendment is essentially the same conduct that was challenged in the original dismissed complaint, the Rule 23.1 demand inquiry must be assessed by reference to the board in place at the time when the amended complaint is filed. *Braddock v. Zimmerman, 906 A.2d 776, 2006 Del. LEXIS 468 (Sept. 12, 2006).*

Which board? — Where, as in this proceeding, a plaintiff's complaint has been dismissed and the plaintiff is given leave to file an amended complaint, the plaintiff must make a demand on the board of directors in place at that time the amended complaint is filed or demonstrate that demand is legally excused as to that board. *Braddock v. Zimmerman, 906 A.2d 776, 2006 Del. LEXIS 468 (Sept. 12, 2006).*

Oversight responsibilities. — In the absence of red flags, good faith in the context of oversight must be measured by the directors' actions to assure a reasonable information and reporting system exists and not by second-guessing after the occurrence of employee conduct that results in an unintended adverse outcome. Accordingly, the state supreme court holds that the Court of Chancery properly applied *Caremark* and dismissed the plaintiffs' derivative complaint for failure to excuse demand by alleging particularized facts that created reason to doubt whether the directors had acted in good faith in exercising their oversight responsibilities. *Stone v. Ritter, 911 A.2d 362, 2006 Del. LEXIS 597 (Nov. 6, 2006).*

II. SHAREHOLDER AT TIME.

Policy behind this rule is to prevent "strike suits" whereby individuals purchase shares in a corporation with litigious motives. *Schreiber v. Bryan, 396 A.2d 512 (Del. Ch. 1978).*

Rule prevents a stockholder from attacking transactions completed before he becomes a stockholder. *Maclary v. Pleasant Hills, Inc., 35 Del. Ch. 39, 109 A.2d 830 (1954).*

It is not to prevent correction of corporate wrongdoing. *Maclary v. Pleasant Hills, Inc., 35 Del. Ch. 39, 109 A.2d 830 (1954); Helfand v. Gambee, 37 Del. Ch. 51, 136 A.2d 558 (1957).*

Rather, it was enacted to prevent what has been considered an evil, namely the purchasing of shares in order to maintain a derivative action designed to attack a transaction which occurred prior to the purchase of the stock. *Helfand v. Gambee, 37 Del. Ch. 51, 136 A.2d 558 (1957).*

This rule was designed principally to prevent the purchasing of stock to be used for the purpose of filing a derivative action attacking transactions occurring prior to such purchase. *Maclary v. Pleasant Hills, Inc., 35 Del. Ch. 39, 109 A.2d 830 (1954).*

And it cannot be construed to cover inexcusable inaction. — There is nothing in the policy behind this rule which would call for a construction favoring its application in situations where inexcusable inaction on the part of corporate personnel might make it less likely that wrongdoing would be discovered. *Maclary v. Pleasant Hills, Inc., 35 Del. Ch. 39, 109 A.2d 830 (1954).*

Stockholder status at time of transaction being attacked and throughout litigation is essential. *Harff v. Kerkorian, 324 A.2d 215 (Del. Ch. 1974),* modified, *347 A.2d 133 (Del. 1975).*

In order to maintain a derivative suit, stockholder status at the time of the transaction being attacked and during the litigation is essential. *Jones v. Taylor, 348 A.2d 188 (Del. Ch. 1975).*

Only individuals who are stockholders at the time of the transaction complained of, or one who thereafter came into possession of the stock by operation of law, have standing to institute a derivative action. *Schreiber v. Bryan, 396 A.2d 512 (Del. Ch. 1978).*

Requirement that plaintiff who brings suit on behalf of corporation must be stockholder of corporation at time he commences suit is not without exception. *Schreiber v. Carney, 447 A.2d 17 (Del. Ch. 1982).*

Additional implicit standing requirements recognized. — While the only explicit standing requirement for maintaining a derivative suit is that the plaintiff be a stockholder of the corporation at the time of the transaction of which he complains, or that his stock thereafter devolves upon him by operation of law, the Court has recognized additional implicit requirements. *Youngman v. Tahmoush, 457 A.2d 376 (Del. Ch. 1983).*

To have post-merger standing to carry on derivative suit, derivative shareholder must not only be stockholder at the time of the alleged wrong and at time of commencement of suit but he must also maintain shareholder status throughout the litigation. *Lewis v. Anderson, 477 A.2d 1040 (Del. 1984); Kramer v. Western Pac. Indus., 546 A.2d 348 (Del. 1988).*

As a result of the cash-out merger and plaintiff's failure to challenge the fairness of the underlying merger itself, the plaintiff was without standing to pursue his stockholder derivative claims. *Kramer v. Western Pac. Indus., 546 A.2d 348 (Del. 1988).*

Exceptions to rule of standing applicable to mergers. — The two recognized exceptions to the rule of standing as applied to mergers are: (1) Where the merger itself is the subject of a claim of fraud; and (2) where the merger is in reality a reorganization which does not affect plaintiff's ownership of the business enterprise. *Lewis v. Anderson, 477 A.2d 1040 (Del. 1984); Kramer v. Western Pac. Indus., 546 A.2d 348 (Del. 1988).*

Former shareholder in a merged company, who had become a shareholder in the successor company, lacked standing to pursue a pre-existing derivative claim under the rule of *Lewis v. Anderson, 477 A.2d 1040 (Del. 1984),* to which the high court adhered; the shareholder had argued that the merger was arranged in a fraudulent attempt to avoid the derivative action, but failed to plead fraud with any particularity. *Lewis v. Ward, 852 A.2d 896 (Del. 2004).*

Plaintiff in derivative action must be qualified to serve in fiduciary capacity as a representative of a class whose interest is dependent upon the representative's adequate and fair prosecution. *Youngman v. Tahmoush, 457 A.2d 376 (Del. Ch. 1983).*

Showing required for disqualification. — Before a plaintiff can be found to be disqualified to maintain an action under this rule, a defendant must show that a serious conflict of interest exists, by virtue of 1 factor or a combination of factors, and that the plaintiff cannot be expected to act in the interests of others because doing so would harm his other interests. *Youngman v. Tahmoush, 457 A.2d 376 (Del. Ch. 1983).*

A plaintiff in a stockholder derivative suit will not be disqualified because he may have interests which go beyond the interests of the class and, as long as the plaintiff's interests are coextensive with the class, his representation of the class will not be proscribed. *Emerald Partners v. Berlin, 564 A.2d 670 (Del. Ch. 1989).*

A defendant has the burden of proof in a motion to disqualify a derivative plaintiff and he must show that a serious conflict exists, and that plaintiff cannot act in the interests of the others because doing so would harm his other interests. *Emerald Partners v. Berlin, 564 A.2d 670 (Del. Ch. 1989).*

Court can and should examine any extrinsic factors which make it likely that the interests of the other stockholders will be disregarded in the prosecution of the suit. *Youngman v. Tahmoush, 457 A.2d 376 (Del. Ch. 1983).*

Purely hypothetical, potential or remote conflicts of interests never disable the individual plaintiff filing a derivative action suit. *Youngman v. Tahmoush, 457 A.2d 376 (Del. Ch. 1983).*

Limitation on derivative actions is estoppel; that is, a stockholder cannot complain of corporate action in which he has concurred. *Schreiber v. Bryan, 396 A.2d 512 (Del. Ch. 1978).*

Fact that wrongs were committed prior to sale precludes holding continuous wrong. — The fact that the allegedly wrongful acts were committed prior to the earliest sale on which the stockholder had acquired stock in the corporation precludes a Court from holding that the wrong was a continuing one, and stockholder is not entitled to proceed. *Elster v. American Airlines, 34 Del. Ch. 94, 100 A.2d 219 (1953).*

However, claim is not barred if the transaction was not completed before becoming stockholder. — Where the transaction of which plaintiff complains is legally completed when the stockholders voted their approval, and this approval is given after the plaintiff became a stockholder, the transaction of which the plaintiff complains is not completed before the plaintiff became

Chancery Court

a stockholder, and his claim is therefore not barred by *8 Del. C. § 327* nor this rule. *Lavine v. Gulf Coast Leaseholds, Inc., 35 Del. Ch. 539, 122 A.2d 550 (1956).*

But stockholder must be continuous owner of stock. — It is implicit in *8 Del. C. § 327* and in this rule that a stockholder-plaintiff must, at the time he files his complaint, have been the continuous owner of some of the stock held at the time of the alleged wrongful transaction. *Dann v. Chrysler Corp., 40 Del. Ch. 103, 174 A.2d 696 (1961).*

Though not the same stock. — Neither *8 Del. C. § 327* nor this rule literally requires that the stockholder bringing a derivative action must allege that he owns the same stock which he owned at the time of the transaction of which he complains. *Dann v. Chrysler Corp., 40 Del. Ch. 103, 174 A.2d 696 (1961).*

Nevertheless, the transaction is not complete until certificates are issued. — Where the issuance of stock is authorized, where certificates are presumably to be issued therefor at once and where such is the very action under attack, the transaction is not complete for purposes of applying this rule until the certificates are issued. *Maclary v. Pleasant Hills, Inc., 35 Del. Ch. 39, 109 A.2d 830 (1954).*

To consider a transaction as having been completed prior to the issuance of the certificates would sanction an application of the rule not required by its language and not fairly required to effectuate its purpose. *Maclary v. Pleasant Hills, Inc., 35 Del. Ch. 39, 109 A.2d 830 (1954).*

But equitable stockholder may maintain suit. — An equitable stockholder, that is, one who owns in a street name, may maintain a stockholder's derivative suit or a representative suit. *Braasch v. Goldschmidt, 41 Del. Ch. 519, 199 A.2d 760 (1964).*

Although this procedural rule was designed to militate against the wrong of buying into a derivative law suit, it should not be allowed to bar an action by a stockholder with a long standing equitable interest in a corporation. *Theodora Holding Corp. v. Henderson, 257 A.2d 398 (Del. Ch. 1969).*

For purposes of a derivative action, an equitable owner is considered a stockholder. *Harff v. Kerkorian, 324 A.2d 215 (Del. Ch. 1974), modified, 347 A.2d 133 (Del. 1975).*

However, stockholders in a corporation involved in a merger may not maintain an action as representatives of either that class of stockholders who sold their shares to another corporation whose subsidiary is a surviving corporation in the merger, pursuant to the offer to buy, or of that class who surrendered their shares on the merger. *Braasch v. Goldschmidt, 41 Del. Ch. 519, 199 A.2d 760 (1964).*

Stockholders who retain their stock on merger cannot represent the class of stockholders who retain their shares and file an appraisal action. *Braasch v. Goldschmidt, 41 Del. Ch. 519, 199 A.2d 760 (1964).*

When there is a pending action by certain of the plaintiffs for an appraisal of the value of their shares, then, since those plaintiffs are not stockholders at the time of the institution of the action, they may not maintain a rep-

resentative action. *Braasch v. Goldschmidt, 41 Del. Ch. 519, 199 A.2d 760 (1964).*

Holder of option to purchase stock is not equitable stockholder of the corporation. *Harff v. Kerkorian, 324 A.2d 215 (Del. Ch. 1974), modified, 347 A.2d 133 (Del. 1975).*

Equitable ownership established. — Plaintiff had sufficient equitable ownership interest in stock to permit her to sue derivatively where she was the equitable owner of shares by virtue of an agreement which obligated her mother to execute a will bequeathing one half of the shares of a company's stock to her. *Jones v. Taylor, 348 A.2d 188 (Del. Ch. 1975).*

Debenture holders are not stockholders. *Harff v. Kerkorian, 324 A.2d 215 (Del. Ch. 1974), modified, 347 A.2d 133 (Del. 1975).*

Holder of convertible bond does not become stockholder, by his contract, in equity any more than at law. *Harff v. Kerkorian, 324 A.2d 215 (Del. Ch. 1974), modified, 347 A.2d 133 (Del. 1975).*

Holders of convertible debentures are creditors of the corporation and simply do not have standing to maintain a stockholder's derivative action under *Delaware law. Harff v. Kerkorian, 324 A.2d 215 (Del. Ch. 1974), modified, 347 A.2d 133 (Del. 1975).*

Stockholder interest in another corporation, in the absence of control, is not an entanglement that is per se antagonistic to the interests of other similarly situated stockholders. *Youngman v. Tahmoush, 457 A.2d 376 (Del. Ch. 1983).*

III. EFFORT TO OBTAIN ACTION.

This rule requires stockholders to first seek redress for corporate wrongs within the corporation before suing derivatively; such rule is clearly procedural. *Aaron v. Parsons, 37 Del. Ch. 184, 139 A.2d 365, aff'd, 144 A.2d 155 (Del. 1958).*

The demand requirements of this rule represent a procedural restatement of the bedrock principles of Delaware corporate governance in the context of standing to maintain a derivative shareholder's suit. *Alabama By-Products Corp. v. Cede & Co. ex rel. Shearson Lehman Bros., 657 A.2d 254 (Del. 1995).*

Effect of rule. — This rule, by excusing demand in certain instances, does not strip a board of its corporate powers; it merely saves the plaintiff the expense and delay of making a futile demand resulting in a probable tainted exercise of that authority in a refusal by the board or in giving control of litigation to the opposing side. *Zapata Corp. v. Maldonado, 430 A.2d 779 (Del. 1981).*

It should be construed so as to reasonably effectuate its primary purpose to discourage a type of strike suit. It should not be construed so as to unduly encourage the camouflaging of transactions or to prevent reasonable opportunities to rectify corporate aberrations. *Maclary v. Pleasant Hills, Inc., 35 Del. Ch. 39, 109 A.2d 830 (1954).*

Properly applied, it should not immunize corporate officers and directors from accounting to their stockholders in a proper case. *Mayer v. Adams, 36 Del. Ch. 466, 133 A.2d 138 (1957).*

Chancery Court

However, a complaint must state with particularity the intracorporate effort made under the rule or the reasons for not making such effort. *Mayer v. Adams, 36 Del. Ch. 466, 133 A.2d 138 (1957).*

Standing. — A plaintiff's standing to sue in a derivative suit, whether based on demand-refused or demand-excused, must be determined on the basis of the well-pleaded allegations of the complaint. *Scattered Corp. v. Chicago Stock Exch., 701 A.2d 70 (Del. 1997).*

"Derivative" versus "direct" claim. — Highest court redefined the test to determine whether a claim was a "direct" shareholder or a "derivative" claim by expressly rejecting a shareholder "special injury" test to determine if a claim was the shareholders' direct claim; additionally, the court stated that a claim was not automatically a derivative one merely if it affected all shareholders the same. *Tooley v. Donaldson, Lufkin, & Jenrette, Inc., 845 A.2d 1031 (Del. 2004).*

With respect to the proper analysis to distinguish between direct and derivative actions, a direct shareholder claim includes: a duty; breach of that duty; and, direct injury to the shareholder (independent of injury to the corporation). *Tooley v. Donaldson, Lufkin, & Jenrette, Inc., 845 A.2d 1031 (Del. 2004).*

Highest court: (1) redefined a test to determine if the shareholders' claim was a separate or a derivative claim under Del. Ch. Ct. R. 23.1; (2) found they did not state a derivative claim; (3) found they did not state a ripe separate claim upon which relief could be granted, but that that issue was not argued; and, (4) affirmed the dismissal, but reversed the judgment and remanded for the trial court to dismiss the case (without prejudice) with leave to replead under Del. Ch. Ct. R. 11. *Tooley v. Donaldson, Lufkin, & Jenrette, Inc., 845 A.2d 1031 (Del. 2004).*

Allegations of corporate misfeasance and malfeasance, while of a type most frequently challenged in derivative suits, may be raised directly in the bankruptcy context without the Plaintiff having first been required to make a Ch. Ct. R. 23.1 demand on the Company's Board of Directors for some corrective action; as such, the court would not entertain a motion to dismiss for failure to comply with the demand requirement of Del. Ch. Ct. R. 23.1, nor were the allegations of the complaint subject to the more exacting standard imposed by Rule 23.1 for derivative actions. *Continuing Creditors' Comm. of Star Telecomms. Inc. v. Edgecomb, — F. Supp. 2d — (D. Del. Dec. 21, 2004).*

Standing to raise demand-related defenses. — Defendant, other than the corporation on whose behalf the derivative action is asserted, has standing to raise demand-related defenses under this rule. *Kaplan v. Peat, Marwick, Mitchell & Co., 540 A.2d 726 (Del. 1988).*

Each case in which there has been no demand before suit must be carefully scrutinized and analyzed according to its own unique set of facts, taking into account the totality of the circumstances and the competing interests. *Lewis v. Aronson, 466 A.2d 375 (Del. Ch. 1983), rev'd on other grounds, 473 A.2d 805 (Del. 1984).*

An unfortunate byproduct of Lewis v. Aronson is that its very application to a specific set of pleaded facts may be misinterpreted as a judicial stamp of approval or disapproval of the transaction itself. *Grobow v. Perot, 526 A.2d 914 (Del. Ch. 1987), aff'd, 539 A.2d 180 (Del. 1988).*

Futility of making demand required by rule must be gauged at the time the derivative action is commenced, not afterward with the benefit of hindsight. *Stepak v. Dean, 434 A.2d 388 (Del. Ch. 1981); Lewis v. Aronson, 466 A.2d 375 (Del. Ch. 1983), rev'd on other grounds, 473 A.2d 805 (Del. 1984).*

Proper time to measure demand futility. — Where the original pleading does not purport to be brought derivatively, the proper time to measure demand futility is when the original pleading is filed and not later when an amended complaint first purports to state a derivative claim based upon the same facts. *Harris v. Carter, 582 A.2d 222 (Del. Ch. 1990).*

Test for determining whether demand for redress before suit would have been futile is whether the board of directors, at the time of the filing of the suit, could have impartially considered and acted upon the demand. *Haber v. Bell, 465 A.2d 353 (Del. Ch. 1983); Lewis v. Aronson, 466 A.2d 375 (Del. Ch. 1983), rev'd on other grounds, 473 A.2d 805 (Del. 1984).*

A demand for redress of a corporate wrong, which ordinarily must be made within the corporation prior to filing suit, is considered futile and therefore unnecessary only if the plaintiff alleges particularized facts which create a reasonable doubt that: (1) the directors are disinterested and independent and (2) the challenged transaction was otherwise the product of a valid exercise of business judgment. *Aronson v. Lewis, 473 A.2d 805 (Del. 1984).*

The test for determining demand futility reflects the interrelationship of business judgment, director independence and interest and requires a bifurcated factual analysis based upon a reasonable doubt standard. Under the demand futility test, the facts alleged in the complaint are examined to determine whether they create a reasonable doubt that: (1) The directors are disinterested and independent and (2) the challenged transaction otherwise was the product of a valid exercise of business judgment. *Pogostin v. Rice, 480 A.2d 619 (Del. 1984).*

Standard or test for determining whether a derivative complaint states a demand futility claim under this rule is: Whether taking the well-pleaded facts as true, the allegations raise a reasonable doubt as to (i) director disinterest or independence or (ii) whether the directors exercised proper business judgment in approving the challenged transaction. *Grobow v. Perot, 539 A.2d 180 (Del. 1988).*

The test for determining whether the complaint alleged facts excusing demand, even though it contained no conclusory allegation that demand was excused, is whether the facts alleged, if true, create a reasonable doubt that: (1) The directors are disinterested and independent, and (2) the challenged transaction was otherwise the product of a valid exercise of business judgment. *Harris v. Carter, 582 A.2d 222 (Del. Ch. 1990).*

If a plaintiff cannot prove that directors are disinterested or otherwise not capable of exercising independent business judgment, a plaintiff in a demand futility case must plead particularized facts creating a reasonable doubt as to the "soundness" of the challenged transaction sufficient to rebut the presumption that the business judgment rule attaches to the transaction. *Levine v. Smith, 591 A.2d 194 (Del. 1991).* But see *Brehm v. Eisner, 746 A.2d 244 (Del. 2000).*

The correct application of the business judgment rule is crucial to a determination of the sufficiency of a derivative complaint to withstand a motion under this rule in both a demand excused and a demand refused context. *Levine v. Smith, 591 A.2d 194 (Del. 1991).* But see *Brehm v. Eisner, 746 A.2d 244 (Del. 2000).*

Criteria for judging derivative claim for demand excusal. — Vice Chancellor's use of a "judicial finding" criterion for judging a derivative claim for demand excusal was erroneous, but not reversible error. *Grobow v. Perot, 539 A.2d 180 (Del. 1988).*

In order to show the futility of a pre-suit demand, a plaintiff must allege facts with particularity that show that a reasonable doubt exists that the directors were not sufficiently disinterested or independent to have entertained a pre-suit demand or that the transaction, for other reasons, cannot be the product of business judgment. *Kaufman v. Belmont, 479 A.2d 282 (Del. Ch. 1984).*

An informed decision to reject a takeover proposal, hostile or friendly, will not excuse demand absent particularized allegations of a breach of fiduciary duty, such as self-dealing, fraud, overreaching, or lack of good faith. It is the plaintiff's burden to allege with particularity that the improper motive in a given set of circumstances, i.e., perpetuation of self in office or otherwise in control, was the sole or primary purpose of the wrongdoer's conduct. *Pogostin v. Rice, 480 A.2d 619 (Del. 1984).*

Board entitled to reasonable time to respond to demand. — Where a shareholder has made a demand upon the board of directors prior to filing a suit under this rule, the board is entitled to a reasonable time to investigate the charges and make a response. Until the board is afforded such a reasonable opportunity to respond, a shareholder making the demand has no standing to commence derivative litigation on the corporation's behalf. *Abbey v. Computer & Communications Technology Corp., 457 A.2d 368 (Del. Ch. 1983).*

Corporation must affirmatively state its position on propriety of derivative litigation. — When a corporation chooses to state its position in regards to the propriety of derivative litigation, it must do so affirmatively; a position of neutrality is viewed as inconsistent with objection to the continued prosecution of the derivative action and thus serves to excuse demand. *Kaplan v. Peat, Marwick, Mitchell & Co., 540 A.2d 726 (Del. 1988).*

Director's mere approval of corporate action would not preclude his reconsidering that action on demand. — The mere approval of a corporate action, absent any allegation of particularized facts supporting a breach of fiduciary duty or other indications of bias, will not disqualify the director from subsequently considering a pre-suit demand to rectify the challenged transaction. *Kaufman v. Belmont, 479 A.2d 282 (Del. Ch. 1984).*

When directors are deemed interested for demand purposes. — Directors will be deemed interested for demand purposes when the complaint alleges specific facts that makes directorial liability a substantial likelihood and not just a mere threat. *Guttman v. Jen-Hsun Huang, 823 A.2d 492 (Del. Ch. 2003).*

Wholesale imputation not permitted. — Delaware law does not permit the wholesale imputation of one director's knowledge to every other for demand excusal purposes. Rather, a derivative complaint must plead facts specific to each director, demonstrating that at least half of them could not have exercised disinterested business judgment in responding to a demand. Plaintiff has not done that, and, therefore, demand is not excused. *Desimone v. Barrows, 924 A.2d 908; 2007 Del. Ch. LEXIS 75 (June 7, 2007).*

Sale of stock does not dictate director is "interested." — Although insider sales are rightly policed by powerful forces — including the criminal laws — to prevent insiders from unfairly defrauding outsiders by trading on non-public information, it is unwise to formulate a common law rule that makes a director "interested" (to determine whether a demand is futile) whenever a derivative plaintiff cursorily alleges that he has made sales of company stock in the market at a time when he has possessed material, non-public information. *Guttman v. Jen-Hsun Huang, 823 A.2d 492 (Del. Ch. 2003).*

Reasonable inference of knowing manipulation. — Defendants argued repeatedly that plaintiff's allegations ultimately rest upon nothing more than statistical abstractions. Nevertheless, the court is required to draw reasonable inferences and need not be blind to probability. True, the report does not state conclusively that options were actually backdated. Rather, it emphatically suggests that either defendant directors knowingly manipulated the dates on which options were granted, or their timing was extraordinarily lucky. Given the choice between improbable good fortune and knowing manipulation of option grants, the court may reasonably infer the latter, even when applying the heightened pleading standards of Rule 23.1. *Ryan v. Gifford, 918 A.2d 341; 2007 Del. Ch. LEXIS 22 (February 6, 2007).*

Board action held not prima facie breach excusing demand. — Board's refusal to accept the premium offered by tender offeror or to negotiate with tender offeror is not prima facie breach of fiduciary duty excusing demand. *Pogostin v. Rice, 480 A.2d 619 (Del. 1984).* But see *Brehm v. Eisner, 746 A.2d 244 (Del. 2000).*

Plaintiff who chooses not to make demand prior to suit is faced with the responsibility of demonstrating with particularity why his demand on the board of directors would have been futile; if the plaintiff fails in meeting this burden, he will find that his suit will be dismissed, in response to a motion to dismiss, even if he has an otherwise meritorious claim. *Haber v. Bell, 465 A.2d 353 (Del. Ch. 1983); Lewis v. Aronson, 466 A.2d 375 (Del. Ch. 1983),* rev'd on other grounds, *473 A.2d 805 (Del. 1984).*

Aronsen's second prong test to excuse demand. — Aronson's second prong is described as a safety valve permitting a derivative plaintiff to not make a demand if he can show with particularity that the board decision under attack is not entitled to business judgment rule protection. *Guttman v. Jen-Hsun Huang, 823 A.2d 492 (Del. Ch. 2003).*

Demand excused under aronson's second prong. — In plaintiff shareholders' derivative action against defendants, a public entertainment corporation as a nominal defendant, the president, the chief executive officer (CEO) (both were directors), and board directors when the president was hired (old directors) and when he was terminated (new directors), which alleged breach (or abdication) of fiduciary duties in his hiring and termination, the Chancery Court decided that the alleged facts excused demand under Aronson's second prong and dismissal under Del. Ch. Ct. R. 23.1, and, if proven true, portrayed directors consciously indifferent to a material corporation issue, the law had to intervene against an abuse of trust, and denied the, less stringent than Rule 23.1, Del. Ch. Ct. R. 12(b)(6) motion to dismiss the claims against (1) board members, concerning fiduciary duty breaches and waste, and (2) the president, for breach of his fiduciary duties by engaging in a self-interested transaction with his friend, the CEO. *In re Walt Disney Co. Derivative Litig., 825 A.2d 275 (Del. Ch. 2003).*

Request for documents under 8 Del. C. § 220. — Stockholder was entitled under *8 Del. C. § 220* to obtain access to corporation's books and records to determine whether there were grounds to assert a claim that his demand to abrogate a compensation package awarded to an officer was wrongfully refused, and if so, to assist him in meeting the pleading requirements of this rule. *Grimes v. DSC Communications Corp., 724 A.2d 561 (Del. Ch. 1998).*

Effect of demand. — A demand, when required and refused, if not wrongful, terminates a stockholder's legal ability to initiate a derivative action, but where demand is properly excused, the stockholder does possess the ability to initiate the action on his corporation's behalf. *Zapata Corp. v. Maldonado, 430 A.2d 779 (Del. 1981).*

Once a shareholder makes a demand upon the board to prevent or remedy an alleged breach of duty, the shareholder is deemed to have conceded that the board is able to function on the question. *Thorpe v. CERBCO, Inc., 611 A.2d 5 (Del. Ch. 1991).*

Claim that demand is excused foreclosed by making demand. — A shareholder who makes a demand can no longer argue that demand is excused. *Spiegel v. Buntrock, 571 A.2d 767 (Del. 1990).*

If stockholders make demand on the board of directors, they are deemed to have waived any claim they might otherwise have had that the board cannot independently act on the demand; however, the stockholders do not, by making demand, waive the right to claim that the demand has been wrongfully refused. *Scattered Corp. v. Chicago Stock Exch., 701 A.2d 70 (Del. 1997).*

Rales test to excuse demand. — When there are allegations that a majority of the board that must consider a demand acts wrongfully, the Rales test sensibly addresses concerns similar to the second prong of Aronson; if the directors face a "substantial likelihood" of personal liability, their ability to consider a demand impartially is compromised under Rales, excusing demand. *Guttman v. Jen-Hsun Huang, 823 A.2d 492 (Del. Ch. 2003).*

Rales standard applies to the determination of whether demand on a corporation's board is excused and an action can proceed and applies where plaintiffs do not challenge any particular business decision made by the corporation's board as a whole and instead allege that the defendant directors individually have breached their fiduciary duties by either purposely trading in their individual capacities while possessing material, non-public information about the corporation's improper accounting practices and financial results and/or by failing to ensure that the corporation has had in place the financial control systems necessary to ensure compliance with applicable accounting standards. *Guttman v. Jen-Hsun Huang, 823 A.2d 492 (Del. Ch. 2003).*

Demand excused. — Since the minority shareholder was to receive the benefit of any recovery, not the corporation, the shareholder's claim that a recapitalization decreased the value of the shareholder's shares because the majority shareholder was given the opportunity to acquire shares for less than fair market value could proceed without the necessity of making a demand on the corporation's board. *Acker v. Transurgical, Inc., (Del. Ch. Apr. 8, 2004).*

Demand was not excused where plaintiffs failed to raise a reasonable doubt as to the absence of self-interest and independence among a majority of members of the board of directors and as to the valid exercise of business judgment of the board directors in approving or honoring an employment agreement. *In re Walt Disney Co. Derivative Litig., 731 A.2d 342 (Del. Ch. 1998).* But see *Brehm v. Eisner, 746 A.2d 244 (Del. 2000).*

A claim the corporation president based on breach of an employment contract was dismissed because of the stockholders' failure to make demand on the board of directors in accordance with this rule. *In re Walt Disney Co. Derivative Litig., 731 A.2d 342 (Del. Ch. 1998).* But see *Brehm v. Eisner, 746 A.2d 244 (Del. 2000).*

Although there were allegations that the interested director and the other directors moved in the same social circles, attended the same weddings, developed business relationships before joining the corporation's board, and described each other as friends, were insufficient, without more, to rebut the presumption of director independence; such affinities, standing alone, did not render pre-suit demand futile. *Beam v. Stewart, 845 A.2d 1040 (Del. 2004).*

Demand upon and refusal by the directors is sufficient. *Mayer v. Adams, 37 Del. Ch. 298, 141 A.2d 458 (1958).*

But if directors are disqualified to give redress, demand is futile and excused. *Mayer v. Adams, 37 Del. Ch. 298, 141 A.2d 458 (1958).*

The fact that at the time a stock appreciation rights plan was approved by the directors, a majority of them were likely to financially benefit from the plan, thereby precluding the assertion that the plan was approved by a majority of disinterested directors, alone is sufficient to

Chancery Court

excuse plaintiffs' failure to have made a demand for action on the board of directors before instituting a derivative suit since plaintiffs were justified in assuming that a demand would have been futile. *Bergstein v. Texas Int'l Co., 453 A.2d 467 (Del. Ch. 1982).*

And it is not to be expected that those charged with fraud or gross negligence would be amenable to a request that they take action against themselves. *Dann v. Chrysler Corp., 40 Del. Ch. 103, 174 A.2d 696 (1961).*

Appointment of special litigation committee not admission that demand is excused. — The decision of a board of directors to appoint a special litigation committee, with a delegation of complete authority to act on a demand, is not, in all instances, an acknowledgement that demand was excused and ergo that a shareholder's lawsuit was properly initiated as a derivative action. *Spiegel v. Buntrock, 571 A.2d 767 (Del. 1990).*

Appointment of special litigation committee. — A disinterested board of directors does not waive its right to control derivative litigation merely by delegating that control to a special committee. For the court to find that a board of directors conceded the futility of demand, a derivative plaintiff must allege particularized facts that support a finding that the board made the concession. *Seminaris v. Landa, 662 A.2d 1350 (Del. Ch. 1995).*

Demand on newly constituted board. — When during the pendency of a derivative litigation there occurs a change in the composition of a board that had been disabled by conflict, and the board as newly constituted is capable of validly exercising judgment concerning that corporate claim, a derivative plaintiff must interrupt litigation, when amending his pleading or otherwise, to make a demand upon such a newly constituted board. *Harris v. Carter, 582 A.2d 222 (Del. Ch. 1990).*

With respect to derivative claims not already validly in litigation, demand upon an independent board that has come into existence after the time of the "challenged transaction" would not be excused if the board that approved the challenged transaction did not qualify for business judgment protection. *Harris v. Carter, 582 A.2d 222 (Del. Ch. 1990).*

But see.

Requirements of particularity in complaint. — Where complaint contained nothing more than bare conclusory allegations that the board acted wrongfully in adopting the recommendation of the committee and rejecting demand, the complaint was not sufficient. The requirements of particularity apply both to plaintiff's efforts to obtain the desired action and the reasons for failing to secure redress. *Levine v. Smith, 591 A.2d 194 (Del. 1991).* But see *Brehm v. Eisner, 746 A.2d 244 (Del. 2000).*

A plaintiff must plead with particularity reasons why demand should be excused, when the reason is that the directors are disabled by a risk of liability; the claim for relief against the directors must also be pled with particularity, although a short and plain statement showing that the pleader is entitled to relief is normally sufficient to

state a claim. *In re Baxter Int'l, Inc. Shareholders Litig., 654 A.2d 1268 (Del. Ch. 1995).*

Where the complaint did not include anything specific about the alleged scheme suggesting that the directors must have known of it, and where it did plead with particularity what obvious danger signs were ignored, defendants' motion to dismiss for failure to comply with this rule was granted. *In re Baxter Int'l, Inc. Shareholders Litig., 654 A.2d 1268 (Del. Ch. 1995).*

To determine whether Del. Ch. Ct. R. 23.1 demand would be futile, the Chancery Court must determine whether the particular facts, as alleged, create a reason to doubt that (1) the directors are disinterested and independent; or (2) the challenged transaction is otherwise the product of a valid exercise of business judgment, and the complaint must plead with sufficient particularity the facts to support demand futility; this is more than the notice pleading requirement under Del. Ch. Ct. R. 8(a), but is not to the level of evidence — the complaint must set forth particularized factual statements that are essential to the claim and mere speculation or opinion is not enough. *In re Walt Disney Co. Derivative Litig., 825 A.2d 275 (Del. Ch. 2003).*

Chancery court granted directors and officers' motion to dismiss derivative suit based on income reports and insider sales; the shareholders did not make demand on board and did not sufficiently plead facts to prove demand futility by the board not being independent. *Guttman v. Jen-Hsun Huang, 823 A.2d 492 (Del. Ch. 2003).*

A ruling by the Court of Chancery that a plaintiff in a derivative suit has not pleaded a claim of wrongful refusal of demand will be reversed only on a showing of abuse of discretion, assuming no legal error led to an erroneous holding. *Scattered Corp. v. Chicago Stock Exch., 701 A.2d 70 (Del. 1997).*

If particularized facts alleged in the complaint (even if pleaded without benefit of an *8 Del. C. § 220* inspection) together with the reasonable inferences from those facts create a reasonable doubt of the independence of a majority of the board of directors, then the complaint is "well-pleaded," despite the fact that a books and records inspection might have gleaned additional facts to support a Del. Ch. Ct. R. 23.1 demand futility claim. *Beam v. Stewart, 845 A.2d 1040 (Del. 2004).*

Non-conclusory factual allegations required. — With respect to a Del. Ch. Ct. R. 23.1 motion to dismiss, the Delaware Chancery Court will consider the motion against a record confined to the well-pleaded allegations of the complaint and will draw all reasonable inferences from the non-conclusory factual allegations of the complaint in the plaintiffs' favor; the Chancery Court cannot accept cursory contentions of wrongdoing as a substitute for the pleading of particularized facts. *Guttman v. Jen-Hsun Huang, 823 A.2d 492 (Del. Ch. 2003).*

Pleading where charter has director excupatory clause. — Threat of liability that directors face can be influenced in a substantial way if the corporate charter contains an exculpatory provision authorized by *8 Del. C. § 102(b)(7)*; in the event that the charter insulates the directors from liability for breaches of the duty of care, then a serious threat of liability may only be found to exist if the plaintiff pleads a non-exculpated claim against the directors based on particularized facts. *Guttman v. Jen-Hsun Huang, 823 A.2d 492 (Del. Ch. 2003).*

Shareholder plaintiff not entitled to discovery. — In a demand refused case, a shareholder plaintiff suing derivatively is not entitled to discovery prior to responding to a motion to dismiss under this rule. *Levine v. Smith, 591 A.2d 194 (Del. 1991).* But see *Brehm v. Eisner, 746 A.2d 244 (Del. 2000).*

Plaintiffs in a derivative suit are not entitled to discovery to assist their compliance with the particularized pleading requirement of this rule in a case of demand refusal. *Scattered Corp. v. Chicago Stock Exch., 701 A.2d 70 (Del. 1997).*

The Court of Chancery properly denied plaintiffs' request for limited discovery in a derivative action alleging wrongful refusal of plaintiffs' pre-suit demand; plaintiffs' failure to take advantage of the opportunity to bring an action under *8 Del. C. § 220* to inspect minutes, reports and other books and records precluded plaintiffs from arguing that they had used the tools at hand to obtain the necessary information before filing a derivative action. *Scattered Corp. v. Chicago Stock Exch., 701 A.2d 70 (Del. 1997).*

"Reasonable doubt" standard properly applied. — The court properly applied the "reasonable doubt" pleading standard to claim of wrongful refusal of demand. *Levine v. Smith, 591 A.2d 194 (Del. 1991).* But see *Brehm v. Eisner, 746 A.2d 244 (Del. 2000).*

With respect to a determination of whether a Del. Ch. Ct. R. 23.1 demand is excused, to create a reasonable doubt about an outside director's independence, a plaintiff must plead facts that would support the inference that because of the nature of a relationship or additional circumstances other than the interested director's stock ownership or voting power, the non-interested director would be more willing to risk the director's own reputation than risk the relationship with the interested director. *Beam v. Stewart, 845 A.2d 1040 (Del. 2004).*

Review of decision to refuse demand. — Stockholders who make a demand which is refused, subject the board's decision to judicial review according to the traditional business judgment rule. *Spiegel v. Buntrock, 571 A.2d 767 (Del. 1990); Thorpe v. CERBCO, Inc., 611 A.2d 5 (Del. Ch. 1991).*

Judicial review of the merits of a special litigation committee's decision to refuse a demand is limited to those cases where demand upon the board of directors is excused and the board has decided to regain control of litigation through the use of an independent special litigation committee. *Spiegel v. Buntrock, 571 A.2d 767 (Del. 1990).*

The issues before the court when reviewing the action or inaction of a board of directors according to the traditional business judgment rule are independence, the reasonableness of its investigation and the board's good faith. By electing to make a demand, a shareholder plaintiff tacitly concedes the independence of a majority of the board to respond; therefore, the only issues to be examined are the good faith and reasonableness of the board's inves-

tigation. *Thorpe v. CERBCO, Inc., 611 A.2d 5 (Del. Ch. 1991).*

IV. DISMISSAL OR COMPROMISE.

A. IN GENERAL.

A prime purpose of this rule is to give the Court meaningful supervision of a derivative settlement and to prevent abuse (such as paying the plaintiff and/or his counsel to discontinue) by requiring judicial supervision of both dismissal and compromise of a derivative suit. *Chickering v. Giles, 270 A.2d 373 (Del. Ch. 1970).*

This rule is intended to guard against surreptitious buy-outs of representative plaintiffs, leaving other class members without recourse. *Wied v. Valhi, Inc., 466 A.2d 9 (Del. 1983),* cert. denied, *465 U.S. 1026, 104 S. Ct. 1284, 79 L. Ed. 2d 687 (1984).*

Applicability of rule contrasted with rule 15(aaa). — In order to give Ch. Ct. R. 15(aaa), limiting a plaintiff's right to amend a complaint, its intended scope, once the time for amendment had passed under that rule, a party-plaintiff was not permitted to resort to Del. Ch. Ct. R. 41(a), 23 or this rule to file a "without prejudice" dismissal of its action. *Stern v. LF Capital Partners, LLC, 820 A.2d 1143 (Del. Ch. 2003).*

Burden of persuasion. — The burden of persuading the court that a settlement proposal is fair and reasonable rests upon the settlement proponents. *NL Indus., Inc. v. MAXXAM, Inc., 659 A.2d 760 (Del. Ch. 1995).*

Only matters referred to in pleadings can be considered in considering a motion to dismiss. *Bergstein v. Texas Int'l Co., 453 A.2d 467 (Del. Ch. 1982).*

In considering a motion to dismiss for failure to make a pre-suit demand the court will only look to the pleadings. *Kaufman v. Belmont, 479 A.2d 282 (Del. Ch. 1984).*

Settlement of derivative action may not be accomplished without judge's participation. — A voluntary settlement of contested issues is favored by the law; but, the Courts having taken cognizance of the fiduciary character of a class action such as a shareholder's derivative action, settlement of such a case may not be accomplished without the participation in such proceeding of the assigned judge to the extent of determining that the proposed settlement is fair. *Steigman v. Berry, 42 Del. Ch. 53, 203 A.2d 463 (1964).*

Court's responsibility to determine if settlement fair. — Under *8 Del. C. § 327* and this rule, the Chancery Court's responsibility is to determine whether or not the proposed settlement terms are fair, reasonable and adequate, a settlement hearing not being in any sense a rehearsal of a trial. *Prince v. Bensinger, 244 A.2d 89 (Del. Ch. 1968).*

Factors to be considered. — In determining whether to approve a settlement of a shareholder derivative action, the court must look to the facts and circumstances upon which the claim is based, the possible defenses thereto, and then exercise its own business judgment to determine the overall reasonableness of the settlement. *NL Indus., Inc. v. MAXXAM, Inc., 659 A.2d 760 (Del. Ch. 1995).*

Interests to be balanced by court. — The court must balance the strong policy favoring the settlement of de-

Chancery Court

rivative suits against the policy of ensuring that the interests of shareholders are properly protected. *NL Indus., Inc. v. MAXXAM, Inc., 659 A.2d 760 (Del. Ch. 1995).*

Court must have fullest disclosure. — In a settlement hearing, when the Court has a responsibility for making a business judgment in what often amounts to an ex parte context, it is entitled to have, and indeed must have, the fullest disclosure so that all significant factors can be weighed. *Paolozzi v. Barber, 260 A.2d 176 (Del. Ch. 1969).*

But only contested issues considered. — On a petition to approve settlement of a derivative suit, the Court's function is to consider contested issues, not those which have been made moot by the parties or by events. *Chickering v. Giles, 270 A.2d 373 (Del. Ch. 1970).*

And approval should not be given when issues moot. — When a settlement has already been consummated without judicial approval and the issues posed by the derivative action are moot, Chancery Court approval should not be given. *Chickering v. Giles, 270 A.2d 373 (Del. Ch. 1970).*

However, it is not necessary in order to determine whether settlement shall be approved that the Court of Chancery try the case which is before it for settlement, for the Court of Chancery is only called upon to consider and weigh the nature of the claim, the possible defenses, the situation of the parties and exercise business judgment in determining whether the proposed settlement is reasonable. *Gladstone v. Bennett, 38 Del. Ch. 391, 153 A.2d 577 (1959).*

And court may look to negative factors. — Although the Court can approve a settlement without approving with res judicata effect each item of expenditure, because fairness of the settlement "considered as a whole" is a common test for approval, it does not follow that the Court does not look to negative factors. *Chickering v. Giles, 270 A.2d 373 (Del. Ch. 1970).*

But it cannot let stand an order for greater claim against a joint defendant. — When the corporation, for whose benefit suits were brought, puts a value on the claims against a defendant many times what the Court approved in settling claims against other defendants who have a joint and several liability, the Court negotiating cannot let the order stand. *Paolozzi v. Barber, 260 A.2d 176 (Del. Ch. 1969).*

And buying-off plaintiffs for dismissal of worthless claims is an undesirable practice. *Hoffman v. Dann, 42 Del. Ch. 123, 205 A.2d 343 (1964), cert. denied, 380 U.S. 973, 85 S. Ct. 1332, 14 L. Ed. 2d 269 (1965).*

However, settlement may be approved although the corporation will not receive immediate tangible benefits upon approval of the proposed settlement, as probable long-term benefits to the stockholders may properly be anticipated. *Prince v. Bensinger, 244 A.2d 89 (Del. Ch. 1968).*

Nonetheless, recovery of monetary damages from director defendants is not a sine qua non to settlement of a derivative action. *Prince v. Bensinger, 244 A.2d 89 (Del. Ch. 1968).*

Special litigation committee may cause corporation to file pretrial motion to dismiss a derivative suit brought on the corporation's behalf. *Kaplan v. Wyatt, 484 A.2d 501 (Del. Ch. 1984), aff'd, 499 A.2d 1184 (Del. 1985).*

Pretrial motion to dismiss by special litigation committee treated as motion for summary judgment. — While a pretrial motion generated by a special litigation committee of the board of directors to dismiss a stockholder's derivative suit is not strictly one for summary judgment pursuant to Rule 56, it is to be handled procedurally in a manner akin to proceedings on summary judgment in some respects. *Kaplan v. Wyatt, 484 A.2d 501 (Del. Ch. 1984), aff'd, 499 A.2d 1184 (Del. 1985).*

Considerations when ruling on motion to dismiss where no demand made before suit filed. — When considering a motion to dismiss where there has been no demand before suit was filed, each case must be carefully scrutinized and analyzed according to its own unique sets of facts, taking into account the totality of the circumstances and the competing interests. *Bergstein v. Texas Int'l Co., 453 A.2d 467 (Del. Ch. 1982).*

Shareholder's derivative action amended complaint was dismissed, pursuant to Del. Ch. Ct. R. 23.1, where the shareholder failed to show either that a demand of the board of directors was made, or alternatively, that demand was excused due to it being futile; conclusory allegations which were not supported by documentary evidence or factual proof from corporate records and sources beyond newspaper articles did not adequately demonstrate that the members of the board of directors were incapable of acting independently and disinterestedly from the corporate founder, who was alleged to have committed wrongdoing at the expense of the corporation. *Beam v. Stewart, 833 A.2d 961 (Del. Ch. 2003), aff'd, 845 A.2d 1040 (Del. 2004).*

Allegations must create reasonable doubt as to whether directors' decision protected by business judgment rule. — In determining the sufficiency of a complaint to withstand dismissal under this rule on wrongful refusal of demand, such complaint must contain well-pleaded allegations of fact which create a reasonable doubt that a board of directors' decision is protected by the business judgment rule. *In re Gen. Motors Class E Stock Buyout Sec. Litig., 790 F. Supp. 77 (D. Del. 1992).*

Evaluation of a plaintiff's contribution and attorneys' fees made. — If the settlement of a derivative action is ultimately consummated, an evaluation of the plaintiffs' contribution and appropriate attorneys' fees thereto will be made by the Court after a duly scheduled hearing. *Prince v. Bensinger, 244 A.2d 89 (Del. Ch. 1968).*

A motion to set aside a settlement will be granted when a plaintiff-stockholder died more than 18 months before the stipulation of settlement was signed, since while the action is derivative, counsel derives its agency and authority from the plaintiff-stockholder. *Paolozzi v. Barber, 260 A.2d 176 (Del. Ch. 1969).*

Propriety of compromise. — Provisions of compromise determined not to be abuse of Court's discretion. *In re Resorts Int'l Shareholders Litig. Appeals, 570 A.2d 259 (Del. 1990).*

Judicial notice of certificate. — The court may take judicial notice of a stock certificate in deciding a motion to dismiss. *In re Baxter Int'l, Inc. Shareholders Litig., 654 A.2d 1268 (Del. Ch. 1995).*

Demand held insufficient. — Shareholder's demand did not state a meritorious legal claim where it argued that leases of property owned by corporate fiduciaries, although reasonable when entered into, had grown unreasonable; although the corporation benefited from the renegotiations spurred by the shareholder's demand, the fact that the leases were reasonable when made prevented an award of attorney fees under this rule. *Bird v. Lida, Inc., 681 A.2d 399 (Del. Ch. 1996).*

Amendment of complaint after dismissal. — Dismissal of a shareholder's derivative action against a pharmaceuticals firm was proper where the shareholder's pleadings failed to sufficiently indicate that directors' conduct in settling sexual harassment suits against the corporation's founder and chief executive was not within the protection of the business judgment rule; there was no exception to the rule precluding amendment of shareholder complaints after dismissal for cases alleging particularly distasteful conduct. *White v. Panic, 783 A.2d 543 (Del. 2001).*

B. NOTICE.

Delaware courts do not adhere to the stringent federal rules governing the use of prospectuses for marketing corporate securities when testing the sufficiency of notices of settlement hearings under *8 Del. C. § 327* and this rule. *Prince v. Bensinger, 244 A.2d 89 (Del. Ch. 1968).*

Moreover, notice to stockholders of "proposed" dismissal or compromise may itself be mooted if parties are free, without waiting for notice, hearing or Court approval, to put through settlement of a claim which belongs to none of them except the beneficiary corporation. *Chickering v. Giles, 270 A.2d 373 (Del. Ch. 1970).*

Notice not required. — A shareholder whose complaint alleges both derivative and individual claims for relief but who shuns any effort to proceed derivatively was not required to comply with notice of dismissal provisions. *Lipton v. News Int'l, 514 A.2d 1075 (Del. 1986).*

Notice held sufficient. — When notice of settlement hearings for a derivative action contained a statement that the file in question would be open for examination, as well as summarized the pleadings, the evidence, plaintiffs' position, the terms of settlement and set forth a new plan in its entirety, it complied with requirements. *Prince v. Bensinger, 244 A.2d 89 (Del. Ch. 1968).*

Notice adequate under this rule. — The form and manner of notice given to the company's stockholders was determined to have been the best notice practicable under the circumstances, to have met the requirements of due process and applicable law, and to have been given in full compliance with this rule. *Seinfeld v. Coker, 847 A.2d 330 (Del. Ch. 2000).*

Notice requirements for settlement hearings. — While Chancery Rule 23(e) and this rule do not specifically address notice requirements with respect to settlement hearings, it is the Delaware Court of Chancery's general practice that settling parties provide notice to class members between 30 and 45 days prior to the settlement hearing. *In re Coleman Co. Shareholders Litig., 750 A.2d 1202 (Del. Ch. 1999).*

CASE NOTES — UNREPORTED

Relitigation of prior determination. — When, in dismissing on demand excusal grounds, another court has denied discovery and leave to amend, it would undermine that decision for this court to permit the same plaintiff to pursue a section 220 action solely targeted at gaining information to relitigate that prior determination. *West Coast Mgmt. & Capital, LLC v. Carrier Access Corp., 2006 Del. Ch. LEXIS 195 (Nov. 14, 2006).*

Specificity of purpose. — Delaware law does not permit section 220 actions based on an ephemeral purpose, nor will this court impute a purpose absent the plaintiff stating one. Simply put, plaintiff must do more than state, in a conclusory manner, a generally accepted proper purpose. Plaintiff must state a reason for the purpose, i.e., what it will do with the information, or an end to which that investigation may lead. Here, it is clear plaintiff's sole purpose and end is to pursue a second derivative suit-an end barred by issue preclusion. *West Coast Mgmt. & Capital, LLC v. Carrier Access Corp., 2006 Del. Ch. LEXIS 195 (Nov. 14, 2006).*

Demand not shown. — Remedial actions sought by plaintiff related to his removal as general counsel and his future employment status at the corporation. The relief would have been for his personal benefit; it would have accomplished little (or nothing) for the shareholders. The

transactions challenged in this litigation are related, at most, tangentially to his termination dispute. In other words, the remedies plaintiff sought in the letter addressed directly his claimed wrongful suspension and likely termination, and the letter cannot fairly be read as an attempt to seek a remedy for the challenged transactions for the good of the corporation or its shareholders. *Khanna v. McMinn, 2006 Del. Ch. LEXIS 86 (Del. Ch. May 9, 2006).*

Demand not excused. — Although board had "cozy" business and social relationships, the plaintiffs have failed to plead particularized allegations that would cast a reasonable doubt on the disinterestedness and independence of at least half of the board. Consequently, the plaintiffs have failed to show that demand was excused under the first prong of Aronson or under Rales. *Khanna v. McMinn, 2006 Del. Ch. LEXIS 86 (Del. Ch. May 9, 2006).*

In concluding that individual must be disqualified as a representative plaintiff, the court relies primarily on his position as corporation's former general counsel and the ethical quagmire that follows. This result is significantly supported, however, by the cloud hanging over the litigation created by the tangential and acrimonious employment dispute between individual and his former employer. Although the existence of a substantial

Chancery Court

relationship between his prior representation of corporation and the matters presently at issue is likely sufficient grounds to deem him inadequate as a representative plaintiff, the court ultimately concludes that, as a consequence of these two intertwined and interrelated considerations, individual must be disqualified as a representative plaintiff in this action. *Khanna v. McMinn, 2006 Del. Ch. LEXIS 86 (Del. Ch. May 9, 2006).*

Too early for weighing analysis. — Chancery court declined to engage in a weighing analysis to determine the disinterestedness of LLC managers for a number of reasons. Plaintiff has pled a significant and material benefit that accrued to the LLC's managers through the allocation of consideration to parent company at the expense of the LLC. Further, allocations to the LLC were subject to certain taxes; these taxes might have diminished the value of an allocation to the LLC, and managers' beneficiary 5% interests in such allocation. Finally, discovery might show that managers had holdings in the parent company greater than 3.125% and 2.054%, as the amended complaint suggests. In other words, it is too early and the facts are not as clear as necessary to engage in such a weighing analysis. Plaintiff has therefore met his burden at this stage in demonstrating the futility of demand. *Bakerman v. Sidney Frank Importing Co., 2006 Del. Ch. LEXIS 180 (Oct. 16, 2006).*

Reasonable doubt surrounds the independence of the managers, raising a specter that their discretion was sterilized. The amended complaint alleges many particularized facts regarding the managers' independence, including: (i) parent company and founder were collectively controlling shareholders of the LLC, holding a 50% interest and 12.5% interest respectively; (ii) founder controlled SFIC as founder, chairman, CEO, and a 70% shareholder, and appointed and employed all of its directors and officers (including the managers; (iii) parent company was a party to and interested in the transaction, and would receive all consideration allocated away from the LLC; (iv) founder was interested in the transaction because he would receive $ 0.70 for every dollar allocated to the parent company, but only $ 0.50 for every dollar allocated to the LLC; and (v) as a result of the transaction, founder received approximately $ 1.6 billion. *Bakerman v. Sidney Frank Importing Co., 2006 Del. Ch. LEXIS 180 (Oct. 16, 2006).*

Direct and derivative harm to plaintiffs found. — There are, however, circumstances which may form the basis for both direct claims and derivative claims. Although the corporation may be harmed, there are times when the consequences of that harm fall disproportionately upon minority stockholders. This is one of those instances. Defendants caused a direct harm to the plaintiffs by the extraction of economic value and residual voting power and a redistribution of the economic value and voting power to themselves as controlling shareholders. *Rhodes v. Silkroad Equity, LLC, 2007 Del. Ch. LEXIS 96 (July 11, 2007).*

Legal counsel not subject to disqualification. — Plaintiff is not challenging a series of transactions in which he was a key participant, but rather is challenging the allocation in a single transaction from whose negotiations he was actively excluded. Additionally, he had a role as an LLC member in approving the transactions, distinct from his role as parent company counsel. Finally, no co-plaintiffs remain to prosecute this action in the event of his disqualification. Therefore, former legal counsel was not subject to disqualification as derivative lead plaintiff. *Bakerman v. Sidney Frank Importing Co., 2006 Del. Ch. LEXIS 180 (Oct. 16, 2006).*

CASE NOTES — OTHER STATES

California

The purpose of Delaware's requirement for contemporaneous ownership is to prevent so-called strike suits, whereby stock in a corporation is purchased with purely litigious motives, that is, for the sole purpose of prosecuting a derivative action to attack transactions that occurred before the stock purchase. The Delaware courts have construed Del. Code Ann. tit. 8, § 327 and Del. Ch. Ct. R. 23.1 as further requiring that the derivative plaintiff retain stock ownership for the duration of the litigation. *Grosset v. Wenaas, 2008 Cal. LEXIS 1414 (February 14, 2008).*

Connecticut

Commencement of suit is not the only acceptable alternative available to a disinterested board which concludes there has been wrongful conduct that needs be addressed. As the cases make clear and as defense counsel stated at argument, a disinterested board might respond to a demand by, for example, authorizing an investigation of company practices and requiring a report of results and recommendations for further action, by instituting immediate policy, administrative, accounting charges, etc. *Fina v. Calarco, 2005 Conn. Super. LEXIS 2984 (Sept. 16, 2005).*

Demand excused. — The failure to filed a demand, pursuant to Del. Ch. Ct. R. 23.1, by the plaintiff in a derivative action suit was excused where the plaintiff showed that all the directors were interested in and participated in the anticompetitive and antitrust violations that the corporation was fined for in the millions of dollars. *Fina v. Calarco, 2005 Conn. Super. LEXIS 2984 (Sept. 16, 2005).*

District of Columbia

Effect of presuit demand. — A rule that a demand concedes for all purposes any claim of bias or lack of independence in the board's action thereafter might discourage presuit demands and work against the goal of promoting judicial economy. Given the logic and benefits of Delaware's approach on this issue, we are persuaded to follow that approach. Therefore, we conclude that appellant-shareholder did not lose his right to allege directors' bias and lack of independence in its action on his demand simply by filing a presuit demand. He retains the right to show, if he can, that the board's bias, lack of independence or failure to conduct a reasonable investigation creates a reasonable doubt that the demand was properly refused. *Behradrezaee v. Dashtara, 910 A.2d 349, 2006 D.C. App. LEXIS 581 (Nov. 9, 2006).*

Adoption of business judgment rule. — If a demand is made and rejected, the board rejecting the demand is entitled to the presumption of the business judgment rule unless the stockholder can allege facts with particularity creating a reasonable doubt that the board is entitled to the benefit of the presumption. This court has not yet adopted the business judgment rule. We do so now consistent with its application in this case. *Behradrezaee v. Dashtara, 910 A.2d 349, 2006 D.C. App. LEXIS 581 (Nov. 9, 2006).*

Reasonable doubt that board acted independently. — Under Federal law, Delaware law, or the principle enunciated by the United States District Court for the District of Columbia above-stated, appellant has made allegations in the second amended complaint sufficient to create a reasonable doubt that board acted independently and to rebut the presumption of the applicability of the business judgment rule. Appellant has alleged with particularity the majority shareholder's personal financial interest in the challenged transactions. He has alleged board control or domination by the majority shareholder, and his wife, who, in addition to her familial relationship with the majority shareholder, is alleged to have obtained through his actions, personal financial benefits to the detriment of the corporation. Any investigation and/or rejection of appellant's demand for action had to be decided by the alleged wrongdoers. Under the circumstances, we cannot agree with the trial court's determination that appellant's derivative action must be dismissed at this stage of the proceedings because of the business judgment rule. *Behradrezaee v. Dashtara, 910 A.2d 349, 2006 D.C. App. LEXIS 581 (Nov. 9, 2006).*

New York

Conclusory allegations. — In the context of futility of demand in a derivative action, the court will not accept as true the conclusory allegations in the complaint that are not supported by allegations of specific facts. *Beebout v. Dolan, 2007 N.Y. Misc. LEXIS 8825; 239 N.Y.L.J. 5 (December 11, 2007).*

Insufficient particularity of nonfeasance pleading. — The motion court, in granting defendants' motion to dismiss for plaintiff's failure to make the prelitigation demand required by Delaware Rules of the Court of Chancery, Rule 23.1, correctly held that plaintiff's conclusory allegations, unsupported by allegations of specific fact, were insufficient to establish that such a demand would have been futile. Where, as here, the derivative claim alleges board nonfeasance, as opposed to a business decision, a court need only determine whether or not the particularized factual allegations create a reasonable doubt that the board of directors could have properly exercised its independent and disinterested business judgment in responding to a demand. Plaintiff failed to sufficiently allege circumstances under which any directors could be considered "interested," i.e., in which they would receive a personal financial benefit, distinct from any benefit enjoyed by shareholders generally, from a transaction respecting which they were called upon to exercise independent business judgment in their capacity as board members. Examples of insufficient particularity pervade plaintiff's pleading, and include plaintiff's general allegations that unnamed executives profited from the challenged compensation scheme and failed to exercise appropriate oversight, and his citation to numerous articles and documents that he claims should have alerted board members to conflicts of interest, but without any allegation that defendants were in fact made aware of such publications. *David Shaev Profit Sharing v. Cayne, 2005 NY Slip Op 9246, 806 N.Y.S.2d 17, 2005 N.Y. App. Div. LEXIS 13713 (Dec. 6, 2005).*

Insufficient wrongdoing demand. — Fifth cause of action should be dismissed because petitioners did not make a procedurally sufficient demand in that there are no specific assertions of wrongdoing upon which the corporation could seek correction or redress. The claim essentially is that the shareholders wish to know why the company went out of business. That factor does not support the necessary claim of breach of fiduciary duties which would give rise to the derivative suit sought here. *Potter v. Arrington, 2006 NY Slip Op 26062; 2006 N.Y. Misc. LEXIS 300 (Feb. 6, 2006).*

Plaintiff has failed to allege sufficient particularized facts to support the allegations that the actions that were the subject of the anti trust division's investigation were undertaken with the specific knowledge and consent of the director defendants, the movants herein. Simply repeating the mantra that the actions were "at the direction of and with the knowledge and approval of the Board" is not sufficient. Some details should be pleaded, i.e. was their approval at a board meeting? Were all the movants present? Do the minutes contain a accurate report of the discussions relating to this matter? Who made the presentation to the Board, on which the Board wrongfully approved the illegal action, etc. *Beebout v. Dolan, 2007 N.Y. Misc. LEXIS 8825; 239 N.Y.L.J. 5 (December 11, 2007).*

North Carolina

Rule 11 sanctions in demand futility context. — Shortcomings in the complaint do raise red flags for the court in connection with the conduct of this litigation by plaintiff's counsel. They demonstrate a disregard for or lack of attention to the rules of procedure as well as court decisions and admonitions. However, the court does not believe that the initial pleadings in this case would, standing alone, support Rule 11 sanctions. The test for demand futility under Delaware law is always fact specific and contextual. The application of the law is done on a case-by-case basis. It is, therefore, an area in which Rule 11 sanctions should be invoked sparingly and with caution. *Egelhof v. Szulik, 2008 NCBC 2; 2008 NCBC LEXIS 3 (February 4, 2008).*

Texas

Shareholders cannot use discovery to satisfy the threshold requirement that they plead particularized facts showing that demand on the board would be futile. Once defendant has responded to the shareholders' request for production, in the absence of sufficient pleading, it will have lost its right to avoid the burden and expense

Chancery Court

of providing the discovery. An appellate remedy is inadequate when the relator stands to lose its substantial rights. Defendant does not have an adequate remedy by appeal. Therefore, the trial court is directed to vacate its order to the extent that it denies defendant's motion for protective order and fails to stay all discovery pending the shareholders' having pleaded adequately that demand on the board of directors is excused. *In re Crown Castle Int'l Corp., 2008 Tex. App. LEXIS 597 (January 29, 2008).*

CASE NOTES — FEDERAL COURTS

First Circuit

Totality of reasons. — When a plaintiff advances numerous reasons supporting his or her claim that demand would be futile, none of which standing alone is sufficient to excuse demand, the court must consider whether the totality of these reasons raises a reasonable doubt as to the directors' disinterest or independence. *In re Sonus Networks, Inc., 422 F. Supp. 2d 281, 294 (D. Mass. Mar. 31, 2006).*

Nonfeasance. — Delaware law requires that in a case such as this, in which the directors are accused of nonfeasance rather than misfeasance, a would-be derivative plaintiff either must make demand on the board to bring the suit or else must allege particular facts which create a reasonable doubt that, as of the time the complaint is filed, the board of directors could have properly exercised its independent and disinterested business judgment in responding to a demand. Demand will be excused only if a majority of the board members are interested or lack independence. *Pisnoy v. Ahmed (In re Sonus Networks, Inc.), 2007 U.S. App. LEXIS 19471 (First Circuit, August 16, 2007).*

Restatement of financials. — The fact that failures of internal controls led to the restatement of financials with worse results than originally reported is not enough under Delaware law to establish demand futility. *Pisnoy v. Ahmed (In re Sonus Networks, Inc.), 2007 U.S. App. LEXIS 19471 (First Circuit, August 16, 2007).*

To show directorial liability where there was a reporting and information system in place, the plaintiffs would need to show that the directors knew of the inadequacies and failed to act. In other words, if the plaintiffs had pleaded that something like the internal investigation report in this case had been presented to the directors *before* the period in question, not after it, and that the directors had failed to address the problems revealed in the report, then the complaint would have met the standards for futility of a demand on that board. However, allegations that the directors became aware of problems and promptly conducted an investigation rooting out the causes for failure does not constitute a showing of conscious neglect and misfeasance, yet those are precisely the sort of allegations the plaintiffs contend would have saved the state complaint. *Pisnoy v. Ahmed (In re Sonus Networks, Inc.), 499 F.3d 47, 2007 U.S. App. LEXIS 19471 (1st Cir., Mass., August 16, 2007).*

Insufficient independence doubt. — Alleging that several directors work together outside the Company and/or serve together on a few boards of unaffiliated companies is not enough because allegations of mere personal friendship or a mere outside business relationship, standing alone, are insufficient to raise a reasonable doubt about a director's independence. *In re First Bancorp Derivative Litig., 2006 U.S. Dist. LEXIS 88966 (D.P.R. Nov. 30, 2006).*

Alleging that director and his father have substantial loan agreements with the company is insufficient to create a reasonable doubt of director independence because plaintiffs have not established that the other directors exercise control over the loans or that the loans are material to director's outside businesses. While the loans' existence may make the board's decision more difficult, the loans do not sterilize the board's ability to decide. Accordingly, the court concludes that plaintiffs' business-relationships allegations do not create a reasonable doubt of director independence. *In re First Bancorp Derivative Litig., 2006 U.S. Dist. LEXIS 88966 (D.P.R. Nov. 30, 2006).*

Second Circuit

Demand futility test. — In determining whether plaintiffs have adequately pled futility, courts must assess whether a reasonable doubt has been created that: (1) the directors are disinterested and independent and (2) the challenged transaction was otherwise the product of a valid exercise of business judgment. *In re Goldman Sachs Mut. Funds Fee Litig., 2006 U.S. Dist. LEXIS 1542 (S.D.N.Y. Jan. 13, 2006).*

Preclusion. — Issue of whether or not the of directors did not lack the disinterestedness and independence needed to consider a demand — albeit technically a procedural issue of standing to proceed derivatively — does constitute a decision on the merits for the purposes of preclusion. *Henik v. LaBranche, 433 F. Supp. 2d 372 (D.N.Y. June 6, 2006).*

Standing. — In the context of standing based upon demand futility, the facts submitted by an individual shareholder to demonstrate that she has standing to sue on behalf of the corporation are facts about the corporation and about members of the corporation's board of directors. Indeed, the demonstration of standing to sue derivatively does not require any showing of the characteristics specific to the individual shareholder who seeks standing, aside from the obvious demonstration that the plaintiff was a shareholder during the relevant period. Given this unique nature of the derivative standing inquiry, assuming the claims are the same, which they are here, the standing analysis for one shareholder will not differ from the standing analysis for another shareholder. Therefore, it is concluded that although plaintiffs in the instance case were not named plaintiffs in the prior action, there is nothing differentiating the standing analysis to be undertaken from that done so in the prior case, and preclusive effect therefore shall be given to the earlier dismissal. *Henik v. LaBranche, 433 F. Supp. 2d 372 (D.N.Y. June 6, 2006).*

Stay granted. — Section 14(a) derivative claims are, like other derivative claims, subject to the demand requirement and business judgment rule. Consequently, the derivative Section 14(a) disclosure claims must be stayed while the special litigation committee conducts its investigation. *St. Clair Shores Gen. Emples. Ret. Sys. v. Eibeler, 2006 U.S. Dist. LEXIS 72316 (D.N.Y. Oct. 4, 2006).*

Third Circuit

Plaintiffs have adequately pled a disabling personal interest of a majority of the directors who sat on the board on the date this suit was filed. The complaint contains particularized factual allegations showing that the demand directors faced a substantial risk of personal liability for their inattention to company's allegedly improper business and clinical testing practices. The wrongdoing detailed in the complaint paints a picture of the kind of sustained and systematic failure of the board to exercise oversight over the company's operations that state a claim for breach of fiduciary duty involving bad faith. The primary business of company - drug trials involving human beings as test subjects - were routinely conducted in an egregiously unethical manner, compromising the data on products that could eventually reach the public and, more immediately, putting the safety of the participants at risk. The complaint also describes a practice of preying on groups particularly vulnerable to company's financial inducements to participate in drug trials without protest regarding the conditions of treatment. As alleged, the violations are not isolated or rare occurrences. The complaint avers that this was company's operating procedure, indeed, that it was the approach that enabled the company to secure and perform contracts for large drug trials. *In re SFBC Int'l, Inc. Sec. & Derivative Litig., 2007 U.S. Dist. LEXIS 53281 (D.N.J. July 24, 2007).*

Failure to exercise oversight sufficiently alleged. — While the Court recognizes that the threshold for pleading a claim against directors based on a sustained failure to exercise oversight is high, it finds that this case is one of those rare occurrences in which the directors have exposed themselves to liability by allegedly ignoring particularly flagrant and reprehensible wrongdoing, which unquestionably resulted in a potentially life threatening situation more immediately to the trials' participants and in the longer-run to public consumers. In re SFBC Int'l, Inc. Sec. & Derivative Litig., 2007 U.S. Dist. LEXIS 53281 (D.N.J. July 24, 2007).

Fourth Circuit

The Delaware standard for distinguishing direct from derivative actions precludes the Virginia shareholders from bringing this suit in their individual capacities. Plaintiffs accuse the board of, inter alia, failing to prevent CEO from absconding with the InvestorAdvice.com software, failing to raise additional capital to keep the corporation from going out of business, and failing to manage the corporation in a businesslike manner. None of these allegations assert the breach of a fiduciary duty owed directly to a shareholder; rather, each allegation asserts a wrong perpetrated against the corporation.

For example, the stolen software was property owned by the corporation and any negligence leading to its conversion constitutes a tort against the corporation. Similarly, the failure to raise enough capital to continue the corporation's business may constitute a breach of the duty of care owed by the board to the corporation, but it is clearly not a direct harm to the shareholders. Mismanaging the corporation is likewise a harm done to AAC. Thus the answer to the first question in *Tooley* — Who was harmed? — is clear: the corporation. *Sykes v. Meyler, 453 F. Supp. 2d 936; 2006 U.S. Dist. LEXIS 70821 (D.Va. Sept. 29, 2006).*

Seventh Circuit

Corporate boards have an obligation to undertake a good faith obligation to ensure that reporting systems are in place that alert board members to significant risks faced by the company. As such, plaintiffs are excused from making a demand upon the board of directors based on the doctrine of demand futility. It is not only the public pronouncements by newspapers, analysts, and litigants that arguably created a duty for the board to act. Instead, if the allegations in the complaint are true, the public pronouncements were merely a symptom of the ills brought upon corporation by massive oversight failures or intentional manipulation of financial and enrollment figures. *McSparran v. Larson, 2006 U.S. Dist. LEXIS 3787 (N.D. Ill. Jan. 27, 2006).*

Director independence. — Complaint provides no substantial reason to question the independence of a majority of board of directors. Plaintiffs have failed to make any allegations that outside directors have their salary set by any board member, or are otherwise financially dependent upon other directors. While most of the board members maintained social and business relationships with other board members, such relationships are de rigueur in today's executive circles; indeed, if these relationships destroyed a board member's independence, few boards would have any independent members. While certain directors are officers of the corporation and therefore have their salaries set by other directors, thereby eliminating their independence, the majority of the directors remain independent. *McSparran v. Larson, 2007 U.S. Dist. LEXIS 14778 (D. Ill. February 28, 2007).*

Ninth Circuit

The Washington State Supreme Court would likely adopt the substantive demand requirement and apply a similar, if not the same, exception for futility as that employed in Delaware. *In re Cray Inc. Derivative Litig., 431 F. Supp. 2d 1114, 1132 (D. Wash. Apr. 28, 2006).*

Audit committee. — In sum, plaintiffs' "demand futility" cases do not stand for the proposition that a committee assigned the general oversight responsibility of the activities underlying a derivative complaint (e.g., establishing accounting controls and guarding against irregularities) is per se "interested." Nor have plaintiffs adequately alleged facts that suggest a substantial likelihood of liability under a *Caremark* duty of care claim. Plaintiffs must allege facts that state "with particularity" the manner in which a given director is interested. The mere threat of personal liability alone is insufficient. Plaintiffs' generic allegation regarding the audit committee directors fails to demonstrate that those directors are interested. *In re Cray Inc. Derivative Litig., 431 F. Supp. 2d 1114, 1132 (D. Wash. Apr. 28, 2006).*

Insider sales. — While the interestedness determination for insider sales is not entirely clear, the cases support defendant's contention that the plaintiffs' allegations are insufficient. Both *Sagent* and *Guttman* analyzed nearly-identical allegations regarding insider sales and found those allegations conclusory and insufficient to demonstrate interestedness. In contrast, the more recent unpublished opinion in *Zimmerman II* held that similar allegations were sufficient to demonstrate interestedness. However, the *Zimmerman II* court gave significant weight to the sheer size of the trades (collectively, approximately $ 248 million dollars), all of which occurred in 45 days. That volume of trading is absent from this case, where the selling defendants sold a total of 161,527 shares of stock for approximately $ 1.71 million in proceeds over a 16-month period. As a result, the weight of authority analogous to this case supports defendants' argument and the court concludes that the selling directors were not interested. *In re Cray Inc. Derivative Litig., 431 F. Supp. 2d 1114, 1132 (D. Wash. Apr. 28, 2006).*

Backdating stock options. — Directors receiving backdated stock options receive a benefit not shared by stockholders. When purchasing the company's stock, the shareholders do not have the benefit of reaching back in time to buy their shares at low-price point. Furthermore, if a corporate decision will have a materially detrimental impact on the director, but not the corporation or its stockholders, a director can be considered interested.. Thus, a decision now to correct the grant dates would have a detrimental impact on the directors by removing the financial benefit of the backdating. The director may be required to pay back the difference in price between the true grant date and the purported grant date. The directors may even face legal exposure. Accordingly, if plaintiffs can plead with particularity that the directors received backdated grants, those directors will be considered interested. *In re Zoran Corp. Derivative Litig., 2007 U.S. Dist. LEXIS 43402 (D. Cal. June 5, 2007).*

Complaint alleges with particularity that defendant is an interested director, because he received a substantial number (approximately 2.5 million) of the backdated options. By receiving a personal financial benefit from the challenged options grants that is not equally shared by the stockholders, he is potentially facing a materially detrimental impact caused by liability or required restitution for the received options that is not shared by the corporation or its stockholders if those grants are found to be wrongful. In re Computer Scis. Corp. Derivative Litig., 2007 U.S. Dist. LEXIS 25414 (D. Cal. March 27, 2007).

The Court does not hold that a plaintiff must allege a pattern of backdating in order to state a claim under Section 10(b), to establish demand futility, or to state a claim for breach of fiduciary duty. For example, a plaintiff likely could proceed past the pleading stage by alleging sufficient factual detail as to the mechanics of an option

backdating scheme, including the specific roles and mental states of the various participants. In such a case, the fact that the defendants only backdated one option grant or did not grant themselves the largest possible benefit (and thus failed to generate a statistically implausible pattern) would not be an automatic bar to liability. In re Ditech Networks, Inc. Derivative Litig., 2007 U.S. Dist. LEXIS 51524 (D. Cal. July 16, 2007).

Ryan and Tyson distinguished. — The federal district court acknowledges the view advanced in those unpublished Delaware Chancery Court cases, Ryan and Tyson, that a director faces a substantial likelihood of liability for options backdating, but notes that this rule only applies to directors who directly approved or received the backdated options, or who are dependent on those who did, and only when plaintiffs allege with particularity that the options backdating occurred. To apply this view as a rule ascribing liability and interest to all directors when the core allegations of backdating are comparatively weak and lack particularity would circumvent the demand requirement in every case where backdating or springloading of options is claimed. Because of these distinctions, the federal district court in the instant case finds it inappropriate to give the analysis and holdings of Ryan and Tyson Foods weight in this case. In re Computer Scis. Corp. Derivative Litig., 2007 U.S. Dist. LEXIS 25414 (D. Cal. March 27, 2007).

Common law insider trading derivative claims. — The individual defendants' argument with regard to the unavailability of insider trading derivative claims has merit. The court finds persuasive the Seventh Circuit's reasoning that *Brophy* is no longer relevant in this context because it was decided well before private causes of action were available to individual shareholders under Rule 10b-5. *In re Cray Inc. Derivative Litig., 431 F. Supp. 2d 1114, 1132 (D. Wash. Apr. 28, 2006).*

Tenth Circuit

Specificity in pleading lacking. — Plaintiffs, along with their generalized averments of culpability, basically quote lengthy blocks from a company press release, a speech from an SEC staff member, sections of the 1934 Securities and Exchange Act, a *Bloomberg* article, and the charter of the audit committee. Noticeably lacking from both the plaintiffs' amended complaint and response are any specific failures of the independent outside director defendants or the audit committee of which they were members. Which specific oversight duties did the independent outside directors neglect? What specific action did these directors fail to take? Which specific red-or even yellow-flags were waved at the outside directors? While plaintiffs claim to have alleged specific facts addressing these questions, the court can find none. *Kenney v. Koenig, 426 F. Supp. 2d 1175, 1187 (D. Colo. Mar. 30, 2006).*

Disclosure in the 10-K/A that company's two founders and plurality stockholders exert significant influence over board elections and stockholder votes simply states the obvious. It does nothing to cast suspicion on the independence of the other directors. On its face, the 10K/A disclosure describes the practical realities of corporate governance when insiders own large but not controlling percentages of company stock. It reveals little if anything about what makes this situation so unusual that outside director independence must be cast into doubt. At most, the disclosure serves as an admission that defendants could exercise a great deal of influence in the election of the other board members. However, in its essence, this statement is not much different than an admission that the two collectively are beneficial owners of a sizable portion of the company's stock, and, without more, is insufficient to create a reasonable doubt that the independent outside directors acted independently from them. *Kenney v. Koenig, 426 F. Supp. 2d 1175, 1187 (D. Colo. Mar. 30, 2006).*

Eleventh Circuit

Delaware courts have clearly held that derivative action plaintiffs do not ring the futility bell merely by including a majority of the directors as defendants. *In re Coca-Cola Enters., 478 F. Supp. 2d 1369; 2007 U.S. Dist. LEXIS 18285 (D. Ga. March 12, 2007).*

The bulk of the plaintiff's "demand futility" allegations are mere conclusions of law masquerading as allegations of fact. Even within the forgiving confines of notice pleading, the court must eschew reliance on bald assertions and unsupported conclusions. In sum, the plaintiff fails to allege any particularized facts raising a reasonable doubt that board member was capable of making corporate decisions on the merits rather than on extraneous considerations or influences. By failing to allege facts sufficient to raise a reasonable doubt as to his independence or disinterestedness as a board member, the plaintiff fails to allege that a majority of board of directors are incapable of impartially considering the demand. *Story v. Kang, 2006 U.S. Dist. LEXIS 4354 (M.D. Fla. Jan. 20, 2006).*

Receipt of customary director compensation does not excuse demand. McCabe v. Foley, 424 F. Supp. 2d 1315, 1325 (D. Fla. Apr. 4, 2006).

Insider trading. — Mere allegations of insider trading do not make a director interested. Rather, a complaint must include particular facts sustaining the two key elements of insider trading, 1) knowledge of material, non-public information, and 2) sales that resulted from the receipt of that information. A well-pled complaint contains particularized allegations of fact detailing the precise roles that the directors played at the company, the information that would have come to their attention in those roles, and any indication as to why they would have perceived the accounting irregularities. Additionally, a complaint should state with particularity the nature of the material, non-public information. Finally, the timing of stock sales is much more important than the amount of stock sales in determining insider trading. A complaint should show inconsistency in trading patterns, and connect the non-public information to those sales. McCabe v. Foley, 424 F. Supp. 2d 1315, 1325 (D. Fla. Apr. 4, 2006).

District of Columbia Circuit

Director independence. — Since it is well established that merely alleging that several directors work together outside the company and/or serve together on a few boards of unaffiliated companies, claiming such is not enough to raise a reasonable doubt about a director's independence; especially where, as here, the directors are individuals whose considerable professional accomplishments had been independently achieved well in advance of their election to the board. Accordingly, these alleged business relationships, as plaintiffs have plead them, do not create a reasonable doubt of director independence. *In re Fannie Mae Sec., 2007 U.S. Dist. LEXIS 39348 (D.D.C. May 31, 2007).*

Rule 23.2.   Actions relating to unincorporated associations

DELAWARE CASE NOTES — REPORTED

This rule does not of itself create equitable jurisdiction in the absence of the threat of a multiplicity of suits or the existence of some other basis for such jurisdiction. *Delaware Bankers Ass'n v. Division of Revenue of Dep't of Fin., 298 A.2d 352 (Del. Ch. 1972).*

Rule 24.   Intervention

DELAWARE CASE NOTES — REPORTED

I. General Consideration.
II. Intervention of Right.
III. Permissive Intervention.
IV. Procedure.

I. GENERAL CONSIDERATION.

This rule clearly applies only to pending actions. *Braasch v. Mandel, 40 Del. Ch. 12, 172 A.2d 271 (1961).*

Jurisdiction over parties and claims. — Court has personal jurisdiction over a party not originally joined, but who meets the test of this rule and who asserts a counterclaim arising out of the same facts as those alleged in the complaint. *In re RJR Nabisco, Inc. Shareholders Litig., 576 A.2d 654 (Del. Ch. 1990).*

Court's ancillary jurisdiction extends to compulsory counterclaims asserted by persons with a right under paragraph (a) to intervene. *In re RJR Nabisco, Inc. Shareholders Litig., 576 A.2d 654 (Del. Ch. 1990).*

When the facts alleged in the intervenor's new "claim" in effect constitute the same factors or transaction as put in issue by the existing pleadings, and when the proposed intervenors, far from being strangers to the existing parties, allegedly acted in the transaction in question at the behest of the defendants, the Court had ancillary jurisdiction over the compulsory and permissive claims of every kind arising from the transaction that could be asserted by the original parties and the intervenors. *In re RJR Na-*

Chancery Court

bisco, Inc. Shareholders Litig., 576 A.2d 654 (Del. Ch. 1990).

Intervention in action no longer pending. — Dismissal of individual claims in an action which also contained derivative claims did not authorize proposed intervenors to intervene to pursue the derivative claims. *Lipton v. News Int'l, 514 A.2d 1075 (Del. 1986).*

II. INTERVENTION OF RIGHT.

The assignee of a contract can intervene in a contract action by the assignor against the other contracting party as of right under paragraph (a) of this rule. *Diner Foods, Inc. v. City of Dover, 43 Del. Ch. 331, 229 A.2d 495 (1967).*

When the applicant's interest is not adequately represented. — If it does not appear that the grounds for complaint can be characterized as frivolous and if the Court cannot conclude to a reasonable certainty that the applicant's interest will be adequately represented by the party in the suit, it follows that the applicant's interest may not be adequately represented within the meaning of this rule. *Schiff v. RKO Pictures Corp., 37 Del. Ch. 21, 136 A.2d 193 (1954).*

"Representation" meaning quality of case plaintiff can present. — The language of this rule concerning representation at least embraces situations where the ability or status of the plaintiff to uphold adequately the rights common to that position may be in doubt. Thus, the word "representation" is defined as including the quality of the case which the plaintiff may be in a position to present, in contrast with the calibre of his attorney. *Young v. Janas, 37 Del. Ch. 14, 136 A.2d 189 (1954).*

But the applicant must show representation inadequate. — In dealing with intervention as a right, whether an applicant has such a right depends upon whether he can show compliance with the requirement in the rule that the representation of the applicant's interest by existing parties is, or may be, inadequate. *Schiff v. RKO Pictures Corp., 37 Del. Ch. 21, 136 A.2d 193 (1954).*

To consider whether one may not adequately represent an applicant's "interest," it is necessary to see what the applicant's interest is. *Schiff v. RKO Pictures Corp., 37 Del. Ch. 21, 136 A.2d 193 (1954).*

Where the applicants have an interest in the subject matter of the litigation and the disposition of the action may impede their ability to protect that interest, but where there is no risk that, due to lack of coordination or limited communication, defendants will overlook or fail to energetically pursue points in which applicants have an interest, intervention of right will not be allowed. *In re RJR Nabisco, Inc. Shareholders Litig., 576 A.2d 654 (Del. Ch. 1990).*

III. PERMISSIVE INTERVENTION.

Demonstration required to be granted leave to intervene. — Where the relevant pleadings in issue are identical, to be granted leave to intervene, a movant must demonstrate either: (1) Collusion between the purported representation and those to whom he is formally opposed in the litigation; (2) a lack of diligence on the part of the present representative; or (3) a conflict of interest between the present representative and movant. *Wier v. Howard Hughes Medical Inst., 404 A.2d 140 (Del. Ch. 1979).*

Time of intervention. — Permitting an individual class member to intervene at any stage of a class action is somewhat antithetical to the representative nature of such a proceeding. *Giammalvo v. Sunshine Mining Co., 644 A.2d 407 (Del. 1994).*

Motions to intervene on appeal are seldom granted, especially when the movant declined to join in the proceedings at trial. *Giammalvo v. Sunshine Mining Co., 644 A.2d 407 (Del. 1994).*

The court must consider whether intervention will unduly delay or prejudice the adjudication of the rights of the original parties. *Campbell v. Loew's, Inc., 37 Del. Ch. 17, 136 A.2d 191 (1957).*

In deciding whether or not to allow an applicant to intervene under paragraph (b) of this rule, the Court must consider whether such intervention will unduly delay or prejudice the adjudication of the rights of the original parties, and, it must also be determined by the Court whether or not the present applicant's claim has a question of law or fact in common with the main action. *Wier v. Howard Hughes Medical Inst., 404 A.2d 140 (Del. Ch. 1979).*

Intervention denied where movant's concern is not directly related to basic issue in litigation. — Where the principal motivation behind movant's application for leave to intervene centers on a concern which is not directly related to the basic issue to be decided in the litigation, and it would not contribute to the resolution of such basic issue but would actually complicate the resolution of such issue to permit applicant to intervene, movant's application for leave to intervene in the litigation will be denied without prejudice. *Wier v. Howard Hughes Medical Inst., 404 A.2d 140 (Del. Ch. 1979).*

Relevant considerations in exercising discretion to permit intervention. — Ordinarily, considerations relating entirely to the litigation itself will determine whether discretion should be exercised to permit intervention. In some circumstances, however, the Court will look beyond the litigation to a larger setting, and in those instances the relevant considerations may involve issues of comity, fairness and efficiency. *In re RJR Nabisco, Inc. Shareholders Litig., 576 A.2d 654 (Del. Ch. 1990).*

IV. PROCEDURE.

Motion not granted unless pleading filed. — If the applicant fails to file an appropriate pleading with his motion to intervene as required by paragraph (c) of this rule and plaintiffs object on that ground, his motion to intervene will not be granted unless and until such a pleading is served and filed. *Schiff v. RKO Pictures Corp., 37 Del. Ch. 21, 136 A.2d 193 (1954).*

V. DEPOSITIONS AND DISCOVERY

Rule 26.   General provisions governing discovery

DELAWARE CASE NOTES — REPORTED

Availability of discovery. — Discovery is available as part of a proceeding to determine whether property should be released after an effective sequestration, it is available in aid of a judgment or execution, it is available as an incident to contempt proceedings and for other purposes not specifically directed to the merits of a controversy. *Kolyba Corp. v. Banque Nationale De Paris, 316 A.2d 585 (Del. Ch. 1973).*

Discovery is available to a party for the purpose of determining whether the Court has subject matter jurisdiction and/or jurisdiction over person or property. *Kolyba Corp. v. Banque Nationale De Paris, 316 A.2d 585 (Del. Ch. 1973).*

Judicial discretion in application of discovery rules. — Where defendant essentially controlled relevant information needed to rebut motion for summary judgment and plaintiffs could only develop facts to contest the motion through the discovery process, to deny them that right and thus extinguish plaintiffs' action at its threshold would not have comported with principles of judicial discretion in the application of discovery rules. *Mann v. Oppenheimer & Co., 517 A.2d 1056 (Del. 1986).*

Discovery should be allowed unless the Court is satisfied that the administration of justice will be impeded by such an allowance. *Fish Eng'g Corp. v. Hutchinson, 39 Del. Ch. 215, 162 A.2d 722 (1960).*

However, discovery is subject to the exercise of the court of chancery's sound discretion. *Dann v. Chrysler Corp., 39 Del. Ch. 437, 166 A.2d 431 (1960).*

And it will not order discovery in criminal case. *Curran v. Craven, 36 Del. Ch. 71, 125 A.2d 375 (1956).*

Moreover, plaintiffs are not entitled to discovery to discover new causes of action. *Dann v. Chrysler Corp., 39 Del. Ch. 437, 166 A.2d 431 (1960).*

Absence showing such may exist. — One is not entitled to discovery to search for a possible cause of action in the absence of a fairly substantial showing that they may possibly exist. *Garbarino v. Albercan Oil Corp., 109 A.2d 824 (Del. Ch. 1954).*

But the court cannot prevent the taking of depositions addressed to merits solely because, in the course thereof, it may provide the plaintiff with information which can be used to obtain an effective seizure of stock of other defendants. *Steinberg v. Shields, 38 Del. Ch. 423, 153 A.2d 599 (1959).*

Furthermore, beliefs, opinions and conclusions as such are not necessarily beyond the scope of the discovery process, as they may lead to admissible evidence under some circumstances. *Hutchinson v. Fish Eng'g Corp., 38 Del. Ch. 414, 153 A.2d 594 (1959),* appeal dismissed, *162 A.2d 722 (Del. 1960).*

However, parties seeking discovery should show a reasonable possibility of the existence of the things they seek in discovery before being permitted to have discovery in that field. *Garbarino v. Albercan Oil Corp., 109 A.2d 824 (Del. Ch. 1954).*

And a corporation is entitled to prevent even its stockholders from engaging in unrestricted discovery in search of "something," even in a derivative suit for the benefit of the corporation. *Garbarino v. Albercan Oil Corp., 109 A.2d 824 (Del. Ch. 1954).*

Discovery may not be had for a "fishing expedition" to find property subject to seizure and thus available for use as a jurisdictional base. *Kolyba Corp. v. Banque Nationale De Paris, 316 A.2d 585 (Del. Ch. 1973).*

But information obtained by proper use of discovery may be used in aid of sequestration process. *Kolyba Corp. v. Banque Nationale De Paris, 316 A.2d 585 (Del. Ch. 1973).*

However, a party who secures a sequestration order cannot have discovery as a matter of course against a garnishee; rather, to get discovery, he must do more than simply assert disagreement with the report by the garnishee or a general desire to test it, as he must make some showing to persuade the court that discovery is reasonable and necessary. *Kolyba Corp. v. Banque Nationale De Paris, 316 A.2d 585 (Del. Ch. 1973).*

Garnishee corporation may respond to discovery through, or by, person of its own choosing. *Kolyba Corp. v. Banque Nationale De Paris, 316 A.2d 585 (Del. Ch. 1973).*

Work product privilege has been formalized by court rule and, in a sense, is now codified under paragraph (b)(3) of this rule. *Riggs Nat'l Bank v. Zimmer, 355 A.2d 709 (Del. Ch. 1976).*

Privilege belongs to attorney. — The work product privilege is not that of the client, but one belonging to the attorney. *Riggs Nat'l Bank v. Zimmer, 355 A.2d 709 (Del. Ch. 1976).*

Actual pending lawsuit not required for work product privilege. — The privilege for trial preparation materials does not require the existence of an actual pending lawsuit but only that materials be written specifically in preparation for threatened or anticipated litigation. *Riggs Nat'l Bank v. Zimmer, 355 A.2d 709 (Del. Ch. 1976).*

Work product privilege applied to subsequent litigation. — Whether actual preparation material under this rule is protected only if prepared in anticipation of litigation or for trial in the same case in which the immunity accorded to such material is sought, or whether the privilege may also apply to subsequent litigation, must turn on the facts of each case, and the decision would depend upon how closely related the prior litigation is to the litigation at hand. *Riggs Nat'l Bank v. Zimmer, 355 A.2d 709 (Del. Ch. 1976).*

Discovery of trade secrets and confidential proprietary information. — Where a plaintiff in a trade secret case seeks to discover the trade secrets and confi-

Chancery Court

dential proprietary information of its adversary, the plaintiff will normally be required first to identify with reasonable particularity the matter which it claims constitutes a trade secret, before it will be allowed, given a proper showing of need, to compel discovery of its adversary's trade secrets. *Engelhard Corp. v. Savin Corp., 505 A.2d 30 (Del. Ch. 1986).*

Curing language of complaint. — If the complaint's language is vague and somewhat uncertain, defendants by discovery can easily cure such uncertainty or ambiguity. *Fish Eng'g Corp. v. Hutchinson, 39 Del. Ch. 215, 162 A.2d 722 (1960).*

Discovery to determine fairness of class action compromise. — The purpose of a hearing on the fairness of a proposed settlement of a class action is not the final determination of the merits of claims or defenses asserted in such litigation, but an assessment of the overall fairness of the compromise, and the full scope of discovery is not appropriate in this setting. A more limited and targeted discovery, if any, is appropriate where the issue is whether a proposed compromise and settlement should be approved. *In re Amsted Indus., Inc. Litig., 521 A.2d 1104 (Del. Ch. 1986).*

Appeals from rulings on discovery fall within the proscription against the appellate review of interlocutory orders. *Lummus Co. v. Air Prods. & Chems., Inc., 243 A.2d 718 (Del. 1968).*

Though such may be appealable where substantive rights are involved. — The rule is settled that in the absence of a determination of legal right and substantial issue, an interlocutory order is unappealable. However, a discovery order involving matters such as privilege, self-incrimination, privacy or trade secrets may determine such rights and issues as to become appealable.

Discovery granted in a given case could be so burdensome as to be ruinous to the party and so disproportionate to the amount in controversy as to amount to deprivation of due process, thus involving substantive rights and issues. *Pepsico, Inc. v. Pepsi-Cola Bottling Co., 261 A.2d 520 (Del. 1969).*

However, a protective order against certain discovery is not an appealable order. *Lummus Co. v. Air Prods. & Chems., Inc., 243 A.2d 718 (Del. 1968).*

Similarly, pretrial indication of an adverse ruling to be expected at trial may not become the basis of an appeal. *Lummus Co. v. Air Prods. & Chems., Inc., 243 A.2d 718 (Del. 1968).*

Lawyer-client communications in stockholder suit. — In the stockholder suit context, if the corporation objects to discovery and successfully establishes that the material sought is a confidential communication as to legal services between it and its attorney, then discovery is not authorized unless the plaintiff stockholder seeking discovery shows "good cause" why the privilege should not attach. *Deutsch v. Cogan, 580 A.2d 100 (Del. Ch. 1990).*

Members of a board of directors who took part in company merger could not use the lawyer-client privilege to block access of shareholders to information and basis of board's decisions. *Deutsch v. Cogan, 580 A.2d 100 (Del. Ch. 1990).*

Good cause for precluding application of the work product doctrine was established where a stockholder showed that he needed access to documents that revealed the deliberative processes of a special committee of the corporation appointed to investigate a pre-suit demand of the stockholder. *Grimes v. DSC Communications Corp., 724 A.2d 561 (Del. Ch. 1998).*

Rule 30.   Depositions upon oral examination

DELAWARE CASE NOTES — REPORTED

Court of Chancery Rule 30(b)(6) is functionally identical to Federal Rule of Civil Procedure 30(b)(6). As is clear from authorities on that rule, an entity asked to designate a Rule 30(b)(6) witness has "an affirmative duty to produce a witness who can answer questions regarding the subject matter listed in the notice. Indeed, as a practical matter, producing a person who knows nothing about the subject matter of the litigation is the functional equivalent of having spurned the deposition altogether. Consequently, Rule 30(b)(6) can be violated when a corporate party literally sends a human being to the deposition but

the person is unequipped to participate meaningfully in the deposition. Further, although Rule 30(b)(6) implicitly restricts the scope of examination by requiring the deposing party to describe 'with reasonable particularity the matters on which examination is requested, courts read the notice broadly to permit substantial inquiry so that the witness does not avoid testimony on the basis of a technicality. *Highland Select Equity Fund, L.P. v. Motient Corp., 906 A.2d 156, 2006 Del. Ch. LEXIS 127 (July 6, 2006).*

Rule 33.   Interrogatories to parties

DELAWARE CASE NOTES — REPORTED

Interrogatories should be allowed unless the Court is satisfied that the administration of justice will be impeded by such an allowance. *Fish Eng'g Corp. v. Hutchinson, 39 Del. Ch. 215, 162 A.2d 722 (1960).*

Nevertheless, the court of chancery has broad discretion in determining whether or not to allow inter-

rogatories under this rule. *Fish Eng'g Corp. v. Hutchinson, 39 Del. Ch. 215, 162 A.2d 722 (1960).*

However, where a party objects, documents need not be produced when the request for production is merely part of an interrogatory. *Hutchinson v. Fish Eng'g Corp., 38 Del. Ch. 414, 153 A.2d 594 (1959), appeal dismissed, 162 A.2d 722 (Del. 1960).*

Likewise, where there is nothing in the record to show any substantial basis that causes of action may exist, such inquiries are not fairly within the discovery provisions. *Garbarino v. Albercan Oil Corp., 109 A.2d 824 (Del. Ch. 1954).*

And same rules apply to corporation. — When a corporation for whose benefit a derivative action is brought objects to requests for interrogatories, the Court of Chancery must apply the same rules of discovery as govern other parties. *Garbarino v. Albercan Oil Corp., 109 A.2d 824 (Del. Ch. 1954).*

In a stockholder's derivative action, interrogators could ask the corporation to describe the nature, terms and subject matter of certain documents called for by the interrogatory, although objection is made to the interrogatory on the ground that it will require the corporation to summarize and to state the effect of the documents referred to where the stockholder asserts that he is only asking for such information as will enable him to identify a paper for the purpose of ordering its production. *Elster v. American Airlines, 34 Del. Ch. 505, 106 A.2d 516 (1954).*

And identity of persons who have knowledge of relevant matters. — In a stockholder's derivative action to enjoin the corporation's activity on a stock option, where the questions propounded under an interrogatory relate to the identity of persons who may have knowledge of relevant facts and to matters relevant to the issue, the interrogatory is proper and should be answered. *Elster v. American Airlines, 34 Del. Ch. 505, 106 A.2d 516 (1954).*

As well as the total number of shares held. — In a stockholder's derivative action to enjoin the corporation's activity, a stockholder in interrogatories could ask for the total number of shares held of record and not of record by each optionee which have been acquired otherwise than by the exercise of the options. *Elster v. American Airlines, 34 Del. Ch. 505, 106 A.2d 516 (1954).*

But answer as to consideration does not require furnishing legal conclusions. — In a stockholder's derivative action to enjoin a corporation's activity on a stock option, where the stockholder asks whether consideration was received from the optionees for the granting of the options, and, if so, the nature of the consideration and whether or not there was an agreement in writing, the answer did not require the furnishing of legal conclusions. *Elster v. American Airlines, 34 Del. Ch. 505, 106 A.2d 516 (1954).*

Though facts upon which consideration theories are based may be elicited. — The fact that the defendant has set forth its theories as to consideration in its briefs and arguments does not deprive the plaintiff of the right to elicit by interrogatories the facts upon which such theories may be based. *Elster v. American Airlines, 34 Del. Ch. 505, 106 A.2d 516 (1954).*

Application for more time may be made. — An affidavit of the appropriate party should be filed prior to the production date showing just what the facts are with respect to the matter; and if it shows the need for more time, an appropriate application can be made. *Carmer v. J. Leo Johnson, Inc., 39 Del. Ch. 171, 161 A.2d 236 (1960).*

And a party who cannot answer should incorporate an explanation in his answer. — A party who cannot answer a particular interrogatory for a reason which would not support a written objection under this rule should incorporate his explanation in the answer to the interrogatories generally. In this way his opponent will have a sworn explanation which he may accept or bring before the Court as he sees fit. *Carmer v. J. Leo Johnson, Inc., 39 Del. Ch. 171, 161 A.2d 236 (1960).*

Rule 34.   Production of documents and things and entry upon land for inspection and other purposes

DELAWARE CASE NOTES — REPORTED

Application of rule is subject to the exercise of the court of chancery's sound discretion. Dann v. Chrysler Corp., 39 Del. Ch. 437, 166 A.2d 431 (1960).

However, a motion for production of documents must relate to allegations of complaint, not independent reports, even though they may cover some of the same subject matter. Dann v. Chrysler Corp., 39 Del. Ch. 437, 166 A.2d 431 (1960).

And party cannot obtain the production of documents by so requesting in a notice of deposition. Steinberg v. Shields, 38 Del. Ch. 423, 153 A.2d 599 (1959).

Rather, the movant must demonstrate a need beyond the relevancy or materiality of the documents and that no other avenue is open to him to obtain discovery. Graham v. Allis-Chalmers Mfg. Co., 41 Del. Ch. 78, 188 A.2d 125 (1963).

Inspection of attorney-client privileged documents cannot be enforced. — Statements taken by the corporate defendant's attorney from the nondirector defendants in connection with its investigation of the antitrust violations and in preparation for the defense of the indictments are privileged documents obtained by reason of an attorney-client relationship, and, as such, an inspection of them cannot be enforced. Graham v. Allis-Chalmers Mfg. Co., 41 Del. Ch. 78, 188 A.2d 125 (1963).

Burden upon respondent to explain failure to comply. — Where a stockholder failed to produce at the request of the corporation certain tax returns and there was nothing to explain the failure and where at the time of production of such returns it is not clear as to whether or not the failure to produce them was due to refusal or negligence or because of his inability to obtain copies from the Bureau of Internal Revenue, the court would not issue an order dismissing the action for failure of the stockholder to comply with the order, although the burden was upon the stockholder to explain satisfactorily the failure to comply. Gottlieb v. McKee, 34 Del. Ch. 537, 107 A.2d 240 (1954).

Chancery Court

DELAWARE CASE NOTES — UNREPORTED

Construction with Section 220. — There is a significant difference in scope between a section 220 action and discovery under Rule 34. The two are, in fact, entirely different procedures. Section 220 is not intended to supplant or circumvent discovery proceedings, nor should it be used to obtain that discovery in advance of the appraisal action itself. If plaintiff wishes to receive the documents it seeks in this action, it must elect to seek appraisal and request them through the discovery process. To now permit plaintiff's additional information beyond the comprehensive disclosure already in the public domain simply because it could receive such information in a later appraisal action through discovery would be putting the cart before the horse. *Polygon Global Opportunities Master Fund v. W. Corp., 2006 Del. Ch. LEXIS 179 (Oct. 12, 2006).*

Rule 36. Requests for admission

DELAWARE CASE NOTES — REPORTED

Unsworn denials of requests for admission sufficient to place facts in issue. — Where plaintiff attempted to carry his burden under Ch. Ct. R. 56 by submitting his sworn affidavit to the Court, and requested defendant to admit to each numbered paragraph in his affidavit pursuant to this rule, and defendant's attorney, on behalf of defendant, provided unsworn responses to plaintiff's request under this rule, the Court of Chancery had those responses before it in considering plaintiff's motion under Ch. Ct. R. 56, and under this rule the unsworn denials of defendant's attorney were sufficient to place the facts stated in the request in issue. *Brown v. Ocean Drilling & Exploration Co., 403 A.2d 1114 (Del. 1979).*

Rule 37. Failure to make discovery: Sanctions

DELAWARE CASE NOTES — REPORTED

An order to compel discovery under paragraph (a) does not give a party a blank check with which to obtain any document or the answer to any question which he might care to ask. Rather, disputes over specific documents and specific questions should be submitted to the Court for resolution by an appropriate motion by either party. *Weinschel Eng'g Co. v. Midwest Microwave, Inc., 297 A.2d 443 (Del. Ch. 1972).*

Jurisdiction to sanction retained notwithstanding separate appeals in action pending before Supreme Court. — Notwithstanding that the action was pending before the Supreme Court of Delaware on separate appeals by the defendants therein, the Court of Chancery, having retained jurisdiction over the action for purposes other than the appeals taken by defendants, had jurisdiction to enter an order sanctioning defendants by striking their pleadings. *Park Oil, Inc. v. Getty Ref. & Mktg. Co., 407 A.2d 537 (Del. 1979).*

Mandatory award of attorney's fees. — Pursuant to this Rule, when a party fails to comply with discovery orders of the Court or otherwise engages in discovery abuses, the award of attorney's fees and expenses to the opposing party is mandatory, absent a showing by the wrongdoer that his actions were substantially justified or that other circumstances make the award unjust. The wrongdoer has the burden to show that his actions were, in fact, justified or that other circumstances make the award unjust. *Bader v. Fisher, 504 A.2d 1091 (Del. 1986).*

Withholding information. — Plaintiff's counsel was found to have prosecuted a purported class action suit against a software company in bad faith by filing false and misleading complaints and by withholding material information during discovery; the trial court ordered plaintiff and counsel jointly and severally to pay $25,000 to the defendant as well as ordered the law firm and lawyers to pay $2,500 to the trial court for the waste of the court's resources and time. *Beck v. Atl. Coast Plc., 868 A.2d 840 (Del. Ch. 2005).*

Sanctions. — Trial courts are obligated to diligently sanction discovery abuse; the burden rests on the trial courts to promptly and effectively take corrective action to secure the just, speedy, and inexpensive determination of every proceeding before them. *Beck v. Atl. Coast Plc., 868 A.2d 840 (Del. Ch. 2005).*

VI. TRIALS

Rule 40. Call of calendar, duty of register; continuances

DELAWARE CASE NOTES — REPORTED

The annual call of calendar serves a salutary purpose of enabling the Court to review both all of its cases and each of its cases. *Michaels v. Lesser, 275 A.2d 797 (Del. Ch. 1971).*

It is primarily for the purpose of determining whether there has been any undue delay in connection with pending matters. *Michaels v. Lesser, 275 A.2d 797 (Del. Ch. 1971).*

Rule 41. Dismissal of actions

DELAWARE CASE NOTES — REPORTED

I. General Consideration.
II. Voluntary Dismissal.
III. Involuntary Dismissal.
IV. Dismissal of Counterclaim, etc.
V. Costs.
VI. Inaction.

I. GENERAL CONSIDERATION.

Scope. In order to give Ch. Ct. R. 15(aaa), limiting a plaintiff's right to amend a complaint, its intended scope, once the time for amendment had passed under that rule, a party-plaintiff was not permitted to resort to subsection (a) of this rule, Ch. Ct. R. 23 or 23.1 to file a "without prejudice" dismissal of its action. *Stern v. LF Capital Partners, LLC, 820 A.2d 1143 (Del. Ch. 2003).*

Applicability. — There was substantial interplay between Ch. Ct. R. 15(aaa), limiting a plaintiff's right to amend its complaint, and subsection (a) of this rule, regarding voluntary dismissal, and those rules were to be construed, to the extent possible, to give effect to both. *Stern v. LF Capital Partners, LLC, 820 A.2d 1143 (Del. Ch. 2003).*

This rule is permissive rather than mandatory. *Smirlock v. Ballard, 280 A.2d 739 (Del. Ch. 1971).*

The doctrine of primary administrative jurisdiction contemplates suspension of judicial proceedings, under Ch. Ct. R. 62 rather than a dismissal thereof under this Rule, pending the action of the administrative agency. *Eastern Shore Natural Gas Co. v. Stauffer Chem. Co., 298 A.2d 322 (Del. 1972).*

Motion to dismiss brought in response to report of special litigation committee is a hybrid motion which takes qualities from a Chancery Rule 41(a)(2) motion to dismiss and a Chancery Rule 56 motion for summary judgment. *Lewis v. Fuqua, 502 A.2d 962 (Del. Ch. 1985).*

Effect of answer or motion for summary judgment. — Once an answer or motion for summary judgment is filed, subdivision (a)(2), and not subdivision (a)(1), applies. *Draper v. Gardner Defined Plan Trust, 625 A.2d 859 (Del. 1993).*

II. VOLUNTARY DISMISSAL.

Paragraph (a)(1) contemplates dismissal of the entire controversy between litigants and not the dropping of a single claim or of a party. *Oil & Gas Ventures, Inc. v. Cheyenne Oil Corp., 43 Del. Ch. 143, 220 A.2d 785 (1966).*

But a party defendant may be dropped on fair terms. — When this Rule is employed to drop a party defendant, the proper function of the Court is to prevent any undue prejudice to the party affected by a motion to drop, and, except where a plaintiff proposes to drop an entire controversy before the filing of an answer or a motion for summary judgment, the Court, while empowered to permit the dropping of a named party defendant, must do so only on terms that are fair and proper and usually in the early stages of the litigation. *Oil & Gas Ventures, Inc. v. Cheyenne Oil Corp., 43 Del. Ch. 143, 220 A.2d 785 (1966).*

Granting of leave for voluntary dismissal is discretionary. — Whether or not to grant leave of court for a voluntary dismissal is a matter for the exercise of discretion by the trial court, and will be reversed by the Superior Court only upon a showing of an abuse of that discretion. *Draper v. Gardner Defined Plan Trust, 625 A.2d 859 (Del. 1993).*

Factors in determining prejudice resulting from voluntary dismissal. — Factors to determine whether a defendant would suffer plain legal prejudice as a result of a voluntary dismissal include: (1) the defendants' effort and expense in preparation for trial; (2) excessive delay and lack of diligence on the part of the plaintiff in prosecuting the action; (3) sufficiency of the explanation for the need to take a dismissal; and (4) whether a motion for summary judgment has been filed by the defendant. *Draper v. Gardner Defined Plan Trust, 625 A.2d 859 (Del. 1993).*

Dismissal of only 1 defendant permitted. — Contrary to the holding in *Oil & Gas Ventures, Inc. v. Cheyenne Oil Corp., Del. Ch., 220 A.2d 785 (1966),* a plaintiff has an absolute right under subdivision (a)(1)(i) of this rule to dismiss one defendant from an action without dismissing any claims against any other defendants. *Pennzoil Co. v. Getty Oil Co., 473 A.2d 358 (Del. Ch. 1984).*

Voluntary dismissal denied in stockholders derivative action. — Voluntary dismissal of an action by derivative plaintiff stockholders was denied where the corporation appointed a special litigation committee, because the dismissal of the action would impinge on the committee's range of action and usurp its function. *In re Oracle Corp. Derivative Litig., 808 A.2d 1206 (Del. Ch. 2002).*

Appraisal action. — Motion by plaintiff, under this rule, to dismiss appraisal action under *8 Del. C. § 262,* made after 60-day limitation, is properly denied. *Dofflemyer v. W.F. Hall Printing Co., 432 A.2d 1198 (Del. 1981).*

Res judicata or collateral estoppel. — Voluntary dismissal in California is more properly analogized to a voluntary dismissal under Del. Ch. Ct. R. 41(a), which cannot be the basis of a res judicata or collateral estoppel defense. *Dieterich v. Harrer, 857 A.2d 1017 (Del. Ch. 2004).*

III. INVOLUNTARY DISMISSAL.

A motion to dismiss the complaint is equivalent to old practice of demurring to the bill. *Du Pont v. Du Pont, 32 Del. Ch. 405, 82 A.2d 376 (1951).*

The court makes a determination of law on the basis of the limited record presented. *Macartor v. Graylyn Crest III Swim Club, Inc., 40 Del. Ch. 53, 173 A.2d 344 (1961).*

But facts alleged in the complaint must be taken to be true. *Taormina v. Taormina Corp.*, 32 Del. Ch. 18, 78 A.2d 473 (1951); *Campbell v. Loew's, Inc.*, 36 Del. Ch. 533, 134 A.2d 565 (1957); *McQuail v. Shell Oil Co.*, 40 Del. Ch. 410, 183 A.2d 581 (1962).

However, only well-pleaded factual allegations are to be taken as admitted. *McQuail v. Shell Oil Co.*, 40 Del. Ch. 410, 183 A.2d 581 (1962).

Notwithstanding, on a motion to dismiss a complaint, all inferences must be construed in favor of the plaintiff. *Jefferson Chem. Co. v. Mobay Chem. Co.*, 253 A.2d 512 (Del. Ch. 1969).

And a complaint is not dismissed if it is not entitled to relief under any state of facts. — A Court should not dismiss a complaint for failure to state a claim unless it appears to a reasonable certainty that under no state of facts which could be proved to support the claim asserted would the plaintiff be entitled to relief. *Fish Eng'g Corp. v. Hutchinson*, 39 Del. Ch. 215, 162 A.2d 722 (1960).

A motion to dismiss can only be granted where the Court finds that under no set of facts would the plaintiff be entitled to recover. *McQuail v. Shell Oil Co.*, 40 Del. Ch. 410, 183 A.2d 581 (1962).

The complaint may not be dismissed unless it appears to a reasonable certainty that the plaintiff would not be entitled to relief under any state of facts which could be proved in support of his claim. *Jefferson Chem. Co. v. Mobay Chem. Co.*, 253 A.2d 512 (Del. Ch. 1969).

Evidence considered. — If a court declines to rule on a subdivision (b) motion to dismiss made at the end of plaintiff's case and then proceeds to hear the remainder of the evidence, the court may consider all the evidence adduced at the trial in reaching its ultimate decision on the merits. *In re Enstar Corp.*, 593 A.2d 543 (Del. Ch. 1991), rev'd on other grounds, 604 A.2d 404 (Del. 1992).

Review of previous dismissal. — Where a vice chancellor denied defendants' motion to dismiss under Rule 12(b)(6) on one ground, another vice chancellor, under subdivision (b), was not precluded from finding on another ground where he simply resolved the ambiguity that the first vice chancellor had identified under a different procedural standard. *Oberly v. Kirby*, 592 A.2d 445 (Del. 1991).

If litigant has not been required to defend on the merits, dismissal with prejudice not presumed. *TWA v. Hughes*, 317 A.2d 114 (Del. Ch. 1974), aff'd, 336 A.2d 572 (Del. 1975), cert. denied, 423 U.S. 841, 96 S. Ct. 72, 46 L. Ed. 2d 61 (1975).

As where acquiesced to entry of default judgment. — In a case where defendants did not defend on the merits but rather acquiesced to the entry of a default judgment, defendants' motion to dismiss a new complaint insofar as it is predicated on Ch. Ct. R. 41(b) must be denied. *TWA v. Hughes*, 317 A.2d 114 (Del. Ch. 1974), aff'd, 336 A.2d 572 (Del. 1975), cert. denied, 423 U.S. 841, 96 S. Ct. 72, 46 L. Ed. 2d 61 (1975).

Curing language of complaint. — If complaint's language is vague and somewhat uncertain, defendants by discovery can easily cure such uncertainty or ambiguity.

Fish Eng'g Corp. v. Hutchinson, 39 Del. Ch. 215, 162 A.2d 722 (1960).

Appeal of denial of motion to dismiss. — Denial of a motion to dismiss a complaint may be an interlocutory decree within the meaning of § 11(4), article 4 of the Constitution and, as such, appealable, provided the denial has determined a substantial issue in the cause and established legal rights. *Du Pont v. Du Pont*, 32 Del. Ch. 405, 82 A.2d 376 (1951).

Error to dismiss for lack of jurisdiction when inadequate remedy at law. — When the answers to the federal issues presented may demonstrate irreparable injury, when it is impossible to compute the continuing damages alleged to be accruing from day to day and when a multiplicity of suits may result, this spells out "inadequate remedy at law," so that it is error to dismiss the action on the ground of lack of equity jurisdiction. *Eastern Shore Natural Gas Co. v. Stauffer Chem. Co.*, 298 A.2d 322 (Del. 1972).

Common-law action not barred by dismissal of federal regulatory case. — Further prosecution of an action on a common-law theory is not barred by dismissal of a companion federal case in a situation in which federal regulatory provisions are paramount and the power to grant immunity from the operation of the laws operates solely to oust the federal courts of jurisdiction to enforce such laws. *TWA v. Hughes*, 317 A.2d 114 (Del. Ch. 1974), aff'd, 336 A.2d 572 (Del. 1975), cert. denied, 423 U.S. 841, 96 S. Ct. 72, 46 L. Ed. 2d 61 (1975).

IV. DISMISSAL OF COUNTERCLAIM, ETC.

If a counterclaim has been answered by the plaintiff, the defendants' motion to dismiss without prejudice must be decided by the Court in the exercise of its sound discretion. *Abercrombie v. Davies*, 36 Del. Ch. 491, 133 A.2d 920 (1957).

V. COSTS.

Having avoided jurisdiction for 3 years, defendants cannot properly ask to be reimbursed for expenses incurred in the case at a time when they were in default, having failed to respond to the Court's order of sequestration for 3 years. *Oil & Gas Ventures, Inc. v. Cheyenne Oil Corp.*, 43 Del. Ch. 182, 222 A.2d 312 (1966).

VI. INACTION.

Good reason for inaction must be shown. — There must be action to prosecute within 1 year unless good reason for inaction is shown. Unless a plaintiff meets that test, then he runs the risk of a dismissal under paragraph (e) of this rule. *Michaels v. Lesser*, 275 A.2d 797 (Del. Ch. 1971).

Because rule is permissive. — The success or failure of the motion for an order of dismissal depends on whether or not the plaintiff has furnished a good reason for inaction, because paragraph (e) of this rule is a permissive rule and should not be employed to bring about a dismissal when good reason for the inaction is given. *Jaeger v. Muscat*, 43 Del. Ch. 178, 221 A.2d 607 (1966).

However, **unwillingness to finance discovery, without more, is not a good reason** for inaction. *Michaels v. Lesser, 275 A.2d 797 (Del. Ch. 1971).*

Dismissal of class action. — Chancery Ct. R. 23(c) dismissal of a class action under the 1962 amendment to the rule normally occurs when a plaintiff who has lost confidence in his case tacitly or actively goes along with a paragraph (e) motion to dismiss for inaction. *Jaeger v. Muscat, 43 Del. Ch. 178, 221 A.2d 607 (1966).*

Rule 42.   Consolidations: Separate trials

DELAWARE CASE NOTES — REPORTED

I. General Consideration.
II. Consolidation.
III. Separate Trials.

I. GENERAL CONSIDERATION.

Cross references. — As to separate trials of counterclaims or cross-claims, see Rule 13(i) of the Court of Chancery. As to third-party claims, see Rule 14 of the Court of Chancery. As to separate trials for parties, see Rule 20(b) of the Court of Chancery. As to separate judgments upon multiple claims, see Rule 54(b) of the Court of Chancery.

II. CONSOLIDATION.

Chancery on the 1 hand discourages splitting up cause into several suits where it can be confined in 1 suit without serious injury to the rights of the parties involved or undue annoyance to them in enforcing or defending them. *Cahall v. Lofland, 12 Del. Ch. 162, 108 A. 752 (1920).*

And on the other hand, it disapproves of combining in 1 suit distinct and independent matters, thereby confounding them. *Cahall v. Lofland, 12 Del. Ch. 162, 108 A. 752 (1920).*

The test is whether justice can be administered between the parties without a multiplicity of suits. *Cahall v. Lofland, 12 Del. Ch. 162, 108 A. 752 (1920).*

III. SEPARATE TRIALS.

Rule expressly provides for order for separate trial. *Auerbach v. Cities Serv. Co., 37 Del. Ch. 381, 143 A.2d 904 (1958).*

But the "trial of a separate issue" device should be used sparingly unless the testimony pertinent to the separate issue can be readily adduced without spreading out over the other issues. *Delaware Chems., Inc. v. Reichhold Chems., Inc., 36 Del. Ch. 8, 124 A.2d 553 (1956).*

However, the practice of separating the issue of the right to an accounting from the account itself is often followed. *Auerbach v. Cities Serv. Co., 37 Del. Ch. 381, 143 A.2d 904 (1958).*

Separate trials on issues of liability and damages are called for when there are complicated issues as to liability and/or "damages" and when those issues can be separated without significant prejudice to any party. *Levien v. Sinclair Oil Corp., 300 A.2d 28 (Del. Ch. 1972).*

An order under paragraph (b) changes neither the character of a lawsuit nor the nature of the relief to be awarded. *Levien v. Sinclair Oil Corp., 300 A.2d 28 (Del. Ch. 1972).*

Rather, ordering separate trials on issues of liability and damages does no more than just that; it divides the trial into 2 different time periods, the first to be devoted to liability and the second to damages. *Levien v. Sinclair Oil Corp., 300 A.2d 28 (Del. Ch. 1972).*

VII. JUDGMENT

Rule 54.   Judgment; costs

DELAWARE CASE NOTES — REPORTED

A party is granted the relief to which he is entitled, even if such relief is not demanded. *Bata v. Hill, 37 Del. Ch. 363, 143 A.2d 728 (1958).*

Conditional relief based upon the existence of "equities" in favor of the losing party comes within this rule. *Bata v. Hill, 37 Del. Ch. 363, 143 A.2d 728 (1958).*

Taxation of all costs is left to the sound discretion of the trial judge, and the exercise of that discretion will not be disturbed in the absence of a showing of abuse. *Consolidated Fisheries Co. v. Consolidated Solubles Co., 35 Del. Ch. 125, 112 A.2d 30, modified on other grounds, 113 A.2d 576 (Del. 1955).*

However, the losing litigant ordinarily must pay his own counsel and bear the burden of costs. *Gottlieb v. Heyden Chem. Corp., 34 Del. Ch. 436, 105 A.2d 461 (1954).*

And expert's fees taxed as part of costs notwithstanding reliance. — It is unwise to hamper the administration of justice by requiring reliance by the trial judge upon each expert witness called before the fees of that witness may be taxed as part of the costs against the losing party; such a rule would unduly restrict counsel preparing for trial who must always be prepared to meet, so far as he is able, the vagaries of the judicial mind and the counter tactics of opposing counsel. *Consolidated Fisheries Co. v. Consolidated Solubles Co., 35 Del. Ch. 125, 112 A.2d 30, modified on other grounds, 113 A.2d 576 (Del. 1955); Weinberger v. UOP, Inc., 517 A.2d 653 (Del. Ch. 1986).*

Costs awarded against prevailing party. — While generally costs are assessed against the losing litigant, the Court of Chancery has discretion to award costs against the prevailing party when justice so requires. This is especially so when the Chancellor finds the prevailing party to have engaged in some impropriety. *Science Accessories Corp. v. Summagraphics Corp., 425 A.2d 957 (Del. 1980).*

While the court's copy of the transcript and depositions are not taxed as costs, this rule does not apply to copies ordered by parties, for the rule is to let the burden with respect to Court copies fall on the parties who saw fit to order copies. In the absence of some compelling special equity, the same approach should apply to copies of the transcript and depositions ordered by parties for their use. *Hutchinson v. Fish Eng'g Corp., 42 Del. Ch. 116, 204 A.2d 752 (1964),* aff'd, *213 A.2d 447 (Del. 1965).*

Rule 56.   Summary judgment

Untimely filing of appeal not attributable to court personnel. — Untimely filing of an appeal was not attributable to Court of Chancery personnel because the appellant had a continuing duty of inquiry to ascertain if the final judgment had been docketed after he expressly asked the Court of Chancery to commence the time to appeal by entering a final judgment pursuant to paragraph (b) of this rule and knew that the executed order had been forwarded to the *Vice-Chancellor. Giordano v. Marta, 723 A.2d 833 (Del. 1998).*

DELAWARE CASE NOTES — REPORTED

I. General Consideration.
II. Motion and Proceedings.
III. Case Not Fully Adjudicated.
IV. Affidavits.

I. GENERAL CONSIDERATION.

It is the chancery court's duty to adopt proper procedure for disposing of a motion for summary judgment; once that is done, it is for the Supreme Court on appeal to determine the propriety of the procedure adopted as well as the appealability of any order entered. *Abercrombie v. Davies, 36 Del. Ch. 102, 125 A.2d 588 (1956),* modified, *130 A.2d 338 (Del. 1957).*

Opportunity to present facts. — When issues are decided on summary judgment, the parties must have a reasonable opportunity to present all facts pertinent to the motion. *Mann v. Oppenheimer & Co., 517 A.2d 1056 (Del. 1986).*

Sua sponte grant of summary judgment against moving party. — In the interests of judicial economy, this rule gives a trial court the inherent authority to grant summary judgment sua sponte against a party seeking summary judgment. *Stroud v. Grace, 606 A.2d 75 (Del. 1992).*

The Court of Chancery should only sua sponte grant summary judgment against a party seeking summary judgment when the state of the record is such that the nonmoving party is clearly entitled to such relief. *Stroud v. Grace, 606 A.2d 75 (Del. 1992).*

Claims against decedent's estate. — When creditors sought to collect a decedent's debt from his estate, and his will specifically directed the payment of this debt from his estate, the failure of the creditors to file a claim against the decedent's estate within 8 months of his death, under *12 Del. C. § 2102,* did not bar their claim, and they were entitled to summary judgment against the estate's executrix, and she was not entitled to summary judgment. *Pamintuan v. Dosado, 844 A.2d 1010 (Del. Ch. 2003).*

II. MOTION AND PROCEEDINGS.

The function of summary judgment is the avoidance of a useless trial where there is no genuine issue as to any material fact. *H. & S. Mfg. Co. v. Benjamin F. Rich Co., 39 Del. Ch. 380, 164 A.2d 447 (1960).*

However, it should be cautiously invoked to the end that parties may always be afforded a trial where there is a bona fide dispute of facts between them. *H. & S. Mfg. Co. v. Benjamin F. Rich Co., 39 Del. Ch. 380, 164 A.2d 447 (1960).*

And summary judgment should not be employed to deprive a litigant of his day in court when the papers on which such a motion is made present genuine issues of material fact. *Guild v. Sterling Drug, Inc., 37 Del. Ch. 357, 143 A.2d 277 (1958).*

Timeliness of motion. — Motion for summary judgment before 20-day period of Del. Ch. Ct. R. 56(a) was permitted by court for plaintiff shareholder, to enforce settlement agreement of disputes underlying an *8 Del. C. § 220* action, as a part of its power to control its docket; the corporation was not prejudiced since (1) material facts were both limited and personally known by the corporation's counsel (the evidence consisting of email exchanges between opposing counsel over the course of only a few days, and (2) the § 220 action was proceeding at an expeditious pace because actions under *8 Del. C.§ 220* are summary in nature. *Loppert v. Windsortech, Inc., 865 A.2d 1282 (Del. Ch. 2004).*

If the facts of the claim are not sufficient, the defendant may move for judgment under paragraph (b) of this rule. *Fish Eng'g Corp. v. Hutchinson, 39 Del. Ch. 215, 162 A.2d 722 (1960).*

And a motion to dismiss supported and opposed by affidavits will be treated as a motion for summary judgment. *Lineberger v. Welsh, 290 A.2d 847 (Del. Ch. 1972).*

Likewise, a motion asserting defense so treated where matters outside pleadings presented. — Chancery Ct. R. 12(b)(6) provides that where matters outside the pleadings are presented and not excluded by the Court, a motion asserting a defense should be treated as one for summary judgment, and all parties should be given reasonable opportunity to present all material matter pertinent to such motion. *Danby v. Osteopathic Hosp. Ass'n, 101 A.2d 308 (Del. Ch. 1953),* aff'd, *104 A.2d 903 (Del. 1955).*

A motion to dismiss supported by matters outside the pleadings. — It is well settled that when a party moves to dismiss for failure to state a claim pursuant to

Court of Chancery Rule 12(b), and submits matters outside the pleadings, the motion will be treated as one for summary judgment under this *Rule. In re Tri-Star Pictures, Inc., 634 A.2d 319 (Del. 1993).*

If a party presents documents in support of its Chancery Ct. R. 12(b)(6) motion and the court considers the documents, it generally must treat the motion as one for summary judgment. *In re Santa Fe Pac. Corp. Shareholder Litig., 669 A.2d 59 (Del. 1995).*

Court not bound by form of pleadings. — When a party moves for summary judgment and the Court concludes that the moving party is not entitled to summary judgment, and the state of the record is such that the nonmoving party clearly is entitled to such relief, the judge may grant final judgment in favor of the nonmoving party; the form of the pleadings should not place a limitation upon the Court's ability to do justice. *Bank of Del. v. Claymont Fire Co. No. 1, 528 A.2d 1196 (Del. 1987).*

Cross-motions. — Even when presented with cross-motions for summary judgment, a trial court is not relieved of its obligation to deny summary judgment if a material factual dispute exists; in evaluating cross-motions for summary judgment, the trial court must examine each motion separately and only grant a motion for summary judgment to one of the parties when there is no disputed issue of material fact and that party is entitled to judgment as a matter of law. *Fasciana v. Elec. Data Sys. Corp., 829 A.2d 160 (Del. Ch. 2003).*

A motion for summary judgment will be granted only when no genuine issue of material fact is in dispute and the moving party is entitled to judgment as a matter of law. *Scureman v. Judge, 626 A.2d 5 (Del. Ch. 1992).*

Summary judgment, where there is no genuine issue as to any material fact, may be entered as a matter of law. *Bader v. Sharp, 35 Del. Ch. 57, 110 A.2d 300 (1954), aff'd, 125 A.2d 499 (Del. 1955).*

If the pleadings and other proofs, if any, show that there is no genuine issue as to any material fact and that the moving party is entitled to judgment, summary judgment will be rendered. *Nash v. Connell, 34 Del. Ch. 20, 99 A.2d 242 (1953).*

If the facts material to an issue are definitive and undisputed on the record which may be employed in connection with summary judgment motions, then the court must ordinarily decide the motion. *Perfect Photo Equities, Inc. v. America Corp., 42 Del. Ch. 372, 212 A.2d 808 (1965).*

Limited partnership was entitled to summary judgment pursuant to Del. Ch. Ct. R. 56 in an action by investment fund holders, seeking to compel a vote that would amend the partnership agreement in order to repeal an ownership cap, where the court could look beyond the agency that held the interests and determine the ownership interests held by the principals. *Sutter Opportunity Fund 2 LLC v. Cede & Co., 838 A.2d 1123 (Del. Ch. Dec. 10, 2003).*

But summary judgment will not be granted if pleadings, affidavits and other proof raise a genuine issue as to any facts material to the dispute between the parties. *Nash v. Connell, 34 Del. Ch. 20, 99 A.2d 242 (1953).*

Where plaintiff stockholder sets forth a legally recognized claim and the pleadings and affidavits raise a substantial factual dispute as to the legal propriety of the motives of the corporate defendant and its controlling stockholder which can only be resolved by a hearing, summary judgment is not proper. *Bennett v. Breuil Petro. Corp., 34 Del. Ch. 6, 99 A.2d 236 (1953).*

A motion for summary judgment will be denied if the affidavits raise a material factual issue. *Macartor v. Graylyn Crest III Swim Club, Inc., 40 Del. Ch. 53, 173 A.2d 344 (1961).*

If the plaintiff's affidavits negate the defendant's pleading claim, it is entitled to summary judgment unless the defendant puts acceptable contravening material in the record by an affidavit or otherwise. *Perfect Photo Equities, Inc. v. America Corp., 42 Del. Ch. 372, 212 A.2d 808 (1965).*

Where vital facts are either lacking or in conflict, it would be inappropriate to assume or to evaluate them on cross-motions for summary judgment. *Gamble v. Penn Valley Crude Oil Corp., 34 Del. Ch. 359, 104 A.2d 257 (1954).*

Discovery to rebut motion. — Where defendant essentially controlled relevant information needed to rebut motion for summary judgment and plaintiffs could only develop facts to contest the motion through the discovery process, to deny them that right and thus extinguish plaintiff's action at its threshold would not have comported with principles of judicial discretion in the application of discovery rules. *Mann v. Oppenheimer & Co., 517 A.2d 1056 (Del. 1986).*

This rule does not contemplate summary judgment for a portion of a single claim in suit. *Abercrombie v. Davies, 36 Del. Ch. 102, 125 A.2d 588 (1956), modified, 130 A.2d 338 (Del. 1957).*

Where other contentions unresolved. — A partial final judgment on 1 claim is not contemplated by this rule where other contentions are unresolved. *Abercrombie v. Davies, 36 Del. Ch. 102, 125 A.2d 588 (1956), modified, 130 A.2d 338 (Del. 1957).*

Unsworn denials to requests for admission sufficient to put facts in issue and deny motion for summary judgment. — Where plaintiff attempted to carry his burden under this rule by submitting his sworn affidavit to the Court, and, pursuant to Ch. Ct. R. 36, requested defendant to admit to each numbered paragraph in his affidavit, and defendant's attorney, on behalf of defendant, provided unsworn responses to plaintiff's Rule 36 request, the Court of Chancery had those responses before it in considering plaintiff's motion under paragraph (c) of this Rule, and under Rule 36 the unsworn denials of defendant's attorney were sufficient to place the facts stated in the request in issue. *Brown v. Ocean Drilling & Exploration Co., 403 A.2d 1114 (Del. 1979).*

Court not to weigh evidence. — The function of the trial judge in passing on a motion for summary judgment is not to weigh evidence and to accept that which seems to him to have the greater weight, it is rather to determine

Chancery Court

whether or not there is any evidence supporting a favorable conclusion to the nonmoving party; and, when that is the state of the record, it is improper to grant summary judgment. *Continental Oil Co. v. Pauley Petro., Inc., 251 A.2d 824 (Del. 1969).*

If the facts set forth in the record are uncontroverted, they must be assumed to be true. Nevertheless, a scrutiny of these facts by the Court is necessary to see if the movant is entitled to judgment. *Tanzer v. International Gen. Indus., Inc., 402 A.2d 382 (Del. Ch. 1979).*

It cannot try the issue. — In a motion for summary judgment a court can determine only whether or not there is a genuine issue as to a material fact, and it cannot try the issue. *Banks v. Cristina Copper Mines, Inc., 34 Del. Ch. 44, 99 A.2d 504 (1953).*

Moreover, it is the province of courts to interpret, not to make, contracts by ascertaining the legal import of the language employed by the parties themselves to express their agreement. *Jefferson Chem. Co. v. Mobay Chem. Co., 267 A.2d 635 (Del. Ch. 1970).*

Motion to dismiss brought in response to report of special litigation committee is a hybrid motion which takes qualities from a Ch. Ct. R. 41(a)(2) motion to dismiss and a motion for summary judgment under this rule. *Lewis v. Fuqua, 502 A.2d 962 (Del. Ch. 1985).*

Court may rely on party's answer to interrogatory in determining summary judgment in favor of that party since, in determining whether there is a dispute of material fact, the trial court must consider all evidence in the record which meets the standards of this rule. *Tate v. Miles, 503 A.2d 187 (Del. 1986).*

A defendant's past inconsistent answers to interrogatories in separate actions do not rise to level of a genuine issue of material fact sufficient to foreclose a defendant's motion for summary judgment. *Church of Religious Science v. Fox, 266 A.2d 881 (Del. 1970).*

But the denial of violating a restrictive covenant poses an issue of fact. — Where defendants have denied that they have erected a structure on their lot, as alleged in the plaintiffs' complaint, in violation of restrictive covenant as to these defendants, there is an issue of fact and a motion for summary judgment will be denied. *Nash v. Connell, 34 Del. Ch. 20, 99 A.2d 242 (1953).*

As does denial of option on stock or appointment of liquidating receiver. — In a suit for specific performance of an agreement to give an option to buy or sell shares of stock or for appointment of a liquidating receiver, the defendant's denial that there was any agreement of option or of the material allegations relied upon by the plaintiff as the basis for the appointment of a liquidating receiver gives rise to a dispute as to material questions of fact which preclude summary judgment. *Vale v. Atlantic Coast & Inland Corp., 34 Del. Ch. 50, 99 A.2d 396 (1953).*

Conflict as to whether a stock price is inadequate cannot be fairly resolved on a motion for summary judgment. *Bennett v. Breuil Petro. Corp., 34 Del. Ch. 6, 99 A.2d 236 (1953).*

And issues of fact material to the validity of the stock transfer may not be resolved in a summary

judgment proceeding. Melson v. Michlin, 43 Del. Ch. 239, 223 A.2d 338 (1966).

But summary judgment should be afforded to a stockholder who meets terms concerning stock ledgers of 8 Del. C. § 220. *Loew's Theatres, Inc. v. Commercial Credit Co., 243 A.2d 78 (Del. Ch. 1968).*

Though no vested interest is disturbed by granting motion against plaintiff-director to inspect. — When any right which a plaintiff may have held in the office of director of the defendant corporation was acquired with actual or implied knowledge that such right could be extinguished by the vote or consent of the holders of a majority of the defendant's common stock, no vested interest is disturbed by granting the defendant's motion for summary judgment of the dismissal of the plaintiff's complaint, made in her capacity as a director, to inspect the defendant's books and records. *Everett v. Transnation Dev. Corp., 267 A.2d 627 (Del. Ch. 1970).*

And motion dismissed where stockholder shows evidence of irrevocable injury. — Where a stockholder has shown evidence of irrevocable injury, a judgment against him on motions to dismiss and for summary judgment will be dismissed. *Elster v. American Airlines, 34 Del. Ch. 94, 100 A.2d 219 (1953).*

Limitation of issues in appraisal actions. — Appraisal actions must be confined to the issues contemplated by *8 Del. C. § 262*; thus, a company was entitled to summary judgment in an action by minority shareholders seeking appraisal rights, because the issue of whether shares beneficially owned by one of the minority shareholders through the company's employee stock option plan (ESOP) should have been eligible for appraisal was beyond the proper scope of relief, where the shareholder conceded that no appraisal demand was made for ESOP shares. *Union Ill. 1995 Inv. L.P. v. Union Fin. Group, Ltd., 847 A.2d 340 (Del. Ch. 2003).*

Summary judgment where a title cannot be conveyed in a specific performance suit. — Where plaintiffs who seek specific performance of a contract for the sale of realty cannot convey a good fee simple marketable title to the defendants, it follows that the plaintiffs' motion for a summary judgment of specific performance must be denied, and a motion for summary judgment dismissing the complaint must be granted. *Anthony v. Harris, 34 Del. Ch. 166, 100 A.2d 229 (1953).*

Also, the defendant is entitled to summary judgment as to alleged interference with customers. — If the plaintiff has neither alleged nor made record proof of interference by the defendant with prospective customers in a way that was "wrongful" and there has been no showing of improper means, illegal restraint or the like, the defendant is entitled to summary judgment as to alleged interference with prospective customers. *Bowl-Mor Co. v. Brunswick Corp., 297 A.2d 61 (Del. Ch.), appeal dismissed, 297 A.2d 67 (Del. 1972).*

However, ordinarily summary judgment is not granted on the defense of laches. *Church of Religious Science v. Fox, 266 A.2d 881 (Del. 1970).*

Unless no issue of material fact exists. — Defendants are entitled to summary judgment on the ground of laches where they have established with sufficient clarity that there is no genuine issue of material fact as to laches. *Church of Religious Science v. Fox*, 266 A.2d 881 (Del. 1970).

But denied where statute of limitations tolled. — Since the doctrine of fraudulent concealment may be applicable to toll the running of the statute of limitations, a motion for summary judgment must be denied. *Bradford, Inc. v. Travelers Indem. Co.*, 301 A.2d 519 (Del. Super. Ct. 1972).

Insufficient facts to grant motion. — Where the affidavits filed in a case do not disclose the circumstances under which the corporate officers are alleged to have appropriated a corporate opportunity and where beyond the naked allegations no information is furnished relative to the circumstances under which the alleged appropriation of a corporate opportunity occurred, then until such evidence is presented, the court can form no conclusion with reference thereto, and a motion for summary judgment will be denied. *Gottlieb v. McKee*, 34 Del. Ch. 537, 107 A.2d 240 (1954).

On a counterclaim for a bonus or interest in a profit-sharing plan, summary judgment is not appropriate if the record is not clear as to exactly what were the terms of the alleged arrangement or to whether the defendant was discharged from employment with cause or without cause. *Keene Corp. v. Hoofe*, 267 A.2d 618 (Del. Ch. 1970), aff'd, 276 A.2d 269 (Del. 1971).

Burden on moving party. — The party moving for summary judgment has the burden of demonstrating clearly the absence of any genuine issue of fact, and any doubt as to the existence of such an issue will be resolved against him. *Nash v. Connell*, 34 Del. Ch. 20, 99 A.2d 242 (1953).

The party asking for summary judgment has the burden of demonstrating that there is no dispute as to any possible issue of fact material to any valid legal theory advanced by the other party. *Warshaw v. Calhoun*, 42 Del. Ch. 437, 213 A.2d 539 (1965), aff'd, 221 A.2d 487 (Del. 1966).

The moving party must satisfy the Court that there is no basis in law on which the opposing party may successfully rely in opposing such a motion for summary judgment. *Leon N. Weiner & Assocs. v. Carroll*, 270 A.2d 539 (Del. Ch. 1970), rev'd on other grounds, 276 A.2d 732 (Del. 1971).

In considering the defendant's motion for summary judgment upon affidavits and depositions, it is fundamental that the defendant have the burden of demonstrating that there is no dispute as to any possible issue of fact material to any valid legal theory advanced by the plaintiff. *Krajewski v. Blair*, 297 A.2d 70 (Del. Ch. 1972).

The proponent of a motion under this rule has the burden to prove clearly the absence of any genuine issue of fact, and any doubt should be resolved against him. *Brown v. Ocean Drilling & Exploration Co.*, 403 A.2d 1114 (Del. 1979).

The moving party, in a motion for summary judgment, has the burden of establishing to the satisfaction of the court the absence of any genuine issue of material fact, and any doubt regarding the existence of such an issue will be resolved against the movant. *Scureman v. Judge*, 626 A.2d 5 (Del. Ch. 1992).

Shifting of burden to defending party. — If the movant puts in the record facts which, if undenied, entitle him to summary judgment, the burden shifts to the defending party to dispute the facts by affidavit or proof of similar weight. *Tanzer v. International Gen. Indus., Inc.*, 402 A.2d 382 (Del. Ch. 1979).

Where a moving party's affidavits in support of a motion pursuant to this rule negate the opposing party's pleadings, the opposing party must submit countervailing evidence or affidavits or judgment may be granted. *Feinberg v. Makhson*, 407 A.2d 201 (Del. 1979).

In a shareholders' derivative action, once the shareholders had made a showing that the corporation's former chief executive officer (CEO) had used stock (the inflated price of which was due entirely to inaccurate financial information that the CEO had signed) in order to pay back a loan from the corporation, the burden of production shifted to the CEO, whose arguments that the board, which was entitled to rely on information supplied by officers, was somehow in pari delicto or that the CEO was the victim of subordinates' misrepresentations, were entirely inadequate; the court therefore entered summary judgment rescinding the stock buyback agreement. *In re HealthSouth Corp. S'holders Litig.*, 845 A.2d 1096 (Del. Ch. 2003).

An application for summary judgment is always addressed to the discretion of the trial judge. *Brunswick Corp. v. Bowl-Mor Co.*, 297 A.2d 67 (Del. 1972).

And denial for insufficient facts will not be disturbed on appeal. — Ordinarily, the denial of a motion for summary judgment, on the ground that there are insufficient facts in the record to determine that under all circumstances the moving party is entitled to summary judgment, will not be disturbed on appeal except in rare circumstances; otherwise, the denial of summary judgment is not appealable. *Brunswick Corp. v. Bowl-Mor Co.*, 297 A.2d 67 (Del. 1972).

However, when rights are adjudicated, denials of summary judgment are appealable; but as the usual denial of summary judgment adjudicates no legal rights, such a result is the exception rather than the rule. Particularly is this so when summary judgment is denied because of the necessity of finding out what the facts are. *Sterling Drug, Inc. v. City Bank Farmers Trust Co.*, 38 Del. Ch. 444, 154 A.2d 156 (1959).

But not where it is desirable to determine issue. — If summary judgment upon any particular issue is denied on the ground that a trial on the merits is desirable to determine the issue, the order denying summary judgment on that issue is clearly not appealable. *Brunswick Corp. v. Bowl-Mor Co.*, 297 A.2d 67 (Del. 1972).

Party opposing summary judgment may not merely deny the factual allegations adduced by the movant. *Tanzer v. International Gen. Indus., Inc.*, 402 A.2d 382 (Del. Ch. 1979).

Or else motion will be granted. — Where claimant to decedent's estate, through counsel, presented the Court

Chancery Court

with her affidavit swearing to the fact that she was the sister of decedent as well as numerous certificates issued by the Bureau of Vital Statistics of the U.S.S.R. relating to her pedigree, and the personal representatives of the estate in their affidavit in opposition to summary judgment stated no more than that they have no information to support or refute that claimant was decedent's sister, the personal representatives' affidavit failed to overcome the admonition of paragraph (e) of this rule that a party opposing summary judgment "may not rest upon the mere allegations or denials of his pleading" and summary judgment was properly granted. *Feinberg v. Makhson, 407 A.2d 201 (Del. 1979).*

III. CASE NOT FULLY ADJUDICATED.

The court will isolate issues to be tried. — While paragraph (d) of this rule appears to be more directly concerned with an order narrating facts, disputed and otherwise, for purposes of future trial, it seems implicit in the rule that the Court will in the order salvage what has been decided on the motion and thus isolate the issues to be tried. *Abercrombie v. Davies, 36 Del. Ch. 102, 125 A.2d 588 (1956),* modified, *130 A.2d 338 (Del. 1957).*

And disregard arguments premised upon dismissal of complaint. — If judgment amounts to the grant of partial summary judgment rather than a dismissal of the complaint, the court disregards all arguments premised upon dismissal of the complaint. *Pomilio v. Caserta, 42 Del. Ch. 535, 215 A.2d 924 (1965).*

Denial of indemnification of bank chairman not adjudication on merits. — Indemnification Regulation, *12 C.F.R. § 545.121,* required indemnification only when a court passed on the substance of a case and entered judgment in favor of the person seeking indemnification, and a judgment obtained as the result of the payment of money in settlement of a claim was not an "on the merits" adjudication; as such, summary judgment, pursuant to Del. Ch. Ct. R. 56(c), was entered in favor of a bank holding company and against a former bank chairman, as there was no claim that the denial of indemnification to the chairman was in bad faith, which the court found was understandable in light of the chairman's criminal conviction and disbarment proceedings. *Conway v. Astoria Fin. Corp., 837 A.2d 30 (Del. Ch. July 16, 2003), aff'd, 840 A.2d 641 (Del. 2004).*

Partial summary judgment. — Partial summary judgment was granted to corporate directors on a dissenting director's claims that they breached their fiduciary duties and acted in bad faith in approving an extension of a merger agreement as: (1) the directors had legitimate reasons for approving the extension that were within the bounds of reasonable judgment; (2) the directors did not have disabling conflicts of interests or approve the extension in bad faith; (3) the directors' decision-making process was adequate; and (4) there was no wrongful act of dominion over the dissenting director's shares and the director did not have any right to an interest in a newly formed corporation; however, the dissenting director raised genuine issues of material fact as to a claim of diversion of corporate opportunity based on the management agreements between the directors' corporation and the newly formed corporation. *McGowan v. Ferro, 859 A.2d 1012 (Del. Ch. 2004).*

IV. AFFIDAVITS.

Paragraph (e) requires affidavits filed under the rule to be made on personal knowledge. *Piekarski v. Smith, 37 Del. Ch. 594, 147 A.2d 176 (1958), aff'd, 153 A.2d 587 (Del. 1959).*

But court may disregard inadmissible parts. — Although an affidavit for summary judgment combines knowledge and argument and is a lamentable admixture of advocacy with fact which violates the spirit of this Rule, it does not necessarily follow that the affidavit must be dismissed in its entirety, since the Court may strike or disregard the inadmissible parts and consider the rest of the affidavit. *Loew's Theatres, Inc. v. Commercial Credit Co., 243 A.2d 78 (Del. Ch. 1968).*

Rule 57.   Declaratory judgments

DELAWARE CASE NOTES — REPORTED

Declaratory judgment jurisdiction exists only in cases of actual controversy. *Wilmington Manor, Inc. v. Grant, 34 Del. Ch. 487, 105 A.2d 783 (1954).*

However, where a valid cause of action exists and further relief is asked, the court does not lose jurisdiction thereof because of a prayer of a declaratory nature. *Whitfield v. Whittington, 34 Del. Ch. 34, 99 A.2d 196 (1953).*

But where the person with an adverse interest declines to act or speak regarding the covenants of a deed, there is no actual controversy to give the Court jurisdiction. *Wilmington Manor, Inc. v. Grant, 34 Del. Ch. 487, 105 A.2d 783 (1954).*

And in an action for declaratory relief upon a deed, the court may not consider surrounding circumstances and construe the language in the light thereof, because to give such evidence legal effect would require a reformation of the quoted language of the deed, and while surrounding circumstances do aid in construction where the language employed is reasonably capable of more than 1 construction, the Court is not free to reform the instrument under the guise of construction. *Cashvan v. Darling, 34 Del. Ch. 570, 107 A.2d 896 (1954).*

Nevertheless, in an action for declaratory judgment upon a deed, it is permissible to plead pertinent portions of a written instrument, and where the opposing party admits such allegations there is no need to prove those portions. *Cashvan v. Darling, 34 Del. Ch. 570, 107 A.2d 896 (1954).*

But in an action for declaratory judgment to quiet title, plaintiffs must recover upon the strength of their own title and cannot rely upon the weakness of the defendant's title. *Marvel v. Barley Mill Rd. Homes, Inc., 34 Del. Ch. 417, 104 A.2d 908 (1954).*

Rule 59.   New trials

DELAWARE CASE NOTES — REPORTED

Applications under this rule are always addressed to the judicial discretion of the Court so that injustice may be prevented, and, accordingly, by a proper exercise of its discretion, it may either grant or deny the motion. *Daniel D. Rappa, Inc. v. Hanson, 42 Del. Ch. 273, 209 A.2d 163 (1965).*

And delay in coming forth with evidence is sufficient justification to refuse to reopen the hearing in a case which already had been long delayed, particularly when that evidence was available to the movant at the time of the first trial. *Daniel D. Rappa, Inc. v. Hanson, 42 Del. Ch. 273, 209 A.2d 163 (1965).*

Where the plaintiff fails to show that with reasonable diligence he could not have discovered evidence before trial, a motion for a new trial should be denied. *Sussex Poultry Co. v. American Ins. Co., 301 A.2d 281 (Del. 1973).*

Basis for newly discovered evidence. — To succeed upon a petition for reargument, the applicant must show that the newly discovered evidence has come to his knowledge since the trial, and that it could not, in the exercise of reasonable diligence, have been discovered for use at the trial. *Bata v. Bata, 39 Del. Ch. 548, 170 A.2d 711 (1961),* cert. denied, *366 U.S. 964, 81 S. Ct. 1926, 6 L. Ed. 2d 1255 (1961).*

Evidence which is only cumulative at best does not justify granting a new trial. *Cashvan v. Darling, 34 Del. Ch. 570, 107 A.2d 896 (1954).*

Motions for reargument are permitted within 5 days after the filing of an opinion or receipt of a decision, which in the context of the rule are synonymous and require the further entry of an order giving effect to the decision announced. *Braasch v. Mandel, 40 Del. Ch. 12, 172 A.2d 271 (1961).*

Effect of timeliness of motion for reargument. — A timely motion for reargument will toll the period for appeal, but an untimely motion will not. *Pinkert v. Wion, 431 A.2d 1269 (Del. 1981).*

Affidavits may not be used to support reargument motion. — Subsection (f) of this Rule does not authorize submission of affidavits in support of motions for reargument; unlike a motion for a new trial based on newly discovered evidence pursuant to Ch. Ct. R. 60(b), a motion for reargument properly seeks only a re-examination of the facts in the record at the time of the decision or the law as it applied to those facts. *Miles v. Cookson, 677 A.2d 507 (Del. Ch. 1995).*

On reargument, new issue may not be raised. — Where having failed to have plaintiffs' complaint dismissed and the relief prayed for denied, defendants may not on motion for reargument seek to raise an issue which they should have raised at trial. *Kern v. NCD Indus., Inc., 316 A.2d 576 (Del. Ch. 1973).*

Following the entry of a final order of dismissal effective immediately there is no pending cause in which intervention can be allowed, even though those seeking intervention petition to intervene within the permissive time under paragraph (b) for the filing of motions for reargument. *Braasch v. Mandel, 40 Del. Ch. 12, 172 A.2d 271 (1961).*

Rule 60.   Relief from judgment or order

DELAWARE CASE NOTES — REPORTED

This rule is designed primarily to shield parties from judgments entered into because of fraud or mistake and it may not be used as a sword to bind a nonparty to a judgment. *Apartment Communities Corp. v. State, 422 A.2d 342 (Del. 1980).*

Paragraph (b) is confined to motions by a party or his legal representative and, consequently, cannot be made by those who have not become parties to the suit. *Braasch v. Mandel, 40 Del. Ch. 12, 172 A.2d 271 (1961).*

And it precisely limits categories for which relief from judgment may be granted, e.g., mistake, new evidence, fraud, voidness and satisfaction. *Swann v. Carey, 272 A.2d 711 (Del. 1970).*

Otherwise, there is no justification for reopening the case. — When failure to present evidence was not the result of mistake, inadvertence, surprise or excusable neglect, and the evidence is not newly discovered, there is no justification for reopening a case. *Poole v. N.V. Deli Maatschappij, 257 A.2d 241 (Del. Ch. 1969).*

Order refusing relief under this rule is an appealable order. *Swann v. Carey, 272 A.2d 711 (Del. 1970).*

But appeal brings up only the correctness of the order; it does not permit the appellant to attack the underlying judgment for an error which he could have complained of on appeal from it. *Swann v. Carey, 272 A.2d 711 (Del. 1970).*

And such motion does not extend time for appeal. — A motion under paragraph (b) of this rule for relief from a judgment does not extend the time for taking an appeal, as distinguished from a motion for new trial. *Swann v. Carey, 272 A.2d 711 (Del. 1970).*

However, a motion under this rule has no time limit. *Swann v. Carey, 272 A.2d 711 (Del. 1970).*

Vacatur available where justice so requires. — In Delaware, the equitable remedy of vacatur is available in only a narrow set of circumstances, and as a general rule, when a case becomes moot at some point during the appellate process, the Supreme Court of Delaware will vacate the judgment below where the interests of justice so requires; this so-called "interests of justice" standard is no doubt met where the party seeking appellate review is thwarted by some event beyond its control, and in such circumstances, vacatur is necessary to prevent the unappealable judgment from obtaining precedential or preclusive res judicata effect. *Tyson Foods, Inc. v. Aetos Corp., 818 A.2d 145 (Del. 2003).*

Chancery Court

Vacatur not available after settlement. — Equitable remedy of vacatur was denied to a corporation that settled its claims without appealing the orders that were entered following a trial, as the corporation voluntarily gave up its statutory right to appeal, without coercion, when it chose to settle; a rule of law which routinely permitted post-settlement vacatur of judgments would actually distort the settlement process, and might encourage litigants to delay settlement until a later stage in the litigation, resulting in a waste of judicial resources. *IBP, Inc. v. Tyson Foods, Inc., 793 A.2d 396 (Del. Ch. 2002)*, aff'd, sub nom. *Tyson Foods v. Aetos Corp., 818 A.2d 145 (Del. 2003)*.

Federal vacatur standard now embodied in *U.S. Bancorp Mortgage Co. v. Bonner Mall, 513 U.S. 18, 130 L. Ed. 2d 233, 115 S. Ct. 386 (1994)*, is not a significant departure from the standard previously provided in *U.S. v. Munsingwear, 340 U.S. 36, 95 L. Ed. 36, 71 S. Ct. (1950)*, and it does not necessarily announce a new federal vacatur standard, but rather it sketches the outer limits of the existing Munsingwear standard; moot cases are disposed of in a manner most consonant to justice, and mootness by reason of settlement does not justify vacatur unless exceptional circumstances exist. In other words, the equitable remedy of vacatur is still available in the federal forum where a party is frustrated by the vagaries of circumstance and justice requires that he not be forced to acquiesce in the judgment, but where a judgment is not unreviewable, but simply unreviewed because of settlement, vacatur is inappropriate. *Tyson Foods, Inc. v. Aetos Corp., 818 A.2d 145 (Del. 2003)*.

United States Supreme Court's discussion of the federal vacatur standard demonstrates the harmony with Delaware's standard; where a party has voluntarily forfeited his legal remedy through settlement he surrenders his claim to the equitable remedy of vacatur, unless exceptional circumstances counsel otherwise. *Tyson Foods, Inc. v. Aetos Corp., 818 A.2d 145 (Del. 2003)*.

Tactical mistake of competent counsel. — The type of mistake contemplated by paragraph (b) of this rule does not include a tactical mistake of competent counsel made in the course of conduct of a case entrusted to his discretion. *TWA v. Summa Corp., 394 A.2d 241 (Del. Ch. 1978)*.

Novel issue of law. — The fact that a case presents a seemingly novel issue of law does not by itself merit the designation of "extraordinary circumstances" and, further, does not automatically raise the suspicion of manifest injustice. *Nakahara v. NS 1991 Am. Trust, 718 A.2d 518 (Del. Ch. 1998)*.

Request for leave to open case below addressed to court's discretion. — A request for leave to open a case below for the purpose of introducing evidence to conform to the rulings contained in a Supreme Court decision may be addressed to the discretion of the Chancery Court under paragraph (b) of this rule. *Poole v. N.V. Deli Maatschappij, 243 A.2d 67 (Del. 1968)*.

Showing required for newly discovered evidence. — Where a party seeks to reopen a trial to introduce newly discovered evidence, he is required to show: That the newly discovered evidence has come to his knowledge since the trial; that it could not in the exercise of reasonable diligence have been discovered for use at the trial; that it is so material and relevant that it will probably change the result if a new trial is granted; that it is not merely cumulative or impeaching in character and that it is reasonably possible that the evidence will be produced at the trial. *Poole v. N.V. Deli Maatschappij, 257 A.2d 241 (Del. Ch. 1969)*.

Material evidence acquired while appeal pending. — The trial court did not abuse its discretion in granting plaintiffs leave to file a Second Amended Complaint even though they had acquired material evidence while appeal was still pending. *Levine v. Smith, 591 A.2d 194 (Del. 1991)*. But see *Brehm v. Eisner, 746 A.2d 244 (Del. 2000)*.

Court's analysis limited to newly discovered evidence. — The Court of Chancery did not abuse its discretion in limiting its second demand futility analysis to plaintiffs' claims based on newly discovered evidence. *Levine v. Smith, 591 A.2d 194 (Del. 1991)*. But see *Brehm v. Eisner, 746 A.2d 244 (Del. 2000)*.

Economic harm not "newly discovered evidence." — Evidence showing economic harm resulting from a stay granted in conjunction with a judgment did not meet the "newly discovered evidence" standard of subsection (b) of this *Rule. Miles v. Cookson, 677 A.2d 507 (Del. Ch. 1995)*.

Rule 62.   Stays by trial court in cases of appeal and motion for new trial

DELAWARE CASE NOTES — REPORTED

Filing an appeal from the court does not automatically stay the judgment of the trial court; a supersedeas bond is necessary under the state Constitution in order to accomplish that result. *Sannini v. Casscells, 401 A.2d 927 (Del. 1979)*.

The doctrine of primary administrative jurisdiction contemplates suspension of judicial proceedings under this rule, rather than a dismissal thereof under Ch. Ct. R. 41, pending the action of the administrative agency. *Eastern Shore Natural Gas Co. v. Stauffer Chem. Co., 298 A.2d 322 (Del. 1972)*.

Constructive trust. — If the parties to an order of the Court involving a constructive trust do not carry out the terms of the order as to the tender of consideration in exchange for the conveyance of legal title to a specific piece of property within the time period specified in the order, and do not stay the order, as specified in Del. Const., art. IV, § 24, and paragraph (d) of this rule, the order, by its express terms, will dissolve the constructive trust and place legal ownership of the property in the original owners, free and clear of any legal or equitable claim of the other parties. *Sannini v. Casscells, 401 A.2d 927 (Del. 1979)*.

Rule 63.   Inability of a judge to proceed

DELAWARE CASE NOTES — REPORTED

Applicability. — Based upon the persuasive rationale of federal precedents, the Court of Chancery held that this rule applies to any proceedings on remand being conducted by a successor trial judge rather than the original jurist who presided. *Cede & Co. v. Technicolor, Inc., 758 A.2d 485 (Del. 2000).*

VIII. PROVISIONAL AND FINAL REMEDIES AND SPECIAL PROCEEDINGS

Rule 65.   Injunctions

I. General Consideration.
II. Preliminary Injunction.
III. Temporary Restraining Order.
IV. Security.
V. Form and Scope.

I. GENERAL CONSIDERATION.

An injunction operates in personam. *Smith v. Biggs Boiler Works Co., 32 Del. Ch. 287, 85 A.2d 365 (1951).*

If defendants fail to appear and have no property in delaware, the chancery court has no jurisdiction to grant injunctive relief against them. *Abercrombie v. Davies, 36 Del. Ch. 445, 131 A.2d 822 (1957).*

And in rem jurisdiction arising from stock alone is not sufficient. — If a nonresident defendant, sought to be enjoined, fails to appear and the only jurisdiction the Court of Chancery has over him arises from its in rem jurisdiction over stock which he owns in a Delaware corporation, the jurisdiction of the res without more does not give the Court of Chancery any personal jurisdiction, and no injunction can issue against such nonresident defendant. *Abercrombie v. Davies, 36 Del. Ch. 445, 131 A.2d 822 (1957).*

Extent of inquiry in contempt proceeding. — In a contempt proceeding based upon the violation of an injunction, the only legitimate inquiry to be made by the Court is whether or not it had jurisdiction of the parties and of the subject matter, and the Court will not listen to an excuse for the contemptuous action based upon an argument that the order in question was imperfect or erroneous, since no person may with impunity disregard an order of the Court having jurisdiction over the subject matter and of the parties. *Mayer v. Mayer, 36 Del. Ch. 457, 132 A.2d 617 (1957).*

Labor disputes. — Although substantially all jurisdiction in labor disputes affecting interstate commerce has been preempted by the federal government, state power may prevent conduct marked by violence and imminent threats to public order by establishing subject matter jurisdiction. *Avisun Corp. v. Oil, Chem. & Atomic Workers Local 8-732, 259 A.2d 389 (Del. Ch. 1969).*

Claim for injunctive relief unsupported. — Attorney General had not pled facts supporting a claim for injunctive relief against a real-estate developer and its affiliates, in the Attorney Generals action claiming they falsely led condominium owners and potential buyers to believe a clubhouse was part of the common area of the condominium complex; by the time the case was filed the developer and affiliates did not even own the clubhouse in question and it had been 4 years since they were last alleged to have made any misrepresentations concerning it. *State ex rel. Brady v. Pettinaro Enters., 870 A.2d 513 (Del. Ch. 2005).*

Recovery for wrongful injunction. — Where a party has been wrongfully enjoined or restrained, recovery is limited to the value of the security. *Emerald Partners v. Berlin, 712 A.2d 1006 (Del. Ch. 1997).*

II. PRELIMINARY INJUNCTION.

The purpose of a preliminary injunction is to maintain the true status quo until the final determination of the case. *Smith v. Delaware Coach Co., 31 Del. Ch. 256, 70 A.2d 257 (1949).*

Injunction affords interlocutory relief. — Protection by injunction of a clear legal right against a continuing wrong, pending final determination of the entire controversy, is one of the most familiar instances of interlocutory relief and is especially appropriate if no serious injury to the other party will follow. *Consolidated Fisheries Co. v. Consolidated Solubles Co., 34 Del. Ch. 24, 99 A.2d 253 (1953).*

And the court has the power to grant an injunction mandatory in form in order to preserve status quo. *Simmons v. Steiner, 34 Del. Ch. 593, 108 A.2d 173 (1954), rev'd on other grounds, 111 A.2d 574 (Del. 1955).*

Nevertheless, an order for preliminary injunction will not order defendants to operate a plant, but it will direct defendants, should they proceed to operate and to sell the product of the plant, that they must not violate the terms of their agreement in doing so. *Consolidated Solubles Co. v. Consolidated Fisheries Co., 34 Del. Ch. 551, 107 A.2d 639 (1954), modified, 112 A.2d 30 (Del. 1955), 113 A.2d 576 (Del. Ch. 1955).*

In order to dispose of the motion for preliminary injunction, it is necessary to state the facts as they appear from the pleadings and affidavits. *Sandler v. Schenley Indus., Inc., 32 Del. Ch. 46, 79 A.2d 606 (1951).*

Injunction will never be issued simply because it will do no harm. *Danby v. Osteopathic Hosp. Ass'n, 101 A.2d 308 (Del. Ch. 1953), aff'd, 104 A.2d 903 (Del. 1954); Bayard v. Martin, 34 Del. Ch. 184, 101 A.2d 329 (1953), cert. denied, 347 U.S. 944, 74 S. Ct. 639, 98 L. Ed. 1092 (1954).*

And it will never issue merely because there is a threat of very great injury. *Bayard v. Martin, 34 Del. Ch. 184, 101 A.2d 329 (1953), cert. denied, 347 U.S. 944, 74 S. Ct. 639, 98 L. Ed. 1092 (1954).*

Rather, a preliminary injunction should not be issued unless it appears that the plaintiff will suffer irreparable injury. *Sandler v. Schenley Indus., Inc., 32*

Del. Ch. 46, 79 A.2d 606 (1951); Turek v. Tull, 37 Del. Ch. 190, 139 A.2d 368, aff'd, 147 A.2d 658 (Del. 1958).

And the same is true for mandatory injunctions. — Relief by mandatory injunction should only be awarded in a clear case, free from doubt, and when necessary to prevent irreparable injury. Richard Paul, Inc. v. Union Imp. Co., 32 Del. Ch. 332, 86 A.2d 744, modified, 91 A.2d 49 (Del. Ch. 1952).

An injunction will not be issued unless necessary for the protection of plaintiff's rights. Danby v. Osteopathic Hosp. Ass'n, 101 A.2d 308 (Del. Ch. 1953), aff'd, 104 A.2d 903 (Del. 1954).

A preliminary mandatory injunction will not issue unless the legal right to be protected is clearly established. Steiner v. Simmons, 35 Del. Ch. 83, 111 A.2d 574 (1955).

Restaurant did not show it was entitled to a preliminary injunction requiring a county to issue it a certificate of occupancy because it did not establish that it had a clear legal right to such a certificate when the owner of the building in which it was to operate had not obtained a certificate of occupancy for that building shell, nor did it show a likelihood of imminent irreparable harm, as there was no reason to expect the county would refuse to issue a certificate of occupancy because the building was smaller than that shown on an approved plan. Bertucci's Rest. Corp. v. New Castle County, 836 A.2d 515 (Del. Ch. 2003).

Reasonable probability of success to be shown. — A preliminary injunction will not issue unless it is apparent that there is reasonable probability of the plaintiff's ultimate success upon final hearing or that the failure to issue a preliminary injunction will work irreparable injury. Sandler v. Schenley Indus., Inc., 32 Del. Ch. 46, 79 A.2d 606 (1951).

An application for a preliminary injunction imposes on the plaintiff the burden of showing a reasonable probability of ultimate success, and this applies whether the improbability of ultimate success is a question of law or a question of fact. Gropper v. North Cent. Tex. Oil Co., 35 Del. Ch. 198, 114 A.2d 231 (1955).

A preliminary injunction will not be issued unless the person seeking it can satisfy the Court that there is at least a reasonable probability that he will achieve ultimate success on final hearing. Arbour Park Civic Ass'n v. City of Newark, 267 A.2d 904 (Del. Ch. 1970).

Where the plaintiff has established a clear legal right to an injunction, he should normally receive what he has prayed for, assuming he has done equity and not misled his opponent. Turek v. Tull, 37 Del. Ch. 190, 139 A.2d 368, aff'd, 147 A.2d 658 (Del. 1958).

But it does not necessarily follow in every case, even though the right may be clear, that the plaintiff is entitled to a mandatory injunction, as the Court will always consider the equities between the parties. Hollingsworth v. Szczesiak, 32 Del. Ch. 274, 84 A.2d 816 (1951).

Hence, parties in an injunctive proceeding should be heard on the scope of the injunction in order to protect both parties' interests. Gronemeyer v. Hunter Mfg. Corp., 34 Del. Ch. 515, 106 A.2d 519 (1954).

And the court has broad discretion in granting or denying a preliminary injunction. Data Gen. Corp. v. Digital Computer Controls, Inc., 297 A.2d 437 (Del. 1972).

But on application for preliminary injunction, the equities must be balanced and the probable ultimate results of the case evaluated. Thomas C. Marshall, Inc. v. Holiday Inn, Inc., 40 Del. Ch. 77, 174 A.2d 27 (1961).

In acting upon applications for preliminary injunctions, a court of equity is bound to balance the conveniences of the respective parties, and the probability of ultimate success, being of obvious practical importance, is one of the elements which must always be weighed in the balance, along with the probability of any harm to be suffered by one party or the other on account of giving the requested temporary relief or by withholding it, as the case may be. Bayard v. Martin, 34 Del. Ch. 184, 101 A.2d 329 (1953), cert. denied, 347 U.S. 944, 74 S. Ct. 639, 98 L. Ed. 1092 (1954).

Where it was found that the board of directors of a corporation that was involved in a potential merger, and had provided misleading information about certain change-in-control agreements in the proxy statement, a preliminary injunction pursuant to Del. Ch. Ct. R. 65 was granted, as it: would remedy the wrong caused to the stockholders' right to cast a vote after a full and fair disclosure of material facts; no harm would be caused to the corporation; and, the balance of hardships tilted in favor of granting the relief. In re MONY Group Inc. S'holder Litig., 852 A.2d 9 (Del. Ch. 2004).

So there is no error in denial when hardship outweighs the benefit. — There is no error in the denial of a preliminary injunction when the hardship to the adverse party which would result from the grant of injunctive relief far outweighs any possible benefit to the applicant. Eastern Shore Natural Gas Co. v. Stauffer Chem. Co., 298 A.2d 322 (Del. 1972).

Or where movant would obtain all relief to be gained. — If to grant the movant's interim prayers would be to allow the movant all the relief it might hope to gain after final hearing, the preliminary injunction will be denied. Thomas C. Marshall, Inc. v. Holiday Inn, Inc., 40 Del. Ch. 77, 174 A.2d 27 (1961).

Irreparable harm. — Shareholder's motion for a preliminary injunction to stop the corporation's annual meeting was granted because the corporation's proxy statement was false and misleading, where the corporation and its board of directors breached their fiduciary duty to disclose fully and fairly to stockholders all material information in seeking stockholder approval of the amendments to the corporation's bylaws; the threat of an uninformed stockholder vote constituted irreparable harm. ODS Techs., L.P. v. Marshall, 832 A.2d 1254 (Del. Ch. 2003).

Injunction against liquidation meeting denied. — Where a corporation would not be able to repay the purchaser of its assets if the Court directed a restoration of the status quo ante, the corporation may hold a stockholders' meeting for the purpose of corporate liquidation, and an injunction to restrain this meeting pending determination of a single stockholders' suit for restoration of the status quo ante will be denied. *Cottrell v. Pawcatuck Co., 34 Del. Ch. 528, 106 A.2d 709 (1954).*

Injunction to prevent filing of merger documents denied. — Where plaintiffs have not established probability of ultimate success, application for a preliminary injunction to prevent the filing of the documents necessary to consummate merger will be denied. *Muschel v. Western Union Corp., 310 A.2d 904 (Del. Ch. 1973).*

When inequitable to grant mandatory injunction. — Where there has been an innocent mistake or a bona fide claim of right on the part of defendants, inexcusable or unconscionable delay on the part of the plaintiffs or where the conduct of the defendants was not willful and inexcusable, courts in some cases have held it to be inequitable to grant a mandatory injunction. *Hollingsworth v. Szczesiak, 32 Del. Ch. 274, 84 A.2d 816 (1951).*

No appeal from dismissal of injunction for photographs and fingerprints. — An appeal from the dismissal by the Court of Chancery of an action for a mandatory injunction requiring the return to the appellant of photographs and record of fingerprints taken in a criminal prosecution cannot be maintained. *Walker v. Lamb, 259 A.2d 663 (Del. 1969).*

Patentee is entitled to injunctive protection against the wrongful use of patterns and drawings disclosing secret information as to the commercial use of the patented product in the form of equitable relief to protect his interest in the knowledge disclosed and to an accounting of profits accrued from its use after election to return the material. *Gronemeyer v. Hunter Mfg. Corp., 34 Del. Ch. 515, 106 A.2d 519 (1954).*

However, information as to the commercial use of a patented product must meet both the novelty and secrecy tests imposed as a condition precedent to injunctive relief. *Gronemeyer v. Hunter Mfg. Corp., 34 Del. Ch. 515, 106 A.2d 519 (1954).*

In an action to enjoin the negotiation of guaranty notes, evidence must be sufficient to show a breach of any condition upon which the guaranty was based. *Danby v. Osteopathic Hosp. Ass'n, 34 Del. Ch. 427, 104 A.2d 903 (1954).*

Where the plaintiff, as guarantor, seeks to enjoin the endorsement of the notes against the defendant and the lending institution and where the lender was not an original party to the guaranty agreement between the plaintiff and defendant, action against the lender will be dismissed. *Danby v. Osteopathic Hosp. Ass'n, 101 A.2d 308 (Del. Ch. 1953), aff'd, 104 A.2d 903 (Del. 1954).*

With burden upon the plaintiffs. — In an action to enjoin a seller from proceeding with the execution of judgment notes, the burden is squarely upon the plaintiffs to make an affirmative showing of whatever is essential to their case. *Bayard v. Martin, 34 Del. Ch. 184, 101 A.2d 329 (1953), cert. denied, 347 U.S. 944, 74 S. Ct. 639, 98 L. Ed. 1092 (1954).*

An injunction against a breach of a contract is likened to a decree for specific performance and, accordingly, governed by the same principles in that relief may be granted or refused in the discretion of the Court. *Turek v. Tull, 37 Del. Ch. 190, 139 A.2d 368, aff'd, 147 A.2d 658 (Del. 1958).*

But no right to cross-claim for specific performance after trial. — After trial, at which he had a full opportunity to participate, a defendant will not be given leave to file a proposed cross-claim for the specific performance of an alleged contract and to have his right to such form of relief preserved by the issuance of a preliminary injunction. *Cook v. Fusselman, 300 A.2d 246 (Del. Ch. 1972).*

And where a party seeks to enforce a bargain which he forced from a badgered board of directors, equity will not lend its aid to the specific performance of such a contract. *Cook v. Fusselman, 300 A.2d 246 (Del. Ch. 1972).*

When a motion for dissolution of injunction should not be granted. — Where the general condition subsequent to the granting of the preliminary injunction is substantially the same as that which existed prior thereto and where no unusual conditions have been called to the court's attention, the rule which provides that unless there is a denial in the answer to the averments of the complaint a motion for the dissolution of a preliminary injunction should not be granted is applicable. *Lionel Corp. v. Klein, 34 Del. Ch. 511, 106 A.2d 525 (1954).*

III. TEMPORARY RESTRAINING ORDER.

Interim injunctive relief is normally granted merely to preserve the status quo and should not be granted unless truly irreparable injury would be suffered by the party seeking such relief were it not to be granted. *Thomas C. Marshall, Inc. v. Holiday Inn, Inc., 40 Del. Ch. 77, 174 A.2d 27 (1961).*

Whether threat is imminent or not. — In cases where possible serious harm or inconvenience can result to a party by action taken before he may have notice thereof, the party seeking a restraining order should not be required to run that risk where he has otherwise made a sufficient showing of interest in such subject matter; otherwise stated, a restraining order is not only issued when the threat is imminent. *Panamanian Sec., Inc. v. Punta Alegre Sugar Corp., 37 Del. Ch. 588, 146 A.2d 808 (1958).*

But laches is ground for denial. — Where a stockholder voluntarily discharged the preliminary injunction rule and stood by for several months with the knowledge that important changes in the corporation were taking place, his failure to press this matter for months while various mutations were taking place does not commend itself to the Court when interim injunctive relief is sought, and thus laches is a ground for denying the application. *Cottrell v. Pawcatuck Co., 34 Del. Ch. 528, 106 A.2d 709 (1954).*

Chancery Court

Reasonable notice of prohibited acts, which may form the basis for a subsequent contempt action, is mandated both by paragraph (b) of this rule and considerations of due process. *Wilmington Fed'n of Teachers v. Howell, 374 A.2d 832 (Del. 1977).*

Motion denied where evidence insufficient to enjoin execution of judgment notes. — In an action to enjoin a seller from proceeding with the execution of judgment notes where evidence was not sufficient to establish that subsequent judgment against the seller would be unavailing, motion for temporary injunction will be denied. *Bayard v. Martin, 34 Del. Ch. 184, 101 A.2d 329 (1953), cert. denied, 347 U.S. 944, 74 S. Ct. 639, 98 L. Ed. 1092 (1954).*

Only probability of prevailing proper to consider. — In an action to enjoin a seller from proceeding with the execution of judgment notes, pending determination of the seller's suit in considering the propriety of the issuance of a temporary injunction, the only probability of prevailing which was proper for the Court of Chancery to consider was the probability of prevailing on the issues which the Court of Chancery itself is to try, and treatment of the fraud issue is not in the jurisdiction of the Court. *Bayard v. Martin, 34 Del. Ch. 184, 101 A.2d 329 (1953), cert. denied, 347 U.S. 944, 74 S. Ct. 639, 98 L. Ed. 1092 (1954).*

No allegation of insolvency as basis for rejection. — The allegation that enforcement of a suit in Superior Court would damage the plaintiffs and limit the ability to collect subsequent claims against the defendant is no allegation of insolvency as a basis for temporary rejection of a suit in *Superior Court. Bayard v. Martin, 34 Del. Ch. 184, 101 A.2d 329 (1953), cert. denied, 347 U.S. 944, 74 S. Ct. 639, 98 L. Ed. 1092 (1954).*

And no showing of sheriff's sale as damaging notoriety. — In an action to enjoin a seller from proceeding with the execution of judgment notes, an allegation that a corporation would be subject to damaging notoriety in connection with a sheriff's sale of its property could not serve as a basis for a temporary injunction where there is no showing in any affidavit of any reason why plaintiffs would ever permit such a sale. *Bayard v. Martin, 34 Del. Ch. 184, 101 A.2d 329 (1953), cert. denied, 347 U.S. 944, 74 S. Ct. 639, 98 L. Ed. 1092 (1954).*

Contempt where violation of order by union. — When there clearly have been violations of a temporary restraining order by picketing employee union members and when in the aggregate they establish a basis for relief, the employer is entitled to a decree finding the union in contempt and with appropriate terms designed to insure future compliance with the order. *Avisun Corp. v. Oil, Chem. & Atomic Workers Local 8-732, 259 A.2d 389 (Del. Ch. 1969).*

Court may determine whether motion to dissolve considered on merits. — Because of the nature of a restraining order, the Court is free to exercise its discretion in determining whether or not a motion to dissolve a restraining order should be considered on its merits even after the entry of a restraining order on notice. In this way the Court of Chancery is free to decide whether the grounds are proper to consider on the motion or whether it should await a preliminary injunction hearing or other developments. *Panamanian Sec., Inc. v. Punta Alegre Sugar Corp., 37 Del. Ch. 588, 146 A.2d 808 (1958).*

But to warrant dissolution of a temporary injunction upon the complaint and answer, the answer should deny the material allegations of the complaint with the same clearness and certainty with which they are charged; and, for the purpose of such a motion, the answer is considered only insofar as it is responsive to the allegations of the complaint. *Lionel Corp. v. Klein, 34 Del. Ch. 511, 106 A.2d 525 (1954).*

A new matter not responsive to allegations of the complaint will not be considered on the hearing of a motion to dissolve a temporary injunction. *Lionel Corp. v. Klein, 34 Del. Ch. 511, 106 A.2d 525 (1954).*

Order dissolved where there is no irreparable injury to stockholders. — Where there is no probability of success by a stockholder to enjoin a corporation from issuing dividends until prior capital impairment has been corrected, the failure to enjoin current dividends on cumulative preferred stock will not irreparably injure the plaintiff and other common stockholders, and a temporary restraining order will be dissolved. *Weinberg v. Baltimore Brick Co., 34 Del. Ch. 586, 108 A.2d 81 (1954), aff'd, Del. Supr., 114 A.2d 812 (1955).*

IV. SECURITY.

The court is without jurisdiction to entertain an application for assessment of damages on an injunction bond. *Morris v. Whaley, 42 Del. Ch. 65, 203 A.2d 618 (1964).*

Although the practice in the federal courts has long permitted assessment of damages in the injunction suit and paragraph (c) of this rule adopted the identical language of *Fed. R. Civ. P. 65(c)* with respect to the requirement of security, this rule contains no provision permitting enforcement of a liability on the bond in the original cause. *Morris v. Whaley, 42 Del. Ch. 65, 203 A.2d 618 (1964).*

"Wrongful injunction." — There is an implicit presumption in favor of awarding damages for a "wrongful injunction" unless good reason evidenced by objective factors supports a contrary view. *Emerald Partners v. Berlin, 726 A.2d 1215 (Del, 1999).*

An injunction is "wrongful" if reversed on appeal or if the enjoined party at all times had the right to do the enjoined act. *Emerald Partners v. Berlin, 726 A.2d 1215 (Del. 1999).*

V. FORM AND SCOPE.

The chancellor may, in his discretion, require the performance of conditions designed to protect temporarily the rights of the parties pending the grant of final relief. *Kahn v. General Dev. Corp., 40 Del. Ch. 83, 174 A.2d 307 (1961).*

Wrongful injunction. — An enjoined party has been "wrongfully enjoined or restrained" when the injunction is later reversed, and a finding of abuse of discretion in the granting of the injunction is not necessary. *Emerald Partners v. Berlin, 712 A.2d 1006 (Del. Ch. 1997).*

Rule 65.1. Security: proceedings against sureties

DELAWARE CASE NOTES — REPORTED

The rule states the procedure on which in personam jurisdiction is based; that is, on a motion without a new action or the issuance of process. *Ellis D.*

Taylor, Inc. v. Craft Bldrs., Inc., 260 A.2d 180 (Del. Ch. 1969).

Rule 70. Judgment for specific acts; vesting title; contempt

DELAWARE CASE NOTES — REPORTED

I. General Consideration.
II. Substitute Performance.
III. Contempt, etc.

I. GENERAL CONSIDERATION.

Cross references. — As to enforcement of judgments, see § 370 of Title 10. As to sale of land to enforce judgment, see § 371 of Title 10. As to attachments generally, see Chapter 35 of Title 10.

II. SUBSTITUTE PERFORMANCE.

The principal process to compel satisfaction of a monetary decree is the writ of sequestration, which is directed to certain persons, called "sequestrators," conferring power upon them to seize the defendant's property. *Greene v. Johnston, 34 Del. Ch. 115, 99 A.2d 627, 42 A.L.R.2d 906 (1953).*

Changes in economic circumstances do not constitute a valid defense to an action for the specific performance of a separation agreement unless provision for such a revision is made in the agreement itself. *J.W.P. v. R.E.P., 301 A.2d 318 (Del. Ch. 1973).*

III. CONTEMPT, ETC.

Actions for contempt of court may be either civil or criminal in nature, or both. *Klein v. State, 36 Del. Ch. 111, 127 A.2d 84 (1956).*

A disclaimer of intent is no defense where the contempt clearly appears from the circumstances constituting the act. *Klein v. State, 36 Del. Ch. 111, 127 A.2d 84 (1956).*

Extent of inquiry in contempt proceeding. — In a contempt proceeding based upon the violation of an injunction, the only legitimate inquiry to be made by the Court is whether or not it had jurisdiction of the parties and of the subject matter. Subject to this limitation, the Court will not listen to an excuse for the contemptuous action based upon an argument that the order in question was imperfect or erroneous, since no person may with impunity disregard an order of the Court having jurisdiction over the subject matter and of the parties. *Mayer v. Mayer, 36 Del. Ch. 457, 132 A.2d 617 (1957).*

Union in contempt for violating restraining order. — When there clearly have been violations of a temporary restraining order by picketing employee union members and when in the aggregate they establish a basis for relief, the employer is entitled to a decree finding the union in contempt and with appropriate terms designed to insure future compliance with the order. *Avisun Corp. v. Oil, Chem. & Atomic Workers Local 8-732, 259 A.2d 389 (Del. Ch. 1969).*

XI. GENERAL PROVISIONS

Rule 81. Applicability in special proceedings

DELAWARE CASE NOTES — REPORTED

When court will not appoint master to conduct stockholders' meeting. — Where plaintiff stockholders have sought judgment on the pleadings and there is nothing alleged in the complaint which attributes any improper conduct or purpose to the present directors of defendant corporation or would indicate futility in requiring the present management to hold the stockholders' meeting to elect directors, the Court will not appoint master to conduct meeting. *Tweedy, Browne & Knapp v. Cambridge Fund, Inc., 318 A.2d 635 (Del. Ch. 1974).*

Rule 88. Allowance for fees, expenses and services

DELAWARE CASE NOTES — REPORTED

Pecuniary compensation may be awarded along with specific performance. — Equity may, when its jurisdiction is invoked to obtain specific performance of a contract, award damages or pecuniary compensation along with specific performance when the decree as awarded does not give complete and full relief. *Tri State Mall Assocs. v. A.A.R. Realty Corp., 298 A.2d 368 (Del. Ch. 1972).*

Although the general rule is that a litigant must defray the costs of his own counsel, and exception is recognized where a suit by 1 member of a class results in the creation of a fund that inures to the benefit of all members of the class, as is the case in stockholder's derivative suits and creditor's bills. *Tri State Mall Assocs. v. A.A.R. Realty Corp., 298 A.2d 368 (Del. Ch. 1972).*

In 1 continuous litigation it is not necessary for counsel to apportion their hours of labor and achievements between the individual parts which together make up 1 whole; it suffices that the entire legal services of counsel are set forth in the affidavit pursuant to this rule. *Cohen v. Cohen, 269 A.2d 205 (Del. 1970).*

Where separate actions are in fact 1 continuous piece of litigation which ultimately results in a settlement of the differences of the parties, it is entirely proper for the Vice-Chancellor to award counsel fees based upon the entire scope of the litigation which is, in reality, one single controversy. *Cohen v. Cohen, 269 A.2d 205 (Del. 1970).*

Award of attorney's fees where party proceded in bad faith. — Where putative shareholder plaintiff's suit proceded in bad faith, the award of attorney fees to defendant, the actual corporate shareholder, was proper under an equity exception to American Rule and plaintiffs' Del. Ch. Ct. R. 59(f) motion to reargue that award was denied. *Rice v. Herrigan-Ferro, — A.2d — (Del. Ch. July 12, 2004).*

XIII. GUARDIANS AND TRUSTEES

Rule 114.   When required to account

DELAWARE CASE NOTES — REPORTED

The accounts of a trustee are subject to regular audit by the Chancery Court, which also calls for state action, under *12 Del. C. § 3521* and this rule. *Milford Trust Co. v. Stabler, 301 A.2d 534 (Del. Ch. 1973).*

Breach of fiduciary duty shown. — The Court of Chancery correctly held that appellants breached their fiduciary duties as trustees under the trust created by the will of their mother because they failed to dispute the incorrect amount of money received to fund the trust from the executor and because they failed to timely file the accountings required by this *Rule. Law v. Law, 753 A.2d 443 (Del. 2000).*

Rule 123.   Exceptions to an account

DELAWARE CASE NOTES — REPORTED

Rule has no application to derivative suit. — Chancery Ct. R. 123-129 fix the procedure to be followed when an exception is taken to an account in a procedure similar to that followed under the old federal equity practice; they have no application to a derivative suit, which is to be considered as if the injured corporation itself were suing the defendants. *Levien v. Sinclair Oil Corp., 300 A.2d 28 (Del. Ch. 1972).*

The stockholder's derivative suit is a distinct and peculiarly equitable action, and nothing about it compels the Chancery Court to follow traditional accounting procedure in what amounts to an action for damages flowing from a breach of contract. *Levien v. Sinclair Oil Corp., 300 A.2d 28 (Del. Ch. 1972).*

Rule 124.   Procedure on hearing exceptions to account

DELAWARE CASE NOTES — REPORTED

Rule has no application to derivative suit. — Chancery Ct. R. 123-129 fix the procedure to be followed when an exception is taken to an account in a procedure similar to that followed under the old federal equity practice; they have no application to a derivative suit, which is to be considered as if the injured corporation itself were suing the defendants. *Levien v. Sinclair Oil Corp., 300 A.2d 28 (Del. Ch. 1972).*

The stockholder's derivative suit is a distinct and peculiarly equitable action, and nothing about it compels the Chancery Court to follow traditional accounting procedure in what amounts to an action for damages flowing from a breach of contract. *Levien v. Sinclair Oil Corp., 300 A.2d 28 (Del. Ch. 1972).*

Rule 125.   Testimony on hearing exceptions to account

DELAWARE CASE NOTES — REPORTED

Rule has no application to derivative suit. — Chancery Ct. R. 123-129 fix the procedure to be followed when an exception is taken to an account in a procedure similar to that followed under the old federal equity practice; they have no application to a derivative suit, which is to be considered as if the injured corporation itself were suing the defendants. *Levien v. Sinclair Oil Corp., 300 A.2d 28 (Del. Ch. 1972).*

The stockholder's derivative suit is a distinct and peculiarly equitable action, and nothing about it compels the Chancery Court to follow traditional accounting procedure in what amounts to an action for damages flowing from a breach of contract. *Levien v. Sinclair Oil Corp., 300 A.2d 28 (Del. Ch. 1972).*

Rule 126.   Guardian or trustee may be examined

DELAWARE CASE NOTES — REPORTED

Rule has no application to derivative suit. — Chancery Ct. R. 123-129 fix the procedure to be followed when an exception is taken to an account in a procedure similar to that followed under the old federal equity practice; they have no application to a derivative suit, which is to be considered as if the injured corporation itself were suing the defendants. *Levien v. Sinclair Oil Corp., 300 A.2d 28 (Del. Ch. 1972).*

The stockholder's derivative suit is a distinct and peculiarly equitable action, and nothing about it compels the Chancery Court to follow traditional accounting procedure in what amounts to an action for damages flowing from a breach of contract. *Levien v. Sinclair Oil Corp., 300 A.2d 28 (Del. Ch. 1972).*

Rule 127.   Account may be referred to Master; procedure

DELAWARE CASE NOTES — REPORTED

Rule has no application to derivative suit. — Chancery Ct. R. 123-129 fix the procedure to be followed when an exception is taken to an account in a procedure similar to that followed under the old federal equity practice; they have no application to a derivative suit, which is to be considered as if the injured corporation itself were suing the defendants. *Levien v. Sinclair Oil Corp., 300 A.2d 28 (Del. Ch. 1972).*

The stockholder's derivative suit is a distinct and peculiarly equitable action, and nothing about it compels the Chancery Court to follow traditional accounting procedure in what amounts to an action for damages flowing from a breach of contract. *Levien v. Sinclair Oil Corp., 300 A.2d 28 (Del. Ch. 1972).*

Rule 128.   Procedure by Court on Master's report as to account

DELAWARE CASE NOTES — REPORTED

Rule has no application to derivative suit. — Chancery Ct. R. 123-129 fix the procedure to be followed when an exception is taken to an account in a procedure similar to that followed under the old federal equity practice; they have no application to a derivative suit, which is to be considered as if the injured corporation itself were suing the defendants. *Levien v. Sinclair Oil Corp., 300 A.2d 28 (Del. Ch. 1972).*

The stockholder's derivative suit is a distinct and peculiarly equitable action, and nothing about it compels the Chancery Court to follow traditional accounting procedure in what amounts to an action for damages flowing from a breach of contract. *Levien v. Sinclair Oil Corp., 300 A.2d 28 (Del. Ch. 1972).*

Rule 129.   Effect of Court approval of account

DELAWARE CASE NOTES — REPORTED

The approval of trustee accounts under this rule is ministerial. *In re Corcoran Trusts, 282 A.2d 653 (Del. Ch. 1971), aff'd, 295 A.2d 725 (Del. 1972).*

Rule has no application to derivative suit. — Chancery Ct. R. 123-129 fix the procedure to be followed when an exception is taken to an account in a procedure similar to that followed under the old federal equity practice; they have no application to a derivative suit, which is to be considered as if the injured corporation itself were suing the defendants. *Levien v. Sinclair Oil Corp., 300 A.2d 28 (Del. Ch. 1972).*

The stockholder's derivative suit is a distinct and peculiarly equitable action, and nothing about it compels the Chancery Court to follow traditional accounting procedure in what amounts to an action for damages flowing from a breach of contract. Levien v. Sinclair Oil Corp., 300 A.2d 28 (Del. Ch. 1972).

Rule 132.   Fiduciary commissions

DELAWARE CASE NOTES — REPORTED

Court may grant full fees. — Although this rule provides that trustees' commissions are "subject in any case to increase or decrease by the Court for cause appearing sufficient to the Court," the Court is justified in granting full fees if it finds the trustee performed its duties faithfully and well. *Cleveland Trust Co. v. Wilmington Trust Co., 258 A.2d 58 (Del. 1969).*

Applicability to inter vivos trusts. — Where the settlor indicated in the trust instrument that the successor trustee of the inter vivos trust was to recover fees as provided for testamentary trustees, the rule setting fees for testamentary trustees, rather than the rule applicable to personal representatives, applied; the court made an upward adjustment, however, to account for the challenges

Chancery Court

encountered by the trustee in dealing with the appraisal and division of the decedent's and difficult personal relationships among the beneficiaries. In re Estate of Howell, — A.2d — (Del. Ch. Dec. 20, 2002).

And parol evidence as to trustee's fees may be considered. — When the provision for a trustee's fees is reasonably susceptible to different meanings, parol evidence as to "pertinent explanatory circumstances" may be considered to resolve the uncertainty and to ascertain the intent of the parties to the trust agreement. *Cleveland Trust Co. v. Wilmington Trust Co., 258 A.2d 58 (Del. 1969).*

Unless trust agreement contains unambiguous provision as to amount. — Where a trust agreement contains a clear and unambiguous provision as to the amount of the fee on principal which would be owing upon transfer of the res to a successor trustee, there is no room for parol evidence as to that issue. *Cleveland Trust Co. v. Wilmington Trust Co., 258 A.2d 58 (Del. 1969).*

Aggregate principal commissions on transfer. — A bank was awarded a termination fee on two trusts after that bank was asked by trustees to resign so the situs of the trust could be moved for tax purposes; pursuant to this rule, upon partial or complete distribution of any trust or upon transfer of a successor trustee, the aggregate principal commissions allowable would be 1 percent of principal over $ 1,000,000. In re Ward, — A.2d — (Del. Ch. Dec. 26, 2001).

"Distribution" and "transfer" are distinguished. — It is clear from this rule that it is customary in banking circles to distinguish between "distribution" to beneficiaries and "transfer" to a successor trustee as words of art. *Cleveland Trust Co. v. Wilmington Trust Co., 258 A.2d 58 (Del. 1969).*

Rule 133.   Appointment and duties of successor guardian or trustee

DELAWARE CASE NOTES — REPORTED

Removal of guardian. — Although there was no doubt that the parent needed a guardian of person and property, the child failed to provide any cause or factual basis to support a *12 Del. C. § 3908(a)* and Del. Ch. Ct. R. 175-180 application to remove a public guardian. *In re Harris,* — *A.2d* — *(Del. Ch. Nov. 14, 2003).*

XIV. MASTERS

Rule 135.   Appointment; removal

DELAWARE CASE NOTES — REPORTED

Review of master's decisions. — A Special Discovery Master's decisions are recommendations which, absent the consent of the parties, are subject to de novo review by the Superior Court. *Playtex FP, Inc. v. Columbia Cas. Co., 609 A.2d 1083 (Del. Super. Ct. 1991).*

XV. RECEIVERSHIPS; RECEIVERS AND TRUSTEES FOR CORPORATIONS

Rule 149.   Appointment on verified complaint; receiver pendente lite

DELAWARE CASE NOTES — REPORTED

Appointment of a receiver pendente lite is discretionary with the court, and so is a decision to continue or to terminate such a receivership. *Liebman & Co. v. Institutional Investors Trust, 406 A.2d 37 (Del. 1979).*

The court will exercise its power to appoint a receiver for a solvent corporation with great restraint. *Vale v. Atlantic Coast & Inland Corp., 34 Del. Ch. 50, 99 A.2d 396 (1953).*

And fraud, gross mismanagement or danger of great loss must be shown. — In order to state a claim for the appointment of a receiver for a solvent corporation, plaintiff must show fraud, gross mismanagement or extreme circumstances causing imminent danger of great loss which cannot be otherwise prevented. *Vale v. Atlantic Coast & Inland Corp., 34 Del. Ch. 50, 99 A.2d 396 (1953).*

But motion to dismiss complaint denied where allegations form basis. — Where the combination of circumstances alleged in a complaint could form the basis for the introduction of evidence of a character which would warrant the appointment of a liquidating receiver, the motion to dismiss must be denied. *Vale v. Atlantic Coast & Inland Corp., 34 Del. Ch. 50, 99 A.2d 396 (1953).*

Receiver subject to court's supervision. — Where receiver of dissolved corporation is an officer of the Court of Chancery, his action in administering the estate is subject to the Court's supervision. *D'Angelo v. Petroleos Mexicanos, 373 F. Supp. 1076 (D. Del. 1974).*

XVI. JUDICIAL ETHICS, ATTORNEYS, ETC

Rule 170.   Attorneys

DELAWARE CASE NOTES — REPORTED

Purpose of rule. — One of the principal purposes of the pro hac vice rules is to assure that, if a Delaware lawyer is not to be present at a deposition, the lawyer admitted pro hac vice will be there. As such, he is an officer of the Delaware court, subject to control of the court to ensure the integrity of the proceeding. *Paramount Communications, Inc. v. QVC Network, Inc., 637 A.2d 34 (Del. 1994).*

Responsibilities of associated attorney. — A Delaware lawyer who moves the admission pro hac vice of an out-of-state lawyer is not relieved of responsibility, is required to appear at all court proceedings (except depositions when a lawyer admitted pro hac vice is present), shall certify that the lawyer appearing pro hac vice is reputable and competent, and that the Delaware lawyer is in a position to recommend the out-of-state lawyer. *Paramount Communications, Inc. v. QVC Network, Inc., 637 A.2d 34 (Del. 1994).*

Rule 174.   Voluntary mediation in the Court of Chancery

DELAWARE CASE NOTES — REPORTED

Enforcement. — Individual's action to enforce an alleged mediation agreement which was only signed by counsel was correctly dismissed; mediation under Del. Ch. Ct. R. 174 was best served by guaranteeing a confidential environment and enforcing an agreement to settle only when there was a writing that complied with Del. Ch. Ct. R. 174(g) by being signed by the parties and the mediator. *Capano v. State ex rel. Brady, 832 A.2d 1250 (Del. 2003).*

XVII. GUARDIANS FOR AGED, MENTALLY INFIRM OR INCAPACITATED PERSONS NOT MENTALLY ILL

Rule 175.   Petition for appointment of guardian

DELAWARE CASE NOTES — REPORTED

Proceeds of taking should be preserved as realty. — When an order is entered by the Chancery Court appointing a guardian for a person's estate under the provisions of former 12 Del. C. § 3914 (see now *12 Del. C. § 3902*), Ch. Ct. R. 176, 178 and this rule, so that lands of the incompetent are then taken by paramount authority, the Court should, to the fullest extent possible, seek to preserve the proceeds of such taking and treat them as if they were realty. *Bank of Del. v. Hargraves, 242 A.2d 472 (Del. Ch. 1968).*

Removal of guardian. — Although there was no doubt that the parent needed a guardian of person and property, the child failed to provide any cause or factual basis to support a *12 Del. C. § 3908(a)* and Del. Ch. Ct. R. 175-180 application to remove a public guardian. *In re Harris, — A.2d — (Del. Ch. Nov. 14, 2003).*

Rule 176.   Appointment of attorney ad litem upon petition for appointment of guardian; service and notice of hearing

DELAWARE CASE NOTES — REPORTED

Proceeds of taking should be preserved as realty. — When an order is entered by the Chancery Court appointing a guardian for a person's estate under the provisions of former 12 Del. C. § 3914 (see now *12 Del. C. § 3902*), Ch. Ct. R. 175, 178 and this rule, so that lands of the incompetent are then taken by paramount authority, the Court should, to the fullest extent possible, seek to preserve the proceeds of such taking and treat them as if they were realty. *Bank of Del. v. Hargraves, 242 A.2d 472 (Del. Ch. 1968).*

Discretion of attorney ad litem. — The language of the attorney ad litem rule provides great latitude to the attorney ad litem to determine the position he or she will advocate. The broad language of that rule, providing that the attorney ad litem should "represent the person as if engaged by such person," clearly does not limit the attorney ad litem to opposing whatever position the guardian takes. *In re Tavel, 661 A.2d 1061 (Del. 1995).*

Termination of medical treatment. — If the attorney ad litem, after careful, independent review, determines that the disabled person he or she represents would have refused or terminated medical treatment, the attorney ad litem may advocate such a position. *In re Tavel, 661 A.2d 1061 (Del. 1995).*

Chancery Court

Rule 178. Petition to exercise powers not granted by Subchapter II of Chapter 39 of Title 12 of the Delaware Code or by the Court

DELAWARE CASE NOTES — REPORTED

Rule preserves incompetent's will as to specified beneficiaries. — This rule provides a procedural basis and guide to the Court in preserving to the fullest extent possible the pattern of the will of an incompetent by avoiding the sale of property intended for specified beneficiaries. *Bank of Del. v. Hargraves, 242 A.2d 472 (Del. Ch. 1968).*

Proceeds of taking should be preserved as realty. — When an order is entered by the Chancery Court appointing a guardian for a person's estate under former 12 Del. C. § 3914 (see now *12 Del. C. § 3902*), Ch. Ct. R. 175, 176 and this rule, so that lands of the incompetent are then taken by paramount authority, the Court should, to the fullest extent possible, seek to preserve the proceeds of such taking and treat them as if they were realty. *Bank of Del. v. Hargraves, 242 A.2d 472 (Del. Ch. 1968).*

Rule 179. Property subject of specific devise or bequest

DELAWARE CASE NOTES — REPORTED

Guardian has right to ask court for permission to take specific action with respect to the ward. *Severns v. Wilmington Medical Ctr., Inc., 421 A.2d 1334 (Del. 1980).*

Assertion of constitutional right of comatose ward regarding medical care. — The Court of Chancery may recognize the right of a guardian of the person to vicariously assert the constitutional right of a comatose ward to accept medical care or to refuse it. *Severns v. Wilmington Medical Ctr., Inc., 421 A.2d 1334 (Del. 1980).*

XVIII. MISCELLANEOUS PROVISIONS

Rule 184. Appeals from registers of wills and exceptions to accounts

DELAWARE CASE NOTES — REPORTED

An appeal to the court of chancery from the register of wills results in a trial de novo on the facts and law, considered in the light of the record as a whole. *In re Estate of Levering, 269 A.2d 260 (Del. Super. Ct.), aff'd, 271 A.2d 42 (Del. 1970), cert. denied, 401 U.S. 976, 91 S. Ct. 1197, 28 L. Ed. 2d 325 (1971).*

Hence, the court, on appeal from the register of wills, may call for the presentation of some or of all of the evidence and testimony which had been considered by the *Register. In re Estate of Levering, 269 A.2d 260* (Del. Super. Ct.), aff'd, *271 A.2d 42 (Del. 1970)*, cert. denied, *401 U.S. 976, 91 S. Ct. 1197, 28 L. Ed. 2d 325 (1971).*

XIX. PROBATE PROCEDURES

Rule 192. Commissions and fees

DELAWARE CASE NOTES — REPORTED

Trust instrument determines applicable fees. — Where the settlor indicated in the trust instrument that the successor trustee of his inter vivos trust was to recover fees as provided for testamentary trustees, the rule setting fees for testamentary trustees, rather than the rule applicable to personal representatives, applied; the court made an upward adjustment, however, to account for the challenges encountered by the trustee in dealing with the appraisal and division of the decedent's assets and difficult personal relationships among the beneficiaries. *In re Estate of Howell, — A.2d — (Del. Ch. Dec. 20, 2002).*

Personal Jurisdiction

TITLE 10.
COURTS AND JUDICIAL PROCEDURE

PART III.
PROCEDURE

CHAPTER 31.
PROCESS; COMMENCEMENT OF ACTIONS

§ 3104.   Personal jurisdiction by acts of nonresidents

DELAWARE CASE NOTES — REPORTED

Purpose. — This long arm statute provides a means for a court to exercise specific and general jurisdiction over parties that cause injuries within *Delaware. E.I. DuPont de Nemours & Co. v. Rhodia Fiber & Resin Intermediates, S.A.S., 197 F.R.D. 112 (D. Del. 2000).*

Intent of this section is to afford Delaware residents a means of redress against persons not subject to personal service with the *State. Harmon v. Eudaily, 407 A.2d 232 (Del. Super. Ct. 1979); 420 A.2d 1175 (Del. 1980).*

Section has its roots in Illinois long-arm statute and under prevailing state law, construction of the Delaware statute may be made by recourse to the legislative and decisional law of *Illinois. Wilmington Supply Co. v. Worth Plumbing & Heating, Inc., 505 F. Supp. 777 (D. Del. 1980); Magid v. Marcal Paper Mills, Inc., 517 F. Supp. 1125 (D. Del. 1981).*

Delaware follows the courts of Illinois in interpreting the Delaware long arm statute, subsection (c) of this section which is based upon the Illinois long arm statute, Ill. Stat. Ann. c. 110 § 17(l). *Wilmington Supply Co. v. Worth Plumbing & Heating, Inc., 505 F. Supp. 777 (D. Del. 1980).*

Delaware long-arm statute was closely modeled on uniform interstate and international procedure act, and a court may look to the Commissioners' Comments on the act in determining how to interpret the law. *Moore v. Little Giant Indus., Inc., 513 F. Supp. 1043 (D. Del. 1981); 681 F.2d 807 (3d Cir. 1982); Magid v. Marcal Paper Mills, Inc., 517 F. Supp. 1125 (D. Del. 1981).*

This section is modeled in most material respects on the Uniform Interstate and International Procedure Act, a so-called "single act" statute which allows jurisdiction to be imposed on a nonresident defendant on the basis of a single transaction in, or contact with, the forum state. *Transportes Aereos De Angola v. Ronair, Inc., 544 F. Supp. 858 (D. Del. 1982).*

Subsection (c)(4) derived from § 1.03 (a)(4) of Uniform Interstate and International Procedure Act (U.I.I.P.A.), 13 U.L.A. § 1.03 (1980). *Waters v. Deutz Corp., 479 A.2d 273 (Del. 1984).*

Construction of section. — This section must be construed as conferring jurisdiction to the maximum perimeters of the due process clause. *Transportes Aereos De Angola v. Ronair, Inc., 544 F. Supp. 858 (D. Del. 1982); Jeffreys v. Exten, 784 F. Supp. 146 (D. Del. 1992).*

Precedent uniformity dictates a liberal construction of this section, favoring the exercise of jurisdiction. *Waters v. Deutz Corp., 460 A.2d 1332 (Del. Super. Ct. 1983).*

Subsection (c) of Delaware's long-arm statute is to be construed liberally, favoring the exercise of jurisdiction. *Mobil Oil Corp. v. Advanced Envtl. Recycling Technologies, Inc., 833 F. Supp. 437 (D. Del. 1993).*

This section should be broadly construed. Mid-Atlantic Mach. & Fabric, Inc. v. Chesapeake Shipbuilding, Inc., 492 A.2d 250 (Del. Super. Ct. 1985).

The 1978 amendment of this section made it possible to bring suit against a nonresident doing business in the State who did not maintain a branch or agency establishment in the *State. Plumb v. Cottle, 492 F. Supp. 1330 (D. Del. 1980).*

Section does not alter any substantive right defendant may have; it merely designates a jurisdiction in which the dispute may be determined. *Eudaily v. Harmon, 420 A.2d 1175 (Del. 1980).*

Interest and expediency. — Delaware has an interest in adjudicating disputes involving contracts based upon its laws, and judicial expediency would not be served by causing another court to duplicate the prior efforts of the *Delaware court. Dentsply Int'l Inc. v. Pentron Corp., 648 F. Supp. 856 (D. Del. 1986).*

Due process requires that defendant have certain minimum contacts with forum. — Due process requires that if a defendant is not present within the territory of the forum, the defendant has certain minimum contacts with it such that the maintenance of the suit does not offend traditional notions of fair play and substantial justice. Whether sufficient minimum contacts exist cannot be answered by reference to any fixed formula, but must be ascertained from close examination of the particular circumstances of

Personal Jurisdiction

each case. *Transportes Aereos De Angola v. Ronair, Inc., 544 F. Supp. 858 (D. Del. 1982).*

Fairness and reasonableness of jurisdiction shown. — Jurisdiction over a foreign manufacturer of asbestos was fair and reasonable in the interests of protecting the health and welfare of Delaware citizens. *Boone v. Oy Partek Ab, 724 A.2d 1150 (Del. Super. Ct. 1997),* aff'd, *707 A.2d 765 (Del. 1998).*

Family court has continuing jurisdiction. — The Family Court has continuing subject matter and in personam jurisdiction over nonresident child support obligors with regard to petitions to modify its own orders; the Family Court's continuing jurisdiction over its own child support orders obviates the need to comply with the requirements of the long-arm statute in a subsequent modification proceeding. *Taylor v. Taylor, 672 A.2d 44 (Del. 1996).*

Trial court has continuing jurisdiction to enforce or modify its own child support order against a nonresident obligor; due process does not require compliance with the provisions of a long-arm statute in such circumstances. *Taylor v. Taylor, 672 A.2d 44 (Del. 1996).*

Federal due process does not preclude Delaware from exercising personal jurisdiction over nonresident defendants that allegedly cause tortious injury in Delaware by an act in Delaware merely because the defendant was acting in a corporate capacity. *Mobil Oil Corp. v. Advanced Envtl. Recycling Technologies, Inc., 833 F. Supp. 437 (D. Del. 1993).*

Inquiry into propriety of jurisdiction over defendant necessarily involves 2-part process: the court must determine, by reference to principles of statutory construction and judicial precedent, whether the Delaware long-arm statute in fact provides for the assertion of in personam jurisdiction. If the answer to this question is in the affirmative, the court must then decide whether the exercise of that jurisdiction would transgress the due process guarantee of fundamental fairness. *Transportes Aereos De Angola v. Ronair, Inc., 544 F. Supp. 858 (D. Del. 1982).*

In determining whether jurisdiction is appropriate under Delaware's long-arm statute and evaluating whether asserting such jurisdiction would offend due process, the court must view all factual disputes in a light most favorable to the plaintiff. *Boone v. Oy Partek Ab, 724 A.2d 1150 (Del. Super. Ct. 1997),* aff'd, *707 A.2d 765 (Del. 1998).*

Act or conduct invoking benefits and protections of forum as basis for jurisdiction. — One of the major requirements for the constitutional application of in personam jurisdiction over a nonresident defendant is that the defendant must act in an affirmative manner to purposefully avail itself of the privilege of conducting activities within the forum state, invoking the benefits and protection of its laws. *Fischer v. Hilton, 549 F. Supp. 389 (D. Del. 1982).*

If a defendant engaged in some act or conduct by which the defendant may be said to have invoked the benefits and protections of the forum, then it is reasonable and just to require the defendant to litigate a dispute arising therefrom in that forum. *Transportes Aereos De Angola v. Ronair, Inc., 544 F. Supp. 858 (D. Del. 1982).*

Personal jurisdiction existed in Delaware as to an international investment bank that created a Delaware subsidiary for the express purpose of facilitating private equity investments in the United States, including Delaware, and the subsidiary, on behalf of the investment bank, sought to acquire through the use of Delaware law a Delaware corporation located in another state, as this was the type of transaction contemplated by the international bank when it created and operated the subsidiary under the benefits and protections of Delaware law; therefore, the totality of the circumstances showed that the investment bank transacted business in the State of Delaware within the meaning of *Delaware's Long Arm Statute. Aeroglobal Capital Mgmt. v. Cirrus Indus., 871 A.2d 428 (Del. 2005).*

Section is "single act" statute which is a type of long-arm statute establishing jurisdiction over nonresidents on the basis of a single act done or transaction engaged in by the nonresident within the *State. Eudaily v. Harmon, 420 A.2d 1175 (Del. 1980); Tabas v. Crosby, 444 A.2d 250 (Del. Ch. 1982).*

The single act of being a party to the contract allegedly signed in Delaware is not sufficient to establish jurisdiction. *Blue Ball Properties, Inc. v. McClain, 658 F. Supp. 1310 (D. Del. 1987).*

Terms "transacting business" and "contracts to supply services or things" construed. — The negotiation of a contract for sale of stock by residents of Pennsylvania did not amount to a "transaction of business" (now "transacts any business") in Delaware under subsection (c)(1) even though a part of the negotiations included a proposed sale of stock of a Delaware corporation which does transact business in Delaware; the contract also did not involve the supplying of "services or things in this State" under subsection (c)(2) even though settlement was to be held in a Delaware law office. *Greenly v. Davis, 486 A.2d 669 (Del. 1984).*

Transaction of business. — As the plaintiff in a patent infringement action failed to set out specific facts on the record indicating that allegedly infringing parts manufactured by the defendant were actually present in the District of Delaware, there was no factual basis for finding that the defendant had transacted business in Delaware indirectly through the stream of commerce. *Intel Corp. v. Silicon Storage Technology, Inc., 20 F. Supp. 2d 690 (1998).*

In an action alleging patent infringement, the defendant corporation's direct contacts with Delaware were sufficient to provide a statutory basis for the assertion of jurisdiction under subsection (c)(1) where the defendant offered to sell (and did sell) two allegedly infringing items in Delaware prior to the commencement of the action. *Intel Corp. v. Broadcom Corp., 167 F. Supp. 2d 692 (D. Del. 2001).*

The defendant pharmaceutical company was not subject to personal jurisdiction under subsection (c)(4) as it did not regularly conduct or solicit business in Delaware where: (1) it had no employees, local telephone listing, bank accounts, or real estate in Delaware; (2) it had a license to sell pharmaceutical products in Delaware, but was not registered with the Secretary of State to do business in Delaware; (3) it had one account manager for the existing Delaware customers who visited Delaware at most three times per year; and

(4) its sales in Delaware amounted to .13 percent of total revenue. *Merck & Co. v. Barr Labs., Inc., 179 F. Supp. 2d 368 (D. Del. 2002).*

Corporation, by itself, did not transact any business in the forum state, nor had it ever engaged in regular business or solicited business in the forum state, as its revenues derived from the forum state were not substantial — less than one percent of its total revenue; thus, long-arm jurisdiction did not exist under subsection (c) of this section. *Bell Helicopter Textron, Inc. v. C&C Helicopter Sales, Inc., 295 F. Supp. 2d 400 (D. Del. 2002).*

In determining whether "minimum contacts" exist, it is the quality and nature of the defendant's activities that control. *Waters v. Deutz Corp., 479 A.2d 273 (Del. 1984).*

Regular solicitation of business. — Making products available in a state through an agent does not amount to regularly soliciting business within the meaning of subsection (c)(4), especially where the agent had no contacts with the state other than a single shipment of goods to the plaintiff's local counsel and the shipment of a data book to a state resident. *Intel Corp. v. Silicon Storage Technology, Inc., 20 F. Supp. 2d 690 (1998).*

Minimum contacts tests. — For nonresident corporations with no direct contacts with the state, the scope of the long-arm statute is analyzed under either the agency theory or the stream of commerce theory. *ICT Pharms., Inc. v. Boehringer Ingelheim Pharms., Inc., 147 F. Supp. 2d 268 (D. Del. 2001).*

In an action alleging patent infringement, the defendant corporation had sufficient minimum contacts with Delaware to support the exercise of personal jurisdiction over it on the basis of the transaction of business within the state since the defendant failed to show that it did not have the resources to fairly litigate the case in Delaware and Delaware had an important interest in protecting the property rights of its citizens, of which the plaintiff was one. *Intel Corp. v. Broadcom Corp., 167 F. Supp. 2d 692 (D. Del. 2001).*

Stream of commerce theory applied to show minimum contacts. — Under the stream of commerce theory, a foreign manufacturer, through its distribution agreement with an American company, engaged in conduct necessary to establish minimum contacts with *Delaware. Boone v. Oy Partek Ab, 724 A.2d 1150 (Del. Super. Ct. 1997), aff'd, 707 A.2d 765 (Del. 1998).*

By selling its products outside Delaware for use in products sold by other manufacturers in Delaware, defendant did not exhibit an intent or purpose to serve the Delaware market and its sales outside Delaware, did not amount to the continuous and substantial activity that subdivision (c)(4) requires. *Siemens Aktiengesellschaft v. LG Semicon Co., 69 F. Supp. 2d 622 (D. Del. 1999).*

"Transactional" jurisdiction does not require regular course of doing business. — Where the court is asked to exercise "transactional" rather than "general" personal jurisdiction (where the claim arises out of a transaction entered into by defendant within the forum state), the absence of a regular course of doing business in Delaware is not controlling. *Speakman Co. v. Harper Buffing Mach. Co., 583 F. Supp. 273 (D. Del. 1984).*

Foreign corporation's status as an affiliate or subsidiary of another was insufficient to confer personal jurisdiction over it in the absence of allegations that it transacted any business or performed any type of work or service in *Delaware. Resource Ventures, Inc. v. Resources Mgt. Int'l, Inc., 42 F. Supp. 2d 423 (D. Del. 1999).*

Purposeful availment. — In a trademark infringement case, a United Kingdom credit card company whose contacts with Delaware arose out of two cardholders who subsequently moved to Delaware from the United Kingdom did not constitute "purposeful availment" of this forum sufficient to invoke jurisdiction over the United Kingdom company under the long arm statute. *Sears, Roebuck & Co. v. Sears, 744 F. Supp. 1289 (D. Del. 1990), supp. op., 744 F. Supp. 1297 (D. Del. 1990).*

The solicitation of business in Delaware in conjunction with the distribution of products in Delaware demonstrates purposeful availment of the protection of Delaware law; it is sufficient that the solicitations, shipment of products, or delivery of free samples are part of this business plan such that each may be considered an act of business within *Delaware. Thorn EMI N. Am., Inc. v. Micron Technology, Inc., 821 F. Supp. 272 (D. Del. 1993).*

Nonresident directors' acts of incorporating and dissolving a corporation were insufficient as contacts that would give rise to jurisdiction over the directors. *Resource Ventures, Inc. v. Resources Mgt. Int'l, Inc., 42 F. Supp. 2d 423 (D. Del. 1999).*

Gratuitous referral of unsolicited purchase order insufficient to support jurisdiction. — A gratuitous referral of an unsolicited purchase order to an affiliate corporation does not constitute a transaction in Delaware under subsection (c)(1) of this section or contracting to supply goods in Delaware under subsection (c)(2) of this section. *O'Neal v. Huxley Dev. Corp., 558 F. Supp. 462 (D. Del. 1983).*

Isolated phone calls do not constitute transacting business within state. — Although isolated phone calls arguably may be related to the constitutional due process question, such phone calls do not constitute a transaction of business within the State for purposes of subsection (c)(1) of this section. *Fischer v. Hilton, 549 F. Supp. 389 (D. Del. 1982).*

Filing of tax forms for a trust by a nonresident bank did not confer jurisdiction over the bank. — The filing of tax forms for a trust was insufficient to confer jurisdiction over a nonresident bank pursuant to subdivision (c)(2) of this section; a mere beneficial interest in a trust was insufficient to assert personal jurisdiction over a nonresident trustee and there was no allegation of the existence of a contract to supply services or things in the forum state. *Walker v. W. Mich. Nat'l Bank & Trust, 324 F. Supp. 2d 529 (D. Del. 2004).*

National advertising. — The placement of advertisements in national magazines is an act performed outside of the jurisdiction and, therefore, does not provide specific jurisdiction under subsection (c)(3). *Intel Corp. v. Silicon Storage Technology, Inc., 20 F. Supp. 2d 690 (1998).*

Billings and advertisements. — Advertising in widely distributed national magazines does not qualify as transact-

Personal Jurisdiction

ing business in *Delaware. Applied Biosystems, Inc. v. Cruachem, Ltd., 772 F. Supp. 1458 (D. Del. 1991).*

The mere mailing of an unknown number of promotional materials to two individuals in Delaware, whose only connection to the corporation arose in the United Kingdom, did not rise to the level of business activity necessary to confer personal jurisdiction on the corporation under subsection (c). *Sears, Roebuck & Co. v. Sears, 744 F. Supp. 1289 (D. Del. 1990),* supp. op., *744 F. Supp. 1297 (D. Del. 1990).*

A United Kingdom credit card company's advertising in international magazines did not qualify as transacting business in Delaware where the company did not seek out Delaware residents by placing the advertisements nor was the magazine required to distribute in Delaware and the advertising contract was entered into in the *United Kingdom. Sears, Roebuck & Co. v. Sears, 744 F. Supp. 1289 (D. Del. 1990),* supp. op., *744 F. Supp. 1297 (D. Del. 1990).*

General supervisory authority. — Subsection (c)(4) does not confer jurisdiction over a company vice president who has general supervisory authority over all of North America, and hence also over transactions in Delaware, without additional specific contacts; to do so would subject every corporate executive with authority over nationwide employees to jurisdiction in Delaware or any of the other fifty states. *Compaq Computer Corp. v. Packard Bell Elecs., Inc., 948 F. Supp. 338 (D. Del. 1996).*

Statements republished in Delaware press. — Defendant who made statements in New York was not "in Delaware" for purposes of subsection (c)(3), and the fact that the Delaware news media republished the offensive statements in Delaware did not alter this conclusion. *Compaq Computer Corp. v. Packard Bell Elecs., Inc., 948 F. Supp. 338 (D. Del. 1996).*

Statute provides for personal service upon nonresident defendant. — Although service under the Delaware long-arm statute may technically be characterized as "substituted," it operates as "personal" service upon a nonresident defendant, empowering the Delaware court to act in personam. *Equitable Trust Co. v. O'Neill, 420 A.2d 1196 (Del. Super. Ct. 1980).*

"Nonresident" construed. — The term "nonresident" refers to the status of the person at the time service is sought to be obtained regardless of whether such persons resided in Delaware at the time the cause of action arose. *Harmon v. Eudaily, 407 A.2d 232 (Del. Super. Ct. 1979); 420 A.2d 1175 (Del. 1980).*

Subsections (c)(1) and (c)(4) provided jurisdiction over a foreign manufacturer who passed title to goods outside of Delaware, based on its intent and purpose to serve the Delaware market and its implicit solicitation of business in the state. *Boone v. Oy Partek Ab, 724 A.2d 1150 (Del. Super. Ct. 1997),* aff'd, *707 A.2d 765 (Del. 1998).*

Subsection (c)(3) is a specific jurisdiction provision; in determining whether the exercise of specific jurisdiction is appropriate, the court must consider the relationship among the defendant, the litigation, and the forum. The relationship would support the exercise of jurisdiction if the defendant purposefully directs his conduct toward the distant forum. *Mobil Oil Corp. v. Advanced Envtl. Recycling Technologies, Inc., 833 F. Supp. 437 (D. Del. 1993).*

Personal jurisdiction over nonresident defendant does not depend upon physical presence of the defendant within the State; where a plaintiff's claims arise from acts or transactions committed by the nonresident defendant, personal jurisdiction over the defendant may be obtained if the acts or transactions have a substantial connection with the forum state. *Wilmington Supply Co. v. Worth Plumbing & Heating, Inc., 505 F. Supp. 777 (D. Del. 1980); O'Neal v. Huxley Dev. Corp., 558 F. Supp. 462 (D. Del. 1983).*

Section is applicable to residents who become nonresidents after the cause of action arose but before the commencement of the suit. *Eudaily v. Harmon, 420 A.2d 1175 (Del. 1980).*

When in personam jurisdiction is challenged by a motion to dismiss, the plaintiff has the burden to show a basis for long-arm jurisdiction; however, this burden is met by a threshold prima facie showing that jurisdiction is conferred by the statute. *Harmon v. Eudaily, 407 A.2d 232 (Del. Super. Ct. 1979); 420 A.2d 1175 (Del. 1980).*

When in personam jurisdiction is challenged by a motion to dismiss, the record is construed most strongly against the moving party. *Harmon v. Eudaily, 407 A.2d 232 (Del. Super. Ct. 1979); 420 A.2d 1175 (Del. 1980).*

This section can be retroactively applied to a cause of action which arose prior to its passage, and to a defendant who departed the State after the alleged tort. *Harmon v. Eudaily, 407 A.2d 232 (Del. Super. Ct. 1979); 420 A.2d 1175 (Del. 1980).*

The prevailing rule regarding single act statutes is that they are procedural in nature, affecting no substantive rights and that they may be applied retroactively. *Eudaily v. Harmon, 420 A.2d 1175 (Del. 1980).*

Consent to jurisdiction. — Valid consent to personal jurisdiction of and venire in "any state or federal court in Delaware" contained in Note and Subscription Agreement is sufficient to permit court to exercise personal jurisdiction over party giving such consent, even where such jurisdiction or venire might not properly exist otherwise. *Chrysler Capital Corp. v. Woehling, 663 F. Supp. 478 (D. Del. 1987).*

A forum selection clause in an agreement between plaintiff and defendant provided consent to jurisdiction of the Delaware courts. *Resource Ventures, Inc. v. Resources Mgt. Int'l, Inc., 42 F. Supp. 2d 423 (D. Del. 1999).*

"Doing business" provision of delaware long-arm statute is broad enough to permit the court of the last matrimonial domicile, in a support action, to acquire jurisdiction over a spouse who has left that domicile. *Prybolsky v. Prybolsky, 430 A.2d 804 (Del. Fam. Ct. 1981).*

"Arising from" language is sufficiently broad to encompass claims in contract, tort or quasi contract. *Moore v. Little Giant Indus., Inc., 513 F. Supp. 1043 (D. Del. 1981); 681 F.2d 807 (3d Cir. 1982).*

Relationship between "jurisdictional act" and cause of action required. — Without a relationship between the "jurisdictional act" and the subsequent cause of action, a court cannot use the "arising from" language of the Delaware long arm statute to exercise personal jurisdiction over a defendant. *Sears, Roebuck & Co. v. Sears PLC, 752 F. Supp. 1223 (D. Del. 1990).*

Personal jurisdiction may be asserted over a nonresident defendant on the basis of a single act related to Delaware if the resulting claim has its basis in the asserted transaction. *Jeffreys v. Exten, 784 F. Supp. 146 (D. Del. 1992).*

Allegations that nonresident defendant father committed a tort in the state by inducing daughter by fraud and intimidation to transfer assets from one trust to another was enough to confer personal jurisdiction over father pursuant to subdivision (c)(3) of this section. *Walker v. W. Mich. Nat'l Bank & Trust, 324 F. Supp. 2d 529 (D. Del. 2004).*

Term "tortious act" is not restricted to the technical definition of a tort, but includes any act committed in Delaware which involves a breach of duty to another and makes the one committing the act liable to respondent in damages. *Magid v. Marcal Paper Mills, Inc., 517 F. Supp. 1125 (D. Del. 1981).*

Acts constituted tortious injury cause of action. — Alleged improper disposal of hazardous wastes is a tortious injury for the purposes of subsection (c)(4). *United States v. Consolidated Rail Corp., 674 F. Supp. 138 (D. Del. 1987).*

Where the claim is one for tortious injury under subsection (c)(3), a single act or omission in the state in which the injury was caused will suffice to establish personal jurisdiction. *E.I. DuPont de Nemours & Co. v. Rhodia Fiber & Resin Intermediates, S.A.S., 197 F.R.D. 112 (D. Del. 2000).*

Tortious injury arising out of trade name violation is a cause of action arising from injuries specified in subsection (c) of this section. *ALTECH Indus., Inc. v. Al Tech Specialty Steel Corp., 528 F. Supp. 521 (D. Del. 1981).*

Each case of trade name or trademark infringement is a separate tort arising where the confusion to the customer occurs. *Sears, Roebuck & Co. v. Sears PLC, 752 F. Supp. 1223 (D. Del. 1990).*

Allegations that non-Delaware subsidiaries of foreign parent company violated plaintiff's trade name were unrelated to the forum state of Delaware, and an exercise of specific jurisdiction over the parent company, based on such out-of-state acts, would violate due process. *Sears, Roebuck & Co. v. Sears PLC, 752 F. Supp. 1223 (D. Del. 1990).*

Subsection (c) confers jurisdiction to maximum extent permitted by due process. *Afros S.P.A. v. Krauss-Maffei Corp., 624 F. Supp. 464 (D. Del. 1985).*

Subsection (c)(4) is "general" rather than a "specific" jurisdiction provision. *Colonial Mtg. Serv. Co. v. Aerenson, 603 F. Supp. 323 (D. Del. 1985).*

Alternative categories of activity described in subsection (c)(4) of this section indicate that either substantial volume of business or continuity of operation in Delaware is sufficient to establish jurisdiction. *Magid v. Marcal Paper Mills, Inc., 517 F. Supp. 1125 (D. Del. 1981).*

"Minimum contacts" test satisfied. — Where a German tractor manufacturer's subsidiary was the sole conduit through which the manufacturer's tractors entered the United States and 40 percent of those tractors entered the country through the port of Wilmington, it did not offend traditional notions of fair play and justice to require the manufacturer to defend itself in an action in *Delaware. Waters v. Deutz Corp., 479 A.2d 273 (Del. 1984).*

A nonresident company that contracted to supply a set of custom-made goods for use in Delaware and derived substantial revenue from these transactions established sufficient contacts with the forum to bring it within the jurisdiction of the Delaware courts. *Mendelson v. Delaware River & Bay Auth., 56 F. Supp. 2d 436 (D. Del. 1999).*

Where a software company acted in consort with licensees or customers to place products containing its softmodems into a nation-wide distribution network and, as a result, many of its products found their way to Delaware, sufficient contacts were established to subject it to personal jurisdiction under both the Delaware long-arm statute and the *Due Process Clause. Motorola Inc. v. PC-Tel, Inc., 58 F. Supp. 2d 349 (D. Del. 1999).*

Indirect shipment of products into state. — Sale of defendant's products outside Delaware for use in products sold by other manufacturers in Delaware was not sufficiently directed at residents of Delaware to constitute "transacting business" in Delaware for the purposes of subdivision (c)(1). *Siemens Aktiengesellschaft v. LG Semicon Co., 69 F. Supp. 2d 622 (D. Del. 1999).*

Nonresident trucking business. — Activities of a nonresident owner of a truck and his nonresident driver who passed through the state on interstate trips did not satisfy any of the jurisdictional thresholds of this section. *McKamey v. Vander Houten, 744 A.2d 529 (Del. Super. Ct. 2000).*

Designation by a nonresident trucking company of an agent to accept service of process, as required by the federal Motor Carrier Act *(49 U.S.C. § 13304*(a)), conferred personal jurisdiction over the company in this state for a tort action occurring in another state. *McKamey v. Vander Houten, 744 A.2d 529 (Del. Super. Ct. 2000).*

Derivation of "substantial revenue" as basis for jurisdiction. — The appropriate inquiry under subsection (c)(4) of this section is whether the nonresident, in absolute dollar amounts, "derives substantial revenue" from *Delaware. Hill v. Equitable Trust Co., 562 F. Supp. 1324 (D. Del. 1983).*

Sale of tractor-trailer does not satisfy substantial revenue requirement of subsection (c)(4) of this section. *Fischer v. Hilton, 549 F. Supp. 389 (D. Del. 1982).*

Persistent or regular course of conduct in state as determining factor. — Even if the nonresident's revenue derived from Delaware is insubstantial, subsection (c)(4) of this section provides for jurisdiction if the defendant's conduct is persistent or regular in Delaware, irrespective of the substantiality of the revenue derived from the *State. Hill v. Equitable Trust Co., 562 F. Supp. 1324 (D. Del. 1983).*

Resident's sporadic activities as an investing partner did not support a finding that a nonresident general partnership regularly did business in, or engaged in a persistent course of conduct, in *Delaware. HMG/Courtland Properties, Inc. v. Gray, 729 A.2d 300 (Del. Ch. 1999).*

Regular shipment of goods to single delaware wholesaler and continuous supervision of certain aspects of the retail sale of products in delaware are more than enough to meet the second requirement of subsection (c)(4) of this section. *Magid v. Marcal Paper Mills, Inc., 517 F. Supp. 1125 (D. Del. 1981).*

Both subsections (c)(2) and (c)(4) may be applied. — It is not inconsistent with the intent of the drafters to apply subsection (c)(2) of this section in a case in which subsection (c)(4) of this section might also have applied. *Moore v. Little Giant Indus., Inc., 513 F. Supp. 1043 (D. Del. 1981); 681 F.2d 807 (3d Cir. 1982).*

Section confers personal jurisdiction over manufacturer who ships goods into Delaware. Moore v. Little Giant Indus., Inc., 513 F. Supp. 1043 (D. Del. 1981); 681 F.2d 807 (3d Cir. 1982).

Where all activities involving product's design and manufacture took place in another state, plaintiff's suggestion that the "tortious act" should be deemed to have occurred where the injury took place would eviscerate the distinction between subsections (c)(3) and (c)(4) of the statute, and must therefore be rejected under generally accepted principles of statutory construction. *Moore v. Little Giant Indus., Inc., 513 F. Supp. 1043 (D. Del. 1981); 681 F.2d 807 (3d Cir. 1982).*

Age discrimination in employment act. — Where a plaintiff's complaint alleges that the employer, a foreign corporation, breached its legal duty under the Age Discrimination in Employment Act, 29 U.S.C. § 621 et seq., the plaintiff has alleged a tortious injury under this section. *Magid v. Marcal Paper Mills, Inc., 517 F. Supp. 1125 (D. Del. 1981).*

Shipment of goods into state by common carrier, without more, does not constitute "transaction of business." *Moore v. Little Giant Indus., Inc., 513 F. Supp. 1043 (D. Del. 1981); 681 F.2d 807 (3d Cir. 1982).*

Nexus between act and injury shown. — In light of the fact that the distribution of allegedly infringing products into Delaware also constituted a business transaction in Delaware, the requisite nexus between defendant's acts and the plaintiff's claimed injuries did in fact exist. *Thorn EMI N. Am., Inc. v. Micron Technology, Inc., 821 F. Supp. 272 (D. Del. 1993).*

Investors alleged facts sufficient to support personal jurisdiction under subdivisions (c)(1)-(2) of this section, to survive a motion to dismiss pursuant to *Fed. R. Civ. P. 12(b)(2)* because a company's wrongdoing arose out of the capitalization of a Delaware assignee, and the breach of contract directly resulted from that act. *CC Investors Corp. v. Raytheon Co., 219 F.R.D. 328 (D. Del. 2003).*

Minimum contacts between defendants and forum state are adequately established by the defendants' interest in, use and possession of property in Delaware, and service and notification met the standards of due process. *Equitable Trust Co. v. O'Neill, 420 A.2d 1196 (Del. Super. Ct. 1980).*

"Minimum contacts" test not satisfied. — Contacts of Massachusetts newspaper with the State were regular and persistent enough to find that jurisdiction existed under this section; however, such contacts were too minimal when examined in the context of Fourteenth Amendment Due Process guarantee to allow the court to maintain jurisdiction where the cause of action was unrelated to the forum-based activities. *United States v. Consolidated Rail Corp., 674 F. Supp. 138 (D. Del. 1987).*

By accepting the check drawn on Wilmington Trust as contemplated by the contract, defendant was not taking an action purposefully to make use of the privilege of conducting activities within Delaware nor did defendant do anything to create a substantial connection with *Delaware. Blue Ball Properties, Inc. v. McClain, 658 F. Supp. 1310 (D. Del. 1987).*

The unilateral activity of cardholders, in their change of residence and in default on their credit account, which established the only contact between their credit card company from the United Kingdom and the State of Delaware did not confer personal jurisdiction over the credit card company. *Sears, Roebuck & Co. v. Sears, 744 F. Supp. 1289 (D. Del. 1990), supp. op., 744 F. Supp. 1297 (D. Del. 1990).*

Where there was no evidence in the record that a magazine containing a potentially trademark-infringing advertisement was ever sold in Delaware, much less that the allegedly infringing company "sustained a promotional campaign" in the State, the advertisements did not establish minimum contacts among defendant, Delaware, and the plaintiff's complaint. *Sears, Roebuck & Co. v. Sears, 744 F. Supp. 1289 (D. Del. 1990), supp. op., 744 F. Supp. 1297 (D. Del. 1990).*

Chancery Court determined that the individual nonresident advisory board members who provided only ideas to Delaware partnership was not to be construed as having the ability to manage the partnership; these actions did not constitute contact with Delaware for the purposes of subsection (c) of this section and the Fourteenth Amendment of the U.S. Constitution, leading to dismissal of the claims under a Ch. Ct. R. 12(b)(2) motion to dismiss. *Werner v. Miller Tech. Mgmt., L.P., 831 A.2d 318 (Del. Ch. 2003).*

Although substituted service by certified mail under a provision applicable only to Family Court proceedings that resulted in a husband's having actual notice of his wife's proceeding seeking an order for protection from abuse satisfied statutory requirements, just as service in accordance with the long-arm statute would have, the court nevertheless determined that it lacked jurisdiction over the husband, because he lacked minimum contacts with Delaware; given that he was located in Ohio, the alleged acts of domestic violence all occurred in Ohio, and the wife sought the order only two days after fleeing to Delaware, so the proper course would be to seek an appropriate order in *Ohio. Long v. Long, 820 A.2d 506 (Del. Fam. Ct. 2003).*

Motion to dismiss for lack of personal jurisdiction under subsection (c) of this section, in a patent infringement claim brought by a French governmental agency, was granted where the Taiwanese corporation had no substantial or continuous contacts with the forum state because there were no operations, employees, property, or licenses to do business in the forum state; the district court had jurisdiction to hear the claim under *28 U.S.C. § 1338. Commissariat a L'Energie Atomique v. Chi Mei Optoelectronics Corp., 293 F. Supp. 2d 423 (D. Del. 2003).*

Contacts insufficient to establish jurisdiction under subsection (c)(4). — Mere selling of cars to Delaware dealers by nonresident defendant does not establish persistent course of conduct in the State or derivation of substantial revenue from the State necessary to justify assertion of personal jurisdiction under subsection (c)(4). *Finkbiner v. Mullins, 532 A.2d 609 (Del. Super. Ct. 1987).*

Mere fact that a general partner of a nonresident partnership had as its general partner a Delaware corporation did not meet the requirements of subsection (c)(4). *HMG/Courtland Properties, Inc. v. Gray, 729 A.2d 300 (Del. Ch. 1999).*

Activity outside of Delaware did not satisfy subsection (c)(4). HMG/Courtland Properties, Inc. v. Gray, 729 A.2d 300 (Del. Ch. 1999).

Execution of separation agreement in Delaware does not confer jurisdiction over nonresident parties. — Though petitioner and respondent, both presently residing in other states, had executed a separation agreement in Delaware in 1962 which provided that Delaware law would govern its provisions as the state of marital domicile, the Family Court lacked jurisdiction to determine liability for the support of their adult indigent nonresident child, either under the separation agreement or under the "poor person" statute (*13 Del. C. § 503*). *Helen B.M. v. Samuel F.D., 479 A.2d 852 (Del. Fam. Ct. 1984).*

Voluntary participation in conspiracy may be sufficient contact for the constitutional exercise of jurisdiction under the standard of *International Shoe Co. v. Washington, 326 U.S. 310, 66 S. Ct. 154, 90 L. Ed. 95 (1945)* where the participation is with knowledge of an act to be taken in furtherance of the conspiracy in this jurisdiction. *Istituto Bancario Italiano SpA v. Hunter Eng'g Co., 449 A.2d 210 (Del. 1982).*

To validly exercise jurisdiction under a conspiracy theory a court must find that a five-part test has been satisfied; the test requires: (1) there is the existence of a conspiracy to defraud; (2) the defendant must be a member of that conspiracy; (3) a substantial act or substantial effect in furtherance of the conspiracy occurs in Delaware; (4) the defendant knows or has reason to know of the act in Delaware or that acts outside Delaware would have an effect in Delaware; and (5) the act in or effect on Delaware is a direct and foreseeable result of the conduct in furtherance of the conspiracy—importantly, this test is a strict test that should be construed narrowly, and therefore, application of personal jurisdiction under the conspiracy theory requires factual proof of each enumerated element; without some showing that some act or effect occurred in Delaware, a plaintiff cannot satisfy the third element of the conspiracy theory test, and his claim for personal jurisdiction on this ground must fail. *Werner v. Miller Tech. Mgmt., L.P., 831 A.2d 318 (Del. Ch. 2003).*

Burden on plaintiff. — Plaintiff has the burden of alleging facts justifying the exercise of jurisdiction. *ALTECH Indus., Inc. v. Al Tech Specialty Steel Corp., 542 F. Supp. 53 (D. Del. 1982).*

Courts should not override plaintiff's choice of forum unless the balance of convenience is strongly in favor of the defendant. *Moore v. Little Giant Indus., Inc., 513 F. Supp. 1043 (D. Del. 1981); 681 F.2d 807 (3d Cir. 1982).*

Where the burden on each party, if required to litigate in the forum of the other party's choice, is comparable, the plaintiff's interest in obtaining convenient and effective relief prevails. *Moore v. Little Giant Indus., Inc., 513 F. Supp. 1043 (D. Del. 1981); 681 F.2d 807 (3d Cir. 1982).*

State's interest in providing forum for litigation is sufficient to support the exercise of jurisdiction and is compatible with the due process clause of the *Fourteenth Amendment. Moore v. Little Giant Indus., Inc., 513 F. Supp. 1043 (D. Del. 1981); 681 F.2d 807 (3d Cir. 1982).*

Allegations of complaint are accepted as true in considering the jurisdictional question. *ALTECH Indus., Inc. v. Al Tech Specialty Steel Corp., 542 F. Supp. 53 (D. Del. 1982).*

Presence in state. — Nonresident's activities in establishing and implementing an insured warranty program for its product was such a persistent course of conduct as to justify the assertion of personal jurisdiction. The warranties, signed in blank, may be viewed as a presence in this State from the moment they are delivered locally with authority to deliver them to ultimate purchasers. *LaNuova D & B, S.p.A. v. Bowe Co., 513 A.2d 764 (Del. 1986).*

In order for a defendant to commit an act in Delaware and be subject to subsection (c)(3), the defendant, or an agent of the defendant, must be present in Delaware when the deed is done. There is no such presence with regard to the mailing of billing statements, promotional material, or the placement of advertisements, from a United Kingdom company to individuals in Delaware. *Sears, Roebuck & Co. v. Sears, 744 F. Supp. 1289 (D. Del. 1990), supp. op., 744 F. Supp. 1297 (D. Del. 1990) Joint Stock Soc'y v. Heublein, Inc., 936 F. Supp. 177 (D. Del. 1996).*

Continuous course of conduct of purchasing supplies on open account from a plaintiff in this State over a long period of time has a substantial enough connection with this forum to make the exercise of jurisdiction over defendant reasonable and consequently, that defendant transacted business in this State within the meaning of this section. *Wilmington Supply Co. v. Worth Plumbing & Heating, Inc., 505 F. Supp. 777 (D. Del. 1980).*

Contacts sufficient where defendant solicited business and sent employees to plaintiff's delaware plant. — Where defendant solicited business in Delaware and where its employee made several trips to plaintiff's Delaware plant, the sufficiency of defendant's contacts within the state for purposes of personal jurisdiction cannot seriously be doubted. *Speakman Co. v. Harper Buffing Mach. Co., 583 F. Supp. 273 (D. Del. 1984).*

Regular and systematic conduct of business activities within state allows that state, without offending due process, to exercise jurisdiction over a cause of action that did not arise in that state and is unrelated to those activities. *Plumb v. Cottle, 492 F. Supp. 1330 (D. Del. 1980).*

Personal jurisdiction. — Personal jurisdiction may be asserted over a nonresident defendant on the basis of a single act related to Delaware if the resulting claim has its basis in the asserted transaction. *Jeffreys v. Exten, 784 F. Supp. 146 (D. Del. 1992).*

Where there is a prima facie showing that an individual personally engaged in substantial contacts in Delaware or with a nexus to Delaware having a clear relationship to the tortious injury alleged, this section permits the exercise of personal jurisdiction over that individual, whether or not

Personal Jurisdiction

the individual was acting in a corporate capacity. *State ex rel. Brady v. Preferred Florist Network, Inc.,* 791 A.2d 8 (Del. Ch. 2001). 07 (D. Del. Aug. 12, 2003).

This section authorizes jurisdiction over foreign manufacturer based on commercial marketing activities of its subsidiary in Delaware. *Waters v. Deutz Corp.,* 460 A.2d 1332 (Del. Super. Ct. 1983).

Section confers jurisdiction where open account maintained and substantial orders placed. — Personal jurisdiction over a nonresident defendant was proper where the defendant had an open-running credit account with a Delaware plaintiff and placed in excess of 500 orders with that plaintiff. *Wilmington Supply Co. v. Worth Plumbing & Heating, Inc.,* 505 F. Supp. 777 (D. Del. 1980).

Long-arm statute held inapplicable. — The Delaware long-arm statute would not apply where plaintiff alleged no facts showing that the defendants transacted any business or performed any work or service within Delaware, or that they contracted to supply services or things in Delaware; where the alleged acts leading to plaintiff's injuries occurred outside Delaware, and plaintiff did not show that defendants engaged in any regular course of business or other conduct within Delaware; and where plaintiff did not allege that defendants have any interest in real property in Delaware, or that they have contracted to insure any person or property within Delaware. *Martin v. Delaware Law Sch.,* 625 F. Supp. 1288 (D. Del. 1985), aff'd, 884 F.2d 1384 (3d Cir. 1989), cert. denied, 493 U.S 875, 110 S. Ct. 212, 107 L. Ed. 2d 165 (1989), 493 U.S. 966, 110 S. Ct. 411, 107 L. Ed. 2d 376 (1989).

A complaint alleging that defendant was the principal spokesperson for the co-defendant corporation, personally promoted the corporation's products throughout the United States via infomercials and other promotional materials, and owned 100% of the corporation's stock was insufficient to establish personal jurisdiction under subdivisions (c)(1) or (c)(3). *Tristrata Technology, Inc. v. Neoteric Cosmetics, Inc.,* 961 F. Supp. 686 (D. Del. 1997).

Jurisdiction not extended on basis of acts of alleged alter ego corporation. — In the absence of a showing of fraud or injustice, the Court will not extend jurisdiction over a corporation for the acts of its alleged alter ego corporation. *O'Neal v. Huxley Dev. Corp.,* 558 F. Supp. 462 (D. Del. 1983).

Personal jurisdiction over nonresident parent in action to modify support decree. — Where Delaware is the last marital domicile of the parties and the mother and children shall live there and the separation agreement, which was executed by nonresident father in another state, provides that Delaware law shall apply, there was sufficient transaction of business to confer personal jurisdiction over the nonresident. *King v. King,* 513 A.2d 773 (Del. Fam. Ct. 1985).

Wrong name. — Service effected upon Allison & Meyer does not reflect service on Meyer Associates and Meyer Associates had no standing to pursue its motion challenging the in personam jurisdiction over *Allison & Meyer. Consolidated Am. Ins. Co. v. Chiriboga,* 514 A.2d 1136 (Del. Super. Ct. 1986).

Incorporation as basis for jurisdiction. — By incorporating a subsidiary in Delaware, a corporation performs an act in the State sufficient to confer personal jurisdiction over it for causes of action related to that act of incorporation. Incorporating a subsidiary is also sufficient to satisfy due process for the court to exercise jurisdiction over claims arising out of that act, because it shows that the corporation "purposefully directed its activity" toward the State of Delaware to avail itself of *Delaware's laws. Sears, Roebuck & Co. v. Sears,* 744 F. Supp. 1297 (D. Del. 1990).

Jurisdiction over affiliated corporations. — It makes no difference for the purpose of long-arm statute jurisdiction that a parent-subsidiary relationship is not present; it is enough that the companies in question are wholly owned affiliates of the larger business group. *Wesley-Jessen Corp. v. Pilkington Visioncare, Inc.,* 863 F. Supp. 186 (D. Del. 1993).

The mere fact that a subsidiary company is a Delaware corporation is not sufficient to confer personal jurisdiction over the parent company, at least in the context of a contract action; where the subsidiary owned no assets in Delaware and the sale of its assets was negotiated and consummated outside of Delaware, there was no jurisdictional conduct to attribute to the parent company. *Ace & Co. v. Balfour Beatty PLC,* 148 F. Supp. 2d 418 (D. Del. 2001).

The foreign affiliate corporation could well expect to be haled into court in Delaware where it entered into an indemnity agreement with a Delaware corporation in which the foreign affiliate stated that it was aware of the use of the accused products, and that it agreed to defend and indemnify the Delaware company in any patent action. *Wesley-Jessen Corp. v. Pilkington Visioncare, Inc.,* 863 F. Supp. 186 (D. Del. 1993).

Jurisdiction over subsidiary. — Jurisdiction over a subsidiary does not necessarily give a court jurisdiction over the parent company. *Dentsply Int'l Inc. v. Pentron Corp.,* 648 F. Supp. 856 (D. Del. 1986).

Owning one subsidiary, where that subsidiary is not the alter-ego or general agent of the parent corporation, is not sufficient to establish substantial activities in the forum to bring the parent corporation under the State's long arm statute. *Sears, Roebuck & Co. v. Sears,* 744 F. Supp. 1297 (D. Del. 1990).

In order for an alien parent corporation's incorporation of its subsidiary in Delaware to constitute an act performed within the State, the cause of action would have to relate to corporate structure or in some way be based on Delaware corporate law. *Outokumpu Eng'g Enters. v. Kvaerner Enviropower, Inc.,* 685 A.2d 724 (Del. Super. Ct. 1996).

A breach of contract claim in no way relates to the organization of a subsidiary corporation in Delaware for purposes of affording jurisdiction pursuant to this section. *Outokumpu Eng'g Enters. v. Kvaerner Enviropower, Inc.,* 685 A.2d 724 (Del. Super. Ct. 1996).

The court would not exercise jurisdiction over a parent corporation based on acts of a subsidiary corporation under the alter ego theory where (1) there was no evidence of fraud in the corporate structure of the corporations, (2) there was no claim that the corporations had ignored the formalities of separate corporate status, and (3) the corporations maintained separate boards and finances. *C.R. Bard. Inc. v. Guidant Corp., 997 F. Supp. 556 (1998).*

The court would not exercise jurisdiction over a parent corporation based on acts of a subsidiary corporation under the agency theory where (1) the parent corporation was merely a holding company and did not engage in any production activities, and (2) the subsidiary corporation made its own decisions about day-to-day activities and designed, manufactured, marketed, and distributed the products at issue. *C.R. Bard. Inc. v. Guidant Corp., 997 F. Supp. 556 (1998).*

The court would not exercise jurisdiction over a parent corporation based on acts of a subsidiary corporation on the basis of a persistent course of conduct by the parent corporation in Delaware since (1) the use of parent corporation's name by the subsidiary corporation did not justify the exercise of jurisdiction over the parent corporation, and (2) the maintenance of a website, whereby the parent corporation provided the entire nation with general information about its company and product line, did not justify a finding that the parent corporation had engaged in a persistent course of conduct in *Delaware. C.R. Bard. Inc. v. Guidant Corp., 997 F. Supp. 556 (1998).*

Where plaintiff invokes this section as basis of jurisdiction in federal court, plaintiff must also show that that court is a proper venue. *Bernstein v. IDT Corp., 582 F. Supp. 1079 (D. Del. 1984).*

Where federal jurisdiction is based upon diversity of citizenship, in personam jurisdiction is determined in accordance with the law of the state in which the court sits, with federal law entering the picture only for the purpose of deciding whether a state's assertion of jurisdiction contravenes a constitutional guarantee. *Wilmington Supply Co. v. Worth Plumbing & Heating, Inc., 505 F. Supp. 777 (D. Del. 1980).*

Undelivered notice requirements not met. — The sending of a second notice by mail to nonresident defendants, more than 60 days after the nonreceipt of a first notice has been noted, does not constitute sufficient compliance with requirements of subsection (g) that such second notice be sent within seven days after the failure of the first notice has been noted. *Greenly v. Davis, 486 A.2d 669 (Del. 1984).*

Trustees of corporation. — In action based on a contract dispute, trustees of dissolved state corporation were subject to jurisdiction of courts sitting within the state under *10 Del.C. § 3104(c)(1)* because the character of their work or service within the state encompassed the resolution of contract disputes and their acceptance of the position of trustee had a sufficient nexus to the defense of claims against the trust to confer jurisdiction and the trustees had sufficient contacts with the state to satisfy due process requirements. *Rollins Envtl. Servs. (FS) Inc. v. Wright, 738 F. Supp. 150 (D. Del. 1990).*

Corporate officers. — Where the law protects a corporate officer from personal liability while acting on behalf of a corporation, it will not base personal jurisdiction over the officer in those same acts; however, in determining whether to disregard the corporate entity and the fiduciary shield defenses to personal jurisdiction over an employee-owner, the test is whether the employee-owner is really acting on behalf of another or is acting on behalf of a shell entity for own behalf. *Plummer & Co. Realtors v. Crisafi, 533 A.2d 1242 (Del. Super. Ct. 1987).*

Defendant's authorization of the filing of a complaint on behalf of a corporation and his presence in Delaware at a deposition in connection with the lawsuit together created sufficient contacts with Delaware to support personal jurisdiction under subsection (c)(3). *Mobil Oil Corp. v. Advanced Envtl. Recycling Technologies, Inc., 833 F. Supp. 437 (D. Del. 1993).*

Fiduciary shield doctrine. — The purpose of the fiduciary shield doctrine is to prohibit acts performed by an individual in the individual's capacity as a corporate employee from serving as the basis for personal jurisdiction over that individual. *Tristrata Technology, Inc. v. Neoteric Cosmetics, Inc., 961 F. Supp. 686 (D. Del. 1997).*

Acts taken in fiduciary capacity. — The fiduciary shield is an absolute bar to personal jurisdiction over a corporate employee; therefore, in interpreting subsection (c) to the maximum allowable limits of due process, the court will consider all forum related contacts of the defendants, even those taken in their fiduciary capacities. *Mobil Oil Corp. v. Advanced Envtl. Recycling Technologies, Inc., 833 F. Supp. 437 (D. Del. 1993).*

"Agent" construed. — It is true that a person who is controlled by a principal may be deemed an agent; however, the Delaware courts have made it clear that as used in this section, the word "agent" is not constricted to that one definition. *Wesley-Jessen Corp. v. Pilkington Visioncare, Inc., 863 F. Supp. 186 (D. Del. 1993).*

Delaware courts have found that an agency relationship may exist between corporate affiliates with close business ties and that a conspirator accepts all coconspirators as agents. *Wesley-Jessen Corp. v. Pilkington Visioncare, Inc., 863 F. Supp. 186 (D. Del. 1993).*

Agency relationship must be alleged in complaint. — While subdivision (c)(4) authorizes jurisdiction even when the tortious acts and the injury occurred outside of Delaware, the defendant or its agent must still be generally present in the state, and where the complaint failed to allege that the corporation, which was generally present in Delaware, should be considered the agent of the defendant, who was not generally present, personal jurisdiction could not be established. *Tristrata Technology, Inc. v. Neoteric Cosmetics, Inc., 961 F. Supp. 686 (D. Del. 1997).*

Presence of agent prevents tolling of statute of limitations. — Although defendant apartment owners were not in Delaware for three years, under this section they were always subject to personal service through a superintendent located at the apartments, so that the statute of limitations had not been tolled. *John J. Molitor, Inc. v. Feinberg, 258 A.2d 295 (Del. Super. Ct. 1969).*

Limited agency relationship. — No statute exists which permits Delaware courts to exercise personal jurisdiction over a nonresident principal based on the mere existence of a limited agency relationship with a Delaware corporation as agent. *Applied Biosystems, Inc. v. Cruachem, Ltd., 772 F. Supp. 1458 (D. Del. 1991).*

Personal Jurisdiction

Finding a limited agency relationship does not obviate the need to apply the Delaware long-arm statute. *Applied Biosystems, Inc. v. Cruachem, Ltd., 772 F. Supp. 1458 (D. Del. 1991).*

Under the agency theory, only acts by the agent which were directed by the principal may provide the basis for jurisdiction. *Applied Biosystems, Inc. v. Cruachem, Ltd., 772 F. Supp. 1458 (D. Del. 1991).*

Attorney as agent. — When a United Kingdom company retained an attorney in Delaware to assist in debt collection from one cardholder, the attorney became an agent of the company who could commit a tortious act and bring the company under the state long arm statute; however, in a trademark and tradename infringement suit there was no tortious conduct on the part of the attorney who used the alleged infringing name to collect the debt but there was no confusion on the part of the indebted as to whom the debt was owed. *Sears, Roebuck & Co. v. Sears, 744 F. Supp. 1289 (D. Del. 1990),* supp. op., *744 F. Supp. 1297 (D. Del. 1990).*

A corporate lawyer and his law firm may be sued in Delaware as to claims arising out of their actions in providing advice and services to a Delaware public corporation, its directors, and its managers regarding matters of Delaware corporate law when the lawyer and law firm: i) prepared and delivered to Delaware for filing a certificate amendment under challenge in the lawsuit; ii) advertise themselves as being able to provide coast-to-coast legal services and as experts in matters of corporate governance; iii) provided legal advice on a range of Delaware law matters at issue in the lawsuit; iv) undertook to direct the defense of the lawsuit; and v) face well-pled allegations of having aided and abetted the top managers of the corporation in breaching their fiduciary duties by entrenching and enriching themselves at the expense of the corporation and its public stockholders. *Sample v. Morgan, 935 A.2d 1046, 2007 Del. Ch. LEXIS 166 (November 27, 2007).* **[For the full text of this case opinion, please see the Appendix at the end of this Volume.]**

Long-arm statute satisfied. — Lawyer and law firm's conduct in arranging the filing of the certificate amendment in Delaware satisfies both *§ 3104(c)(1)* and *§ 3104(c)(3)* of Delaware's long-arm statute. That certificate amendment was integral to an alleged scheme by the top managers of the corporation to have issued to themselves at an unfair price a large bloc of voting stock that would secure their control over the corporation. Thus, the scheme not only involved an act in Delaware, it also involved an injury in Delaware to the Delaware corporation. *Sample v. Morgan, 935 A.2d 1046, 2007 Del. Ch. LEXIS 166 (November 27, 2007).* **[For the full text of this case opinion, please see the Appendix at the end of this Volume.]**

Motion to intervene in action pending in federal district court may be denied where it appears likely that the proposed intervenor may obtain jurisdiction over the parties in a Delaware court under this section. *Jet Traders Inv. Corp. v. Tekair, Ltd., 89 F.R.D. 560 (D. Del. 1981).*

Creation of subsidiary in Delaware was sufficient for jurisdiction. — Even though the complaint was based on violations of federal law, the Delaware court had jurisdiction to hear the claim because defendant company's act of creating a subsidiary in Delaware for the purposes of the merger was sufficient to establish personal jurisdiction. *Friedman v. Alsthom, 752 A.2d 544 (Del. Ch. 1999).*

DELAWARE CASE NOTES — UNREPORTED

Jurisdiction based upon contract. --Personal jurisdiction did not exist over a controlling stockholder, which was a foreign corporation, as a consent to jurisdiction clause in a lockup contract into which the stockholder entered did not provide a valid basis for the exercise of personal jurisdiction in a suit brought by the corporation for an alleged breach by the stockholder of its fiduciary duties; additionally, the controlling stockholder had no other substantive contacts with the *State of Delaware. Multi-Fineline Electronix v. WBL Corp., 2007 Del. Ch. LEXIS 21 (Del. Ch. Feb. 2, 2007).*

§ 3111. Actions against corporations; service of process

DELAWARE CASE NOTES — REPORTED

Foreign corporation "doing business" in Delaware subject to delaware jurisdiction. — Migration of a foreign corporation to a state other than that of its domicile, evidenced by the doing of business in that state, makes the foreign corporation for jurisdictional purposes as liable to suit as though it were a domestic corporation. *Klein v. Sunbeam Corp., 47 Del. 575, 95 A.2d 460 (1953).*

Ownership by a foreign corporation of stock in a domestic corporation does not constitute doing business in the state where the domestic corporation is located. *Mazzotti v. W.J. Rainey, Inc., 31 Del. Ch. 47, 77 A.2d 67 (1950).*

Foreign corporation suing on contract submits to delaware jurisdiction. — A foreign corporation can bring suit in Delaware upon a contract entered into in Delaware even though it has neglected to register under the statute, however, the permission thus granted an unregistered foreign corporation carries with it the obligation of submitting to suit in the courts of this State and to the laws of which it may resort for its protection. *Klein v. Sunbeam Corp., 47 Del. 575, 95 A.2d 460 (1953).*

Federal due process must be satisfied. — The requirements of federal due process are satisfied if at the time of the service of process the jurisdictional fact of doing business exists; the cause of action asserted need not necessarily arise from the jurisdictional fact. *Klein v. Sunbeam Corp., 47 Del. 575, 95 A.2d 460 (1953).*

Any agent of a foreign corporation may be served with process. — The language of this section shows that it was enacted to cover cases where a foreign corporation was a party to something which had taken place in Delaware and the foreign corporation did not have any agents within the State of the type who could normally be served with process; in such cases the section makes service on any agent of the foreign corporation sufficient. *Mazzotti v. W.J. Rainey, Inc., 31 Del. Ch. 47, 77 A.2d 67 (1950).*

Service on the vice-president of a corporation is valid if the vice-president is in Delaware, and no president or head officer is a resident of *Delaware. Klein v. Sunbeam Corp., 47 Del. 575, 95 A.2d 460 (1953).*

The phrase "any corporation" in this section authorizing service of process will be construed to include foreign corporations as well as domestic. *Klein v. Sunbeam Corp., 47 Del. 575, 95 A.2d 460 (1953).*

§ 3114. Service of process on nonresident directors, trustees, members of the governing body or officers of Delaware corporations

DELAWARE CASE NOTES — REPORTED

Enactment of section was legislative response to Shaffer v. Heitner, 433 U.S. 186, 97 S. Ct. 2569, 53 L. Ed. 2d 683 (1977). Pestolite, Inc. v. Cordura Corp., 449 A.2d 263 (Del. Super. Ct. 1982).

This section evidences legislative recognition of need for consistency and certainty in the interpretation and application of Delaware corporation law and the desirability of providing a definite forum in which shareholders can challenge the actions of corporate management without having to overcome certain procedural barriers which can be particularly onerous in the context of derivative litigation. *Armstrong v. Pomerance, 423 A.2d 174 (Del. 1980).*

Design of section. — This section is designed to protect Delaware's substantial interest in defining, regulating and enforcing the fiduciary obligations which directors of Delaware corporations owe to such corporations and the shareholders who elected them. *Pestolite, Inc. v. Cordura Corp., 449 A.2d 263 (Del. Super. Ct. 1982).*

Jurisdiction over nonresident director of insolvent corporation. — Fiduciary duties to creditors arise when one is able to establish the fact of insolvency; thus, this section provides a statutory basis for jurisdiction over a nonresident director of an insolvent corporation. *Geyer v. Ingersoll Publications Co., 621 A.2d 784 (Del. Ch. 1992).*

Delaware has significant and substantial interest in actively overseeing conduct of those owing fiduciary duties to shareholders of Delaware corporations and such interest far outweighs any burden to defendants, who have voluntarily associated themselves with such corporations by accepting directorships, in being required to submit to the jurisdiction of the courts. *Armstrong v. Pomerance, 423 A.2d 174 (Del. 1980).*

This section does not limit or affect any existing method of service of process. Bank of Am. Nat'l Trust & Sav. Ass'n v. GAC Properties Credit, Inc., 389 A.2d 1304 (Del. Ch. 1978).

Statute must authorize jurisdiction over nonresident defendant. — In order for a Delaware court to exercise personal jurisdiction over a nonresident defendant, a Delaware statute must authorize the obtaining of jurisdiction over that defendant. *Geyer v. Ingersoll Publications Co., 621 A.2d 784 (Del. Ch. 1992).*

Jurisdictional reach of section is no broader than necessary for its purpose. — The jurisdictional reach of this section is no broader than necessary to oversee, define, regulate and enforce the statutory and nonstatutory fiduciary duties and obligations of nonresident directors to their Delaware corporation and its shareholders. *Pestolite, Inc. v. Cordura Corp., 449 A.2d 263 (Del. Super. Ct. 1982).*

Jurisdiction authorized only where Delaware law is inextricably involved and where Delaware has strong interest in providing forum for redress of injuries inflicted upon or by a Delaware domiciliary, i.e., the Delaware corporation. The constitutional inquiry must focus on the quality and nature of the relationship between the defendants, the forum and the litigation. *Pestolite, Inc. v. Cordura Corp., 449 A.2d 263 (Del. Super. Ct. 1982).*

Jurisdiction not shown. — In a declaratory judgment action by an excess carrier to determine its liability under directors and officers policy, court could not exercise jurisdiction over nonresident directors of a Delaware corporation where the contract was not executed in Delaware and probably would not be interpreted under *Delaware law. Mt. Hawley Ins. Co. v. Jenny Craig, Inc., 668 A.2d 763 (Del. Super. Ct. 1995).*

This section was not applicable to confer jurisdiction on a nonresident director of a Delaware corporation because the plaintiff was not a stockholder of the defendant corporation. *Resource Ventures, Inc. v. Resources Mgt. Int'l, Inc., 42 F. Supp. 2d 423 (D. Del. 1999).*

This is an implied consent statute whereby a director, by accepting election or appointment as a director of a Delaware corporation, is deemed to have consented to personal jurisdiction being obtained in suits which relate to acts as a director. *Tabas v. Crosby, 444 A.2d 250 (Del. Ch. 1982).*

This section applies to trustees of liquidating trusts. Rollins Envtl. Servs. (FS) Inc. v. Wright, 738 F. Supp. 150 (D. Del. 1990).

Defendants who agreed to serve as trustees of a dissolved Delaware corporation which transferred all of its property to them are subject to the jurisdiction of courts sitting in Delaware and the exercise of such jurisdiction comports with due process requirements. *Rollins Envtl. Servs. (FS) Inc. v. Wright, 738 F. Supp. 150 (D. Del. 1990).*

When this section is applied to trustees of liquidating trusts, it is not necessary that a breach of fiduciary duty be alleged, but only that the dispute be "related to" the trustees' role as trustees. *Rollins Envtl. Servs. (FS) Inc. v. Wright, 738 F. Supp. 150 (D. Del. 1990).*

Mere status as director of Delaware corporation, standing alone, insufficient basis for jurisdiction. — Delaware does not have a significant and substantial interest in overseeing each and every tort and contract claim that may be asserted against the directors of a Delaware corporation no matter where the contract was made or performed or the tort occurred. In the absence of such substantial interest or legitimate state purpose, the mere

Personal Jurisdiction

status as director of a Delaware corporation, standing alone, is not a significant basis for an individual defendant to reasonably anticipate being haled into Delaware court. To rest jurisdiction solely on that basis would violate traditional notions of fair play and substantial justice. *Pestolite, Inc. v. Cordura Corp., 449 A.2d 263 (Del. Super. Ct. 1982).*

Section does not contemplate consent by director for acts not performed in capacity as director. *Istituto Bancario Italiano SpA v. Hunter Eng'g Co., 449 A.2d 210 (Del. 1982).*

Application of section is limited to actions directed against a director of a Delaware corporation for director's acts performed only in capacity as a director. *Hana Ranch, Inc. v. Lent, 424 A.2d 28 (Del. Ch. 1980); Pestolite, Inc. v. Cordura Corp., 449 A.2d 263 (Del. Super. Ct. 1982).*

This section is applicable only when a nonresident director is a necessary or proper party to an action brought by or on behalf of or against a Delaware corporation, or where the cause of action against the nonresident director of a Delaware corporation is based on such director's alleged breach of a fiduciary duty to the corporation and its stockholders in capacity as director. *Istituto Bancario Italiano SpA v. Hunter Eng'g Co., 428 A.2d 19 (Del. Ch. 1981),* modified on other grounds, *449 A.2d 210 (Del. 1982).*

Director's alter ego or agent. — Implied consent of a nonresident Delaware director to the jurisdiction of Delaware courts pursuant to this section may not be imputed to others who act as the director's alter ego or agent. *HMG/Courtland Properties, Inc. v. Gray, 729 A.2d 300 (Del. Ch. 1999).*

Valid cause of action against nonresident for acts within scope of directorship is a sine qua non to the successful assertion of a claim against such a nonresident in capacity as a stockholder. *Hana Ranch, Inc. v. Lent, 424 A.2d 28 (Del. Ch. 1980).*

Absence of substituted service upon personal representative of deceased director evinces a legislative intent not to apply this section to nonresident directors who die before suit is commenced or service of process is commenced. *Tabas v. Crosby, 444 A.2d 250 (Del. Ch. 1982).*

Actions in capacity as a director. — Merely selling shares of stock in a company on whose board one sits is not a directorial act within the meaning of the statute. But where the director is involved also in a negligent transfer of corporate control this section authorizes service of process. *Harris v. Carter, 582 A.2d 222 (Del. Ch. 1990).*

Where the directors of the corporate general partner owed duties to the partnership in the nature of a duty of loyalty, and that that duty was owed in the "capacity" of director of the corporation, service of process was duly authorized by this section with respect to those claims. *In re USACafes, 600 A.2d 43 (Del. Ch. 1991).*

Service upon nonresident elected as director of corporation prior to September 1, 1977, does not confer jurisdiction under subsection (a) of this section. *Armstrong v. Pomerance, 423 A.2d 174 (Del. 1980).*

Section applicable where wrong relates to continuing transaction commenced before section's effective date. — This section is applicable where the alleged wrong relates to a continuing transaction which commenced before the section's effective date but was only consummated after Sept. 1, 1977. *Kaufman v. Albin, 447 A.2d 761 (Del. Ch. 1982).*

Subsection (d) of this section is clear and unambiguous and there is therefore no room for judicial interpretation of it. *Bank of Am. Nat'l Trust & Sav. Ass'n v. GAC Properties Credit, Inc., 389 A.2d 1304 (Del. Ch. 1978).*

And language of subsection (d) specifically preserves right to use § 366 of this title in appropriate circumstances. *Bank of Am. Nat'l Trust & Sav. Ass'n v. GAC Properties Credit, Inc., 389 A.2d 1304 (Del. Ch. 1978).*

Creditor's rights actions. — Creditors' rights arise from contract and do not, by themselves, implicate the fiduciary duties officers owe their own corporations and shareholders so as to bring within the scope of this section a creditor's cause of action against the director of a corporation. *Prudential-Bache Sec. v. Franz Mfg. Co., 531 A.2d 953 (Del. Super. Ct. 1987).*

For due process purposes, there is no distinction between a stockholder derivative suit against a director, with respect to which jurisdiction under this section has been found constitutional, and a suit based on breach of fiduciary duty brought by corporate creditors. *Kidde Indus., Inc. v. Weaver Corp., 593 A.2d 563 (Del. Ch. 1991).*

This section provides jurisdiction over a defendant who is alleged to have violated a fiduciary duty that the defendant, as a director or trustee, owed to a creditor of the corporation upon dissolution. *Kidde Indus., Inc. v. Weaver Corp., 593 A.2d 563 (Del. Ch. 1991).*

Section 18-109 of title 6, like this section, is a consent statute, providing that when a nonresident accepts a position as a manager of a Delaware limited liability company the nonresident consents that service upon his statutory agent will amount to in personam jurisdiction over him for any claims covered by the statute. *Assist Stock Mgt. L.L.C. v. Rosheim, 753 A.2d 974 (Del. Ch. 2000).*

DELAWARE CASE NOTES — UNREPORTED

Individual creditors of a Delaware corporation that is either insolvent or in the zone of insolvency have no right to assert direct claims for breach of fiduciary duty against corporate directors. Creditors may nonetheless protect their interest by bringing derivative claims on behalf of the insolvent corporation or any other direct nonfiduciary claim that may be available for individual creditors. *N. Am. Catholic Educ. Programming Found., Inc. v. Gheewalla, 2007 Del. LEXIS 227 (May 18,. 2007).*

ESCHEAT

TITLE 12.
DECEDENTS' ESTATES AND FIDUCIARY RELATIONS

PART III.
DESCENT AND DISTRIBUTION; ESCHEAT

CHAPTER 11.
ESCHEATS

Subchapter IV.
Other Unclaimed Property

§ 1197.   Other property escheated.

DELAWARE CASE NOTES — REPORTED

State Escheator lacked standing to maintain action to escheat ownership interests in stock and accumulated dividends of Delaware corporation, which corporation was holding after last record owner, a non Delaware resident, denied ownership on assertion that stock was transferred to a party whose identity could not be determined. *Nellius v. Tampax, Inc., 394 A.2d 233 (Del. Ch. 1978).*

DELAWARE CHOICE OF LAW STATUTE

TITLE 6
COMMERCE AND TRADE

SUBTITLE II.
OTHER LAWS RELATING TO COMMERCE AND TRADE

CHAPTER 27.
CONTRACTS

Subchapter I.
General Provisions

§ 2708.   Choice of law

CASE NOTES — OTHER STATES

Missouri

Waiver. — While agreement contained a choice of law clause providing that Delaware law is to govern, both parties have cited only Missouri law in their arguments on the enforceability of the nonsolicitation clause. Parties to a contract may waive the provisions of their contract by their conduct. Therefore, by not citing any Delaware law on customer nonsolicitation clauses, the parties have waived the Delaware choice of law clause in the operating agreement. *JTL Consulting, L.L.C. v. Shanahan, 2006 Mo. App. LEXIS 92 (Jan. 24, 2006).*

UNIFORM COMMERCIAL CODE

TITLE 6
COMMERCE AND TRADE

SUBTITLE I.
UNIFORM COMMERCIAL CODE

ARTICLE 1.
GENERAL PROVISIONS

PART 1.
GENERAL PROVISIONS

§ 1-103.   Construction of Uniform Commercial Code to promote its purposes and poli-
            cies; applicability of supplemental principles of law.

DELAWARE CASE NOTES — REPORTED

Use of Official Comments to UCC. — While Delaware has not adopted the Official Comments prepared by
the drafters of the Uniform Commercial Code, these
Comments are nevertheless useful in interpreting the
Code as it is to be applied in Delaware, in view of the
Code's expressed purpose of making uniform the law
among the various jurisdictions. In re Copeland, 531 F.2d
1195 (3d Cir. 1976).

Applicability. — In Delaware, the UCC does not apply
to transactions entered into before June 30, 1967. The fact
that the alleged injury occurred after the enactment of the
UCC is irrelevant under Delaware law when the alleged

sale or delivery occurred before 1967. Elmer v. Tenneco
Resins, Inc., 698 F. Supp. 535 (D. Del. 1988).

**Common-law remedy not barred where UCC's
policy is furthered thereby.** — Where the UCC provides a comprehensive remedy for parties to a transaction,
a common-law action is barred, but a remedy in tort will
be recognized where the Code's policy is furthered by
"placing the risk of loss on the party most able to minimize
that risk." Yahn & McDonnell, Inc. v. Farmers Bank, 708
F.2d 104 (3d Cir. 1983).

**UCC does not bar claim based on theory of negli-
gence.** Yahn & McDonnell, Inc. v. Farmers Bank, 708
F.2d 104 (3d Cir. 1983).

PART 2.
GENERAL DEFINITIONS AND PRINCIPLES OF INTERPRETATION

§ 1-201.   General definitions.

CASE NOTES — REPORTED

**"Good faith" definition applies to § 9-307 of this
title.** — For the purposes of § 9-307 of this title, "good
faith" is defined in subdivision (19) [now (20)] of this
section. Sherrock v. Commercial Credit Corp., 290 A.2d
648 (Del. 1972).

Conspicuousness. — Warranty disclaimer did not
meet the statutory requirement that the disclaimer must
be conspicuous. Norman Gershman's Things to Wear, Inc.
v. Mercedes-Benz of N. Am., 558 A.2d 1066 (Del. Super.
Ct. 1989), aff'd, 596 A.2d 1358 (Del. 1991).

Delivery — Article 8, as it existed in 1979, did not
displace the doctrine of constructive delivery that was part

of the Delaware common law. Kallop v. McAllister, 678
A.2d 526 (Del. 1996).

"Notice." — Creditor failed to meet its burden of demonstrating that it fully complied with the reasonable
notice requirements of this section and former § § 9-504(3)
and 9-506 of this title where creditor sent notice to debtors
at the wrong street address, a former residence, and sent
notice to their current address with the wrong zip code.
Friendly Fin. Corp. v. Bovee, 702 A.2d 1225 (Del. 1997).

Burden on creditor to show notice sent. — While
Article 9 did not require a creditor to show that the debtor
received actual notice, a creditor seeking a deficiency

judgment after sale had the burden to establish that it complied with subsection (38) [now (36)] of this section and former § 9-504(3) of this Title. Friendly Fin. Corp. v. Bovee, 702 A.2d 1225 (Del. 1997).

Punitive damages. — Although the UCC imposes a duty of good faith and fair dealing, punitive damages generally are not awarded for a breach of this duty. E.I. DuPont de Nemours & Co. v. Pressman, 679 A.2d 436 (Del. 1996).

§ 1-202.   Notice; knowledge.

DELAWARE CASE NOTES — REPORTED

"Good faith" definition applied to former § 9-307 of this title. — For the purposes of former § 9-307 of this title, "good faith" was defined in subdivision (19) of this section (see now 6 Del.C. § 1-201(20)). Sherrock v. Commercial Credit Corp., 290 A.2d 648 (Del. 1972).

Conspicuousness. — Warranty disclaimer did not meet the statutory requirement that the disclaimer must be conspicuous. Norman Gershman's Things to Wear, Inc. v. Mercedes-Benz of N. Am., 558 A.2d 1066 (Del. Super. Ct. 1989), aff'd, 596 A.2d 1358 (Del. 1991).

Delivery — Article 8, as it existed in 1979, did not displace the doctrine of constructive delivery that was part of the Delaware common law. Kallop v. McAllister, 678 A.2d 526 (Del. 1996).

"Notice." — Creditor failed to meet its burden of demonstrating that it fully complied with the reasonable notice requirements of this section and former § § 9-504(3) and 9-506 of this title where creditor sent notice to debtors at the wrong street address, a former residence, and sent notice to their current address with the wrong zip code. Friendly Fin. Corp. v. Bovee, 702 A.2d 1225 (Del. 1997).

Burden on creditor to show notice sent. — While Article 9 did not require a creditor to show that the debtor received actual notice, a creditor seeking a deficiency judgment after sale had the burden to establish that it complied with subsection (38) of this section (see now 6 Del.C. § 1-201(36)) and former § 9-504(3) of this title. Friendly Fin. Corp. v. Bovee, 702 A.2d 1225 (Del. 1997).

Punitive damages. — Although the UCC imposes a duty of good faith and fair dealing, punitive damages generally are not awarded for a breach of this duty. E.I. DuPont de Nemours & Co. v. Pressman, 679 A.2d 436 (Del. 1996).

§ 1-203.   Lease distinguished from security interest.

DELAWARE CASE NOTES — REPORTED

Exercise of an express power in a written contract may constitute a breach of the duty of good faith if the external circumstances demonstrate, for example, overreaching or undue interference in the other party's performance, and the presence of important business consideration does not automatically insulate a party from a finding of bad faith. Coca-Cola Bottling Co. v. Coca-Cola Co., 668 F. Supp. 906 (D. Del. 1987).

Burden of proof. — The buyer bore the burden of proving a breach of the covenant of good faith in a contract with a supplier/manufacturer who refused to accept the return of unsold inventory. Gates Eng'g Co. v. Standard Roofing, Inc. (In re GEC Indus., Inc.), 123 Bankr. 714 (Bankr. D. Del. 1991).

PART 3.
TERRITORIAL APPLICABILITY AND GENERAL RULES

§ 1-301.   Territorial applicability; parties' power to choose applicable law.

DELAWARE CASE NOTES — REPORTED

Subsection (1) allows for a choice of law by the parties to a sales transaction. Falcon Tankers, Inc. v. Litton Sys., 300 A.2d 231 (Del. Super. Ct. 1972).

Law applicable in sequestration of a security. — Where an alleged interest in a security arises in a foreign jurisdiction, the law of that jurisdiction governs the existence of the interest and presumably its nature, and the law of Delaware determines whether the interest is one which may be sequestered. Baker v. Gotz, 387 F. Supp. 1381 (D. Del. 1975); 523 F.2d 1050 (3d Cir. 1975).

§ 1-303.   Course of performance, course of dealing, and usage of trade.

DELAWARE CASE NOTES — REPORTED

Usage of trade. — Buyer failed to show by a preponderance of the evidence that a usage of trade existed allowing it to return its inventory to the manufacturer where the buyer itself had a return policy with respect to its customers that allowed it to refuse returns based on factors similar to those the manufacturer employed. Gates Eng'g Co. v. Standard Roofing, Inc. (In re GEC Indus., Inc.), 123 Bankr. 714 (Bankr. D. Del. 1991).

§ 1-304.   Obligation of good faith.

DELAWARE CASE NOTES — REPORTED

Exercise of an express power in a written contract may constitute a breach of the duty of good faith if the external circumstances demonstrate, for example, overreaching or undue interference in the other party's performance, and the presence of important business consideration does not automatically insulate a party from a finding of bad faith. Coca-Cola Bottling Co. v. Coca-Cola Co., 668 F. Supp. 906 (D. Del. 1987).

Burden of proof. — The buyer bore the burden of proving a breach of the covenant of good faith in a contract with a supplier/manufacturer who refused to accept the return of unsold inventory. Gates Eng'g Co. v. Standard Roofing, Inc. (In re GEC Indus., Inc.), 123 Bankr. 714 (Bankr. D. Del. 1991).

§ 1-305.   Remedies to be liberally administered.

DELAWARE CASE NOTES — REPORTED

Diminution in business value. — Diminution in business value is a type of consequential damages and therefore may not be awarded under this title. True N. Composites, LLC v. Trinity Indus., Inc., 191 F. Supp. 2d 484 (D. Del. 2002).

§ 1-308.   Performance or acceptance under reservation of rights.

DELAWARE CASE NOTES — REPORTED

Accord and satisfaction. — The adoption of this section by the Delaware General Assembly did not displace the common law doctrine of accord and satisfaction; it remains a part of the law. Acierno v. Worthy Bros. Pipeline Corp., 656 A.2d 1085 (Del. 1995).

ARTICLE 8.
INVESTMENT SECURITIES

PART 1.
SHORT TITLE AND GENERAL MATTERS

§ 8-102.   Definitions

DELAWARE CASE NOTES — REPORTED

Public trading not essential for investment security. — The fact that notes were never publicly traded is not important since all this section requires for an instrument to qualify as an investment security is that it be of a type commonly dealt in upon securities exchanges or markets. *Baker v. Gotz, 387 F. Supp. 1381 (D. Del. 1975); 523 F.2d 1050 (3d Cir. 1975).*

PART 3
TRANSFER OF CERTIFICATED AND UNCERTIFICATED SECURITIES

§ 8-301.   Delivery

DELAWARE CASE NOTES — REPORTED

Transfer to person designated by purchaser. — Relinquishment shares employed as collateral to an agent to hold as an accommodation for both parties would constitute a transfer under this section as it existed prior to the 1997 revision of Article 8. *Haft v. Haft, 671 A.2d 413 (Del. Ch. 1995).*

Conditions of possession. — Although there was a question whether law firm represented seller alone when it took possession of the shares of stock, or whether it represented both purchaser and seller, the record did not create a triable issue on the assertion that law firm never took possession of the collateral on behalf of the seller, and thus summary judgment was appropriate. *Haft v. Haft, 671 A.2d 413 (Del. Ch. 1995).*

Constructive delivery. — Transfer of a share of stock held valid even though only a constructive delivery of the share took place. *Kallop v. McAllister, 678 A.2d 526 (Del. 1996).*

This article, as it existed in 1979, did not displace the doctrine of constructive delivery that is part of the Delaware common law. *Kallop v. McAllister, 678 A.2d 526 (Del. 1996).*

UCC

PART 4
REGISTRATION

§ 8-401.   Duty of issuer to register transfer

DELAWARE CASE NOTES — REPORTED

"Register the transfer" construed. – It is reasonable to construe the term "register the transfer," to include those ministerial acts that normally accompany such registration, including, where applicable, the issuance of a new certificate. *Bender v. Memory Metals, Inc., 514 A.2d 1109 (Del. Ch. 1986).*

Liability of corporation under duty to register transfer. – Where a corporation is under a duty to "register a transfer of a security" it is also liable in damages to the person presenting it for registration "for loss resulting from any unreasonable delay in registration or from failure or refusal to register the transfer." *Reeves v. Transport Data Communications, Inc., 318 A.2d 147 (Del. Ch. 1974).*

Basis required for refusal to register. – A refusal to register a transfer of stock must be based on a legitimate ground supported by some credible evidence. *Loretto Literary & Benevolent Inst. v. Blue Diamond Coal Co., 444 A.2d 256 (Del. Ch. 1982).*

Defense by issuer. – The apparently unconditional right of a holder of a valid stock certificate to require a transfer of the stock on the company's books to the holder and the issuance of a new certificate is, in Delaware,

subject to a possible defense by the issuer: That the shares were adjudicated lost, stolen or destroyed, and the bond required under *8 Del. C. § 168* and which was fixed in that adjudication would be insufficient fully to cover the cost, somehow measured, of the prospective double issuance. *Castro v. ITT Corp., 598 A.2d 674 (Del. Ch. 1991).*

Actions which may be maintained individually. – Actions based on a wrongful refusal to issue a stock certificate or a refusal to recognize a proper transfer of stock may be maintained individually by stockholders rather than derivatively. *Reeves v. Transport Data Communications, Inc., 318 A.2d 147 (Del. Ch. 1974).*

Election of remedies upon failure to register. – When an issuer fails to register a transfer, as required by this section, a plaintiff must elect a remedy, whether to proceed at law for the value of the stock in the law courts, or to proceed in equity seeking to compel recordation and ancillary damages. *Loretto Literary & Benevolent Inst. v. Blue Diamond Coal Co., 444 A.2d 256 (Del. Ch. 1982).*

Attorneys' fees are not generally a cognizable loss under subsection (b) of this section. *Loretto Literary & Benevolent Inst. v. Blue Diamond Coal Co., 444 A.2d 256 (Del. Ch. 1982).*

§ 8-404.   Wrongful registration

DELAWARE CASE NOTES — REPORTED

Suit for delivery of new certificates after originals submitted for transfer. – The Chancery Court has subject-matter jurisdiction of a claim for delivery of new stock certificates based upon improper indorsement of the original certificates even when a bona fide purchaser has

submitted the original securities for transfer, and the plaintiff in such case is not limited to an action at law for money damages. *Scott v. Ametek, Inc., 277 A.2d 714 (Del. Ch. 1971).*

§ 8-405.   Replacement of lost, destroyed, or wrongfully taken security certificate

DELAWARE CASE NOTES — REPORTED

Evidence of ownership as prerequisite for replacement certificates. – Requiring independent credible evidence of beneficial ownership as a prerequisite to the issuance of replacement certificates is a reasonable requirement under this section. *Merrill Lynch Pierce Fenner & Smith, Inc. v. North European Oil Royalty Trust, 490 A.2d 558 (Del. 1985).*

Suit for delivery of new certificates after originals submitted for transfer. – The Chancery Court has subject-matter jurisdiction of a claim for delivery of new stock certificates based upon improper indorsement of the original certificates even when a bona fide purchaser has submitted the original securities for transfer, and the

plaintiff in such case is not limited to an action at law for money damages. *Scott v. Ametek, Inc., 277 A.2d 714 (Del. Ch. 1971).*

Defense by issuer. – The apparently unconditional right of a holder of a valid stock certificate to require a transfer of the stock on the company's books to holder and the issuance of a new certificate is, in Delaware, subject to a possible defense by the issuer: That the shares were adjudicated lost, stolen or destroyed, and the bond required under *8 Del. C. § 168* and which was fixed in that adjudication would be insufficient fully to cover the cost, somehow measured, of the prospective double issuance. *Castro v. ITT Corp., 598 A.2d 674 (Del. Ch. 1991).*

ARTICLE 9
SECURED TRANSACTIONS

PART 1
GENERAL PROVISIONS

SUBPART 1
SHORT TITLE, DEFINITIONS, AND GENERAL CONCEPTS

§ 9-101.   Short title

DELAWARE CASE NOTES — REPORTED

Effect of article. – This article simplifies pre-Code secured financing by providing for the unitary treatment of all security arrangements. *In re Copeland, 531 F.2d 1195 (3d Cir. 1976)* (decided under prior law).

This article eliminates many of the antiquated distinctions between various security devices in favor of a single

"security interest," and a single set of rules regarding creation and perfection, designed to govern any transaction (regardless of its form) which is intended to create a security interest in personal property or fixtures including goods, documents and instruments. *In re Copeland, 531 F.2d 1195 (3d Cir. 1976)* (decided under prior law).

§ 9-102.   Definitions and index of definitions

DELAWARE CASE NOTES — REPORTED

"Account" includes accounts receivable. – "Account" is defined as "any right to payment for goods sold or leased or for services rendered which is not evidenced by an instrument or chattel paper," including accounts receivable in this definition. *Bramble Transp., Inc. v. Sam Senter Sales, Inc., 294 A.2d 97 (Del. Super. Ct. 1971)* (decided under prior law).

Description of collateral in financing statement. – Where a financing statement set forth a lien on "equipment" and the debtor bought the equipment for the business of farming, a description of the collateral in the financing statement was sufficiently informative as to constitute notice as was required by former § 9-402(1), in that it indicated the "types" of collateral by which the security agreement was secured. *Maryland Nat'l Bank v. Porter-Way Harvester Mfg. Co., 300 A.2d 8 (Del. 1972)* (decided under prior law).

"Debtor." – Where a car owner and family members alleged that a repossessor harassed them, the seller was

entitled to summary judgment as to the family members' Uniform Commercial Code claims because, inter alia, they were not "debtors" for purposes of recovering for violations of U.C.C. Article 9. *Robertson v. Horton Bros. Recovery, Inc., — F. Supp. 2d —, 2005 U.S. Dist. LEXIS 5256 (D. Del. Mar. 31, 2005).*

Default arrangement for pledgee as security agreement. – Agreements which include the right of the pledgee to sell stock upon default and use the proceeds in payment of the debt, constitute a security agreement. *In re Copeland, 391 F. Supp. 134 (D. Del. 1975)* (decided under prior law); *531 F.2d 1195 (3d Cir. 1976)* (decided under prior law).

Prerequisite to a security interest is a security agreement. *In re Copeland, 391 F. Supp. 134 (D. Del. 1975) (decided under prior law); 531 F.2d 1195 (3d Cir. 1976) (decided under prior law).*

§ 9-108.   Sufficiency of description

DELAWARE CASE NOTES — REPORTED

A financing statement should have been read in the context of the provisions of former § 9-110, which shed light upon an adequate description under Article 9.

Maryland Nat'l Bank v. Porter-Way Harvester Mfg. Co., 300 A.2d 8 (Del. 1972) (decided under prior law).

SUBPART 2
APPLICABILITY OF ARTICLE

§ 9-109.　　Scope

DELAWARE CASE NOTES — REPORTED

Determination of whether agreement is lease or secured transaction within meaning of this article requires the court to look beyond the face of the agreement and view the nature of the transaction in its entirety. *Computer Sciences Corp. v. Sci-Tek, Inc., 367 A.2d 658 (Del. Super. Ct. 1976)* (decided under prior law).

Lease was one intended as security, and secured party, not having complied with the terms of the Delaware Uniform Commercial Code, did not have a perfected security interest. *Telmark, Inc. v. Schwartz (In re Johnson), 1 Bankr. 689 (Bankr. D. Del. 1979)* (decided under prior law).

Creation of security interest shown. – Intent required for the creation of a security interest held established where contract contained a paragraph entitled "Collateral" in which it stated that the note "shall be secured solely by the collateral, the Shares." *Haft v. Haft, 671 A.2d 413 (Del. Ch. 1995)* (decided under prior law).

Purpose of excluding assignments of accounts for collection. – The exclusion of subdivision (f) of former § 9-105, which stated that this article did not apply "to . . . an assignment of accounts . . . which is for the purpose of collection only . . .," was for the purpose of removing from the Uniform Commercial Code assignments of a noncommercial nature such as those to a collection agency for the sole purpose of facilitating collection of the debt. It did not purport to exclude transactions generally considered "financing in nature." *Bramble Transp., Inc. v. Sam Senter Sales, Inc., 294 A.2d 97 (Del. Super. Ct. 1971)* (decided under prior law); *294 A.2d 104 (Del. 1972)* (decided under prior law).

PART 2
EFFECTIVENESS OF SECURITY AGREEMENT; ATTACHMENT OF SECURITY INTEREST; RIGHTS OF PARTIES TO SECURITY AGREEMENT

SUBPART 1
EFFECTIVENESS AND ATTACHMENT

§ 9-202.　　Title to collateral immaterial

DELAWARE CASE NOTES — REPORTED

Location of title to collateral is immaterial with respect to the rights and obligations of the parties to a security transaction. *In re Copeland, 531 F.2d 1195 (3d Cir. 1976)* (decided under prior law).

SUBPART 2
RIGHTS AND DUTIES

§ 9-207.　　Rights and duties of secured party having possession or control of collateral

DELAWARE CASE NOTES — REPORTED

Failure to exercise reasonable care. – Defendants failed to carry their burden of proof that plaintiff failed to exercise reasonable care in the custody and preservation of the collateral in plaintiff's possession. *FDIC v. Blue Rock Shopping Ctr., Inc., 676 F. Supp. 552 (D. Del. 1987)* (decided under prior law); *849 F.2d 599, 600 (3d Cir. 1988)* (decided under prior law).

PART 3
PERFECTION AND PRIORITY

SUBPART 1
LAW GOVERNING PERFECTION AND PRIORITY

§ 9-301. Law governing perfection and priority of security interests

DELAWARE CASE NOTES — REPORTED

Florida law on validity applies where assignors' offices are located there. – This provision dictates that Florida law applies to determine the validity of assignments where the offices of the assignors are located in Florida. The Florida legislature adopted the Uniform Commercial Code. Inasmuch as the Florida choice of laws provision is the same as that found in the Delaware version of the Uniform Commercial Code, the court will turn to Florida law to determine the validity of the assignments. *Bramble Transp., Inc. v. Sam Senter Sales, Inc., 294 A.2d 97 (Del. Super. Ct. 1971)* (decided under prior law); *294 A.2d 104 (Del. 1972)* (decided under prior law).

SUBPART 2
PERFECTION

§ 9-308. When security interest or agricultural lien is perfected; continuity of perfection

DELAWARE CASE NOTES — REPORTED

Interest becomes attached when property becomes subject to security interest. *In re Copeland, 391 F. Supp. 134 (D. Del. 1975)* (decided under prior law); *531 F.2d 1195 (3d Cir. 1976)* (decided under prior law).

But security interest in personal property attaches only when parties agree that it shall attach. *In re Copeland, 391 F. Supp. 134 (D. Del. 1975)* (decided under prior law); *531 F.2d 1195 (3d Cir. 1976)* (decided under prior law).

§ 9-309. Security interest perfected upon attachment

DELAWARE CASE NOTES — REPORTED

Perfection of interest in automobile. – Claimant did not show that claimant properly perfected claimant's purchase money security interest in an automobile where claimant relied only on possession of the vehicle; at most, the claimant had an unperfected interest in the car, only enforceable against the owner. *United States v. One 1987 Cadillac DeVille, 774 F. Supp. 221 (D. Del. 1991)* (decided under prior law).

§ 9-312. Perfection of security interests in chattel paper, deposit accounts, documents, goods covered by documents, instruments, investment property, letter-of-credit rights, and money; perfection by permissive filing; temporary perfection without filing or transfer of possession

DELAWARE CASE NOTES — REPORTED

Secured party can perfect a security interest through possession of a bailee. – Former § 9-305 (now § 9-313) of this title modified the rule of former § 9-304 that a security interest in instruments could only be perfected by the secured party's taking possession, by permitting a secured party to perfect a security interest through the possession of a bailee. *In re Copeland, 531 F.2d 1195 (3d Cir. 1976)* (decided under prior law).

§ 9-313. When possession by or delivery to secured party perfects security interest without filing

DELAWARE CASE NOTES — REPORTED

Secured party can perfect a security interest through possession of a bailee. – Former § 9-305 modified the rule of former § 9-304 of this title (now § 9-312) that a security interest in instruments could only be perfected by the secured party's taking possession, by permitting a secured party to perfect a security interest through the possession of a bailee. *In re Copeland, 531 F.2d 1195 (3d Cir. 1976)* (decided under prior law).

Possession by debtor insufficient. – Where the UCC requires perfection by possession of the secured party or the secured party's bailee, possession by the debtor or an individual closely associated with the debtor is not sufficient to alert prospective creditors of the possibility that the debtor's property is encumbered. *In re Copeland, 531 F.2d 1195 (3d Cir. 1976)* (decided under prior law).

Perfection by possession of motor vehicle. – While it is true Delaware law provides that a lien can be perfected against a motor vehicle only by noting its existence on the certificate of title, Delaware law also provides that possession of the collateral by a secured party perfects a

security interest even though there had been no prior perfection because there had been no prior filing; this perfection does not relate back to the time the security interest was created under the agreement but attaches at the time of repossession, and continues so long as possession is retained. *In re Boogaard, 89 Bankr. 397 (Bankr. D. Del. 1988)* (decided under prior law).

§ 9-315. Secured party's rights on disposition of collateral and in proceeds

Sale of inventory to purchasers. – A secured party with a security interest in the inventory of a retail seller may be assumed to have authorized the sale of inventory to purchasers. *GECC v. Gayl (In re Darling's Homes, Inc.), 46 Bankr. 370 (Bankr. D. Del. 1985)* (decided under prior law).

Although the terms of a security agreement are effective only between the parties to the agreement, they are effective against purchasers of the collateral in the context of protecting a security interest. *GECC v. Gayl (In re Darling's Homes, Inc.), 46 Bankr. 370 (Bankr. D. Del. 1985)* (decided under prior law).

The failure of a condition subsequent to the sale of collateral, such as a requirement that the proceeds must be paid to the secured party, does not prevent the authorization to sell from terminating the security interest at the time of the sale. *GECC v. Gayl (In re Darling's Homes, Inc.), 46 Bankr. 370 (Bankr. D. Del. 1985)* (decided under prior law).

Proceeds of insurance payment to cover loss of collateral payable to bankruptcy estate. – Where debtor-in-possession purchased an insurance policy, which was issued to the debtor, to cover bankruptcy estate assets after filing for bankruptcy, proceeds of an insurance payment to cover the loss of a combine destroyed by fire were, in fact, payable to the bankruptcy estate, which was the real beneficiary of the policy, as the debtor-in-possession was simply performing a duty to preserve the estate when the debtor in possession purchased the policy with estate funds. The proceeds of the policy, therefore, were payable to a person other than a party to the security agreement, which debtor had entered, covering the combine, and the secured party was not entitled to the proceeds despite a perfected security interest. *John Deere Co. v. Patton (In re Durham), 100 Bankr. 711 (D. Del. 1989)* (decided under prior law).

SUBPART 3
PRIORITY

§ 9-317. Interests that take priority over or take free of security interest or agricultural lien

Perfected interest superior to debtor-in-possession. – If a security interest is perfected prior to the time of filing of a petition in bankruptcy, then such interest is superior to that claimed by the debtor-in-possession. *In re Copeland, 391 F. Supp. 134 (D. Del. 1975)* (decided under prior law); *531 F.2d 1195 (3d Cir. 1976)* (decided under prior law).

But if no security interest exists or if a security interest exists but is not perfected on the date of filing of a petition, the debtor-in-possession has rights to the collateral to that of the secured party. *In re Copeland, 391 F. Supp. 134 (D. Del. 1975)* (decided under prior law); *531 F.2d 1195 (3d Cir. 1976)* (decided under prior law).

§ 9-320. Buyer of goods

This article applies to rights and obligations of buyer and creditor of cars. – A transaction concerned with the rights and obligations of a buyer of two cars and the secured creditor of the cars, one to the other, is a transaction expressly controlled by this article. *Sherrock v. Commercial Credit Corp., 290 A.2d 648 (Del. 1972)* (decided under prior law).

In order to qualify for protection under former § 9-307(1) (now subsection (a) of this section), a purchaser must buy from a seller who is in the business of selling goods of the kind involved. *GECC v. Gayl (In re*

Darling's Homes, Inc.), 46 Bankr. 370 (Bankr. D. Del. 1985) (decided under prior law).

Buyer in ordinary course is protected against secured creditor. Under this article, the policy of the Uniform Commercial Code is to protect the "buyer in ordinary course of business" when the seller sells out of trust in violation of contractual duty to the secured party. *Sherrock v. Commercial Credit Corp., 277 A.2d 708 (Del. Super. Ct. 1971)* (decided under prior law); *290 A.2d 648 (Del. 1972)* (decided under prior law); *GECC v. Gayl (In re*

Darling's Homes, Inc.), 46 Bankr. 370 (Bankr. D. Del. 1985) (decided under prior law).

But secured creditor prevails over buyer not buying in ordinary course. – The "buyer in ordinary course of business" is not expected to foresee and guard against the risk of a seller selling out of trust. If, however, the buyer cannot qualify as a "buyer in ordinary course of business," the Uniform Commercial Code dictates that as between the buyer and the secured creditor, the secured creditor shall prevail. *Sherrock v. Commercial Credit Corp., 277 A.2d 708 (Del. Super. Ct. 1971)* (decided under prior law); *290 A.2d 648 (Del. 1972).*

A merchant-buyer may be a "buyer in the ordinary course of business" under this section, which is not limited to consumer-buyers. *Sherrock v. Commercial Credit Corp., 290 A.2d 648 (Del. 1972)* (decided under prior law).

§ 9-322.   Priorities among conflicting security interests in and agricultural liens on same collateral

DELAWARE CASE NOTES — REPORTED

Priority of federal liens. – The absence of a controlling federal statute establishing priority between small business administration's lien and landlord's lien does not mean that lien of chattel mortgage held by an agency of the United States is subordinate to plaintiffs' subsequently perfected rent lien because federal common law is determinative where the question involved is the priority to be accorded to a lien of the federal government what-ever its source. *Stein v. Moot, 297 F. Supp. 708 (D. Del. 1969)* (decided under prior law).

In the absence of a federal statute, the priority of federally created tax liens is determined by the common-law rule that a lien first in time is the first in right and not by state law. *Stein v. Moot, 297 F. Supp. 708 (D. Del. 1969)* (decided under prior law).

PART 4
RIGHTS OF THIRD PARTIES

It was the intent of the general assembly to forbear concerning the enactment of any statutory provision for the "appropriate process" contemplated by § 9-311, in order that case law remain determinative of the issue of alienability of debtor's rights. *Maryland Nat'l Bank v. Porter-Way Harvester Mfg. Co., 300 A.2d 8 (Del. 1972)* (decided under prior law).

Creditor may levy on secured property in the possession of a debtor with the proceeds being distributed according to the priority of interests. *Computer Sciences Corp. v. Sci-Tek, Inc., 367 A.2d 658 (Del. Super. Ct. 1976)* (decided under prior law).

§ 9-401.   Alienability of debtor's rights

DELAWARE CASE NOTES — REPORTED

Chattels sold at an execution sale should be sold free and clear of all encumbrances in order to ensure the highest price and to stimulate bidding; the creditor with the highest priority is not prejudiced in creditor's reliance on the value of the chattel to secure the debt since he or she is satisfied first from the proceeds. *Maryland Nat'l Bank v. Porter-Way Harvester Mfg. Co., 300 A.2d 8 (Del. 1972)* (decided under prior law).

Right to return of stock on fulfillment of debt obligation. – Where pledger of stock in a Delaware corporation retained, under Florida law, right to return of stock on fulfillment of debt obligations, such right is expressly transferable, either voluntarily or involuntarily under this section. *U.S. Indus., Inc. v. Gregg, 348 F. Supp. 1004 (D. Del. 1972)* (decided under prior law); *540 F.2d 142 (3d Cir. 1976)* (decided under prior law); *433 U.S. 908, 97 S. Ct. 2972, 53 L. Ed. 2d 1091 (1977)* (decided under prior law).

§ 9-404.   Rights acquired by assignee; claims and defenses against assignee

DELAWARE CASE NOTES — REPORTED

Construction of section. – To hold that waiver of defense clauses are enforceable against all Article 9 account debtors who agree not to assert defenses or claims would require, in effect, qualifying language of the section be excised. *Suburban Trust & Sav. Bank v. University of Del., 910 F. Supp. 1009 (D. Del. 1995)* (decided under prior law).

Former § 9-318(1) expressly delineated only one specific exception from its general treatment of the rights of an assignee, i.e., account debtors whose status has arisen pursuant to a sales agreement governed by former § 9-206; to allow parties to vary their contractual terms beyond the scope of the legislated exception would have done violence to that very limitation. *Suburban Trust & Sav. Bank v. University of Del., 910 F. Supp. 1009 (D. Del. 1995)* (decided under prior law).

PART 5
FILING

SUBPART 1
FILING OFFICE; CONTENTS AND EFFECTIVENESS OF FINANCING STATEMENT

§ 9-502.   Contents of financing statement; record of mortgage as financing statement; time of filing financing statement

DELAWARE CASE NOTES — REPORTED

This section is a "notice" type statute rather than a "document" type statute; it is designed to give public notice of the existence of a security agreement and to give enough information as to permit interested persons to make inquiries to the parties of the secured transaction to ascertain details regarding the debtor's encumbered assets. *Maryland Nat'l Bank v. Porter-Way Harvester Mfg. Co., 300 A.2d 8 (Del. 1972)* (decided under prior law).

Restrictive construction not to be given section. – Taking into consideration the broad purposes of the Uniform Commercial Code, a restrictive construction should not be given to this section setting forth the requisites of a sufficient financing statement. *Maryland Nat'l Bank v. Porter-Way Harvester Mfg. Co., 300 A.2d 8 (Del. 1972)* (decided under prior law).

A financing statement should be read in the context of the provisions of former § 9-110 (now § 9-108), which shed light upon an adequate description under

Article 9. *Maryland Nat'l Bank v. Porter-Way Harvester Mfg. Co., 300 A.2d 8 (Del. 1972)* (decided under prior law).

Describing the "item" of collateral. – A financing statement is not incomplete or inadequate merely because it does not follow the alternate offered by this section describing the "item" of collateral. *Maryland Nat'l Bank v. Porter-Way Harvester Mfg. Co., 300 A.2d 8 (Del. 1972)* (decided under prior law).

Description constitutes notice of types of collateral. – If a financing statement sets forth a lien on "equipment" and the debtor bought the equipment for the business of farming, a description of the collateral in the financing statement is sufficiently informative as to constitute notice as required by this section, in that it indicates the "types" of collateral by which the security agreement is secured. *Maryland Nat'l Bank v. Porter-Way Harvester Mfg. Co., 300 A.2d 8 (Del. 1972)* (decided under prior law).

PART 6
DEFAULT

SUBPART 1
DEFAULT AND ENFORCEMENT OF SECURITY INTEREST

§ 9-601.   Rights after default; judicial enforcement; consignor or buyer of accounts, chattel paper, payment intangibles, or promissory notes

DELAWARE CASE NOTES — REPORTED

Section specifically recognizes the right of parties to a security agreement to agree among themselves as to the duties and responsibilities of a secured party when default occurs. *In re Copeland, 531 F.2d 1195 (3d Cir. 1976)* (decided under prior law).

Secured party permitted to pursue alternative remedies. – Under this section, the secured party is permitted to pursue alternative remedies until the

obligation is satisfied. *Shultz v. Delaware Trust Co., 360 A.2d 576 (Del. Super. Ct. 1976)* (decided under prior law).

And not required to elect one remedy to exclusion of another. – Because this section provides that upon a default, the secured party's remedies are cumulative, a secured party is not required to elect one remedy to the exclusion of another. *Shultz v. Delaware Trust Co., 360 A.2d 576 (Del. Super. Ct. 1976)* (decided under prior law).

§ 9-609.   Secured party's right to take possession after default

DELAWARE CASE NOTES — REPORTED

This section does not constitute the creation by the state of a new right in a secured creditor which

the secured creditor would not theretofore have had but for the statute, but rather it is merely a statutory recognition of the law which has existed for almost a century, namely, that if the parties so provide in their agreement, a secured party may privately retake collateral upon default by private means and without the necessity of judicial action, provided the secured creditor can do so peacefully. *Giglio v. Bank of Del., 307 A.2d 816 (Del. Ch. 1973)* (decided under prior law).

The enactment of this section is not sufficient "state action" to make the standards of the due process clause applicable to "self-help" repossession of collateral by a secured party. *Giglio v. Bank of Del., 307 A.2d 816 (Del. Ch. 1973)* (decided under prior law).

A private repossession pursuant to a contract recognized as valid by this section is not such conduct as to be "impregnated with a governmental character" to such extent as would cause it to fall under the Fourteenth Amendment coverage of state action. *Giglio v. Bank of Del., 307 A.2d 816 (Del. Ch. 1973)* (decided under prior law).

Standing to contest repossession after default. – Where a car owner and family members alleged that a repossessor harassed them, the seller was entitled to summary judgment as to three family members' *6 Del. C. § 9-609* claims because, inter alia, those parties were not "debtors" for purposes of recovering for violations of U.C.C. Article 9; however, factual issues regarding whether the seller committed wrongful repossession against the car owner prevented summary judgment as to the car owner's claim under *6 Del. C. § 9-609. Robertson v. Horton Bros. Recovery, Inc., — F. Supp. 2d —, 2005 U.S. Dist. LEXIS 5256* (D. Del. Mar. 31, 2005).

§ 9-610.   Disposition of collateral after default

DELAWARE CASE NOTES — REPORTED

Intent of section. – The intent of this section is to protect the debtor's right to redemption under former § 9-506 (now § 9-623) of this title, to market the collateral to other buyers, and to oversee the sale and maximize the potential for obtaining a fair market price. *Friendly Fin. Corp. v. Bovee, 702 A.2d 1225 (Del. 1997)* (decided under prior law).

Retention of collateral not contemplated disposition. – Retention of collateral is not the type of disposition which is contemplated by the language of this section permitting a secured party to "otherwise dispose of" collateral in the absence of a disposition by sale or lease. *In re Copeland, 531 F.2d 1195 (3d Cir. 1976)* (decided under prior law).

Reassignment of collateral. – A reassignment of collateral from a bank back to the seller, pursuant to the repurchase agreement, is not a sale or disposition of the collateral under the Code and does not activate the notice provision of this section. *Stoppi v. Wilmington Trust Co., 518 A.2d 82 (Del. 1986)* (decided under prior law).

Sale of collateral by secured party must be "commercially reasonable." –The Delaware U.C.C. requires every aspect of a sale or other disposition of repossessed collateral by a secured party after default to be commercially reasonable, including the method, manner, time, place and terms. *MacDonald v. First Interstate Credit Alliance, Inc., 100 Bankr. 714 (Bankr. D. Del. 1989)* (decided under prior law).

The law does not require that the purchase price be at least equivalent to an estimated quick sale value. *MacDonald v. First Interstate Credit Alliance, Inc., 100 Bankr. 714 (Bankr. D. Del. 1989)* (decided under prior law).

In selling inventory, a dealer is not constrained by this section as is a repossessing finance company; such a creditor must dispose of the equipment within a reasonable time. The creditor cannot wait until a buyer willing to pay the price is found, as a dealer might. *MacDonald v. First Interstate Credit Alliance, Inc., 100 Bankr. 714 (Bankr. D. Del. 1989)* (decided under prior law).

Commercial reasonableness of creditor's actions must include consideration of delay in proceeding with sale after coming into possession of the collateral and after giving notice of private sale. *Associates Fin. Servs. Co. v. DiMarco, 383 A.2d 296 (Del. Super. Ct. 1978)* (decided under prior law).

Effect of debtor's objection to secured party's proposal to retain collateral. – The requirement under former § § 9-504 and 9-507 (now this section and § 9-627, respectively) of this title that secured creditors proceed in a commercially reasonable manner does not displace the specific provision of this section which requires a secured party to "sell, lease or otherwise dispose of" collateral, if the debtor properly objects to the secured party's proposal to retain the collateral in satisfaction of the secured party's claim. *In re Copeland, 531 F.2d 1195 (3d Cir. 1976)* (decided under prior law).

CASE NOTES – FEDERAL

Seventh Circuit

Impermissible disposition. – Simply taking shares and keeping them (retention) is not a permissible means of disposing of collateral under Delaware's version of the Uniform Commercial Code. A secured party does not acquire ownership of pledged collateral simply because the debtor defaults on a loan. There is a process for transferring ownership that must be followed. *Weinstein v. Schwartz, 2005 U.S. App. LEXIS 18976 (7th Cir. 2005).*

UCC

§ 9-611.   Notification before disposition of collateral

DELAWARE CASE NOTES — REPORTED

Notice of private sale by previous secured party. – Seller did not have the rights and responsibilities of previous secured party; thus notice of private sale given by previous secured party could not be relied on by current secured party to satisfy duty to notify under this section. *Stoppi v. Wilmington Trust Co., 518 A.2d 82 (Del. 1986)* (decided under prior law).

Usual method of giving notice. – The usual method of giving public notice is to place an advertisement in a newspaper of general circulation enough times for the general public to become aware of the sale; to require actual notice to a particular segment of the public would place an unreasonable burden on a creditor. *MacDonald v. First Interstate Credit Alliance, Inc., 100 Bankr. 714 (Bankr. D. Del. 1989)* (decided under prior law).

Purpose of requiring notice under is threefold: (1) It gives the debtor an opportunity to exercise the right of redemption of the repossessed collateral provided for by former § 9-506 (now § 9-623) of this title; (2) it gives the debtor the chance to challenge any aspect of the disposition before it is made; and (3) it offers the debtor the opportunity to seek out persons who might be interested in purchasing the collateral. Particularly the last 2 of these purposes serve the ultimate goal of allowing the debtor to maximize the sale price of the collateral and, thus, minimize any deficiency for which the debtor will be liable. *Rushton v. Shea, 423 F. Supp. 468 (D. Del. 1976)* (decided under prior law).

The purpose of the requirement of "reasonable notification" in former § 9-504 was threefold: (1) It gave the debtor the opportunity to exercise redemption rights under former § 9-506 (now § 9-623) of this title; (2) it affords the debtor an opportunity to seek out buyers for the collateral; and (3) it allowed the debtor to oversee every aspect of the disposition, thus maximizing the probability that a fair sale price would be obtained. *Wilmington Trust Co. v. Conner, 415 A.2d 773 (Del. 1980)* (decided under prior law).

Purpose of written notice. – Written notice gives greater protection to the debtor, eliminates the problems of proof associated with oral notice, and establishes exactly what notice has been given in a particular instance. *Stoppi v. Wilmington Trust Co., 518 A.2d 82 (Del. 1986)* (decided under prior law).

"Reasonable notice" a subjective determination. – This section requires only reasonable notice to a debtor. It does not specify, nor should courts read, a specific number of days into the statute. Time must be tailored to the circumstances of a particular situation. *MacDonald v. First Interstate Credit Alliance, Inc., 100 Bankr. 714 (Bankr. D. Del. 1989)* (decided under prior law).

Failure to comply with notice provisions is "absolute bar" to recovery of deficiency judgment. – The apparent majority rule under the Uniform Commercial Code as concerns failure to fully comply with its notice provisions is the "absolute bar" theory: Failure to comply strictly with the notice provisions of the Code acts as an absolute bar to recovery of a deficiency judgment by the creditor. *Wilmington Trust Co. v. Conner, 415 A.2d 773 (Del. 1980)* (decided under prior law).

Delaware adheres to the "absolute bar" rule. *Wilmington Trust Co. v. Conner, 415 A.2d 773 (Del. 1980)* (decided under prior law).

Burden on creditor to show compliance. – While Article 9 does not require a creditor to show that the debtor received actual notice, a creditor seeking a deficiency judgment after sale has the burden to establish that it complied with this section and § 1-201(38) (now § 1-201(36)) of this title. *Friendly Fin. Corp. v. Bovee, 702 A.2d 1225 (Del. 1997)* (decided under prior law).

Failure to account for rebate of unearned charges and premiums is defect in notice. – Plaintiff's failure to account in the notice required in this section for the rebate of unearned finance charges and insurance premiums constituted a defect in the notice. *Wilmington Trust Co. v. Conner, 415 A.2d 773 (Del. 1980)* (decided under prior law).

And is manifestly unreasonable. – Where plaintiff's notice pursuant of this section failed to take into account possible rebates due the buyer, in light of the plaintiff's statutory duty under former *5 Del. C. § 2908* (see now *5 Del. C. § 2909(b)*) and under *5 Del. C. § 2906(g)* (now *5 Del. C. § 2907(g)*) to rebate unearned finance charges and insurance premiums, a blatant assertion in the notice that the total amount under the contract was due, without reference to such possible rebates, was manifestly unreasonable. *Wilmington Trust Co. v. Conner, 415 A.2d 773 (Del. 1980)* (decided under prior law).

Notice containing inflated balance due is not "reasonable notification". – Where the notice required by of this section contained a stated balance that was inflated $654.61 above the amount actually owed, this notice was not "reasonable notification." *Wilmington Trust Co. v. Conner, 415 A.2d 773 (Del. 1980)* (decided under prior law).

Mere delay in effecting private sale after giving notice does not violate the notice requirements, provided the test of commercial reasonableness can be met. *Associates Fin. Servs. Co. v. DiMarco, 383 A.2d 296 (Del. Super. Ct. 1978)* (decided under prior law).

Notice of private sale cannot be given as preliminary step culminating in public sale. *Associates Fin. Servs. Co. v. DiMarco, 383 A.2d 296 (Del. Super. Ct. 1978)* (decided under prior law).

Holding that creditor failed to meet notice requirements. – Creditor failed to meet its burden of demonstrating that it fully complied with the reasonable notice requirements of this section and §§ 1-201 and former 9-506 (now 9-621) of this title where creditor sent notice to debtors at the wrong street address, a former residence, and sent notice to their current address with the wrong zip code. *Friendly Fin. Corp. v. Bovee, 702 A.2d 1225 (Del. 1997)* (decided under prior law).

§ 9-620. Acceptance of collateral in full or partial satisfaction of obligation; compulsory disposition of collateral

DELAWARE CASE NOTES — REPORTED

Length of time secured party holds collateral must be reasonable. – There must be a reasonable limit to the length of time a secured party is permitted to hold collateral before it is deemed to have exercised its right to retain that collateral in satisfaction of the obligation. *Shultz v. Delaware Trust Co., 360 A.2d 576 (Del. Super. Ct. 1976)* (decided under prior law).

And determination of reasonableness is for trier of fact. – The determination of the question of reasonableness of length of time a secured party holds collateral is for the trier of fact. *Shultz v. Delaware Trust Co., 360 A.2d 576 (Del. Super. Ct. 1976)* (decided under prior law).

§ 9-621. Notification of proposal to accept collateral

DELAWARE CASE NOTES — REPORTED

Notice may not be waived. – Notice guarantee in this section may not be waived. *Shultz v. Delaware Trust Co., 360 A.2d 576 (Del. Super. Ct. 1976)* (decided under prior law).

And damages are recoverable under former § 9-507 (now § 9-625) of this title for violation of the notice guarantee of this section. *Shultz v. Delaware Trust Co., 360 A.2d 576 (Del. Super. Ct. 1976)* (decided under prior law).

§ 9-623. Right to redeem collateral

DELAWARE CASE NOTES — REPORTED

Intent of former *6 DEL. C. § 9-504* (NOW § 9-610). – The intent of former § 9-504 (now § 9-610) of this title was to protect the debtor's right to redemption under this section, to market the collateral to other buyers, and to oversee the sale and maximize the potential for obtaining a fair market price. *Friendly Fin. Corp. v. Bovee, 702 A.2d 1225 (Del. 1997)* (decided under prior law).

SUBPART 2
NONCOMPLIANCE WITH ARTICLE

§ 9-625. Remedies for secured party's failure to comply with article

DELAWARE CASE NOTES — REPORTED

Applicability of section. – This section imposes damages only upon secured parties who violate this part. *Stoppi v. Wilmington Trust Co., 518 A.2d 82 (Del. 1986)* (decided under prior law).

Damages are recoverable under this section for violation of the notice guarantee of former § 9-505 (now § 9-621) of this title. *Shultz v. Delaware Trust Co., 360 A.2d 576 (Del. Super. Ct. 1976)* (decided under prior law).

§ 9-627. Determination of whether conduct was commercially reasonable

DELAWARE CASE NOTES — REPORTED

Effect of debtor's objection to secured party's proposal to retain collateral. – The requirement under former § 9-504 of this title and this section that secured creditors proceed in a commercially reasonable manner does not displace the specific provisions of former § 9-504 (now § 9-610) of this title which require a secured party to "sell, lease or otherwise dispose of" collateral, if the debtor properly objects to the secured party's proposal to retain the collateral in satisfaction of the secured party's own claim. *In re Copeland, 531 F.2d 1195 (3d Cir. 1976)* (decided under prior law).

Adequacy of sales price in foreclosure sales. – Absent unusual circumstances, foreclosure sales will be set aside only if the sale price is so grossly inadequate as to shock the conscience of the court. In general, the standard has been met where the sale price represented 50% of fair market value. *MacDonald v. First Interstate Credit Alliance, Inc., 100 Bankr. 714 (Bankr. D. Del. 1989)* (decided under prior law).

UCC

APPENDIX: CASES

DAVID PORTNOY, Plaintiff, v. CRYO-CELL INTERNATIONAL, INC., A Delaware corporation, MERCEDES WALTON, GABY W. GOUBRAN, JAGDISH SHETH, Ph.D., ANTHONY P. FINCH and SCOTT CHRISTIAN, Defendants.

C.A. No. 3142-VCS

COURT OF CHANCERY OF DELAWARE, NEW CASTLE

2008 Del. Ch. LEXIS 6*

November 30, 2007, Submitted

January 15, 2008, Decided

NOTICE:

THIS OPINION HAS NOT BEEN RELEASED FOR PUBLICATION. UNTIL RELEASED, IT IS SUBJECT TO REVISION OR WITHDRAWAL.

COUNSEL: [*1] Richard D. Heins, Esquire, Philip Trainer, Jr., Esquire, Carolyn S. Hake, Esquire, Richard L. Renck, Esquire, Tiffany G. Lydon, Esquire, ASHBY & GEDDES, Wilmington, Delaware, Attorneys for Plaintiff.

Srinivas M. Raju, Esquire, Blake K. Rohrbacher, Esquire, Jennifer J. Veet, Esquire, RICHARDS, LAYTON & FINGER, P.A., Wilmington, Delaware; Robert S. Faxon, Esquire, Geoffrey J. Ritts, Esquire, Louis A. Chaiten, Esquire, Adrienne M. Ferraro, Esquire, Andrew G. Fiorella, Esquire, JONES DAY, Cleveland, Ohio, Attorneys for Defendants.

JUDGES: STRINE, Vice Chancellor.

OPINION BY: STRINE

OPINION:

STRINE, Vice Chancellor.

This case involves a challenge to the results of a contested corporate election. Cryo-Cell International, Inc. ("Cryo-Cell" or the "Company") is a small public company that has struggled to succeed. By early 2007, several of its large stockholders were considering mounting a proxy contest to replace the board.

One of those stockholders, Andrew Filipowski, used management's fear of replacement to strike a deal for himself to be included in the management slate for the 2007 annual meeting. Another stockholder, plaintiff David Portnoy, filed a dissident slate (the "Portnoy Slate").

Going into the week of the annual [*2] meeting, Cryo-Cell's chief executive officer, defendant Mercedes Walton, was desperate because, in her words, "the current board and management [were] losing by huge margins."[1] Aside from actually asking the FBI

to intervene in the proxy contest on the side of management, Walton ginned up a plan with Filipowski to win the proxy contest. That plan involved Walton acting as a "matchmaker" by finding stockholders willing to sell their shares to Filipowski. In exchange for this alliance, Walton promised Filipowski that if their "Management Slate" prevailed, Cryo-Cell's board would, using their power as corporate directors, expand the board to add another seat that Filipowski's designee would fill. That designee was a subordinate who had within the recent past resolved an SEC insider trading investigation by agreeing to disgorge trading profits and to be jointly liable for trading profits made by his tippees. This plan was not disclosed to the Cryo-Cell stockholders, who did not realize that if they voted for management, they would in fact be electing a seven, not six member board, with two, not one, Filipowski representatives.

In an effort to secure another key [*3] bloc of votes, Walton used a combination of threats (the ending of cooperation on key projects) and inducements (the long-sought but never before granted removal of a restrictive legend) to secure the vote of Saneron CCEL Therapeutics Inc. That leverage was enhanced by the fact that Cryo-Cell owned 38% of Saneron's shares and that Saneron depended on Cryo-Cell's laboratory space to conduct many of its own operations. Notwithstanding that, Saneron had gone into the week before the meeting undecided about how to vote. Walton "locked up" Saneron only after employing these persuasive strategies involving the threatened withholding and actual granting of concessions on the part of Cryo-Cell as a corporation.[2]

Even after employing these methods, Walton and her board went into the day of the annual meeting fearing defeat. They had rented the meeting room from the 11 a.m. start time only until 1 p.m. But Walton did not want to close the polls and count the vote when the scheduled presentations at the meeting were over. So she had members of her manage-

---

[1] Joint Exhibit ("JX") 189.

[2] JX 218.

ment team make long, unscheduled presentations to give her side more time to gather votes and ensure that they had locked in two key [*4] blocs. She overruled motions to close the polls.

Even after the filibusters, Walton still harbored doubt that the Management Slate would prevail if the vote was counted and the meeting was concluded. So, at around 2 p.m., Walton declared a very late lunch break, supposedly in response to a request made much earlier.

In fact, Walton desired the break so that she would have more time to seek votes and so that she could confirm that the major blockholders had switched their votes to favor the Management Slate. Only after confirming the switches did Walton resume the meeting at approximately 4:45 p.m., declare the polls closed, and have the vote counted.

The post-meeting vote count resulted in the Management Slate squeaking out a victory by an extremely small margin. Immediately after that, Walton began preparing to add Filipowski's designee to the Cryo-Cell board. Only after this challenge was brought to the election by Portnoy did that process slow down, and only for the obvious reason that the litigation was brought.

In this opinion, I decline Portnoy's request to declare his side the victor in the election process. But I do agree with him that the election results were tainted by inequitable [*5] behavior by Walton and her allies and must be set aside. In particular, I conclude that the Cryo-Cell stockholders cast their votes in ignorance of material facts regarding the promise made to Filipowski regarding a second board seat and the pressure that Walton was exerting on Saneron — both of which involved the use by Walton of corporate resources and fiduciary authority motivated by the desire to protect herself from the risk of losing her corporate offices.

Rather than seating a board for the Cryo-Cell stockholders, I believe the more appropriate remedy to be a requirement that Cryo-Cell have another election at a special meeting to be held promptly. Because the stockholders should not be required to bear extra expense because of management's misconduct, the Management Slate will be required to fund their own re-election campaign and to pay any costs incurred by the Company to hold the special meeting, including the cost of a special master to preside over the meeting.

I. Factual Background

A. Cryo-Cell's Business

Cryo-Cell is a Delaware corporation with its primary business being the cryopreservation of umbilical cord stem cells of its clients for possible later medical use by their [*6] family members. Cryo-Cell was founded in 1989 by Dan Richard. Richard's

resignation from his positions as CEO and Chairman of Cryo-Cell in 2002 signaled the beginning of a troublesome period for the Company. In 2003, Cryo-Cell incurred a net loss of $7.5 million on $7.5 million in revenues, the Company's stock was delisted from NASDAQ, the Company went through three different audit firms, and the Company was the defendant in several lawsuits.[3] During that same time period, Mercedes Walton, who had served as a Cryo-Cell director since 2000, began to play a dominant role at the Company. She replaced Richard as Chairman after he left in 2002 and was later appointed as Cryo-Cell's interim CEO in 2003 after the CEO who succeeded Richard resigned. In 2005, Walton was appointed as CEO on a non-interim basis.

Although Cryo-Cell's current situation is not as dim as it was in 2003, it continues to struggle as a company. In 2006, Cryo-Cell incurred a net loss of $2.8 million on $17 million in revenue. It again lost money in 2007. Moreover, Cryo-Cell, which was the first company to enter the now fragmented cord blood industry, is losing market share to its [*7] competitors. According to the Company, however, its future prospects look brighter, at least in part based on the launch of a new product line, C'elle. C'elle, which was launched on November 1, 2007, is Cryo-Cell's proprietary menstrual stem cell collection and storage service.

Before the 2007 annual meeting, Cryo-Cell's board of directors had five directors. Those directors join Cryo-Cell as the defendants in this action. Walton, Cryo-Cell's Chairman and CEO, was the lone inside director. The outside directors were Gaby W. Goubran, Jadish Sheth, Anthony P. Finch, and Scott Christian. Walton, Sheth, and Christian were used to working together — they were directors together at Norstan, Inc., a Minnesota telecommunications company, before it was acquired by Black Box Corporation in 2005.[4] Other than the options that they held as compensation for their service at Cryo-Cell, the directors did not own large equity positions in Cryo-Cell.[5]

B. Stockholder Discontent With Cryo-Cell

By late 2006, Cryo-Cell's stockholders [*8] were unhappy with the Company's performance. That discontent was amplified when Cryo-Cell's board of directors amended the Company's bylaws in December 2006 (the "Bylaw Amendments"). The Bylaw Amendments imposed additional requirements on stockholders seeking to bring business before the board or nominate directors, restricted stockholders' ability to call special meetings of stockholders,

---

[3] Trial Transcript ("Tr.") at 313.

[4] Tr. at 264-65; JX 117 at CRYO 491-92.

[5] JX 117 at CRYO 500. The directors owning the largest positions in Cryo-Cell were Finch with 104,500 shares and Walton with 40,000 shares.

limited the ability of stockholders to act by written consent, and purported to place a supermajority requirement on the stockholders' ability to amend the new bylaw provisions.[6]

The first group of stockholders to communicate its unhappiness with Cryo-Cell's performance and the Bylaw Amendments to Cryo-Cell's board in writing was the "Filipowski Group." The Filipowski Group, a collection of Cryo-Cell stockholders who owned approximately 6% of the Company at that time, is composed of SilkRoad Equity, the private investment firm of Andrew Filipowski, a wealthy entrepreneur, and Matthew Roszak; Filipowski and Roszak individually; and the Andrew J. Filipowski Revocable Trust (the "Filipowski Trust"). Filipowski is the top dog at SilkRoad. Roszak is his key subordinate.

In its January 9, 2007 letter, [*9] the Filipowski Group wrote that the Bylaw Amendments were "a way for existing management to entrench itself and to perpetuate its role with the Company and the economic benefits that go along with that."[7] In addition, the letter "question[ed] the sincerity and ability of the current directors to provide leadership and support stockholders' interests."[8] The letter threatened legal action against the board and stated that the Filipowski Group was "considering proposing a slate of directors to replace" the current board.[9] In concluding the letter, the Filipowski Group noted that it was available to meet with the board to discuss its concerns. Filipowski and Roszak would meet with Walton in February 2007 — more on that meeting later.

The Filipowski Group was not the only stockholder group to express its negative reaction to the Bylaw Amendments. The "Portnoy Group"[10] — a group of affiliated stockholders led by David Portnoy that owned approximately 12% of Cryo-Cell at that time — filed a Schedule 13 D/A on January 31, 2007, voicing its dissatisfaction with management and the Bylaw Amendments.[11] The Portnoy Group letter, similar to the Filipowski Group letter, [*10] indicated the possibility of litigation over the Bylaw Amendments and other issues and expressed a willingness to have further discussions with the Cryo-Cell board. Cryo-Cell, however, did not respond to that invitation because Walton had concluded that Portnoy "was not

a reasonable person to deal with."[12] Walton formed this opinion of Portnoy based on a meeting in 2004, just after Portnoy became an investor in Cryo-Cell, as well as from subsequent telephone calls.

The Filipowski Group and the Portnoy Group were not acting entirely independently of one another — they were sharing their concerns about Cryo-Cell during late 2006 and early 2007.[13] In fact, Filipowski would later claim that the content of the Filipowski [*11] Group's letter criticizing Cryo-Cell's management was primarily the result of input from Portnoy.[14] The communication between the Filipowski and Portnoy Groups would continue, but they would ultimately align on opposite sides of the ensuing proxy contest.

C. The Portnoy Group Decides To Wage A Proxy Contest

After receiving no response from Cryo-Cell to its January letter expressing disappointment with the Company's results and the Bylaw Amendments, the Portnoy Group decided to solicit proxies to elect its own slate of directors at the upcoming Cryo-Cell annual meeting. In hope of putting together a competitive slate and garnering support from another large stockholder, Portnoy had discussions with the Filipowski Group about combining forces. Specifically, Portnoy and Roszak exchanged emails in the week before the deadline for filing a proxy statement in advance of the Cryo-Cell annual meeting.[15] Roszak suggested that the Filipowski Group put up two directors and the Portnoy Group put up two directors with the fifth director being either Walton [*12] or a mutually acceptable candidate. Portnoy responded that the Portnoy Group would only offer one board seat to Filipowski and only if the Filipowski Group paid a portion of the proxy solicitation costs and agreed to vote its shares in favor of the Portnoy Group slate.

The Filipowski Group never responded to the Portnoy Group's proposal for two reasons. One was that Filipowski had doubts about the experience, qualifications, and intentions of the proposed members of the Portnoy Group slate. The Filipowski Group was especially concerned about the proposed board member that the Filipowski Group believed that the Portnoy Group intended to have serve as CEO.[16]

The Filipowski Group's concerns about the Portnoy Group's slate were not irrational. The slate ultimately proposed by the Portnoy Group on March 26, 2007 was David Portnoy, Mark Portnoy, Craig

---

[6] JX 16.
[7] JX 22.
[8] JX 22.
[9] JX 22.
[10] The Portnoy Group is composed of David Portnoy; Visual Investment Corp., a Delaware corporation; PartnerCommunity, Inc., a Delaware corporation; Jamie H. Zidell; Mayim Investment Limited Partnership, a Delaware limited partnership; David Ruttenberg; Liza Amar; Lynne Portnoy; Gilbert Portnoy; Mark Portnoy; Capital Asset Fund Limited Partnership, a Delaware limited partnership; George Gaines; Scott D. Martin; and Steven Berkowitz. JX 25 at 16.
[11] JX 25 at 30.

[12] Tr. at 321.
[13] See JX 15 (November 2006 email chain between Portnoy and Roszak) and JX 43A (March 2007 email chain between Portnoy and Roszak).
[14] Tr. at 168.
[15] JX 43A.
[16] Tr. at 155.

Fleishman, M.D., Harold Berger, and Scott Martin (the "Portnoy Slate").[17] Later, when Cryo-Cell expanded its slate, John Yin was added to the Portnoy Slate.[18] No members of the Portnoy Slate had ever served as a director of a public company.[19] Moreover, none of the members of the Portnoy Slate had any experience in the [*13] stem cell industry. David Portnoy and his brother, Mark Portnoy, the individuals primarily responsible for making the strategic decisions for the Portnoy Group, are private investors. Fleischman is a cardiologist. Berger is Mark Portnoy's accountant. Yin is the CEO of a privately held technology company in which David Portnoy is a major investor. Martin, the proposed board member that the Filipowski Group believed would be installed as CEO,[20] had the most relevant experience managing an operating company, having served as CEO of a very large HVAC company with revenues and profits far in excess of Cryo-Cell's. But that corporation was in a very different industry and was not a public company. The Portnoy Slate's lack of expertise in the stem cell industry and inexperience with public companies and proxy contests was evident in the vague business plan they ultimately presented in their proxy statement, which consisted of generic statements about eliminating unnecessary costs and considering strategic alternatives to increase stockholder value.[21]

But even more than Filipowski's doubts about Portnoy's [*14] proposed slate, another more important reason inspired Filipowski to eschew an alliance with Portnoy: He was cutting his own deal with Cryo-Cell management that would give him the influence he sought.

D.   The Filipowski Group Joins Forces With Management

Turned off by Portnoy, the Filipowski Group decided to consider supporting Cryo-Cell's management in the proxy contest but subject to a very important condition — which was that Filipowski get a seat at the board table.

The Filipowski Group and Cryo-Cell's management began to form this alliance at a February 2007 meeting held at Cryo-Cell's headquarters. At that meeting, held in response to the Filipowski Group's January letter, Filipowski and his chief aide, Roszak, discussed their concerns about Cryo-Cell with Walton, Jill Taymans, Cryo-Cell's Vice President of Finance, and other members of Cryo-Cell's management team. Walton characterized it as "a very positive meeting."[22] The Filipowski Group was also pleased with the meeting. Filipowski described his view of management after the meeting as follows: "I felt that they were very much on top of their business, knew where the future of the business lay, and were very much anxious to [*15] pursue what I thought was a very logical appropriate strategy."[23] Filipowski's take on the appropriate strategy for Cryo-Cell — focusing on upgrading their services to collect and store additional types of stem cells — differed materially from what Filipowski understood the Portnoy Group's strategy to be — focusing only on collecting and storing stem cells from cord blood.[24]

Despite the positive tone of the February meeting, the Filipowski Group did not immediately join forces with management. Instead, the Filipowski Group continued discussions with the Portnoy Group about a possible joint slate into late March.[25] At the same time that the Filipowski Group was considering the Portnoy Group's offer of a position on its slate for Filipowski, the Filipowski Group was negotiating with Walton about a separate slate. Early in the negotiations, Roszak suggested a Filipowski Group slate that would include four new outside directors plus Walton as the management representative.[26] In the board meeting held the week after Roszak's suggestion of a separate Filipowski Slate, Walton informed the board of her discussions with the Filipowski Group.[27] [*16] The board's response was to consider whether anyone from the Filipowski Group should be invited to join the Management Slate. The board assigned Walton to continue discussions with Roszak. The day of that board meeting Walton emailed Roszak the board's required profile for new board members: "we're looking for a combination of healthcare and business background (preferably women's healthcare); stem cell industry (huge plus); P&L; public company board experience; marquee recognition in their field. The board is unanimous in our belief that this profile is a requisite."[28] During the discussions over adding board members, Roszak provided Walton with the names and profiles of several board candidates. Ultimately, however, the negotiations between the Filipowski Group and Walton centered on increasing the size of the board of directors by one seat effective the date of the annual meeting and adding Filipowski to the Management Slate to fill that seat. This focus on Filipowski was somewhat of a reversal for the board because, as defendant Christian admitted at trial, Filipowski did not fit the board's required profile.[29]

In mid-April, [*17] once the board was focused on the tactical utility of adding Filipowski to the Management Slate, it followed its normal protocol for

[17] JX 46 at CRYO 114.
[18] JX 126 at CRYO 317.
[19] Tr. at 28.
[20] Tr. at 155.
[21] JX 126 at CRYO 318.
[22] Tr. at 323.

[23] Tr. at 153.
[24] Tr. at 155-56.
[25] JX 43A.
[26] Tr. at 171; JX 44.
[27] JX 54.
[28] JX 55.
[29] Tr. at 269.

considering a new board member. Cryo-Cell had Filipowski sign a confidentiality agreement and fill out the usual directors and officers and director independence and committee compliance questionnaires.[30] Cryo-Cell also had a private investigator perform a background investigation on Filipowski.[31] On May 21, 2007, the corporate governance committee of Cryo-Cell's board met to discuss the procedures that would be used to evaluate Filipowski's candidacy and determine whether to add him as a nominee on the Management Slate. At that meeting, Walton emphasized the importance of the decision and the need for an expeditious decision so that Filipowski could be included in the proxy statement in advance of the annual meeting. Walton also told the committee members that "although initially Mr. Filipowski had proposed the names of other nominees, he had subsequently confirmed that his agreement to support management's slate *was conditioned on his nomination to the Board*."[32] The committee members proceeded on to discuss "the possible results of a proxy contest, [*18] with or without Mr. Filipowski's support."[33]

In addition to its conversations about the proxy contest, the committee discussed Filipowski's qualifications and reputation. Cryo-Cell considered Filipowski an interesting candidate for its board for several reasons. Filipowski had extensive entrepreneurial experience, having founded and developed several technology companies, including one that sold for nearly $4 billion.[34] Filipowski had served as chairman of the Wake Forest Institute for Regenerative Medicine and was knowledgeable and passionate about the stem-cell industry.[35] Moreover, Filipowski's ability to represent the perspective of a large shareholder was attractive.[36] Filipowski's background, however, was not without blemish. The committee members were concerned about litigation and bankruptcies involving the companies with which Filipowski was previously associated.[37] In addition, the committee was concerned about an SEC investigation of Roszak for insider trading in Blue Rhino Corporation stock. That SEC investigation involved whether Roszak had traded on and tipped others about non-public information that Roszak [*19] garnered from Filipowski, who was a director of Blue Rhino.[38] The resolution of that investigation resulted

in Roszak entering into a consent decree with the SEC whereby he (without admitting liability) disgorged the profits from his own trades in Blue Rhino's shares, accepted joint and several liability for disgorgement of the profits of his tippees for their trading in Blue Rhino shares, and paid a civil penalty.[39]

In light of the committee's concerns about Filipowski and its desire to add Filipowski to the Management Slate if those concerns could be allayed, the committee set up a conference call with Filipowski. The conference call involved a detailed discussion of Filipowski's prior activities and what he could contribute to the board.[40] The committee satisfied itself that there were not any criminal or ethical problems with Filipowski's prior business dealings and that the SEC's investigation and imposition of agreed sanctions against Roszak for insider trading and tipping violations of Rule 10b-5 did not implicate Filipowski in any wrongdoing.[41] The committee then decided that a face-to-face meeting with Filipowski would be beneficial before making a final determination on his candidacy.

On May 24, 2007, Gaby Goubran, the chair of the committee, flew in from Europe and met with Filipowski. Goubran had a positive meeting with Filipowski, and after [*21] he reported the results of the meeting to the committee later that day, the committee unanimously approved Filipowski's candidacy.[42] The following day the entire Cryo-Cell board approved the expansion of the board and Filipowski's inclusion on the Management Slate, subject to the negotiation of a suitable standstill and voting agreement with Filipowski.[43] Thus, the Management Slate of directors that Cryo-Cell would put forth for election at the annual meeting would include the five incumbent directors and Filipowski.

The contemplated standstill and voting agreement between Filipowski and the Company (the "Voting Agreement") was executed and filed with the SEC on June 4, 2007.[44] The Voting Agreement stated that Cryo-Cell would expand the board by one seat, effective at the date of the 2007 annual meeting, and that it would include Filipowski as the nominee for that seat on the Management Slate. In return, Filipowski, Roszak, and the Filipowski Trust agreed

---

[30] JX 64; JX 76.

[31] JX 73.

[32] JX 84 (emphasis added).

[33] JX 84.

[34] JX 80.

[35] Tr. at 329-30.

[36] Tr. at 330.

[37] JX 84.

[38] Tr. 476-80; JX 74. The defendants contend that Joint Exhibit 74, which includes information about Roszak's SEC litigation, is inadmissible under Delaware Uniform Rules of Evidence 402, 403, 404, and 608. Their objection is overruled for the same reasons I overruled their objection to testimony about Roszak's SEC litigation at trial — the defendants affirmatively put that information at issue

by alleging the Portnoy Slate is unqualified and by touting the credibility of the deliberative process the Cryo-Cell board undertook before adding Filipowski to the Management Slate. *See* Tr. at 389-90. The defendants also defended their decision to add (or in their view, to consider) Roszak as a board member. The final judgment in Roszak's [*20] SEC litigation is a publicly filed court document, which incorporates the consent decree that was voluntarily entered into by Roszak, and is reliable, relevant evidence. JX 74 at CRYO 3111-14.

[39] JX 74 at CRYO 3112.

[40] JX 93.

[41] Tr. at 249-50; 476-80.

[42] JX 100.

[43] JX 100.

[44] JX 119.

Appendix

to vote any shares they controlled in favor of the Management Slate. In addition, they agreed to standstill on various matters until after the 2008 annual meeting.

Despite the (non-credible) insistence [*22] of defendant Scott Christian, one of Cryo-Cell's outside directors, that Filipowski's nomination "[h]ad nothing to do with the proxy contest,"[45] Filipowski was clearly added to the Management Slate to increase the odds that the Management Slate would prevail in the upcoming proxy contest. As Walton explained to the Director of the Wake Forest Institute for Regenerative Medicine, Filipowski and the incumbent directors on the Management Slate were "very strange bedfellows indeed."[46] Immediately after the public disclosure of the agreement with Filipowski, Walton underscored the connection between the proxy contest and adding Filipowski to the Management Slate by emailing the following message board post to Taymans, Cryo-Cell's counsel, and its proxy solicitor with the comment that she hoped the author was "right on the money": "No Greater Coup . . . Could Possibly have been accomplished!!! [Filipowski] joining the board 'lays to waste' considerable efforts and monies squandered on the 'overthrow' . . . Game, Set, Match?? Me thinks so. JMHFO."[47]

I also find that as Walton told the committee on May 21, 2007, Filipowski would not have supported the Management [*23] Slate unless he was a candidate on that Slate. Absent the board's willingness to include him, Filipowski almost certainly would have bargained with Portnoy over the shape of a unified insurgent slate and cast his lot with the outsiders.

E.   The Proxy Contest Begins

On June 8, 2007, Cryo-Cell filed its definitive proxy statement which indicated the Cryo-Cell annual meeting would be held on July 16.[48] Although the Cryo-Cell 2007 annual meeting had been scheduled for June 28, the meeting was delayed until July 16 because, among other things, both sides were late in getting out their definitive proxy statements. The Cryo-Cell board delayed the meeting "to allow more time for both sides to get their proxy materials out and allow shareholders to conscientiously consider each side's positions."[49]

The Portnoy Group filed its definitive proxy statement on June 13, 2007.[50] After that filing, both sides began a vigorous proxy solicitation process. Both sides hired experienced proxy solicitors to help with election tactics and call stockholders to solicit votes. In addition, both sides sent several fight

letters to Cryo-Cell's stockholders, detailing why those stockholders should [*24] return their proxy card instead of their opponent's proxy card.

Both sides also attempted to personally solicit Cryo-Cell's largest stockholders. Ki Yong Choi, the president of a San Francisco hotel operations and management company, was one of those stockholders. Choi was the beneficial owner of approximately 3% of Cryo-Cell's shares at the beginning of the proxy contest. Walton solicited Choi over the phone on June 18, 2007. Walton described the call as "delightfully uplifting" and Choi as "most supportive," indicating that Choi "asked for assistance in buying more shares."[51] In early July, Mark Portnoy traveled to San Francisco to solicit Choi's vote. According to Mark Portnoy, that meeting "went ok . . . [b]ut [Choi] wants to be the one in control."[52] Although Choi's allegiance appeared up for grabs to Mark Portnoy, Choi would later join Filipowski in siding with management.

F.   Cryo-Cell's Plan To Come From Behind And Win The Election

As the July 16 annual meeting approached, the status of the early vote became clear — the Portnoy Group held a big lead over the Management Slate. Of Cryo-Cell's 11,669,629 million shares outstanding, the July 12, 2007 vote [*25] report from Cryo-Cell's proxy solicitor showed 4,106,441 shares voting for the Portnoy Slate compared to only 2,098,579 shares voting for the Management Slate.[53] Walton was rendered desperate and, frankly, irrational at this state of affairs.

I do not say this lightly, but it is undisputed that Walton sought to have the Federal Bureau of Investigation intervene in the proxy fight. She emailed the July 12 vote report to an FBI agent who was investigating (at her instance) whether Dan Richard had stolen Cryo-Cell client data and explained that the vote report showed that "the current board and management are losing by huge margins."[54] Walton then requested that "[i]f there is any evidence that Dan Richard was involved in corporate theft of CCEL client's [sic] data; and is in turn corroborating with Portnoy to get control of CCEL, the SEC Enforcement Division must be notified immediately. . . . We are running out of time, literally."[55]

On a somewhat more traditional front, Walton developed a two-prong strategy to overcome the vote deficit. The first prong was to intensify the cam-

---

[45] Tr. at 267.
[46] JX 134.
[47] JX 115.
[48] JX 117.
[49] JX 122.
[50] JX 126.

[51] JX 143.
[52] JX 163.
[53] JX 187.
[54] JX 189. By referencing this unsubstantiated accusation levied by Walton, the court by no means suggests that it is true. Richard is not a party to the case and Walton produced no evidence suggesting that Richard ever engaged in wrongdoing of [*26] any kind.
[55] JX 189.

paigning efforts.[56] The second prong was for Walton to act as a "matchmaker" by putting prospective sellers of shares in touch with "shareholders with significant financial resources [who] had expressed to management their opposition to the Portnoy Group's attempt to take over control of the Company."[57] Those shareholders were Filipowski and Choi.[58] The prospective sellers "were only those who had either not voted or had already voted but voted for the Portnoy slate."[59] Walton disclosed her plan to the Cryo-Cell board at a July 12, 2007 telephone meeting. She asked the board to postpone the annual meeting a few days to allow her matchmaking plan time to take effect, but counsel advised the board that the meeting could not be postponed.[60] The board members did, however, "generally express[] their support for taking valid actions that would increase the likelihood that management's slate of directors would be elected."[61]

Walton formulated her matchmaking [*27] plan in the days before the July 12 board meeting based on discussions she had with Filipowski and his operative Roszak. Those discussions centered on the Filipowski Group buying additional Cryo-Cell shares to vote them in favor of the Management Slate.[62] Filipowski explained that he "wanted to accumulate as many shares as possible in order to be able to vote [his] opinion on how the company should proceed."[63] But the Filipowski Group wanted concessions in return for buying more Cryo-Cell shares. Roszak demanded two things on Filipowski's behalf: (1) that management, the incumbent directors, and the Company use their own resources to purchase additional Cryo-Cell shares, and (2) that the Filipowski Group be given additional board seats beyond the seat that would be held by Filipowski if the Management Slate prevailed.[64] As to the first request for participation in buying additional shares, Walton's response was an "emphatic 'no way.'"[65] Her response to the request for additional board representation was much warmer, and, I find, signaled very clearly that the answer would be yes.[66] [66] That

is, I find that Walton made clear that Filipowski would get a second board seat if the share [*28] buying plan resulted in a Management Slate victory.

The difficulty for Walton and Roszak was how to deal with Choi. They wanted him to buy more shares and support the Management Slate but not to give him board seats. So Walton played coy with Choi. Therefore, Walton called Choi the night of the board meeting to discuss and confirm the matchmaking plan.[67] Choi, according to Cryo-Cell's proxy solicitor, requested two board seats and Walton indicated to Choi that although she could not grant his request, the board would consider it.[68]

After confirming Choi's participation in her plan, Walton emailed the Filipowski Group to let them know that "[t]he board has a proposed strategy [*29] on turning the plurality in our favor — some aspects include what you and Flip proposed earlier this week; but other elements have been added as well."[69] Those other elements were the addition of Choi to the buying effort.[70] When Roszak responded "[l]ove the energy here and sounds like a plan," Walton told him that "'[w]e will either find a way, or make one.'"[71] The following morning, Friday, July 13, 2007, Walton held a conference call with the Filipowski Group to further discuss the matchmaking plan. That same day, Walton ensured that those involved in the matchmaking plan — the Filipowski Group and Choi and his broker, Chris Kovarik — had each other's contact information and the contact information for Cryo-Cell's executives, its proxy solicitor, and its counsel. More importantly, Walton made sure that Choi and Filipowski had the contact information for the large Cryo-Cell stockholders who had either voted for the Portnoy slate or were undecided. Three of those large stockholders would turn out to be particularly important to the election — Lewis Asset Management, Saneron, and Apollo Capital.

G.   The Lewis Shares

Lewis Asset Management owned approximately [*30] one million shares of Cryo-Cell stock during the time leading up to the Cryo-Cell annual meeting — almost 9% of the shares outstanding.[72] Before July 14, 2007, the Saturday before the Cryo-Cell annual meeting, the proxy for the Lewis shares had been submitted in favor of the Portnoy Slate. The vote attached to the Lewis shares would change, however, after Choi entered an agreement to purchase the Lewis shares with a proxy attached on July 14. Walton, who had brokered the deal by putting Kovarik in touch with Lewis Asset Management, would later be surprised by how those votes would

---

[56] Tr. at 347-48.
[57] JX 190.
[58] Tr. at 348.
[59] Tr. at 424.
[60] Tr. at 417.
[61] JX 190.
[62] Tr. at 418; JX 194.
[63] Tr. at 161.
[64] Tr. at 354-55, 418-19.
[65] Tr. at 355.
[66] Tr. at 355. This response was consistent with Walton's perhaps feigned, but overtly effusive relationship with Filipowski. A June 13 email from Walton to Filipowski and Roszak captures that dynamic:

  Flip . . . you are most definitely CCEL's "Earth Angel"! A million thanks to you and Matt for being there when it counts the most. *We will never disappoint you* . . . Big Hugs, Mercedes

JX 125 (emphasis added).

[67] Tr. at 422.
[68] Tr. at 214-15, 424-25.
[69] JX 194.
[70] Tr. at 424.
[71] JX 194.
[72] JX 266 at 3.

Appendix

change. On Monday, July 16, only hours before the annual meeting, Walton would find out that Choi had submitted the proxies for the Lewis shares and the other shares he owned in favor of the Management Slate, but withheld proxies on three of the directors.[73] That turn of events would have later consequences.

H. The Saneron Shares

Saneron is a research firm with a focus on cellular therapy. Cryo-Cell owns 38% of Saneron and Saneron owns 253,800 shares of Cryo-Cell (about 2% of the outstanding shares). Cryo-Cell and Saneron are involved in many collaborative projects.[74] In addition, [*31] Saneron uses Cryo-Cell's clinical lab and regulated manufacturing facility, which Saneron needs to get into clinical trials.[75]

Despite the close relationship between Cryo-Cell and Saneron, Walton was concerned about how Saneron would vote its shares in the proxy contest.[76] This concern was the result of Saneron not voting its shares in favor of the Management Slate early in the proxy contest and a "weird" conversation that Taymans had with Nicole Kuzmin-Nichols, Saneron's Vice President of Business Development, on June 18 when she asked about how Saneron was going to vote its shares.[77] Walton's immediate response was to forward Taymans' email to Dr. Julie Allickson, Cryo-Cell's Vice President of Research and Development and Laboratory Operations, instructing her that "we can not move forward with any agreements with Saneron until this matter is positively closed."[78]

Walton's concerns and frustration grew with time. She repeatedly tried without success to contact Dr. Paul Sanberg, Saneron's Chairman and co-founder, about Saneron's vote and still had no proxy card from Saneron. Therefore, on June 27, Walton instructed [*32] Allickson to "pause communication with [Saneron] on the project until this matter is positively addressed."[79] Although Walton claimed that her emails about withholding cooperation from Saneron were only internal emails, the silence on the joint projects combined with the requests for Saneron to submit its vote in favor of the Management Slate sent a clear message to Saneron — its vote in favor of the Management Slate was required if it wanted to continue working with Cryo-Cell. This signal's strength was undoubtedly enhanced by Cryo-Cell's ownership of 38% of Saneron.

In addition to withholding its cooperation on joint projects, Cryo-Cell had another means to coerce Saneron's vote — the restrictive legend on Saneron's Cryo-Cell shares. That restrictive legend stated that the shares could not be sold without a registration statement or "an opinion of company counsel that such registration was not required."[80] Saneron had been requesting a counsel opinion authorizing removal of the restriction since January 2005.[81] Cryo-Cell had stonewalled, never agreeing to Saneron's request. Although the defendants now contend that Saneron was not interested in a counsel opinion from [*33] Cryo-Cell removing the restriction because it did not need that action to sell, Saneron's and Cryo-Cell's actions belie that.[82] During the discussions Saneron had with Cryo-Cell about how it would vote in the proxy contest, Saneron's desire to have the restrictive legend removed was an important and frequently discussed topic. For example, removal of the restrictive legend was discussed in a June 27, 2007 email from Kuzmin-Nichols to Taymans[83] and at Saneron's own annual meeting on July 12.[84]

Despite Saneron's requests, Cryo-Cell withheld the counsel opinion lifting the restrictive legend. Instead, Walton, discouraged that Sanberg had not returned her numerous phone calls, attempted to arrange for Choi and Filipowski to purchase the Saneron shares.[85] On July 14, even after she learned that Choi had acquired the Lewis shares, Walton still was concerned about the Saneron shares. She explained her concern in an email to Roszak: "Without Saneron we are at risk. No news this a[.]m[.] on Saneron — working every angle with [Kovarik, Choi's broker] to get to [Sanberg]."[86] On July 15, Walton learned that the efforts by Filipowski and Choi to purchase the Saneron shares had fallen through.[87] In response, she called Sanberg and offered what Saneron had sought [*35] from Cryo-Cell for the previous several years, the counsel opinion removing the restriction on Saneron's shares. Walton had Cryo-Cell's counsel draft and fax the opinion letter to Saneron that Sunday.[88] That coun-

---

[80] JX 2.

[81] JX 4.

[82] The defendants' arguments that the counsel opinion lifting the restriction on the Saneron shares was not meaningful to Saneron because it could obtain a similar opinion from its own counsel and that Saneron did not intend to sell its shares for less than $5 per share, which was materially above the prevailing market price, are similarly unconvincing. If the opinion lifting the restriction were so unimportant, why did Saneron keep asking for it? Likely because, as a practical matter, any prospective purchaser would request that the restrictive legend be removed because the legend, which was typed on the face of the stock certificate, explicitly stated that the shares could only [*34] be transferred if they were effectively registered or Cryo-Cell's counsel issued an opinion that registration was not required. In addition, Kuzmin-Nichols indicated that Saneron needed capital and that one of the options being considered for obtaining that capital was selling its Cryo-Cell stock, even though it was trading at less than $5 per share. Kuzmin-Nichols Dep. at 60-61.

[83] Tr. at 401-02.

[84] Kuzmin-Nichols Dep. at 22.

[85] Tr. at 407-08.

[86] JX 212.

[87] Tr. at 408.

[88] JX 219.

---

[73] Tr. at 443.

[74] Tr. at 335, 342.

[75] Sanberg Dep. at 17.

[76] Tr. at 339-40.

[77] JX 136.

[78] JX 136.

[79] JX 146.

sel opinion, which was also faxed to Cryo-Cell's transfer agent, informed the transfer agent that Cryo-Cell had no objection to the transfer agent reissuing a stock certificate to Saneron without the restrictive legend.[89] In return, Walton demanded that Saneron vote its shares immediately rather than follow its prior plan of voting the shares at the annual meeting.[90] Kuzmin-Nichols made a special trip into Saneron's office that Sunday afternoon just to vote the shares.[91] After Kuzmin-Nichols voted the Saneron shares, Walton emailed Filipowski that "we just locked up Saneron."[92]

The parties dispute whether Saneron's vote was improperly influenced by Walton. I have no difficulty in finding that Saneron's vote was influenced by Cryo-Cell's decision to withhold both cooperation on the companies' joint projects and the counsel opinion lifting the restriction on Saneron's [*36] shares. The defendants argue that Saneron was never going to vote for the Portnoy Slate because Sanberg was unimpressed by the Portnoy Slate. In this as in other respects, the defendant's disparagement of the Portnoy Slate casts a mirrored reflection of ineptitude on the Management Slate because it is very clear that Walton, whose board controlled 38% of Saneron, genuinely feared that Saneron would vote for the Portnoy Slate. Walton's fear that Saneron would not go her way was supported by Saneron's own expressed desire to wait until the meeting day to make its final decision. Sanberg claims to have favored the Management Slate because Portnoy did not know anything about Saneron when he called to solicit Sanberg and because the Portnoy Slate did not include any scientists.[93] Those after-the-fact explanations are contrary to Saneron's desire to wait until the annual meeting to vote its shares and are at odds with Walton's clear discomfort over Saneron's refusal to commit to vote for her slate.

In concluding that Saneron's voting decision was influenced by Walton's combination of threats and inducements, I acknowledge that Sanberg, Kuzmin-Nichols, and Bernard Skerkowski [*37] of Saneron have testified otherwise.[94] But that is, of course, unsurprising. Cryo-Cell owns 38% of Saneron and it is not to be expected that its executives would suggest that Saneron's vote was in essence paid for by a removal of a restrictive legend and the necessity of obtaining Cryo-Cell management's cooperation in projects vital to Saneron. The objective facts, in my view, support the conclusion that Saneron did not commit to vote for the Management Slate until the counsel opinion authorizing the removal of the

restrictive legend was issued and after it was made clear that if Saneron voted no and the Management Slate won, the likelihood of future strategic relations between the companies would have been rendered much more doubtful.

I. The Apollo Shares

During the time leading up to the Cryo-Cell annual meeting, Apollo Capital owned approximately 323,000 shares of Cryo-Cell stock (almost 3% of the shares outstanding). Kyle Krueger, Apollo's decision maker with respect to the Cryo-Cell shares, was the subject of an intense lobbying effort in the days preceding the annual meeting. On July 13, Walton and Taymans [*38] had an hour-long discussion with Krueger in an attempt to convince him to vote in favor of the Management Slate.[95] As part of that discussion, Krueger asked Walton to have Filipowski contact him. Walton arranged for Filipowski to speak with Krueger that Friday afternoon, and after that conversation Krueger voted his shares in favor of the Management Slate.[96]

The following day, Saturday, July 14, Krueger emailed Portnoy to let him know that he had decided to vote for the Management Slate.[97] Portnoy, who had been in contact with Krueger since February, did not give up on soliciting Krueger's vote. He emailed Krueger asking him to reassess his vote and consider calling some of Cryo-Cell's former employees to find out more about "the reality of the situation" at Cryo-Cell.[98] Portnoy also contacted Susan Archibald, a former Cryo-Cell employee with whom he had been in contact since February, and asked her to call Krueger. Archibald called Krueger on Sunday, July 15, and answered the questions Krueger had about Cryo-Cell.[99] After Archibald spoke to Krueger, Krueger changed Apollo's vote to favor the Portnoy Group.[100]

J. The Annual Meeting

The Management Slate was greeted with surprising and unpleasant news on the morning of July 16, the day of the annual meeting. Walton learned that the Apollo shares that she thought had been voted in favor of the Management Slate had flipped in favor of the Portnoy Slate. She and Roszak then changed course and Roszak set out to buy the Apollo shares for Filipowski. Roszak purchased the Apollo shares for SilkRoad Equity sometime before the 11 a.m. start to the annual meeting.[101] As part of that

---

[89] JX 219.
[90] Tr. at 409-10.
[91] Kuzmin-Nichols Dep. at 44-46.
[92] JX 218.
[93] Sandberg Dep. at 8.
[94] Sanberg Dep. at 14-15; Kuzmin-Nichols Dep. at 54; Skerkowski Dep. at 18-19.

[95] Tr. at 369-70.
[96] JX 202; JX 203.
[97] JX 193.
[98] JX 193.
[99] Archibald Dep. [*39] at 133.
[100] Tr. at 56.
[101] Roszak Dep. at 130. The transaction between Roszak and Krueger was agreed to on July 16 and Krueger processed the change in the votes based on Roszak's word that they had a deal at $3 per

transaction, Krueger agreed to switch the vote attached to the Apollo shares from the Portnoy Slate to the Management Slate. But it would take time for the change to be processed.

Even more important than the Apollo shares was the news that Choi had withheld giving his proxy as to three of the members of the Management Slate. Walton called Choi at around 9 a.m., two hours before the start of the annual meeting, to ask why he had withheld his proxy as to those candidates. Choi explained that he "thought that by withholding votes for three of the Cryo-Cell directors that I would be able to create vacancies to effectively fill them with my own candidates, my own nominees." [102] Walton informed Choi that rather than creating vacancies for Choi's own nominees, his decision to withhold his proxy as to certain Management Slate candidates would likely result in a split slate of directors.[103] Choi then asked Walton how he could fix his "mistake."[104] Walton put Choi in touch with Chris Hayden, Cryo-Cell's proxy solicitor, who explained the process for switching the votes, and Choi set to work changing his votes. Hayden informed Walton that it "could take us [*41] quite a while to fix Mr. Choi's mistake," especially the votes for the approximately 135,000 shares held at Charles Schwab.[105]

As the time for the 11 a.m. annual meeting approached, Walton knew that the outcome of the election was uncertain and that the Management Slate needed time for the Choi votes to be switched. The Management Slate also needed time for the votes attached to the Apollo shares Roszak was acquiring to be switched.[106]

The agenda for the annual meeting called for the following items: (i) welcome and meeting procedures; (ii) the election of directors; (iii) the ratification of the appointment of independent registered accountants; (iii) consideration of a shareholder proposal; (iv) a presentation by Walton; and (v) general shareholder questions.[107] On July 13, the Friday before the annual meeting, the Portnoy Slate agreed to the rules of conduct proposed by Cryo-Cell's counsel.[108] Those rules included the [*42] rule that "the Chair-

man has the authority to decide all procedural issues regarding the conduct of the meeting, including adjournment."[109] But Portnoy's counsel warned in an email sent to Cryo-Cell's counsel early the morning of the annual meeting, that the Chairman's procedural authority, regardless of the agreement between the competing slates, "must be exercised in accordance with the By-laws of the company, and may not be arbitrary or capricious."[110] That belated attempt to add to the prior agreement on the rules of conduct never was communicated to Walton before the start of the annual meeting."[111]

The annual meeting started at 11 a.m. with a welcome and an explanation of the agenda and the rules of conduct. The meeting then proceeded as would be expected, with Portnoy introducing the Portnoy Slate, Walton introducing the Management Slate, and the polls opening for the election of directors. The ratification of auditors and the shareholder proposal were also introduced and the polls opened on those issues. Walton provided the stockholders with the opportunity to ask questions and have them answered by both her and Portnoy. [*43] Several Cryo-Cell stockholders, including Dan Richard, asked numerous questions. After the stockholder questions subsided, Portnoy attempted to introduce a motion to close the polls.[112] The time was approximately 12:30 p.m. and all the agenda items had been addressed.[113] Walton responded to Portnoy by ruling him "out of order."[114] Walton "ruled [Portnoy] out of order because [she] wanted the polls to remain open."[115] She admits, however, that while keeping the polls open was what she wanted to achieve, that is not what she explained to the Cryo-Cell stockholders.[116]

After rejecting Portnoy's motion to close the polls, Walton deviated from the agenda. She "decided at the meeting on the spot" to have Allickson, Cryo-Cell's Vice President of Research and Development and Laboratory Operations, give an unscheduled presentation on Cryo-Cell's research and development.[117] After Allickson's presentation concluded at approximately 1 p.m., Portnoy again attempted to move to close the polls.[118] Walton's response was the same as before — ruling Portnoy "out of order" without providing any information about what that meant [*44] or explaining that she was using her procedural authority to keep the polls open. Walton then had Rob Doll, Cryo-Cell's Vice President of Corporate Marketing, Sales & Services, give an impromptu presentation on Cryo-Cell's sales. The

---

share. Roszak Dep. at 133. Roszak, however, did not close the transaction until July 31. Rosak Dep. at 150. The reason for the delay was that the Cryo-Cell stock price dropped materially after the election and Roszak was trying to see if he could negotiate a better deal with Krueger. Roszak [*40] Dep. at 150-51. Roszak only closed the deal at $3 per share after Krueger sent an email stating that Roszak "procured [his] vote by fraud" and that he was "going to seek reversal of [his] vote." Roszak Dep. at 163.

[102] Tr. at 357-58.

[103] Tr. at 357.

[104] Tr. at 358.

[105] Tr. at 359.

[106] Walton claims she did not know until late afternoon that Roszak — her collaborator in the vote acquisition plan — had forged a deal to buy those shares that very morning. I find that denial incredible.

[107] JX 228.

[108] JX 197.

[109] JX 228.

[110] JX 240.

[111] Tr. at 361.

[112] Tr. at 9.

[113] Tr. at 8-9.

[114] Tr. at 365.

[115] Tr. at 365.

[116] Tr. at 365.

[117] Tr. at 447.

[118] Tr. at 9-10.

Allickson and Doll presentations took over an hour in total.[119]

After Doll's presentation and at some time between 1:30 p.m. and 2:00 p.m., Walton declared that there would be a "break for lunch" until 4:45 p.m. and that the polls would remain open during that break.[120] The issues of the exact time that Walton announced there would be a break in the meeting, the exact words she used in making that announcement, and whether that break was an "adjournment" of the meeting are highly contested. What is uncontroverted is that Walton was not forthright with the Cryo-Cell stockholders in announcing the purpose for the break. The defendants, speaking through the testimony of defendant Christian and their pre-trial brief, attempted to justify the break as a response to several requests for a lunch by stockholders, including Mark Portnoy, the fact that the meeting had run through the normal lunch hour, and, Christian's [*45] determination that the meeting "obviously wasn't going to conclude very soon."[121] Christian buttressed his conclusion that the meeting was not going to end soon with testimony that stockholders were still asking questions as of the break.[122] Later, Christian had to acknowledge that he had no direct knowledge of why Walton decided a lunch break was necessary and that his direct testimony had misrepresented what was occurring at the meeting just before the break.[123]

As a matter of fact, I conclude that Walton was stalling for time, seeking to ensure not only that the Choi and Apollo votes had been switched, but to troll for even more votes, not sure that those blocs would suffice to prevail. Mark Portnoy's request for food was a request for food to be brought in rather than to stop the meeting for a lunch break. In any event, that request was made more than an hour before Walton decided that a three-hour, mid-afternoon lunch was appropriate.[124] Moreover, Christian admitted that stockholder questions had ceased before the unplanned (and I find intentionally filibustering) [*46] presentations by Allickson and Doll.[125] When pressed, Walton admitted the "real reason" for the break was to make sure that Choi's votes had been switched and that absent the issue with Choi's votes, she probably would not have taken a break.[126]

During the break, Walton was not just waiting for the changes in Choi's and Apollo's votes to be processed — she was actively soliciting votes and continuing her matchmaking plan. For example, Walton had Irene Smith, her executive assistant,

give Charles Northcutt, a Cryo-Cell stockholder who had the proxies for approximately 100,000 shares, her business card with Roszak's name and phone number written on its face.[127]

By the end of the break, the vote changes that Walton was waiting for had been processed. As Hayden had anticipated, the votes for the non-Schwab Choi shares were changed relatively quickly, with the changes having been processed by the 11:16 a.m. voting report from Broadridge (formerly ADP).[128] At the time of that Broadridge report, proxies for the Choi shares held at Charles Schwab were still withheld for three [*47] directors. In addition, that report showed the Apollo shares were still voted in favor of the Portnoy Slate. The next Broadridge report, which showed the reversal of the Choi withholds for the Schwab shares and the change in the vote for the Apollo shares, was not issued until 3:41 p.m.[129] Thus, the exact time at which the votes for the Schwab and Apollo shares changed cannot be identified. Hayden suggests that that the change of the votes for the Schwab shares was processed by approximately 1:55 p.m.[130] Neither Hayden nor Paul Schulman, the Portnoy Slate's proxy solicitor, could estimate the time the change of the votes for the Apollo shares was processed.[131]

At 4:45 p.m., having received the 3:41 p.m. Broadridge report and now knowing that the Management Slate held a lead of approximately 600,000 votes, Walton reconvened the meeting.[132] Walton asked if any stockholders who wanted to vote had not voted, and when no stockholders indicated that they still needed an opportunity to vote, Walton quickly closed the polls.[133] The entire post-break activities took approximately five minutes.[134]

The six-hour length of the annual meeting, primarily due to the three-hour lunch break and the approximately one hour of impromptu presentations by Allickson and Doll was surprising. Cryo-Cell's annual meeting typically only lasted one hour, and the hotel conference room where the annual meeting took place was only reserved until 1 p.m.[135] Cryo-Cell's own proxy solicitor, Hayden, was scheduled on a flight leaving at 2:10 p.m. from Tampa.[136]

Even after the close of the extended annual meeting, the day was not over for Cryo-Cell's stockholders. Only minutes after the annual meeting ended, Cryo-Cell filed its 10-Q with the SEC.[137] That document disclosed that Cryo-Cell lost $1.4 million in

---

[119] Tr. at 302.
[120] Tr. at 366-67.
[121] Tr. at 258, 299-300; Def. Op. Pre-Trial Br. at 28-29.
[122] Tr. at 262.
[123] Tr. at 297-98, 301-02.
[124] Mark Portnoy Dep. at 25.
[125] Tr. at 302.
[126] Tr. at 367, 448.

[127] Smith Dep. at 36-39; Northcutt Dep. at 13, 27; JX 284.
[128] JX 230; Tr. at 191.
[129] JX 237; Tr. at 98-100.
[130] Tr. at 193.
[131] Tr. at 99-100, 220-221.
[132] Tr. [*48] at 104-05, 450.
[133] Tr. at 368-69.
[134] Tr. at 222.
[135] Tr. at 430.
[136] Tr. at 222-23.
[137] Tr. at 450-51; JX 234.

Appendix

the previous quarter.[138] The market's response following the annual meeting and the 10-Q was not positive — Cryo-Cell stock dropped from a close of $2.35 per share on July 16 to $1.48 per share on July 31.[139]

K.   The Results Of The Election

On July 31, the Inspectors of Election issued their final report, showing that all six directors on the Management Slate had prevailed [*49] in the proxy contest.[140] After adjusting the election results for approximately 30,000 shares that the parties have stipulated were improperly recorded for the Management Slate, the Management Slate candidate with the most votes exceeded the Portnoy Slate candidate with the least votes by 613,977 votes.[141]

L.   The Second Filipowski Group Board Seat

After it became clear that the Management Slate had prevailed, Walton and the board immediately began to follow through on their agreement to give the Filipowski Group an additional board seat. On August 2, 2007, Walton emailed Cryo-Cell's counsel about a phone call she had with Roszak about the promised board seat: "Roszak called today and among other matters indicated that [Filipowski] had chosen him to fill *their* second board seat."[142] That email also contained a fig leaf designed to suggest that this was not a sealed deal: "I asked [Roszak] to e-mail me his profile along with one or two other potential candidates, recognizing that the board is obligated to conduct our established process for consideration and due diligence review of nominees. He agreed to provide. [Counsel for the board], please add the [*50] background check for Roszak to the project."[143] I view those statements as just what I said, a fig leaf to conceal the prior deal, especially from counsel.

Carrying out their side of this game of creating a good appearance, the Filipowski Group filed an amendment to its Schedule 13D on August 3, 2007. That amendment disclosed that "[p]ursuant to its discussions with management, SilkRoad Equity intends to seek to put a person on the Board of Directors of the Company." [144] That same day, Roszak also emailed Walton three profiles for prospective board candidates, including his own, and asked Walton to "[p]lease let [him] know what our next steps are in this regard."[145] Walton responded to Roszak's email with the following: "Thanks for your follow-up. I'll get things rolling on this with [counsel

for the board] and the board. I'll keep you posted as we progress. Please note that the BOD dinner is on 9/26 and the meeting itself is on 9/27--two dates to reserve. More to follow."[146] The process of adding Roszak to the board was halted, however, with the filing of the complaint in this action on that same Friday, August 3, 2007.

The defendants claim that the exchange of emails above does not indicate that the Filipowski Group had been promised a second board seat. Instead, Walton argues that her email to Cryo-Cell's counsel about "their second board seat" only "referr[ed] to the fact that counsel knew that Mr. Roszak and Mr. Filipowski had requested a second board seat."[147] Walton claims that her later email to Roszak about the dates of the next board dinner and meeting was not sent to Roszak because he was being added to the board but rather to inform Filipowski of the dates. Walton alleges that Roszak was Filipowski's "chief administrator" and sending him information for Filipowski was not unusual.[148] Walton's alternate after-the-fact explanation is that she was informing Roszak that the governance committee, which was not mentioned in the email, would be meeting on that date and that it might be a possible date for that committee to interview Roszak.[149] I find that the email to counsel about "their second board seat" and the email to Roszak about the dates of the upcoming board events, when combined with facts described above about Roszak's request for a second board seat, support my conclusion that [*52] Walton had promised the Filipowski Group a second board seat before the election.

The defendants' explanations of the Walton's emails are, candidly, implausible. Sadly, that is consistent with a good deal of the defendants' testimony. The defendants, rather than coming into court and honestly explaining what occurred in the heat of a close proxy contest, presented me with numerous half-truths and implausible tales. Defendant Christian, for example, implausibly said that the proxy contest had nothing to do with adding Filipowski to the Management Slate. He also claimed to have knowledge of the reasons for the decision to take a lunch break at the annual meeting when he had no role in making that decision. Moreover, Christian gave misleading and then retracted testimony about whether stockholders were asking questions immediately before the lunch break. Walton, who sat through Christian's misleading testimony and saw the truth come out on cross-examination, was undeterred from making implausible assertions. Her claim that the email about "their second board seat" does not mean what it plainly says is unbelievable. Equally as implausible [*53] is her claim that her

---

[138] JX 234 at 5.
[139] JX 290.
[140] JX 275.
[141] Stip. Facts 23-24.
[142] JX 279 (emphasis added).
[143] JX 279.
[144] JX 278.
[145] JX 280.

[146] JX [*51] 281.
[147] Tr. at 466-67.
[148] Tr. at 460-61.
[149] Tr. at 466.

reply email to Roszak about the dates of the next board events, which did not copy or even reference Filipowski and was clearly made in the context of an email chain discussing adding Roszak to the board, was merely intended to give notice to Filipowski about those events. Perhaps, in an odd way, the best argument in favor of Walton's improbable explanations that her emails really mean something different than what they seem to plainly state is that whether giving testimony in court or explaining to Cryo-Cell's stockholders why she was declaring a break in the annual meeting, Walton has been consistent in making statements that differ from what I perceive to be the underlying realities of the situation.

II.   The Merits Of Portnoy's Claims

Portnoy has brought this claim under 8 *Del. C.* § 225 challenging the seating of the Management Slate. He claims that the election results should be overturned because the Management Slate would not have been elected had the following alleged breaches of duty not occurred:

1) A supposedly improper agreement by the Cryo-Cell board to include Filipowski on the Management Slate, not because they believed that was in the best interests [*54] of Cryo-Cell and its stockholders, but merely as consideration for Filipowski's agreement to vote for the incumbent board members in the proxy fight;

2) A supposedly improper promise by Walton that the incumbent board members would, if re-elected, add another Filipowski designee, Roszak, to the board if Filipowski continued to buy up more shares and if that conduct resulted in the Management Slate winning the election;

3) A course of conduct by Walton employing both threats and an inducement to influence Saneron to cast its vote for the Management Slate;

4) An adjournment of the annual meeting without a vote of the Cryo-Cell stockholders as Portnoy contends was required by the corporation's bylaws, and, in any event, an inequitably motivated and falsely justified "lunch break" that was designed to give the Management Slate more time to gather votes because they feared defeat if the vote was counted in accordance with the original schedule.

As a [*55] remedy for these supposed breaches, Portnoy argues that I should simply seat his Slate because, but for these breaches, they would have prevailed. He also seeks reimbursement for his fees

and expenses, not only in the proxy fight, but in this litigation.

For their part, the defendants contend that they at all times acted properly. As they see it, all of their conduct was fair. They vehemently deny most of Portnoy's factual allegations, but then alternatively argue that even if they did what he alleges, no remedy should ensue. Proxy fights are full of rough and tumble, in their estimation, and the fact that their side's elbows were sharper is no basis to upset the election results. As a backstop, the defendants argue that I should deny Portnoy any right to contest the election because they view his communications with a former Cryo-Cell employee bound by a confidentiality agreement during the proxy fight to be inequitable behavior disqualifying him from equitable relief.

I begin my consideration of these arguments, with Portnoy's claims regarding the relationship between the incumbent board members on the Management Slate (led by Walton) and Filipowski. I then move on to briefly address [*56] the Saneron issue. I conclude with the claim related to the conduct of the meeting itself.

A.   The Addition Of Filipowski To The Management Slate

Portnoy claims that all aspects of the incumbents' dealings with Filipowski are tainted by fiduciary misconduct. As he sees it, the incumbents had already marked out the key characteristics they were looking for in additional board members — healthcare industry and stem cell industry experience — and that Filipowski did not have those. Walton, and a board that Portnoy rightly portrays as having every appearance of largely following her lead without much question, simply made a bargain to add Filipowski to the Management Slate, not because they thought his service would help Cryo-Cell but because it would ensure that the large bloc of votes Filipowski controlled would vote for their re-election. That is, this was an entrenchment-motivated decision. Portnoy contends that the deal struck between Walton and the other incumbents, on the one hand, and Filipowski, on the other, to add Filipowski to the Management Slate in exchange for his support in the proxy fight constituted an illegal vote-buying arrangement.

On this claim, which has some color, [*57] I find in favor of the defendants. My conclusion rests on several grounds. Initially, I note that an arrangement of this kind fits comfortably, as a linguistic matter, within the traditional definition of so-called "vote buying" used in our jurisprudence. As defined by Vice Chancellor Hartnett in his important decision in *Schreiber v. Carney,* "[v]ote-buying . . . is simply a voting agreement supported by consideration personal to the stockholder, whereby the stockholder divorces his discretionary voting power and votes as directed by the offeror."[150] In this case, I have no doubt that the voting agreement between the Filipowski Group and the incumbents was only assented to by Filipowski after he was offered a candidacy on the Management Slate. What I am more doubtful about is whether an arrangement of this kind — where the incumbents offer a potential insurgent a seat on the management slate in exchange for the potential insurgent's voting support — should trigger the sort of heightened scrutiny rightly given to more questionable arrangements.

To say that the law of corporations has struggled with how to address the subject of so-called "vote buying" [*58] is no insult to judges or corporate law scholars, the question of what inducements and agreements may legitimately be forged to cement a voting coalition is doubtless as old as the concept of a polity itself. For these very real-world reasons, *Schreiber* refused to say that any sort of arrangement involving the exchange of consideration in connection with a stockholder's agreement to vote a particular way was forbidden vote buying.[151] Indeed, distinguished scholars have anguished (the adjective I take away from their work) over how to deal with such arrangements, with most concluding that flat-out prohibitions are neither workable nor of utility to diversified stockholders.[152] The absence of a per se ban on such arrangements is unsurprising for another obvious reason, voting agreements with respect to corporate stock are actually contemplated by our statutory corporate law.[153] Often such agreements have the intended effect of forming a voting coalition between stockholders that involves the requirement that the contracting parties vote to elect each other to the board.

To deal with these complexities, *Schreiber* declined to find that vote buying was, in the first instance, per se improper.[154] Rather, *Schreiber* articulated a two-pronged analysis.[155] In the first instance, if the plaintiff can show that the "object or purpose [of the vote buying was] to defraud or in some way disenfranchise the other stockholders," the arrangement would be "illegal per se."[156] Putting this in terms that I think are truer to the way our corporate law works, what I take from this is that if the plaintiff proved that the arrangement under challenge was improperly motivated, then the arrange-

ment would be set aside in equity, irrespective of its technical compliance with the DGCL.[157] That is, in keeping with the traditional vigilance this court has displayed in ensuring the fairness [*60] of the corporate election process, and in particular the process by which directors are elected, purposely inequitable conduct in the accumulation of voting power will not be tolerated.[158] Even when a vote buying arrangement cannot be found, in the first instance, to be motivated by a fraudulent, disenfranchising, or otherwise inequitable intent, *Schreiber* concluded that "because vote-buying is so easily susceptible of abuse it must be viewed as a voidable transaction subject to a test for intrinsic fairness."[159]

Subjecting an agreement to add a potential insurgent to a management slate to the *Schreiber* intrinsic fairness test would, in my view, be an inadvisable and counterproductive precedent. If one takes a judicial standard of review seriously, as the members of this court do, the decision to subject all such arrangements to the entire fairness standard could result in creating litigable factual issues about a large number of useful compromises that result in the addition of fresh blood to management slates, new candidates who will [*62] tend to represent actual owners of equity and might therefore be more independent of management and more useful representatives of the interests of stockholders generally. I emphasize "litigable factual issues" because a judicial standard that by definition imposes on the defendants an onerous burden of persuasion is one that largely eliminates any possible use of Rule 12(b)(6) motion practice to get rid of the case. Beyond the pleading stage, it is also difficult to meet a substantive fairness standard by invoking Rule 56, because any material factual question relevant to fairness will result in the need for a trial.

In being chary about extending *Schreiber's* reach to this context, I do not underestimate the value of

---

[150] 447 A.2d 17, 23 (Del. Ch. 1982).

[151] *Id.* at 25-26.

[152] *See, e.g.,* Thomas J. Andre, Jr., *A Preliminary Inquiry into the Utility of Vote Buying in the* [*59] *Market for Corporate Control,* 63 S. CAL. L. REV. 533, 636 (1990); Robert Charles Clark, *Vote Buying and Corporate Law,* 29 Case W. RES. L. REV. 776, 806-07 (1979). *But see* Frank H. Easterbrook & Daniel R. Fischel, *Voting in Corporate Law,* 26 J.L. & ECON. 395, 410-11 (1983) (arguing against allowing vote-buying agreements).

[153] *See* 8 *Del. C.* § 218 (permitting voting trusts and voting agreements).

[154] 447 A.2d at 25-26.

[155] *Id.*

[156] *Id.*

[157] *See Schnell v. Chris-Craft Indus., Inc.,* 285 A.2d 437, 439 (Del. 1971) (holding that "inequitable action does not become permissible simply because it is legally possible"); *see also* Adolphe A. Berle, *Corporate Powers As Powers In Trust,* 44 HARV. L. REV. 1049, 1049 (1931) ("[I]n every case, corporate action must be twice tested: first, by the technical rules having to do with the existence and proper exercise of the power; second, by equitable rules somewhat analogous to those which apply in favor of a cestui que trust to the trustee's exercise of wide powers granted to him in the instrument making him a fiduciary.").

[158] *E.g., MM Cos. v. Liquid Audio, Inc.,* 813 A.2d 1118, 1127 (Del. 2003) [*61] ("This Court and the Court of Chancery have remained assiduous in carefully reviewing any board actions designed to interfere with or impede the effective exercise of corporate democracy by shareholders, especially in an election of directors."); *Schnell,* 285 A.2d at 439 (Del. 1971); *State of Wisconsin Inv. Bd. v. Peerless Sys. Corp.,* 2000 Del. Ch. LEXIS 170, 2000 WL 1805376, at *7 (Del. Ch. 2000); *Chesapeake Corp. v. Shore,* 771 A.2d 293, 297 (Del. Ch. 2000); *Agranoff v. Miller,* 1999 Del. Ch. LEXIS 78, 1999 WL 219650, at *11-12, *18 (Del. Ch. 1999); *Blasius Indus., Inc. v. Atlas Corp.,* 564 A.2d 651, 663 (Del. Ch. 1988); *Lerman v. Diagnostic Data, Inc.,* 421 A.2d 906, 914 (Del. Ch. 1980).

[159] 447 A.2d at 25-26.

being included in the management slate. An offer to be on the management slate will often promise a near certainty of eventual election. At the very least, it will relieve the insurgent of having to pay for his own candidacy and to run a contested election against corporate insiders who do not have to pay their own solicitation costs. Instead, the insurgent would be on the inside track, so to speak.

But being on the inside track is different than being on the board, and [*63] that difference suggests that employing an entire fairness standard to such arrangements is overkill. If the only arrangement at issue is a promise to add a potential insurgent to the management slate in exchange for the insurgent's voting support, then the arrangement is subject to stockholder policing in an obvious, but nonetheless, potent form. That policing occurs at the ballot box itself.

Here, to be specific, the Cryo-Cell stockholders went to the polls knowing that Filipowski had been added to the Management Slate. Those stockholders also knew that Filipowski had contracted to vote the Filipowski Group's shares for the Management Slate. Although it was not publicly disclosed that Filipowski's agreement to vote for the Management Slate had been conditioned on his addition to that Slate, and that the incumbents had added Filipowski to the Management Slate in exchange for his support, that inference was, I think, unmistakable to any rational stockholder. Surely it was known by Portnoy, who knew that Filipowski had been unhappy about the Company's performance, and had flirted with running a slate with Portnoy, only to secure a place for himself on the Management Slate. Therefore, [*64] Portnoy was well-positioned to point out that Filipowski had committed to support incumbents whose wisdom and fidelity to stockholders Filipowski himself had only recently called into serious question.

Given that the electorate's own opportunity to decide for itself whether Filipowski should serve, I think it unwise, as a matter of our common law, to apply the intrinsic fairness test to this situation. As Portnoy would have it, I should make a judgment about whether Walton and the other incumbents would have ever thought Filipowski a board member beneficial to Cryo-Cell *but for* their entrenchment-motivated desire to secure his vote. I have little hesitancy in concluding that Walton was not anxious to have Filipowski on her board. She and her colleagues warmed to that idea only when confronted with the reality of almost certain defeat if Filipowski joined Portnoy in running a dissident slate, and were at great risk even if Filipowski supported the Management Slate. In other words, I have no doubt Filipowski was added to the Management Slate primarily to secure his vote. But I also have no doubt that Walton and the board determined that Filipowski was a credible candidate with some useful [*65] attributes.

The notion that judges should chew over the complicated calculus made by incumbent boards considering whether to add to the management slate candidates proposed by a large blockholder whose velvety suggestions were cloaking an unmistakably clenched fist seems to run against many of the sound reasons for the business judgment rule.[160] There is, thankfully, a practical and civic dynamic in much of our nation's human relations, including in commerce, by which clashes of viewpoint are addressed peaceably through give and take. When stockholders can decide for themselves whether to seat a candidate who obtained a place on a management slate by way of such bargaining, it seems unwise to formulate a standard that involves the potential for excessive and imprecise judicial involvement.[161]

In expressing concerns about over-breadth in this area, this decision echoes concerns voiced by the Supreme Court and this court about the difficulty of applying the compelling justification test articulated in *Blasius* in a manner that works sensible results.[162] But like those decisions, this decision is rooted in the premise that the *Schnell* doctrine, authorizing this court to set aside conduct that is inequitably motivated and that unfairly tilts the [*67] electoral playing field, is itself a potent tool of equity. That is, the first order review required by *Schreiber* and that suggested in this court's recent decisions in *Mercier v. Inter-Tel (Del.), Inc.*[163] and *In re MONY Group, Inc. Shareholder Litigation,*[164] which looks to the subjective motivations of the defendants is an extremely important safeguard of the stockholder voting rights whose importance were so eloquently articulated in *Blasius,* particularly when insiders are undertaking

---

[160] *See, e.g., In re Caremark Int'l Inc. Derivative Litig.,* 698 A.2d 959, 967 (Del. Ch. 1996) ("To employ a different rule — one that permitted an 'objective' evaluation of the decision — would expose directors to substantive second guessing by ill-equipped judges or juries, which would, in the long-run, be injurious to investor interests.").

[161] The doctrine of ratification is not a satisfactory [*66] answer to this problem. Under our law, ratification has to be accomplished by a vote of the disinterested shares. That is, even if one assumes that the election of the nominee on the management slate by the electorate is a ratification of that nominee's placement on that slate by way of the agreement under challenge, the nominee would have to win a majority of the shares not subject to the agreement. Because the very purpose of voting alliances is to pool voting power, disqualification of those shares for these purposes would render them less effective. Here, for example, Filipowski would not have won absent the shares he and the other Management Slate members voted in his favor. That is also true for the rest of the Management Slate.

[162] *See, e.g., Williams v. Geier,* 671 A.2d 1368, 1376 (Del. 1996) ("*Blasius'* burden of demonstrating a 'compelling justification' is quite onerous, and is therefore applied rarely."); *Mercier v. Inter-Tel (Del.), Inc.,* 929 A.2d 786, 809-10 (Del. Ch. 2007); *In re MONY Group, Inc. S'holder Litig.,* 853 A.2d 661, 674 (Del. Ch. 2004); *Chesapeake,* 771 A.2d at 319-20.

[163] 929 A.2d at 810.

[164] 853 A.2d at 676-77.

actions designed to aid their own efforts to retain office.[165]

The second order questions of what good faith actions affecting the voting and the election process (and which elections) trigger what form of heightened scrutiny are important and controversial. But the debate over those questions should not obscure the potency of a good old-fashioned inquiry under precedent such as *Schnell,* which proscribes conduct that is disloyal in the well-understood sense that it was undertaken not to advance corporate interests, but to entrench managers in office.[166]

In my view, a mere offer of a position on a management slate should not be considered a vote-buying arrangement subject to a test of entire fairness, and for that reason, I see no reason to condemn the addition of Filipowski to the Management Slate.[167]

---

[165] *See Inter-Tel,* 929 A.2d at 807 ("Because there is a burden on the party in power to identify its legitimate objectives and to explain its actions as necessary to advance those objections, flimsy pretense stands a greater chance of being [*68] revealed.").

[166] *See Cede & Co. v. Technicolor, Inc. ("Cede II"),* 634 A.2d 345, 363 (Del. 1993) (stating that action taken for the purpose of entrenchment is disloyal).

[167] In expressing concerns about subjecting the addition of a candidate to a management slate to a fairness test, I also acknowledge that the recent decision in *Inter-Tel* articulating a method for addressing behavior influencing the conduct of a corporate election resembles the *Schreiber* test in important ways. That decision applied, consistent with *Unocal,* a two-part review. *Inter-Tel,* 929 A.2d at 810-11 (referencing *Unocal Corp. v. Mesa Petroleum Co.,* 493 A.2d 946 (Del. 1985)). In the first instance, that review required the directors to show that their election-directed conduct was motivated by "a legitimate corporate objective." *Id.* at 810. That is, as a minimum, the directors had to show that they acted in good faith to advance proper corporate, not personal interests. *Id.* ("[T]he directors should bear the burden of persuasion to show that their motivations were proper [*70] and not selfish."). Even if they made that showing, they then had to demonstrate that their actions were reasonable, in the sense that they did not have the effect of precluding the stockholders from voting contrary to management's wishes or coercing the stockholders in their voting calculus. *Id.* at 810-11.

> As with the *Schreiber* test, the first layer of the test remains focused where it should, on the question of whether the actions of the defendants were well-motivated, i.e., a straightforward *Schnell* inquiry. Applied to actions like that of adding someone to the management slate (rather than say, how an election was conducted), that first layer is difficult to apply because if the defendants believed in good faith that their continued board service is useful to stockholders and that the new addition to the management slate will help in the election process and be a credible director, then condemning their decision without some other troubling effect or evidence would have the effect of chilling voluntary solutions to stockholder unrest.
>
> The second-stage of the *Inter-Tel* standard would be advantageous, because it would likely be less litigation-intensive and judicially-intrusive to [*71] consider the objective effect of an arrangement of this kind. Because such arrangements would rarely, one thinks, preclude stockholders from electing someone else or coerce them out of doing so, use of a standard of this kind would provide more possibility for low-cost resolution of weak claims, while still requiring defendants to survive review under a plaintiff-friendly standard of review. In so suggesting, I confess to believing it awkward and not particularly useful for a judge to inquire into whether it was "entirely fair" for incumbent directors to add a

As an alternative matter, the defendants have convinced me that there was nothing unfair about joining forces with Filipowski in this manner. In this regard, I note that there is not a hint that Filipowski sought to receive financial payments from Cryo-Cell in the form of contracts [*69] or consulting fees or other such arrangements. What he sought was influence on the board of a company in which he owned a large number of shares, an ownership interest that gave him an incentive to increase the company's value. Stockholders knew he sought a seat and he had to obtain their votes to get on the board.

For all these reasons, I conclude that Portnoy's attack on this aspect of the incumbents' dealings with Filipowski fails.

B.   The Promise Of A Second Board Seat For The Filipowski Group

I reach a different conclusion, however, about the later arrangement that was reached with Filipowski shortly before the annual meeting. As I found previously, Walton (acting at the very least with the apparent authority of her board colleagues, who were extremely deferential to her leadership) promised Filipowski that if the Management Slate won, the incumbent board majority [*72] would use its powers under the Company's bylaws to expand the Cryo-Cell board from six members to seven and to fill the new seat with Filipowski's designee, Roszak. That promise was made in response to Roszak's request — as Filipowski's negotiator — and made in exchange for Filipowski's promise to go out and buy more shares (and therefore votes).

Although the defendants deny that this deal was made, I find their denial lacking in credibility. I also have no doubt that Walton had sufficient dominion over the Cryo-Cell board to deliver on the deal and that she and her fellow incumbents would have placed Roszak on the board had not this suit by Portnoy intervened and made that inadvisable, from a litigation and perceptual standpoint.

I believe that this arrangement differed in materially important respects from the prior agreement to place Filipowski on the Management Slate. For starters, Walton did not merely promise someone a shot at getting elected by the stockholders by running in the advantaged posture of being a member of a management slate. She promised that she and her incumbent colleagues would use their powers as directors of Cryo-Cell to increase the size of the board and seat [*73] Roszak. This was therefore a promise that would not be, for the duration of the term, subject to prior approval by the electorate.

In noting this difference, however, I wish to be mindful of the continuing relevance of the color grey.

---

certain person to a management slate in exchange for her voting support.

As is well known, it is hardly unusual for boards to address the concerns of unsettled stockholders by using their powers to fill a vacancy (whether newly created or pre-existing) with a director suggested by the stockholders. Indeed, many stockholder advocates believe that developments of this kind should be more common. There is therefore some non-trivial basis to be concerned about labeling such arrangements as vote buying arrangements subject to *Schreiber,* or as inequitable under *Schnell,* even if the incumbents' motivations for the arrangements include (as they almost always will) a desire to remain in office.

In voicing this concern, I recognize that there is a rather obvious retort, which is that incumbents should not be adding new candidates only on the condition that those who suggest them agree to vote for the management slate at the next election. But if one is going to address the issue maturely — in the sense of actually realistically considering [*74] the human, business, and practical considerations that motivate pragmatic settlements of difficult problems — then that is no answer at all. From the subjective view of the incumbents, one of the benefits they are accomplishing by a settlement of that kind is to protect the company from the distraction of a costly and fractious battle over control. The incumbents may well believe, in good faith, that their continuance in office is best for the stockholders. They may prefer not to add members to the board but may come to believe that, on balance, it would better serve the interests of stockholders to add new representation at the instance of vocal stockholders and avoid a high-stakes fight for control than to be confrontational. In that circumstance, though, it seems logical that the incumbent board majority might well, and with entire fidelity, expect that the stockholders who asked for new representation commit in exchange to support the newly composed board at the next election, if not for some longer period of service. Absent such an agreement, no appreciable period of peace would be secured during which the newly composed board could focus on simply making the business hum.

In [*75] view of these concerns, I am chary about addressing the promise of a second board seat that was made to Filipowski on broader grounds than is necessary. For me, there is a very clear and important, but narrow, reason why this later arrangement with Filipowski was improper and inequitably tainted the election process: it was a very material event that was not disclosed to the Cryo-Cell stockholders.

"[D]irectors of Delaware corporations are under a fiduciary duty to disclose fully and fairly all material information within the board's control when it seeks

shareholder action."[168] That disclosure "obligation attaches to proxy statements and any other disclosures in contemplation of stockholder action."[169] "An omitted fact is material if there is a substantial likelihood that a reasonable shareholder would consider it important in deciding how to vote."[170]

On the day they voted, the Cryo-Cell stockholders knew that a vote for the Management [*76] Slate would seat six directors, including Filipowski. They had to know that Filipowski's support for the Management Slate was in large measure motivated by his own inclusion.

What the Cryo-Cell stockholders did not know was that Walton had promised that the board would use its fiduciary powers to expand the board to seven members and seat another person designated by Filipowski. Problematically, the Cryo-Cell stockholders did not know that Filipowski clearly intended to designate Roszak, a person whose recent past would have weighed heavily on the mind of a rational stockholder considering whether to seat him as a fiduciary. Indeed, at trial, the defendants went out of their way to say that they decided to include Filipowski only after concluding that Roszak's conduct in the Blue Rhino situation did not cast doubt on *Filipowski's* own good character.

In so concluding, I do not hesitate to note my belief that Walton knew that Roszak was going to be Filipowski's designee before the meeting, but also that my ultimate conclusion that this was a material agreement that should have been disclosed would not change if that was not so. Stockholders would have found it material to know that corporate [*77] management's cooperation with Filipowski had now extended to a bargain whereby he would buy up more shares and votes in exchange for having two seats on the board. A reasonable stockholder could have come to the conclusion that they did not want Filipowski to have so much influence — and certainly not if Roszak, his employee with a dubious track record, was going to be his guaranteed echo on the board.

In this regard, it is worth observing that even those academic commentators who have endeavored to justify tolerance of forms of vote buying as having benefits to diversified investors have emphasized the need for fair disclosure of such arrangements.[171] For

---

[168] *Arnold v. Soc'y for Savings Bancorp., Inc.,* 650 A.2d 1270, 1277 (Del. 1994) (quoting *Stroud v. Grace,* 606 A.2d 75, 84 (Del. 1992)).

[169] *Id.*

[170] *Zirn v. VLI Corp.,* 621 A.2d 773, 778 (Del. 1993) (quoting *TSC Indus. v. Northway,* 426 U.S. 438, 449, 96 S. Ct. 2126, 48 L. Ed. 2d 757 (1976)).

[171] *See* Thomas J. Andre, Jr., *A Preliminary Inquiry into the Utility of Vote Buying in the Market for Corporate Control,* 63 S. CAL. L. REV. 533, 625 (1990) (observing that disclosure is a constraint on the agency costs that might result from vote buying by management); Robert Charles Clark, *Vote Buying and Corporate Law,* 29 CASE W. RES. L. REV. 776, 799 (1979) (suggesting that disclosure of vote-buying arrangements provides protection against looters); *cf. Schreiber,* 447 A.2d at 26 ("[T]he subsequent ratification of the [vote-

reasons I have described, it is prudent not to jump too quickly to the conclusion that voting pacts of this kind should automatically be seen as inequitable, although one could do so and find credible support for such a finding.[172] For many of the reasons that supported my earlier decision regarding Filipowski's inclusion on the Management Slate, an agreement of this kind that was made and disclosed in advance of an election is subject to the important fairness check of the stockholder vote itself. By contrast, the disinterested [*78] Cryo-Cell electorate voted in ignorance of the actual board that would govern them in the event the Management Slate won.

This finding is not affected by the defendants' argument that all stockholders were free to go out and acquire shares with voting rights before the polls closed and that that was all that Filipowski did. Well no, it wasn't. He went out and bought more shares only on the promise that the incumbents would appoint another designee of his to the board. What Filipowski did with his own bought shares is less the point than that the disinterested electorate voted in a razor-thin election without knowledge of very material facts. Absent that deal, the Management Slate would have lost. If the deal was disclosed, it might well have lost due to the reaction of unaffiliated stockholders to the deal itself.

C. Management's [*80] Influence Over Saneron's Vote

Because of my conclusions regarding the Filipowski issues, I need not dwell at length on the Saneron bloc. Even absent Walton's conduct toward Saneron, I would set aside the election results.

In my view, threats and promises of the kind directed at Saneron are much less problematically dealt within the *Schreiber* framework than properly disclosed agreements that involve give-and-take about the shape of a board slate. When what an agreement involves is not an accommodation about board service itself, but the use of a corporate asset (such as a contractual concession) by the management slate to secure a vote for itself, it is much more natural to consider that agreement "vote buying" in

the traditional sense and to employ *Schreiber's* backstop fairness analysis. For the following reasons, I find that the defendants fail both the prong requiring Walton's actions to have been motivated by a good faith desire to advance corporate interests, rather than to entrench herself, and the prong requiring the defendants, even if Walton had acted in good faith, to justify their dealings with Saneron as entirely fair to Cryo-Cell.[173]

I begin [*81] with my conclusion that Walton breached her fiduciary duties by intentionally using corporate assets to coerce Saneron in the exercise of its voting rights. As I have found, Walton both threatened Saneron (with the loss or at least cooling of a strategic partnership vital to it) and granted it an inducement (the lifting of a restrictive legend on its shares) in order to extract a commitment from Saneron to vote for the Management Slate.

There is no doubt that threatening Saneron was improper conduct by Walton, whereby she used her power as a fiduciary to control assets of Cryo-Cell for the purpose of entrenching herself in office. I, of course, do not rest my conclusion on a finding that Saneron formally agreed to vote for the Management Slate in response to Walton's inducements and threats. As Chancellor Chandler observed in his important decision in *Hewlett-Packard,* it would be naive to expect that dealings of this kind would manifest themselves in a formal contract.[174] Just as [*82] was the case with her dealings with Filipowski, Walton's dealings with Saneron were conducted in a different vernacular than that of executed contracts, but one that was just as easy, or even easier, to understand.

Hewlett-Packard recognized that management controls powerful tools that, if misused for entrenchment purposes, can inequitably tilt the election process. For that reason, Chancellor Chandler held a trial to determine whether the CEO of Hewlett-Packard had put pressure on a key stockholder to vote in favor of management on a merger by implying that the stockholder, which had important commercial relationships with Hewlett-Packard, would not get future business if it voted against management's favored position.[175] He rejected that claim only after a searching factual inquiry into whether such pressure had been exerted and after concluding that it had not.[176] In his earlier decision concluding that a trial was necessary, he stated:

> Shareholders are free to do whatever they want with their votes, including selling them to the highest bidder. Management, on the

---

buying] transaction by a majority of the independent stockholders, *after a full disclosure of all germane facts with complete candor* precludes any further judicial inquiry of it.") (emphasis added); Henry T.C. Hu & Bernard Black, *The New Vote Buying: Empty Voting and Hidden (Morphable) Ownership,* 79 S. CAL. L. REV. 811, 877 (2006) ("The history of ownership disclosure suggests that, precise thresholds and delay periods aside, our society will not tolerate hidden control of major companies, nor control contests waged behind closed doors. So disclosure [*79] of major positions there will be.").
[172] *See* RESTATEMENT OF CONTRACTS § 569 (1932) ("A bargain by an official or shareholder of a corporation for a consideration enuring to him personally to exercise or promise to exercise his powers in the management of the corporation in a particular way is illegal."); *see also* N.Y. BUS. CORP. LAW § 609(e) (McKinney 2003) (stating that a "shareholder shall not sell his vote or issue a proxy to vote to any person for any sum of money or anything of value").

[173] *Schreiber,* 447 A.2d at 25-26.
[174] *See Hewlett v. Hewlett-Packard Co.,* 2002 Del. Ch. LEXIS 35, 2002 WL 549137, at *4 (Del. Ch. 2002).
[175] 2002 Del. Ch. LEXIS 35, [WL] at *3, *5.
[176] *Hewlett v. Hewlett-Packard Co.,* 2002 Del. Ch. LEXIS 44, 2002 WL 818091, at *15 (Del. Ch. 2002).

other hand, may not use corporate assets [*83] to buy votes in a hotly contested proxy contest about an extraordinary transaction that would significantly transform the corporation, unless it can be demonstrated, as it was in *Schreiber,* that management's vote-buying activity does not have a deleterious effect on the corporate franchise.[177]

Chancellor Chandler's serious concerns about overreaching of this kind is understandable. As a practical matter, it is to be expected that stockholders who have ongoing commercial relationships with the corporation are likely to fear crossing management. When management asks for the vote of such a stockholder by appealing to the stockholder at its highest level of authority in a hotly contested, high-stakes situation, the very act of asking can be perceived as carrying with it the idea that the stockholder's answer will have implications for the future relationship of the stockholder and the corporation, on all levels.

Therefore, what is perhaps most surprising about the Saneron situation is that the Saneron vote was in such serious doubt that Walton felt the need to and did apply [*84] overt pressure on Saneron. Clearly, Saneron's leadership was frightened of being on the wrong side of a proxy fight, at a company that controlled 38% of its own shares. It was afraid of tilting either way. Although Walton would now have me believe that her instructions to her subordinates to end cooperation with Saneron until Saneron committed to vote for the Management Slate should simply be seen as Nixonian ramblings her staff was wise enough to ignore, I don't believe that was the case. Rather, I believe that Walton and her aides did what was found not to have occurred in *Hewlett-Packard,* which was to use the threat that a vote contrary to management's wishes would injure a stockholder's commercial relationship with the corporation in order to extract its vote.[178] And, as I noted previously, to expect that Saneron would admit after the fact that Walton's improper behavior influenced its vote is unrealistic, given the very reasons that gave Walton leverage over it in this first instance.

Given that Walton clearly used company resources to coerce Saneron in the voting process and thereby breached her duty of loyalty, it was the defendants' burden [*85] to show that Saneron's vote was not influenced by her misbehavior.[179] They have

not convinced me of that at all. Rather, the circumstances surrounding Saneron's decision to vote for the Management Slate are more consistent with a bargained-for exchange, in which Saneron got a removal of the restrictive legend and the hope of future cooperation from Cryo-Cell in exchange for casting an early and important vote for the Management Slate. Walton's own words regarding the effect of her tactics said it best: those tactics "locked up" Saneron's vote.[180]

In concluding that Walton's conduct was improper, it is relevant that Cryo-Cell had refused to remove the restrictive legend from Saneron's shares for two years. One has to presume that the refusal was properly motivated by Cryo-Cell's best interests and legal rights. For Walton to relent in exchange for a vote for the Management Slate involved the conversion of a corporate asset into a tool of personal entrenchment. Likewise, there is no reason to believe that Saneron had any motive to misuse its strategic relationship with Cryo-Cell so as to injure Cryo-Cell as a corporation and advantage itself. Making the future of that strategic relationship dependent on Saneron's vote was clearly a use by Walton of a valuable asset of the corporation for personal ends. I am not saying that voting decisions of this kind do not always have real world ramifications on relationships. But when a corporate manager's only reason for casting doubt on a strategic partner's ongoing relationship with the corporation has nothing to do with the best interests of the corporation, except insofar as the manager believes [*87] her own re-election is critical, using the threat of future non-cooperation is the simple use of a corporate, not personal, asset as leverage to extract a vote. That is inequitable behavior.

Although a change in the voting of the Saneron bloc alone would not have turned the election, Walton's improper conduct and its non-disclosure contributes to my overall sense that the election was tainted by misbehavior by insiders who could not win an election simply using the traditionally powerful advantages afforded incumbents. Our law has no tolerance for unfair election tactics of this kind.[181]

D.   The Annual Meeting

I now come to Portnoy's last complaint. That is about how Walton conducted the meeting.

[177] 2002 Del. Ch. LEXIS 35, 2002 WL 549137, at *4.

[178] *Hewlett,* 2002 Del. Ch. LEXIS 44, 2002 WL 818091, at *15.

[179] *See In re RJR Nabisco, Inc. S'holders Litig.,* 1989 Del. Ch. LEXIS 9, 1989 WL 7036, at *1159 (Del. Ch. 1989) (When "a director . . . place[s] his own interests, preferences or appetites before the welfare of the corporation" it is "apparent that such a director would be required to demonstrate that the corporation had not been injured . . . ."); *see also Cede II,* 634 A.2d at 371 ("A breach of . . . the duty of loyalty . . . requires the directors to prove that the transaction was entirely fair."); *Hewlett,* 2002 Del. Ch. LEXIS 35, 2002 WL 549137, at

*4; *Rainbow Navigation, Inc. v. Yonge,* 1989 Del. Ch. LEXIS 41, 1989 WL 40805, at *10 (Del. Ch. 1989) (finding no forbidden vote buying because defendants had persuaded [*86] the court that an inducement, as a factual matter, had not influenced the votes).

[180] JX 218.

[181] *See, e.g., Schnell,* 285 A.2d at 439; *Blasius,* 564 A.2d at 651; *see also Peerless,* 2000 Del. Ch. LEXIS 170, 2000 WL 1805376, at *11-12, *15; *Chesapeake,* 771 A.2d at 297 (Del. Ch. 2000); *Lerman,* 421 A.2d at 914; *Schroder v. Scotten, Dillon Co.,* 299 A.2d 431, 437 (Del. Ch. 1972).

Appendix

As an initial matter, I decline to use this as an excuse to probe the difference between a lunch break and a formal adjournment. The language of the Cryo-Cell bylaws creates a colorable argument that a formal adjournment could not have been declared [*88] without stockholder approval and there is doubt whether Walton had sufficient proxies in hand for that purpose.[182] In my view, Portnoy is not positioned to contest Walton's authority to "decide all procedural issues regarding the conduct of the meeting, including adjournment," so long as she did so in good faith.[183] The contending Slates, through their representatives, reached agreement three days before the meeting on certain procedures. That sort of agreement can be thought to have utility, insofar as it provides the contestants with a reliable set of assumptions about how the meeting will be conducted.[184] To have one of the agreeing parties later carp about a provision he assented to undermines the utility of such agreements and creates a risk of electoral uncertainty over trivial missteps in what can be the technically challenging process of running a meeting. Nor, in my view, does a general letter sent on the very morning of the meeting purporting to impose, after the fact, a caveat that the Slates' agreement was subject to the bylaws help Portnoy. That "oh by the way" was more than a tad late and did not even reach Walton by meeting time. Moreover, the fact that the agreement [*89] could not bar another stockholder from complaining does not mean that Portnoy was free to complain about an act that he agreed Walton could undertake.[185]

What, however, is more uncertain is that Walton acted inequitably in her conduct of the meeting. The reality is that she did not take a "lupper" break of nearly three hours at 2 p.m. so that the attendees at the meeting could eat. Because Walton undertook action that affected the conduct of an election of directors in a potentially important way,[186] the

defendants bear the burden to show that Walton's actions were "motivated by a good faith concern for the stockholders' best interests, and not by a desire to entrench [herself.]"[187] They have failed to prove that Walton's tactics were undertaken in selfless good faith.

Walton's behavior during the day was analogous to a corrupted soccer referee, intent on adding extra time so that the game would end only when her favored team had a sure lead. Very early in the meeting, the scheduled course of events had run and all stockholder questions had been answered.

When Walton was asked to count the vote, she replied with the jejune response that the request was out of order. At trial, she could not explain what that response was supposed to mean. It sounds to the court like something out of Robert's Rules of Order that Walton had heard invoked by someone trying to fake their way through a local town council meeting or had seen when watching a congressional debate on C-Span.

This is not to say that Walton had no discretion to keep the polls open. But what she did was to stall without being honest about why she was acting.

If she were being candid, she would have admitted that she was waiting for confirmation that two large blockholders' votes had been switched before having the vote counted. Indeed, if she were being perfectly candid, she would have admitted that she was keeping the polls [*92] open so that the Management Slate could continue its efforts to secure more votes by purchase because she was concerned that it would lose even with their votes. Even with less candor, she could have straightforwardly said that she was keeping the polls open to a time certain so that the parties could continue their contest for votes.

Instead, she first tried to pull off a filibuster, subjecting the stockholders to unscheduled bloviation from her management subordinates. Particularly disturbing is Walton's choice to have presentations made on laboratory research and sales when she might have instead released the company's 10-Q, which was already prepared, and had the CFO, who was at the meeting, explain Cryo-Cell's disappointing financial results. But providing the stockholders with information such as actual up-to-date financial results that might have been material to how they chose to vote their shares was not Walton's concern. Stalling was. During the filibuster, Walton rejected another request to hold the vote. Again, she ruled that request "out of order" for no articulated reason.

[182] Portnoy argues that Article II § 8(b) of Cryo-Cell's bylaws provides the exclusive means to adjourn a stockholder meeting. That section, which is titled "Quorum," states: "Despite the absence of a quorum at any annual or special meeting of shareholders, the shareholders, by a majority of the votes cast by holders entitled to vote thereon, may adjourn the meeting." JX 16 at CRYO 989.
[183] JX 228.
[184] DAVID A. DREXLER, LEWIS S. BLACK, JR. & A. GILCHRIST SPARKS, III, DELAWARE CORPORATE LAW AND PRACTICE § 24.05[1] (2007) ("[T]here are no statutory guidelines for such routine matters as . . . the rules of procedure, if any, which must be followed. . . . For this reason, parties anticipating a contested vote often find it to their mutual advantage to agree in advance upon procedural details in order to avoid the potential degeneration of proceedings into confusion, if not chaos.").
[185] See Stengel v. Rotman, 2001 Del. Ch. LEXIS 22, 2001 WL 221512, at *7 (Del. Ch. 2001) (holding, in the alternative, that when a removed officer waited one month after an election of [*90] directors to contest its validity for an alleged breach of the corporations bylaws, that former officer was barred from asserting his claims by laches, acquiescence, waiver, and ratification).
[186] Accipiter Life Scis. Fund, L.P. v. Helfer, 905 A.2d 115, 125 (Del. Ch. 2006) ("In deciding whether an act is an inequitable restraint on the stockholder's franchise, this court has looked closely at the

circumstances of each case. Obviously, our courts have been more likely to find an action impermissible if the board acted with the intent of influencing or precluding a proxy [*91] contest for control of the corporation.").
[187] Inter-Tel, 929 A.2d at 807.

It was then that she used the pretense that everyone needed lunch to delay the vote. That move gave [*93] her side time, which they used, to ensure that they had the votes to prevail. And lest anyone be moved by the attendees' need for sustenance, by any measure they would have dined earlier — at the traditional time of lunch, in fact — had Walton closed the polls when the events scheduled to precede the vote had concluded.

The defendants, of course, say that the Portnoy Slate should have recognized the need to keep searching for votes during the period when Walton was delaying, and that the Portnoy Slate was less than assiduous in ensuring that its early lead was secured by faithful tending of its proxy-giving flock. And one cannot be but reluctant to set a precedent that helps creates justiciable issues out of delays measured in hours, rather than days or weeks.[188]

---

[188] The only Delaware case of which I am aware that has explicitly dealt with the issue of a tactical adjournment in a convened stockholder meeting involved a 30-day adjournment while keeping the polls open on only one of three issues presented to the stockholders for a vote. *See Peerless*, 2000 Del. Ch. LEXIS 170, 2000 WL 1805376, at *3; *see also* DAVID A. DREXLER, LEWIS S. BLACK, JR. & A. GILCHRIST SPARKS, III, DELAWARE CORPORATE LAW AND PRACTICE § 24.05[6][b] [*94] (2007) ("The *Peerless* decision represents for the present the only judicial direction on tactical adjournments.").

In a recent decision, this court held that directors had not breached their fiduciary duty by postponing a vote on an arms-length merger before a meeting was convened. *Inter-Tel*, 929 A.2d at 818-19. The directors believed that they would lose the vote if it was held that day but had reason to believe that stockholder sentiment was changing, especially in view of changes in the economy's credit markets. A delay ensued during which it was clear to both sides that they needed to continue to press their case, pro and con the merger. As noted in that decision, when directors advocate an affirmative vote on a transaction, they are supposed to do so because they believe in good faith that the transaction will benefit the stockholders. *Id.* at 819. That context is importantly distinct from an actual election of directors, in which the insiders delay because they believe the stockholders are making a mistake in choosing new leadership. In the former case, directors who face no risk of removal are asking for more time to make their case that a non-self-dealing transaction should receive [*95] approval. In the latter case, the directors are trying to insulate themselves from ouster, by forcing the insurgents to continue the fight beyond when the election was supposed to be held. Even in that context, room for some discretion has been recognized as necessary, but the court rightly looks at director moves with a deeply furrowed brow. *See Stahl v. Apple Bancorp, Inc.*, 579 A.2d 1115, 1122-23 (Del. Ch. 1990) (Chancellor Allen concluding that a board's properly motivated decision to hold an annual meeting *several months later* than it had originally intended because it was facing a proxy contest for board control should not be enjoined).

In this case, unlike in *Inter-Tel*, Walton gave the assembled stockholders false reasons for delay and was not acting in good faith to ensure that stockholders had more time to consider an arms-length transaction that was at danger in a time of economic tumult. Rather, she misled the meeting attendees about the reasons for delay, did not use the period of delay to release a quarterly report that was adverse, and closed the polls as soon as she knew her side would win. Given these facts, Walton's delaying conduct was arguably

Nonetheless, it is impossible to ignore the unfairness of Walton's behavior, a justification by reference to effect being no defense to actions affecting a director election that are undertaken for "an inequitable purpose" and in an inequitably deceptive manner.[189] If an electoral contestant assumes the role of presiding over the meeting, she has an obligation to do so fairly. Walton did not do so. She stalled so that her side could win the game, knowing that if the game ended when it was scheduled to end, her side would lose. Then she was dishonest about the reasons for delay.

* * *

For all these reasons, I find that Portnoy has proven that serious breaches of fiduciary duty tainted the election. Before considering what remedy to impose, I must briefly address the defendants' contention that the inequitable conduct [*97] of their side should be ignored because Portnoy has unclean hands. After doing that, I address the remedial implications of my findings.

III. Unclean Hands

The defendants argue that Portnoy seeks equitable relief, yet he comes to court with unclean hands. The defendants allege that Portnoy has unclean hands based on his communications with Susan Archibald, a former Cryo-Cell employee. Specifically, the defendants allege that Portnoy induced Archibald to provide him confidential information in violation of a confidentiality agreement that she signed with the company.

Archibald, a former quality systems specialist at Cryo-Cell who was fired in February 2007,[190] contacted Portnoy later same month after she learned that he was seeking to wage a proxy contest.[191] Archibald shared with Portnoy her view that misconduct and misuse of corporate assets was occurring at Cryo-Cell. Portnoy then attempted to communicate that information to the four outside directors on Cryo-Cell's board. Soon after his first contact with Archibald, Portnoy wrote a letter to the outside directors, dated February 20, 2007, which stated:

> [A]s a result of the publicity surrounding [the Portnoy Group's] letter and related [*98] amendment of our Form 13d, we received several bits of unsolicited, unsubstantiated, but nevertheless troubling information from individuals purporting to be prior employees of

---

less fair in effect than [*96] if she had adjourned the meeting for several weeks. At that stage, she would have had to face the consequences of the electorate's reaction to the 10-Q and the possible revelation of her new deal with Filipowski. Moreover, it would have been clear to the Portnoy Slate that they needed to continue to fight for every vote.

[189] *Inter-Tel*, 929 A.2d at 807; *Schnell*, 285 A.2d at 439.
[190] Archibald Dep. at 15-16.
[191] Tr. at 12; Archibald Dep. at 24.

the Company. We have no way of knowing whether these assertions are accurate, but we feel duly-bound to pass them along to you, who are charged with the stewardship of the Company's assets, supervision of its officers, and obligations to its shareholders.

Therefore, we would like to meet with you, in order to share this information, so that you can determine the best course of action, and whether additional information is warranted.[192]

The response of the Cryo-Cell outside directors to a whistle blower letter by a large group of stockholders was to ask Walton, the only management director, to "handle it in the way she felt best."[193] The outside directors did not even follow up with a letter to Portnoy.[194]

After the Cryo-Cell outside directors failed to consider the allegations of wrongdoing at the Company, Portnoy continued to communicate with Archibald despite the fact that Archibald had signed a confidentiality [*99] agreement with the Company.[195] As Portnoy explained at trial, he did not believe that Archibald was violating her confidentiality agreement because she "was looking to, I believe, protect the assets of the company by providing me with that information."[196] Portnoy, for his part, did not publicly disclose any information that he received from Archibald other than disclosing in a June 14 fight letter that the Cryo-Cell directors had not investigated Portnoy's February 20 letter about receiving unsubstantiated, troubling information from a purported former Cryo-Cell employee.[197]

The defendants seize upon the fact that Portnoy asked Archibald to call Krueger the day before [*100] the annual meeting, pointing to Archibald's discussion with Krueger as evidence of wrongdoing by Portnoy. The defendants, however, have provided no evidence of what Archibald and Krueger discussed. When Archibald was asked if she told Krueger "all the negative inside information that [she] had previously provided to Mr. Portnoy," she answered: "No, I don't believe so. I answered the questions that Mr. Krueger asked. That was pretty much about it."[198] The defendants chose not to depose Krueger to

find out more information about that conversation.[199] Rather, they merely speculate that "[t]here can be little doubt" that Archibald communicated negative inside information to Krueger.[200] Moreover, Archibald had not worked at Cryo-Cell for over five months at the time she spoke with Krueger, and the only potentially sensitive information that the defendants were able to show that Archibald possessed, that the Company had decided to indefinitely postpone the launch of its Plureon placental stem cell service, had been publicly disclosed months before Archibald spoke to Krueger.[201]

The defendants have failed to identify any confidential information of Cryo-Cell possessed by Archibald that was truly of a sensitive nature, much less that it was misused by Portnoy or even communicated to him. There is at least as much reason to believe that the defendants were wielding the confidentiality agreement against Archibald, not to keep her from revealing trade secrets or business strategies in a way that could aid Cryo-Cell's competitors, but to keep her from discussing improper conduct she observed while at Cryo-Cell. In any event, the defendants' showing on this issue will not support the immunizing effect they desire.

The doctrine of "unclean hands" provides that "a litigant who engages in reprehensible conduct in relation to the matter in controversy . . . forfeits his right to have the court hear his claim, regardless of its merit."[202] "[T]he purpose of the clean hands maxim is to protect the court against misuse by one who, because of his conduct, has forfeited his right to have the court consider his claims, regardless of their merit. As such it is not a matter of defense to be applied on behalf of a litigant; [*102] rather it is a rule of public policy."[203] Therefore, "[t]he question raised by a plea of unclean hands is whether the plaintiff's conduct is so offensive to the integrity of the court that his claims should be denied, regardless of their merit."[204] "This court has consistently refused to apply the doctrine of unclean hands to bar an otherwise valid claim of relief where the doctrine would work an inequitable result."[205]

I do not agree that Portnoy comes to this court with hands dirty enough to deny him any relief. Portnoy's conduct was far from ideal. Although one can understand his frustration at the board's refusal

---

[192] JX 33.

[193] Tr. at 235.

[194] Tr. at 264.

[195] JX 3.

[196] Tr. at 16. Archibald did ask Portnoy if she could get her job back if Portnoy prevailed in the proxy contest. Tr. at 47. Portnoy refused, promising only that "she would be given the opportunity to interview for the job and, if she was the most capable person, then she would be entitled to the job." Tr. at 48. Archibald's email response to Portnoy's offer to consider her for her old position expressed disappointment, but Archibald continued her communication with Portnoy anyway. JX 38 at Archibald 50.

[197] JX 131.

[198] Archibald Dep. at 133.

[199] It is likely that the defendants feared what Krueger might say. See supra [*101] note 101.

[200] Def. Op. Post-trial Br. at 33.

[201] Tr. at 44-45.

[202] Nakahara v. The NS 1991 American Trust, 739 A.2d 770, 791-92 (Del. Ch. 1998) (internal quotation omitted).

[203] Skoglund v. Ormand Indus., Inc., 372 A.2d 204, 213 (Del. Ch. 1976).

[204] Gallagher v. Holcomb & Salter, 1991 Del. Ch. LEXIS 148, 1991 WL 158969, at *4 (Del. Ch. 1991).

[205] Dittrick v. Chalfant, 2007 Del. Ch. LEXIS 47, 2007 WL 1039548, at *5 n.18 (Del. Ch. 2007) (citing Cole v. Kershaw, 2000 Del. Ch. LEXIS 117, 2000 WL 1206672, at *4 (Del. Ch. 2000)).

to undertake a disinterested review of the concerns Archibald brought to his attention, Portnoy responded by engaging in conversations that, I have little doubt, involved literal violations [*103] of Archibald's confidentiality agreement. Had he behaved most scrupulously, Portnoy could have pressed Cryo-Cell to take her concerns more seriously, by filing suit if necessary. Responding to one perceived wrong with a furtive course of contractually-questionable conduct is not laudable.

That said, unclean hands is a doctrine designed to protect the integrity of a court of equity, not a weapon to be wielded by parties seeking to excuse their own inequitable behavior by pointing out a trifling instance of impropriety by their counterpart, especially when the defendants cannot show that Portnoy's conduct caused any harm to Cryo-Cell as a corporation or to its disinterested stockholders.[206] Portnoy's conduct, while being far from pristine, falls well short of disqualifying him from seeking relief.

Denying Portnoy [*104] relief on the basis of unclean hands would work an inequitable result by denying Cryo-Cell's stockholders the right to fairly conducted election of directors, something that DGCL § 225 was enacted to ensure.[207] It would be unjust to permit the defendants to invoke the confidentiality agreement, which was designed to protect Cryo-Cell, to shield themselves from accountability for their inequitable behavior. That said, I do take Portnoy's behavior into account in shaping the final relief I award to him, but in a manner that is more proportionate and that does not injure the Cryo-Cell electorate.

IV. The Remedy

I come now to the question of the appropriate remedy. Although Portnoy would have me simply declare his slate the victor, I do not believe [*105] that is the most appropriate remedy. Given how close the contest was and the reality that Filipowski actually acquired beneficial ownership of the shares he voted, I think the remedy that best vindicates the interests of Cryo-Cell stockholders as a class is to order a prompt special meeting at which a new election will be held and presided over by a special

master.[208] Until that time, the incumbents who sat on the Cryo-Cell board before the 2007 annual meeting will continue in office; Filipowski's claim to office has no pre-existing legitimacy and he shall leave the board until he is elected by the stockholders.

For their part, the defendants carp about the holding of a special meeting, supposedly out of a concern for the financial interests of Cryo-Cell. Although that concern is legitimate, it does not lie gracefully in their mouths to voice as an excuse to insulate themselves from a fair election challenge. The defendants' desire to wait for an annual meeting in the summer is self-serving and inequitable, given that it is their Slate's behavior that tainted the election held last year.

A more fitting way to address the cost concerns is to require the Management Slate to bear the costs of their own proxy solicitation efforts, the costs to the corporation of holding the meeting, and the costs of a special master to conduct the meeting.[209] This will ensure that the Cryo-Cell stockholders are not injured by the requirement for an extra meeting. Given the [*107] misconduct by the Management Slate, this is a fitting and proportionate remedy. Nor will the remedy place the Management Slate at a disadvantage to any insurgent slate, it will simply level the playing field.

Not surprisingly, the defendants pull out an old tool of corporate incumbents whose electoral shenanigans requires this court to order a special meeting — that the corporation's annual report is not ready and the SEC will not let them solicit proxies. That is their problem and they should seek relief, if necessary, from the SEC. Having felt free to delay a meeting through the presentation of time-wasting presentations that did not include quarterly results contained a 10-Q that they filed a half hour after the polls closed, the defendants are unusual champions of the need for full disclosure before stockholder votes. As this court has indicated previously, the

---

[206] To be clear, my decision is based on my determination that Portnoy's conduct does not rise to the level of inequity where he should be denied relief. Harm, of course, is not strictly required for the doctrine of unclean hands to bar relief. See *Nakahara*, 739 A.2d at 794 ("Equity does not reward those who act inequitably, even if it can be said that no tangible injury resulted.").

[207] Cf. *Belle Isle Corp. v. Corcoran*, 29 Del. Ch. 554, 49 A.2d 1, 4 (Del. 1946) (refusing to apply the doctrine of unclean hands to bar relief, even if for the sake of argument, the plaintiff who was seeking to having a voting trust agreement declared invalid was guilty of misconduct because "the public policy of this State, as announced under [the DGCL section on voting trust agreements], will not be disturbed by the application of [the unclean hands] doctrine.").

[208] The DGCL gives this court wide discretion to craft a remedy in the case of a tainted election. Section 225(a) provides:

> [T]he Court of Chancery may hear and determine the validity of any election, appointment, removal or resignation of any director . . . and the right of any person to hold or continue to hold such office, and in the case any such office is claimed by more than 1 person, may determine the person entitled thereto; *and to that end make such order or decree in any such case as may be just and proper . . . . In case it should be determined that no valid election [*106] has been held, the Court of Chancery may order an election* to be held in accordance with § 211 [the DGCL section on stockholder meetings]
> . . . .

8 *Del. C.* § 225(a) (emphasis added); *see also* 8 *Del. C.* § 227(b) (allowing the court to appoint a master to conduct an election ordered under § 225 "under such orders and powers as it deems proper").

[209] See 8 *Del. C.* § 225(a) (allowing the court to "make such order or decree in any such case as may be just and proper").

Appendix

SEC's requirements are well-intended ones designed to protect stockholders; they are no basis to insulate corporate insiders from their obligations under the corporation law governing their company's relations [*108] to its stockholders.[210]

In terms of the financial obligations imposed on the defendants, I note that I focus their responsibilities on remediating the harm they have caused to the corporation in a proportionate and constructive manner. I reject Portnoy's request to have the defen-

---

[210] *See Esopus Creek Value LP v. Hauf,* 913 A.2d 593, 606 (Del. Ch. 2006) (observing with respect to sections 14(a) and 14(c) of the 1934 Act that "'[n]othing in . . . that statute . . . suggests any purpose to interfere with the power of state courts to require that stockholder meetings be held in accordance with the requirements of state corporation law in situations where the registrant corporation is delinquent in its SEC filings obligations.'") (quoting *Newcastle Partners, L.P. v. Vesta Ins. Group, Inc.,* 887 A.2d 975, 980-81 (Del. Ch. 2005)).

dants or Cryo-Cell pay his litigation and proxy solicitation costs. I do so in deference both to the traditional American Rule approach our jurisprudence embraces and as a fitting consequence for Portnoy's dalliance with Archibald, a course of conduct that I do not believe disentitles him to a remedy but that ought to have some consequence. By rejecting Portnoy's request [*109] for reimbursement of his litigation and proxy costs, I limit the defendants' exposure to paying the costs of holding a special meeting, which should not be onerous if the parties are sensible, which the special master will ensure.

The parties shall collaborate on the appropriate date and location for a prompt special meeting and present a conforming order, in advance of seeking a conference this week with the court at which the order will be finalized and a special master appointed.

GARY L. SAMPLE, on behalf of himself and all persons similarly situated on Counts I, IV, V, and VI and on behalf of Nominal Defendant RANDALL BEARINGS, INC., on Counts II, III, and VI, Plaintiff, v. KENT P. MORGAN, JEFFREY L. HAGER, DAVID L. WIERWILLE, KENNETH C. HARROD, STEPHEN M. RICHMOND, BAKER & HOSTETLER LLP, and JOSEPH P. BOECKMAN, Defendants, and RANDALL BEARINGS, INC., Nominal Defendant.

C.A. No. 1214-VCS

COURT OF CHANCERY OF DELAWARE

935 A.2d 1046*; 2007 Del. Ch. LEXIS 166**

September 6, 2007, Submitted

November 27, 2007, Decided

PRIOR HISTORY: Sample v. Morgan, 914 A.2d 647, 2007 Del. Ch. LEXIS 16 (Del. Ch., 2007)

COUNSEL: [**1] Pamela S. Tikellis, Esquire, Robert J. Kriner, Jr., Esquire, A. Zachary Naylor, Esquire, Daniel J. Brown, Esquire, CHIMICLES & TIKELLIS LLP, Wilmington, Delaware, Attorneys for Plaintiff.

David A. Jenkins, Esquire, Michele C. Gott, Esquire, SMITH KATZENSTEIN & FURLOW LLP, Wilmington, Delaware, Attorneys for Defendants Baker & Hostetler LLP and Joseph P. Boeckman.

James J. Merkins, Jr., Esquire, BLANK ROME LLP, Wilmington, Delaware; Attorneys for Kent P. Morgan, Jeffrey L. Hager, and David L. Wierwille.

Joanne Pileggi Pinckney, Esquire, Susan E. Poppiti, Esquire, PINCKNEY HARRIS & POPPITI, LLC, Wilmington, Delaware, Attorneys for Defendants Kenneth C. Harrod and Stephen M. Richmond.

S. Mark Hurd, Esquire, Samuel T. Hirzel, II, Esquire, MORRIS, NICHOLS, ARSHT & TUNNEL, Wilmington, Delaware, Attorney for Nominal Defendant Randall Bearings, Inc.

OPINION:

[*1047] **STRINE,** Vice Chancellor.

I. Introduction

The question presented is a straightforward one. May a corporate lawyer and his law firm be sued in Delaware as to claims arising out of their actions in providing advice and services to a Delaware public corporation, its directors, and its managers regarding matters of Delaware corporate law when the lawyer and [**2] law firm: i) prepared and delivered to Delaware for filing a certificate amendment under challenge in the lawsuit; ii) advertise themselves as being able to provide coast-to-coast legal services and as experts in matters of corporate governance; iii) provided legal advice on a range of Delaware law matters at issue in the lawsuit; iv) undertook to direct the defense of the lawsuit; and v) face well-pled allegations of having aided and abetted the top managers of the corporation in breaching their fiduciary duties by entrenching and enriching themselves at the expense of the corporation and its public stockholders? The answer is yes.

The lawyer and law firm's conduct in arranging the filing of the certificate amendment in Delaware satisfies both § 3104(c)(1) and § 3104(c)(3) of Delaware's long-arm statute.[1] That Certificate Amendment was integral to an alleged scheme by the top managers of the corporation to have issued to themselves at an unfair price a large bloc of voting stock that would secure their control over the [*1048] corporation. Thus, the scheme not only involved an act in Delaware, it also involved an injury in Delaware to the Delaware corporation.

Likewise, [**3] it is constitutionally permissible to exercise jurisdiction over the lawyer and his law firm. Having directed their legal practice toward Delaware by regularly providing advice about Delaware law matters to the corporation, these defendants should have reasonably expected that they might face suit here if the managers and directors they were advising were sued for a breach of fiduciary duty related to that advice. These sophisticated defendants had to know of the strong interest Delaware has in ensuring that Delaware corporations and their stockholders have access to this court to hold corporate fiduciaries and their advisors accountable for honoring their legal and fiduciary obligations. Given their Delaware-directed conduct and the tight nexus between that conduct and this suit, these defendants have no basis to object to having to appear in Delaware to defend this suit.

Their motion to dismiss for lack of personal jurisdiction will therefore be denied.

---

[1] 10 *Del. C.* § 3104.

II.   Factual Background

These are the relevant facts from the record, with inferences drawn in the plaintiff-friendly manner required in this procedural context. [2]

In [**4] 2004, the three "Top Managers" of Randall Bearings, Inc., an Ohio-headquartered bronze ball bearings concern incorporated in Delaware, received 200,000 shares of the company's stock. [3] Although the Top Managers' right to ownership of the shares was subject to a vesting schedule, the shares could be voted immediately, had dividend rights, and all of the shares vested immediately in the event of a "proposed or actual change in control" of the company. [4] The 200,000 shares amounted to nearly a third of the company's voting power. The Top Managers comprised three of the board of directors' five members.

The Top Managers paid a total of $200 in exchange for the shares, $199,800 less than if the corporation had not amended its certificate of incorporation to lower the par value of its shares from $1.00 to $0.001. That "Certificate Amendment" was put to the Randall Bearings stockholders at the [**5] same time as the stockholders voted to authorize an "Equity Incentive Plan," by which up to 200,000 shares of stock could be issued by the board to employees or officers for the purposes of — or so the stockholders were told — "attracting and retaining key employees for the company." [5]

Before the full board and stockholders approved these items, the Top Managers sought advice from the company's outside counsel, defendant Joseph Boeckman of the Columbus, Ohio office of defendant Baker & Hostetler LLP. Although being paid at all relevant times by Randall Bearings to act as the company's counsel, Boeckman developed options for the Top Managers that would facilitate their objectives of voting control. These options always involved in part the issuance of [*1049] shares by the company to the Top Managers. In providing his advice to the Top Managers, Boeckman noted that the amount of shares that the Top Managers would need to be a serious obstacle to any change of control exceeded the amount of shares that boards were typically authorized to grant to employees in compensation plans.

In the end, Boeckman and the Top Managers [**6] agreed to seek board and stockholder approval for a Certificate Amendment that would, as noted, lower the par value of the company's stock from $1.00 to $0.001 and for an Equity Incentive Plan that would authorize the board to issue up to 200,000 shares — or some 31.7% of the company's voting power — to officers and managers. The pled facts suggest that the Top Managers and Boeckman intended from the get-go for all 200,000 shares to be issued to the three Top Managers — 100,000 shares to Morgan, 75,000 to Hager, and 25,000 to Wierwille — so as to accomplish their entrenchment objectives. [6] The reduction in par value would allow the Top Managers to receive the shares for a total of $200 rather than $200,000. This reduction, one can infer, was not chump change to the Top Managers, who later sought and accomplished having the company pay the taxes they owed on their receipt of the shares.

At the time Boeckman was providing advice about these issues, the Top Managers were insecure because the company's former CEO and largest stockholder had died. A relative of the founder and Chairman of the Board at the time of his death, Bruce Dickerson, owned [**7] a bloc of nearly 30%. The leader of the Top Managers, defendant Kent Morgan, had succeeded Bruce Dickerson as Chairman and CEO and had joined the company only a few years earlier.

The Top Managers feared that the Dickerson stock could end up in hands that were unfriendly to management. Boeckman aided the Top Managers in their efforts to manage this risk. Boeckman sent two memoranda to Morgan in late May of 2003. At first, Boeckman recommended securing an agreement from Bruce Dickerson's widow, Susan Dickerson, to put the family's shares in a voting trust whereby she would pledge support for management. At that point, Boeckman contemplated using a combination of a voting trust and the grant of a smaller, but still sizable, number of shares to the Top Managers as a method for achieving their entrenchment objectives.

When the voting trust option became either unattractive or unavailable, Boeckman altered tactics. For one thing, he then recommended that a much larger grant of shares — the 200,000 shares ultimately granted — be authorized for issuance to the Top Managers. [7] When the Randall Bearings board approved the Certificate Amendment and the Equity Incentive Plan some months later, [**8] neither the Top Managers nor Boeckman — who was acting as the board's counsel — disclosed the memoranda Boeckman had written to the Top Managers discussing the options they had to achieve their entrench-

---

[2] *Outokumpu Eng'g Enters. v. Kvaerner Enviropower*, 685 A.2d 724, 727 (Del. 1996).

[3] The Top Managers included CEO Kent P. Morgan, Treasurer and CFO David L. Wierwille, and Vice President of Manufacturing Jeffrey L. Hager. Kenneth C. Harrod and Stephen M. Richmond rounded out the board at the time the grant of shares under the Equity Incentive Plan was approved.

[4] Naylor Aff. Ex. 19.

[5] Third Amended Class Action and Derivative Complaint ("Compl.") Ex. 1, at 4.

[6] Compl. P 30; *see* Naylor Aff. Ex. 7.

[7] The second of the two memoranda from Boeckman to Morgan, sent May 22, 2003, is substantially identical to the first, sent two days earlier. *Compare* Compl. P 26 *with id.* P 29. It downplays the voting control protection afforded against third parties, and omits discussion of the smaller size of most equity incentive plans and the voting trust with Susan Dickerson, subjects that were all covered in the May 20, 2003 memo. *Id.* PP 26, 29, 30.

ment objectives. Nor did they disclose to the non-management director who was present that the number of shares to be included in [*1050] the Equity Incentive Plan far exceeded that which was standard.[8]

Boeckman also [**9] helped the Top Managers ensure that the Dickerson bloc ended up in hands friendly to management. Around the same time as the Randall Bearings Board approved the Certificate Amendment and Equity Incentive Plan, Boeckman told the board that Susan Dickerson wanted to sell her stake in Randall Bearings. Boeckman immersed himself in the negotiations over the terms of sale for Susan Dickerson's bloc of shares to the A Cubed Corporation. Once billed to the court by counsel to the defendants as "an entity that the Dickersons were familiar with" which "do[es]n't have a relationship with the company,"[9] the defendants finally and belatedly admitted — through counsel for the nominal defendant, Randall Bearings, at oral argument on this motion — that A Cubed is affiliated with Randall Bearings' principal supplier of raw materials, Concast.[10] Taken together with the contemplated grant of 200,000 shares to the Top Managers, the sale of the 127,442-share Dickerson bloc to A Cubed would place a majority of Randall Bearing's voting power under the control of the Top Managers and A Cubed, if they acted concertedly.

In this respect, A Cubed's supplier relationship was not the only tie that would bind together the 58% voting bloc. Notably, the arrangement with A Cubed also involved a contractual commitment on Randall Bearings' part not to issue more than 200,000 shares of stock during the next five years. That number was not coincidental. It was precisely the larger number of shares the Top Managers sought to have issued to them under the Equity Incentive Plan once the option of securing a voting trust agreement with Susan Dickerson had evaporated. Also in connection with the negotiations over the sale of the Dickerson bloc, Boeckman had the Top Managers execute a "Term Sheet" reflecting an agreement in principle with the sole owner of A Cubed, Alfred Barbour, that was signed on November 21, 2003, along with the Stock Purchase Agreement.[11] Months before stockholder approval, the Term Sheet specified that the 200,000 shares would

be distributed to the Top Managers in certain proportions, stating that those shares [**11] "will be awarded" to the Top Managers.[12] Of course, as of November 21, 2003, the Randall Bearings stockholders had not yet been informed of, much less voted to approve, the Equity Incentive Plan.

The Term Sheet also contemplated two future agreements among the Top Managers, Barbour, and A Cubed to be executed when the Top Managers were awarded stock under the Equity Incentive Plan. One would require the Top Managers to vote their shares for a board nominee of Barbour's choosing if he requested they do so. Another agreement governed the future sale of Randall Bearings' stock by the [*1051] signatories to the Term Sheet. This "Co-Sale Rights Agreement" included a term prohibiting any of the Top Managers, A Cubed, or any affiliate of A Cubed from selling less than all of its stock to a third party.[13] Another related term provided that if any party covered by that restriction found a buyer for its holdings then all parties would have equal rights to sell to that buyer for the same price and on the same terms and conditions. It also granted an assignable option to the Top Managers that would allow them to purchase the Randall Bearings shares owned by A Cubed in [**12] the event Barbour ever transferred away his majority voting control over A Cubed.[14]

When Boeckman reported the consummation of the A Cubed transaction to the board, the meeting minutes indicate he told them that: "The company's participation in the transaction was solely to facilitate the transaction."[15] It is not clear how informed the only non-management director in attendance was about these side arrangements.

After the board approved [**13] the Certificate Amendment and Equity Incentive Plan, Boeckman prepared and sent to Morgan a checklist listing what needed to be done to implement the Equity Incentive Plan.[16] That checklist included executing stock award agreements and stock certificates reflecting the 200,000 shares the Top Managers would receive.[17] This was in March 2004, two and a half months

---

[8] Randall Bearing's board then included two members who were not managers. One was Susan Dickerson, who had stopped attending meetings by that point because she was feuding with the company over a contractual benefits package. The other was Kenneth Harrod, who had retired in 1997 as a senior executive at Randall Bearings after 30 years of service.

[9] Transcript of Oral Argument on Defendant's Motion to Dismiss the Second Amended Complaint [**10] (Nov. 6, 2006) ("Nov. 6, 2006 Tr.") at 15, 16-17.

[10] Transcript of Oral Argument on Defendant's Motion to Dismiss the Third Amended Complaint (Aug. 29, 2007) ("Aug. 29, 2007 Tr.") at 59-60.

[11] Naylor Supp. Aff. Ex. 16.

[12] Id.

[13] Id. For the purposes of this provision, the Co-Sale Rights Agreement treats A Cubed and all of its affiliates as a single stockholder.

[14] Although the Term Sheet mentions an option being granted in favor of the Top Managers and the company, its other terms seem to make clear that the Top Managers control its exercise. For example, the option was assignable by the Top Managers to a third party. Moreover, the board minutes for the November 17, 2003 meeting indicate that the company's involvement in the transaction with A Cubed was "to make certain representations in the stock purchase agreement concerning corporate matters beyond the knowledge of the Dickerson Family . . . solely to facilitate the transaction." Naylor Aff. Ex. 10.

[15] Naylor Aff. Ex. 10.

[16] Naylor Aff. Ex. 7. The checklist was attached to an email sent from Boeckman to Morgan on March 11, 2004.

[17] Id.

Appendix

before Randall Bearings held a meeting for its stockholders to vote on the Certificate Amendment and the Equity Incentive Plan. Boeckman played the key role in drafting the proxy statement for that meeting, too.

The proxy statement is remarkable for what it did not say. It told the Randall Bearings stockholders that the purpose of the Equity Incentive Plan was to enable the company to "attract[] and retain[] key employees."[18] But it failed to mention that the Top Managers already contemplated that all 200,000 shares would be granted to the Top Managers, leaving no shares left for the "attract[ion]" of anyone, and no shares left to help "retain[]" any but the three Top Managers on the board itself. Likewise, the [**14] proxy statement failed to disclose anything about the contractual arrangements Randall Bearings had entered into with A Cubed. By those arrangements, Randall Bearings had bound itself not to issue any more equity for five years other than the shares contemplated by the Equity Incentive Plan. As important, the proxy statement did not disclose that A Cubed — an affiliate of Randall Bearings' major supplier — and the Top Managers would, if their plans were implemented, control over 50% of the company's voting power. And, as noted, the A Cubed agreements evidenced a plan for [*1052] the immediate grant of all the Equity Incentive Plan shares to the Top Managers and the Top Managers' contemplated right to purchase A Cubed's shares if A Cubed sought to sell its shares. These subjects were not addressed at all in the proxy statement.

After the stockholders approved the Certificate Amendment and the Equity Incentive Plan in a close vote, a Baker & Hostetler employee under Boeckman's supervision played the key role in ensuring the Certificate Amendment he drafted was filed in Delaware with the Secretary of State.[19] The pled facts support the inference that Boeckman's firm, Baker [**15] & Hostetler, engaged the Corporation Service Company ("CSC") to accomplish the filing. Indeed, a list of "Action Items" Boeckman himself prepared for Randall Bearings identified himself as the "Responsible Party" for filing the Certificate Amendment[20] and other evidence belatedly produced in discovery demonstrates that Baker & Hostetler transmitted the Certificate Amendment to CSC in Delaware for filing.[21]

Once the Certificate Amendment and the Equity Incentive Plan became effective, Boeckman then acted as the sole source of advice to the board committee that was charged with determining how and on what terms to allocate the shares authorized by the Equity Incentive Plan. Boeckman presented the committee with a proposal to grant all 200,000 shares to the Top Managers.[22] After brief meetings at which Boeckman [**16] provided the only advice, the committee agreed to do what he recommended — grant the Top Managers all the shares, with immediate voting power and dividend rights, and accelerated vesting in the event of a change of control. Not only that, the committee decided to have the company pay the $930,000 in taxes that the Top Managers owed on the shares they had received. This was a sizable sum that Randall Bearings could not pay out of available funds. Rather, it was forced to take out a five year loan to acquire the funds. During the committee's deliberations, Boeckman did not disclose his discussions with or memoranda to the Top Managers regarding their voting control objectives.

In a prior decision in this case, I denied the defendant-directors' motion to dismiss.[23] In that decision, I concluded that the plaintiff Sample had pled viable claims for breach of fiduciary duty against all the directors of Randall Bearings who served during the period relevant to the grant of 200,000 shares to the Top Managers. In so holding, I noted that the amended complaint pled facts supporting the inference "that the [Certificate] Amendment and the Equity Incentive Plan resulted from [**17] a conscious scheme of entrenchment and personal self-enrichment by the [Top Managers], facilitated by the advice of Boeckman, which was purposely concealed from the Randall Bearing stockholders when they were asked to vote on the Amendment and the Plan."[24]

After the court's decision, the plaintiff sought to further amend the complaint to [*1053] state claims for aiding and abetting breaches of fiduciary duty against Boeckman and Baker & Hostetler.[25]

Boeckman and Baker & Hostetler have now moved to dismiss the claims against them solely on the grounds that personal jurisdiction over them cannot be had in this court. Before addressing that motion's legal merits, it is worth noting that Boeckman and Baker & Hostetler were involved in this litigation long before the third amended complaint added them as parties.

III. The Litigation To Date

Since the inception of this litigation, Boeckman and Baker & Hostetler have played a major role in shaping the defense strategy, although no Baker & Hostetler lawyer sought admission pro hac vice.

---

[18] Compl. Ex. 1, at 4.

[19] *See* Naylor Supp. Aff. Exs. 1, 2 (evidencing "preparations for and transmissions with the CSC regarding filing certificate of amendment with the Delaware Secretary of State"); Boeckman Aff. P 10 (acknowledging he "supervised all legal services performed in connection with the transactions giving rise to" the claims in this suit).

[20] Naylor Aff. Ex. 7.

[21] Naylor Supp. Aff. Exs. 1, 2.

[22] Naylor Aff. Ex. 13.

[23] *Sample v. Morgan*, 914 A.2d 647 (Del. Ch. 2007).

[24] *Id.* at 675.

[25] *See* Compl. PP 91, 92.

Oddly, until a few months ago, counsel for Randall Bearings itself (a nominal party [**18] in this derivative and class action) and for the defendant-directors (who themselves were until recently represented by a single counsel purporting to represent both the Top Managers and the outside directors) seem to have relied almost entirely upon Baker & Hostetler to do the key work required in connection with the production of documents. The defendant-directors' compliance with their discovery obligations has been, to put it mildly, woefully and repeatedly inadequate.

A full recitation of the repeated discovery violations committed by the defendants in this litigation could go on for dozens of pages. One glaring example is worth mentioning. Before this court issued its first decision rejecting the defendant-directors' motion to dismiss, the defendant-directors had been under an obligation to produce documents, including documents relating to the Dickerson shares and any arrangements made in connection with the sale of those shares. But it was not until July 20, 2007 — six months after the prior decision was issued — that the defendants finally produced documents revealing the Top Managers' negotiations over voting, sale rights, and other issues with A Cubed. Even worse, the defendants [**19] continued to dribble out documents, and only in the same time period did they finally produce documents indicating that the Top Managers, Boeckman, and A Cubed had already planned for the Top Managers to receive all 200,000 shares under the Equity Incentive Plan — with immediate voting and dividend rights — before the Randall Bearings stockholders were asked to vote on the Plan. The omission of these material documents from the earlier production has, to date, not been explained.

IV.   A "Coast-To-Coast" Platform

This substantial direction of the legal work by Baker & Hostetler for its clients regarding Delaware law matters is, of course, not surprising. Baker & Hostetler touts itself as a "Counsel to Market Leaders," including businesses that "are leaders globally, nationally, regionally[,] and locally."[26] With the strength of being "one of the nation's largest law firms" with "more than 600 lawyers" and a "unique [10 office] coast-to-coast platform" consisting of "[c]oordinated national and international practice groups," Baker & Hostetler advertises itself as being able to handle the full range of any corporation's legal needs, regardless of its location in the United States.[27] [**20] In fact, as to corporations in [*1054] particular, Baker & Hostetler says that it has "200 business lawyers in all ten of [its] offices [who] work

with clients in every region in the United States and many parts of the world providing comprehensive and experienced business counsel to large and small . . . corporations of . . . all sizes."[28] As to corporate law itself, Baker & Hostetler promotes as "practice strengths" its expertise in understanding the "evolving requirements and actions necessary to maintain or achieve compliance with fiduciary duty obligations . . . and [corporate] disclosure requirements."[29]

V.   The Motion To Dismiss

Boeckman and Baker & Hostetler have not moved to dismiss the claims [**21] against them under Rule 12(b)(6). Rather, they have only challenged the complaint on the ground that they are not subject to personal jurisdiction in Delaware.

Frankly, their opening brief was an odd one in that it entirely ignored the fact that they had prepared the Certificate Amendment and caused it to be filed in Delaware. In support of that brief, Boeckman filed an affidavit that, although true in the most literal of senses, seems intended to distract attention from Baker & Hostetler's role in the Certificate Amendment filing. In Boeckman's words:

> 10. I was the Baker Hostetler attorney who supervised all legal services performed in connection with the transactions giving rise to Plaintiff's alleged claims in the above captioned matter.
>
> * * *
>
> 13. I had no cause to enter Delaware in connection with my representation, nor did I file any documents with any court or agency in Delaware in connection with this representation.[30]

When the plaintiff's answering brief was filed, it understandably featured the Certificate Amendment. After that brief was submitted, more late-produced documents came in when Baker & Hostetler finally produced its billing [**22] records. The records demonstrated that a paralegal under Boeckman's supervision at Baker & Hostetler sent the Certificate Amendment to CSC in Delaware for filing.[31] Confronted with the reality — which they might have thought to disclose up-front — that they not only drafted the Certificate Amendment, but sent it to CSC *in Delaware* for filing, the moving defendants retreated to the contention that although they sent

---

[26] Baker Hostetler — About Us, http://www. bakerlaw.com/ AboutUs.aspx?Abs_WP_ID=56b84b31-3f37-41eb-8960-e42b349976f6 (last visited Nov. 27, 2007).

[27] Id.

[28] Baker Hostetler — Practice Strengths — Business, http://www. bakerlaw.com/BDs.aspx?Abs_BD_ID=116896b2-50a8-4fde-88c9-21f4fa0cab48 (last visited Nov. 27, 2007).

[29] Baker Hostetler — Practice Strengths — Business — Corporate Governance, http://www. bakerlaw.com/BDs.aspx?Abs_BD_ID=9fd65ea7-8a93-4a79-afa9-acceafd19e24 (last visited Nov. 27, 2007).

[30] Boeckman Aff. PP 10, 13 (emphasis added).

[31] Naylor Supp. Aff. Ex. 1.

the Certificate Amendment to CSC in Delaware, CSC was the registered agent who actually filed the Certificate Amendment with the Secretary of State. Why this matters as a jurisdictional matter, they do not make clear.

Recognizing that their direct role in filing the Certificate Amendment undercut most of the arguments made in their opening brief, the moving defendants then resorted to a panoply of implausible and strained new arguments, which, if accepted, would undermine the purposes of our state's long-arm statute and the ability of stockholders of Delaware corporations to avail themselves of this court as a forum to hold parties responsible for aiding and abetting breaches of fiduciary duty. Consistent [*1055] with the pattern of this litigation, it [**23] turns out that the briefs on this motion were drafted by attorneys at Baker & Hostetler, but filed and signed only by Delaware counsel, who argued the motion. At oral argument, Delaware counsel conceded that at least one of the arguments in the Baker & Hostetler briefs lacked any plausible basis in law or logic.[32]

Distilled down, the arguments made by Boeckman and Baker & Hostetler go essentially as follows. For starters, they note that all the legal work they did was done in offices [**24] of Baker & Hostetler outside Delaware. The only potentially relevant act that they directed toward Delaware itself as a physical place was the transmission of the Certificate Amendment to CSC in Delaware. But that action was, they say, not sufficient to constitute a qualifying act under the long-arm statute because the reduction in the Top Managers' cost of acquisition from $200,000 to $200 was simply a nice extra of the overall scheme alleged by the plaintiff. Absent the Certificate Amendment, the approval of the Equity Incentive Plan would still have enabled the Top Managers to obtain voting control over 200,000 shares, although at a much richer price.

In addition, they argue that because the Certificate Amendment was filed by the company, albeit by Baker & Hostetler sending it to CSC, the filing cannot be attributable to any of the Top Managers with whom Boeckman and Baker & Hostetler allegedly conspired. Rather, the filing was a corporate act, and a corporation cannot, say the moving parties, conspire with its own officers, directors, and lawyer. In that same vein, Boeckman and Baker & Hostetler

argue that a lawyer who is simply acting for a client with only the hope of getting [**25] paid for his work cannot conspire with that client and therefore the conspiracy theory of jurisdiction cannot be used against the lawyer to hold him accountable for acts of the client in the forum state.

Finally, Boeckman and Baker & Hostetler contend that it would offend notions of due process for them to have to defend this suit in Delaware. Although they admit to having acted as outside general counsel to a Delaware corporation on matters of Delaware law as to the very matters at dispute in this lawsuit, and to regularly giving clients advice on matters of Delaware law, the fact that their "coast-to-coast" platform of offices does not include a Delaware office makes it constitutionally offensive for them to have to face suit in this state, even as to claims challenging the propriety, as a matter of Delaware law, of board actions on which they gave advice about Delaware law and of a Certificate Amendment they caused to be filed in Delaware.

VI. Legal Analysis

In considering a motion to dismiss for lack of personal jurisdiction under Court of Chancery Rule 12(b)(2), I am not limited to the pleadings. Rather, I am "permitted to rely upon the pleadings, proxy statement, affidavits, and [**26] briefs of the parties in order to determine whether [*1056] the defendants are subject to personal jurisdiction."[33] In evaluating the record, I must draw reasonable inferences in favor of the plaintiff.[34]

There are two legal questions to be answered in considering a motion under Rule 12(b)(2). The first is whether there is a statutory basis for serving the defendants with process.[35] The second is whether this court's exercise of personal jurisdiction over the defendants is consistent with the Due Process Clause of the Fourteenth Amendment of the United States Constitution.[36]

Here, the first question is, I suppose, modestly more difficult to answer than the second, which is not close at all. Before beginning, it is useful to reiterate that the moving defendants have not challenged the viability of the claims pled against them. They accept the proposition that the plaintiff has alleged well-pled facts supporting the inference that Boeckman consciously assisted the Top Managers [**27] in conceiving and implementing a scheme to enrich and entrench the Top Managers at the expense of Randall Bearings and its stockholders. The sole determination I must now make is whether the moving

---

[32] That argument contended that because the director-defendants, including the Top Managers, had been served under 10 *Del. C.* § 3114, the plaintiff could not utilize the so-called "conspiracy" theory of jurisdiction to obtain jurisdiction over Boeckman and Baker & Hostetler under 10 *Del. C.* § 3104. Why this was so was not something counsel for Boeckman and Baker & Hostetler could explain. And for good reason, it makes no sense. The fact that the director-defendants were served under § 3114 does not mean that they could not have engaged in a civil conspiracy with a co-conspirator who was not subject to service under § 3114 in order to determine whether that person could be served under the long-arm statute.

[33] *Crescent/Mach I Partners, L.P. v. Turner*, 846 A.2d 963, 974 (Del. Ch. 2000).

[34] *Outokumpu Eng'g Enter., Inc.*, 685 A.2d at 727.

[35] *AeroGlobal Capital Mgmt., LLC v. Cirrus Indus., Inc.*, 871 A.2d 428, 438 (Del. 2005).

[36] *Id.*

defendants must defend that claim on the merits in this court.

Boeckman and Baker & Hostetler were served under Delaware's long-arm statute, 10 *Del. C.* § 3104. That statute provides in pertinent part that:

> (c) As to a cause of action brought by any person arising from any of the acts enumerated in this section, a court may exercise personal jurisdiction over any nonresident, or a personal representative, who in person or through an agent:

> (1) Transacts any business or performs any character of work or service in the State; [or]

> * * *

> (3) Causes tortious injury in the State by an act or omission in this State 37

The Delaware Supreme Court has made clear that trial courts must give a broad reading to the terms of the long-arm statute, in order to effectuate the statute's intent to ensure that this state's court may exercise jurisdiction to the full limits permissible under the Due Process Clause.38 In other words, the Supreme Court has instructed that trial courts should [**28] permit service under § 3104 if the statutory language plausibly permits service, and rely upon a Due Process analysis to screen out uses of the statute that sweep too broadly.39

[*1057] Here, the parties initially joined issue over whether Boeckman [**29] and Baker & Hostetler could be served under § 3104 because well-pled facts support the inference that Boeckman engaged in concerted activity with the Top Managers to entrench and enrich the Top Managers at the unfair expense of Randall Bearings and its stockholders. As an element of that scheme, Boeckman and the Top Managers proposed and obtained approval for the Certificate Amendment, which was filed in Delaware. That Certificate Amendment permitted the Top Managers to receive the disputed shares for only $200, saving themselves $199,800. Using the so-called conspiracy theory of jurisdiction, the plaintiff argues that the act of filing the Certifi-

cate Amendment can be imputed to Boeckman and Baker & Hostetler, thereby satisfying both § 3104(c)(1) and § 3104(c)(3) of the long-arm statute.

As things turn out, the inquiry is much simpler. Discovery has since revealed that Boeckman and Baker & Hostetler themselves prepared and sent the Certificate Amendment to CSC in Delaware for filing with the Secretary of State.40 That is, the moving defendants themselves directly transacted business in Delaware for purposes of § 3104(c)(1).41 The involvement of a defendant in arranging, either [**30] directly or through an agent such as CSC, for the filing of a corporate instrument in Delaware that facilitated transactions under challenge in litigation in this court has been repeatedly recognized as sufficient to constitute the transaction of business under § 3104(c)(1).42 The Certificate Amendment is directly at issue in the claims against the moving defendants, and therefore the use of § 3104(c)(1) to serve the moving defendants is permissible.43 Likewise, the moving defendants' filing of the Certificate Amendment in Delaware satisfies § 3104(c)(3) because that action injured Randall Bearings, a Delaware corporation. When a Delaware corporation is financially injured by faithless conduct of its directors, the corporation is injured in its legal home, this State, for purposes of § 3104(c)(3). As this court has previously observed:

> When conspirators commit a breach of fiduciary duty against a Delaware corporation [*1058] that causes cognizable injury to the entity (as an unfair dilution is deemed to do)

---

37 10 *Del. C.* § 3104.

38 *See Hercules Inc. v. Leu Trust and Banking (Bahamas) Ltd.*, 611 A.2d 476, 480-81 (Del. 1992) ("[Section] 3104(c) is to be broadly construed to confer jurisdiction to the maximum extent possible under the Due Process Clause.") (internal citations omitted).

39 *See Chandler v. Ciccoricco*, 2003 Del. Ch. LEXIS 47, 2003 WL 21040185, at *10-11 (Del. Ch. 2003) ("Under [the *Hercules*] mandate, my task should be to give the words of the statute a liberal construction and to conclude that [a filing in Delaware] is a transaction of business if that can be reasonably done. Any problems of overbreadth by such a liberal construction can be policed by application of the minimum contacts analysis under the due process clause of the Fourteenth Amendment."); *cf. Assist Stock Mgmt. L.L.C. v. Rosheim*, 753 A.2d 974, 980 (Del. Ch. 2000) (advocating the use of the Due Process analysis to temper potentially overbroad application of the terms of Delaware's director consent statute, 10 *Del. C.* § 3114).

40 Naylor Aff. Exs. 1, 2.

41 *Benihana of Tokyo, Inc. v. Benihana, Inc.*, 2005 Del. Ch. LEXIS 19, 2005 WL 583828, at *6, *8 (Del. Ch. 2005); *Gibralt Capital Corp. v. Smith*, 2001 Del. Ch. LEXIS 68, 2001 WL 647837, at *6 (Del. Ch. 2001).

42 *E.g., In re General Motors (Hughes) S'holder Litig*, 2005 Del. Ch. LEXIS 65, 2005 WL 1089021, at *22 (Del. Ch. 2005) (certificate of merger); *Benihana*, 2005 Del. Ch. LEXIS 19, 2005 WL 583828, at *8 (certificate of designation); *Chandler*, 2003 DEl. Ch. LEXIS 47, 2003 WL 21040185, at *11 (certificate of designation); *Parfi Holding AB v. Mirror Image Internet, Inc.*, 794 A.2d 1211, 1229 (Del. Ch. 2001) (charter amendments), *rev'd on other grounds*, 817 A.2d 149 (Del. 2002); *Gibralt*, 2001 Del. Ch. LEXIS 68, 2001 WL 647837, at *6 (charter amendment and certificate of designation); *Kahn v. Lynch Commc'n Sys., Inc.*, 1989 Del. Ch. LEXIS 102, 1989 WL 99800, at *4 (Del. Ch. 1989) ("negotiating [**32] and consummating the merger at issue" constituted transaction of business under 10 *Del. C.* § 3104(c)(1) when the merger's consummation required a filing with the Secretary of State).

43 The "single act" or specific jurisdiction subsections of § 3104(c), such as § 3104 (c)(1), only allow jurisdiction over causes of action that are closely intertwined with the jurisdictional contact. DONALD J. WOLFE, JR. & MICHAEL A. PITTENGER, CORPORATE AND COMMERCIAL PRACTICE IN THE DELAWARE COURT OF CHANCERY § 3-5[a][1][iii] (2005); *accord* 10 *Del. C.* § 3104(c). When service is premised on these subsections, the Delaware-related conduct must form a source of the claim. *E.g., Arnold v. Soc'y for Sav. Bancorp., Inc.*, 1993 Del. Ch. LEXIS 275, 1993 WL 526781, at *3 (Del. Ch. 1993). Here, the tight nexus between the Certificate Amendment and the entrenchment scheme forming the cause of action make service under the single act provisions of the long-arm statute unproblematic.

Appendix

... it is fair to say that the entity was injured in its chosen home — Delaware — the situs that reflects the center of gravity of the corporation for all issues involving its internal [**31] affairs. The balance sheet and voting dilution injuries that result in fiduciary duty cases are in some sense metaphysical, but that reality strengthens the argument that the corporation at the very least suffers these injuries in its chosen domicile. Any problems with this common sense approach are best policed by the minimum contacts tests or by the other aspects of § 3104, which for the most part require that an actual act take place in Delaware.[44]

Because Boeckman and Baker & Hostetler were the parties responsible for filing the Certificate Amendment, there is, as noted, no need to impute the conduct of the Top Managers to them by using the conspiracy theory. But the moving defendants make another odd argument that I must consider. That argument — improperly advanced for the first time in the moving defendants' reply brief — consists in the [**35] notion that because the Certificate Amendment was filed on behalf of Randall Bearings as a corporation, Boeckman and Baker & Hostetler cannot be held personally responsible for the filing, for purposes of a personal jurisdiction inquiry under the long-arm statute. That is, even though the moving directors in fact were the parties who prepared the Certificate Amendment, retained CSC to

file it as registered agent, and transmitted the Amendment to CSC in Delaware for filing with the Secretary of State, the fact that the Certificate Amendment was filed on behalf of Randall Bearings immunizes the moving defendants.[45] In its broadest form, a form that [*1059] the moving defendants did not shy from advancing, the moving defendants posit that the filing of a charter amendment or other key corporate instrument with the Secretary of State in Delaware may never form the basis for serving a party sued for aiding and abetting a breach of fiduciary duty in Delaware. Why? Because such documents are formally filed by the corporation itself and thus respect for the corporation's separate legal identity requires that the individuals who caused the corporation to make the filings cannot be held personally [**36] accountable for those filings for purposes of § 3104.

One can sleep soundly at night confident that rejection of this argument is not at odds with either logic or sound public policy. When a claim for breach of fiduciary duty is at issue, the underlying conduct almost always involves formal action of the corporation itself. After all, the very essence of a breach [**37] of corporate law fiduciary duty claim is the misuse of corporate control.[46] For example, an unfair squeeze out merger by a controlling stockholder quintessentially involves the corporation entering into a merger agreement allowing the controlling stockholder to purchase the corporation for an unfair price.[47] That is, claims of fiduciary duty ultimately rest on the proposition that a corporate fiduciary has caused the corporation to do something at odds with its own best interests, typically so that the fiduciary could secure an improper personal benefit.[48] Indeed,

---

[44] *Chandler v. Ciccoricco*, 2003 Del. Ch. LEXIS 47, 2003 WL 21040185, at *11 n.46 (Del. Ch. 2003). This court noted in *Chandler v. Ciccoricco* that the mandate to construe § 3104(c) to the constitutional limits of Due Process should warrant treatment of Delaware as the situs of injury to [**33] a Delaware corporation. *Id.* As *Chandler* mentioned, the seminal conspiracy jurisdiction case in Delaware, *Istituto Bancario Italiano SpA v. Hunter Engineering Co., Inc.*, 449 A.2d 210, 228 (Del. 1982), may seem at first blush to preclude a holding that the situs of injury to a Delaware corporation not headquartered in Delaware that is victimized by a breach of fiduciary duty is in Delaware for purposes of § 3104(c)(3). *Chandler*, 2003 Del. Ch. LEXIS 47, 2003 WL 21040185, at * 11 n.46. Upon close examination, there is not as much tension between this conclusion and the Supreme Court's decision in *Istituto* as the *Chandler* decision perceived. In that case, an Italian holding company in financial difficulty pledged its entire 10,000 shares of a wholly-owned Delaware subsidiary to an Italian bank. *Istituto*, 449 A.2d at 214-15. When it appeared that the loan would not be repaid, the subsidiary's board authorized additional shares and distributed 190,000 shares as a stock dividend that was then transferred to another owner, thus diluting the security interest from 100% to 5% of the subsidiary's assets. *Id.* On those facts it appeared clear to the Supreme Court that the situs of the injury to the pledgee's security interest [**34] in a direct suit by the Italian bank was either the location of the pledge, or the home of the pledgee Italian bank. *Id.* at 228. In other words, *Istituto* did not involve a derivative claim. By contrast, when a Delaware resident — a Delaware corporation — is injured by a breach of fiduciary duty, it is easy to conceive of the corporation as having been injured in its chosen place of legal residence. After all, it is precisely for purposes of internal affairs that corporations — which are not physical beings — choose a legal domicile. When they suffer financial injury, that injury should, consistent with the instruction of *Hercules* and other Delaware public policies favoring a broad construction of § 3104's reach, be deemed to have been suffered in Delaware for purposes of § 3104(c)(3).

[45] The defendants cite cases which advance a fairness-based policy rationale for protecting corporate fiduciaries from being sued personally when jurisdiction over them is based solely on contacts initiated in their fiduciary capacity. *See Plummer & Co. Realtors v. Crisafi*, 533 A.2d 1242, 1246 (Del. Super. 1987) ("The underpinning of this fiduciary shield doctrine is the notion that it is unfair to force an individual to defend a suit brought against him personally in a forum with which his only relevant contacts are acts performed not for his own benefit but for the benefit of his employer.") (quoting *Marine Midland Bank, N.A. v. Miller*, 664 F.2d 899, 902 (2d Cir. 1981)); *Mktg Prods Mgmt, LLC v. HealthandBeautyDirect.com, Inc.*, 2004 Del. Ch. LEXIS 26, 2004 WL 249581, at *3 (Del. Super. 2004) (citing *Plummer & Co. Realtors*, 533 A.2d at 1246).

[46] *E.g., Guth v. Loft, Inc.*, 23 Del. Ch. 255, 5 A.2d 503, 510 (Del. 1939) ("Corporate officers and directors are not permitted to use their position of trust and confidence to further their private interests.").

[47] E.g., *Weinberger v. UOP, Inc.*, 457 A.2d 701 (Del. 1983).

[48] *E.g., Zahn v. Transamerica Corp.*, 162 F.2d 36, 46 (3d Cir. 1947) ("[T]he directors of Axton-Fisher ... were [**38] the instruments of [a controlling stockholder,] Transamerica[,] ... voting in favor of their special interest, that of Transamerica, [and they] could not and did not exercise an independent judgment in calling the Class A stock, but made the call for the purpose of profiting their true principal, Transamerica. In short a puppet-puppeteer relationship existed between the directors of Axton-Fisher and Transamerica. The act of the board of directors in calling the Class A stock, an act which could have been legally consummated by a disinterested board of directors, was here effected at the direction of the principal Class B stockholder in order to profit it."); *Sinclair Oil Corp. v. Levien*, 280

in fiduciary duty cases, the relief that is sought often involves enjoining or rescinding official corporate action. That is in fact the situation presented by this case, in which the plaintiff seeks rescission of the grant of the disputed shares to the Top Managers.

Although there are sound public policy reasons for limiting the ability of contract [*1060] and tort claimants to file certain claims against corporate officers and directors for conduct of the corporation itself,[49] those reasons have little to do with this case or other cases involving the internal affairs of corporations. When well-pled facts support the inference that a person caused a corporation to take jurisdictionally-significant conduct in Delaware and that conduct is an element in a scheme by corporate fiduciaries to unfairly advantage themselves at the expense of a Delaware corporation and its stockholders, our case law has consistently held that the long-arm statute may be used to serve that person.[50] It would be surprising were it otherwise, because a contrary ruling would turn the very essence of faithless conduct — the abuse of corporate power — into an immunity from accountability, precisely because the disloyal fiduciaries derived their wrongful gains from actions of the corporation itself, albeit corporate actions that [**40] their own conduct brought about.[51] Such an accountability-destroying

reading of the long-arm statute would itself be entirely disloyal to the statute's purpose, as articulated by our Supreme Court in its *Hercules* decision.[52]

Boeckman [**42] and Baker & Hostetler assert a narrower version of the prior argument to protect them from application of the conspiracy theory of jurisdiction — that is, that the filing of the Certificate Amendment, although brought about by humans at Baker & Hostetler, was a corporate act of Randall Bearings, for which those humans may not be held responsible for purposes of a personal jurisdiction analysis under § 3104. This narrower version centers on considerations supposedly unique to the legal profession. According to the moving defendants, case law in some other jurisdictions says that lawyers cannot be sued simply for performing services for a client if all that the lawyers get out of [*1061] those services is a fee.[53] That is, if the only benefit of the lawyer's actions is getting a fee for the work he did, this doctrine supposedly gives the lawyer a free pass from being held civilly responsible for his actions to those who would sue their clients. The moving defendants refer to this doctrine as a version of the "intra-corporate conspiracy doctrine" or the "agent's immunity rule," whereby corporate officials acting in their official capacity are usually deemed incapable of conspiring with the [**43] corporation.[54]

Again, the problem with the moving defendants' argument is that they seek to wrench notions that

A.2d 717, 721 (Del. 1971) ("Self-dealing occurs when the parent, by virtue of its domination of the subsidiary, causes the subsidiary to act in such a way that the parent receives something from the subsidiary to the exclusion of, and detriment to, the minority stockholders of the subsidiary."); *Bennett v. Propp*, 41 Del. Ch. 14, 187 A.2d 405, 408 (Del. 1962) (Chairman of the board caused a corporation to engage in unauthorized stock purchases in anticipation of a hostile tender offer. Share "purchases were made [**39] to preserve the control of the corporation in [the chairman] and his fellow directors. . . . The use of corporate funds for such a purpose is improper.").

[49] *See Allied Capital Corp. v. GC-Sun Holdings, L.P.*, 910 A.2d 1020, 1044 n.63 (Del. Ch. 2006) ("When corporations commit intentional torts or breaches of contract, they obviously do so at the behest of some human agent and often more than one. Therefore, if corporate agents were generally capable of conspiring among themselves and with their corporate employer, many claims against corporations for their own acts could also regularly be supplemented by claims against corporate managers for conspiring with each other to cause the corporation to act illegally."); Martin H. Pritikin, *Toward Coherence in Civil Conspiracy Law: A Proposal to Abolish the Agent's Immunity Rule*, 84 NEB. L. REV. 1, 25 (2005) (explaining that because corporate principals can only act through their agents, agency relationships and breaches of contract by the corporate principal would be chilled if agents "were to absorb the cost of tort liability for inducing a breach of their principals' [**41] contracts — or, more accurately, if they internalized the risk of such liability ex ante").

[50] *See, e.g., Benihana*, 2005 Del. Ch. LEXIS 19, 2005 WL 583828, at *8; *In re General Motors (Hughes) S'holder Litig.*, 2005 Del. Ch. LEXIS 65, 2005 WL 1089021, at *22; *Gibralt*, 2001 DEl. Ch. LEXIS 68, 2001 WL 647837, at *6 (Del. Ch. 2001).

[51] This is not a novel observation. In *U.S. v. Montreal Trust Co.*, for example, a New York federal court asserted jurisdiction over a corporate officer of a publicly-owned Canadian company who had been diverting funds through New York agents. 358 F.2d 239, 243 (2d Cir. 1966). The officer claimed that because his only contacts with New York were in an official corporate role on behalf of the Canadian company he was charged with victimizing, he was

protected by the fiduciary shield doctrine. In rejecting his argument on appeal, the Court of Appeals for the Second Circuit stated: "It would be ironic, indeed, if the very corporations whose funds [the officer] is charged with diverting were to supply him with a shield against suit for tax liability allegedly incurred in connection with this purported breach of his fiduciary duty." *Id; see also Marine Midland Bank*, 664 F.2d at 902 (2d Cir. 1981) (summarizing *Montreal Trust*, 358 F.2d at 243).

[52] 611 A.2d 476, 480-81 (Del. 1992).

[53] *See, e.g., In re County of Orange*, 203 B.R. 983, 999-1000 (Bankr. C.D. Cal. 1996), *rev'd on other grounds* ("The gain must be more than the fees received from the fiduciary-defendant that the nonfiduciary is accused of conspiring with."); *Cooper v. Equity Gen. Ins. Co.*, 219 Cal. App. 3d 1252, 268 Cal. Rptr. 692, 696-97 (Cal. Ct. App. 1990) (holding that an attorney working on a contingency basis did not have an independent financial stake because plaintiff did not allege that the attorney "stood to gain anything more than a fee for his work as an attorney."); *see also General Refractories Co. v. Fireman's Fund Ins. Co.*, 337 F.3d 297, 313 (3d Cir. 2003) ("[T]he mere fact that attorneys have 'mixed motives' such as 'enhancing' their reputation by aggressive representation, does not remove their conduct from the scope of the agency.").

[54] *See, e.g., Superior Court Chain Store Maint., Inc. v. Nat'l Glass & Gate Serv. Inc.*, 2004 R.I. Super. LEXIS 81, 2004 WL 877599, at *11 (R.I. Super. 2004) ("It is well-settled that 'a conspiracy between a corporation and its agents, acting within the scope of their employment, is a legal impossibility.' . . . The policy behind the intracorporate conspiracy doctrine "is to preserve independent [**44] decision-making by business entities and their agents free of the pressure that can be generated by allegations of conspiracy.") (quoting *Marmott v. Maryland Lumber Co.*, 807 F. 2d 1180, 1184 (4th Cir. 1986) and *Fairley v. Andrews*, 300 F. Supp. 2d 660, 668 (N.D. Ill. 2004)); *see also Roth v. La Societe Anonyme Turbomeca France*, 120 S.W.3d 764, 778 (Mo. App. 2003) ("Because an attorney is an alter ego of his or her client, a conspiracy between the attorney and the client is not possible.").

Appendix

are logical in some contexts into a context in which they make no sense. For certain purposes — for example, claims of tort or antitrust violations brought against a corporation and its officers — it makes little sense to describe the officers as conspiring with the corporation.[55] After all, corporations make decisions through humans, usually humans involved in collaborative activity. Indeed, if one assumes that every corporate action must involve some human actor, every corporate act could be a conspiracy between the corporation and the human causing its act.[56] This area of the law is complex and freighted [**45] with important policy questions regarding the circumstances in which both the corporation and those who cause it to act should be held accountable to third-parties and society for corporate conduct. Unsurprisingly, for example, there are distinctions in this area between civil and criminal responsibility and among various kinds of civil claims.[57]

[*1062] Here, however, those complications are not present. The alleged conspiracy does not include Randall Bearings; Randall Bearings is one of the alleged victims. The conspiracy is among the Top Managers, allegedly with the knowing assistance of Boeckman and Baker & Hostetler, who were being paid to represent Randall Bearings, not the Top Managers. The conspiracy was intended to entrench and enrich the Top Managers.

Given the nature of this conspiracy, the doctrine on which [**47] the moving defendants rely does not even apply on its own terms. Well-pled facts support the inference that the moving defendants were not acting within the appropriate scope of their agency. That is, there are well-pled allegations that the moving defendants were in fact acting to unfairly advantage the Top Managers at the expense of their real client, the company. As the moving defendants admit, when an agent is alleged to have breached its duty to its principal, the so-called agent's immunity they rely upon does not apply.[58] Furthermore, it is not the case, as the moving defendants allege, that the only benefit the moving defendants got was the fees they were paid for their work. By assisting in an entrenchment scheme, the moving defendants got a benefit similar to that obtained by the Top Managers, securing their position as company counsel against the risk of displacement in a takeover. I perceive no Delaware public interest that would be served by adopting a rule that insulates advisors of managers of a Delaware corporation from accountability if can be proven that those advisors, although being paid by the corporation to advise the managers in their official capacity, consciously [**48] assisted the managers in breaching their fiduciary duties.

Put simply, the use of § 3104 to serve the moving defendants is entirely consistent with the language and evident purpose of that statute, and with the precedent interpreting it. The requirement that there be a statutory basis for service is therefore [**49] met.

The second step in the personal jurisdiction analysis is a simple one. The United States Supreme Court has held that it is constitutionally permissible to exercise personal jurisdiction over a non-resident defendant when that defendant should have "reasonably anticipated ... that his ... actions might result in the forum state exercising personal jurisdiction over him in order to adjudicate disputes arising from [*1063] those actions."[59] To satisfy this test, the defendant need not have ever entered the forum state physically because the Supreme Court has rightly focused the test on the more relevant question of whether the defendant has engaged in such conduct directed toward the forum state that makes it reasonably foreseeable that that conduct could give rise to claims against the defendant in the forum state's courts.[60]

---

[55] See Allied Capital Corp., L.P., 910 A.2d at 1044 n.63 (discussing the complexities of using the tort of civil conspiracy to apply to concerted action among corporate officials); see also Kathleen F. Brickey, Conspiracy, Group Danger and the Corporate Defendant, 52. U. CIN. L. REV. 431, 432-33 (1983).

[56] See Allied Capital Corp., 910 A.2d at 1044 n.63 ("[I]f corporate agents were generally capable of conspiring among themselves and with their corporate employer, many claims against corporations for their own acts could regularly be supplemented by claims against corporate managers for conspiring with each other to cause the corporation to act illegally.").

[57] See Pritikin, supra note 49 at 4-5 ("[T]he single legal actor theory — the fiction that the agent's acts are those of the principal, and thus that the 'plurality' element of conspiracy [**46] is absent — arose where policy considerations regarding the underlying offense supported its application. The fiction is accepted in the antitrust context, on the rationale that proscribing certain intracorporate combinations that restrain trade could chill legitimate business conduct. However, the same fiction is rejected in the context of criminal conspiracy, on the rationale that the increased danger arising from a group of criminal actors that justifies punishing conspiracy generally exists even where the conspirators are all agents and employees of a single entity."); see also Brickey, supra note 55 at 438-40 ("The incongruity of these rules is attributable to the disparate policy considerations that shaped them.").

[58] E.g., Amaysing Techs. Corp v. CyberAir Commc'ns, Inc., 2005 Del. Ch. LEXIS 35, 2005 WL 578972, at *7 (Del. Ch. 2005) ("An exception exists to this general rule, however, when the officer or agent of the corporation steps out of her role as an officer or agent and acts pursuant to personal motives.... Courts interpreting the 'personal reasons' exception ... have read it to mean a personal animus and/or desire for financial benefit other than one's corporate salary.") (internal citations and quotations omitted); Pritikin, supra note 49 at 25 (The agent's privilege is "based on the agent's value to the principal in accomplishing its legitimate business goals.... [I]f benefiting the principal is no longer the sole or primary purpose of the agent in inducing a breach, the social interest in the agent's inducement no longer outweighs the interest in upholding the contract, so the privilege is vitiated.").

[59] In re USACafes, L.P. Litig., 600 A.2d 43, 50 (Del. Ch. 1991) (citing World-Wide Volkswagen Corp. v. Woodson, 444 U.S. 286, 292, 100 S. Ct. 559, 62 L. Ed. 2d 490 (1980)).

[60] E.g., Asahi Metal Indus. Co. Ltd. v. California, 480 U.S. 102, 110, 107 S. Ct. 1026, 94 L. Ed. 2d 92 (1987); Burger King Corp. v. Rudzewicz, 471 U.S. 462, 475, 105 S. Ct. 2174, 85 L. Ed. 2d 528 (1985); see also William M. Richman, Understanding Personal Jurisdiction, 25 ARIZ. ST. L.J. 599, 617-18 (1993) [**50] ("The Court

That test is easily satisfied here. As noted previously, Baker & Hostetler advertises itself as a national, indeed, international, firm that regularly advises public corporations in matters of corporate and securities law. It touts its coast-to-coast platform.

As sophisticated practitioners of corporate law, the moving defendants realize that Delaware, as a chartering state, has an important interest in regulating [**51] the internal affairs of its corporations, in order to ensure that the directors and officers of Delaware corporations honor their obligations to operate the corporation lawfully and in the best interest of the corporation's stockholders. The United States Supreme Court has long recognized the legitimacy and importance of a state's interest in regulating the internal affairs of its corporations.[61] It can also be no surprise to the moving defendants that this important interest is given life in our state by providing stockholders with access to Delaware's court system in order to assert claims of breach of fiduciary duty; after all, decisions too numerous to cite make this clear.[62] So too does § 3114 of Title 10,

which makes clear that the directors [*1064] and officers of Delaware corporations, accept, as a condition of office, the responsibility for answering official capacity suits in the court of this State.[63] Therefore, the moving defendants had to know that if the Top Managers and other defendant-directors engaged in conduct that gave rise to fiduciary duty claims, that the Top Managers and other defendant-directors were likely to be sued in Delaware.[64]

Given [**55] these realities, it is difficult to conceive how it would shock the conscience to require the moving defendants to defend a lawsuit in Delaware. As is clear, the moving defendants purported to provide a wide range of advice and services to the board and officers of a Delaware corporation about important issues of Delaware law.[65] That advice and

Delaware's "compelling interest in the efficient and consistent application of its laws governing business entities").

[63] *HMG/Courtland Properties, Inc. v. Gray* explains why Delaware's director consent statute is constitutionally valid:

> [T]he power of defendant directors to act in their director capacity arises exclusively under the Delaware corporation laws; defendant directors avail themselves of important privileges and legal powers and protections when they accept office as directors of Delaware corporations; by virtue of § 3114, defendant directors who accept such privileges are put on notice that [**54] they can be haled into court here to answer for breaches of Delaware corporation laws; Delaware has a legitimate interest in enforcing those laws; § 3114 is narrowly tailored to serve that legitimate interest and to compel the appearance of defendant directors only where that purpose is served; that the state's legitimate interest outweighs any burden to defendant directors; and, as a result, defendant directors served in conformity with § 3114 can fairly be expected to defend suits here.

729 A.2d 300, 304 n.3 (Del. Ch. 1999) (summarizing *Armstrong v. Pomerance*, 423 A.2d 174 (Del. 1980)).

[64] *See HealthTrio, Inc. v. Margules*, 2007 Del. Super. LEXIS 34, 2007 WL 544156, at *6 (Del. Super. 2007) (finding that a non-Delaware attorney's provision of legal services for a client in filing its certificate of incorporation in Delaware and in acting for it in connection with a prior Delaware litigation, including calls and letters to corresponding counsel in Delaware, satisfied the long-arm statute and the Due Process Clause when the lawyer was sued in Delaware for malpractice relating to the prior Delaware litigation even though the attorney never appeared in the prior Delaware litigation or physically entered Delaware).

[65] In fact, during the period when the Certificate Amendment and the Equity Incentive Plan were being devised and implemented, Boeckman was representing Randall Bearings in connection with a books and records request made by the lead plaintiff in this action, Gary Sample. *See* Naylor Supp. Aff. Exs. 9, 10, 11, 12, 13, 14. In the § 220 litigation, Boeckman appeared on pleadings and a response to interrogatories filed in this court as of counsel and took the lead in jousting with Sample's Delaware-based counsel over the books and records that the company would produce [**56] to Sample. *See* Answer, *Sample v. Randall Bearings, Inc.*, C.A. 491-N; Defendant Randall Bearing, Inc.'s Responses to Plaintiff's First Set of Interrogatories, *Sample v. Randall Bearings, Inc.*, C.A. 491-N; Naylor Aff. Exs. 25, 26, 28, 30. In the course of that jousting, Baker & Hostetler also gave its view on the propriety and scope of Sample's right to books and records under Delaware law. *See* Naylor Aff. Exs. 25, 26, 28. Notably, in a memorandum that Boeckman wrote to Top Manager and Randall Bearings CEO Kent Morgan relating to the grants issued under the Equity Incentive Plan, Boeckman reminded Morgan that there are "stockholders like Gary Sample out there." Naylor Aff. Ex. 7.

has realized that 'it is an inescapable fact of modern commercial life that a substantial amount of business is transacted solely by mail and wire communication across state lines, thus obviating the need for physical presence.' *Burger King*, 471 U.S. at 476. It is enough if defendant's conduct is 'purposefully directed' at the forum. *Keeton v. Hustler Magazine, Inc.*, 465 U.S. 770, 774, 104 S. Ct. 1473, 79 L. Ed. 2d 790 (1984).... Also, defendant may be amenable when her actions outside the state have foreseeable effects inside the state. Indeed, if the defendant's out-of-state activity is purposeful and geographically targeted at the forum state, jurisdiction can be based on a single transaction or occurrence — the most minimal of contacts. *McGee v. Int'l Life Ins. Co.*, 355 U.S. 220, 223, 78 S. Ct. 199, 2 L. Ed. 2d 223 (1957).").

[61] *E.g., CTS Corp. v. Dynamics Corp. of America*, 481 U.S. 69, 91, 93, 107 S. Ct. 1637, 95 L. Ed. 2d 67 (1987) [**52] (recognizing that "[a] State has an interest in promoting stable relationships among parties involved in the corporations it charters" and "a substantial interest in preventing the corporate form from becoming a shield for unfair business dealing."); *cf. Edgar v. MITE Corp.*, 457 U.S. 624, 645-46, 102 S. Ct. 2629, 73 L. Ed. 2d 269 (1982) (observing that no state has a legitimate interest "in regulating the internal affairs of foreign corporations").

[62] *E.g., Sternberg v. O'Neil*, 550 A.2d 1105, 1125 (Del. 1988) ("The Delaware courts and legislature have long recognized a 'need for consistency and certainty in the interpretation and application of Delaware corporation law and the desirability of providing a definite forum in which shareholders can challenge the actions of corporate management without having to overcome certain procedural barriers which can be particularly onerous in the context of derivative litigation.'") (quoting *Armstrong v. Pomerance*, 423 A.2d 174, 178 (Del. 1980)); *In re Topps Co. S'holders Litig*, 924 A.2d 951, 960 (Del. Ch. 2007) ("[I]n Delaware's system of corporate law, the adjudication of cases involving the fiduciary duties of directors in new business dynamics is one of the most important methods [**53] of regulating the internal affairs of corporations, as these cases articulate the equitable boundaries that cabin directors' exercise of their capacious statutory authority."); *Ryan v. Gifford*, 918 A.2d 341, 349-50 (Del. Ch. 2007) (Delaware has a "significant and substantial interest in overseeing the conduct of those owing fiduciary duties to shareholders of Delaware corporations.") (quoting *In re Chambers Dev. Co. S'holders Litig*,1993 Del. Ch. LEXIS 79, 1993 WL 179335, at *8 (Del. Ch. 1993)); *see also Diedenhofen-Lennartz v. Diedenhofen*, 931 A.2d 439, 451 n.26 (Del. Ch. 2007) (citing numerous cases evidencing

Appendix

assistance included the conception, preparation, and [*1065] filing of the Certificate Amendment, which culminated in a filing in Delaware. Indeed, it is difficult to find a part of the scheme attacked by the plaintiff that did not involve substantial participation by the moving defendants.

For sophisticated counsel to argue that they did not realize that acting as the de facto outside general counsel to a Delaware corporation and regularly providing advice about Delaware law about matters important to that corporation and its stockholders might expose it to this court's jurisdiction fails the straight-face test. The moving defendants knew that the propriety of the corporate action taken in reliance upon its advice and through its services would be determined under Delaware corporate law, and likely [**57] in a Delaware court.

As a more general matter, the moving defendants are poorly positioned to claim a violation of Due Process. Given its own self-proclaimed national reach, Baker & Hostetler is in a graceless position to claim to be constitutionally aggrieved by an exercise of jurisdiction by this court over it in a case where the claims against it entirely rest on its actions in providing Delaware law advice to a Delaware corporation. That is especially so when Baker & Hostetler has taken the role of quarterbacking the defense of this action by drafting pleadings and briefs filed by other lawyers with this court, directing the defendants' (inadequate, incomplete, and untimely) responses to discovery, and even drafting the briefs in support of this motion.

Lastly, I reject the idea that denying the moving defendants' motion somehow will undermine the public policy of this state, by causing law firms that provide advice to Delaware corporations to fear that they will be regularly hauled into court here. This is a highly unusual case. In most fiduciary duty cases, it will be exceedingly difficult for plaintiffs to state an aiding and abetting claim against corporate counsel. But in this [**58] case, the moving defendants have conceded — as frankly the record makes clear they must — the pleading-stage viability of the claims against them.

More importantly, Delaware has no public policy interest in shielding corporate advisors from responsibility for consciously assisting the managers of Delaware corporations in breaching their fiduciary duties. If well-pled facts can be pled that support the inference that a corporate advisor knowingly assisted corporate directors in breaching their fiduciary duties, Delaware has a public policy interest in ensuring that its courts are available to derivative plaintiffs who wish to hold that advisor accountable to the corporation. The precise circumstances when corporate advisors should be deemed responsible to the corporation or its stockholders for their role in advising directors and officers should be determined by decisions addressing the merits of aiding and abetting claims, not by decisions about motions to dismiss for lack of personal jurisdiction. Lawyers and law firms, like other defendants, can be sued in this state if there is a statutory and constitutional foundation for doing so.

VII. Conclusion

Both the statutory and constitutional [**59] bases for jurisdiction over defendants Boeckman and Baker & Hostetler are obvious. Their motion to dismiss is denied. IT IS SO ORDERED.

UNITED RENTALS, INC., Plaintiff, v. RAM HOLDINGS, INC., and RAM ACQUISITION CORP., Defendants.

Civil Action No. 3360-CC

COURT OF CHANCERY OF DELAWARE

937 A.2d 810*; 2007 Del. Ch. LEXIS 181**

December 19, 2007, Submitted

December 21, 2007, Decided

December 21, 2007, EFiled

PRIOR HISTORY: United Rentals, Inc. v. Ram Holdings, Inc., 2007 Del. Ch. LEXIS 180 (Del. Ch., Dec. 17, 2007)

COUNSEL: [**1] Collins J. Seitz, Jr., Matthew F. Boyer, and Christos T. Adamopoulos, of CONNOLLY BOVE LODGE & HUTZ LLP, Wilmington, Delaware; OF COUNSEL: Richard D. Bernstein, Tariq Mundiya, and John R. Oller, of WILLKIE FARR & GALLAGHER LLP, New York, New York; Leslie A. Lupert, Thomas A. Brown II, and Timothy D. Sini, of ORANS, ELSEN & LUPERT LLP, New York, New York; Roger E. Schwed, of UNITED RENTALS, INC., Greenwich, Connecticut, Attorneys for Plaintiff.

Gregory P. Williams, Raymond J. DiCamillo, Richard P. Rollo, and John D. Hendershot, of RICHARDS, LAYTON & FINGER, P.A., Wilmington, Delaware; OF COUNSEL: Michael L. Hirschfeld, Scott A. Edelman, and Daniel M. Perry, of MILBANK, TWEED, HADLEY & MCCLOY LLP, New York, New York; Stuart L. Shapiro, of SHAPIRO, FORMAN, ALLEN, SAVA & MCPHERSON LLP, New York, New York, Attorneys for Defendants.

OPINION:

[*813] CHANDLER, Chancellor

In classical mythology, it took a demigod to subdue Cerberus, the beastly three-headed dog that guarded the gates of the underworld.[1] In his twelfth and final labor, Heracles[2] journeyed to Hades to battle, tame, and capture the monstrous creature. In this case, plaintiff United Rentals, Inc. journeyed to Delaware to conquer a more modern obstacle [**2] that, rather than guards the gates to the afterlife, stands in the way of the consummation of a merger. Nevertheless, like the three heads of the mythological Cerberus, the private equity firm of the same name presents three substantial challenges to plaintiff's case: (1) the language of the Merger Agreement, (2) evidence of the negotiations between the parties, and (3) a doctrine of contract interpretation known as the forthright negotiator principle. In this tale the three heads prove too much to overcome.

First, the language of the Merger Agreement presents a direct conflict between two provisions on remedies, rendering the Agreement ambiguous and defeating plaintiff's motion for summary judgment. Second, the extrinsic evidence of the negotiation [**3] process, though ultimately not conclusive, is too muddled to find that plaintiff's interpretation of the Agreement represents the common understanding of the parties. Third, under the forthright negotiator principle, the subjective understanding of one party to a contract may bind the other party when the other party knows or has reason to know of that understanding. Because the evidence in this case shows that defendants understood this Agreement to preclude the remedy of specific performance and that plaintiff knew or should have known of this understanding, I conclude that plaintiff has failed to meet its burden and find in favor of defendants.

I. FACTUAL AND PROCEDURAL BACKGROUND[3]

On November 19, 2007, plaintiff United Rentals, Inc. ("URI" or the "Company") filed its complaint in this action. Thereafter, on November 29, 2007, URI moved for summary judgment. In its motion for summary judgment, URI sought an order from this Court specifically enforcing the terms of the July 22, 2007 "Agreement and Plan of Merger" (the "Merger Agreement" or the "Agreement") among URI and defendants RAM Holdings, [**4] Inc. ("RAM Holdings") and RAM Acquisition Corp. ("RAM Acquisition" and, together with RAM Holdings, "RAM" or the "RAM Entities").[4]

---

[1] Ancient sources disagree on the precise description of Cerberus. Homer's terse description in the *Iliad* labels it simply the hound of Hades. Apollodorus describes Cerberus as having three dog heads, the tail of a dragon, and a backside covered with snakes. In Hesiod's *Theogony*, Cerberus is characterized as a relentless, fifty-headed, flesh-eating, brazen-voiced hound.

[2] Heracles is also commonly known as "Hercules," the Latin equivalent of Heracles.

[3] These facts either are undisputed by the parties or are as found by the Court at trial.

[4] Both because RAM is controlled by Cerberus, as defined below, and because the witnesses' testimony often does not distinguish among these Cerberus-controlled entities, I will sometimes refer to defendants as "Cerberus," though Cerberus is *not* a party to this

[*814] On December 13, 2007, this Court denied plaintiff's motion for summary judgment, finding that the question was exceedingly close.[5] A trial was therefore necessary to ascertain the meaning of the Agreement.

A.   The Parties

URI is a Delaware corporation with its principal place of business in Greenwich, Connecticut. Founded in 1997, it is a publicly traded company listed on the New York Stock Exchange. URI is the largest equipment rental company in the world based on revenue, earning $3.64 billion in 2006. The Company consists of an integrated network of over 690 [**5] rental locations in forty-eight states, ten Canadian provinces, and one location in Mexico. The Company serves construction and industrial customers, utilities, municipalities, homeowners and others. On or about May 18, 2007, URI offered itself up for sale through a draft merger agreement sent to potential buyers, including Cerberus Capital Management, L.P. ("CCM"). As a result of the negotiation process (discussed below), URI entered into the Merger Agreement. URI is a signatory to both the Merger Agreement and the Limited Guarantee.

Defendants RAM Holdings and RAM Acquisition are shell entities with *de minimis* assets that were formed solely to effectuate transactions contemplated under the Merger Agreement. Defendant RAM Holdings is a Delaware corporation. Defendant RAM Acquisition is also a Delaware corporation and is a direct, wholly-owned subsidiary of defendant RAM Holdings. RAM Acquisition, identified as "Merger Sub" in the Merger Agreement, the Limited Guarantee, and the Equity Commitment Letter, is a direct, wholly owned subsidiary of RAM Holdings, which is identified as "Parent" in the Agreements. The RAM Entities are controlled by funds and accounts affiliated with CCM, a [**6] major New York private equity buyout firm, which is not a party to the Merger Agreement or this lawsuit.

Cerberus Partners, L.P. ("Cerberus Partners"), an investment fund, is a limited partnership organized under the laws of the State of Delaware with its principal offices in New York, New York. Cerberus Partners, identified as the "Guarantor" in the Limited Guarantee, is a signatory only to the Limited Guarantee, under which it is the guarantor of certain payment obligations of the RAM Entities up to a maximum amount of $100 million plus incidental solicitation costs. Cerberus Partners is not a party to the Merger Agreement or to the Equity Commitment Letter, and it is not a defendant in this action. Venue

and jurisdiction for any claim under the Limited Guarantee are exclusively in New York.[6]

CCM is a limited partnership organized under the laws of the State of Delaware with its principal offices in New York, New York. CCM is a management company that, together with other affiliated entities, manages investment funds, including Cerberus Partners [**7] (and, together with CCM, "Cerberus"). CCM, identified as the "Equity Sponsor" in the Equity Commitment Letter, is a signatory to only the Equity [*815] Commitment Letter, under which it agreed on behalf of one or more of its affiliated funds or managed accounts (which had not yet been designated) to purchase or cause to be purchased shares of capital stock of RAM Holdings for an aggregate purchase price of $1.5 billion (the "Equity Financing"), subject to the satisfaction of various conditions as more specifically set forth in the letter. CCM is not a party to the Merger Agreement or to the Limited Guarantee, and it is not a defendant in this action. The Equity Commitment Letter provides that venue and jurisdiction for any claim under the Limited Guarantee are exclusively in New York.

B.   The Merger Agreement

In the spring of 2007, URI's board of directors decided to explore strategic alternatives to maximize stockholder value, including by soliciting offers from third parties to buy the Company. After an exhaustive effort that lasted several months, the board of directors authorized URI to execute the Merger Agreement, which it did on July 22, 2007.[7] Under the Merger Agreement, RAM committed [**8] to purchase all of the common shares of URI for $34.50 per share in cash, for a total transaction value of approximately $7 billion, which includes the repayment or refinance of URI's existing debt. Under the Merger Agreement, RAM Acquisition is to be merged into URI, which will be the surviving corporation.

C. Relevant Provisions of the Agreements

The Merger Agreement contemplates that, in order to fund a portion of the Merger consideration, RAM Holdings will obtain financing through the sale of equity to CCM for an aggregate purchase price of not less than $1.5 billion under the Equity Commitment Letter. The signatories to the Equity Commitment Letter are CCM and RAM Holdings. The terms of the Equity Commitment Letter were negotiated with and accepted by URI, but URI is neither a party to nor a beneficiary of the Equity Commitment Letter.[8]

---

action; only RAM Holdings and RAM Acquisition are defendants in this case. *See* Section II of this opinion.

[5] *United Rentals, Inc. v. RAM Holdings, Inc.,* C.A. No. 3360-CC, 2007 Del. Ch. LEXIS 179, slip. op. at 1 (Del. Ch. Dec. 13, 2007) (letter denying summary judgment).

---

[6] Cerberus Partners and CCM filed an action against URI on November 12, 2007, in the Supreme Court of the State of New York, County of New York.

[7] *See* URI Proxy Statement at 22-32.

[8] *See* Equity Commitment Letter at 1.

1.   The Merger Agreement

The Merger Agreement contains two key provisions at issue in this case.[9] Section 9.10, entitled "Specific Performance," provides:

> The parties agree that irreparable damage would occur in the event that any of the provisions of this Agreement were not performed [**9] in accordance with their specific terms or were otherwise breached. Accordingly, (a) [RAM Holdings] and [RAM Acquisition] shall be entitled to seek an injunction or injunctions to prevent breaches of this Agreement by the Company and to enforce specifically the [*816] terms and provisions of this Agreement, in addition to any other remedy to which such party is entitled at law or in equity and (b) the Company shall be entitled to seek an injunction or injunctions to prevent breaches of this Agreement by [RAM Holdings] or [RAM Acquisition] or to enforce specifically the terms and provisions of this Agreement and the Guarantee to prevent breaches of or enforce compliance with those covenants of [RAM Holdings] or [RAM Acquisition] that require [RAM Holdings] or [RAM Acquisition] to (i) use its reasonable best efforts to obtain the Financing and satisfy the conditions to closing set forth in Section 7.1 and Section 7.3, including the covenants set forth in Section 6.8 and Section 6.10 and (ii) consummate the transactions contemplated by this Agreement, if in the case of this clause (ii), the Financing (or Alternative Financing obtained in accordance with Section 6.10(b)) is available to be drawn [**10] down by [RAM Holdings] pursuant to the terms of the applicable agreements but is not so drawn down solely as a result of [RAM Holdings] or [RAM Acquisition] refusing to do so in breach of this Agreement. *The provisions of this Section 9.10 shall be subject in all respects to Section 8.2(e) hereof, which Section shall govern the rights and obligations of the parties hereto (and of [Cerberus Partners], the Parent Related Parties, and the Company Related Parties) under the circumstances provided therein.*[10]

Section 8.2(e), referred to in the specific performance provision in section 9.10, is part of Article VIII, entitled "Termination, Amendment and Waiver." [**11] Article VIII provides specific limited circumstances in which either RAM or URI can terminate the Merger Agreement and receive a $100 million termination fee.[11] The relevant portion of section 8.2(e) of the Merger Agreement provides:

> Notwithstanding anything to the contrary in this Agreement, including with respect to Sections 7.4 and 9.10, (i) the Company's right to terminate this Agreement in compliance with the provisions of Sections 8.1(d)(i) and (ii) and its right to receive the Parent Termination Fee pursuant to Section 8.2(c) or the guarantee thereof pursuant to the Guarantee, and (ii) [RAM Holdings]'s right to terminate this Agreement pursuant to Section 8.1(e)(i) and (ii) and its right to receive the Company Termination Fee pursuant to Section 8.2(b) shall, in each case, be the sole and exclusive remedy, including on account of punitive damages, of (in the case of clause (i)) the Company and its subsidiaries against [RAM Holdings], [RAM Acquisition], [Cerberus Partners] or any of their respective affiliates, stockholders, general partners, limited partners, members, managers, directors, officers, employees or agents (collectively "Parent Related Parties") and (in the case [**12] of clause (ii)) [RAM Holdings] and [RAM Acquisition] against the Company or its subsidiaries, affiliates, stockholders, directors, officers, employees or agents (collectively "Company Related Parties"), for any and all loss or damage suffered as a result thereof, and upon any termination specified in clause (i) or (ii) of this Section 8.2(e) and payment of the Parent Termination Fee or Company Termination Fee, as the case may be, none of [RAM Holdings], [RAM Acquisition], [Cerberus Partners] or any of their respective Parent Related Parties or the Company or any of the Company Related Parties shall have any further liability or obligation of any kind or nature relating to or arising out of this Agreement or the transactions contemplated [*817] by this Agreement as a result of such termination.
>
> . . .
>
> In no event, whether or not this Agreement has been terminated pursuant to any provision hereof, shall [RAM Holdings], [RAM Acquisition], [Cerberus Partners] or the Parent Related Parties, either individually or in the aggregate, be subject to any liability in excess of the Parent Termination Fee for any or all losses or damages relating to or arising out of this Agreement or the transactions contemplated [**13] by this Agreement, including breaches by [RAM Holdings] or [RAM Acquisition] of any representations, warranties, covenants or agreements contained in this Agreement, and *in no event shall the Company seek equitable relief or seek to recover any*

---

[9] The Merger Agreement permits RAM to walk away from the deal in the event of a material adverse change in URI's business, but prohibits RAM from doing so based on the condition of the credit markets in this country. Section 3.1 of the Merger Agreement expressly provides that "Material Adverse Effect shall not include facts, circumstances, events, changes, effects or occurrences (i) generally affecting the economy or the financial, debt, credit or securities markets in the United States . . . ."

[10] Merger Agreement § 9.10 (emphasis added).

[11] Denominated the "Parent Termination Fee" when payable by RAM to URI, and the "Company Termination Fee" when payable by URI to RAM.

money damages in excess of such amount from [RAM Holdings], [RAM Acquisition], [Cerberus Partners] or any Parent Related Party or any of their respective Representatives.[12]

The parties dispute the effect of section 8.2(e) on section 9.10.

2.   The Equity Commitment Letter and Limited Guarantee

The Equity Commitment Letter states that URI is not a third-party beneficiary:

> There is no express or implied intention to benefit any third party including, without limitation, [URI] and nothing contained in this Equity Commitment Letter is intended, nor shall anything herein be construed, to confer any rights, legal or equitable, in any Person other than [RAM Holdings].[13]

The Equity Commitment Letter also provides that any claim against CCM with respect to the transactions contemplated [**14] by the Merger Agreement or the Equity Commitment Letter be made only pursuant to the Limited Guarantee:

> Under no circumstances shall [CCM] be liable for any costs or damages including, without limitation, any special, incidental, consequential, exemplary or punitive damages, to any Person, including [RAM Holdings] and [URI], in respect of this Equity Commitment Letter; and any claims with respect to the transactions contemplated by the Merger Agreement or this Equity Commitment Letter shall be made only pursuant to the Guarantee to the extent applicable.[14]

In executing the Merger Agreement with the RAM Entities, URI was contracting with shell companies that effectively had no assets.[15] Accordingly, to ensure that there would be some level of financial backing for the RAM Entities' obligations under the Merger Agreement accessible to URI, URI entered into the Limited Guarantee with Cerberus Partners. The execution of such a guarantee is "market practice" in LBO transactions sponsored by private equity firms. The Limited Guarantee provides that Cerberus Partners will guarantee payment, up to a maximum amount of $100 million plus certain solicitation [**15] expenses, of the enumerated payment obligations of the RAM Entities under the Merger Agreement.[16] Before accepting the Limited Guarantee, URI inquired into the financial resources of Cerberus Partners and satisfied itself that Cerberus Partners had the ability to make good on a claim thereunder. The Limited [*818] Guaran-

tee contains a representation by Cerberus Partners to this effect. The Limited Guarantee provides, in relevant part:[17]

> (a) . . . The Company, by its acceptance of the benefits hereof, agrees that it has no right of recovery in respect of a claim arising under the Merger Agreement or in connection with any documents or instruments delivered in connection therewith, including this Limited Guarantee, against any former, current or future officer, agent, affiliate or employee of [Cerberus Partners] or [RAM Holdings] (or any of their successors' or permitted assignees'), against any former, current or future general or limited partner, member or stockholder of the [Cerberus Partners] or [RAM Holdings] (or any of their successors' or permitted assignees'), notwithstanding that Guarantor is or may be a partnership, or any affiliate thereof or against any former, current or future [**16] director, officer, agent, employee, affiliate, general or limited partner, stockholder, manager or member of any of the foregoing (collectively, "Guarantor/Parent Affiliates"; it being understood that the term Guarantor/Parent Affiliates shall not include [Cerberus Partners], [RAM Holdings], or [RAM Acquisition]), whether by or through attempted piercing of the corporate veil, by or through a claim by or on behalf of [RAM Holdings] or [RAM Acquisition] against the Guarantor/Parent Affiliates, or otherwise, except for its rights under this Limited Guarantee and subject to the limits contained herein . . . .

> (b) Recourse against [Cerberus Partners] under this Limited Guarantee shall be the sole and exclusive remedy of the Company and all of its affiliates against [Cerberus Partners] and any Guarantor/Parent Affiliates in respect of any liabilities or obligations arising under, or in connection with, the Merger Agreement or the transactions contemplated thereby including in the event [RAM Holdings] or [RAM Acquisition] breaches any covenant, representation or warranty under the Merger Agreement or [Cerberus Partners] breaches a covenant, representation or warranty hereunder.[18]

These provisions were the result of negotiations that began from a May 18 bid contract and culminated in the final, executed Merger Agreement of July 22.

3.   Negotiation of the Merger Agreement[19]

Throughout the course of negotiation of the Merger Agreement, URI contends that it communicated to RAM's principal attorney contract negotia-

---

[12] Merger Agreement § 8.2(e) (emphasis added).
[13] Equity Commitment Letter at 1.
[14] *Id.*
[15] Limited [**17] Guarantee P 4(a).
[16] *See id.* at P 1(a).

[17] *Id.* at P 4(a).
[18] Limited Guarantee P 4.
[19] As explained later, an ambiguity in the contract requires the Court to consider extrinsic evidence.

tor, Peter Ehrenberg of Lowenstein Sandler PC ("Lowenstein"), that URI wanted to restrict RAM's ability to breach the Merger Agreement and unilaterally refuse to close the transaction. URI further maintains that URI's counsel, Eric Swedenburg of Simpson Thacher & Bartlett LP ("Simpson"), made clear to Ehrenberg that it was very important to URI that there be "deal certainty" so that RAM could not simply refuse to close if debt financing was available.[20]

[*819] On the other side of the negotiation table, the RAM entities argue that Ehrenberg consistently communicated that Cerberus had a $100 million walkway right and [**18] that URI knowingly relinquished its right to specific performance under the Merger Agreement.

a.   The Initial May 18, 2007 Draft of the Merger Agreement

On May 18, 2007, UBS Investment Bank ("UBS") provided bidders, including Cerberus Partners, with an initial draft of a Merger Agreement prepared by URI's deal counsel, Simpson.[21] Simpson's initial draft contemplated that two corporations, referred to as "Parent" and "Merger Sub," would be formed to effect a merger with URI, that a separate "Guarantor" would provide a guarantee "with respect to certain obligations of Parent and Merger Sub," and that Parent would supply an "equity commitment letter" between it and a third party.[22] The initial draft further provided that URI would be entitled "to enforce specifically the terms and provisions of this Agreement ... the Equity Commitment Letter and the Guarantee" that require Parent or Merger Sub to, *inter alia,* "pay the Equity Financing and consummate the transactions contemplated by this [Merger] Agreement ..."[23] This draft also required Parent to "consummate the Financing at or prior to the Closing (including by taking enforcement actions against the lenders and other persons providing [**19] the Financing to fund such Financing)."[24]

As is typical when a private equity sponsor (like Cerberus Partners) makes an acquisition, the initial draft of the Merger Agreement contemplated that the buyer under the merger agreement would be one or more newly formed "shell acquisition entities" formed by the sponsor.[25] The ability of these shell entities to consummate the transaction depends entirely upon their ability to obtain financing commitments — for both debt and equity — from other persons. The seller (here, URI) recognizes that its leverage to force a closing of the transaction depends entirely upon the

rights it obtains under the equity commitment and/or guarantee. Simpson's draft of the Merger Agreement proposed to accomplish this by giving URI the right to seek specific performance of the equity commitment letter and by requiring the guarantee, and by requiring Parent to do so with respect to all financing commitments.[26]

b.   The June 18, 2007 Draft of the Merger Agreement

On June 18, 2007, CCM's counsel, [**20] Lowenstein, responded to URI, delivering to Simpson a mark-up of the initial draft Merger Agreement.[27] In that mark-up, Lowenstein indicated, among other things, that CCM would not provide a guarantee[28] and removed all references to the proposed guarantee. Lowenstein also removed the provisions stating that URI would have the right to enforce the equity commitment letter, and that Parent would [*820] be required to take action against the Financing sources to compel them to fund.[29]

In the June 18, 2007 draft of the Merger Agreement proffered by RAM, Ehrenberg explicitly deleted the very detailed specific performance provisions of section 9.10 that ultimately appears in the final version.[30]

c.   The June 25, 2007 Draft of the Merger Agreement

On June 25, 2007, Simpson provided Lowenstein with a revised draft of the proposed form of Merger Agreement.[31] In that revised draft, Simpson sought to encourage CCM to alter its position in one of two ways: (1) provide a guarantee of the obligations of Parent to pay a reverse [**21] break-up fee (defined in the Merger Agreement as the "Parent Termination Fee") in the event that Parent or Merger Sub failed to close the transaction by the stated deadline (URI's sole and exclusive remedy in such circumstances); or (2) provide an unconditional equity commitment letter in favor of URI. Footnote 1 of Simpson's June 25, 2007 draft informed CCM as follows:

> In the event that Parent's obligations with respect to the Parent Termination Fee are not supported by a Guarantee from the prospective purchaser's fund, the prospective purchaser's bid will be significantly disadvantaged. This disadvantage would be less significant, however, if prospective purchaser's equity commitment letter unconditionally obligates purchaser's fund to fund any amount necessary to satisfy Parent's obligations and

Appendix

---

[20] Swedenburg Dep. 44-51. *See also* McNeal Dep. 105-08; Kochman Dep. 60.

[21] UBS was retained by URI to help facilitate its sale.

[22] Defs.' Ex. 6 at 1, 22 (Draft Merger Agreement, May 18, 2007).

[23] *Id.* at 48-49.

[24] *Id.* at 36.

[25] *See id.*

[26] *Id.* at 48-49, 36-39.

[27] Defs.' Ex. 9 (Draft Merger Agreement, June 18, 2007).

[28] *Id.* at 1.

[29] *Id.* at 50, 66, 67.

[30] Ehrenberg Test., Trial Tr. vol. 2, 333-35, Dec. 19, 2007 [hereinafter "Ehrenberg Test. at "].

[31] Defs.' Ex. 11 (Draft Merger Agreement, June 25, 2007).

provides third-party beneficiary rights to [URI] to enforce such letter.[32]

Simpson's June 25 draft also restored URI's ability to seek specific performance of the equity commitment letter and the obligation of Parent to take action against the Financing sources to compel them to fund.[33]

d.   The July 1, 2007 [**22] Draft of the Merger Agreement

On July 1, 2007, while waiting for a response to its June 25 draft, Simpson provided Lowenstein with a form of guarantee that it represented to be "consistent with what we have seen executed in a large number of recent sponsor-led deals."[34] Simpson's cover email explained:

> As discussed, in the event that Parent's obligations with respect to the Parent Termination Fee are not supported by a Guarantee that will significantly disadvantage your client's bid, although the disadvantage may be less significant if the equity commitment letter is along the lines discussed.[35]

The draft guarantee provided by Simpson was limited to a fixed payment amount, with the amount to be determined in negotiation. It also provided that the Guarantor would deliver an Equity Commitment Letter to Parent, that URI would be "an express third party beneficiary under [*821] the Guarantor's Equity Commitment Letter," and that URI, as "the express [**23] third party beneficiary under the Guarantor's Equity Commitment Letter to Parent, may specifically enforce the terms of such letter agreement in connection with [URI's] exercise of" its specific performance rights under section 9.10 of the Merger Agreement.[36]

e.   The July 2, 2007 and July 4, 2007 Drafts of the Merger Agreement

On July 2, 2007, Lowenstein sent a revised draft of the Merger Agreement to Simpson. In its covering email, Lowenstein advised that CCM was reconsidering its prior unwillingness to provide a guarantee, although no final decision had been made.[37] Accordingly, although Lowenstein did not provide comments to the form of Guarantee received from Simpson the previous day, its July 2 draft of the Merger Agreement bracketed for further attention the text indicating that a Guarantor would provide a guaran-

tee "of certain obligations of Parent and Merger Sub."[38] Lowenstein's July 2 draft again deleted from the Merger Agreement language that would have permitted URI to seek specific performance of the equity commitment letter and that would have required Parent to take action against the Financing sources to compel them [**24] to fund.[39]

On July 4, 2007, Simpson sent a revised draft Merger Agreement to Lowenstein.[40] Again, Simpson "reversed" Lowenstein's deletion of the text allowing URI to enforce the equity commitment letter and requiring Parent to pursue action to compel the Financing sources to fund.[41]

In oral communications during this period between the two law firms, Simpson indicated to Lowenstein that URI wanted to make sure it could collect the full amount of the equity commitment letter in the event that Parent had its debt financing available but refused to close. Lowenstein told Simpson that such an arrangement was not acceptable, and that the buyer was unwilling to accept any exposure in the event Parent did not close the transaction other than payment of a fee.[42] With the negotiations thus stalled, on July 10, 2007, Lowenstein attorneys Ehrenberg and Jeffrey Shapiro met with Simpson lawyers, including Swedenburg, and Emily McNeal, an Executive Director at UBS. At that meeting, Lowenstein again made clear that the buyer [**25] and its affiliates were unwilling to have any exposure beyond the payment of a break-up fee in the event that Parent failed to close the transaction. Swedenburg was not willing to agree, and this fundamental issue remained open.[43]

f.   The July 12, 2007 Meeting at UBS

On the evening of July 12, 2007, Ehrenberg and representatives of the buyer met in person and telephonically with Swedenburg, and McNeal and Cary Kochman, URI's lead investment banker at UBS, at the UBS offices in New York City. During this meeting, Swedenburg and Kochman enumerated a number of open deal issues, including the impasse over the interrelated Guarantee, Equity Commitment Letter, [*822] and buyer's exposure in the event buyer did not close the transaction. Though the parties agree that reverse break-up fees were discussed, they dispute whether this issue was resolved at the meeting. According to defendants, Swedenburg and Kochman indicated that URI would accept payment of a reverse break-up fee as its sole and exclusive remedy in the event the buyer did not proceed with the transaction.[44] Plaintiff rejoins that

---

[32] *Id.* at 1.

[33] *Id.* at 40, 53.

[34] Defs.' Ex. 12 at 1 (Draft Guarantee, July 1, 2007).

[35] *Id.* In prior discussions, Simpson had indicated to Lowenstein that it was looking for an equity commitment letter with express third-party beneficiary rights in favor of URI. (Ehrenberg Test. at 344.)

[36] Defs.' Ex. 12 at 4 (Draft Guarantee, July 1, 2007).

[37] Defs.' Ex. 13 (Draft Merger Agreement, July 2, 2007).

[38] *Id.*

[39] *Id.* at 48, 62, 63 (of black-lined draft).

[40] Defs.' Ex. 14 (Draft Merger Agreement, July 4, 2007).

[41] *Id.* at 42, 64.

[42] Ehrenberg Test. at 349.

[43] *Id.*

[44] Ehrenberg Test. at 352.

Ehrenberg, who said he made notes of that meeting he has been unable to locate, [**26] now asserts that "URI's representatives told us that they were in agreement to the receipt of that fee being URI's sole and exclusive remedy in the event of breach of the merger agreement," but does not recall any actual words used or who said them.[45] Plaintiff further argues that, though Swedenburg acknowledged that the reverse break-up fee issues were discussed, there was certainty that no such "agreement" was reached and his notes of the July 12 meeting, which have been produced, do not reflect any such agreement.[46]

Following this July 12 meeting, Lowenstein revised Simpson's July 4 draft to reflect the understandings reached, including what Cerberus felt was an agreement that the buyer and all of its affiliates would have no obligation beyond payment of the reverse break-up fee in the event that they decided not to go forward with the merger transaction. On July 15, 2007, [**27] Lowenstein sent a full package of deal documents — including a revised draft of the Merger Agreement, a revised draft of the Guarantee, now identified as a "Limited Guarantee," and a draft of the Equity Commitment Letter — to Simpson and UBS.[47]

g.   The July 15, 2007 Draft of the Merger Agreement and the July 16, 2007 Conference Call

The July 15 draft of the Merger Agreement included, for the first time, the two key provisions that defendants say gave effect to the parties' agreement on July 12 that URI's sole and exclusive remedy against the buyer and all of its affiliates would, in all circumstances, be limited to payment of the reverse break-up fee. First, Lowenstein provided new language in the final sentence of section 8.2(e), which provided:

> In no event, whether or not this Agreement has been terminated pursuant to any provision hereof, shall Parent, Merger Sub, Guarantor or the Related Parties, either individually or in the aggregate, be subject to any liability in excess of the Parent Termination Fee for any or all losses or damages relating to or arising out of this [**28] Agreement or the transactions contemplated by this Agreement, including breaches by Parent or Merger Sub of any representations, warranties, covenants or agreements contained in this Agreement, *and in no event shall the Company seek equitable relief* or seek to recover any money damages in excess of such amount from Parent, Merger Sub, Guarantor or any Related

Party or any of their respective Representatives or Affiliates.[48]

[*823] Second, Lowenstein also added a sentence at the end of section 9.10 that expressly provided that section 8.2(e) subrogated section 9.10. Thus, the final sentence of section 9.10, as drafted by Lowenstein, provided as follows:

> The provisions of this Section 9.10 shall be subject in all respects to Section 8(e) [sic] hereof, which Section shall govern the rights and obligations of the parties hereto (and of the Guarantor, the Related Parties, and the Company Related Parties) under the circumstances provided therein.[49]

Consistent with the text of the form of Equity Commitment Letter it transmitted [**29] on July 15, which specified that URI was not a third-party beneficiary thereunder, Lowenstein also deleted from the July 15 drafts of the Merger Agreement and the Guarantee all of Simpson's language referring to URI's rights under, and ability to obtain specific enforcement of, the Equity Commitment Letter.[50] Because there had been no agreement regarding the amount of the reverse break-up fee, no figure was specified in the July 15 drafts of the Merger Agreement or the Limited Guarantee.

As noted, Lowenstein also supplied a draft of the Equity Commitment Letter on July 15, which made clear that URI would not be a third-party beneficiary:

> There is no express or implied intention to benefit any third party including, without limitation, the Company and nothing contained in this Equity Commitment Letter is intended, nor shall anything herein be construed, to confer any rights, legal or equitable, in any Person other than Parent.[51]

This provision appears unchanged in the Equity Commitment Letter that ultimately was executed as part of the transaction.[52] Lowenstein's draft also provided that the party making the [**30] commitment would not be liable to any person, including the RAM Entities or URI, for costs or damages in the event that CCM breached the Equity Commitment Letter. The draft further provided that "any claims with respect to the transactions contemplated by the Merger Agreement or this Equity Commitment Letter shall be made only pursuant to the Guarantee

Appendix

---

[45] Ehrenberg Aff. P 27; Ehrenberg Dep. 67-71.

[46] Swedenburg Test., Trial Tr. vol.1, 141-43, Dec. 18, 2007 [hereinafter "Swedenburg Test. at "]; Pl.'s Ex. 98 (Swedenburg July 12, 2007 notes). *See also* McNeal Test., Trial Tr. vol.1, 86, Dec. 18, 2007 [hereinafter "McNeal Test. at "].

[47] Defs.' Ex. 20 (Draft Merger Agreement, July 15, 2007; Draft Equity Commitment Letter and Guarantee, July 15, 2007).

[48] *Id.* at 61, 62 of the black-lined draft (Draft Merger Agreement, July 15, 2007) (emphasis added).

[49] *Id.* at 66, 67 of the black-lined draft (Draft Merger Agreement, July 15, 2007).

[50] *Id.* at 66 of the black-lined draft (Draft Merger Agreement, July 15, 2007).

[51] Defs.' Ex. 20 at 1 (Draft Equity Commitment Letter, July 15, 2007).

[52] Defs.' Ex. 36 (Equity Commitment Letter, July 22, 2007).

to the extent applicable."[53] Again, these provisions were not disputed by URI and are included in the final version of the Equity Commitment Letter.

Following delivery of the July 15 Lowenstein drafts, lawyers from the two firms participated in a conference call to discuss what the parties perceived as "major issues" remaining to be resolved. During that call, defendants say Swedenburg again confirmed that URI was willing to agree that receipt of the break-up fee, from either the RAM Entities or the Guarantor, would be URI's "sole and exclusive" remedy if the buyer failed to close. Contemporaneous notes of the call taken [**31] by Lowenstein attorney Ethan Skerry reflect [*824] Swedenburg's purported confirmation.[54] Contemporaneous notes of the call taken by Ehrenberg do so as well.[55]

URI argues that the July 15, 2007 drafts of the Merger Agreement, Limited Guarantee, and Equity Commitment Letter proffered by RAM's lawyers provide the best evidence of what, if anything, the parties had agreed to on July 12, 2007. Late on the evening of July 15, 2007, Ehrenberg sent to Swedenburg drafts of the Merger Agreement, the Limited Guarantee, and the Equity Commitment Letter.[56] The July 15 draft made numerous revisions to Swedenburg's July 3 draft of the Merger Agreement.[57]

The words "sole and exclusive remedy" appear in the July 15 draft in only two parts of section 8.2(e).[58] In the first sentence, the "sole and exclusive remedy" language (which was already in an earlier draft circulated by URI) applies only to "all loss or damage . . . upon *any termination* in accordance with clause (i) or (ii) of this section 8.2(e)."[59] And the second sentence — newly added by Ehrenberg [**32] in response to the July 12 meeting[60] — makes clear that "[t]he parties acknowledge and agree that the Parent Termination Fee . . . constitute liquidated damages and are not a penalty and shall be the *sole and exclusive remedy* for recovery by the Company . . . in the *event of termination of this Agreement by [URI]* in compliance with the provisions of Section 8.1(d)(i) or (ii). . ."[61]

As demonstrated by Ehrenberg's redline of section 9.10, he made one change — to delete URI's right to itself obtain specific performance of the Equity Commitment Letter — but he left untouched URI's express specific performance rights to compel

RAM to make reasonable best efforts to obtain the Financing, and consummate the Merger if the Financing was available but was not drawn down by RAM. Most important, despite having stricken section 9.10(b) in previous drafts, he chose not to delete section 9.10(b) on July 15 but rather to edit it by deleting the words "the Equity Commitment Letter" and the "pay the Equity [**33] Financing" from section 9.10(b).[62] He then added the last sentence, which he claims rendered section 9.10(b), with its detailed provisions of specific performance, a nullity.[63] But Ehrenberg could provide no real explanation why he did not delete, but rather edited, section 9.10(b).[64] Ehrenberg conceded that it might have been clearer to just delete it.[65]

On July 16, Ehrenberg (and his colleagues) and Swedenburg discussed Ehrenberg's [*825] July 15 draft.[66] Swedenburg testified that he was generally agreeable with the draft "as written."[67]

h.   The July 18, 2007 Draft of the Merger Agreement

On July 18, 2007, Simpson circulated a responsive draft of the Merger Agreement, marked to show changes from the Lowenstein July 15 draft.[68] Simpson deleted the phrase "equitable relief" from the final sentence of Section 8.2(e).[69] Simpson did not propose to restore in either the Merger Agreement or the Limited Guarantee, or to add to the Equity Commitment Letter, any reference to a specific performance right with respect to the equity financing.[70]

i.   The July 19, 2007 Meeting

On July 19, 2007, representatives of the parties and their advisors met at Lowenstein's New York offices. Those in attendance included McNeal of UBS, Ehrenberg, Shapiro, and Skerry of Lowenstein, and Holt, a Cerberus in-house attorney. Steven Mayer, RAM's President and Chief Executive [**35] Officer

---

[53] Draft Equity Commitment Letter and Guarantee, July 15 at 1 of Equity Commitment Letter.

[54] Defs.' Ex. 23 (Notes, July 16, 2007).

[55] Defs.' Ex. 22 (Notes, July 16, 2007).

[56] Swedenburg Dep. 124, 129.

[57] Ehrenberg Dep. 73-75; Ehrenberg Aff. Ex. H2.

[58] Ehrenberg Aff. Ex. H2 at 61-62.

[59] Defs.' Ex. 20 (Draft Merger Agreement, July 15, 2007) (emphasis added).

[60] Ehrenberg Dep. 72-77.

[61] Defs.' Ex. 20 (Draft Merger Agreement, July 15, 2007) (emphasis added).

[62] Ehrenberg Dep. 59-64.

[63] Ehrenberg Dep. 229-33.

[64] Ehrenberg Dep. 60-64. On July 15, 2007, Ehrenberg also provided his comments to the Limited Guarantee. There, unlike his revision to section 9.10 of the Merger Agreement (in which URI's right to seek specific performance was preserved), he deleted the provision investing URI with a direct right to seek specific performance of the Equity Commitment Letter. (Ehrenberg Aff. PP 33-34 and Ex. I; Ehrenberg Dep. 60-61).

[65] Ehrenberg Test. at 391-92.

[66] Ehrenberg Dep. 88-92; Swedenburg Dep. 120-21.

[67] Swedenburg Dep. 123-26 ("I intended to convey that we were okay with those sections as written in the draft subject [**34] to wordsmithing . . . [w]hen it comes to the reverse breakup fee construct the way that 9.10 was written and generally the way that 8.2(e) was written, although like I said, both of them I said subject to some wordsmithing.").

[68] Draft Merger Agreement, July 18.

[69] Defs.' Ex. 24 at 66 of the black-lined draft (Draft Merger Agreement, July 18, 2007).

[70] *Id.* at 70 of the black-lined draft.

on behalf of the buyer, and Swedenburg, of Simpson, participated by telephone. Lowenstein had circulated to URI's representatives in advance of the meeting an agenda based upon Simpson's July 18 draft, listing what it saw as open issues.[71] The agenda included, in pertinent part, items about "fee issues" (company termination; reverse termination; go shop; other fees payable at the time of termination) and "limitation of liability in 8.2(e)."[72]

A principal point of discussion at the meeting concerned the size of the break-up fee that the buyer would have to pay if it chose not to proceed with the merger. Swedenburg explained that URI would require a reverse break-up fee of sufficient size to ensure that it would be "scary" and "painful" for the RAM Entities to walk away from the transaction.[73] Swedenburg noted that URI was not content merely to rely upon the reputational fallout that would ensue if the RAM entities and their affiliates failed to close. Swedenburg's remarks are reflected in notes taken contemporaneously at the meeting by Holt.[74]

Testimony from McNeal, one of URI's bankers at UBS, confirms that the parties discussed that URI wanted a large break-up fee in light of the buyer's ability to walk away from the deal, and that URI was counting on the combination of that fee and the buyer's concerns about its reputation as a basis for believing that the buyer would not elect to walk away from the transaction.[75] McNeal recalled that UBS representatives stated, "We want a high break-up fee so you'll feel a lot of pain if [*826] you walk from this deal."[76] Similarly, McNeal testified that there was also a discussion of reputational damage to the purchaser if it walked away from this transaction in breach of the merger agreement.[77]

As reflected in Holt's notes, the parties then proceeded to debate the appropriate amount of the break-up fee, including a discussion of what would be a "market" fee, with the buyer offering $75 million (up from $50 million it had contemplated earlier), and URI demanding $110 million. There was also a discussion of expenses payable in the event either side chose not to complete the merger. Holt's notes captured [**37] the discussion as follows: "If CCM stepping away, willing to pay expenses plus break-up fee at $75 MM."[78]

Later during the night of July 19, attorneys from Lowenstein had a number of calls with Swedenburg to review specific language in the July 18 Simpson draft of the Merger Agreement, in an effort to come to agreement on text to reflect the various agreements reached during the broader discussion that had preceded. During a discussion of Simpson's changes to section 8.2(e) — specifically, their removal of the phrase "equitable relief" — Lowenstein attorney Skerry recalls that it was reiterated to Swedenburg that the documents must reflect the agreement that URI's only remedy in the event the buyer did not proceed would be payment of the so called Parent Termination Fee. In that context, the Lowenstein attorneys explained that the bar on "equitable relief" had to be put back into section 8.2(e), and Swedenburg stated in response, "I get it."[79]

j.   The July 20, 2007 Draft of the Merger Agreement

Lowenstein then circulated a revised draft of the Merger Agreement [**38] on July 20, 2007. Among other things, that revised draft reinserted the language in section 8.2(e) barring URI from seeking "equitable relief."[80] The final sentence of section 8.2(e) thus read exactly as it does in the final Merger Agreement, and contains the admonition that "in no event shall the Company seek equitable relief or seek to recover any money damages in excess of such amount from Parent, Merger Sub, Guarantor or any Related Party or any of their respective Representatives or Affiliates."[81]

k.   The July 21, 2007 Conversation

On July 21, 2007, in a conversation between Mayer, Kochman, and McNeal, Mayer indicated that he thought RAM was purchasing an "option," Kochman strongly disagreed with the contention. Kochman testified about that conversation:

> A. He said, you know, "Gee, that's a lot of money. You know, I view this as an option. And my LPs would be very unhappy if I, you know, burnt that 100 million plus dollars." And I was taken aback by that.
>
> Q. And what did you say to him?
>
> A. I said, "You know, that's crazy. That's a nonstarter. This is not an option. That's something I would never [**39] [*827] take back to the board." And I laid into him fairly good and said that this is a board that has concerns about your ability to consummate transactions. They see what's going on with Chrysler. They don't view you in the same breaths as KKR or Blackstone. And, you know, it's a complete nonstarter.
>
> Q. Did he respond to that?

---

[71] Defs.' Ex. 28 (Agenda, July 19, 2007).

[72] Id.

[73] Holt Test., Trial Tr. vol. 2, 542, Dec. 19, 2007 [hereinafter "Holt Test. at "].

[74] Defs.' [**36] Ex. 30 at 1 (Notes, July 19, 2007).

[75] McNeal Test. at 112-113.

[76] Id. at 113.

[77] Id. at 114.

[78] Defs.' Ex. 38 at 1 (Notes, July 19. 2007).

[79] Skerry Test., Trial Tr. vol. 2, 497, Dec. 19, 2007 [hereinafter "Skerry Test. at "].

[80] Defs.' Ex. 31 (Draft Merger Agreement, July 20, 2007).

[81] Id. at 58 of black-lined draft.

A. He backed away. He said, "Time out. You know, I'm 100 percent committed to this transaction. I'm going to take you — I'm going to tell you right now that the debt financing and the commitment letters we have in hand are designed exactly for difficult markets. We'll get this deal done. I'm going to take you under the tent."[82]

4. RAM's Repudiation and Breach of the Merger Agreement

On November 14, 2007, RAM Holdings notified URI that it would not proceed with the acquisition of URI on the terms stated in the Merger Agreement, but would be prepared to enter into discussions with URI about revised terms. RAM repudiated via letter, which stated, in part:

> . . . this is to advise that Parent and Merger Sub [RAM] are not prepared to proceed with the acquisition of URI on the terms contemplated by the Agreement.
>
> Given [**40] this position and the rights and obligations of the parties under the Agreement and the ancillary documentation, we see two paths forward. If URI is interested in exploring a transaction between our companies on revised terms, we would be happy to engage in a constructive dialogue with you and representatives of your choosing at your earliest convenience. We could be available to meet in person or telephonically with URI and its representatives for this purpose immediately. In order to pursue this path, we would need to reach resolution on revised terms within a matter of days.
>
> If, however, you are not interested in pursuing such discussions, we are prepared to make arrangements, subject to appropriate documentation, for the payment of the $100 million Parent Termination Fee.
>
> We look forward to your response.[83]

Citing sources "close to the deal," several news stories beginning around 9:30 a.m. and published throughout the day on November 14, 2007 indicated that RAM was not intending to consummate the merger in accordance with the terms of the Merger Agreement. URI's shares fell by more than 30% to $23.50 per share, $10.29 less than the opening price. URI's stock was the NYSE's largest [**41] decliner of the day.

URI argues that it is plain that RAM's actions are directed at putting pressure on the board of directors of URI to renegotiate a price below $34.50 per share. Indeed, on the evening of November 14,

the same day that RAM sent its letter, a senior executive of RAM initiated contact with URI's investment banker, UBS, to offer a substantially reduced price. URI promptly rejected this "offer" and, on November 19, 2007, filed the present lawsuit seeking specific performance of the Merger Agreement.

II. RAM'S STANDING ARGUMENT

RAM has, both in its briefing and at trial, suggested that this case should be dismissed because URI lacks standing to [*828] assert its claims. Viewing this action as a mere pretense, RAM argues that URI, in reality, is attempting to compel performance by CCM of the Equity Commitment Letter. Specifically, RAM contends that URI cannot do this because (1) URI is not an intended third party beneficiary of the Equity Commitment Letter, and (2) URI agreed to refrain from bringing this action in the Limited Guarantee. Neither argument is successful.

A. That URI Is Not a Third Party Beneficiary Under the Equity Commitment [**42] Letter Is Irrelevant

The Equity Commitment Letter explicitly disclaims that it confers rights on any third parties. Indeed, under New York and Delaware law, persons who are neither parties nor intended third party beneficiaries of a contract may not sue to enforce the contract's terms.[84] Accordingly, URI probably lacks the ability to sue CCM under the Equity Commitment Letter. As is quite clear from the caption of this case, however, URI here brings an action against the RAM Entities; CCM is not a party. URI is unquestionably a party to the Merger Agreement, and it is the Merger Agreement that URI seeks to enforce in this action.

B. The Limited Guarantee Does Not Bar an Action Against RAM [**43] by URI

Defendants also rely on the Limited Guarantee to support their contention that URI may not bring this suit. In paragraph 4(a), URI agrees "that it has no right of recovery in respect of a claim arising under the Merger Agreement . . . against any former, current, or future officer, agent, affiliate, or employee of [Cerberus Partners or RAM] . . . ."[85] That subparagraph further states that URI agrees it will not bring any such action "by or through attempted piercing of

---

[82] Kochman Test. at 303-305. *See also* McNeal Test. at 94-96.
[83] Pl.'s Ex. 169 (Nov. 14, 2007 letter).

[84] *NAMA Holdings, LLC v. Related World Market Center, LLC,* 922 A.2d 417, 434 (Del. Ch. 2007) ("As a general rule, only parties to a contract and intended third-party beneficiaries may enforce an agreement's provisions."); *Nepco Forged Prods., Inc. v. Consol. Edison Co. of N.Y., Inc.,* 99 A.D.2d 508, 470 N.Y.S.2d 680, 681 (N.Y. App. Div. 1984) ("Where a provision exists in an agreement expressly negating an intent to permit enforcement by third parties, as exists in the agreement at bar, that provision is decisive.").
[85] Limited Guarantee P 4(a).

the corporate veil, by or through a claim by or on behalf of [RAM] against [Cerberus Partners], except for its rights under this Limited Guarantee ...."[86] Subparagraph (b) proclaims that

> Recourse against [Cerberus Partners] under this limited guarantee shall be the sole and exclusive remedy of the Company and all of its affiliates against [Cerberus Partners and RAM] in respect of any liabilities or obligations arising under, or in connection with, the Merger Agreement ... including in the event [RAM] breaches any covenant, representation or warranty under the Merger Agreement or [Cerberus Partners] breaches a covenant, representation or warranty hereunder.[87]

RAM [**44] suggests that URI is attempting to "pierce the corporate veil" or make a claim by or on behalf of RAM against Cerberus Partners in contravention of paragraph 4(a). The "corporate veil" is a legal term of art that stands for the proposition "that the acts of a corporation are not the actions of its shareholders, so that the shareholders are exempt from [*829] liability for the corporation's actions."[88] To "pierce" the corporate veil is to disregard that legal assumption and to go directly after a corporation's shareholders rather than the corporation itself.[89] URI is doing no such thing in this case. On the contrary, it steadfastly clings to the legal fact that the RAM Entities are independent, legal "persons." URI has brought this case against them — not against Cerberus Partners — and the RAM Entities are explicitly carved out in the Limited Guarantee.[90] Additionally, URI is clearly not bringing a claim "by or on behalf" of RAM; it is bringing a claim *against* RAM.

Finally, RAM's reliance on the "sole and exclusive remedy" language of paragraph 4(b) is untenable. RAM's reading of that paragraph omits a key sentence: "Nothing set forth in this Limited Guarantee shall affect or be construed to affect any liability of Parent or Merger Sub to the Company ...." The Limited Guarantee — by its own explicit terms — does not affect the liability of RAM to URI; the Limited Guarantee cannot, then, be read to preclude this action.

RAM's fundamental point is not lost on this Court: the evidence of these agreements and their negotiation does indeed suggest that RAM/Cerberus Partners worked mightily to limit drastically URI's

ability to seek recourse against Cerberus Partners. Those same agreements, however, repeatedly carve out exceptions that preserve URI's ability to seek recourse against RAM. When something goes wrong in these sorts of transactions, lawsuits are sure to follow.[91] Cerberus Partners availed itself of the protections of the corporate veil by creating the RAM Entities. The mere creation of a new corporate form does not, however, eviscerate liability, it merely shifts it. Though [**46] URI may harbor dreams of compelling performance by Cerberus Partners and CCM. that is not what they seek in this action, and the agreements at issue in this case in no way prevent URI from suing RAM directly for its admitted breach.

III. SUMMARY JUDGMENT

A.   *Legal Standards*

A trial is merely a vehicle for the act of fact finding. To the extent this Court needs to resolve a legal question alone, no trial is necessary.[92] Summary judgment under Rule 56 allows resolution of a legal issue without the "delay and expense of a trial."[93] Summary judgment [*830] is only granted, however, when the movant can demonstrate that there are no genuine issues of material fact.[94] Indeed, the burden is on the movant, and the Court reviews all of the evidence in the light most favorable to the non-moving party.[95]

When the issue before the Court involves the interpretation of a contract, summary judgment is appropriate only if the contract in question is unambiguous. Therefore, the threshold inquiry when presented with a contract dispute on a motion for summary judgment is whether [**48] the contract is ambiguous.[96] Ambiguity does not exist simply be-

---

[86] *Id.*

[87] *Id.* at P 4(b).

[88] BLACK'S LAW DICTIONARY 365 (8th ed. 2004).

[89] *See Albert v. Alex. Brown Mgmt. Servs., Inc.,* C.A. Nos. 762-N, 763-N, 2005 Del. Ch. LEXIS 133, 2005 WL 2130607, at *9-10 (Del. Ch. Aug. 26, 2005).

[90] *See* Limited Guarantee at P 4(a) ("the term Guarantor/Parent [**45] Affiliates shall not include the Guarantor, Parent or Merger Sub").

[91] *Cf.* Robert B. Thompson & Randall S. Thomas, *The New Look of Shareholder Litigation: Acquisition-Oriented Class Actions,* 57 VAND. L. REV. 133 (2004) (discussing the significant rise of acquisition-oriented class action lawsuits).

[92] Fact finding leads to the best reconstruction of the parties' intentions while drafting the contract, and the purpose of contract interpretation is to discover the common intent [**47] of the parties. Nevertheless, the fact finding process is fulsome and costly. Courts can and should interpret unambiguous contracts without recourse to extrinsic evidence when possible in order to provide for the efficient resolution of disputes. *See* Richard A. Posner, *The Law and Economics of Contract Interpretation,* 83 TEX. L. REV. 1581, 1590, 1592 (2005).

[93] *In re Maull,* C.A. No. 1533, 1994 Del. Ch. LEXIS 94, 1994 WL 374302, at *2 (Del. Ch. June 9, 1994) ("The purpose of summary judgment is to avoid the delay and expense of a trial where there is nothing for the fact finder to decide."); *N & W Dev. Co. v. Carey,* C.A. No. 6885, 1983 Del. Ch. LEXIS 410, 1983 WL 17997, at *3 (Del. Ch. Jan. 27, 1983) ("The purpose of summary judgment is the avoidance of a useless trial where there is no genuine issue as to any material fact."), *aff'd,* 474 A.2d 138 (Del. 1983).

[94] Ct. Ch. R. 56(c).

[95] *HIFN, Inc. v. Intel Corp.,* C.A. No. 1835-VCS, 2007 Del. Ch. LEXIS 58, 2007 WL 1309376, at *9 (Del. Ch. May 2, 2007).

[96] *Nw. Nat'l Ins. Co. v. Esmark, Inc.,* 672 A.2d 41, 43 (Del. 1996); *see also* Lawrence M. Solan, *Pernicious Ambiguity in Contracts and*

cause the parties disagree about what the contract means.[97] Moreover, extrinsic, parol evidence cannot be used to manufacture an ambiguity in a contract that facially has only one reasonable meaning.[98] Rather, contracts are ambiguous "when the provisions in controversy are reasonably or fairly susceptible of different interpretations or may have two or more different meanings."[99] Stated differently, to succeed on its motion for summary judgment, URI must establish that its construction of the merger agreement is the *only* reasonable interpretation.[100] Guided by "Delaware's well-understood principles of contract interpretation,"[101] this Court concludes that URI has not succeeded in establishing that its interpretation of the disputed provisions is the only reasonable one. Because the Court concludes that the provisions are fairly susceptible to at least two reasonable interpretations, the contract is ambiguous and summary judgment is inappropriate.

B. [**50] URI's Interpretation of the Merger Agreement is Reasonable

URI argues that the plain and unambiguous language of the merger agreement allows for specific performance as a remedy for the Ram Entities' breach. Section 9.10 expressly invests URI with a right to seek specific performance to enforce the Merger Agreement and to obtain an order [*831] enjoining RAM to (i) make reasonable best efforts to obtain financing and satisfy the Merger Agreement's closing conditions, and (ii) consummate the transactions when financing is available and has not been drawn down by RAM as a result of its breach of the Merger Agreement.

Section 9.10, however, explicitly states that it is "subject in all respects to Section 8.2(e) hereof, which Section shall govern the rights and obligations of the parties ... under the circumstances provided

therein." Section 8.2(e) describes the $100 million Parent Termination Fee payable to URI as the "sole and exclusive" remedy against RAM under the Agreement when there has been a termination of the Merger Agreement by URI. Further, section 8.2(e) provides that

> In no event, whether or not this Agreement has been terminated pursuant to any provision hereof, shall [RAM or Cerberus [**51] Partners] ... be subject to any liability in excess of the Parent Termination Fee for any or all losses or damages relating to or arising out of this Agreement or the transactions contemplated by this Agreement, ... and in no event shall the Company seek equitable relief or seek to recover any money damages in excess of such amount from [RAM or Cerberus Partners] ....

Relying heavily on the canon of construction that requires harmonization of seemingly conflicting contract provisions,[102] URI contends that specific performance under section 9.10 remains a viable remedy despite the language of section 8.2(e). URI offers two chief reasons in support of this position. First, section 8.2(e)'s $100 million Parent Termination Fee operates as the "sole and exclusive" remedy only if one of the parties terminates the agreement. Termination is a defined term in the Agreement, however, and it is not equivalent to a breach. URI contends (and RAM does not dispute) that neither party has terminated the agreement pursuant to section 8. Thus, the Termination Fee is not necessarily the "sole and exclusive remedy" in this case. Second, URI submits that the outright prohibition of equitable remedies [**52] in the last sentence of section 8.2(e) is limited to equitable remedies that involve monetary compensation like restitution or rescission. The sentence commands that "in no event shall [URI] seek equitable relief or seek to recover any money damages in excess of [the $100 million Termination Fee] from [RAM or Cerberus]." URI argues that the prepositional phrase ("in excess of the" termination fee) modifies *both* "equitable relief" and "money damages." This reading is required, URI says, because otherwise this sentence would render section 9.10 "mere surplusage"[103] devoid of any meaning in violation of longstanding principles of

---

Statutes, 79 CHI.-KENT L. REV. 859, 862 (2004) [**49] ("Thus, a court acts like a gatekeeper in making its initial inquiry into whether an ambiguity exists."); Gregg L. Weiner, *But is it Clear? Avoiding Ambiguous Contracts*, 10 BUS. L. TODAY 33, 34-35 (2001).

[97] *Esmark*, 672 A.2d at 43; *Seidensticker v. Gasparilla Inn, Inc.*, C.A. No. 2555-CC, 2007 Del. Ch. LEXIS 155, 2007 WL 4054473, at *2 (Del. Ch. Nov. 8, 2007); *accord John v. United States*, 247 F.3d 1032, 1041 (9th Cir. 2001) ("[S]tatutory ambiguity cannot be determined by referring to the parties' interpretations of the statute. Of course their interpretations differ. That is why they are in court.").

[98] *Eagle Indus., Inc. v. DeVilbiss Health Care, Inc.*, 702 A.2d 1228, 1232 (Del. 1997) ("If a contract is unambiguous, extrinsic evidence may not be used to interpret the intent of the parties, to vary the terms of the contract or to create an ambiguity."); *Seidensticker*, 2007 Del. Ch. LEXIS 155, 2007 WL 4054473, at *2-3; *Lions Gate Entm't Corp. v. Image Entm't Inc.*, C.A. No. 2011-N, 2006 Del. Ch. LEXIS 108, 2006 WL 1668051, at *6 (Del. Ch. June 5, 2006).

[99] *Rhone-Poulenc Basic Chems. Co. v. Am. Motorists Ins. Co.*, 616 A.2d 1192, 1196 (Del. 1992).

[100] *See Modern Telecomms., Inc. v. Modern Talking Picture Serv.*, C.A. No. 8688, 1987 Del. Ch. LEXIS 438, 1987 WL 11286, at *3 (Del. Ch. May 27, 1987).

[101] *HIFN, Inc. v. Intel Corp.*, C.A. No. 1835-VCS, 2007 Del. Ch. LEXIS 58, 2007 WL 1309376, at *9 (Del. Ch. May 2, 2007).

---

[102] *See, e.g., Counsel of the Dorset Condo. Apartments v. Gordon*, 801 A.2d 1, 7 (Del. 2002) ("A court must interpret contractual provisions in a way that gives effect to every term of the instrument, and that, if possible, reconciles all of the provisions of the instrument when read as a whole."); *Delta & Pine Land Co. v. Monsanto Co.*, C.A. No. 1970-N, 2006 Del. Ch. LEXIS 171, 2006 WL 1510417, at *4 (Del. Ch. May 24, 2006) ("It is, of course, a familiar principle that contracts must be interpreted in a manner that does not render any provision 'illusory or meaningless.'").

[103] *W. Willow-Bay Court, LLC v. Robino-Bay Court Plaza, LLC*, C.A. No. 2742-VCN, 2007 Del. Ch. LEXIS 154, 2007 WL 3317551, at *11 (Del. Ch. Nov. 2, 2007) ("Delaware courts do prefer to interpret contracts to give effect to each term rather than to construe them in a way that renders some terms repetitive or mere surplusage.").

contractual interpretation. Moreover, URI points to the final sentence of section 8.2(a) as proof that the Agreement contemplates a right to specific performance: "The parties acknowledge and agree [*832] that, subject to Section 8.2(e), nothing in this Section 8.2 shall be deemed to affect their right to specific performance under Section 9.10." According to URI, section 8.2(a) shows that the parties were aware of the "specific performance" remedy and could have expressly eliminated it. The Merger Agreement does not do so; instead, it explicitly provides that both [**53] specific performance and injunctive relief are available remedies.

The RAM Entities counter that URI's interpretation is unreasonable. First, they argue, it is URI's position that would render portions of the Agreement "mere surplusage." If the operation of section 8.2(e) were in fact limited, as URI asserts, to circumstances in which the Merger [**54] Agreement had been properly terminated by either party, there would be no need to include a sentence in section 9.10 subjecting the specific performance provisions of section 9.10 to section 8.2(e) because specific performance, by law, would be unavailable in those circumstances; one cannot specifically perform an agreement that has been terminated. Thus, section 8.2(e) must have applicability outside the context of termination. Second, the RAM Entities argue that is unreasonable to limit the phrase "equitable relief" to those equitable remedies that include monetary damages.

Reading the Agreement as a whole and with the aid of the fundamental canons of contract construction, I conclude that URI's interpretation is reasonable. The parties explicitly agreed in section 9.10 that "irreparable damage would occur in the event that any of the provisions of this Agreement were not performed in accordance with their specific terms or were otherwise breached." They further agreed that "the Company shall be entitled to see an injunction or injunctions . . . to enforce compliance." Given this clarion language supporting the existence and availability of specific performance, it is reasonable to [**55] read the limitations of section 8.2(e) in the manner URI has championed. RAM's arguments to the contrary are ultimately unpersuasive. Neither party has terminated the Agreement pursuant to the termination provisions of section 8.1, and the context of the final sentence of section 8.2(e) allows one to reasonably conclude that "equitable relief" in that sentence means only equitable relief involving monetary damages. URI's interpretation thus represents a reasonable harmonization of apparently conflicting provisions.

C.   RAM's Interpretation of the Merger Agreement Also Is Reasonable

Though defendants fail to demonstrate that plaintiff's interpretation of the Merger Agreement is unreasonable as a matter of law, defendants do succeed in offering a reasonable alternative interpretation.[104] In opposing URI's motion for summary judgment, defendants deny that the provisions of the Merger Agreement conflict so as to require harmonization. The relationship between sections 9.10 and 8.2(e), as set forth in section 9.10 is, defendants contend, clear: section 9.10 is "subject to" [*833] section 8.2(e).[105] Section 8.2(e) then provides that "in no event shall [URI] seek equitable relief or seek to recover [**56] any money damages in excess of such amount [i.e., the $100 million termination fee] from [RAM or Cerberus]." RAM argues that section 8.2(e) operates to prohibit URI from seeking any form of equitable relief (including specific performance) under all circumstances, relegating URI's relief to only the $100 million termination fee. Relying on *Penn Mutual Life Insurance Co. v. Oglesby*[106] and *Supermex Trading Co., Ltd. v. Strategic Solutions Group, Inc.,*[107] defendants contend that Delaware law specifically permits the parties to establish supremacy and subservience between provisions such that, where the terms of one provision are expressly stated to be "subject to" the terms of a second provision, the terms of the second provision will control, even if the terms of the second provision conflict with or nullify the first provision. Additionally, RAM argues, unlike plaintiff's interpretation, RAM's interpretation utilizes only the plain meaning of "equitable relief." As described above, plaintiff, in proposing a reconciliation of the section 8.2(e) limitation on equitable relief with the right of specific performance in section 9.10, urges this Court to read the words "equitable relief" [**57] and "money damages" as modified by the phrase "in excess of" the termination fee. Defendants' interpretation of this portion of the provision is, however, at least as reasonable as (if not more than) that of plaintiff. The phrase "in excess of"

---

[104] If defendants had filed a cross-motion for summary judgment and, therefore, borne the burden to demonstrate that their interpretation was, in fact, the *only* reasonable interpretation as a matter of law, this Court would not have hesitated to deny defendants' motion. Here, however, in opposing plaintiff's motion, defendants need only to meet the lesser burden of demonstrating that their interpretation was *a* reasonable interpretation and that, therefore, plaintiff's interpretation of the Merger Agreement is not the sole reasonable interpretation. I find that defendants have satisfied this burden, concluding that their proffered interpretation is not unreasonable as a matter of law and that, therefore, the agreement is ambiguous. This was, however, as I indicated in my letter opinion denying plaintiff's motion, an exceedingly close question.

[105] The relevant portion of section 9.10 provides: [**58] "The provisions of this Section 9.10 shall be subject in all respects to Section 8.2(e) hereof, which Section shall govern the rights and obligations of the parties hereto (and of the Guarantor, the Parent Related Entities, and the Company Related Parties) under the circumstances provided herein." Merger Agreement § 9.10.

[106] 695 A.2d 1146, 1150 (Del. 1997) (finding that the phrase "subject to all provisions" operated to "sublimate or 'trump'" other provisions).

[107] No. 16183, 1998 Del. Ch. LEXIS 66, 1998 WL 229530 (Del. Ch. May 1, 1998).

appears, grammatically, to modify only "money damages."[108]

Plaintiff argues that if RAM had wanted to eliminate URI's rights to specific performance in all circumstances, it could have simply stricken out clause (b) of section 9.10. Though the Court has no doubt that this simple (and seemingly obvious) drafting approach would have been superior, on a motion for summary judgment, I cannot look beyond the text [**59] of the agreement to inquire into the motivations of the parties or to consider ways in which a particular end may have been more efficiently achieved and more clearly articulated. An interpretation of the Agreement that relies on the parties' addition of hierarchical phrases, instead of the deletion of particular language altogether, is not unreasonable as a matter of law.

Having considered all of plaintiff's arguments, I must conclude that plaintiff has not shown that defendants' interpretation is unreasonable as a matter of law. The contracting parties here chose terms, such as "subject to," that impose a hierarchy among provisions. Defendants' interpretation of those terms and the provisions they affect is not, I conclude, unreasonable.

[*834] D. Because Both Interpretations of the Merger Agreement are Reasonable, the Agreement is Ambiguous and Summary Judgment Is Inappropriate

It is probably unlikely that a single, *unambiguous* agreement can simultaneously affirm and deny the availability of a specific performance remedy. If there is such an unambiguous contract, it is certainly not the contract at issue in this case. Both URI and RAM have proffered reasonable readings of the Merger Agreement, [**60] and because "provisions in controversy are fairly susceptible of different interpretations or may have two or more different meanings, there is ambiguity."[109] Thus, plaintiff's and defendants' arguments suffer the same flaw, which is fatal at this stage: each party is unable to demonstrate that its proposed interpretation of the Merger Agreement is the *only* interpretation of the Agreement that is reasonable as a matter of law. In such a case, summary judgment is inappropriate because the court is presented with a genuine issue of material fact: what was the intent of the parties?[110]

Therefore, I must consider extrinsic evidence to ascertain the meaning of the Merger Agreement.

IV. TRIAL

The Court heard testimony from seven witnesses over a two-day trial in order to resolve the factual issue of what was the common understanding [**61] of the parties with respect to remedies in the Merger Agreement. The Merger Agreement, of course, is a contract, and the Court's goal when interpreting a contract "is to ascertain the shared intention of the parties."[111] Thus, URI, which seeks to specifically enforce the Merger Agreement, bore the burden of persuasion in demonstrating that the common understanding of the parties was that this contract allowed for the remedy of specific performance and that URI is entitled to such a remedy.[112] URI has failed to meet its burden.

A. Legal Standards

Having determined that the contract is ambiguous on account of its conflicting provisions, the Court permitted the parties to introduce extrinsic evidence of the negotiation process.[113] Such extrinsic [*835] evidence may include "overt statements and acts of the parties, the business context, prior dealings between the parties, [and] business custom and usage in the industry."[114] This evidence may lead to "a single 'correct' or single 'objectively reasonable' meaning."[115] Restated, the extrinsic evidence may

---

parties have set forth 'more than one plausible construction of the meaning of' a key term in the contract).

[111] *W. Willow-Bay Court, LLC v. Robino-Bay Court Plaza, LLC,* 2007 Del. Ch. LEXIS 154, 2007 WL 3317551, at *9.

[112] The burden of persuasion with respect to the existence of the contractual right is a "preponderance of the evidence" standard. *Carlson v. Hallinan,* 925 A.2d 506. 524 (Del. Ch. 2006); *Bell Atl. Meridian Sys. v. Octel Commc'ns Corp.,* C.A. No. 14348, 1995 Del. Ch. LEXIS 156, 1995 WL 707916, at *6 (Del. Ch. Nov. 28, 1995) ("[I]t becomes incumbent upon the party seeking judicial enforcement of their [sic] interpretation of the ambiguous language to show by a preponderance of the evidence that the other party knew or had reason to know of the meaning they [sic] attached to the language."). The burden of [**62] persuasion with respect to the entitlement to specific performance is by a "clear and convincing evidence" standard. *In re IBP, Inc., S'holders Litig.,* 789 A.2d 14, 52 (Del. Ch. 2001).

[113] *E.g., Pellaton v. Bank of N.Y.,* 592 A.2d 473, 478 (Del. 1991); *Nw. Nat'l Ins. Co. v. Esmark, Inc.,* 672 A.2d 41, 43 (Del. 1996); *Brandywine River Props., LLC v. Maffett,* C.A. No. 2655-VCN, 2007 Del. Ch. LEXIS 173, 2007 WL 4327780, at *3-4 (Del. Ch. Dec. 5, 2007) [**63] (considering extrinsic evidence to ascertain the parties' common understanding of an ambiguous contract term); *see also* Eric. A. Posner, *The Parol Evidence Rule, the Plain Meaning Rule, and the Principles of Contractual Interpretation,* 146 U. PA. L. REV. 533, 535 (1998) ("A court will refuse to use evidence of the parties' prior negotiations in order to interpret a written contract unless the writing is (1) incomplete, (2) ambiguous, or (3) the product of fraud, mistake, or a similar bargaining defect.").

[114] *Supermex Trading Co. v. Strategic Solutions Group, Inc.,* C.A. No. 16183, 1998 Del. Ch. LEXIS 66, 1998 WL 229530, at *3 (Del. Ch. May 1, 1998); *see also Eagle Indus., Inc. v. DeVilbiss Health Care, Inc.,* 702 A.2d 1228, 1233 (Del. 1997) ("In construing an ambiguous contractual provision, a court may consider evidence of prior agreements and communications of the parties as well as trade usage or course of dealing.").

[115] *U.S. West, Inc. v. Time Warner, Inc.,* C.A. No. 14555, 1996 Del.

---

[108] The relevant portion of 9.10 provides: "and in no event shall the Company seek equitable relief or seek to recover any money damages in excess of such amount . . . ." The natural reading of this clause, given the usage of the verb "seek" with both "equitable relief" and "monetary damages" seems to be the reading suggested by RAM.

[109] *Eagle Indus., Inc. v. DeVilbiss Health Care, Inc.,* 702 A.2d 1228, 1232 (Del. 1997).

[110] *Cf. Bae Sys. N. Am. Inc. v. Lockheed Martin Corp.,* C.A. No. 20456, 2004 Del. Ch. LEXIS 119, 2004 WL 1739522 (Del. Ch. Aug. 3, 2004) (denying a motion for judgment on the pleadings because "[t]he

render an ambiguous contract clear so that an "objectively reasonable party in the position of either bargainer would have understood the nature of the contractual rights and duties to be."[116] In such a case, the Court would enforce the objectively reasonable interpretation that emerges.

The Court must emphasize here that the introduction of extrinsic, parol evidence does not alter or deviate from Delaware's adherence to the objective theory of contracts.[117] As I recently [**64] explained to counsel in this case, the private, subjective feelings of the negotiators are irrelevant and unhelpful to the Court's consideration of a contract's meaning,[118] because the meaning of a properly formed contract must be shared or common.[119] That is not to say, however, that a party's subjective understanding is never instructive. On the contrary, in cases where an examination of the extrinsic evidence does not lead to an obvious, objectively reasonable conclusion, the Court may apply the forthright negotiator principle.[120] Under this principle, the Court considers the evidence of what one party *subjectively* "believed the obligation to be, coupled with evidence that the other party knew or should have known of such belief."[121] In [*836] other words, the forthright negotiator principle provides that, in cases where the extrinsic evidence does not lead to a single, commonly held understanding of a contract's meaning, a court may consider the subjective understanding of one party that has been objectively manifested and is known or should be known by the other party.[122] It is with

these fundamental legal principles in mind that I consider the factual record developed at trial.

B. Analysis

The evidence presented at trial conveyed [**67] a deeply flawed negotiation in which both sides failed to clearly and consistently communicate their client's positions. First, I find that the extrinsic evidence is not clear enough to conclude that there is a single, shared understanding with respect to the availability of specific performance under the Merger Agreement. Second, I employ the forthright negotiator principle to make two additional findings. With respect to URI, I find that even if the Company believed the Agreement preserved a right to specific performance, its attorney Eric Swedenburg categorically failed to communicate that understanding to the defendants during the latter part of the negotiations. Finally, with respect to RAM, although it could have easily avoided this entire dispute by striking section 9.10(b) from the Agreement, I find that its attorney did communicate to URI his understanding that the Agreement precluded any specific performance rights. Consequently, I conclude that URI has failed to meet its burden and determine that the Merger Agreement does not allow a specific performance remedy.

1.   The Extrinsic Evidence Presented at Trial Does Not Lead to an Obvious, Reasonable Interpretation of This Hopelessly [**68] Conflicted Contract

As discussed above, this Merger Agreement simultaneously purports to provide and preclude the remedy of specific performance.[123] Despite the plaintiff's well-argued motion for summary judgment, the conflicting provisions of this contract render it decidedly ambiguous. At trial, both sides attempted to show that the extrinsic evidence led ineluctably to that party's respective interpretation. This was an exercise in futility.

The parties began their negotiations very far apart. URI circulated a draft that included numerous provisions favorable to their side, including several mechanisms by which URI could specifically enforce the merger against Cerberus.[124] RAM responded with a "heavy-handed" mark-up.[125] Early conversa-

---

Ch. LEXIS 55, 1996 WL 307445, at *10 (Del. Ch. June 6, 1996).

[116] *Id.*

[117] *See* [**65] *Seidensticker v. Gasparilla Inn, Inc.,* C.A. No. 2555-CC, 2007 Del. Ch. LEXIS 155, 2007 WL 4054473, at *1 (Del. Ch. Nov. 8, 2007) (recognizing Delaware's objective theory of contracts).

[118] *See United Rentals, Inc. v. RAM Holdings, Inc.,* C.A. No. 3306-CC, 2007 Del. Ch. LEXIS 180, letter decision at 2 (Del. Ch. Dec. 17, 2007) ("Evidence of one side's undisclosed, private mental impressions or understandings is useless."); *see also Bell Atl. Meridian Sys. v. Octel,* 1995 Del. Ch. LEXIS 156, 1995 WL 707916, at *5 n.4 ("[I]t is generally not the parties' unexpressed intent or understanding that is relevant.").

[119] *See* RESTATEMENT (SECOND) OF CONTRACTS § 201 cmt. c (1981). Indeed, this is precisely why constructs like the parol evidence rule and the statute of frauds exist: "the fear that the more we allow the words of a contract to be challenged in the name of the parties' actual intent, the more we produce disorder or even chaos, waiting to be exploited by unscrupulous litigants who demand a bonus to do what they already promised to do." Peter Linzer, *The Comfort of Certainty: Plain Meaning and the Parol Evidence Rule,* 71 FORDHAM L. REV. 799, 804 (2002).

[120] Comrie v. Enterasys Networks, Inc., 837 A.2d 1, 13 (Del. Ch. 2003).

[121] *U.S. West, Inc. v. Time Warner, Inc.,* C.A. No. 14555, 1996 Del. Ch. LEXIS 55, 1996 WL 307445, at *11 (Del. Ch. June 6, 1996); [**66] *see also id.* at *10 ("Only an objectively reasonable interpretation that is in fact held by one side of the negotiation and which the other side *knew or had reason to know that the first party held* can be enforced as a contractual duty."); *accord Alland v. Consumers Credit Corp.,* 476 F.2d 951, 956 (2d Cir. 1973).

[122] *See Supermex Trading Co. v. Strategic Solutions Group, Inc.,* C.A. No. 16183, 1998 Del. Ch. LEXIS 66, 1998 WL 229530, at *3 (Del. Ch. May 1, 1998) ("It is the law of Delaware that subjective understandings of a party to a contract which are not communicated

to the other party are of no effect."); RESTATEMENT (SECOND) OF CONTRACTS § 201(2) (1981) ("Where the parties have attached different meanings to a promise or agreement or a term thereof, it is interpreted in accordance with the meaning attached by one of them if at the time the agreement was made (a) that party did not know of any different meaning attached by the other, and the other knew the meaning attached by the first party; or (b) that party had no reason to know of any different meaning attached by the other, and the other had reason to know the meaning attached by the first party.").

[123] *Compare* Merger Agreement § 9.10 ("the Company shall be entitled to seek an injunction"), *with* Merger Agreement § 8.2(e) ("in no event shall the Company seek equitable relief").

[124] Defs.' Ex. 6 (May 18 draft of Agreement).

[125] Pl.'s Ex. 3; Swedenburg Test. at 127, Dec. 18, 2007.

Appendix

tions led to no agreement, and URI simply ignored many [*837] of the proposed changes that RAM initially made.[126] Although RAM ultimately succeeded in striking many of the provisions entitling URI to specific performance,[127] and although RAM did modify section 8.2(e) to try to [**69] limit the availability of equitable relief, section 9.10 in the final agreement continued to speak of the Company's right to specific performance. Testimony revealed that communications between the parties routinely skirted the issue of equitable relief and only addressed it tangentially or implicitly.[128] The defendants put forth some evidence suggesting that by mid to late July Swedenburg had agreed to give up specific performance,[129] but it was not conclusive. Mr. Seitz, URI's attorney, deftly questioned RAM's chief negotiator Ehrenberg about the clarity and wisdom of his curious editing of section 9.10, a provision Ehrenberg also contends he nullified, but this did not uncover "a single 'correct' or single 'objectively reasonable' meaning'"[130] for the Agreement. Indeed, because "a review of the extrinsic evidence does not lead the Court to an 'obvious' conclusion,"[131] I must apply the forthright negotiator principle to determine the proper interpretation of this contract.

2. **Even if URI Understood the Agreement to Provide a Specific Performance Remedy, Defendants Did Not Know and Had No reason to Know of This Understanding**

Swedenburg, the primary draftsman and contact at Simpson, drafted the initial bid contract as part of the auction process.[132] Once the bid contract was drafted, Swedenburg sent it to Emily McNeal of UBS, who then circulated it to purchasers. This May 18 bid contract contained a specific performance provision.[133] On June 18, Ehrenberg [**71] returned a "heavy handed" mark-up.[134] After receiving Ehren-

berg's comments, Swedenburg spoke with Ehrenberg in what Swedenburg described as a "largely one way conversation" in which Swedenburg articulated what URI cared about the most.[135] During this conversation, Swedenburg described to Ehrenberg the "construct" included in the draft.[136] Acknowledging that the inclusion of the reverse break-up [*838] fee/specific performance construct in the draft was not "market" relative to other recent LBO transactions,[137] Swedenburg explained to Ehrenberg that this construct made sense in terms of what URI wanted to accomplish: "the deal was supposed to be that if the financing was there, that the RAM entities should have to access the financing and close the transaction. And that's why we have the specific performance the way we have it."[138] Swedenburg then told Ehrenberg that he did not expect to include "a lot" of Ehrenberg's changes in Swedenburg's revised version of the agreement.[139] No one disputes that, as of this time, URI understood the agreement under negotiation to include a specific performance remedy, which was highly valued by URI, and that RAM knew of this. After the bid contract [**72] and throughout, Swedenburg and Ehrenberg discussed changes to terms of the Agreement[140] and exchanged revised drafts.[141] No agreements were reached on these issues and the discussions continued. At this point, there is no dispute that the parties had not reached an agreement as to whether URI had a right of specific performance and that both Swedenburg and Ehrenberg were aware of each other's position.[142]

On July 16, Swedenburg discussed the July 15 version of the contract.[143] In this conversation, Swedenburg testified that the amount of the reverse break-up fee contemplated by the construct was not discussed and that he told Ehrenberg that, with respect to the rest of the construct, "we were okay

---

[126] Ehrenberg Test. at 335-36, Dec. 19, 2007.

[127] See, e.g., id. at 336.

[128] See, e.g., id. at 380 ("In my discussions [**70] with Mr. Swedenburg, I don't recall us using the words 'specific performance.'"); id. at 403 ("We never talked to the issue of specific performance of the guarantee."); Skerry Test. at 512 ("But to your question, did somebody specifically say equitable relief, I don't recall."); McNeal Test. at 90 ("Q: Do you remember any discussion involving the words 'specific performance'? A: No."); Swedenburg Test. at 149 ("I don't ever recollect those words being used.").

[129] See Defs.' Ex. 23 (Ethan Skerry's notes of July 16, 2007); Defs.' Ex. 30 (Christopher Holt's notes of July 19, 2007).

[130] U.S. West, Inc. v. Time Warner, Inc., 1996 Del. Ch. LEXIS 55, 1996 WL 307445, at *10.

[131] Comrie v. Enterasys Networks, Inc., 837 A.2d 1, 13 (Del. Ch. 2003).

[132] Swedenburg Test. at 123-24. Swedenburg testified that Gary Horowitz was the supervising partner at Simpson on this transaction. Id. at 124; see also Horowitz Dep. 8:2-5, Dec. 11, 2007. Horowitz engaged in no negotiations with the buyer. Id., 8:8-12.

[133] See Pl.'s Ex. 3, at LS00019717 (Merger Agreement Draft, June 18, 2007).

[134] Swedenburg Test. at 127. See also Pl.'s Ex. 3 (Email from Ehrenberg to Horowitz re: attached marked copy of Merger Agreement).

[135] Swedenburg Test. at 127.

[136] Id. at 128.

[137] Id. at 158 ("[W]e are asking for an off-market contract when it came to the specific performance, because most LBOs these days, or at least the large majority of them, have no rights of specific performance against the shell entities or otherwise. It's just a one-way specific performance against [**73] the company. So that's what I was trying to articulate to Peter in terms of why we viewed our contract as being off-market in that respect.").

[138] Id. at 128-130.

[139] Id. at 130.

[140] See id. at 133-34.

[141] See Pl.'s Ex. 176 (Merger Agreement Draft, July 2, 2007).

[142] See Swedenburg Test. at 136 ("It's — it's kind of — it was a broken record on both sides at this point in terms of what was said. I again articulated our view of why we thought [specific performance] was important the way we had it drafted and why it made sense. And Mr. Ehrenberg again expressed unwillingness to go in that direction and couldn't agree to that at this point.").

[143] Pl.'s Ex. 166 (Merger Agreement Draft, July 15, 2007). "[T]his is a revised version of the merger agreement that was marked against the draft that we had sent back on July 3rd right before the bid [**75] date. This was the first time the contract had been turned since July 3rd." Swedenburg Test. at 144.

with" the July 15 draft.[144] At this point, the evidence begins to reveal that URI's apparent belief that it had a specific performance right was not effectively communicated to defendants such that defendants either knew or should have known of URI's understanding [**74] of the Merger Agreement. The July 15 draft, which contains Ehrenberg's edits to Swedenburg's July 3 draft, is a pivotal moment in the drafting history of the Merger Agreement: Ehrenberg added both the "in no event shall the Company seek equitable relief" to section 8.2(e) and the infamous "subject to" section 8.2(e) language to the end of section 9.10.[145] Lest it be somehow lost in the details, it is worthwhile to highlight the potential effect of this additional language: section 8.2(e), to which URI's [*839] section 9.10 right to specific performance is subject (under Ehrenberg's revision), *purports to specifically prohibit URI from seeking equitable relief*. Yet, to such a substantive revision that attempts to eviscerate the right to specific performance (the importance of which Swedenburg understood and had previously communicated during negotiations),[146] Swedenburg simply told Ehrenberg that "we were okay with the contract as written regarding those [specific performance] provisions."[147]

In the next draft of the Agreement, despite this statement to Ehrenberg, Swedenburg struck the words "equitable relief" in section 8.2(e).[148] Though this might indicate that Swedenburg had realized that Ehrenberg's language could be interpreted to eliminate URI's right to specific performance, the next conversation regarding the agreements shows this was not the case. For the July 19 conversation, "limitation of liability at 8.2(e)" is identified as an item on the agenda.[149] Swedenburg testified [**76] that, regarding his striking "equitable relief" from section 8.2(e), he told Ehrenberg that he "thought all of the changes were — that I had made to the last version of the contract in that section were *technical* and *non-substantive*."[150] Ehrenberg objected to this deletion and the language was reinserted.[151]

At this point, even if URI in fact believed that it had a right to specific performance or I could conclude that such a belief were reasonable, I find that

defendants had no reason to know of this understanding.[152] Though URI, through Swedenburg, had many opportunities throughout the negotiation process to clearly vocalize its understanding of its rights for specific performance under the Merger Agreement, URI consistently failed to communicate this to Cerberus representatives.[153] Particularly damning [*840] is the Mayer conversation on July 19, 2007.

McNeal and Kochman testified that, on July 19, they had a conversation in which Mayer said Cerberus thought that it was buying an option in URI.[154] McNeal and Kochman were taken aback by this assertion and immediately relayed this conversation to Horowitz, URI's attorney at Simpson.[155] Horowitz, however, did nothing to dissuade Ehrenberg that Mayer's understanding of the transaction was erroneous. Horowitz stated that when he spoke with Ehrenberg, Horowitz made no reference to *any* of the following: the position that had been relayed to Horowitz that Cerberus could pay $100 million and walk away from the contract; Mayer's position that

---

[144] Swedenburg Test. at 145.

[145] *See* Pl.'s Ex. 166, at LS00018623, LS00018628.

[146] *See, e.g.*, Swedenburg Test. at 128 (identifying the reverse breakup fee/specific performance construct as an issue "we cared about in the contract in particular"); *id.* 134 ("we thought [specific performance] was important").

[147] *Id.* at 145-46 ("Q: By the way, just to go back on the conversation you had on the 16th, was specific performance discussed in that conversation? A: No, it wasn't discussed. I just — like I said, I just told Mr. Ehrenberg that we were okay with the contract as written regarding those provisions.").

[148] *See* Defs.' Ex. 24, at LS 00018448 (Merger Agreement Draft, July 17, 2007).

[149] Pl.'s Ex. 82 (Agenda, July 19, 2007).

[150] Swedenburg Test. at 147 (emphasis added).

[151] *Id.* at 148 ("[Ehrenberg] said he needed that to go back in, the sentence where it was, to which I said 'Okay. That's fine.'").

---

[152] URI's counsel failed to provide a basis upon [**77] which defendants reasonably could form such an understanding. *See, e.g.*, Ehrenberg Test. at 373.

> Q: At any point during the meeting, when there were discussions about incentives for Cerberus to walk away or not walk away from the deal, did anybody on the URI side ask any questions about what the Cerberus and RAM representatives were talking about?
>
> A: No.
>
> Q: Did anybody on the URI side say anything about walking away didn't make any sense because they had a specific performance right?
>
> A: No.
>
> Q: Did anybody on the URI side challenge the assertions that Cerberus would have a right to walk away from this deal?
>
> A: No.

[153] URI's counsel's equivocal testimony regarding issues that both sides agree were important to their respective clients perhaps is indicative of the apparent deficiencies in communication and supports this Court's conclusion that URI did not give defendants a reason to know that their understanding of the Merger Agreement was different than that of URI.

> Q: Are you sure it wasn't said at that meeting: we're okay with the reverse break-up fee being the sole and exclusive remedy here?
>
> A: I would be surprised if I said it. But you can't be sure, I suppose.
>
> Q: So it's possible that that's [**78] what was said?
>
> A: Anything is possible.

Swedenburg Test. at 250. *See also id.* at 265 ("Q: At any time did you say to any of the Cerberus representatives, 'I don't know why you're talking about a right to walk away from the transaction; we have a right to specific performance'? A: No, I did not.").

[154] McNeal Test. at 94; Kochman Test. at 303-04.

[155] McNeal Test. at 109; Horowitz Dep. at 26:11-25.

Cerberus had the right to pay $100 million and walk away from the contract; whether or not Horowitz agreed with the position that Mayer had expressed to McNeal and Kochman; whether or not there was a specific performance right under the Merger Agreement; whether [**79] or not the parties disagreed about the interpretation of the contract.[156] Horowitz also said that he did not recall that Ehrenberg said anything about these issues, except to state that Cerberus was not repudiating the contract.[157] It is unclear what, if anything, was said during this conversation but it is clear that nothing was said or done to enable this Court to find that defendants should have known that URI believed it was entitled to specific performance. I therefore conclude that the evidence demonstrates that, even if URI did believe it had a right to specific performance, defendants did not know and had no reason to know of URI's understanding of the Merger Agreement.[158]

3.   Defendants Understood the Agreement to Bar Specific Performance and URI Either Knew or Should Have Known of This Understanding

Based on the evidence presented at trial, I find that the defendants understood the agreement to eliminate any right to specific performance and that URI either knew or should have known of defendants' understanding. Cerberus seems to have [*841] come to this transaction halfheartedly and unenthusiastic about committing. It took issue with a great deal of the initial draft agreement URI circulated[159] and failed to submit a bid by the proposed deadline.[160] The defendants offered a go-shop period with a lower break fee to allow URI [**81] to shop itself to other bidders without the fear of paying a huge termination fee.[161] Moreover, Cerberus lowered its bid significantly.[162] Cerberus was not acting like an eager buyer and was not willing to do this deal on the terms initially proposed by URI.

Testimony from two of Cerberus's leaders, CEO Stephen Feinberg and managing director Steven Mayer, demonstrated that the firm believed it had the ability to walk away from this agreement relatively unscathed. Indeed, Feinberg, though evidently unsure of what "specific performance" means,[163] did think "very clearly that to the extent we didn't complete the merger, that our — our liability and our — what we'd have to come up with was a hundred million and that we could not be forced to close the deal."[164] Mayer, who participated more directly in the negotiations and who reviewed the Merger Agreement both in drafts and in final form,[165] testified that he "believe[s] there was an explicit [**82] understanding that Cerberus could choose not to close the transaction for any reason or no reason at all and pay a maximum amount of a hundred million dollars."[166] In addition to the Cerberus executives, lawyers for Cerberus testified to and produced contemporaneous notes corroborating their subjective understanding that the $100 million termination fee was the "sole and exclusive" recourse available to URI in the event of a failure to close.[167]

I also find that defendants communicated this understanding to URI in such a way that URI either knew or should have known of their understanding. Initially, Cerberus conveyed its position by means of the drafts and mark-ups it sent to Swedenburg. For example, on June 18, 2007, Ehrenberg sent Simpson his initial mark-ups to the draft circulated by URI. In that mark-up, Ehrenberg wrote, "OUR CLIENT WILL NOT AGREE TO A GUARANTEE."[168] Ehrenberg also removed a provision from section 6.10 "that would have required the buyer to take enforcement actions against the lenders [*842] and other persons providing the financing."[169] Finally, Ehrenberg struck portions of section 9.10(b) that would have allowed URI to specifically enforce the Equity Commitment Letter and the Guarantee and to specifically enforce the consummation of the transaction.[170] While discussing these, Swedenburg told Ehrenberg that he would likely not incorporate many of the

---

[156] Horowitz Dep. at 26:23-29:2.

[157] Id. at 27:6-8.

[158] URI contends that the post-Agreement conduct of the parties was consistent with the existence of a valid and enforceable right of specific enforcement under section 9.10 of the Merger Agreement. URI, in proffering this evidence to show that it communicated its understanding of the Agreement to defendants, specifically highlights the description of the merger [**80] in the preliminary and final proxy statement filed by URI with the SEC. See Proxy Statement at 69, 70. Though the final proxy may be consistent with the interpretation of the Agreement urged by URI, in light of the fact that the original draft omitted any mention of the right of specific performance and the fact that the drafting and execution of the proxy statement occurred after the signing of the Merger Agreement, I cannot conclude that this post-Agreement extrinsic evidence is indicative of the common understanding of the parties.

[159] Ehrenberg Test. at 332-36.

[160] McNeal Test. at 76-77.

[161] See id. at 85.

[162] Compare id. at 77 ("they had verbally given us a price range of around $35 to $37 a share"), with Kochman Test. at 292-93 (noting that Cerberus lowered its offer to $33).

[163] Stephen Feinberg Test., Trial Tr. vol.1, 47, Dec. 18, 2007 [hereinafter "Feinberg Test. at "] ("I'm not an attorney and I'm not really knowledgeable what exactly 'specific performance' means.").

[164] Id. at 47-48.

[165] Steven Mayer Test., Trial Tr. vol. 2, 452, Dec. 19, 2007 [hereinafter "Mayer Test. at "].

[166] Id. at 446-47; see also id. at 466 ("As of July 22nd, specific performance wasn't even a concept that I had even entertained as being a possibility.").

[167] See Defs.' Ex. 22 (Ehrenberg's notes of July 16, 2007; Defs.' Ex. 23 (Skerry's notes of July 16, 2007); Defs.' Ex. 30 (Holt's notes of July 19, 2007). These notes all reflect their authors' understanding that URI was "OK" with the "sole and exclusive remedy" of the termination fee. [**83] See also Ehrenberg Test. at 401 ("8.2(e) was designed to say no specific performance of the merger agreement").

[168] Defs.' Ex. 9, at LS0019728; Ehrenberg Test. [**84] at 333.

[169] Ehrenberg Test. at 334; Defs.' Ex. 9, at LS0019777.

[170] Ehrenberg Test. at 334; Defs.' Ex. 9, at LS0019793.

changes, would send it back, and would expect
Cerberus's next mark-up to be "less voluminous."[171]

Nevertheless, Ehrenberg persisted. In a conversation that occurred sometime between June 25 and
July 10, Ehrenberg and Swedenburg discussed the
extent of the defendants' potential liability. During
this conversation, Swedenburg indicated "that it was
important for his client to assure that . . . Cerberus
and the RAM entities showed up at the closing."[172]
Ehrenberg "explained to Mr. Swedenburg that that
was a significant problem."[173] At a July 10 meeting of
the attorneys, it was decided that the issue of liability needed to be decided by the principals, but that
Cerberus would be willing to enter a limited guarantee agreement.[174]

The next important meeting occurred on July 12,
2007. There, via telephone, Mayer represented to the
URI team that "Cerberus would not proceed with the
negotiations or with the deal unless there was an
arrangement where, if the Cerberus parties, to
include RAM, failed to close, the obligation would be
to pay a fee."[175] Both Ehrenberg and Mayer testified
that [**85] the URI team agreed to this point on the
twelfth.[176]

After this meeting, Ehrenberg and his team returned to the Merger Agreement and made several
important revisions. The draft they produced was
circulated early in the morning on July 15, 2007
along with new versions of the Equity Commitment
Letter and the Limited Guarantee.[177] I find several
edits significant in these documents:

    1. the Equity Commitment Letter expressly
disclaims any third-party beneficiaries and
exceptions to allow for suit against the Cerberus entities were removed;[178]

    2. the "no recourse" provisions of the Lim-
ited Guarantee were expanded to make them
farther reaching;[179]

    3. section 9.10 was edited to remove refer-
ences to the Equity Commitment Letter and
the final sentence was added to make the provision subservient to section 8.2(e);[180] and

    4. section 8.2(e) was substantially rewrit-
ten to include a limitation on liability and to
provide explicitly that "in no event shall the
Company seek equitable relief . . . ."[181]

[*843] Although, as discussed above, these edits do
not provide a [**86] perfectly clear expression of
RAM's position that the agreement bars specific
performance, they are substantial enough that they
should have at least put Swedenburg and URI on
notice that RAM had a different understanding than
URI did. Subsequent communications between the
parties go substantively beyond this, and unquestionably convey RAM's position.

Swedenburg made very few changes to this draft.
He struck the provision about the Company's ability
to "seek equitable relief,"[182] but he ultimately did not
stand by this revision. When Ehrenberg received
Swedenburg's edits, he circulated an agenda for a
meeting to discuss the Merger Agreement. On that
agenda, Ehrenberg listed "limitation of liability in
8.2(e)" as a topic for discussion,[183] and by this he
"intended to address the deletion of the words equity
relief."[184] At that meeting, Mr. Swedenburg spent his
time lobbying for a higher break-up fee, one that
would be "painful," because the potential reputational harm Cerberus would suffer from walking
away would not be enough to deter [**87] them from
doing so.[185] Perhaps more importantly, the RAM
attorneys also explained to Swedenburg the importance of the words "equitable relief" that Swedenburg
had stricken from the Merger Agreement: "it was
important for us that the language that he struck be
restored to reflect the agreement that the only
remedy available to United Rentals, if Cerberus
didn't proceed with the closing, was the break-up
fee — reverse break-up fee."[186] Testimony indicated
that Swedenburg put up no fight on this issue. He
tersely replied, "I get it."[187]

I find this testimony to be credible and I find that
it is supported by certain of defendants' exhibits and
by Swedenburg's testimony. First, the agenda that
Ehrenberg circulated specifically references section
8.2(e).[188] Second, Holt's notes from the July 19
meeting support the proposition that this conversation happened and that Swedenburg assented.[189]
Third, Swedenburg essentially capitulated on this

[171] Swedenburg Test. at 131.
[172] Ehrenberg Test. at 338.
[173] Id. at 339.
[174] Id. at 348-49.
[175] Id. at 352; Mayer Test. at 428-29.
[176] Ehrenberg Test. at 352; Mayer Test. at 429-30. But see McNeal
Test. at 86; Swedenburg Test. at 142.
[177] See Defs.'Ex. 20.
[178] Id. at LS0056180; Ehrenberg Test. at 360-61.
[179] Defs.' Ex. 20, at LS00056185-86.
[180] Id. at LS00056095-96.
[181] Id. at LS00056091.

[182] See Defs.' Ex. 24, at LS00018448.
[183] Defs.' Ex. 28, at RAM00092282.
[184] Ehrenberg Test. at 370.
[185] Id. at 372; Skerry Test. at 494-95; Mayer Test. at 431-33. This
Court has previously noted the importance of reputation in the
private equity field. See Abry Partners V, L.P. v. F&W Acquisition
LLC, 891 A.2d 1032, 1061 (Del. Ch. 2006) ("Although there are a lot
more private equity firms today than there were a decade ago, the
nature of that market is still such that reputational factors are likely
to be important."). Given the fact, however, that Cerberus so readily
balked on this deal, query how well the firm will be able to rely on its
reputation in the [**88] future. See Andrew Ross Sorkin, If Buyout
Firms Are So Smart, Why Are They So Wrong?, N.Y. TIMES, Nov.
18, 2007, at 38 (criticizing Cerberus's buyer's remorse and claiming
that "Cerberus just proved itself to be the ultimate flighty, hot-
tempered partner").
[186] Skerry Test. at 497.
[187] Id.
[188] See Defs.' Ex. 28, at RAM00092282.
[189] See Defs.' Ex. 30, at RAM00004472.

point during cross examination. Conceding that he quickly assented to the reinsertion of the language he had removed from section 8.2(e), Swedenburg then testified that he knew "equitable relief included specific performance,"[190] that this was "probably why [he] did strike it,"[191] admitted that Ehrenberg conveyed how important [*844] that provision was to Cerberus,[192] and then concluded by suggesting he knew it would have been a good idea to inquire further about why this provision was so important to Cerberus, [**89] but that he failed to so inquire because it "was at the end of an agenda, there was [sic] more negotiations to go, et cetera, et cetera."[193] I find it frankly incredible that Swedenburg could have recognized the import of the language he was striking and that Cerberus considered that language key but manifestly failed to make any further inquiry. Swedenburg, the original architect of this transaction, testified that one lynchpin of his "construct" was the seller's ability to force the sale to close.[194] By the end of this July 19 meeting, Swedenburg either knew or should have known that Cerberus's understanding of the Agreement was fundamentally inconsistent with that construct.

If Swedenburg's faltering on July 19 were not enough to put URI on notice of Cerberus's understanding, the July 21 telephone conversation between the UBS representatives (McNeal and Kochman) and Mayer surely was. On that call, Mayer mentioned something about Cerberus's ability to walk away from the deal.[195] Kochman responded forcefully, declaring that his client, [**90] URI, would never agree to this deal if it were merely an option.[196] Mayer reassured him that Cerberus was committed to the deal, but never conceded that the contract amounted to anything other than an option.[197] McNeal and Kochman reported this conversation to Horowitz, and Brad Jacobs, then-CEO/Chairman of URI.[198] Horowitz, who evidently cannot remember much of this deal, failed to raise this issue with Swedenburg,[199] the chief negotiator, or with Ehrenberg.[200] On July 22, the very next day, the Agreement was executed. At that time, I conclude that URI had ample reason to know that Cerberus understood the Agreement to bar the remedy of specific performance.

V. CONCLUSION

Although some in the media have discussed this case in the context of Material Adverse Change ("MAC") clauses,[201] the dispute between URI and Cerberus is a good, old-fashioned contract [**91] case prompted [*845] by buyer's remorse.[202] As with many contract disputes, hindsight affords the Court a perspective from which it is clear that this case could have been avoided: if Cerberus had simply deleted section 9.10(b), the contract would not be ambiguous, and URI would not have filed this suit. The law of contracts, however, does not require parties to choose optimally clear language; in fact, parties often riddle their agreements with a certain amount of ambiguity in order to reach a compromise.[203] Although the language in this Merger Agreement remains ambiguous, the understanding of the parties does not.

One may plausibly upbraid Cerberus for walking away from this deal, for favoring their lenders over their targets, or for suboptimal contract editing, but one cannot reasonably criticize the firm for a failure to represent its understanding of the limitations on remedies provided by this Merger Agreement. From the beginning of the process, Cerberus and its attorneys have aggressively negotiated this contract, and along the way they have communicated their [**93] intentions and understandings to URI. Despite the Herculean efforts of its litigation counsel at trial, URI could not overcome the apparent lack of communication of *its* intentions and understandings to defendants. Even if URI's deal attorneys did not affirmatively and explicitly agree to the limitation on specific performance as several witnesses allege they did on multiple occasions, no testimony at trial rebutted the inference that I must reasonably draw from the evidence: by July 22, 2007, URI knew or should have known what Cerberus's understanding of the Merger Agreement was, and if URI disagreed with that understanding, it had an affirmative duty to clarify its position in the face of an ambiguous contract with

---

[190] Swedenburg Test. at 252.

[191] *Id.*

[192] *Id.* at 255.

[193] *Id.* at 256.

[194] *Id.* at 128-30.

[195] Mayer Test. at 434-35; Kochman Test. at 303.

[196] Kochman Test. at 303-04.

[197] *Id.* at 313-15; Mayer Test. at 436 (admitting he tried to reassure the UBS team by telling them "just because we had a walk-away right, didn't mean we intended to exercise it").

[198] McNeal Test. at 109.

[199] Swedenburg Test. at 268.

[200] Horowitz Dep. 27:2-29:10.

[201] *See, e.g.,* Jack Welch & Suzy Welch, *Behind all those Undone Deals: Nervous Dealmakers are Trying to Use Loosely Written Escape Clauses to Bail Out,* BUSINESS WEEK, Dec. 17, 2007, at 84 ("Fast forward, then, to an adverse change — like the subprime crisis — and you understand why so many companies are engaged in legal slugfests over what their MAC clauses technically allow. Sallie Mae and the private equity firm J.C. Flowers could be in court for years, for instance, as could Cerberus and United Rentals."). This Court has, of course, served as the forum for several disputes [**92] over MAC clauses. *See, e.g., Frontier Oil v. Holly Corp.,* C.A. No. 20502, 2005 Del. Ch. LEXIS 57, 2005 WL 1039027 (Del. Ch. Apr. 29, 2005) (interpreting a material adverse effect ("MAE") clause); *In re IBP, Inc., S'holders Litig.,* 789 A.2d 14, (Del. Ch. 2001).

[202] Indeed, defendants have admitted that they have breached the Merger Agreement and seek no protection from the Agreement's MAC clause.

[203] *See* Richard A. Posner, *The Law and Economics of Contract Interpretation,* 83 TEX. L. REV. 1581, 1583 (2005) ("Deliberate ambiguity may be a necessary condition of making the contract; the parties may be unable to agree on certain points yet be content to take their chances on being able to resolve them, with or without judicial intervention, should the need arise.").

Appendix

glaringly conflicting provisions. Because it has failed to meet its burden of demonstrating that the common understanding of the parties permitted specific performance of the Merger Agreement, URI's petition for specific performance is denied.

IT IS SO ORDERED.

JONATHAN BERNSTEIN, Plaintiff, v. TRACTMANAGER, INC., a Delaware corporation, Defendant.

C.A. No. 2763-VCL

COURT OF CHANCERY OF DELAWARE

2007 Del. Ch. LEXIS 172*

August 2, 2007, Submitted

November 20, 2007, Decided

COUNSEL: [*1] Joel Friedlander, Esquire, John M. Seaman, Esquire, BOUCHARD MARGULES & FRIEDLANDER, P.A., Wilmington, Delaware, Attorneys for the Plaintiff.
Ian Connor Bifferato, Esquire, Chad J. Toms, Esquire, BIFFERATO GENTILOTTI LLC, Wilmington, Delaware; Thomas J. Fleming, Esquire, OLSHAN GRUNDMAN FROME ROSENZWEIG & WOLOSKY LLP, New York, New York, Attorneys for the Defendant.

OPINION:

MEMORANDUM OPINION

LAMB, Vice Chancellor.

This advancement action arose after the conversion of a limited liability company into a corporation. In that context, the court is asked to determine whether the corporation's bylaws providing a mandatory right of advancement to its officers and directors should be read to apply equally to the former managers of the LLC, even where the LLC's operating agreement provided for indemnification but not for mandatory advancement.

The court concludes that the right to indemnification or advancement for claims that arose during the life of the LLC continues to be governed by the terms of the old operating agreement. Thus, to the extent a claim is made against an officer or director of the corporation arising out of actions taken pre-conversion in his or her capacity as an officer [*2] or manager of the LLC, he or she has no mandatory right to advancement with respect thereto. While rights created by the LLC's operating agreement may be enforced against the corporation into which the LLC was converted, the corporation's bylaws do not govern the rights of former officers or managers of the LLC.

I.

The plaintiff, Jonathan Bernstein, was a manager and co-founder of MediTract, LLC, a Delaware limited liability company formed in 1999. In 2001, MediTract, LLC changed its name to TractManager, LLC, and Bernstein retained his title after the name change. Effective January 2, 2003, TractManager, LLC was converted into TractManager, Inc., a Delaware corporation that provides contract management services utilizing proprietary software. Bernstein has been a director of TractManager, Inc. since that date, and was an officer of TractManager, Inc. until late 2004. In addition, Bernstein is, and at all relevant times was, a member of the New York Bar, practicing at the law firm of Pryor Cashman Sherman & Flynn, LLP ("Pryor Cashman"). Bernstein and his firm have provided legal services to TractManager, Inc. and its predecessors since 1999, including formation of MediTract, LLC in 1999 [*3] and its 2003 conversion into a corporation.

In 2006, Bernstein and Pryor Cashman brought suit in the Supreme Court of the State of New York against TractManager, Inc. seeking recovery of legal fees allegedly owed to them. TractManager, Inc. counterclaimed against Bernstein with three causes of action: (1) constructive trust; (2) legal malpractice; and (3) unjust enrichment.[1]

On or about February 5, 2007, Bernstein served TractManager, Inc. with a demand for advancement of litigation expenses incurred in defending the New York litigation. Bernstein also provided an undertaking to repay all amounts advanced if it were ultimately determined he was not entitled to indemnification under TractManager, Inc.'s bylaws.

Less than two weeks later, on February 16, 2007, TractManager, Inc.'s board of directors met, allegedly without giving advance notice to Bernstein, and rejected the demand.[2] On March 1, 2007, Bernstein filed this action pursuant to 8 *Del. C.* § 145 asserting two counts for relief. Count I seeks advancement, pursuant to TractManager, Inc.'s [*4] bylaws and Delaware law, of litigation expenses incurred in the New York action. Count II seeks an award of ex-

---

[1] TractManager, Inc. also brought several counterclaims against Pryor Cashman that are not at issue in this litigation and have been settled.

[2] Bernstein does not ask this court to invalidate the process by which the board denied advancement. Rather, he argues that he is entitled to mandatory advancement, and challenges the board's right to deny it.

Appendix

penses incurred in connection with prosecuting this action for advancement.

TractManager, Inc. concedes its bylaws provide for mandatory advancement to directors and officers of the corporation.[3] It argues, however, that the allegations in the counterclaim concern activities Bernstein took prior to TractManager, LLC's 2003 conversion into a corporation, and, therefore, concern acts he took as a manager of the limited liability company, not a director of the corporation. TractManager, Inc. concludes that Bernstein is not entitled to mandatory advancement because nothing in TractManager, LLC's bylaws provided for mandatory advancement to its managers, and nothing in TractManager, Inc.'s bylaws plainly specifies an intent to extend mandatory advancement to managers of the limited liability company. TractManager, Inc. further argues the claims against Bernstein are brought "by [*5] reason of the fact" that he was the corporation's attorney, not a director of the corporation.

Bernstein argues that the bylaws [*7] should be read to provide mandatory advancement for managers of the limited liability company as well as for

---

[3] Article VIII, Section 1 contains the indemnification provision, and states in pertinent part:

> SECTION I. RIGHT TO INDEMNIFICATION - Each person who was or is made a party or is threatened to be made a party to or is otherwise involved in any action, suit or proceeding, whether civil, criminal, administrative or investigative (hereinafter a "proceeding"), by reason of the fact that he or she is or was a director or an officer of the corporation or is or was serving at the request of the corporation as a director, officer, employee or agent of another corporation or of a partnership, joint venture, trust or other enterprise, including service with respect to an employee benefit plan (hereinafter an "indemnitee"), whether the basis of such proceeding is an alleged action in an official capacity as a director, officer, employee or agent or in any other capacity while serving as a director, officer, employee or agent, shall be indemnified and held harmless by the corporation to the fullest extent authorized by the Delaware General Corporation Law, as the same exists or may hereafter be amended [*6] . . . against all expense, liability and loss . . . reasonably incurred or suffered by such indemnitee in connection therewith . . . .

Article VIII, Section 2 contains the advancement provision, and states in pertinent part:

> SECTION 2. RIGHT TO ADVANCEMENT OF EXPENSES - In addition to the right to indemnification conferred in Section 1 of this ARTICLE VIII, an indemnitee shall also have the right to be paid by the corporation the expenses (including attorneys' fees) incurred in defending any such proceeding in advance of its final disposition . . . .

A third clause in the by-laws extends indemnification and advancement, on a discretionary basis, to the corporation's employees and agents. Article VIII, Section 6 provides:

> SECTION 6. INDEMNIFICATION OF EMPLOYEES AND AGENTS OF THE CORPORATION - The corporation may, to the extent authorized from time to time by the Board of Directors, grant rights to indemnification and to the advancement of expenses to any employee or agent of the corporation to the fullest extent of the provisions of this Article with respect to the indemnification and advancement of expenses of directors and officers of the corporation . . . .

directors and officers of the corporation. He also argues that TractManager, Inc.'s bylaws grant mandatory advancement for suits brought against a director or officer in "any capacity," not simply those brought "by reason of the fact" that the individual is a director or officer.

II.

The parties cross-move for summary judgment. To prevail on summary judgment, the moving party must "demonstrate that no genuine issue of material fact exists and that it is entitled to judgment as a matter of law."[4] "The court must view the evidence presented in the light most favorable to the non-moving party, and the moving party bears the burden of demonstrating the absence of a material factual dispute."[5] Once the moving party has demonstrated such facts, and such facts entitle it to summary judgment, the burden shifts to the non-moving party to present "specific facts showing that there is a genuine issue of fact for trial."[6] The non-moving party "may not rest upon the mere allegations or denials [contained in the pleadings]."[7]

The existence of cross-motions does not necessarily make summary judgment for either party inappropriate, nor does it change the standard for summary judgment.[8] Rather, the court examines each motion separately,[9] and "if the pleadings, depositions, answers to interrogatories and admissions on file, together with the affidavits, if any, show that there is no genuine issue as to any material fact and that the moving party is entitled to a judgment as a matter of law, then summary judgment is appropriate."[10]

---

[4] Levy v. HLI Operating Co., Inc., 924 A.2d 210, 219 (Del. Ch. 2007).

[5] Id.

[6] Id. [*8] (citing Court of Chancery Rule 56(e)).

[7] Id.

[8] See Mehiel v. Solo Cup Co., No. 851-N, 2005 Del. Ch. LEXIS 66, 2005 WL 1252348, at *3 (Del. Ch. May 13, 2005); United Vanguard Fund, Inc. v. Takecare, Inc., 693 A.2d 1076, 1079 (Del. 1997); see also Rochester v. Katalan, 320 A.2d 704 (Del. 1974); Levy, 924 A.2d at 219. The court notes that the filing of cross-motions will often trigger Court of Chancery Rule 56(h). That rule treats cross-motions for summary judgment as a stipulation for decision on the merits based on the record submitted. In this case, however, each party argues that material factual issues exist that preclude summary judgment in the other's favor. Bernstein alleges that if the court concludes [*9] TractManager, Inc.'s bylaws are ambiguous, he is entitled to discovery into how TractManager, Inc. interprets its bylaws with respect to other directors. TractManager, Inc. alleges that if the court awards advancement for only a portion of Bernstein's claims, there is a material issue as to the claims and allegations to which he is entitled to advancement. "Because both sides have alleged that there are outstanding issues of fact material to the resolution of the other's motion, Rule 56(h) does not apply by its own terms." Chambers v. Genesee & Wyoming, Inc., 2005 Del. Ch. LEXIS 118, 2005 WL 2000765, at *5 n.21 (Del. Ch. Aug. 11, 2005).

[9] See Union Oil Co. of Calif. v. Mobil Pipeline Co., No. 19395, 2006 Del. Ch. LEXIS 213, 2006 WL 3770834, at *9 (Del. Ch. Dec. 15, 2006).

[10] Mehiel, 2005 Del. Ch. LEXIS 66, 2005 WL 1252348 at *3; see

In this case, the court must determine whether Bernstein is due advancement pursuant to Tract-Manager, Inc.'s bylaws. The rules that govern the interpretation of statutes and contracts "apply to the interpretation of corporate charters."[11] Thus, "[i]t is settled Delaware law that if a corporate bylaw is unambiguous, the Court shall not attempt to interpret it or search for the [*10] parties' intent behind the bylaw."[12] Words and phrases used in the bylaw are to be given their commonly accepted meaning "unless the context clearly requires a different one or unless legal phrases having a special meaning are used."[13] Further, the bylaw is not made ambiguous merely because the parties disagree on the proper construction.[14] Rather, it is ambiguous only if reasonably susceptible to different constructions or interpretations.[15]

III.

A.   Advancement For Acts Taken As A Manager Of TractManager, LLC

As an initial matter, absent a clearly worded bylaw or contract making advancement mandatory, Delaware law leaves the decision whether to advance expenses to the business judgment of the board.[16] In this case, TractManager, LLC's governing document (the "Operating Agreement") [*11] provided indemnity for managers and officers, but contained no provision for advancement of expenses. The indemnity clause was amended and restated in the Third Amendment, executed June 1, 2001. This amended indemnity provision did not provide for mandatory advancement for expenses. Therefore, Bernstein has no mandatory advancement rights under the Operating Agreement.

Bernstein's right to indemnification (but not mandatory advancement) in his capacity as a manager of TractManager, LLC was preserved in the conversion. 6 *Del. C.* § 18-216(h) states:

> When any conversion shall have become effective under this section, for all purposes of the laws of the State of Delaware . . . all debts, liabilities and duties of the limited liability company that has converted shall remain at-

tached to the other business form to which such limited liability company has converted, and may be enforced against it to the same extent as if said debts, liabilities and duties had originally been [*12] incurred or contracted by it in its capacity as such other business form.

Thus, upon conversion, TractManager, Inc. became liable to satisfy any contractual indemnification obligation found in the Operating Agreement. The scope of that liability is that defined in the Operation Agreement and does not include a right of mandatory advancement.

Bernstein tries to avoid this result by arguing that the language of the corporation's bylaws should be read broadly enough to confer rights on the former managers or officers of TractManager, LLC. Despite the fact that the bylaws do not refer to TractManager, LLC's managers or officers, he argues that the extension of rights of advancement to any person made a party to an action "by reason of the fact that he or she is or was a director or an officer of the corporation" in Article VIII, Section 1 of TractManager, Inc.'s bylaws should be read to include managers of TractManager, LLC.[17] In support, Bernstein cites to *Bowen Engineering v. Reeve* for the proposition that a corporate indemnification bylaw can be read to imply rights to persons who formerly served as directors of a predecessor corporation.[18] *Bowen Engineering* is highly authoritative, [*13] yet it does not support the result Bernstein seeks.

In *Bowen Engineering*, the company was originally incorporated in Idaho ("Bowen of Idaho") in 1949. In 1973, the Bowen of Idaho board of directors authorized the formation of a new corporation under the same name in New Jersey ("Bowen of New Jersey"). Bowen of Idaho later dissolved after the two corporations entered into a broad agreement of assignment and assumption. In 1977, the corporation (Bowen of New Jersey) amended its bylaws to include [*14] an indemnification provision granting "all costs and expenses, including attorneys' fees" to any person who "shall be or who has been involved in or who has been made a party to any claim, action, suit or proceeding by reason of the fact that he, his testator or his intestate is or was a director, officer or employee of the company, whether or not then in office."[19] The defendant, an estate of a former direc-

---

also Rochester, 320 A.2d 704; *Levy,* 924 A.2d at 219.

[11] *Gentile v. Singlepoint Fin., Inc.,* 788 A.2d 111, 113 (Del. Ch. 2001) (citing *Hibbert v. Hollywood Park, Inc.,* 457 A.2d 339, 343 (Del. 1983)); *Sundlun v. Executive Jet Aviation, Inc.,* 273 A.2d 282, 285 (Del. Ch. 1970).

[12] *Salaman v. Nat'l Media Corp.,* No. 92C-01-161, 1994 Del. Super LEXIS 376, 1994 WL 465535, at *4 (Del. Ch. July 22, 1994) (citing *Hibbert,* 457 A.2d 339).

[13] *See Hibbert,* 457 A.2d at 343 (citations omitted).

[14] *Id.*

[15] *Id.*

[16] *See Majkowski v. Amer. Imaging Mgmt. Serv.,* 913 A.2d 572, 580 (Del. Ch. 2006); *Havens v. Attar,* No. 15134, 1997 Del. Ch. LEXIS 12, 1997 WL 55957, at * 13 (Del. Ch. Jan. 30 1997); *Adv. Mining Sys., Inc. v. Fricke,* 623 A.2d 82, 84 (Del. Ch. 1992).

[17] As Bernstein points out, bylaws can apply to acts taken before their adoption. *See, e.g., Salaman v. Nat'l Media Corp.,* 1994 Del. Super. LEXIS 376, [WL] at *6 (noting that where, as here, the bylaws define the indemnified event as "a claim asserted against the executive by reason of his service or actions in his position," the indemnified event is the claim itself, "not . . . the actions leading up to the claim"). Therefore, if Bernstein can establish that TractManager, Inc. intended its bylaws to apply to managers of TractManager, LLC, he can obtain advancement for expenses incurred in defending acts taken before those bylaws were adopted.

[18] 799 F. Supp. 467 (D.N.J. 1992).

[19] *Id.* at 486-87.

tor of both Bowen of Idaho and Bowen of New Jersey, was subsequently sued under the Comprehensive Environmental Response, Compensation, and Liability Act and related laws for acts taken by its decedent as a director of both corporations.

Ruling on the defendant's counterclaim for indemnification, the United States District Court for the District of New Jersey held that the indemnification provision in Bowen of New Jersey's amended bylaws, which were obviously intended to apply retroactively, applied to acts the defendant's decedent took as a director of both Bowen of Idaho and Bowen of New Jersey. The court reasoned that the directors who decided to reincorporate in New Jersey thought of the two corporations as identical in virtually every respect; "[t]he *only* change [*15] to occur was the state of incorporation."[20] Moreover, this change "was considered technical and without impact on the identity of the corporation."[21] Because Bowen of New Jersey was a "mere continuation" of Bowen of Idaho, it was "clear" that the directors intended changes in Bowen of New Jersey's bylaws (adopted some three years after the reincorporation) to "apply equally to the corporation throughout its history, whether incorporated in Idaho or reincorporated in New Jersey."[22]

The court's holding in *Bowen Engineering* was predicated upon the virtually absolute identity of the two corporations. Here, by contrast, the conversion from a limited liability company to a corporation accomplished a more fundamental change in identity. Limited liability companies and corporations differ in important ways, most pertinently in regard to indemnification: mandating it in the case of corporate directors and officers who successfully defend themselves, but leaving the indemnification of managers or officers of limited liability companies to private contract.[23] While the business of TractManager, LLC continued on in the corporate form following the 2003 conversion, [*16] there is no reason to infer that the directors who approved the new certificate of incorporation and bylaws intended to change,

adjust, or expand any of the existing rights or duties governing TractManager, LLC.[24]

This point would, perhaps, be more easily understood if the tables were turned and it was the later adopted [*18] bylaw that contained more restrictive provisions applicable on their face only to the corporate officers and directors. In that case, there is little likelihood that a court would infer a silent intention to alter the more generous contractual arrangements previously enjoyed by the managers or officers of a predecessor limited liability company. Instead, the court would look to the terms of the limited liability company's operating agreement or other contracts to determine the rights and duties of the parties. The same result should apply here.

In sum, TractManager, Inc.'s bylaws provide for mandatory advancement only for directors and officers of the corporation. Its authors could have employed words granting the managers or officers of TractManager, LLC this right but did not. This court will not rewrite a contract by reading words into it that the parties clearly did not intend.[25] Therefore, Bernstein is entitled only to advancement for acts occurring after he became a director and officer of TractManager, Inc. on January 2, 2003.[26]

B. "By Reason Of The Fact"

TractManager, Inc. argues that Bernstein is not entitled to advancement under its bylaws because he is not being sued by reason of the fact that he is or was a director or officer of the corporation. In *Homestore v. Tafeen,* the Delaware Supreme Court held that "if there is a nexus or causal connection between any of the underlying proceedings . . . and one's official capacity, those proceedings are 'by

---

[20] *Id.* at 488.
[21] *Id.*
[22] *Id.* at 489.
[23] *Compare* 8 Del. C. § 145 (mandating indemnification of successful directors and officers) *with* 6 Del. C. § 18-108 (leaving the decision to indemnify even successful directors and officers to the limited liability company); *see also* 2 R. Franklin Balotti & Jesse A. Finkelstein, THE DELAWARE LAW OF CORPORATIONS & BUSINESS ORGANIZATIONS, §§ 20.1, 20.8 (3d ed. 2007) (noting that a key advantage of an LLC over a corporation is the broad freedom of contract allowed in its formation and structure, including with regard to duties and liabilities of managers); Martin I. Lubaroff & Paul M. Altman, DELAWARE LIMITED PARTNERSHIPS § 13.1 (2006) (noting that "the concept of freedom of contract, which is a core concept recognized by Delaware law with respect to a partnership . . . is also recognized as a cornerstone of the formation of an LLC"). Indeed, Bernstein admits that, upon conversion, TractManager, Inc. drafted indemnification provisions that were far more generous than TractManager, [*17] LLC's, and provided wholly new advancement rights. *See* Pl.'s Reply Br. 12.

[24] Bernstein also argues that Article VIII, Section 1 should be read as having a retrospective application since it grants indemnification (and therefore mandatory advancement) to individuals sued "by reason of the fact that he or she is or was a director or an officer of the corporation." Because, Bernstein argues, TractManager, Inc. had no directors or officer prior to January 2, 2003, and therefore no one existed who "was" a director or officer on that date, the bylaw should be read as applying retrospectively to TractManager, LLC since any other reading would render meaningless the word "was" in the phrase "by reason of the fact that he or she is or was a director or an officer of the corporation." TractManager, Inc. easily refutes this bizarrely hyper-technical argument, noting that the use of the word "was" is clearly included to ensure only that a director's departure from TractManager, Inc. at some time in the future does not eliminate his or her right to indemnification and mandatory advancement.

[25] *Morgan v. Grace,* No. 20430, 2003 Del. Ch. LEXIS 113, 2003 WL 22461916, at *3 (Del. Ch. Oct. 29, 2003).

[26] *Radiancy, Inc. v. Azar,* No. 1547, 2006 Del. Ch. LEXIS 113, 2006 WL 224059, at *3 (Del. Ch. Jan. 23, 2006) [*19] (stating "in the absence of any facts on the record indicating [an individual] was appointed as a director or officer . . . before [engaging in the acts underlying the action against him], he is not entitled to any earlier advancement"); *see also FGC Holdings Ltd. v. Teltronics, Inc.,* No. 883, 2007 Del. Ch. LEXIS 14, 2007 WL 241384, at * 13-14 (Del. Ch. Jan. 22, 2007) (finding an individual not entitled to indemnification under 8 Del. C. § 145(c) because he did not become a director until after engaging in the acts underlying the claim against him).

reason of the fact' that one was a corporate officer, without regard to one's motivation for engaging in that conduct."[27] This connection is established if the corporate powers were used or necessary for the commission of the alleged misconduct. [*20][28] Further, the requisite nexus can be established even if the cause of action does not specify a claim of breach of fiduciary duty owed to the corporation.[29] Of course, the conduct complained of must occur at a time when one is a corporate officer or director.

TractManager's counterclaims in the New York action against Bernstein allege three causes of action: (1) constructive trust; (2) legal malpractice; and (3) unjust enrichment. The first seeks to impose a trust over equity interests Bernstein obtained before January 2, 2003.[30] The unjust enrichment claim concerns these same equity interests, but also concerns Bernstein's retention [*21] of legal fees for work done between 1999 and 2004.[31] The legal malpractice claim covers, generally, Bernstein's representation of TractManager from 1999 to 2004. Thus, only the unjust enrichment claim and legal malpractice claim involve conduct post-dating January 2, 2003 that could satisfy the "by reason of the fact" requirement.

Further, reading the New York counterclaims as a whole and viewing the evidence presented in a light most favorable to Bernstein, the court identifies three allegations relevant to the New York counterclaims that occurred after Bernstein became a director and officer of TractManager, Inc. First, TractManager, Inc. alleges that "[b]etween 2001 and 2004 ... Bernstein ... advised and represented TractManager[, Inc.] in a series of private placements and corporate transactions."[32] Second, Tract-

Manager, Inc. alleges that, in the latter half of 2003, Bernstein advised TractManager, Inc. it owed Pryor Cashman $700,000 in legal fees. TractManager, Inc. asserts that this advice was improper for two reasons: (1) the legal fees were not valid because Pryor Cashman had allegedly failed to provide TractManager, Inc. with a written letter of engagement as required by New York ethics rules; and (2) the $700,000 bill included fees for services Bernstein personally provided and for which he agreed not to charge TractManager, Inc.

Third, TractManager, Inc. alleges that after it indicated it could not pay the $700,000 in legal fees, it entered into a detrimental contract with Pryor Cashman called the Conditional Agreement.[33] TractManager, Inc. alleges that Bernstein did not advise it to seek outside counsel before signing this agreement.

In essence, TractManager, Inc.'s claims are that Bernstein drafted legal documents and agreements in violation of legal ethics rules, advised his client to enter into those agreements, and attempted to recover legal fees to which he was not entitled. These claims bear no nexus to Bernstein's status as a director or officer. There are no allegations that Bernstein relied on information he obtained as a director or officer in order to render legal advice.[34] Nor are there allegations that Bernstein used his corporate powers to force the company to follow his legal advice. Nothing indicates that Bernstein used his corporate powers to draft the relevant documents, to advise TractManager, Inc. to enter into them, or to recover legal fees from TractManager, Inc.

Bernstein makes no serious attempt to argue that the claims were brought [*25] against him "by reason of the fact" that he is or was a director or officer of TractManager, Inc. Instead, Bernstein responds that Article VIII, Section 1 provides indemnification to anyone made a party to an action by reason of the fact that he or she was a director or an officer of the corporation "whether the basis of such proceeding is alleged action in an official capacity ...

---

[27] 888 A.2d 204, 215 (Del. 2005).

[28] *Brown v. Liveops, Inc.,* 903 A.2d 324, 329 (Del. Ch. 2006); *Perconti v. Thornton Oil Corp.,* No. 18630, 2002 Del. Ch. LEXIS 51, 2002 WL 982419, at *6 (Del. Ch. May 3, 2002).

[29] *Perconti,* 2002 Del. Ch. LEXIS 51, 2002 WL 982419, at *7 & n.35 (finding criminal indictment against officer was an action brought "by reason of the fact" he was an officer, even though he was not charged with breaching any fiduciary duty owed to the corporation, because "conduct which falls within the scope of a federal criminal statute can also be a breach of a corporate officer's fiduciary duty").

[30] The pleading references interests that Bernstein acquired in 2000 upon the formation of MediTract, LLC and shortly thereafter, specifically, the 19% of MediTract, LLC's equity Bernstein obtained in 2000 for $3,625. It also alleges that other investors had to spend $100,000 for each one percent equity interest. The pleading alleges that Bernstein obtained his interests in violation of N.Y. Disc. R. 5-104.

[31] On March 9, 2007, the Supreme Court for the State of New York dismissed TractManager, Inc.'s claims for constructive trust and unjust enrichment based upon the interest Bernstein obtained in MediTract, LLC through an entity he owned called Everest, LP. *See* Bernstein Aff. Ex. 11 at 25-26. In a letter dated May 29, 2007, Bernstein's counsel informed the court that the New York court had dismissed all of TractManager, Inc.'s claims against Bernstein on [*22] May 18, 2007. On June 1, 2007, Bernstein's counsel informed the court that on May 29, 2007, TractManager, Inc. had filed a notice of appeal of the May order.

[32] This is [*23] one of only two post-January 2, 2003 allegations

that Bernstein identifies in his brief. *See* Pl.'s Opening Br. 7 (characterizing TractManager, Inc.'s counterclaims as based on four allegations against Bernstein, only two of which date after 2003). The other post-January 2, 2003 allegation Bernstein identifies is that he "sought to use his improperly obtained board positions for his enrichment [by making] groundless charges [to other directors] regarding Rizk and sought to induce his fellow board members to remove Rizk." Bernstein Aff. Ex. 9 P 166. However, Bernstein is not being sued for this act. Rather, the allegation is included in support of the breach of fiduciary duty claim against Pryor Cashman, which has been settled. *See* Bernstein Aff. Ex. 9 P 204.

[33] In the Conditional Agreement, Pryor Cashman allegedly agreed to waive TractManager, Inc.'s fees in return for a payment [*24] of $1.85 million if the company were sold. *See* Bernstein Aff. Ex. 8 P 29.

[34] *Heffernan v. Pacific Dunlop GNB Corp.,* 965 F.2d 369, 374 (7th Cir. 1992) (finding suit was brought "by reason of the fact" that an individual was a director because the individual sold shares without disclosing inside information he learned of by virtue of being a director of the company).

Appendix

or *any other capacity* while serving as a director, officer, employee or agent . . . ."[35] Bernstein argues the phrase "or any other capacity" entitles directors and officers to mandatory advancement for defending proceedings brought against them in any capacity, including suits wholly unrelated to his or her corporate capacity.

Such an interpretation, however, clearly was not what the parties intended and must be rejected. Under Bernstein's reading, even a director fighting a speeding ticket he or she received on the way to a board meeting is entitled to advancement. As Tract-Manager, Inc. points out, this reading renders meaningless the words "by reason of the fact." Rather, the phrase "or any other capacity" is better read as clarifying the term "proceeding by reason of the fact he or [*26] she is or was a director or an officer of the corporation." It assures, for example, that a director receives advancement for defending a criminal action brought against him because of something he did as a director — even though such an action is brought against him as an individual rather than in his "official" capacity as a director of a corporation. The post-January 2, 2003 factual allegations against Bernstein arise solely out of acts taken by him in his capacity as the corporation's attorney, and Bernstein has pointed to nothing in the bylaws extending mandatory advancement to directors or officers facing such claims.

Nor does the fact that Bernstein was TractManager, Inc.'s attorney make him an "agent" entitled to discretionary advancement under Article VIII, Section 6 of TractManager, Inc.'s bylaws. As this court explained in *Fasciana v. Electronic Data Systems Corporation:*

> Although it is true that attorneys are often described as agents of their clients, this loose general usage is not a helpful or sensible as-

cription to use in implementing [indemnification provisions]. Otherwise, outside attorneys retained by corporations would be able to seek advancement whenever they are accused [*27] of malpractice so long as their employing corporations have adopted a maximal bylaw extending coverage to the limits of [8 *Del. C*] § 145.[36]

IV.

Bernstein's claim for advancement must be denied because he seeks advancement for claims premised on acts taken before he became a director of TractManager, Inc., and TractManager, LLC bylaws did not provide for mandatory advancement of its managers. Further, as to those few acts occurring after January 2, 2003 for which Bernstein is sued, he is not sued by reason of the fact that he was or is a director or officer of TractManager, Inc. Because the bylaws are unambiguous, Bernstein's request for discovery into how TractManager, Inc. interprets its bylaws with respect to other directors will be denied.[37] Further, this court need not address TractManager, Inc.'s argument that the bylaws are to be construed against Bernstein.[38] For the foregoing reasons, Bernstein's motion for summary judgment is DENIED, and TractManager, Inc.'s motion for summary judgment is GRANTED. IT IS SO ORDERED.

---

[35] (emphasis added).

[36] 829 A.2d 160, 163 (Del. Ch. 2003).

[37] *See Hibbert,* 457 A.2d at 343 n.4; *Telephone and Data Sys. Inc. v. Eastex Cellular LP,* No. 12888, 1993 Del. Ch. LEXIS 182, at *38-39 (Del. Ch. Aug. 27, 1993); [*28] *see also NBC Universal, Inc. v. Paxson Commcn's Corp.,* No. 650-N, 2005 Del. Ch. LEXIS 56, 2005 WL 1038997, at *5 (Del. Ch. Apr. 29, 2005) (stating that summary judgment is particularly appropriate in a dispute over an unambiguous contract "because there is no need to resolve material disputes of fact").

[38] *Weinstock v. Lazard Debt Recovery GP, LLC,* No. 20048, 2003 Del Ch. LEXIS 83, at * 21 n. 14 (Del. Ch. Aug. 1, 2003).

JAMES FORSYTHE and ALAN TESCHE, Individually and derivatively on behalf of CIBC EMPLOYEE PRIVATE EQUITY FUND (U.S.) I, L.P., Plaintiffs, v. ESC FUND MANAGEMENT CO. (U.S.), INC., PETER H. SORENSEN, DEAN A. CHRISTIANSEN, VERNON L. OUTLAW, ORLANDO FIGUEROA, ALBERT FIORAVANTI, CIBC ESC ADVISORS, LLC, CIBC ESC SLP, LLC; and CANADIAN IMPERIAL BANK OF COMMERCE, Defendants, and CIBC EMPLOYEE PRIVATE EQUITY FUND (U.S.) I, L.P., Nominal Defendant.

C.A. No. 1091-VCL

COURT OF CHANCERY OF DELAWARE, NEW CASTLE

2007 Del. Ch. LEXIS 140*

June 12, 2007, Submitted

October 9, 2007, Decided

NOTICE:

THIS OPINION HAS NOT BEEN RELEASED FOR PUBLICATION. UNTIL RELEASED, IT IS SUBJECT TO REVISION OR WITHDRAWAL.

PRIOR HISTORY: Forsythe v. CIBC Emple. Private Equity Fund, 2006 Del. Ch. LEXIS 60 (Del. Ch., Mar. 22, 2006)

COUNSEL: [*1] Robert Kriner, Jr., Esquire, A. Zachary Naylor, Esquire, CHIMICLES & TIKELLIS LLP, Wilmington, Delaware; Lynda J. Grant, Esquire, Jonathan Gardner, Esquire, LABATON SUCHAROW & RUDOFF, LLP, New York, New York, Attorneys for the Plaintiffs.

Michael D. Goldman, Esquire, Stephen C. Norman, Esquire, Melony R. Anderson, Esquire, Scott B. Czerwonka, Esquire, Jennifer A. Chamagua, Esquire, POTTER ANDERSON & CORROON, LLP, Wilmington, Delaware, Attorneys for the Defendants.

OPINION:

MEMORANDUM OPINION AND ORDER

LAMB, Vice Chancellor.

A major bank offered to its most highly paid employees partnership interests in a fund intended to co-invest with the bank in its proprietary investments. In accordance with the partnership agreement, the corporate general partner, owned by its three unaffiliated directors, delegated the responsibility for the fund's management to affiliates of the bank. After the fund suffered extreme losses, a group of limited partners brought suit against, the bank, the general partner, its directors and the bank's affiliates for breach of fiduciary duty and breach of the partnership agreement.

The defendants have moved to dismiss on various grounds, including failure to make pre-suit demand [*2] on the general partner. The issue raised by this aspect of the motion is whether the general partner's oversight duty is governed by the familiar standard of *Caremark* or by a higher standard rooted in the partnership agreement itself.

The court concludes the partnership agreement provides the relevant standard. Particularly in light of the general partner's full delegation of its managerial duties to conflicted persons, the residual duty of oversight found in the agreement imposes a duty upon the general partner to take active steps to satisfy itself that the conflicted delegates actually discharge their powers loyally to the fund and in conformity with the partnership agreement. Because the complaint adequately alleges facts which, if true, show that the general partner did not fulfill that duty, demand will be excused.

I.

Litigation before this court began on August 23, 2004, when the plaintiffs filed a complaint seeking access to the defendants' books and records. On February 11, 2005, the plaintiffs filed their first derivative complaint in the present fiduciary duty action. The parties mutually agreed to stay proceedings pending the outcome of the books and records action. The court [*3] held a one-day trial on April 1, 2005 and issued an opinion on July 7, 2005 granting the plaintiffs limited access to the defendants' books and records.

The plaintiffs filed an amended derivative complaint in the fiduciary duty action on November 6, 2006.[1] The complaint seeks damages in connection with mismanagement of CIBC Employee Private Equity Fund (U.S.) I, LP (the "Fund").[2] The defendants now move to dismiss the complaint on the grounds that: (1) the plaintiffs did not make demand and demand is not excused; (2) the plaintiffs have failed to state a claim upon which relief can be

---

[1] The second amended complaint is the operative complaint referred to herein.

[2] The complaint also seeks dissolution of the Fund. The plaintiffs, however, have since indicated that they "are not pursuing their claims for dissolution at this time." See Pls.' Br. 45.

granted; (3) the plaintiffs' claims are barred by laches and/or the statute of limitations; and (4) the plaintiffs have waived their right to bring suit.

II.

A. The Parties

The plaintiffs in this matter are limited partners in the Fund. The plaintiffs name as defendants ESC Fund Management Co. (U.S.), Inc., a Delaware corporation and the Fund's [*4] general partner (the "General Partner"); Peter H. Sorensen, Dean A. Christiansen, Vernon L. Outlaw, Orlando Figueroa, and Albert Fioravanti, the General Partner's current and former individual directors (the "Individual Defendants"); CIBC ESC Advisors, LLC, a Delaware corporation and the Fund's investment advisor (the "Investment Advisor"); CIBC ESC SLP, LLC, a Delaware corporation and the Fund's special limited partner (the "Special Limited Partner"); and Canadian Imperial Bank of Commerce, a Canadian banking operation ("CIBC").

B. Creation And Terms Of The Fund

According to the complaint, CIBC made a strategic decision to expand its United States investment banking operations in the late 1990s. The plaintiffs allege that by late 2000, CIBC's U.S. operations were under pressure from the "dramatic softening" in market conditions and "commenced a number of schemes" to combat these market conditions.[3] One of those schemes, the plaintiffs allege, involved creation of the Fund. To this end, the plaintiffs describe the Fund as a vehicle created by CIBC to "continue to fund high risk, high yield ventures," "free[] up [CIBC's] capital from underperforming and low return investment, decreasing [*5] its market risk exposure and removing large sources of credit risk from its balance sheet," while at the same time allowing CIBC "an additional way to earn management and other fees including interest on leverage."[4]

The Fund was sold in November 1999 through a Confidential Private Placement Memorandum (the "PPM"),[5] which was supplemented in early 2000 with the Supplement to Private Placement Memoranda (collectively the "Offering Documents"). The Offering Documents provide a more benign explanation for CIBC's creation of the Fund — IBC created the Fund

in late 1999 to enable a select group of the bank's employees to invest alongside CIBC.[6]

The PPM states that the goal of the Fund is to achieve long-term capital [*6] appreciation for investors through investments in three categories: (1) the Trimaran Fund; (2) the Fund of Funds; and (3) Merchant Banking. The Trimaran Fund is a private equity fund run by three senior members of CIBC's high yield investment banking unit. According to the PPM, Trimaran investments are intended to represent between 33% and 50% of the Fund's total capital commitment. The Fund of Funds is a diversified portfolio of primarily private equity investment funds that invest in equity securities. The Fund of Funds is intended to represent between 40% and 57% of the Fund's total capital commitment. Merchant Banking invests in equity securities, typically on a side-by-side basis with CIBC. These investments are intended to represent 10% of the Fund's total commitment. Limited partners are allowed to leverage their investment by taking out loans offered by CIBC. The decision to take out loans is completely voluntary.[7] In addition, CIBC earns a 7% finder's fee for every investment it transfers to the Fund.

In March 2000, the Fund closed with total investor commitments [*7] of $561 million and approximately 490 investors.

C. Governance Of The Fund

The governing document of the Fund is the Amended and Restated Agreement of Limited Partnership, dated March 10, 2000 (the "Partnership Agreement"). Under the Partnership Agreement, the General Partner has the "sole right and power to manage and administer the affairs of the Fund."[8] As outlined in the Partnership Agreement and the PPM, the General Partner is 100% owned by three individuals who make up the General Partner's board of directors (the "Independent Board"). According to the Partnership Agreement and the PPM, each director receives $15,000 per year for serving on the Independent Board. Lord Securities Corporation, which is in the business of providing director services for corporate clients, selected the initial members of the Independent Board. From its inception until October 2004, Sorensen, Christiansen, and Outlaw were the three directors. In October 2004, Sorensen and Christiansen resigned, and Figueroa and Fioravanti replaced them.

Under the terms of section 4.1(a) of the Partnership Agreement, the General Partner must delegate certain of its responsibilities. Pursuant [*8] to this section, the General Partner delegated its authority

---

[3] Compl. PP 36, 39, 42.

[4] Compl. PP 43, 44.

[5] The court may consider documents referred to in the complaint when ruling on motions to dismiss when, as here, those documents are integral to a plaintiff's claim. *See, e.g., In re Santa Fe Pac. Corp. S'holder Litig.,* 669 A.2d 59, 69 (Del. 1995); *In re General Motors (Hughes) S'holder Litig,* No. 20269, 2005 Del. Ch. LEXIS 65, 2005 WL 1089021, at *6-7 (Del. Ch. May 4, 2005); *O'Reilly v. Transworld Healthcare, Inc.,* 745 A.2d 902, 909 n.1 (Del. Ch. 1999).

[6] PPM 1.

[7] *Forsythe v. CIBC Employee Private Equity Fund (U.S.) I, L.P.,* No. 657, 2005 Del. Ch. LEXIS 104, 2005 WL 1653963, at *1 (Del. Ch. July 7, 2005).

[8] P'ship Agmt. § 4.1(a).

to select and dispose of the Fund's investments to the Special Limited Partner. The General Partner also delegated other investment management and related powers, such as exercising the Fund's voting rights in its investments, to the Investment Advisor, pursuant to the terms of an investment advisory services agreement between the Fund and the Investment Advisor (the "Investment Advisory Agreement"). Under the Investment Advisory Agreement, the Investment Advisor also has authority to develop investment policies and strategies and to recommend particular investments for the Fund. The Investment Advisor delegated much of this investment decision authority to CIBC's Investment Committee, which consists of upper level CIBC executives. The Investment Advisor can also buy investments for the Fund, but only with approval of the Special Limited Partner.

According to the Partnership Agreement, the General Partner retains at least one important duty — the delegatees exercise their powers and "perform their duties subject to the oversight of the General Partner."[9] The Partnership Agreement also provides that the General Partner, Investment [*9] Advisor, Special Limited Partner, Independent Board, directors, sub-advisors, and employees of the Independent Board are liable only for actions or omissions resulting from bad faith, willful misconduct, gross negligence, or a material breach of the Partnership Agreement.

D. The Plaintiffs' Allegations

As noted in this court's earlier order, "the Fund did not prosper. This is something of an understatement, as the Fund lost over 75% of its initial value, and over half of its investments have been written down or written off."[10] The complaint alleges that these losses resulted from the defendants' breaches of fiduciary duties.

Generally, the plaintiffs allege that the Fund is designed so that it can "co-invest" with CIBC. Under this design, CIBC's Investment Committee decides on CIBC's behalf to make a particular investment. The Investment Advisor or Special Limited Partner then decides if the investment meets the Fund's eligibility requirements. If the investment meets the Fund's eligibility [*10] requirements, the Investment Advisor or Special Limited Partner invests alongside CIBC on behalf of the Fund.

According to the complaint, however, since late 2000 and continuing to the present, the individuals serving as the Investment Advisor and Special Limited Partner have caused the Fund to make worthless investments. Specifically, the plaintiffs

allege that the CIBC senior executives serving on CIBC's Investment Committee are the same individuals who make up the Investment Advisor and Special Limited Partner. According to the complaint, these CIBC senior executives, sitting as the CIBC Investment Committee, make and continue to make investment decisions for CIBC. When investments lose significant value, these same executives change hats and, sitting as the Special Limited Partner or the Investment Advisor, allegedly approve the Fund's purchase of the same investments from CIBC. The plaintiffs allege the Fund is forced to buy these investments from CIBC at prices equal to CIBC's original cost of investment and pay CIBC a 7% finder's fee. The complaint alleges that CIBC, the Special Limited Partner, and the Investment Advisor have violated and continue to violate their fiduciary [*11] duties to the Fund through this activity.

At the same time, the plaintiffs allege that the General Partner and the Individual Defendants have violated their fiduciary duties to the Fund by abdicating their oversight responsibilities, "[n]ever once question[ing] either the Special Limited Partner, the Investment Advisor, or any other person or entity regarding the investments being made or transferred to the Fund."[11] The plaintiffs further allege that the Investment Advisor, Special Limited Partner, and CIBC have aided and abetted the General Partner's and the Individual Defendants' violations of their fiduciary duties.

1. Merchant Banking

The plaintiffs contend that CIBC initially chose to transfer to the Fund high risk, losing merchant banking investments it purchased in 1999.[12] CIBC's supposed motivation was to move these underperforming investments off its balance sheets and "free up capital" so it could invest that money in "other lucrative" investments,[13] and collect a 7% finder's fee from each transfer. Not only were these investments losing money at the time of the transfers, they allegedly violated the six-year time horizon established for [*12] the Fund, which required that any investments transferred to the Fund be purchased between 2000 and 2006. According to the complaint, the Investment Advisor ratified these transfers "without even a question as to their value," and in violation of its fiduciary duties to the Fund.[14] The plaintiffs similarly allege that the Special Limited Partner ratified other transfers of worthless investments to the Fund. In support, the plaintiffs cite to, among other things, the minutes of the first meeting of the "Co-Invest Advisory Board," which allegedly show that the members of the Special Limited

---

[9] P'ship Agmt. § 4.1(a); see also Inv. Adv. Agmt. P 2(a) (stating that the Investment Advisor provides its services "[s]ubject to the oversight of the General Partner").
[10] Forsythe, 2005 Del. Ch. LEXIS 104, 2005 WL 1653963 at *5.

[11] Compl. PP 76, 182(b-c), (k), (l).
[12] Compl. PP 99, 102.
[13] Compl. P 104.
[14] Compl. P 100.

Partner and Investment Advisor approved, without discussion, the transfer of investments to Merchant Banking.[15] Finally, the plaintiffs allege the Fund has not divested side by side with CIBC, in violation of the Offering Documents.

2. The Fund Of Funds

The plaintiffs allege that CIBC has, through the General Partner and Special Limited Partner, caused the Fund to purchase investments "worth significantly less than the consideration paid by the Fund to CIBC,"[16] invested in the same companies as Merchant Banking, thus violating the restriction [*13] that only 10% of the Fund be in Merchant Banking, and made an investment with a 20-year time horizon, even though the Fund has a time horizon of only six years. In support, the plaintiffs again point to, among other things, the minutes of the first meeting of the "Co-Invest Advisory Board," which allegedly show that the members of the Special Limited Partner and Investment Advisor approved, without discussion, the transfer of investments to the Fund of Funds.[17] The plaintiffs also allege that the Fund has not divested alongside CIBC, in violation of the Offering Documents.

The plaintiffs [*14] allege CIBC has made these investment decisions in order to secure fees from the underlying portfolio companies, and to obtain finder's fees from the Fund.

3. The Trimaran Fund

Turning to the Trimaran Fund, the plaintiffs allege that in 2001, the Trimaran principals, who earned CIBC millions of dollars in profit with their investment in Global Crossing, threatened to leave CIBC if they were not provided with additional seed money for the establishment of a new fund. Confusingly, the complaint states that CIBC decided to appease these demands in 2000, a full year before the threats were even made, by providing the Fund with the opportunity to invest in Trimaran. Regardless of CIBC's motive, the plaintiffs allege that CIBC and the General Partner allowed the Fund to invest in the Trimaran Fund, as well as worthless telecommunications investments, even as CIBC divested itself of them. The complaint, in somewhat conclusory language, alleges that the Fund would not have made these "worthless" telecommunications invest-

ments had the General Partner and the Individual Defendants "properly exercised" their supervisory obligations.[18]

In addition, the plaintiffs allege that in early [*15] 2002, CIBC cut Trimaran off from CIBC's deal flow, in violation of the terms of the PPM. The General Partner, in violation of its fiduciary duties, allegedly did nothing to change the level of the Fund's capital committed to Trimaran.

III.

The plaintiffs sue derivatively, but did not make pre-suit demand. Title 6, section 17-1003 of the Delaware Code therefore requires that the complaint "set forth with particularity . . . the reasons for not making" demand. Delaware courts look to pleading standards developed in the corporate context to determine whether a limited partner has alleged particularized facts satisfying section 17-1003 requirements.[19] The requirement of particularized facts means a "[p]laintiff's pleading burden [in the demand excused context] is more onerous than that required to withstand a Rule 12(b)(6) motion."[20] At this stage in the proceedings, "only well-pleaded allegations of fact must be accepted as true; conclusory allegations of fact or law not supported by allegations of specific facts may not be taken as true."[21]

The Delaware Supreme Court has articulated a two-part test, first developed in *Aronson v. Lewis,* for determining whether demand is excused in a given case.[22] The first step is to determine "whether under the particularized facts alleged, a reasonable doubt is created that . . . the directors are disinterested and independent."[23] The second step is to determine whether the pleading creates a reasonable doubt that "the challenged transaction was otherwise the product of a valid exercise of business judgment."[24]

As the court in *Rales v. Blasband* held, however, where the complaint challenges a board's failure to exercise business judgment, the business judgment rule has no [*17] application and it is impossible to perform the second inquiry.[25] In that situation, "a court must determine whether or not the particularized factual allegations of a derivative stockholder

---

[15] Compl. P 79.

[16] Compl. PP 143, 151.

[17] Compl. P 79. Oddly, the plaintiffs raise no claims against the Investment Advisor with regard to the Fund of Funds, even though the Investment Advisory Agreement provides that "[t]he Investment Advisor shall be responsible for choosing Portfolio Funds and all activities relating to holding such Investments." *Compare* Compl. PP 63-64, 143 (alleging the Investment Advisor delegated its investment authority to CIBC's merchant banking investments and the Trimaran Fund, and that the General Partner and Special Limited Partner made Fund of Funds investments) *with* Inv. Adv. Agmt. P 2(c)(ii).

[18] Compl. P 127.

[19] *Gotham Partners v. Hallwood Realty Partners, L.P.,* No. 15754, 1998 Del. Ch. LEXIS 226, 1998 WL 832631, at *4 (Del. Ch. Nov. 10, 1998) (noting that the limited partner [*16] demand futility pleading standard is "substantially the same as the pleading standard for shareholder plaintiffs") (citing *Littman v. Prudential-Bache Prop., Inc.,* No. 12137, 1993 Del. Ch. LEXIS 13, at *7 (Del. Ch. Jan. 4, 1993)); *Seaford Fund L.P. v. M&M Assoc. II, L.P.,* 672 A.2d 66, 69 (Del. Ch. 1995).

[20] *Levine v. Smith,* 591 A.2d 194, 207 (Del. 1991).

[21] *Grobow v. Perot,* 539 A.2d 180, 187 (Del. 1988).

[22] *Brehm v. Eisner,* 746 A.2d 244, 256 (Del. 2000) (citing *Aronson v. Lewis,* 473 A.2d 805, 814 (Del. 1984)).

[23] *Id.*

[24] *Id.*

[25] 634 A.2d 927, 933 (Del. 1993).

Appendix

complaint create a reasonable doubt that, as of the time the complaint is filed, the board of directors could ... properly exercise[] its independent and disinterested business judgment in responding to a demand."[26] Importantly for this case, allegations of specific facts establishing that "the potential for liability is not 'a mere threat' but instead may rise to 'a substantial likelihood'" create a reasonable doubt as to the board's disinterestedness.[27] The same test will be applied in the context of a demand on the general partner of a limited partnership.[28]

Here, the parties agree that the plaintiffs do not challenge any business judgment made by the General Partner. Rather, the plaintiffs allege that the General Partner failed to act when necessary, and by that failure to act violated its duties to the Fund.[29] Therefore, the *Rales* test applies, and demand will be excused because the particularized facts alleged in the complaint establish that the potential for the General Partner's liability is not a mere threat, but instead rises to a substantial likelihood.

To determine whether the allegations contained in the complaint establish a substantial likelihood of liability, it is essential to first determine the standard of liability governing the General Partner's duty of oversight. The defendants argue that *In re Caremark International Derivative Litigation*[30] provides the applicable standard of liability in this case. As the court in *Stone v. Ritter* stated, *Caremark* "articulates the necessary conditions predicate for director oversight liability."[31] "[I]mposition of liability requires a showing that the directors knew that they were not discharging their [*19] fiduciary obligations."[32]

The plaintiffs argue that *Davenport Group MG, L.P. v. Strategic Investment Partners, Inc.*[33] governs, and imposes a lower standard of oversight liability in the partnership context. According to the plaintiffs, *Davenport* establishes that general partners are "always ultimately responsible for the proper administration of their limited partnerships and their limited partnership agreements, even where they have delegated certain responsibilities."[34] Therefore, the plaintiffs argue, the complaint need not allege that the defendants had knowledge of wrongdoing in

order to establish a substantial likelihood of liability. Rather, the plaintiffs rely on *Davenport* and agency law for the proposition that "the misconduct of a general partner's delegatees is imputed to the general partner, even when notice of such acts is never actually communicated to the general partner."[35]

The defendants respond that *Davenport* is consistent with *Caremark,* and does not create a new standard of oversight liability [*20] applicable to the partnership context.[36] Rather, the defendants argue, the court in *Davenport* merely assumed the general partner's knowledge of wrongdoing, and proceeded to the second prong of *Caremark,* finding that the general partner took no steps to prevent or remedy the situation.[37] As such, they argue, *Davenport* did nothing more than apply the *Caremark* test, even if it did not explicitly say it was doing so (if only because *Davenport* preceded *Caremark* by approximately eight months).

Neither *Caremark* nor *Davenport,* however, is determinative. In this case, the Partnership Agreement, not the common law, provides the proper standard of liability. "[W]here the parties have a more or less elaborated statement of their respective rights and duties, absent fraud, those rights and duties, where they apply by their terms, and not the vague language of a default fiduciary duty, will be the metric for determining breach of duty."[38]

Here, the structure contemplated by the Partnership Agreement and the PPM leave the General Partner with only one substantive duty, *i.e.* the duty to oversee the activities of the CIBC-related entities that actually manage the affairs of the partnership. Section 4.1 of the Partnership Agreement states that the Investment Advisor and Special Limited Partner, *inter alia,* "exercise [their] powers and perform [their] duties subject to the oversight of the General Partner." Similarly, paragraph [*22] 2 of the Investment Advisory Agreement states that the Investment Advisor performs its duties "[s]ubject to the oversight of the General Partner." The Partnership Agreement also outlines the standard that governs the General Partner's discharge of its duty of oversight. Specifi-

---

[26] *Id.* at 934.

[27] *Id.* at 936.

[28] Cf. *In re Cencom Cable Income Partners,* No. 14634, 2000 WL 130629, at *4 (Del. Ch. Jan. 27, 2000) (applying the *Aronson* test in a partnership context); *Dean v. Dick,* No. 16566, 1999 WL 413400, at *2 (Del. Ch. June 10, 1999) (same); *Katell v. Morgan Stanley Group Inc.,* No. 12343, 1993 WL 10871, at *5 (Del. Ch. Jan. 14, 1993) (applying "the demand excused analysis in our corporation [*18] law" to a claim brought against a partnership).

[29] Defs.' Br. 20; Pls.' Br. 21-22.

[30] 698 A.2d 959 (Del. Ch. 1996).

[31] 911 A.2d 362, 370 (Del. 2006) (emphasis added).

[32] *Id.*

[33] 685 A.2d 715, 721 (Del. Ch. 1996).

[34] June 12, 2007 Letter from Plaintiffs at 6.

---

[35] *Id.* at 7.

[36] June 7, 2007 Letter from Defendants at 3.

[37] *Id.*

[38] *Cantor Fitzgerald, L.P. v. Cantor,* No. 18101, 2001 Del. Ch. LEXIS 137, at *17 (Del. Ch. Nov. 5, 2001) (citing *In re Marriott Hotel Prop. II L.P. Unitholders Litig.,* No. 14961, 1996 Del. Ch. LEXIS 60, at *16 (Del. Ch. June 12, 1996)); [*21] see also *Gotham Partners,* 2000 WL 1476663 at *10 ("Where the Partnership Agreement provides the standard that will govern the duty owed by a General Partner to his partners in self-dealing transactions, it is the contractual standard and not the default fiduciary duty of loyalty's fairness standard that exclusively controls."); *Wilmington Leasing, Inc. v. Parrish Leasing Co., L.P.,* No. 15202, 1996 Del. Ch. LEXIS 155, at *44 (Del. Ch. Dec. 23, 1996) ("Where, as here, a Partnership Agreement specifically addresses the rights and duties of the partners, any fiduciary duty that might be owed by the Limited Partners is satisfied by compliance with the applicable provisions of the partnership agreement.").

cally, section 12.1 states the General Partner is liable for acts or omissions resulting from bad faith, willful misconduct, gross negligence, or a material breach of the Partnership Agreement.

The defendants argue that the complaint does not adequately allege that the General Partner breached its duty of oversight. They urge the court to adopt a *Caremark*-based standard requiring well-pleaded allegations of fact reasonably supporting an inference that the General Partner knowingly failed to discharge its fiduciary obligations. *Caremark* requires such a showing in the context of a board of directors generally involved in the management of the business and affairs of a corporate enterprise. But there is less reason to insist on such a showing of knowing misconduct in the case of a general partner whose only substantial duty is to monitor the faithful performance of third parties who themselves occupy inherently conflicted [*23] positions.

Caremark rests importantly on the observation that corporate boards sit atop command-style management structures in which those to whom management duties are delegated generally owe their loyalty to the corporation.[39] In that context, boards of directors are presumed to discharge their oversight responsibilities by adopting internal reporting and compliance systems that function to bring problems to the attention of senior managers and the directors themselves.[40] As the Delaware Supreme Court recently held, where such a system is implemented, directors will be potentially liable for breach of their oversight duty only if they ignore "red flags" that actually come to their attention, warning of compliance problems.[41] That is to say that, with an effective compliance system in place, corporate directors are entitled to believe that, unless red flags surface, corporate officers and employees are exercising their delegated corporate powers in the best interest of the corporation.

In the context presented in this case, the *Caremark* duty of oversight analysis is missing one or more major premise. Instead of a board of directors sitting atop a command-style management structure of persons legally required to act loyally to the corporation, there is a nominally independent general partner that has delegated nearly all of its managerial responsibilities to conflicted entities who act through persons employed by and loyal to a third [*25] party. There is no command-style system of management reporting up to the General Partner, and the General Partner had no reason to believe that the Special Limited Partner or the Investment Advisor, entities made up of persons whose primary loyalty was and is to CIBC, would likely exercise their delegated duties in a manner that was loyal to the partnership. In the circumstances, the duty of oversight created by the Partnership Agreement is better understood as imposing on the General Partner an active obligation, at a minimum, to take steps to satisfy itself that the Special Limited Partner and the Investment Advisor actually discharge their delegated duties in compliance with the Partnership Agreement and in a manner loyal to the partnership.

Albert v. Alex Brown Management Services is instructive in this regard.[42] In *Alex Brown*, this court denied the defendants' motion to dismiss two complaints that alleged the general partners of two funds had failed to discharge their supervision and oversight duties. Those complaints alleged that both funds were faced with "exceptional challenges, first by the sharply rising value of the securities that made up the Funds, and second by the rapid [*26] fall in value of those same securities."[43] Those complaints alleged that the general partners met less than once a year during this time of turmoil, and took no action to protect the unitholders' investments. At the same time, the complaints alleged, the general partners received millions of dollars in fees for "doing almost nothing."[44] The partnership agreements in *Alex Brown* made the general partners liable for, among other things, gross negligence. This court, while recognizing that "whether the [general partners of a partnership] exercised the requisite amount of due care in managing the Funds is, of course, a fact sensitive inquiry," found that those alleged facts raised a duty of care claim sufficient to survive a motion to dismiss.[45]

Here, the allegations in the complaint paint a more particular and detailed picture of possible gross negligence or material breach of the Partnership Agreement than the allegations in *Alex Brown*. The facts alleged in the complaint indicate that the General Partner knew of its duty to oversee [*27] its delegatees — that duty is clearly stated in the Offering Documents and the Partnership Agreement. Further, as in *Alex Brown*, the complaint alleges that, despite a precipitous drop in the Fund's value and annual compensation of $15,000 to each Individual Defendant, the General Partner took no steps to

---

[39] As Chancellor Allen observed in *Caremark*, "[m]ost of the decisions that a corporation, acting through its human agents, makes are, of course, not the subject of directors' attention. Legally, the [*24] board will be required only to authorize the most significant corporate acts or transactions: mergers, changes in capital structure, fundamental changes in business, appointment and compensation of the CEO, etc." 698 A.2d at 968.

[40] *See Caremark*, 698 A.2d at 970 (expressing the view that corporate boards cannot be properly informed "without assuring themselves that information and reporting systems exist in the organization that are reasonably designed to provide to senior management and to the board itself timely, accurate information sufficient to allow management and the board, each in its own scope, to reach informed judgments concerning both the corporation's compliance with law and its business performance").

[41] *Stone*, 911 A.2d at 370.

[42] *See* No. 762, No. 763, 2005 Del. Ch. LEXIS 133, at *19-20 (Del. Ch. Aug. 26, 2005).

[43] *Alex Brown*, 2005 Del. Ch. LEXIS 133 at *19-20.

[44] 2005 Del. Ch. LEXIS 133 at *20.

[45] 2005 Del. Ch. LEXIS 133 at *19.

inquire into the investment decisions of the Investment Advisor and Special Limited Partner.[46] The defendants' argument that the plaintiffs "have no basis for alleging that the General Partner 'did nothing' other than the fact that there were no documents demonstrating otherwise produced in the Books and Records Action"[47] is incorrect. Rather, the plaintiffs allege that the General Partner has "[n]ever once questioned either the Special Limited Partner, the Investment Advisor, or any other person or entity regarding the investments being made or transferred to the Fund" and "[n]ever once asked for any of the underlying material to determine whether the investments in effect being sold to the Fund were being transferred at a fair and reasonable price, or [took] any steps to determine whether the Investment Advisor was fulfilling its duty of ensuring that any transactions with CIBC [*28] were transferred at a fair and reasonable price . . . ."[48] The plaintiffs also allege that the General Partner allowed the Fund to continue investing in Trimaran even after CIBC cut Trimaran off from CIBC's deal flow, in violation of the PPM.

Additionally, the plaintiffs allege that the General Partner at most had only annual meetings at which its directors signed off on the Fund's tax returns, and otherwise took action only in one instance of a defaulting limited partner. Moreover, the complaint alleges that the General Partner allowed the Investment Advisor and Special Limited Partner to be composed of high level CIBC officers without, until February 4, 2004, implementing formal policies governing conflict management. And the plaintiffs allege that the General Partner, as a creation of Lord Securities and partially owned by Lord Securities' president, had a motive to abdicate its duties, namely, to curry more business [*29] from its regular client, CIBC.[49]

Finally, contrary to the defendants' argument that the plaintiffs have failed to identify a single overvalued investment sold to the Fund, or a proposed investment that did not meet the Fund's criteria, the plaintiffs identify at least two investments the defendants approved even though the investments were clearly outside the Fund's time horizon. The plaintiffs also allege the Fund lost 75% of its value quickly after its inception. While in general the decrease in value of a fund is, without

more, insufficient on its own to support an inference of mismanagement, the decline in this case, when considered with the rest of the plaintiffs' allegations, supports such an inference.

The General Partner was required to make at least some effort to oversee the Fund in order to properly discharge its duties. The facts [*30] alleged in the complaint are sufficient to support an inference that the General Partner exercised no oversight, and create a substantial likelihood of the General Partner's liability for gross negligence in discharging its oversight duty, or material breach of the Partnership Agreement. For these reasons, demand will be excused.

IV.

The defendants argue that the facts of the complaint do not state a claim for which relief can be granted. In order to dismiss a claim under Court of Chancery Rule 12(b)(6), a court "'must determine with reasonable certainty that, under any set of facts that could be proven to support the claims asserted, the plaintiffs would not be entitled to relief.'" [50] "When making its decision, a court must accept as true all well pleaded factual allegations in the complaint and all reasonable inferences to be drawn from those facts."[51] Still, a court need not "'blindly accept as true all allegations, nor must it draw all inferences from them in plaintiff's favor unless they are reasonable inferences.'"[52]

A.   [*31] Claims Against The Investment Advisor And The Special Limited Partner

The defendants argue that the plaintiffs have failed to state a claim for breach of fiduciary duty against the Special Limited Partner because the plaintiffs have not identified a single individual investment that was overvalued at the time of its transfer to the Fund. Therefore, the defendants conclude, the plaintiffs have not alleged facts with sufficient particularity to support an inference that they are entitled to relief.

As noted above, the Partnership Agreement, not the common law, provides the proper standard of liability in this case.[53] Section 12.1 of the Partnership Agreement makes the Special Limited Partner liable for acts or omission resulting from bad faith, willful misconduct, gross negligence, or in material breach of the Partnership Agreement or the Investment Advisory Agreement. In order to survive a motion to dismiss, the complaint must contain facts that, if taken as true, support an inference that the Special

---

[46] Compl. P 182(b).

[47] Defs.' Reply 14; Defs.' Br. 20 n.8. The defendants rightly point out that the reason the plaintiffs have no such documents is simply because the plaintiffs did not ask for them in the Books and Records Action. *Id.*

[48] Compl. PP 76, 182(b-c), (k), (l).

[49] Pls.' Br. 32 n.32; *Guttman v. Huang,* 823 A.2d 492, 498, 503 (Del. Ch. 2003) (finding that plaintiff was required to make demand because complaint failed to allege, among other things, how often or when the audit committee met, how often and how long it met, who advised the committee, or a reasonable motive for the allegedly wrongful behavior).

[50] *Orloff v. Shulman,* No. 852, 2005 Del. Ch. LEXIS 184, 2005 WL 3272355, at *7 (Del. Ch. Nov. 23, 2005) (quoting *Grobow,* 539 A.2d at 187 n.6).

[51] *Id.*

[52] *Id.* (quoting *Grobow,* 539 A.2d at 187).

[53] *Cantor Fitzgerald,* 2001 Del. Ch. LEXIS 137 at *17.

Limited Partner acted with gross negligence or in material breach of the Partnership Agreement.

The plaintiffs have alleged such facts. [*32] For instance, the plaintiffs have alleged, with some specificity, that the Special Limited Partner ratified investments without independent discussion or consideration.[54] The plaintiffs also allege that the Special Limited Partner has not divested the Fund's assets alongside CIBC, as the Offering Documents contemplate.[55] Additionally, the plaintiffs have identified two investments in which the Special Limited Partner allowed the Fund to invest even though the investments did not fit the time horizon of the Fund. These facts, taken as true, support a reasonable inference that the Special Limited Partner acted grossly negligently or in contravention of the Partnership Agreement. The plaintiffs need not, at least at the pleading stage, also identify a specific overvalued investment in order to survive a motion to dismiss. For these reasons, the motion to dismiss Count I against the Special Limited Partner will be denied.

The defendants also argue that the Investment Advisor does not owe fiduciary duties to the Fund. A fiduciary relationship arises in a situation where one person reposes special trust in, and reliance on, the judgment of another, or where a special duty exists on the part of one person to protect the interests of another.[56] In contrast, a straightforward, arm's-length commercial relationship arising from contract does not give rise to fiduciary duties.[57] The defendants argue that, likewise, Delaware fiduciary duties are not implicated where "there is an express agreement that one party is acting in the capacity of 'independent contractor.'"[58] Because the Investment Advisor is identified in the Investment Advisory Agreement as an independent contractor, the defendants argue, it cannot owe fiduciary duties to the Fund.

Neither case cited by the defendants, however, creates such a per se rule. Indeed, the court in Total Care Physicians v. O'Hara imposed fiduciary duties

on a defendant even though he was an independent contractor.[59] The plaintiffs allege in the complaint, and the Offering Documents show, that the Investment Advisor, as a delegatee of the General Partner, ratified investment decisions, and had authority to purchase and sell investments for the Fund. This case is analogous, then, to Goodrich v. E.F. Hutton Group, Inc., which held that "a broker with the authority to buy and sell securities" is a fiduciary.[60] The plaintiffs have therefore adequately alleged that the Investment Advisor owes a fiduciary duty to the Fund.[61]

Defendants make no other arguments as to Count I against the Investment [*35] Advisor, and the facts alleged, if true, support a reasonable inference that the Investment Advisor breached its fiduciary duty. Specifically, as in the allegations against the Special Limited Partner, the plaintiffs allege with some specificity that the Investment Advisor ratified investments without independent discussion or consideration.[62] It is alleged that the Investment Advisor has not divested the Fund's assets alongside CIBC, as the Offering Documents contemplate. And the plaintiffs have identified two investments in which the Investment Advisor allowed the Fund to invest even though the investments did not fit the time horizon of the Fund. For these reasons, the motion to dismiss Count I against the Investment Advisor will be denied.

Finally, the defendants point out that the plaintiffs failed to brief their claims that the Investment Advisor and Special Limited Partner aided and abetted the General Partner's breach of its oversight duties.[63] The plaintiffs have waived these claims by failing to brief them in their opposition to the motion to dismiss.[64] For these reasons, the motion to dismiss these claims will be granted.

B. Claims Against The General Partner And Individual Defendants

The defendants argue that the claims against Individual Defendants Figueroa and Fioravanti must be dismissed because all of the alleged wrongdoing, namely, making investments at the time around the Fund's inception, occurred before they became Independent Directors. Therefore, the defendants argue, there are no allegations that they committed any wrongdoing. The court agrees. Nothing in the complaint supports an inference of wrongdoing after

---

[54] See Compl. PP 72, 79 (referring to testimony of Tanya Carmichael, a CIBC employee, that the Special Limited Partner and Investment Advisor relied on the CIBC Investment Committee's initial approval when making investment decisions for the Fund).

[55] Although the Offering [*33] Documents do say that the Fund may divest and invest apart from CIBC and may make investments with no operating history, a fair reading of those provisions show these situations are to be the exception, not the rule.

[56] Prestancia Mgt. Group, Inc. v. Virginia Heritage Found., II L.L.C., No. 1032-S, 2005 Del. Ch. LEXIS 80, 2005 WL 1364616, at *6 (Del. Ch. May 27, 2005) (citing Metro Ambulance Inc. v. E. Med. Billing, Inc., No. 13929, 1995 WL 409015, at *2-3 (Del. Ch. July 5, 1995)).

[57] Wal-Mart Stores, Inc. v. AIG Life Ins. Co., 901 A.2d 106, 113-114 (Del. 2006) [*34] (discussing difference between duties owed by a broker that can bind its principal and duties arising from a "normal, arm's-length business relationship"); McMahon v. New Castle Assoc., 532 A.2d 601, 605 (Del. Ch. 1987).

[58] Defs.' Reply 16.

[59] 798 A.2d 1043, 1058-59 (Del. Super. 2001).

[60] No. 8279, 1991 Del. Ch. LEXIS 93, 1991 WL 101367, at *2 (Del. Ch. June 7, 1991) (citing Warwick v. Addicks, 35 Del. 43, 5 W.W. Harr. 43, 157 A. 205 (Del. Super. 1931)).

[61] Id.

[62] Compl. PP 64-66, 79.

[63] Defs.' Reply 19 n.9; Pls.' [*36] Br. 40-41.

[64] See Emerald Partners v. Berlin, No. 9700, 2003 WL 21003437, at *43 (Del. Ch. Apr. 28, 2003) (stating "[i]t is settled Delaware law that a party waives an argument by not including it in its brief").

2004. In fact, the only specific allegation identified in the complaint that post-dates 2004 is that the Fund developed policies governing conflict management in February 2004, an allegation running counter to Figueroa and Fioravanti's liability. Count I against them will be dismissed.

The motion to dismiss Count I against the General Partner, however, will be denied. As noted previously, a "[p]laintiff's pleading burden [in the demand excused context] is more onerous than that [*37] required to withstand a Rule 12(b)(6) motion."[65] Having pled allegations with regard to the General Partner's gross negligence or material breach of the Partnership Agreement in overseeing the Fund sufficient to excuse demand, the complaint also withstands a Rule 12(b)(6) attack. Further, for the same reasons discussed earlier with regard to demand, the facts alleged in the complaint support a reasonable inference that the remaining Individual Defendants (Sorensen, Christiansen, and Outlaw) breached their duties, and the motion to dismiss Count I against them will be denied.

Finally, the plaintiffs failed to brief their claim that the Individual Defendants aided and abetted the General Partner's breach of its oversight duties.[66] The plaintiffs have waived this claim by failing to brief it in their opposition to the motion to dismiss, and the claim will be dismissed.[67]

C. Claims Against CIBC

The plaintiffs assert that CIBC acts as the Fund's investment advisor, and therefore owes fiduciary duties to the Fund. Their lone allegation supporting this position is that the Special [*38] Limited Partner's decisions are "subject to approval by CIBC's Investment Committee."[68] The defendants are correct that the plaintiffs' assertion is at odds with the language of the Offering Documents.[69] The Offering Documents require only that the CIBC Investment Committee invest in an investment before the Special Limited Partner does the same. Nothing in the Offering Documents subjects the Special Limited Partner's decisions to the CIBC Investment Committee's approval. Therefore, the plaintiffs' allegation does not support an inference that CIBC functioned as an investment advisor, or in any other relationship of trust, to the Fund.

The plaintiffs also allege that CIBC is the *de facto* general partner of the Fund and owes the Fund fiduciary duties because CIBC controls the Investment Advisor and the Special Limited Partner.[70] The plaintiffs point to *Tapps of Nassau Supermarkets,*

Inc. v. Linden Boulevard L.P.[71] in support of their assertion that a party not named as a general partner nonetheless assumes the liabilities of the general partner if it controls the limited partner's activities. *Tapps,* however, is inapposite.

Tapps involved a limited partnership that subleased real estate. There, the limited partner was not only the sole stockholder of the general partner, but also conducted business for the limited partnership on behalf of the general partner. Specifically, the limited partner negotiated leases for the partnership, acted as the partnership's attorney, collected rent on behalf of the partnership, referred to herself in negotiations with sub-lessees as the "landlord," and arranged for repairs of the limited partnership's properties.[72] Because she conducted all the partnership's activities, she could not shield herself from liability by claiming status as a limited partner.

In this case, however, CIBC is not a stockholder of the General Partner. In fact, as this court has previously found, the General Partner is independent of CIBC.[73] Most importantly, in contrast to *Tapps,* there are no allegations that CIBC conducts all of the Fund's activities. Specifically, the General Partner has the duty to monitor and oversee the Fund. Also, the General Partner can remove the Investment Advisor on 120 days notice. Although [*40] the plaintiffs claim that CIBC has used the Fund to off-load non-performing investments, the plaintiffs have made no allegations sufficient to infer that there was a "pervasive disregard of corporate formalities" such that the court should pierce the corporate veil between the Fund and CIBC.[74] Therefore, the plaintiffs have not established that CIBC is the Fund's *de facto* general partner, or that CIBC owes the Fund fiduciary duties. For these reasons, Count I against CIBC for breach of fiduciary duty will be dismissed.

Finally, the plaintiffs allege that CIBC aided and abetted the breaches of the General Partner, the Investment Advisor, and the Special Limited Partner.[75] In order to establish aiding and abetting liability, the plaintiffs must allege: (1) a fiduciary

---

[65] *Levine,* 591 A.2d at 207.

[66] Defs.' Reply 19 n.9; Pls.' Br. 40-41.

[67] *See Emerald Partners,* 2003 WL 21003437 at *43.

[68] Pls.' Br. 38.

[69] Pls.' Br. 38; Defs.' Reply 17.

[70] Compl. PP [*39] 169-173.

[71] 242 A.D.2d 235, 661 N.Y.S.2d 223 (N.Y. App. Div. 1997) (applying Delaware law).

[72] *Id.* at 237.

[73] *Forsythe,* 2005 Del. Ch. LEXIS 104, 2005 WL 1653963 at *7.

[74] *Id.* (citing *Mobil Oil Corp. v. Linear Films, Inc.,* 718 F. Supp. 260, 268 (D. Del. 1989)).

[75] In fairness, the plaintiffs allege in the complaint that CIBC aided and abetted only the General Partner's breach of fiduciary duty, not the Individual Defendants', Investment Advisor's or Special Limited Partner's breach of fiduciary duty. However, the parties have briefed the claim that CIBC aided and abetted the Special Limited Partner's and Investment Advisor's breaches of fiduciary duty. *See* Pls.' Br. 40. As there is no prejudice to the defendants, and because "the facts pled in the complaint clearly support such a theory of relief," the court treats Count II of the complaint as implicitly raising such a claim. *RGC Int'l Invest., LDC v. Greka Energy Corp.,* No. 17674, 2000 WL 1706728, at *1 n.1 (Del. Ch. Nov. 8, 2000) (citing *Brehm,* 746 A.2d at 267). The parties have not, however, briefed whether CIBC aided and abetted the Individual Defendants' breaches, and therefore this claim is not considered.

Appendix

relationship; (2) the fiduciary breached its duty; (3) knowing participation in a breach; and (4) damages.[76] The defendants argue that the plaintiffs have failed to establish that CIBC knowingly participated in the breaches of the General Partner, the Investment Advisor, and the Special Limited [*41] Partner. The plaintiffs respond that the court in *In re Nantucket Island Associates L.P. Unitholders Litigation* found "knowing participation" in even more attenuated circumstances than these.[77]

Knowing [*42] participation in a fiduciary's breach of its duties "requires that the third party act with the knowledge that the conduct advocated or assisted constitutes such a breach."[78] A court can infer a non-fiduciary's knowing participation if "a fiduciary breaches its duty in an inherently wrongful manner, and the plaintiff alleges specific facts from which that court could reasonably infer knowledge of the breach."[79]

In *Nantucket,* limited partners brought suit against the limited partnership's general partner. The limited partnership owned a portfolio of properties on Nantucket Island, Massachusetts, but was struggling under $25 million of debt. To raise cash and eliminate debt, the general partner decided to offer the limited partners the opportunity to purchase "preferred units" in the limited partnership. These preferred units received priority in distributions from the limited partnership, and sold for $13,333 each. The general partner then purchased 83% of the preferred units through an entity it owned called "Zero Main."

When the limited partnership [*43] sold its property, the general partner received an overwhelming percentage of the sale price because it owned, through Zero Main, 83% of the preferred shares. The limited partners sued the general partner for, *inter alia,* self-dealing, and sued Zero Main for knowing participation in the general partner's breaches. The court found it could infer Zero Main's knowledge of the general partner's breaches because: (1) the general partner created Zero Main to purchase the preferred units; and (2) the general partner was the primary investor in Zero Main.[80] In other words, the persons who made Zero Main's decision to purchase the preferred units were the same persons who caused the general partner to breach its duty to disclose. Therefore, the court could infer Zero Main's knowledge of the general partner's breaches of fiduciary duty.

This is analogous to the relationship between the Special Limited Partner, the Investment Advisor,

and CIBC. CIBC created the Fund and populated the Fund's decision-making entities with CIBC's own employees. Thus, the same individuals who have made the Fund's investment decisions are also high-level CIBC executives. These investment [*44] decisions form the basis of the plaintiffs' breach of fiduciary duty claims. Therefore, the court may infer CIBC's knowledge of the Special Limited Partner's and Investment Advisor's breaches of fiduciary duty. The court may not, however, infer CIBC's knowledge of the General Partner's breaches because, as already discussed, the General Partner is independent of CIBC.[81] For these reasons, the motion to dismiss Count II as to CIBC will be denied in part, and granted in part.

V.

The defendants next argue that the plaintiffs' claims are barred by the statute of limitations, or by laches. The plaintiffs, however, advance two bases on which the court should toll the statute of limitations: equitable tolling and fraudulent concealment.

As the plaintiffs point out, the Court of Chancery, a court of equity, "does not strictly apply statutes of limitations."[82] The court instead applies the doctrine of laches and "uses analogous statutes of limitations as a presumptive time period for application of laches to bar [*45] a claim."[83] A three-year statute of limitations applies to breach of fiduciary duty claims.[84] However, the court avoids inflexible or arbitrary application of a statute of limitations.[85] Therefore, the limitations period will be tolled where "the facts of the underlying claim [are] so hidden that a reasonable plaintiff could not timely discover them."[86]

The doctrine of equitable tolling "stops the statute from running while a plaintiff has reasonably relied upon the competence and good faith of a fiduciary."[87] No evidence of actual concealment is necessary, "but the statute is only tolled until the investor 'knew or had reason to know of the facts constituting the [*46] wrong.'"[88] Reasonable reliance

---

[76] *In re General Motors (Hughes),* 2005 Del. Ch. LEXIS 65, 2005 WL 1089021 at *23.

[77] 810 A.2d 351 (Del. Ch. 2002).

[78] *Malpiede v. Townson,* 780 A.2d 1075, 1097-98 (Del. 2001).

[79] *Nebenzahl v. Miller,* No. 13206, 1996 WL 494913, at *7 (Del. Ch. Aug. 29, 1996).

[80] *In re Nantucket,* 810 A.2d at 376.

[81] For the same reason, a claim against CIBC for aiding and abetting the Individual Defendants' breaches of fiduciary duty, had it been briefed or considered in this motion, would fail.

[82] *Franklin Balance Sheet Inv. Fund v. Crowley,* No. 888, 2006 Del. Ch. LEXIS 188, 2006 WL 3095952, at *6 (Del. Ch. Oct. 19, 2006) (citing *U.S. Cellular Inc. Co. of Allentown v. Bell Atl. Mobile Sys., Inc.,* 677 A.2d 497, 502 (Del. 1996)).

[83] *Id.* (citing *Orloff,* 2005 Del. Ch. LEXIS 184, 2005 WL 3272355 at *10).

[84] *In re Tyson Foods, Inc. Consl. S'holder Litig.,* 919 A.2d 563, 584 (Del. Ch. 2007).

[85] *Franklin Balance Sheet,* 2006 Del. Ch. LEXIS 188, 2006 WL 3095952 at *6 (citing *Orloff,* 2005 Del. Ch. LEXIS 184, 2005 WL 3272355 at *10).

[86] *In re Dean Witter P'ship Litig.,* No. 14816, 1998 Del. Ch. LEXIS 133, 1998 WL 442456, at *5 (Del. Ch. July 17, 1998).

[87] *In re Tyson Foods,* 919 A.2d at 586.

[88] *Id.* (citing *In re Dean Witter,* 1998 Del. Ch. LEXIS 133, 1998 WL 442456 at *6).

on the competence and good faith of fiduciaries can toll the running of the statute of limitations, but "the trusting plaintiff must still be *reasonably attentive* to his interests."[89] Thus, a plaintiff is on inquiry notice "when the information underlying [the] plaintiff's claim is readily available."[90]

Fraudulent concealment exists where a defendant "knowingly acted to prevent a plaintiff from learning facts or otherwise made misrepresentations intended to 'put the plaintiff off the trail of inquiry.'"[91] This requires an "affirmative act of concealment by a defendant."[92]

"A court considering timeliness as a basis for a motion to dismiss must draw the same plaintiff-friendly inferences required in a [Rule] 12(b)(6) analysis."[93] This, however, "does not govern [the] assertion of tolling exceptions to the operation of a statute of limitations (or the running of the analogous period for purposes of a laches analysis). [*47] . . ."[94] Rather, "[a] plaintiff asserting a tolling exception must plead facts supporting the applicability of that exception."[95] Further, on a motion to dismiss an action as untimely, the court may consider two types of evidence outside the complaint without converting the motion to dismiss into a motion for summary judgment: "(a) documents expressly referred to and relied upon in the complaint itself, and (b) documents that are required by law to be filed, and are actually filed, with federal or state officials."[96]

In this case, the plaintiffs have shown that, for the purposes of this motion, the statute of limitations was tolled until April 2002. The plaintiffs allege they had no knowledge or reason to know that the Fund purchased worthless or improper investments at its inception because the Offering Documents provided names of the Fund's investments, but did not include valuation or time horizon information for these investments. Indeed, the plaintiffs allege they could not obtain [*48] this valuation and time horizon information from the Offering Documents or elsewhere because of the unique nature of the investments.[97] Instead, the plaintiffs allege they reasonably relied upon the Offering Documents' promises that the Fund's fiduciaries would make investments

competently and in good faith. As indicated earlier, the plaintiffs were entitled to rely on their fiduciaries in this respect.[98] Therefore, the plaintiffs were not on inquiry notice at the inception of the Fund.

The defendants contend, however, that the General Partner's quarterly reports put the plaintiffs' on notice of their claims as early as May 2001.[99] In support, the defendants note that the General Partner made all the disclosures it was obligated to make under the Partnership Agreement, and the reports showed that the Fund was losing money. The defendants' argument that equitable tolling cannot apply because the General Partner made all the disclosures the Partnership [*49] Agreement obligated it to make, however, misses the mark. The issue is not whether the General Partner improperly failed to make some disclosure. Indeed, the court is reluctant to find that the General Partner acted improperly simply by making disclosures consistent with the Partnership Agreement's mandates. Rather, the question is when were the plaintiffs on notice that the Fund was making worthless and improper investments.

In this case, the disclosures the defendants point to were made on an income tax basis and did not put the plaintiffs on inquiry notice. Those disclosures did not tell the plaintiffs what they needed to know — the real value of the investments.[100] The defendants do not argue otherwise. Thus, prior to the substantial write-offs reported in April 2002, the plaintiffs knew only what the Fund had paid for its investments, not what those investments were worth on a GAAP basis. Moreover, to the extent these quarterly reports disclosed that the Fund was losing money, the plaintiffs point out that the markets were generally depressed and the reports explicitly blamed the losses on this fact. The quarterly reports, therefore, only put the plaintiffs on [*50] notice that the Fund's investments were suffering losses because of market conditions, not because the Fund had overpaid for improper or worthless investments. Nor is this a case, as in *Dean Witter,* where the Fund's valuation information was public information, or was alleged to be properly disclosed but then contradicted elsewhere by the fiduciary.

The plaintiffs have alleged facts supporting the conclusion that it was not until April 2002, when they received the first annual report indicating the Fund had taken substantial write-offs of the investments (meaning the investments had been sold at a loss, thereby revealing the true value of those investments), that they had facts sufficient to put them on notice of wrongdoing with regard to management of the Fund. Only at this point should the plaintiffs have known to inquire whether the Special Limited

---

[89] *In re Dean Witter,* 1998 Del. Ch. LEXIS 133, 1998 WL 442456 at *8.

[90] *Id.*

[91] *State ex rel. Brady v. Pettinaro Enters.,* 870 A.2d 513, 531 (Del. Ch. 2005).

[92] *In re Dean Witter,* 1998 Del. Ch. LEXIS 133, 1998 WL 442456 at *5.

[93] *Pettinaro Enter.,* 870 A.2d at 524-25.

[94] *Id.* at 525; *In re Dean Witter,* 1998 Del. Ch. LEXIS 133, 1998 WL 442456 at *6 n.44.

[95] *Id.* at 525 (citing *In re Dean Witter,* 1998 Del. Ch. LEXIS 133, 1998 WL 44256 at *6).

[96] *In re Tyson Foods,* 919 A.2d at 585.

[97] Compl. P 237; *see also Forsythe,* 2005 Del. Ch. LEXIS 104, 2005 WL 1653963 at *5 (stating "the Fund is comprised of several non-typical investments which make valuing the plaintiffs' interest in the Fund difficult").

[98] *In re Dean Witter,* 1998 Del. Ch. LEXIS 133, 1998 Del. Ch. LEXIS 133, 1998 WL 442456 at *8.

[99] Defs.' Br. 44.

[100] The disclosures on the website did not put plaintiffs on notice for the same reason. *See* Compl. PP 197-198, 217.

Partner and Investment Advisor had breached their duties by recommending improper or worthless investments for the Fund, and whether the General Partner and Individual Defendants had allowed them to do so by abdicating their [*51] duties of oversight. Therefore, for purposes of this motion, the statute of limitations in this case was equitably tolled until April 2002 and the plaintiffs' February 11, 2005 filing was timely. "At trial, [the] defendants will have the opportunity to present evidence to show that [the] plaintiffs were, in fact, on inquiry notice."[101]

Having found that the claims were equitably tolled, this court need not address the fraudulent concealment issue. The court points out, however, its reluctance to hold, as the plaintiffs request, that the defendants committed affirmative acts of concealment simply by making disclosures on an income tax basis as the Partnership Agreement mandated.

VI.

Finally, the defendants argue that the Offering Documents and Partnership Agreement disclosed the investments the Fund intended to make, the terms of the loans and management fees, that certain transactions would involve conflicts of interest, and that the Fund might not invest and divest alongside CIBC in every instance. Therefore, the defendants conclude, the plaintiffs have waived their right to object to alleged wrongdoing in connection with these issues because they [*52] had "complete" knowledge prior to investing.

"Waiver is the voluntary and intentional relinquishment of a known right."[102] As the court in *Werner, M.D. v. Miller Technology Management, L.P.* explained, "in some instances, disclosure . . . may preclude a claim for breach of the duty of loyalty [or care]."[103] The disclosure, however, must be specific. "It is well established that a stockholder cannot complain of corporate action in which, *with full knowledge of all the facts,* he or she has concurred."[104] "[I]t cannot be said . . . that the boiler plate disclosures . . . convey full knowledge of all the facts."[105]

The defendants' arguments that the plaintiffs have waived their rights are unpersuasive. Here, as in *Werner,* it cannot be said that the disclosures conveyed full knowledge of all the facts. Specifically, the plaintiffs have not waived their right to challenge that the investments were improper or worthless when made because, as [*53] the plaintiffs point out, they lacked knowledge as to the investments' propriety or worth. As noted previously, the plaintiffs saw only a list of investments, not values or time horizons, prior to investing in the Fund. The court declines to accept the defendants' invitation to impose upon the plaintiffs a duty to investigate, absent some indication of wrongdoing, whether the investments the Fund chose were proper. Rather, the limited partners were entitled to rely on the good faith and competence of the Fund's fiduciaries in selecting investments, as the Offering Documents contemplate.[106] This is especially so where, as here, the nature of the investments makes it particularly difficult for the limited partners to obtain valuation and time horizon information on their own. The plaintiffs did not waive their right to challenge the investments, then, because they lacked full knowledge of the right allegedly waived.

Moreover, although the Offering Documents disclosed the existence of conflicts, the Offering Documents, as plaintiffs note, did not disclose that CIBC would [*54] cause the Fund to make inappropriate investments or violate the Fund's investment criteria because of these conflicts. It cannot be said that the disclosures in the Partnership Agreement and the Offering Documents conveyed full knowledge of all the facts. The defendants' arguments that the plaintiffs have waived their right to challenge the management fees and loans fail for the same reason. The Offering Documents did not disclose that CIBC would receive management fees and interest on loans in return for making worthless or improper investments. The defendants' motion as to waiver will be denied.

VII.

For the foregoing reasons, the defendants' motion to dismiss is GRANTED as to Count I against CIBC, Figueroa, and Fioravanti, and Count II against the Individual Defendants, Investment Advisor, and Special Limited Partner. The defendants' motion to dismiss is DENIED as to Count I against Sorensen, Christiansen, and Outlaw, the General Partner, the Special Limited Partner, and the Investment Advisor. The defendants' motion to dismiss is DENIED as to Count II against CIBC for aiding and abetting the Special Limited Partner's and Investment Advisor's breaches of fiduciary duty, and is GRANTED [*55] as to Count II against CIBC for aiding and abetting the General Partner's breach of fiduciary duty. IT IS SO ORDERED.

---

[106] *In re Tyson Foods,* 919 A.2d at 588; *In re Healthsouth Corp. S'holders Litig.,* 845 A.2d 1096, 1106 (Del. Ch. 2003).

---

[101] *In re Tyson Foods,* 919 A.2d at 591.

[102] *Realty Growth Investors v. Council of Unit Owners,* 453 A.2d 450, 456 (Del. 1982).

[103] 831 A.2d 318, 334 (Del. Ch. 2003).

[104] *Id.* (citing *Boxer v. Husky Oil Co.,* No. 6261, 1983 WL 17937 (Del. Ch. June 28, 1983), *aff'd,* 483 A.2d 633 (Del. 1984)).

[105] *Id.*

MARTIN MELZER, and ROLLIN LINDERMAN, Plaintiffs, v. CNET NETWORKS, INC., a Delaware corporation, Defendant.

Civil Action No. 3023-CC

COURT OF CHANCERY OF DELAWARE, NEW CASTLE

934 A.2d 912*; 2007 Del. Ch. LEXIS 163**

November 13, 2007, Submitted
November 21, 2007, Decided

PRIOR HISTORY: Meltzer v. CNET Networks, Inc., 2007 Del. Ch. LEXIS 132 (Del. Ch., Sept. 6, 2007)

COUNSEL: [**1] David L. Finger and Charles Slanina, of FINGER & SLANINA, LLC, Wilmington, Delaware; OF COUNSEL: Travis E. Downs III, Randall J. Baron, Kathleen A. Herkenhoff, Benny C. Goodman III, and Mary Lynne Calkins, of COUGHLIN, STOIA, GELLER, RUDMAN & ROBBINS LLP, San Diego, California, Attorneys for Plaintiffs.
Kevin G. Abrams and Nathan A. Cook, of ABRAMS & LASTER LLP, Wilmington, Delaware; OF COUNSEL: Patrick E. Gibbs, Philip J. Wang, and Andrew M. Farthing, of LATHAM & WATKINS LLP, Menlo Park, California, Attorneys for Defendant.

OPINION:

[*913] CHANDLER, Chancellor

This should have been a very easy case. Plaintiffs, who are shareholders of CNET, initiated this action under 8 *Del. C.* § 220 to seek books and records relating to stock options backdating — a practice in which the company has already admitted it engaged — after being ordered to do so by a federal judge in California. This seeming simplicity notwithstanding, CNET opposed the demand for inspection, the parties battled over discovery via a contentious motion to compel, and only on the brink of trial did CNET agree to share certain documents with plaintiffs. This agreement was not, however, all encompassing, and now the parties dispute the scope of [**2] books and records to which plaintiffs are entitled. Summarized as succinctly as possible, the issue is whether plaintiffs are entitled to documents relating to options granted before plaintiffs owned stock in CNET. Because plaintiffs' purpose in this action is to obtain the particularized facts they need to adequately allege demand futility (rather than to investigate potential claims that plaintiffs have no standing to assert), plaintiffs may have access to certain documents pertaining to options granted before they owned shares.

[*914] I. FACTUAL AND PROCEDURAL BACKGROUND

This case, like so many others concerning backdated stock options, found its genesis in a March 18, 2006 article in the *Wall Street Journal* that suggested many large corporations were engaging in an options-granting practice that contravened corporate charters far and wide.[1] That article and its findings have led to the filing of numerous federal and state law actions and to well over one hundred SEC investigations.[2] This case is somewhat unique, however, because here the defendant corporation has admitted that it engaged in backdating stock options granted from the time of its IPO in 1996 through at least 2003.

CNET's options issues first came to light in May 2006, when the Center for Financial Research and Accountability ("CFRA") published an analysis of option-granting practices of one hundred publicly traded companies. The CFRA report specifically identified CNET as a company whose pattern of granting options indicated backdating. On June 27, 2006, CNET disclosed that its option granting practices were under investigation by the U.S. Attorney for the Northern District of California and by the Securities and Exchange Commission. The next month, CNET announced that an internal investigation conducted by a special committee confirmed the CFRA report and announced that the company would need to restate its financial statements from 2003-05. In mid-October 2006, CNET released further, more specific findings from the special committee, which concluded backdating had been a problem for the company from the time of its IPO in 1996.

---

[1] *See* Charles [**3] Forelle & James Bandler, *The Perfect Payday*, WALL ST. J., Mar. 18, 2006, at A1.

[2] See David I. Walker, Unpacking Backdating: Economic Analysis and Observations on the Stock Option Scandal, 87 B.U. L. REV. 561, 563 (2007).

On June 19, 2006, plaintiffs filed their initial [**4] complaint in the District Court for the Northern District of California alleging federal securities and state law claims against CNET and its directors relating to backdated stock options.[3] After CNET's disclosures in the fall, plaintiffs amended their derivative complaint, and the defendants moved to dismiss for failure to make a demand on the CNET board. Applying the *Aronson*[4] test for demand futility, the district court granted the motion to dismiss. [5]

Plaintiffs had alleged several theories to support their contention that demand on the CNET board would have been futile. First, to the extent a director materially benefited from a backdated option, he or she would not be disinterested under the first prong of the *Aronson* test.[6] Thus, to the extent that plaintiffs could plead with particularity facts demonstrating that a majority of the directors received backdated options, demand would be excused. Second, to the extent a director knowingly backdated a stock option in violation of the company's charter, that director's action [**5] is *ultra vires* and is not the product of valid business judgment.[7] If a majority of the [*915] current board engaged in backdating, demand would be excused.[8]

Thus, key to establishing demand futility was particularized facts demonstrating that backdating occurred and either that (1) a majority of the current board received backdated options or (2) a majority of the current board engaged in backdating itself. The district court analyzed [**6] individually the eight option grants that plaintiffs alleged were backdated and concluded that plaintiffs successfully pleaded particularized facts with respect to only the grants on June 3, 1998, April 17, 2000, and October 8, 2001.[9] Consequently, plaintiffs had demonstrated that only *one* member of the then-current board received backdated options.[10] Judge Alsup also found unpersuasive plaintiffs' attempts to show demand futility under the second prong of *Aronson*, concluding that plaintiffs failed to allege the particularized facts

necessary to demonstrate that board members actually engaged in the process of backdating.[11]

After dismissing plaintiffs' amended complaint, however, Judge Alsup granted further leave to amend,[12] and issued a stay pending a books and records demand in Delaware.[13] The stay specifically requested that CNET cooperate [**7] and expedite the inspection because "CNET itself raised the availability of such an inspection in its recent memoranda."[14] Judge Alsup listed four categories of books and records that would be helpful in the California action:

> 1. All books and records showing the extent to which the CNET compensation committee delegated (or did not delegate) to management, either expressly or by custom and practice, the authority to select the exercise price or grant date of stock options under the 1997 plan and, if such delegation occurred, the extent to which the compensation committee was made aware of the exercise prices and dates selected.
>
> 2. All books and records establishing the specific chronology and events leading to the stock-option grants alleged in the complaint and exercise prices and grant dates associated therewith.
>
> 3. All books and records needed to determine whether Messrs. Colligan and Robison received stock options that were backdated.
>
> 4. [**8] All books and records necessary to show the extent to which any minutes [*916] or unanimous written consents for the compensation committee (while Colligan and Robison were members) were backdated, at least as to those minutes involving stock-option grants.

Judge Alsup also noted that those categories were without prejudice to other possible requests, and ordered plaintiffs to make their books and records demand by May 14, 2007.

Indeed, on May 14, 2007, plaintiffs sent their demand to inspect books and records to CNET via certified mail. In this demand letter, plaintiffs made six requests:

> 1. All books and records created by, distributed to, or reviewed by CNET's Board of Directors (the "Board"), or any member or committee thereof, showing the extent to

---

[3] *In re CNET Networks, Inc.,* 483 F. Supp. 2d 947, 953 (N.D. Cal. 2007).

[4] *Aronson v. Lewis,* 473 A.2d 805 (Del. 1984).

[5] *CNET Networks,* 483 F. Supp. 2d at 954-55.

[6] *See Grimes v. Donald,* 673 A.2d 1207, 1216 (Del. 1996) ("The basis for claiming excusal would normally be that . . . a majority of the board has a material financial or familial interest").

[7] *See In re infoUSA, Inc. S'holders Litig.,* C.A. No. 1956-CC, 2007 Del. Ch. LEXIS 123, 2007 WL 2419611, at *15 (Del. Ch. Aug. 20, 2007) ("demand will be excused if a majority of the board that allegedly pursued the *ultra vires* action remains on the defendant board at the time demand is made").

[8] *Ryan v. Gifford,* 918 A.2d 341, 354-55 (Del. Ch. 2007) (finding demand futile under the second prong of *Aronson* where the complaint's particularized facts showed that a majority of the current board sat on the compensation committee that granted backdated options in violation of the company's stock option plan).

[9] *CNET Networks,* 483 F. Supp. 2d at 962.

[10] That one member, co-founder Shelby Bonnie, resigned in October 2006. *See SEC Clears CNET,* CFO MAGAZINE, Sept. 5, 2007, at 2.

[11] *CNET Networks,* 483 F. Supp. 2d at 965 ("Plaintiffs' allegations that because they were on the compensation committee, they must have known, do not constitute particularized facts.").

[12] *In re CNET Networks, Inc. S'holder Derivative Litig.,* No. C 06-03817 WHA (N.D. Cal. Apr. 30, 2007) (order allowing leave to amend and denying motion for reconsideration).

[13] *In re CNET Networks, Inc. S'holder Derivative Litig.,* No. C 06-03817 WHA (N.D. Cal. May 9, 2007) (stay pending books and records demand).

[14] *Id.*

which the CNET Compensation Committee delegated (or did not delegate) to management, either stock options under CNET's 1997 Stock [**9] option Plan ("1997 Plan") and, if such delegation occurred, the extent to which the Compensation Committee was made aware of the exercise prices and dates selected.

2. All books and records establishing the specific chronology and events leading to the stock option grants alleged in the Amended Consolidated Verified Shareholder Derivative Complaint and exercise prices and grant dates associated therewith.

3. All books and records needed to determine whether John C. Colligan and/or Eric Robison received stock options that were backdated, misdated, mispriced or incorrectly dated.

4. All books and records necessary to show the extent to which any minutes or unanimous written consents for the Compensation Committee (while Colligan and Robison were members) were backdated, at least as to those minutes involving or relating to stock option grants.

5. The written report and findings of the Special Committee of the CNET Board on the Company's option granting practices and procedures.

6. All documents that CNET provided to the Securities and Exchange Commission ("SEC") in connection with the SEC's investigation into the stock option granting practices and procedures at CNET.

In this demand letter, [**10] the plaintiffs identified their purpose as "investigating possible violations of law . . . in connection with the Company's granting practices" and "determining whether the Company's officers and directors are independent and/or disinterested and whether they have acted in good faith."

CNET, unmoved by Judge Alsup's request for cooperation, did not comply, and plaintiffs initiated the present action in this Court on June 14, 2007. The parties battled over discovery in a motion to compel and motion for protective order, bickered through letter submissions about a requested continuance, and barreled headlong towards trial. Finally, on November 5, 2007, the parties submitted a stipulation cancelling the trial, which was scheduled for November 14, 2007. Despite this agreement, the parties were unable to resolve the precise scope of the documents to which plaintiffs are entitled under section 220. Specifically, the parties disagree about whether plaintiffs may properly inspect books and records predating plaintiffs' ownership of stock. It is that question this opinion now resolves.

II.   LEGAL ANALYSIS

A.   *Investigation of admitted stock option back-dating constitutes a proper purpose under Section 220.*

Section 220 [**11] provides shareholders of Delaware corporations with a qualified [*917] right to inspect corporate books and records.[15] In relevant part, the statute reads:

> Any stockholder, in person or by attorney or other agent, shall, upon written demand under oath stating the purpose thereof, have the right during the usual hours for business to inspect for any proper purpose, and to make copies and extracts from: (1) The corporation's stock ledger, a list of its stockholders, and its other books and records . . . .[16]

The statute is an expansion of the common law right of shareholders to protect themselves by keeping abreast of how their agents were conducting corporate affairs,[17] but it does not permit unfettered access. Before shareholders may inspect books and records, they must (1) comply with the technical requirements of section 220 and (2) demonstrate a proper purpose for seeking inspection. There is no shortage of proper purposes under Delaware law,[18] but perhaps the most common "proper purpose" is the desire to investigate potential corporate mismanagement, wrongdoing, or waste. Merely stating that one has a proper purpose, however, is necessarily insufficient. For example, a shareholder seeking [**12] a books and records inspection under section 220 in order to investigate mismanagement or wrongdoing "must present 'some evidence' to suggest a 'credible basis' from which a court can infer that mismanagement, waste or wrongdoing may have occurred."[19]

---

[15] *La. Mun. Police Employees' Ret. Sys. v. Countrywide Fin. Corp.,* C.A. No. 2608-VCN, 2007 Del. Ch. LEXIS 138, 2007 WL 2896540, at *9 (Del. Ch. Oct. 2, 2007).

[16] 8 *Del. C.* § 220.

[17] *Saito v. McKesson HBOC, Inc.,* 806 A.2d 113, 116 (Del. 2002).

[18] *See* 1 EDWARD P. WELCH, ANDREW J. TUREZYN, & ROBERT SAUNDERS, FOLK ON THE DELAWARE GENERAL CORPORATION LAW § 220.6.3 (supp. 2007-2) (listing well over ten examples of broad categories of proper purposes under section 220).

[19] *Seinfeld v. Verizon Commc'ns, Inc.,* 909 A.2d 117, 118 (Del. 2006). Delaware courts have been harshly criticized for this requirement. *See, e.g.,* J. Robert Brown's *Inspection Rights under Delaware Law,* http://www.thereacetothebottom.org (Nov. 20, 2007, 6:16 a.m.) (arguing that the *Seinfeld* decision "illustrates that courts deliberately discourage the use of inspection rights by shareholders, using not the language in the statute but excessive pleading standards"). Such sensationalized criticism may make for [**13] an entertaining blog, but it is both unfair and incorrect. First, there is nothing "excessive" about requiring a petitioner to plead the elements of the statute under which he or she petitions the court. Section 220 makes inspection available only for shareholders with a "proper purpose." If a shareholder could satisfy this burden by conclusorily repeating words previously used to describe a proper purpose, the requirement would be rendered meaningless, and well settled canons of statutory construction prevent such absurd results. Second, as Justice Holland

Here, as noted above, the plaintiffs have identified two purposes, but both really relate to plaintiffs' desire to bring [**14] derivatively in California a suit alleging a breach of fiduciary duty in connection with backdated options granted by CNET.[20] Defendant does not dispute this characterization. In fact, defendant relies on this characterization [*918] to support its chief argument: plaintiffs are not entitled to books and records from the time period before plaintiffs owned stock in CNET, because plaintiffs lack standing under 8 *Del. C.* § 327 to bring a derivative suit for any claims that accrued before they owned such stock. Thus, all parties agree that plaintiffs have a proper purpose. At issue, however, is the scope of the investigation that plaintiffs' proper purpose will permit.

B.   *A stockholder must be given sufficient access to books and records to effectively address the problem of backdating through derivative litigation.*

Section 220 does not sanction a "broad fishing expedition,"[21] but "where a § 220 claim is based on alleged corporate wrongdoing, ... the stockholder should be given enough information to effectively address the problem . . . ."[22] Generally, this Court has "wide [**15] latitude in determining the proper scope of inspection," and this Court must "tailor the inspection to the stockholder's stated purpose."[23]

Defendant argues that plaintiffs should be barred from inspecting any books and records that predate plaintiffs' ownership of CNET stock. Because plaintiffs are only seeking to bring a derivative claim, defendant argues, and because plaintiffs can only bring claims for wrongs that occurred after plaintiffs purchased stock, there is no reason for plaintiffs to inspect documents before the purchase date. In so arguing, defendant relies heavily on *Polygon Global Opportunities Master Fund v. West Corp.*[24] and *West Coast Management & Capital, LLC v. Carrier Access Corp.*[25] In *Polygon,* Vice Chancellor Lamb refused to grant an investigation under section 220 where the shareholder, an arbitrage fund, purchased shares in the West Corporation *after* an announced reorganization and then sought a books and records inspection [**16] to look into potential derivative claims in connection with the proposed reorganization plan.[26] Because the fund could not possibly have standing to challenge any breach it purportedly wanted to investigate, allowing an inspection of books and records under section 220 was improper.[27] In *West Coast,* shareholders attempted to conduct a section 220 inspection after their federal derivative claim was dismissed for failure to adequately plead demand futility.[28] There, however, the federal judge "specifically denied the plaintiffs' request for leave to replead."[29] With this explicit ruling in hand, Vice Chancellor Lamb concluded that the shareholders were estopped from relitigating demand futility and, therefore, lacked a proper purpose under section 220.[30] Finally, defendant also cites language [*919] from the Supreme Court's opinion in *Saito* that indicates "if the stockholder's only purpose [in pursuing a section 220 books and records inspection] was to institute derivative litigation," one might reasonably question "whether the stockholder's purpose was reasonably related to his or her interest as a stockholder."[31]

However, *Polygon* and *West Coast* are distinguishable, and *Saito,* while instructive, mandates a different result than what defendant proposes. Plaintiffs here do not seek the pre-2000 books and records in order to investigate potential *new* causes of action — claims plaintiffs would admittedly have no standing to assert. Rather, plaintiffs seek access to those documents in order to plead demand futility with respect to the causes of action plaintiffs *do* have standing to bring.

Judge Alsup told plaintiffs to go to Delaware to find the particularized facts they needed to properly plead demand futility. There are several ways plaintiffs can attempt to accomplish this, one of which is the second prong of *Aronson v. Lewis.* To plead demand futility under the second prong of *Aronson,* a shareholder must allege particularized facts that create a reasonable doubt that the "challenged transaction was ... the product of a valid exercise of business [**18] judgment."[32] This invites an inquiry "into the substantive nature of the challenged transaction and the board's approval thereof."[33] One potential way to show that the board was not exercising valid business judgment is to

---

explained in *Seinfeld,* permitting a single shareholder to hound a corporation with exclusively personal requests for books and records is a waste of corporate resources that engenders no benefit for the shareholders in general. The proper purpose requirement protects against such wealth-reducing outcomes. Finally, the "credible basis" standard is "the lowest possible burden of proof" in Delaware jurisprudence, and this can hardly be characterized as an excessive pleading standard. *Seinfeld,* 909 A.2d 117 at 123.

[20] By virtue of CNET's admission of backdating, there is sufficient evidence to support a credible basis of wrongdoing.

[21] *Freund v. Lucent Techs., Inc.,* C.A. No. 18893, 2003 Del. Ch. LEXIS 3, 2003 WL 139766, at *4 (Del. Ch. Jan. 9, 2003).

[22] *Saito v. McKesson HBOC, Inc.,* 806 A.2d 113, 115 (Del. 2002).

[23] *Security First Corp. v. U.S. Die Casting & Dev. Co.,* 687 A.2d 563, 569 (Del. 1997).

[24] C.A. No. 2313-N, 2006 Del. Ch. LEXIS 179, 2006 WL 2947486 (Del. Ch. Oct. 12, 2006).

[25] 914 A.2d 636 (Del. Ch. 2006).

[26] 2006 Del. Ch. LEXIS 179, [WL] at *5.

[27] *Id.*

[28] 914 A.2d at 639.

[29] *Id.*

[30] *Id.* at 646 [**17] (noting that because West Coast's "sole purpose is to use the information it seeks to replead demand futility" — an action it is precluded from doing — it lacks a proper purpose under section 220).

[31] *Saito v. McKesson HBOC, Inc.,* 806 A.2d 113, 117 (Del. 2002).

[32] 473 A.2d 805, 814 (Del. 1983).

[33] *Id.*

show that there was a "sustained or systematic failure of the board to exercise oversight"[34] — a violation of the board's duty of loyalty by way of bad faith.[35] To show a "sustained or systematic failure of the board to exercise oversight," the plaintiffs might reasonably need to consult documents that predate their ownership of CNET stock.

In *Polygon,* the shareholder's articulated purpose was solely to investigate potential claims — claims that the shareholder would be barred from bringing. Here, plaintiffs are seeking particularized facts to replead demand futility; they are not fishing for new claims. [**19] In *West Coast,* the federal judge overseeing the derivative action explicitly barred the shareholder from repleading demand futility. Here, Judge Alsup explicitly asked plaintiffs to do just that. Indeed, *Saito* is ultimately controlling. There, Justice Berger defined the appropriate scope of a books and records investigation as "enough information to *effectively address the problem. . . .*"[36] Here, plaintiffs cannot effectively address the alleged problem through a derivative suit unless they can properly plead demand futility. Because *Stone v. Ritter* held that a violation of the duty of loyalty/good faith described in *Caremark* can, in theory, excuse demand,[37] and because plaintiffs might need older documents to establish a "sustained or systematic failure" [*920] of oversight,[38] I must conclude that plaintiffs' request for the documents here is reasonably related to their proper purpose as shareholders of CNET.

III. CONCLUSION

Plaintiffs should have access to books and records that predate their purchase of stock in order to allow them to explore a potential lapse in the good faith of the CNET board that would excuse demand in the California derivative suit. The outer bounds of this disclosure are defined by plaintiffs' demand letter itself; not by plaintiffs' interrogatories.[39] It is about time defendant takes Judge Alsup's advice, provides the requested documents, and gets "going, going / back, back / to Cali, Cali."[40]

IT IS SO ORDERED.

---

[34] *Stone v. Ritter,* 911 A.2d 362, 372 (Del. 2006) (quoting *In re Caremark Int'l, Inc. Derivative Litig.,* 698 A.2d 959, 971 (Del. Ch. 1996)).

[35] Indeed, the plaintiffs here specifically stated that one of their purposes for seeking a books and records inspection under section 220 was to investigate the good faith of the CNET directors.

[36] 806 A.2d at 115 (emphasis added).

[37] 911 A.2d at 372-73.

[38] *See Desimone v. Barrows,* 924 A.2d 908, 940 (Del. Ch. 2007) ("[I]n order to state a viable *Caremark* claim, and to predicate a substantial likelihood of director liability on it, a plaintiff must plead the existence of facts [**20] suggesting that the board knew that internal controls were inadequate, that the inadequacies could leave room for illegal or materially harmful behavior, and that the board chose to do nothing about the control deficiencies that it knew existed."); *Guttman v. Jen-Hsun Huang,* 823 A.2d 492, 506 (Del. Ch. 2003) (noting that a *Caremark* claim is successful "on a showing that the directors were conscious of the fact that they were not doing their jobs").

[39] *See Kaufman v. CA, Inc.,* 905 A.2d 749, 753-54 (Del. Ch. 2006) ("[R]elief under Section 220 is limited only to the inspection of books and records that are necessary and essential to the satisfaction of the stated purpose. To summarize [**21] the meaning of our cases as to this latter prong, when a books and records action is brought with the goal of evaluating a possible derivative suit, the books and records that satisfy the action are those that are required to prepare a well-pleaded complaint. Of course, this means that Section 220 is not meant as a replacement for discovery under Rule 34.").

[40] THE NOTORIOUS B.I.G., *Going Back to Cali,* on LIFE AFTER DEATH (Bad Boy Records 1997).

Appendix

Notes

Notes

Notes

Notes

Notes

Notes

Notes

Notes

Notes

Notes

Notes

Notes

Notes

Notes

CORPORATION SERVICE COMPANY®

The leading provider of Registered Agent Services for over 100 years

Corporation Service Company is the leading registered agent providing representation and transactional services, plus a valuable suite of industry-related services. Headquartered in Wilmington, Delaware, CSC operates in all 50 states and internationally.

CSC® Services:
- Registered Agent
- Compliance & Governance
- Charitable Registration and Compliance
- Litigation & Matter Management
- Corporate and Transaction Legal Services
- UCC & Motor Vehicle Services
- Intellectual Property Management
- Trust & Financial Services

Registered Agent

Corporation Service Company provides representation services both domestically and internationally to meet all of your representation needs, including:
- **Registered Agent Services**
- **Special Agency Services**
- **Contract Agent Services**

Compliance & Governance

CSC RecordsCenter℠
CSC is the only registered agent to offer a complete platform containing the entity information you need to oversee and manage your company records, domain names and trademark registrations. The CSC RecordsCenter℠ system allows real-time monitoring of the status of your entities, along with tools to assist with corporate compliance, as required by your board of directors and shareholders.

CSC Compliance Calendar℠
CSC Compliance Calendar℠ was the first web-based compliance management application specifically designed to help ensure jurisdictional good standing at the Secretary of State level. This application includes annual report, franchise tax, and related filing information for corporations, limited liability companies, and limited partnerships.

CSC Virtual Boardroom℠
This CSC web-based application is specifically designed to streamline document management and communication among board of directors or team members.

Charitable Registration and Compliance

CSC is a leading provider of public record document filing and retrieval services. We can prepare, file, and register your charitable organization wherever you need to register, and can assist your charitable organization or charitable clients with compliance obligations.

For more information call 1.800.927.9800 or visit us at www.cscglobal.com.

Litigation & Matter Management

CSC Custom SOPᔆᴹ allows you to receive email notification of legal process; next-day delivery; custom notification, delivery and processing; online access to your service of process details and history, online acknowledgement of document delivery, real-time electronic tracking, and email alerts of newly filed court cases. You decide how you want to be notified about your SOP and how you'd like to receive it.

Corporate and Legal Transaction Services

CSC prepares and files the documents required to incorporate or form an entity, checking the name for availabiity, and recording and publishing when necessary. CSC then prepares and files the documents required to keep the entity in compliance.

UCC & Motor Vehicle Services

UCC Services

Now the largest provider of secured transaction services, CSC is the single source for all your asset-related document searching and filing needs across the U.S. and Canada. We deliver complete support for all of your Revised Article 9 (RA9) UCC needs, from single filings to a portfolio of projects.

Our online solution UCCXpress® makes it easy to conduct lien searches, prepare and file UCC forms and file electronically, direct to the jurisdiction. Manage your portfolio with FileWatch ᔆᴹ, the automated notification system, as well as provide timely delivery of searches on real property.

Motor Vehicle Services

CSC provides nationwide titling and registration services for virtually any type of vehicle, from passenger cars and trucks to modular buildings and recreational equipment. We've streamlined the process by maintaining ongoing relationships with motor vehicle departments throughout the country. In addition to titling and registering your vehicles, CSC can obtain duplicate titles, add or release lien holders, renew registrations and search motor vehicle records.

Intellectual Property Management

One of the most important assets a company can possess is its name. However, with the evolution of the Internet, managing and protecting a company's name has become more costly, complex and time-consuming. Corporation Service Company now offers a comprehensive suite of name management services tailored to the unique needs of corporations and law firms. Integrated on CSC's web-based corporate compliance and governance platform, CSC RecordsCenter ᔆᴹ , our suite of name management services helps companies acquire, consolidate, manage and proactively monitor name assets worldwide.

Domain Name Management

Avoid the confusion and cost of utilizing multiple domain name registrars by consolidating all your general top-level domain names (gTLDs) and all country code top-level domain names (ccTLDs) with CSC.

For more

information call

1.800.927.9800

or visit us at

www.cscglobal.com.

Trademarks

Conduct online trademark queries and populate search results to your portfolio, dramatically decreasing data entry and potential errors. Link your trademarks to particular entities within your organization, saving time and confusion at the time of a merger or acquisition.

IP Watch Services

Our IP Watch Services help you monitor your trademarks on the Internet to protect them from misuse, cybersquatters, traffic diversion and parody. Corporation Service Company offers a unique collection of clientside, real time search tools (Quick Tools™), as well as monthly, delivered reports (SmartReports™) to help corporations and law firms monitor their domain and trademark portfolios on the Internet.

Trust & Financial Services

Independent Director Services from CSC Entity Services®

You can rely on the truly independent status of our directors and managers provided through CSC Entity Services. Personnel are totally independent of any lender, underwriter, bank, insurance company or securitization administrator. We can provide both natural person and non-natural person appointments.

Trust Services

CSC Trust Company℠ offers institutional trust services including Delaware Statutory Trust Services, Escrow Agency Services and Specialized Agency Services. These fiduciary and agency services support myriad business and commercial transactions.

For more information about these and other CSC® services, visit www.cscglobal.com or contact a customer service representative at 1.800.927.9800.

CSC CORPORATION SERVICE COMPANY®

CSC® Publications. Your point of departure. *Where you go is up to you*℠.

The CSC® Library of Publications offers you a wide array of valuable resources. Whether you're looking for important jurisdictional updates or forming a limited liability company, these books offer you the information you need most—in a format that is compact, concise and convenient.

The CSC® Business Entity Jurisdiction Library

You'll appreciate the valuable resources offered by the CSC® Jurisdiction Library. Each book offers the state's key business statutes, including: Corporation, LLC, LLP, LP and Nonprofit Laws. The books also include annotations, amendments, and the statutes' legislative history. Softbound for portability, updated annually—no filing required.

Delaware Laws Governing Business Entities (Spring and Fall Editions)

Volume 1 (Annotated Statutes and Rules) features a corporate fees and taxes payable chapter, the full text of the Chancery Court Rules, and Articles 1, 8 and 9 of the Uniform Commercial Code, plus the Delaware General Corporation Law, Limited Liability Act, and more. This title also includes Blackline Notes showing the effect of the most recent amendments, and a complete analysis of amendments.

Volume 2 (Annotations from All State and Federal Courts) contains annotations of cases decided under Delaware business entity law in all state and federal courts; case annotations are organized by statute, section-by-section, then by state and federal court.

Companion Website

With your subscription to Delaware Laws Governing Business Entities you have online access to the full text of the two-volume set, as well as all opinions cited in the books, in a convenient searchable format.

Business Entity Jurisdiction Books from CSC
Select the jurisdictions you need.

- **California** Laws Governing Business Entities
- **Delaware** Laws Governing Business Entities Volumes 1 & 2 (Spring and Fall)
- **Florida** Laws Governing Business Entities
- **Illinois** Laws Governing Business Entities
- **Maryland & District of Columbia** Laws Governing Business Entities
- **Massachusetts** Laws Governing Business Entities
- **Nevada** Laws Governing Business Entities
- **New Jersey** Laws Governing Business Entities
- **New York** Laws Governing Business Entities (Spring and Fall)
- **Pennsylvania** Laws Governing Business Entities
- **Virginia** Laws Governing Business Entities